# Lecture Notes in Computer Science 7495

Commenced Publication in 1973
Founding and Former Series Editors:
Gerhard Goos, Juris Hartmanis, and Jan van Leeuwen

T0224173

Georgios Ch. Sirakoulis   Stefania Bandini (Eds.)

# Cellular Automata

10th International Conference on Cellular Automata
for Research and Industry, ACRI 2012
Santorini Island, Greece, September 24-27, 2012
Proceedings

 Springer

Volume Editors

Georgios Ch. Sirakoulis
Democritus University of Thrace
Department of Electrical and Computer Engineering
67100 Xanthi, Greece
E-mail: gsirak@ee.duth.gr

Stefania Bandini
University of Milano-Bicocca
CSAI - Complex Systems and Artificial Intelligence Research Center
20134 Milano, Italy
E-mail: stefania.bandini@disco.unimib.it

ISSN 0302-9743                          e-ISSN 1611-3349
ISBN 978-3-642-33349-1                  e-ISBN 978-3-642-33350-7
DOI 10.1007/978-3-642-33350-7
Springer Heidelberg Dordrecht London New York

Library of Congress Control Number: 2012947014

CR Subject Classification (1998): F.1.1, F.1, F.2.2, I.6, I.4, C.2

LNCS Sublibrary: SL 1 – Theoretical Computer Science and General Issues

*Typesetting:* Camera-ready by author, data conversion by Scientific Publishing Services, Chennai, India

Printed on acid-free paper

Springer is part of Springer Science+Business Media (www.springer.com)

# Preface

This volume collects the papers selected for presentation at the 10th International Conference on Cellular Automata for Research and Industry (ACRI 2012), held on Santorini Island (Greece), September 24–27, 2012. ACRI 2012 was organized by the Democritus University of Thrace as a forum for the presentation and discussion of specialized results as well as general contributions to the growth of the cellular automata approach and its application. Cellular automata represent a very powerful approach to the study of spatio-temporal systems where complex phenomena are built up out of many simple local interactions. The ACRI conference series was first organized in Italy, namely ACRI 1994 in Rende, ACRI 1996 in Milan, and ACRI 1998 in Trieste, and followed by ACRI 2000 in Karlsruhe (Germany), ACRI 2002 in Geneva (Switzerland), ACRI 2004 in Amsterdam (The Netherlands), ACRI 2006 in Perpignan (France), ACRI 2008 in Yokohama (Japan), and ACRI 2010 in Ascoli Piceno (Italy).

ACRI conferences have been offering since 1994 a biennial scientific meeting to both scientists and innovation managers in academia and industry to express and discuss their viewpoints on current and future trends, challenges, and state-of-the-art solutions to various problems in the fields of arts, biology, chemistry, communication, cultural heritage, ecology, economy, geology, engineering, medicine, physics, sociology, traffic control, etc. The ACRI conferences have been traditionally focused on challenging problems and new research, not only on theoretical but also on applicational aspects of cellular automata, including cellular automata tools and computational sciences. The conference sereis is also concerned with applications and solutions of problems from the fields of physics, engineering, environment science, social science, and life sciences. Its primary goal is to discuss problems from a variety of scientific fields, to identify new issues, and to enlarge the research fields of cellular automata. Since its inception, the ACRI conference has attracted an ever-growing community and has raised knowledge and interest in the study of cellular automata for both new entrants into the field as well as researchers already working on particular aspects of cellular automata.

In order to give a perspective in which both theoretical and applicational aspects of cellular automata contribute to the growth of the area, this book mirrors the structure of the conference, grouping the 88 papers into two main parts. The first part collects papers presented as part of the main conference and organized according to six main topics: (1) theoretical results on cellular automata, (2) cellular automata dynamics, control and synchronization, (3) cellular automata and networks, (4) modeling and simulation with cellular automata, (5) cellular automata-based hardware and architectures, and (6) codes, pseudorandom number generators and cryptography with cellular automata. The second part of the volume is dedicated to contributions presented during the ACRI 2012 workshops on theoretical advances, specifically Asynchronous Cellular Automata (2$^{nd}$ workshop, chairs: Alberto Dennunzio, Enrico Formenti, and Nazim Fatès), and challenging application contexts for cellular automata: Crowds and Cellular Automata (4$^{th}$ workshop, chairs: Sara Manzoni, Ioakeim Georgoudas, and Georgios Sirakoulis), Traffic and Cellular Automata (2$^{nd}$ workshop, chairs: Katsuhiro Nishinari and Andreas Schadschneider), and the satellite workshop on Cellular Automata of Cancer Growth and Invasion (chairs: Michael Meyer-Hermann, Andreas Deutsch, and Haralampos Hatzikirou).

Many people contributed to the success of ACRI 2012 and to the creation of this volume, from the initial idea to its implementation. Our first acknowledgement goes to all the scientists that submitted their works, and to all Program Committee members and reviewers for their precious collaboration. A special thanks for their hospitality to the Municipality of Santorini, Petros Nomikos Conference Center, and for its generous contribution to the realization of this volume to the Research Committee of the Democritus University of Thrace. A special acknowledgement also to all the people involved in the organization of ACRI 2012 (in particular, alphabetically ordered, to: Prodromos Chatziagorakis, Savvas Chatzichristofis, Konstantinos Ioannidis, Michail-Antisthenis Tsompanas, Ioannis Vourkas, and especially to Christos Mavrakis as well to Giuseppe Vizzari) whose work was really fundamental for the actual success of the event.

Finally, we would like to thank the Department of Electrical and Computer Engineering of Democritus University of Thrace as well as the Complex Systems and Artificial Intelligence (CSAI) research center of the University of Milano-Bicocca, and all those institutes and organizations that financially supported the congress.

September 2012

Georgios Ch. Sirakoulis
Stefania Bandini

# Organization

ACRI 2012 was organized by the Laboratory of Electronics of the Department of Electrical and Computer Engineering of the Democritus University of Thrace.

## Conference Chairs

Georgios Ch. Sirakoulis      Democritus University of Thrace, Greece
Stefania Bandini      University of Milano-Bicocca, Italy

## Workshop Chairs

### Asynchronous CA

Alberto Dennunzio      University of Milano-Bicocca, Italy
Nazim Fatès      INRIA Nancy - Grand Est - France
Enrico Formenti      University of Nice - Sophia Antipolis, France

### Crowds and CA

Ioakeim Georgoudas      Democritus University of Thrace, Greece
Sara Manzoni      University of Milano-Bicocca, Italy
Georgios Sirakoulis      Democritus University of Thrace, Greece

### Traffic and CA

Katsuhiro Nishinari      University of Tokyo, Japan
Andreas Schadschneider      University of Cologne, Germany

### CA of Cancer Growth and Invasion

Michael Meyer-Hermann      Helmholtz Centre for Infection Research Braunschweig, Germany
Andreas Deutsch      Dresden University of Technology, Germany
Haralampos Hatzikirou      Helmholtz Centre for Infection Research Braunschweig, Germany

## Organizing Committee

Prodromos Chatziagorakis      Christos Mavrakis
Ioakeim Georgoudas      Michail-Antisthenis Tsompanas
Konstantinos Ioannidis      Ioannis Vourkas

## International Steering Committee

| | |
|---|---|
| Stefania Bandini | University of Milano-Bicocca, Italy |
| Bastien Chopard | University of Geneva, Switzerland |
| Giancarlo Mauri | University of Milano-Bicocca, Italy |
| Hiroshi Umeo | University of Osaka, Japan |
| Thomas Worsch | University of Karlsruhe, Germany |

## Program Committee

| | |
|---|---|
| Andrew Adamatzky | UK |
| Ioannis Andreadis | Greece |
| Franco Bagnoli | Italy |
| Stefania Bandini | Italy |
| Olga Bandman | Russia |
| Belgacem Ben Youssef | Canada |
| Bastien Chopard | Switzerland |
| Alberto Dennunzio | Italy |
| Andreas Deutsch | Germany |
| Salvatore Di Gregorio | Italy |
| Pedro de Oliveira | Brazil |
| Michel Droz | Switzerland |
| Samira El Yacoubi | France |
| Nazim Fatès | France |
| Teijiro Isokawa | Japan |
| Francisco Jiménez | Spain |
| Ioannis Karafyllidis | Greece |
| Toshihiko Komatsuzaki | Japan |
| Martin Kutrib | Germany |
| Anna T. Lawniczak | Canada |
| Jia Lee | China |
| Joseph Lizier | Germany |
| Danuta Makowiec | Poland |
| Sara Manzoni | Italy |
| Maurice Margenstern | France |
| Genaro J. Martínez | Mexico |
| Nobuyuki Matsui | Japan |
| Giancarlo Mauri | Italy |
| Michael Meyer-Hermann | Germany |
| Angelo Mingarelli | Canada |
| Shin Morishita | Japan |
| Katsuhiro Nishinari | Japan |
| Hidenosuke Nishio | Japan |
| Ferdinand Peper | Japan |
| Franciszek Seredynski | Poland |
| Roberto Serra | Italy |

| | |
|---|---|
| Biplab K. Sikdar | India |
| Georgios Sirakoulis | Greece |
| Furio Suggi Liverani | Italy |
| Domenico Talia | Italy |
| Marco Tomassini | Switzerland |
| Leen Torenvliet | The Netherlands |
| Hiroshi Umeo | Japan |
| Giuseppe Vizzari | Italy |
| Burton Voorhees | Canada |
| Thomas Worsch | Germany |

# Table of Contents

## Theoretical Results on Cellular Automata

Topological Perturbations and Their Effect on the Dynamics of
Totalistic Cellular Automata .................................... 1
   *Jan M. Baetens and Bernard De Baets*

Counting Cycles in Reversible Cellular Automata .................... 11
   *Sukanta Das, Avik Chakraborty, and Biplab K. Sikdar*

Propagative Mode in a Lattice-Grain CA: Time Evolution and
Timestep Synchronization ........................................ 20
   *Dominique Désérable*

Limit Cycle for Composited Cellar Automata ....................... 32
   *Toshikazu Ishida and Shuichi Inokuchi*

Iterative Arrays: Little Resources Big Size Impact ................... 42
   *Martin Kutrib and Andreas Malcher*

Generating Expander Graphs Using Cellular Automata ............... 52
   *Debdeep Mukhopadhyay*

Analysis of Reachability Tree for Identification of Cyclic and Acyclic
CA States......................................................... 63
   *Nazma Naskar, Avik Chakraborty, Pradipta Maji, and Sukanta Das*

Confliction-Like Dynamics of Rule 20 ECA of Wolfram Class II ........ 73
   *Fumio Ohi and Takanori Ichikawa*

## CA Dynamics, Control and Synchronization

Determining the Critical Temperature of the Continuous-State Game
of Life ........................................................... 83
   *Susumu Adachi, Jia Lee, Ferdinand Peper, Teijiro Isokawa, and
Katsunobu Imai*

The Dynamics of Disproportionality Index for Cellular Automata
Based Sociophysical Models ....................................... 91
   *Tomasz M. Gwizdałła*

A Spatio-temporal Algorithmic Point of View on Firing Squad
Synchronisation Problem.......................................... 101
   *Luidnel Maignan and Jean-Baptiste Yunès*

A Coevolutionary Approach to Cellular Automata-Based Task
Scheduling . . . . . . . . . . . . . . . . . . . . . . . . . . . . . . . . . . . . . . . . . . . . . . . . . . . . . .   111
    Gina M.B. Oliveira and Paulo M. Vidica

Searching Cellular Automata Rules for Solving Two-Dimensional
Binary Classification Problem . . . . . . . . . . . . . . . . . . . . . . . . . . . . . . . . . . . . .   121
    Anna Piwonska, Franciszek Seredynski, and Miroslaw Szaban

Multi-objective Cellular Automata Optimization . . . . . . . . . . . . . . . . . . . . .   131
    Epaminondas Sidiropoulos

Behavior of Social Dynamical Models I: Fixation in the Symmetric
Cyclic System (with Paradoxical Effect in the Six-Color Automaton) . . .   141
    Stylianos Scarlatos

Behavior of Social Dynamical Models II: Clustering for Some Multitype
Particle Systems with Confidence Threshold . . . . . . . . . . . . . . . . . . . . . . . . .   151
    Adam Adamopoulos and Stylianos Scarlatos

Investigation of Stable Patterns Formed by Totalistic Cellular
Automata Evolution. . . . . . . . . . . . . . . . . . . . . . . . . . . . . . . . . . . . . . . . . . . . . . .   161
    Anastasiya Sharifulina

Recent Developments in Constructing Square Synchronizers . . . . . . . . . . .   171
    Hiroshi Umeo and Keisuke Kubo

Structural Operational Semantics for Cellular Automata . . . . . . . . . . . . . .   184
    Baltasar Trancón y. Widemann

Controlling the Opacity of a Building Envelope by a Triangular
Two-Color Two-Dimensional Cellular Automaton . . . . . . . . . . . . . . . . . . . .   194
    Machi Zawidzki and Katsuhiro Nishinari

## Cellular Automata and Networks

Community-Detection Cellular Automata with Local and Long-Range
Connectivity . . . . . . . . . . . . . . . . . . . . . . . . . . . . . . . . . . . . . . . . . . . . . . . . . . . . . . .   204
    Franco Bagnoli, Emanuele Massaro, and Andrea Guazzini

Cellular Automaton as Sorting Network Generator Using Instruction-
Based Development . . . . . . . . . . . . . . . . . . . . . . . . . . . . . . . . . . . . . . . . . . . . . . . .   214
    Michal Bidlo and Zdenek Vasicek

Network View of Binary Cellular Automata . . . . . . . . . . . . . . . . . . . . . . . . .   224
    Yoshihiko Kayama

A Cellular Automata Based Scheme for Energy Efficient Fault
Diagnosis in WSN. . . . . . . . . . . . . . . . . . . . . . . . . . . . . . . . . . . . . . . . . . . . . . . . .   234
    Nasiruddin Khan, Ilora Maity, Sukanta Das, and Biplab K. Sikdar

Noise-Induced Emergent Hierarchies in a CA Model ..................     244
    *Marco Villani, Roberto Serra, Stefano Benedettini, Andrea Roli, and*
    *David Lane*

Introducing Innovation in a Structured Population ...................     254
    *Burton Voorhees*

Spreading Patterns of Mobile Phone Viruses Using Cellular
Automata.............................................................     263
    *Ioannis Vourkas, Dimitrios Michail, and Georgios Ch. Sirakoulis*

## Modeling and Simulation with Cellular Automata

A Preliminary Cellular Model for Sand Coastal Erosion and
Experimental Contrast with Porto Cesareo Case ....................     273
    *Maria Vittoria Avolio, Claudia Roberta Calidonna,*
    *Marco Delle Rose, Salvatore Di Gregorio, Valeria Lupiano,*
    *Tiziano Maria Pagliara, and Anna Maria Sempreviva*

Simulation of Wildfire Spread Using Cellular Automata with
Randomized Local Sources ...........................................     279
    *Maria Vittoria Avolio, Salvatore Di Gregorio, Valeria Lupiano, and*
    *Giuseppe A. Trunfio*

A Theorem about the Algorithm of Minimization of Differences for
Multicomponent Cellular Automata ..................................     289
    *Maria Vittoria Avolio, Salvatore Di Gregorio, William Spataro, and*
    *Giuseppe A. Trunfio*

Generation of Pedestrian Groups Distributions with Probabilistic
Cellular Automata ..................................................     299
    *Stefania Bandini, Lorenza Manenti, and Sara Manzoni*

Coupling Method for Building a Network of Irrigation Canals on a
Distributed Computing Environment .................................     309
    *Mohamed Ben Belgacem, Bastien Chopard, and Andrea Parmigiani*

Urban Cellular Automata with Irregular Space of Proximities: A Case
Study ..............................................................     319
    *Ivan Blecic, Arnaldo Cecchini, Giuseppe A. Trunfio, and*
    *Emmanuil Verigos*

Efficient Robot Path Planning in the Presence of Dynamically
Expanding Obstacles ................................................     330
    *Konstantinos Charalampous, Angelos Amanatiadis, and*
    *Antonios Gasteratos*

Image Encryption Using the Recursive Attributes of the eXclusive-OR
Filter on Cellular Automata .................................... 340
  *Savvas A. Chatzichristofis, Oge Marques, Mathias Lux, and*
  *Yiannis Boutalis*

Agent-Based Model to Simulate Groundwater Remediation with
Nanoscale Zero Valent Iron .................................... 351
  *Davide De March, Alessandro Filisetti, Elisabetta Sartorato, and*
  *Emanuele Argese*

Theory and Application of Restricted Five Neighborhood Cellular
Automata (R5NCA) for Protein Structure Prediction ................. 360
  *Soumyabrata Ghosh, Nirmalya S. Maiti, and Parimal Pal Chaudhuri*

Multi Agent-Based Simulation on Technology Diffusion of China ....... 370
  *Gaoxiang Gu, Zheng Wang, and Jing Wu*

An Edge Preserving Image Resizing Method Based on Cellular
Automata ..................................................... 375
  *Konstantinos Ioannidis, Ioannis Andreadis, and*
  *Georgios Ch. Sirakoulis*

Modelling of Incident Sound Wave Propagation around Sound Barriers
Using Cellular Automata ....................................... 385
  *Toshihiko Komatsuzaki, Yoshio Iwata, and Shin Morishita*

Path Tracing on Polar Depth Maps for Robot Navigation ............. 395
  *Ioannis Kostavelis, Evangelos Boukas, Lazaros Nalpantidis, and*
  *Antonios Gasteratos*

Modeling Development and Disease in Our "Second" Brain ............ 405
  *Kerry A. Landman, Benjamin J. Binder, and Donald F. Newgreen*

A 2D Cellular Automaton Biofilm Detachment Algorithm ............. 415
  *Chrysi S. Laspidou, Antonis Liakopoulos, and*
  *Marios G. Spiliotopoulos*

Creature Learning to Cross a CA Simulated Road .................... 425
  *Anna T. Lawniczak, Jason B. Ernst, and Bruno N. Di Stefano*

An Electro-Mechanical Cardiac Simulator Based on Cellular Automata
and Mass-Spring Models ....................................... 434
  *Ronan Mendonça Amorim, Ricardo Silva Campos, Marcelo Lobosco,*
  *Christian Jacob, and Rodrigo Weber dos Santos*

Swii2, a HTML5/WebGL Application for Cellular Automata Debris
Flows Simulation ............................................. 444
  *Roberto Parise, Donato D'Ambrosio, Giuseppe Spingola,*
  *Giuseppe Filippone, Rocco Rongo, Giuseppe A. Trunfio, and*
  *William Spataro*

Effects of Initial Concentration and Severity of Infected Cells on
Stochastic Cellular Automaton Model Dynamics for HIV Infection . . . . .     454
  *Monamorn Precharattana and Wannapong Triampo*

Decentralized Method for Traffic Monitoring . . . . . . . . . . . . . . . . . . . . . . . .     464
  *Guillaume Sartoretti, Jean-Luc Falcone, Bastien Chopard, and
  Martin J. Gander*

Improving a Project Management by Use of Cellular Automata . . . . . . . .     474
  *Kenichiro Shimura and Katsuhiro Nishinari*

Use of Cellular Automata to Create an Artificial System of Image
Classification and Recognition . . . . . . . . . . . . . . . . . . . . . . . . . . . . . . . . . . .     483
  *Stepan Belan and Nikolay Belan*

Modeling of Recrystallization with Recovery by Frontal Cellular
Automata . . . . . . . . . . . . . . . . . . . . . . . . . . . . . . . . . . . . . . . . . . . . . . . . . . . . . .     494
  *Dmytro S. Svyetlichnyy, Jarosław Nowak, and Łukasz Łach*

A CA-Based Model Describing Fat Bloom in Chocolate . . . . . . . . . . . . . .     504
  *Pieter Van der Weeën, Nathalie De Clercq, Koen Dewettinck, and
  Bernard De Baets*

Scene Text Detection on Images Using Cellular Automata . . . . . . . . . . . .     514
  *Konstantinos Zagoris and Ioannis Pratikakis*

A Novel Cellular Automaton Model for Traffic Freeway Simulation . . . . .     524
  *Marcelo Zamith, Regina Célia P. Leal-Toledo, and Esteban Clua*

## CA-Based Hardware and Architectures

Scintillae: How to Approach Computing Systems by Means of Cellular
Automata . . . . . . . . . . . . . . . . . . . . . . . . . . . . . . . . . . . . . . . . . . . . . . . . . . . . . .     534
  *Gabriele Di Stefano and Alfredo Navarra*

Cellular Automata Analysis on Self-assembly Properties in DNA Tile
Computing . . . . . . . . . . . . . . . . . . . . . . . . . . . . . . . . . . . . . . . . . . . . . . . . . . . . .     544
  *Miki Hirabayashi, Syunsuke Kinoshita, Shukichi Tanaka,
  Hajime Honda, Hiroaki Kojima, and Kazuhiro Oiwa*

Quantum–Dot Cellular Automata Design for Median Filtering and
Mathematical Morphology Operations on Binary Images . . . . . . . . . . . . . .     554
  *Fotios K. Panagiotopoulos, Vassilios A. Mardiris, and
  Vassilios Chatzis*

A 3-State Asynchronous CA for the Simulation of Delay-Insensitive
Circuits . . . . . . . . . . . . . . . . . . . . . . . . . . . . . . . . . . . . . . . . . . . . . . . . . . . . . . .     565
  *Oliver Schneider and Thomas Worsch*

On Construction by Worm-Like Agents on a Self-timed Cellular
Automaton.................................................... 575
    Daichi Takata, Teijiro Isokawa, Jia Lee, Ferdinand Peper, and
    Nobuyuki Matsui

Periodicity in Quantum Cellular Automata.......................... 585
    Georgios I. Tsormpatzoglou and Ioannis G. Karafyllidis

## Codes, Pseudorandom Number Generators and Cryptography with Cellular Automata

CSHR: Selection of Cryptographically Suitable Hybrid Cellular
Automata Rule ................................................ 591
    Kaushik Chakraborty and Dipanwita Roy Chowdhury

CASTREAM:A New Stream Cipher Suitable for Both Hardware and
Software ..................................................... 601
    Sourav Das and Dipanwita Roy Chowdhury

Evolution of 2-Dimensional Cellular Automata as Pseudo-random
Number Generators ........................................... 611
    Bernard Girau and Nikolaos Vlassopoulos

Countermeasures of Side Channel Attacks on Symmetric Key Ciphers
Using Cellular Automata....................................... 623
    Sandip Karmakar and Dipanwita Roy Chowdhury

## ACA - Int. Workshop on Asynchronous CA

First Steps on Asynchronous Lattice-Gas Models with an Application
to a Swarming Rule ........................................... 633
    Olivier Bouré, Nazim Fatès, and Vincent Chevrier

Synthesis of Reversible Asynchronous Cellular Automata for Pattern
Generation with Specific Hamming Distance....................... 643
    Sukanta Das, Anindita Sarkar, and Biplab K. Sikdar

m-Asynchronous Cellular Automata .............................. 653
    Alberto Dennunzio, Enrico Formenti, Luca Manzoni, and
    Giancarlo Mauri

Cellular Automata and Random Field: Statistical Analysis of Complex
Space-Time Systems........................................... 663
    Mario Di Traglia

Limit Cycle Structure for Block-Sequential Threshold Systems ......... 672
    Henning S. Mortveit

A Study of Stochastic Noise and Asynchronism in Elementary Cellular
Automata . . . . . . . . . . . . . . . . . . . . . . . . . . . . . . . . . . . . . . . . . . . . . . . . . . . . . . . . . . . . .    679
    Fernando Silva and Luís Correia

(Intrinsically?) Universal Asynchronous CA . . . . . . . . . . . . . . . . . . . . . . . .    689
    Thomas Worsch

## C&CA - Int. Workshop on Crowds and CA

Data Collection for Modeling and Simulation: Case Study at the
University of Milan-Bicocca . . . . . . . . . . . . . . . . . . . . . . . . . . . . . . . . . . . . . . . .    699
    Mizar Luca Federici, Andrea Gorrini, Lorenza Manenti, and
    Giuseppe Vizzari

Cellular Model of Room Evacuation Based on Occupancy and
Movement Prediction . . . . . . . . . . . . . . . . . . . . . . . . . . . . . . . . . . . . . . . . . . . . . .    709
    Pavel Hrabák, Marek Bukáček, and Milan Krbálek

On Validation of the SIgMA.CA Pedestrian Dynamics Model with
Bottleneck Flow . . . . . . . . . . . . . . . . . . . . . . . . . . . . . . . . . . . . . . . . . . . . . . . . . . .    719
    Ekaterina Kirik and Tat'yana Vitova

Modeling of Walking through Pathways and a Stairway by Cellular
Automata Based on the Guideline for Evacuation . . . . . . . . . . . . . . . . . . . .    728
    Shigeyuki Koyama, Nobuhiko Shinozaki, and Shin Morishita

Cellular Automata, Agents with Mobility and GIS for Practical
Problems . . . . . . . . . . . . . . . . . . . . . . . . . . . . . . . . . . . . . . . . . . . . . . . . . . . . . . . . . .    738
    Alexander Makarenko, Anton Musienko, Anna Popova,
    Gennadiy Poveshenko, Evgeniy Samorodov, and
    Alexander Trofimenko

Evacuation Simulation from Rooms through a Pathway and a Stairway
by Cellular Automata Based on the Public Guideline . . . . . . . . . . . . . . . .    743
    Nobuhiko Shinozaki, Shigeyuki Koyama, and Shin Morishita

Follow-the-Leader Cellular Automata Based Model Directing Crowd
Movement . . . . . . . . . . . . . . . . . . . . . . . . . . . . . . . . . . . . . . . . . . . . . . . . . . . . . . . . .    752
    Christos Vihas, Ioakeim G. Georgoudas, and Georgios Ch. Sirakoulis

A Spatially Explicit Migration Model for Pike . . . . . . . . . . . . . . . . . . . . . . .    763
    Steffie Van Nieuland, Jan M. Baetens, Ine S. Pauwels,
    Bernard De Baets, Ans M. Mouton, and Peter L.M. Goethals

Proxemics in Discrete Simulation of Evacuation . . . . . . . . . . . . . . . . . . . . . .    768
    Jarosław Wąs, Robert Lubaś, and Wojciech Myśliwiec

## T&CA - Int. Workshop on Traffic and CA

Metastability in Pedestrian Evacuation .......................... 776
   Takahiro Ezaki and Daichi Yanagisawa

Modeling and Simulation of a Car Race .......................... 785
   Rolf Hoffmann and Maurice Margenstern

Construction of Cellular Automata Lattice Based on the Semantics of
an Urban Traffic Network ...................................... 795
   Vedran Ivanac, Bojana Dalbelo Bašić, and Zvonimir Vanjak

Calibration of Traffic Simulation Models Using Vehicle Travel Times.... 807
   Pavol Korcek, Lukas Sekanina, and Otto Fucik

Cellular Automata Model Properties: Representation of Saturation
Flow .......................................................... 817
   Ioanna Spyropoulou

A Traffic Cellular Automaton with Time to Collision Incorporated ..... 827
   Yohei Taniguchi and Hideyuki Suzuki

A Cellular Automata-Based Network Model for Heterogeneous Traffic:
Intersections, Turns and Their Connection ....................... 835
   Jelena Vasic and Heather J. Ruskin

## CACGI - Int. Workshop on CA of Cancer Growth and Invasion

A Metaphor of Complex Automata in Modeling Biological
Phenomena ..................................................... 845
   Rafał Wcisło and Witold Dzwinel

Author Index .................................................. 857

# Topological Perturbations and Their Effect on the Dynamics of Totalistic Cellular Automata

Jan M. Baetens* and Bernard De Baets

KERMIT, Department of Mathematical Modelling, Statistics and Bioinformatics,
Ghent University, Coupure links 653, Gent, Belgium
{jan.baetens,bernard.debaets}@ugent.be

**Abstract.** Although several studies addressed the dynamical properties of cellular automata (CAs) in general and the sensitivity to the initial condition from which they are evolved in particular, only minor attention has been paid to the interference between a CA's dynamics and its underlying topology, by which we refer to the whole of a CA's spatial entities and their interconnection. Nevertheless, some preliminary studies highlighted the importance of this issue. Henceforth, in contrast to the sensitivity to the initial conditions, which is frequently quantified by means of Lyapunov exponents, to this day no methodology is available for grasping this so-called topological sensitivity. Inspired by the concept of classical Lyapunov exponents, we elaborate on the machinery that is required to grasp the topological sensitivity of CAs, which consists of topological Lyapunov exponents and Jacobians. By relying on these concepts, the topological sensitivity of a family of 2-state irregular totalistic CAs is characterized.

## 1 Introduction

Ever since cellular automata (CAs) have been found capable of evolving striking spatio-temporal patterns in spite of their overly simple formulation, researchers in various branches of science have been desirous to comprehend their intriguing dynamics. For that purpose, several methods have been proposed during the last two decades [7,11,12,20], among which Lyapunov exponents are probably the most popular seen their successful application within the framework of continuous dynamical systems [8,9,15,16,17]. Notwithstanding several papers on Lyapunov exponents of 1-dimensional CAs stick to directional Lyapunov exponents [15], namely right and left exponents that quantify the rate with which perturbations or defects in such CAs propagate to right or left, respectively, recent studies have shown the strengths of direction-independent Lyapunov exponents [4,7]. The latter are preferred in case of higher-dimensional CAs because the directionality that is inherent to defect propagation in 1-dimensional CAs gets blurred if higher-dimensional CAs are at stake [4,5,6]. Moreover, it has been shown that an upper bound on non-directional Lyapunov exponents

---

* Corresponding author.

G.C. Sirakoulis and S. Bandini (Eds.): ACRI 2012, LNCS 7495, pp. 1–10, 2012.

can be obtained by resorting to Jacobians whose elements constitute Boolean derivatives [18], and which express the sensitivity of CAs to their inputs [5,6].

Although several papers address the sensitivity of CAs to the initial conditions from which they evolve [4,5,6,8,17], it is rather surprising to notice that only a handful of papers address the interference between a CA's dynamical properties, on the one hand, and its topology, on the other hand, since the dynamics of a CA is inherently determined by both the states of its cells and its topology, *i.e.* the way its cells are interconnected. Indeed, only a few studies touch upon this topological sensitivity in the framework of CAs [10,13,14], but these largely discard its quantification. Nonetheless, the importance of the underlying topology has long been acknowledged for closely-related dynamical systems, such as neural networks, [1] and coupled-map lattices [2].

This stimulated us to formulate so-called topological Lyapunov exponents that measure the rate by which phase space trajectories diverge following the insertion of a topological perturbation, which may be envisaged as either the breaking up of the connectivity between two neighbouring cells, or as the establishment of a connection between two not yet neighbouring cells. Parallel to the framework that has been developed for classical Lyapunov exponents, we conceive topological Jacobians and derivatives to get a grip on the origin of the numerically obtained topological Lyapunov exponent for a given CA. Finally, we resort to these constructs for quantifying the topological sensitivity of a family of 2D 2-state irregular totalistic CAs.

In Sec. 2, we elaborate on the preliminaries that are indispensable for a clear understanding of the constructs that are presented in Sec. 3, and which allow for a quantification of the topological sensitivity of CAs. These constructs are employed to assess the topological sensitivity of a family of 2D 2-state irregular totalistic CAs.

## 2 Preliminaries

As a family of 2D totalistic CAs is considered throughout the remainder of this paper, we first state its definition after which we introduce a nomenclature that is applicable to the CA family at stake. It should be emphasized that this definition deviates from the original CA paradigm by von Neumann [19] because it is not restricted to hypercube tessellations.

**Definition 1.** *(Totalistic cellular automaton)*
*A totalistic cellular automaton (CA) $\mathscr{C}$ can be represented as a quintuple*

$$\mathscr{C} = \langle \mathcal{T}, S, s, N, \Omega \rangle \, ,$$

*where*

  (i) $\mathcal{T}$ *is a countably infinite tessellation of an $n$-dimensional Euclidean space $\mathbb{R}^n$, consisting of cells $c_i$, $i \in \mathbb{N}$.*
  (ii) $S$ *is a finite set of $k$ states, here $S \subset \mathbb{N}$.*

(iii) *The output function $s : \mathcal{T} \times \mathbb{N} \to S$ yields the state value of cell $c_i$ at the $t$-th discrete time step, i.e. $s(c_i, t)$.*

(iv) *The neighborhood function $N : \mathcal{T} \to \bigcup_{p=1}^{\infty} \mathcal{T}^p$ maps every cell $c_i$ to a finite sequence $N(c_i) = (c_{i_j})_{j=1}^{|N(c_i)|}$, consisting of $|N(c_i)|$ distinct cells $c_{i_j}$.*

(v) *The transition function $\Omega : \mathbb{N} \to S$ governs the dynamics of each cell $c_i$, i.e.*

$$s(c_i, t + 1) = \Omega(\sigma_i),$$

*where $\sigma_i = \sum_{j=1}^{|N(c_i)|} s(c_{i_j}, t)$.*

In order to identify every $\Omega$ that can be formulated for a given number of states $k$ by means of an unique number, commonly referred to as a rule number, we set up a numbering convention. The rule number of a $k$-state, $\theta$-sum irregular totalistic CA, denoted $R_\theta^T$, can then be found from its base-$k$ representation, containing $\theta + 1$ digits, $z_\theta z_{\theta-1} \cdots z_2 z_1 z_0$ as

$$R_\theta^T = z_\theta k^\theta + z_{\theta-1} k^{\theta-1} + \ldots + z_2 k^2 + z_1 k^1 + z_0, \tag{1}$$

where $\theta$ is an upper bound on $\sigma_i$ such that $\Omega(\sigma_i) = \Omega(\theta)$ if $\sigma_i \geq \theta$ and $z_f \in \{0, 1, \ldots, k-1\}$ represents the state value assigned to $c_i$ at the following time step if $\sigma_i = f$. This upper bound $\theta$ is introduced to overcome the unboundedness of the sum $\sigma_i$ that naturally arises if CAs are built upon irregular tessellations of $\mathbb{R}^n$. A total of $k^{\theta+1}$ different rules can be enumerated for this family of irregular CAs. For reasons of brevity, we refer in the remainder of this paper to $k$-state, $\theta$-sum irregular totalistic CAs as $(k, \theta)$ irregular totalistic CAs.

## 3    Quantifying Topological Sensitivity

In the remainder of this section, we consider both topological Lyapunov exponents and Jacobians for 2-state totalistic CAs, for which $S = \{0, 1\}$. The former are relied upon for measuring the rate by which two phase space trajectories diverge upon the introduction of a topological perturbation, while the latter characterizes the sensitivity of $\Omega$ to the underlying topology. By restricting the scope of this paper to totalistic CAs, of which the dynamics does not depend on the ordering imposed on $N(c_i)$, a topological perturbation may be simply contemplated either as the breaking up of the connectivity between two neighbouring cells, or as the establishment of a connection between two not yet neighbouring cells. Essentially, totalistic CAs enable one to investigate the consequences of such a true topological perturbation, whereas CAs of which the dynamics depends on the ordering of its neighbouring cells, such as elementary CAs, only allow for investigating the impact of substituting one of the neighbouring cells by an other cell. Hence, since our goal is to assess the effect of a true topological perturbation on the stability of CAs, we adhere to the family of totalistic CAs throughout the remainder of this paper. It should be emphasized that the measures introduced in the remainder of this section, may equally well be used for any kind of two-state discrete dynamical system that is based upon either a tessellation or a graph, which indicates the wide applicability of the proposed constructs.

## 3.1   Topological Lyapunov Exponents

In line with the definition of classical Lyapunov exponents that express a CA's sensitivity to the initial condition from which it evolves [4,7], we can contemplate topological Lyapunov exponents that express the sensitivity of a CA to topological perturbations, and hence to its topology. By resorting to a graph representation of a totalistic CA $\mathscr{C} = \langle \mathcal{T}, S, s, N, \Omega \rangle$, which boils down to identifying $\mathcal{T}$ as the graph's vertex set $V_G$ and by setting $\{c_i, c_j\} \in D_G$ if $c_j \in N(c_i)$, where $D_G$ is the graph's edge set, such perturbations may be envisaged as either the deletion or establishment of an edge in an undirected graph $G$. As such, we can consider a CA $\mathscr{C} = \langle G, S, s, \Omega \rangle$ that is built upon the original topology embodied in $G$ and the one built upon a perturbed topology $G^*$, i.e. $\mathscr{C}^* = \langle G^*, S, s^*, \Omega \rangle$. The sensitivity of a given transition function $\Omega$ to the underlying topology can then be assessed by tracking the number of cells $c_i$ for which $s(c_i, t) \neq s^*(c_i, t)$, further referred to as defects, that emerge during the evolution $\mathscr{C}$ and $\mathscr{C}^*$. If we denote the number of defects at the $t$-th time step during the evolution of a CA as $\epsilon_t$, the maximum topological Lyapunov exponent (MTLE) of a 2-state totalistic CA can be defined as

$$\lambda_\tau = \lim_{t \to \infty} \frac{1}{t-1} \log \left( \frac{\epsilon_t}{\epsilon_1} \right). \tag{2}$$

Clearly, since $\mathscr{C}$ and $\mathscr{C}^*$ evolve from the same $s_0$, it holds that $\epsilon_0 = 0$. Yet, $\epsilon_1$ is possibly strictly positive as a topological perturbation may give rise to either zero, one or two defective cells at $t = 1$. Naturally, in every subsequent time step additional defects may be introduced by the topological perturbation, which must be tracked separately since multiple defects can cancel each other due to the utter discrete nature of the dynamical systems at stake. It should be emphasized that practical considerations restrict the assessment of $\lambda_\tau$ to finite $T$, and, likewise, to finite tessellations $\mathcal{T}^*$.

Based upon the numerically calculated $\lambda_\tau$, we have a means to identify a CA as topologically insensitive if $\epsilon_t = 0$ for all $t \geq t^*$ such that $\lambda_\tau = -\infty$, where $t^*$ represents the number of time steps constituting the CA's transient period, or as topologically sensitive if $\lambda_\tau > 0$ since a positive MTLE entails exponentially diverging phase space trajectories as a consequence of the topological perturbation. Clearly, the topological sensitivity becomes more pronounced as $\lambda_\tau$ increases. Some CAs might evolve towards $\lambda_\tau = 0$, which entails that $\epsilon_1 t^{-m} \leq \epsilon_t \leq \epsilon_1 t^m$ where $m \in \mathbb{N}$ and means that polynomial growth of the number defects will give rise to a zero MTLE as the number of time steps becomes infinitely large. In the remainder of this paper, such CAs will also be referred to as topologically insensitive.

## 3.2    Topological Jacobians

Similarly to the study of classical Lyapunov exponents of a CA $\mathscr{C}$, which relies on a statistical measure $\bar{\mu}_\alpha$ that quantifies the sensitivity of $\Omega$ to its inputs using a Jacobian matrix $J^\alpha$ of which the elements are Boolean derivatives (see Eq. (13) in [4]), we can set up topological Jacobians to encode the sensitivity of $\Omega$ to the topology upon which it is based. Therefore, let us first define the topological derivative of $\Omega$ with respect to the independent variable $c_j$ as

$$\frac{\partial \Omega\big(\tilde{s}(N(c_i),t)\big)}{\partial c_j} = \begin{cases} \Omega\big(\tilde{s}(N(c_i),t)\big) \oplus \Omega\big(\tilde{s}(N^{-j}(c_i),t)\big) \text{ , if } c_j \in N(c_i), \\ \Omega\big(\tilde{s}(N(c_i),t)\big) \oplus \Omega\big(\tilde{s}(N^{+j}(c_i),t)\big) \text{ , if } c_j \notin N(c_i), \end{cases} \quad (3)$$

where $\tilde{s}(N(c_i),t) = \big(s(c_{i_j},t)\big)_{j=1}^{|N(c_i)|}$, $N^{-j}(c_i) = N(c_i) \setminus \{c_j\}$, $N^{+j}(c_i) = N(c_i) \cup \{c_j\}$ and $\oplus$ is the addition modulo 2 operator. By restricting this paper to 2-state totalistic CA, $\frac{\partial \Omega}{\partial c_j}$ can be either one or zero, depending on whether or not the computation of $s(c_i, t+1)$ is affected by perturbing the connectivity between $c_i$ and $c_j$. It should be stressed that the formalization of topological derivatives becomes much more intricate in case of CAs for which the transition function depends on the ordering of the neighbours because a cell can then only be excluded from the neighbourhood if it is replaced by an other one. We refer the reader to [3] for more details on this issue.

Using these topological derivatives, we can construct a $|\mathcal{T}^*| \times |\mathcal{T}^*|$ topological Jacobian matrix $J^\tau$ with elements

$$J_{ij}^\tau = \frac{\partial s(c_i, t+1)}{\partial c_j}, \quad (4)$$

which can then be exploited to obtain a mean-field estimate of the proportion of connections between $c_i$ and any other $c_j \in \mathcal{T}^*$ that affects the determination of $s(c_i, t+1)$, and which is given by

$$\mu_\tau(t) = \frac{1}{|\mathcal{T}^*|} \sum_{c_i} \left( \frac{1}{|N(c_i)|} \sum_{c_j \in N(c_i)} J_{ij}^\tau + \frac{1}{|\mathcal{T}^*| - |N(c_i)|} \sum_{c_j \notin N(c_i)} J_{ij}^\tau \right). \quad (5)$$

In this equation, the first term represents the contribution from the topological connections $(c_i, c_j) \in D_G$ that alter $s(c_i, t+1)$ if broken, whereas the second term is the contribution from topological connections $(c_i, c_k)$, where $(c_i, c_k) \notin D_G$, which alter $s(c_i, t+1)$ if $c_k$ belongs to $N(c_i)$. Clearly, $\mu_\tau(t) = 1$ if and only if $J_{ij}^\tau = 1$ for all $c_i, c_j$ in $\mathcal{T}^*$, whereas $\mu_\tau(t) = 0$ can occur if and only if the determination of $s(c_i, t+1)$ is completely independent from the CA's underlying topology. In order to get an idea of $\mu_\tau(t)$ throughout a CA's evolution, we consider its geometric mean after a large number of time steps $T$

$$\bar{\mu}_\tau = \left( \prod_{t=1}^{T} \mu_\tau(t) \right)^{T^{-1}}, \quad (6)$$

which yields that higher values of $\bar{\mu}_\tau$ indicate a higher sensitivity to topological perturbations.

# 4    Topological Sensitivity of $(2, 6)$ Irregular Totalistic CA

## 4.1    Simulation Setup

In this section we consider the CAs within the family of $(2, 6)$ irregular totalistic CAs, for which $S = \{0, 1\}$. We opt to focus on this family because it allows for assessing the impact of a true topological perturbation, its set of states complies with the main presumption underlying Section 3, namely $S = \{0, 1\}$, and finally, its upper bound $\theta = 6$ is such that it does not interfere with the CAs' stability as pointed out in [4]. All together, 128 distinct rules can be listed for this CA family in accordance with the numbering convention presented in Section 2. The results presented in this section were obtained numerically for $T = 500$, since by then $\lambda_\tau$, $\bar{\mu}_\tau$ and $\bar{\mu}_\alpha$ showed convergence in the sense that an increase of the number of time steps did not significantly alter the numerically assessed values. Furthermore, periodic boundary conditions were applied in order to minimize boundary effects owing to the finiteness of $\mathcal{T}^*$, which consisted of 675 irregular cells covering a unit square, and were generated from random seeds in $[0, 1]^2$ using a Voronoi tessellation. Further, it should be stressed that the values of $\lambda_\tau$ represent averages obtained over an ensemble $E_\tau = \{_e G^* \mid e = 1, \ldots, 8\}$ of eight different topological perturbations, while $\bar{\mu}_\tau$ and $\bar{\mu}_\alpha$ are calculated from an ensemble of $E_\alpha = \{_e s_0 \mid e = 1, \ldots, 8\}$ of eight different initial conditions. Hereafter, $_e\lambda_\tau$ denotes the MTLE found for the $e$-th member of the ensemble $E_\tau$. Figure 1 depicts the exemplary Voronoi tessellation used throughout this paper, on which an exemplary initial condition is superimposed.

**Fig. 1.** Exemplary Voronoi tessellation used throughout this paper on which an exemplary initial condition is superimposed where cells with states zero and one, are coloured white and black, respectively

## 4.2   Simulation Results

In order to verify whether the numerically obtained MTLE converges to a steady value as the number of time steps upon which its assessment is based increases, Fig. 2 depicts the MTLE versus the number of time steps upon which the evaluation of Eq. (2) is based for rules 49, 65 and 83. The plots in this figure clearly illustrate that the MTLE steadily converges to a limit value as $t$ becomes increasingly large. Moreover, it shows that the limit value is approached already quite closely after not more than 200 time steps, which indicates that the convergence is not caused by saturation effects that might come into play due to the finiteness of the underlying Voronoi tessellation and the predefined number of time steps. The consistency of the MTLE over $E_\tau$'s elements is supported by the small standard deviation $\sigma_{\lambda_\tau}$ observed on $\lambda_\tau$ for all but a few totalistic rules (Fig. 3(a)). Similar observations apply to $\bar{\mu}_\tau$ (Fig. 3(b)). More pronounced $\sigma_{\lambda_\tau}$ (*i.e.* $\sigma_{\lambda_\tau} > 0.01$) are sometimes found for rules leading to $\lambda_\tau = -\infty$ for several members of the ensemble $E_\tau$.

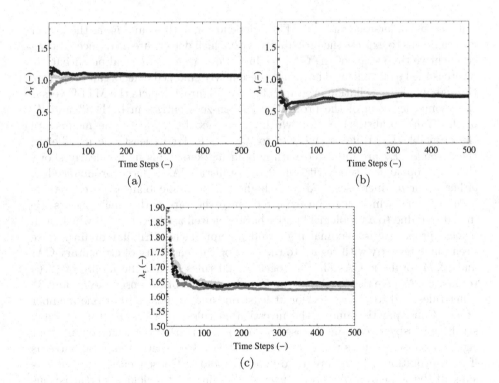

**Fig. 2.** MTLE obtained for three members of the ensemble of topological perturbations $E_\tau = \{_e s_0^* \mid e = 1, \ldots, 8\}$ versus the number of time steps for rules (a) 49, (b) 65 and (c) 83

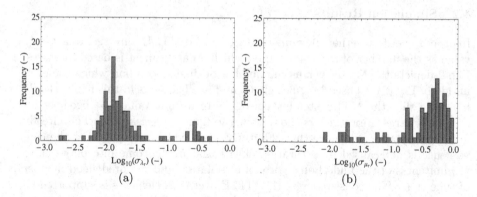

**Fig. 3.** Frequency distribution of the standard deviation (base 10 logarithm) of (a) $\lambda_\tau$ ($\sigma_{\lambda_\tau}$), and (b) $\bar{\mu}_\tau$ ($\sigma_{\bar{\mu}_\tau}$) calculated over the ensemble of topological perturbations $E_\tau = \{es_0^* \mid e = 1, \ldots, 8\}$ and an ensemble of initial conditions $E_\alpha = \{es_0 \mid e = 1, \ldots, 8\}$, respectively

It can be understood that the MTLE depends on both $\bar{\mu}_\tau$ and $\bar{\mu}_\alpha$ as the former gives a means to express the probability with which defects are introduced during consecutive time steps of the CA's evolution due to a topological perturbation, whereas the latter indicates how easy these newly emerged defects can propagate throughout the tessellation or graph at stake, Figure 4 depicts the MTLE versus the geometric mean of the proportion of non-zero entries in both $J^\alpha$ and $J^\tau$ of the $(2, 6)$ totalistic CAs for which $\lambda_\tau \neq -\infty$ for at least one member of the ensemble $E_\tau$. Rules giving rise to $\lambda_\tau = -\infty$ for at least one member of the ensemble $E_\tau$ are indicated with cuboid markers. This figure clearly shows that the topological sensitivity of $(2, 6)$ totalistic CAs is more pronounced as either $\bar{\mu}_\tau$ or $\bar{\mu}_\alpha$ increases, and $\lambda_\tau$ is highest if both Jacobian-based constructs approach one, which is to be expected since the rate with which defects are introduced due to a topological perturbation as well as the rate with which such defects propagate is maximal if $\bar{\mu}_\tau$ and $\bar{\mu}_\alpha$ approach 1. Similar findings have been made recently with regard to the topological sensitivity of elementary CAs and $(2, 7)$ totalistic CAs [3]. All together, 20 rules within the family of $(2, 6)$ totalistic CAs give rise to $_e\lambda_\tau = -\infty$ for all members of the ensemble $E_\tau$ and 31 other rules lead to $_e\lambda_\tau = -\infty$ for at least one and at most all but one member of $E_\tau$. Consequently, among the investigated rules, 77 rules are topologically sensitive irrespective of the imposed topological perturbation, which entails that significant discrepancies will arise between the evolved spatio-temporal patterns if their evolution is based upon a different topology. Consequently, our findings support the claim of earlier preliminary studies, in that topological perturbations might have a severe impact on the dynamics, and hence the stability, of CAs [3,10,13,14].

Further, this figure indicates that the majority of the depicted data points seemingly lies on a smooth trend surface such that it is to be expected that there exists an upper bound on $\lambda_\tau$ that is determined by $\bar{\mu}_\tau$ and $\bar{\mu}_\alpha$, which is in line with the existence of an upper bound on the classical Lyapunov exponent of CAs that depends on $\bar{\mu}_\alpha$ [4]. For comprehensiveness, it should be remarked that the data points which deviate from the overall trend are largely located in the region where both $\bar{\mu}_\tau$ and $\bar{\mu}_\alpha$ are relatively low, and often originate from rules that either give rise to $_e\lambda_\tau = -\infty$ for some members of the ensemble $E_\tau$ or for which the standard deviation among $_e\lambda_\tau$ is relatively high as opposed to the data points from which a trend can be inferred.

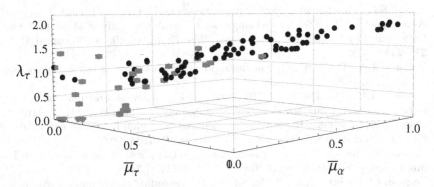

**Fig. 4.** Maximum topological Lyapunov exponent ($\lambda_\tau$) versus the geometric mean of the proportion of non-zero entries in both $J_\alpha$ ($\bar{\mu}_\alpha$) and $J_\tau$ ($\bar{\mu}_\tau$) after 500 time steps, starting from a random initial condition. Results are averages calculated over an ensemble of different topological perturbations $E_\tau = \{_eG^* \mid e = 1, \ldots, 8\}$ for $\lambda_\tau$ and over an ensemble of initial conditions $E_\alpha = \{_es_0 \mid e = 1, \ldots, 8\}$ for both $\bar{\mu}_\alpha$ and $\bar{\mu}_\tau$, and are only shown for those $(2,6)$ irregular totalistic CAs for which $\lambda_\tau \neq -\infty$ for all members of $E_\tau$ (spheres), and for rules giving rise to $\lambda_\tau = -\infty$ for at most all but one member of $E_\tau$ (cuboids)

Actually, a closer inspection of Fig. 4 reveals that there exists an ellipsoidal region in the $\bar{\mu}_\alpha \bar{\mu}_\tau$ plane, which encloses all topologically sensitive rules within the CA family at stake. Hence, only rules for which $(\bar{\mu}_\alpha, \bar{\mu}_\tau)$ are located in this region might be sensitive to topological perturbations and, as a consequence of the ellipsoidal shape of the concerned region, a lower $\bar{\mu}_\tau$ may to some extent be compensated by a higher $\bar{\mu}_\alpha$ so that the CA can still evolve diverging phase space trajectories, and vice versa.

## 5 Conclusions and Further Work

Following the formulation of Lyapunov exponents for assessing the sensitivity of CAs to the initial condition, we defined topological Lyapunov exponents for quantifying the topological sensitivity of CAs, which, to this day, deserved only minor attention notwithstanding the dynamics of a CA is explicitly determined by the interconnection between its cells. Further, these topological Lyapunov exponents were compared with a quantity expressing the sensitivity of a CA's transition function to topological perturbations. Simulations suggest that the topological Lyapunov exponent is upper bounded somehow by both this construct and a construct quantifying the sensitivity of a CA's transition function to its inputs, but further research should aim at retrieving the functional relationship defining this upper bound.

# References

1. Amari, S.I.: A method of statistical neurodynamics. Kybernetik 14, 201–215 (1974)
2. Atmanspacher, H., Filk, T., Scheingrabe, H.: Stability analysis of coupled map lattices at locally unstable fixed points. The European Physical Journal B 44, 229–239 (2005)
3. Baetens, J.M., De Baets, B.: On the topological sensitivity of cellular automata. Chaos 21, 023108 (2011)
4. Baetens, J.M., De. Baets, B.: Phenomenological study of irregular cellular automata based on Lyapunov exponents and Jacobians. Chaos 20, 033112 (2010)
5. Bagnoli, F., Rechtman, R.: Synchronization and maximum Lyapunov exponents of cellular automata. Physical Review E 59, R1307–R1310 (1999)
6. Bagnoli, F., Rechtman, R.: Thermodynamic entropy and chaos in a discrete hydrodynamical system. Physical Review E 79, 041115 (2009)
7. Bagnoli, F., Rechtman, R., Ruffo, S.: Damage spreading and Lyapunov exponents in cellular automata. Physics Letters A 172, 34–38 (1992)
8. Courbage, M., Kamiński, B.: Space-time directional Lyapunov exponents for cellular automata. Journal of Statistical Physics 124, 1499–1509 (2006)
9. Courbage, M., Kamiński, B.: On Lyapunov exponents for cellular automata. Journal of Cellular Automata 4, 159–168 (2009)
10. Fatès, N., Morvan, M.: Perturbing the Topology of the Game of Life Increases Its Robustness to Asynchrony. In: Sloot, P.M.A., Chopard, B., Hoekstra, A.G. (eds.) ACRI 2004. LNCS, vol. 3305, pp. 111–120. Springer, Heidelberg (2004)
11. Ilachinski, A.: Cellular Automata. A Discrete Universe. World Scientific, London (2001)
12. Langton, C.: Computation at the edge of chaos. Physica D 42, 12–37 (1990)
13. O'Sullivan, D.: Graph-based Cellular Automaton Models of Urban Spatial Processes. Ph.D. thesis, University of London, London, United Kingdom (2000)
14. Rouquier, J.B., Morvan, M.: Combined Effect of Topology and Synchronism Perturbation on Cellular Automata: Preliminary Results. In: Umeo, H., Morishita, S., Nishinari, K., Komatsuzaki, T., Bandini, S. (eds.) ACRI 2008. LNCS, vol. 5191, pp. 220–227. Springer, Heidelberg (2008)
15. Shereshevsky, M.: Lyapunov exponents for one-dimensional cellular automata. Journal of Nonlinear Science 2, 1–8 (1991)
16. Tisseur, P.: Cellular automata and Lyapunov exponents. Nonlinearity 13, 1547–1560 (2000)
17. Urías, J., Rechtman, R., Enciso, A.: Sensitive dependence on initial conditions for cellular automata. Chaos 7, 688–693 (1997)
18. Vichniac, G.: Boolean derivatives on cellular automata. Physica D 45, 63–74 (1990)
19. von Neumann, J.: Theory of Self-Reproducing Automata. University of Illnois Press, Urbana (1966)
20. Wolfram, S.: Universality and complexity in cellular automata. Physica D 10(1-2), 1–35 (1984)

# Counting Cycles in Reversible Cellular Automata

Sukanta Das[1], Avik Chakraborty[1], and Biplab K. Sikdar[2]

[1] Dept. of Information Technology
sukanta@it.becs.ac.in, avikjis27@gmial.com
[2] Dept. of Computer Science & Technology
Bengal Engineering & Science University, Shibpur, West Bengal, India, 711103
biplab@cs.becs.ac.in

**Abstract.** This paper reports characterization of 1-D cellular automata (CA) state space to count the cycles of reversible CA. The reachability tree provides theoretical framework to identify number of cycles in reversible CA. However, we concentrate here on a special class of reversible CA that follow *right independence* property. The right independence property implies, the cells of CA are independent of right neighbor. To our knowledge, no work till now has been done to find the number cycles of reversible CA by analyzing the CA state space.

**Keywords:** Reversible celular automata, cycle, reachability tree.

## 1 Introduction

In the early 1980s, Stephen Wolfram studied behavior of a family of 1-dimensional 3-neighborhood cellular automata (CA) that could model complex systems [6]. The CA structure was viewed as a discrete lattice of two-state per cell. This structure attracted a large section of researchers working in diverse fields and a special class of CA, called linear/additive CA, had gained the primary attention [1]. The linear/additive CA are amenable to detailed characterization through algebraic tools [1,4]. The analysis to find cycle structure is done through the algebraic tool based on primitive/irreducible polynomial. However, this framework can not support analysis of cycle structure of nonlinear CA.

This scenario motivates us to enact a theoretical framework so that the nonlinear CA behavior can also be expressed as far as possible. In this work we develop a framework based on CA state space analysis. It enables counting of cycles in a CA state space. The reachability tree, introduced in [2,3] provides the basis of this analysis. We process the reachability tree in parallel to find the number of cycles in a specific class of hybrid CA. We, however, primarily focus on a special class of CA that follow *right independence* property. We define the right independence property as the facts that the cells of CA are independent of their right neighbors. We propose an algorithm that can efficiently count the cycles of such reversible CA. To our knowledge, this work is the first target to find the cycles of nonlinear reversible CA.

G.C. Sirakoulis and S. Bandini (Eds.): ACRI 2012, LNCS 7495, pp. 11–19, 2012.
© Springer-Verlag Berlin Heidelberg 2012

The paper is organized as follows. The next section introduces the CA, relevant for our work. The reachability tree is introduced in this section. Section III provides the state space analysis of reversible CA based on the reachability tree. Section 4 reports the proposed technique for counting the cycles.

## 2   CA Preliminaries

The cellular automaton (CA) is a lattice of cells. The cells update states based on their neighbors. In the current work, we concentrate on the 3-neighborhood (self, left and right neighbors) CA, where a CA cell is having two states - 0 or 1. The next state of the $i^{th}$ cell of such a CA is,

$$S_i^{t+1} = f_i(S_{i-1}^t, S_i^t, S_{i+1}^t) \tag{1}$$

where $f_i$ is the next state function; $S_{i-1}^t$, $S_i^t$ and $S_{i+1}^t$ are the present states of left neighbor, self and right neighbor of the $i^{th}$ cell. $S^t(S_1^t, S_2^t, \cdots, S_n^t)$ is the present state of an $n$-cell CA and its next state is

$$S^{t+1} = (f_1(S_0^t, S_1^t, S_2^t), f_2(S_1^t, S_2^t, S_3^t), \cdots, f_n(S_{n-1}^t, S_n^t, S_{n+1}^t)) \tag{2}$$

For the null boundary CA $S_0^t = S_{n+1}^t = 0$ (null). In this work we concentrate only on null boundary CA.

The next state function $f_i$ of $i^{th}$ CA cell can be expressed in the form of a truth table (Table 1). The decimal equivalent of the 8 outputs is called 'Rule' $R_i$ [5]. In a two-state 3-neighborhood CA, there can be a total of $2^8$ (256) rules. Three rules namely 60, 195, and 102 are illustrated in Table 1. The first row of the table lists the possible $2^3$ (8) combinations of the present states of $(i-1)^{th}$, $i^{th}$ and $(i+1)^{th}$ cells at time t. Each combination is also referred to as RMT (rule mean term). The last three rows indicate the next states of $i^{th}$ cell at (t + 1) for different combinations of the present states of its neighbors. The column 011 in Table 1 is the $3^{rd}$ RMT; the next states corresponding to this RMT are 1 for Rule 60 , and 0 for Rule 195 and 102. Out of 256, only 14 rules are linear/additive rules.

The set of rules $\mathcal{R} = \langle \mathcal{R}_1, \mathcal{R}_2, \cdots, \mathcal{R}_i, \cdots, \mathcal{R}_n \rangle$ configure the cells of a CA. If $\mathcal{R}_1 = \mathcal{R}_2 = \cdots = \mathcal{R}_n$, the CA is a **uniform** CA, otherwise it is **non-uniform** or **hybrid** CA. If all the $\mathcal{R}_i$s $(i = 1, 2, \cdots, n)$ are linear/additive, the CA is referred to as **Linear/Additive** CA, otherwise the CA is a **Nonlinear** one.

**Table 1.** Truth table for rule 60, 195 and 102

| Present state : | 111 | 110 | 101 | 100 | 011 | 010 | 001 | 000 | Rule |
|---|---|---|---|---|---|---|---|---|---|
| (RMT) | (7) | (6) | (5) | (4) | (3) | (2) | (1) | (0) | |
| (i) Next State : | 0 | 0 | 1 | 1 | 1 | 1 | 0 | 0 | 60 |
| (ii) Next State : | 1 | 1 | 0 | 0 | 0 | 0 | 1 | 1 | 195 |
| (iii) Next State : | 0 | 1 | 1 | 0 | 0 | 1 | 1 | 0 | 102 |

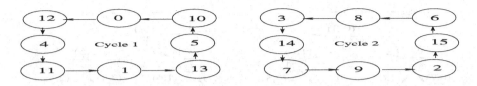

**Fig. 1.** Cyclic states of a reversible CA $\langle 195, 60, 195, 60 \rangle$

The sequence of states generated (transitions), during its evolution, directs the CA behavior.

The state transition diagram (Fig.1) of a CA may contain *cyclic* and *non-cyclic* states (a state is called *cyclic* if it lies in a cycle; the states of Fig.1). In a reversible CA, each CA state repeats after certain number of time steps (Fig.1). That is, each state of a reversible CA has exactly one predecessor as well as have a single successor [2].

**Reachability Tree:** The Reachability Tree (RT) is introduced in [2,3] to characterize the CA states. It is a binary tree. Each node of the tree is constructed with *RMT(s)* of a rule. The left and right edges are called 0-edge and 1-edge. 0-edge represents the *RMT(s)* that produce 0 and 1-edge is for *RMT(s)* producing 1. For an $n$-cell CA, the number of levels in *RT* is $(n+1)$. The root node is at Level 0 and the leaves are at Level $n$. The number of leaf nodes in the RT denotes the number of reachable states of the CA. A sequence of edges from the root to a leaf, representing an $n$-bit binary string, is a reachable state, where 0-edge and 1-edge denote 0 and 1 respectively.

Fig.2 is the *RT* for the CA $\langle 102, 102, 102, 102 \rangle$. Its state transition diagram is in Fig.3. The decimal numbers within a node in Fig.2 at Level $i$ represent the RMTs of the CA rule $R_{i+1}$ following which the cell $(i+1)$ may change its state. The root node has only 4 valid RMTs for a null boundary CA. It is constructed with RMTs 0, 1, 2 and 3 as cell 1 can change its state following any one of those RMTs. The state of left neighbor of cell 1 is always 0, therefore, RMTs 4, 5, 6 and 7 are don't cares for cell 1. Now RMT 0 and RMT 3 follow the 0-edge as cell 1 changes its state following 011 or 000 RMTs (Table 1). On the other hand, RMT 1 and 2, follow the 1-edge. Therefore, at Level 1, the 0-edge of level 0 connects a node with RMTs 0, 1, 6 & 7 and 1-edge to a node with RMTs 2, 3, 4 & 5 [2,3]. All other nodes of the *RT* follow the same logic.

For an $n$-cell reversible CA, there are $2^n$ leaves in the *RT*. For null boundary, at leaf level there can be only four possible even RMTs (RMT 0, 2, 4 and 6).

In a reversible CA, each state must have only one predecessor and one successor. The set of RMTs corresponding to a path from the root to leaf points to the immediate predecessor state. That is, if $f(f_1(), f_2(), ...f_n())$ is a function representing a mapping from the set of possible states of an $n-$ cell CA to itself and $f_i()$ performs a mapping from the set of all possible RMTs to a binary value such that

$$S^{t+1} = f(f_1(S_0^t, S_1^t, S_2^t), f_2(S_1^t, S_2^t, S_3^t), \cdots, f_n(S_{n-1}^t, S_n^t, S_{n+1}^t)) \tag{3}$$

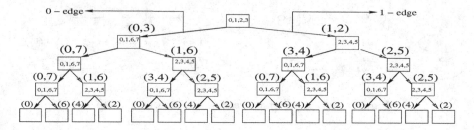

**Fig. 2.** Reachability Tree of a 4-cell uniform CA with *Rule−102*

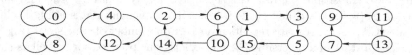

**Fig. 3.** State transitions of a reversible CA $\langle 102, 102, 102, 102 \rangle$

then $\mathcal{S}^t$ represent the path from the root to a leaf which is pointed by the path represented by the set of $RMT$ corresponding to $\mathcal{S}^{t+1}$. Now, if a path in the reachability tree denotes the Next state $\mathcal{S}^{t+1}$, then the path should consist of RMT sequence as $\langle RMT'_1, RMT'_2, RMT'_3, \cdots, RMT'_n \rangle$ from root to the leaf, representing the present state $\mathcal{S}^t$. For example in Fig.2, the state (0111) ($7_{10}$) consist of the RMT sequence $\langle 3, 6, 5, 2 \rangle$ -that is, the neighborhood configuration for the cells are $\langle 011, 110, 101, 010 \rangle$ that represent the state (1101) ($13_{10}$) which is the predecessor to the state $7_{10}$ (Fig.3).

The above considerations are the basis of our current state-space-analysis methodologies.

## 3   State Space Analysis

To find the number of cycles in a CA, we figure out the group of states that belongs to the same cycle (Fig.4). Finally we keep a single state for each cycle. By counting those single states, one can get the number of cycles of the reversible CA.

Let us consider the CA of Fig.1 ($\langle 195, 60, 195, 60 \rangle$). Processing of state space of the CA is shown in Fig.4. Here, 0 is the predecessor of state 12. That is 0 and 12 belong to the same cycle. To summarize we remove either state (i.e the RMTs) 0 or 12. In Fig.4(a) 12 is removed. This is to reduce the problem through selection of a single representative for each group -that is, for each cycle. The number of such representatives gives the cycle count. In Fig.4, the number of such representative is two (0 and 2) (Fig.4(c))

Hence, to keep a single representative for a cycle, we *merge* the CA states. Reachability tree helps to perform such operations.

## 3.1   Identification of Representative of a Cycle

We define merging to find the predecessor of a state. In Fig.5, it can be noticed that the state represented by $\langle i'\ j'\ k'\ l' \rangle$ is the predecessor of state represented by the set of $RMTs \langle i\ j\ k\ l \rangle$. However, if we wipe out a state, all the links related to that state are vanished. For example if we delete state 12 (Fig.1), then to get the state 4 from state 0 is difficult. The solution is we have to replace RMTs to represent the state 12 so that in further processing we could replace the state 4 keeping the state 0 as representative of cycle 1 (Fig.4(a)). That is, after removal of state 12, it should appear in the state space that state 4 is the predecessor of state 0. So, the representative state (state 0) of a cycle forms a single length cycle in the processed state space. Therefore, the terminating condition of the processing is, all the states form single length cycle in the processed state space. Following property dictates the condition of forming single length cycles.

**Property 1:** A rule can contribute in formation of single length cycle if at least one of the RMTs 0, 1, 4, and 5 is 0, or the RMTs 2, 3, 6, and 7 is 1.

We say an RMT follows Property 1, if its value is equal with the middle bit of the 3-bit RMT. That is, if a cell is configured with the RMT, the cell does not change its state.

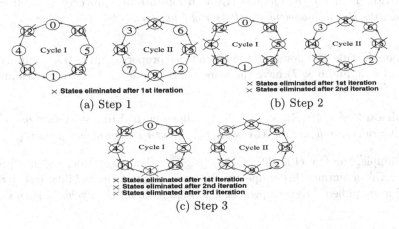

(a) Step 1

(b) Step 2

(c) Step 3

**Fig. 4.** Elimination of states of a CA $\langle 195, 60, 195, 60 \rangle$

## 3.2   Processing Reachability Tree to Analyze the State Space of CA

A reachability tree gives a vivid description of all the reachable states. In a reversible CA, all the states have their own predecessor as well as the successor. On the other hand, in the $RT$ a particular path from the root to the leaf defines a state that can be reached from a given initial state ($S$). If we process a tree in such a way that we can predict a successor or predecessor of a state (i.e a path from the root node to the leaf), then we can retain the corresponding path of the

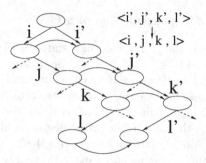

**Fig. 5.** Tree merging

state and discard all the paths pertaining to the successor or predecessor states. Now, we can get a tree can be formed having paths that are the representative of a particular cycle. If the number of remaining leaf nodes are counted, it can give the number of cycles. However, for some CA, it becomes difficult to maintain the proper intermediate tree structure. The complexity depends on the property of CA rule. In this work, we target a special class of CA that follow the *right independence* property.

**Definition 1** *A rule* $(\mathcal{R}_i)$ *follows* **right independence** *property, if a cell, configured with* $\mathcal{R}_i$, *is independent of its right neighbor while the cell changes its state.*

For example, rule 60 follows right independence property. RMTs 0 & 1 (similarly, 2 & 3, 4 & 5, and 6 & 7) have the same value (Table 1). Few such rules are 0, 15, 51, 195, 204, etc.

**Definition 2** *A CA* $(\langle \mathcal{R}_1, \mathcal{R}_2, \cdots, \mathcal{R}_n \rangle)$ *follows* **right independence** *property, if all the rules, configure the CA cells, follow right independence property.*

For example, the CA $\langle 195, 60, 195, 60 \rangle$ (Fig.1) follow right independence property. If CA maintain this property, the processing of reachability tree (state space) is simplified. We next present a scheme to count the cycles of such CA.

## 4    Cycle Counting Algorithm

The proposed algorithm constructs the reachability tree, and then processes the tree by replacing RMTs on edges. By such replacement, we actually modify the values of RMTs. This action in effect eliminates some states from cycles (Fig.4). The replacement of an RMT (on an edge at level $i$) depends on two factors – whether the RMT (say $r$) maintains Property 1, and how the RMT on some edge at level $i - 1$ that derives $r$, is merged on some edge at level $i - 1$.

While we start processing of the tree, we mark all the nodes as 'ACTIVE'. However, during processing some nodes may become 'INACTIVE', which are not further processed. The terminating condition of the algorithm is, whether all the RMTs of ACTIVE nodes follow Property 1. It can be summarized as following:

We say a reachability tree has reached its final position if the RMTs 0, 1, 4, and 5, and RMTs 2, 3, 6, and 7, of all ACTIVE nodes are on 0-edge and 1-edge respectively.

Before formally describing the algorithm, we present following example which illustrates the tree processing.

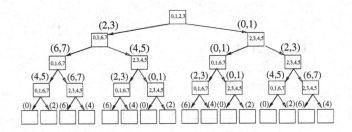

**Fig. 6.** Reachability Tree with Rule $\langle 195, 60, 195, 60 \rangle$

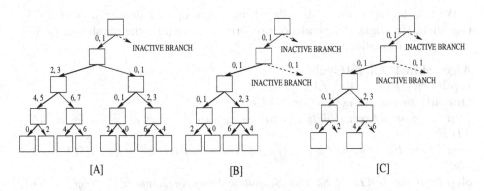

**Fig. 7.** Steps of tree merging for the CA $\langle 195, 60, 195, 60 \rangle$

Let us take the CA $\langle 195, 60, 195, 60 \rangle$. The $RT$ of the CA is in Fig. 6. From the root node (at level 0), we get two sets namely $S_0^0 = \{2, 3\}$ and $S_1^0 = \{0, 1\}$. Here, the $S_0^0$ ($S_1^0$) contains the RMTs that are 0 (1) for rule 195 (the first cell rule). The RMTs of both the sets do not follow Property 1. So, the RMTs of set $S_0^0$ is replaced by that of $S_1^0$, and we set the node, coming from set $S_0^0$ at level 1, as INACTIVE (dotted node at level 1 of Fig. 8). The nodes, coming from that INACTIVE node, also become INACTIVE. Now, we make a link from edge associated with $S_0^0$ to that of $S_1^0$ to indicate merging (Fig. 8). For the only ACTIVE node at level 1, we define two sets – $S_0^1 = \{6, 7\}$ and $S_1^1 = \{4, 5\}$. The RMTs of these two sets do not maintain Property 1. So we exchange $S_0^{1A}$ with $S_1^{1B}$, and $S_1^{1A}$ with $S_0^{1B}$, where $S_0^{1A}$ and $S_0^{1B}$ ($S_1^{1B}$ and $S_1^{1B}$) are the sets coming from node A and node B at level 1 respectively (Fig. 8). The edge incident to node A is merged with edge that of node B. After the processing, we get a tree like Fig. 7[A], where we get rid off half of the RT, as one node at level 1 is INACTIVE. In Fig. 7[B], we further get rid off $\frac{1}{4}$ of the RT. In Fig. 7[C], we get the processed RT which follows the termination condition. Fig. 7[C] also indicates that the CA ($\langle 195, 60, 195, 60 \rangle$) contains only two cycles.

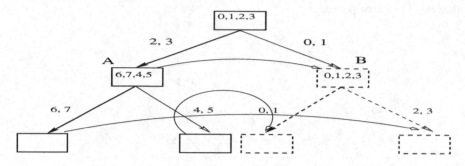

**Fig. 8.** Root merging

We next formally present the algorithm. The proposed algorithm takes a CA that maintains right independence property, and outputs the number of cycles of the given reversible CA.

**Algorithm 1. CountCycle**
**Input:** $\langle \mathcal{R}_1, \mathcal{R}_2, \cdots, \mathcal{R}_n \rangle$ *(An n-cell CA)*
**Output:** *Number of cycles if reversible.*
Step 1: *Construct reachability tree for the given CA. Mark all the nodes ac AC-TIVE.*
Step 2: *For the root, find $S_0^0 = \{i : RMT\ i \in 0\text{-}edge\}$, $S_1^0 = \{i : RMT\ i \in 1\text{-}edge\}$*
Step 3: *If the RMTs of $S_0^0$ and $S_1^0$ follow Property 1, mark the edge as 'self merged'.*

*Otherwise, exchange contents of the sets, and make a link from 0-edge to 1-edge of the root.*
Step 4: *For $i = 2$ to $n$, repeat Step 5 to Step 7*
Step 5: *Suppose there is link from node A to node B at level $i - 1$. Then find*
$S_0^{iA} = \{k : RMT\ k$ *is on 0-edge of node A*$\}$
$S_1^{iA} = \{k : RMT\ k$ *is on 1-edge of node A*$\}$
$S_0^{iB} = \{k : RMT\ k$ *is on 0-edge of node B*$\}$
$S_1^{iB} = \{k : RMT\ k$ *is on 1-edge of node B*$\}$
Step 6: *If the RMTs of $S_0^{iA}$ and $S_1^{iA}$ (or, $S_0^{iB}$ and $S_1^{iB}$) do not simultaneously follow or deny Property 1, report the CA as irreversible.*
Step 7: *If the RMTs of $S_0^{iA}$ and $S_0^{iB}$ follow (or deny) Property 1, then*
$S_0^{iA} \leftarrow S_0^{iB},\ S_1^{iA} \leftarrow S_1^{iB}$
*Else $S_0^{iA} \leftarrow S_1^{iB},\ S_1^{iA} \leftarrow S_0^{iB}$*
*Mark the node derived from $S_0^{iB}$ and $S_1^{iB}$ as INACTIVE.*

Step 8: *If the processed tree does not follow the termination condition, then goto Step 2.*
Step 9: *Count the ACTIVE leaves to report the number of cycles of reversible CA.*

Algorithm 1 assumes that the given CA is reversible. However, the algorithm is capable enough to report irreversibility of the given CA, if it is so.

## 5   Conclusion

This paper has reported an analysis of state space to get the number of cycles of reversible CA that follow the right independence property. We have utilized the reachability tree in the analysis. The proposed algorithm can slightly be modified to count the number of cycles (attractors) of an irreversible CA (that maintains right independence property). This work is an initiation of the finding of cycle structure of nonlinear CA. Our next target is to find the cycle structure of reversible CA that do not even follow the right independence property.

## References

1. Pal Chaudhuri, P., Roy Chowdhury, D., Nandi, S., Chatterjee, S.: Additive Cellular Automata – Theory and Applications, vol. 1. IEEE Computer Society Press, California (1997) ISBN 0-8186-7717-1
2. Das, S.: Theory and Applications of Nonlinear Cellular Automata In VLSI Design. PhD thesis, Bengal Engineering And Science University, Shibpur, West Bengal, India 711103 (2006)
3. Das, S., Sikdar, B.K.: Classification of *CA* Rules Targeting Synthesis of Reversible Cellular Automata. In: El Yacoubi, S., Chopard, B., Bandini, S. (eds.) ACRI 2006. LNCS, vol. 4173, pp. 68–77. Springer, Heidelberg (2006)
4. Ganguly, N.: Cellular Automata Evolution: Theory and Applications in Pattern Recognition and Classification. PhD thesis, Bengal Engineering College (a Deemed University), India (2004)
5. Wolfram, S.: Statistical mechanics of cellular automata. Rev. Mod. Phys. 55(3), 601–644 (1983)
6. Wolfram, S.: Universality and complexity in cellular automata. Physica D 10, 1–35 (1984)

# Propagative Mode in a Lattice-Grain CA: Time Evolution and Timestep Synchronization

Dominique Désérable

INSA – Institut National des Sciences Appliquées,
Laboratoire de Génie Civil & Génie Mécanique,
20 Avenue des Buttes de Coësmes, 35043 Rennes, France
deserable@insa-rennes.fr
http://www.insa-rennes.fr

**Abstract.** The void propagation defines a long-range interaction in granular matter. We detail a logic scheme simulating the propagation and implemented in a $2d$ cellular automata applied to granular flow. The CA belongs to the family of "lattice-grain" automata (LGrA) with one particle per cell. We focus first on the influence of inertia, or "memory effect", on the flow patterns. The propagative mode is presented afterwards: it implies that transition and timestep must be considered at two different time scales. Although a CA is usually driven by local, nearest-neighbor communications, it follows here that the timestep termination must be detected at each transition, that involves a perpetual and global communication within the network to synchronize the timestep. An all-to-all "systolic gossiping" underlies the framework of this void propagation model.

**Keywords:** lattice-grain (cellular) automata (LGrA), void propagation, memory effect, time evolution, timestep synchronization, systolic gossiping.

## 1 Introduction

Cellular automata may capture the essence of physical phenomena resulting from elementary factors and make a suitable and powerful tool to catch the influence of the microscopic scale onto the macroscopic behavior of complex systems [1]. Known as "lattice-gas" (cellular) automata (LGA) in hydrodynamics, they are an extreme simplification of molecular dynamics and have been widely developed over the last forty years. Concerning granular media, there was a number of attempts which in turn make a relative simplification of granular dynamics and which are often known as "lattice-grain" (cellular) automata (LGrA); they have yielded some interesting results especially for hopper flows, flows around obstacles, segregation or stratification phenomena during free surface multiphase flows or the formation of density waves in channel flows [2,3,4,5,6,7,8]. A state of the art for lattice-grain models is given in [9] with references therein.

We focus here on a specific feature of our LGrA [10,11] concerning its capability of handling long-range interactions resulting from the phenomenon of void

G.C. Sirakoulis and S. Bandini (Eds.): ACRI 2012, LNCS 7495, pp. 20–31, 2012.
© Springer-Verlag Berlin Heidelberg 2012

propagation in a granular assembly. The time evolution is governed by a "request-exchange" synchronous mode which simulates a two-stage interaction-advection process. The transition rule follows a simple logic including three physical components: an external field, a set of kinematical exclusion rules and an inertial effect. Our model is inspired by the first discrete, analytic model of Litwiniszyn-Müllins [12,13] dealing with granular flow under gravity and including a "memory" effect of inertia.

Section 2 recalls our LGrA logic that defines how the time evolution is driven by the local interaction law acting on the hexavalent lattice. The inertial, memory effect is illustrated through a case study in Section 3. Section 4 describes the logic of the propagative mode acting on the void. After a short reference to the works upon the intensive communication protocols in coarse-grain and fine-grain massively parallel architectures, Section 5 explains how the timestep synchronization scheme induced by the long-range propagative logic is carried out by means of a perpetual "systolic gossiping". We conclude in Section 6 by asking the question of the consistency of our model with the physical time as an open problem.

## 2  LGrA Logic

### 2.1  Topology and Local Interaction Law

The LGrA is constructed on the 6-*valent* grid. This 2*d* topology offers the greatest number of symmetries for a regular lattice: herein it maximizes the number of *degrees of freedom* (or directions) for a displacement as well as the upper bound of the *coordination number* (the number of contacts of a particle with its vicinity). The concise notation "$\nu$df" ($0 \leq \nu \leq 6$) will be used for a law with $\nu$ degrees of freedom. Each site is connected to its six nearest neighbors denoted $NE, N, NW, SW, S, SE$. The order $N_s$ stands for the number of sites of the network. Since the graph is regular with degree 6, the number of links connecting a pair of adjacent sites is clearly $3N_s$.

The *space occupancy* principle allows one and only one particle per site, whether it is a solid, liquid or gaseous one, the term "particle" being a purely formal denotation. Multiphase flows are considered, where a phase $\phi_i$, indexed in the set $N_\phi = \{1, 2, \ldots, n_\phi\}$ for a system of $n_\phi$ phases, denotes a set of particles provided with identical properties.

The *interaction-advection* process is performed by a two-stage transition according to an original "request-exchange" mechanism. In the *request* stage, each cell autonomously performs a computation composed of a precalculation followed by a random choice. The result is a *potential* direction of displacement which becomes the direction of request. In the *exchange* stage, a test is performed for each link of the network in order to detect whether an agreement has been reached between the potential directions yielded by both adjacent sites (*interaction*). In this case, a cell-to-cell exchange is performed (*advection*).

The behavior of a *phase* in a multiphase system is defined by three "physical" components: an external field, a set of exclusion rules and an inertial effect. It should be pointed out that it is not so much the autonomous behavior law of a given phase that must be taken into account but the *interaction* law with its local neighborhood: a phase component is meaningful, only when embedded into the interaction law.

## 2.2   Time Evolution Equations and Transition Rule

A set $K = (0, 1, 2, 3, 4, 5)$ is assigned to the six directions $NE, N, NW, SW, S, SE$. For a given timestep, a cell contains a particle of phase $\phi_i$ ($i \in N_\phi$) characterized by the three following components:

– the action of an *external field*, depicted by a "$\nu$df" law with a 6–fold vector

$$W_i = (w_i^{(k)})_{k \in K} \tag{1}$$

where weights $w_i^{(k)}$ are non-negative integers and $\nu$ is the number of positive weights.

– the action of *exclusion rules*, precluding some direction or other depending on the state of the local vicinity and acting according to a *mode* from which the exclusion will be applied before (*pre*-exclusion) or after (*post*-exclusion) the request. This action is depicted by the 6–fold binary vector

$$\tilde{\mathcal{E}}_i = (\tilde{\varepsilon}_i^{(k)})_{k \in K} : \quad \tilde{\varepsilon}_i^{(k)} = r_i \, \varepsilon_i^{(k)} + (1 - r_i) \tag{2}$$

where $\varepsilon_i^{(k)} = 0$ (or 1) whenever the site in direction $k$ is excluded (or not) and $r_i = 1$ (resp. 0) for a pre (resp. post) mode assigned to the phase. In the sequel, a pre-exclusion will always be assumed, that simplifies (2) into

$$\mathcal{E}_i = (\varepsilon_i^{(k)})_{k \in K} . \tag{3}$$

– the action of *inertia*, or "memory" effect, depicted by the 6–fold vector

$$\mathcal{M}_i = (\mu_i^{(k)})_{k \in K} \tag{4}$$

where $\mu_i^{(k)} = c_i$ if $k$ was the displacement direction at the previous timestep and $\mu_i^{(k)} = 1$ otherwise. Coefficient $c_i$ takes on positive integer values and $c_i = 1$ means no inertia for the phase.

Prior to computing a request, a precalculation yields the corrected distribution

$$W_i^* = (w_i^{*(k)})_{k \in K} : \quad w_i^{*(k)} = \mu_i^{(k)} \, \varepsilon_i^{(k)} \, w_i^{(k)} \tag{5}$$

and the probability of sending a request in direction $k$ is then given by

$$p_i^{*(k)} = \frac{w_i^{*(k)}}{\sum_K w_i^{*(k)}} \tag{6}$$

on condition that the sum of the corrected distribution be positive ($p_i^{*(k)} = 0$ otherwise). Direction $k$ is selected at random by a pseudorandom sequence generated from a user-defined seed.

Let $(p_j^{*(k)})_{k \in K}$ be now the distribution of probabilities of the neighboring particle of phase $\phi_j$ in direction $k$ and let $X_k$ be the representative event of a displacement in direction $k$ for the current particle. The probability of this event is finally

$$P(X_k) = p_i^{*(k)} p_j^{*(k+3 \bmod 6)} \tag{7}$$

according to the exchange protocol.

For brevity's sake, the reader is referred to [10,11] for a more detailed description of our LGrA logic.

## 3   Inertia and Memory Effect

Modeling inertia consists in saving the *memory* of the particle's displacement direction at the previous timestep, to reintroduce it with a user-defined weight into the new weighted distribution for the current timestep. An *inertial* coefficient $c_i$, which takes on a positive integer value, is assigned to each phase $\phi_i$ and $c_i = 1$ means no inertial effect for this phase.

### 3.1   A Case Study

The memory effect will be illustrated through a simple granular system simulating a silo emptying process. A silo is a container provided with an outlet through which bulk grain falls down. A two-phase system $N_\phi = \{1, 2\}$ is considered, where $\phi_1$ denotes the "grain" phase and $\phi_2$ the "void" phase. Let us recall the set $K = (0, 1, 2, 3, 4, 5)$ assigned to the six directions $NE, N, NW, SW, S, SE$. Regarding the gravity axis, we adopt two scenarios:

- a "2df–2df" law (shortly denoted "2df") with $W_1 = (1, 0, 0, 0, 0, 1)$, $W_2 = (0, 0, 1, 1, 0, 0)$ where the pattern $NE$–$SE$ means "downwards", the sense of the main axis being $W \rightarrow E$;
- a "3df–3df" law (shortly denoted "3df") with $W_1 = (0, 0, 0, 1, 1, 1)$, $W_2 = (1, 1, 1, 0, 0, 0)$ where the pattern $SW$–$S$–$SE$ means "downwards", the sense of the main axis being $N \rightarrow S$.

A "frontal" exclusion rule $R_1$ is assigned to $\phi_1$ and $\phi_2$: this rule prohibits two particles with the same phase to exchange. That is, neither a grain-grain nor a void-void exchange may occur.

The size of the container is defined by its height $H = 101$, its width $L = 57$, giving a volume $V_0$ of 5707 or 5729 cells, respectively for the "2df" or the "3df" law; the negligible deviation (of 0.4%) results from a side-effect of the lattice. The container is flat-bottomed and has no hopper, namely, its shape is rectangular. The outlet, centered in the bottom, has a diameter $D = 7$ cells. The cells in the outlet play a special role of "source" cells generating a void when a grain exits. The instantaneous "flow rate" is defined as the number of exiting grains (or generated voids) per timestep. Initially, the silo is fully filled with grains. The "porosity", in this context, is defined from the ratio void/grain, namely zero at initial state. A qualitative observation of the flow is made easier by zoning the material into horizontal colored layers.

## 3.2   Influence of Inertia on Flow Patterns

Figure 1 highlights the action of inertia for the "2df" law under rule $R_1$ after $T = 600$ timesteps. In (a), no inertia is applied and a "funnel flow" is observed where the upper layers fall down first. In (b), an inertial coefficient $c_2 = 10$ is applied to the void phase and a "mass flow" is observed with a strong dissymmetry in the emptying process. The dissimilarity between both patterns results only from two distinct values assigned to the seed of the pseudorandom sequence, that reveals here a sensitive dependence on initial conditions. A hopper-shaped pattern between two shear bands separates the dynamic flow from a static "dead zone", with an angle of stability of 60° induced by the "2df" law. Moreover, the chaotic free surface is induced by the flow above the outlet, which periodically alternate from one shear band to the other. This kind of flow pattern was experimentally observed [14]. A *propagative* effect acting on the voids upgoing from the outlet appears on both sides of the hopper, though with an abnormally high porosity.

The action of inertia for the "3df" law is displayed in Fig. 2 at state $T = 1000$. In (a), no inertia is applied and a (last-in first-out) "funnel flow" is again observed but with a reduction of the funnel's depth. In (b-c), an inertial coefficient

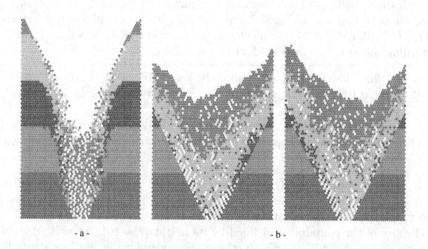

- a -                                      - b -

**Fig. 1.** "2df" law with rule $R_1$ governing $\phi_1$ and $\phi_2$. States at $T = 600$ (a) without inertial action (b) with inertial coefficients $c_1 = 1$ and $c_2 = 10$ and two distinct values of the seed of the pseudorandom sequence

$c_2 = 10$ is applied to the void and a (first-in first-out) "mass flow" is again observed but with a non-chaotic behavior and only weak instabilities appearing on the free surface. A hopper-shaped pattern between two shear bands still separates the dynamic flow from a static dead zone, but with an angle of stability of $30°$ induced by the "3df" law. As a consequence, the void phase is distributed throughout the entire bulk, possibly with a porosity ratio higher than the normal average, compared with which could be experimentally observed. Besides, while a same value $c_1 = c_2$ is assigned to the grain phase in (b), no significant behavioral discrepancy can be observed. Therefore, it should be pointed out that the impact of a "memory" assigned to the void is significant whereas a "memory" assigned to the grain is irrelevant in a dense packing.

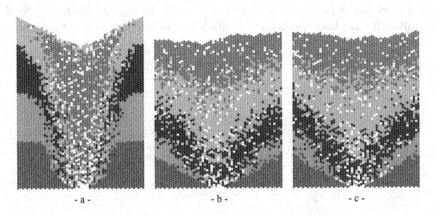

- a -     - b -     - c -

**Fig. 2.** "3df" law with rule $R_1$ governing $\phi_1$ and $\phi_2$. States at $T = 1000$ (a) without inertial action (b) with inertial coefficients $c_1 = c_2 = 10$ (c) with $c_1 = 1$, $c_2 = 10$.

From the above observations, it may be asked what *physical* meaning could be attributed to the artifact giving inertia to the *void*. Whenever a high value is assigned to the "memory" of the void phase, this tends to induce, when the void moves in a dense packing, an "indraught" to the particle located in the active direction. During a sequence of transitions, this void will move a row of grains one at a time but in the same direction. Although the row only moves at a rate of one particle per timestep, a sort of effect of void *propagation* may occur. Let us recall that a phase component is meaningful, only when embedded into the *interaction* law.

## 4   Modeling a Propagative Mode

### 4.1   Limitation of the Transition Rule

In spite of the above remark, the transition rule as detailed in Sect. 2.2 is unable to move two contiguous grains when one sends a request to the site of the other.

To illustrate this deficiency, let us consider the scenario in Fig. 3 (for simplicity, an isolated system is assumed). At state $t$ of a one-dimensional system, $m + 1$ solid particles lie in sites denoted here $x$, $x - 1$, ..., $x - m$ while a void lies in site $x + 1$. A downward request is sent by sites $x$, $x - 1$, ..., $x - m$ while an upward request is sent by site $x + 1$. An exchange $x \leftrightarrow x + 1$ is then activated while the $m$ grains above stay at rest. So a void has been inserted in site $x$, for state $t + 1$, although all grains above have emitted a downward request (case (a)). This elementary transition rule does not allow the void to *propagate* and the grains to tumble down *simultaneously* (as in case (b)).

The question of propagating the void (or more generally the fluid phase) implies that the transition rule be reconsidered. This problem has been dealt with for automata models applied to gravity flows, but the sequential nature of the approach which processes particles from bottom to top violates the principle of simultaneity and Galilean invariance [3]. The solution proposed hereafter leads to a strictly *synchronous* algorithm.

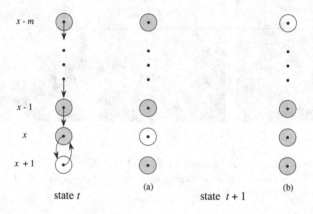

**Fig. 3.** State $t$: isolated $1d$-system of $m + 1$ solid particles in sites $x$, $x - 1$, ..., $x - m$ acting under gravity; one void in site $x+1$. State $t+1$: (a) Elementary (non-propagative) mode: void in site $x$. (b) Propagative mode: void in site $x - m$.

## 4.2   Time Evolution: Transition and Timestep

Including a propagative mode leads us to consider transition and timestep at two different scales. In Fig. 3, case (a) represents the outcome of one transition but no longer a state $t + 1$, and case (b) the outcome of $m + 1$ transitions at state $t + 1$ which defines the new timestep. The transition will be said to be *instantaneous* within this timestep.

A first problem is to set up a criterion to stop this transitional sequence, namely a criterion of *termination* for the current timestep. The "physical" principle we adopt is as follows:

- a *grain* is allowed to move at the most one time during a timestep,
- a *void* stayed at rest during a transition remains locked until completion of the current timestep.

It follows that the cell should contain an "activity" signal, to be *disabled* when locking a grain or a void in one of both situations. It is easy to show that this process terminates because the medium is of finite size. Moreover, according to rule $R_1$, a void will stop upon reaching the free surface. Consequently, after a finite number of transitions, the scene will no longer contain any active void. Therefore, since only grain-void exchanges are allowed from $R_1$, that ensures the end of the current timestep.

A second problem that now arises is to *detect* the termination, a global state which should be perceived at the local scale, namely at the cell level. The detection algorithm runs as follows: at each transition, each cell *broadcasts* over the whole network the binary signal "I have an active void" (true for an active void, false otherwise); conversely, each cell will detect the timestep completion whenever the predicate "There exists one active void!" becomes false; at this time, all the cells will *enable* their activity signal synchronously and initiate the next timestep.

Let us note that this synchronization problem differs from the Myhill-Moore Firing Squad [15,16] because we have no General.

## 5    Timestep Synchronization

### 5.1    Systolic Gossiping

The previous action consisting in broadcasting a message from any cell to any other one follows an all-to-all *gossiping* scheme [17]. It should be observed that, in general, gossiping is a more consuming task, in space and time, than broadcasting. For example, given a message of length $L$ and a network of order $N$, broadcasting requires a buffer of size $L$ whereas gossiping may require a buffer of size $NL$. But the coarse-grained communications protocols are seldom appropriate for cellular automata. For this reason, further investigations were derived under a "systolic" form (this metaphor was borrowed from H.T. Kung [18]). For fine-grained systolic gossiping, we can refer in particular to [19] and references therein.

For our specific case, this task is much easier to achieve, and this for two reasons: the first one is due to the symmetries of the graph, the second because our buffer is far from exploding. Recall first that our LGrA is constructed on the hexavalent grid, that provides a maximal symmetry for a $2d$ lattice. More precisely, the underlying graph belongs to the family of so-called "rotational" Cayley graphs [20,21] and it is shown therein that this nice property leads to effective gossip schemes. It is beyond the scope of this paper to describe them. Let us just say that there exists a half-duplex 3-port systolic protocol that gossips through the $N$–$SW$–$SE$ pattern in a time bounded by $\sqrt{N_s}$ steps [22]. For the second reason, let us assume the cell having a 1-bit buffer. When receiving the 3-fold signal "There exists one active void!" from its $N$–$SW$–$SE$ neighbors, it can immediately reduce it by an "OR" operation. Therefore, a 1-bit buffer suffices to achieve the timestep termination detection.

## 5.2   The Case Study Revisited

Figure 4 resumes the study of the emptying process with the "3df" law and the same inertial coefficients of Fig. 2c for two different timesteps at $T = 400$ and $T = 1000$ (observe for this state the identical snapshots of Fig. 2c and Fig. 4a). The propagative mode is applied in Fig. 4b. A decrease of porosity appears in this second case as well as the corresponding ebb of the free surface level.

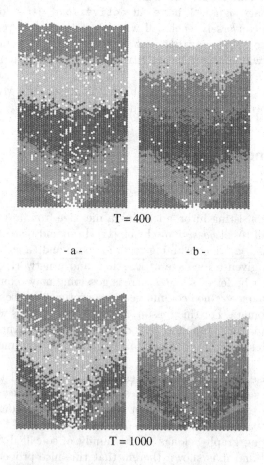

T = 400

- a -                              - b -

T = 1000

**Fig. 4.** The "3df" law with rule $R_1$ governing $\phi_1$ and $\phi_2$ and inertial coefficients $c_1 = 1$, $c_2 = 10$. States at $T = 400$ and $T = 1000$ (a) without propagative law (b) with propagative law.

Since the snapshots are captured at the end of the timestep, it might seem surprising that all the voids did not reach the free surface. Indeed, if we consider a single void isolated in the bulk, the action of $R_1$ on both phases implies that a grain-void exchange must occur within the transition and therefore that the void moves up surely. However, it should be pointed out that the grain's site requested by the void is likely to be locked. This means that the void would be about to cross the path of another void that has already spread to the upper layers. Disabling the grain's site caused a lack of response and consequently the retention of the void, which stays at rest. This phenomenon explains how the state of non-zero porosity observed during the silo's emptying process follows from the definition of the criterion of propagation.

**Table 1.** Impact of the propagative mode on the flow process

| | | | | | |
|---|---|---|---|---|---|
| $3df$   $H = 101$   $L = 57$   $V_0 = 5729$   $V_0^* = 5391$   $D = 7$ | | | | | |

| | Mode | | | | Ratios |
|---|---|---|---|---|---|
| | Non propagative | | Propagative | | |
| Timestep | $T = 400$ | $T = 1000$ | $T = 400$ | $T = 1000$ | |
| Voids: $N_v$ | 326 | 240 | 72 | 48 | |
| Grains: $N_g$ | 4848 | 3528 | 4620 | 2994 | |
| Flow rate $Q$:<br>$\frac{N_g(t)-N_g(t+\Delta t)}{\Delta t}$ | $Q = 2.20$ | | $Q' = 2.71$ | | $Q'/Q = 1.23$ |
| Void index:<br>$e = \frac{N_v}{N_g}$ | $e = 0.0676$ | | $e' = 0.0158$ | | $e'/e = 0.235$ |
| Porosity:<br>$\phi = \frac{e}{1+e}$ | $\phi = 0.0633$ | | $\phi' = 0.0156$ | | $\phi'/\phi = 0.246$ |
| Relaxation time:<br>$\Delta t_r = \frac{\phi V_0}{Q}$ | $\Delta t_r = 165$ | | $\Delta t_r' = 33$ | | $\frac{\Delta t_r'}{\Delta t_r} = 0.2$ |
| Discharge time:<br>$\Delta t_v = \frac{V_0^*}{Q}$ | $\Delta t_v = 2451$ | | $\Delta t_v' = 1990$ | | $\frac{\Delta t_v'}{\Delta t_v} = \frac{Q}{Q'} = 0.81$ |
| Free surface ebb:<br>$U = \frac{H(t+\Delta t)-H(t)}{\Delta t}$ | $U = -0.0411$ | | $U' = -0.0482$ | | $U'/U = 1.17$ |
| Void mean speed:<br>$u = \frac{H}{\Delta t_r}$ | $u = 0.6121$ | | $u' = 3.075$ | | $u'/u = 5.02$ |

The impact of the propagative mode on the flow process in Fig. 4 is analyzed in Tab. 1. $V_0^*$ denotes the dynamical volume of a "hopper" induced by the $3df$ law and out of which a granular dead zone of $V_0 - V_0^* = 338$ cells will stay at rest on both sides of the outlet in the bottom corners of the container. The flow rate remains constant on average from the beginning to the end of the emptying process. As soon as the outlet is opened, the process enters a transient state during a relaxation time before the porosity reaches a maximal threshold and until the first voids emerge from the free surface. Then the process enters a steady state and the descent of the free surface is activated with constant velocity until completion of a mass flow discharge; note that the "mass flow" pattern is only a consequence of inertial coefficient $c_2$. The ratios of the macroscopic quantities between propagative and non propagative modes are given, respectively for flow rate, void index, porosity, relaxation and total discharge times, velocity of the descent of the free surface and vertical mean speed of the void.

# 6    Conclusion

This paper dealt with the various logical problems induced by the simulation of the physical phenomenon of void propagation in a lattice-grain automata, illustrated with a case study of a silo emptying process. After a short presentation of the transition rule underlying the time evolution in our LGrA, the logic of an inertial memory effect was tackled as well as its influence on the diversity of resulting flow patterns. This background introduced the core of this study: from a simple "physical" criterion governing the void propagation within the medium, a logical framework is proposed to solve the successive problems of synchronization and intensive communications yielded in the cellular automata by this long-range interaction.

Further issues should be pursued. Firstly, the question of "memory effect" must be tackled from its generic sense and in the context of other alternative memory mechanisms [23]. We let also open the question of consistency of our model with the physical time: the time evolution is the main point and, of course, our physical criterion of termination of the void propagation within a row of grains, the perception of the instantaneous transition as well as the transition-timestep duality should be discussed. More precisely, the property of our model regarding Galilean invariance will be examined elsewhere and Lamport's paradigm [24] between logical clocks and real-time clocks in a distributed system appears as an appropriate startpoint. Besides, a more detailed explanation about the physical results in Tab. 1 will be examined elsewhere [25].

# References

1. Chopard, B., Droz, M.: Cellular automata modeling of physical systems. Cambridge University Press, Cambridge (1998)
2. Baxter, G.W., Behringer, R.P.: Cellular automata models of granular flow. Phys. Rev. A 42, 1017–1020 (1990)
3. Fitt, A.D., Wilmott, P.: Cellular-automaton model for segregation of two-species granular flow. Phys. Rev. A 45(4), 2383–2388 (1992)
4. Peng, G., Herrmann, H.J.: Density waves of granular flow in a pipe using lattice-gas automata. Phys. Rev. E 49, R1796–1799 (1994)
5. Károlyi, A., Kertész, J., Havlin, S., Makse, H.A., Stanley, H.E.: Filling a silo with a mixture of grains: friction-induced segregation. Europhys. Lett. 44(3), 386–392 (1998)

6. Ktitarev, D.V., Wolf, D.E.: Stratification of granular matter in a rotating drum: cellular automaton modelling. Granular Matter 1, 141–144 (1998)
7. Désérable, D., Masson, S., Martinez, J.: Influence of exclusion rules on flow patterns in a lattice-grain model. In: Kishino, Y. (ed.) Powders and Grains 2001, Balkema, pp. 421–424 (2001)
8. Cisar, S.E., Ottino, J.M., Lueptow, R.M.: Geometric effects of mixing in 2D granular tumblers using discrete models. AIChE Journal 53(5), 1151–1158 (2007)
9. Désérable, D., Dupont, P., Hellou, M., Kamali-Bernard, S.: Cellular automata in complex matter. Complex Systems 20(1), 67–91 (2011)
10. Désérable, D.: A versatile two-dimensional cellular automata network for granular flow. SIAM J. Applied Math. 62(4), 1414–1436 (2002)
11. Cottenceau, G., Désérable, D.: Open Environment for $2d$ Lattice-Grain CA. In: Bandini, S., Manzoni, S., Umeo, H., Vizzari, G. (eds.) ACRI 2010. LNCS, vol. 6350, pp. 12–23. Springer, Heidelberg (2010)
12. Litwiniszyn, J.: Application of the equation of stochastic processes to mechanics of loose bodies. Archivuum Mechaniki Stosowanej 8(4), 393–411 (1956)
13. Müllins, W.W.: Stochastic theory of particle flow under gravity. J. Appl. Phys. 43, 665–678 (1972)
14. Sakaguchi, H., Ozaki, E., Igarashi, T.: Plugging of the flow of granular materials during the discharge from a silo. Int. J. Mod. Phys. 7(9,10), 1949–1963 (1993)
15. Moore, E.F.: The firing squad synchronization problem. In: Moore, E.F. (ed.) Sequential Machines, Selected Papers, pp. 213–214. Addison-Wesley, Reading (1964)
16. Umeo, H.: Firing squad synchronization problem in cellular automata. Encyclopedia of Complexity and Systems Science, 3537–3574 (2009)
17. Liestman, A.L., Richards, D.: Perpetual gossiping. Parallel Processing Letters 3(4), 347–355 (1993)
18. Kung, H.T., Leiserson, C.E.: Systolic arrays for VLSI. In: Mead, Conway (eds.) Introduction to VLSI systems, pp. 271–292. Addison-Wesley, Reading (1980)
19. Flammini, M., Pérennes, S.: Lower bounds on systolic gossip. Information and Computation 196(2), 71–94 (2005)
20. Désérable, D.: A family of Cayley graphs on the hexavalent grid. Discrete Applied Math. 93, 169–189 (1999)
21. Heydemann, M.C., Marlin, N., Pérennes, S.: Complete rotations in Cayley graphs. European Journal of Combinatorics 22(2), 179–196 (2001)
22. Désérable, D.: Systolic dissemination in the arrowhead (unpublished)
23. Alonso-Sanz, R., Martin, M.: Elementary cellular automata with memory. Complex Systems 14(2), 99–126 (2003)
24. Lamport, L.: Time, clocks, and the ordering of events in a distributed system. Comm. ACM 21(7), 558–565 (1978)
25. Désérable, D., Lominé, F., Dupont, P., Hellou, M.: Propagative mode in a lattice-grain CA: time evolution and Galilean invariance (to be submitted to) Granular Matter

# Limit Cycle for Composited Cellar Automata

Toshikazu Ishida[1] and Shuichi Inokuchi[2]

[1] Center for Fundamental Education, Kyushu Sangyo University,
Fukuoka, 813-8503, Japan
`tishida@ip.kyusan-u.ac.jp`
[2] Faculty of Mathematics, Kyushu University, Fukuoka, 819-0395, Japan
`inokuchi@math.kyushu-u.ac.jp`

**Abstract.** We know that a few uniform cellular automata have maximum cycle lengths. However, there are many uniform cellular automata, and checking the cycles of all uniform cellular automata is impractical. In this paper, we define a cellular automaton by composition and show how its cycles are related.

## 1 Introduction

The study of cellular automata was initiated by von Neumann in the 1940s[6]. Cellular automata have cells on a lattice, and the states of their cells (configuration) are determined by a transition function that references the states of neighboring cells in the previous time step. When all cells evolve according to the same local transition function, the cellular automaton is called a uniform cellular automaton, otherwise, it is called a hybrid cellular automaton. Cellular automata have been developed by many researchers as computational models for simulating physical systems. For example, cellular automata with maximum cycle length have been used to make pseudo-random pattern generators [1]. By defining the transition function and cell size of uniform cellular automata well enough, cellular automata can be made to have long cycle lengths[11]. Moreover, the necessary and sufficient conditions for having a maximum cycle length have been shown for a hybrid cellular automata[2], and methods for finding it have been devised by Tezuka and Fushimi[8]. For uniform cellular automata, Matsumoto showed that five uniform cellular automata have a maximum cycle length[5]. However, there are many uniform cellular automata, and comparatively little is known about their maximum cycle lengths because checking the lengths of all of them would take so long.

Cellular automata have been defined on groups[3][7][12]. For instance, we introduced cellular automata on groups in [4]. A configuration is defined as being a function from the group into the set of states. Thus, a configuration is a way of attaching a state to each element of the group. There is a natural action of the group on the set of configurations, which is called the shift action. A cellular automaton is thus a self-mapping of the set of configurations defined from a system of local transition functions commuting with the shift.

G.C. Sirakoulis and S. Bandini (Eds.): ACRI 2012, LNCS 7495, pp. 32–41, 2012.

In this paper, we define a cellular automaton that is made from a composition of two cellular automata, and show how it is related to its composing automata. In fact, for two cellular automata $CA_1, CA_2$ with global transition functions $F_1, F_2$, we can define a composited cellular automaton $CA$ that has a global transition function $F = F_1 \circ F_2$. Moreover, we show how $CA_1$, $CA_2$ and $CA$ are associated.

## 2   Cellular Automata and Composited Cellular Automata

In this section, we shall review the definitions of cellular automata and compositions[4].

**Definition 1.** *Let $G$ be a group. A cellular automaton on $G$ is a triple $CA = (G, V, V')$, in which $V \subset G$ and $V' \subset 2^V$ are finite subsets of $G$. For $V'$, we define a function $f : 2^V \to \{\phi, \{e\}\}$ by*

$$f(A) = \begin{cases} \phi & (A \notin V') \\ \{e\} & (A \in V') \end{cases}$$

*and for all $X \in 2^G$ and a function $F : 2^G \to 2^G$ by $F(X) = \bigcup_{g \in G} gf(g^{-1}X \cap V)$.*

*We call $f$ a local transition function and $F$ a global transition function.*

The set $2^G$ is called the set of *configurations*.
  Now let us define the operation $+$.

**Definition 2.** *For $X, Y \in 2^G$ and $A \in 2^V$, we define*

- $\phi + \phi = \phi$ , $\phi + \{e\} = \{e\} + \phi = \{e\}$ , $\{e\} + \{e\} = \phi$
- $X + Y = \bigcup_{g \in G} g((g^{-1}X \cap \{e\}) + (g^{-1}Y \cap \{e\}))$.

The following lemma holds for the operation $+$.

**Lemma 1.** *Let $X, Y, Z$ be elements of $2^G$.*

1.  $X + X = \phi$,
2.  $X + Y = Y + X$,
3.  $(X + Y) \cap Z = Z \cap (X + Y) = (X \cap Z) \cup (Y \cap Z)$,
4.  $\forall g \in G, g(X + Y) = gX + gY$.

Now let us define the composition of cellular automata.

**Definition 3.** *For cellular automata $CA_1 = (G, V_1, V_1')$ and $CA_2 = (G, V_2, V_2')$ on $G$, the cellular automaton $CA_1 \Diamond CA_2 = (G, V_1 \cdot V_2, V_1' \Diamond V_2')$ is defined by*

- $V_1 \cdot V_2 = \{v_1 v_2 \in G | v_1 \in V_1, v_2 \in V_2\}$
- $V_1' \Diamond V_2' = \{X \in 2^{V_1 \cdot V_2} | \{v \in V_1 | v^{-1}X \cap V_2 \in V_2'\} \in V_1'\}$

For $CA_1 \Diamond CA_2$, the following theorem hold [4].

**Theorem 1.** *For global transition functions $F_{CA_1}, F_{CA_2}, F_{CA_1 \Diamond CA_2}$,*

$$F_{CA_1} \circ F_{CA_2} = F_{CA_1 \Diamond CA_2}.$$

In the following, $CA_1 \Diamond CA_2$ is called a composited cellular automaton.

**Definition 4.** *Let $C$ be a subset of $2^G$ and $F$ be a global transition function of a cellular automaton on $G$. We define $F^\infty(C)$ by*

$$F^\infty(C) := \{c \in C | \exists n > 0 \ \ c = F^n(c)\}.$$

*We call $c \in F^\infty(C)$ an element of the limit cycle (LC) of $F$.*

**Definition 5.** *The local transition function $f$ of a cellular automaton $CA = (G, V, V')$ is linear, if $f(A + B) = f(A) + f(B)$ for all $A, B \in 2^V$. So is $CA$. For the local transition function $f$ of $CA$ and $A \in 2^V$, if there exists a linear local transition function $q$ satisfying $f(A) = q(A) + \{e\}$, then $f$ is affine. So is $CA$.*

**Lemma 2.** *For all $X, Y \in 2^G$, if a cellular automaton $CA = (G, V, V')$ is linear, then $F(X + Y) = F(X) + F(Y)$.*

**Theorem 2.** *Let $f_1, f_2$ be local transition functions of $CA_1 = (G, V_1, V_1')$ and $CA_2 = (G, V_2, V_2')$. If $f_1, f_2$ are linear, then the local transition function $f_1 \diamond f_2$ of $CA_1 \diamond CA_2$ is linear.*

**Definition 6.** *If no cellular automaton $CA_2 = (G, V_2, V_2')$ satisfying $F_{CA_1} = F_{CA_2}$ and $V_2 \subsetneq V_1$ exists, then $CA_1 = (G, V_1, V_1')$ is called the minimum cellular automaton.*

**Definition 7.** *For a cellular automaton $CA = (G, V, V')$, we define the cellular automaton $CA_m = (G, V_m, V_m')$ by*

- $V_m = \{v \in V | \{v\} \in V'\}$,
- $V_m' = \{A \subset V_m | A \in V'\}$.

**Lemma 3.** *For all $X \in 2^G$, if a cellular automaton $CA = (G, V, V')$ is linear, then*

$$X \cap V_m \in V_m' \Longleftrightarrow X \cap V \in V'.$$

**Corollary 1.** *If a cellular automaton $CA = (G, V, V')$ is linear, then $F_{CA} = F_{CA_m}$. Hence, $CA \cong CA_m$.*

**Lemma 4.** *If a cellular automaton $CA = (G, V, V')$ is linear, then the cellular automaton $CA_m$ is a minimum.*

**Definition 8.** *For a linear cellular automaton $CA = (G, V, V')$, we can form $CA_m = (G, V_m, V'_m)$. If $\sharp V_m$ is even, then $CA$ is called even linear. If $\sharp V_m$ is odd, then $CA$ is called odd linear. We assume the local transition function $f$ of an affine cellular automaton $CA = (G, V, V')$ satisfies $f(A) = q(A) + \{e\}$ $(\forall A \in 2^V)$ for the local transition function $q$ of a linear cellular automaton $CA'$. If $CA'$ is even linear, then $CA$ is called even affine. Moreover, if $CA'$ is odd linear, then $CA$ is called odd affine.*

# 3   Commutativity Condition of Compositions

In this section, we discuss commutativity of transition functions. B. Voorhees proved that the set of all local transition functions commuting with given local transition functions is obtained by solving nonlinear Diophantine equations [9]. We state propositions for composited cellular automata and the commutativity conditions for linear and affine cellular automata.

First, we shall consider linear cellular automata. Two simple linear cellular automata commute as follows.

**Proposition 1.** *For cellular automata $CA_1 = (G, V_1, V_1')$ and $CA_2 = (G, V_2, V_2')$, the following hold.*

- *If $V_1' = \emptyset$ and $\emptyset \notin V_2'$, then $CA_1 \diamond CA_2 = CA_2 \diamond CA_1$.*
- *If $\sharp V_1 = 1$ and $V_1' = \{V_1\}$, then $CA_1 \diamond CA_2 = CA_2 \diamond CA_1$ for all $CA_2$.*

**Lemma 5.** *Let $CA = (G, V, V')$ be a minimum linear cellular automaton. For $A \subset V$,*
$$A \in V' \iff \sharp A \text{ is odd.}$$

Using this lemma, we can prove the following theorem.

**Theorem 3.** *Let $CA_1 = (G, V_1, V_1')$ and $CA_2 = (G, V_2, V_2')$ be minimum linear cellular automata. If $G$ is commutative for the composition, $CA_1 \diamond CA_2 = CA_2 \diamond CA_1$.*

Now let us consider affine cellular automata. Affine cellular automata are not linear.

**Lemma 6.** *For all $A \in 2^V$, we define $\overline{A} = \bigcup_{v \in V} v((v^{-1}A \cap \{e\}) + \{e\})$.*

1. *If $CA$ is even linear, then $f(\overline{A}) = f(A)$.*
2. *If $CA$ is odd linear, then $\overline{f(A)} = f(\overline{A})$.*

Let $F_1$ and $F_2$ be global transition functions of even linear and odd linear cellular automata, respectively. We define $\overline{X} = \bigcup_{g \in G} g((g^{-1}X \cap \{e\}) + \{e\})$. From this lemma and the definition of the global transition function, $F_1(\overline{X}) = F_1(X)$ and $\overline{F_2(X)} = F_2(\overline{X})$.

In the following, we define a cellular automaton $CA_{rev}$ by $CA_{rev} = (G, V, V'), V = \{e\}, V' = \{\phi\}$. This cellular automaton corresponds to $\overline{@}$.

**Lemma 7.** *Let $CA_{even}$ be even linear, and let $CA_{odd}$ be odd linear. Then the following hold.*

- *$CA_{even} \diamond CA_{rev} \cong CA_{even}$,*
- *$CA_{odd} \diamond CA_{rev} \cong CA_{rev} \diamond CA_{odd}$.*

*Proof.* For $X \in 2^G$,

1.

$$\overline{F(X)} = \bigcup_{g \in G} gf\overline{(g^{-1}(X) \cap V)}$$

$$= \bigcup_{g \in G} gf(g^{-1}(X) \cap V)$$

$$= F(X).$$

2.

$$\overline{F(X)} = \bigcup_{g \in G} g\overline{f(g^{-1}(X) \cap V)}$$

$$= \bigcup_{g \in G} gf\overline{(g^{-1}(X) \cap V)}$$

$$= F(\overline{X}).$$

□

**Lemma 8.** *If* $CA_{rev} \diamond CA_2 \cong CA_2 \diamond CA_{rev}$ *and* $CA_1 \diamond CA_2 \cong CA_2 \diamond CA_1$, *then* $CA_1 \diamond CA_{rev} \diamond CA_2 \cong CA_2 \diamond CA_1 \diamond CA_{rev}$.

The above leads us to the following theorem.

**Theorem 4.** *Let* $CA_1, CA_2$ *be even affine cellular automata. Then* $CA_1 \diamond CA_2 \cong CA_2 \diamond CA_1$.

*Proof.* Let $F_1, F_2$ be global transition functions of $CA_1$ $CA_2$. Then there are global transition functions $F_1', F_2'$ of even linear cellular automata such that $F_1 = \overline{F_1'}$ and $F_2 = \overline{F_2'}$. For all $X \in 2^G$,

$$F_1 F_2(X) = \overline{F_1' \overline{F_2'(X)}} = \overline{F_1' F_2'(X)} = \overline{F_2' F_1'(X)} = \overline{F_2' \overline{F_1'(X)}} = F_2 F_1(X).$$ □

**Theorem 5.** *Let cellular automata* $CA_1, CA_2$ *be odd affine and let a cellular automaton* $CA_3$ *be odd linear. Then* $CA_1 \diamond CA_2 \cong CA_2 \diamond CA_1$ *and* $CA_1 \diamond CA_3 \cong CA_3 \diamond CA_1$.

**Corollary 2.** *For* $CA_1 = (G, V_1, V_1') A C A_2 = (G, V_2, V_2')$, *if* $V_1' = 2^{V_1}$ *and* $V_2 \in V_2'$, $CA_1 \diamond CA_2 = CA_2 \diamond CA_1$.

## 4  Cycles of Composited Cellular Automata

In this section, we discuss the circumstances under which a limit cycle (LC) exists and the cycles for composited cellular automata.

In the following, we assume cellular automata compositions are commutative. Let $CA = (G, V, V')$ be a composited cellular automaton of $CA_1 = (G, V_1, V_1')$ and $CA_2 = (G, V_2, V_2')$. Thus $CA$ satisfies $CA = CA_1 \diamond CA_2 = CA_2 \diamond CA_1$ and the global transition function $F$ is defined as $F = F_1 \circ F_2 = F_2 \circ F_1$.

**Lemma 9.** *Following hold.*

- $F(C) \subseteq F_1(C)$,
- $F(C) \subseteq F_2(C)$.

$c \in C - F(C)$ is called a configuration of the Garden of Eden (GOE). This lemma show $C - F_1(C) \cup C - F(C) \subseteq C - F(C)$. Therefore if $c \in C$ is a configuration of GOE of $F_1$ or $F_2$, then $c$ is a configuration of GOE of $F$.

**Lemma 10.** *For the set of configurations of LC, the following lemma holds.*

1. $F_1^\infty(C) \cap F_2^\infty(C) \subset F^\infty(C)$,
2. $F^\infty(C) \subset F_1^\infty(C) \cup F_2^\infty(C)$.

*Proof.*
(1)    Let $c$ be a configuration of $F_1^\infty(C) \cap F_2^\infty(C)$. Then there exist $n_1, n_2 > 0$ that satisfy $c = F_1^{n_1}(c) = F_2^{n_2}(c)$. Thus, $F^{n_1 \times n_2}(c) = (F_1 \circ F_2)^{n_1 \times n_2}(c) = F_1^{n_1 \times n_2}(F_2^{n_1 \times n_2}(c)) = c$ by $F_1 \circ F_2 = F_2 \circ F_1$. Therefore, $c \in F^\infty(C)$.
(2)    Let $c$ be a configuration of $F^\infty(C)$. Then, there exists $n > 0$ that satisfies $c = F^n(c)$. Hence there exists an integer $m$ that satisfies $n \times m > \sharp C$. Therefore $c = F^{n \times m}(c) = F_1^{n \times m}(F_2^{n \times m}(c))(= F_2^{n \times m}(F_1^{n \times m}(c)))$ and $c \in F_1^\infty(C)(c \in F_2^\infty(C))$. (For $t > \sharp C$ and $\forall c \in C, F^n(c) \in F^\infty(C)$.)    □

This lemma means that if $c \in C$ is a configuration of LC of $F_1$ and LC of $F_2$, then $c$ is a configuration of LC of $F$.

From the commutativity of compositions, the following lemma holds.

**Lemma 11.**    1. *If $c \in F_1^\infty(C)$, then $F_2(c) \in F_1^\infty(C)$.*
2. *If $c \in F^\infty(C)$, then $F_1(c) \in F^\infty(C)$.*

**Corollary 3.**

$$(C - F_1^\infty(C)) \cap (C - F_2^\infty(C)) \subseteq (C - F^\infty(C)).$$

If the configuration $c$ is not an element of the set of configurations LC of $F_1$ or $F_2$, then this corollary guarantees that $c$ is not an element of LC of $F$.

Let us discuss the cycles of each transition function of cellular automata and composited cellular automaton.

**Lemma 12.** *For any $c \in C$, if there exists integers $n_1, n_2 > 0$ satisfying $c = F_1^{n_1}(c) = F_2^{n_2}(c)$, then $c = F^{LCM(n_1, n_2)}(c)$.*

In the following, we define $c \in F_1^\infty(C) \cap F_2^\infty(C)$, $C_1 = \{F_1^t(c) | t \geq 0\}$, $C_2 = \{F_2^t(c) | t \geq 0\}$, $\sharp C_1 = n_1$, $\sharp C_2 = n_2$, $\sharp(C_1 \cap C_2) = m$.

**Lemma 13.** *$m | n_1$ and $m | n_2$ hold.*

*Proof.* We will show the proof of $m | n_1$. Assume $m \nmid n_1$. Let the integer $t$ be $t = min\{t' > 0 | F_1^{t'}(c) \in C_2\}$. Then, $c \in C_2, F_1^t(c) \in C_2$ and $F_1^{t'}(c) \notin C_2$ for $1 < t' < t$. Thus, $F_1^s(c) \in C_2$ and there exist $s > 0, s' > 0$ that satisfy $F_1^{s+s'}(c) \in C_2 \wedge F_1^{s+t'}(c) \notin C_2$ $(1 \geq t' < s') \wedge t \neq s'$. Let $c = (F_2^k F_1^s)(c)$ for any integer $k$.

1. If $t > s'$,

$$C_2 \not\ni F_1^{s'}(c)$$
$$= F_1^{s'}(F_2^k F_1^s)(c)$$
$$= F_2^k(F_1^{s+s'}(c)).$$

By $F_1^{s+s'}(c) \in C_2$, this runs counter to our assumption.
2. We can apply the same method as above to $t < s'$.

Therefore, $m|n_1$.  □

**Corollary 4.** *We have* $F_1^{\frac{n_1}{m}}(C_2) = C_2$ *and* $F_2^{\frac{n_2}{m}}(C_1) = C_1$.

- *For* $0 < t < \frac{n_1}{m}$, $F_1^t(C_2) \neq C_2$.
- *For* $0 < t < \frac{n_2}{m}$, $F_1^t(C_1) \neq C_1$.

**Theorem 6.** *If* $C_1 \cap C_2 = \{c\}$, *then*

$$\min\{t|t > 0, c = F^t(c)\} = LCM(n_1, n_2).$$

*Proof.* The fact $c = F^{LCM(n_1,n_2)}(c)$ is well defined. $C_1 \cap C_2 = \{c\}$ implies that $C_1 \neq F_2^t(C_1)$ for $t > 0$ satisfying $n_1|t$. Thus, $c \neq F^t(c)$ $(1 \leq t < LCM(n_1, n_2))$. Therefore, $\min\{t > 0|c = F^t(c)\} = LCM(n_1, n_2)$.  □

**Theorem 7.** *Let* $m$ *be* $\sharp(C_1 \cap C_2) = m > 1$ *and let* $t$ *be* $t = \min\{t' > 0|F_1^{\frac{n_1}{m}}(c) = F_2^{\frac{n_2}{m}t'}(c)\}$.

$$\min\{i|F^i(c) = c\} = LCM(\frac{n_1 + n_2 t}{m}, n_2) \times \frac{n_1}{(n_1 + n_2 t)}.$$

*Proof.* By $F^{\frac{n_1}{m}}(c) = F_2^{\frac{n_1}{m}}(F_1^{\frac{n_1}{m}}(c)) = F_2^{\frac{n_1+n_2t}{m}}(c)$,

$$= F^{LCM(\frac{n_1+n_2t}{m},n_2) \times \frac{n_1}{(n_1+n_2t)}}(c)$$
$$= F^{LCM(\frac{n_1+n_2t}{m},n_2) \times \frac{m}{n_1+n_2t} \times \frac{n_1}{m}}(c)$$
$$= F_2^{LCM(\frac{n_1+n_2t}{m},n_2)}(c)$$
$$= c.$$

We assume there exists $k$ satisfying $F^k(c) = c$ and $0 < k < LCM(\frac{n_1+n_2t}{m}, n_2) \times \frac{n_1}{(n_1+n_2t)}$. By corollary 4, $k$ is a multiple of $\frac{n_1}{m}$. Let $k$ be $k = \frac{n_1}{m}h$.

$$c = F^{\frac{n_1}{m}h} = F_2^{\frac{n_1+n_2t}{m}h}(c).$$

Thus $\frac{n_1+n_2t}{m}h$ must be a multiple of $n_2$. We have $LCM(\frac{n_1+n_2t}{m}, n_2) < \frac{n_1+n_2t}{m}h$. Thus $LCM(\frac{n_1+n_2t}{m}, n_2) \times \frac{n_1}{(n_1+n_2t)} < \frac{n_1}{m}h = k$. Then this is in conflict with the assumption. Therefore $\min\{i|F^i(c) = c\} = LCM(\frac{n_1+n_2t}{m}, n_2) \times \frac{n_1}{(n_1+n_2t)}$.  □

**Corollary 5.** *Let* $\sharp C_1 = \sharp C_2 = n$ *and* $\sharp(C_1 \cap C_2) = m > 1$. *Then let* $t = \min\{t' > 0|F_1^{\frac{n}{m}}(c) = F_2^{\frac{n}{m}t'}(c)\}$.

$$\min\{i > 0|F^i(c) = c\} = \frac{n}{m} \times \frac{LCM(m, t+1)}{t+1}.$$

## 5   Examples of Composited Cellular Automata

In this section, we present examples of compositions of one-dimensional two-state cellular automata that have periodic boundary conditions. We express the local transition functions by their Wolfram number [10]. We represent a configuration as a binary number and show it as a decimal number.

Let us being with an example in which the cycle length of composited cellular automaton is lowest common multiple of the cycle lengths of each cellular automaton. Figure 1, 2 and 3 correspond to CA90(5), CA240(5) and the composited cellular automaton. For the configuration $c = 9$, $C_1 = \{6, 9, 15\}, C_2 = \{5, 9, 10, 18, 20\}$ and $\min\{t > 0 | F^t(9) = 9\} = 15$.

Next, let us show an example in which the cycle length of a composited cellular automaton is the maximum cycle length for a linear cellular automaton

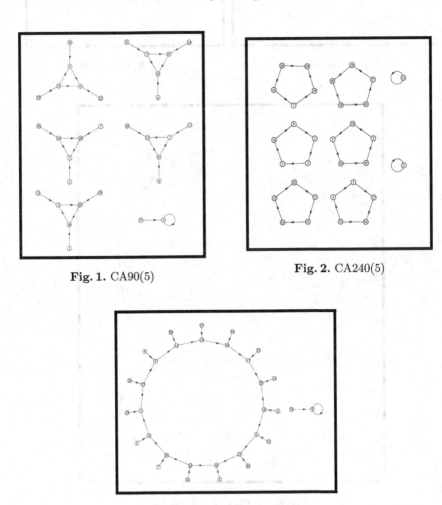

**Fig. 1.** CA90(5)

**Fig. 2.** CA240(5)

**Fig. 3.** CA90(5) × CA240(5)

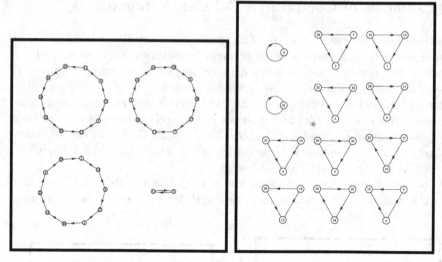

**Fig. 4.** CA15(5)     **Fig. 5.** CA150(5)

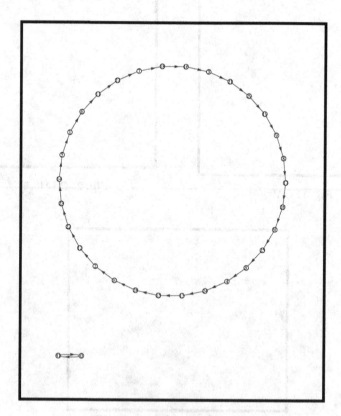

**Fig. 6.** CA15(5) × CA150(5)

and a non-linear cellular automaton. Figure 4, 5 and 6 correspond to CA15(5), CA150(5) and the composited cellular automaton. For the configuration $c = 6$, $C_1 = \{3, 6, 7, 12, 14, 17, 19, 24, 25, 28\}, C_2 = \{6, 9, 15\}$ and $\min\{t > 0 | F^t(6) = 6\} = 30$.

# 6  Conclusion

In this paper, we discussed the commutativity conditions of composition and behavior of composited cellular automata. We presented the commutativity conditions of compositions of linear cellular automata and affine cellular automata. In addition, we showed the relations of cycles of cellular automata and their composited cellular automaton. We presented that a cellular automaton made by composition of cellular automata has a maximum cycle length.

In the future, we will study more commutativity conditions of compositions and the behaviors of all cellular automata. In addition, we would like to show a systematic way to define cellular automata with maximum cycle lengths.

# References

1. Pal Chaudhuri, P., Chowdhury, D.R., Nandi, S., Chattopadhyay, S.: Additive Cellular Automata, Theory and Applications, vol. 1. John Wiley & Sons (1997)
2. Elspas, B.: The Theory of Autonomous Linear Sequential Networks Circuit Theory. IRE Transactions on Issue Date 6(1), 45–60 (1959)
3. Fujio, M.: XOR2 = 90 - graded algebra structure of the boolean algebra of local transition rules. Papers Res. Inst. Math. Sci. 1599, 97–102 (2008)
4. Ito, T., Fujio, M., Inokuchi, S., Mizoguchi, Y.: Composition, union and division of cellular automata on groups. In: Proc. of the 16th International Workshop on Cellular Automata and Discrete Complex Systems, Automata 2010, pp. 255–264 (2010)
5. Matsumoto, M.: Simple Cellular Automata as Pseudorandom m-Sequence Generators for Bulit-In Self-Tes. ACM Transactions on Modeling and Computer Simulation 8(1), 31–42 (1988)
6. von Neumann, J.: Theory of self-reproducing automata. Univ. of Illinois Press (1966)
7. Pries, W., Thanailakis, A., Card, H.: Group properties of cellular automata and VLSI applications. IEEE Trans. on Computers C-35(12), 1013–1024 (1986)
8. Tezuka, S., Fushimi, M.: A method of designing cellular automata as pseudorandom number generators for built-in self-test for VLSI. Finite Fields: Theory, Applications, and Algorithms 168, 363–367 (1994)
9. Voorhees, B.: Commutation of Cellular Automata Rules. Complex Systems 7, 309–325 (1993)
10. Wolfram, S.: Statistical Mechanics of Cellular Automata. Reviews of Modern Physics 55, 601–644 (1983)
11. Wolfram, S.: Random Sequence Generation by Cellular Automata. Advances in Applied Mathematics 7, 123–169 (1986)
12. Yukita, S.: Dynamics of Cellular Automata on Groups. IEICE Trans. Inf. & Syst. E82-D(10), 1316–1323 (1999)

# Iterative Arrays:
# Little Resources Big Size Impact

Martin Kutrib and Andreas Malcher

Institut für Informatik, Universität Giessen
Arndtstr. 2, 35392 Giessen, Germany
{kutrib,malcher}@informatik.uni-giessen.de

**Abstract.** We investigate the descriptional complexity of little resources added to deterministic one-dimensional real-time iterative arrays. More precisely, we study the impact of adding sublinearly more time obtaining time complexities strictly in between real time and linear time, adding dimensions, allow the communication cell to perform a few nondeterministic steps, and increase the number of bits that may be communicated to neighboring cells slightly. In all cases it is shown that there are arbitrary savings in the size of the descriptions of the arrays which cannot be bounded by any computable function.

## 1 Introduction

The approach to analyze the descriptional complexity, that is, the size of systems as opposed to the computational complexity seems to originate from [24], where the relative succinctness of regular languages represented by deterministic finite state and deterministic pushdown machines is studied. In general, suppose that a set of syntactical patterns, in our terms a formal language, has to be stored or transmitted. Then there is a natural interest to represent the patterns as succinctly as possible. As a simple example, we consider the representation of a regular language over the symbols $a$ and $b$ by a minimal deterministic finite state machine having, say $n$ states. Then the size of the machine, that is, the length of its description given by a fixed set of, say $x$ symbols, is roughly $2 \cdot n \cdot \log_x(n)$, since for any state and input symbol we have to write down the next state using the $x$ symbols. It is well known, that any regular language can be represented by a nondeterministic finite state machine as well. Moreover, there are examples where the minimal deterministic machine equivalent to an $n$-state nondeterministic device requires $2^n$ states. So, the representation can be exponentially more succinct, when the resource 'nondeterminism' is added to finite state machines. Can we do better? What if deterministic pushdown machines are used to represent regular languages? In [26] it has been shown that in this case the order of magnitude of the size can be reduced double exponentially. So, adding the resource 'pushdown store' to finite state machines has a big impact on the size of the representation. Can we do still better? What if we add nondeterminism *and* a pushdown store? In [21] as one of the cornerstones of descriptional complexity theory it is shown that in this case there is no computable

G.C. Sirakoulis and S. Bandini (Eds.): ACRI 2012, LNCS 7495, pp. 42–51, 2012.

function serving as upper bound for the possible gain in economy of description. With other words, when regular languages are represented by nondeterministic pushdown machines, one can choose an arbitrarily large computable function $f$ but the gain in economy of description eventually exceeds $f$. This qualitatively phenomenon is called *non-recursive trade-off* (see, for example, [9,10,11,15]).

Here we start with one of the simplest models for massively parallel computations, that is, with deterministic one-dimensional iterative arrays (IA), which sometimes are called cellular automata with sequential input, operating in real time. In connection with formal language processing IAs have been introduced in [7], where it was shown that the language family accepted by real-time IAs forms a Boolean algebra not closed under concatenation and reversal. In [6] it is shown that for every context-free language a two-dimensional linear-time IA parser exists. In [8] a real-time acceptor for prime numbers has been constructed. Pattern manipulation is the main aspect in [1]. A characterization of various types of IAs by restricted Turing machines and several results especially speed-up theorems are given in [12,13,14]. Several more results concerning formal languages can be found in [22,23,25]. We study here the impact on the descriptional complexity of deterministic one-dimensional real-time iterative arrays when little resources are added. In particular, we add sublinearly more time obtaining time complexities strictly in between real time and linear time. Then we add dimensions, allow the communication cell to perform a few nondeterministic steps, and increase the number of bits that may be communicated to neighboring cells slightly. In all cases non-recursive trade-offs are proved. So, from a compressibility point of view it is worthwile to add them.

In the next section we recall the necessary definitions and notions, and the basics of descriptional complexity theory. In the following four sections we present our results. The proofs are omitted here owing to space restrictions.

## 2    Preliminaries and Definitions

We denote the rational numbers by $\mathbb{Q}$ and the non-negative integers by $\mathbb{N}$. The empty word is denoted by $\lambda$, the reversal of a word $w$ by $w^R$, and for the length of $w$ we write $|w|$. The cardinality of a set $M$ is denoted by $|M|$ and its powerset by $2^M$. We write $\subseteq$ for set inclusion, and $\subset$ for strict set inclusion.

An iterative array is an infinite linear array of finite automata, sometimes called cells. We identify the cells by natural numbers. Each cell except the origin is connected to its both nearest neighbors (one to the left and one to the right). The input is supplied sequentially to the distinguished communication cell at the origin which is connected to its immediate neighbor to the right only. For this reason, we have two different local transition functions. The state transition of all cells but the communication cell depends on the current state of the cell itself and the current states of its both neighbors. The state transition of the communication cell additionally depends on the current input symbol (or if the whole input has been consumed on a special end-of-input symbol). The finite automata work synchronously at discrete time steps. Initially they are in the so-called quiescent state.

**Definition 1.** *An* iterative array *(IA) is a system* $\langle S, A, \#, F, s_0, \delta, \delta_0 \rangle$*, where*

1. $S$ *is the finite, nonempty set of* cell states,
2. $A$ *is the finite, nonempty set of* input symbols,
3. $\# \notin A$ *is the* end-of-input symbol,
4. $F \subseteq S$ *is the set of* accepting states,
5. $s_0 \in S$ *is the* quiescent state,
6. $\delta : S^3 \to S$ *is the* local transition function for non-communication cells *satisfying* $\delta(s_0, s_0, s_0) = s_0$,
7. $\delta_0 : (A \cup \{\#\}) \times S^2 \to S$ *is the* local transition function for the communication cell.

Let $M$ be an IA. A configuration of $M$ at some time $t \geq 0$ is a description of its global state which is actually a pair $(w_t, c_t)$, where $w_t \in A^*$ is the remaining input sequence and $c_t : \mathbb{N} \to S$ is a mapping that maps the single cells to their current states. The configuration $(w_0, c_0)$ at initial time 0 is defined by the input $w_0$ and the mapping $c_0(i) = s_0$, $i \geq 0$, while subsequent configurations are chosen according to the global transition function $\Delta$. Let $(w_t, c_t)$, $t \geq 0$, be a configuration. Then its successor configuration $(w_{t+1}, c_{t+1}) = \Delta((w_t, c_t))$ is defined as $c_{t+1}(i) = \delta(c_t(i-1), c_t(i), c_t(i+1))$, $c_{t+1}(0) = \delta_0(a, c_t(0), c_t(1))$, where $i \geq 1$, and $a = \#$, $w_{t+1} = \lambda$ if $w_t = \lambda$, and $a = a_1$, $w_{t+1} = a_2 a_3 \cdots a_n$ if $w_t = a_1 a_2 \cdots a_n$. Thus, the global transition function $\Delta$ is induced by $\delta$ and $\delta_0$.

An input $w$ is accepted by an IA $M$ if at some time $i$ during its course of computation the communication cell enters an accepting state. The *language accepted* by $M$ is defined as $L(M) = \{ w \in A^* \mid w$ is accepted by $M \}$. Let $t : \mathbb{N} \to \mathbb{N}$ be a mapping. If all $w \in L(M)$ are accepted with at most $t(|w|)$ time steps, then $L(M)$ is said to be of time complexity $t$. The family of all languages that are accepted by IAs with time complexity $t$ is denoted by $\mathscr{L}_t(\text{IA})$. The index is omitted for arbitrary time. If $t$ is the function $n + 1$, acceptance is said to be in *real time* and we write $\mathscr{L}_{rt}(\text{IA})$.

## 2.1 Descriptional Complexity

We recall some notation for descriptional complexity. Following [11] we say that a *descriptional system* $\mathcal{S}$ is a set of finite descriptors such that each $D \in \mathcal{S}$ describes a formal language $L(D)$, and the underlying alphabet alph$(D)$ over which $D$ represents a language can be read off from $D$. The *family of languages represented* (or *described*) by $\mathcal{S}$ is $\mathscr{L}(\mathcal{S}) = \{ L(D) \mid D \in \mathcal{S} \}$. For every language $L$, the set $\mathcal{S}(L) = \{ D \in \mathcal{S} \mid L(D) = L \}$ is the set of its descriptors in $\mathcal{S}$. A *complexity measure* for a descriptional system $\mathcal{S}$ is a total computable mapping $c : \mathcal{S} \to \mathbb{N}$.

*Example 2.* Iterative arrays can be encoded over some fixed alphabet such that their input alphabets can be extracted from the encodings. The set of these encodings is a descriptional system $\mathcal{S}$, and $\mathscr{L}(\mathcal{S})$ is $\mathscr{L}(\text{IA})$.

Examples for complexity measures for IAs are the total number of symbols, that is, the *length of the encoding* (length), or the total *number of transitions* (trans) in $\delta$ and $\delta_0$. $\qquad\square$

Here we only use complexity measures that (with respect to the underlying alphabets) are related to length by a computable function. If there is a total computable function $g : \mathbb{N} \times \mathbb{N} \to \mathbb{N}$ such that, for all $D \in \mathcal{S}$, $\text{length}(D) \leq g(c(D), |\text{alph}(D)|)$, then $c$ is said to be an *s-measure*. If, in addition, for any alphabet $A$, the set of descriptors in $\mathcal{S}$ describing languages over $A$ is recursively enumerable in order of increasing size, then $c$ is said to be an *sn-measure*. Clearly, length and trans are sn-measures for iterative arrays.

Whenever we consider the relative succinctness of two descriptional systems $\mathcal{S}_1$ and $\mathcal{S}_2$, we assume the intersection $\mathcal{L}(\mathcal{S}_1) \cap \mathcal{L}(\mathcal{S}_2)$ to be non-empty. Let $\mathcal{S}_1$ and $\mathcal{S}_2$ be descriptional systems with complexity measures $c_1$ and $c_2$, respectively. A total function $f : \mathbb{N} \to \mathbb{N}$ is an *upper bound* for the increase in complexity when changing from a descriptor in $\mathcal{S}_1$ to an equivalent descriptor in $\mathcal{S}_2$, if for all $D_1 \in \mathcal{S}_1$ with $L(D_1) \in \mathcal{L}(\mathcal{S}_2)$, there exists a $D_2 \in \mathcal{S}_2(L(D_1))$ such that $c_2(D_2) \leq f(c_1(D_1))$.

If there is no recursive, that is, computable function serving as upper bound, the *trade-off is said to be non-recursive*. That is, whenever the trade-off from one descriptional system to another is non-recursive, one can choose an arbitrarily large recursive function $f$ but the gain in economy of description eventually exceeds $f$ when changing from the former system to the latter. In fact, the non-recursive trade-offs are independent of particular sn-measures, as any two sn-measures $c_1$ and $c_2$ for some descriptional system $\mathcal{S}$ are related by a recursive function. So, a non-recursive trade-off exceeds any difference caused by applying two sn-measures. For establishing non-recursive trade-offs the following general result is useful.

**Theorem 3 ([11]).** *Let $\mathcal{S}_1$ and $\mathcal{S}_2$ be two descriptional systems for recursive languages such that any descriptor $D$ in $\mathcal{S}_1$ and $\mathcal{S}_2$ can effectively be converted into a Turing machine that decides $L(D)$, and let $c_1$ be a measure for $\mathcal{S}_1$ and $c_2$ be an sn-measure for $\mathcal{S}_2$. If there exists a descriptional system $\mathcal{S}_3$ and a property $P$ that is not semi-decidable for descriptors from $\mathcal{S}_3$, such that, given an arbitrary $D_3 \in \mathcal{S}_3$, (i) there exists an effective procedure to construct a descriptor $D_1$ in $\mathcal{S}_1$, and (ii) $D_1$ has an equivalent descriptor in $\mathcal{S}_2$ if and only if $D_3$ does not have property $P$, then the trade-off between $\mathcal{S}_1$ and $\mathcal{S}_2$ is non-recursive.*

In the following we show all non-recursive trade-offs between iterative arrays having little additional resources and those that do not have these resources by reduction of the finiteness problem for linearly space bounded Turing machines. In order to apply Theorem 3, we use the family of deterministic linearly space bounded one-tape one-head Turing machines, so-called linear bounded automata (LBA), as descriptional system $\mathcal{S}_3$. Property $P$ is *infiniteness*, which is not semi-decidable for LBAs. Next, given an arbitrary LBA $M$, that is, a descriptor $D_3 \in \mathcal{S}_3$, we must construct an iterative array with the additional resources, that is, a descriptor $D_1$ in $\mathcal{S}_1$, that has an equivalent iterative array without the resources, that is, a descriptor in $\mathcal{S}_2$, if and only if $M$ accepts a finite language, that is, $D_3$ does not have property $P$.

For the reduction, we consider strings which record all configurations of an accepting computation of a given LBA. Without loss of generality and for technical reasons, one can assume that any accepting computation has at least three and, in general, an odd number of steps. Therefore, it is represented by an even number of configurations. Moreover, it is assumed that the LBAs get their input in between two endmarkers, and that a configuration is halting if and only if it is accepting.

Let $Q$ be the state set of some LBA $M$, where $q_0$ is the initial state, $T \cap Q = \emptyset$ is the tape alphabet containing the endmarkers $\rhd$ and $\lhd$, and $\Sigma \subset T$ is the input alphabet. A configuration of $M$ can be written as a string of the form $\rhd T^* Q T^* \lhd$ such that, $\rhd t_1 t_2 \cdots t_i q t_{i+1} \cdots t_n \lhd$ is used to express that $\rhd t_1 t_2 \cdots t_n \lhd$ is the tape inscription, $M$ is in state $q$, and scans tape symbol $t_{i+1}$. We consider words of the form $w_1 \$ w_3 \$ \cdots \$ w_{2k-1} \math0 w_{2k}^R \$ \cdots \$ w_4^R \$ w_2^R$, where $w_i$ are configurations, $\$$ and $\mathcent$ are symbols not appearing in $w_i$, $w_1$ is an initial configuration of the form $q_0 \Sigma^*$, $w_{2k}$ is an accepting, that is, halting configuration, and $w_{i+1}$ is the successor configuration of $w_i$, for $1 \leq i \leq 2k$. Let $\$'$ and $\mathcent'$ be new symbols and $T'$ and $Q'$ primed copies of $T$ and $Q$. The set of *valid computations* VALC($M$) is now defined to be the set of words $\varphi^{-1}(w)$, where $w$ is a word of the form above and $\varphi$ is the homomorphism defined by $\varphi(a) = a$ if $a \in T \cup Q \cup \{\$, \mathcent\}$, and $\varphi(a') = a$ if $a' \in T' \cup Q' \cup \{\$', \mathcent'\}$. The set of *invalid computations* INVALC($M$) is the complement of VALC($M$) with respect to the *coding alphabet* $\Lambda_M = \{\$, \$', \mathcent, \mathcent'\} \cup T \cup T' \cup Q \cup Q'$. By using the redundant primed symbols we ensure that for any $u \in$ VALC($M$) there are are at least $2^{|u|}$ further strings of length $|u|$ in VALC($M$)) [19].

Since the language class $\mathscr{L}_{rt}$(IA) is closed under inverse homomorphisms, essentially, the following crucial theorem has been shown in [18].

**Theorem 4.** *Let $M$ be an LBA. Then real-time iterative arrays that accept VALC($M$) and INVALC($M$) can effectively be constructed.*

## 3  Time

Basically, for any non-trivial computation an iterative array has to read at least one end-of-input symbol. Therefore, real time is defined to be $(n+1)$-time. In [2] it has been shown that there exists an infinite dense and strict time hierarchy between real time and linear time. So adding a little bit more time yields a strictly stronger class of iterative arrays. Here we consider the differences of their descriptional complexities.

In order to deal with infinite dense time hierarchies in almost all cases reasonable time bounding functions are required. Usually the notion reasonable is substantiated in terms of the computability or constructibility of the function with respect to the device in question. Here we consider so-called *IA-constructible* functions. A strictly increasing function $f : \mathbb{N} \to \mathbb{N}$ is IA-constructible, if there exists an IA such that on empty input the leftmost cell enters an accepting state exactly at all time steps $f(i)$, $1 \leq i$. Note that since all IA-constructible functions $f$ are necessarily strictly increasing, for their inverses we have $f^{-1}(n) \leq n$, for all $n \geq 1$.

The family of IA-constructible functions is very rich. It includes $n!$, $k^n$, $n^k$, $n + \lfloor \sqrt{n} \rfloor$, $n + \lfloor \log \rfloor$, etc., where $k \geq 1$ is an integer. It is closed under the operations such as addition of constants, addition, iterated addition, multiplication, composition, minimum, maximum etc. [20]. Further results can be found in [4,5].

Now, let $M$ be an LBA, $r^{-1}$ be an IA-constructible function, and define a function $h_r$ as $h_r(n) = r^{-1}((n+1)^2)$, and a language

$$L_{r,M} = \{ \$^{h_r(m)-(m+1)^2+1} w_1 \$ w_2 \$ \cdots \$ w_m \mathbb{¢} y \mid m \geq 1, w_i \in \Lambda_M^m, 1 \leq i \leq m,$$
$$y \in \text{VALC}(M) \text{ and } \exists 1 \leq j \leq m : y = w_j \}.$$

**Lemma 5.** *Let $M$ be an LBA and $r_1, r_2 : \mathbb{N} \to \mathbb{N}$ be two increasing functions so that $r_2 \in o(r_1)$ and $r_1^{-1}$ is IA-constructible. Then $L_{r_1,M} \in \mathscr{L}_{n+r_2(n)}(IA)$ if and only if $L(M)$ is finite.*

In order to apply Theorem 3 to show the non-recursive trade-off between iterative arrays with time complexity $n + r_1(n)$ and $n + r_2(n)$ as mentioned above, it now suffices to show $L_{r_1,M} \in \mathscr{L}_{n+r_1(n)}(IA)$. In [2] an $(n + r_1(n))$-time IA for a language $L_{r_1}$ has been constructed, where essentially, $L_{r_1}$ is derived from $L_{r_1,M}$ by defining the subwords $w_i$ over a binary alphabet and omitting the condition that the suffix following $\mathbb{¢}$ has to belong to VALC($M$). By Theorem 4 it is not hard to extend the construction to language $L_{r_1,M}$. A corresponding IA simply can check the suffix on another track. So, the next theorem follows.

**Theorem 6.** *Let $r_1, r_2 : \mathbb{N} \to \mathbb{N}$ be two increasing functions so that $r_2 \in o(r_1)$ and $r_1^{-1}$ is IA-constructible. Then the trade-off between $(n+r_1(n))$-time IAs and $(n + r_2(n))$-time IAs is non-recursive.*

## 4    Nondeterminism

This section is devoted to nondeterministic iterative arrays, where the nondeterminism is regarded as a limited resource. The ability to perform nondeterministic transitions is restricted to the communication cell, all the other automata are deterministic ones. Moreover, the number of allowed nondeterministic transitions is limited dependent on the length of the input. Such iterative arrays with limited nondeterministic communication cell have been introduced and investigated in [3]. In particular, it has been shown that the number of nondeterministic transitions can be reduced by any constant without decreasing the computational capacity, and that there is a strict and dense infinite hierarchy of language classes dependent on sublogarithmic limits of the nondeterminism.

In order to define so-called $g$G-IA ($g$ guess IA) the transition function $\delta_0$ for the communication cell is replaced by a nondeterministic local transition function $\delta_{nd} : (A \cup \{\#\}) \times S^2 \to 2^S$ and a deterministic local transition function $\delta_d : (A \cup \{\#\}) \times S^2 \to S$. The number of allowed nondeterministic transitions is given by a mapping $g : \mathbb{N} \to \mathbb{N}$ dependent on the length $n$ of the input, such that the first $g(n)$ transitions of the communication cell are nondeterministic according to $\delta_{nd}$, and all subsequent transitions are deterministic according to $\delta_d$. The fact that the nondeterministic transitions have to be applied before the deterministic ones is not a serious restriction since nondeterministic transitions for later time steps can be guessed and stored in advance.

Now, let $M$ be an LBA, $r \in o(\log)$ and $r^{-1}$ be an IA-constructible function, and define a function $h_r$ as $h_r(n) = 2^{r(n)}$ and a language

$$\tilde{L}_{r,M} = \{\, \$^{l+1}w_1\$w_2\$\cdots\$w_j\mathord{\text{¢}}y \mid \exists n \geq 1 : j = h_r(n), l = n - (j+1)\cdot(|y|+1),$$
$$y \in \mathrm{VALC}(M), w_i \in \Lambda_M^{|y|}, 1 \leq i \leq j, \text{ and } \exists 1 \leq i \leq j : y = w_i^R \,\}.$$

Clearly, function $h_r$ is increasing since $r$ is. Moreover, since $r \in o(\log)$, it follows $\lim_{n\to\infty}\frac{h_r(n)}{n^k} = \lim_{n\to\infty}\frac{2^{r(n)}}{2^{\log(n)\cdot k}} = 0$ and, thus, $h_r(n) \in o(n^k)$, for all $k \in \mathbb{Q}$, $0 < k$. Therefore, the function $\frac{n}{2h_r(n)}$ is unbounded and for all $m$ there is an $n$ so that $m+1 \geq \frac{n}{2h_r(n)} \geq m$, which implies $n \geq m \cdot 2 \cdot h_r(n) \geq (h_r(n)+1)\cdot(m+1)$, for $m$ large enough. This in turn implies that $\tilde{L}_{r,M}$ includes at least one word for every word in $\mathrm{VALC}(M)$.

**Lemma 7.** *Let $M$ be an LBA and $r_1, r_2 : \mathbb{N} \to \mathbb{N}$ be two increasing functions so that $r_2 \in o(r_1)$, $r_1 \in o(\log)$, and $r_1^{-1}$ is IA-constructible. Then $\tilde{L}_{r_1,M} \in \mathscr{L}_{rt}(r_2\,G\text{-}IA)$ if and only if $L(M)$ is finite.*

Similar as in Section 3, now Theorem 3 can be applied to show the non-recursive trade-off between iterative arrays with $r_1(n)$ and $r_2(n)$ guesses as mentioned above.

**Theorem 8.** *Let $r_1, r_2 : \mathbb{N} \to \mathbb{N}$ be two increasing functions so that $r_2 \in o(r_1)$, $r_1 \in o(\log)$, and $r_1^{-1}$ is IA-constructible. Then the trade-off between real-time $r_1\,G\text{-}IA$ and real-time $r_2\,G\text{-}IA$ is non-recursive.*

## 5   Dimensions

In this section, we will show that there exist non-recursive trade-offs between $(d + 1)$-dimensional and $d$-dimensional real-time iterative arrays. To define a multidimensional IA we adopt Definition 1 by replacing the local transition functions $\delta$ and $\delta_0$ by $\delta : S^{2d+1} \to S$ satisfying $\delta(s_0, s_0, \ldots, s_0) = s_0$, and $\delta_0 : (A \cup \{\#\}) \times S^{d+1} \to S$. Configurations of $d$-dimensional IAs (denoted by $\mathrm{IA}^d$) and the global transition function are straightforwardly defined, where $c_t$ is now a mapping from $\mathbb{N}^d$ to $S$.

In [17], a dimension hierarchy is shown for IAs with restricted communication. Let us first describe the witness languages used there for the dimension hierarchy. We will then modify these languages suitably to obtain non-recursive trade-offs between real-time $\mathrm{IA}^{d+1}$ and real-time $\mathrm{IA}^d$, for all $d \geq 1$.

For any dimension $d \geq 2$, a language $L_d$ is defined as follows. First, consider the following series of regular sets: $X_1 = \${a,b}^+$ and $X_{i+1} = \$X_i^+$, for $i \geq 1$ Due to the separator symbol $\$$, every word $u \in X_{i+1}$ can uniquely be decomposed into its subwords from $X_i$. So, the projection on the $j$th subword can be defined as usual: Let $u = \$u_1 \cdots u_m$, where $u_j \in X_i$, for $1 \leq j \leq m$. Then $u[j]$ is defined to be $u_j$, if $1 \leq j \leq m$, otherwise $u[j]$ is undefined. Now define the language

$$M_d = \{\, u\mathrm{¢}e^{x_d}\$ \cdots \$e^{x_1}\$e^{2x}\$v \mid u \in X_d \text{ and } 1 \leq x_i, 1 \leq i \leq d,$$
$$\text{and } x = x_1 + \cdots + x_d \text{ and } v = u[x_d][x_{d-1}] \cdots [x_1] \text{ is defined} \,\}.$$

Finally, the language $L_d$ is defined as the homomorphic image of $M_d$ using a suitable homomorphism $h$. It is shown in [17] that $L_{d+1}$ can be accepted by a $(d+1)$-dimensional real-time IA with restricted communication, but not by any $d$-dimensional real-time IA.

Now, we modify the set $M_d$ in such a way that the prefix $u$ is interleaved symbol by symbol with some word from the set $\mathrm{VALC}(M)$ for some LBA $M$. The remaining symbols $\mathrm{¢}, \$, e$ and the suffix $v \in \{a, b\}$ are repeated once. Additionally, the prefix $u$ may end with some dummy symbols $c$. Thus, we obtain

$$L_{d,M} = \{\, u_1 w_1 u_2 w_2 \cdots u_t w_t \mathrm{¢¢} e^{2x_d} \$\$ \cdots \$\$ e^{2x_1} \$\$ e^{4x} \$\$ vv \mid u_j \in \{a, b, c, \$\},$$
$$w_j \in \Lambda_M, 1 \leq j \leq t, u = u_1 u_2 \cdots u_t \in X_d\, c^*, w = w_1 w_2 \cdots w_t \in \mathrm{VALC}(M),$$
$$1 \leq x_i, 1 \leq i \leq d, x = x_1 + \cdots + x_d, \text{ and } v = u[x_d][x_{d-1}] \cdots [x_1] \text{ is defined} \,\}.$$

**Lemma 9.** *Let $M$ be an LBA and $d \geq 1$ be a constant. Then $L_{d+1,M} \in \mathscr{L}_{rt}(\mathrm{IA}^d)$ if and only if $L(M)$ is finite.*

**Lemma 10.** *Let $M$ be an LBA and $d \geq 1$ be a constant number. Then language $L_{d+1,M}$ belongs to $\mathscr{L}_{rt}(\mathrm{IA}^{d+1})$.*

Lemma 9, Lemma 10, and Theorem 3 show the following result.

**Theorem 11.** *Let $d \geq 1$ be a constant number. Then the trade-off between real-time $\mathrm{IA}^{d+1}$ and real-time $\mathrm{IA}^d$ is non-recursive.*

## 6   Communication

Now we turn to consider $d$-dimensional real-time $\mathrm{IA}^d$ with restricted communication. Basically, these are real-time $\mathrm{IA}^d$ whose bandwidth of the inter-cell communication links is limited. In the general case, in every step the states of the cells are transmitted. Here the limitation is modeled by a set of messages that can be sent, where the number $k$ of different messages is independent of the number of states. We denote these devices by $\mathrm{IA}_k^d$. Formally, we add to the definition the set of messages $B$ and communication functions $b_i : S \to B, 1 \leq i \leq 2d$, that determine the messages to be sent to neighbors. Furthermore, we replace $\delta$ and $\delta_0$ by $\delta : S \times B^{2d} \to S$ satisfying $\delta(s_0, (b_1(s_0), b_2(s_0), \ldots, b_{2d}(s_0))) = s_0$, and $\delta_0 : (A \cup \{\#\}) \times S \times B^d \to S$.

It is shown in [17] that for real-time $\mathrm{IA}^d$ with $d \geq 1$ there exists a proper hierarchy dependent on the number of possible messages, that is, real-time $\mathrm{IA}^d$

that can communicate $k + 1$ different messages are more powerful than those that can communicate $k$ different messages, for $k \geq 1$. For $d \geq 1$ and any number of messages $k \geq 2$ we define an alphabet $A_{d,k} = \{a_0, \ldots, a_{k^d-1}\}$ and a language $\hat{L}_{d,k}$ as

$$\hat{L}_{d,k} = \{ e^x \$ u_1 u_2 \cdots u_m \mid x \geq 1 \text{ and } m \geq 2x - 1$$
$$\text{and } u_i \in A_{d,k}, 1 \leq i \leq m, \text{ and } u_j = u_{j+2x-1}, 1 \leq j \leq m - (2x - 1) \}.$$

Then, it is shown [17] for $d \geq 1$ and $k \geq 2$ that $\hat{L}_{d,k+1}$ belongs to $\mathscr{L}_{rt}(\text{IA}_{k+1}^d)$, but cannot be accepted by any real-time $\text{IA}_k^d$. Now, we modify these languages in order to obtain non-recursive trade-offs. For a constant $c \geq 1$ and an alphabet $A$, let $h_c$ be the homomorphism $h_c(a) = a^c$, for all $a \in A$. For an LBA $M$, let $S$ be the state set of the real-time IA accepting $\text{VALC}(M)$ constructed in Theorem 4. Now set $c = \lceil \log_2(|S|) \rceil$ and consider the set $h_c(\text{VALC}(M))$. It has been shown in [16] that a real-time $\text{IA}_2$ accepting $h_c(\text{VALC}(M))$ can effectively be constructed. The main idea is to simulate one transition of the IA accepting $\text{VALC}(M)$ by $c$ transitions. During these transitions the binary encoded states of the cells are communicated. A cell that receives the $c$th bit with the $c$th transition, then simulates the original transition. Finally, the communication cell can verify whether each input symbol is repeated $c$ times. With these prerequisites, we define the languages

$$L_{d,k,M} = \{ e w_1 e w_2 \cdots e w_x \$^{2x} u_1 u_2 \cdots u_m \mid x \geq 1 \text{ and } m \geq 2x - 1$$
$$\text{and } u_i \in A_{d,k}, 1 \leq i \leq m, \text{ and } u_j = u_{j+2x-1}, 1 \leq j \leq m - (2x - 1),$$
$$w_t \in \Lambda_M, 1 \leq t \leq x, \text{ and } w_1 w_2 \cdots w_x \in h_{c+1}(\text{VALC}(M)) \}.$$

**Lemma 12.** *Let $M$ be an LBA and $d, k \geq 1$ be constants. Then language $L_{d,k+1,M}$ belongs to $\mathscr{L}_{rt}(\text{IA}_k^d)$ if and only if $L(M)$ is finite.*

**Lemma 13.** *Let $M$ be an LBA and $d, k \geq 1$ be constant numbers. Then language $L_{d,k+1,\dot{M}}$ belongs to $\mathscr{L}_{rt}(\text{IA}_{k+1}^d)$.*

Lemma 12, Lemma 13, and Theorem 3 show the following result.

**Theorem 14.** *Let $d, k \geq 1$ be constant numbers. Then the trade-off between real-time $\text{IA}_{k+1}^d$ and real-time $\text{IA}_k^d$ is non-recursive.*

# References

1. Beyer, W.T.: Recognition of topological invariants by iterative arrays. Tech. Rep. TR-66. MIT, Cambridge, Proj. MAC (1969)
2. Buchholz, T., Klein, A., Kutrib, M.: Iterative Arrays with Small Time Bounds. In: Nielsen, M., Rovan, B. (eds.) MFCS 2000. LNCS, vol. 1893, pp. 243–252. Springer, Heidelberg (2000)
3. Buchholz, T., Klein, A., Kutrib, M.: Iterative arrays with limited nondeterministic communication cell. In: Words, Languages and Combinatorics III, pp. 73–87. World Scientific Publishing (2003)

4. Buchholz, T., Kutrib, M.: Some relations between massively parallel arrays. Parallel Comput. 23, 1643–1662 (1997)
5. Buchholz, T., Kutrib, M.: On time computability of functions in one-way cellular automata. Acta Inform. 35, 329–352 (1998)
6. Chang, J.H., Ibarra, O.H., Palis, M.A.: Parallel parsing on a one-way array of finite-state machines. IEEE Trans. Comput. C-36, 64–75 (1987)
7. Cole, S.N.: Real-time computation by $n$-dimensional iterative arrays of finite-state machines. IEEE Trans. Comput. C-18, 349–365 (1969)
8. Fischer, P.C.: Generation of primes by a one-dimensional real-time iterative array. J. ACM 12, 388–394 (1965)
9. Goldstine, J., Kappes, M., Kintala, C.M.R., Leung, H., Malcher, A., Wotschke, D.: Descriptional complexity of machines with limited resources. J. UCS 8, 193–234 (2002)
10. Gruber, H., Holzer, M., Kutrib, M.: On measuring non-recursive trade-offs. J. Autom., Lang. Comb. 15, 107–120 (2010)
11. Holzer, M., Kutrib, M.: Descriptional complexity – An introductory survey. In: Scientific Appl. of Language Methods, pp. 1–58. Imperial College Press (2010)
12. Ibarra, O.H., Jiang, T.: On one-way cellular arrays. SIAM J. Comput. 16, 1135–1154 (1987)
13. Ibarra, O.H., Palis, M.A.: Some results concerning linear iterative (systolic) arrays. J. Parallel Distributed Comput. 2, 182–218 (1985)
14. Ibarra, O.H., Palis, M.A.: Two-dimensional iterative arrays: Characterizations and applications. Theoret. Comput. Sci. 57, 47–86 (1988)
15. Kutrib, M.: The phenomenon of non-recursive trade-offs. Int. J. Found. Comput. Sci. 16, 957–973 (2005)
16. Kutrib, M., Malcher, A.: Computations and decidability of iterative arrays with restricted communication. Parallel Process. Lett. 19, 247–264 (2009)
17. Kutrib, M., Malcher, A.: Cellular automata with limited inter-cell bandwidth. Theoret. Comput. Sci. 412, 3917–3931 (2011)
18. Malcher, A.: On the descriptional complexity of iterative arrays. IEICE Trans. Inf. Syst. E87-D(3), 721–725 (2004)
19. Malcher, A., Mereghetti, C., Palano, B.: Sublinearly space bounded iterative arrays. Int. J. Found. Comput. Sci. 21, 843–858 (2010)
20. Mazoyer, J., Terrier, V.: Signals in one-dimensional cellular automata. Theoret. Comput. Sci. 217, 53–80 (1999)
21. Meyer, A.R., Fischer, M.J.: Economy of description by automata, grammars, and formal systems. In: Symposium on Switching and Automata Theory, SWAT 1971, pp. 188–191. IEEE (1971)
22. Seiferas, J.I.: Linear-time computation by nondeterministic multidimensional iterative arrays. SIAM J. Comput. 6, 487–504 (1977)
23. Smith III, A.R.: Real-time language recognition by one-dimensional cellular automata. J. Comput. System Sci. 6, 233–253 (1972)
24. Stearns, R.E.: A regularity test for pushdown machines. Inform. Control 11, 323–340 (1967)
25. Terrier, V.: On real time one-way cellular array. Theoret. Comput. Sci. 141, 331–335 (1995)
26. Valiant, L.G.: Regularity and related problems for deterministic pushdown automata. J. ACM 22, 1–10 (1975)

# Generating Expander Graphs Using Cellular Automata

Debdeep Mukhopadhyay

Department of Computer Science and Engineering,
Indian Institute of Technology Kharagpur, India
debdeep@cse.iitkgp.ernet.in

**Abstract.** The paper characterizes a special class of Cellular Automaton (CA) called Two Predecessor Single Attractor CA (TPSA-CA). We show that the transition graphs of the TPSA-CA can be used to realize pseudo-random regular graphs with good expansion properties. The elegance of the scheme lies in the fact that the storage required to capture the graph is $O(logN)$, where $N$ is the total number of vertices in the graph.

**Keywords:** expander graphs, Cellular Automata (CA), Two-Predecessor Single Attractor CA (TPSA-CA).

## 1 Introduction

Expander Graphs have been a significant tool both in theory and practice. It has been used in solving problems in communication and construction of error correcting codes as well as a tool for proving results in number theory and computational complexity. The combinatorial properties of the expander graphs can also lead to the construction of one-way functions [1] and hash functions [2] for cryptography.

The present work characterizes a special class of Cellular Automata (CA) [3], known as the *Two Predecessor Single Attractor Cellular Automata* (TPSA-CA). Next the work shows that the transition graphs generated by the TPSA-CA can be composed to realize pseudo-random regular graphs with expansion properties. Informally, a pseudo-random graph $G = (V, E)$ is a graph that behaves like a truly random graph. The paper shows that the CA based transition graphs have uniform edge distributions, if the graveyard states are chosen uniformly and independently. We provide both theoretical and experimental evidence to show that the pseudo-randomness of the generated graphs can be utilized to demonstrate good expansion properties. The elegance in the scheme lies in the fact that the storage required for the generation of the graphs is $O(logN)$, where $N$ is the number of vertices in the graph.

The outline of the paper is as follows: *Section 2* describes some of the preliminaries of expander graphs. The TPSA-CA is characterized in *section 3* and the state transitions of the machine is employed to generate pseudo-random regular graphs. In *section 4* we present experimental evidence of the expansion properties of the generated graphs. The work is concluded in *section 5*.

G.C. Sirakoulis and S. Bandini (Eds.): ACRI 2012, LNCS 7495, pp. 52–62, 2012.

## 2 Preliminaries on Expander Graphs

Informally *expander graphs* are a class of graphs $G = (V, E)$ in which every subset $S$ of vertices expands quickly, in the sense that it is connected to many vertices in the set $\overline{S}$ of complementary vertices. It may be noted that the graph may have self loops and multiple edges. The following definition states formally the *expansion property* of these class of graphs [4].

**Definition 1.** *The edge boundary of a set $S \in G$, denoted $\delta(S)$ is $\delta(S) = E(S, \overline{S})$ is the set of outgoing edges from $S$. The* expansion parameter *of $G$ is defined as:*

$$h(G) = min_{S:|S|\leq N/2} \frac{|\delta(S)|}{|S|}$$

*where $|S|$ denotes the size of a set $S$ and $N$ is the total number of vertices in the graph.*

There are other notions of expansion, the most popular being counting the number of neighbouring vertices of any small set, rather than the number of outgoing edges.

Random graphs have been utilized to develop expander graphs. A random graph $G(N, p)$ is a probability distribution of all the labeled graphs on $N$-vertices where for each pair $1 \leq i, j \neq N$, $(i, j)$ is an edge of $G(N, p)$ with probability $p = p(N)$, independently of any other edges.

Although $d$-regular random graphs on $N$ vertices define an expander, for real life applications it is necessary to have more explicit constructions on $O(2^n)$ vertices, where $n$ is the parameter defining the problem size. This is because to store a description of a random graph on so many vertices requires exponential time and space. Two well known constructions are found in [5,6,7].

The properties of the eigenvalue spectrum of the adjacency matrix $A(G)$ can also be used to understand properties of the graph $G$.

The **adjacency matrix** of a graph $G$, denoted by $A(G)$ is an $n \times n$ matrix such that each element $(u, v)$ denotes the number of edges in $G$ between vertex $u$ and vertex $v$[4]. For a $d$-regular graph, the sum of each row and column in $A(G)$ is $d$. By definition the matrix $A(G)$ is symmetric and therefore has an orthonormal base $v_0, v_1, \ldots, v_{n-1}$, with eigenvalues $\mu_0, \mu_1, \ldots, \mu_{n-1}$ such that for all $i$ we have $Av_i = \mu_i v_i$. Without loss of generality we assume the eigenvalues sorted in descending order $\mu_0 \geq \mu_1 \geq \ldots \geq \mu_{n-1}$. The eigenvalues of $A(G)$ are called the spectrum of $G$. The following two results are important in estimating the expansion properties of the graph.

1. $\mu_0 = d$
2. $\frac{d-\mu_1}{2} \leq h(G) \leq \sqrt{2d(d - \mu_1)}$

Thus, the parameter $d - \mu_1$, also known as the *Spectral Gap* gives a good estimate on the expansion of the graph $G$. The graph is an expander if the spectral gap has a lower bound $\epsilon'$ such that $d - \mu_1 > \epsilon'$.

A graph $G_1$ has better expansion properties than graph $G_2$, implies that for any subset $S$, $|S| \leq n/2$ of the graph $G_1$ has a larger number of neighbouring elements outside the set $S$, compared to that in $G_2$. Mathematically, the value of $h(G_1) > h(G_2)$. Informally, it implies that the graph $G_1$ expands faster compared to graph $G_2$. A random regular graph has good expansion properties. However the problem of realizing such a graph is in its description which grows exponentially with the number of vertices.

For the proposed construction of expander graphs, we use graphs which are parameterized by a shorter *seed*. These pseudo-random graphs, posses properties like edge-density, identical to random graphs, if the seed is generated by a pseudo-random generator.

In the next section we present the construction of random $d$ regular graph using the properties of a special class of CA, known as the Two Predecessor Single Attractor Cellular Automaton (TPSA CA). The transition graphs of the CA is at the heart of the proposed construction.

# 3 Expander Graphs Using TPSA CA

TPSA CA are a special class of non-group CA in which the state transition graph forms a single inverted binary routed tree at all zero state (**Fig. 1**). Every reachable state in the state transition graph has exactly two predecessors. The only cyclic state is the all zero state (for a non-complemented TPSA CA), which is an attractor (or graveyard). If $T_n$ is the characteristic matrix of an $n$ cell automaton then the necessary and sufficient conditions to be satisfied by the Transition matrix for the CA to be TPSA CA are[3]:

1. Rank$(T_n)=n-1$
2. Rank$(T_n \oplus I_n)=n$, $I_n$ being an $n \times n$ identity matrix
3. Characteristic Polynomial $= x^n$
4. Minimal Polynomial $= x^n$

The following results [3] characterize the state transition of the non-complemented TPSA CA.

**Lemma 1.** *[3] For an $n$ cell TPSA CA with characteristic polynomial $x^n$ and minimal polynomial $x^n$, (i) the number of attractors is 1, the all zero state, (ii) the number of states in the tree is $2^n$.*

**Lemma 2.** *For an $n$ cell TPSA CA having $m(x) = x^n$ the depth of the tree is $n$.*

Next, we develop a method to recursively synthesize an $n$ cell TPSA. The state transition matrix of the $n$ cell TPSA is denoted by $T_n$ and is generated from an $n-1$ cell TPSA CA characterized by the matrix $T_{n-1}$. The following theorem describes the property exploited in the construction.

**Theorem 1.** *Given that $T_{n-1}$ is the characteristic matrix of an $(n-1)$ cell TPSA, the matrix $T_n$ denoted by:*

$$T_n = \begin{pmatrix} & & & & | & 0 \\ & & T_{n-1} & & | & \vdots \\ & & & & | & 0 \\ - & - & - & - & - & - \\ 0 & \cdots & 0 & 1 & | & 0 \end{pmatrix}$$

*represents the characteristic matrix of an $n$ cell TPSA.*

*Proof.* We prove the result using mathematical induction. Let us assume that the theorem holds for $n-1$. We have to prove that the result holds true for $n$ cell as well. Thus, $T_{n-1}$ represents the characteristic matrix of an $(n-1)$ cell TPSA CA. Thus, the four properties which $T_{n-1}$ satisfy are: i) Rank($T_{n-1}$)=$n-2$, ii) Rank($T_{n-1} \oplus I_{n-1}$)=$n-1$, $I_{n-1}$ being an $n-1 \times n-1$ identity matrix, iii) Characteristic Polynomial = $x^{n-1}$, iv) Minimal Polynomial = $x^{n-1}$.

It is evident that since the element at the $n^{th}$ row and $(n-1)^{th}$ column is 1 and by the construction methodology all the other rows have 0 in the $(n-1)^{th}$ columns the row added is linearly independent from the other rows of $T_n$. Hence it adds by 1 to the rank of $T_{n-1}$. Thus, $rank(T_n) = rank(T_{n-1})+1 = n-2+1 = n-1$.

Similarly, using the fact that $rank(T_{n-1} \oplus I_{n-1}) = n-1$ (where $I_{n-1}$ is the identity matrix of order $n-1$), we have $rank(T_n \oplus I_n) = n$. The characteristic polynomial of the matrix $T_n$, denoted by $\phi_n(x)$ is evaluated as $det(T_n \oplus xI_n)$, where $det$ denotes the determinant. Thus we have,

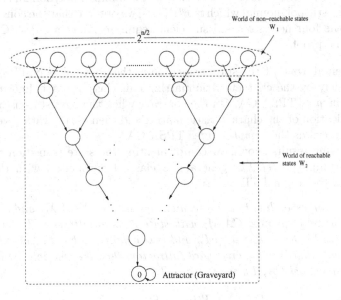

**Fig. 1.** The state transition graph of a non-complemented TPSA CA

$$\phi_n(x) = \det \begin{pmatrix} & & & & | & 0 \\ & & & & | & 0 \\ & & & & | & \vdots \\ & T_{n-1} & \oplus & xI_{n-1} & | & 0 \\ & & & & | & \vdots \\ & & & & | & 0 \\ & & & & | & 0 \\ - & - & - & - & - & - \\ 0 & \cdots & 0 & 1 & | & x \end{pmatrix}$$

$$= x\phi_{n-1}(x), (\phi_{n-1}(x) \text{ denotes}$$

the characteristic polynomial of $T_{n-1}$)

$$= x.x^{n-1} = x^n$$

In order to evaluate the minimal polynomial we make use of the following proposition.

**Lemma 3.** *Let $\phi_n(x)$ and $\psi_n(x)$ be the characteristic polynomial and the minimal polynomial of the matrix $T_n$, respectively. Let the greatest common divisor (gcd) of the matrix $(T_n \oplus I_n x)^\vee$ that is the matrix of algebraic complements of the elements of the matrix $(T_n \oplus I_n x)$ be $d(x)$. Then, $\phi_n(x) = d(x)\psi_n(x)$.*

From the matrix $(T_n \oplus I_n x)^\vee$ it may be observed that the element at the position $(0, n)$ is 1 and thus the gcd $d(x)$ is also 1. Thus the minimal polynomial is equal to the characteristic polynomial which is $x^n$. Thus, we observe that the construction follows all the four necessary and sufficient requirements of a TPSA CA. This completes the proof.

We have seen above that the state transition in the above class of TPSA CA is governed solely by the characteristic matrix. This class of CA is known as the *non-complemented* TPSA CA. On the contrary when the next state is obtained by the application of the characteristic matrix and then xoring with a vector $F$, the CA is known as the *complemented* TPSA CA.

The following results show how complementing the state transition function of the non-complemented CA generates a class of automaton with the same properties as the original TPSA CA.

**Lemma 4.** *Corresponding to a non-complemented TPSA CA $M_1$ and a state $Z$, there exists a complemented CA $M_2$ with state $Z$ as an attractor. If the characteristic matrix $M_1$ be indicated by $T_n$ and it is required to build a complemented TPSA CA such that $Z$ is the graveyard (attractor) then the characteristic matrix of the complemented CA, $\overline{T}_n$ is related to $T_n$ by*

$$\overline{T}_n(X) = T_n(X) \oplus (I_n \oplus T_n)Z$$

*where $X$ is the seed to the CA and $I_n$ is the identity matrix of order $n$.*

**Lemma 5.** *A complemented TPSA CA has the same structure as a non-complemented TPSA CA. To emphasize*

- *Number of attractors in the complemented CA is the same as that in the original non-complemented CA.*
- *Number of reachable states and non-reachable states are same as that in the original non-complemented CA.*

**Lemma 6.** *If any state $Z$ in the non-reachable world of a non-complemented CA is made the graveyard in a complemented TPSA, then the non-reachable elements become elements of the reachable world in the complemented CA and viceversa. Thus the non-reachable world $(W_1)$ and the reachable world $(W_2)$ exchange themselves (**Fig. 2**).*

*Proof.* Let $X$ and $Z$ be two non-reachable elements in the $n$ cell non-complemented CA with characteristic matrix $T_n$. Let $X$ be the $l^{th}$ level sister of $Z$. In all cases $l < n$. Thus, we have:

$$T_n^l(X) = T_n^l(Z)$$

Let us consider the state transition diagram of the complemented CA with $Z$ as the graveyard. The state transition of the complemented CA is indicated by $\overline{T}_n$. We shall prove that in this state transition graph $X$ is a reachable state. Let, the depth of $X$ in the graph of the complemented CA be $t$. If $t$ is less than $n$ then $X$ is a reachable state. Since, $Z$ is the graveyard of this graph we have:

$$\overline{T}_n^t(X) = Z$$
$$T_n^t(X) \oplus (I_n \oplus T_n^t)Z = Z$$
$$T_n^t(X) = T_n^t(Z)$$

Thus, $X$ and $Z$ are $t^{th}$ level sisters in the state transition graph of the non-complemented CA. But we know that they are $l^{th}$ level sisters. Thus $t = l < n$. Thus, the depth of $X$ is lesser than $n$ and hence $X$ is a reachable state in the state transition graph of the complemented CA.

**Lemma 7.** *If the state $Z$ is chosen independently as the graveyard in a complemented TPSA from a uniform distribution, then the state transition graph is a pseudo-random graph.*

*Proof.* Given any input state $X$, the output $Y$ is governed by the equation: $Y = \overline{T}_n(X) = T_n(X) \oplus (I_n \oplus T_n)Z$.

Now, since $Z$ is chosen independently and randomly from a uniform distribution, the probability that $Z$ equals a particular $Z_1$ is given by $Pr[Z = Z_1] = \frac{1}{2^n}$. Here $n$ is the size of the TPSA CA.

Let, when $Z_1$ is the graveyard, the next state of a state $X_1$ is say $Y_1$. Thus, $Y_1 = T_n(X_1) \oplus (I_n \oplus T_n)Z_1$. We compute the probability that for any arbitrary graveyard, $Z$, the next state of $X_1$ is $Y_1$. That is we compute:

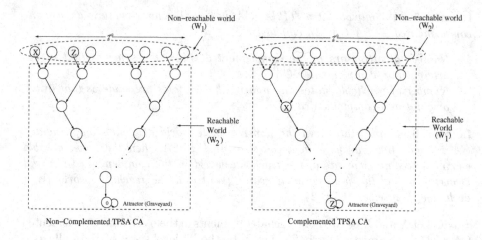

**Fig. 2.** The exchange of the worlds in a complemented TPSA CA

$$Pr[\overline{T_n}(X_1) = Y_1] = Pr[T_n(X_1) \oplus (I_n \oplus T_n)Z = Y_1]$$
$$= Pr[Z = Z_1]$$
$$( \text{ since, } rank(I_n \oplus T_n) = n)$$
$$= \frac{1}{2^n}$$

Thus the probability that there is an edge from $X_1$ to $Y_1$ is $Pr[X_1 \to Y_1] = \frac{1}{2^n} = \frac{1}{N}$, where $N$ is the number of vertices in the graph.

Thus for a given $X$, all the $Y$'s are equally probable and hence the distribution of $Y$ for a given $X$ is indistinguishable from a random distribution. Thus, the state transition graph of the TPSA CA *looks like* a random graph when the graveyard is chosen randomly and independently.

## 3.1 Construction of a Random $d$ Regular Graph Using the TPSA CA

We have seen in the previous discussion that the TPSA CA is capable of generating pseudo-random graphs. In this section we present a method to generate pseudo-random $d$ regular graphs by composing the random graphs. It may be noted that the adjacency of the graph is stored in the graveyard state, thus leading to a very compact storage of the graph. This is because given the graveyard state, the entire transition graph can be obtained. If there are $N$ vertices in the graph, the graveyard state has a size $logN$ and thus the storage required to store the graph is $O(logN)$.

In order to construct the $d$ regular graph we proceed as follows. We first present the construction of a 4 regular graph. Let $Z_1 \in W_1$ (non-reachable world in the non-complemented TPSA CA) and $Z_2 \in W_2$ (reachable world in the non-complemented TPSA CA). Let, $G_1$ and $G_2$ be the state transition graphs with $Z_1$ and $Z_2$ as the graveyards respectively.

Clearly, in $G_1$ if $X \in W_1$, $degree(X) = 3$ and if $X \in W_2$, $degree(X) = 1$. Similarly, in $G_2$ if $X \in W_1$, $degree(X) = 1$ and if $X \in W_2$, $degree(X) = 3$. Here $degree$ is defined as the sum of the $indegree$ and the $outdegree$ in the corresponding graph.

Thus, in the graph $G$ obtained by a union operation in the graphs $G_1$ and $G_2$, allowing multiple edges and self loops, we have for $X \in G$, $degree(X) = 4$. If we continue the union operation in the above method we have $degree(X) = d = 2(t+1)$, where $t$ is an odd integer and represents the number of union operations. Thus we can construct a $d$ regular graph from the TPSA CA. In fact we argue that we have a pseudo-random $d$ regular graph, if the graveyards are properly chosen.

For each of the graphs, we choose the graveyard states independently in a random fashion. We have seen previously, that the probability than an edge exists from any $X$ to any $Y$ is $\frac{1}{N}$. After performing the union operation we obtain a $d$ regular graph, where there are $d$ neighbors of each vertex. If we divide the graveyards into two sets:

$$Z = \{Z_1, Z_3, \ldots, Z_{d/2-1}\} \in W_1$$
$$Z^* = \{Z_2, Z_4, \ldots, Z_{d/2}\} \in W_2$$

Thus the $d$ regular graph is formed by the union of $d/4$ graphs, each of which is the union of two graphs formed with the graveyards chosen as the pairs $(Z_1, Z_2), \ldots, (Z_{d/2-1}, Z_{d/2})$. Then in the final graph, if $X \in W_1$, there are $d/2$ incoming edges and $d/4$ outgoing edges belonging to graphs with graveyards from $Z$ and $d/4$ outgoing edges belonging to graphs with graveyards from $Z^*$. Similarly, if $X \in W_2$, there are $d/2$ incoming edges and $d/4$ outgoing edges belonging to graphs with graveyards from $Z^*$ and $d/4$ outgoing edges belonging to graphs with graveyards from $Z$.

We note that $Y$ cannot be on the other side of two edges $e$ and $e^*$ if:

1. $e$ and $e^*$ are both outgoing edges and $e$ belongs to a graph with graveyard from $Z$ and $e^*$ belongs to a graph with graveyard from $Z^*$ or both belongs to either $Z$ or $Z^*$.
2. $e$ and $e^*$ are both incoming edges and $e$ belongs to a graph with graveyard from $Z$ and $e^*$ belongs to a graph with graveyard from $Z^*$ or both belongs to either $Z$ or $Z^*$.

The above properties hold because $rank(I_n \oplus T_n) = n$ and $Z \cap Z^* = \Phi$. Thus, the only possibility is if $e$ is say an incoming edge with graveyard from $Z$ and $e^*$ is an outgoing edge with graveyard from $Z^*$. Let the graveyards be respectively, $Z_i$ and $Z_j$, where $i$ is an odd integer such that $1 \leq i \leq d/2 - 1$ and $j$ is an even integer such that $2 \leq j \leq d/2$. Note that $Y$ cannot be opposite two pairs of edges, as then it implies that we also have two pairs of edges which have $Y$ and each pair belongs to the graphs with graveyard from $Z$ or $Z^*$. This is not permitted from our previous discussion. Thus, the node $Y$ can be opposite only one pair of edges, in which one edge belongs to a graph with graveyard $Z_i \in Z$ and the other belongs to a graph with graveyard $Z_j \in Z^*$. Suppose, there is an edge from $Y$ to $X$ in the graph with graveyard $Z_i$. Thus, $X = T_n(Y) \oplus (I_n \oplus T_n)Z_i$. Also if there is an edge from $X$ to $Y$ in the graph with graveyard $Z_j$ we have, $Y = T_n(X) \oplus (I_n \oplus T_n)Z_j$. Thus, we have $Y = (I_n \oplus T_n)^{-1}(T_n Z_i \oplus Z_j)$. Thus for each pair of $Z_i$ and $Z_j$ we have one such $Y$ which may have two edges with an $X$. From the enumeration of $Z$ and $Z^*$ we can have $(d/4)^2$ pairs and thus $(d/4)^2$ values of $Y$ which may form 2 multiple edges with $X$. For these values of $Y$, using inclusion-exclusion principle, the probability that $Y$ is a neighbor of a given $X$ is $p = d/N - (d/4)^2(1/N)^2$. If we set $d = N/c$, for some integer $c > 0$ we have $p = \frac{1}{c}(\frac{16c-1}{16c}) \approx 1/c$, for $c > 4$. For some chosen values of $N = 128$ and $d = 16$, we have $p = 0.124$ which is almost equal to $1/8 = 0.125$.

For other cases of $Y$, $Y$ can be a neighbor of $X$ in only one of the $d$ edges, so the probability that $Y$ is the neighbor of $X$ is $\frac{d}{N}$. Thus, we can fairly state that for all cases the probability that $Y$ is a neighbor of $X$ has a probability of $d/N$. Thus we have indeed a $d$ regular graph which has its edge distributions like a random graph with $d$ regularity.

## 4   Experimental Observations on the Expansion Properties

We present some experimental results on the expansion properties of the constructed graph in **Table 1**. It measures the value of the two largest eigen values for the TPSA based graphs for degree $4, 8, 12$ and $16$. The difference between the largest two eigen values is known as the spectral gap and should be large for good expansion of the graph. Results show that the spectral gap and hence the expansion increases proportionately with the number of union operations ($t$).

**Table 1.** Spectrum of a 4 cell TPSA based regular graph

| No. of Union (t) | Graveyards | Degree | First Eigen Value | Second Eigen Value | Spectral Gap (g) | g/t |
|---|---|---|---|---|---|---|
| 1 | {0},{4} | 4 | 4 | 3.2361 | 0.76 | 0.76 |
| 3 | {0,15},{4,8} | 8 | 8 | 4.899 | 3.10 | 1.03 |
| 5 | {0,15,3},{4,8,10} | 12 | 12 | 6.3440 | 5.66 | 1.14 |
| 7 | {0,15,3,2},{4,8,10,9} | 16 | 16 | 5.2263 | 10.77 | 1.54 |

The lower bound of the expansion of the generated graphs may be computed using Tanner's Theorem[8,9].

**Theorem 2. (Tanner)** Let $M$ be the adjacency matrix of a $d$-regular graph $G$ with $N$ vertices and let $\lambda_2$ be its second largest eigenvalue. Then, for all sets $A$,

$$N(A) \geq \frac{d^2 N}{d^2 |A| + N\lambda_2^2(1 - |A|/N)}|A|$$

*,where $N(A)$ is the neighbourhood of $A$ outside $A$.*

Let, $G$ be the expander graph with $n$ nodes, generated by the TPSA based method. The expansion of the graph $G$ may be computed as follows:

$$E(G) = max_{A \in [N]} min_{A \subseteq G; |A| = x}(|N(A)| - |A|)$$

$$\geq max_{A \in [N]} \frac{d^2}{d^2 x/N + \lambda_2^2(1 - x/N)} x - x$$

$$= max_{A \in [N]} \frac{Nx}{(1 - \frac{\lambda_2^2}{d^2})x + \frac{\lambda_2^2}{d^2}N} - x$$

$$= max_{A \in [N]} \frac{Nx}{(1 - c)x + cN} - x,$$

$$\text{where } c = \frac{\lambda_2^2}{d^2}$$

The expression in the variable $x$ becomes maximum at $x = x_{max}$, where

$$\frac{x_{max}}{N} = \frac{\sqrt{c} - c}{1 - c}$$

$$= \frac{\lambda - \lambda^2}{1 - \lambda^2}, \text{ where } \lambda = \sqrt{c}$$

Thus the lower bound of the expansion of the graph $G$ is

$$E(G) \geq \frac{\lambda(1 + \lambda^2) - 2\lambda^2}{\lambda(1 - \lambda^2)} N$$

Using the above result we obtain lower bounds of the expansion of the generated expander graphs and tabulate them in **Table 2**.

**Table 2.** Expansion of the expander graphs generated by 4 cell TPSA CA

| No. of nodes ($N$) | Degree ($d$) | First Eigenvalue ($\lambda_1$) | Second Eigenvalue ($\lambda_2$) | $\lambda = \frac{\lambda_2}{\lambda_1}$ | Expansion Bound ($E(G)$) |
|---|---|---|---|---|---|
| 16 | 4 | 4 | 3.2361 | 0.809 | 1.688 |
| 16 | 8 | 8 | 4.899 | 0.6124 | 3.85 |
| 16 | 12 | 12 | 6.3440 | 0.5287 | 7.84 |
| 16 | 16 | 16 | 5.2263 | 0.3266 | 8.12 |

As expected the expansion increases with the increase in the degree of the graphs. The results may be compared with the expansion rates of other constructions of expander graphs, with similar parameters as mentioned in [8]. It is mentioned in [1], that the best results are from the random construction of the expander graphs. A typical value of the expansion bound of the random expander constructions mentioned in [8,1] is $N = 20, d = 8$ and $E(G) = 6.49$. This is quite similar to the expansion bound of the proposed construction. The storage required to store the $d$ graphs is that of storing $d$ graveyard states, and is thus $O(logN)$, and is thus possible to be realized by efficient implementations.

# 5    Conclusion

We have proposed a new construction method of expander graphs using a special class of Cellular Automata, called TPSA-CA. We have characterized the CA and have theoretically explained its various properties. Finally, we show that the transition graphs of the CA can be composed to realize random regular graphs which also has good expansion properties. The storage required to store the expander graph of $N$ vertices is $O(logN)$.

# References

1. Goldreich, O.: Candidate One-Way Functions Based on Expander Graphs. Cryptology ePrint Archive, Report 2000/063 (2000)
2. Charles, D.X., Lauter, K.E., Goren, E.Z.: Cryptographic Hash Functions from Expander Graphs. Journal of Cryptology (2007)
3. Chaudhuri, P.P., Chowdhury, D.R., Nandi, S., Chattopadhyay, S.: Additive Cellular Automata Theory and its Application, vol. 1. IEEE Computer Society Press (1997)
4. Linial, N., Wigderson, A.: Expander graphs and their applications, (2003), http://www.math.ias.edu/boaz/ExpanderCourse/
5. Lubotzky, A., Phillips, R., Sarnak, P.: Ramanujan graphs. Combinatorica 8(3), 261–277 (1988)
6. Margulis, G.A.: Explicit constructions of expanders. Problemy Peredači Informacii 9(4), 71–80 (1973)
7. Margulis, G.A.: Explicit group-theoretic constructions of combinatorial schemes and their applications in the construction of expanders and concentrators. Problemy Peredachi Informatsii 24(1), 51–60 (1988)
8. Panjwani, S.K.: An Experimental Evaluation of Goldreich's One-Way Function, Cryptology ePrint Archive, Report 2000/063 (2001)
9. Alon, N.: Eigen Values, Geometric Expanders, Sorting in Rounds and Ramsey Theorem. Combinatorica 6, 207–219 (1986)

# Analysis of Reachability Tree for Identification of Cyclic and Acyclic CA States[*]

Nazma Naskar[1], Avik Chakraborty[2], Pradipta Maji[3], and Sukanta Das[2]

[1] Dept. of Information Technology, Seacom Engineering College,
Howrah, 711302, India
naskar.preeti@gmail.com
[2] Dept. of Information Technology, Bengal Engg and Sci University,
Shibpur, 711103, India
avikjis27@gmail.com, sukanta@it.becs.ac.in
[3] Machine Intelligence Unit,Indian Statistical Institute, Kolkata, 700108, India
pmaji@isical.ac.in

**Abstract.** This paper reports a scheme to identify cyclic/acyclic states from the state space of cellular automata (CA). We analyze the reachability tree to do this. An algorithm is presented to count the cyclic states. We introduce a concept of tree merging for identifying cyclic and acyclic states. To our knowledge, this is the first work to efficiently identify cyclic/acyclic states from the state space of nonlinear CA. Since cyclic states can only form attractors, the identification of cyclic states would help us to characterize CA attractors.

**Keywords:** Attractor, multi attractor cellular automata (MACA), reachability tree, cyclic states.

## 1 Introduction

Reachability tree was proposed to characterize reachable/non-reachable states of 1-dimensional cellular automata (CA) [6]. The tree was utilized in analysis and synthesis of reversible CA [2,4], and also in exploring a few aspects of irreversible CA [3,5]. The aim of this work is to analyze reachability tree to distinguish *cyclic* states from *acyclic* states of a given automaton, and count the number of cyclic states of the automaton.

In the state space of a CA, a few states form cycles (attractors). Such states are cyclic, and the rest states in the CA state space are acyclic. To our knowledge, there is no efficient method till now to identify cyclic and acyclic CA states. It requires exponential time to directly recognize a state as cyclic/acyclic from CA state space. Here we present an efficient method to recognize, as well as to count the cyclic states. However, the attractors may be formed with a single cyclic state (single length cycle) or with more than one cyclic state (multi-length cycle). The

---

[*] This work is supported by AICTE Career Award fund (F.No. 1-51/RID/CA/29/ 2009-10), awarded to Sukanta Das.

G.C. Sirakoulis and S. Bandini (Eds.): ACRI 2012, LNCS 7495, pp. 63–72, 2012.
© Springer-Verlag Berlin Heidelberg 2012

CA with only single length cycle attractors attracted the CA researchers due to their utility in several applications, like pattern classification, design of associative memory, etc. [1,7,8]. To get such type of CA, however, the researchers concentrated on linear/additive CA, which have limited search space. Due to the unavailability of proper characterization, the wide search space of nonlinear CA could not be utilized for those applications. Recently, a work on such characterization has been reported [3]. The work, however, has not explored the whole search space of nonlinear CA. Moreover, it has not addressed the issue of identifying cyclic and acyclic states separately.

In this scenario, this work targets to identify cyclic states from the CA state space. The identification of cyclic states would enable us to recognize CA having only single length cycle attractors. In the current work, we process reachability tree of a given CA to declare a state as cyclic/acyclic. An algorithm is also presented to count the cyclic states of an arbitrary CA.

## 2  Cellular Automata and Reachability Tree

The cellular automata (CA), the discrete dynamical systems, consist of a lattice of cells. The states of cells are affected by their neighbors. In the current work, we concentrate on the two-state 3-neighborhood (self, left and right neighbors) CA. The next state of the $i^{th}$ cell of such CA is $S_i^{t+1} = f_i(S_{i-1}^t, S_i^t, S_{i+1}^t)$, where $f_i$ is the next state function; $S_{i-1}^t$, $S_i^t$ and $S_{i+1}^t$ are the present states of the left neighbor, self and right neighbor of the $i^{th}$ CA cell.

The collection of states $\mathcal{S}^t(S_1^t, S_2^t, \cdots, S_n^t)$ of cells at time $t$ is the present state of CA having $n$ cells. If $S_0^t = S_{n+1}^t = 0$ (null), the CA are null boundary. The function $f_i$ can be expressed in the form of truth table (Table 1). The decimal equivalent of the 8 outputs is traditionally called as 'rule' [9]. In a two-state 3-neighborhood CA, there can be a total of $2^8$ (256) rules. The first row of the Table 1 lists the possible $2^3$ (8) combinations of the present states of $(i-1)^{th}$, $i^{th}$ and $(i+1)^{th}$ cells at time t. The last four rows indicate the next states of the $i^{th}$ cell at $(t+1)$ for different combinations of the present states of its neighbors, forming the rules 10, 69, 204 and 68 respectively. Out of 256, only 14 rules are linear/additive rules [1]. The rest are nonlinear rule.

**Rule Min Term (RMT):** From the view point of Switching Theory, a combination of the present states (as noted in the 1st row of Table 1) of a CA cell can be viewed as the min term of a 3-variable $(S_{i-1}^t, S_i^t, S_{i+1}^t)$ switching function. Therefore, each column of the first row of Table 1 is referred to as Rule Min Term (RMT). The column 011 is the RMT 3. The next states corresponding to this RMT are 1 for rules 10 and 204, and 0 for rules 69 and 68.

The set of rules $\mathcal{R} = \langle \mathcal{R}_1, \mathcal{R}_2, \cdots, \mathcal{R}_i, \cdots, \mathcal{R}_n \rangle$ that configure the cells of CA is called the rule vector. If $\mathcal{R}_1 = \mathcal{R}_2 = \cdots = \mathcal{R}_n$, the CA are uniform, otherwise they are non-uniform or hybrid CA. This work deals with hybrid null-boundary CA.

The sequence of states generated (state transitions), during their evolution (with time), directs the CA behavior. The state transition diagram (Fig. 1) of

**Table 1.** Truth table for rule 10, 69, 204 and 68

| Present state : | 111 | 110 | 101 | 100 | 011 | 010 | 001 | 000 | *Rule* |
|---|---|---|---|---|---|---|---|---|---|
| (*RMT*) | (7) | (6) | (5) | (4) | (3) | (2) | (1) | (0) | |
| (i) Next State : | 0 | 0 | 0 | 0 | 1 | 0 | 1 | 0 | 10 |
| (ii) Next State : | 0 | 1 | 0 | 0 | 0 | 1 | 0 | 1 | 69 |
| (iii) Next State : | 1 | 1 | 0 | 0 | 1 | 1 | 0 | 0 | 204 |
| (iv) Next State : | 0 | 1 | 0 | 0 | 0 | 1 | 0 | 0 | 68 |

a CA may contain *cyclic* and *acyclic* states. A state is called *cyclic* if it lies on some cycle. Cyclic states form attractors. The states 4, 3, 11 and 12 (considering first bit of a CA state as LSB) of Fig. 1 are the cyclic states that form attractors; whereas the states 7, 6, 1, 9, 14 and 15 are the non-reachable states.

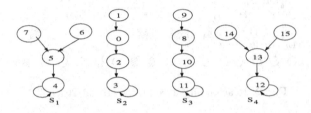

**Fig. 1.** State transitions of a CA with rule vector $\langle 10, 69, 204, 68 \rangle$

**Reachability Tree:** Reachability tree [2,6] is a logical device to characterize nonlinear CA. It is a binary tree that represents the reachable states of the CA. Each node of the tree is constructed with RMT(s) of a rule. The left edge of a node is considered as the 0-edge and the right edge is the 1-edge. The number of levels of a reachability tree for an $n-$cell CA is $(n+1)$. Root node is at level 0 and the leaf nodes are at level $n$. The nodes of level $i$ are constructed by the RMTs of $\mathcal{R}_{i+1}$. The number of leaf nodes in the tree denotes the number of reachable states of the CA. A sequence of edges from the root to a leaf node, representing an $n-$bit binary string, is a reachable state, where 0-edge and 1-edge represent 0 and 1 respectively. The RMTs of two consecutive cell rules $\mathcal{R}_i$ and $\mathcal{R}_{i+1}$ are related while the CA changes its state [2]. The relationship between the RMTs of $\mathcal{R}_i$ and $\mathcal{R}_{i+1}$, while computing the next state of a CA, is noted in Table 2 [2]. The relations, noted in the table, play an important role in characterizing the CA behavior configured with different cell rules. We say two RMTs are **equivalent** if they produce same set of RMTs for the next level. For example 0 and 4 are equivalent RMT. Two RMTs at level $i$ are sibling if they are resulted from an RMTs of level $(i-1)$. For example, RMTs 0 and 1 are sibling RMT.

Fig. 2 shows the reachability tree for the CA $\langle 10, 69, 204, 68 \rangle$ (the RMTs of the CA rules are noted in Table 1). The decimal numbers within a node (Fig. 2) at level $i$ represent the RMTs of the CA cell rule $\mathcal{R}_{i+1}$ following which the cell $(i+1)$ may change its state. The RMTs of a rule for which we follow 0-edge

**Table 2.** Relationship between RMTs of cell $i$ and cell $(i+1)$ for next state computation

| RMT at $i^{th}$ rule | RMTs at $(i+1)^{th}$ rule |
|----------------------|---------------------------|
| 0/4 | 0, 1 |
| 1/5 | 2, 3 |
| 2/6 | 4, 5 |
| 3/7 | 6, 7 |

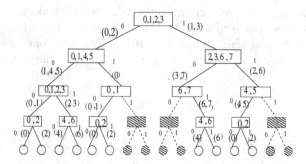

**Fig. 2.** Reachability Tree of CA $\langle 10, 69, 204, 68 \rangle$

or 1-edge are noted in the bracket. The dotted edges represent non-reachable edges, The state 0110 is non reachable state indicated by dotted edge. The root node (level 0) is constructed with RMTs 0, 1, 2 and 3. Since we consider only null boundary CA, the RMTs 4, 5, 6 and 7 are the *don't cares* for first cell rule. Similarly, RMTs 1, 3, 5 and 7 of last cell rule are the don't cares.

**Definition 1.** *A sequence of n RMTs those derive a reachable state of an n-cell CA is called* **RMT Sequence (RS).**

For example, the sequence $\langle 2412 \rangle$ is an RS which derives the state 0001 (8 of Fig. 2), where 2, 4, 1 and 2 are the RMTs corresponding to rules 10, 69, 204 and 68 respectively (Table 1). However, another RS $\langle 0012 \rangle$ points to the next state of 0001. Therefore, we get a sequence of RSs that represents a sequence of states in state transition diagram. The RSs 2412, 0012, 1252, 3652 derive the states 8, 10, 11, 11 in sequence (Fig. 2). The sequence of RS plays an important role in analysis of reachability tree.

## 3    Cyclic States in State Transition Diagram

In a state transition diagram, three types of states are found – (i) cyclic, (ii) acyclic but reachable and (iii) non-reachable. All the reachable states (cyclic and acyclic) can be reached from the non-reachable states. So, we first identify the non-reachable (hence, acyclic) states in a state transition diagram, and remove

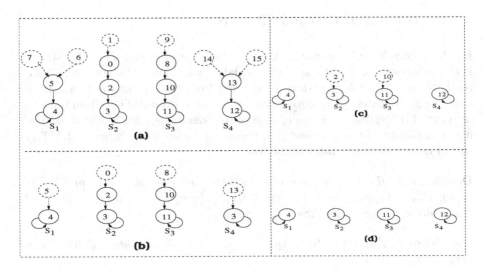

**Fig. 3.** Processing of State Transition Diagram of CA $\langle 10, 69, 204, 68 \rangle$

them from the diagram. Therefore, we get a new set of non-reachable states. These states are also acyclic. This process is repeated to identify all acyclic states. However, if a state is cyclic, it is not possible to convert it a non-reachable one by the above process (see the example below). So, the processing is stopped if no non-reachable states are found. The rest states are the cyclic states. We can itemize the steps as following.

1. Process the state space of CA and remove the non-reachable states.
2. Identify new non-reachable (which are originally acyclic but reachable) states in the processed state space.
3. Repeat (1) and (2) until no new non-reachable states can be identified.

To illustrate the above process, consider the CA of Fig. 1. We process state transition diagram of the CA to identify the cyclic/acyclic states (Fig. 3). The non-reachable states of the CA are identified first (dotted circle states of Fig. 3(a)). These states are removed from the diagram, and we get a new set of non-reachable states – 5, 0, 8 and 13 (Fig. 3(b)). Now we remove these non-reachable states and get a new diagram (Fig. 3(c)). In this new diagram, however, states 4 and 12 are not non-reachable, as they are cyclic states. Finally, we get a diagram having only cyclic states (Fig. 3(d)). So we stop further processing of the diagram. If we even further process, no more states can be removed. The remaining states are the cyclic states. Those states form single length cycle attractors (point states).

Therefore, our task is (a) to identify non-reachable states, and (b) to remove non-reachable states from the state transition diagram. The non-reachable states can efficiently be identified by utilizing reachability tree [6]. However, any state may not be directly removed from the state transition diagram, because it may affect other states. To achieve this, we process the reachability tree of the CA.

## 4    Processing of Reachability Tree

By the processing of reachability tree, we find the predecessors of CA states. If the processors of a state are non-reachable, we convert the state to a non-reachable one. That is, the state is removed from the tree as the tree depicts only reachable states. To remove a state, we need to drop RMT(s) from the tree or move RMT(s) from one node/edge to another node/edge of the tree. The major challenge of this processing is, the dropping or reorientation of RMT(s) should not affect other states of the tree.

**Definition 2.** *RMT $x_i$ ($y_i$) is said to be the predecessor (successor) of RMT $y_i$ ($x_i$) if $RS_t = \langle x_1 x_2 \cdots x_i \cdots x_n \rangle$ and $RS_{t+1} = \langle y_1 y_2 \cdots y_i \cdots y_n \rangle$, and $RS_t$ and $RS_{t+1}$ are two consecutive RSs in a sequence.*

**Definition 3.** *An RMT x0y (x1y) is said to be self replicating if RMT x0y (x1y) is 0 (1).*

For example, RMT 3 (011) of rule 10 is self replicating, whereas all the RMTs of rule 204 are self replicating (Table 1). An RS points to a single cycle attractor if all the RMTs of the RS are self replicating. The RS $\langle 3652 \rangle$ derives the point state 1101 (11 of Fig. 1) because RMTs 3, 6, 5 and 2 are self replicating. We move an RMT from one edge to another in a level of tree depending upon the fact that the RMT is self replicating or not.

We presume in the processing of tree that all the cyclic states form single length cycle attractors. So, only self replicating RMTs are to be present in the finally processed tree. We call a position of an RMT on the tree is *stable* if the RMT is self replicating. During processing, if an RMT is not in its stable position, we *make* the RMT self replicating by moving it from one edge to another. We call such movement of an RMT as *merging*. However, the merging of an RMT depends on the RMT value and the merging of its predecessor RMT. For the RMTs of root, merging depends only on the RMT values. By the process of merging, we actually find the predecessor RMT of an RMT.

Let us consider a subtree TR with $i^{th}$ and $(i + 1)^{th}$ levels (Fig. 4). Suppose, RMT $k$ and RMT $y$ are not in their stable positions. To get their stable positions, RMT $k$ (RMT $y$) should be on right (left) edge. We make a link for RMT $k$ (RMT $y$) from left to right (right to left), and call it forward merging (backward merging). The RMTs $x$ and $l$ are on their stable positions and form self merging (Fig. 4).

Now, we consider $(i + 1)^{th}$ level for merging $k_1$, $k_2$ (both have value 0). We have to find where RMT $k$ is merged at $i^{th}$ level. In this case, RMT $k$ is merged at subtree $TR_2$. So RMTs $k_1$, $k_2$ are to be merged at anywhere at $TR_2$. However both $k_1$ and $k_2$ both of them finally merges at left edge of $TR_2$. In Fig. 4, RMT $k$ is merged to right edge at $i^{th}$ level. However, RMT $y$ and $l$ are already in the right edge. This implies, if RMT $k$ exists at $i^{th}$ position of $RS_t$, then the $i^{th}$ position of $RS_{t-1}$ contains either RMT $l$ or RMT $y$. By this process, therefore, we can get predecessor RMT(s) of an RMT.

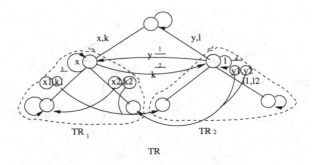

**Fig. 4.** Basics of tree merging

If the predecessor(s) of a state is non-reachable, we remove the state from the tree. To do this, we find predecessor RMT of an RMT. However, we can not directly remove an RMT, because that may affect other states. For example, RMTs 2 and 3 in level 2 of Fig. 2 generate four RSs – $\langle 0136 \rangle$, $\langle 2536 \rangle$, $\langle 0124 \rangle$ and $\langle 2524 \rangle$. If we remove RMT 3 then the cyclic state 0011 (pointed by RS $\langle 0136 \rangle$) is also removed, which is not desirable. To handle this situation, we introduce the concept of *predecessor weight* and *successor weight*.

At $i^{th}$ level say RMT $x$ has predecessor weight $W_p$ ($W_p$ is number of predecessors of RMT $x$) and successor weight $W_s$ ($W_s$ is number of successors of RMT $x$). So each RMT at some level has some $W_p$ and $W_s$. In an $n$-cell CA, $W_p=0$ and $W_s=2$ for the root. For second level to $(n-2)^{th}$ level, $W_p = 1$ and $W_s = 2$; for $(n-1)^{th}$ level, $W_p =1$ and $W_s = 1$; and for last level, $W_p = 1$ and $W_s$ is invalid. Predecessor weights and successor weights are decreased by 1 and 2 respectively when the respective RMT is merged to some non-reachable edge. The $W_s$ and $W_p$ become zero if it is not a part of some cycle. The edge/node are said to be non-reachable edge/node if at that edge/node, $W_s= W_p=0$. The following example illustrates the scheme in detail.

*Example 1.* Let take an example of $CA\langle 10, 69, 204, 68 \rangle$. Fig. 5 depicts the tree merging technique for finding cyclic and acyclic states. At root RMTs 0 and 3 form self merging. RMT 1 makes backward merging whereas RMT 2 forms forward merging. $W_p$ and $W_s$ of all RMTs are 0 and 2 respectively. At second level, all RMTs are merged as per merging rule and we proceed for next level, because no non-reachable state is encountered till now. Here, $W_p = 1$ and $W_s = 2$ for all RMTs. At $3^{rd}$ level, only RMTs 0 and 1 have default predecessor and successor weights as 1 ($(n-1)^{th}$ level) as their parent equivalent RMT 0 and 4 are on different edge at $2^{nd}$ level. However rest 6 RMTs have predecessor and successor weights as 2, because their parent RMTs are equivalent and appear at the same edge in $2^{nd}$ level. In this level, we encounter non-reachable node (shaded node). Here for RMTs 0 and 1, $W_p$ and $W_s$ are decremented by 1. Based on merging of RMTs 6 and 7, $W_p$ and $W_s$ of them are decremented by 2. After decrementing, the edges as well as nodes become non-reachable. This is shown in Fig. 5(b). However, RMTs 2 and 3 lose their both weights by 1.

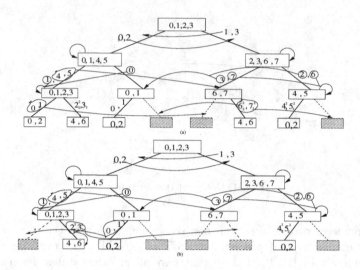

**Fig. 5.** Tree merging for getting cyclic states. RMTs have $W_p$ and $W_s$, not shown here.

The decrement of weight of any RMT implies, some more states become non-reachable. After previous step we can't decrement weights of any RMT further so we go for next level (leaf). In next level we cannot perform the operation as they are all self merged. So, the remaining states the cyclic states. One can count the cyclic states by observing the weights.

## 5    Counting Cyclic States

We now formally present an algorithm to calculate the number of cyclic states of CA, based on the theory developed in the last section. Input to the algorithm is CA rule vector and output of the algorithm is number of cyclic states. We do not form the reachability tree separately. Rather, we construct just 2 levels and do the required processing. Variables like *oldcount, newcount* store the number of non-reachable state. We report the number of cyclic state by subtracting final value of oldcount from total number states. We use other two variable $W_p$ and $W_s$ with its usual meaning, discussed earlier.

**Algorithm 1. FindNoOfCyclicState**
**Input:** $\langle \mathcal{R}_1, \cdots, \mathcal{R}_i, \cdots, \mathcal{R}_n \rangle$ ($n$-cell CA).
**Output:** number of cyclic state.
*Step 1:* Form the root node and identify the left and right edge of the root (based on $\mathcal{R}_1$).
For each RMT, set $W_p \leftarrow 0, W_s \leftarrow 2$.
    *(i)* Form a link from the edge of an RMT to the edge which is the stable position of the RMT.
    *(ii)* If the stable position does not exist on the tree (non-reachable edge),

decrement $W_s$ by 2 and mark the RMT as non-reachable.
Set $oldcount \leftarrow$ number of non-reachable RMT $\times 2^{n-2}$
*Step 2*: Repeat Step 3 to Step 5 for $i = 2$ to $n$.
*Step 3*: Get the nodes of reachability tree for level $(i - 1)$.
*Step 4*: For each RMT $(r)$ on each edge of level $(i - 1)$,
      *(i)* identify number of RMTs $(p)$ of previous level that derive $r$,
      *(ii)* set $W_p \leftarrow p$ and $W_s \leftarrow p \times 2$ (for $i = n - 1$, $W_s \leftarrow p \times 1$ and $i = n$, $W_s$
is invalid),
      *(iii)* find stable position of the RMT on an edge and make a link from the
current position (edge) to the final edge (the link determines the RMTs, derived
from $r$, will be linked with an edge which is proceed by the previously linked
edge),
      *(iv)* if the stable position does not exist on the tree (non-reachable edge),
decrement $W_p$ by 1 and $W_s$ by 2 (for $i = n - 1$, decrement $W_s$ by 1; and for
$i = n$, $W_s$ is invalid) and mark the RMT as non-reachable,
      *(vi)* if $W_s = 0$ and $W_p = 0$, then
            Mark the RMT as non-reachable for its current edge position.
*Step 5*: Set $newcount \leftarrow$ number of non-reachable RMTs $\times 2^{n-i}$.
      If newcount $\neq$ oldcount, then
      *(i)* set oldcount = newcount,
      *(ii)* Find some stable positions of level $(i - 1)$ have already become non-
reachable.
      *(iii)* If such positions exist, decrement $W_p$ by 1 and $W_s$ by 2.
      *(iv)* If $W_s = 0$ and $W_p = 0$ then,
            Mark RMT as non-reachable.
      *(v)* Repeat Step 5.
*Step 6*: Report number of cyclic state $\leftarrow$ $(2^n$ - oldcount$)$.
*Performance analysis:* This algorithm's complexity depends on the level in which
we first encounter non reachable state. We need to store the information about
$i^{th}$ level and $(i - 1)^{th}$ level. The worst case happen when any CA is reversible,
as we have to store exponential information. However when we dealing with
irreversible CA some states may be removed at $i^{th}$ level, so storage and time
complexity may get reduced. For example in case of CA $\langle 10, 60, 204, 204, 0 \rangle$ we
do not need exponential time or space to identify the cyclic states.

Since the cyclic states can only form the attractors, the number of attractors
are less than or equal to the number of of cyclic states (which is the output of
the Algorithm 1). If all the attractors are single length cycle attractors, then the
number of cyclic states is equal to the number of attractors. We have already
reported a scheme in [5] to find the number of single length cycle attractors.
Using that scheme and Algorithm 1, we can answer whether all attractors are
of cycle length 1.

# 6    Conclusion

This paper has reported a novel scheme to identify cyclic/acyclic states in the
state space of CA. To do this, reachability tree for CA is explored. An algorithm

is also reported to count the the number of cyclic states. The scheme, reported here, may be utilized to characterize the CA attractors.

# References

1. Pal Chaudhuri, P., Roy Chowdhury, D., Nandi, S., Chatterjee, S.: Additive Cellular Automata – Theory and Applications, USA, vol. 1. IEEE Computer Society Press (1997) ISBN 0-8186-7717-1
2. Das, S.: Theory and Applications of Nonlinear Cellular Automat. In: VLSI Design. PhD thesis, Bengal Engineering and Science University, Shibpur, India (2007)
3. Das, S., Mukherjee, S., Naskar, N., Sikdar, B.K.: Characterization of single cycle ca and its application in pattern classification. Electr. Notes Theor. Comput. Sci. 252, 181–203 (2009)
4. Das, S., Sikdar, B.K.: Classification of CA Rules Targeting Synthesis of Reversible Cellular Automata. In: El Yacoubi, S., Chopard, B., Bandini, S. (eds.) ACRI 2006. LNCS, vol. 4173, pp. 68–77. Springer, Heidelberg (2006)
5. Das, S., Shaw, C., Sikdar, B.K.: Exploring CA State Space to Synthesize Cellular Automata with Specified Attractor Set. In: Umeo, H., Morishita, S., Nishinari, K., Komatsuzaki, T., Bandini, S. (eds.) ACRI 2008. LNCS, vol. 5191, pp. 152–159. Springer, Heidelberg (2008)
6. Das, S., Sikdar, B.K., Pal Chaudhuri, P.: Characterization of Reachable/Nonreachable Cellular Automata States. In: Sloot, P.M.A., Chopard, B., Hoekstra, A.G. (eds.) ACRI 2004. LNCS, vol. 3305, pp. 813–822. Springer, Heidelberg (2004)
7. Maji, P., Shaw, C., Ganguly, N., Sikdar, B.K., Pal Chaudhuri, P.: Theory and Application of Cellular Automata For Pattern Classification. Special issue of Fundamenta Informaticae on Cellular Automata 58, 321–354 (2003)
8. Maji, P.: Cellular Automata Evolution for Pattern Recognition. PhD thesis, Jadavpur University, Kolkata, India (2005)
9. Wolfram, S.: Theory and Application of Cellular Automata. World Scientific (1986)

# Confliction-Like Dynamics of Rule 20 ECA
# of Wolfram Class II

Fumio Ohi and Takanori Ichikawa

Nagoya Institute of Technology, Gokiso-cho, Showa-ku, Nagoya 466-8555, Japan

**Abstract.** In this paper, we examine rule 20 elementary cellular automaton of Wolfram class II and show that the rule has 2-step 2-right and 2-step 2-left shift dynamical subsystems, and combining these two subsystems moving in the opposite direction, we have a confliction-like dynamical sub-system which cannot be imagined from that the rule belongs to Wolfram class II. Furthermore we show $g_{20}^2 = \max\{f_{20RE}, f_{20LE}\}$ suggesting that the rule 20 is composed of two simpler cellular automata $f_{20RE}$ and $f_{20LE}$ corresponding to 2-step 2-right and 2-step 2-left shift dynamical subsystems, respectively. We also mention that there exist several rules of class II showing confliction-like dynamics similar to rule 20 but all of them have not yet been fully examined. Rule 14, one of them, especially shows an interesting movement called reversing and right shift.

From these observations we know that even a single cellular automaton has not necessarily only one dynamical property but also includes several entirely different subsystems and each of them emerges depending on patterns of initial configurations. And furthermore we may say that there exist some basic cellular automata and methods, perhaps Boolean functions, to combine them to generate other cellular automata.

## 1 Introduction

It is well known that Wolfram [6] has classified cellular automata into four classes according to space-time patterns emerged from randomly given initial configurations, by intensive computer simulations. This classification gives us a perspective over cellular automata, but does not figure out complicated relationships among local rules, patterns of configurations and emerged space-time patterns. One cellular automaton may have diverse dynamical properties, which are not uniquely characterized by the class to which it belongs.

The space-time patterns generated by the cellular automata of Wolfram's class I are said to die out eventually or in a finite time steps [7]. But for example, rule 40 ECA(elementary cellular automaton) of the class I shows a right shift dynamics on a set of configurations having a special pattern and then is shown to be Devaney chaos on the set [2]. These configurations cannot be given randomly, since the Bernoulli measure of the set is proved to be 0 [5]. Rule 168 ECA, also a member of class I, is observed to have a right shift dynamical subsystem [3], similarly to rule 40.

Rule 56 ECA of class II shows confliction-like or wave-like movements for configurations having a special pattern. This dynamics cannot be imagined from

G.C. Sirakoulis and S. Bandini (Eds.): ACRI 2012, LNCS 7495, pp. 73–82, 2012.
© Springer-Verlag Berlin Heidelberg 2012

that the rule belongs to class II, of which cellular automata are said to emerge periodic space-time patterns [7]. It is also shown that rule 56 is composed of rules 40 and 48, and $g_{56} = \max\{g_{40}, g_{48}\}$ [4]. Rule 56 is equivalent to rule 40 and is right shift on a set of configurations of a particular pattern, and is equivalent to rule 48 and is left shift on a set of ones of another pattern. The confliction-like dynamics are shown on a set of configurations composed by combining the above two kinds of configurations [4].

We have found 0-quiescent ECAs of class II that show a glimpse of confliction-like dynamics as $6 \leftrightarrow 20$, $14 \leftrightarrow 84$, $56 \leftrightarrow 98$, $58 \leftrightarrow 114$, $74 \leftrightarrow 88$, $134 \leftrightarrow 148$, $142 \leftrightarrow 212$, $158 \leftrightarrow 214$, $168 \leftrightarrow 224$, $184 \leftrightarrow 226$, where for example, $6 \leftrightarrow 20$ means that rules 6 and 20 are mutually symmetric. We notice that there exist ECAs dual to the above rules, which are omitted here. Examinations of these cellular automata suggest us that even a single cellular automaton has not necessarily only one dynamical property but also several entirely different subsystems and the emergence of each of them is depend on the patterns of initial configurations. We may also infer that there may exist some basic cellular automata and many other cellular automata could be composed of them by Boolean functions.

Examinations of cellular automata from the above point of view clarify dynamical properties of them along with patterns of configurations, and give us a prospect for problems of choosing cellular automata with which we face when applying cellular automata to modeling complex phenomena. But we need to accumulate more case studies in order to build a general framework for this problem. In this paper, focusing on rules 20 and 14, we show 2-step confliction-like dynamical properties of them, a decomposition of rule 20, and reversing and right shift property of rule 14, which are not seen for rule 56.

**Definition 1.** *A one-dimensional cellular automaton is defined to be a triplet $(S, r, g)$ satisfying the following conditions.*

*(1) $S = \{0, 1, \cdots, n\}$, called a state space,*
*(2) $r$ is a positive integer, called a radius of neighborhood,*
*(3) $g : S^{2r+1} \to S$, called a local transition function.*

A cellular automaton is called 0−quiescent when the local transition function $g$ satisfies $g(0, \cdots, 0) = 0$ and an elementary cellular automaton(ECA) when $S = \{0, 1\}$ and $r = 1$. There exist $2^8 = 256$ ECAs, each of which is well known to have the rule number defined as $\sum_{a,b,c \in \{0,1\}} g(a, b, c) \cdot 2^{4a+2b+c}$.

For a cellular automaton $(S, r, g)$, a global transition function $\boldsymbol{g} : S^{\boldsymbol{Z}} \to S^{\boldsymbol{Z}}$ is defined as

$$\forall \boldsymbol{x} \in S^{\boldsymbol{Z}}, \forall i \in \boldsymbol{Z}, ((\boldsymbol{g}(\boldsymbol{x}))_i = g(x_{i-r}, \cdots, x_i, \cdots, x_{i+r}),$$

where $\boldsymbol{Z}$ is the set of all the integers. An element $\boldsymbol{x} = (\cdots, x_{-1}, x_0, x_1, \cdots)$ of $S^{\boldsymbol{Z}}$ is called a configuration. Defining a metric $d_n$ on $S^{\boldsymbol{Z}}$ as $d_n(\boldsymbol{x}, \boldsymbol{y}) = \sum_{i=-\infty}^{\infty} \frac{|x_i - y_i|}{(n+1)^{|i|}}$ for $\boldsymbol{x}, \boldsymbol{y} \in S^{\boldsymbol{Z}}$, we have a topological dynamical system $(S^{\boldsymbol{Z}}, \boldsymbol{g})$.

An orbit for an initial configuration $x \in S^Z$ is a series $\{g^t(x)\}_{t \geq 0}$ given by applying $g$ iteratively to $x$ as

$$t \geq 0 \ , \ g^{t+1}(x) = g(g^t(x)) = g^t(g(x)) \ , \ g^0(x) = x.$$

When for a positive integer $n$,

$$x = g^n(x) \ , \ g^t(x) \neq x \ , \ \forall t \ (0 < t < n)$$

are satisfied, the orbit $\{g^t(x)\}_{t \geq 0}$ is called a periodic orbit having period $n$, and the configuration $x$ is called periodic. An orbit $\{g^t(x)\}_{t \geq 0}$ is said to be transitive, when the orbit is dense in $S^Z$.

For a cellular automaton $(S, r, g)$, a dynamical system $(S^Z, g)$ is called Devaney chaos [1], when the set of periodic configurations is dense in $S^Z$ and the dynamical system has a transitive orbit.

When $W \subseteq S^n$ is a set of words of length $n$, a language generated by $W$ is defined to be $\mathcal{L}(W) \stackrel{def}{=} \{ x \in S^Z \mid \forall i \in Z, \ (x_i, x_{i+1}, \cdots, x_{i+n-1}) \in W \}$. For words $w_1 = (w_1^1, \cdots, w_n^1)$ and $w_2 = (w_1^2, \cdots, w_n^2)$ of $W$, $w_2$ is transitioned from $w_1$, written as $w_1 \rightarrow w_2$, when $w_{i+1}^1 = w_i^2$ for $1 \leq i \leq n - 1$.

## 2    Rule 20 ECA

The local transition function of rule 20 ECA is given by the following table.

Table 1. Local transition function of rule 20

| $(a,b,c)$ | (1,1,1) | (1,1,0) | (1,0,1) | (1,0,0) | (0,1,1) | (0,1,0) | (0,0,1) | (0,0,0) |
|---|---|---|---|---|---|---|---|---|
| $g_{20}(a,b,c)$ | 0 | 0 | 0 | 1 | 0 | 1 | 0 | 0 |

From Table 1, for every $\alpha, \beta \in \{0, 1\}$ we have the next transitions.

$$\cdots \alpha\, 0\, 1\, 0\, 1 \cdots \qquad \cdots \alpha\, 0\, 1\, 0\, 0\, \beta \cdots$$
$$\cdots \cdot 0\, 1\, 0 \cdot \cdots \qquad \cdots \cdot 0\, 1\, 1\, 0 \cdot \cdots$$

$$\overbrace{\phantom{\cdots}}^{\geq 2} \qquad\qquad \overbrace{\phantom{\cdots}}^{\geq 2}$$

$$\cdots \alpha\, 0\, 1 \cdots 1\, 0\, 1 \cdots \qquad \cdots 0\, 1 \cdots 1\, 0\, 0\, \alpha \cdots$$
$$\cdots \cdot 0\, 0 \cdots 0\, 0 \cdot \cdots \qquad \cdots 0\, 0 \cdots 0\, 1\, 0 \cdot \cdots$$

Then we have

$$\forall x \in S_{1(\geq 2), 0(1)} \ , \ g_{20}(x) = 0 = (\cdots, 0, 0, 0, 0, \cdots) \ ,$$

$$\forall x \in \{0, 1\}^Z \setminus S_{1(\geq 2), 0(1)} \ , \ g_{20}(x) \in S_{1(1,2)},$$

where $S_{1(\geq 2), 0(1)}$ is the set of configurations of which 1-state blocks have length at least two and 0-state sites are isolated. $S_{1(1,2)}$ is the set of configurations of which 1-state blocks have length one or two.

Dynamical properties of $g_{20}$ on $S_{1(1,2)} \setminus S_{1(\geq 2),0(1)}$ are complicated and show 2-step 2-left shift, 2-step 2-right shift and furthermore 2-step confliction-like dynamics which are not predictable from that rule 20 belongs to Wolfram class II. We show detailed examinations of these properties.

We first clarify the 1-step dynamical properties of $g_{20}$. It is easily shown that

$$\mathcal{W}_R(g_{20}) \overset{def}{=} \{ (a,b,c) \mid g_{20}(a,b,c) = a \} = \{ (1,0,0),(0,1,1),(0,0,1),(0,0,0) \},$$

$$\mathcal{W}_L(g_{20}) \overset{def}{=} \{ (a,b,c) \mid g_{20}(a,b,c) = c \} = \{ (0,0,0),(1,1,0) \},$$

$$\mathcal{L}(\mathcal{W}_R(g_{20})) = \mathcal{L}(\mathcal{W}_L(g_{20})) = \{ \mathbf{0} \}.$$

Noticing that $\mathbf{0}$ is a fixed point, there is no configuration which is truly right or left shift for $g_{20}$.

**Dynamical properties of $g_{20}^2$**  The 2-step local transition function $g_{20}^2$ : $\{0,1\}^5 \to \{0,1\}$ is defined to be $g_{20}^2(a,b,c,d,e) = g_{20}(g_{20}(a,b,c),g_{20}(b,c,d),g_{20}(c,d,e))$, and is given by Table 2.

**Table 2.** Table of $g_{20}^2$, $f_{20RE}$ and $f_{20LE}$. $f_{20RE}$ is the simplest 2-step 2-right shift transition function on $\mathcal{L}(\mathcal{W}_{2R}(g_{20}^2))$. $f_{20LE}$ is the simplest 2-step 2-left shift transition function on $\mathcal{L}(\mathcal{W}_{2L}(g_{20}^2))$.

| $(a,b,c,d,e)$ | 11111 | 11110 | 11101 | 11100 | 11011 | 11010 | 11001 | 11000 |
|---|---|---|---|---|---|---|---|---|
| $g_{20}^2(a,b,c,d,e)$ | 0 | 0 | 0 | 0 | 0 | 0 | 1 | 1 |
| $f_{20RE}(a,b,c,d,e)$ | 0 | 0 | 0 | 0 | 0 | 0 | 1 | 1 |
| $f_{20LE}(a,b,c,d,e)$ | 0 | 0 | 0 | 0 | 0 | 0 | 1 | 0 |
| $(a,b,c,d,e)$ | 10111 | 10110 | 10101 | 10100 | 10011 | 10010 | 10001 | 10000 |
| $g_{20}^2(a,b,c,d,e)$ | 0 | 0 | 1 | 0 | 1 | 0 | 1 | 1 |
| $f_{20RE}(a,b,c,d,e)$ | 0 | 0 | 1 | 0 | 1 | 0 | 1 | 1 |
| $f_{20LE}(a,b,c,d,e)$ | 0 | 0 | 1 | 0 | 1 | 0 | 1 | 0 |
| $(a,b,c,d,e)$ | 01111 | 01110 | 01101 | 01100 | 01011 | 01010 | 01001 | 01000 |
| $g_{20}^2(a,b,c,d,e)$ | 0 | 0 | 0 | 0 | 1 | 0 | 0 | 0 |
| $f_{20RE}(a,b,c,d,e)$ | 0 | 0 | 0 | 0 | 0 | 0 | 0 | 0 |
| $f_{20LE}(a,b,c,d,e)$ | 0 | 0 | 0 | 0 | 1 | 0 | 0 | 0 |
| $(a,b,c,d,e)$ | 00111 | 00110 | 00101 | 00100 | 00011 | 00010 | 00001 | 00000 |
| $g_{20}^2(a,b,c,d,e)$ | 0 | 0 | 1 | 0 | 0 | 0 | 0 | 0 |
| $f_{20RE}(a,b,c,d,e)$ | 0 | 0 | 0 | 0 | 0 | 0 | 0 | 0 |
| $f_{20LE}(a,b,c,d,e)$ | 0 | 0 | 1 | 0 | 0 | 0 | 0 | 0 |

(1) The case of $g_{20}^2 = \sigma_R^2$  Letting

$$\mathcal{W}_{2R}(g_{20}^2) \overset{def}{=} \{ (a,b,c,d,e) \mid g_{20}^2(a,b,c,d,e) = a \}$$

$$= \{ (0,0,0,0,0),(0,0,0,0,1),(0,0,0,1,0),(0,0,0,1,1),(0,0,1,0,0),$$

$$(0,0,1,1,0),(0,0,1,1,1),(0,1,0,0,0),(0,1,0,0,1),(0,1,0,1,0),$$

$$(0,1,1,0,0),(0,1,1,0,1),(0,1,1,1,0),(0,1,1,1,1),(1,0,0,0,0),$$

$$(1,0,0,0,1),(1,0,0,1,1),(1,0,1,0,1),(1,1,0,0,0),(1,1,0,0,1) \},$$

$g_{20}^2 = \sigma_R^2$ on $\mathcal{L}(\mathcal{W}_{2R}(g_{20}^2))$. It is easily verified that there is no word transitioned from (01101), (01110) and (01111). (01110) and (01111) can be transitioned from (00111). Fig. 1 shows the transitions among the words of $\mathcal{W}_{2R}(g_{20}^2)$ except these four words. Any configuration of $\mathcal{L}(\mathcal{W}_{2R}(g_{20}^2))$ is shown to have the pattern $\cdots 010101 \cdots$ or to be composed of four blocks 1000, 1100, 100 and 0, for example $\cdots 1000100011000100110000100110001000100 \cdots$. Fig. 2 shows the connecting relations among the four blocks, for example the block 100 should have the block 1100 on its right hand side.

For the time developments of the configurations of $\mathcal{L}(\mathcal{W}_{2R}(g_{20}^2))$, only the underlined bits in the raw of $f_{20RE}$ of Table 2 are used, which are common to those of $g_{20}^2$. Then we have

$$(\mathcal{L}(\mathcal{W}_{2R}(g_{20}^2)) \, , \, g_{20}) \; = \; (\mathcal{L}(\mathcal{W}_{2R}(g_{20}^2)) \, , \, f_{20RE}) \; = \; (\mathcal{L}(\mathcal{W}_{2R}(g_{20}^2)) \, , \, \sigma_R^2).$$

We may say that $g_{20}^2$ includes a cellular automaton $f_{20RE}$, which emerges when it faces the configurations of $\mathcal{L}(\mathcal{W}_{2R}(g_{20}^2))$.

(2) The case of $g_{20}^2 = \sigma_L^2$    Letting

$$\mathcal{W}_{2L}(g_{20}^2) \stackrel{def}{=} \{ \, (a,b,c,d,e) \mid g_2^2(a,b,c,d,e) = e \, \}$$
$$= \{ \, (0,0,0,0,0), (0,0,0,1,0), (0,0,1,0,0), (0,0,1,0,1), (0,0,1,1,0),$$
$$(0,1,0,0,0), (0,1,0,1,0), (0,1,0,1,1), (0,1,1,0,0), (1,0,0,0,1),$$
$$(1,0,0,1,0), (1,0,0,1,1), (0,1,1,1,0), (1,0,1,0,0), (1,0,1,0,1),$$
$$(1,0,1,1,0), (1,1,0,0,1), (1,1,0,1,0), (1,1,1,0,0), (1,1,1,1,0) \, \},$$

$g_{20}^2 = \sigma_L^2$ holds on $\mathcal{L}(\mathcal{W}_{2L}(g_{20}^2))$. Following the examinations similar to those of the case (1), the configurations of $\mathcal{L}(\mathcal{W}_{2L}(g_{20}^2))$ except for **0** are composed of blocks $1000, 1100, 10$, the connecting relations among these blocks are shown in Fig. 3. Furthermore $g_{20}^2$ is equivalent to $f_{20LE}$ on $\mathcal{L}(\mathcal{W}_{2L}(g_{20}^2))$, which is given by Table 2, i.e.

$$(\mathcal{L}(\mathcal{W}_{2L}(g_{20}^2)), g_{20}) \; = \; (\mathcal{L}(\mathcal{W}_{2L}(g_{20}^2)), f_{20LE}) \; = \; (\mathcal{L}(\mathcal{W}_{2L}(g_{20}^2)), \sigma_L^2).$$

A cellular automaton $f_{20LE}$ embedded in $g_{20}^2$ emerges when it faces the configurations of $\mathcal{L}(\mathcal{W}_{2L}(g_{20}^2))$.

(3) A decomposition and a composition of $g_{20}^2$    From Table 2, we have $g_{20}^2 = \max\{ \, f_{20RE} \, , \, f_{20LE} \, \}$, which means that $g_{20}^2$ is decomposed into $f_{20RE}$ and $f_{20LE}$, and can be composed by taking maximum of these two local transition functions. Following Wolfram's class classification, $f_{20LE}$ belongs to class I and $f_{20RE}$ to class II.

## 3    Confliction-Like Dynamics of Rule 20

**Configurations of Pattern I.**    We consider configurations having a pattern as shown in Fig 4. The left hand of FL is a left infinite configuration truncated from a configuration of $\mathcal{L}(\mathcal{W}_{2R}(g_{20}^2))$ composed of 1100 and 00. The right hand

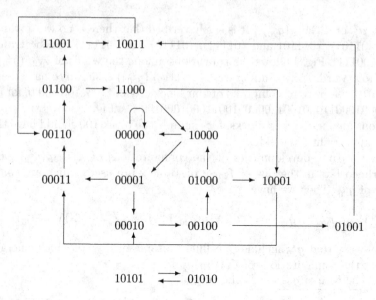

**Fig. 1.** Transitions among the words of $\mathcal{W}_{2R}(g_{20}^2)$ except (00111), (01101), (01110) and (01111)

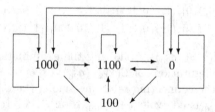

**Fig. 2.** Relation of connections among blocks 1000, 1100, 100 and 0 composing the configurations of $\mathcal{L}(\mathcal{W}_{2R}(g_{20}^2))\backslash\{(\cdots,0,1,0,1,0,1,\cdots)\}$

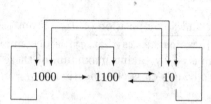

**Fig. 3.** Relation of connections among blocks 1000, 1100 and 10 composing the configurations of $\mathcal{L}(\mathcal{W}_{2L}(g_{20}^2))\backslash\{0\}$

is a right infinite configuration truncated from a configuration of $\mathcal{L}(\mathcal{W}_{2L}(g_{20}^2))$ composed of 1100 and 10.

We denote the set of the configurations having this pattern as $S_{even}^I$ or $S_{odd}^I$ according to $m$ is even or odd, respectively. FL is the front line at which these two groups face with each other, and there happen to be some conflictions between the two groups around FL.

The conflictions are caused by the interactions between 00 and 10, 00 and 1100, 1100 and 10, which are checked after this, denoting 0 and 1 as $\bigcirc$ and $\bullet$ in the Fig.'s 5 to 7, respectively.

(1) When 00 faces 10 with the front line between them, both of them disappear in two steps, and the front line does not move. See Fig. 5.

(2) When 00 faces 1100 with the front line between them, the block 1100 is erased in two steps and the front line moves to the right by two sites. See Fig. 6

(3) When 1100 faces 10 with the front line between them, the block 1100 is erased in two steps and the front line moves to the left by two sites. See Fig. 7. Then $g_{20}^2(S_{even}^I) \subseteq S_{even}^I$ and $g_{20}^2(S_{odd}^I) \subseteq S_{odd}^I$ hold and we have two dynamical sub-systems, $(S_{even}^I, g_{20}^2)$ and $(S_{odd}^I, g_{20}^2)$.

From the interactions (1), (2) and (3), Fig. 9 shows a typical time development of a configuration of the type given in Fig. 4. FL moves to the right or the left by $\left|2\sum_{i=1}^{l_1} n_i - 2k_1\right|$ sites according to the quantity in the absolute value symbol is positive or negative, respectively. Then it is seen that FL moves like a wave along with time, and this movement is determined by the number of blocks composing the left and the right half infinite configurations, and hence, for any configuration of $S_{even}^I$ or $S_{odd}^I$ and for any neighborhood of the configuration, adjusting the number of blocks 1100, 00 and 10, we may construct a periodic configuration in the neighborhood. And also for each of $S_{even}^I$ and $S_{odd}^I$, a transitive configuration can be constructed. Thus we have the following theorem, which is easily proved by following the idea similar to that of [4]. But the proof is tedious and therefore omitted here.

**Theorem 1.** $(S_{even}^I, g_{20}^2)$ and $(S_{odd}^I, g_{20}^2)$ are Devaney chaos.

**Configuration of Pattern II.** We consider configurations having a pattern as shown in Fig 8. The left hand is a left infinite configuration truncated from a configuration of $\mathcal{L}(\mathcal{W}_{2R}(g_{20}^2))$ composed of 1000 and 00. The right hand is a right infinite configuration truncated from a configuration of $\mathcal{L}(\mathcal{W}_{2L}(g_{20}^2))$ composed of 1000 and 10. We denote the set of the configurations having the pattern of Fig. 8 as $S_{even}^{II}$ or $S_{odd}^{II}$ according to $m$ is even or odd, respectively. It is easily verified that $g_{20}^2(S_{even}^{II}) \subseteq S_{even}^{II}$ and $g_{20}^2(S_{odd}^{II}) \subseteq S_{odd}^{II}$.

For a configuration $x \in S_{even}^{II} \cup S_{odd}^{II}$, we have the following transitions, where F means FL;

$$x = \cdots, 1, 0, 0, 0, 0, 0, 0, 0, 1, 0, 0, 0, 0, 0, F, 1, 0, 1, 0, 0, 0, 1, 0, 0, 0, 1, 0, 1, 0, \cdots$$
$$g_{20}(x) = \cdots, 1, 1, 0, 0, 0, 0, 0, 0, 1, 1, 0, 0, 0, 0, F, 1, 0, 1, 1, 0, 0, 1, 1, 0, 0, 1, 0, 1, 0, \cdots$$
$$g_{20}^2(x) = \cdots, *, *, 1, 0, 0, 0, 0, 0, 0, 0, 1, 0, 0, 0, F, 1, 0, 0, 0, 1, 0, 0, 0, 1, 0, 1, 0, *, *, \cdots$$
$$g_{20}^3(x) = \cdots, *, *, 1, 1, 0, 0, 0, 0, 0, 0, 1, 1, 0, 0, F, 1, 1, 0, 0, 1, 1, 0, 0, 1, 0, 1, 0, *, *, \cdots$$

FL

$$\cdots (1100)_{k_i}(00)_{l_i} \cdots (1100)_{k_2}(00)_{l_2}(1100)_{k_1}(00)_{l_1}\left|\overset{m}{1}\ 0(1100)_{n_1}10(1100)_{n_2}\cdots 10(1100)_{n_j}\cdots\right.$$

**Fig. 4.** A configuration of pattern I

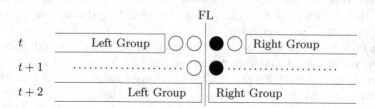

**Fig. 5.** Confliction between 00 and 10

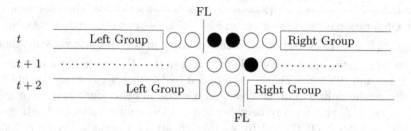

**Fig. 6.** Confliction between 00 and 1100

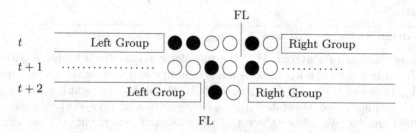

**Fig. 7.** Confliction between 1100 and 10

FL

$$\cdots (1000)_{k_i}(00)_{l_i} \cdots (1000)_{k_2}(00)_{l_2}(1000)_{k_1}(00)_{l_1}\left|\overset{m}{1}\ 0(1000)_{n_1}10(1000)_{n_2}\cdots 10(1000)_{n_j}\cdots\right.$$

**Fig. 8.** A configuration of pattern II

from which, considering predecessors of each block, it is shown that

$$g_{20} : S^I_{even} \rightarrow S^{II}_{even} , \quad g_{20} : S^{II}_{even} \rightarrow S^I_{even} ,$$
$$g_{20} : S^I_{odd} \rightarrow S^{II}_{odd} , \quad g_{20} : S^{II}_{odd} \rightarrow S^I_{odd}$$

are bijections. Then we have the next theorem from Theorem 1.

**Theorem 2.** $(S^{II}_{even}, g^2_{20})$, $(S^{II}_{odd}, g^2_{20})$, $(S^I_{even} \cup S^{II}_{even}, g_{20})$ and $(S^I_{odd} \cup S^{II}_{odd}, g_{20})$ are Devaney chaos.

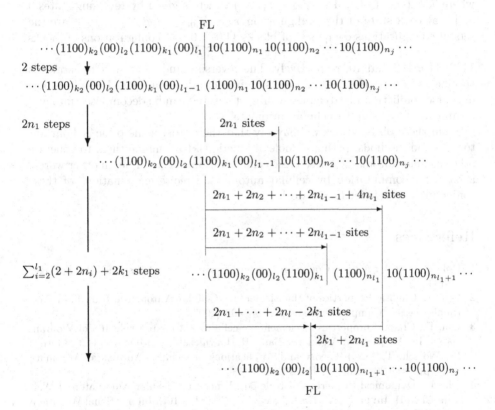

**Fig. 9.** Typical time development of the configuration of pattern I

## 4   Rule 14 and Concluding Remarks

In this paper, following an argument similar to the one about rule 56 [4], we examined rule 20 of Wolfram class II and found out that the rule has 2-step 2-right and 2-step 2-left shift dynamical subsystems, and combining the two oppositely moving subsystems, we have a confliction-like dynamical sub-system which we cannot imagine from that the rule belongs to Wolfram class II. Furthermore we have shown $g_{20}^2 = \max\{\ f_{20RE}\ ,\ f_{20LE}\ \}$ suggesting that the rule 20 is composed of two simpler cellular automata $f_{20RE}$ and $f_{20LE}$ corresponding to 2-step 2-right and 2-step 2-left shift dynamical subsystems, respectively.

In the introduction we mentioned that there exist several rules of class II showing confliction-like dynamics, but all of them have not yet been fully examined. Rule 14 especially shows an interesting movement that

$$\forall \boldsymbol{x} \in S_{1(2),0(\geq 2)},\ \boldsymbol{g}_{14}(\boldsymbol{x}) = \sigma_L(\boldsymbol{x}),$$
$$\forall \boldsymbol{x} \in S_{1(2,1),0(1,2)},\ \boldsymbol{g}_{14}(\boldsymbol{x}) = \sigma_R(\overline{\boldsymbol{x}}),$$

where $\overline{\boldsymbol{x}} = (\cdots, 1 - x_1, 1 - x_0, 1 - x_1, \cdots)$ which is given by reversing states 0 and 1 at each state of the configuration $\boldsymbol{x}$. $S_{1(2),0(\geq 2)}$ and $S_{1(1,2),0(1,2)}$ are the sets of configurations composed of blocks $11\underbrace{0\cdots 0}_{\geq 2}$ and configurations of blocks 1100, 110, 100 and 10, respectively. The reversing and right shift dynamics is specific to rule 14, the dual and the symmetric to it in the class II. Rule 14 has of course confliction-like dynamical subsystems and can be decomposed into and composed of two simpler cellular automata.

From these observations we may say that there exist some basic cellular automata and methods, perhaps Boolean functions, to combine them to generate other cellular automata. These basic cellular automata could be, in other words, a basis for computation by cellular automata. Precise examinations of these conjectures are left for future work.

# References

1. Holmgren, R.A.: A First Course in Discrete Dynamical Systems, 2nd edn. Springer (1991)
2. Ohi, F.: Chaotic Properties of the Elementary Cellular Automaton Rule 40 in Wolfram's Class I. Complex Systems 17, 295–308 (2007)
3. Ohi, F.: Chaotic properties of elementary cellular automaton rule 168 of Wolfram class I. In: Adamatzky, A., Alonso-Sanz, R., Lawniczak, A., Martinez, G.J., Morita, K., Worsch, T. (eds.) Theory and Applications of Cellular Automata, Automata 2008, pp. 196–206. Luniver Press (2008)
4. Ohi, F.: Dynamical Properties of Rule 56 Elementary Cellular Automaton of Wolfram Class II. In: Fatès, N., Kari, J., Worsch, T. (eds.) 16th International Workshop on Cellular Automata and Discrete Complex Systems, Automata 2010, pp. 287–298 (2010)
5. Ohi, F.: Exact Calculation of Lyapunov Exponents and Spreading Rates for Rule 40. Complex Systems 19, 323–341 (2011)
6. Wolfram, S.: Statistical mechanics of cellular automata. Review of Modern Physics 55, 601–644 (1983)
7. Wolfram, S.: Universality and Complexity in Cellular Automata. Physica 10D, 1–35 (1984)
8. Wolfram, S. : A New Kind of Science. Wolfram Media, Inc.(2002)

# Determining the Critical Temperature of the Continuous-State Game of Life

Susumu Adachi[1], Jia Lee[1,2], Ferdinand Peper[1],
Teijiro Isokawa[3], and Katsunobu Imai[4]

[1] Nano ICT Group, National Institute of Information and Communications Technology, Japan
[2] College of Computer Science, Chong Qing University, China
[3] Division of Computer Engineering, University of Hyogo, Japan
[4] Faculty of Engineering, Hiroshima University, Japan

**Abstract.** This paper proposes a simple algorithm to find the critical temperature of the continuous-state Game of Life (GoL). The algorithm conducts the transitions of cells and the update of the temperature parameter alternatingly. The temperature starts from a low value and it increases gradually, while a fixed GoL pattern evolves. This process continues, but before the temperature exceeds the critical temperature, the update algorithm acts to decrease it, so as to prevent overshoot of the temperature, which would make the cell states deviate from the normal GoL behavior. An oscillatory value of the temperature can be observed, but it converges towards a fixed value, indicating that its critical point is being approached.

## 1 Introduction

Cell states in conventional Cellular Automata (CA) assume discrete values, but when continuous states are allowed [9], it becomes possible to investigate dynamics that is chaotic or at the edge of chaos [1,10,11,12,13] or to apply it to biological modeling [2], the coupled map lattice [4,5], etc.

One model with continuous cell states is the so-called Game of Life at finite temperature [3]. A cell state in this model lies in the range $[0 - 1]$ and it is updated in a synchronous way at discrete time steps, such that a cell's state after update is determined by its own state and the sum of the neighbouring cell states at the previous time, as well as by a temperature parameter.

It has been observed [3] that the temperature parameter plays an important role in the behavior of the model. When it is below a certain value, which we call the *critical value*, the model behaves like the traditional (discrete-state) GoL [6,7,14], but once this critical value is exceeded, different behavior emerges. The degree at which the behavior differs from the traditional GoL tends to be proportional with the difference of the actual temperature and the critical temperature below it. Though the use of the term *critical temperature* implies that it is at a unique point, the reality is more complicated. It turns out that the critical temperature is somewhat dependent on the actual configurations

G.C. Sirakoulis and S. Bandini (Eds.): ACRI 2012, LNCS 7495, pp. 83–90, 2012.

in cell space, and in fact it is a range of values. The minimum of these values represents a critical point below which every configuration behaves as if it were in the traditional GoL, and we are interested in this particular value. We call this the *critical point* of the model.

In this paper we formulate an algorithm that determines this critical point by adapting the temperature over the course of iterations. The algorithm employs two phases in alternation: cell update and temperature update. The temperature update is based on a steepest descent algorithm, whereby the gradient of the transition function is updated with a limiting value of 1. The algorithm then selects a target cell in the cell space, which distinguishes itself from other cells by having the largest gradient. The meaning of a cell's gradient being the largest is that that cell will start to decay first, i.e., behave in a different way than it would in the traditional GoL. It is demonstrated that when the temperature starts from a low value and increases gradually, a fixed GoL pattern evolves. This process continues, but before the temperature exceeds the critical temperature, the update algorithm acts to decrease it, so as to prevent overshoot of the temperature, which would make the cell states deviate from the normal GoL behavior.

This paper is organized as follows. In Section 2, the continuous-state GoL is explained. The methods and the results of the algorithm used to find the critical temperature are shown in Section 3. Conclusions are drawn in Section 4.

## 2   Continuous State Game of Life

The transition rule of the continuous state Game of Life [3] is described by

$$f(C_i) = 1/\left[1 + \exp(-2E(C_i)/T)\right] \tag{1}$$

$$E(C_i) = E_0 - \left(C_i + 2\sum_{j \neq i} C_j - x_0\right)^2 \tag{2}$$

where, $C_i$ is the continuous state ($0 \leq C_i \leq 1$) of the $i$-th cell, $j$ varies over the Moore neighbourhood, $T$ is the temperature, $E(C_i)$ is the local energy, and $E_0$ and $x_0$ are constants. All cells are selected in an iteration and their states undergo transitions according to this function $f$ synchronously, i.e., $C_i(t+1) = f(C_i(t))$. Note that the transition function has 3 variables, the center cell's state, the summation of the neighbouring cells' states, and the temperature. If the constants are $E_0 = 2.25$ and $x_0 = 6$, this function is identical to the rule of the Game of Life at zero temperature limit, as can be shown. For this reason, these typical values are used in this paper.

A *pattern* is defined as a set of living cells that is a subset of the cell space, whereby a cell is called *alive* when its state is larger than 0.5, and dead otherwise. The patterns of the model decay above the critical temperature $T_c$, and sustain their typical Game of Life forms below $T_c$. The critical temperatures are different for different patterns, for example, 0.53 is the critical temperature for a 'beehive',

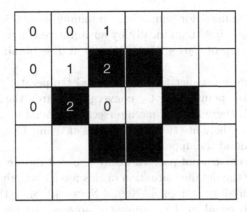

**Fig. 1.** A beehive pattern. Cells with the same indexes take about the same value at a stable situation.

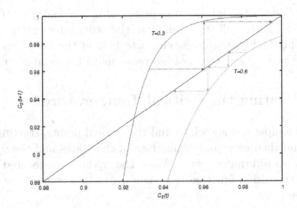

**Fig. 2.** A part of the map of the cell state $C_2$ at time $t$ and $t+1$

0.61 for a 'glider gun', 0.66 for an 'eater', 0.7 for a 'glider', and 0.8 for a 'block', respectively. Since glider guns, eaters, and gliders are required as logic gates for computing [7,8], this model is computational universal at $T < 0.61$.

We show the dynamics of how a pattern decays above the critical temperature $T_c$. Below the critical temperature, the beehive pattern is stable as shown in Fig.1. In the figure, we assume that the cells with the same indexes take about the same value.

Relations of the states of cells denoted by 1 and 2 at the stable situation can be expressed as follows,

$$E_1 = E_0 - (3C_1 + 4C_2 - x_0)^2 \tag{3}$$
$$C_1 = 1/\left[1 + \exp(-2E_1/T)\right] \tag{4}$$
$$E_2 = E_0 - (5C_2 + 6C_1 - x_0)^2 \tag{5}$$
$$C_2 = 1/\left[1 + \exp(-2E_2/T)\right] \tag{6}$$

where, $C_0 \sim 0$ is assumed for simplicity. Assuming $T \sim 0.5$, then we obtain $C_1 \sim 0.0005$ and $C_2 \sim 0.99$ numerically by an iterative computation. Based on this value of $C_1$, a map of $C_2(t+1) = f(C_2(t))$ at $T$ is obtained that is shown in Fig.2.

If the temperature is smaller than the critical temperature $(T < T_c)$, there are three intersection points, and $C_2$ converges towards the largest of them. Otherwise $(T > T_c)$, there is only one intersection around 0, and $C_2$ converges towards it. If $T = T_c$, there are two intersections at 0 and 1, and the gradient of the function is 1 around the upper intersection.

Generally the mechanism of pattern decay is based on the disappearance of bistability. However the detailed situation of this model is slightly different from the Ising model in physics (or Hopfield Neural Network). Since the magnetization of the Ising model is equal to the solutions of an equation like $x = \tanh(x/T)$, which is derived by using mean field approximation, the disappearance of the bistability occurs continuously towards $x \to 0$ at $T \to 1$, which is a so-called phase transition.

In this model, since the intersection points of $y = x$ and $y = f(x)$ around 1 disappear at $T > T_c$, the cell state jumps to the other intersection point around 0. In general, this highly non-linear characteristic of the transition function of the model guarantees the survival of life patterns at low temperatures.

## 3   Approximating the Critical Temperature

We introduce a simple framework to find the critical points, starting with a low temperature, and then carry out transitions of cell states and the update of the temperature in an alternating way. When the update is executed so that the gradient of the transition function is 1, then it can be expressed by the steepest descent as follows.

$$T \to T - \mu \frac{\partial g}{\partial T} \tag{7}$$

$$g = \left(1 - \frac{\partial f}{\partial C_i}\right)^2 \tag{8}$$

where $\mu$ is a constant and $g$ is the error function. The index $i$ of cell $C_i$ is chosen as the point where the gradient $\partial f/\partial C_i$ takes its maximum value in the cell space. The reason of taking this $i$ is that if the gradient of a cell is larger than 1, the cell starts to decay as shown in the previous section. In other words, a critical temperature is the maximum value at which the weakest cell does not decay. In the example of Fig. 1, the left cell of two cells $C_2$ labeled 2 is the weakest cell (since the pattern is symmetric, there are two of such weakest cells).

There is a problem in this framework that if the temperature becomes larger than the critical point at a certain time and it becomes smaller according to Eq. (7), it is too late to recover the cell state. This situation can be understood by investigating the gradient being dependent on the temperatures at the stable situation, as shown in Fig.3 (a). In the figure, the gradient is 0.177 at $T = 0.539$,

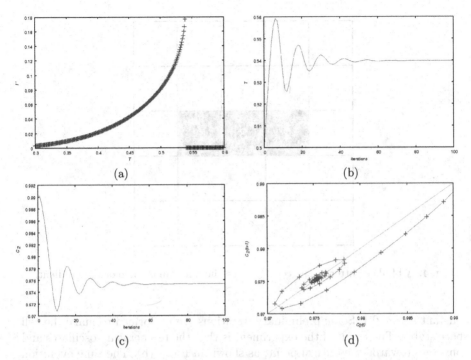

**Fig. 3.** Gradient of a living cell as a function of $T$ (a), dynamics of temperature (b), dynamics of the cell state (c) and its map representation (d). The size of the cell space is $20 \times 20$, the initial configuration is beehive, the initial temperature is 0.5, and the constants are $\mu = 0.1$ and $\theta = 0.2$.

and $\sim 0$ at $T = 0.54$. Although the critical point must be between them, the gradient does not exceed 0.2 within the double precision of $T$ due to sensitivity considerations. The problem of an overshooting temperature can be solved in the following ways:

1. replace double precision of $T$ with quadruple precision.
2. asymmetric update (decrease the temperature more than in the original algorithm).
3. replace $g = (1 - f')^2$ with $g = (\theta - f')^2$, whereby $\theta$ is an appropriately chosen threshold.

We adopt option 3 above, because of reasons of simplicity: it only requires the change of the constant 1 into $\theta$ in Eq. (8). Since we have the knowledge that the gradient does not exceed 0.2, we can safely choose $\theta = 0.2$. Then the expression Eq. (8) can be rewritten as follows.

$$g = \left( \theta - \frac{\partial f}{\partial C_i} \right)^2 \tag{9}$$

The experiment is carried out as follows. The size of the cell space is $20 \times 20$, the initial configuration is the beehive pattern, the initial temperature is 0.5, and the

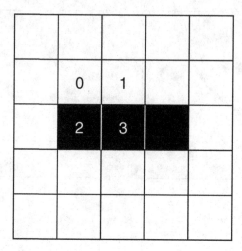

**Fig. 4.** A blinker pattern. The cell $C_3$ takes the maximum value of the gradient.

constant is $\mu = 0.1$. Some preliminary iterations are performed to make the cell space stable. The result of the experiment is that the temperature oscillates and converges towards the critical point, as shown in Fig. 3 (b). The time evolution of the cell state $C_2$ and its map representation are illustrated in Fig. 3 (c) and (d).

The next example concerns the blinker pattern shown in Fig. 4. It is known that the blinker is a period 2 oscillator. The center cell of the blinker $C_3$ is the weakest cell, which means its gradient has the maximum value. The gradient plotted as a function of $T$ is shown in Fig. 5 (a). In the figure, the maximum value is 0.715 at $T = 0.976$, so in this case it is possible to set $\theta = 0.7$.

The experiment is carried out as follows. The size of cell space is $20 \times 20$, the initial configuration is the blinker pattern, the initial temperature is 0.9, and the constant is $\mu = 0.01$. Some preliminary iterations are performed to make the cell space stable at every even steps. As a result, the temperature oscillates and converges to the critical point, as shown in Fig. 5 (b). The time evolution of the cell state $C_3$ and its map representation are illustrated in Fig. 5 (c) and (d).

In both cases of the beehive and the blinker, the algorithm can work well, because the constant $\theta$ plays a role of an early stopping to increase the temperatures. There are also some cases it fails. If $\mu$ is large, the cell's states can not follow the updated temperature, then the states can not converge and in the end the temperatures continue to oscillate. On the other hand, if $\mu$ is small, the temperature converges below the critical point or oscillates periodically tracking a hysteresis loop.

Finally, the results of the critical temperatures for some famous patterns including the above patterns can be shown in Table.1.

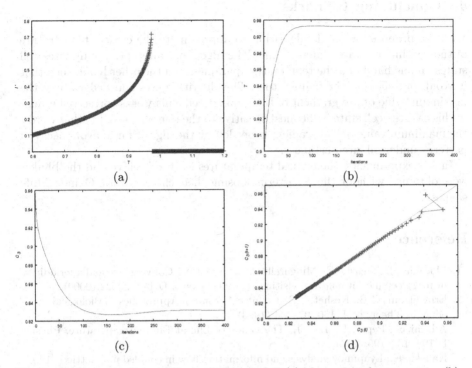

**Fig. 5.** Gradient of a living cell as a function of $T$ (a), dynamics of temperature (b), dynamics of the cell state (c), and its map representation (d). The size of the cell space is $20 \times 20$, the initial configuration is a blinker, the initial temperature is 0.9, and the constants are $\mu = 0.01$ and $\theta = 0.7$.

**Table 1.** Threshold values of the gradient and critical temperatures for some patterns are listed

| pattern | $\theta$ | $T$ |
|---------|----------|-----|
| beehive | 0.2 | 0.539694 |
| paperclip | 0.3 | 0.577207 |
| loaf | 0.3 | 0.597193 |
| boat | 0.35 | 0.612362 |
| tub | 0.195 | 0.639911 |
| eater | 0.454 | 0.665002 |
| pond | 0.28 | 0.680342 |
| barge | 0.3 | 0.696146 |
| blinker | 0.7 | 0.975632 |

# 4   Concluding Remarks

We have proposed a simple algorithm to approximate the critical temperature of the continuous-state Game of Life. The algorithm alternatingly updates cell states on one hand and the temperature parameter on the other hand, such that it avoids overshoot of the temperature. The algorithm uses knowledge about the maximum value of the gradient of the weakest cell; this works correctly because in this case the cell state is the most sensitive to the temperature. In other words, the maximum value of the gradient is needed by the algorithm to avoid decay of patterns under all circumstances.

In our experiments, the critical temperatures for the beehive and the blinker were obtained without these patterns loosing their characteristic Game of Life shapes.

# References

1. Flocchini, P., Geurts, F., Mingarelli, A., Santoro, N.: Convergence and aperiodicity in fuzzy cellularautomata: revisiting rule 90. Physica D 142, 20–28 (2000)
2. Ermentrout, G.B., Keshet, L.E.: Cellular Automata Approaches to Biological Modeling. J. Theor. Biol. 160, 97–133 (1993)
3. Adachi, S., Peper, F., Lee, J.: The Game of Life at Finite Temperature. Physica D 198, 182–196 (2004)
4. Kaneko, K.: Lyapunov analysis and information flow in coupled map lattices. Physica D 23, 436–447 (1986)
5. Ding, M., Yang, W.: Stability of synchronous chaos and on-off intermittency in coupled map lattices. Phys. Rev. E 56, 4009–4016 (1997)
6. Berlekamp, E.R., Conway, J.H., Guy, R.K.: Wining Ways For Your Mathematical Plays. Academic Press, New York (1982)
7. Poundstone, W.: The Recursive Universe. Morrow, New York (1985)
8. Schiff, J.L.: Cellular Automata: A Discrete View of the World. Wiley & Sons (2007)
9. Ilachinski, A.: Cellular Automata. World Scientific Publishing, Singapore (2001)
10. Wolfram, S.: Cellular Automata and Complexity. Addison-Wesley, Reading (1994)
11. Langton, C.G.: Computation at the edge of chaos: phase transitions and emergent computation. Physica D 42, 12–37 (1990)
12. Ninagawa, S., Yoneda, M., Hirose, S.: $1/f$ fluctuation in the Game of Life. Physica D 118, 49–52 (1998)
13. Alstrøm, P., Leão, J.: Self-organized criticality in the "game of Life". Phys. Rev. E 49, 2507–2508 (1994)
14. Blok, H.J., Bergersen, B.: Effect of boundary conditions on scaling in the "game of Life". Phys. Rev. E 55, 6249–6252 (1997)

# The Dynamics of Disproportionality Index for Cellular Automata Based Sociophysical Models

Tomasz M. Gwizdałła

Dept. of Solid State Physics, University of Łódź,
Pomorska 149/153, 90-236 Łódź, Poland
tomgwizd@uni.lodz.pl

**Abstract.** The cellular automata approach to the analysis of the electorate voting is presented. We show the analysis of the proportionality of elections by using different update rules for the cellular automata representing the voters space. There exist many methods of performing system update which can be generally classified into two classes: outward, when the individual's opnion is spread over his neighbors and inward when the individual is under pressure of his environment. In the paper we show the relaxation, stability and the Gallagher index value for at the successive stages of CA simulation run. We find that the majority of methods leads to similar results however few of them is promising when trying to reproduce some social phenomena.

**Keywords:** Cellular automata, Sociophysical models, Disproportionality.

## 1 Introduction

Among different characteristics of the voting process, one of the fundamental is the question about the representativeness of the results of elections. In this general notion we encompass especially the problem of proportionality of elections. There exist a lot of different numerical indexes which try to describe this effect [1]. One of the most popular is the Gallagher index

$$G = \sqrt{\frac{1}{2}(V_i^2 - S_i^2)} \tag{1}$$

In the above equation $V$ is the percentage number of votes obtained by the given party while $S$ is the number of mandates (seats) awarded to this party. The value of $G$ index depends mainly on the voting system (FPTP, proportional) and the stability of political system. Some typical values can be found in our previous paper where the problem was studied using CA method [2].

In the paper we are going to study the dynamics of $G$ index changes. We will consider the typical multi-seat constituency where 11 deputies are elected. This value corresponds to the typical constituency in Poland. For such a constituency

G.C. Sirakoulis and S. Bandini (Eds.): ACRI 2012, LNCS 7495, pp. 91–100, 2012.

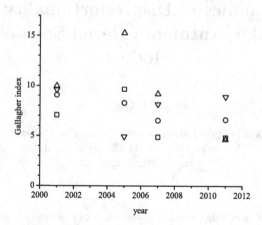

**Fig. 1.** The dynamics of Gallagher index changes for selected 11-mandate constituencies in Poland. Private calculations.

the disproportionality index can be also calculated and its value is higher than for the whole country. In the Fig.1 we show the changes of Gallagher index for the 4 selected polish constituencies during the last 4 elections (proportional system).

We do not call here the detailed locations of these constituencies but they significantly differ one from another according to the sociological structure of electors. We took into account only those parties which exceeded 1% of votes in the particular constituency.

It is hard to present unambiguous conclusions related to the observed results. The most stable case is represented by circles, for all others it exist minima or maxima and their positions are uncorrelated.

We will try to find whether we can find the Cellular Automata system which can, even approximately, reproduce the effects visible in the Fig.1.

## 2  Model

The details of the calculation model has been presented in our earlier paper [2]. Let us mention here only main features of this model as well as those assumptions which are different from the ones presented there. We use here only two-dimensional sample. Its size equals $81 \times 99$ what corresponds to the 8019 cells. There are several reasons to make such a choice. We can directly compare the results to those obtained in earlier paper, the number is divisible by 11 what enables to study the system with equal division into one-seat constituencies and finally among the samples with equal sizes we consider this one for which the stabilization is fastest.

We study the 4-state model which corresponds to the division of the space of opinions by the Nolan's diagram. Every person's opinion is located in the selected quadrant of two-dimensional plane divided according to the economic and social beliefs. Certainly, such a description should involve more detailed analysis related to the actual, exact position of person on the chart, but for simplicity reasons often just 4-state approach enabling only general localization is used. Such an approach is similar to the mentioned in [3] ACLS model (authoritarian/conservative/libertarian/socialist).

Originally we have studied four different methods of performing the assignment of mandates(seats) to the parties according to the number of votes they obtained and according to the political system. There were: (1) FPTP, (2) two-round majority system, (3) d'Hondt system and (4) d'Hondt with the threshold 5%. It turned out that the results obtained by using similar methods of seats assignment (1 and 2, 3 and 4) do not differ much therefore in the current paper we perform the calculations only for (1) and (3) methods.

For the proportional system of mandates assignment, the further method of dividing the sample into constituencies is certainly not important. We want however to study the influence of such division on the results obtained for majority system. Also following our earlier study [2] we introduce four types of divisions according to the two features: number of cells in each constituency and their compactness. In the further part of paper this option will be also restricted but some initial plots are prepared for all four possibilities.

The crucial algorithm determining the behavior of system is the method of performing the cell content update. Earlier we applied only the so-called Stauffer's rule III [4]. In the paper authors presented three rules for two-dimensional CA update. They are indeed the tries of generalization of seminal Sznajd's scheme [5] onto the two-dimensional case. With the first two schemes it is assumed that a structure constructed of several cells is considered. According to the rule I we consider the "plaquette" $2 \times 2$ and the opinion of cells from inside the plaquette is expanded onto 8 neighboring cells only if all cells has the same state. According to the version a (rule Ia) the same state as possessed by the plaquette cells is expanded while with the rule Ib we use the opposite one. Since in the Stauffer's paper only two-state CA was used, here we have to redefine the notion opposite. As the opposite state we understand the state which lies in the opposite (not in the neighboring) quadrant. By using the rule II we consider the $1 \times 2$ set of cells trying to persuade their opinions into 6 neighbors. Here, the distinction into 3 possibilities (IIa, IIb, IIc) is related to the behavior of CA in situation where two initial states are different. If initial states are same always their state is copied, it doesn't exist the situation when the oppositions are copied. The rule III is the direct enhancement of typical one-dimensional behavior [5] for the $2 \times 2$ subset of cells where the chosen state influences the cells in the same row and column.

The Sznajd/Stauffer's update is the example of method where the opinion is spread into its neighbors. In order to take into account also another class of update algorithms we take into account the Glauber mechanism which considers the state cell as dependent on the state of its neighbors. The discussion about the difference between both techniques, usually called outward/inward (or outflow/inflow) can be often observed [6,7]. The Glauber mechanism is connected to the physical image of interactions between different states when the probability of state change is given by the formula

$$prob = \frac{1}{1 + exp(\frac{\Delta E}{k_B T})}.$$

(2)

It shows the next difference between both methods used. While Stauffer's rules are purely deterministic, the Glauber's rule is probabilistic. As it can be seen in the formula 2 we have some physically interpreted quantities like energy change, Boltzmann constant and temperature. Actually the energy change ($\Delta E$) has to be calculated in the way similar to some magnetic multi-state models (e.g Potts model). For simplicity let us consider the formula which enables to calculate the energy change when the state $s_i$ is changed

$$\Delta E = J * \sum_j \Delta s_i * s_j$$

(3)

where summation is over neighboring states and $\Delta s_i$ equals 1 if we change between the states neighboring on the Nolan chart, and $\Delta s_i = 2$ if states are opposite. The dynamics of the system depends on the parameter $\beta = \frac{J}{k_B T}$ which has to be defined for every run.

Additionally we decided to study two time regimes of update. According to the first one we work always on the same array. The "Monte Carlo Sweep" is then the number of successive updates performed on the sample. In our approach the number equals the size of array. In the second method, let us call it synchronous, we try to simulate the concurrent update therefore the states of cells are set according to the array remembered at the beginning of the Monte Carlo Sweep. This mechanism is used only for Stauffer's update rules.

## 3   Results and Conclusions

The presentation of results we start from the analysis of the relaxation time. In the Fig. 2 there is shown the percentage number of runs which are unrelaxed after given Monte Carlo Sweeps. The plots are shown only for the Stauffer's update since for all simulations with the Glauber dynamics, independently on the $\beta$ parameter the system does not relax to the steady state. The maximum number of sweeps equals 100000. The data in Fig.2 and Tab.1 are collected from the 100 independent runs for every version of rule.

In the Table 1 we summarize the data concerning the relaxation time. All values are shown in Monte Carlo sweeps. The main conclusion which follows the analysis of Fig.2 and Tab.1 is that except of just a few cases, the course of curves is similar. The relaxation point is usually about $10^3 - 10^4$, except of Stauffer's rule Ib. This effect can be expected since the lack of fixed points for this particular rule has been mentioned in earlier paper [4]. Certainly, our model is a little more complicated than the one used in the original paper due to increase of number of states. We can expect however the similar features where taking into account the existence or nonexistence of fixed points.

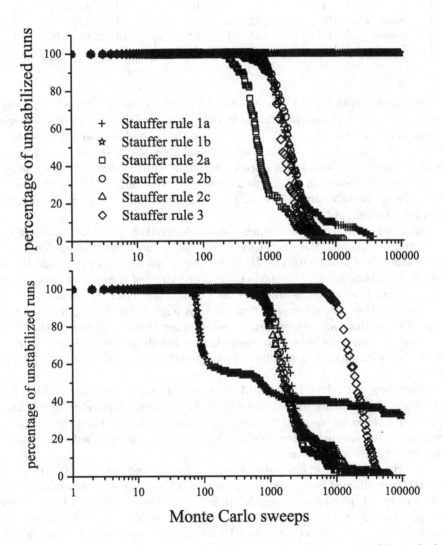

**Fig. 2.** The percentage number of runs which are unrelaxed after given Monte Carlo Sweeps. Upper plot - unsynchronized update. Lower plot - synchronized update.

**Table 1.** Average relaxation time for different versions of system update

|  | unsynchronized | synchronized |
|---|---|---|
| Stauffer rule Ia | $(4.3 \pm 7.3) * 10^3$ | $(4.5 \pm 7.7) * 10^3$ |
| Stauffer rule Ib | $- - -$ | $(3.5 \pm 4.6) * 10^4$ |
| Stauffer rule IIa | $(1.1 \pm 1.0) * 10^3$ | $(2.5 \pm 2.8) * 10^3$ |
| Stauffer rule IIb | $(2.5 \pm 1.7) * 10^3$ | $(3.1 \pm 3.8) * 10^3$ |
| Stauffer rule IIc | $(2.2 \pm 1.2) * 10^3$ | $(3.4 \pm 4.5) * 10^3$ |
| Stauffer rule III | $(1.84 \pm 0.9) * 10^3$ | $(2.14 \pm 1.0) * 10^4$ |

The fixed points for the 4-state model belong to the two types: all states can be the same and the two states can occupy approximately half of cells each (please note that the size of sample is odd, so these numbers can not be equal). We do not want here to use the magnetic analogy and call the ferro- antiferro- or ferrimagnetic configurations since for the multi-state systems the description is more complicated than for simple 2-state and the additional interpretation of states should be taken into account. The majority of runs (about 80%) leads to a uniform ordering of states.

The three interesting cases which can be observed on plots are: both implementations of rule Ib (the unsynchronized case has been described before) and the synchronized update for rule III. For the synchronized update of rule Ib we obtain the relaxation and the ratio of final orderings of states conforms to the one mentioned before (80% uniform - 20% two-state). The extrapolation of the curve shows that we can expect that all runs lead to the fixed point but the time of relaxation can be even few decades longer than presented on the plot. The shape of curve for rule III presents the similar dependence as other curves but the average lifetime is significantly longer (the difference is of order of one decade).

Comparing the values from Tab.1 we can point some differences which are the effects of the change of update method. The analysis of standard deviations shows that these values are for synchronized update larger when compared to averages as for unsynchronized update. It is the effect of so-called long tails of relaxation time distributions.

The crucial interest in our paper is related to the study of disproportionality generated by different update schemes. Figures 3-5 shows the values of Gallagher index averaged over all runs which are active at the particular Monte Carlo sweep. They are not averaged over sweeps what could smooth the curves. In Fig.3 we show the results for rule III and different methods of constituency construction. The upper plot is indeed the repetition of plots from our paper [2]. The plots confirm that the crucial process influencing the result is the coherence of constituencies and not their strength. Further we will present only one plot for compact and one for spread type of constituency.

The results for different methods of update are shown in Figs.4 and 5

We can observe that qualitative behavior which was noticed when considering rule III is repeated for almost all rules visible in figures. Usually, shortly after

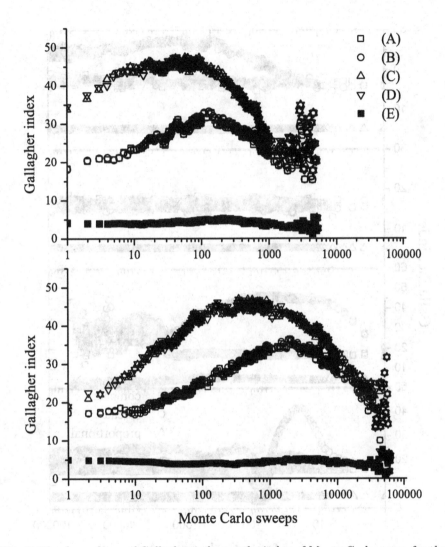

**Fig. 3.** The dependence of Gallagher index on the index of Monte Carlo sweep for the Stauffer's rule III. (A)-compact and equal constituencies; (B)-compact and not equal; (C)-spread and equal; (D)-spread and not equal. Upper plot - unsynchronized update. Lower plot - synchronized update.

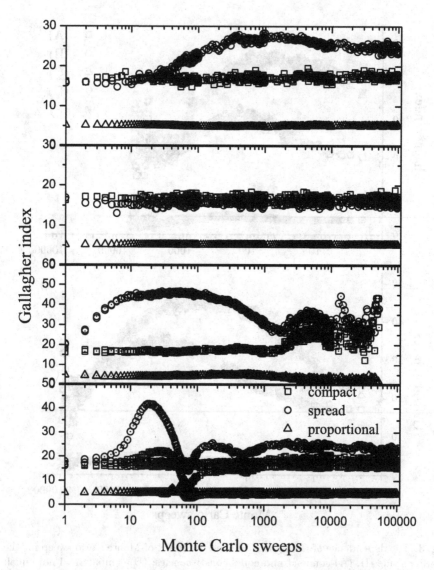

**Fig. 4.** The dependence of Gallagher index on the index of Monte Carlo sweep for different update rules. From upper: Glauber rule $\beta = 1$; Glauber rule $\beta = 0.5$; Stauffer rule Ia; Stauffer rule Ib. Open symbols correspond to the unsynchronized, dotted - synchronized update.

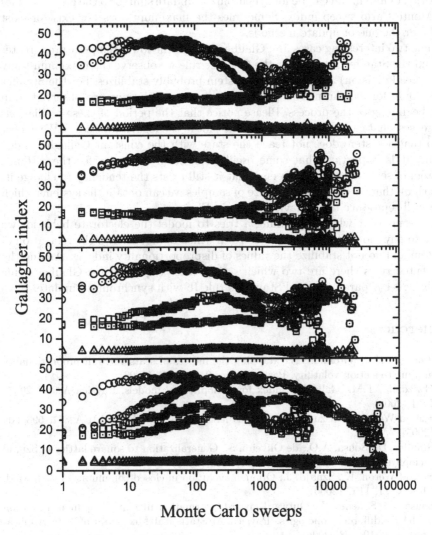

**Fig. 5.** The dependence of Gallagher index on the index of Monte Carlo sweep for different update rules. From upper: Stauffer rule IIa; Stauffer rule IIb; Stauffer rule IIc; Stauffer rule III. Open symbols correspond to the unsynchronized, dotted - synchronized update.

simulation starts, there exist a maximum. Afterwards the short oscillations occur just before the relaxation. Actually, it seems that these oscillations should be rather related to the still decreasing number of data which undergo averaging, that to the real effect. There certainly exist some quantitative differences. The compact division leads to the lower Gallagher values than the spread ones. The position of maximum can be for synchronized update shifted to the greater values of Monte Carlo sweep index. Sometimes the maximum does not exist or exist only for the one of update methods.

The two interesting cases are: Glauber rule for the lower temperature (greater $\beta$)and the Stauffer rule Ib. For the Glauber rule we observe the maximum (only for spread division) and further the system probably stabilizes. For the Stauffer rule (only for synchronized update) the strong oscillations are observed from the beginning of the process. Please notice that the period of these oscillations increases what can be not obvious on the plot in the logarithmic scale. We expect also that a system does not reach the state with the constant Gallagher index value. It is important that some oscillations occur here also for the d'Hondt system of seats awarding. It seems that it still exists the tendency to change it. We think that by enhancing the size of samples we can obtain the systems which can well reproduce the behavior shown in Fig.1.

It seems that when performing a tries to model the electorate behavior we have to pay more attention to these rules which do not lead to the relaxation of system and do not stabilize the values of disproportionality indexes. Among the presented rules there are two which satisfy these requirements: Glauber's rule with higher $\beta$ parameter and Stauffer's rule Ib with synchronized update.

# References

1. Taagepera, R., Grofman, B.: Mapping the indices of seats-votes disproportionality and inter-election volatility. Party Politics 9, 659–677 (2003)
2. Gwizdałła, T.M.: Gallagher index for sociophysical models. Physica A 387, 2937–2751 (2008)
3. Sznajd-Weron, K., Sznajd, J.: Who is left, who is right? Physica A 351, 593–604 (2005)
4. Stauffer, D., Sousa, A.O., de Oliveira, S.: Generalization to square lattice of Sznajd sociophysics. Int. J. Mod. Phys. C 11, 1239 (2000)
5. Sznajd-Weron, K., Sznajd, J.: Opinion evolution in closed community. Int. J. Mod. Phys. C 11, 1157 (2000)
6. Sousa, A., Sanchez, J.: Outward-inward information flux in an opinion formation model on different topologies. Physica A: Statistical Mechanics and its Applications 361, 319–328 (2006)
7. Galam, S.: Local dynamics vs. social mechanisms: A unifying frame. Europhys. Lett. 70, 705–711 (2005)

# A Spatio-temporal Algorithmic Point of View on Firing Squad Synchronisation Problem

Luidnel Maignan and Jean-Baptiste Yunès

LIAFA, Université Paris-Diderot, France

**Abstract.** Firing Squad Synchronization Problems are well known to be solvable by voluminous transition tables describing signals traveling and colliding. In this paper, we show that it is possible to solve it by expressing directly the fact that we want a recursive division of the space into two parts of equal size, and a notification when no further division is possible. Using fields – objects associating a value to every point in space and time – as primitive objects, the solution is designed algorithmically by a semantically-intuitive decomposition of the global evolution into simpler evolutions.

The system we obtain has several interesting characteristics : it is understandable, time-optimal, tackles many initial configurations, and allows a new interpretation of the traditional signals and collisions point of view. We will quickly sketch how we can obtain a finite state automaton by reduction of the system using the Lipschitz-continuity of involved fields, and a kind of tail-recursivity property of the dependencies.

## 1 Introduction

Cellular automata are often described as signal machines, i.e. sets of signals or particles that move, bounce and collide in a continuous space. However, if this description is commonly sufficient to convince that a cellular automaton really computes what is wanted, it is far from clear how this continuous model helps to obtain a discrete realization in terms of a cellular automaton. But worse, it is much more unclear that a continuous idealization of a cellular automaton really helps to prove its correctness.

A typical example of this is the well-known firing squad synchronization problem (FSSP) [2,12,13], its great variety of solutions, [1] and the very poor number of proofs of their correctness [11,14,20]. It can be described as follows:

> Find a local evolution rule defined on a finite set such that, starting from arbitrary sized initial configurations where all but one cell (the general) are in a sleeping (quiescent) state, all cells synchronously enter, and for the first time, a given (fire) state.

Being quiescents at the beginning, cells will wake up one after the other from the non-quiescent one, which means that they are originally "desynchronized", and this explains why it is considered as a "synchronization" problem. This problem

G.C. Sirakoulis and S. Bandini (Eds.): ACRI 2012, LNCS 7495, pp. 101–110, 2012.

is as old as the cellular automaton model is and many solutions exist for the original problem or to variations or generalizations of it. For example, one can consider synchronizing with arbitrary general [21] at any arbitrary position [19], many generals synchronous or not [16], synchronizing 2D-spaces [3,6,18], 3D-spaces [17], graphs [15,5], and variants with different constraints on shape of the space. There are also solutions involving spaces that are dynamic to some extent [4]. As already said, the design and dynamics of these solutions are often explained in terms of signals. For example, in many papers one can read things like:

> [...] we launch two signals from the general: one at maximum speed 1 which bounces on the border and another one at speed $\frac{1}{3}$ that both collide right at the middle of the space. From this collision other signals may be generated [...] and as more signals are added to the process, quarters of the space, eighth of the space and so on are detected. At some point, a kind of saturation which corresponds to the fire state is obtained [...]

Such continuous intuition explains beautifully the fractal patterns that appears on the space time diagrams of the solutions. But starting from it, it is not clear how to discretize it.

In this paper, we focus only on cellular automata and discrete related objects and we will never use any continuous object or argument. Instead we propose to design a cellular automaton by decomposing the problem into easier sub-problems and compose their solutions into a global solution. To do so, we introduce the concept of dynamic fields which allow to express composable partial solutions. Informally speaking, fields are kinds of partial cellular automata. Their main interest is to have clear semantics relevant to the computation. To demonstrate their benefits, we use them to design a solution for the firing squad synchronization problem. Ultimately, we show that we recover the classical concepts of modularity, reusability, semantic decomposition, etc. All of this can be seen as an algorithmic methodology useful to synthesize cellular automata and to manage proofs of these algorithms.

But first, let us consider the simple example of Pascal's triangle modulo 2, in order to introduce and define the necessary concepts in a natural way.

## 1.1  Fields and Pascal's Triangle Modulo 2

Here, the goal is to synthesize a solution for the parity of the Pascal's triangle using fields. But first, let us make clear what fields are. They are defined using a local evolution rule uniformly dispatched over the space, and that has the same locality properties as CA rules (finite neighborhood, finite time dependency). In fact a cellular automaton is a particular field, but in the more general case a field may have infinite domains and may also depend on other fields.

Now, we will decompose our problem into two sub-problems: the first one being the problem of building the Pascal's triangle, and the other one to compute the parity. The first is solved defining the field $T$ of Pascal's triangle integers which given $N(x) = \{x - 1, x + 1\}$, the neighborhood of cell $x$, is simply defined as :

$$T_0(x) = \begin{cases} 1 & \text{if } x = 0, \\ 0 & \text{otherwise.} \end{cases} \qquad T_{t+1}(x) = \sum_{y \in N(x)} T_t(y)$$

The second is solved defining $P$ as a filtering field, i.e. a field that only depends on other fields and not on its own values at $t - 1$. $P$ operates on any arbitrary given field $X$ of integers, extracting the parity of the values of $X$:

$$P[X]_t(x) = X_t(x) \mod 2$$

Now we are able to compose the two fields $P$ and $T$ into a field $F$ defined as:

$$F = P[T]$$

We obviously obtain the field of the parity of Pascal's triangle, but it remains to construct a cellular automaton. The problems are that the first field is not defined over a finite set, and it is not clear at first sight that the field $F$ is computable by a cellular automata. But, if we remark that:

$$
\begin{aligned}
F_{t+1}(x) &= P[T]_{t+1}(x) \\
&= \sum_{y \in N(x)} T_t(y) \mod 2 \\
&= \sum_{y \in N(x)} (T_t(y) \mod 2) \mod 2 \\
&= \sum_{y \in N(x)} P[T]_t(y) \mod 2 \\
&= \sum_{y \in N(x)} F_t(y) \mod 2
\end{aligned}
$$

we are now able to easily construct a cellular automaton which computes $F$.

Of course in the general case, many problems remain, but these considerations are out of scope of this paper. We would rather like to show how these tools can be successfully applied with benefits to some more complex problem such as the FSSP.

## 2   A Field-Based Description of the FSSP

In this section, we will first explain how the FSSP can be decomposed into simpler problems, how these elementary problems are represented as fields, how these fields are finally composed and then how we will be able to obtain a cellular automaton by overcoming the unbounded number of states and fields generated.

## 2.1   An Algorithmic Solution

We recall that the main idea is to divide the space into two equals regions and to proceed recursively until all regions have size 1.

Naturally, the first step is to *identify the middle of the physical space*. To do this we introduce three fields. The first field, $R^0$, represents the discovery of the region to be cut. The second field, $D^0$, will provide some distance information deduced from $R^0$, such that this distance will eventually allows us to detect the middle. The third one is a boolean field, $F^0$ that indicates the correctness of the values of $R^0$ and $D^0$. Indeed, $R^0$ and $D^0$ are dynamic fields, which means that $R^0$ discovers the space from time to time and so its derived field $D^0$ also updates accordingly. Eventually $R^0$ stabilizes when it corresponds to the whole physical space and leading in turn to the stabilization of $D^0$ (see Section 2.2).

Now that we have a region and its middle, we introduce another collection of three fields: $R^1$ that represents the discovery of the two regions induced by the previous cut of the space, $D^1$ the distance field deduced from $R^1$ such that the middles of the two regions will be detected, and $F^1$ the corresponding correctness field. As the reader might guess, this extends to a recursive schema which defines $R^\ell$, $D^\ell$ and $F^\ell$ in terms of $R^{\ell-1}$, $D^{\ell-1}$ and $F^{\ell-1}$ (see Section 2.3).

This obviously implies that we need an unbounded number of fields. However, we will later explain how this can be reduced to a finite system (see Section 2.4).

## 2.2   Initial Region and Its Middle

The *initial region field* $R^0$ is defined using three states $O$ (*"outside"*), $B$ (*"border"*) and $I$ (*"inside"*). $O$ is the quiescent state of the field. A cell in state $O$ will turn into $B$ as soon as one of its neighbors is in state $B$. The "border" state is used to mark the border of the region currently discovered, which at this step must finally correspond the whole physical space. A cell in state $B$ which does not coincide with a physical border of the space updates its state to $I$. With the help of a given static boolean field $Border^0(x)$ that states for each $x$ if it is a physical border or not, the field $R^0$ is formally defined by:

$$R_t^0(x) = \begin{cases} B & \text{if } R_{t-1}^0(x) = O \wedge \exists y \in N(x); R_{t-1}^0(y) = B \\ I & \text{if } R_{t-1}^0(x) = B \wedge \neg Border^0(x) \\ R_{t-1}^0(x) & \text{otherwise.} \end{cases} \quad (1)$$

From any initial condition of the form $BO\ldots O$, the evolution of $R^0$ produces a space-time diagram like the one depicted in Fig. 1(a).

Now that we have the field that, after some time, represents the whole initial region, we want to determine its middle point. To do so, we use the fact that the middle of a region is the inner point farthest from both "borders". So, we build the *distance field* $D^0$, which associates to each cell its distance to latest observed nearest "borders" of the region. As the middle is necessarily an inner cell, the value of $D^0$ of any cell that is not inside is defined as 0. One can note that this is consistent with the fact that a "border" is obviously at distance 0

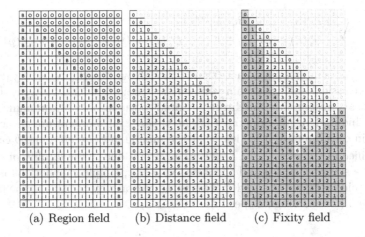

(a) Region field       (b) Distance field       (c) Fixity field

**Fig. 1.** The three fields describing the initial region and its middle

from a "border". For an inner cell its distance to the latest observed nearest "border" is obviously 1 plus the smallest distance to the latest observed nearest "border" of its neighbors. This is formally defined by:

$$D_t^0(x) = \begin{cases} 0 & \text{if } R_t^0(x) \neq I \\ \min_{y \in N(x)} 1 + D_{t-1}^0(y) & \text{otherwise} \end{cases} \qquad (2)$$

This rule has been extensively studied as a generic building block in cellular automata that solve different geometric problems (see [7,8,9,10]). It is sufficient to detect non-strict local maxima from the distance field to obtain the middle cell(s) of the region. This is illustrated in Fig. 1(b) which shows how region and distance fields evolve.

A final piece is required with respect to synchronization: we need to know when values provided by the region and distance fields are finals. Hence, we define a boolean field $F^0$ which associates to each cell a boolean indicating if its respective region and distance values are definitely correct. It is possible to determine the appropriate value by a simple case analysis. First, no field's value of an "outside" cell is considered correct (it has not been discovered yet). "Border" cell field's values are correct only if they coincide with a physical border. For "inside" cells, we know by construction that they are really inside so this value is always correct, but we still need to ensure that the distance value is also correct. To determine the distance value correctness, we use the fact that the region only grows, which implies that distance values only increase. And, from the point of view of a cell $x$, this means that once a neighbor is both correct and minimaly-valued in its neighborhood, it will remain such forever. This ensures that the distance value of $x$ will not evolve anymore since it correspond to this fixed value $+ 1$ as specified in Eq. (2). Altogether, this leads to the following formal definition, whose evolution is illustrated in Fig. 1(c).

$$F_t^0(x) = \bigvee \begin{cases} R_t^0(x) = B \wedge Border^0(x) \\ R_t^0(x) = I \wedge \exists y \in N(x); \ D_t^0(x) = 1 + D_{t-1}^0(y) \wedge F_{t-1}^0(y) \end{cases} \quad (3)$$

*Remark 1.* It is interesting to note that, although our description is very different from the classical one, we obtain very similar spatio-temporal patterns. Indeed, they appear because they are directly related to the locality of communications, and the induced delay. Suppose that at time $t$, the borders are respectively located in cells $a$ and $b$. It is clear that the middle in between $a$ and $b$ can only be identified at time $t + \frac{d(a,b)}{2}$. This is an invariant due to the locality of system, and if the speed of $a$ is 0 and the speed of $b$ is 1, simple calculations indicate that the middle moves at speed $\frac{1}{3}$. This is the reason why one side of the triangle has slope 3 (classical signal speed $\frac{1}{3}$).

## 2.3  Subsequent Regions and Divisions

Now that the initial region is identified and that enough information has been built to divide it, let us proceed by adding new fields to obtain the division and provide sufficient information to recurse.

First, let us clearly identify what we want to build. From Fig. 1, it should be clear that we are going to build one region starting from the left and another starting from the right. However, we shall prevent ourselves to trust our eyes too much, but try to describe what we want by definition.

Let us come back on what we have done for the initial region and do nearly the same here. Given the predicate $Border^0(x)$, what we built is a region field whose values are, after some time, $R^0(x) = B$ for $x$'s that are physical borders, and $R^0(x) = I$ for $x$'s that are not physical borders and so inner cells.

In the region field $R^1$, we want to obtain as borders all the "borders" obtained at the previous level and new ones corresponding to the middle(s) cell(s) finally obtained at the previous level. Thus, we consider as borders of the two regions all correct $x$'s such that $R^0(x) = B$, and all $x$'s that correspond to correct non-strict local maxima of $D^0$. We also want to have $R^1(x) = I$ everywhere $x$ is correct and is neither a "border" nor a maximum among its neighbors in $D^0$. This naturally leads to the following recursive formal definition of the two predicates *Border* and *Inside* for any level $l > 0$ :

$$Border_t^{\ell+1}(x) = \bigvee \begin{cases} R_t^\ell(x) = B \wedge F_t^\ell(x) \\ \forall y \in \{x\} \cup N(x); \ D_{t-1}^\ell(x) \geq D_{t-1}^\ell(y) \wedge F_{t-1}^\ell(y) \end{cases} \quad (4)$$

$$Inside_t^{\ell+1}(x) = F_t^\ell(x) \wedge R_t^\ell(x) \neq B \wedge \exists y \in N(x); \ D_{t-1}^\ell(y) > D_t^\ell(x) \quad (5)$$

Given these two boolean fields, we can apply the same reasoning as before and, obtain nearly the same evolution rule as the initial region. We only need to change the use of $\neg Border^0(x)$ in Eq. 1 into $Inside_t^1(x)$ and the use of $Border^0(x)$ in Eq. 3 into $Border_t^1(x)$. Thus, we obtain the three additional fields

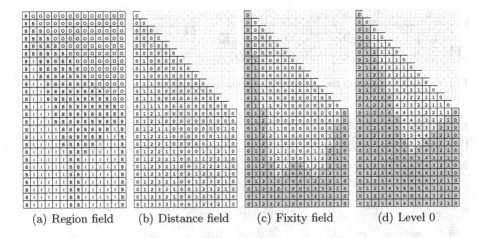

(a) Region field     (b) Distance field     (c) Fixity field     (d) Level 0

**Fig. 2.** The three fields describing the level 1

describing the first level of division, and iterating this construction, for any level $l > 0$ we obtain the following recursive definition:

$$R_t^\ell(x) = \begin{cases} B & \text{if } R_{t-1}^\ell(x) = O \wedge \exists y \in N(x); R_{t-1}^\ell(y) = B \\ I & \text{if } R_{t-1}^\ell(x) = B \wedge Inside_t^\ell(x) \\ R_{t-1}^\ell(x) & \text{otherwise.} \end{cases} \qquad (6)$$

$$D_t^\ell(x) = \begin{cases} 0 & \text{if } R_t^\ell(x) \neq I \\ \min_{y \in N(x)} 1 + D_{t-1}^\ell(y) & \text{otherwise.} \end{cases} \qquad (7)$$

$$F_t^\ell(x) = \bigvee \begin{cases} R_t^\ell(x) = B \wedge Border_t^\ell(x) \\ R_t^\ell(x) = I \wedge \exists y \in N(x); D_t^\ell(x) = 1 + D_{t-1}^\ell(y) \wedge F_{t-1}^\ell(y) \end{cases} \qquad (8)$$

Fig. 2 shows how the three fields evolve at level 1 of the algorithm. In Fig. 2(a) we have one region that grows from the left and starts at the initial time, and another one that grows from the right and starts at time $n - 1$ ($n$ is the number of cells). The distance field $D^1$ evolves inside each region described by $R^1$.

One can observe that while in $D^0$ the non-strict local maxima spanned two cells, then in $D^1$ there is two non-strict local maxima that both span only one cell. This depends on whether the region's length is odd or even (Fig. 2(b)).

## 2.4 Reduction to a Finite Number of States

Now we face two problems. The first one is that distance fields are defined over integers and the other one that we obtained an unbounded number of fields. Altough a complete and detailed explanation of the reducability in finite state is out of the scope of this paper, let us sketch the more important steps.

The first problem can be solved using a special property. If an integer field is Lipschitz-continuous, i.e. the difference of values between two neighbors is

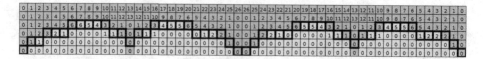

**Fig. 3.** Stack (level 0 on top) of all field values computed at time 96. Line length is 54.

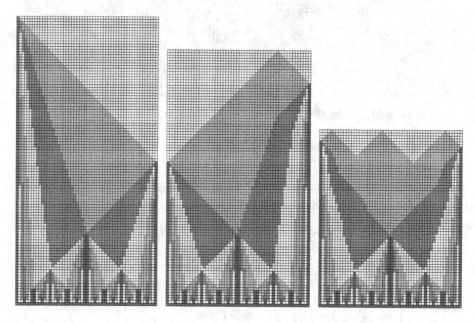

**Fig. 4.** Evolution of the complete system with different set of generals

bounded, and the information used in the system only depends on this difference, then it can be transformed into a finite-state field (refer to [8] for all the details). An application of this result is that when the difference is at most 1, then only 3 states are required. With definitions given in Eq. 2 and Eq. 7, it's easy to remark that all the distance fields $D^\ell$ can therefore be represented with only 3 states each.

To solve the second problem we remark that *in some sense* the recursive schema is "tail-recursive". Indeed, tail-recursiveness is about conserving only the information that are required but the subsequent recursive calls. From the point of view of a cell $x$, if its field values at given level $\ell$ are correct, this means that they do not evolve anymore. If furthermore its field values at $\ell + 1$ are also correct and so are the values of its neighbors, then its values at level $\ell$ are no more useful and can be discarded. This is observable in Fig. 3 where fields values are represented for all cells at a given time. Values $(x, \ell)$ in darker gray are correct ($F_t^\ell(x)$ is true), and if the whole neighborhood at the next level is also gray, then $(x, \ell)$ can be "forgotten". By discarding all these gray values (and a little bit more with a much finer analysis), we obtain for each cell a *lowest useful level* represented by a bold surround in the figure. In fact, these are the only necessary values that need to be stored, along with their associated lowest level number (which can be represented with only three state thanks to the Lipschitz-continuous argument).

Altogether, this shows that field values are uniformly bounded, and that only a finite number of fields is required. This implies that we finally describe the behavior of a cellular automaton.

## 3 Conclusion

Without any modification, the system described in this paper is much more general than one can think. Indeed, in our whole description we never use the property that there is only one general on the left. Since nothing such has been assumed in the design of the solution, we can naturally expect that it is agnostic to such particularities, and this is exactly the case as one can observe in Fig. 4. We also never assumed that the wake-up of the cells happens one after the other from the general, so that removing the corresponding sub-system, one obtains a solution for arbitrary initial desynchronized configurations.

It seems also possible to compose the same fields in slightly different ways to obtain different kind of solutions or to extend this solution to higher dimensions. We can also expect that a proof of correctness of the solution for all sizes and all initial desynchronized configurations seems to be much easier than for classical solutions, each field is simple and almost correct by construction, and so is their composition.

Finally, what we propose is a semantic-oriented framework which let anyone describe cellular machines in very natural modular way, which is a very common point of view in classical algorithmic and computer programming. Each of these composable fields, expressed in their original form, can be reused in many other different contexts. We think that this method is really helpful and so powerful that many things previously considered as hard to manage and to understand now appear to be clearer and easier.

## References

1. Culik, K.: Variations of the firing squad problem and applications. Information Processing Letters 30, 153–157 (1989)
2. Goto, E.: A minimum time solution of the firing squad synchronization problem. Courses Notes for Applied Mathematics, vol. 298. Harvard University (1962)
3. Grasselli, A.: Synchronization of cellular arrays: The firing squad problem in two dimensions. Information and Control 28, 113–124 (1975)
4. Herman, G.T., Liu, W., Rowland, S., Walker, A.: Synchronization of growing cellular automata. Information and Control 25, 103–122 (1974)
5. Jiang, T.: The synchronization of nonuniform networks of finite automata. Information and Control 97, 234–261 (1992)
6. Kobayashi, K.: The firing squad synchronisation problem for two-dimensional arrays. Information and Control 34, 177–197 (1977)

7. Maignan, L., Gruau, F.: Integer gradient for cellular automata: Principle and examples. In: Proceedings of the 2008 Second IEEE International Conference on Self-Adaptive and Self-Organizing Systems Workshops, pp. 321–325. IEEE Computer Society, Washington, DC (2008)

8. Maignan, L., Gruau, F.: A 1D cellular automaton that moves particles until regular spatial placement. Parallel Processing Letters 19(2), 315–331 (2009)

9. Maignan, L., Gruau, F.: Convex Hulls on Cellular Automata. In: Bandini, S., Manzoni, S., Umeo, H., Vizzari, G. (eds.) ACRI 2010. LNCS, vol. 6350, pp. 69–78. Springer, Heidelberg (2010)

10. Maignan, L., Gruau, F.: Gabriel graphs in arbitrary metric space and their cellular automaton for many grids. ACM Trans. Auton. Adapt. Syst. 6, 12:1–12:14 (June 2011)

11. Mazoyer, J.: A six states minimal time solution to the firing squad synchronization problem. Theoretical Computer Science 50, 183–238 (1987)

12. Minsky, M.: Computation: Finite and Infinite Machines. Prentice-Hall (1967)

13. Moore, E.E.: Sequential machines, Selected papers. Addison-Wesley (1964)

14. Noguchi, K.: Simple 8-state minimal time solution to the firing squad synchronization problem. TCS 314, 303–334 (2004)

15. Rosenstiehl, P., Fiskel, J.R., Holliger, A.: Intelligent Graphs: Networks of Finite Automata capable of Solving Graph Problems. In: Read, R.C. (ed.) Graph Theory and Computing. Academic Press (1972)

16. Schmid, H., Worsch, T.: The firing squad synchronization problem with many generals for one-dimensional CA. In: Lévy, J.-J., Mayr, E.W., Mitchell, J.C. (eds.) IFIP TCS, pp. 111–124. Kluwer (2004)

17. Shinahr, I.: Two and three dimensional firing squad synchronization problems. Information and Control 24, 163–180 (1974)

18. Szwerinski, H.: Time-optimal solution of the firing-squad synchronization problem for $n$-dimensional rectangles with the general at an arbitrary position. Theoretical Computer Science 19, 305–320 (1982)

19. Varshavsky, V.I., Marakhovsky, V.B., Peshansky, V.A.: Synchronization of interacting automata. Mathematical System Theory 4(3), 212–230 (1969)

20. Yunès, J.-B.: An intrinsically non minimal-time Minsky-like 6-states solution to the firing squad synchronization problem. RAIRO ITA/TIA 42(1), 55–66 (2008)

21. Yunès, J.-B.: Known CA synchronizers made insensitive to the initial state of the initiator. JCA 4(2), 147–158 (2009)

# A Coevolutionary Approach to Cellular Automata-Based Task Scheduling

Gina M.B. Oliveira and Paulo M. Vidica

Faculdade de Ciencia da Computacao - Universidade Federal de Uberlandia (UFU)
Av. Joao Naves de Avila, 2121- Campus Santa Monica, Bloco B, sala 1B60
CEP: 38400-902 Uberlandia, MG, Brazil
gina@facom.ufu.br

**Abstract.** Cellular Automata (CA) have been proposed for task scheduling in multiprocessor architectures. CA-based models aim to be fast and decentralized schedulers. Previous models employ an off-line learning stage in which an evolutionary method is used to discover cellular automata rules able to solve an instance of a task scheduling. A central point of CA-based scheduling is the reuse of transition rules learned for one specific program graph in the schedule of new instances. However, our investigation about previous models showed that evolved rules do not actually have such generalization ability. A new approach is presented here named multigraph coevolutionary learning, in which a population of program graphs is evolved simultaneously with rules population leading to more generalized transition rules. Results obtained have shown the evolution of rules with better generalization abilitywhen they are compared with those obtained using previous approaches.

**Keywords:** Cellular automata, task scheduling, coevolution.

## 1    Introduction

Scheduling tasks in multiprocessor architectures is known to be a NP-complete problem [4] and it is still a challenge in parallel computing field. Approaches to explore task scheduling typically employ specific heuristics [11] or metaheuristics, like genetic algorithms and simulated annealing [12]. A computational effort is used to solve an instance of the problem in these approaches and when a new instance is presented to the algorithm, the process needs to start again from scratch. Besides, the majority of scheduling algorithms is sequential and they are not appropriate to be implemented in parallel hardware. Promising results obtained with the join use of genetic algorithms (GA) [1] and cellular automata [3] have shown a new perspective direction in developing fast and parallel scheduling algorithms [4-8].

Cellular automata (CA) are discrete dynamical systems that consist of a large number of simple components with local connectivity. It is necessary to design an appropriate neighborhood structure to use CA for scheduling. This neighborhood must reflect the structure of a program graph, which contains all the relevant information of the parallel application such as precedence of tasks, their computational costs and communication

G.C. Sirakoulis and S. Bandini (Eds.): ACRI 2012, LNCS 7495, pp. 111–120, 2012.

costs between pairs of tasks. In the present work a nonlinear structure named *Selected Neighborhood* [4] is used to capture the intrinsic characteristics of program graphs. CA model applies an asynchronous updating of cells since it has returned better results in previous works [4, 10].

Some CA-based approaches had presented good results when applied to schedule tasks for given program graphs [4, 8]. These approaches have a learning phase characterized by the use of a standard GA to find the correct distribution of the tasks considering a single program graph. The population of such GA is formed by CA transition rules aiming to schedule tasks over architecture processors. Later on, evolved CA rules can be used to schedule the same program graph or they can be applied to find optimal or suboptimal solutions to other parallel programs. However, as we will show in Section 4, the rules evolved using previous schemes [4, 8] have shown almost none generalization ability, that is, they cannot find reasonable makespam for new program graphs not seen during learning, even if these instances are very similar to the one used to find them.

A new approach is proposed here, in which a coevolutionary .algorithm is used during learning to search for good scheduling not only for the target program graph but also for some similar graphs generated applying some mutations on the target graph. The goal is to find CA rules with better generalization ability. Therefore, a second population formed by variations of the target graph is evolved simultaneously with the transition rule population. We call this new approach as multigraph coevolutionary learning.

Seredynski and Zomaya [5] have also investigated a coevolutionary approach in the learning phase of CA-based schedulers. However, in their approach the second population was formed by different initial configurations of the CA lattice to be used as initial allocations to evaluate rules for a single program graph. The goal of coevolutionary search in [5] is not to improve the generalization ability of the discovered rules as we are seeking here, but to improve the performance of these rules in relation to the proper target program. Other related works investigated CA models to task scheduling [7, 13, 14]. However, they employed a different kind of neighborhood (linear), while selected neighborhood used here and in references [4, 5, 6, 8] have shown more efficient to solve scheduling.

The paper is organized as follows. Section 2 contextualizes the problem of scheduling tasks on multiprocessor systems. Section 3 reviews previous CA models on scheduling. Section 4 discusses the generalization ability of CA rules – a key point of this work. Section 5 presents the multigraph coevolutionary learning proposed here. Section 6 presents some experiments accomplished with the new approach. Section 7 shows the main conclusions of this work.

## 2     Multiprocessor Task Scheduling

A parallel application is represented by a program graph which is a weighted directed acyclic graph $G_p = (V_p, E_p)$. $V_p$ is the set of $N_p$ tasks of the parallel program. It is assumed that each task is a computational indivisible unit. There is a precedence constraint relation between tasks $k$ and $l$ if the result produced by task $k$ has to be available to task $l$, before it starts. $E_p$ is the set of precedence relations between tasks. A program graph has weights associate to nodes and edges: $b_k$ describes the processing time required to execute a given task on any processor and $a_{kl}$ describes the communication time between pairs of tasks $k$ and $l$, when they are located in distinct processors. The purpose of scheduling is to distribute the tasks of a parallel program among the processors in such a way that the precedence constraints are preserved and the total execution time (or makespan) $T$ is minimized. $T$ depends on tasks allocation between processors and on some scheduling policy that defines the order for executing tasks within processors. Attributes can be associated with each node $k$ in a program graph such as: the level $h_k$ is defined as the maximal length of the longest path from a node $k$ to an exit node and the co-level $d_k$ is defined as the length of the longest path from the starting node to node $k$. If they are calculated depending on tasks allocation they are called dynamic level and dynamic co-level [4]. Some special sets are defined in relation to a given task $k$: *predecessors(k)*, *brothers(k)* (nodes that have at least one common predecessor) and *successors(k)*. The multiprocessor architecture used in the present work is composed by two identical processors: it is assumed that both processors have the same computational power and communications between channels do not consume any extra time.

# 3    Cellular Automata-Based Scheduling

Cellular automata are discrete complex systems that possess both a dynamic and a computational nature. Basically, a cellular automaton consists of two parts: the cellular space and the transition rule. Cellular space is a regular lattice of $N$ cells, each one with an identical pattern of local connections to other cells, and subjected to some boundary conditions. CA are characterized by a transition rule, that determines which will be the next configuration of the lattice, from their current one. Cells interact locally in a discrete time $t$: for each cell $i$, a neighborhood of radius $r$ is defined; the state of the cell $i$ at time $t + 1$ depends only on the states of its neighborhood at time $t$ and its current state. Cells updating is usually performed in a synchronous way. However, asynchronous updating is also possible. In sequential updating, only one cell is update at each time step, starting from the first cell.

A scheduler model was presented in [4] where each lattice cell is associated with a task. Considering two-processor architectures, the lattice is binary and each cell state indicates that the corresponding task is allocated either in the processor P0 or P1. Each lattice configuration corresponds to a different allocation of the tasks in the processors. Makespam $T$ associated to a given lattice is calculated using a scheduling policy that defines the order of the tasks within each processor. The scheduling policy used is: the task with the highest dynamic level is performed first.

CA evolve according to their transition rules. The goal is to find a CA rule able to converge the lattice to a final allocation of tasks, which minimizes $T$, starting from any initial allocation. The nonlinear structure of a program graph is represented in [4] by a nonlinear CA neighborhood named Selected Neighborhood. Only two selected representatives of each set of predecessors, brothers and successors are used to create the neighborhood of a cell associated with a task $k$ [4]. The two representative tasks are selected on the basis of maximal and minimal values of a chosen attribute. The neighborhood for a cell $k$ consists of 7 cells (including cell $k$). The length of a rule is 250 bits and there are $2^{250}$ possible rules [4]. Although sequential updating of cells is not usual as the synchronous one, considering CA broad context, it has returned interesting results in previous works involving CA-based scheduling [4, 6] and it is also investigated in the present work.

CA-based scheduler presented in [4] has two stages: a learning phase and an operating phase. In the learning phase, a GA [1] is used to search for CA rules able to schedule a specific program graph. GA begins with a population of $P$ rules randomly generated, encoded as binary strings. Rule's fitness is calculated by: (i) using a set of initial configurations (ICs) corresponding to initial allocations of a program graph; (ii) applying the rule starting from each IC for $M$ time steps and calculating the makespam $T$ for each final allocation; (iii) adding the values of $T$ calculated for all the ICs evaluated to obtain the fitness. The smaller is the fitness the better is the rule. GA is simple and it is based on the framework to evolve rules to solve density classification task [12]. At the end, population is stored in a repository of rules. In operating phase, it is expect that, for any initial allocation of tasks, stored rules will be able to find an allocation providing the optimal $T$ (or near to). It is also expected that rules evolved in the learning phase can be used in other graphs different from the one for which they were learned providing a good performance. The scheduler model in [4] was further investigated in references [5, 6, 8].

## 4     Generalization Ability of Previous Models

In previous CA-based schedulers [4, 8], a single program graph was used to discover CA rules in learning phase. GA evolves the rules calculating their fitness based only on this target graph. Published results have shown that the CA-based scheduler was able to discover rules that can successfully schedule several program graphs investigated in literature. However, when the discovered rules evolved for a specific graph were applied to other programs, conclusive results about the generalization ability of rules have not been published as we argument in the following.

It is interesting to point out that this generalization ability of evolved rules is crucial to CA-based scheduling. The huge computational effort necessary to discover the CA rules is justified only if these rules are able to be reused in new problems. Otherwise, a GA can be directly used in the search for optimal configurations of each graph independently, without the need to involve CA rules in the model. The idea behind the application of transition rules is the possibility of reusing them in new instances, without the need of a new process of evolutionary learning.

The generalization ability was evaluated in [4] using graphs Gauss 18 and Tree15. It was presented that rules evolved for Gauss18 were successfully applied to schedule Tree 15. However, when the rules evolved for Tree15 were applied to schedule Gauss 18, the results were not good: the best makespam found was 62 and the optimum is 44 (time units). Besides, the rules evolved for Tree 15 in [4] were applied to "similar" graphs Tree63 and Tree127. In this last test, the rules were able to schedule the two new graphs obtaining the optimum time. What is important to point here is that the family Tree*x* is formed by graphs with a very regular structure (binary trees), which are easy to schedule. We performed a simple test to evaluate the difficulty of solving the scheduling of Tree15: 10,000 random lattices of CA were sorted and $T$ associated to each allocation was calculated. The optimum $T$ is 9: average $T$ found was close to 9.8 and in approximately 40% of the random allocations optimum was obtained. So, even using a random allocation it is relatively easy to obtain the best scheduling for this kind of graph. The same test was performed for Gauss18, which has the optimal makespam equal to 44. In this case the average makespam obtained was close to 75 and none of the 10,000 random allocations returns the optimum. It is clear that for Gauss18, which represents a real parallel program, the scheduling problem is actually difficult to solve. Therefore, the results obtained reusing rules evolved for Gauss18 in the scheduling of Tree15 presented in [4] must be taken in a relative sense: the results are as good as if one uses a random allocation.

In subsequent works, few results about the generalization ability were presented. In [5] the generalization results refer again to the application of rules in family Tree*x*. In [6] this generalization ability was tested using rules evaluated for two program graphs separately (g18 and rnd25) in a new graph formed by joining these two graphs. Using a model based on an artificial immune system, the rules were able to schedule the mixed graph. Although these results are interesting, the learning phase was applied again to obtain the new rules. The related studies [4-8] are promising but just a little information about generalization ability was shown.

Aiming to better investigate such desirable ability, we realized experiments based on the model described in [4] and [8] applying the evolved rules to graphs totally different from the one used in the learning phase. In these experiments we used four graphs also applied in [4-8]: Gauss18, G18, Tree15 and G40 with optimum equal to 44, 46, 9 and 80, respectively. Each one of these graphs was used in learning phase as the target graph and then evolved rules were applied to the target graph and to the other three graphs in the operating phase. It was possible to observe that for each evaluated target graph the best rule evolved is able to find the optimal makespam for all the initial configurations tested. However, when the best evolved rules were applied to a graph different from the target one the results were not good in general. The unique exception is graph Tree15: the average makespam (considering all IC) when the target graph used as an input for the learning phase was Gauss18, G18 and G40 is 9.84, 9.63 and 9.39, respectively. For the other graphs, the results are not reasonable. For Gauss18 the optimum is 44 and it was found 72.78, 62.85 and 58.36 using rules evolved for target graphs G18, Tree15 and G40, respectively; no rules was able to find the optimal time. For G18 the optimum is 46 and it was found 58.46, 59.08 and 61.27 using rules evolved for target graphs Gauss18, Tree15 and G40, respectively; no rules were able to find the optimal time. For G40 the optimum is 80 and it was found 97.51, 87.41 and 105.2 for the target graphs Gauss18, Tree15 and G40, respectively. Due to the arguments and results presented we concluded that reasonable results about the generalization ability of the evolved rules were found only in graphs in which an optimal solution was relatively easy to obtain.

Another kind of investigation of generalization ability of previous CA-models [4, 8] were performed in [10]. This study concentrates on the following question: if CA rule evolved based on a specific program graph has some kind of generalization ability, this rule should return reasonable results (near to the optimal) at least when it is applied to new graphs that are similar variations of the original. Simple tests were carried out to evaluate if rules evolved for Gauss18 return reasonable results when they are applied to other graphs very similar to it, using fifteen graphs with 18 tasks very similar to Gauss18. Experiments using a simple GA (without CA rules) were conducted to find reference values for the similar graphs, since their optima are unknown. Besides, 10,000 random allocations were used to calculate average makespam considering all allocations for each similar graph. Best reference values were not easy to obtain using random allocations, as we expected for graphs closely to Gauss18. Finally, the best rules evolved for Gauss18 using the model in [4] in the learning phase was reused to schedule the fifteen new graphs.

Comparing the average time found in reuse with the average time found using 10,000 random allocations, it was possible to verify evolved rules indeed perform a kind of scheduling in all the graphs, because it was possible to reduce the makespam, starting from a random initial configuration. However, if one considers the average makespam found in operation phase with the best reference value for each graph, the makespam obtained with the CA rules is around 20% above the best value, considering the fifteen graphs. Therefore, considering CA-based model described in [4, 8], rules evolved using Gauss18 as the target graph when applied to new similar graphs were able to return makespam better than random allocations. But these values are still distant from the best possible. Besides, in reference [10], an approach called *joint evolution* was proposed, which also uses more graphs besides the target one during the learning phase. However, this set of graphs is kept frozen during the evolution and no coevolutionary strategy is employed. These previous results were promising and they inspired us to propose the multigraph coevolutionary learning discussed here which returned the best results of our investigation.

## 5    Multigraph Coevolutionary Learning

In the new approach to the learning phase proposed here, a coevolutionary environment [2] is used to evolve CA rules able to schedule program graphs. In this model, coevolutionary interactions are modeled as predator and prey metaphor. Coevolutionary algorithms evolve different populations during the evolutionary process (one of possible solutions and another of instances to solve) and mutual feedback mechanisms between the individuals of both populations provide a strong driving force towards complexity. Two populations involved in CA-based scheduler are: $P_1$ formed by possible solutions to the problem (CA rules) and $P_2$ formed by different program graphs. $P_2$ is composed by the target program graph (for example, Gauss18) and its random variations, i.e., program graphs very similar to the target one. We employed a total coevolutionary model in which both populations are modified by genetic operators during the evolutionary search [9] (another model is the partial coevolutionary in which only one population is actually evolved with operators). Considering $P_1$, selection, crossover and mutation operators are applied in the transition rules evolution. Considering $P_2$, only selection and mutation are applied:

selection decides which program graph will be discarded at each generation step and mutation operator creates a new variation of the target graph.

Let $T_{p1}$ and $T_{p2}$ be the size of populations $P_1$ and $P_2$, respectively. $P_2$ is composed by the target graph and $T_{p2} - 1$ program graphs randomly generated based on the target one. The other individuals of $P_2$ are variations of the target program, each one having 1 to 4 mutations in relation to original graph. The possible modifications can be: ($i$) a different computational cost associated to a task; ($ii$) a different communication cost associated to an edge from task $k$ to task $j$; ($iii$) exclusion of an edge from task $k$ to task $j$; ($iv$) inclusion of a new edge from task $k$ to task $j$, being the order of $k$ lesser than the order of $j$ and the cost associated to the new edge will be randomly generated between the biggest and the smallest communication cost of the target program.

In each generation, $T_{p2}$ program graphs – including the target one – are used to evaluate all $T_{p1}$ transition rules. In this evaluation, $I$ initial configurations (IC) of the lattice are used to evaluate the ability of each CA rule of $P_1$ to schedule one program graph of $P_2$. Starting from each IC (representing an initial allocation), CA rule is applied over the lattice by $M$ time steps and makespam $T$ associated to the final configuration is computed. The rule fitness is given by the sum of $T$ for all $I$ tests.

$P_1$ individuals are evolved as in [4]: ($i$) randomly sorting a initial population of $T_{p1}$ rules; ($ii$) randomly sorting a set of $I$ initial configurations of the lattice, different for each generation and testing them on each rule as described above; ($iii$) copying the $E_1$ best rules (elite) without modification to the next generation. Forming the remaining $T_{p1}$- $E_1$ rules for the next generation applying the single-point crossover operator to randomly sorted pairs of elite rules, which are submitted to mutation (subject to a given rate); ($iv$) the process returns to step $ii$ and continues a predefined number of generations $G$; ($v$) the population of the last generation is stored in a repository of rules. $P_2$ is also modified during the evolutionary process. The selection strategy adopted here is simple: the target graph is kept in $P_2$ during all execution and each program graph in $P_2$ participates of the evaluation of $P_1$ for at least 10 generations. As a consequence, the initial $T_{p2}$ individuals are frozen in the first 10 generations. Starting from generation 11, the variation with the worst fitness in the last 10 generations is eliminated and substituted by a new one: a mutation forming by applying 1 to 4 modifications on the target graph. In operating phase, the discovered rules are applied to schedule different variations of the target graph to test the quality of discovered rules. It is expect the coevolved rules have good generalization ability.

## 6    Experiments

The target graph used in the experiments described here is Gauss18. We used in the operating phase 40 different variations to evaluate the rules found with coevolutionary learning. All theses variations have 18 tasks and there are 10 graphs with 2 modifications in relation to Gauss18, 10 graphs with 3 modifications, 10 graphs with 4 modifications and 10 graphs with 5 modifications.

Initially, we reproduce the environment described in [4] and explained in Section 3, where a standard GA was used to search for CA rules; we named it *GA_Learning*. A second environment was implemented using the multigraph coevolutionary learning described in last section and we named it *CO_Learning*. Both environments were implemented in C language. We choose the Selected Neighborhood because it has shown more appropriated to Gauss18 graph as presented in [4] and as observed in our own experiments. The chosen attributes for this neighborhood were the same adopted in [4]: static co-level for predecessors, computational cost for brothers and communication cost for successors. Both environments use the scheduling policy "the task with the highest dynamic level is performed first". As reported in [4] sequential updating mode has shown to be more appropriate to deal with *Gauss18*, due to its intrinsic non-linearity [5]. Some initial experiments using *GA_learning* environment confirmed it. Thus, we performed the experiments described here using sequential updating. CA and GA parameters were $T_{p1} = 100$, $T_{p2} = 10$. $E_1 = 10$, $p_{cross} = 0.90$, $p_{mut} = 0.012$, $G = 100$, $I = 25$ and $M = 50$.

The first experiment was carried out with 30 runs of *GA_learning* performing the search for CA rules able to schedule *Gauss18*. Initially, the quality of the discovered rules was evaluated in the operation phase based only on Gauss18 as in [4]. A hundred initial configurations randomly sorted were used to test each rule of the final GA population. About fifty rules were able to find an optimal scheduling ($T = 44$) in all the 100 ICs evaluated. The results found were compatible with [4]. Aiming to evaluate the generalization ability of these rules, we use them as schedulers in the 40 random variations of Gauss18. In these tests we also use 100 ICs to evaluate the rules for each program graph. The results are presented in Table 1, where the 40 graphs were categorized in 4 groups according to the number of variations of the graphs in respect to Gauss18: Group_2 (10 graphs with 2 modifications), Group_3 (10 graphs with 3 modifications), and so on. Table 1 presents average results of the best rule found with each environment, for each group of graphs. $T_{average}$ is the average makespam obtained using the best evolved rule to schedule the respective graph starting from 100 different IC; $T_{min}$ is the minimum value of $T$ found starting from 100 different IC. The table presents the average values of these metrics associated to each set of 10 graphs: $\overline{T}_{average}$ and $\overline{T}_{min}$. It also presents the average values considering the 40 graphs as a whole. Using these values we calculated the confidence interval associated to *GA_Learning*: we have 95% of confidence that average makespam is between 52.25 and 53.63.

**Table 1.** Operation Phase: results found aplying rules evolved in learning phase for each group of variations of Gauss18

| GRAPH | GA_Learning | | CO_Learning | |
|---|---|---|---|---|
| | $\overline{T}_{average}$ | $\overline{T}_{min}$ | $\overline{T}_{average}$ | $\overline{T}_{min}$ |
| Group_2 | 51,75 | 50,4 | 47,96 | 45,4 |
| Group_3 | 51,03 | 48,2 | 48,02 | 45,5 |
| Group_4 | 54,32 | 49,6 | 50,29 | 46,6 |
| Group_5 | 54,69 | 51 | 51,15 | 47,1 |
| Average | 52,94 | 49,8 | 49,35 | 46,15 |
| Conf. Int. | (52,25 to 53,63) | | (48,49 to 50,10) | |

Subsequently, a new experiment was conducted using the new coevolutionary approach presented in section 5. It was named CO_Learning and it was also formed by 30 runs. The operation phase was also tested to evaluate the generalization ability of the discovered rules, as presented in Table 1. Comparing the performance of the rules found in each learning environment, one can see that rules found by *CO_Learning* overcame those found by *GA_Learning* in all groups of 10 graphs, both in the best makespan as in the average makespan found by the best rules. This superiority reflects in the average of *T* found considering the 40 graphs: 49.35 and 52.94, for *CO-Learning* and *GA-Learning*, respectively. The confidence interval associated to the *CO_Learning* environment was also calculated: we have 95% of confidence that makespan is between 48.49 and 50.10. Comparing with the confidence interval calculated with the rules evolved with *GA_Learning* (52.25, 53.63), one can see that the coevolutionary environment returns a better performance.

We used the null hypothesis to evaluate if the rules of the second experiment are better than the first: there are significant evidences that a coevolved rule returns lower than a single evolved rule. We have 95% of confidence that this improvement is between 2.87 and 4.31 time units. As the best makespan found for these variations are close to 44 time units (optimum for Gauss18), it represents a decrease of 10% in respect to the previous model. We understand that these results qualify the coevolved rules as more general than the single evolved rules.

# 7    Conclusions

Starting from the multiprocessor scheduler model proposed in [4], we investigated a new approach to the learning phase, in which a coevolutionary genetic algorithm is used to search for CA rules able to schedule tasks over a parallel architecture. The coevolutionary algorithm evolves two populations simultaneously: the first formed by CA transition rules and the second formed by a target program graph and some random graphs that are similar to the target one, generated applying simple modifications in the original graph.

An important observation that we made about the related studies in [4-8] is that just a little information about the generalization ability related to the evolved rules was available and just few examples of successful reusing of such rules were indeed verified. We realized experiments applying the rules evolved in the learning phase to graphs different from the target graph and we concluded that reasonable results were found only in graphs where an optimal solution was easy to reach.

Rules evolved by the coevolutionary method proposed here have presented better generalization ability. They returned a better performance to schedule new graphs similar to the target one. It was possible to verify such ability in experimental results. These rules outperformed the scheduling accomplished by rules obtained through the strategy used in [4], that we called single evolution.

Such generalization ability is primordial to a CA-based scheduling model. The evolved rules should be able to schedule not only the target program graph but they must have an intrinsic scheduling strategy in such a way that when they are applied to a new program, optimal or suboptimal allocations are returned without the need for a new evolution. Although CA-based schedulers have been proposed with the aim to find rules with a high level of generalization, such ability was not easy to obtain in previous work [4-7]. Using the proposed coevolutionary approach, this ability was obtained at least for program graphs similar to the target one.

The results presented in the present work focus on the generalization ability of the evolved rules in respect to schedule graphs similar to the target one. Nevertheless, the desirable skill of these evolved rules is to have generalization ability not only in respect to these graphs but also for graphs more different from the graphs used to evolve the rules. We are working in this problem now but we face the results using the similar graphs as an important step to achieve this goal.

**Acknowledgments.** GMBO thanks to CNPq and Fapemig financial support.

# References

1. Goldberg, D.E.: Genetic Algorithms in Search, Optimization, and Machine Learning. Addison-Wesley (1989)
2. Hillis, D.: Co-evolving parasites improves simulated evolution as an optimization procedure. Physica D 42(1-3), 228–234 (1991)
3. Wolfram, S.: Universality and complexity in cellular automata. Physica D 10, 1–35 (1984)
4. Seredynski, F.: Evolving cellular automata-based algorithms for multiprocessor scheduling. In: Zomaya, A., Ercal, F. (eds.) Solutions to Parallel and Distributed Computing Problems: Lessons from Biological Sciences, pp. 179–207 (2001)
5. Seredynski, F., Zomaya, A.Y.: Sequential and parallel cellular automata-based scheduling algorithms. IEEE Trans. Parallel Distrib. Syst. 13(10), 1009–1023 (2002)
6. Swiecicka, A., Seredynski, F., Zomaya, A.Y.: Multiprocessor scheduling and rescheduling with use of cellular automata and artificial immune system support. IEEE Trans. Parallel Distrib. Syst. 17(3), 253–262 (2006)
7. Swiecicka, A., Seredynski, F.: Cellular automata approach to scheduling problem. In: Proc. of the International Conference on Parallel Computing in Electrical Engineering, PARELEC 2000, Washington, DC, USA, p. 29 (2000)
8. Seredynski, F., Swiecicka, A., Zomaya, A.Y.: Discovery of parallel scheduling algorithms in cellular automata-based systems. In: IPDPS, p. 132 (2001)
9. Paredis, J.: Coevolutionary computation. Artificial Life Journal 2(3) (1996)
10. Vidica, P.M., Oliveira, G.M.B.: Cellular Automata-Based Scheduling: A New Approach to Improve Generalization Ability of Evolved Rules. In: Proc. of Brazilian Symposium on Neural Networks, pp. 18–23 (2006)
11. Kwok, Y.K., Ahmad, I.: Benchmarking and comparison of the task graph scheduling algorithms. Journal of Parallel and Distributed Computing 59(3), 381–422 (1999)
12. Pinedo, M.L.: Scheduling: Theory, Algorithms, and Systems, 3rd edn. Springer Science (2008)
13. Carneiro, M.G., Oliveira, G.M.B.: Cellular automata based model with synchronous updating for task static scheduling. In: Proc. of 17th International Workshop on Cellular Automata and Discrete Complex System, AUTOMATA 2011, pp. 263–272 (2011)
14. Carneiro, M.G., Oliveira, G.M.B.: SCAS-IS: Knowledge Extraction and Reuse in Multiprocessor Task Scheduling based on Cellular Automata. Accepted for Brazilian Symposium on Neural Networks (2012, preprint)

# Searching Cellular Automata Rules for Solving Two-Dimensional Binary Classification Problem

Anna Piwonska[1], Franciszek Seredynski[2,3], and Miroslaw Szaban[4]

[1] Bialystok University of Technology, Computer Science Faculty, Poland
[2] Polish-Japanese Institute of Information Technology, Poland
[3] Cardinal Stefan Wyszynski University in Warsaw, Poland
[4] Siedlce University of Natural Sciences and Humanities, Poland
a.piwonska@pb.edu.pl, sered@pjwstk.edu.pl, mszaban@uph.edu.pl

**Abstract.** This paper proposes a cellular automata-based solution of a two-dimensional binary classification problem. The proposed method is based on a two-dimensional, three-state cellular automaton (CA) with the von Neumann neighborhood. Since the number of possible CA rules (potential CA-based classifiers) is huge, searching efficient rules is conducted with use of a genetic algorithm (GA). Experiments show an very good performance of discovered rules in solving the classification problem. The best found rules perform better than the heuristic CA rule designed by a human and also better than one of the most widely used statistical method: the k-nearest neighbors algorithm (*k-NN*). Experiments show that CAs rules can be successfully reused in the process of searching new rules.

**Keywords:** Cellular Automata, Binary Classification Problem, Genetic Algorithm.

## 1 Introduction

CA is a discrete, dynamical system composed of many identical cells arranged in a regular grid, in one or more dimensions [9]. Each cell can take one of a finite number of states and has an identical arrangement of local connections with other cells called a neighborhood, which also includes the cell itself. After determining initial states of all cells (an initial configuration of a CA), states of cells are updated synchronously at discrete time steps, according to a local rule defined on a neighborhood, with the assumption of particular boundary conditions.

CAs were intensively studied in many science disciplines, including computability theory, mathematics, physics, theoretical biology, etc. The reason is that in spite of their simple construction and principle of operation, these relatively simple systems can exhibit complex global behavior.

In spite the fact that CAs have the potential to efficiently perform complex computations, the main problem is a difficulty of designing CAs producing a desired behavior. One must not only select a neighborhood type and size, and

G.C. Sirakoulis and S. Bandini (Eds.): ACRI 2012, LNCS 7495, pp. 121–130, 2012.

above all the appropriate rule (or rules). Since the number of possible rules is usually huge, this is the extremely hard task. In some applications of CAs one can design an appropriate rule by hand based on partial differential equations describing a given phenomenon, see for example [7]. However, it is not always possible. In the 90-ties of the last century Mitchell and collaborators proposed to use GAs to find CAs rules able to perform one-dimensional density classification task [6] and the synchronization task [2].

Statistical classification is the problem of determining to which class new observations belong, based on the training set of data containing observations whose class is known. The binary classification deals with only two classes, whereas in a multiclass classification observations belong to one of several classes. The well-known classifiers are neural networks, support vector machines, $k - NN$ algorithm, decision trees and others.

The idea of using CAs in the classification problem was described by Maji et al. [5], Povalej et al. [8] and recently by Fawcett [3]. Fawcett designed the heuristic rule based on the von Neumann neighborhood (so-called voting rule) and tested its performance on different data sets. This paper proposes a different approach: finding appropriate CAs rules by a GA. The effectiveness of rules discovered by a GA will be compared with the effectiveness of the hand-designed voting rule. Both CA-based approaches will be compared with the $k - NN$ algorithm.

This paper is organized as follows. Section 2 defines the classification problem and describes the proposed CAs-based algorithm. Experimental results are presented in Section 3. The last section contains conclusions.

## 2     Binary Classification Problem and Cellular Automata

### 2.1     Two-Dimensional Binary Classification Problem

In this paper we deal with the classification problem described in [4] in the context of fuzzy rule-based classification system. Let us assume that the data space is the unit square $[0, 1] \times [0, 1]$. Suppose that $m$ data-points $\mathbf{x}_p = (x_{p1}, x_{p2})$, $p = 1, 2, ..., m$ are given as a training set from two classes: class 1 and class 2. That is, the classification of each $\mathbf{x}_p = (x_{p1}, x_{p2})$, $p = 1, 2, ..., m$ is known as one of two classes. The classification problem can be stated as follows. Given $m$ training data find a rule (or "classifier") which divides the data space into two disjoint decision areas (class 1 or 2) such that the class number can be assigned to any new observation.

### 2.2     Proposed CA-Based Classifier

The idea of using CAs to solve the binary classification problem is based on the construction of a CA and finding an appropriate rule which can perform the classification task. Since the problem is defined in the two-dimensional space, our CA will also be the two-dimensional. The CA works on a grid of cells, so we must partition our data space $[0, 1] \times [0, 1]$ into a grid of cells. Let us assume that the considered CA has an equal number of cells in each dimension ($N = M$).

Our CA is a three-state automaton ($k = 3$). The initial state of each cell is set by training points belonging to this cell and is determined in the following way:

- if there is no point in a cell (an empty cell), then a cell is in state 0 (a cell is marked in grey color),
- if there are points only from class 1 in a cell, then a cell is in state 1 (a cell is marked in white color),
- if there are points only from class 2 in a cell, then a cell is in state 2 (a cell is marked in black color),
- if there are points from both classes (class 1 and 2) in a cell, then a cell is in state 0 (a cell is marked in grey color).

The interpretation of the above mentioned rules is simply and intuitive. The class of training points determines the state of a cell. If the state of a cell cannot be assigned, a cell is in state 0 (unknown class). This can happen in two situations: either there are no training points in a cell or there are points from both classes in it. The performance of the CA-based classifier depends on the size of a partition. If a partition is too coarse, the performance of the system may be low (many observations may be misclassified). On the other hand, if a partition is too fine, one can observe the lack of training points in corresponding cells.

The next step is to determine the neighborhood type, along with boundary conditions. We assumed the von Neumann neighborhood and null boundary conditions: border cells have dummy neighbors always in state 0.

After determining initial states of all cells (i.e. the initial configuration of the CA), cells change their states synchronously according to a certain rule which must be found. An appropriate rule transforms, during $T$ time steps, the initial configuration of the CA into the final configuration in which there are no empty cells and for which the correct class number can be assigned to any new observation. Finding an appropriate rule is a key factor for performance of CA-based classifier.

Let us first consider the heuristic rule for the classification problem designed by Fawcett [3]. The rule, called n4V1nonstable, is a non-stable update rule defined on the von Neumann neighborhood with $k = 3$, in which a cell may change its state if the majority changes. According to this rule, the state of a cell at the next time step is determined in the following way:

- if $neigh1 + neigh2 = 0$, then a cell state will be 0,
- if $neigh1 > neigh2$, then a cell state will be 1,
- if $neigh1 < neigh2$, then a cell state will be 2,
- if $neigh1 = neigh2$, then a cell state will be rand$\{1, 2\}$,

where $neigh1$ and $neigh2$ denote the number of a cell's neighbors, respectively in state 1 and 2, and rand$\{1, 2\}$ selects randomly 1 or 2 with equal probability. After determining initial states of all cells, the CA runs for a maximum number of $T$ time steps (if two subsequent CA's configurations are identical, the run is stopped). The intention is that cells will organize themselves into regions of similar class assignment (class 1 or 2). Details of this approach along with the extension to multi-dimensional data mining are described in [3].

In our approach there is the same goal but we want to discover such rules by the GA and compare them with the hand-designed n4V1nonstable rule and with the $k - NN$ algorithm. The quality of a given CA rule (n4V1nonstable rule and rules discovered by the GA) is determined on the base of a final configuration of the CA. We generate $l$ new observations of the classification problem and test if new points fall into cells with right states. If a cell is in state 1 then "the answer" of the CA is: "the class of all points falling into this cell is 1" (and similarly with state 2). In rare cases, when a final configuration contains cells in state 0, new points falling into these cells cannot be classified. The score of a CA rule is the sum of the correctly classified points.

## 2.3   A Genetic Algorithm for Searching Efficient Rules

Assuming the von Neumann neighborhood, with three possible cell states and the neighborhood size equal to 5 we have $3^5 = 243$ possible neighborhood states. Thus, the length of a CA rule is equal to 243 and the number of possible rules is equal to $3^{243}$. We use the neighborhood coding described below.

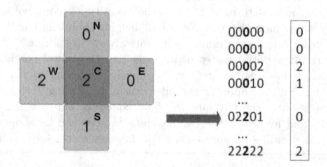

**Fig. 1.** The neighborhood coding (on the left) and the fragment of the rule - the chromosome of the GA (on the right, in the rectangle)

Five cells of the von Neumann neighborhood are usually described by directions on the compass: North (N), West (W), Central (C), East (E), South (S). Fig. 1 (left) presents the example of such a neighborhood: 02201. It also lists possible neighborhood states and presents the example of CA rule (on the right, in the rectangle). The value at position 0 in the rule (the value at the top in the rectangle) denotes a state of the central cell of the neighborhood 00000 at the next time step, the value at position 1 in the rule denotes a state of the central cell of the neighborhood 00001 at the next time step and so on, in lexicographic order of neighborhoods. One can see that the central cell of the neighborhood 02201 will be in state 0 at the next time step.

The next step is to evaluate individuals in the initial population for the ability to perform the classification task. For this purpose each rule in the population is run on the initial configuration of a CA for $T$ time steps. The initial configuration corresponds to the given problem instance and is determined as described in Section 2.2. The final configuration of a CA is used to compute the following fitness function components:

- $n0$ - the number of cells in state 0,
- $nc$ - the number of cells in correct state (1 or 2),
- $ni$ - the number of cells in incorrect state (1 or 2),
- $nb$ - the number of cells with a "suspicious neighbor".

Cells in correct states are these cells in state 1 or 2 whose states in the initial configuration remained unchanged in the final configuration. Cells in incorrect states are these cells in state 1 whose state in the initial configuration was 2 and vice versa: these cells in state 2 whose state in the initial configuration was 1. A cell with a "suspicious neighbor" is a cell which has at least one neighbor in different state than cell's own state. These values are used to compute the fitness $f$ of a rule $i$, denoted as $f_i$:

$$f_i = nc - ni - n0 - w \cdot nb , \tag{1}$$

where $w \in \langle 0, 1 \rangle$ is a coefficient used to adjust the influence of the number of cells with a "suspicious neighbor" on the fitness. Omitting $nb$ factor causes that the GA tends to evolve CA rules which change states of empty cells into the state 1 or 2 randomly: in the final configuration cells in states 1 and 2 do not form consistent regions, as one would expect.

Once we have the genetic representation and the fitness function defined, the GA starts to improve the initial population of rules through repetitive application of selection, crossover and mutation operators. In our experiments we used the selection scheme described by Mitchell [6] in which $E$ best individuals (the elite) are copied without modifications to the next generation. The remaining $P - E$ rules are formed by crossover and mutation from the elite rules. Crossover between two rules involves randomly selecting a single crossover point in the rules and exchanging parts of the rules before and after this point. Mutation is performed for each individual in the population (with the exception of the elite rules) with the probability $p_m$. When a given gene is to be mutated, we replace the current value of this gene by the value 1 or 2, with equal probability. Omitting the value 0 prevents from evolving rules with many 0s. Such rules are more likely to produce configurations containing cells with state 0. It would be unfavorable situation.

These steps are repeated through $G$ generations. Then, the quality of the final population of rules is tested on $l = 1000$ randomly generated new points of the classification problem. A new point is classified correctly if it falls into a cell whose state is the same as the class of a point. The quality of a rule is measured by the number of correct classifications. The higher score a rule obtains, the better classifier it represents. The result of the best rule is considered as the result of the proposed method.

## 3   Experimental Results

As test problems, we took two classification problems. In each problem the data space $[0,1] \times [0,1]$ is divided into two classes according to the value of the function $g(\mathbf{x})$, i.e. if $g(\mathbf{x}) \geq 0$ then $\mathbf{x}$ belongs to class 1, else $\mathbf{x}$ belongs to class 2. The functions used in experiments are:

- Problem 1: $g(\mathbf{x}) = -sin(2\pi x_1)/4 + x_2 - 0.5$ [4]
- Problem 2: $g(\mathbf{x}) = -x_1^3 + x_2 - 0.3$

For both problems we randomly generated 10 problem instances, where each of them had 50 points in class 1 and 50 points in class 2 ($m = 100$). Each problem instance was used to determine the initial configuration of the CA, with the number of cells in each dimension equal to 10 (grid $10 \times 10$).

The parameters of the CA and the GA were the following: $T = 50$, $P = 200$, $E = 50$, $p_m = 0.05$, $w = 0.1$, $G = 500$. The parameters were tuned during many experiments and these values were chosen to final runs.

Since the GA and the n4V1nonstable rule are probabilistic, five runs of each of them were performed. The best of five runs of the GA (CA-GA ($10 \times 10$)) were compared with the best five runs of the n4V1nonstable rule (n4V1 ($10 \times 10$), $T = 50$) and with the best results obtained by the distance weighted $k - NN$ method $(k - NN)$ [1]. The $k - NN$ was allowed to use up to five neighbors and the best $k$ was determined experimentally. Results of these experiments are presented in Table 1 and Table 2.

**Table 1.** Problem 1: the number of correct classifications, $l=1000$

| instance | CA-GA $10 \times 10$ | CA-GA $20 \times 20$ | $k - NN$ | n4V1 $10 \times 10$ | n4V1 $20 \times 20$ |
|---|---|---|---|---|---|
| 1 | 938 | 974 | 926 | 908 | 928 |
| 2 | 965 | 974 | 981 | 951 | 977 |
| 3 | 956 | 967 | 951 | 914 | 951 |
| 4 | 936 | 943 | 944 | 917 | 944 |
| 5 | 966 | 975 | 962 | 942 | 953 |
| 6 | 943 | 965 | 952 | 950 | 964 |
| 7 | 951 | 961 | 961 | 955 | 947 |
| 8 | 951 | 964 | 956 | 917 | 953 |
| 9 | 967 | 971 | 967 | 934 | 936 |
| 10 | 953 | 923 | 927 | 939 | 925 |
| average | 952.6 | **961.7** | 952.7 | 932.7 | 947.8 |

The structure of these tables is as follows. The first column lists the number of a problem instance, the second and the third present results obtained by the GA on grids $10 \times 10$ and $20 \times 20$, the fourth lists results obtained by the $k - NN$ and the last two columns present results obtained by n4V1nonstable rule on grids $10 \times 10$ and $20 \times 20$.

**Table 2.** Problem 2: the number of correct classifications, $l=1000$

| instance | CA-GA $10 \times 10$ | CA-GA $20 \times 20$ | $k-NN$ | n4V1 $10 \times 10$ | n4V1 $20 \times 20$ |
|:---:|:---:|:---:|:---:|:---:|:---:|
| 1 | 964 | 975 | 959 | 952 | 956 |
| 2 | 954 | 976 | 973 | 966 | 973 |
| 3 | 969 | 970 | 962 | 964 | 963 |
| 4 | 967 | 964 | 962 | 943 | 965 |
| 5 | 970 | 972 | 972 | 957 | 963 |
| 6 | 975 | 977 | 966 | 963 | 959 |
| 7 | 961 | 965 | 945 | 956 | 939 |
| 8 | 941 | 978 | 939 | 970 | 946 |
| 9 | 965 | 972 | 947 | 937 | 941 |
| 10 | 972 | 990 | 967 | 939 | 962 |
| average | 963.8 | **973.9** | 959.2 | 954.7 | 956.7 |

As it was mentioned, in the first experiment we compared the results obtained by both CA-based methods on grid $10 \times 10$ with the results obtained by the $k-NN$.

In the case of Problem 1, the CA-GA approach received better results than the $k-NN$ and n4V1nonstable rule in four instances (instances: 1, 3, 5, 10). In the case of instance 9, the CA-GA obtained the same result as the $k-NN$. The $k-NN$ received better results than both CA-based methods in other five instances. The n4V1nonstable was never the best. Looking at the average results one can see that the best values were obtained by the $k-NN$. However, the CA-GA algorithm performed significantly better than the n4V1nonstable rule.

In the case of Problem 2, the CA-GA method gained higher score than the $k-NN$ and the n4V1nonstable rule in seven cases (instances: 1, 3, 4, 6, 7, 9, 10). In two cases (instances 2 and 5) the $k-NN$ received better results than both CA-based methods. N4V1nonstable was the best in instance 8. The best average result was obtained by the CA-GA which also performed better than n4V1nonstable.

However, it is worth to notice that the CA-based methods perform on a grid of cells (in contrast to the $k-NN$) and the performance of these methods strongly depends on the size of the partition (the number of cells in each dimension). In the second series of experiments we tested the quality of n4V1nonstable rule on the same problem instances, but on the grid size $20 \times 20$. Results of these experiments are presented in the sixth column in Table 1 and Table 2 (n4V1 $(20 \times 20)$).

The CA-GA method was also tested on the grid size $20 \times 20$. We performed two series of experiments. In the first case the initial population of rules was created fully randomly. In the second case, we took five best rules from the final populations obtained for the grid size $10 \times 10$ for each problem instance and then inserted them into initial populations of the GA (grid size $20 \times 20$). Experiments showed that the GA (grid size $20 \times 20$) with the initial population containing

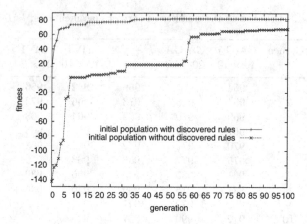

**Fig. 2.** Problem 2, instance 10: fitness of the best individual

previously discovered rules evolved better solutions than the GA with randomly generated initial population. Moreover, inserting the best rules into the initial population caused that the efficient rules were discovered very quickly.

As the example, let us look at the instance 10 of Problem 2. Fig. 2 presents two runs of the GA (with the grid size 20 × 20, first 100 generations marked) in the case of randomly generated initial population and in the case of inserting previously discovered rules into it. In the first case, the GA needs 500 generations (not shown in the figure) to evolve the best rule. In the second case, one of the best rules found for the grid size 10 × 10 receives high fitness value on the double grid size (15.80 in the generation 0). The GA quickly improves the best rule and as early as in the sixtieth generation the final, best rule is discovered. This rule obtained the high score equal to 990 (see, Table 2, instance 10).

Fig. 3 and 4 present final configurations of the best rules during selected generations of the GA in the case of randomly generated initial population (Fig. 3) and inserting previously discovered rules into the initial population (Fig. 4). One can see the best rule in the random initial population performs chaotically (the first picture in the first row, Fig. 3). On the contrary, the best rules found for the grid size 10 × 10 performs quite good on the double grid size (the first picture in the first row, Fig. 4). This is the evidence of the scalability of CAs rules: rules discovered for a given problem instance can be used to solve the same problems on denser grids. Results of the experiment in which previously discovered rules are inserted into the initial population of the GA are presented in the third column of both tables (CA-GA (20 × 20)). One can see that this approach usually improves results for both problems in comparison with the CA-GA performing on the grid 10 × 10. Only in two cases (Problem 1, instance 10 and Problem 2, instance 4) obtained results were worse. In the case of Problem 1 the average result has improved from 952.6 to 961.7 and in the case of Problem 2 from 963.8 to 973.9.

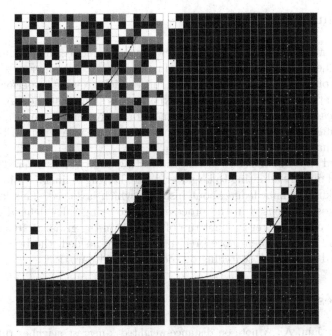

**Fig. 3.** Problem 2, instance 10, random initial population: the final configurations of the best rule in the GA generations: 0, 20, 150, 500

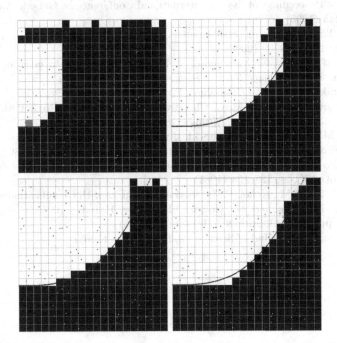

**Fig. 4.** Problem 2, instance 10, initial population with discovered rules: the final configurations of the best rule in the GA generations: 0, 8, 20, 60

# 4    Conclusions

In this paper we have presented the new approach concerning binary classification in the context of CAs. The main purpose of the paper was to study possibilities of the GA in discovering CA rules which are able to perform binary classification task. Results of presented experiments show that the GA is able to discover rules appropriate to solve this task for a given instance of a problem. The best found rules perform better than the heuristic rule designed by human and better than the $k - NN$ algorithm.

Conducted experiments showed very interesting ability of discovered rules, i.e. the ability of quickly adopting to larger grid size. During artificial evolution rules store some kind of knowledge about instance which is solved. This knowledge can be successfully reused in the process of discovering rules defined on larger grid size. We can interpret the first run of the GA on the grid size $10 \times 10$ as the preprocessing phase. When more precise results are needed, the best rules can be again used by the GA searching on more fine grid partition.

# References

1. Bailey, T., Jain, A.: A note on distance-weighted k-nearest neighbor rules. IEEE Transactions on Systems, Man and Cybernetics 8(4), 311–313 (1978)
2. Das, R., Crutchfield, J., Mitchell, M.: Evolving globally synchronized cellular automata. In: Proceedings of the 6th International Conference on Genetic Algorithms, pp. 336–243 (1995)
3. Fawcett, T.: Data mining with cellular automata. ACM SIGKDD Explorations Newsletter 10(1), 32–39 (2008)
4. Ishibuchi, H., Nozaki, K., Yamamoto, N.: Selecting fuzzy rules by genetic algorithm for classification problems. Fuzzy Systems 2, 1119–1124 (1993)
5. Maji, P., Sikdar, B.K., Pal Chaudhuri, P.: Cellular Automata Evolution for Pattern Classification. In: Sloot, P.M.A., Chopard, B., Hoekstra, A.G. (eds.) ACRI 2004. LNCS, vol. 3305, pp. 660–669. Springer, Heidelberg (2004)
6. Mitchell, M., Hraber, P., Crutchfield, J.: Revisiting the edge of chaos: Evolving cellular automata to perform computations. Complex Systems 7, 89–130 (1993)
7. Omohundro, S.: Modelling cellular automata with partial differential equations. Physica 10D 10(1-2), 128–134 (1984)
8. Povalej, P., Lenič, M., Kokol, P.: Improving Ensembles with Classificational Cellular Automata. In: Gallagher, M., Hogan, J.P., Maire, F. (eds.) IDEAL 2005. LNCS, vol. 3578, pp. 242–249. Springer, Heidelberg (2005)
9. Wolfram, S.: A New Kind of Science Wolfram Media (2002)

# Multi-objective Cellular Automata Optimization

Epaminondas Sidiropoulos

Faculty of Engineering, Aristotle University of Thessaloniki, Greece
nontas@topo.auth.gr

**Abstract.** The role of cellular automata in optimization is a current area of research. This paper presents a multi-objective approach to cellular optimization. A typical nonlinear problem of spatial resource allocation is treated by two alternative methods. The first one is based on a specially designed operative genetic algorithm and the second one on a hybrid annealing – genetic procedure. Pareto front approximations are computed by the two methods and also by a non-cellular version of the second approach. The better performance of the cellular methods is demonstrated and questions for further research are discussed.

**Keywords:** Cellular automata, multi-objective optimization, genetic algorithm, simulated annealing, resource allocation.

## 1 Introduction

Cellular automata are being used for the simulation of a great variety of phenomena encompassing both natural processes and evolution of anthropogenic systems. In all those cases the system to be modeled is represented as a set or a lattice of discrete cells, to each one of which a certain "state" is assigned, coming from a set of possible states. The states of the individual cells are evolved according to a local transition rule. The local rule determines the next state of the cell as a function of the current states of the cells that are confined to the neighborhood of the cell in question.

The formulation of the transition rule is the key issue in modeling the evolution of a system. A suitable transition rule is determined, such that the produced overall simulation will be satisfactory, according to preset criteria. This determination can be achieved by means of evolutionary methods, such as genetic algorithms. A multitude of such simulations have been presented ranging from physical to social and economic, such as forest fire propagation [1], urban development [2], adsorption - diffusion processes [3], traffic flow [4].

An alternative view of the cellular automaton concept is its use and role in optimization. Indeed, cellular automata can play a significant role as conceptual tools in optimization, if the system to be optimized can be modeled as a discrete set of cells with a well defined neighborhood structure and with certain properties, that can be identified as states. Then, suitable local rules have to be found, such that, starting from an arbitrary initial configuration, the system will be guided toward optimal arrangements. Clearly, in this case the functioning of the transition rule will not be to

G.C. Sirakoulis and S. Bandini (Eds.): ACRI 2012, LNCS 7495, pp. 131–140, 2012.
© Springer-Verlag Berlin Heidelberg 2012

produce a simulation, but to act as an adaptive local operator in an iterative procedure that aims at the optimum.

The concept of cellular automaton has been utilized in order to deal with a problem of groundwater management by Sidiropoulos and Tolikas [5]. Two alternative approaches were followed for that purpose: First, a genetic algorithm was embedded into a cellular automaton in order to effect the desired optimization. The chromosomes of the genetic algorithm reflected directly the local transition rules of the cellular automaton and an efficient solution was demonstrated. The second approach consisted in the application of simulated annealing. The perturbation involved in simulated annealing was chosen to take place inside the neighborhoods of the individual cells, thus forming the requisite local transition rule.

An idea similar to the above genetic algorithm was later applied to a problem of spatial groundwater allocation [6]. The typical chromosome expressed the local transition rule of the cellular automaton and thus it acted as an operator transforming a base configuration. Hence, the genetic algorithm presented was characterized as an operative genetic algorithm [7]. The same process was generalized and reinforced with local search by Sidiropoulos [8].

The simulated annealing approach described above was applied by Sidiropoulos [9] to a similar spatial resource allocation problem. Both an annealing and a mixed annealing - genetic approach were presented, always on a cellular background. In all cases the introduction of the cellular automaton mechanism and concept contributed to more efficient numerical procedures in addition to a more appealing and realistic representation of the problem.

This paper presents multi-objective versions of the above spatial groundwater allocation problems. The cellular automaton concept plays the central role in the proposed algorithms. The genetic algorithm of the previous cited works is extended to a multi-objective version retaining the operative character of the typical chromosome and incorporating the basic characteristics of Pareto front development. On the other hand, an extension of the simulated annealing approach is given in the form of a hybrid annealing – genetic algorithm with the local transition rule activating the perturbation of the annealing method. The same approach without the local aspect in the perturbation is shown to produce inferior results.

## 2    Problem Formulation

The single-objective versions of the present problem have been presented elsewhere ([6] and [9]). The problem is briefly reviewed here. A two-dimensional terrain is divided into land blocks as shown in Figure 1. Each one of the blocks is occupied by a certain cultivation and it receives irrigation water form one of three wells placed as shown in the same Figure. The land blocks can be considered to be the cells of the cellular automaton and the state of each cell will be identified with the well from which the cell (block) is irrigated. Each block is assumed to receive water from only one well and the set of possible states coincides with the set of the existing wells.

Contrary to the above references, two separate objective functions will be considered: $f_P$ denoting the cost of pumping water at the sites of the wells and $f_T$ denoting the cost of transporting water from the wells to the individual cells.

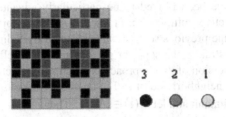

**Fig. 1.** Problem definition. The color of each cell signifies the well (1,2 or 3) to which the cell is connected

The cells are numbered consecutively according to the scheme presented by Sidiropoulos and Fotakis [6].

Let $\mathbf{C} = \{1, 2, ...\ell\}$ be the set of cells numbered consecutively.

Let $\mathbf{W} = \{P, Q, R,...\}$ be the set of wells. Also, let w: $\mathcal{C} \rightarrow \mathcal{W}$ be a function assigning to each one of the cells the well to which it is connected, i.e. w(i) $\in \mathcal{W}$, $i = 1, 2,..., \ell$. The individual values w(i) will be identified as the states of the cells i (i=1,2,.., $\ell$). The function w will determine the whole configuration, which is defined as

$$\mathcal{L} = \{w(1), w(2), ..., w(\ell)\} \tag{1}$$

The two objective functions associated with each configuration are now denoted more precisely as

$$f_P[\mathcal{L}] \in \mathbb{R}^+ \text{ and } f_T[\mathcal{L}] \in \mathbb{R}^+ \tag{2}$$

Both these costs are to be considered as functionals mapping the set of all possible configurations to the set of positive reals. The values of the functional $f_P$ are determined with the help of a groundwater model that governs the function of an underlying aquifer, while the values of $f_T$ are computed on the basis of the distances of the cell-blocks from the wells. From the nature of these objective functions it can be seen that the problem is both non linear and non-separable with respect to individual cell contributions. The details of the physical model and of the objective functions have been given elsewhere ([6], [7]) and will not be repeated here.

The problem is to determine the configuration (1) that minimizes the pair of functionals (2). According to the multi-objective optimization methodology, the Pareto front of non-dominated solutions will be sought (e.g.[10]). For this purpose, two alternative algorithms will be presented in the following sections, bearing a cellular automaton mechanism as their basic ingredient.

# 3     Method of Solution

## 3.1     A Genetic Algorithm Approach

Genetic algorithms have been proved to be particularly advantageous for the management of multi-objective optimization problems. A single-objective version of the problem described in the previous section was presented by Sidiropoulos and Fotakis [6], along with demonstrating the superior performance of a cell-based genetic algorithm. A bi-objective version of that approach is given in this section.

Let $\mathcal{N}(i)$ denote the neighborhood of cell i., i.e. the set of cells neighboring to cell i in the sense of von Neumann and let $n(i) \in \mathcal{N}(i)$. Then the set

$$\mathcal{O} = \{n(1), n(2), ..., n(\ell)\} \tag{3}$$

can be considered as an operator acting on the configuration $\mathcal{L}$ of Equation (1), as follows: Let $\bar{w}(i) = w(n(i))$. Then the new configuration

$$\bar{\mathcal{L}} = \{\bar{w}(1), \bar{w}(2), ..., \bar{w}(\ell)\} \tag{4}$$

may be thought of as the product of an operation of the set $\mathcal{O}$ of Equation (3) on the configuration $\mathcal{L}$ of Equation (1) and thus be denoted as

$$\bar{\mathcal{L}} = \mathcal{O} \otimes \mathcal{L} \tag{5}$$

$\mathcal{O}$ obviously represents the rule that, for each one of the cells, picks out one of their neighboring cells. The cell in question will then adopt the state of the neighbor thus selected. In order to determine rules that iteratively lead to "better" configurations a genetic algorithm will be employed. This genetic algorithm will be called an operative genetic algorithm (OGA) [7] and the set $\mathcal{O}$ of Equation (3) will be its typical chromosome.

An initial base configuration $\mathcal{L}$ is formed with a random selection of the cell states. A population

$$\mathcal{O}_i \ (i=1,2,...,N) \tag{6}$$

of such chromosomes will be formed and an equal number of new configurations will result according to the operation of Equation (5):

$$\bar{\mathcal{L}}_i = \mathcal{O}_i \otimes \mathcal{L}, \ i=1,2,..,N \tag{7}$$

Each one of the new configurations of Equation (7) will be evaluated according to Equation (2):

$$\mathbf{f}_i = (f_{Pi}, f_{Ti}) = \left( f_P[\bar{\mathcal{L}}_i], f_T[\bar{\mathcal{L}}_i] \right) \tag{8}$$

The pairs $f_i$, i=1,2,..,N of Equation (8) are considered as points on the two-dimensional space of the objective functions and they will be used for the selection of the new base configuration. In the single-objective version of the problem, the new base configuration was selected as the one with the best value of the objective function. In the present multi-objective problem, the selection will be done on the basis of two criteria: domination and isolation.

More specifically, from the set of points

$$\mathcal{F} = \{f_i \mid i=1,2,..,N\} \tag{9}$$

of Equation (8), the non-dominated ones are separated. The concept of domination is defined in textbooks on multi-objective optimization (e.g.[10]). The notation $i \prec j$ is used to indicate that a point i dominates a point j, where $i, j \in \{1, 2, .., N\}$. Thus the subset $\mathcal{F}_0$ of $\mathcal{F}$ that contains the non-dominated points can be written as

$$\mathcal{F}_0 = \{f_j \in \mathcal{F} \mid \neg \exists \ i \in (1,2,..,N\} \ \text{ with } \ i \prec j\} \tag{10}$$

On the other hand, for each one of the $f_j$ pairs belonging to the set $\mathcal{F}_0$ of Equation (10), the distances $d_j$ are formed from all other points of the set $\mathcal{F}$ of Equation (9):

$$d_{ji} = \left[ (f_{Pi} - f_{Pj})^2 + (f_{Ti} - f_{Tj})^2 \right]^{1/2} \tag{11}$$

where j and i are such that $f_j \in \mathcal{F}_0$ and $f_i \in \mathcal{F}$.

From the above distances the smallest is chosen:

$$d_j = \min_i \{d_{ji}\} \tag{12}$$

The distance $d_j$ of Equation (12) is the distance of point j to the one nearest to it, on the objective space. Finally, among the non-dominated points, the one is found with the largest $d_j$:

$$d_{base} = \max_j \{d_j\} \tag{13}$$

The point of the objective space with the index "base" of Equation (13) is characterized by a relative isolation with respect to the other points of the non-dominated set $\mathcal{F}_0$. Among the configurations $\mathcal{L}_i$ of Equation (7), the one with the index "base" will now replace the old base configuration $\mathcal{L}$:

$$\mathcal{L} \leftarrow \bar{\mathcal{L}}_{base} \tag{14}$$

The population of operators of the type given by (3), is the current population of chromosomes for the genetic algorithm. Therefore, they will now be subjected to the genetic operations of selection, crossover and mutation. Tournament selection will be adopted for this problem. Two points i and j are picked at random from the whole population. If one of them dominates the other, then the dominant is selected. Otherwise the distances $d_i$ and $d_j$ are considered. If $d_i > d_j$, then i is selected. Otherwise j is selected.

Crossover and mutation are executed in the standard fashion on the chromosomes of the type (3) and finally a renewed population is produced, whose members act as operators on the base configuration that was defined above. It needs to be noted here that distance was found to be a convenient way of characterizing isolation in the present approach. Other alternatives can be found in the literature, such as sharing distance [11] and crowding distance [10]

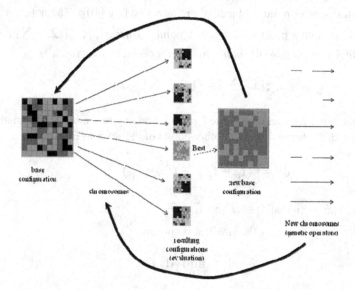

**Fig. 2.** Outline of the multi-objective algorithm. The adjective best in front of the new base configuration means superior with respect to the criteria of domination and isolation as defined above.

The present algorithm is summarized as follows:

(a) An initial base configuration or mosaic is formed by randomly assigning a well to each one of the blocks.
(b) An initial population of operator-chromosomes is formed by randomly assigning to each block one of its neighbors.
(c) The chromosomes operate on the base configuration and generate an equal number of new configurations.
(d) Non-domination sorting is performed and the non-dominated configurations are kept separately.
(e) Out of all configurations of step (d) one is selected on the basis of domination and isolation and it becomes the new base configuration

(f)  The current population of operator-chromosomes is subjected to tournament selection, crossover and mutation

(g)  The renewed population of chromosomes of step (f) will operate on the base configuration of step (d) and new configurations are generated, just as in step (c).

(h)  To the new configurations of step (g) the non-dominated ones of step (d) are added as elites.

(i)  Control is transferred to step (d).

## 3.2    A Hybrid Annealing – Genetic Approach

An alternative approach to the genetic algorithm of the previous section is a scheme based on simulated annealing, but still retaining the characteristic of a population of solutions with a certain degree of genetic interaction. The concept of cellular automaton again plays a central role in the crucial step of perturbing the current base configuration. As with the operative genetic algorithm, there is also here a predominant base configuration, which does not stand separately, but it is a member of a population of configurations. This base configuration is perturbed, according to the annealing method.

In order for the resulting perturbed configuration to be subjected to the annealing test of acceptance, a certain value or fitness needs to be defined for a configuration. For multi-objective problems this is an open issue. In the present approach, the so called energy function is adopted for the evaluation of the possible solutions in multi-objective optimization [12]. The energy function is defined as follows:

```
For i=1,2,..,N
  E_i = 1
  For j=1,2,..,N
    If j≺ithen E_i = E_i+1
    End If
  End For
End For
```

Extensive use of the concept of energy is made in reference [12], where more details are given. Below $E_i$ denotes the energy of configuration $\mathcal{L}_i$:

$$E_i = E[\mathcal{L}_i].\tag{15}$$

The above definition means that the lower the energy, the higher the value or fitness of the configuration. Thus the non-dominated points will have an energy value equal to 1. The proposed algorithm consists of the following steps:

(a)  An initial population of configurations $\mathcal{P}= \{\mathcal{L}_i|\ i=1,2,..,N\}$ is formed according to the type given by Equation (1). These configurations give rise to a set $\mathcal{I}$ of N corresponding points $(f_{Pi}, f_{Ti})$ on the objective space.

(b)  The initial base configuration is chosen at random from the N configurations.

(c)  The current base configuration is set equal to the initial one of step (b).

The annealing double loop starts at this step:

(d)  The current base configuration $\mathcal{L}$ is perturbed and a new configuration $\mathcal{L}_1$ results.

(e)  The respective energies $E[\mathcal{L}]$ and $E[\mathcal{L}_1]$ are computed as above.

(f)  Let $\delta E = E[\mathcal{L}_1] - E[\mathcal{L}]$.

If $\delta E < 0$, then $\mathcal{L}_1$ is accepted and $\mathcal{L} \leftarrow \mathcal{L}_1$

      Else    let $r = \mathrm{Random}(0,1)$ and $p = \exp(-\delta E/T)$

               If $r < p$ then $\mathcal{L}_1$ is accepted and $\mathcal{L} \leftarrow \mathcal{L}_1$

                  Else $\mathcal{L}_1$ is not accepted and $\mathcal{L}$ remains

           End If

    End If

(g)  By means of domination sorting algorithms, the subset $\mathcal{P}_d \subset \mathcal{P}$ of points is found that are dominated by the current base configuration $\mathcal{L}$. These points will eventually be removed from the population. Let the number of these points be equal to $l_{dom}$.

(h)  A randomly chosen subset $\mathcal{P}_r \subset \mathcal{P}$ is formed with cardinality equal to $l_{dom}-1$

(i)  The base configuration $\mathcal{L}$ is recombined with each one of the configurations that generated the points of $\mathcal{P}_r$. The recombination consists in an ordinary crossover with a single random separator. Out of the three new individuals involved in the crossover (one member of $\mathcal{P}_r$ and two offspring) the one is kept with the smallest energy function value (Equation 15). Thus $l_{dom}-1$ members are now available. The set thus resulting is denoted as $\mathcal{P}_c$

(j)  Finally, the new population will be composed as $\mathcal{P} \leftarrow (\mathcal{P} \backslash \mathcal{P}_d) \cup \mathcal{P}_c \cup \{ \mathcal{L} \}$, thus retaining the same number of configurations.

    The annealing loop is completed with step (j) and control is transferred to step (d).

    The temperature T that appears in step (f) is decreased every time a specified number of iterations are completed.

    The idea of removing from the population the members dominated by the current point is known from the literature (Smith et al., 2008). The way of replacing the removed elements is different in the present approach.

    The concept of cellular automaton comes into the algorithm when perturbing the current base configuration in step (d). Perturbation is carried out in two different ways. According to the first option, every cell will exchange states with one of its neighbors in a von Neumann neighborhood (Figure 3a). This is in full accord with the concept of cellular automaton and the method may be called cellular simulated annealing (CSA). Another mode of perturbation consists in an exchange of states between the current cell and another one anywhere in the space covered by the cells (Figure 3b). This is clearly incompatible with the notion of cellular automaton and it will be interesting to compare its performance to that of the CSA.

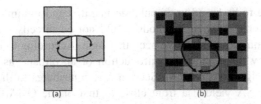

**Fig. 3.** Modes of perturbation

## 4    Results - Discussion

A fictive rectangular area was considered with an underlying aquifer of infinite extent. It was divided into 100 blocks and the specific data concerning the aquifer and the positions of the wells have been given in [6] and in [7]. As pointed out in the section on problem formulation, the problem is both nonlinear and non-separable. In previous works it was demonstrated that the operative genetic algorithm produced clearly superior results compared to more conventional, non-cellular approaches for the single-objective problem ([6] and [7]). Also, the application of simulated annealing on a cellular background gave results comparable to those of the operative genetic algorithm for the problem examined by Sidiropoulos and Tolikas [5] and clearly superior results compared to a more conventional version of simulated annealing for the problem treated by Sidiropoulos [9].

In the present multi-objective approach the operative genetic algorithm is compared to the CSA and to the non-cellular SA described in the previous section.

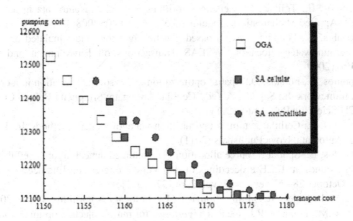

**Fig. 4.** Comparison of methods

All three methods produced approximations to the Pareto front. It is demonstrated in Figure 4 that OGA produced a clearly better front in comparison to the simulated annealing methods. The data depicted on the figure are not scaled, because classical scaling would have to be based on population maxima and minima. But in that case the results of the three different methods would not be directly comparable, as the respective populations could not have been the same. According to numerical experiments conducted by the author, the introduction of an elitism, as explained in the description of the algorithm given in Section 3.1, contributes to the performance of OGA. The cellular SA yielded a front close to that of the OGA, but not covering clearly the whole range of OGA.

Multi-objective cellular automata optimization has not been studied extensively as yet and a lot of research is needed regarding various methodological possibilities, as well as more extensive comparisons among methods. For instance, in the case of simulated annealing there are more alternatives to be considered with respect to the replacement of points removed due to being dominated by the current configuration.

# References

1. Karafyllidis, I.: Design of a dedicated parallel processor for the prediction of forest fire spreading using cellular automata and genetic algorithms. Engineering Applications of Artificial Intelligence 17, 19–36 (2004)
2. Jennerette, G.D., Wu, J.: Analysis and simulation of land use change in the central Arizona – Phoenix region, USA. Landscape Ecology 16, 611–626 (2001)
3. Chopard, B., Droz, M., Kolb, M.: Cellular automata approach to non-equilibrium diffusion and gradient percolation. Journal of Physics, A: Mathematical and General 22, 1609–1619 (1989)
4. Salcido, A.: Equilibrium Properties of the Cellular Automata Models for traffic Flow in a Single Lane. Cellular Automata, Simplicity behind Complexity. In: Salcido, A. (ed.) INTECH (2011)
5. Sidiropoulos, E., Tolikas, P.: Genetic algorithms and cellular automata in aquifer management. Applied Mathematical Modelling 32(4), 617–640 (2008)
6. Sidiropoulos, E., Fotakis, D.: Cell-based genetic algorithm and simulated annealing for spatial groundwater allocation. WSEAS Transactions on Environment and Development 4(5) (2009)
7. Sidiropoulos, E., Fotakis, D.: Spatial optimization and resource allocation in a cellular automata framework. In: Salcido, A. (ed.) Cellular Automata: Simplicity Behind Complexity. INTECH Scientific Publishing (2011)
8. Sidiropoulos, E.: Cellular automata optimization via evolutionary methods. In: Li, T. (ed.) Cellular Automata. Nova Publishers (2011)
9. Sidiropoulos, E.: Spatial resource allocation via simulated annealing on a cellular automaton background. In: IEEE Proceedings of the World Congress on Engineering and Technology, October 28 –November. 2, vol. 2, p. 137 (2011)
10. Deb, K.: Multi-Objective Optimization using Evolutionary Algorithms. Wiley (2001)
11. Fonseca, C.M., Fleming, P.J.: Genetic algorithms for multi-objective optimization: Formulation, discussion and generalization. In: Proceedings of the 5th International Conference on Genetic Algorithms, pp. 416–423 (1993)
12. Smith, K.I., Everson, R.M., Fieldsend, J.E., Murphy, C., Misra, R.: Dominance-Based Multiobjective Simulated Annealing. IEEE Transactions on Evolutionary Computation 12(3) (2008)

# Behavior of Social Dynamical Models I: Fixation in the Symmetric Cyclic System (with Paradoxical Effect in the Six-Color Automaton)

Stylianos Scarlatos*,**

Department of Mathematics, Center for Research and Applications of Nonlinear
Systems, University of Patras, 265 00 Patra, Greece
stylian.scarlatos@gmail.com

**Abstract.** We modify the transition rule of the $N$-color cyclic particle
system, such that the arising system is applied for social dynamics. An
asynchronous update is examined, where each two neighboring sites of a
social network interact at exponential rate, and one of the sites adopts
the color (opinion) of a randomly chosen neighbor, provided that their
colors are adjacent on the cycle $C_N$ that represents the colors. We show
that starting from independent and uniformly distributed colors on the
integer lattice, each site fixates to a final color with probability 1 if $N \geq 5$,
which is sharp due to Lanchier (2012). Moreover, we conduct simulations
with appropriate cellular automata and find that the frequency of the
long observed Condorcet's paradox of voting increases in the fixation
region of the six-color automaton.

**Keywords:** Cyclic particle systems, two-feature two-trait Axelrod model, social dynamics, fixation phenomena, Condorcet's paradox of voting.

## 1 Introduction

Motivated by the study of nonlinear multitype particle systems, Bramson and
Griffeath proposed cyclic particle systems, which is a stochastic spatial model
with cyclic and hierarchical interactions between types/colors [6]. Initially, each
site of the lattice of integers $\mathbb{Z}$ is independently and uniformly distributed with
one of $N$ colors labeled $0, 1, \cdots, N - 1$. At independent exponential times with
rate 1, each site of color $u$ picks and paints with its color a random neighboring
site of color $v$, provided that $u, v$ are adjacent in cyclic hierarchy

$$u - v = 1 \mod N .$$

The exhibited behavior is complex: (a) each site fluctuates at arbitrary large
times if $N \leq 4$, and (b) each site fixates to a final color if $N \geq 5$. A remarkable

---

* The author would like to express gratitude towards two scientists for accepting him
as almost equal and teaching him many things through research. The one is Adam
Adamopoulos for the experimental part. The other is Nicolas Lanchier for the theoretical part. The dedication is to late fair father Stavros.
** Present Address: Kabouridou 44, 552 36 Thessaloniki, Greece.

G.C. Sirakoulis and S. Bandini (Eds.): ACRI 2012, LNCS 7495, pp. 141–150, 2012.

fact about these stochastic processes is that they are emulated by a completely deterministic counterpart, namely cyclic cellular automata [10]. That is, both systems exhibit the same qualitative behavior in the asymptotic limit of time.

Motivated by the study of social dynamical models, we modify the transition rule of cyclic particle systems. Specifically, we substitute the hierarchical interactions of colors with symmetric interactions, i.e., two colors can change each other with equal probability. This assumption is inherent within well-known models of social influence, such as the voter model, where transitions occur at rate proportional to the number of neighboring sites with a different type [18, Chapter V], or the model of Axelrod, where additionally *homophily* is incorporated [4, two sites tend to interact more frequently if they are more similar]. Social dynamical models are mostly nonlinear systems, where analytical tools usually fall short and research relies on simulations and mean-field approaches. Although much has been learned through such efforts [7], spatial simulations are usually difficult to interpret [15]. A formal study of social dynamical models is dictated through the field of interacting particle systems within probability theory. Henceforth, a more robust argument is presented for the fixation of symmetric cyclic particle systems. In a second installment, Adam Adamopoulos and the author present a more robust argument for the fluctuation and clustering for some multitype systems with confidence threshold [2]. The prerequisites are elementary graph theoretical notions and a graduate level course in probability theory.

Let $\eta_t$ denote the configuration (state) of the system at time $t$, $\eta_t(x)$ denote the color of site $x$ at time $t$, and $(\eta_t)_{t \geq 0}$ be a continuous-time Markov process with state space $\{0, 1 \cdots, N-1\}^G$, where graph $G$ with site set $V(G)$ and edge set $E(G)$ represents the social network. One may think of individuals or agents located at the sites of $G$, and they neighbor each other if they are connected by an edge of $G$. Thinking of the $N$ colors as all possible individual opinions that are represented by the vertices of the cycle graph $C_N$, dynamics is described by the following transition rule that specifies the transition rates of the examined process. Starting from a random configuration, at independent exponentially distributed times with rate 2 for each edge $\{x, y\}$, one of the sites $x, y$ of colors $u, v$, respectively, paints the other site with its color with equal probability $1/2$, provided that their colors are adjacent on $C_N$. Labeling colors in cyclic hierarchy with $0, 1, \cdots, N-1$, this transition rule is formally described in Section 2, first paragraph. Once one considers the multidimensional integer lattice $\mathbb{Z}^d$ as a social network, this homogeneous for all transitions rule of local interactions between neighboring sites describes not only an agent-based dynamic system, but a random asynchronous cellular automaton as well, where both the initial configuration and the transition rule is random [11].

Our first finding, Theorem 1, is on the behavior of the one-dimensional system on the integers $\mathbb{Z}$. The combination of [15, Theorem 1] and Theorem 1 offers one more emulation up to fluctuation and fixation of one-dimensional cyclic particle [6] and cellular automata systems [10].

**Theorem 1.** *In the one-dimensional symmetric cyclic particle system with $N$ colors, starting from independently and uniformly distributed colors, fixation* *occurs if $N \geq 5$. That is, there exists a random (possibly deterministic) limiting configuration $\eta_\infty$ such that, for each site $x$*

$$\lim_{t \to \infty} P[\eta_t(x) = \eta_\infty(x)] = 1 \ . \tag{1}$$

Our second finding is experimental by the use of a random cellular automaton with double clock, which was employed recently in discrete-time simulations of alternatives of the Axelrod model [1]. In particular, we employ a system with six-colors and estimate the probability of Condorcet's paradox of voting, thus extending the static approach of Klahr [14] to a dynamic scheme. It has been long discovered, that the aggregation of individual rankings over alternatives may result in a cyclical social ranking with no majority winner. If the alternatives to be ordered by the individuals are three, they can be represented by the six-cycle $C_6$ [1]. We incorporate as well a confidence threshold $\varepsilon = 1, 2, 3$, i.e., two colors can interact if their distance on the cycle $C_6$ is at most $\varepsilon$. Our interesting finding is the *dependence of the probability of the paradox of voting on $\varepsilon$, in the sense that this probability increases in the region of fixation (small $\varepsilon$ compared to $N$) on finite $\Lambda \subset \mathbb{Z}$, the complete graph, and a small-world network.*

## 2   Proof of Theorem 1

The process $(\eta_t)$ with $N$ colors is graphically represented on space-time lattice $\mathbb{Z} \times [0, \infty)$ following a widespread technique by Harris [12]. A graphical representation is an equivalent description of $(\eta_t)$ to the description with the transition rates. At $t = 0$, label independently the sites of $\mathbb{Z}$ with random colors $0, 1, \cdots, N-1$ according to the uniform product distribution with densities $P[\eta(x) = i] = 1/N$ for each site $x$ and color $i$. For $t > 0$ and each edge $\{x-1, x\}$, assign independent Poisson processes with rate $2 N_t(x-1, x)$ whose $n$-th arrival time is denoted by $T_n(x-1, x)$, $n \geq 1$, and independent i.i.d. (independent and identically distributed) sequences of fair coin tosses $\{U_n(x-1, x), n \geq 1\}$ with $P[U_n(x-1, x) = 1] = P[U_n(x-1, x) = -1] = 1/2$. At each time $T_n(x-1, x)$, allocate an arrow from $x$ to $x-1$ if $U_n(x-1, x) = -1$, or from $x-1$ to $x$ if $U_n(x-1, x) = 1$. Thinking of an arrow as representing an interaction, an arrow from $y = x \pm 1$ to $x$ is called active and the head $x$ of color $u = \eta(x)$ assumes the color $v = \eta(y)$ of the tail $y$, if

$$\min \left\{ \pm (u - v) \mod N \right\} = 1 \ , \tag{2}$$

which means that colors $u, v$ are adjacent on cycle $C_N$ with vertices labeled hierarchically as $0, 1, \cdots, N-1$.

Important in this construction is the concept of *an active path*, which is a directed path from $(z, s)$ to $(x, t)$ if there is a sequence of times $s = t_0 < t_1 < \cdots < t_n \leq t_{n+1} = t$ and a sequence of sites $z = z_0, z_1, \cdots, z_n = x$ such that, for all $i = 1, 2, \cdots, n$,

1. There is active arrow from $z_{i-1}$ to $z_i$ at time $t_i$.
2. The time segment $\{z_i\} \times (t_i, t_{i+1})$ does not cross the head of an active arrow.

For each point $(x, t)$ there is a unique $(z, 0)$, such that there is an active path from $(z, 0)$ to $(x, t)$ and $z$ is called the *ancestor of* $x$ *at time* $t$, $\alpha_t(x) = z$. Using this construction, $(\eta_t)$ is defined inductively for each $x$ by writing $\eta_t(x) = \eta_0(\alpha_t(x))$.

To show fixation, it suffices to show that any given site changes color finitely often, which is satisfied if it cannot have ancestors at arbitrary large distance. This fixation condition is formally stated in Lemma 1, which extends the applicability of [6, Lemma 2]. In a straightforward manner, the fixation condition of Lemma 1 has generality to systems with symmetric interactions - such as those encountered in social dynamical modeling - and with types/colors represented by other graphs than the cycle $C_N$. A generalization of Lemma 1 has been prepared for the fixation of the Axelrod model [17].

**Lemma 1 (Fixation Condition).** *Let* $T(z) = \min\{t : \alpha_t(0) = z\}$ *be the first time that the ancestor of site 0 is* $z$. *The process* $(\eta_t)$ *fixates if*

$$\lim_{n \to \infty} P[T(z) < \infty \text{ for some } z < -n] = 0 . \tag{3}$$

*Proof.* We follow [6] in proving that there cannot be infinitely often change at the origin 0 caused by ancestors in a finite interval. The apparent difficulty is that an ancestor can cause more than one change at site 0, which is not true in cyclic particle systems. Note that, our argument depends on the symmetry of interactions that does not hold for cyclic particle systems; therefore, our proof is different from the one in [6]. The details are as follows.

For each point $(x, 0)$, we define the set of descendants of $x$ at time $t$,

$$\Lambda_t(x) = \{y \in \mathbb{Z} : \alpha_t(y) = x\} .$$

The set of descendants of an ancestor is an interval, and in particular, the number of descendants of $x$ at time $t$, $\#\Lambda_t(x)$, is a non-negative martingale with respect to the $\sigma$-field $\mathcal{F}_0$ generated by the configuration at time $t = 0$. This fact follows from the definition of a martingale with respect to the $\sigma$-field $\mathcal{F}_s$ generated by $\eta_0$ and the graphical representation of $(\eta_t)$ through time $s \geq 0$ (see, e.g., [8]). Since for all $y$ and $n$, $P(U_n(y - 1, y) = 1) = P(U_n(y - 1, y) = -1) = 1/2$, the number of descendants of point $(x, s)$ at time $t > s$ is a martingale with respect to $\mathcal{F}_s$, $s \geq 0$ with conditional expectation constantly equal to 1.

By the martingale convergence theorem, for almost all realizations of the process, the number of descendants of $x$ converges to a finite number $\#\Lambda_\infty(x)$. Since this martingale is integer-valued, there is a finite time $S(x)$ such that

$$\#\Lambda_t(x) = \#\Lambda_\infty(x) \quad \text{for all } t \geq S(x) . \tag{4}$$

Let $\tau(j)$ be the time of the $j$-th change at site 0, and define the event that there is infinitely often change at site 0, $B = \{\tau(j) < \infty \text{ for all } j\}$, and the event that all changes at site 0 are caused by ancestors in the interval $[-n, n]$,

$G_n = \{|\alpha_{\tau(j)}(0)| \le n \text{ for all } j\}$. On the one hand, (3) and reflection symmetry imply

$$P(G_n) = 1 \qquad \text{for some } n . \tag{5}$$

On the other hand, on $G_n$, (4) implies that the last change at site 0 must occur before finite time $T = \max\{S(x) : |x| \le n\}$; hence, for each $n$

$$P(B \cap G_n) = 0 . \tag{6}$$

From (5) and (6) one obtains that $P(B) = 0$, which implies fixation.     □

Coupled with $(\eta_t)$ there is a system of edge processes $(e_t)$, which instead of keeping track of the color at each site $x$, they keep track of the weight at each edge $\{x - 1, x\}$

$$e_t(x - 1, x) = \min\left\{ \pm\left[\eta_t(x - 1) - \eta_t(x)\right] \mod N \right\} .$$

Alternatively, $e_t(x - 1, x)$ calculates the distance on the cycle $C_N$ between the colors of adjacent sites $x - 1$ and $x$. Say that edge $\{x - 1, x\}$ is vacant, active, blockade (resp.) at time $t$, if $e_t(x - 1, x)$ is 0, 1, or in $\{2, 3, \cdots, d(C_N)\}$ (resp.), where $d(C_N)$ is the diameter of $C_N$. As Bramson and Griffeath insightfully observed and exploited, active edges follow the motion of active paths and collide with each other and with the blockades [6]. Recently, Nicolas Lanchier analyzed the system of edge processes in the two-feature two-trait Axelrod model [15] that coincides up to time change with the symmetric cyclic particle system with $N = 4$ colors. His interesting discovery, fully supported in a joint work for two-trait models [16], is that active edges form a system of non-independent annihilating symmetric random walks. Contrary to this, if $N \ge 5$, a collision of an active edge with another edge particle of certain weight is more complicated.

Define that, *a jump occurs at time $t$ if edge $\{x - 1, x\}$ is active and moves to edge $\{x, x + 1\}$ at time $t$.* However, blockades and vacant edges do not move - although their incident sites may have descendants. By the fair coin tosses in a graphical representation, an active edge *attempts to jump* either to the left or to the right with equal probability $1/2$. By the exponential clocks of rate 2 in a graphical representation, an edge particle at $\{x - 1, x\}$ attempts to jump at rate 1 provided that $e_t(x - 1, x) = 1$. The jump occurs if the nearest neighbor edge is vacant. Otherwise, collisions of active edges with non-vacant edges, which may result in active edge jumps, are defined as follows.

Define that, *a collision occurs at time $t$ if edge $\{x - 1, x\}$ is active, edge $\{x, x+1\}$ is not vacant, and edge $\{x-1, x\}$ attempts to jump to $\{x, x+1\}$ at time $t$.* The last step in the construction is to understand the two possible outcomes of a collision. Suppose that the weight of $\{x, x+1\}$ is $e > 0$. Upon collision, if the color of the middle site $x$ is not in the geodesic of $C_N$ that connects the colors of $x - 1$ and $x + 1$, the outcome is that the weight of $\{x, x + 1\}$ decreases by 1, which we call an "annihilating" event. If the color of the middle site $x$ is in the geodesic of $C_N$ that connects the colors of $x - 1$ and $x + 1$, the outcome is that the weight of $\{x, x + 1\}$ increases by 1, which we call a "coalescing" event, with the exception that if $e = d(C_N)$ and $N$ is odd, the outcome is that the weight of $\{x, x + 1\}$ remains the same.

The induced systems of symmetric edge processes are not independent, owing to the discrepancy between the motion of active edges and blockades or vacant edges. However, collision events are independent and occur with fixed probabilities as in the following lemma. One can prove the lemma by the fact that three active paths cannot cross one another to show that independent of the realization of edges processes, the colors at $x - 1$, $x$, $x + 1$ just before a collision at time $\sigma_-$ are determined by the initial colors at $\alpha_{\sigma_-}(x - 1)$, $\alpha_{\sigma_-}(x)$, $\alpha_{\sigma_-}(x + 1)$ (consult [17, Lemma 3]).

**Lemma 2.** *Conditional on a realization of* $(e_t)$ *until time* $\sigma_-$, *and the event that a collision occurs at time* $\sigma$:

1. *If* $e < d(C_N)$ *or* $N$ *is odd, an "annihilating" event occurs with probability* $1/2$.
2. *If* $e < d(C_N)$ *or* $N$ *is odd, a "coalescing" event occurs with probability* $1/2$.
3. *If* $e = d(C_N)$ *and* $N$ *even, an "annihilating" event occurs with probability* $1$.

From this point, fixation stems from the construction of a comparison function $\phi(x)$, which compares the initial density of active edges with their eliminated density upon collisions. For another application of this technique, see [10]. Suppose that every site changes color at arbitrary large times (fluctuation hypothesis), and define effects $E_i$, $i = 1, 2$, which occur with probabilities $p_i$ and eliminate $r_i$ active edges at some random times $\sigma$:

$E_1$. Initially edge $\{x, x + 1\}$ is blockade of weight $e \geq 2$, and throughout $j$ collisions at $x$ or $x + 1$ at times $\sigma_1 < \sigma_2 < \cdots < \sigma_j = \sigma$, each outcome is such that $\{x, x + 1\}$ remains a blockade (of possibly different weight than $e$). $j$ active edges are eliminated in this sequence of collisions, $r_1 = j$.

$E_2$. Two initial active edges collide with any outcome. Two active edges are eliminated in this collision, $r_2 = 2$.

Then, implicitly define for each site $x$ a comparison function $\phi(x)$ through the following two-step construction. Initially, if edge $\{x - 1, x\}$ is active then set $\phi(x) = -1$, and otherwise set $\phi(x) = 0$. For $t > 0$, adjust $\phi(x)$ by $r_i$ upon occurrence of effect $E_i$ for each $i = 1, 2$:

$$\begin{aligned}
\phi(x) &= r_i, & &\text{if } E_i, \ i = 1, 2 \text{ occurs} \\
&= -1, & &\text{if } e_0(x - 1, x) = 1 \\
&= 0, & &\text{otherwise.}
\end{aligned}$$

If the sum of $\phi(x)$ over an interval is strictly positive, this has the meaning that there are not enough active edges to eliminate the blockades in the interval. Specifically, the event in condition (3) is included in the event

$$\left\{ \sum_{x=l}^{m} \phi(x) \leq 0 \text{ for some } l \leq -n, m \geq 0 \right\},$$

shown as in [6, page 33]. Therefore, to show fixation, it suffices to show that

$$\lim_{n\to\infty} P[\sum_{x=-l}^{m} \phi(x) \leq 0 \text{ for some } l \geq n, m \geq 0] = 0 . \tag{7}$$

For $N \geq 6$, effect $E_1$ is exploited. If $e = 3$ and $j = 1$, Lemma 2 implies that the probability of effect $E_1$ is equal to the probability of an initial blockade of weight at least three, $p_1 = (N-5)/N$. If $e = 2$ and $j = 2$, the probability of effect $E_1$ is calculated exactly as follows. The probability of an initial blockade of weight 2 is $2/N$ and by Lemma 2 with chance $1/2$ its weight increases (upon occurrence of a "coalescing" event), and then there is one more collision ("annihilating" or "coalescing" event) with probability 1; thus, $p_1 = (1/2)(2/N)$. By construction of function $\phi(x)$, before any adjustments we have $E[\phi(x)] = -P[e_0(x-1,x) = 1] = -2/N$, and after adjustments from the occurrence of $E_1$ we have $E[\phi(x)] = (N-5)/N + 2/N - 2/N > 0$.

Finally, $\phi(x)$ are i.i.d. for each $x$, and standard large deviations estimates show that the probability of the event in (7) exponentially tends to 0 as $n \to \infty$ (Cramer's Theorem can be applied, see for instance the lecture notes [9, pages 43-51]). Therefore, by contradiction of the fluctuation hypothesis, fixation occurs if $N \geq 6$ with probability 1.

For $N = 5$, effect $E_2$ is also exploited. Consider initial states at $x-1, x, x+1$ with two active edges at $\{x-1, x\}$ and $\{x, x+1\}$, and define the independent exponential variable with rate four, $T^{(4)}$; the event that there is an arrow from $x-1$ to $x$ or from $x+1$ to $x$ at $T^{(4)}$, $G$; the time of the first change at $x-1$ from the left, $T^-$; and, the time of the first change at $x+1$ from the right, $T^+$. Since event $G$ is independent of $T^-, T^+$ and has probability $\frac{1}{2}$, the probability that two initial active edges collide with each other, and before their collision is prevented by a collision with other active particles, is at least

$$p_2 \geq (2/5)^2 P_*[G, T^{(4)} < T^-, T^{(4)} < T^+] \geq (2/5)^2(1/2)(1 - 2P_*[T^- \leq T^{(4)}])$$

where $P_*[T^+ \leq T^{(4)}]$ is conditional probability on the initial state at $x-1, x, x+1$

$$P_*[T^+ \leq T^{(4)}] \leq (2/5)(\lambda+2)^{-1} + (3/5)(\lambda+2)^{-2}, \qquad \lambda = 4 ,$$

where the first term is an upper bound of the probability that there is an active arrow from $x-2$ to $x-1$ before an active arrow from $x-1$ to $x-2$ and before $T^{(4)}$, and the second term is an upper bound of the probability that there are two active arrows, each before before $T^{(1)}$ and before $T^{(4)}$. A "coalescing" collision with an initial blockade which eliminates one active edge with probability $p_1 = (1/2)(2/5)$, a sequence of two "coalescing" collisions with an initial blockade which eliminates one additional active edge with probability $p_1 = (1/2)^2(2/5)$, and the above estimate of $p_2$ guarantee $E[\phi(x)] > 0$ with clearance 0.0333. By construction the evaluations of $\phi(x)$ are statistically independent for each $x$, and standard large deviations estimates provide fixation.

# 3   Paradoxical Effect

We apply a random cellular automaton with double clock in discrete-time $t = 0, 1, \cdots, T$ [1]. The initial state is according to the uniform product distribution on finite lattice $\Lambda \subset \mathbb{Z}$ over six colors represented by cycle $C_6$. At odd time steps all odd sites are updated simultaneously, while at even times steps all even sites are updated simultaneously. Each updated site of color $u$ chooses equiprobable a neighbor of color $v$ and mimics her, provided that colors $u, v$ are adjacent on $C_6$ (confidence condition (2) holds). Below we report some experimental findings.

In simulations we observed only highly fragmented final states, which indicate that the proposed doubly synchronous automaton emulates the six-color symmetric cyclic particle system. One can extend the automaton with confidence parameter $\varepsilon > 1$, i.e., two neighboring sites can interact if their colors have distance at most $\varepsilon$. The case $\varepsilon = 3$ is the well studied multitype voter model that converges to consensus, which corresponds to clustering of the infinite system. In the case $\varepsilon = 2$, the exhibited qualitative behavior is very similar to the constrained voter model [21] (on a complete $G$, see also [13]) with two possible spatial scales present at equilibrium (large and small regions of different colors). Figure 1 depicts three realizations of the automaton for each $\varepsilon$.

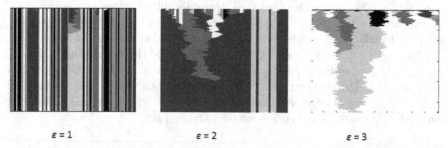

$\varepsilon = 1$          $\varepsilon = 2$          $\varepsilon = 3$

**Fig. 1.** Three typical realizations of the one-dimensional six-color symmetric cyclic cellular automaton for three different values of confidence $\varepsilon$. Fixation to highly fragmented configuration ($\varepsilon = 1$), two spatial scales at equilibrium ($\varepsilon = 2$), convergence towards consensus ($\varepsilon = 3$). Time is running from top to bottom of the page.

We briefly report our interesting finding. Let $A$ and $B$ be alternatives, and $AB$ denote that $A$ is preferred to $B$. Then consider a third alternative $C$ and three individuals to rank the three alternatives according to their preferences, say $ABC$, $BCA$, and $CAB$. In this example, by majority $A$ is preferred to $B$, $B$ is preferred to $C$, but also $C$ is preferred to $A$. Even though the individual rankings in the example are transitive, in the sense that $AB$ and $BC$ implies $AC$ for any alternatives $A, B, C$, the outcome is intransitive (cyclical) with no majority winner. This paradox has been observed since the times of Condorcet in the 18th century, was rediscovered by Black [5], and described by the Theorem of Arrow [3]. Klahr estimated *the probability of intransitive majority $P(m, n)$* for small number of alternatives $m$ and size of population $n$, and for equally likely and transitive individual rankings [14]. If $m, n \geq 3$, the experimental evidence in [14] shows that $P(m, n)$ is strictly positive and increasing in $m$ and $n$. For further reading on the paradox of voting, see for instance [20].

By applying the Monte Carlo techniques in [14] on the absorbing states of the automaton with $\varepsilon = 1$, we estimated probability $P(3, n)$ at absorption, $P_\infty(3, n)$. We have respected in the simulations all political theoretic assumptions in [14]: (i) individual rankings are strong (an individual can either prefer $A$ to $B$, or $B$ to $A$ for all alternatives $A, B$), (ii) individual rankings are transitive, and (iii) the parity of population $n$ is odd. Figure 2 compares our estimates that match Klahr's estimates at $t = 0$, with estimates obtained at absorption time $T > 0$ on complete graph, one-dimensional torus, and a version of the Watts-Strogatz's small-world model [19] [where the social network is one-dimensional torus, and additionally to nearest-neighbor edges, there is a density $p$ of random long-range edges; in the set of our experiments, $p = 0.01$]. We would also like to report that for $\varepsilon > 1$, no simulation run produced any intransitive outcome (ensemble size $10^5$). Therefore, there is dependence of probability $P_\infty(3, n)$ on $\varepsilon$, in the sense that $P_\infty(3, n)$ increases in the region of fixation (small $\varepsilon$ compared to the number of colors) on finite $\Lambda \subset \mathbb{Z}$, the complete graph, and a small-world network.

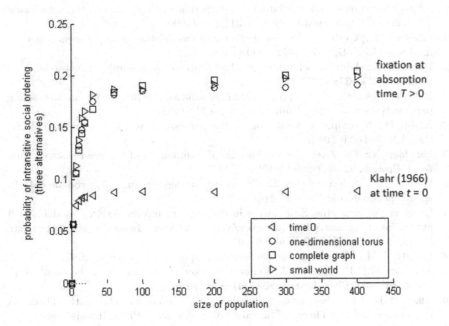

**Fig. 2.** Comparison of the probability of intransitive majority at time $t = 0$, $P(3, n)$, versus population $n$ ($\triangleleft$) with the probability of intransitive majority at absorption time $T > 0$, $P_\infty(3, n)$, versus population $n$ on complete graph ($\square$), one-dimensional torus ($\circ$), and a small-world network ($\triangleright$). The ensemble size of the simulations was $10^5$.

# References

1. Adamopoulos, A., Scarlatos, S.: Emulation and complementarity in one-dimensional alternatives of the Axelrod model with binary features. Complexity 17, 43–49 (2012)
2. Adamopoulos, A., Scarlatos, S.: Behavior of Social Dynamical Models II: Clustering for Some Multitype Particle Systems with Confidence Threshold. In: Sirakoulis, G.C., Bandini, S. (eds.) ACRI 2012. LNCS, vol. 7495, pp. 151–160. Springer, Heidelberg (2012)
3. Arrow, K.J.: Social Choice and Individual Values. Wiley & Sons, New York (1951)
4. Axelrod, R.: The dissemination of culture: A model with local convergence and global polarization. J. Conflict Res. 41, 203–226 (1997)
5. Black, D.: On the rationale of group decision-making. J. Pol. Econ. 56, 23–34 (1948)
6. Bramson, M., Griffeath, D.: Flux and fixation in cyclic particle systems. Ann. Probab. 17, 26–45 (1989)
7. Castellano, C., Fortunato, S., Loreto, V.: Statistical physics of social dynamics. Rev. Modern Phys. 81, 591–646 (2009)
8. Durrett, R.: Probability Theory and Examples. Brooks/Cole-Thomson Learning, Belmont (2005)
9. Ellis, R.S.: The theory of large deviations and applications to statistical mechanics. In: Lectures for the International Seminar on Extreme Events in Complex Systems, Max-Planck-Institut für Physik Komplexer Systeme, Dresden (2006)
10. Fisch, R.: The one-dimensional cyclic cellular automaton: a system with deterministic dynamics that emulates an interacting particle system with stochastic dynamics. J. Theoretical Probab. 3, 311–338 (1990)
11. Griffeath, D.: Cyclic random competition: A case history in experimental mathematics. AMS Notices 35, 1472–1480 (1988)
12. Harris, T.E.: Additive set-valued Markov processes and graphical methods. Ann. Probab. 6, 355–378 (1978)
13. Itoh, Y., Mallows, C., Shepp, L.: Explicit sufficient invariants for an interacting particle system. J. Appl. Probab. 35, 633–641 (1998)
14. Klahr, D.: A computer simulation of the paradox of voting. American Pol. Sc. Rev. LX, 384–390 (1966)
15. Lanchier, N.: The Axelrod model for the dissemination of culture revisited. Ann. Appl. Probab. 22, 860–880 (2012)
16. Lanchier, N., Schweinsberg, J.: Consensus in the two-state Axelrod model. To appear in Stochastic Process. Appl.
17. Lanchier, N., Scarlatos, S.: Fixation in the one-dimensional Axelrod model (2012) http://math.la.asu.edu/~lanchier/articles/20xxb_lanchier_scarlatos.pdf (accessed August 7, 2012) (submitted)
18. Liggett, T.M.: Interacting Particle Systems. Springer, New York (1985)
19. Newman, M.E.J., Watts, D.J.: Renormalization group analysis of the small-world network model. Phys. Lett. A 263, 341–346 (1999)
20. Riker, W.H.: Liberalism against Populism: A confronation between the Theory of Democracy and the Theory of Social Choice. Waveland Press, Illinois (1988)
21. Vázquez, F., Krapivsky, P.L., Redner, S.: Constrained opinion dynamics: freezing and slow evolution. J. Phys. A 36, L61–L68 (2003)

# Behavior of Social Dynamical Models II: Clustering for Some Multitype Particle Systems with Confidence Threshold

Adam Adamopoulos[1] and Stylianos Scarlatos[2,*,**]

[1] Department of Medicine, Medical Physics Laboratory,
Democritus University of Thrace, 681 00 Alexandroupolis, Greece
adam@med.duth.gr
[2] Department of Mathematics, Center for Research and Applications of Nonlinear Systems, University of Patras, 265 00 Patra, Greece
stylian.scarlatos@gmail.com

**Abstract.** We generalize the clustering theorem by Lanchier (2012) on the infinite one-dimensional integer lattice $\mathbb{Z}$ for the constrained voter model and the two-feature two-trait Axelrod model to multitype biased models with confidence threshold. Types are represented by a connected graph $\Gamma$, and dynamics is described as follows. At independent exponential times for each site of type $i$, one of the neighboring sites is chosen randomly, and its type $j$ is adopted if $i, j$ are adjacent on $\Gamma$. Starting from a product measure with positive type densities, the clustering theorem dictates that fluctuation and clustering occurs, i.e., each site changes type at arbitrary large times and looking at a finite interval consensus is reached asymptotically with probability 1, if there is one or two vertices of $\Gamma$ adjacent to all other vertices but each other. Additionally, we propose a simple definition of clustering on a finite set, in which case one can apply the clustering theorem that justifies known previous claims.

**Keywords:** Multitype biased voter models, Axelrod model, confidence threshold, fluctuation phenomena.

## 1 Introduction

One of the most popular and interesting social dynamical models is the model of Axelrod for the evolution of cultural domains [2]. It is formulated as a stochastic spatial model, where each site is characterized by $f$ features and each feature by $q$ possible traits. Two assumptions are employed in the description of the dynamics. Pairs of neighboring sites interact at rate equal to the number of features they share (homophily assumption), and the one site adopts a feature

* Present Address: Kabouridou 44, 552 36 Thessaloniki, Greece.
** The second author would like to express his gratitude towards Moses Boudourides for introducing him to social dynamics, and advisor Professor Tassos Bountis for his support and fairness. He would also like to thank Yioshiaki Itoh and Frederico Vázquez for interesting discussions, and especially Nicolas Lanchier for accepting him as coworker and teaching him many things for the theoretical part of his research.

G.C. Sirakoulis and S. Bandini (Eds.): ACRI 2012, LNCS 7495, pp. 151–160, 2012.

of its neighboring site they do not share (social influence assumption). After more than a decade of interdisciplinary research primarily by computer simulation and mean-field approximation [3], Nicolas Lanchier [9,10] with Jason Schweinsberg [11] and the second author [12] has recently achieved analytical findings in one-dimensional lattices. The infinite model clusters to a monopolar configuration (consensus is reached) whenever $q = 2$ [10,11], and the finite model converges to a highly fragmented configuration for $f \leq cq$ where the slope satisfies the equation $e^{-c} = c$ [10] (see also, [12, Introduction]). For the same parameter region as in the latter result or if $f = 2$ and $q \geq 3$ each site of the infinite model fixates to a final cultural type with probability 1 [12].

In the first installment, the second author showed fixation in symmetric cyclic particle systems [14]. In this article, we examine the behavior of social dynamical models with respect to fluctuation and clustering for alternatives of the Axelrod model, which generalize systems presented in [16,10,1] and also appear as discrete analogues of certain models with continuous types [9].

The investigated dynamics is described as continuous-time Markov processes $(\xi_t)_{t \geq 0}$ with state space $\{0, 1, \cdots, N-1\}^{\mathbb{Z}}$, where $\mathbb{Z}$ represents the one dimensional integers. Types are represented by a connected graph $\Gamma$ with vertex set $V(\Gamma)$ of cardinality $\#V(\Gamma) = N$, and edge set $E(\Gamma)$. Let $d_{z,w}^F$ denote the distance of two vertices $z, w$ of a graph $F$. The initial configuration (state) is $\xi$ according to a product measure with positive type densities. From then on, for each site $x$, type $\xi(x)$ independently becomes of the type $\xi(y)$ at an exponential rate proportional to the number of $neighbors$ $y$ that satisfy $d_{x,y}^{\mathbb{Z}} = 1$, provided that the $weight$ of edge $\{x, y\}$ is equal to 1, that is, $d_{\xi(x),\xi(y)}^{\Gamma} = 1$. For each site $x$, the transition rule is formally written as

$$\xi(x) \to c \quad \text{at rate} \quad \#\{y \in \mathbb{Z} : d_{x,y}^{\mathbb{Z}} = 1, \ d_{\xi(x),\xi(y)}^{\Gamma} = 1, \ \xi(y) = c\} . \tag{1}$$

For example, suppose that graph $\Gamma$ is the hypercube $Q_f$ with $2^f$ vertices. If $f = 1$, rates (1) describe linear dynamics of a voter model, where transitions occur at rate proportional to the number of neighboring sites with a different type [7,4]. If $f = 2$, the four-type system with rates (1) coincides with the two-feature two-trait Axelrod model, which alike the voter model fluctuates and clusters [10]. For $f > 1$, rates (1) describe conditionally attractive dynamics on bounded confidence. A central problem is to determine the phase transition from fluctuation to fixation in the asymptotic limit of time, and full qualitative or asymptotically sharp results are valuable. The exhibited qualitative behaviors are formally defined as follows.

$(\xi_t)$ $fixates$ if there exists a random (possibly deterministic) limiting configuration $\xi_\infty$ such that for each $x$,

$$\lim_{t \to \infty} P[\xi_t(x) = \xi_\infty(x)] = 1 . \tag{2}$$

$(\xi_t)$ $fluctuates$ if for each $x$,

$$P[\xi_t(x) \text{ changes at arbitrarily large times } t] = 1 . \tag{3}$$

$(\xi_t)$ *clusters* if for each $x, y$,

$$\lim_{t \to \infty} P[\xi_t(x) = \xi_t(y)] = 1 \,. \tag{4}$$

The eccentricity of a vertex in a connected graph is the maximum distance from it to any other vertex, the center of the graph is the set of all vertices of minimum eccentricity, and a peripheral vertex has eccentricity equal to the diameter of the graph, which is the maximum eccentricity of any vertex in the graph. Starting from any product measure with positive type densities, as the diameter of graph of types $\Gamma$ increases, by increasing the number of types $N$ and adding accordingly vertices and edges on $\Gamma$, edges in $\mathbb{Z} + 1/2$ with types that cannot interact with each other are more probable at $t = 0$. Furthermore, it is more likely that most types will have no neighbors to interact with for $t > 0$, so that the system fixates. Definition (2) does not a priori exclude the more sophisticated regime of clustering, and particularly, fixation of the examined systems corresponds to convergence to a highly fragmented configuration. Depending on the interaction mechanism and the dimension of the integer lattice, fluctuation may be accompanied with clustering, which is the case in systems with rates (1).

In this article, we present a generalization of [10, Theorem 1] formulated in Theorem 1 below for the clustering of systems with many types represented by an arbitrary connected graph $\Gamma$. Our motivation, and excuse at the same time, is to attack arbitrary multitype particle systems with confidence threshold to the hopes of understanding asymptotic behavior with respect to graph theoretic properties of the structure of types. For asymptotic results which consider the structure of the social network in systems with continuous types in the interval $[0, 1]$, see [9]. We believe that part (i) of Theorem 1 is asymptotically sharp, and we mention that it seems more potent than part (ii) if the center of $\Gamma$ is a strict subset of the full graph (for all confidence values different from the diameter of $\Gamma$), while the converse seems to hold otherwise. The previous statement is explained in Section 2, where additionally simulations are conducted and corollaries of Theorem 1 are obtained. In Section 3 we sketch a proof Theorem 1. In Section 4 we provide applications for finite systems.

**Theorem 1 (Generalized Lanchier's Theorem).** *Consider a voter model with $N \geq 3$ types and confidence 1 as follows. Each type is in the vertex set $V(\Gamma)$ of a connected graph $\Gamma$, and two types can interact if they are adjacent in $\Gamma$. Starting from a product measure on $V(\Gamma)^{\mathbb{Z}}$ with positive type densities, fluctuation and clustering occurs if (i) there is a vertex of $\Gamma$ adjacent to all other vertices, or (ii) there are two vertices of $\Gamma$ adjacent to all other vertices but each other.*

## 2 Discussion

In this Section we discuss Theorem 1 by providing corollaries and conducting simulations for special cases. Our discussion is accommodated by the consideration of a conditional convergent interaction (see, rates (5)).

The substitution in rates (1) of graph $\Gamma$ with graph $\Gamma^\varepsilon$, where $\Gamma^\varepsilon$ is induced from the original graph by linking each two vertices within distance $\varepsilon$, defines a certain multitype particle system with confidence parameter. If $\Gamma = Q_f$ is the hypercube with $2^f$ vertices, the following corollary of Theorem 1(ii) holds, which was given a sketch of proof up to fluctuation in [1].

**Corollary 1.** *The hypercubic particle system with $2^f$ types represented by hypercube $Q_f$ and confidence $\varepsilon$, starting from a product measure on $V(Q_f)^{\mathbb{Z}}$ with positive type densities, fluctuates and clusters if $\varepsilon \geq f - 1$.*

The substitution in rates (1) of graph $\Gamma$ with graph $P_N^\varepsilon$, where $P_N^\varepsilon$ is induced from path $P_N$ with $N$ vertices by linking each two vertices within distance $\varepsilon$, defines a certain constrained voter model with confidence parameter and implies the following corollary of Theorem 1(i).

**Corollary 2.** *The constrained voter model with $N \geq 3$ types represented by path $P_N$ and confidence $\varepsilon$, starting from a product measure on $V(P_N)^{\mathbb{Z}}$ with positive type densities, fluctuates and clusters if $N \leq 2\varepsilon + 1$.*

Similarly, if $\Gamma = C_N$ is the $N$-cycle, one can define a symmetric cyclic particle system [14] with arbitrary confidence threshold. In addition, we define a *convergent transition rule* for certain particle systems with confidence threshold, and for each site $x$

$$\xi(x) \to c \quad \text{at rate} \quad \#\{y \in \mathbb{Z} : d_{x,y}^{\mathbb{Z}} = 1, \ 0 < d_{\xi(x),\xi(y)}^\Gamma \leq \varepsilon, \ d_{c,\xi(y)}^\Gamma = d_{\xi(x),\xi(y)}^\Gamma - 1\} \tag{5}$$

where $c$, depending on graph $\Gamma$, may be random (uniformly chosen among all possible vertices of $\Gamma$ which satisfy rates (5)). The confidence parameter $\varepsilon$ is positive with maximum value equal to the diameter $d(\Gamma) = \max_{z,w \in V(\Gamma)} d_{z,w}^\Gamma$.

Figure 1 compares conditional convergent and conditional attractive interactions on bounded confidence, the former following rates (5) for a graph $\Gamma$, and the latter following rates (1) for induced graph $\Gamma^\varepsilon$. This comparison is with respect to the mean size of clusters at absorption versus the confidence parameter (hundred-site torus, ensemble size $10^4$). Small cluster sizes compared to the size of the torus correspond to highly fragmented configurations, while cluster sizes that equal the size of the torus correspond to consensus. For models with rates (1) all evidence so far is that, these two regimes match in an infinite setting the behaviors of fixation and fluctuation accompanied with clustering, respectively. Although there may be exceptions, a similar statement holds according to the rigorous findings for certain systems with a more sophisticated rates than (5) which include the assumption of homophily as well - viz., the model of Axelrod.

Paying attention on models with conditional attractive interactions on confidence, Figure 1(blue circle marks) shows the mean cluster size at absorption versus confidence in a fifteen-type constrained voter model. The center of graph $P_N^\varepsilon$ is a strict subset of the full graph for all nontrivial values of confidence that do not produce a linear multitype voter model $\varepsilon \neq d(P_N) = N - 1$. In particular,

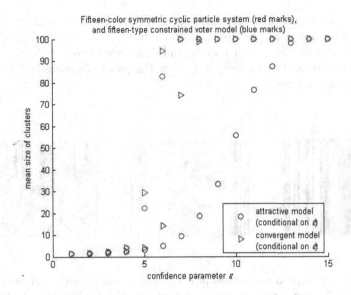

**Fig. 1.** Mean size of clusters at absorption versus confidence parameter $\varepsilon$ in models with convergent or attractive interactions, conditional on bounded confidence: the constrained voter model with confidence threshold (blue marks) and the symmetric cyclic particle system with confidence threshold (red marks). A hundred-site torus, and a $10^4$ ensemble was used.

if $N = 15$ and $\varepsilon = (N-1)/2 = 7$, Theorem 1(i) implies clustering on the infinite lattice, which is clearly more potent than Theorem 1(ii) in the sense that part (i) of the theorem provides clustering while part (ii) does not. Comparing with the data for conditional convergent interactions on $\varepsilon = 7$ (blue triangle marks), there seems like a huge contradiction between the qualitative behavior of the two finite models, since the mean cluster size is a lot smaller in the former case, while clustering is indicated in the latter case. However, as Nicolas Lanchier spoke it "spatial simulations are usually difficult to interpret" [10]. In our particular case, no contradiction between the qualitative behaviors of two finite models with the same parameters is somewhat suggested in simulations by the not atypical two spatial scales at absorption, Figure 2. To further strengthen this view, one needs to consider larger lattices in simulations, or prove it analytically as in the next Section.

Furthermore, the center of graph $C_N^\varepsilon$ is the full graph for all $N, \varepsilon$. If $N$ is even, Theorem 1(ii) is more potent than Theorem 1(i) in the sense that part (ii) of the theorem provides an asymptotically sharper condition $\varepsilon \geq N/2 - 1$ than the one provided by part (i) $\varepsilon = N/2$. Moreover, if $N$ is odd and $\varepsilon \geq d(C_N)$, Theorem 1 implies clustering of the infinite model. In particular, if $N = 15$ and $\varepsilon \geq d(C_{15}) = 7$, based on the mean cluster sizes of Figure 1 the condition $\varepsilon \geq 7$ does not seem asymptotically sharp, since clustering is highly indicated for $\varepsilon = 6$, and less clearly for $\varepsilon = 5$. Based on such simulations, we conjecture that the one-dimensional symmetric cyclic particle system with confidence threshold fixates if $\varepsilon < N/3$, and fluctuates and clusters if $\varepsilon > N/3$. In writing the previous two paragraphs, we had the faith that infinite and finite models with the same parameters should exhibit no essential difference in their behavior, which we attempt to strengthen in Section 4, after the proof of generalized Lanchier Theorem in the next Section.

**Fig. 2.** Three not atypical realizations of a fifteen-type constrained voter model with confidence $\varepsilon = 7$ using a random cellular automaton with double clock [1]. Fixation to a fragmented configuration (a), two spatial scales near equilibrium (b), convergence towards consensus (c). Time is running from top to bottom of the page.

## 3    Proof of Theorem 1

Reference [10] starts from the two-feature two-trait Axelrod model, and employs a coupling observed by Vázquez and Redner [16]. One recovers the voter model from the two-feature two-trait Axelrod model by identifying the cultural types that have no feature in common. Using fluctuation and clustering of the two-type voter model, Lanchier showed clustering of a four-type Axelrod model. Then, the constrained voter model with three types represented by the path graph $P_3$ clusters as well, since the mean size of clusters is stochastically larger in the latter case.

The following proof of Theorem 1 briefly reviews and generalizes by the mapping of [8] steps within the proof of the first theorem in [10]. We work in opposite, starting from the constrained voter model $(\zeta_t)$ with rates (1) and types represented by path $P_3$. As a side note, the non-spatial models in references [8] and [17] deal independently with the same system, and arrive at the same result through a different proof.

The three-type $(\zeta_t)$ can be graphically constructed on space-time lattice $\mathbb{Z} \times [0, \infty)$ following a versatile technique by Harris [6], which is applicable for any dimension $d$ of the multidimensional integers. At $t = 0$, label independently the sites of $\mathbb{Z}$ with random types $0, 1, 2$ according to a product measure $\mu$ with positive type densities $\mu(\zeta(x) = i) = \theta_i > 0$ and $\theta_0 + \theta_1 + \theta_2 = 1$ . The types are hierarchically labeled, that is, for two vertices $u, v$ in $P_3$, $d_{u,v}^{P_3} = |u - v|$.

For $t > 0$, assign independent Poisson processes with parameter 1 $\{T_n^x, n \geq 1\}$ for each site $x$, together with independent sequences of i.i.d. fair coin tosses $\{U_n^x, n \geq 1\}$ ($P(U_n^x = 1) = \frac{1}{2}$, $P(U_n^x = -1) = \frac{1}{2}$). At each arrival time $T_n^x$, allocate a directed edge that is called arrow $yx$ from $y = x + U_n^x$ to $x$, which has the metaphorical meaning that the voter at $x$ at time $T_n^x$ considers the opinion of a random neighboring voter $y$. The voter at head $x$ of an *active arrow* $yx$ assumes the type/opinion of the voter at tail $y$ provided that $d_{\zeta(y),\zeta(x)}^{P_3} = 1$. An arrow $yx$ is inert and induces no change at head $x$, if $d_{\zeta(y),\zeta(x)}^{P_3} \neq 1$. To distinguish the two kinds of arrows, one can mark inert arrows, for instance, with an 'x'. Active arrows and fixed-site increasing time segments give rise to directed paths, which connect different points in $\mathbb{Z} \times [0, \infty)$. Important in this construction is the concept of *an active path*, which is a directed path that does not coincide with the head of an active arrow. For each point $(x, t)$ there is always a unique $(z, 0)$, such that there is an active path from $(z, 0)$ to $(x, t)$ and $z$ is called the *ancestor of $x$ at time $t$*, $\alpha_t(x) = z$. Using this construction, $(\zeta_t)$ is defined inductively for each $x$ by writing $\zeta_t(x) = \zeta_0(\alpha_t(x))$.

Looking at a finite interval $A \subset \mathbb{Z}$, the configuration at time $t$ is then determined by the process $(\alpha_t)$ that keeps track of the ancestor of each $x$ in $A$. To compute configuration $\zeta_t(x)$ one has to invert all arrows and follow backwards in time the active path from $(x, t)$ to $(\alpha_t(x), 0)$. Note that while computing $\zeta_t(x)$ backwards, to avoid following an inert arrow at a given time, one needs to have constructed the process up to this time. Therefore, the construction of $(\alpha_t)$ depends on the initial configuration, which differs from the construction of dual paths in the voter model.

However, if $\zeta_t(x) = 1$, all arrows in backward computations are followed, and the process can be constructed regardless of the initial configuration. Thus, a connection with coalescing random walks can be exploited as in the voter model. In this case, $(\alpha_t)$ is a dual process of $(\zeta_t)$ defined exclusively for type 1 as a system of coalescing symmetric random walks, which start from $A \subset \mathbb{Z}$. By well know results in linear particle systems, the density of type 1 is preserved for any dimension $d$ of multidimensional integers, and in one and two dimensions $d = 1, 2$ clustering occurs for type 1 with positive probability

$$\lim_{t \to \infty} P[\zeta_t(x) = \zeta_t(y) = 1] = \theta_1 > 0 . \tag{6}$$

The obtained duality with coalescing random walks for type 1 suggests a particular mapping of the types. We consider an imbedded Markov process $(i_t)$ within $(\zeta_t)$, which cannot distinguish types that are different from type 1. If we identify types $u$ such that $u \neq 1$, $(i_t)$ is the two-type voter model, which fluctuates on $\mathbb{Z}$ owing to known results. It is crucial that the voter model fluctuates for rather general initial configurations [15, Remark]. Therefore, each site of the three-type process fluctuates between type 1 and type 0 or 2. This idea is applicable for any connected $\Gamma$, if there is a vertex of $\Gamma$ adjacent to all other vertices. In this case, the $N$-type process clusters for a central vertex of $\Gamma$, and each site fluctuates between this central vertex and one of the remaining vertices of $\Gamma$, which shows fluctuation in Theorem 1(i).

Fluctuation in Theorem 1(ii) can be proved by the mapping of Itoh, Mallows, and Shepp [8, Section 3], which obtains quantitative results for the asymptotic distributions of constrained models with more than three types from the distributions of the three-type model. We employ the mapping of [8] to obtain a qualitative result. If there are two vertices $u, v$ of $\Gamma$ at distance 1 from all other vertices but each other, one can identify all $j \neq u, v$. By the first part of the theorem, the imbedded three-type system within the $N$-type system fluctuates. Therefore, each site of the $N$-type system fluctuates among types $u, v$ and one of the types $j \neq u, v$.

Following [10], clustering for all three types is a result of the key facts of fluctuation and clustering for type 1, together with the analysis of the evolution of weights of edges $\{x, x+1\}$ using the edge process $(e_t)$ for each $x$

$$e_t(x) = d^{P_3}_{\zeta_t(x), \zeta_t(x+1)},$$

which keeps track of the type distances along the edges of $\mathbb{Z}$ rather than the types of the sites. We say that edge $x_+$ is vacant, active, blockade (resp.) at time $t$, if $e_t(x) = 0, 1, 2$ (resp.). Following the motion of an active path, an active edge jumps to one of two nearest neighbor vacant edges with equal probability, unless the nearest neighbor edge is blockade or active in which case a collision occurs. Taking into account symmetry, all possible transitions of edge pairs are collisions of two active edges, which annihilate $(1, 1) \rightarrow (0, 0)$ or annihilate thus creating a blockade $(1, 1) \rightarrow (0, 2)$, and jumps of an active edge to a nearest neighbor vacant edge $(1, 0) \rightarrow (0, 1)$ or to a nearest neighbor blockade $(1, 2) \rightarrow (0, 1)$. The edge pair transitions show that active edges cannot be created, and that they evolve as a system of annihilating symmetric random walks. Moreover, clustering for type 1 implies almost sure extinction of active edges

$$\lim_{t \to \infty} P[e_t(x) = 1] = 0 .\tag{7}$$

Letting $0 < s < t < \infty$, where $s$ is large, on the one hand, the probability of a blockade at time $t$ that has been created after time $s$ is at most $\epsilon$, for all small $\epsilon > 0$ (as a consequence of (7), and the fact that a blockade can only be created by the annihilation of two active edges). On the other hand, the probability of a blockade at time $t$ that has been created by time $s$ fixed is at most $\epsilon$, for some $t > s$ (as a consequence of fluctuation). Then, the combination of the previous two estimates implies almost sure extinction of blockades

$$\lim_{t \to \infty} P[e_t(x) = 2] = 0 .\tag{8}$$

By (7) and (8), the three-type process clusters (4) for all types and each $x, y$:

$$\lim_{t \to \infty} P[\zeta_t(x) \neq \zeta_t(y)] \leq \lim_{t \to \infty} P[e_t(x) \neq 0] = 0 .$$

In any $N$-type process, if a vertex of $\Gamma$ is adjacent to all other vertices, clustering occurs for this central vertex with positive probability. In addition, all possible transitions of edge pairs are as in the three-type process (it suffices that in both processes the initial type densities are positive). As previously, the combination of clustering for a particular type and the already established fluctuation of the $N$-type process implies clustering (4) in Theorem 1(i).

In any $N$-type process, if there are two vertices $u, v$ of $\Gamma$ adjacent to all other vertices but each other, then the mapping of [8] identifies all $j \neq u, v$. As already shown, the imbedded three-type process $(\zeta_t)$ clusters with probability 1. It is crucial that clustering of $(\zeta_t)$ occurs for any positive initial densities. Therefore, the $N$-type process clusters for types $u, v$ with positive probability. The combination of clustering for particular types and the already established fluctuation of the $N$-type process implies clustering (4) in Theorem 1(ii).

## 4    Applications

In this section, we provide applications of Theorem 1, which are grounded on a simple definition and justify previous claims of fluctuation until absorption of certain finite systems and their generalizations in the present article.

Any stationary distribution of a finite system with rates (1) is supported on the set of absorbing states. Apparently, definition (2) implies that any finite system fixates with probability 1 for any number of types and confidence threshold, which contradicts observations from simulations that a model seems to exhibit different qualitative behaviors for complementary ranges of its parameters. We clarify this discrepancy and justify the understanding in [1], by proposing a definition of fluctuation on a finite set, which is also applicable for the systems in [16] and [9], and seems to be applicable for all systems with rates (1) that fluctuate and cluster according to Theorem 1.

The definition of fluctuation on a finite set is slightly more involved than definition (3). Suppose that the process $(\xi_t)$ has rates (1) on finite connected $G \subset \mathbb{Z}$ for an induced graph $\Gamma^\varepsilon$. Then, define the process $(g_t)$ on $G \cup \{l, r\}$, which starts from finite configuration $g$ that is obtained from $\xi$ by adding two peripheral sites on $G$, $l = \min\{x \in V(G)\} - 1$ and $r = \max\{x \in V(G)\} + 1$, and evolves as $(\xi_t)$ except that all arrows towards the leftmost site $l$ and the rightmost site $r$ of initial types $g(l)$ and $g(r)$, respectively, are deleted.

We say that, $(\xi_t)$ *fluctuates until absorption on $G$* if for each site $x$ different from $l$ and $r$, conditional on the event that $g(l)$ and $g(r)$ have distance $\varepsilon$,

$$P\big[g_t(x) \text{ changes at arbitrary times } t \mid x \neq l, r, \, d^\Gamma_{g(l),g(r)} = \varepsilon\big] = 1 . \quad (9)$$

Definition (9) has the interpretation that, by deactivating all arrows towards the end sites of a finite interval with types that can change one another, the definition of fluctuation assimilates the idea of definition (3) of the infinite system.

Suppose that $\Gamma$ is a tree graph. Under the imposed conditions by definition (9), if Theorem 1 holds for the infinite model, then for the finite model with the same parameters there is large time $t$ such that the ancestor of each site $x \neq l, r$ is either $l$ or $r$ and the edge of the two domains with types $\xi(l)$ and $\xi(r)$ is a symmetric random walk with jump rate $1/2$ which bounces at the end sites of the interval. Therefore, the following application holds.

**Application 1.** *Consider a voter model with $N \geq 3$ types, confidence $\varepsilon$, and rates (1) for an induced graph $\Gamma^\varepsilon$ where $\Gamma$ is a tree. Starting from a product measure on $V(\Gamma)^{\mathbb{Z}}$ with positive type densities, if the infinite model fluctuates and clusters according to Theorem 1, then the finite model fluctuates until absorption (which may be either consensus or a fragmented configuration).*

Considering more applications, the graph of types $\Gamma$ can be a hypercube or a cycle graph, whence the underlaid claim of Application 1 holds.

# References

1. Adamopoulos, A., Scarlatos, S.: Emulation and complementarity in one-dimensional alternatives of the Axelrod model with binary features. Complexity 17, 43–49 (2012)
2. Axelrod, R.: The dissemination of culture: A model with local convergence and global polarization. J. Conflict Res. 41, 203–226 (1997)
3. Castellano, C., Fortunato, S., Loreto, V.: Statistical physics of social dynamics. Rev. Modern Phys. 81, 591–646 (2009)
4. Clifford, P., Sudbury, A.: A model for spatial conflict. Biometrika 60, 581–588 (1973)
5. Fisch, R.: The one-dimensional cyclic cellular automaton: a system with deterministic dynamics that emulates an interacting particle system with stochastic dynamics. J. Theoretical Probab. 3, 311–338 (1990)
6. Harris, T.E.: Additive set-valued Markov processes and graphical methods. Ann. Probab. 6, 355–378 (1978)
7. Holley, R.A., Liggett, T.M.: Ergodic theorems for weakly interacting infinite systems and the voter model. Ann. Probab. 3, 643–663 (1975)
8. Itoh, Y., Mallows, C., Shepp, L.: Explicit sufficient invariants for an interacting particle system. J. Appl. Probab. 35, 633–641 (1998)
9. Lanchier, N.: Opinion dynamics with confidence threshold: an alternative to the Axelrod model. ALEA Lat. Am. J. Probab. Math. Stat. 7, 1–18 (2010)
10. Lanchier, N.: The Axelrod model for the dissemination of culture revisited. Ann. Appl. Probab. 22, 860–880 (2012)
11. Lanchier, N., Schweinsberg, J.: Consensus in the two-state Axelrod model. To appear in Stochastic Process. Appl.
12. Lanchier, N., Scarlatos, S.: Fixation in the one-dimensional Axelrod model (2012), http://math.la.asu.edu/~lanchier/articles/20xxb_lanchier_scarlatos.pdf (accessed August 7, 2012) (submitted)
13. Liggett, T.M.: Interacting Particle Systems. Springer, New York (1985)
14. Scarlatos, S.: Fixation in the Symmetric Cyclic System (with Paradoxical Effect in the Six-Color Automaton). In: Sirakoulis, G.C., Bandini, S. (eds.) ACRI 2012. LNCS, vol. 7495, pp. 141–150. Springer, Heidelberg (2012)
15. Schwartz, D.: On hitting probabilities for an annihilating particle model. Ann. Probab. 6, 398–403 (2004)
16. Vázquez, F., Krapivsky, P.L., Redner, S.: Constrained opinion dynamics: freezing and slow evolution. J. Phys. A 68, L61–L68 (2003)
17. Vázquez, F., Redner, S.: Ultimate fate of constrained voters. J. Phys. A 37, 8479–8494 (2004)

# Investigation of Stable Patterns Formed by Totalistic Cellular Automata Evolution[*]

Anastasiya Sharifulina

The Institute of Computational Mathematics and Mathematical Geophysics,
SB RAS Prospekt Akademika Lavrentieva 6, Novosibirsk, Russia
sharifulina@ssd.sscc.ru

**Abstract.** The stable patterns formed as a result of evolution of totalistic cellular automata (CA) with weighed templates are investigated. A formal definition of the CA with the weighed templates is presented. As a result of simulation by synchronous and asynchronous CA, various stable patterns emerging from one nucleation cell are obtained and classified. The influence of weight matrix entries on stable patterns is studied. The theorem about the stable patterns dependence on the ratio of positive to negative entries of a weight matrix is proved. Stable patterns formed of two nucleation cells are also investigated.

**Keywords:** stable patterns formation, totalistic cellular automata, weighted templates, synchronous and asynchronous mode, nucleation cell.

## 1   Introduction

Many of the phenomena and processes in physics, chemistry, biology and sociology are associated with emergence of stable patterns. Concentric, spiral spatial waves are observed in different chemical reactions. Well-known examples of stable patterns in living systems are the pigment spots and stripes on the animals' skin. Studying the stable patterns arising in self-organizing complex systems is important both from fundamental and practical points of view. For example, in chemistry, the investigation of self-organizing processes on catalysts makes possible to develop new materials with unique properties, in medicine studying self-organization of neurons has great importance to diagnostics of the brain activity.

There are many publications devoted to studying the patterns formation in dissipative non-equilibrium systems. The foundations of spatially stable patterns are laid by A.Turing in his study of reaction-diffusion morphogen systems in 1952 [1]. The first CA of the Turing pattern formation based on an activator-inhibitor interaction was proposed by D.A Young [2]. The pattern formation occurs in

---

[*] Supported by 1)Presidium of Russian Academy of Sciences, Basic Research Program 15.9-5, 2)Siberian Branch of Russian Academy of Sciences, Interdisciplinary Project 47 3)Russian Fund for Basic Research grant 1-01-0567a.

G.C. Sirakoulis and S. Bandini (Eds.): ACRI 2012, LNCS 7495, pp. 161–170, 2012.

many well-known catalytic reactions, for instance, the carbon monoxide oxidation reaction over platinum metal [3] and the Belousov-Zabotinskii reaction [4]. Many examples of the stable patterns formation in different physical, chemical and biological systems are presented in [5] and [6]. In [7] and [8], the cellular automata (CA) approach to describing the self-organizing processes and patterns formation is proposed. Cellular automata are most suitable for describing the complex systems dynamics, because they make possible to simulate spatial heterogeneous nonlinear processes by simple local transition rules.

The objective of the paper is to investigate the stable patterns formed by evolution of cellular automata with weighted templates with a single initial nucleation cell.

Apart from Introduction and Conclusion, the paper contains three sections. The second section contains a formal definition of cellular automata with weighted templates. The third section presents the dependence of stable patterns formation on weight matrix entries. Results of computing experiments performed by synchronous and asynchronous CA are given in the fourth section.

## 2   Definition of Cellular Automaton with Weighted Templates

The totalistic cellular automaton (CA) with weighted templates is defined by the four notions [9]:

$$\aleph = \langle A, X, \Theta, \rho \rangle, \tag{1}$$

where $A = \{0, 1\}$ is a cells *state alphabet*, $X = \{(i, j) : i = 1, \ldots, M_i, j = 1, \ldots, M_j\}$ is a *set of names*, $\Theta$ is a *local operator* defined by the cells transition rules, $\rho \in \{\sigma, \alpha\}$ is a *mode of operations*. *Cell* is a pair $(u, (i, j))$, where $u \in A$ is a state of a cell, $(i, j)$ is a name of a cell. On the set of names $X$, the *template* $T(i, j)$ is introduced. The template defines the nearest neighbours of each cell. Further, the template $T_R(i, j)$ having the size of $R \times R$ cells is used:

$$T_R(i, j) = \{(i, j), (i + a, j + b) : a, b = -\lfloor R/2 \rfloor, \ldots, 0, \ldots, \lfloor R/2 \rfloor\}. \tag{2}$$

In the CA model, a *weight matrix* $W_{R \times R}$ is associated with the template $T_R(i, j)$. The weight matrix $W_{R \times R}$ contains positive and negative entries. The positive entries are called *activators* and are responsible for the growth of patterns. The negative entries are *inhibitors*, they impede the pattern growth. The structure of a weight matrix, used in the sequel, is the following:

$$w_{kl} = \begin{cases} n, & \text{if } |k|, |l| = \lfloor R/2 \rfloor, \\ p, & \text{if } |k|, |l| < \lfloor R/2 \rfloor, \end{cases} \Rightarrow W_{R \times R} = \begin{pmatrix} n\,n \ldots n\,n \\ n\,p \ldots p\,n \\ \cdots \cdots \cdots \\ n\,p \ldots p\,n \\ n\,n \ldots n\,n \end{pmatrix}, \tag{3}$$

where $n < 0$ is an inhibitor, $p > 0$ is an activator. The presence of activators and inhibitors in a system allows supporting the process in an equilibrium state, and provides conditions for the stable patterns formation [2, 5].

The local operator $\Theta$ changes a cell state $(i, j)$ depending on the states of the neighboring cells allocated by the template $T_R(i, j)$:

$$\Theta(i, j) : (a_0, (i, j)) \to (a'_0, (i, j)),$$

$$\text{where } a' = \begin{cases} 0, & \text{if } s \leq 0, \\ 1, & \text{if } s > 0, \end{cases} \qquad s = \sum_{k,l=0,\ldots,R} w_{kl} \cdot a_{kl}. \tag{4}$$

Here $w_{kl}$, $k, l = 0, \ldots, R$ are defined by (3) and $a_{kl}$, $k, l = 0, \ldots, R$ are states of cells allocated by the $T_R(i, j)$. The term *totalistic CA* means that a new cell state is a function of the sum or a weighted sum of states of the cells belonging to the template.

There are two modes of application of a local operator to the cells of a CA: synchronous $\sigma$ and asynchronous $\alpha$ modes. In the synchronous mode, a local operator is applied to all the cells of the CA, all being updated simultaneously. Whereas the asynchronous mode of CA prescribes a local operator to be applied to a randomly chosen cell, changing its state immediately. Application of a local operator to all the cells of the CA is named *iteration*. An iteration transfers the cellular array $\Omega(t)$ into $\Omega(t + 1)$, where $t$ is an iteration number. The sequence $\sum(\Omega) = \Omega(0), \ldots, \Omega(t), \Omega(t + 1), \ldots, \Omega(t_{fin})$ is named *evolution*.

Simulation is performed for the initial cellular array $\Omega(0)$ with one and two nucleation cells. A nucleation cell is a cell in a state $a = 1$. A nucleation cell is situated in the center of the cellular array, other elements of the array being equal to zero.

## 3    The Stable Patterns Formation by CA Evolution

The above-defined CA exhibits self-organization properties. This means that after a number of iterations, the CA evolves to a *steady state*, notably, such that does not change or changes in no more than some number of cells [10]. Here, steady state may be one stable state of cellular array (fixed point) or pair of states which are alternated on each iteration (limit cycle). If the states $a = 1$ in $\Omega(t)$ are marked with black color, $a = 0$ – with white one, then $\Omega(t)$ is displayed as different black-and-white patterns which are named *motifs*. Some motifs of $\aleph$ evolution are shown in Fig. 1.

The main parameters affecting the CA evolution are the initial state $\Omega(0)$ and the weight matrix. The number of initial nucleation cells essentially affects the patterns formation. Further, the patterns formed with a single initial nucleation cell are investigated, although some patterns formed of two nucleation cells are presented below in Sect. 4. It is revealed that for fixed array size and initial state, the pattern motif is uniquely determined by the ratio of activator to inhibitor. This statement is proved by the following theorem.

**Theorem 1.** *Evolution of the totalistic CA with weighted templates for a specified initial state and a cellular array size is uniquely determined by the ratio $\frac{p}{n}$. Identical patterns are formed for the same value of $\frac{p}{n}$.*

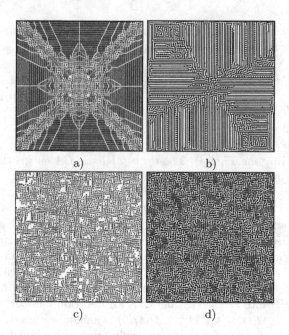

**Fig. 1.** Motifs are formed by $\aleph$ evolution from one nucleation cell with $M_i \times M_j = 500 \times 500$ cells and $R = 7$ for the synchronous mode: a) $n = -1, p = 0.56$, b) $n = -1, p = 0.9$ and asynchronous mode: c) $n = -1, p = 0.5$, d) $n = -1, p = 1$

*Proof.* Let us consider application of $\Theta(i,j)$ to a cell $(i,j) \in X$. According to (4), a new state of the cell $(i,j)$ depends on the sum $s$:

$$
s = n \cdot \left( \sum_{|k| \leq \lfloor R/2 \rfloor} a_{(i-\lfloor R/2 \rfloor),k} + \sum_{|k| \leq \lfloor R/2 \rfloor} a_{k,(j-\lfloor R/2 \rfloor)} + \sum_{|k| \leq \lfloor R/2 \rfloor} a_{k,(j+\lfloor R/2 \rfloor)} + \right.
$$
$$
\left. + \sum_{|k| \leq \lfloor R/2 \rfloor} a_{(i+\lfloor R/2 \rfloor),k} \right) + p \cdot \left( \sum_{|k| < \lfloor R/2 \rfloor} \sum_{|l| < \lfloor R/2 \rfloor} a_{k,l} \right) = n \cdot OUT + p \cdot IN
$$

$$(5)$$

Then a new state of the cell $(i,j)$ is as follows:

$$
a' = \begin{cases} 0, \text{ if } (n \cdot OUT + p \cdot IN) > 0 \\ 1, \text{ otherwise.} \end{cases} \Rightarrow \begin{cases} 0, \text{ if } -\dfrac{p}{n} \leq \dfrac{OUT}{IN} \\ 1, \text{ otherwise.} \end{cases} \quad (6)
$$

Consequently, a new value of the cell state depends on the ratio $\dfrac{p}{n}$ and does not depend on the specific values of activator and inhibitor. The theorem is proved.                                                                    □

## 4    Results of Computational Experiments

Computational experiments were performed for a cellular array of the size of $M_i \times M_j = 500 \times 500$ cells and template size $R = 7$, $T_7(i, j)$. The initial state is a single nucleation cell in the center of cellular array. Periodic boundary condition is used. Both synchronous and asynchronous modes were tested.

As a result of the CA simulation, many different stable patterns such as fancy figures, spots, strips, diamonds, crosses and other geometric figures are formed. *Stable patterns* are named the motifs obtained in a steady state of the CA evolution. To analyze and to classify these patterns, the following quantitative characteristics are introduced:

- The number of ones $N(1)$ and the number of zeros $N(0)$.
- Convergence time $Conv$ is the number of iterations which is needed for the evolution to become stable;
- The number of connected components for ones $L(1)$ and zeros $L(0)$. A connected component is a maximal subset of cells in the state "one" ("zero"), all having a path to each cell in this subset. Here the path is a sequence of cells in the state "one" ("zero") such that each next cell is neighboring for a previous one.
- Percolation along ones $Per(1)$ and zeros $Per(0)$ in the vertical and horizontal directions. Percolation is the number of connected components containing two cells belonging to different borders of a cellular array.
- Tortuosity $Tor$ is the number of angles on the borders of the connected components.

According to Theorem 1, the key parameter of the patterns formation process is the absolute value of the coefficients ratio $\frac{p}{n}$. Identical ratios form identical patterns. Therefore, it is sufficient to investigate the dependence of CA evolution on values $p$ assuming $n = -1$.

Stable patterns formed as a result of the evolution of *the synchronous CA* ($\aleph_\sigma$) for different values $p$ are shown in Fig. 2.

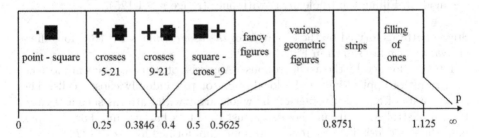

**Fig. 2.** Stable patterns formed as a result of the synchronous CA evolutions for different values of $p$

A steady state of the synchronous CA $\aleph_\sigma$ is alternation of two patterns on each iteration. For example, alternation of two geometric figures: a square and a cross, arises at $p \in (0.4; 0.5]$. In this case evolution is as follows. On first iteration, a square is formed of a nucleation cell. On the next iteration, a cross is formed of the square. Then the square is formed again, et cetera. Such an alternation occurs also for fancy figures and strips, though in this case a few cells states change, but not the whole pattern (Fig. 3). Many different crosses are formed by the evolution of $\aleph_\sigma$. These crosses are named as it is shown in Fig. 3. For example, the pattern name "crosses 5-21" denotes alternation of the cross of 5 ones and the cross of 21 ones. The range $p \in (0.5625; 0.8751)$ comprises a some small ranges of various geometric figures alternation.

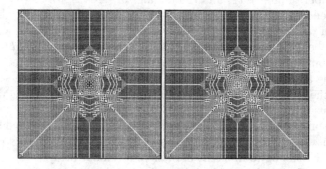

**Fig. 3.** Alternation of two fancy figures for $p = 0.501$

Analyzing the evolutions of $\aleph_\sigma$, three modes of behavior can be defined:

- mode 1. Alternation of two geometric figures (range $p \in [0; 0.5] \bigcup (0.5625; 0.8751)$);

- mode 2. Formation of various fancy figures and strips spreading over the whole cellular array (range $p \in (0.5; 0.5625] \bigcup [0.8751; 1.125]$);

- mode 3. Filling the whole array with ones (range $p > 1.125$).

Stable patterns formed by the evolution of *the asynchronous CA* ($\aleph_\alpha$) for different values of $p$ are shown in Fig. 4.

Patterns formed by the asynchronous CA consist of strokes, which are formed as a result of application of the local operator to randomly chosen cells. The steady state of $\aleph_\alpha$ is a coverage of the whole array with patterns such as figures formed of strokes, strips and points against the black background. For example, fancy figures consisting of strokes and points are formed for $p < 0.1429$.

Analyzing the evolutions of $\aleph_\alpha$, the following modes of behavior are defined:

- mode 1. Formation of black patterns against the white background, $N(0) > N(1)$, $p \in [0; 1]$;

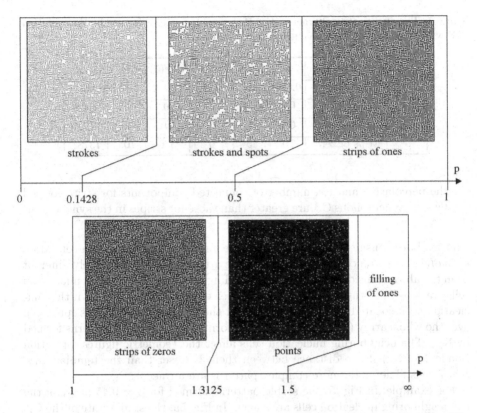

**Fig. 4.** Stable patterns formed as a result of the asynchronous CA evolutions for different values of $p$

- mode 2. Formation of white patterns against the black background, $N(0) < N(1)$, $p \in (1; 1.5]$;

- mode 3. Filling the whole cellular array with ones, $p > 1.5$.

In Table 1, some quantitative characteristics of the stable patterns are presented. For the synchronous mode, characteristics of fancy figures and strips are shown. For the asynchronous mode, characteristics of strips of ones and strips of zeros are given.

As a result of comparing characteristics of stable patterns formed by the evolutions of synchronous and asynchronous CA (Table 1), the following conclusions are made:

1. the convergence time of the CA with asynchronous mode is less than the convergence time of the CA with synchronous mode;

2. the number of connected components and the tortuosity for fancy figures formed by the synchronous CA are greater than those for other patterns formed by the synchronous and asynchronous CA;

**Table 1.** The quantitative characteristics of the stable patterns formed by the evolution of ℵ with synchronous $\sigma$ and asynchronous $\alpha$ modes

| mode | stable pattern | $p$ | $Conv$ | $Per(0)$ | $Per(1)$ | $L(1)$ | $Tor$ |
|---|---|---|---|---|---|---|---|
| $\sigma$ | fancy figures | 0.501 | 293 | 206 | 0 | 40637 | 162117 |
| $\sigma$ | strips | 0.9 | 524 | 3 | 51 | 105 | 5098 |
| $\alpha$ | strips of ones | 0.9 | 86 | 230 | 0 | 2699 | 21035 |
| $\alpha$ | strips of zeros | 1.1 | 45 | 0 | 336 | 105 | 13781 |

3. the percolation and the number of connected components for strips formed by the asynchronous CA are greater than those for stripes in the synchronous CA.

All the above-considered stable patterns are formed of one nucleation cell. More than one nucleation cell allows us to create patterns that are absolutely different from the above-considered patterns. Depending on a distance between nucleation cells, various patterns are formed. Computer experiments have shown that nucleation cells, located at any distance, affect the formation of patterns spreading over the whole array (fancy figures, stripes formed by ℵ$_\sigma$ and all patterns formed by ℵ$_\alpha$). The neighboring nucleation cells affect the geometric figures formation (mode 1 of ℵ$_\sigma$) if the distance between them is lesser than the template size $S \leq 7$ cells. Therefore, more complex patterns are formed.

For example, in Fig. 5, the stable patterns formed for $p = 0.45$ of ℵ$_\sigma$ of the two neighboring nucleation cells are shown. In Fig. 5a, the stable state of the CA evolution for the nucleation cells located at the distance along a horizontal axis $S_x = 2$ and along a vertical axis $S_y = 3$ is given. Alternation of two CA states on even and odd iterations is observed. In Fig. 5b, alternation of geometric figures, formed of nucleation cells situated at $S_x = 3$ and $S_y = 4$, is presented.

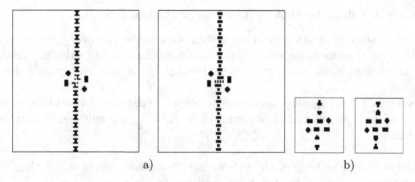

a)                                                              b)

**Fig. 5.** Stable patterns formed of the two neighboring nucleation cells located at the distance a) $S_x = 2$ and $S_y = 3$; b) $S_x = 3$ and $S_y = 4$

# 5    Conclusion

In this paper the evolution of the totalistic CA with weighted templates for one nucleation cell in the initial condition is investigated. The variety of stable patterns such as fancy figures, spots, strips, diamonds, crosses and other geometric figures is obtained by computer experiments. The dependence of stable patterns on values of weight matrix coefficients is studied. It has been revealed and proved that for the fixed array size and initial state, the pattern formation is uniquely determined by the ratio $\frac{p}{n}$ (Theorem 1).

To analyze stable patterns, the quantitative characteristics such as convergence time, the number of connected components, the percolation and the tortuosity were calculated for various values of $p$. As a result of studying evolutions of $\aleph$, three modes of behavior for $\aleph_\sigma$ and $\aleph_\alpha$ have been defined.

The stable patterns formed by $\aleph_\sigma$ and $\aleph_\alpha$ essentially differ. A distinguishing feature of stable patterns formed by the asynchronous mode is the pattern spreading over the whole cellular array for any value of $p$. Whereas in terms of the synchronous mode, for the majority of values $p$, formation of bounded geometric figures is observed.

The stable patterns formation for two neighboring nucleation cells is studied as well. It is obtained that stable patterns formed of two nucleation cells are essentially different from those formed of one cell. The dependence of the nucleation cells location on the patterns formation is investigated.

Studying patterns formed by the evolution of CA with weighted templates is useful for understanding the basic mechanisms of the formation of spatial structures in complex non-equilibrium systems.

# References

[1]   Turing, A.M.: The Chemical Basis of Morphogenesis. Philosophical Transactions of the Royal Society of London. Series B, Biological Sciences 237(641), 37–72 (1952)

[2]   Young, D.A.: A local activator-inhibitor model of vertebrate skin patterns. In: Wolfram, S. (ed.) Theory and Applications of Cellular Automata. Advanced series on complex systems, vol. 1, pp. 320–327 (1986)

[3]   Imbihl, R., Ertl, G.: Oscillatory kinetics in heterogeneous catalysis. Chemical Reviews 95, 697–733 (1995)

[4]   Zaikin, A.N., Zhabotinsky, A.M.: Concentration wave propogation in a two-dimensional, liquid phase self-oscillating system. Nature 225, 535 (1970)

[5]   Vanag, V.K.: Dissociative structures in reaction-diffusion systems. In: Regular and Chaotic Dynamics. Institute of computer researches, M - Izhevsk, p. 300 (2008)

[6]   Deutsch, A., Dormann, S.: Cellular Automaton Modeling of Biological Pattern Formation. In: Modeling and Simulation in Science, Engineering and Technology, Boston, p. 331 (2005)

[7]   Chua, L.O.: CNN: a paradigm for complexity. World scintific series on nonlinear scince, Series A, vol. 31, p. 320 (1998)

[8]   Wolfram, S.: A New Kind of Science. Wolfram Media (2002) ISBN 1-57955-008-8
[9]   Bandman, O.L.: Cellular Automatic Models of Spatial Dynamics. System Informatics - Methods and Models of Modern Programming 10, 59–113 (2006)
[10]  Bandman, O.L.: Method of construction of cellular-automatic models of stable patterns formation processes. Prikladnaya Diskretnaya Matematika 4, 91–99 (2010)

# Recent Developments in Constructing Square Synchronizers

Hiroshi Umeo* and Keisuke Kubo

Univ. of Osaka Electro-Communication,
Neyagawa-shi, Hastu-cho, 18-8, Osaka, 572-8530, Japan
umeo@cyt.osakac.ac.jp

**Abstract.** The firing squad synchronization problem (FSSP) on cellular automata has been studied extensively for more than fifty years, and a rich variety of synchronization algorithms have been proposed. In the present paper, we focus our attention to two-dimensional square synchronizers that can synchronize square arrays and construct a survey on recent developments in their designs and implementations of optimum-time synchronization algorithms for square arrays. A new generalized square synchronization algorithm with an initial general at any position is also presented.

## 1 Introduction

The synchronization in cellular automata has been known as a firing squad synchronization problem (FSSP) since its development, in which it was originally proposed by J. Myhill in Moore [1964] to synchronize all parts of self-reproducing cellular automata. The problem has been studied extensively for more than fifty years [1-22].

In the present paper, we focus our attention to two-dimensional square synchronizers that can synchronize square arrays and construct a survey on recent developments in designs and implementations of optimum-time synchronization algorithms for square arrays. The square is a special class of two-dimensional arrays. For a long time there exists only one FSSP algorithm: an algorithm based on rotated L-shaped mapping on 2-D square arrays proposed by Beyer [1969] and Shinar [1974]. However, nowadays we have a rich variety of square synchronizers, which will be discussed in this paper. Specifically, we attempt to consider the following questions:

- Is there any new FSSP algorithm other than the classical Shinahr's one?
- What is the smallest, i.e. smallest number of states in its realization, square synchronizer?
- How can we synchronize squares with the general at any position?

The square synchronization algorithms discussed herein are the first seventeen-state algorithm proposed by Shinahr [1974], its nine-state improved version

---

* Corresponding author.

G.C. Sirakoulis and S. Bandini (Eds.): ACRI 2012, LNCS 7495, pp. 171–183, 2012.

given in Umeo, Maeda, and Fujiwara [2002], and a seven-state implementation presented in Umeo and Kubo [2010], which is a smallest implementation of the optimum-time square FSSP algorithm, known at present. In addition, two optimum-time synchronization algorithms for square arrays are also discussed, where the algorithmic design schema employed is quite different from previous ones. The first one is based on a diagonal mapping and the second is based on one-sided recursive-halving marking presented in Umeo, Uchino and Nomura [2011]. In the last, we present a new generalized square synchronization algorithm that can synchronize any square arrays of size $n \times n$ in $2n - 2$ step, where an initial general is situated at any position in the array. The proposed generalized algorithm includes Shinahr's classical square FSSP algorithm (Shinahr [1970]) as a special case where the initial general is on one corner of the array. Due to the space available we omit the details of those algorithms and their implementations.

## 2    Firing Squad Synchronization Problem

### 2.1    FSSP on One-Dimensional Array

The firing squad synchronization problem (FSSP, for short) is formalized in terms of the model of cellular automata. Consider a one-dimensional (1-D) array of finite state automata. All cells (except the end cells) are identical finite state automata. The array operates in lock-step mode such that the next state of each cell (except the end cells) is determined by both its own present state and the present states of its right and left neighbors. Thus, we assume the nearest left and right neighbors. All cells (*soldiers*), except one *general* cell, are initially in the *quiescent* state at time $t = 0$ and have the property whereby the next state of a quiescent cell having quiescent neighbors is the quiescent state. At time $t = 0$ the *general* cell is in the *fire-when-ready* state, which is an initiation signal to the array.

The FSSP is stated as follows: Given a one-dimensional array of $n$ identical cellular automata, including a *general* at one end that is activated at time $t = 0$, we want to design the automaton $M = (Q, \delta)$ such that, *at some future time*, all the cells will *simultaneously* and, *for the first time*, enter a special *firing* state, where $Q$ is a finite state set and $\delta : Q^3 \to Q$ is a next-state function. The tricky part of the problem is that the same kind of soldier having a fixed number of states must be synchronized, regardless of length $n$ of the array. The set of states and the next state function must be independent of $n$.

The problem was first solved by J. McCarthy and M. Minsky who presented a $3n$-step algorithm for one-dimensional cellular array of length $n$. In 1962, the first optimum-time, i.e. $(2n - 2)$-step, synchronization algorithm was presented by Goto [1962], with each cell having several thousands of states. Afterward, Waksman [1966], Balzer [1967], Gerken [1987], and Mazoyer [1987] presented a 16-state, an 8-state, a 7-state, and a 6-state optimum-time synchronization algorithm, respectively, thus decreasing the number of states required for the synchronization. In the sequel we use the following theorem as a base algorithm in the design of square algorithms.

**Theorem 1.** Goto [1962], Waksman [1966] There exists a cellular automaton that can synchronize any one-dimensional array of length $n$ in optimum $2n - 2$ steps, where an initial general is located at a left or right end.

### 2.2  FSSP on Two-Dimensional Square Cellular Array

A finite two-dimensional (2-D) square array consists of $n \times n$ cells. Each cell is an identical (except the border cells) finite-state automaton. The array operates in lock-step mode in such a way that the next state of each cell (except border cells) is determined by both its own present state and the present states of its north, south, east and west neighbors. Thus, we assume the von Neumann-type four nearest neighbors. All cells (*soldiers*), except the north-west corner cell (*general*), are initially in the quiescent state at time $t = 0$ with the property that the next state of a quiescent cell with quiescent neighbors is the quiescent state again. At time $t = 0$, the north-west corner cell $C_{11}$ is in the *fire-when-ready* state, which is the initiation signal for synchronizing the array. The firing squad synchronization problem is to determine a description (state set and next-state function) for cells that ensures all cells enter the *fire* state at exactly the same time and for the first time.

One can easily see that it takes $2n - 2$ steps for any signal to travel from $C_{11}$ to $C_{nn}$ due to the von Neumann neighborhood. Concerning the time optimality of the two-dimensional square synchronization algorithms, the following theorems have been established.

**Theorem 2.** Beyer [1969], Shinahr [1974] There exists no cellular automaton that can synchronize any two-dimensional square array of size $n \times n$ in less than $2n - 2$ steps, where the general is located at one corner of the array.

**Theorem 3.** Shinahr [1974] There exists a 17-state cellular automaton that can synchronize any two-dimensional square array of size $n \times n$ at exactly $2n - 2$ optimum steps.

## 3  Time-Optimum Square Synchronization Algorithms

### 3.1  Rotated L-Shaped Mapping Based Algorithm $\mathcal{A}_1$

The first square synchronization algorithm was developed independently by Beyer [1969] and Shinahr [1974]. It is based on a simple mapping which embeds a 1-D optimum-time FSSP algorithm onto rotated L-shaped sub-arrays composing a square. We refer the embedding as *rotated L-shaped mapping*. The algorithm operates as follows: By dividing an entire square array of size $n \times n$ into $n$ rotated L-shaped 1-D arrays, shown in Fig. 1 (left), in such a way that the length of the $i$th (from outside) L-shaped array is $2n - 2i + 1$ $(1 \leq i \leq n)$. One treats the square synchronization as $n$ independent 1-D synchronizations with the general located at the bending point of the L-shaped array. We denote the $i$th L-shaped array by $L_i$ and its horizontal and vertical segment is denoted by $L_i^h$ and $L_i^v$, respectively. Note that a cell at each bending point of the L-shaped array is shared for each synchronization by the two segments. Concerning the synchronization of $L_i$, it can be easily seen that a general is generated by the cell $C_{ii}$ at time $t = 2i - 2$ with the four nearest von-Neumann neighborhood communication, and the general initiates the horizontal (row) and vertical (column) synchronizations on $L_i^h$ and $L_i^v$, each of length $n - i + 1$ using an optimum-time synchronization algorithm which can synchronize arrays of length $\ell$ in $2\ell - 2$ steps (Theorem 1). For each $i$, $1 \leq i \leq n$, the $i$th L-shaped array $L_i$ can be synchronized at time $t = 2i - 2 + 2(n - i + 1) - 2 = 2n - 2$. Thus the square array of size $n \times n$ can be synchronized at time $t = 2n - 2$ in optimum-steps. In Fig. 1 (left), each general is represented by a black circle • in a shaded square and a wake-up signal for the synchronization generated by the general is indicated by a horizontal and vertical arrow.

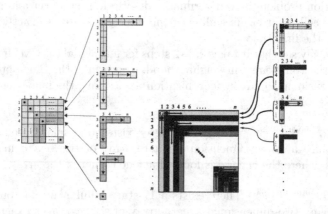

**Fig. 1.** A synchronization scheme based on *rotated L-shaped mapping* (left) and its variant: *zebra mapping* (right) for an $n \times n$ square cellular automaton

Shinahr [1974] gave a 17-state implementation based on Balzer's eight-state synchronization algorithm (Balzer [1967]). Later, it has been shown in Umeo, Maeda and Fujiwara [2002] that nine states are sufficient for the optimum-time square synchronization:

**Theorem 4.** [Umeo et al. 2002] There exists a nine-state 2-D CA that can synchronize any $n \times n$ square array in $2n - 2$ steps.

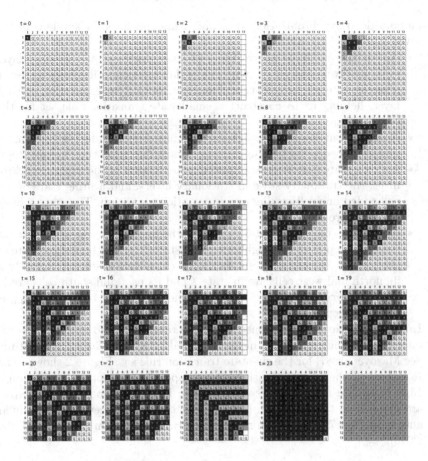

**Fig. 2.** Snapshots of the seven-state synchronizer on a $13 \times 13$ array

## 3.2   Zebra Mapping Based Algorithm $\mathcal{A}_2$

In this section we consider a state-efficient optimum-time square synchronization algorithm $\mathcal{A}_2$ proposed in Umeo and Kubo [2010]. The algorithm is a variant of the L-shaped mapping.

– **Zebra Mapping**

The proposed algorithm is basically based on the rotated L-shaped mapping scheme presented in the previous section. However, it is quite different from it in the following point. The mapping onto square arrays consists of two types of configurations: one is a one-cell smaller synchronized configuration and the other is a filled-in configuration with a stationary state. The stationary state remains unchanged once filled-in by the time before the final synchronization. Each configuration is mapped alternatively onto an L-shaped array *in a zebra-like fashion*. The mapping is referred to as *zebra mapping*. Figure 1 (right) illustrates the zebra mapping which consists of an embedded synchronization layer and a filled-in layer. A key idea of the seven-state implementation is:

- Alternative mapping of two types of configurations. A stationary layer separates two consecutive synchronization layers and it allows us to use a single state set for the vertical and horizontal synchronization on each layer, helping us to construct a small-state transition rule set for the synchronization layers.
- A one-cell smaller synchronization configuration than the L-shaped mapping is embedded, where we can save synchronization time by two steps.
- A single state X is used as an initial general state of the square synchronizer, the stationary state in stationary layers, and a firing state of the embedded one-cell-smaller synchronization algorithm. The state X itself acts as a pre-firing state.
- Any cell in state X, except $C_{n,n}$, enters the final synchronization state at the next step if all its neighbors are in state X or the boundary state of the square. The cell $C_{n,n}$ enters the synchronization state if and only if its north and west cells are in state X and its east and south cells are in the boundary state. A cell in state X that is adjacent to the cell $C_{n,n}$ is also an exception.

- **Implementation:** In our construction we take the Mazoyer's 6-state one-dimensional synchronization rule as an embedded synchronization algorithm. See Mazoyer [1987] for the six-state transition rule set. Figure 2 shows some snapshots of the synchronization process operating in optimum-steps on a $13 \times 13$ square array. The readers can see how those configuration layers are mapped in the zebra-like fashion. The constructed seven-state cellular automaton has 787 transition rules, which can be found in Umeo and Kubo [2010].

We have:

**Theorem 5.** [Umeo and Kubo [2010]] The seven-state synchronization algorithm $\mathcal{A}_2$ can synchronize any $n \times n$ square array in optimum $2n - 2$ steps.

## 3.3   Diagonal Mapping Based Algorithm $\mathcal{A}_3$

In this section we study a synchronization algorithm based on diagonal mapping. With the diagonal mapping, configurations of 1-D cellular array with a general located at its center can be embedded onto a square array divided along the principal diagonal. We divide $n^2$ cells on a square array of size $n \times n$ into $2n - 1$ groups $g_k$, $-(n-1) \leq k \leq n-1$ along the principal diagonal such that:

$$g_k = \{C_{i,j} | j - i = k\}, \ -(n-1) \leq k \leq n-1.$$

Each cell in $g_k$ on the 2-D square simulates the state of its corresponding cell $C_k$ in the 1-D array of length $2n - 1$, $-(n-1) \leq k \leq n-1$. It has been shown in Umeo, Hisaoka, and Akiguchi [2005] that any 1-D generalized FSSP algorithm with an Inner-Independent Property $\mathcal{Z}$ (below) can be easily embedded onto two-dimensional rectangle arrays *without introducing additional states*. The statement can also be applied to square arrays.

*Inner-Independent Property $\mathcal{Z}$*: Let $S_i^t$ denote the state of $C_i$ at step $t$. We say that an FSSP algorithm has *Inner-Independent Property $\mathcal{Z}$*, where any state $S_i^t$ appearing *in the area $\mathcal{Z}$* can be computed from its left and right neighbor states $S_{i-1}^{t-1}$ and $S_{i+1}^{t-1}$ but it never depends on its own previous state $S_i^{t-1}$.

It can be shown that there exists a 15-state cellular automaton with the *Inner-Independent Property $\mathcal{Z}$* that can synchronize any 1-D arrays of length $2n - 1$ in $2n - 2$ steps, where an initial general is situated at the center of the 1-D array. The 15-state algorithm with the property $\mathcal{Z}$ can be embedded on any square arrays without introducing additional states, yielding an optimum-time square synchronization algorithm.

**Theorem 6.** The synchronization algorithm $\mathcal{A}_3$ can synchronize any $n \times n$ square array in optimum $2n - 2$ steps.

### 3.4 One-Sided Recursive-Halving Marking Based Algorithm $\mathcal{A}_4$

We present an optimum-time square synchronization algorithm $\mathcal{A}_4$ which is quite different from the previous designs. The algorithm is based on a marking called *one-sided recursive-halving marking*. The marking scheme prints a special mark on cells in a cellular space defined by one-sided recursive-halving.

Let $S$ be a one-dimensional cellular space consisting of cells $C_i$, $C_{i+1}$, ..., $C_j$, denoted by $[i...j]$, where $j > i$. Let $|S|$ denote the number of cells in $S$, that is $|S| = j - i + 1$ for $S = [i...j]$. A cell $C_x$ in $S$, where $x = (i + j)/2$, is a center cell of $S$, if $|S|$ is odd. Otherwise, two cells $C_x$ and $C_{x+1}$, $x = (i + j - 1)/2$, are center cells of $S$.

The one-sided recursive-halving marking for a given cellular space $[1...n]$ is defined as follows:

```
┌─ One-sided Recursive-Halving Marking ──────────────────

     begin
        S := [1...n];
        while |S| > 1 do
           if |S| is odd then
              mark a center cell Cₓ in S
                 S := [x...n];
           else
              mark center cells Cₓ and Cₓ₊₁ in S
                 S := [x + 1...n];
     end

└──────────────────────────────────────────────
```

It can be easily seen that any 1-D cellular space of length $n$ with the one-sided recursive-halving marking initially can be synchronized in optimum $n-1$ steps.

Now we consider a square array of size $n \times n$ with an initial general G on $C_{11}$. The square is regarded as consisting of two triangles: upper and lower halves separated by a diagonal. Each upper and lower half triangle consists of $n$ columns and $n$ rows, each denoted by $c_k$ and $r_k$, $1 \leq k \leq n$, such that:

$$c_k = \{C_{ik} \mid 1 \leq i \leq k\}, \qquad r_k = \{C_{kj} \mid 1 \leq j \leq k\}.$$

An overview of the algorithm $\mathcal{A}_4$ is:

- Each upper and lower half triangle is synchronized independently.
- At time $t = 0$ the array begins to prepare printing the one-sided recursive halving mark on each column and row, each starting from top of each column and a left end of each row, respectively, in the triangles. The marking operation will be finished before the arrival of the first wake-up signal for the synchronization.
- Simultaneously, the general generates two signals $s_H$ and $s_V$ at time $t = 0$. Their operations are as follows:

  • **Signal $s_H$:**  The $s_H$-signal travels along the 1st row at 1/1-speed and reaches $C_{1n}$ at time $t = n - 1$. Then it reflects there and returns the same route at 1/1-speed, and reaches $C_{11}$ again at time $t = 2n - 2$. On the return way, it generates a general on $C_{1i}$ at time $t = n - 1 + n - (i - 1) = 2n - i$, at every visit of $C_{1i}$, where $1 \leq i \leq n$. The general initiates a synchronization for the $i$th column, and yields a successful synchronization at time $t = 2n - 2$. Note that the length of the $i$th column is $i$ and the synchronization is started at time $t = 2n - i$, for any $1 \leq i \leq n$. In this way, the upper half triangle can be synchronized in $2n - 2$ steps.

  • **Signal $s_V$:**  The $s_V$-signal travels along the 1st column at 1/1-speed and reaches $C_{n1}$ at time $t = n-1$. Then it reflects there and returns the same route at 1/1-speed, and reaches $C_{11}$ again at time $t = 2n - 2$. On the return way, it generates a general on $C_{i1}$ at time $t = n-1+n-(i-1) = 2n - i$, at every visit of $C_{i1}$, where $1 \leq i \leq n$. The general initiates a synchronization for the $i$th row. Note that the length of the $i$th row is $i$. The $i$th row can be synchronized at time $t = 2n-2$, for any $i$, $1 \leq i \leq n$. Thus, the lower half triangle can be synchronized in $2n - 2$ steps.

We have implemented the marking scheme for the upper half triangle on a two-dimensional cellular automaton. The constructed cellular automaton has 14 internal states and 540 transition rules. See Umeo, Uchino and Nomura [2011] for details. It can be seen that all cells in the upper half are synchronized in $2n - 2$ steps. The synchronization in the lower half can be done similarly. Thus we have:

**Theorem 7.** Umeo, Uchino, and Nomura [2011] The synchronization algorithm $\mathcal{A}_4$ can synchronize any $n \times n$ square array in optimum $2n - 2$ steps.

We implemented the algorithm $\mathcal{A}_4$ on a two-dimensional cellular automaton. The constructed cellular automaton has 37 internal states and 3271 transition rules.

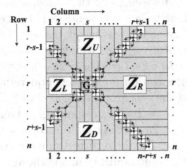

**Fig. 3.** A square array of size $n \times n$ with a general $C_{r,s}$ is decomposed into four sub-arrays by two perpendicular lines intersecting at $C_{r,s}$

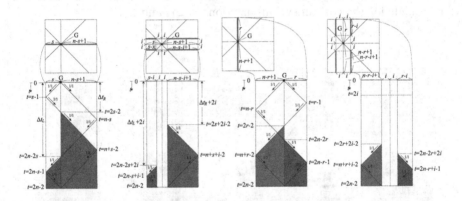

**Fig. 4.** Space-time diagram for the row and column synchronizations in each sub-array

### 3.5   Generalized Synchronization Algorithm $\mathcal{A}_5$

In this section, we propose a generalized square synchronization algorithm $\mathcal{A}_5$ that can synchronize any square arrays of size $n \times n$ with a general at an arbitrary position $C_{r,s}$ in the square in exactly $2n - 2$ steps, where $1 \leq r, s \leq n$. An overview of the algorithm $\mathcal{A}_5$ is as follows: A square array of size $n \times n$ with an initial general $C_{r,s}$, $1 \leq r, s \leq n$, is decomposed into four sub-arrays by two perpendicular lines which intersect at $C_{r,s}$. See Fig. 3. We consider the synchronization in the case $1 \leq s \leq r, s + r \leq n + 1$, where the general is situated in the left quarter triangle area circulated by two perpendicular diagonals of the square. Other cases can be treated in a similar way. We denote those four sub-arrays by $\mathcal{Z}_U$, $\mathcal{Z}_R$, $\mathcal{Z}_D$, $\mathcal{Z}_L$ in the clockwise direction, respectively, shown in Fig. 3. The right and left sub-arrays $\mathcal{Z}_R$, $\mathcal{Z}_L$ are regarded as $n$, $2s + 1$ rows, respectively. The upper and lower sub-arrays $\mathcal{Z}_U$, $\mathcal{Z}_D$ are regarded as $r + s - 1$, $n - r + s$ colums, respectively. At time $t = 0$, the general sends out a 1/1-speed signal in each diagonal direction in order to decompose the square into four sub-arrays shown in Fig. 3. First we consider the synchronization for the $r$th row in $\mathcal{Z}_R$ and $\mathcal{Z}_L$. The general, at time $t = 0$, sends a 1/1-speed signal along the $r$th row in both directions. The signal reaches at the left and right border at time $t = s - 1$ and $t = n - s$, respectively, and it reflects there and returns back to the general at time $t = \Delta t_L = 2n - 2s$, $t = \Delta t_R = 2s - 2$, respectively. Each returned signal initiates the synchronization for the left and right row segment each of length $s$, $n - s + 1$, yielding the synchronization at time $t = \Delta t_L + 2s - 2 = 2n - 2$, $t = \Delta t_R + 2(n - s + 1) - 2 = 2n - 2$, respectively. Thus, the $r$th row can be synchronization at time $t = 2n - 2$. As for the rows which are located $i$ rows apart from the $r$th row in $\mathcal{Z}_R$, $\mathcal{Z}_L$, the returned signal travels along each diagonal at 1/1-speed to initiate the synchronizations for those $r - i$, $(r + i)$th rows. It takes additional $2i$ steps to reach the row segments of length $s - i$, $n - s - i + 1$, yielding the synchronization at time $t = \Delta t_L + 2i + 2(s - i) - 2 = 2n - 2$, $t = \Delta t_R + 2i + 2(n - s - i + 1) - 2 = 2n - 2$, respectively. Thus, the $r - i$, $(r + i)$th rows can be synchronization at time $t = 2n - 2$. A similar discussion can be made for the column synchronizations in $\mathcal{Z}_U$ and $\mathcal{Z}_D$

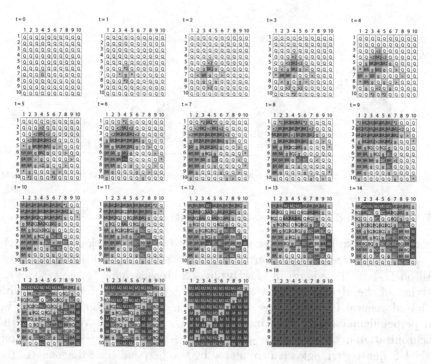

**Fig. 5.** Snapshots of the synchronization process in $\mathcal{A}_5$ on $10 \times 10$ array. The initial general is on $C_{7\ 4}$.

Figure 4 shows the space-time diagram for those row and column synchronizations. All of the row and column segments are synchronized at time $t = 2n - 2$. No generalized square synchronization algorithm has been known so far. It is noted that the synchronization time required by the algorithm $\mathcal{A}_5$ is independent of the general's position. It remains an open problem whether the time complexity $2n - 2$ is a lower bound for the generalized square synchronization problem. A finite-state implementation of the algorithm $\mathcal{A}_5$ has been made. The constructed cellular automaton has 40 internal states and 11210 transition rules. Figures 5 shows some snapshots of the synchronization process with an initial general at $C_{7\ 4}$ on $10 \times 10$ square arrays. Our generalized square synchronization algorithm $\mathcal{A}_5$ includes Shinahr's classical square FSSP algorithm (Shinahr [1970]) as a special case where the initial general is on one corner of the array.

**Theorem 8.** The generalized synchronization algorithm $\mathcal{A}_5$ can synchronize any $n \times n$ square array in $2n - 2$ steps.

## 4   Conclusions

In this paper, we have presented a survey on recent developments of optimum-time square synchronizers that can synchronize any $n \times n$ two-dimensional square arrays in $2n - 2$ steps. Umeo and Yanagihara [2011] presented an optimum-time FSSP algorithm for 1-bit communication cellular automata. The 1-bit communication model is a subclass of the O(1)-bit model, in which inter-cell communication is restricted to 1-bit communication. The O(1)-bit communication model, discussed in this paper, is a usual cellular automaton in which the amount of communication bits exchanged in one step between neighboring cells is assumed to be O(1) bits. Most of the algorithms presented are based on efficient mapping schemes for embedding some one-dimensional optimum-time firing squad synchronization algorithms onto 2-D square arrays. Similar ideas can be employed for the 1-bit communication models. The readers can see how a rich variety of 2-D FSSP algorithms exists, even in the square case. Some algorithms can be easily extended to three-dimensional arrays, yielding an optimum-time $(3n - 3)$-step FSSP algorithm for cubes of size $n \times n \times n$. The embedding schemes developed in this paper would be useful for state-efficient implementation of multi-dimensional synchronization algorithms.

**Acknowledgments.** A part of this work is supported by Grant-in-Aid for Scientific Research (C) 21500023.

## References

1. Balzer, R.: An 8-state minimal time solution to the firing squad synchronization problem. Information and Control 10, 22–42 (1967)
2. Beyer, W.T.: Recognition of topological invariants by iterative arrays. Ph.D. Thesis, MIT, pp. 144 (1969)

3. Goto, E.: A minimal time solution of the firing squad problem. Dittoed course notes for Applied Mathematics, vol. 298, pp. 52–59. Harvard University (1962)
4. Gruska, J., Torre, S.L., Parente, M.: The firing squad synchronization problem on squares, toruses and rings. Intern. J. of Foundations of Computer Science 18(3), 637–654 (2007)
5. Mazoyer, J.: A six-state minimal time solution to the firing squad synchronization problem. Theoretical Computer Science 50, 183–238 (1987)
6. Moore, E.F.: The firing squad synchronization problem. In: Moore, E.F. (ed.) Sequential Machines, Selected Papers, pp. 213–214. Addison-Wesley, Reading (1964)
7. Schmid, H.: Synchronisationsprobleme für zelluläre Automaten mit mehreren Generälen. Diplomarbeit, Universität Karsruhe (2003)
8. Schmid, H., Worsch, T.: The firing squad synchronization problem with many generals for one-dimensional CA. In: Proc. of IFIP World Congress, pp. 111–124 (2004)
9. Shinahr, I.: Two- and three-dimensional firing squad synchronization problems. Information and Control 24, 163–180 (1974)
10. Szwerinski, H.: Time-optimum solution of the firing-squad-synchronization-problem for $n$-dimensional rectangles with the general at an arbitrary position. Theoretical Computer Science 19, 305–320 (1982)
11. La Torre, S., Napoli, M., Parente, M.: Firing Squad Synchronization Problem on Bidimensional Cellular Automata with Communication Constraints. In: Margenstern, M., Rogozhin, Y. (eds.) MCU 2001. LNCS, vol. 2055, pp. 264–275. Springer, Heidelberg (2001)
12. Umeo, H.: Firing squad synchronization algorithms for two-dimensional cellular automata. Journal of Cellular Automata 4, 1–20 (2008)
13. Umeo, H.: Firing squad synchronization problem in cellular automata. In: Meyers, R.A. (ed.) Encyclopedia of Complexity and System Science, vol. 4, pp. 3537–3574. Springer (2009)
14. Umeo, H., Hisaoka, M., Akiguchi, S.: A Twelve-State Optimum-Time Synchronization Algorithm for Two-Dimensional Rectangular Cellular Arrays. In: Calude, C.S., Dinneen, M.J., Păun, G., Jesús Pérez-Jímenez, M., Rozenberg, G. (eds.) UC 2005. LNCS, vol. 3699, pp. 214–223. Springer, Heidelberg (2005)
15. Umeo, H., Hisaoka, M., Teraoka, M., Maeda, M.: Several New Generalized Linear- and Optimum-Time Synchronization Algorithms for Two-Dimensional Rectangular Arrays. In: Margenstern, M. (ed.) MCU 2004. LNCS, vol. 3354, pp. 223–232. Springer, Heidelberg (2005)
16. Umeo, H., Kubo, K.: A Seven-State Time-Optimum Square Synchronizer. In: Bandini, S., Manzoni, S., Umeo, H., Vizzari, G. (eds.) ACRI 2010. LNCS, vol. 6350, pp. 219–230. Springer, Heidelberg (2010)
17. Umeo, H., Maeda, M., Hisaoka, M., Teraoka, M.: A state-efficient mapping scheme for designing two-dimensional firing squad synchronization algorithms. Fundamenta Informaticae 74, 603–623 (2006)
18. Umeo, H., Nishide, K., Yamawaki, T.: A New Optimum-Time Firing Squad Synchronization Algorithm for Two-Dimensional Rectangle Arrays: One-Sided Recursive Halving Based. In: Löwe, B., Normann, D., Soskov, I., Soskova, A. (eds.) CiE 2011. LNCS, vol. 6735, pp. 290–299. Springer, Heidelberg (2011)
19. Umeo, H., Uchino, H.: A new time-optimum synchronization algorithm for rectangle arrays. Fundamenta Informaticae 87(2), 155–164 (2008)

20. Umeo, H., Uchino, H., Nomura, A.: How to synchronize square arrays in optimum-time. In: Proc. of the 2011 International Conference on High Performance Computing and Simulation (HPCS 2011), pp. 801–807. IEEE (2011)
21. Umeo, H., Yanagihara, T.: Smallest Implementations of Optimum-Time Firing Squad Synchronization Algorithms for One-Bit-Communication Cellular Automata. In: Malyshkin, V. (ed.) PaCT 2011. LNCS, vol. 6873, pp. 210–223. Springer, Heidelberg (2011)
22. Waksman, A.: An optimum solution to the firing squad synchronization problem. Information and Control 9, 66–78 (1966)

# Structural Operational Semantics
# for Cellular Automata

Baltasar Trancón y. Widemann

Computer Science & Ecological Modelling, University of Bayreuth, Germany

**Abstract.** The structural operational semantics approach to the dynamic meaning of formal models has been immensely influential as a foundation of both theoretical calculi and practical programming languages, and is a viable alternative to automata-oriented approaches. We report on an effort to apply the approach to cellular automata, in particular of the two-dimensional, regular finite grid kind that underlies many agent-based simulation models. We summarize previous, intensively category-theoretic work in more general terms, and discuss how various interesting properties are made (more) explicit by the semantical analysis of cellular automata in terms of novel mathematical structures.

## 1 Introduction

### 1.1 The Role of Semantics for Formal Models

Semantics is the mathematical study of the meaning of both concrete programming languages and abstract models of computation. As such, semantics assigns to one mathematical structure (the syntax of a language or the representation of a computing model) another mathematical structure (the intended conceptual objects, processes and/or propositions). Quite often multiple complementary semantics are given for a single language or model. If any one of them already captures the meaning, why would one do such a thing?

The main reason is that often one wants to make abstract universal statements about instances of a model, whether predicative such as "all expressions have property $P$" or relational such as "any expression of the form $f$ is behaviorally equivalent to the transformed expression $f'$". For such properties, being *determined* by a semantics is not at all the same as being *easily provable* by it. It is therefore the role of semantics to guide and inform the selection and application of mathematical reasoning adequate to the problem at hand.

Finding new and more useful mathematical structures for semantics has been a driving force behind disciplines of mathematics and theoretical computer science such as *domain theory*. When new structures or novel applications of known structures are discovered, it may be worthwhile to reconsider well-established models in a new semantical light. Of particular interest as generators of novel semantics are emerging concepts of the discipline of *category theory*, two of which have been applied very recently to cellular automata, and form the methodological context for the present article.

G.C. Sirakoulis and S. Bandini (Eds.): ACRI 2012, LNCS 7495, pp. 184–193, 2012.

## 1.2   Research Context

The earlier of the two related studies is the application of *comonads* to *one-dimensional* cellular automata by Capobianco and Uustalu [1]. Defining comonads in an accessible form is way beyond the scope of this article. All we can say is that they are the categorical dual (conceptual mirror image) of the more familiar, but likewise categorical concept of *monads*, which have been used pervasively in semantics during the last two decades, starting with the seminal work of Moggi [4].

The later, more closely related work by ourselves [8] is the application of *bialgebras* to *two-dimensional* cellular automata and, by extension, to a class of *agent-based models* (ABMs) popular in complex system sciences. In a nutshell, bialgebras are compatible pairs of certain appropriate algebras and *coalgebras* (again, the categorical dual of algebras). The purpose of the present article is to summarize the findings of [8] in a form that is accessible without extensive knowledge of category theory.

## 2   Structural Operational Semantics (SOS)

Structural operational semantics (SOS), due to Plotkin [5], is one of the most popular and influential approaches to *operational* semantics, where the process character of meaning is emphasized over the object and proposition aspects. SOS differs from the other dominant approach, *abstract machines*, by its rule-based and compositional flavour. Plotkin [6] cautions against machine approaches:

> *I recall not much liking this way of doing operational semantics. It seemed far too complex, burying essential semantical ideas in masses of detail; further, the machine states were too big. The lesson I took from this was that abstract interpreting machines do not scale up well when used as a human-oriented method of specification for real languages [...]*

While this judgement certainly pertains more to programming languages than to abstract computation models such as cellular automata, the present article intends to demonstrate that rule-based approaches have some merits over automata-theoretic ones for cellular automata (despite the suggestive name) as well.

### 2.1   Classical Approach

The classical approach to SOS takes the form of a logical calculus in the Hilbert style. System behaviour is specified by a collection of deduction rules of the form

$$\frac{P_1 \quad \cdots \quad P_n}{Q}$$

where the antecedents $P_i$ and the conclusion $Q$ are all logical propositions about system events. The conclusions of a rule set form a case distinction over the available state-combining operations. The rules can then be applied inductively over the syntactic structure of composite system states, in order to predict events and future states. For instance, in a calculus with sequential composition (;) and interleaved parallel composition ($\parallel$), we would find rules such as

$$\frac{X \xrightarrow{t} X'}{X \parallel Y \xrightarrow{t} X' \parallel Y}\text{PAR}_1 \qquad\qquad \frac{Y \xrightarrow{u} Y'}{X \parallel Y \xrightarrow{u} X \parallel Y'}\text{PAR}_2$$

for parallelism and

$$\frac{X \xrightarrow{t} X'}{X \,;Y \xrightarrow{t} X' \,;Y}\text{SEQ}_1 \qquad\qquad \frac{X \nrightarrow \quad Y \xrightarrow{u} Y'}{X \,;Y \xrightarrow{u} Y'}\text{SEQ}_2$$

for sequentiality. Rule $\text{SEQ}_1$, for example, reads as: "If the state $X$ can make a transition to $X'$, producing the observable event $t$ in the process, then the sequential composite $(X \,; Y)$ can make an equivalent transition to $(X' \,; Y)$, thus deferring potential transitions of $Y$." Rule $\text{SEQ}_2$ deals with the case that $X$ cannot make any transition in analogous fashion.

Note that $X$, $X'$, $Y$, $Y'$, $t$ and $u$ are variables for states and events that need not be atomic, but can have arbitrary complex inner structure. This simple observation is the key difference to abstract machine semantics, and turns out to entail enormous power of abstraction. In particular, SOS encourages *compositional* models where state-combining operations can be applied in arbitrary nesting order, and *modular* analysis and evaluation, where just one layer of state structure is dealt with at a time, to the effect that constructs can be designed and understood independently.

These discussions remain necessarily abstract at present, but in sections 3 and 4 the concrete applications to cellular automata will be investigated.

## 2.2   Bialgebraic Approach

It is of course easy to give a collection of rules in the SOS style that does *not* define the behaviour of the model in question consistently and completely. In the classical SOS approach, sufficient criteria (termed *formats*) for consistence and completeness of rules are given syntactically. The seminal idea of Turi and Plotkin [9], that raised the interest for SOS in the theoretical computer science community considerably, is to switch from a syntactical to a semantical perspective on the meta-model of SOS rules themselves. They give a mathematical structure that is the precise meaning of a certain, fairly general SOS format.

Unfortunately, the adequate mathematical structure, namely a *distributive law of a monad over a comonad*, is a rather heavy-weight concept from category theory. This makes the proofs of meta-semantical properties in [9] extremely concise end elegant, but also thoroughly inaccessible to non-experts in the field. Klin [3] gives a retrospective and much gentler introduction, but some basic training in category theory is still presupposed. In the present article, we attempt to restate both the SOS approach and our own SOS-based results for cellular automata in a form accessible to a general computer science audience. Of course, many technical details have to be omitted because of space limitations.

The main concept of categorical approaches to both syntax and semantics is the notion of a *functor*, which for the present discussion can be understood as a mapping that takes sets to other sets with extra structure. The bialgebraic approach involves two such functors: One, usually labelled $\Sigma$, that specifies the abstract syntax of the model in set theoretic terms, and another, usually labelled $B$, that specifies the range of possible behavior.

As an example for the syntactic side, consider a calculus comprising the sequential and parallel composition detailed above, plus atomic operations that explicitly cause some event $e \in E$. Abstract syntax specified by the grammar rule

$$Term ::= (Term \, ; \, Term) \mid (Term \parallel Term) \mid \mathrm{do} \, E$$

can also be modelled in terms of Cartesian product ($\times$) and disjoint union ($+$) of sets

$$\Sigma(X) = (X \times X) + (X \times X) + E$$

where the injections into the disjoint sum take the place of term constructors.

Any such signature functor $\Sigma$ entails uniquely, up to isomorphism, an *initial algebra*, that is a pair $(\mu\Sigma, \mathrm{in})$, where the set $\mu\Sigma$ is the least fixpoint solution of the domain equation $X \cong \Sigma(X)$, and in $: \Sigma(\mu\Sigma) \to \mu\Sigma$ is the corresponding isomorphism. This object can be shown to coincide with, and is in fact the categorization of, the *algebra of terms* of classical universal algebra. Initial algebras come with a proof principle of *structural induction*: any predicate that is inherited over the constructs from $\Sigma$ holds for all $\mu\Sigma$.

As an example for the behavioral side, consider the following functor:

$$B(X) = (I \to X) \times O$$

Pairs $(S, \sigma)$ of a set $S$ and a map $\sigma : S \to B(S)$ are called *B-coalgebras*. For the given functor $B$, they coincide with total Moore semiautomata (automata without fixed initial state) with input alphabet $I$ and output alphabet $O$, seeing as $\sigma$ assigns to every pre-state $s \in S$ a pair of a reaction function from inputs ($I$) to post-states ($S$), and an output ($O$). See [7] for a thorough introductory discussion of automata as coalgebras. Functors are more precise about behavioral options than the arrow notation for transitions from the classical SOS rule format. For instance, the question of determinism, that is whether the possibility of one transition implies the impossibility of others, is answered explicitly: the formula for $B$ given above is fully deterministic, and hence cannot be used in ambiguous rules such as $\mathrm{PAR}_1$ and $\mathrm{PAR}_2$ together. Alternative formulas include $(I \to \mathcal{P}(X)) \times O$, where only post-states are nondeterministic, and $\mathcal{P}((I \to X) \times O)$, where output is nondeterministic too. Here $\mathcal{P}$ denotes the set of finite subsets.

Any such behavior functor $B$ entails uniquely, up to isomorphism, a *final coalgebra*, that is a pair $(\nu B, \mathrm{out})$, where the set $\nu B$ is the greatest fixpoint solution of $X \cong B(X)$ and out $: \nu B \to B(\nu B)$ is the corresponding isomorphism. Elements of $\nu B$ can be thought of as universal, nonredundant equivalence classes of global automaton behavior (comprising all potential future transitions), and hence as an ideal semantics of concrete automaton states. In the case of the example functor $B$ given above, the elements of $\nu B$ can be understood as the infinite trees with $O$-labelled nodes and a full set of $I$-labelled outgoing arcs for every node, thus specifying the full future reactive behavior ensuing from a Moore automaton state. Final coalgebras come with a proof principle dual to induction, namely *coinduction*: Let a *bisimulation* be a relation between states of the same or different systems such that the assumption of any pair of states $(s, s') \in R$ being behaviorally indistinguishable is consistent with locally observable events. Then for all such pairs $(s, s') \in R$ their interpretations in the final coalgebra, and hence their global behavior, actually coincide.

Besides the two functorial formalizations of syntactic and behavioral structure, the key ingredient is what is called a *distributive law* in category theory. It is a collection of maps of a certain type, in the simplest case $\lambda_X : \Sigma(B(X)) \to B(\Sigma(X))$ for all sets $X$, although slightly more complex types are required for some of the example rules given above; cf. [3]. Any such a distributive law $\lambda$, of which there may be many, gives rise to a unique map from $A$ (the set of syntactic state descriptions) to $\Omega$ (the set of behavioral meanings), hence the name *bialgebra*, thus defining a full semantical theory.

SOS rule systems in certain formats can be rephrased as distributive laws, with the desired type governing the form of logical propositions. The type given above, which shall be used for cellular automata, can be read as "infer, from any system description that gives the top-level combining operator and the behavior of its operands $(\Sigma(B(\_)))$, the behavior of the whole in terms of combined future states $(B(\Sigma(\_)))$." See section 3.2 for a solution of this riddle characterizing cellular automata.

# 3    Cellular Automata and SOS

## 3.1    Model Perspectives

In a programming calculus or language, it is fairly obvious what actually constitutes syntax, since that is the dominating theme of any description. For cellular automata, many answers are possible. We have demonstrated in [8] that an elegant separation of concerns arises when syntax is equated with *space*, and behavior with *time*.

In order to define two-dimensional cellular automata as they appear as a basis for animated models such as Conway's Game of Life and ABM simulations, we assume without loss of generality a regular rectangular grid. The base case is a single cell with local state space $L$. Global states $G$ are constructed by horizontal ($|$) or vertical ($/$) juxtaposition. In order to avoid shape checks, we assume that $L$ contains a distinguished default element $\star$ used for padding the smaller subgrid. Finally, in order to allow for nontrivial topologies, we allow both the whole and arbitrary subgrids to have *torsion* along the horizontal ($\leftrightarrow$) and/or vertical

($\updownarrow$) axis, whereby the left and right, or top and bottom edges are connected, respectively. In summary, as a grammar rule and syntactic functor:

$$G \quad ::= \quad (G \mid G) \quad | \quad (G \mathbin{/} G) \quad | \quad G^{\leftrightarrow} \quad | \quad G^{\updownarrow} \quad | \quad [L]$$
$$\Sigma(X) = (X \times X) + (X \times X) + \; X \; + \; X \; + \; L$$

Note that many ABM platforms allow for torsion, but only at the global boundaries of an otherwise plain grid. For SOS, however, compositional syntax is always preferrable. Other topological operators such as Möbius or solenoidal torsion (with a simultaneous orthogonal flip/rotation, respectively) could be added modularly.

In cellular automata, interaction takes place by each cell simultaneously consuming the pre-states of its neighbors as input, and producing its own pre-state as output, while transiting to its post-state, according to a shared local transition function. For the behavioral functor, we may hence specialize the total Moore automaton case discussed above, by setting $I = O^k$ where $k$ is the number of neighbors for each cell.

$$B(X) = (O^k \to X) \times O$$

This automaton view applies to both locally individual cells (with $O = L$) and globally composite grids (with $O = A$). In the global case, the input is boundary conditions rather than proper neighbors.

## 3.2 Semantic Rules

The third and final ingredient of bialgebraic SOS for cellular automata, a distributive law, distinguishes syntactic cases as usual. The base case for single cells encodes the local transition function. The composite cases are concerned with the issue of topology, namely how neighborhoods of cells are arranged. Fig. 1 depicts the rules in classical format. The function $u(n, \ell)$ denotes the local transition rule for cell state $\ell \in L$ with neighbors $n \in L^k$. The vertical cases have been omitted, but are exactly analogous to the horizontal ones. For the only extra feature, the operation names below transition arrows, see the immediately following discussion.

$$\frac{}{[\ell] \xrightarrow[\text{cosingleton}]{[\ell]} [u(\_,\ell)]} \qquad \frac{X \xrightarrow{t} X' \quad Y \xrightarrow{u} Y'}{X \mid Y \xrightarrow[\text{cobeside}]{t \mid u} X' \mid Y'} \qquad \frac{X \xrightarrow{t} X'}{X^{\leftrightarrow} \xrightarrow[\text{cohwrap}]{t} X'^{\leftrightarrow}}$$

**Fig. 1.** SOS rules for cellular automata

How the rules work can best be understood in relation to classical evaluation algorithms for cellular automata that are organized around array data structures, and establish neighborhoods by relative indexing of cells. Fig. 2 depicts a snapshot of a flat $(2 \times 2)$-grid (left, gray center) and its decomposition into

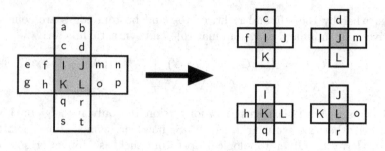

**Fig. 2.** Full decomposition of $(2 \times 2)$-grid with four-point (Moore) neighborhood

individual cells with four-point (Moore) neighborhood (right). Boundary conditions are given by adjacent virtual grids (left, white perimeter). From each of the pre-state cells-in-context, a post-state of the center cell is computed, for instance in a two-dimensional loop.

The basic idea of the described evaluation algorithm, namely the decomposition of data flow from global states-in-context to local ones, can be salvaged and reused in the SOS framework. But instead of proceeding from whole arrays to individual cells in a single conceptual step, the decomposition is done inductively over the syntax. In fact, each of the syntax operations admits a kind of inverse, such that the single-step behavior of a syntactically composite state with respect to its neighborhood can be expressed equivalently as the behavior of the operand substates with respect to appropriately transformed neighborhoods. These neighborhood transformations are denoted here as cosingleton, cobeside, coabove, cohwrap and covwrap, respectively. Their appearance in Fig. 1 below transition arrows specifies that they are to be composed with the reaction functions denoted by the respective right hand sides.

Fig. 3 depicts the functioning of inverse horizontal juxtaposition and torsion intuitively for the Moore neighborhood. Precise definitions for this and other neighborhood types are rather technical, but the idea is simple and elegant nevertheless, and worthy of human-centric semantics: For instance, torsion can be understood as overwriting opposing neighbors with copies of the center (top), and juxtaposition can be understood as a combination of shared neighbors and mutual neighborhood (bottom).

## 4   Semantic Properties

We have claimed that semantics need to be chosen for adequacy with respect to particular properties of interest. This claim shall be illustrated by briefly discussing various semantical properties that are clearly apparent from the SOS presentation, either for cellular automata in particular or for SOS models in general.

*Compositionality.* As already stressed before, compositionality is a hallmark of SOS models: No restriction is placed on the nesting order or depth of syntactic

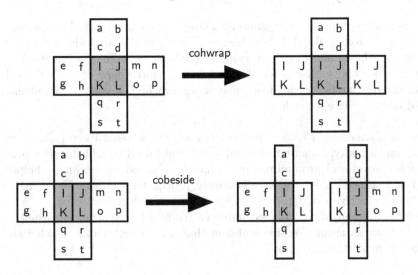

**Fig. 3.** Inductive deconstruction (horizontal) for four-point (Moore) neighborhood

constructs; parts and the whole of system states are treated the same. This allows for constructs to be added and removed modularly, as well as for automatic generalization of existing constructions. For instance, by nesting torsion within juxtaposition, weird grid topologies can be constructed, such as the trouser shape specified in the form $A^{\leftrightarrow} / (B^{\leftrightarrow} | C^{\leftrightarrow})$.

*Conservation of Grid Shape.* All rules in Fig. 1 have the same syntactic operators on both sides of a transition. This trivially implies that the grid shape remains constant over time. Rules that diverge from that behavior could be devised to give semantics to hybrid cellular/Lindenmayer systems.

*Parallelism.* None of the rules in Fig. 1 is of the form of $\text{SEQ}_1$ or $\text{SEQ}_2$, calling for suspension or resumption of computations, respectively. Hence the only limitation on the evaluation order of states is given by data flow. Parts of a single global state may be computed in parallel, by reading the SOS rules as a divide-and-conquer parallel algorithm. Parts of several global states can even be computed out of order by demand-driven algorithms, such as a literal implementation of the SOS rules in a lazy functional programming language; see below.

*Full Abstraction.* By the coinduction principle that comes for free with final coalgebras, bialgebraic models are by construction *fully abstract*; they do not posit spurious semantical inequalities which are not reflected in distinguishable observed behavior.

*Executability.* The type of distributive law used here, $\lambda_X : \Sigma(B(X)) \to B(\Sigma(X))$, has a direct implementation in terms of structurally recursive and corecursive functions in a lazy functional programming language, such as Haskell, as has been noted by Jaskelioff et al. [2]. It is therefore a simple matter to derive a formally verifiable, mathematically faithful, generic simulator of cellular automata from the SOS rules. The sophisticated demand-driven control flow of Haskell, both sequential and parallel, is an ideal match for the high degree of parallelism ensured by the SOS approach.

*Behavioral Equivalence Proofs.* Proofs of behavioral theorems about cellular automata can be tricky, because they need to account for all possible future states. The rather novel and groundbreaking principle of coinduction can be helpful here. For instance, in [8] we have concisely proven the equivalence of array-based and inductive evaluation (cf. Figs. 2 and 3, respectively), by straight-forward fleshing out of the coupled inductive–coinductive scheme suggested by the bialgebraic situation. We are confident that other proofs can be guided and abridged in much the same way.

## 5    Conclusion

We have outlined the SOS approach to semantics and how it relates to the fundamentals of category theory: functors, algebras and coalgebras. We have sketched, although many questions must be left unanswered in limited space, the analysis of cellular automata into spatial, temporal and topological aspects. We have indicated how the most complex aspect, the topology, can be modularized by the inverse-syntax approach. The specific local transition rule is plugged into the topological distributive law as the base case. As a first validation of the approach, we have enumerated various properties, some more theoretical, some truly operational in nature, that are clearly apparent from the SOS presentation. We conjecture that we have merely grazed the surface of the potential of this powerful semantical methodology for the study of cellular automata, and predict that future work will uncover many additional useful findings.

**Acknowledgments.** Michael Hauhs, Jan Rutten and Milad Niqui have supported this work through valuable discussions and suggestions at various stages of development.

## References

1. Capobianco, S., Uustalu, T.: A categorical outlook on cellular automata. In: Kari, J. (ed.) Proceedings 2nd Symposium on Cellular Automata (JAC 2010), pp. 88–99. Turku Center for Computer Science (2010)
2. Jaskelioff, M., Ghani, N., Hutton, G.: Modularity and implementation of mathematical operational semantics. Electronic Notes in Theoretical Computer Science 229(5), 75–95 (2011)
3. Klin, B.: Bialgebras for structural operational semantics: an introduction. Theoretical Computer Science 412(38), 5043–5069 (2011)

4. Moggi, E.: Notions of computation and monads. Information and Computation 93(1), 55–92 (1991)
5. Plotkin, G.D.: A structural approach to operational semantics. Tech. Rep. DAIMI FN-19, Computer Science, Aarhus University, Denmark (1981)
6. Plotkin, G.D.: The origins of structural operational semantics. J. Log. Algebr. Program, 60–61, 3–15 (2004)
7. Rutten, J.: Universal coalgebra: a theory of systems. Theoretical Computer Science 249(1), 3–80 (2000)
8. Trancón y Widemann, B., Hauhs, M.: Distributive-Law Semantics for Cellular Automata and Agent-Based Models. In: Corradini, A., Klin, B., Cîrstea, C. (eds.) CALCO 2011. LNCS, vol. 6859, pp. 344–358. Springer, Heidelberg (2011)
9. Turi, D., Plotkin, G.D.: Towards a mathematical operational semantics. In: Proceedings 12th International Conference on Logic in Computer Science (LICS 1997), pp. 280–291. IEEE (1997)

# Controlling the Opacity of a Building Envelope by a Triangular Two-Color Two-Dimensional Cellular Automaton

Machi Zawidzki[*] and Katsuhiro Nishinari

Research Center for Advanced Science and Technology, University of Tokyo, Japan
{umachu,tknishi}@mail.ecc.u-tokyo.ac.jp

**Abstract.** This paper presents the system based on cellular automata (CA) for controlling the average opacity of any triangulated surface, in particular serving as a building envelope. The concept is based on the emergent and modular qualities of CAs and is proposed for a practical application in the field of architecture. The concept of triangular cellular automata (TCA) is explained, followed by application of totalistic (tTCA) and semi-totalistic (stTCA) TCA on an imperfect test mesh, that is a mesh with voids and nodes of various degrees. Preliminary analysis of the behavior of these TCAs at various types of initial conditions in the context of shading purposes is presented.

**Keywords:** triangular CA, triangulated surface, surface state control.

## 1    Introduction

It is intuitive for every architect that an ideal building envelope should allow to cover any three-dimensional shape and its state should be controllable. So far, universal, feasible and affordable solutions for neither of these two problems have been successfully realized, particularly for the combination of the two. The main reason is the cost – free-form shapes almost always require high level of customization and therefore are usually far more expensive than simple modular systems that result in also simple overall form. For the discussion on the "free-form vs. modularity" in the field of architecture see [1]. A number of mechanical systems that adjust the physical properties, in particular opacity of a facade, have been realized. However, due to their lack of robustness often amplified by the problems with maintenance they fail to operate, or their applications are much reduced comparing to the designers' intentions. The idea of a modular shading system for a flat surface that changes the average opacity of a building facade [2] and takes visual advantage of the emerging qualities of a cellular automaton (CA) has been proposed in [3], and a simplified, small scale prototype based on LCD technology has been built [4]. The extension of this idea to any triangulated surface in space has been introduced in [5]. This paper clarifies the criteria for triangular cellular automata (TCA) for this particular application, introduces a method

---

[*] Corresponding author.

G.C. Sirakoulis and S. Bandini (Eds.): ACRI 2012, LNCS 7495, pp. 194–203, 2012.

for their preliminary evaluation, and briefly analyzes the applicability of totalistic (tTCA) and semi-totalistic (stTCA) nearest-neighbor two-color TCA.

## 2    Triangulated 3D Surface

Triangulation is a simple and intuitive method of approximating any three-dimensional surface by topologically identical facets – triangles. Unlike other polygons, triangles are rigid in $\mathbb{R}^2$, which is a particularly practical property in the fields of architecture and engineering. This commonly known fact can be demonstrated formally using graph theory, based on the combinatorial properties [6] of this skeletal structure. The mathematical model of such constructions is considered to be a finite graph $S$ without loops and multiple edges [7]. According to Laman's theorem [8], such a graph $S$ is generically, minimally rigid in plane, that is becomes flexible after an edge is removed, if and only if:

1. it has $2n - 3$ edges, where $n$ is the number of vertices, and
2. no subgraph of $k$ vertices has more than $2k - 3$ edges.

In the case of a triangle, the first condition is met since it has three edges ($3=2\times3-3$). The second condition is also met for two possible types of subgraphs. For a simple bar (one edge with two nodes): $1 \leq 2\times2 - 3$, and for two connected bars (two edges with three nodes): $2 \leq 2\times3 - 3$.

Although each triangle is rigid in its own plane, in general, a triangular mesh is not rigid in $\mathbb{R}^3$. Therefore the mesh as a whole needs to be designed structurally.

## 3    CA and TCA

CAs combine two unique qualities that make their use in the field of architecture particularly interesting – the emergent aesthetics and modularity. For the discussion on the CAs in the context of design see [5]. The most commonly used lattice for CAs is an orthogonal grid (1D, 2D or 3D), however, several studies have been carried out to test the properties of other tessellations such as triangular, hexagonal [9–11], for an interactive demonstration see [12]. TCA are applied on a triangular tessellation with each regular cell having three immediate neighbors. Further details on this implementation can be found in [5]. In the case of a general CA, the information from every cell is taken, for a totalistic one – the sum of all the values (the main + neighboring cells), for semi-totalistic (also called outer-totalistic) CAs – the value in the main cell and the sum of the values in the neighboring cells is used as an input. Unlike the other two types, the general CAs depend not only on the topology, but also on the geometry of a mesh – the relative position of neighbor cells to the main cell is important. On a regular grid, where each node has the same degree the application of general CAs is straightforward. However, in this paper the most universal case of a mesh is considered – where the degree of the nodes may vary and facets may be missing. For these reasons the applicability of general CAs is not considered here. The test mesh (TM) is shown in figure 1.

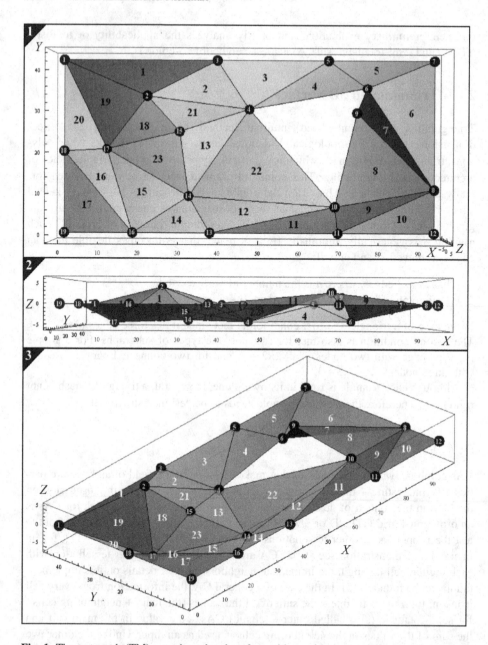

**Fig. 1.** The test mesh (TM) – a triangulated surface with a void – two missing facets spanned on vertices {4,9,10} & {4,6,9}. From the top: 1) top view, 2) front view, and 3) isometric view.

Each facet of the mesh can have two states – white, equivalent to transparency (value 0) or black – corresponding to opacity (value 1). The fixed boundary conditions are used, with 0 as the assumed value for any cell beyond the actual mesh. For practicality, the initial conditions (ICs) are set on the perimeter of the mesh. As an example, stTCA rule no. 250 is applied on TM as shown in table 1. For ICs in the following example, a single 1 is assigned to the cell no. 17.

**Table 1.** The top view of TM. IC with 1 at the cell no. 17 is the step 0, followed by 9 consecutive steps of the evolution of stTCA rule. 250. The explicit local state transition rules (explained further in text) are: $\{1,3\}\rightarrow1$, $\{1,2\}\rightarrow1$, $\{1,1\}\rightarrow1$, $\{1,0\}\rightarrow1$, $\{0,3\}\rightarrow1$, $\{0,2\}\rightarrow0$, $\{0,1\}\rightarrow1$, $\{0,0\}\rightarrow0$. The state of TM stabilizes after the 8th step, with no further fluctuations. The facets 6 and 22 are not affected by this evolution.

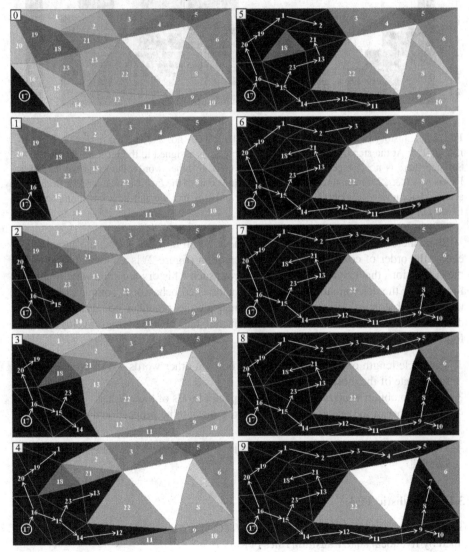

This two-dimensional dynamic process can be concisely represented by a history of evolution analog to the convention commonly used for one-dimensional CAs. The history of TCA evolution from table 1 is presented in figure 2.

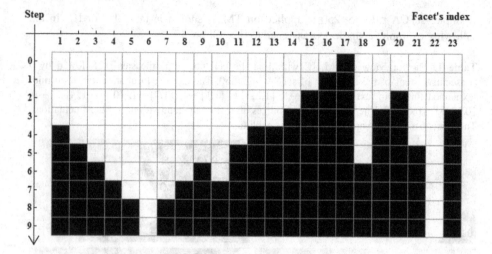

**Fig. 2.** The history of evolution of the semi-totalistic TCA no. 250 applied to the 23-facet surface of TM. At the step 0, equivalent to IC, a single 1 is assigned to the facet no. 17. After the 8th step there is no change to the state of any cells, in other words, the cycle has period 1. Facets nos. 6 & 22 remain unaffected. Note: the indexing of the facets is independent from their actual adjacency – for example facets nos. 17 & 18 in fact are not adjacent (compare with figure 1).

Since the order of indices of the facets in the mesh may not reflect the actual adjacency, the order of columns in such representation (figure 2) is accidental. Therefore the conclusions that can be drawn directly from such a history are somewhat limited – for example the determination whether the manifested behavior is complex or chaotic may be problematic. However, at this stage, all the practical conclusions can be derived from it. The criteria for controlling the state of a building envelope are as follows:

1. The cycle length of after stabilization to be 1, in other words – no further changes to the state of the mesh.
3. Ability to obtain wide range of average opacity levels of the mesh.
4. The number of the opaque cells in the entire mesh to be proportional to the number of the opaque cells in IC.
5. The transitions between consecutive steps of CA evolution to appear not overly chaotic.

## 3.1    Totalistic TCA

Totalistic two-state nearest neighbor TCA (tTCA) are the simplest 2D automata, defined by five local state transition rules (TRs):

$$(4) \rightarrow a, (3) \rightarrow a, (2) \rightarrow a, (1) \rightarrow a, (0) \rightarrow a, \text{ where } a : \{0,1\}.$$

In order to distinguish the sums from the actual values in cells, the former are brack-eted. There are 32 tTCAs. The histories of evolution on TM for all of them starting from the same IC are shown in table 2.

**Table 2.** 20 steps of evolution of all tTCAs from the same IC – 1 in position 17. Under each rule number, the step at which the pattern becomes periodic and the length of the cycle are given. In this experiment tTCA nos. 5, 10, 11 & 21 show enormous stabilization time and/or the cycle length after the stabilization.

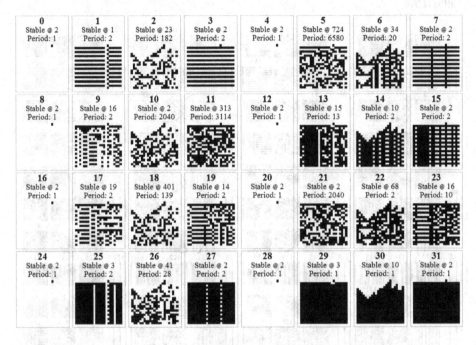

As table 2 indicates, the applicability of tTCA for controlling the state of a triangu-lated mesh seems very limited, for the following reasons:

1. Quite surprisingly, for some of them the stabilization takes enormous number of steps – over 700 for tTCA no. 724, and the cycle length at the stable state – 6580 (for the same automaton).
6. Only 11 of them stabilize to period length 1.
7. Among these 11 ones, 8 quickly or instantly all cells converge to 0s.
8. Only three tTCAs, that is nos. 29, 30 & 31, (almost) instantly converge to all black.

If the objective was to switch all the cells from 0s to 1s, and vice versa, the rule no. 30 would be the most appropriate since the state of the entire mesh gradually changes from complete transparency to opacity. However, in such a case the emergent proper-ties of automata are not used to a meaningful extent, and such a simple task can be realized in a straightforward way.

## 3.2    Semi-totalistic TCA

Semi-totalistic TCA (stTCA) are defined by 10 TRs:

$$\{1,(4)\} \to a, \{1,(3)\} \to a, \{1,(2)\} \to a, \{1,(1)\} \to a, \{1,(0)\} \to a,$$
$$\{0,(4)\} \to a, \{0,(3)\} \to a, \{0,(2)\} \to a, \{0,(1)\} \to a, \{0,(0)\} \to a, \text{ where } a : \{0,1\}.$$

**Table 3.** 20 steps of evolution starting from the same IC (1s assigned to cells nos. 1,6,11 & 17) of all stTCAs.

Although stTCAs are quite simple automata, they already demonstrate a variety of behaviors. The representative examples are shown in table 4.

**Table 4.** Histories of evolution of selected stTCAs starting from the same IC with a single 1 in the cell no. 17. Under the rule number, the step at which the pattern becomes periodic and the length of the cycle are given respectively.

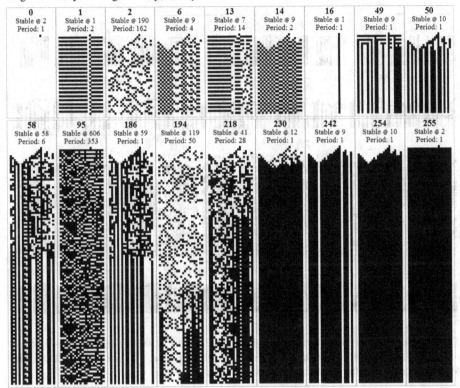

All of the stTCAs at given IC become periodic, however, sometimes the stabilization takes a relatively large number of cycles (e.g. rule nos. 2 & 95 from table 4). As mentioned above the only automata that can be used for controlling the state of a building envelope have the length of the stabilized cycle equal to 1, in other words, they do not fluctuate. The most promising stTCAs for controlling the state of TM are nos. 49, 50, 186 & 242. Table 5 shows the histories of stTCA evolution where initial configurations have from 1 to 12 1s in ICs set on the perimeter of TM. For the mesh state control in this project, controlling the average density (AD), in other words the rate of black cells of the entire mesh, is the most crucial, however, under condition that the state of cells is stable. Therefore, AD has meaning only if the state of cells does not change after being once affected by the CA evolution. As table 5 indicates, since at certain ICs the state of entire mesh does not stop fluctuating, some of these promising stTCAs may not be applicable. However, perhaps it is possible to set up specific sequences of ICs to avoid this problem. In the examples shown in table 5, only rule 49 and 242 clearly demonstrate stable behavior. However, ADs of the patterns seems to be rather independent from the rate of 1s in the given sequence of ICs which changes from a single (approx. 0%) to 12 1s (44%). For rule 49 the number of 1s remains approximately 11 (40%), and for rule 242 – 20 (74%).

**Table 5.** Evolution of the selected stTCAs at 12 consecutive ICs – from 1 to 12 1s. "T" stands for the total number of 1s in the entire mesh after stabilization to period of length 1. Otherwise the automaton does not stop to fluctuate, as indicated. TRs for each rule are shown on the right.

**Table 6.** 14 steps of evolution of stTCAs: 49 and 242 at all ICs with a single 1 placed in each of the 23 facets of TM. Although rule 242 stabilizes in each case, for 1 set in the 9th facet rule 49 does not stabilize (the 9th pattern in the top row).

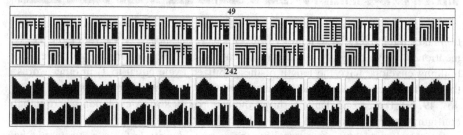

## 4    Conclusions

Although CAs have been studied for well over half of a century, there are no robust and universal methods of designing them to perform predefined actions. According to [13]: *interesting CAs currently known have typically been found through stepwise and careful thought-out engineering; exhaustive searches in very restricted domains; formal methods in extremely particular problems; and specialized search methods in constrained spaces.* Moreover, due to the computational irreducibility, an experiment is the most common method for drawing conclusions regarding CAs. This preliminary study demonstrated that the proposed triangulated surface control system has the following advantages: it can be applied on any 3D surface; it is highly modular; the dynamics of the changes of its state is organic, which is desirable from designer's perspective. Some rules, e.g.: 242 & 250 demonstrate consistent behavior that can be used for shading. Others, such as 49, although demonstrate more complex behavior, sometimes do not stabilize, as shown in table 6. To generalize the conclusions beyond this particular TM, further analysis, in particular experiments are to be performed. For example determination whether rule 242 would always stabilize on TM with ICs set on the boundary facets which have only two neighbors requires 986,409 experiments (there are 9 such facets: 1,3,5,6,10,11,14,17&20). The future research will also include: the role and optimization of the ICs and boundary conditions, implementation of general TCAs, analysis of TCAs with more than two states and with a higher range and building a prototype.

**Acknowledgments.** This is part of a postdoctoral project grant-funded by the Japanese Society for the Promotion of Science: "Improvements of the Seniors' Quality of Life through Application of Innovative Computational Systems to the problems of Accessibility, Ergonomics and Housing & Living Environment".

# References

1. Zawidzki, M., Nishinari, K.: Modular Truss-Z system for self-supporting skeletal freeform pedestrian networks. Advances in Engineering Software 47(1), 147–159 (2012)
2. Zawidzki, M.: A Cellular Automaton Mapped on the Surface of a Cuboid. Wolfram Demonstrations Project (Published: January 17, 2010),
   http://demonstrations.wolfram.com/ACellularAutomatonMappedOn
   TheSurfaceOfACuboid/
3. Zawidzki, M.: Implementing Cellular Automata for Dynamically Shading a Building Facade. Complex-Systems 18(3), 287–305 (2009)
4. Zawidzki, M., Fujieda, I.: The prototyping of a shading device controlled by a cellular automaton. Complex-Systems 19(2), 157–175 (2010)
5. Zawidzki, M.: Application of Semitotalistic 2D Cellular Automata on a triangulated 3D surface. International Journal of Design & Nature and Ecodynamics 6(1), 34–51 (2011)
6. Crapo, H.: Structural Rigidity: Structural Topology 1, 26–45 (1979)
7. Kaveh, A.: Topological Properties of Skeletal Structures. Computers and Structures 29(3), 403–411 (1988)
8. Laman, G.: On Graphs and Rigidity of Plane Skeletal Structures. J. Engineering Math. 4, 331–340 (1970)
9. Bays, C.: Cellular automata in the triangular tessellation. Complex Sys. 8, 127–150 (1994)
10. Imai, K.: A computation-universal two-dimensional 8 state triangular reversible cellular automaton. Theoretical Computer Science 231(2), 181–191 (2000)
11. Alonso-Sanz, R.: A structurally dynamic cellular automaton with memory in the triangular tessellation. Complex Systems 17(1), 1–15 (2007)
12. Zawidzki, M.: One-Dimensional Cellular Automata on the Regular Tessellations. Wolfram Demonstrations Project: (Published February 20, 2012),
    http://demonstrations.wolfram.com/OneDimensionalCellularAuto
    mataOnTheRegularTessellations/
13. Wolz, D., de Oliveira, P.: Very Effective Evolutionary Techniques for Searching Cellular Automata Rule Spaces. Journal of Cellular Automata 3(4), 289–312 (2008)

# Community-Detection Cellular Automata
# with Local and Long-Range Connectivity

Franco Bagnoli[1,2,*], Emanuele Massaro[1,**], and Andrea Guazzini[3,***]

[1] Dept. Energy and CSDC, Università di Firenze,
via S. Marta, 3 50139 Firenze, Italy
[2] Also INFN, sez. Firenze
[3] Dept. Psychology and CSDC, Universitá di Firenze, and Institute for Informatics
and Telematics (IIT), National Research Council (CNR),
via G. Moruzzi, 1 56124 Pisa, Italy

**Abstract.** We explore a community-detection cellular automata algorithm inspired by human heuristics, based on information diffusion and a non-linear processing phase with a dynamics inspired by human heuristics. The main point of the methods is that of furnishing different "views" of the clustering levels from an individual point of view. We apply the method to networks with local connectivity and long-range rewiring.

**Keywords:** Graph theory, Community, Clustering.

## 1  Introduction

Detecting communities is a task of great importance in many disciplines, namely sociology, biology and computer science [23,20,6,21,1], where systems are often represented as graphs. Community detection is linked to clustering of data: many clustering methods establish links among representative points that are nearer than a given threshold, and then proceed in identifying communities on the resulting graphs [3,2]. Given a graph, a community is a group of vertices "more linked" than between the group and the rest of the graph. This is clearly a poor definition, and indeed, on a connected graph, there is not a clear distinction between a community and a rest of the graph. In general, there is a continuum of nested communities whose boundaries are somewhat arbitrary: the structure of communities can be seen as a hierarchical dendogram [16].

The problem of community detection is fundamental for social simulations: human decisions (for instance, cooperation vs. exploitation) often depends on the detection of the community in which one is embedded [12].

Community detection relies on global quantities like betweenness, centrality, etc. [16,15] and the most algorithms require that the graph be completely known. This constraint is problematic for networks like the World Wide Web, which for

---

\* franco.bagnoli@unifi.it
\*\* emanuele.massaro@unifi.it
\*\*\* andrea.guazzini@iit.cnr.it

G.C. Sirakoulis and S. Bandini (Eds.): ACRI 2012, LNCS 7495, pp. 204–213, 2012.
© Springer-Verlag Berlin Heidelberg 2012

all practical purposes is too large and too dynamic to ever be known fully. In 2005 Clauset [4] introduced the concept of *local modularity* in order to find a local measure to remedy at the global character of the *modularity* defined by Girvan and Newman in 2004 [16].

For instance, let us suppose to be an internet user, who wants to know, at a certain time, which community he belongs to. He/she has no possibility of calculating gloabal quantities like the network betweenness (for example) of the World Wide Web. He/she has to rely on individual-based heuristics to infer, from the knowledge obtainable from the nearest neighbour nodes (assuming a certain degree of collaboration), the structure of the network, at least up to a certain distance.

At a superficial level, most of our information processing concerns the evaluation of probabilities. When faced with insufficient data or insufficient time for a rational processing, we humans have developed algorithms, denoted heuristics, that allows to take decisions in these situations. Basically, the cognitive heuristics program proposed by Goldstein and Gigerenzer suggests to start from fundamental psychological mechanisms in order to design the models of heuristics [9].

Here we propose a new tool for detecting communities in complex networks using a local algorithm, applied as an (irregular) cellular automaton. In our previous work we shown an information dynamics algorithm, inspired by human heuristics, capable to discover communities in regular networks [14].

In our approach an individual (node) is simply modelled as a memory and a set of connections to other individuals. The information about neighbouring nodes is propagated using a standard diffusion process, and elaborated locally using a non-linear competition process among the pieces of information. This process can be considered an implementation of the "take the best" heuristic [8], which is simply the assumption that the most vivid or easily recallable information give an accurate estimate of the frequency of the related event in the population.

The applicability of community detection algorithms to a network with local connectivity is rather problematic. Let us consider for illustration the small-world effect [24]: starting from a regular network with pure local connectivity a small fraction of links is rewired to other sites. What is generally observed is that local quantities (like the clustering level) do not change until the fraction of rewiring is quite large, while global quantities (like network diameter) essentially take the values of random networks as soon as the fraction if rewiring is greater than zero. What happens to community detection?

## 2    The Cellular Automata Network

We shall consider $N$ individuals, labelled from 1 to $N$. The nodes are divided in a number $G$ of groups, and each group in a number $C$ of communities. The nodes in each community are connected using a local connection scheme, like in standard cellular automata of connectivity $K$: node $i$ is connected to nodes $j = i - K/2, i - K/2 + 1, \ldots, i + K/2$, with periodic boundary conditions inside each community. The communities are therefore initially separated.

With probability $p$, each link can be rewired. Once detached it is reattached to a random node inside the group the community belongs to with probability $q$, or to a random node extracted from the whole network with probability $1-q$. In this way we can build networks with a three-level structure: community, groups of communities, whole network.

The network is represented by the adjacency matrix $A_{ij} = 1$ (0) if nodes $i$ takes information from node $j$ (the matrix $A$ needs not to be symmetric). An example of the adjacency matrix is reported in Figure 2.

We assume that each individual spends the same amount of time in gathering information, so that people with more connections dedicate less time to each of them. Since the amount of available time is limited, we normalize the adjacency matrix on the index $i$ (*i.e.*, we assign at each link the inverse of the input degree of the incoming node), forming a Markov communication matrix $M$,

$$M_{ij} = \frac{A_{ij}}{\sum_k A_{ik}}. \tag{1}$$

## 3  The Community Detection Algorithm

The community detection algorithm is implemented in each node and is updated in parallel, it is therefore a kind of cellular automaton rule.

Each individual $i$ is characterized by a knowledge vector a state vector $S^{(i)}$, representing his knowledge of the outer world.

The vector $S^{(i)}$ is a probability distribution, assuming that $S_j^{(i)}$ is the probability that individual $i$ belongs to the community $j$. Thus, $S_j^{(i)}$ is normalized over the index $j$. We shall denote by $S = S(t)$ the state of the all network at time $t$, with $S_{ij} = S_j^{(i)}$. We shall initialize the system by setting $S_{ij}(0) = \delta_{ij}$, where $\delta$ is the Kronecker delta, $\delta_{ij} = 1$ if $i = j$ and zero otherwise. In other words, at time 0 each node knows only about itself.

The dynamics of the network is given by an alternation of communication and elaboration phases. The communication is implemented as a simple diffusion process, with memory $m$. The memory parameter $m$ allows us to introduce some limitations to the human cognitive power, such as the mechanism of oblivion and the timing effects: indeed the most recent informations have more relevance than informations gained in the past [22,7].

In the communication phase, the state of the system evolves as

$$S_{ij}(t + 1/2) = mS_{ij}(t) + (1 - m) \sum_k M_{ik} S_{kj}(t), \tag{2}$$

where $M$ is the communication matrix. In this phase an individual becomes aware of neighbouring individuals.

The elaboration phase is modelled trying to implement a "take the best" heuristics [8]. When real people are asked to take a decision, very rarely they weight all available pieces of information. If there is some aspect that has a higher importance than others, and one item exhibits it, than the decision is taken, otherwise, the second most important factor is considered, etc. In order to implement an adaptive scheme, we exploit a similarity with a competition dynamics among species.

If two populations $x$ and $y$ are in competition for a given resource, their total abundance is limited. After normalization, we can assume $x + y = 1$, i.e., $x$ and $y$ are the frequency of the two species, and $y = 1 - x$. The reproduction phase is given by $x' = f(x)$, which we assume to be represented by a power $x' = x^\alpha$. For instance, $\alpha = 2$ models birth of individuals of a new generation after binary encounters of individuals belonging to the old generation, with non-overlapping generations (eggs laying) [17].

After normalization

$$x' = \frac{x^\alpha}{x^\alpha + y^\alpha} = \frac{x^\alpha}{x^\alpha + (1 - x)^\alpha}. \tag{3}$$

Introducing $z = (1/x) - 1$ $(0 \le z < \infty)$, we get the map

$$z(t + 1) = z^\alpha(t), \tag{4}$$

whose fixed points (for $\alpha > 1$) are 0 and $\infty$ (stable attractors) and 1 (unstable), which separates the basins of the two attractors. Thus, the initial value of $x$, $x_0$, determines the asymptotic value, for $0 \le x < 1/2$ $x(t \to \infty) = 0$, and for $1/2 < x < 1$ $x(t \to \infty) = 1$.

By extending to a larger number of components for a probability distribution $S^{(i)}$, the competition dynamics becomes

$$S_{ij}(t + 1) = \frac{S_{ij}(t + 1/2)^\alpha}{\sum_j S_{ij}^\alpha(t + 1/2)}, \tag{5}$$

and the iteration of this mapping, for $\alpha > 1$, leads to a Kronecker delta, corresponding to the largest component. However, the convergence time depends on the relative differences among the components and therefore, when coupled with the information propagation phase, it can originate interesting behaviours.

The model therefore has two free parameters, the memory $m$ and the exponent $\alpha$.

Using a simple synthetic network, Figure 1(a), it is possible to explain our algorithm; it faces with a very simple task and converges to an optimal solution in few iterations and for a wide range of model's parameters $m$ and $\alpha$. Analysing the state matrix S(t), it is possible to identify two different communities characterized by nodes 5 and 9.

In Figure 1 (c) it is possible to identify two different communities highlighted by upper values in the graph. The first community is composed by node 1-2-3-4-5 and the second one by 6-7-8-9. Our algorithm is capable also to detect overlapping nodes (4 and 6) as "middle" values between grey lines. In this way each node knows exactly its role in the network.

In order to summarize the amount of information gathered by all nodes, we compute the Shannon entropy of the knowledge of nodes: we build the

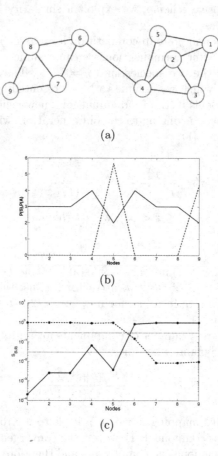

(a)

(b)

(c)

**Fig. 1.** (a) *Synthetic network* composed by of 9 nodes and 13 links divided in 2 communities. It is possible to identify two different communities: the first one composed by nodes 1-2-3-4-5 and the second one by 6-7-8-9. (b) On the x-axis of both figures there is the node index. On the y-axis there are the cumulative distributions $P^{(S)}$ (dashed black line, $P_j^{(S)} = \sum_i S_{ij}$, multiplied by five) and $P^{(A)}$ (grey line, $P_j^{(A)} = \sum_i A_{ij}$, connectivity). The information propagation algorithm identifies communities by leaves (nodes 5 and 9 with lower connectivity) with $m = 0.3$ and $\alpha = 1.4$. (c) The value of state vectors, at the final asymptotic time, of node 5 (dashed black line) and node 9 (black line). We can observe upper values identifying communities: the first one composed by nodes 1-2-3-4-5 and the second one by nodes 6-7-8-9. The algorithm is capable also to detect the *communication nodes* 4 and 6 between the grey lines. In this way we can identify the overlap between the communities and also define a sort of *objective vision* of nodes. It is clear that the upper nodes know very well which is their community as well as nodes 4 and 6 that know that they are in a middle state between two communities.

distribution of labels $P_j$ by summing the knowledge matrix $S_{ij}$ over the index $i$ ($S_{ij}$ is the amount of information of site $i$ about site $j$),

$$P_j = \frac{1}{N} \sum_i S_{ij}$$

and compute

$$H = -\sum_j P_j \log(P_j).$$

In case of a population formed by $n$ communities of the same size, each character-ized by a different label (so that only $n$ values $P_j = 1/n$ are different from zero), we get $H = \log(n)$. There are therefore four characteristic values of $H$: $\log(N)$ if each node knows only about itself (this is the starting value), $\log(N/(GC))$ is the nodes organize their information at the level of communities, $\log(N/G)$ if the nodes cluster their knowledge at the level of groups, and zero if the nodes share a common label (only one big community).

In order to make the results more easily readable, we plot $\exp(H)$ as a function of time, so that the reference values are now $N$, $N/(GC)$, $N/G$ and 1.

## 3.1  Results

We have generated matrices as defined in Section 2, with $K = 5$, $N = 120$, $G = 3$, $C = 2$ (3 groups of 40 nodes, and communities of 20 nodes). After having generated the networks with uniform local connectivity $K$, links are rewired with probability $p_r$. If rewired, the site is connected to another one (possibly already connected) in the same community with probability $p_c$, in the same group with probability $(1 - p_c)p_g$ and to a random node with probability $(1 - p_c)(1 - p_g)$.

An example of such matrix is reported in Figure 2-a. The rewiring probabilities ($p_r = 0.2$, $p_c = 0.9$, $p_g = 0.7$) are such that the local structure is extremely evident, followed by the community structure. The group structure is almost invisible.

In order to reveal all structures of communities, we have slowly varied $m$, for a given value of $\alpha$. The community structure for $\alpha = 1.04$ is reported in Figure 2-b. The levels of $\exp(H)$ corresponding to the group and community structures are marked. By changing the value of the memory $m$, nodes tend to accumulate more knowledge about the external world, and, due to the competition phase, their memory becomes dominated in general by just one label, that marking the community the node belongs to. There are occasional transitions when two com-munities fuse together, in the sense that a label from one community invades the other. It is possible to see these transitions. In particular, plateaus corresponding to a structure in six and three communities are evident for large intervals of $m$. The final state corresponds to just one community (we have not reported the trivial initial phase, with $H \simeq \log(120)$).

Since the matrices are generated stochastically, it may happen that two com-munities are more connected in one realization, and therefore the plateaus may happen for slightly different values of $H$.

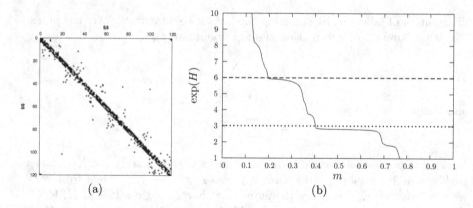

(a)                                          (b)

**Fig. 2.** (a) One adjacency matrix for $K = 5$, $N = 120$, $G = 3$, $C = 2$, $p_r = 0.2$, $p_c = 0.9$, $p_g = 0.7$. Black dots corresponds to $A_{ij} > 0$. (b) The plot of $\exp(H)$ vs $m$ for the network of Figure 2(a). The dotted line marks the value of $\exp(H)$ corresponding to the three groups level and the dashed line marks the value corresponding to the six communities level.

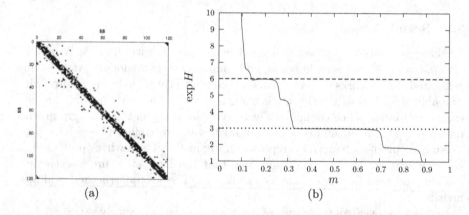

(a)                                          (b)

**Fig. 3.** (a) One adjacency matrix for $K = 7$, $N = 120$, $G = 3$, $C = 2$, $p_r = 0.2$, $p_c = 0.9$, $p_g = 1.0$. Black dots corresponds to $A_{ij} > 0$. (b) The plot of $\exp(H)$ vs $m$ for the network of Figure 3(a). The dotted line marks the value of $\exp(H)$ corresponding to the three groups level and the dashed line marks the value corresponding to the six communities level.

Actually, the long-range connections at the network levels are not strictly needed: due to the local connectivity all nodes are connected, and we can set $p_g = 1$ and still have the transition to a single community, but this is favored by a larger local connectivity $K$. See for instance the Figure 3 .

We have also applied our method to two real networks, the well-known Zachary *karate club* network, Figure 4-a [25], and the social interaction of bottlenose dolphins observed by Leusseau, Figure 4-b [13].

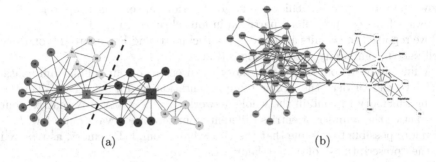

(a)                (b)

**Fig. 4.** (a) Zachary's karate club network ($m = 0.2$ and $\alpha = 1.4$). (b) Bottlenose dolphin network ($m = 0.5$ and $\alpha = 1.03$).

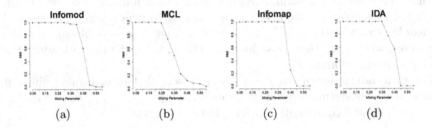

(a)        (b)        (c)        (d)

**Fig. 5.** Test of the algorithm on the GN benchmark based on normalized mutual information (NMI) on the y axes, and the mixing parameter $\mu$ on the x axes. (a) Infomod [18], (b) MCL [5] (c) Infomap [19], (d) our model.

For the Zachary club, our algorithm identifies four communities with different overlapping nodes between them. Considering the hierarchical structure of the network it is possible to merge together two sub-communities. Diamonds denote the overlapping nodes between the two principal communities. Triangles mark the overlapping nodes between the two sub-communities while square are the overlapping nodes between both subcommunities and communities.

The bottlenose dolphin network has a size of 62 nodes and was obtained by direct observation. Our algorithm detects 2 principal communities but also 7 overlapping nodes (diamonds) between them.

Finally, in order to evaluate our algorithm's performance we computed the normalized mutual information (NMI) on a Girvan-Newman (GN) benchmark graph [10] varying the mixing parameter $\mu$, see Figure 5. The graph consists of 128 nodes, each with expected degree 16, which are divided into four groups of 32. The GN benchmark is regularly used for testing algorithms for community detection.

We created 11 networks varying the mixing parameters $\mu$, and compared the results with other well knows community-detection algorithms. We performed simulations with different values of parameters $m$ and $\alpha$. Results (Figure 5-(d)) show that our algorithm achieves very good performance: in fact, up to $\mu = 0.35$ it always finds the predefined partition in four clusters. In the Figure 5-(a)-(b)-(c) we reported the results achieved by Lancichinetti and Fortunato [11] on three well-known community detection algorithms.

A final remark concerns the memory requirement of our cellular automata. We have chosen here the simplest implementation by furnishing to all nodes enough memory to contain the whole network (*i.e.*, $S$ is a $N \times N$ matrix), but in practice the number of entries different from zero are always quite few. It is therefore possible to assume that the nodes have bounded memory, as required by the "prescriptions" of human heuristics.

## 4    Conclusions

We have implemented a community-detection algorithms inspired by human heuristics, as a cellular automaton with some long-range rewiring. In spite of a possible "small world effect", we have seen that it is possible to tune the parameters so to have "windows" in which the nodes of the network adopt the label of different communities.

The main advantage of our method is precisely that of furnishing different "views" of the clustering levels from an individual point of view, *i.e.*, reveal the structure of nested communities an individual belongs to.

**Acknowledgements.** We acknowledge fruitful discussions with P. Lió and Dr. A. Lancichinetti. This work is financially supported by Recognition Project RECOGNITION, a 7th Framework Programme project funded under the FET initiative.

## References

1. Albert, R., Barabasi, A.L.: Rev. Mod. Phys. 74, 47 (2002)
2. Blatt, M., Wiseman, S., Domany, E.: Superparamagnetic clustering of data. Phys. Rev. E 76, 3251–3254 (1996)
3. Brandes, U., Delling, D., Gaertler, M., Görke, R., Hoefer, M., Nikoloski, Z., Wagner, D.: On Finding Graph Clusterings with Maximum Modularity. In: Brandstädt, A., Kratsch, D., Müller, H. (eds.) WG 2007. LNCS, vol. 4769, pp. 121–132. Springer, Heidelberg (2007)
4. Clauset, A.: Finding local community structure in networks. Phys. Rev. E 72, 026132 (2005)
5. Van Dongen, S.: Graph clustering via a discrete uncoupling process. SIAM. J. Matrix Anal. and Appl. 30, 121–141 (2009)
6. Dorogovtesev, S.N., Mendes, J.F.F.: Evolution of Networks. Oxford University Press, Oxford (2003)
7. Forster, K.I., Davis, C.: Repetition priming and frequency attenuation. Journ. Exp. Psyc.: Learning Memory and Cognition 10(4) (1984)
8. Gigerenzer, G., Goldstein, D.G.: Reasoning the fast and frugal way: Models of bounded rationality. Psychological Review 103, 650–669 (1996)

9. Gigerenzer, G., Goldstein, G.: Models of ecological rationality: The recognition heuristic. Psyc. Rev. 109(1), 75–90 (2002)
10. Girvan, M., Newman, M.E.J.: Community structure in social and biological networks. PNAS 99, 7821–7826 (2002)
11. Lancichinetti, A., Fortunato, S.: Community detection algorithms: A comparative analysis. Phys. Rev. E 80, 056117 (2009)
12. Lieberman, E., Hauert, C., Nowak, M.A.: Evolutionary dynamics on graphs. Nature 433(7023), 312–316 (2005)
13. Lusseau, D., Schneider, K., Boisseau, O.J., Haase, P., Slooten, E., Dawson, S.M.: Behavioral Ecology and Sociobiology 54, 396–405 (2003)
14. Massaro, E., Bagnoli, F., Guazzini, A., Lió, P.: Information dynamics algorithm for detecting communities in networks. Communications in Nonlinear Science and Numerical Simulation 17(11), 4294–4303 (2012)
15. Newman, M.E.J.: Detecting community structure in networks. Europ. Phys. J. B 38, 331–330 (2004)
16. Newman, M.E.J., Girvan, M.: Finding and evaluating community structure in networks. Phys. Rev. E 69, 026113 (2004)
17. Nicosia, V., Bagnoli, F., Latora, V.: Impact of network structure on a model of diffusion and competitive interaction. EPL 94(68009) (2011)
18. Rosvall, M., Bergstrom, C.T.: An information-theoretic framework for resolving community structure in complex networks. PNAS 18(104), 7327–7331 (2007)
19. Rosvall, M., Bergstrom, C.T.: Maps of random walks on complex networks reveal community structure. PNAS 105(4), 1118 (2008)
20. Scott, J.: Social Networks Analysis: A Handbook, 2nd edn. Sage, London (2000)
21. Strogatz, S.H.: Nature (London) 410, 268 (2001)
22. Tulving, E., Schacter, D.L., Stark, H.A.: Priming effects in word fragment completion are independent of recognition memory. Journ. Exp. Psyc.: Learning Memory and Cognition 8(4) (1982)
23. Wasserman, S., Faust, K.: Social Networks Analysis. University Press, Cambridge (1994)
24. Watts, D.J., Strogatz, S.H.: Collective dynamics of 'small-world' networks. Nature 393(6684), 409–410 (1998)
25. Zachary, W.W.: An information flow model for conflict and fission in small groups. Journal of Anthropological Research 33, 452–473 (1977)

# Cellular Automaton as Sorting Network Generator Using Instruction-Based Development

Michal Bidlo and Zdenek Vasicek

Brno University of Technology, Faculty of Information Technology
IT4Innovations Centre of Excellence
Božetěchova 2, 61266 Brno, Czech Republic
{bidlom,vasicek}@fit.vutbr.cz

**Abstract.** A new cellular automaton-based approach allowing to generate sorting networks is presented. Since the traditional table-based transition function in this case involves excessive number of rules, a program-based representation of the transition function is applied. The sorting networks are encoded by the cell states and generated during the cellular automaton development. The obtained results are compared with our previous approaches utilizing cellular automata.

**Keywords:** cellular automaton, sorting network, instruction-based development, evolutionary design.

## 1 Introduction

In nature, development is a biological process of ontogeny representing the formation of a multicellular organism from a zygote. It is influenced by the genetic information of the organism and the environment in which the development is carried out. In the area of computer science and evolutionary algorithms in particular, the artificial (or computational) development has been inspired by this biological phenomena. Computational development is usually considered as a non-trivial and indirect mapping from genotypes to phenotypes in an evolutionary algorithm to provide a more flexibility in the construction process of a candidate solution than that is achievable by direct mappings. In such case the genotype has to contain a prescription for the construction of target object. While the genetic operators work with the genotypes, the fitness calculation (evaluation of the candidate solutions) is applied on phenotypes created by means of the development. The principles of the computational development together with a brief biological background and selected application of this bio-inspired approach are summarized in [13]. There are several approaches to perform the development, for example Miller's developmental cartesian genetic programming [11], Koza's developmental genetic programming [8], instruction-based development [5] or cellular automata [12].

This paper proposes a method for the evolutionary design of cellular automata allowing to generate functional structures encoded by the states produced during the cellular automaton development. In order to overcome the problem of

G.C. Sirakoulis and S. Bandini (Eds.): ACRI 2012, LNCS 7495, pp. 214–223, 2012.

scale when evolving CAs with higher number of cell states, the instruction-based approach to represent the local transition function of the CA will be applied. The concept of instruction-based CA was introduced in [3] and demonstrated on non-trivial problems such as replication and pattern development problem. An encoding will be introduced that allows to represent parts of a sorting network by means of cell states in a given development step of the CA. The hypothesis we will work on in this paper is that if a suitable development algorithm (local transition function) is found, then various patterns of cell states may be generated in a series of CA steps that encode a working sorting network. The obtained results will be compared to the sorting networks developed using our previous methods [4].

## 2   Related Work

In this paper, one-dimensional uniform cellular automata (CA) will be applied whose concept was introduced in [12]. To calculate the next cell states, the cellular neighborhood will involve the investigated cell and its left and right immediate neighbors. Since a finite CA dimension will be considered, zero boundary conditions will be considered to determine the states of boundary cells.

Cellular automata have been applied to solve many complex problems in different areas. For example, Miller investigated the problem of evolving a developmental program inside a cell to create multicellular organism of an arbitrary size and characteristic [10]. Tufte and Haddow utilized a FPGA-based platform of Sblocks [7] for the online evolution of digital circuits. The evolutionary algorithm was utilized to design the rules for the development of the CA [14].

Cellular automata have also been successfully applied as a developmental method for generating digital circuits. Although both the uniform and non-uniform CA demonstrated the ability to generate combinational circuits, the non-uniform approach requires several times higher chromosome length which in many cases exceeds the amount of information needed to encode the candidate solution directly (e.g. using CGP) [1,2]. This issue is caused by the need of encoding different local transition function for each cell of the CA. Therefore, our next research has mainly been devoted to uniform CAs and advanced techniques of encoding of the local transition function allowing to reduce the search space for the increasing number of cell states [3]. A method for generating sorting networks by means of cellular automata was introduced in [4].

## 3   Sorting Networks and Their Design

A sorting network [9] is defined as a sequence of compare–swap operations (comparators) that depends only on the number of elements to be sorted, not on the values of the elements. A compare–swap of two elements $(a, b)$ compares and exchanges $a$ and $b$ so that we obtain $a \leq b$ after the operation (a comparator possesses 2 inputs and 2 outputs). Sorting networks represent a class of digital circuits consisting of a finite sequence of comparators. Therefore, a pair $(a, b)$,

$a < b$ represents a comparator whose first input is connected to wire of index $a$ and the second input to wire of index $b$ of a sorting network. Figure 1 shows an example of a 3-input sorting network. For the purposes of this paper we will define the "width" of a comparator as the difference of the indices of wires the comparator is connected to. As evident, all comparators of the width 0 or the value exceeding the number of wires (inputs) of the sorting network are meaningless according to the previous specification.

The number of compare–swap components and the circuit delay are two crucial parameters of any sorting network. By delay we mean the minimal number of groups of compare–swap components that can be executed sequentially. Designers try to minimize the number of comparators, delay or both parameters.

## 4    Sorting Network Development from Cell States

In [4], two different techniques were introduced for the development of sorting networks by means of cellular automata: (1) an absolute encoding and (2) a relative encoding. Each method is based on a suitable enhancement of the local transition function of the CA. The fundamental principle of this enhancement is based on including an additional information to the local transition function (together with the new cell state) that represents a prescription for generating a compare–swap component. In summary, this information includes connection of a compare–swap element to the specific wires of the target sorting network. During the process of the CA development, each cell determines its next state according to a specific rule of the local transition function. The additional information associated with this rule specifies a comparator to be generated by a cell in a development step. Whilst the absolute encoding directly specifies connection of a comparator generated by a given cell after calculating its next state, the relative encoding involves position of the cell and the additional information in the transition function is used to calculate the comparator connection with respect to the cell position. The initial state of the CA together with the enhanced local transition function is a subject of the evolutionary design process. Those experiments have shown the possibility of involving the cellular automata development to generate working sorting networks.

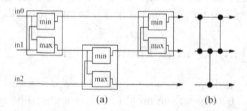

(a)    (b)

**Fig. 1.** (a) A three-input sorting network consists of three comparators connected in an appropriate way to three wires. (b) Alternative symbol. This network can be described using the sequence of integer pairs (0,1)(1,2)(0,1).

This section introduces a new approach to developing sorting networks by means of cellular automata that encodes the compare–swap operations by the cell states rather than the additional information of the local transition function. However, if the number of inputs of the sorting network increases, the number of cell states increases too in order to be able to encode the connection of the comparators to all the wires of the sorting network (which is needed to generate a working solution). For example, the development of an 8-input sorting network requires 8 cell states. If 3-cell neighborhood is considered, there are $8^3 = 512$ rules of the transition function in total and in this case the search space (the space of all the local transition functions) contains $8^{512} = 2.41 \times 10^{462}$ candidate solutions and the exploration of so huge search space using an evolutionary algorithm becomes extremely difficult. In order to overcome this issue, the concept of instruction-based development was adopted to cellular automata [3]. The key idea of this approach is to evolve a program (a sequence of application-specific instructions) for calculating the transition function rather than the complete sequence of transition rules. Since the length of the chromosome encoding the program is shorter, the size of the search space can be reduced substantially as demonstrated in [3].

For the purposes of this paper the following rules will be considered for generating comparators from the cell states. Let $p$ denote the position (index) of a cell in the CA. Then $p$ corresponds to the index of a wire of target sorting network the first input of a comparator will be connected to. Let $s$ denote the state of a cell. Then $s$ corresponds to the width of the comparator, thus its second input will be connected to the wire of index $p+s$. A comparator $(p, p+s)$ is generated by the cell in a development step of the CA if (1) $s$ is different from state 0, (2) $p+s$ does not exceed the index of the last wire of the target sorting network and (3) neither wire $p$ nor wire $p+s$ is occupied by other comparator generated in the same development step (The comparators generated in a development step are independent each other and thus can be executed in parallel. It means that the delay of the target sorting network may be reduced). The order of comparators generated in a given development step is determined by the increasing cell position which ensures the development process is deterministic.

For example, consider a 4-cell cellular automaton whose cells can possess one of the states 0, 1, 2, 3. Assume that the CA performs three development steps and the goal is to generate a 4-input sorting network as shown in Figure 2a. After

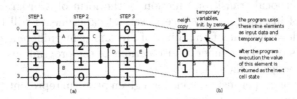

**Fig. 2.** An example of generating 4-input sorting network by means of a cellular automaton

the first development step, the state of the CA is 1010. Therefore, comparator A (0, 1) will be generated by the cell at position 0 because this cell possesses non-zero state. According to the position of this cell, the first input of the comparator will be connected to wire 0 and the cell state corresponds to the width of the comparator (1), i.e. its second input will be connected to wire of index $0 + 1 = 1$. At the same time, comparator B is generated by the cell at position 2. Similarly, the cell position 2 corresponds to the wire of connecting the first comparator input and the cell state 1 determines width of the comarator, i.e. the second input will be connected to wire 3. No other comparator is generated in this development step because all the remaining cells possess state 0. After the second development step the CA exhibits state 2210. Comparator C (0, 2) is generated by the cell at position 0 – it is a comparator of width 2 because it is generated by the cell possessing state 2. Similarly, comparator D (1, 3) is generated by the cell at position 1. In the second development step of the CA, the cell at position 2 does not generate any comparator because the appropriate wires have already been occupied by the comparators generated from cells 0 and 1. The last development step takes the CA into state 0111. In this step only the cell at position 1 generates the comparator E (1, 2). The cell at position 2 does not generate any comparator because the wire 2 has already been occupied and the cell at position 3 also can not generate its comparator since it would exceed the last wire of the sorting network. As evident, the 4-input sorting network can be fully generated in 3 development steps. If more than one comparator is generated in a single step, such comparators can be executed in parallel which reduces the delay of the resulting network. It is a case of step 1 in which comparators $(0, 1)$ and $(2, 3)$ were generated and step 2 that produced comparators $(0, 2)$ and $(1, 3)$.

The cell states are calculated by the program that represents the local transition function and is a subject of evolution. In order to determine the next state of a cell, the states of cells in the cellular neighborhood are copied into the first three elements of a temporary program memory (see Fig. 2b). Then the program is executed and its instructions modify the program memory. Then the value of the memory cell 3 is returned as the next state.

## 5   Evolutionary System Setup

The simple genetic algorithm (GA) will be utilized for the evolutionary design of the cellular automaton that generates a target sorting network. The CA is represented by a local transition function in the form of a program consisting of a sequence of instructions [3]. Several sets of experiments will be presented regarding the development of this kind of circuits using different setup of the CA (the initial state, the number of instructions of the program and the number of development steps of the CA).

The selection of proper instructions for a given problem represent a challenging task. Experiments were performed with a wide range of arithmetic, logic and conditional instructions. However, one of the most promising instruction set for generating sorting networks showed to be a modulo addition operation with

**Table 1.** The set of instructions utilized for the development. $N[a1], N[a2]$ denote the cell states from the neighborhood positions determined by the instruction arguments $a1, a2$. $S[a1], S[a2], S[a3]$ represent state values specified directly by the arguments $a1, a2$ and $a3$. $|S|$ represents the number of cell states. $W, C$ and $E$ specifies the cell state in the West, Central and East position in the cellular neighborhood respectively. *mod* represents the modulo division.

| Instruction | Operation |
|---|---|
| IFW $a1$ $a2$ $a3$ | $if\ (N[a1] == W)\ N[a1] = N[a2]\ else\ N[a1] = N[a3]$ |
| IFC $a1$ $a2$ $a3$ | $if\ (N[a1] == C)\ N[a1] = N[a2]\ else\ N[a1] = N[a3]$ |
| IFE $a1$ $a2$ $a3$ | $if\ (N[a1] == E)\ N[a1] = N[a2]\ else\ N[a1] = N[a3]$ |
| IFSW $a1$ $a2$ $a3$ | $if\ (S[a1] == W)\ W = S[a2]\ else\ W = S[a3]$ |
| IFSC $a1$ $a2$ $a3$ | $if\ (S[a1] == C)\ C = S[a2]\ else\ C = S[a3]$ |
| IFSE $a1$ $a2$ $a3$ | $if\ (S[a1] == E)\ E = S[a2]\ else\ E = S[a3]$ |
| IFG $a1$ $a2$ $a3$ | $if\ (N[a1] == N[a2])N[a1] = N[a3]$ |
| IFGS $a1$ $a2$ $a3$ | $if\ (N[a1] == S[a2])N[a1] = S[a3]$ |
| IFNG $a1$ $a2$ $a3$ | $if\ (N[a1]\ ! = N[a2])N[a1] = N[a3]$ |
| IFNGS $a1$ $a2$ $a3$ | $if\ (N[a1]\ ! = S[a2])N[a1] = S[a3]$ |
| ADDM $a1$ $a2$ $a3$ | $N[a1] = (N[a2] + N[a3])\ mod\ |S|$ |
| NOP | empty operation |

some conditional instructions for modifying the cell states. Each instruction is encoded as a 4-tuple $[op, a1, a2, a3]$, where $op$ denotes the operation code of the instruction and $a1, a2$ and $a3$ represent its arguments. The description of the complete instruction set considered for the experiments is shown in Table 1.

In a single evolutionary experiment, a chromosome of the genetic algorithm contains a fixed number of instructions that undergo changes during evolution in order to create a suitable program for calculating the local transition function. A gene of the chromosome is considered as a single element of the instruction. In all the experiments, the population consists of 100 chromosomes which are initialized randomly at the beginning of evolution. The chromosomes are selected by means of the tournament operator with the base 4. Experiments have shown that the crossover operator is not very suitable to evolve programs using linear encoding, however, in this case a larger change in the chromosomes allows to increase the convergence of the GA, therefore we use one-point crossover operator with the probability 5%. Mutation represents a basic genetic operation to evolve the programs and is performed by generating a new random value for a given gene. In this paper four genes of the chromosome are selected randomly, each of which is mutated with the probability 80%.

Each chromosome is evaluated as the complete test of the sorting network generated by the corresponding CA. The fitness is calculated as the number of correct output bits of the sorting network using all the binary input test vectors. For example, there are $2^{16}$ test vectors in case of 16-input sorting network. Therefore, the fitness value of a perfect solution is $F_{max} = 16 \cdot 2^{16} = 1048576$. If the maximum fitness is not reached until 100k generations, then the evolutionary run is terminated and considered as unsuccessful.

# 6   Experimental Results and Discussion

The experiments were focused of the evolutionary development of 16-input sorting networks by means of one-dimensional uniform cellular automata. 16-input networks were chosen as a benchmark problem for the proposed developmental encoding. This section presents the obtained results and discusses their properties as well as the features of the proposed approach. Note that the analysis of results (i.e. the number of generations and properties of obtained sorting networks) is performed for successful runs only (in which the fitness reached the maximal value $F_{max}$).

**Table 2.** Statistical results of the CA-based sorting network development using the homogeneous 0-valued initial state. The success rate is calculated as the number of successful experiments out of 100 independent evolutionary runs.

| parameters | | | comparators | | | generations [$\times 10^3$] | | | program length | | | success |
|---|---|---|---|---|---|---|---|---|---|---|---|---|
| initial st. | prog. len. | steps | average | max | min | average | max | min | average | max | min | rate |
| 0000 | 10 | 13 | – | – | – | – | – | – | – | – | – | 0 |
| 0000 | 16 | 13 | – | – | – | – | – | – | – | – | – | 0 |
| 0000 | 20 | 13 | 99.2 $\pm 2.8$ | 104 | 97 | 39.2 $\pm 21.1$ | 63.9 | 7.6 | 17.2 $\pm 0.8$ | 18 | 16 | 4 |
| 0000 | 26 | 13 | 99.7 $\pm 0.9$ | 101 | 99 | 68.1 $\pm 21.9$ | 94.9 | 41.2 | 25.0 $\pm 0.8$ | 26 | 24 | 3 |
| 0000 | 10 | 14 | 104.0 $\pm 0.0$ | 104 | 104 | 32.3 $\pm 29.1$ | 72.3 | 3.8 | 9.7 $\pm 0.5$ | 10 | 9 | 3 |
| 0000 | 16 | 14 | 106.2 $\pm 4.4$ | 112 | 99 | 43.9 $\pm 24.8$ | 84.7 | 7.6 | 15.2 $\pm 0.9$ | 16 | 13 | 13 |
| 0000 | 20 | 14 | 109.1 $\pm 2.8$ | 112 | 104 | 42.1 $\pm 30.4$ | 98.3 | 3.7 | 18.8 $\pm 1.0$ | 20 | 17 | 12 |
| 0000 | 26 | 14 | 106.8 $\pm 4.2$ | 112 | 99 | 27.5 $\pm 23.1$ | 82.7 | 2.4 | 24.3 $\pm 0.8$ | 25 | 23 | 20 |

The experiments have shown that the initial CA state represents a crucial parameter to achieve working results with a reasonable success rate. Table 2 shows the statistical results for a set of experiments considering a homogeneous initial state consisting of only 0-state cells. In some cases the evolution has succeeded and found programs that generate sorting networks using this initial state. We have determined that the zero boundary conditions of the CA play an important role in this set of experiments. If the CA state changes to an other homogeneous state after the first development step, the zero boundary conditions provide different state values in the cellular neighborhood allowing the cell states to diverse during the subsequent steps and to generate suitable comparator arrangements. As evident from Table 2, the success rate depends especially on the number of development steps and the length of the program to be evolved. We have determined that 20 instruction in a chromosome and 13 development steps are required to develop a working sorting network in this set of experiments. As expectable, more development steps allows to generate sorting networks with a higher success rate because more comparators can be generated. However, no clear dependence has been observed for increasing the program length for a given number of development steps. In some cases the success rate is even lower for larger number of instructions in the chromosome. This may be caused by increasing the cardinality of the search space in which the evolution probably needs more generations to find a working solution.

**Table 3.** Statistical results of the CA-based sorting network development using the alternating initial state consisting of values 2 and 0. The success rate is calculated as the number of successful experiments out of 100 independent evolutionary runs.

| parameters | | | comparators | | | generations [$\times 10^3$] | | | program length | | | success |
|---|---|---|---|---|---|---|---|---|---|---|---|---|
| initial st. | prog. len. | steps | average | max | min | average | max | min | average | max | min | rate |
| 2020 | 10 | 13 | 94.0 ±0.0 | 94 | 94 | 95.4 ±0.0 | 95.4 | 95.4 | 10.0 ±0.0 | 10 | 10 | 1 |
| 2020 | 16 | 13 | 96.4 ±3.1 | 100 | 90 | 28.2 ±27.2 | 89.4 | 5.9 | 14.4 ±0.7 | 16 | 14 | 7 |
| 2020 | 20 | 13 | 96.3 ±2.4 | 99 | 94 | 40.7 ±13.6 | 57.2 | 19.2 | 19.3 ±0.9 | 20 | 18 | 6 |
| 2020 | 26 | 13 | 95.5 ±1.5 | 97 | 94 | 48.7 ±35.3 | 84.1 | 13.3 | 24.5 ±0.5 | 25 | 24 | 2 |
| 2020 | 10 | 14 | 102.6 ±2.9 | 108 | 90 | 34.8 ±27.2 | 93.9 | 0.5 | 9.3 ±1.0 | 10 | 7 | 31 |
| 2020 | 16 | 14 | 102.5 ±2.8 | 106 | 90 | 35.0 ±27.2 | 89.4 | 1.6 | 15.0 ±1.0 | 16 | 13 | 45 |
| 2020 | 20 | 14 | 103.8 ±4.0 | 112 | 90 | 38.7 ±31.5 | 98.8 | 0.4 | 18.8 ±1.2 | 20 | 15 | 43 |
| 2020 | 26 | 14 | 103.1 ±3.1 | 110 | 90 | 28.3 ±25.4 | 83.6 | 0.8 | 24.1 ±1.2 | 26 | 21 | 36 |

Table 3 shows the statistical results for the experiments considering an initial state with alternating values 2 and 0 (an alternating initial state). It is interesting to observe that the success rate has increased in most cases just by changing the initial CA state. Moreover, the evolution was able to find a solution even for 10 or 16 instructions in the chromosomes. Although the success rate is not very high for 13 development steps, it has increased substantially for 14 steps (Table 3). This fact indicates that the conditions for generating working sorting networks are highly dependent on the initial state of the CA. However, it is very difficult to identify the optimal initial state for 16-cell CA in which each cell may possess one of 16 different values. The proposed initial states were determined experimentally and the evolution has not optimized them in this stage of research.

Another interesting feature can be observed in the number of comparators of the resulting sorting networks which exhibits lower values for the alternating initial state (Table 3) in comparison with the experiments considering the homogeneous state (Table 2). This fact supports the hypothesis that the initial state does not only influence the success rate but also the properties of the target sorting networks. Note that the delay of the sorting networks are determined by the number of development steps of the CA because the proposed encoding ensures that the comparators generated in a single step can be performed in parallel.

The approach proposed in this paper exhibits the following features in comparison with other techniques. In [4], two techniques were applied: (1) the absolute encoding provided a sorting network with 75 comparators whose delay is 16 and (2) the relative encoding provided a sorting network with 92 comparators whose delay is 14. In this paper, the best resulting sorting network consists of 78 comparators and its delay is 13. This network has been obtained by removing redundant comparators from a SN consisting of 104 comparators. The resulting sorting network and the corresponding program according to which the CA generated that network is shown in Figure 3. However, the average delay achieved for different developmental setups in [4] was greater than 20 whilst in this paper the delay is limited by the number of development steps of the CA (i.e. for 13 development steps the delay can not be larger). The currently best-known

16-input sorting network consists of 60 comparators and its delay is 10 (e.g. see [6]). Note that the significant difference in the proposed approach is that we have used a developmental encoding whilst the currently best known result was obtained using a direct representation with an explicit area/delay optimization mechanism.

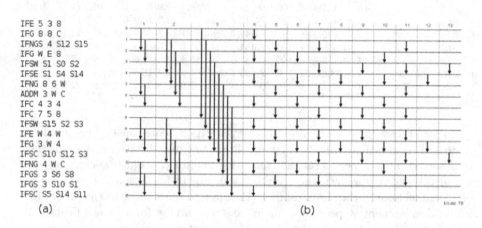

Fig. 3. (a) Evolved program for calculating the transition function of cellular automaton, (b) a sorting network developed by the CA (redundant comparators were removed)

## 7    Conclusions

A generative approach was introduced for the development of sorting networks by means of cellular automata. The encoding of sorting network comparators is based on the positions of cell in the cellular automaton and the cell states. The transition function of the cellular automaton is represented by a program (consisting of simple application-specific instructions) that is a subject of evolutionary design process. It was shown that the proposed method is able to generate sorting networks whose properties are significantly influenced by the initial state of the cellular automaton. Since the identification of a proper initial state represents a difficult task, it was performed experimentally for the presented case studies. In order to increase the success rate and the quality of the resulting solutions, more research is needed. Therefore, the design of initial states by means of evolution as well as the utilization of advanced evolutionary techniques for the design of the transition function represent areas in which the future experiments will be performed.

**Acknowledgment.** This work was supported by the Czech science foundation project P103/10/1517.

# References

1. Bidlo, M., Vasicek, Z.: Gate-level evolutionary development using cellular automata. In: Proc. of The 3nd NASA/ESA Conference on Adaptive Hardware and Systems, AHS 2008, pp. 11–18. IEEE Computer Society (2008)
2. Bidlo, M., Vasicek, Z.: Comparison of the uniform and non-uniform cellular automata-based approach to the development of combinational circuits. In: Proc. of The 4th NASA/ESA Conference on Adaptive Hardware and Systems, AHS 2009, pp. 423–430. IEEE Computer Society (2009)
3. Bidlo, M., Vasicek, Z.: Instruction-based development of cellular automata. In: Proc. of The 2012 IEEE Congress on Evolutionary Computatio, CEC 2012, IEEE Computer Society (2012)
4. Bidlo, M., Vasicek, Z., Slany, K.: Sorting Network Development Using Cellular Automata. In: Tempesti, G., Tyrrell, A.M., Miller, J.F. (eds.) ICES 2010. LNCS, vol. 6274, pp. 85–96. Springer, Heidelberg (2010)
5. Bidlo, M., Škarvada, J.: Instruction-based development: From evolution to generic structures of digital circuits. International Journal of Knowledge-Based and Intelligent Engineering Systems 12(3), 221–236 (2008)
6. Choi, S.S., Moon, B.R.: Isomorphism, normalization, and a genetic algorithm for sorting network optimization. In: GECCO 2002: Proceedings of the Genetic and Evolutionary Computation Conference, pp. 327–334. Morgan Kaufmann Publishers Inc., San Francisco (2002)
7. Haddow, P.C., Tufte, G.: Bridging the genotype–phenotype mapping for digital FPGAs. In: Proc. of the 3rd NASA/DoD Workshop on Evolvable Hardware, pp. 109–115. IEEE Computer Society, Los Alamitos (2001)
8. Koza, J.R., Keane, M.A., Streeter, M.J., Mydlowec, W., Yu, J., Lanza, G.: Genetic Programming IV: Routine Human-Competitive Machine Intelligence. Kluwer Academic Publishers (2003)
9. Knuth, D.E.: The Art of Computer Programming: Sorting and Searching, 2nd edn. Addison Wesley (1998)
10. Miller, J.F.: Evolving Developmental Programs for Adaptation, Morphogenesis, and Self-Repair. In: Banzhaf, W., Ziegler, J., Christaller, T., Dittrich, P., Kim, J.T. (eds.) ECAL 2003. LNCS (LNAI), vol. 2801, pp. 256–265. Springer, Heidelberg (2003)
11. Miller, J.F., Thomson, P.: A Developmental Method for Growing Graphs and Circuits. In: Tyrrell, A.M., Haddow, P.C., Torresen, J. (eds.) ICES 2003. LNCS, vol. 2606, pp. 93–104. Springer, Heidelberg (2003)
12. von Neumann, J.: The Theory of Self-Reproducing Automata. In: Burks, A.W. (ed.) University of Illinois Press (1966)
13. Kumar, S., Bentley, P.J. (eds.): On Growth, Form and Computers. Elsevier Academic Press (2003)
14. Tufte, G., Haddow, P.C.: Towards development on a silicon-based cellular computing machine. Natural Computing 4(4), 387–416 (2005)

# Network View of Binary Cellular Automata

Yoshihiko Kayama

Department of Media and Information, BAIKA Women's University
2-19-5 Shukuno-sho, Ibaraki 567-8578, Osaka, Japan
y_kayama@ieee.org

**Abstract.** The network view of cellular automata focuses on the effective relationships between cells rather than the states themselves. In this article, we review a network representation presented in previous papers and present network graphs derived from all independent rules of one-dimensional elementary cellular automata and totalistic five-neighbor cellular automata. Removal of the transient effects of initial configurations improves the visibility of the dynamical characteristics of each rule. Power-law distributions of lifetimes and sizes of avalanches caused by one-cell perturbations of an attractor are exhibited by the derived network of Rule 11 (or 52) of totalistic five-neighbor cellular automata.

**Keywords:** Cellular Automaton, Complex Network, Scale-free.

## 1 Introduction

Originally proposed by von Neumann [1], cellular automata (CA) have been studied and applied to investigate complex phenomena in various kinds of research fields. The parallelism of CA rules and their ability to form complex patterns can be characterized by four kinds of patterns called Wolfram's classes: homogeneous (class I), periodic (class II), chaotic (class III), and complex (class IV) [2]. In particular, Conway's Game of Life, or simply Life, can generate a wide range of interesting behaviors and simulate a universal computer [3,4]. Alternatively, complex networks have been studied extensively in the wake of papers by Watts and Strogatz on small-world networks [5] and by Barabási and Albert on scale-free networks [6]. The small-world or scale-free topologies can be identified ubiquitously in social relationships, biological and chemical systems, the Internet, etc. Complex systems composed of some fundamental elements frequently organize such complex networks. Motivated by this point of view, we proposed a method to derive a network from a binary CA rule, called a "network representation." The networks derived from elementary CA (ECA) and five-neighbor totalistic CA (5TCA) rules can visualize the dynamical characteristics of each rule and their network parameters show behaviors corresponding to Wolfram's classes [7,8]. The network representation of Life was discussed in the previous article [9]. Life is not only a member of class IV but also one of the simplest examples of *self-organized criticality* (SOC). Bak, Tang and Wiesenfeld [10] discovered that critical behavior can emerge spontaneously from simple local interactions

G.C. Sirakoulis and S. Bandini (Eds.): ACRI 2012, LNCS 7495, pp. 224–233, 2012.

without any fine tunings of variable parameters. As in the case of the sandpile model discussed by the above-mentioned authors, scale invariance is also exhibited by the distributions of the lifetimes and sizes of avalanches launched in Life's rest state [11]. Our network representation can visualize the underlying tension causing the avalanches and correspondingly exhibit a scale-free nature in its degree distributions.

In this article, we review our network representation of binary CA and present network graphs derived from all independent ECA and 5TCA rules. In contrast to the previous study [8], one-cell perturbations are applied after a sufficiently long initial time in order to remove the transient effects of initial configurations. The characteristic parameters of derived networks, namely efficiency and cluster coefficients (CCs), exhibit more obvious correspondence with Wolfram's classes than previously observed. The size of an avalanche catalyzed by the one-cell perturbation of a rest state, i.e., an attractor, is defined by the total changes in out-degrees during its lifetime [12]. The derived network of a class IV candidate, rule 11 (equivalent to rule 52) of 5TCA, exhibits power-law distributions of the lifetimes and sizes of the avalanches.

The next section reviews our network representation of binary CA. Section three consists of two parts: the first presents sample network graphs of all the independent rules of ECA and 5TCA, and the second introduces Life networks of typical patterns and a rest state. Section four reports the characteristic parameters of derived networks and the power-law distributions of the 5TCA rule.

## 2   Network Representation

Now we consider a regular 1D grid of cells, each characterized by binary states that are updated synchronously in discrete time steps according to a CA rule. Each cell has $2r + 1$ neighbors which consist of the cell itself and its $r$ local neighbors on both sides, where $r$ denotes the radius. The state of a cell at the next time step is determined from the current states of the neighboring cells:

$$x_i(t + 1) = f_R(x_{i-r}(t), ..., x_i(t), ..., x_{i+r}(t)), \tag{1}$$

where $x_i(t)$ denotes the state of the cell $i$ at time $t$, and $f_R$ is the transition function of a rule $R$. The term *configuration* refers to an assignment of states to all cells for a given time step; a configuration is given by $\boldsymbol{x}(t) = \sum_{i=0}^{N-1} x_i(t)\boldsymbol{e}_i$, where $\boldsymbol{e}_i$ denotes the $i$-th unit vector: $\boldsymbol{e}_i = (0, \cdots, 0, \overset{i}{1}, 0, \cdots, 0)$, and $N$ is the grid size. Thus, the time transition of configuration $\boldsymbol{x}(t)$ with some boundary conditions is given by $\boldsymbol{x}(t + 1) = \boldsymbol{f}_R(\boldsymbol{x}(t))$, where $\boldsymbol{f}_R$ represents a mapping on the configuration space $\{\boldsymbol{x}\}_N$ induced from the rule function $f_R$. After $t$ time steps, the configuration of cells obtained from an initial configuration $\boldsymbol{\varphi}$ is given by $\boldsymbol{x}(t, \boldsymbol{\varphi}) = \boldsymbol{f}_R^t(\boldsymbol{\varphi})$.

After $t_0$ time steps from the initial configuration, a perturbation is given to the configuration $\boldsymbol{\varphi}_0 \equiv \boldsymbol{x}(t_0, \boldsymbol{\varphi})$. The perturbation effect after $t_I$ time steps can be written as

$$\Delta\boldsymbol{x}(t_I, \boldsymbol{\varphi}_0) \equiv \boldsymbol{f}_R^{t_I}(\boldsymbol{\varphi}_0 + \Delta\boldsymbol{\varphi}_0) + \boldsymbol{f}_R^{t_I}(\boldsymbol{\varphi}_0) \,(\text{mod } 2). \tag{2}$$

If we denote $\Delta_i \varphi_0$ as a one-cell perturbation of cell $i$, then $\Delta_i \varphi_0 = e_i$ in the binary case, and Eq. (2) leads to

$$\Delta_i \boldsymbol{x}(t_I, \boldsymbol{\varphi_0}) \equiv \Delta_i \boldsymbol{f}_R^{t_I}(\boldsymbol{\varphi_0}) = \boldsymbol{A}_R(t_I, \boldsymbol{\varphi_0}) \bullet e_i, \tag{3}$$

where the product of the right-hand side is the inner product, and

$$\boldsymbol{A}_R(t_I, \boldsymbol{\varphi_0}) \equiv \sum_{i=0}^{N-1} \Delta_i \boldsymbol{f}_R^{t_I}(\boldsymbol{\varphi_0}) e_i \tag{4}$$

has an $N \times N$ matrix representation. If $\mathcal{N} \equiv \{e_i\}$ defines a set of nodes, then each component $(\Delta_i \boldsymbol{f}_R^{t_I}(\boldsymbol{\varphi_0}))_j$ defines a one-to-one mapping: $\mathcal{N} \to \mathcal{N}$. Therefore, we call $(\Delta_i \boldsymbol{f}_R^{t_I}(\boldsymbol{\varphi_0}))_j$ a *directed edge* from node $i$ to node $j$. Then, $(\mathcal{N}, \mathcal{N}, \Delta_i \boldsymbol{f}_R^{t_I}(\boldsymbol{\varphi_0}))$ defines a directed graph connecting node $i$ to other nodes. Taking all the graphs into consideration, we define a network representation of binary CA as $(\mathcal{N}, \mathcal{N}, \boldsymbol{A}_R(t_I, \boldsymbol{\varphi_0}))$, and a matrix representation of $\boldsymbol{A}_R(t_I, \boldsymbol{\varphi_0})$ is the adjacency matrix $[\boldsymbol{A}_R]_{i,j} = (\Delta_i \boldsymbol{f}_R^{t_I}(\boldsymbol{\varphi_0}))_j$.

In CA, the network view focuses on the effective relationships between cells rather than their states. The directed graph $(\mathcal{N}, \mathcal{N}, \Delta_i \boldsymbol{f}_R^{t_I}(\boldsymbol{\varphi_0}))$ illustrates the effective information flow from a one-cell perturbation of the cell $i$ after $t_I$ time steps. The symmetries of the network representation were discussed in the previous papers [7,8], in which we defined a transformation of a rule function called the *diminished-radix complement* $\hat{f}_R$ in addition to the mirror (left-right reflection), complement (0-1 exchange), and mirror-complement: $\hat{f}_R(x_{i-r}, ..., x_i, ..., x_{i+r}) \equiv f_R(\bar{x}_{i-r}, ..., \bar{x}_i, ..., \bar{x}_{i+r})$, where $\bar{x}$ is the complement of $x$. The transformation defines a new pairing of rules and if the two rules are self-complementary, their network representations are equivalent.

## 3    Sample Networks

– ECA and 5TCA rules

ECA are the simplest nontrivial CA with $r = 1$ and the $2^3 = 8$ different neighborhood configurations result in $2^8 = 256$ possible rules. Although five-neighbor $(r = 2)$ CA contain $2^{32}$ rules, the totalistic CA (5TCA) are more restricted and contain $2^6 = 64$ rules. We follow a standard naming convention invented by Wolfram [2,13] that gives each rule in ECA and 5TCA a number from 0 to 255 and 0 to 63, respectively. To avoid confusion, we add the letter "$T$" to the Wolfram code of the 5TCA rules, e.g., rule $T52$. Taking all symmetries into consideration, we obtained the number of rules having non-trivial and independent networks as 73 in ECA and 26 in 5TCA [8]. The diminished-radix complement pairs of self-complement rules were also listed.

Sample networks of the independent rules are listed in the Appendix with $N = 41$ and $t_0 = 1000$. In order to ensure that each cell has causal relationships with all the other cells and to avoid repetitions, the time interval $t_I$ was set to $[N/2]$ and $[N/4]$ for ECA and 5TCA, respectively, where [n] represents the maximum integer not exceeding n. The red and gray dots on the circumference of the graphs represent the active and inactive cells, respectively. Directed links are drawn with a color gradient from red to blue. Red indicates that the link is exiting the node (out-link), and blue indicates that the link is entering the node (in-link). Bilateral links are drawn in black. In this study, each rule could be classified to its corresponding Wolfram class more easily than in our previous study [8]. Networks of class II rules contain localized or thin and striped links. Class III rules have thick and complex networks. The network representation of additive rules, e.g., rule 90 and $T42$, is independent of an initial configuration, and it is equivalent to the rules and not merely a perturbed result. Consequently, the symmetric and geometric graphs in Tables 1 and 2 are all additive rules. Their geometric patterns drastically change depending on the time interval $t_I$. The networks of some class II rules and class IV candidates, rule 110 and $T11(T52)$, are sensitive to changes in an initial configuration. Such characteristics are represented by a large value of one of their clustering coefficient components, as described in the next section.

– Conway's Game of Life

The typical patterns of Life are known as still lifes, oscillators, and spaceships [14,15]. Although Block (Fig. 1a) and Beehive (Fig. 1b) are both typical still lifes, their networks show different behaviors to stop or continue their growth with $t_I$. Because the outermost in-links of Beehive indicate the spreading of the

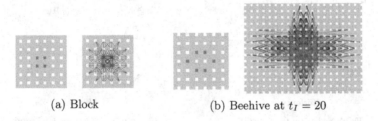

(a) Block                    (b) Beehive at $t_I = 20$

**Fig. 1.** Typical Life patterns and their networks. Still lifes: (a) Block and (b) Beehive.

perturbations from the inner cells to the outer area, if a large value of $t_I$ is considered, the blue edges may spread widely into the outer area. These edges represent the underlying tension in the Life rest state, leading to avalanches from one-cell perturbations (Fig. 2). Networks derived from other famous patterns such as Blinker and Glider can be found in our previous article [9] or a web site [16].

## 4    Network Parameters

Here, we use the efficiency [17,18] and the clustering coefficients (CCs) [19] to investigate the characteristics of the derived CA networks. The efficiency is the

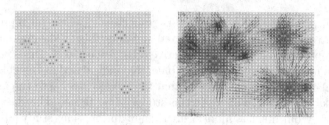

**Fig. 2.** Life in rest state and its network at $t_I = 25$

harmonic mean of the shortest path lengths from one node to the other nodes. The CCs of directed networks are divided into several types: cycle ($C^{cyc}$), middleman ($C^{mid}$), in ($C^{in}$), out ($C^{out}$), and the sum total of all the CCs ($C^{all}$) [20]. Graphs of the efficiency and $C^{all}$ of the derived networks show a relation between network connectivity and Wolfram's classes. Radar charts of the efficiency and other CC components also illustrate characteristic figures reflecting the global and local connection properties of the derived networks. Typical class III rules, which can produce highly random bit sequences, have a pentagonal figure. The rules that are regarded as candidates for class IV occupy the area

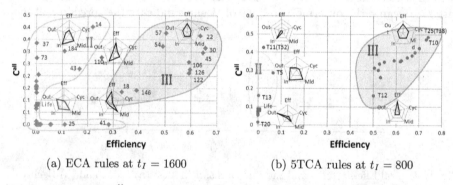

(a) ECA rules at $t_I = 1600$          (b) 5TCA rules at $t_I = 800$

**Fig. 3.** Efficiency/$C^{all}$ graphs of networks derived from (a) ECA and (b) 5TCA rules, representing the average of networks obtained from ten pseudo-randomly generated initial configurations with $N = 3201$ and $t_0 = 10^4$. Efficiency/$C^{all}$ value of Life network is also plotted with $N = 101 \times 101$, $t_0 = 10^5$, and $t_I = 50$. Radar charts show efficiency-CC components of networks derived from the typical rules, (a) 184, 110, 22, Life, and 18; and (b) T11(T52), T10, T5, T20 and T12 (from left top to right bottom). The five axes are (clockwise from the top) efficiency, $C^{cyc}$, $C^{mid}$, $C^{in}$, and $C^{out}$.

between class II and III rules (Fig. 3). Rule 184, which is known for its high-dependency on initial configurations [13], and similar class II rules, 14, 43 and $T5$, are represented by a large $C^{in}$ relative to the other CC components [8]. The class IV candidates, rule 110 and $T11(T52)$, are also sensitive to changes in an initial configuration. The elimination of transients allows us to clearly observe the large value of $C^{in}$ in their radar charts (Fig. 4). On the contrary, the large

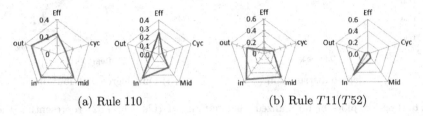

(a) Rule 110                    (b) Rule $T11(T52)$

**Fig. 4.** Changes in radar charts of efficiency-CC components of class IV candidates, (a) rule 110 and (b) rule $T11(T52)$, with $N = 3201$. The left and right graphs in each figure are at $t_0 = 0$ and $10^4$, respectively.

$C^{in}$ figure of rule $T30$ changes to a pentagonal one which can be recognized as a class III characteristic (Fig. 5).

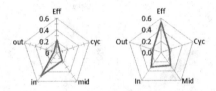

**Fig. 5.** Change in radar chart of efficiency-CC components of rule $T30$ with $N = 3201$. The left and right graphs are at $t_0 = 0$ and $10^4$, respectively.

As reported in the previous paper [9], the Life rest-state network has a scale-free nature in its degree distribution. Seeking such a scale-free network in the ECA and 5TCA rules, we have found that a rule $T11(T52)$ network has scale-free-like degree distributions (Fig. 6). Although the power-law was not a plausible fit to the distributions according to a goodness-of-fit test [21], we checked the distributions of the lifetimes and sizes of the avalanches caused by one-cell perturbations of an attractor. The lifetime $l$ can be defined by the number of time steps before the configuration returns to an attractor [11]. The size $s$ is defined as the space-time sum of the changes in the out-degrees [12]:

$$s_i \equiv \sum_{t=1}^{l_i} | n_{out}^i(t) - n_{out}^i(t-1) |, \qquad (5)$$

where $l_i$ is the lifetime of the avalanche launched from the cell at $i$, and the out-degree of the cell is given by $n_{out}^i(t) = \sum_{j=0}^{N-1} [A_R(t)]_{i,j}$. Fig. 7 shows the

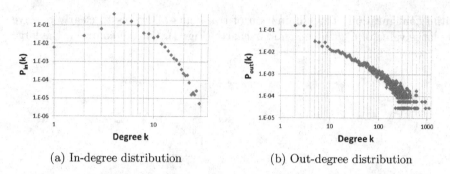

(a) In-degree distribution          (b) Out-degree distribution

**Fig. 6.** Log-log plots of normalized distributions of rule $T11(T52)$ representing the average of networks obtained from ten pseudo-randomly generated initial configurations with $N = 20001$, $t_0 = 2 \times 10^5$, and $t_I = 5000$.

power-law distributions of the lifetimes and sizes of avalanches. The statistical tests gave $p$-values larger than 0.1 at $l_{min}$ and $s_{min}$ larger than 200.

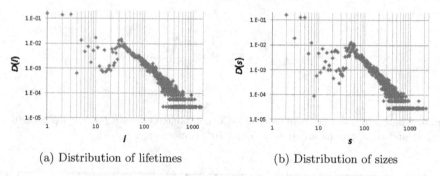

(a) Distribution of lifetimes          (b) Distribution of sizes

**Fig. 7.** Log-log plots of normalized distributions of the lifetimes and sizes of the avalanches of rule $T11(T52)$ representing the average of networks obtained from ten pseudo-randomly generated initial configurations with $N = 20001$, $t_0 = 2 \times 10^5$, and $t_I = 5000$.

## 5   Conclusions

Our network representation provides us with a new visualization scheme of binary CA rules. The networks derived from the independent ECA and 5TCA rules illustrate the symmetrical and dynamical features more clearly than in the previous study [8]; this is because of the removal of the transient effects of initial configurations. The network representation allows the techniques of the network theory to be used for the investigation of CA dynamics. The efficiency/CC graphs and the characteristic radar charts of the efficiency and the

CC components are useful for studying the global and local connection properties of derived networks. Similar to the Life rest-state network, the residual patterns of an attractor of class IV candidates may be connected to each other by the expansion of links, which creates the underlying tension that is the cause of avalanches, whose lifetimes and sizes show power-law distributions. In fact, the derived network of rule $T11(T52)$ has the power-law distributions of the lifetimes and sizes of the avalanches. Although Rule 110 is well-known as a class IV rule, thus far, we have not found such a scale-free nature in its distributions. If class IV behavior requires some fractal structures inside the system, a scale-free nature would be detected in its network representation. Further investigations will be required to clarify a relation between scale invariance and class IV behavior.

# References

1. von Neumann, J.: The theory of self-reproducing automata. In: Burks, A.W. (ed.) Essays on Cellular Automata. University of Illinois Press (1966)
2. Wolfram, S.: Statistical mechanics of cellular automata. Rev. Mod. Phys. 55, 601–644 (1983)
3. Gardner, M.: Mathematical games. Scientific American 223, 120–123 (1970)
4. Berlekamp, E.R., Conway, J.H., Guy, R.K.: Winning Ways for Your Mathematical Plays, vol. 2. Academic Press, New York (1982)
5. Watts, D.J., Strogatz, S.H.: Collective dynamics of 'small-world' networks. Nature 393, 440–442 (1998)
6. Barabási, A.L., Albert, R.: Emergence of scaling in random networks. Science 286, 509–512 (1999)
7. Kayama, Y.: Complex networks derived from cellular automata. arXiv:1009.4509 (2010)
8. Kayama, Y.: Network representation of cellular automata. In: 2011 IEEE Symposium on Artificial Life (IEEE ALIFE 2011) at SSCI 2011, pp. 194–202 (2011)
9. Kayama, Y., Imamura, Y.: Network representation of the game of life. Journal of Artificial Intelligence and Soft Computing Research 1 (3), 233–240 (2011)
10. Bak, P., Tang, C., Wiesenfeld, K.: Self-organized criticality: an explanation of 1/f noise. Physical Review Letters 59 (4), 381–384 (1987)
11. Bak, P., Chen, K., Creutz, M.: Self-organized criticality in the 'game of life'. Nature (London) 342, 780 (1989)
12. Kayama, Y.: Network representation of the game of life and self-organized criticality (extended abstract). To be appeared in the Proceedings of the 13th International Conference on the Simulation & Synthesis of Living Systems (2012)
13. Wolfram, S.: A New Kind of Science. Wolfram Media, Inc. (2002)
14. Callahan, P.: Patterns, programs, and links for conway's game of life (1995), http://www.radicaleye.com/lifepage/ (retrieved at February 1, 2011)
15. Flammenkamp, A.: Achim's game of life page (1998), http://wwwhomes.uni-bielefeld.de/achim/gol.html (retrieved at December 12, 2011)
16. Kayama, Y.: Network View of Conway's Game of Life. Wolfram Demonstrations Project (2012), http://demonstrations.wolfram.com/NetworkViewOfConwaysGameOfLife/
17. Latora, V., Marchiori, M.: Efficient behavior of small-world networks. Phys. Rev. Lett. 87, 198701–198704 (2001)

18. Boccaletti, S., Latora, V., Moreno, Y., Chavez, M., Hwang, D.U.: Complex networks: Structure and dynamics. Physics Reports 424, 175–308 (2006)
19. Wasserman, S., Faust, K.: Social Network Analysis. Cambridge University Press (1994)
20. Fagiolo, G.: Clustering in complex directed networks. Phys. Rev. E 76, 026107–026114 (2007)
21. Clauset, A., Shalizi, C.R., Newman, M.E.J.: Power-law distributions in empirical data. SIAM Review 51, 661–703 (2009)

## Appendix: Sample Networks of ECA and 5TCA

All independent and non-trivial network graphs of ECA and 5TCA rules are shown in Table 2 and Table 1, respectively. The initial configurations of each of the 41 cells are pseudo-randomly generated, and their initial time $t_0$ is set to 1000.

**Table 1.** Independent networks of 5TCA rules obtained from pseudo-randomly generated initial configurations with $N = 41$, $t_0 = 1000$, and $t_I = 10$. The rules inside the square brackets are the diminished-radix complement to the one outside the brackets. It is hard to find a non-trivial network in rule $T20$ because of the small lattice size.

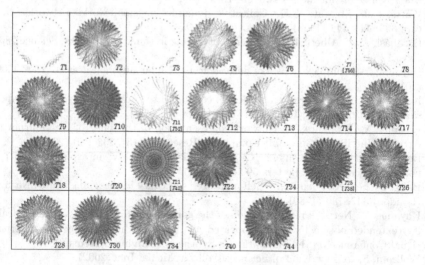

**Table 2.** Independent and non-trivial networks of ECA rules obtained from pseudo-randomly generated initial configurations with $N = 41$, $t_0 = 1000$, and $t_I = 20$. The rules inside the square brackets are the diminished-radix complement to the one outside the brackets.

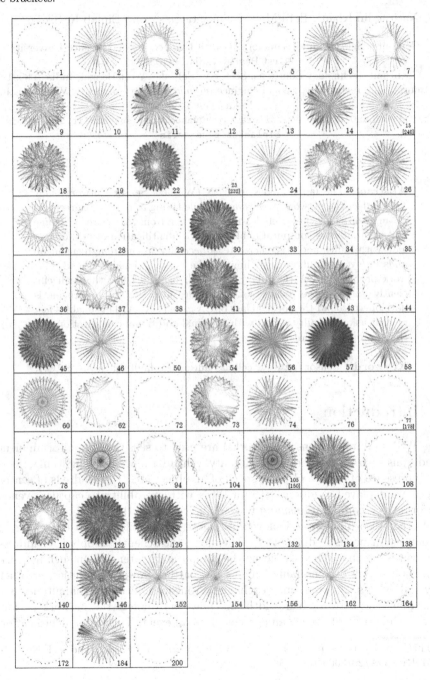

# A Cellular Automata Based Scheme for Energy Efficient Fault Diagnosis in WSN*

Nasiruddin Khan[1], Ilora Maity[2], Sukanta Das[3], and Biplab K. Sikdar[1]

[1] Computer Science and Technology, Bengal Engineering and Science University,
West Bengal, India 711103
[2] Cognizant Technology Solutions, Sector-V, Saltlake, West Bengal, India 700091
[3] Information Technology, Bengal Engineering and Science University, West Bengal,
India 711103
nasiruddinkhan07@gmail.com, ilora_maity@yahoo.com, sukanta@it.becs.ac.in,
biplab@cs.becs.ac.in

**Abstract.** The faulty nodes in WSN (Wireless Sensor Network) may
badly affect the network performance while trying to reach an agreement
on an event. This effectively leads to deviation from the desired outcome
and unproductive computational overhead. Identification of network region with faulty nodes is, therefore, a necessity to ensure agreement on
an issue/event simultaneously limiting the computational overhead. This
work proposes a CA (Cellular Automata) based scheme that can efficiently diagnose the region of faulty nodes in a WSN. The scheme is
developed around the special class of CA called SACA. This enables fast
identification of faulty region with marginal additional computation and
the network bandwidth.

**Keywords:** Sensor network, cellular automata, fault diagnosis, SACA.

## 1   Introduction

The WSNs (Wireless Sensor Networks) are used to sense and monitor ambient
conditions such as: temperature, humidity, vehicular movement, lightning, noise
level, presence of certain objects, speed of an object etc. [1]. Hundreds of sensor
nodes are deployed randomly [1] in a WSN with the ability to capture events,
perform some computations, and to communicate with the neighbors.

As the sensor nodes are deployed in remote and hostile areas, the recharging
of battery in nodes is difficult [1]. Therefore, the schemes adopted to address
different issues in a WSN should not be computation intensive. In such network
some nodes may become faulty due to low battery power, calamities, or other
physical defects [2]. These may exchange erroneous information simultaneously
consuming the network bandwidth and may badly affect the network performance while trying to reach an agreement on an event. Therefore, identification

* This work is supported by AICTE Career Award fund (F.No. 1-
51/RID/CA/29/2009-10).

G.C. Sirakoulis and S. Bandini (Eds.): ACRI 2012, LNCS 7495, pp. 234–243, 2012.
© Springer-Verlag Berlin Heidelberg 2012

of such faulty nodes/region of faulty nodes is a necessity to avoid the destructive malfunctioning.

In centralized fault detection approach [3], a geographically or logically centralized node takes responsibility for monitoring the misbehaved nodes of the network. The major drawback of centralized approaches is the high volume of message traffic and quick energy depletion in some nodes. On the other hand, the distributed fault detection approaches target self-detection and self-correction [4], [5]. Some of these approaches consider that the nodes are equipped with expensive costly GPS like technology.

The CA (cellular automata) based solutions are established as the effective methodology in VLSI design [6]. Design of fault detection and diagnosis schemes for VLSI circuits around cellular automata have also been reported [7][8]. The effectiveness of CA based diagnosis scheme in VLSI circuits encourages us to address the issue of diagnosis of faulty nodes in sensor network, in CA framework, so that the solution should not rely on expensive designs as well as can avoid the intensive computation.

The proposed CA based scheme employs the SACA (Single Attractor Cellular Automata). The theory is developed to design a CA model for WSN that enable identification of the network region concentrated (clustered) with the faulty nodes, simultaneously satisfying the requirements of minimum computation overhead as well as the network bandwidth. Each base station (BS)/coordinator of a WSN runs a CA, configured for the BS, on the data received dynamically from the nodes under control of the BS. The outcome of this run (attractor) points to the network region with one or more faulty nodes.

## 2   CA Preliminaries

A Cellular Automaton $(CA)$ can be viewed as an autonomous finite state machine $(FSM)$. A $CA$ cell is having two states - 0 or 1 and the next state (NS) of $i^{th}$ $CA$ cell is $S_i^{t+1} = f_i(S_{i-1}^t, S_i^t, S_{i+1}^t)$, where $S_{i-1}^t$, $S_i^t$ and $S_{i+1}^t$ are the present states (PS) of the left neighbor, self and right neighbor of the $i^{th}$ cell at time $t$. $f_i$ is the next state function. On the other hand, the states of cells $S^t = (S_1^t, S_2^t, \cdots, S_n^t)$ at $t$ is the present state of $CA$.

The $f_i$ can be expressed in the form of a truth table ($Table 1$). The decimal equivalent of the 8 outputs is called Rule $R_i$ [9]. In a 2-state 3-neighborhood CA, there can be $2^8$ (256) rules. Three such rules 192, 207, and 240 are illustrated in $Table 1$. The first row lists the possible $2^3$ (8) combinations of present states of $(i-1)^{th}$, $i^{th}$ and $(i+1)^{th}$ cells at t.

A combination of the present states ($1^{st}$ row of $Table 1$) can be considered as Min Term of a 3-variable $S_{i-1}^t, S_i^t, S_{i+1}^t$ switching function and called RMT (rule min term). Column 011 of $Table 1$ is the $3^{rd}$ RMT. The next state corresponding to this RMT is 1 for Rule 207 and 0 for Rule 192 & 240.

The set R $=<R_1, R_2, \cdots, R_i, \cdots, R_n>$ configures the cells of a CA. If all the $R_i$s are same, the CA is a uniform CA; otherwise it is a non-uniform/hybrid CA. For the current work, we consider null boundary CA as in $Fig.1(a)$.

**Table 1.** $RMTs$ of the $CA < 192, 207, 240 >$

| PS | 111 | 110 | 101 | 100 | 011 | 010 | 001 | 000 | Rule |
|---|---|---|---|---|---|---|---|---|---|
| RMT | (7) | (6) | (5) | (4) | (3) | (2) | (1) | (0) | |
| NS | 1 | 1 | 0 | 0 | 0 | 0 | 0 | 0 | 192 |
| NS | 1 | 1 | 0 | 0 | 1 | 1 | 1 | 1 | 207 |
| NS | 1 | 1 | 1 | 1 | 0 | 0 | 0 | 0 | 240 |

A CA is reversible if its states form only cycles in the state transition diagram; otherwise, the CA is irreversible (*Fig.1(b)*). The set of states that forms cycle ($7{\to}7$ and $9{\to}1{\to}9$ of *Fig.1(b)*) is referred to as the *attractor*. The attractors of single length cycle, that is, $7{\to}7$ of *Fig.1(b)* is of our current interest.

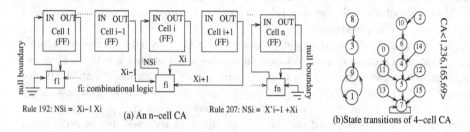

Rule 192: NSi = Xi−1 Xi          (a) An n−cell CA          Rule 207: NSi = X'i−1 +Xi          (b)State transitions of 4−cell CA

**Fig. 1.** Null boundary CA

# 3  The SACA

Since the next state of a single length cycle attractor is the attractor itself, there should be at least one RMT of each cell rule $R_i$ of R for which the cell $i$ does not change its state in the next time step. For example, to get a single length cycle attractor, the RMT xdx of $R_i$ is to be $d(0/1)$. It implies that the state change in cell $i$ is $d \to d$. That is, for rule $R_i$, if the RMT 0(000), 1(001), 4(100), 5(101) are 0, then the CA cell $i$, configured with $R_i$, does not change its state. Similarly, if the RMTs 2 (010), 3(011), 6(110) or 7(111) are 1 in a rule $R_i$, a cell configured with $R_i$ can stick to its current state in the next time step.

*Property 1*: [10] A rule $\mathcal{R}_i$ can contribute to the formation of single length cycle attractor(s) if at least one of the $RMTs$ 0, 1, 4 or 5 is 0, and/or at least one of the $RMTs$ 2, 3, 6 or 7 is 1.

A $CA$ synthesized with arbitrary rules may result in one or more attractors with multi-length cycles (*Figure 1(b)*). To synthesize an $SACA$, in [10] the 256 $CA$ rules are classified in 9 groups (group 0-8) based on *Property1*. The rule 200 (11001000) is in group 7 as it follows *Property1* for 7 RMTs.

A $CA$ configured with the rules that maintain *Property1* for most of the RMTs can have better chances of forming single length cycle attractors.

**Observation 1.** Most of the rules of group 6 form single length cycle attractor $CA$. Out of these 136,192 form single graph -that is, $SACA$ (*Fig. 2(a)*).

**Observation 2.** In group 2, out of 28 rules [10] the uniform $CA$ designed only with the rule 34/48 can form SACA (*Figure 2(b)*).

**Observation 3.** The uniform $CA$ designed with the rules of group 3 form single length cycle attractors only. Among those - 2, 16, 32, 42, 56, 98, 112, 162, and 176 form SACA.

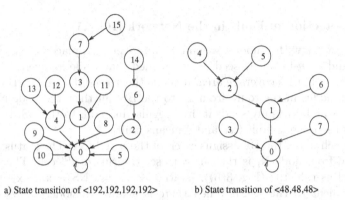

a) State transition of <192,192,192,192>          b) State transition of <48,48,48>

**Fig. 2.** State transition diagrams of <192,192,192,192> and <48,48,48>

The above observations point to the fact that to form an SACA, the CA rule should follow Property 1. However, a rule (e.g. rule 204) that maintains Property 1 for all its RMTs can't form an SACA. This leads to the following property.

Property 2: To form a uniform SACA with rule 'r', the 'r' must deny Property 1 for some RMTs.

**Example 1.** *The rule 48 of group 2 denies Property 1 for 6 RMTs. On the other hand, rule 192 of group 6 denies Property 1 only for 2 RMTs. Each of these rules forms SACA for all lengths.*

Table 2 displays the rules that form SACA of any arbitrary length. The SACA is employed to develop the proposed diagnosis scheme.

## 4   The Diagnosis Scheme

In this section, we propose an SACA based scheme to identify the faulty/defective nodes clustered in a network area. The solution developed considers the design of a CA structure that analyzes the status of network nodes and then can identify the location of the faulty nodes affected possibly due to natural calamities or intervention of intruder.

**Table 2.** CA rules for uniform SACA

| group | Rule for SACA |
|-------|---------------|
| 2 | 34, 48 |
| 3 | 2, 16, 32, 42, 56, 98, 112, 162, 176 |
| 4 | 0, 10, 15, 24, 40, 66, 80, 85, 96 |
|   | 130, 144, 160, 170, 184, 226, 240, 255 |
| 5 | 8, 64, 128, 138, 143, 152, 168, 194, 208, 213, 224 |
| 6 | 136, 192 |

## 4.1  Detection of Fault in the Network [10] [11]

For a network with $n$ nodes, we employ an $n$-cell CA, placed at the base station (BS), and an $n$-bit all 1s seed. It is assumed that while an event is sensed by a node $N_i$ within its coverage area, it sends the sensed data to its BS via a set of network nodes in the route from $N_i$ to the BS. Further, the node $N_i$ can check its status and faithfully sends it, in a regular interval, to the BS. Here, status 1 implies the node is fault free and 0 means faulty.

For each node, the BS assigns a cell of the $n$-cell CA. The status information received from node $N_i$ is then used to set the rule of $i^{th}$ cell. The status '1' is encoded as rule 192 (Fig. 3(b)), (status $M_i=1 \Rightarrow NS_i = x_{i-1} \, x_i$- that is, $NS_i$ is equivalent to rule 192). When there is a fault in node $N_i$, $M_i=0$ -that is, $NS_i = x'_{i-1} + x_i$. Therefore, rule 207 is set for the $i^{th}$ cell. The following theorem justifies the application of rule 207 for Cell $i$ when node $N_i$ is faulty. The n-cell uniform CA constructed with rule 192 is an SACA (*Table 2*).

**Theorem 1.** *The attractor of n-cell SACA constructed with rule 192 is the all 0s state. The length of longest path from a state to the attractor is $<= n$.*

**Theorem 2.** *If a uniform SACA with rule $R_o$ is hybridized by a cell rule $R_h$, it can generate new attractors only if the set of RMTs of $R_o$, for which Property 1 is denied, is not a subset of the set of RMTs of $R_h$, for which also the Property 1 is denied.*

The RMTs of rule 192 ($R_o$) for which Property 1 is denied are {2, 3} and the similar set for rule 207 ($R_h$) is {0, 1} (Fig. 3(a)). Therefore, the CA resulted from an uniform SACA (with rule 192), due to faults at single or multiple nodes, is a hybrid CA (hybridized with 207).

**Theorem 3.** *The CA resulted out of hybridization with rule 207 at one or more number of cells of an n-cell uniform CA, designed with rule 192, settles to an attractor with LSB 1 after $t <= n$ time steps if initialized with all 1s seed.*

Once the status bits from all the nodes are received, the CA at BS is run for $t <= n$-steps, initialized with all 1s seed. The CA for a fault free network is a uniform SACA constructed with rule 192 and it reaches the attractor state 0 (Fig. 2(a)). On the other hand, for fault at one or more nodes the CA at BS is a hybrid CA and it reaches a non-zero attractor with LSB=1 after t-steps (Fig. 4). Therefore, by sensing the LSB of the CA the BS can identify a faulty network.

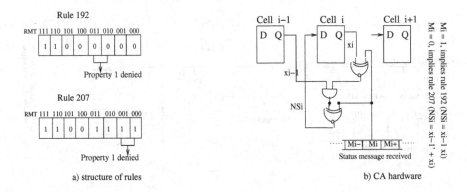

Fig. 3. CA rule setting for fault detection in a WSN

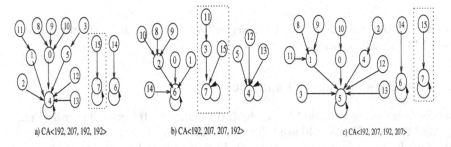

Fig. 4. State transition diagrams of the CA resulted due to presence of faults in WSN

## 4.2 Fault Diagnosis

In a WSN, when a bunch of network nodes are malfunctioning/faulty, these may seriously affect the network performance as well as the decision on an event in consideration. Therefore, in the current realization, we assume that the affected/faulty sensor nodes are clustered within a network region.

For diagnosis of region of faulty nodes, we choose rule 143 and 240. The status bit $(M_i)$ of a node $N_i$ is encoded as rule 143 if $M_i = 1$ (Fig. 5(c)) -that is, $i^{th}$ node fault free (as $M_i=1$, $NS_i = x_i \; x_{i+1} + x'_{i-1}$, equivalent to rule 143). On the other hand, if $M_i=0$, rule 240 is set for the $i^{th}$ CA cell, to specify a faulty node (In Fig. 5(c), as $M_i=0$, $NS_i= x_{i-1}$ -that is, equivalent to rule 240).

Once rule setup is done, based on the states received, the CA (either a uniform CA with rule 143, or non-uniform CA hybridized with 240) is run for t-steps ($t <= (2n-3)$), considering all 1s seed. It then settles to a single length cycle attractor. By sensing a specific set of bit positions (check bits) of the attractor, the BS can decide the region (location) of faulty nodes in the WSN.

The $\frac{n}{2}^{th}$ and $(\frac{n}{2}+1)^{th}$ bits (from left) of the attractor can be the check bits. If one of the check bits is 0 -that is, check bit pair is **01/10** (*Table 3*), the faulty nodes are in the left half of the network. On the other hand, if the checkbits are

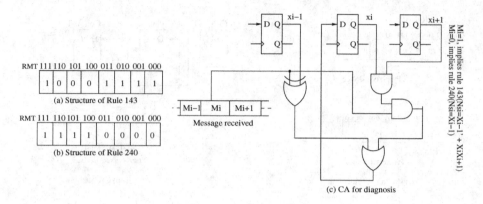

**Fig. 5.** CA rule setting for fault diagnosis in a WSN

11 (*Table 3*), the faulty nodes are in the right half. It follows from the properties of rule 143 and 240, described next.

### 4.3 Properties of Rule 143 and 240

The NSs (next states) of rule 143 for the RMTs 0dx (d=0/1, x=0/1) are 1 (Fig. 5(a)) and the NSs of rule 240 are 0 for the RMTs 0dx, d=0/1 and x=0/1 (Fig. 5(b)). On the other hand, the NSs for RMTs 1dx (d=0/1, x=0/1) of rule 240 are 1 (Fig.5(b)). However, the NSs for the RMTs 1x0 (x=0/1) and RMT 101 of rule 143 are 0 and for RMT 111 it is 1 (Fig. 5(a)).

**Case 1:** Let faulty nodes reside successively in the leftmost part, in between 1 to $\frac{n}{2}^{th}$ positions of the network. As the left most node is faulty, the NS of $1^{st}$ CA cell is always 0 (Fig. 6(a), for rule 240, NSs of the RMTs 0dx, x=0/1,d=0/1 are 0). If the CA runs, the 0 is propagated right till the CA cell corresponding to the fault free node $N_{ff}$ is reached. The NS of $N_{ff}$ is always 1 (Fig. 6(a)) as for rule 143, the NS of RMT 0dx (d=0/1,x=0/1) is 1 (Fig. 5(a)). The right most CA cell's NS (follows rule 143) is 0, as for rule 143 the NS of the RMT 1x0 (x=0/1) is 0. It can be shown that after (n-1) time-steps, an attractor is generated. The attractor contains a string 1010.... starting from the bit position corresponding to the first fault free node $N_{ff}$ ($4^{th}$ from left in Fig. 6(a)).

If the faulty nodes do not reside successively then the attractor contains a string 1111.... starting from cell position against the $1^{st}$ node to the last faulty node of the n-node network. Starting from the $1^{st}$ fault free node $N_{ff}$, after the last faulty node, the attractor contains a sub-string 0101....($5^{th}$ from left in Fig. 7). That is, the $\frac{n}{2}^{th}$ and $(\frac{n}{2}+1)^{th}$ bit pair of the attractor is **10/01** and can act as the check bits (*Table 3*).

**Case 2:** When the faulty nodes reside in between $((\frac{n}{2}+1)^{th}$ to $n^{th})$ positions of the WSN, then the attractor contains 1s at positions corresponding to the $1^{st}$ node to the last faulty node. The rest bits of the attractor is 0101.... If the

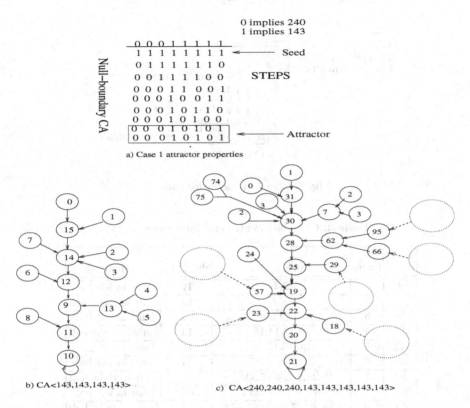

**Fig. 6.** CA state transitions

right most node is faulty of the n-node network, then we get all 1s (that is, seed) attractor (Fig. 7(b)). So, the $\frac{n}{2}^{th}$ and $(\frac{n}{2}+1)^{th}$ bit pair of the attractor is **11** and can conclude that the faulty nodes are in the right part of the network. In this case, the nodes in between 1 to $\frac{n}{2}^{th}$ positions are fault-free. The NS of $1^{st}$ node is 1, as for rule 143 the NSs of the RMTs odx (d=0/1,x=0/1) are 1.

For succeeding fault free nodes NSs are 1. This is because for rule 143 the NS of the RMT 111 is always 1. But if the rightmost node is fault free (follows rule 143), then its NS is 0 (for rule 143, NS of RMT 1x0 (x=0/1) is 0). Therefore, the cells corresponding to the last faulty node settles to pattern 0101... However, if the last node is faulty (follows rule 240), its NS is 1 as for rule 240 the NSs of the RMTs 1dx (d=0/1,x=0/1) are 1. Therefore, the attractor generated in this case is the all 1s -that is, the seed. So, the $\frac{n}{2}^{th}$ and $(\frac{n}{2}+1)^{th}$ bit pair of the attractor is **11** (Fig. 7(b)) and can act as the check bits.

**Example 2.** *When $4^{th}$, $8^{th}$, $9^{th}$ and $15^{th}$ (from left) nodes of a 32-node WSN is faulty. That is, the status message received at the BS is **11101110011111101111 111111111111** (Fig.8(a)). Now if the CA constructed, considering the message, and runs with all 1s seed, it settles to an attractor **1111111111111110**101010*

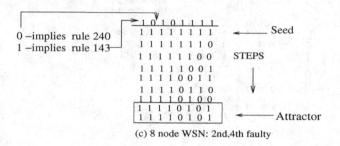

0 —implies rule 240
1 —implies rule 143

(c) 8 node WSN: 2nd,4th faulty

**Fig. 7.** Case 1 attractor formation

**Table 3.** Checkbits of attractor for various faults

| # nodes | # faults | faulty nodes | checkbits | remarks |
|---|---|---|---|---|
| 8 | 2 | 2,4 | **10** | fault in left half |
| 8 | 3 | 6,7,8 | **11** | fault in right half |
| 16 | 3 | 2,4,5 | **01** | fault in left half |
| 16 | 4 | 10,12,14,15 | **11** | fault in right half |
| 32 | 5 | 1,6,10,12,16 | **10** | fault in left half |
| 32 | 6 | 2,3,7,8,14,15 | **01** | fault in left half |
| 32 | 7 | 18,20,21,24,27,30,31 | **11** | fault in right half |
| 64 | 8 | 1,4,8,9,10,20,23,29 | **01** | fault in left half |
| 64 | 9 | 34,38,39,47,49,50,55,57,62 | **11** | fault in right half |

*1010101010. The check bits (01) in the $16^{th}$ and $17^{th}$ bit positions determine that the faults are in the left half of the network.*

**Example 3.** *When $18^{th}$, $23^{rd}$, $26^{th}$ and $32^{th}$ (from left) nodes of the 32-node WSN are faulty, then the status message received at the BS is **1111111111111111 11011110110111110**. In this case, the attractor is 11111111111111111111111111 11111111 (Fig.8(b)). The check bit pair -that is, the $16^{th}$ and $17^{th}$ bit positions is (11) and it determines that the faults are in the right half of the network.*

*Table 3* records the experimental observations considering WSN with n = 8, 16, 32 and 64 nodes. Column 2 of the table represents the number of faults in the WSN. The locations of faulty nodes are noted in Column 3. In Column 4, the $\frac{n}{2}^{th}$ and $(\frac{n}{2}+1)^{th}$ bit pair (check bits) of the resulting attractor is shown and Column 5 describes the diagnosed of faulty network region. A WSN can consist of thousands of sensor nodes. The scheme described in this section requires a CA run for t <= 2n-3 time steps (clock cycles) for an n-node network to diagnose the network region with faulty nodes. It avoids checking of individual status bit of the n-nodes and, thereby, realize fast diagnosis. Once a region is identified the scheme can applied hierarchically to diagnose the faulty sub-region.

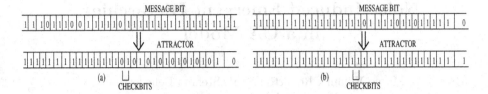

**Fig. 8.** CA attractor formation in 32-node WSN

## 5  Conclusion

This work proposes an efficient scheme to diagnose the location of faulty nodes in a wireless sensor network (WSN) without major computational overhead, that is desired for power constrained WSN. The solution is developed around the regular structure of CA (Cellular Automata). A special class of CA called SACA is chosen for the reported scheme. The characterization of SACA has been reported to realize the proposed diagnosis methodology.

## References

1. Megerian, S., Polkonjak, M.: Wireless Sensor Network. In: Proakis, J.G. (ed.) Wiley Encyclopedia of Telecommunications (December 2002)
2. Chen, J., Kher, S., Somani, A.: Distributed fault detection of wireless sensor networks. In: DIWANS, pp. 65–72 (2006)
3. Yu, M., Mokhtar, H., Merabti, M.: A Survey on Fault Management in Wireless Sensor Networks. School of Computing and Mathematical Science, PGNET (2007)
4. Varshney Ruixin Niu, P.K., Michael Moore, D.K.: Decision Fusion in a Wireless Sensor Network with a Large Number of Sensors. In: IF 2004, Stockholm, Sweden (2004)
5. Harte, S., Rahman, A., Razeeb, K.M.: Fault Tolerance In Sensor Networks using Self-Diagnosing Sensor Nodes. In: IEEE IE 2005 (2005)
6. Pal Chaudhuri, P., Roy Chowdhury, D., Nandi, S., Chatterjee, S.: Additive Cellular Automata – Theory and Applications, vol. 1. IEEE Computer Society Press, California (1997) ISBN 0-8186-7717-1
7. Hortencius, P.D., McLeod, R.D., Pries, W., Card, H.C.: Cellular Automata Based Pseudo-random Number Generators for Built-In Self-Test. IEEE TCAD 8(8), 842–859 (1989)
8. Sikdar, B.K., Ganguly, N., Chaudhuri, P.P.: Fault diagnosis of VLSI circuits with cellular automata based pattern classifier. IEEE TCAD 24(7), 1115–1131 (2005)
9. Wolfram, S.: Cellular Automata and Complexity — Collected Papers. Addison Wesley (1994)
10. Das, S., Naskar, N.N., Mukherjee, S., Dalui, M., Sikdar, B.K.: Characterization of CA Rules for SACA Targeting Detection of Faulty Nodes in WSN. In: Bandini, S., Manzoni, S., Umeo, H., Vizzari, G. (eds.) ACRI 2010. LNCS, vol. 6350, pp. 300–311. Springer, Heidelberg (2010)
11. Maity, I., Bhattacharya, G., Das, S., Sikdar, B.K.: A Cellular Automata based Scheme for Diagnosis of Faulty Nodes in WSN. In: SMC 2011 (2011)

# Noise-Induced Emergent Hierarchies
# in a CA Model

Marco Villani[1], Roberto Serra[1], Stefano Benedettini[2],
Andrea Roli[3], and David Lane[4]

[1] Faculty of Mathematical, Physical and Natural Sciences
Università di Modena e Reggio Emilia &
European Centre for Living Technology, Venezia
{rserra,marco.villani}@unimore.it
[2] European Centre for Living Technology, Venezia
stefano.benedettini@gmail.com
[3] DEIS-Cesena
*Alma Mater Studiorum* Università di Bologna
andrea.roli@unibo.it
[4] Department of Social, Cognitive and Quantitative Sciences
Università di Modena e Reggio Emilia &
European Centre for Living Technology, Venezia
davidavra.lane@unimore.it

**Abstract.** This paper introduces the notion of noise-induced emergent hierarchies and analyses the influence of the topology of the underlying network on these hierarchies. By developing upon a previous model of cell differentiation based on noisy random Boolean networks, we show that the adoption of a regular topology such that of cellular automata can lead to interesting effects, the most remarkable one being that, *ceteris paribus*, the resulting hierarchies have a larger number of levels and could therefore describe more "structured" complex systems.

## 1 Introduction

A major feature of most complex systems is the presence of hierarchical structures, so that it is possible to identify different levels. While the naïve view of a hierarchy is that represented by a tree, in most complex systems this is not the case, and one has to deal with tangled hierarchies, where the tree structure is only an approximate description of the actual relationships. Moreover, it is also frequent that multiple hierarchies coexist, so that the same subsystem can belong to different hierarchical descriptions (for example, in multicellular organisms, an organ can be classified as a member of a functional hierarchy but also as a member of a spatial one). In spite of these remarks, the notion of level remains useful to describe the properties of many complex systems [1].

Hierarchies can be generated in different ways, e.g. by forcing such structures from the outside, like it is often the case in artificial systems that are explicitly designed in that way, or in social organizations like, for instance, companies,

G.C. Sirakoulis and S. Bandini (Eds.): ACRI 2012, LNCS 7495, pp. 244–253, 2012.

where the organization is designed to achieve the desired goals. But the most interesting cases, from a complex systems theoretical perspective, are those where the hierarchies are spontaneously formed by the system own dynamics. An outstanding example of this kind is provided by emergent spatio-temporal patterns (sometimes referred to as "dissipative structures") like those exhibited for example in the well-known Bénard-Marangoni hexagonal convection cells, which can be observed in a shallow cylindrical container, filled with liquid and heated from below, when the heat flow exceeds a certain threshold [2]. This is an example of a two-level hierarchy, where the micro-level can be associated to the water molecules, while the upper level is the set of hexagonal cells in the container. Emergent structures can be also observed in many kinds of dynamical models: let it suffice to mention, among the Cellular Automata (CA) models, the well-known examples of gliders in the Game of Life [3], and the vortices in the FHP model [4].

However, it usually happens that the hierarchies that are spontaneously formed in dynamical models are composed by a very small number (typically, two) of levels, while on the other hand natural and social systems display many-level hierarchies. Therefore, a major challenge for a dynamical theory of hierarchical systems is that of identifying models where several hierarchical layers can emerge. In this paper we indeed introduce a dynamical model that is able to spontaneously give rise to a large number of different levels.

The initial version of this model was created for a different purpose, i.e., that of describing cell differentiation, but this is precisely a case where a multi-level hierarchy is formed: there are stem cells, which can give rise to all the various cell types, then there are various kinds of multipotent and pluripotent cells, that can give rise to a certain number of cell types, and finally there are the mature cell types. In the model we developed, differentiation is associated to a reduction in the noise level in the cells: a stem cell can freely wander, under the action of noise, among many attractors of its genetic regulatory network, while a reduction of the level of cellular noise makes some transitions among attractors unlikely, and thereby limits the wandering to a smaller portion of phase space. When the noise level is very low the cell is bound to remain in a single attractor, which corresponds to a final cell type.

A key concept here is that of a threshold ergodic set (TES), which are sets of attractors that the system can not leave (at a given noise level, specified by the threshold that is mentioned in the name) [5]. TESs, which will be precisely defined in Sec. 2, are disjoint sets of attractors, and their number ranges from a very small amount (typically, just one) at zero threshold to a maximum that equals the number of attractors at high threshold. The term "attractors" refers here to those of the (deterministic) model of the genetic network. While the model has been able to describe a wealth of phenomena related to cell differentiation [5,6], its principles are fairly general and might be at work in different systems: the idea is that noise can induce jumps between the attractors of a dynamical system; if the "observable states" are related to the sets of attractors that the system can visit, then as noise is reduced new observables appear, giving rise to a hierarchical structure.

The purpose of this paper is to provide a contribution towards the analysis of these general properties, so we will not be concerned here with cell differentiation. The "parent" model will be briefly reviewed in Sec. 2, referring the reader to the original papers for further information. This "parent" model was based on a well-known model of gene regulatory networks—Random Boolean Networks (RBNs)—whose topology is random. These networks exhibit three different dynamical behaviours (i.e., ordered, critical and chaotic), characterised by different reactions to attractor perturbations. In particular, there are theoretical reasons, as well as partial experimental evidence, that biological genetic networks tend to be critical (or perhaps ordered, but near the critical region) [7,8,9] so we will concentrate on this kind of networks. The issue of the number of attractors in critical networks has been thoroughly investigated, and some initial claims have later been modified. So it is now accepted that the number of attractors in critical networks scales superlinearly with the network size [10]. However, most theoretical results are valid for infinitely large networks, and are obtained using the so-called "annealed" approximation [11]. When one comes to considering finite networks, comprising a number of genes up to a few tens of thousands, he observes that the attractors with a significant basin of attraction (i.e., those that can be found in actual simulations, that necessarily involve a strong undersampling of the $2^N$ initial conditions) *do* scale sublinearly with $N$ [12]. Having in mind the application of RBNs to biological or artificial systems, these attractors are those that actually matter, as they are reachable with an appreciable probability. In practice, therefore, critical RBNs have a limited number of attractors, which implies that also the number of TESs is limited (it never exceeds the number of attractors). It is therefore interesting to explore models with a higher number of different attractors, that could display more TESs and therefore a richer hierarchical structure. Note however that the number of different attractors must not be, loosely speaking, too large, because each attractor must still have a significant basin of attraction (otherwise the self-organization properties of the system dynamics, that depend upon the fact that many initial conditions are mapped onto the same attractors, would be lost). A more practical concern is having a huge number of attractors can make the search for TESs prohibitively long.

We therefore explore here the opportunities to achieve such a rich hierarchical structure by changing the topology from random (as in RBNs) to that of a regular CA. For the reasons given above, the structure of the CA model that has been chosen has been driven by the goal of having a number of attractors significantly higher that that of RBNs, while still keeping them to a manageable number. The structure of the chosen model is presented and discussed in Sec. 3. Note that this work does not only concern the effects on the number of attractors but, more important, on the number and structure of the TESs. Sec. 4 reports (still preliminary) results concerning TESs and the hierarchical structure induced by the increase of the threshold. Finally, Sec. 5 is devoted to discussion and indications for further work.

## 2    Threshold Ergodic Sets and Hierarchical Structures

We have already developed a dynamical model of cell differentiation, i.e., the process whereby stem cells, which can develop into different types, become more and more specialized [6,5]. The model is an abstract one (it does not refer to a specific organism or cell type) and it aims at reproducing the most relevant features of the process: (i) different degrees of differentiation, that span from totipotent stem cells to fully differentiated cells; (ii) stochastic differentiation, where populations of identical multipotent cells stochastically generate different cell types; (iii) deterministic differentiation, where signals trigger the progress of multipotent cells into more differentiated types, in well defined lineages; (iv) limited reversibility: differentiation is almost always irreversible, but there are limited exceptions under the action of appropriate signals; (v) induced pluripotency: fully differentiated cells can come back to a pluripotent state by modifying the expression of some genes; and (vi) induced change of cell type: modification of the expression of few genes can directly convert one differentiated cell type into another.

Surprisingly enough, a single model has been able to describe all these phenomena, whereas previously only models that make use of continuous descriptions and take into account the contributions of only few genes had been proposed. In our model, differentiation is rather an emerging property due to the interactions of very many genes: its main features therefore should be shared by a variety of different organisms. The differentiation model is based on a noisy version of a well-known model of gene networks, that is, the RBN model, which, in spite of its discrete approach, has been proven to describe important experimental facts concerning gene expression [13]. While we refer to [5] for more details, let us recall that RBNs are deterministic Boolean models with synchronous updating. In their "classical" version, used in this study, each node has the same number of input links, 2 in our case, coming from two of the remaining $N - 1$ nodes, chosen at random. Double connections and self-loops are prohibited. The transition function is randomly chosen among a set of allowed functions (typically, all the 16 two-input Boolean functions). The dynamics of "classical" RBNs is discrete and synchronous, so fixed points and cycles are the only possible asymptotic states in finite networks; typically a single RBN owns more than one attractor. Note nevertheless that attractors of RBNs are unstable with respect to noise even at low levels, as for example transient flips of randomly chosen nodes. In fact, even if the flips last for a single time step one sometimes observes transitions from that attractor to another one (see Tab. 1 and further discussion). Therefore, because noise is known to play a role in key cellular processes, single attractors can no longer be associated to cell types, as proposed in the past.

Ribeiro and Kauffman [14] observed that it is possible to identify in the attractor landscape subsets of attractors, which they called Ergodic Sets, entrapping the system in the long time limit, so the system continues to jump between attractors which belong to the set. Unfortunately it turns out that most noisy RBNs have just one such set: this observation rules out the possibility to associate them to cell types. A possible solution to this problem was proposed in [5,6], by observing that flips are a kind of a fairly intense noise, as they amount to silencing an expressed gene or to express a gene that would otherwise be inactive: this may well be an event too rare to happen with significant probability in the cell lifetime. It is possible therefore to introduce a threshold $\theta$, and neglect all the transitions whose occurrence probability is lower than it. In such a way, the notion of Ergodic Set has to be modified into that of Threshold Ergodic Set (briefly, $TES_\theta$): a set of attractors linked only by jumps having a probability higher than $\theta$, which entrap the system in the long time limit. A $TES_\theta$ is therefore a subset of attractors that are each either directly or indirectly $\theta$-reachable (reachable by means of transition whose probability exceeds the threshold $\theta$), and from which no transition can allow escaping. The threshold clearly is related to the level of noise in the cell, and scales with its reciprocal (the frequency of flips).

We proposed to associate cell types to TESs, which represent coherent stable ways of functioning of the same genome even in the presence of noise. According to this framework RBNs can host more than one TES, avoiding in such a way the problem that hampered the straightforward association of cell types to Ergodic Sets. At high noise level the system can jump among all the attractors, thus modelling stem cells, while as the threshold is increased (and the noise reduced) the cell becomes entrapped in a smaller TES, which represents a multipotent cell. At very low noise levels all attractors are also TESs, a condition likely to describe final cell types. There are experimental indications in favour of the key hypothesis that noise in stem cells is higher than in more differentiated ones.

We have proven that this model does not only reproduce stochastic differentiation but also deterministic differentiation; such process, triggered by chemical signals coming from outside the cell (sometimes from other cells), is often observed and is at the heart of the regulation of embryo development. Deterministic differentiation is related to the presence of "switch" genes such that, when they are in a given state, the transition to a more differentiated state, induced by a change of the threshold, always leads to the same TES, irrespectively of the dynamical state of the system. This property has been found to be widespread in RBNs. Moreover, the model has also been able to describe induced pluripotency and change of cell type, obtained by overexpressing some genes without acting on the threshold [5,6]. The model suggests experimental tests, so its application to real cell differentiation processes is open to judgements (there are some positive but not yet definitive experimental data). Nevertheless, in this work we are more interested in the properties of the model, that could be the basis of a general mechanism for generating levels (which are related to the changes in the TES landscape brought about by threshold changes). The mechanism at work here (i.e., noise-induced emergent hierarchies) seems indeed a rather general one, and there is no reason to limit it to differentiation.

## 3    The Quasi-CA Model

Let us first recall our goal: modifying the topology of the model described in Sec. 2 in such a way as to increase the number of attractors and of TESs, while leaving the dynamical rules unchanged. In order to do so we first consider the deterministic Boolean model, ignoring noise, and look for its long term dynamics. Moreover, the results summarised in Sec. 2 were obtained using a model with 2 input connections per node, so we keep this feature also in these new experiments. The model we propose will have local interactions, synchronous updating and a regular topology as is typical of cellular automata, but it will retain the presence of different transition functions at different nodes (i.e., we work with *inhomogeneous cellular automata*).

Preliminary simulations show that a 2D square lattice gives rise to a huge, unmanageable number of attractors, so we focused on 1D automata, with a circular topology. One input comes from the nearest neighbour, say in a clockwise way. Therefore, the only choice left concerns the second input. We checked different possibilities (say, from the other nearest neighbour, from the second nearest neighbour on the right, etc.). Precisely: let us number the nodes in a clockwise way, from 1 to $N$, and let us suppose that node $k$ receives an input from its left neighbour, $k - 1$. Then the various topologies will be called $1D_1$ if the second input to node $k$ comes from the node to the right $k + 1$, $1D_2$ if it comes from node $k + 2$, etc.

We observed that the number of attractors is prohibitively large for $1D_1$ topology, and that it begins to attain more satisfying values when the second input comes from the second neighbour, i.e., for $1D_2$ topology. Obviously, the classical random topology (in which each node has exactly two randomly chosen inputs) is our reference, and in the following it will be denoted by the term RND (see Figs. 1 and 2).

Formally, our CA is defined by:

- its state space $S = \{0, 1\}^N$;
- its topology: linear with wrap around (i.e., circular);
- its neighbourhood: each node $k$ ($0 \leq k \leq N$) gets an input from node $k - 1$ and one from node $k + d \mod N, d = 2, 3, 4$;
- its transition function: for each node, it is chosen at random among the 16 two-input Boolean functions.

Note that, since networks are built with random transition functions, the statistics is not performed only on different initial conditions, but also by considering different network realizations. In total, we generated 250 networks with $N = 100$ nodes for each of the four topologies and simulated each one starting from $10^6$ random initial conditions.

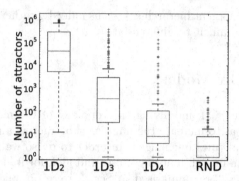

**Fig. 1.** Number of attractors for various 1D alternatives. The central line denotes the median number of attractors across the set of 250 networks; the box outlines the first and third quartile, and crosses mark the outliers. Note that the number of attractors is actually underestimated (we sampled $10^6$ initial conditions for each network).

**Fig. 2.** The $1D_3$ topology: a 1D structure in which each node receives a signal from its directly upstream node, and a signal from the downstream node at distance 3. Note that in order to close the structure the first three nodes (node 1, 2 and 3) send their "upstream" signals respectively to nodes $N-2$, $N-1$ and $N$, and that node $N$ sends its "downstream" signal to node 1.

## 4    Results

In this paragraph we discuss the main features of the attractor landscape that emerges from the different 1D topologies and from the RND one, and of the hierarchical structures of TESs that result from it.

The first interesting observations concerns the attractor landscape, which is defined as a weighted graph in which nodes are the different attractors of the underlying BN and two nodes are linked, with weight $p$, if, with probability $p$, the system can transit between the corresponding attractors because of the presence of noise. As we can see from the results in Tab. 1, attractors of RND topologies are significantly more stable than those of 1D topologies. Stability, in our context, means the probability to return to the same attractor after a bit-flip perturbation occurs, hence, the weight of the self-loops in the attractor landscape. The same observation holds also for the average connectivity, defined as the ratio between the number of nodes and the number of links in the attractor landscape, which is considerably higher for 1D topologies. Despite being directed graphs with a large number of nodes (Fig. 1), attractor landscapes of 1D topologies have almost always a single $TES_0$ that encompasses all nodes (Fig. 3).[1] Let us observe

---

[1] It is actually possible to have networks with more than one TES at threshold level 0, but in our experiments such occurrence happened only once in 1000 networks tested.

**Table 1.** Main characteristics of the attractor landscape and of the resulting hierarchical structures of TESs, for 1D and RND topologies. For each measure, figures report mean and standard error of the mean

|  | $1D_2$ | $1D_3$ | $1D_4$ | RND |
|---|---|---|---|---|
| Median stability | $0.75 \pm 0.01$ | $0.73 \pm 0.01$ | $0.851 \pm 0.007$ | $0.885 \pm 0.007$ |
| Average connectivity | $16.5 \pm 0.4$ | $11.2 \pm 0.4$ | $7.5 \pm 0.4$ | $4.6 \pm 0.5$ |
| Effective Differentiation tree depth | $2.94 \pm 0.04$ | $2.54 \pm 0.06$ | $1.95 \pm 0.05$ | $1.46 \pm 0.06$ |
| Effective Differentiation tree size | $3400 \pm 800$ | $1300 \pm 300$ | $300 \pm 70$ | $10 \pm 4$ |

that this situation is very different from what observed in the RND topology, where there are several networks in which $TES_0$ contains only a subset of all the attractors. Note that for $1D_d$ topologies the values of the measures shown in Tab. 1 monotonically approaches that of the RND topology as the "upstream" links connect more and more distant nodes, i.e., as the $d$ value increases. In Tab. 1 you can see that the same holds also for the measures defined on the differentiation trees (explained below) emerging from BN dynamics.

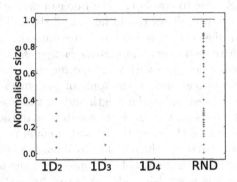

**Fig. 3.** The normalised size of the $TES_0$ for 1D and RND topologies. Note that the distribution of 1D topologies is practically a delta function, with only very few exceptions, whereas the RND distribution, although very peaked, has a significant number of outliers.

The differences in the attractor landscape between the topologies of interest have huge influence on the resulting hierarchical structures of TESs, induced by the process of threshold increase. In order to characterise these trees we propose two measures: the Effective Differentiation Tree Depth (EDTD) and the Effective Differentiation Tree Size (EDTS). The EDTD is simply the number of levels of the differentiation tree, whereas EDTS is the number of TESs present at each threshold level, summed across all the levels, and provides indication about the number of objects involved during the differentiation process. Both these measures are performed on *effective trees*. In fact it often happens that, during subsequent threshold increases, a TES breaks into another smaller TES, losing some attractors in the process that cannot be reached starting from the new TES, but that have nevertheless connected paths toward it. In other word, these attractors constitute the "basin of attraction" of the new TES: the cells whose pattern of activation lies on these attractors sooner or later will leave it, moving toward the new TES. In brief, these attractors will be depleted of their cell population and cease in such a way to have biological meaning. For this reason, the TESs emerging from these attractors are ignored by our analyses, which focuses only on the trees composed by populated TES (the "effective" trees). As we can see in Tab. 1, 1D topologies have deeper trees, involving a very large number of elements.

## 5  Discussion

The purpose of this paper is to provide a contribution towards the analysis of the factors that can give birth to noise-induced emergent hierarchies; among these factors, the topology of the underlying system can have a big influence, and it is the focus of this work. We presented an already existing model of cell differentiation based on noisy RBNs, and implemented it on random and regular topologies. We showed that a regular topology can give raise to the presence of an all-embracing $TES_0$ able to envelop all the Boolean networks' attractors: the emergence of this structure allows the formation of deep differentiation trees, more articulated than the corresponding structures emerging in random topologies. This circumstance constitutes an interesting fact *per se* (if we want to design noise-induced emergent hierarchies with some specific characteristics), and could have interesting consequences also on the topic of the emergence of cell differentiation itself. In fact, presumably the length and/or the size of differentiation trees have significant effects on the survival probabilities of the living organisms they help to develop. If it is the case, the evolution could take advantage from these differences in order to select the fittest individuals, and therefore the fittest hierarchies—through the modification of the topology of the underlying generic networks. Further work is needed in order to better understand the processes that affect the features of the emergent hierarchies, and further measures of their properties should also be considered, Moreover, it would be interesting to consider different topologies, like for example that of the Watts-Strogatz models of small world [15], or various networks of the scale-free type.

**Acknowledgements.** The authors gratefully acknowledge useful discussions with Stuart Kauffman, Alex Graudenzi and Chiara Damiani. This article has been partially funded by the UE project "MD – Emergence by Design", Pr.ref. 284625, under the 7th FWP - FET programme.

## References

1. Pumain, D.: Hierarchy in natural and social sciences. Methodos series, vol. 3. Springer (2006)
2. Bragard, J., Velarde, M.: Bénard–Marangoni convection: planforms and related theoretical predictions. Journal of Fluid Mechanics 368, 165–194 (1998)

3. Berlekamp, E., Conway, J., Guy, R.: Winning ways for your mathematical plays, vol. 2. Academic Press, New York (1982)
4. Frisch, U., Hasslacher, B., Pomeau, Y.: Lattice-gas automata for the navier-stokes equation. Phys. Rev. Lett. 56, 1505–1508 (1986)
5. Serra, R., Villani, M., Barbieri, A., Kauffman, S., Colacci, A.: On the dynamics of random Boolean networks subject to noise: Attractors, ergodic sets and cell types. Journal of Theoretical Biology 265(2), 185–193 (2010)
6. Villani, M., Barbieri, A., Serra, R.: A dynamical model of genetic networks for cell differentiation. PLoS ONE 6(3), e17703:1–e17703:9 (2011)
7. Kauffman, S.: The Origins of Order: Self-Organization and Selection in Evolution. Oxford University Press, Oxford (1993)
8. Kauffman, S.: At home in the universe: the search for laws of self-organization and complexity. Oxford University Press (1995)
9. Aldana, M., Coppersmith, S., Kadanoff, L.: Boolean dynamics with random couplings. In: Kaplan, E., Marsden, J., Sreenivasan, K. (eds.) Perspectives and Problems in Nonlinear Science. A Celebratory Volume in Honor of Lawrence Sirovich. Springer Applied Mathematical Sciences Series. Springer, Heidelberg (2003)
10. Drossel, B., Mihaljev, T., Greil, F.: Number and length of attractors in a critical Kauffman model with connectivity one. Phys. Rev. Lett. 94, 088701:1–088701:4 (2005)
11. Derrida, B., Pomeau, Y.: Random networks of automata: a simple annealed approximation. Europhysics Letters 1(2), 45–49 (1986)
12. Samuelsson, B., Troein, C.: Superpolynomial growth in the number of attractors in Kauffman networks. Physical Review Letters 90(9) (2003)
13. Serra, R., Villani, M., Graudenzi, A., Kauffman, S.: Why a simple model of genetic regulatory networks describes the distribution of avalanches in gene expression data. Journal of Theoretical Biology 246, 449–460 (2007)
14. Ribeiro, A., Kauffman, S.: Noisy attractors and ergodic sets in models of gene regulatory networks. Journal of Theoretical Biology 247, 743–755 (2007)
15. Watts, D.J., Strogatz, S.H.: Collective dynamics of 'small-world' networks. Nature 393(6684), 440–442 (1998)

# Introducing Innovation in a Structured Population

Burton Voorhees

Center for Science, Athabasca University,
1 University Drive, Athabasca, Alberta, CANADA T9S 3A3
burt@athabascau.ca

**Abstract.** Given a population with internal structures determining possible interactions between population members, what can be said about the spread of innovation? In genetics, this is a question of the spread of a favorable mutation
within a genetically homogeneous population. In a model society, it is the question of rumors, beliefs, or innovation [1,2,3,4,5]. This paper sketches a simple
iterative model of populations with structure represented in terms of edge
weighted graphs. Use of such graphs has become a powerful tool in evolutionary dynamics [e.g. 6]. The model presented here employs a Markov process on
a state space isomorphic to the vertex set of the N-hypercube. In analogy to genetics, spread of innovation is first modeled as a biased birth-death process in
which the innovation provides a fitness r as compared to the fitness of 1 assigned to non-innovative individuals. Following on this, a probabilistic model is
developed that, in the simplest cases, corresponds to an elementary probabilistic
cellular automata.

## 1 The Birth-Death Model

Consider a population of N individuals evolving in discrete time, consisting of m
innovators with fitness r and N – m non-innovators with relative fitness 1. At each
iteration a random individual is chosen to communicate its state (innovative or non-
innovative) and another (or the same) individual is chosen to receive and be converted
by this communication. When the same individual is chosen to communicate and to
receive, this corresponds to lack of receptivity of other individuals with whom that
individual is in contact. This is represented by a graph with N vertices, with edges
(including loops at each vertex) given a weight indicating the probability of an individual at any given vertex i transmitting their state to an individual at an adjacent
vertex j. Choice of the communicating individual is biased by fitness: for r > 1, innovators are more likely to be chosen to communicate, corresponding to the tendency to
imitate successful innovation. If individual i is chosen to communicate choice of the
receiving individual j is limited to those for whom there is an edge directed from vertex i to vertex j and the choice of which such vertex is to receive the communication
is based on the probability weight attached to the corresponding edges.

A length N binary vector $\vec{v} = (v_1, ..., v_N)$ represents the population state, where $v_k$
is 0 or 1 respectively as vertex k is occupied by a non-innovator or an innovator. If the
population graph is complete and all edges are assigned probability 1/N this is a

G.C. Sirakoulis and S. Bandini (Eds.): ACRI 2012, LNCS 7495, pp. 254–262, 2012.
© Springer-Verlag Berlin Heidelberg 2012

biased version of the birth-death Moran process [7]. Two questions of immediate interest are: given an initial distribution of innovators in a population, what is the probability the innovation fixes in the population as a whole; and the related question, what is the best way to introduce an innovation into a population given limited resources [5]?

For an N-vertex directed graph G with row stochastic edge-weight matrix W the full state space is $V(H^N)$, the vertex set of the N-hypercube. The matrix $W = (w_{ij})$ defines a state transition matrix T on $V(H^N)$: for each state $\vec{v} = (v_1,...,v_N)$ define vectors $\vec{a}(\vec{v}), \vec{b}(\vec{v})$ by

$$a_j(\vec{v}) = \sum_{i=1}^N v_i w_{ij}, b_j(\vec{v}) = \sum_{i=1}^N (1-v_i)w_{ij} \tag{1}$$

Theorem 1

Let vectors $\vec{a}(\vec{v}), \vec{b}(\vec{v})$ be defined as in equation (1) where $\vec{v}$ ranges over $V(H^N)$. Then for all j, $1 \le j \le N$:

1. The probability of a transition from the state $\vec{v} = (v_1,...,v_{j-1},0,v_{j+1},...,v_N)$ to the state is $(v_1,...,v_{j-1},1,v_{j+1},...,v_N)$ is equal to

$$\frac{ra_j(\vec{v})}{N-m+rm} \tag{2}$$

2. The probability of a transition from the state $\vec{v} = (v_1,...,v_{j-1},1,v_{j+1},...,v_N)$ to the state $(v_1,...,v_{j-1},0,v_{j+1},...,v_N)$ is equal to

$$\frac{b_j(\vec{v})}{N-m+rm} \tag{3}$$

3. The probability that $\vec{v}$ remains in the same state is equal to

$$\frac{r\vec{a}(\vec{v}) \cdot \vec{v} + b(\vec{v}) \cdot v'}{N-m+rm} \tag{4}$$

Proof follows from equation (1) and the definition of the birth-death process.

The state transition diagram, constructed with use of Theorem 1, is an edge-weighted directed graph on $2^N$ vertices. The transition matrix T is row stochastic and has an eigenvalue 1 with eigenvector $\vec{x} = \underline{1}$, the $2^N$-dimensional vector of all ones. To avoid confusion, the indices i,j are used to indicate vertices of the graph, and the elements of state vectors while the indices u,v will be used for the state transition matrix $T = (T_{uv})$, indicating that the rows and columns of this matrix are labeled by states in the state space.

The introduced innovation goes to extinct or to fixation, hence the birth-death process has two absorbing states represented by the N-dimensional vectors $\underline{0}$ and $\underline{1}$. Since $T_{uv}^k$ is the probability of a k-step transition from state u to state v, the matrix $T^* = \lim_{k\to\infty} T^k$ consists of initial and final non-zero columns with all other entries equal to zero. Further, $T^*\vec{x} = \vec{x}$, and the solution of $(I-T)\vec{x} = 0$ is given by

$$x_u = \alpha T_{u0}^* + \beta T_{u,2^N-1}^* \equiv \alpha\eta_u + \beta\mu_u \tag{5}$$

with $\alpha$ and $\beta$ as free parameters. With this definition, $\eta_u$ is the probability that state u goes to extinction and $\mu_u$ is the probability that it goes to fixation.

For the general case, with $v'_j = (1 - v_j)$ define v as the denary form of the binary number $(v_1,...,v_N)$: $v = \sum_{k=1}^{N} v_k 2^{N-k}$. Then, for $\vec{v} \in V(H^N)$, the system of equations for $\vec{x}$ is summarized in the master equation

$$[N + (r-1)m - r\vec{a}(\vec{v})\cdot\vec{v} - \vec{b}(\vec{v})\cdot\vec{v}']x_v$$
$$- r\sum_{j=1}^{N} a_j(\vec{v})v'_j x_{v+2^{N-j}} - \sum_{j=1}^{N} b_j(\vec{v})v_j x_{v+2^{N-j}} = 0 \tag{6}$$

From the definition of v, the single vertex fixation probability is

$$\rho = \frac{1}{N}\sum_{k=0}^{N-1} x_{2^k} \tag{7}$$

Since T is row stochastic, $I - T$ is the graph Laplacian L of the state transition diagram and the vectors $\vec{\eta}$ and $\vec{\mu}$ span the null space of L.

The determinacy $\delta(G)$ of the population graph is defined as

$$\delta(G) = 1 - \frac{\vec{\eta}\cdot\vec{\mu}}{|\vec{\eta}||\vec{\mu}|} \tag{8}$$

Clearly $0 \leq \delta(G) \leq 1$. This quantity measures the degree to which extinction or fixation is determined, starting from a randomly chosen initial state. If $\delta(G) = 1$, for example, each state always goes either to fixation or to extinction.

Solution of equation (6) is generally difficult since there will be $2^N - 2$ equations in an equal number of unknowns. If the Graph G has a large automorphism group, however, the number of equations can be substantially reduced by partitioning states into equivalence classes [11,14]. The easiest case is the Moran process: the graph is a complete graph and all states containing m innovators are equivalent. The state space is isomorphic to $\{1,2,...,N\}$ and equations (6) reduce to

$$(r+1)x_m - x_{m-1} - rx_{m+1} = 0 \quad 1 \le m \le N-1 \tag{9}$$

with solution

$$x_m = \left[\sum_{k=0}^{N-1} r^k\right]^{-1}\left(\alpha \sum_{k=0}^{N-m-1} r^k + \beta\sum_{k=1}^{m} r^{N-k}\right) \tag{10}$$

For single vertex fixation probabilities $\alpha = 0$, $\beta = 1$. The Moran process provides a standard of comparison for inhomogeneous populations. Recent work in evolutionary dynamics has discovered graphs that suppress selective effects, and graphs that enhance such effects relative to a structurally homogeneous population [8,9]. In addition, surprisingly, there are graphs where suppression or enhancement of selection depending on the value of the fitness parameter[10]. Graphs for which a subset of vertices are inaccessible from the remaining vertices will suppress selection while graphs in which there are hubs or centers from which all other vertices are accessible tend to enhance selection. The graph shown below is the simplest example of a graph that suppresses selection.

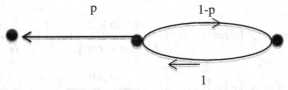

This graph consists of a two cycle with a link out to an isolated third vertex. Vertices are labeled right to left as $(v_1, v_2, v_3)$. The solution to equation (6) is:

$$\bar{\eta} = (1,1,1/(1+rp),1/(1+rp), p/(r+p), p/(r+p),0,0))$$
$$\bar{\mu} = (0,0, rp/(1+rp), rp/(1+rp), r/(r+p), r/(r+p),1,1) \tag{11}$$

Components of these vectors correspond respectively to the states (000), (001), (010), (100), (011), (101), (110), and (111) Thus, if the individual at $v_1$ is an innovator (100) the probability that all three individuals will become innovators is $rp/(1+rp)$ and the probability that $v_1$ will give up innovation is $1/(1+rp)$. On the other hand, a simple graph enhancing the effect of selection is:

Setting $P(r) = 2r^2 + r + 2$ and defining equivalence classes of states {000}, {001,100}, {010}, {101}, {110,011}, and {111}, solution of equation (6) gives

$$\bar{\eta} = \left(1,(r+2)/P(r),4(1+r+r^2)/(r+2)P(r),(r+2)/(1+2r)P(r),2/P(r),0\right)$$

$$\bar{\mu} = \left(0,2r^2/P(r),r^2(1+2r)/(r+2),4r(1+r+r^2)/(1+2r)P(r),r(1+2r)/P(r),1\right)$$

(12)

## 2    Synchronic Probabilistic Updating

In the birth-death process, at each iteration a single vertex is selected for reproduction. In this section a synchronic updating process is introduced, based on probabilities derived from the incoming edge labels for each vertex. All vertices are simultaneously updated with a value of 0 or 1 assigned based on the weighted probabilities of incident edges from vertices with value 0 and vertices with value 1. The model can be thought of as a probabilistic cellular automata with vertex (cell) neighborhoods determined by the graph topology.

As in Section 1, a Markov process is defined on the state space and a new transition matrix is constructed for equation (5). Using Theorem 1, the probabilities for a state transition $\vec{u} \to \vec{v}$ are determined in two stages. For given $u_j$ the probabilities that $v_j$ is 0 or 1 are given by

$$v_j = 1 : p_j(\vec{v}) = (1-u_j)\left[\frac{ra_j(\vec{u})}{N-m+rm}\right] + u_j\left[1 - \frac{b_j(\vec{u})}{N-m\_rm}\right]$$

$$v_j = 0 : q_j(\vec{v}) = (1-u_j)\left[1 - \frac{ra_j(\vec{u})}{N-m+rm}\right] + u_j\left[\frac{b_j(\vec{u})}{N-m\_rm}\right]$$

(13)

For the specific transition $\vec{u} \to \vec{v}$ the transition probability is the product of probabilities for each component of $\vec{v}$:   .

$$T_{uv} = \prod_{j=1}^{N}\left[v_j p_j(\vec{v}) + (1-v_j)q_j(\vec{v})\right]$$

(14)

If the matrix W is circulant, having the form $W = circ(s_0, s_1, 0, ...0, s_{-1})$ with $s_{-1}, s_0, s_1$ and each non-zero term equal to $1/(s_{-1}+s_0+s_1)$, this is a probabilistic version of a one-dimensional nearest neighbor additive cellular automata with periodic boundary conditions. Synchronic updating for the Moran process has $w_{ij} = 1/N$ for all i,j.

## 3    Examples

This section shows some simple results for both birth-death and probabilistic updating. Figure 1 shows the birth-death fixation probability for synchronic updating of the 2-star (SD) and the N = 3 complete graph (MS3), together with this probability for the N = 3 Moran birth-death process (M3) and the birth-death 2-star (S2). Figure 2 shows differences between the single vertex fixation probabilities for four cases:

$\rho_{SD} - \rho_{S2}$, $\rho_{MS3} - \rho_{M3}$, $\rho_{SD} - \rho_{MS3}$, and $\rho_{S2} - \rho_{M3}$. Inspection of these graphs shows that for birth-death updating the 2-star enhances selection slightly for $r > 1$ while for synchronic updating this effect is significantly greater. The fixation probabilities for $r > 1$ are substantially larger for synchronic updating.

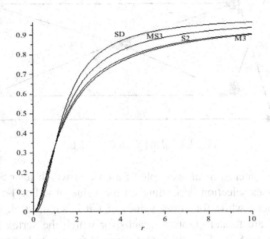

**Fig. 1.** Synchronically Updated 2-Star, Complete Graph, Birth-Death 2-Star, Moran Process

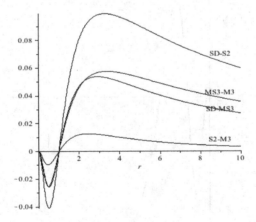

**Fig. 2.** Difference Between Fixation Probabilities for Synchronic 2-Star and Complete Graphs with Synchronic or Birth-Death Updating

As a final example, consider the birth-death process on the graph of Figure 3, a width two cycle with a constriction. Figure 4 shows the difference between the fixation probability for this graph and the fixation probability for a Moran process on five vertices.

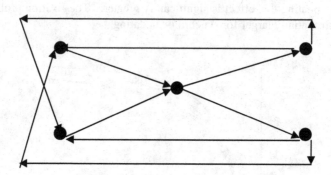

**Fig. 3.** Channel With Constriction

This graph is of interest as an example of a case in which for r > 1 the graph enhances or suppresses selection depending on the value of r. For 1< r <2.267235117 selection is enhanced while for larger values of r it is suppressed. Other graphs for which this occurs are funnel graphs – graphs for which the vertex set can be partitioned into subsets $S_0$, $S_1$,...,$S_{k-1}$ with edges directed from $S_j$ to $S_{j-1}$ and from $S_0$ to $S_{k-1}$ with $S_j$ containing more vertices than $S_{j-1}$ .

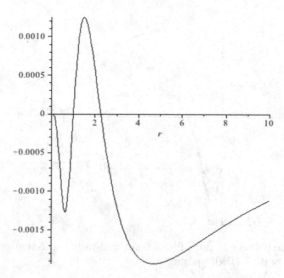

**Fig. 4.** Difference Between Birth-Day Fixation Probability for Graph of Figure 3 and Moran Process

# 4    Discussion

The birth-death process on graphs has been used to study fixation probability for distributions of genetic mutants in structured populations [e.g., 10,11,12] and applied more generally to birth-death diffusion processes in populations. Several significant applications have been studied in the literature. For example, in epidemics, or in cases such as the spread of a virus through a computer network, structures that suppress selection are important [2], while attempts to spread a favorable idea or new product are assisted by population structures that enhance selection [5]. The discovery that for some graphs suppression or enhancement of selection can depend on the value of the fitness parameter suggests that fitness, taken as a measure of "fit" between a requirement and a state, can act as a control parameter [10].

In addition to the birth-death process, a synchronic model related to probabilistic cellular automata is introduced. In comparison to the birth-death process, this model increases the influence of selection (see Figure 2). The synchronic model would seem to fit more with the spread of a computer virus, as compared to spread of a genetic mutation.

One potential application of interest arises from the behavior of columns in the matrix $T^k$ as k becomes large. Entries in these columns provide asymptotic probabilities for initial states that produce specific distributions of innovators, providing a means of addressing the question of how to best spread an innovation given limited resources.

Mathematically, the fact that the matrix $I - T$ is a graph Laplacian provides a link to research in spectral graph theory [e.g., 13]. If the Laplacian eigenvalues of an N-vertex graph are ordered from smallest to largest, the first is 0, the remaining eigenvalues satisfy $0 \leq \lambda_1 \leq \lambda_2 \leq \ldots \leq \lambda_{N-1} \leq 2$, and the number of 0 eigenvalues equal the number of connected components of the graph. In particular, $\lambda_1$ – called the algebraic connectivity of the graph – is non-zero if and only if the graph is connected and its value provides information about the difficulty of cutting the graph into disconnected parts, giving a measure of the degree of integration or connectivity of a population. If this eigenvalue is found to be decreasing in time it may suggest an increasing polarization or conflict in the represented population.

**Acknowledgements.** This research is supported by NSERC Discovery Grant OGP-0024871. Discussions on graph theory with Gary MacGillivray of the University of Victoria were seminal in developing ideas used in this paper. An initial version of the paper was presented in the Mathematical Biology Seminar at the University of Victoria, September 27, 2011.

# References

1. Barbour, A.D., Reinert, G.: Asymptotic behavior of gossip processes and small world networks. arXiv: 1202.5895v2 (2012)
2. Shah, D., Zaman, T.R.: Rumors in a network: Who's the culprit? IEEE Transactions on Information Theory 57, 5163–5181 (2011)

3. Tanimura, E.: Diffusion of innovations on community based Small Worlds: the role of correlation between social spheres. FEEM working paper 126 (2010), working.papers@feem.it
4. Wang, Y., Xiao, G., Liu, J.: Dynamics of competing ideas in complex social networks. ar-Xiv: 1112.5534v1 (2011)
5. Kempe, D., Kleinberg, J., Tardos, E.: Maximizing the spread of influence through a social network. In: Proceedings of KDD 2003, Washington DC (2003)
6. Nowak, M.A.: Evolutionary Dynamics. Cambridge. Harvard University Press, Cambridge (2006)
7. Moran, P.: Random processes in genetics. In: Mathematical Proceedings of the Cambridge Philosophical Society, vol. 54(01), pp. 60–71 (1958)
8. Liberman, E., Hauert, C., Nowak, M.A.: Evolutionary dynamics on graphs. Nature 433(7023), 312–316 (2005)
9. Hauert, C.: Evolutionary dynamics. In: Skjeltorp, A.T., Belushkin, A.V. (eds.) Proceedings of the NATO Advanced Study Institute on Evolution From Cellular to Social Scales, pp. 11–44. Springer, Dordrecht (2008)
10. Voorhees, B.: Birth-death fixation probabilities for structured populations (preprint, 2012)
11. Broom, M., Rychtár, J.: An analysis of the fixation probability of a mutant on special classes of non-directed graphs. Proceedings of the Royal Society A 464, 2609–2627 (2008)
12. Nowak, M.A., Tarnita, C.E., Antal, T.: Evolutionary dynamics in structured populations. Philosophical Transactions of the Royal Society B 365, 19–30 (2010)
13. Banerjee, A.: The Spectrum of the Graph Laplacian as a Tool for Analyzing Structure and Evolution of Networks. Dissertation (Dr. rer. nat.), University of Leipzig (2008)

# Spreading Patterns of Mobile Phone Viruses Using Cellular Automata

Ioannis Vourkas, Dimitrios Michail, and Georgios Ch. Sirakoulis

Department of Electrical & Computer Engineering,
Democritus University of Thrace (DUTh), Xanthi, Greece
{ivourkas,gsirak}@ee.duth.gr, michailjim@gmail.com

**Abstract.** Major technology progress and evolution of human living standards have led to wide development of mobile telecommunications. Nowadays, classic mobile phones tend to be replaced by more complex devices that show similar abilities to personal computers (PCs), known as smartphones. Rapid spreading of smartphone technology, as well as significant resemblance to PCs, gave rise to the appearance of mobile phone viruses, and the first attacks have already been recorded. In this work, the study of methods for the spreading of mobile phone viruses using Cellular Automata (CAs) is presented. The dependence of spreading patterns on time and on the operating system (OS) market share is examined with the use of a mathematical model designed for the prediction of such future situations. Simulation results are compared to published results based on real communication patterns, proving that the proposed model effectively captures the dynamics of mobile virus spreading.

**Keywords:** Cellular Automata, complex networks, virus spreading patterns, mobile phones.

## 1 Introduction

Wide development of mobile telecommunications boosted the production of advanced mobile phone devices, known as smartphones, which nowadays tend to replace classic devices. They are mobile devices with abilities similar to PCs, including a central processing unit and memory for the execution of programs, also using OS software to facilitate better utilization of available resources. Evolution and rapid spreading of the PC technology gave rise to the appearance of computer viruses. Significant resemblance between smartphones and PCs has recently opened a new field of work for authors of malicious software (malware) [1], [2], although so far attacks to PCs outnumber attacks on smartphones, which is attributed to the fact that smartphones are still fewer than PCs. User preferences related to OS software has steered malware authors towards the most well-known OS types. Continuously expanding variety of OS solutions for smartphones resulted in the division of the corresponding software market share. Taking into consideration also that the market share of smartphones was recently announced to be almost 5% of existing mobile devices [3], smartphones still

G.C. Sirakoulis and S. Bandini (Eds.): ACRI 2012, LNCS 7495, pp. 263–272, 2012.

constitute a tiny portion of susceptible devices for the spreading of mobile phone viruses, though these percentages change rapidly over time.

In this work, the study and development of methods for the spreading of mobile phone viruses using CAs is presented. CAs have been extensively used in the past for the modeling of spreading epidemics as an alternative to mathematical models based on ordinary differential equations. In specific, CAs overcome the drawbacks of the aforementioned models and have been used by several researchers as an efficient alternative method to simulate epidemic spreading [4], [5]. Such drawbacks include individual contact processes, effects of individual behavior, spatial aspects of the epidemic spreading, and effects of mixing patterns of individuals. Usually, when CAs are used for modeling of an epidemic spreading, individuals are assumed to be distributed in the cellular space so that each cell corresponds to one or more individuals of the population [4]. In the approach presented here, we focus explicitly on the presentation of spreading patterns of mobile viruses and their dependence on time and market share of OS, with the use of a mathematical model designed for the prediction of such future situations. Moreover, the proposed here model uses the aforementioned CA approach where CA cell states refer to portions of the population owning smart mobile devices potential to get infected. The derived simulations have been compared with published work on spreading patterns of mobile phone viruses based on real communication patterns of mobile phone users and simulations using the susceptible infected (SI) model [3], and it is proved that the proposed here CA-based model captures effectively the complex dynamics of mobile phone virus spreading. Such a model could be part of a future decision support system for telecommunication companies to aid risk estimation and facilitate better response in case of a potential virus outbreak.

## 2    CA-Based Modeling of Mobile Phone Virus Spreading

In our work we consider that all individuals own mobile phone devices that have active the Bluetooth (BT) device detection service and are able to receive multimedia messages (MMS), therefore all constitute vulnerable devices for infection. The population over which the virus propagation is modeled is assumed to be homogeneously distributed in a two dimensional space, divided into a matrix of identical square cells with specific side length, represented by a CA. Each CA cell includes a number of individuals, owners of mobile phone devices, who reside there, an assumption also mentioned in [4]. The widths of the two sides of the CA array are taken to be equal. The size of the array is defined by the user of the model and it is a compromise between accuracy and computation time. Larger array sizes result in more CA cells with smaller side length, increasing in this way the model's accuracy at the expense of computation time. The state $C^t_{i,j}$ of the CA cell with coordinates $(i,j)$ at time $t$ is the following:

$$C^t_{i,j} = \{P^t_{i,j}, INF^t_{i,j}, OS^t_{i,j}\}. \tag{1}$$

$INF^t_{i,j}$ is a flag indicating whether infected devices exist in the specific cell at time $t$. If $INF^t_{i,j} = 1$ then the cell includes individuals owning infected devices, whereas if $INF^t_{i,j} = 0$ then no infected devices are present. $P^t_{i,j}$ is the fraction of the number of infected devices found in the specific cell at time $t$, which may take any value between 0 and 1, and it is defined as follows:

$$P^t_{i,j} = I^t_{i,j}/T^t_{i,j}. \tag{2}$$

$I^t_{i,j}$ is the infected part of the local population and $T^t_{i,j}$ is the total population in the $(i,j)$ cell. Moreover, the proposed model supports the existence of different OS for the population of mobile phones. Particularly, we take into account existence of two different OS whose distributions are based on the actual market share, defined by the user, for which the study of the virus spreading patterns takes place [3]. All individuals, residents of a cell, are considered users of the same OS, and the specific type of the supported OS is denoted in the model using another flag, namely $OS^t_{i,j}$, found in the set of parameters forming the state of the CA cells described in Eq. 1. Thus, during initialization of the CA, the virus OS compatibility is also defined, which is a necessary condition for a potential change of a cell's state to take place.

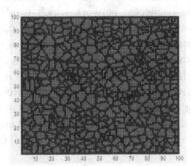

**Fig. 1.** The CA grid and approximation of each phone tower's service area with Voronoi cells

After studying the model's behavior, we decided to use a square matrix of size 100x100 cells to cover the area under consideration, without reducing the model's generality. Each mobile phone tower's service area is approximated by a Voronoi cell to facilitate visual representation, as it is shown in Fig. 1. The Voronoi diagram is calculated for a number of uniformly distributed points inside the grid and then, according to their coordinates, each CA cell is assigned a specific Voronoi cell. The cells located on the cells' border lines are deliberately painted black, and are not taken into account in the visual representations presented later in Section 3. Initial CA cell states are globally set to zero and fixed boundary conditions set also at zero are considered, which is the value corresponding to cells comprising only healthy devices. Any other given value within the range (0, 1] corresponds to a local infection percentage. The only cell which is given initial value of infection equal to one is the cell from where the start of the virus spread is studied.

Complex networks theory [6] is applied to mobile telecommunication networks in this paper's framework. Operation of complex networks is based mostly on the interconnection patterns between the network components. A significant feature of these patterns is their robustness to the removal of network nodes [7], which can be modeled as a percolation process on a network graph [8] whose vertices are considered occupied or not, depending on whether the corresponding network nodes are functioning normally. Percolation models built on networks have been used in the past also for the simulation of the effect of population movement on epidemic propagation and can be used also for the simulation of computer/mobile phone virus spreading The study of the giant component ($G_m$) for networks is the present work is necessary for the case of infection propagation via MMS, provided that the process depends on the contact list found inside each device. The $G_m$ of a network is formed by the remaining connections after a subset of nodes has been removed. This removal is related to the OS parameter introduced to the model to define software compatibility with the virus. More specifically, when a network is fully connected, i.e. in the case of having only one OS and thus 100% compatibility, then $G_m$ is the same with the OS market share, which is 100%, thus a potential virus outbreak could lead to the infection of the entire network. If the OS market share is smaller than 100%, the $G_m$ substantially affects the final number of infected devices. Moreover, this number is always smaller than the OS market share, which is attributed to the inability of finding the appropriate path in the connected network which would lead to all vulnerable devices. In other words, not all users of a particular region can be reached, even indirectly, through intermediate devices. Furthermore, there is an important constraint related to the OS market share which indicates the existence of $G_m$. It is a threshold value below which $G_m$ is eliminated (market share cut off - $m_c$). Above this threshold there is a $G_m$, therefore infection propagation is possible. Recent measurements have shown that a $G_m$ exists for market share values greater than 0.095. The value of $m_c$ and $G_m$ for market share values above $m_c$ can be calculated using the generating function formalism [9], requiring only as input the degree distribution of the network under consideration.

## 2.1    Bluetooth (BT) Virus

One of the possible ways for the spreading of a mobile phone virus is via BT service. Interaction between CA cells takes place in a cell's neighborhood, which is chosen to be the Moore's neighborhood, and is used for the simulation of the BT access range from the source device to the recipients. Inside the CA grid we consider that all cells adjacent to the reference cell inside the Moore's neighborhood are found within the BT access range, whereas the rest of the cells are not affected. Moreover, human mobility is taken into account given that all individuals frequently move to different places for a variety of reasons. This mobility contributes to the continuous change of the actual neighbors of a cell where infected devices are found. In the cellular space, human mobility is simulated by copying the whole set of the state parameters of the initial cell to the destination cell, considering that the total population of a cell is moving, introducing in this way potential new infection outbreaks in the grid. More specifically, we defined at each simulation time step a randomly selected 3% of the total number of cells to move to random destinations, where the randomness of selection is based on a discreet uniform distribution. The evolution rule chosen for the CA is summarized as follows, where only dynamic component $P$ of Eq. 1 is present:

$$P^{t+1} = k_1 P^t + k_2(P_N^t + P_S^t + P_E^t + P_W^t) + k_3(P_{NE}^t + P_{NW}^t + P_{SE}^t + P_{SW}^t). \qquad (3)$$

$P^{t+1}$ is the next cell state and $P^t$ is the actual cell state. In the used notation, $t$ and $t+1$ are not exponents but indexes of the particular simulation time step. Also, sub-indexes $N$, $S$, $E$, and $W$, as well as combinations $NE$, $NW$, $SE$ and $SW$ indicate the eight nearest neighboring cells found in the corresponding geographic location around the central cell. The state $P^{t+1}_{i,j}$ of the $(i,j)$ cell at the next time step $t+1$ is affected by the states of all eight cells in its neighborhood, as well as by its own state at the present time step $t$. In the CA local rule, described by Eq. 3, the adjacent neighbors of the cell, i.e. the cells that have a common side with the central cell, and the diagonal adjacent cells are grouped respectively together. The weight coefficients $k_2$ and $k_3$ found in the rule's formula define each neighboring cell's contribution depending on its location around the reference cell. It is expected that the $(i,j)$ cell will receive greater influence by an infected adjacent nearest cell than by an infected diagonal adjacent cell, because of the more extensive contact between populations. Therefore it is $k_2>k_3$. Coefficient $k_1$ defines how much each cell by itself contributes to its own state evolution. The spreading of the virus is homogeneous if the initial properties of the population of CA cells are the same for all cells. In this case, the resulting virus propagation fronts should be circular. After application of the model to a matrix of 100x100 cells, it was found that in order to produce circular propagation fronts away from the initial out-break point, the values of the set of parameters $\{k_2, k_3\}$ of the local CA rule should be $\{0.44, 0.04\}$. For all conducted simulations, coefficient $k_1$ was given a value 0.11, i.e. $k_2/4$, because it is considered that a cell by itself contributes equally with any nearest neighboring cell. At every simulation time step the presented rule is applied to all CA cells, taking into account OS compatibility with the virus. CA evolution finishes when all susceptible devices compatible to the virus are infected.

## 2.2    Multimedia Message Service (MMS) Virus

Another way of mobile phone virus transmission studied in this work is via MMS. Modeling of this infection process is a fairly simple task compared to the BT case presented before. When a device is infected, the virus is stored in the device's memory and starts browsing the phone contacts trying to send an MMS to all of them without the user's consent. This results in a potential infection of all message recipi-ents. During simulation, interaction between CA cells does not involve the cells found in the Moore's neighborhood, as in the BT case, but instead a number of randomly chosen cells from the entire cellular grid, based on a discreet uniform distribution, as shown in Fig. 2. This is because the infection spreads according to the found number of phone contacts, which correspond to different grid coordinates, provided that the residents of a cell build relationships with individuals who live in either close (e.g. relatives, neighbors, etc) or in distant places (e.g. colleagues, partners, friends, etc). For all conducted simulations it was considered that each cell is associated with ten other cells of the cellular grid, i.e. 0.1% of the total number of cells. Therefore, at every simulation time step, each infected cell communicates via MMS with ten potentially infected recipients, residents of other CA cells. The coordinates of these cells are found in the randomly created contact list assigned to each particular cell. Higher contact list numbers were also simulated but it was found that they dramatically shorten the total computation steps needed for this particular grid size. Definition of the infection process using MMS considers as potential infected devices the ones found inside each phone's contact list. Human mobility does not alter the final outcome if inserted in the computational model for the MMS virus, because the exact position of device owners does not affect the infection process.

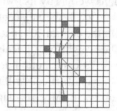

**Fig. 2.** Random CA neighborhood in the case of infection via MMS

In the MMS virus case, the giant component ($G_m$) needs to be calculated because it plays an important role in the infection propagation, unlike the BT case where it does not exist. $G_m$ depends on the market share and is the maximum network segment which may be infected. Inclusion of the $G_m$ in the model takes place in the processing of the values regarding the supported OS in each CA cell. In this way, prevention of infection propagation in spite of OS compatibility with the target cells is possible. The CA evolution rule used in this case is summarized as follows:

*If a cell with value 1 (one) is found, then in the next time step its state is copied to ten other cells whose coordinates are found inside the particular contact list of the cell, provided that there is OS compatibility between the target cells and the virus.*

This time the values used for the CA cell state definition are only 0 (zero), for healthy local population, and 1 (one) for a fully infected cell. This is because we consider that all individuals residing in a cell are familiar with each other, thus they all communicate between with their phones. Furthermore, a significant dependence of the total infected cells on the actual market share used in each simulation scenario is observed and it is discussed later in the simulations section. CA evolution finishes when all cells with susceptible devices compatible to the virus that also belong to the $G_m$ are fully infected.

## 2.3   Hybrid Virus

The last method of infection studied in this work is the hybrid mode which combines the aforementioned methods, i.e. BT and MMS, in order to overcome any imposed limitations and give better virus propagation results. More specifically, for virus infection via BT the existence of susceptible devices within the BT access range is necessary, whereas infected devices simultaneously use their contact list in order to infect other devices via MMS. The CA neighborhood used this time is the combination of the neighborhoods used is the separate cases of BT and MMS virus types. Particularly, we take into account both the Moore's neighborhood for the infection via BT and the randomly selected cells as well for the infection via MMS. In order to define OS compatibility the $G_m$ is necessary for the calculation of the maximum potentially infected network fraction by virus propagation via MMS. On the other hand, for the BT case we simulate human mobility, which is the main factor that creates new infection outbreaks, although it does not affect the infection via MMS. The CA evolution rule for the case of hybrid infection is a combination of the earlier discussed rules and is summarized as follows:

*If a cell with infected devices is found, then in the next time step its state is copied to ten other cells whose coordinates are found inside the particular contact list of the cell, provided that there is OS compatibility between the target cells and the virus. Afterwards, human mobility is simulated and the BT virus spreading rule is applied as well, both in the same time step t.*

The CA cell states are updated according to this combined logic and the infection percentage in each cell is given values inside the range [0, 1]. Simulation ends when all susceptible devices using OS compatible to the virus are infected.

# 3    Simulation Results

In this section, simulation results regarding spreading and spatial patterns of BT, MMS and hybrid modes of infection propagation are summarized and discussed. The changes in the ratio of infected and susceptible devices with time in the case of a BT and an MMS virus affecting devices for different market share values are presented in Fig. 3. A comparison is made with the work of Wang *et al.* [3] where spreading patterns of mobile phone viruses are studied. The published results are found in Fig. 3(a1) and 3(a2), whereas simulation results based on our model are presented in Fig. 3(b1), 3(b2) and 3(b3), for all studied cases of infection. The most important difference between BT and MMS infection is the required time scale for their spreading. An MMS epidemic reaches saturation very fast compared to a BT virus. The observed saturation of the reached ratio in Fig. 3(a2) and 3(b2) indicates that an MMS virus can reach only a finite fraction of all susceptible phones. The origin of this saturation is the fragmentation of the underlying call network. Different required time scales are made obvious in the corresponding time-dependent infection curves for BT and MMS virus types given in Fig. 4. A comparison is made again between published results derived using the SI model [3] and simulation results based on the proposed here model showed in Fig. 4(a) and Fig. 4(b) respectively. Qualitative agreement between the graphs in all presented cases proves that the proposed CA-based model successfully captures the evolution dynamics of a virus spreading among mobile devices for different infection scenarios.

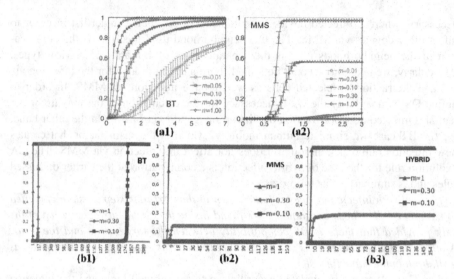

**Fig. 3.** Changes in the ratio of infected and susceptible devices with time for different OS market share ($m$) values. Presentation of spreading patterns for (a1) BT and (a2) MMS virus types results in [3], and our simulation results for (b1) BT, (b2) MMS and (b3) hybrid virus types.

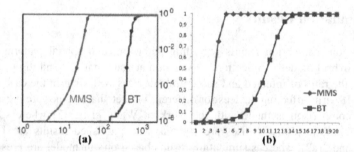

**Fig. 4.** Corresponding time-dependent infection curves for BT and MMS virus types. Comparison between (a) published SI-based [3] and (b) the proposed model's simulation results.

Moreover, spatial patterns in the spread of BT, MMS and hybrid viruses are extracted from simulations conducted based on the proposed model and are presented in Fig. 5. In all scenarios, just for comparison reasons, infection starts from the same point in the CA grid with coordinates $(x,y)=(50, 50)$. The panels in the three columns show the percentage of the infected devices in the vicinity of each phone tower, denoted by a Voronoi cell that approximates each tower's service area. Over the simulation time, a color change in the areas that correspond to different phone towers is used to indicate different percentages of infection. White color denotes that no infected devices exist in the specific region, whereas any other color indicates the average value of the local infected devices. In this comparative presentation it is obvious that all types of infection differ in their spatial spreading as well. A BT virus follows a wave-like spreading pattern infecting users in the vicinity of the virus's release point, whereas an MMS virus follows a more delocalized pattern. Both BT and MMS viruses have their limitations. For example, spreading of a BT virus is relative slow, because of human mobility, whereas an MMS virus can reach only a small fraction of users due to the fragmentation of the call graph and the existence of the $G_m$. These limitations can be avoided by hybrid viruses which take advantage of the potential of both types of infection and perform better, achieving the fastest infection of the total of the susceptible devices. An important observation in the scenario of a hybrid virus is the elimination of the effect that $G_m$ has to the devices susceptible to the MMS virus, because of the global infectious ability of the BT process. The derived spatial patterns for the BT and MMS infection types are in accordance with the patterns presented by Wang et al. [3] where a Voronoi diagram is used as well to approximate phone towers' service areas. This underlines our model's performance and ability to appropriately simulate mobile virus spreading under different infection conditions with a CA approach, which requires less computational effort and leads to fast execution, taking advantage of the inherent parallelism of the CA structure.

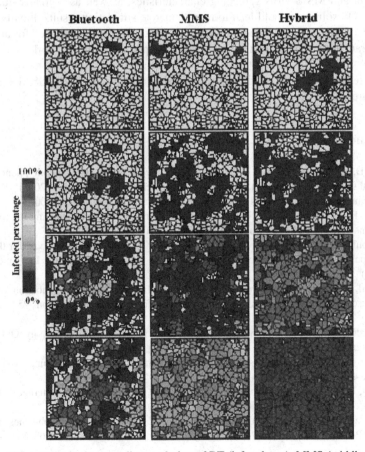

**Fig. 5.** Spatial patterns in the spreading evolution of BT (left column), MMS (middle column) and hybrid (right column) viruses for OS market share $m=100\%$

## 4     Conclusions and Future Work

In this work we presented a CA-based model for the simulation of spreading of mobile phone viruses via BT, MMS and hybrid infection processes. Simulation results indicate the substantial differences between different infection scenarios and their impact on their spreading characteristics. Our model's results are compared to published results and a qualitative agreement was found. The spatial evolution dynamics of mobile virus spreading are captured using the CA approach which requires less computational effort and leads to fast execution, exploiting inherent parallelism of the CAs. Our model could be included as a component of a future decision support system for the case of a potential virus outbreak, aiding better reaction and facilitating estimation of the realistic risks carried by mobile viruses, also helping the development of proper measures so as to avoid severe costly impacts. Further extensions of the proposed model could include different infection conditions and support of immune devices. Also, exploration of some more realistic aspects regarding population movement and MMS virus spreading characteristics, as well as a greater number of available OS solutions could lead to more concrete simulation results. Finally, alteration of the duration of the infection process, along with the time needed for an antivirus program to react and cure the device could be part of our future work.

**Acknowledgement.** This work was supported in part by the BODOSSAKI Foundation in Greece.

## References

1. Shih, D.-H., Lin, B., Chiang, H.-S., Shih, M.-H.: Security aspects of mobile phone virus: a critical survey. Industrial Management & Data Systems 108(4), 478–494 (2008)
2. Hypponen, M.: Malware Goes Mobile. Scientific American 295, 70–77 (2006)
3. Wang, P., González, M.-C., Hidalgo, C.-A., Barabási, A.-L.: Understanding the Spreading Patterns of Mobile Phone Viruses. SCIENCE 324, 1071–1075 (2009)
4. Sirakoulis, G.C., Karafyllidis, I., Thanailakis, A.: A cellular automaton model for the effect of population movement on epidemic propagation. Ecological Modeling 133(3), 209–223 (2000)
5. Ahmed, E., Agiza, H.N.: On modeling epidemics. Including latency, incubation and variable susceptibility. Physica A: Statistical Mechanics and its Applications 253, 247–352 (1998)
6. Caldarelli, G.: Scale-Free Networks Complex Webs in Nature and Technology. Oxford Uni. Press (2007)
7. Albert, R., Jeong, H., Barabási, A.-L.: Error and Attack Tolerance of Complex Networks. Nature 406, 378–382 (2000)
8. Cohen, R., Erez, K., ben-Avraham, D., Havlin, S.: Resilience of The Internet to Random Breakdowns. Phys. Rev. Lett. 85, 4626–4628 (2000)
9. Callaway, D.S., Newman, M.E.J., Strogatz, S.H., Watts, D.J.: Network Robustness and Fragility: Percolation on Random Graphs. Physical Review Letters 85(25), 5468–5471 (2000)

# A Preliminary Cellular Model for Sand Coastal Erosion and Experimental Contrast with Porto Cesareo Case

Maria Vittoria Avolio[1], Claudia Roberta Calidonna[2],
Marco Delle Rose[3], Salvatore Di Gregorio[1], Valeria Lupiano[4],
Tiziano Maria Pagliara[5], and Anna Maria Sempreviva[2]

[1] Dept. of Mathematics, University of Calabria (UNICAL), 87036 Rende (CS), Italy
[2] CNR-ISAC Inst. of Climate and Atmospheric Science, Industrial Area Comp.
15,88046 Lamezia Terme (CZ), Italy
[3] CNR-IBAM Ins. for Archaeological and Monumental Heritage, Prov.le
Lecce-Monteroni,73100 Lecce, Italy
[4] Dept. of Earth Science, UNICAL, 87036 Rende (CS), Italy
[5] Nautilus Puglia, Campi Salentina (LE), Italy
cr.calidonna@isac.cnr.it

**Abstract.** The phenomenon of sand erosion is recently spreading in Mediterranean beaches in a worrisome way. Cellular Automata modelling such a phenomenon involves many difficulties for adopting a convenient time and space scale (minute and decimeter), that can permit temporally reasonable simulations. A very preliminary model RUSICA was developed in association with an experimental work in order to test hypotheses, to receive suggestion separately for some basic processes and to learn from past occurred cases. During this contamination phase, some experimental applications were succesfully projected in order to contrast sand erosion on the coast. This paper presents the current initial version of RUSICA for sand erosion/transport/deposition and describes the results obtained at Porto Cesareo coast in the Italian Apulia Region. Complete simulations by RUSICA will soon follow this preparatory work.

## 1   Introduction

An extension of classical Cellular Automata (CA), the Macroscopic CA [5], were developed in order to model many complex macroscopic fluid-dynamical phenomena, that seem difficult to be modeled in other CA frames (e.g. the lattice Boltzmann method), because they take place on a large space scale. Macroscopic CA can need a large amount of states describing properties of the cells (e.g. temperature of bottom sea, thickness of sand cover,...); such features may be formally represented by means of substates, that specify the characteristics to be attributed to the state of the cell and determining the CA evolution. In the case of surface flows, quantities concerning the third dimension, i.e. the height, may be easily included among the CA substates (e.g. the altitude). This is an easier and effective way to deal with third dimension and simplifying the problem in a two dimensional one. The phenomenon is very complex as it includes

G.C. Sirakoulis and S. Bandini (Eds.): ACRI 2012, LNCS 7495, pp. 273–278, 2012.

granular flows problem class, in this case, time dynamics is very important. In the past the erosion problem by CA approach was described and modeled by: [3] soil erosion by rain (SCAVATU model); [2] transport, deposit and erosion by sand and snow; [2,6], subaerial-subaqueous flow-like landslides [1]. We can summarize consideration in the previous approaches as follows: phenomenon, when approached as *sandpile* + waves, requires naturally a microscopic approach. That means cells smaller than *mm* and time step smaller than *s*, i.e. problems about data precision and validation. Two-dimensional Chopard model for snow/sand transport, deposit and erosion would be extended.

The aim of this contribution is to show, how, by means of CA, to model and simulate dynamics of the coastal erosion complex phenomenon. In the following sections the CA RUSICA (RUdimental SImulation of Coastal erosion by cellular Automata) model is introduced and then experimental results are described. Finally some conclusions and perspectives of this work are outlined.

## 2    The Model RUSICA

### 2.1    Phenomenological Considerations and Hypothesis

The underlying ideas in modeling coastal erosion is to approach it according a macroscopic view on the base of a simplified phenomenology. Equivalent sand cover (an average type of sand) may be assumed without a continuous variation of sand properties.

Water covers the shore on the sea level up to a height dependent on *wind intensity* and *direction* or/and *tide height* or/and *sea current intensity* and *direction* without explicit wave movement. Sand flows are averaged in time (no explicit turbulence and movement alternation), but along a computed direction between slope, wind and current directions.

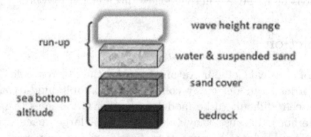

**Fig. 1.** Vertical scheme according to model substates, expliciting the third dimension

The wind transmits energy from the sea surface possibly up to the sea bottom, depending on its intensity, type and depth of sea bottom. Shallow sandy/porous/rock-solid but irregular bottom involves larger energy loss. Such an energy permits (by turbulence) sand suspension in water up to a maximum possible quantity, if the wind intensity is not sufficient, sand sedimentation occurs. Sand erosion occurs when enough wind energy passes on sandy bottom sea. Sand sedimentation and erosion may occur contemporary.

Free wind generates surface wind by propagation from the borders of CA: it implies that updating needs a shortest time step (less than a minute) only when the wind changes: this problem may be solved by introducing a coupled CA, that works only when wind changes. Obstacles (cliffs, artificial barriers of different type) can locally affect wind direction-intensity and sea current direction-intensity.

Third dimension substates are made explicit as depicted in the Fig. 1.

## 2.2   The CA Model

The RUSICA model is a two-dimensional CA with hexagonal cells, with substates and the transition function defined as follows:

$$RUSICA = \langle \mathcal{R}, \mathcal{G}, X, S, P, \tau, \Gamma \rangle$$

- $\mathcal{R}$ identifies the set of regular hexagons, where the phenomenon evolves.
- $\mathcal{G}$ represents the cell at the border of $\mathcal{R}$, where the wind could be generated.
- $X = \{(0,0),(0,1)(0,-1)(1,0)(-1,0),(1,1),(-1,-1)\}$ are the neighbors of the central cell according to hexagonal grid.
- $S = \{S_A \times S_D \times S_{TH} \times S_{WE} \times S_{SWE} \times S_C \times S_F \times S_{XC} \times S_{YC} \times S_{XFW} \times S_{YFW} \times S_{XSW} \times S_{YSW} \times S_{WL} \times S_{WA} \times S_{XWC} \times S_{YWC}\}$ is the finite set of states (of the finite automaton embedded in the cell) respectively: the cell altitude (or sea bottom depth), the cell sea water depth, the sand layer thickness, the average (for a step) kinetic energy of wind inside the cell, the average kinetic energy of sea water inside the cell, the sea water average sand concentration, the suspended sand flows, normalized to a thickness, from the central cell toward any adjacent cell, the $x - y$ components of sea current speed, the $x - y$ components of free wind speed, the $x - y$ components of surface wind speed. Furthermore wavelenght, wave amplitude, and x-component and y-component wave celerity address for sea waves considered properties.
- $P = \{p_a, p_t, p_d, p_{et1}, p_{et2}, p_{slv}, p_{sm}, p_{sd}\}$ is the set of the global physical and empirical parameters, which account for the general frame of the model and the physical characteristics of the phenomenon, respectively considering: the apothem of the cell, the time interval corresponding to a CA step, is the decay parameter for kinetic energy variation according the sea depth, the two energy transfer coefficients; parameter for sea level variation; two parameters of sand mobilization and deposit.
- $\tau : S^7 \to S$ is the deterministic transition function, composed by the following *elementary* processes:
    - $\sigma_1$ suspended sand outflows determination; the motion of a suspended sand particle may be described as a combination of an elliptical and translational motion with a drift along the composed wind and sea current directions, ellipsis and translation size increase depending on wave

energy and decrease top-down, ellipsis (a circle for deep waters) flattens in shallow waters; sand outflows are computed by accounting of back and forth motion and by considering the hexagonal discretization of plane and variations in height: $\sigma_1 : (S_A \times S_D \times S_{TH})^7 \times S_{SWE} \times S_C \times S_{XC} \times S_{YC} \times S_{XSW} \times S_{YSW} \times S_{WL} \times S_{WA} \times S_{XWC} \times S_{YWC} \to S_F^6$

- $\sigma_2$ variation of sand cover thickness and suspended sand concentration by sand cover mobilization and sand deposit; if the water energy of sea bed overcomes a threshold $p_{sm}$ dependent on sand granulosity, a sand quantity proportional to energy overcoming the threshold (this is a first rough approximation [3]) is added to suspended sand, then the sand deposit is computed by considering that sea water energy density in the cell can proportionally (by $p_{sd}$ dependent on sand granulosity) support a maximum suspended sand concentration, if the concentration overcomes such a maximum, sand deposit occurs in order to re-establish equilibrium; sand deposit and mobilization may occur simultaneously:
$\sigma_2 : S_A \times S_D \times S_{TH} \times S_{SWE} \times S_C \to S_A \times S_D \times S_{TH} \times S_C$

- $\sigma_3$ variation of suspended sand concentration in the water inside the cell; it consists trivially by composition of new suspended sand concentration from remaining (because of outflows) suspended sand in the cell more suspended sand from the inflows; control of possible deposits is performed according the sand deposit computation in $\sigma_2$ and correspondent variation in sand layer thickness, depth etc.:
$\sigma_3 : S_A \times S_D \times S_{TH} \times S_{SWE} \times S_C \times S_F^6 \to S_A \times S_D \times S_{TH} \times S_C$

- $\sigma_4$ surface wind intensity, direction variation by free wind intensity, direction and altitude (if rocks or structures emerge from the sea, then the other coupled CA must work when at most direction and/or intensity changes of wind occur, otherwise free and surface wind coincide without coupled CA): $\sigma_4 : (S_A \times S_D \times S_{TH})^7 \times S_{XSW} \times S_{YSW} \to S_{YWC} \times S_{XWC}$

- $\sigma_5$ water depth variation by altitude, wind and sea current; wind and sea current involve wave formation, that is complicated by form (altitude) of sea bed: $\sigma_5 : (S_A \times S_D \times S_{TH})^7 \times S_{XC} \times S_{YC} \times S_{XSW} \times S_{YSW} \to S_A \times S_D \times S_{TH} \times S_{WA}$

- external influences $\Gamma : \gamma_1 \bullet \gamma_2$ account for generating step by step (historical, statistical, hypothetical) data of:

  - sea current velocity components offshore: $\gamma_1 : \mathcal{N} \times G \to S_{XC} \times S_{YC}$ , ($\mathcal{N}$ is the set of natural number accounting for CA steps).
  - free wind velocity components: $\gamma_2 : \mathcal{N} \times G \to S_{XFW} \times S_{YFW}$

## 3    The Experimental Site: Porto Cesareo

The study area, Porto Cesareo site, is a special Italian coastal zone in Apulia, on the east side, Jonian sea, which represents a significant example of Mediterranean type low-lying coastal landscape with different kinds of human activities and some important areas of environmental and archaeological interest. Such a region, similar in geomorphology to some second-order physiographic unit in south-western Apulia Adriatic coast, is particularly prone to coastal erosion and marine inundation [4]. From a morpho-sedimentological characteristic, gently sloping carbonate ramp are present as well as discontinues dunes, coastal do-lines and water basin along the coast.

The coastal site was in equilibrium for several decades not showing particular and intense erosion phenomenon until 2009 year (see Fig. 2.a). The intertidal bars and coastal line were at first modified and then destroyed in a very short temporal range. Analising meteorological and oceanographic data (2009-2011) some observation arised: 1)there was not an evident correlation between wind intensity and direction and wave height in the open sea and erosion events/sand deposit, 2)different wind direction from south direction in some cases arised in erosion or sand accumulation.

**Fig. 2.** A particular of sand deposition after experimental intervention and turbulence effect after slopes a) before erosion b)eroded beach c) removable contrast barrier d) erosion after a storm e) sand deposit after barrier intervention f) turbulence effect

At beginning of 2011 year a contrast intervention was experimented, in the south zone of the bay, for three months in order to allow the intertidal bar reconstruction. It was built a barrier under sea level with some controlled ex-its in order to modulate outflow currents (see Fig 2.b). The removable barrier (height 70 cm considering a 90 cm height bathymetry) was built with special bags (propylene 1000 lt capacity) filled with sands (2,1 t each weight). After about 45 days, in which the barrier was stable, the estimation of accumulated sands in the bay was about $2500m^3$ (see Fig. 2.e). The accumulation occurred during three main severe storms (February - April 2011) with Southern direc-tion winds whose intensity was $17Kn$. In particular during one of them there was an additional effect as the sea level was very high (+ 0,17 m on zero eleva-tion IGM). With removable bags it was possible to tune the suitable control of outflows currents in the bay. The experimental intervention was guided by the turbulence behavior in presence of obstacles/slopes (see Fig 2.f). The measured bathymetry allow us to refine the model described in the previous section and actually still in development.

## 4  Observations and Future Works

Adopting an interdisciplinary approach and analysing the complex phenomenon of the sand erosion/transport/deposition allowed us to project and experiment a low impact method. This gave us such results in contrasting erosion and also individuating emerging processes for the whole complex system. CA RUSICA is a new preliminary empirical way to approach and simulate the coastal erosion complex phenomenon and tacking into account its emerging phenomena. This permits to define a simplified model when opportune temporal scale and discrete steps in order to overcome turbulence regimes. Considering turbulence regime and related dynamics gave us the way to exploit the properties of the turbulent energy when a slope is present (see Fig 2.f). Taking into account this last issue, according the shoreline orientation and wind and marine currents directions, it was possible to put opportunely the contrast disposable structures in order to transform a usual erosive event into an accumulation one. Our first experimentation results comfort us; there is an ongoing work on data elaboration to populate the RUSICA model input. That will permit to tune, refine and validate RUSICA on the base of other site experimentations.

**Acknowledgements.** This research was partially funded by PON (Operational National Plan) 2007 − 2013 from MIUR (Italian Research Ministry of Research) project "SIGIEC: Integrated management system for Coastal erosion " ID: PON01_02651.

## References

1. Avolio, M.V., Lupiano, V., Mazzanti, P., Di Gregorio, S.: Modelling combined subaerial-subaqueous flow-like landslides by Cellular Automata. In: Umeo, H., Morishita, S., Nishinari, K., Komatsuzaki, T., Bandini, S. (eds.) ACRI 2008. LNCS, vol. 5191, pp. 329–336. Springer, Heidelberg (2008)
2. Chopard, B., Masselot, A., Dupuis, A.: A lattice gas model for erosion and particles transport in a fluid. Computer Physics Communications 129, 167–176 (2000)
3. D'Ambrosio, D., Di Gregorio, S., Gabriele, S., Gaudio, R.: A Cellular Automata Model for Soil Erosion by Water. Phys. Chem. Earth (B) 26(1), 33–39 (2001)
4. Delle Rose, M., Beccarisi, L., Elia, T.: Short-Medium term assessments of coastal erosion and marine inundation effects on natural and anthropic environments (Apulia, southern Italy). Marine Research At CNR (CNR Ed.), pp. 1149–1163 (2011) ISBN-2239-5172
5. Di Gregorio, S., Serra, R.: An empirical method for modelling and simulating some complex macroscopic phenomena by cellular automata. FGCS 16, 259–271 (1999)
6. Kubo, Y., Syvitski, J.P.M., Hutton, E.W.H., Paola, C.: Advance and application of the stratigraphic simulation model 2D-SedFlux: From tank experiment to geological scale simulation. Sedimentary Geology 178, 187–195 (2005)
7. Salles, T., Lopez, S., Cacas, M.C., Mulder, T.: Cellular automata model of density currents. Geomorphology 88, 1–20 (2007)

# Simulation of Wildfire Spread Using Cellular Automata with Randomized Local Sources

Maria Vittoria Avolio[1], Salvatore Di Gregorio[1],
Valeria Lupiano[2], and Giuseppe A. Trunfio[3]

[1] Department of Mathematics, University of Calabria, 87036 Rende (CS), Italy
[2] Department of Earth Sciences, University of Calabria, 87036 Rende (CS), Italy
[3] DADU, University of Sassari, 07041 Alghero (SS), Italy

**Abstract.** The accuracy of Cellular Automata (CA) methods for simulating wildfires is limited by the fact that spread directions are constrained to the few angles imposed by the regular lattice of cells. To mitigate such problem, this paper proposes a new CA in which a local randomization of the spread directions is explicitly introduced over the lattice. The suggested technique, inspired by a method already used for simulating lava flows, is empirically investigated under homogeneous conditions and by comparison with the vector-based simulator FARSITE. According to the presented results, the adopted randomization seems to be able to significantly improve the accuracy of CA based on a standard center-to-center ignition scheme.

**Keywords:** Modelling and Simulation, Cellular Automata, Wildfire.

## 1 Introduction

Most algorithms for simulating wildfire spread through Cellular Automata (CA) are based on a mono-dimensional fire behaviour model (FBM), which allows the CA to determine the head fire rate of spread as a function of the relevant cell-level variables (i.e., fuel, humidity, wind speed, terrain slope). An additional component is often included, that is a suitable assumption about the shape of the two-dimensional spread under homogeneous conditions (i.e., spatially and temporally constant fuels, wind and topography). Among the different proposals, the most common model of fire shape is a simple ellipse the eccentricity of which increases with both the wind strength and terrain slope. Therefore, in such models the main task of the CA transition function consists of automating the FBM together with the shape model, for leading to a suitable discrete sequence of cells' ignitions in a heterogeneous landscape.

Approaches different from CA exist for the computation of the areas burned by wildland fires. For example, the vector algorithms adopted in simulators like FARSITE [1] and PROMETHEUS [2] are known to be very accurate. However, it has been proved that CA-based methods can be computationally much more convenient than other simulation algorithms [3]. Unfortunately, such greater efficiency is often achieved at the cost of a lower accuracy. In fact, a typical problem

G.C. Sirakoulis and S. Bandini (Eds.): ACRI 2012, LNCS 7495, pp. 279–288, 2012.

of CA-based algorithms for fire spread simulation is the distortion that may affect the produced fire shape. For example, under homogeneous conditions and in presence of wind, the shape of the heading portion of the fire is often angular rather than rounded as in the expected ellipse [4],[5]. Obviously, such systematic errors under homogeneous conditions typically give rise to inaccurate results also in operational contexts [6],[3].

As is well known, such distorted shapes are caused by the fire only being able to propagate along the fixed directions imposed by the raster [4],[1],[7],[3]. In the literature, many different approaches have been adopted to mitigate the problem. In most cases, the increase of the number of neighbouring cells towards which the fire can propagate, so that to allows more spread directions, is adopted [8],[5]. A different technique for mitigating distortions has been proposed in [7], which describes the use of an irregular grid that has the effect of a randomization of the discrete spread directions. Another approach, proposed by [3], consists of a modification of the ellipse equation through a suitable *adjustment factor*. Also, a recent approach proposed in [9] devised a spreading algorithm in which the fire is not forced to travel only along the few fixed directions imposed by both the lattice and neighbourhood.

This paper describes a CA for wildfire simulations which provides a satisfactory level of accuracy thanks to some of the ideas above, namely extending the size of the neighbourhood and randomizing the spread directions. However, instead of using an irregular grid as in [7], here the randomization is explicitly introduced over the regular lattice according to the approach proposed in [10] for simulating lava flows through CA. Moreover, the model is characterized by a high run time efficiency thanks to: ($i$) an adaptive time step strategy [3], which simulates the progression of the fire by avoiding unnecessary computation; ($ii$) the use of a list of *active cells* which allows to apply the transition function only to the cells on the current fire front.

## 2   Model Description

The approach adopted in this paper is based on the semi-empirical FBM of Rothermel [11],[12], which is one of the most commonly adopted and widely studied [13],[14],[1],[15],[3]. As in different CA-based wildfire simulation models [16],[3], the two-dimensional fire propagation is locally modelled through a growing ellipse having the semi-major axis along the direction of maximum spread, the eccentricity related to the intensity of the so-called *effective wind* and one focus acting as a 'fire source'. At each time step the ellipse's size is incremented according to both the duration of the time step and maximum rate of spread (see Figure 1). Afterwards, a neighbouring cell invaded by the growing ellipse is considered a candidate to be ignited by the spreading fire. In case of ignition, a new ellipse is generated according to the amount of overlapping between the invading ellipse and the ignited cell. More formally, the model is a two-dimensional CA with square cells defined as:

$$CA = \langle \mathcal{K}, \mathcal{N}, \mathcal{S}, \mathcal{P}, \eta, \Psi \rangle \tag{1}$$

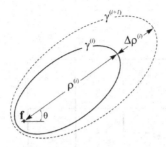

**Fig. 1.** Growth of the ellipse $\gamma$ locally representing the fire front. The symbol $\rho$ denotes the forward spread which is incremented by $\Delta\rho$ at the $i$-th time step.

where:

- $\mathcal{K}$ is the set of points in the finite region where the phenomenon evolves. Each point represents the centre of a square cell;
- $\mathcal{Q}$ is a set of *random local sources* (RLSs), one point for each cell; they are generated at the beginning of the simulation within an assigned radius $\delta$ from each of the centres in $\mathcal{K}$, as shown in Figure 2. As detailed later, a new ignition in a cell consists of a new ellipse having its rear focus on the local source $\mathbf{q} \in \mathcal{Q}$;
- $\mathcal{N}$ is the set that identifies the pattern of cells influencing the cell state change (i.e the neighbourhood);
- $\mathcal{S}$ is the finite set of the states of the cell, defined as the Cartesian product of the sets of definition of all the cell's substates;
- $\mathcal{P}$ is the finite set of global parameters, which affect the transition function and are constant in the overall cellular space. Some relevant parameters in set $\mathcal{P}$ are the current time $p_t$, the size of the cell's side $d$, the time corresponding to a single CA step $p_{\Delta t}$. Additional parameters in $\mathcal{P}$ define the reference values of weather conditions and the fuel models (fuel bed characteristics are specified according to the fuel models used in BEHAVE [17]);
- $\eta : \mathcal{S}^{|\mathcal{N}|} \to \mathcal{S}$ is the transition function accounting for the fire ignition, spread and extinction mechanisms;
- $\Psi$ is the set of global functions, activated at each step before the application of the transition function $\eta$ to modify either the values of model parameters in $\mathcal{P}$ or the cells' substates. Among these, the function $\phi_\tau$ adapts the size $p_{\Delta t}$ of the time step according to both the size of the cells $d$ and maximum spread among the cells on the current fire front. The value of $p_{\Delta t}$ is then used by another function, $\phi_t$, for keeping the current time $p_t$ up to date.

The cell's substates include all the local quantities used by the transition function for modelling the local interactions between the cells (i.e. the fire propagation to neighbouring cells) as well as its internal dynamics (i.e. the fire ignition and growth). In particular, among the substates that define the state of each cell, there are:

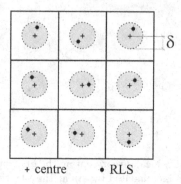

+ centre    • RLS

**Fig. 2.** An example of RLSs arrangement in a subset of the automaton. Each RLS occupy a random position within a distance $\delta$ from the cell centre.

- the altitude $z \in \mathbb{R}$ of the cell;
- the fuel model $\mu \in \mathbb{N}$, which is an index referring to one of the mentioned fuel models that specify the characteristics of vegetation relevant to Rothermel's equations;
- the combustion state $\sigma \in S_\sigma$, which takes one of the values *unburnable, not ignited, ignited* and *burnt*.
- the accumulated forward spread $\rho \in \mathbb{R}_{\geq 0}$, that is the current distance between the focus $\mathbf{f}$ of the local ellipse and the farthest point on the semi-major axis (see Figure 1);
- the angle $\theta \in \mathbb{R}$ (see Figure 1), giving the direction of the maximum rate of spread. In the context of the semi-empirical Rothermel's approach, such an angle is obtained through the composition of two vectors, namely the so-called *wind effect* and *slope effect* [11], both obtained on the basis of the local wind vector, local terrain slope and fuel model;
- the maximum rate of spread $r \in \mathbb{R}_{\geq 0}$, also provided by Rothermel's equations on the basis of the relevant local characteristics [11];
- the eccentricity $\varepsilon \in [0, 1]$ of the ellipse $\gamma$ representing the local fire front, which is obtained as a function of both the wind and terrain slope through the empirical relation proposed in [18],[1].

Among the remaining substates are the local wind vector and the relative humidity value of the cell, both provided as external input to the model.

In order to speed up the computation, the transition function $\eta$ is only applied to cells that are in the *burning* state. To this purpose, a list of *active cells*(i.e., the cells on the current fire front) is maintained during the simulation. The first step of $\eta$ consists of checking the condition that triggers the transition to the *burnt* state. The latter is verified when all the neighbouring cells are in either the *ignited* or in the *unburnable* state, that is when the cell's contribution is no longer necessary to the fire spread mechanism.

Then, if the cell still belongs to the fire front, $\eta$ updates the size of the local ellipse $\gamma$. This is accomplished by adding to the accumulated forward spread $\rho$ the product of the rate of spread $r$ and the step size $\Delta t$. The latter is dynamically

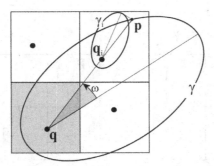

**Fig. 3.** The $i$-th neighbouring cell intersected by the ellipse $\gamma$ locally representing the fire front

established by the global function $\phi_\tau$ according to a procedure similar to that proposed in [3]. In particular, the value of $\Delta t$ is computed as the minimum amount of time that elapses before the fire may have travelled from an RLS on the current fire front to a neighbouring RLS.

The next statement of $\eta$ consists of testing if the fire is spreading towards other cells $c_i$ of the neighbourhood that are in the *not ignited* state. Since in the current cell the fire front is represented by a local ellipse $\gamma$, such a spread test is carried out through checking if $\gamma$ includes the RLS $q_i$ of the cell $c_i$ (see Figure 3). To this purpose the current spread $|\mathbf{qp}|$ in direction of $\mathbf{q}_i$ can be easily computed using the mathematical properties of the ellipse as:

$$|\mathbf{qp}| = \rho\,\frac{1-\varepsilon}{1-\varepsilon\,\cos\omega} \qquad (2)$$

Also, in order to account for sloping terrains, all distances are computed along the ground surface as in [3], [9]. If $\mathbf{q}_i$ is inside $\gamma$, then a new ellipse $\gamma_i$ is generated for the cell $c_i$, having the following characteristics:

- both the intensity $r_i$ of the maximum spread rate vector and its direction $\theta_i$ are computed through the proper Rothermel's equations [11];
- the eccentricity $\varepsilon_i$ is determined using the empirical formula used in [1], which accounts for both the effect of wind and topography through the previously mentioned *effective wind speed* [19].
- as shown in Figure 3, the local spread $\rho_i$ is initialized with the the amount of the invading spread that exceeds the RLS $\mathbf{q}_i$ of the newly ignited cell (i.e., the distance $|\mathbf{q}_i\mathbf{p}|$ in Figure 3);
- the RLS $\mathbf{q}_i$ is assumed as rear focus.

Is is worth noting that $\phi_\tau$ computes the the step size in order to avoid a large $|\mathbf{q}_i\mathbf{p}|$ (see Figure 3), which would determine the accumulation of simulation errors in terms of under-estimation or over-estimation burned area.

When compared with a typical CA algorithm for simulating wildland fires, the main advantage of the approach based on the RLSs, lies in its ability to

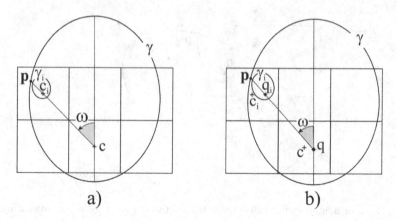

**Fig. 4.** a) In the typical center-to-center ignition mechanism, the angular coordinate $\omega$ in which ignition occur is forced to a few falues; b) in the proposed approach based on the RLSs the value of $\omega$ varies as the fire propagates

increase the directions of spread. As shown in the next section, this leads to an improved accuracy. The reason can be highlighted by considering Figure 4-a, which exemplifies the mechanism of a typical CA-based spread technique. As shown, the rear focus of the ellipse locally representing the fire front occupies the same position in each cell (i.e., the center of the cell, in this case). Consequently, the process of ignition of the neighbouring cells is always along one of the fixed directions given by the neighbourhood. For example, suppose that the Moore's neighbourhood is used and let **p** be the generic point of the ellipse from which, as depicted in Figure 4, a new ignition is originated. Then, the angular coordinate $\omega$ of **p** is restricted to the set $\{0°, \pm45°, \pm90°, 180°\}$. Therefore, since the derivative of the distance $|\mathbf{c}\,\mathbf{p}|$ with respect to $\omega$ is largest for small values of $\omega$, the front portion of the ellipse is likely to be under-sampled, regardless of both the cell size and step duration [3]. Conversely, in the case of Figure 4-b, representing the proposed mechanism based on the RLSs, an angular coordinate $\omega$ associated with the point **p** would not be forced to take only a few fixed values. As a consequence, during a long simulation in which many cells of the landscape are burned, the front portion of the ellipse turns out to be better sampled.

## 3   Numerical Experiments

The model described above has been implemented using the MAGI C++ class library described in [20]. The approach was first empirically investigated using a constant rate and direction of spread, i.e. under homogeneous conditions. In the latter case, the expected fire perimeter after a given time from the ignition can be easily computed from the assumed fire and shape models. In other words, an exact solution to be taken as reference is known.

The simulations were carried out for two different main directions of spread (i.e. the angle $\theta$ in Figure 1) and for different values of the parameter $\delta$ shown

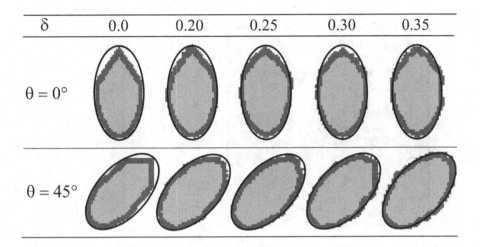

| $\delta$ | 0.0 | 0.20 | 0.25 | 0.30 | 0.35 |

**Fig. 5.** A comparison between the simulated fire shapes obtained under homogeneous condition with different values of the parameter $\delta$ (see Figure 2) and for two main directions of spread. The value $\delta = 0$ corresponds to a standard CA based on a center-to-center ignition scheme (see for example [3]). All the simulations were carried out using cells with side 10 m and an extended Moore neighbourhood composed of 24 cells. The continuous line represents the expected shape.

in Figure 2. The automaton was made of cells with sides of $10\,m$ and adopted an extended Moore neighbourhood composed of 24 cells. Also, the simulated fire had a fixed rate of spread $r = 1.7\,m/min$ and lasted $8.3\,hours$.

In Figure 5 the simulation results are shown. As expected, the standard CA based on the typical center-to-center ignition scheme (i.e., $\delta = 0$) gave the typical kite-shaped burned area instead of the expected ellipse with eccentricity 0.83. However, increasing the value of $\delta$ lead to a slightly randomized burned area much more similar to the expected ellipse. In particular, in Figure 5 the improved accuracy is particular evident for $\delta = 0.30$.

A further numerical experiment was carried out, which consisted of a comparison with the results provided by FARSITE [1] on a real landscape and under realistic weather conditions. To this purpose, an area of the Ligury region, in Italy, historically characterized by a high frequency of serious wildfires was chosen. The landscape, shown in Figure 6 was modelled through a Digital Elevation Model composed of $461 \times 445$ square cells with side of $40\,m$. In the area, the terrain is relatively complex with an altitude above sea level ranging from 0 to 250 m. The heterogeneous fuel bed depicted in Figure 6, was described by the 1:25000 land cover map from the CORINE project. The land-cover codes were mapped on the standard fuel models used by the CA model (i.e., the substate $\mu$). Plausible values of fuel moisture content were obtained from literature data. Also, a domain-averaged open-wind vector from the North direction, having an intensity of $20\,km\,h^{-1}$, was used for producing time-constant gridded winds

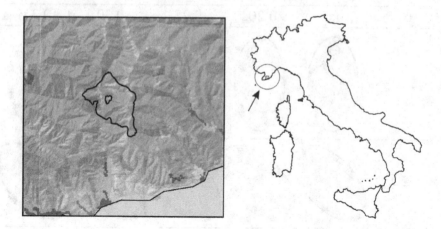

**Fig. 6.** The landscape under study (in Ligury, Italy) and the burned area simulated by FARSITE. Colors refer to the standard CORINE land-cover data.

through WindNinja [21], a computer program that simulates the effect of terrain on the wind flow. The simulated fire, which is shown in Figure 6, lasted 12 hours.

A direct comparison with FARSITE was made possible because the CA uses the same fire and eccentricity models described by [1]. In addition, crown fire together with the spotting and acceleration modules, were disabled in FARSITE. In order to ensure a fair comparison, FARSITE's spatial and temporal resolutions were set to values similar to those used by the CA-based simulator. However, it should be considered that FARSITE adapts the step size according to the complexity of the fire perimeter introducing some sub-steps when necessary. Also, maps of fuel moisture and mid-flame wind speed computed by FARSITE were exported and used by the CA algorithms.

For the CA simulations two different values of $\delta$ were used, namely $\delta = 0$ (corresponding to a standard center-to-center ignition scheme) and $\delta = 0.3\,d$, being $d$ the size of the cell. In Figure 7, the results of the comparisons are shown. As already observed in other studies (e.g. [3], [9]), the standard ignition scheme lead to an underestimation of the burned area. Instead, as can be seen in Figure 7, a significant improvement was found using the method proposed in this paper. To measure the agreement between the simulated fire shapes, the following metric was adopted:

$$\lambda_s = \frac{|R \cap S|}{|R \cup S|} \tag{3}$$

where $R$ is the set of cells defining the fire shape simulated by FARSITE, $S$ is the set of cells defining the spread simulated by the CA model and the operator $|\cdot|$ gives the size of a set. Quantitatively, the CA simulation with $\delta = 0$ lead to $\lambda_s = 0.87$ while the agreement between the CA with $\delta = 0.3\,d$ and FARSITE was $\lambda_s = 0.93$. The discrepancies that still exist can be partly motivated by

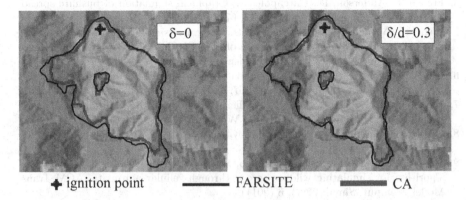

+ ignition point    ———— FARSITE    ▬▬▬▬ CA

**Fig. 7.** The results obtained for $\delta = 0$ (i.e., standard CA) and $\delta = 0.3\,d$, where $d$ is the size of the CA square cell. The continuous line represent the burned area simulated by FARSITE

the consideration that FARSITE is based on a completely different solution approach (e.g., it is impossible to control how FARSITE automatically adapts the step size). Also, it is worth noting that the observed differences between FARSITE and the improved CA are acceptable for practical purposes, especially considering the significant uncertainties that usually affect input data used for simulating wildfires.

## 4    Conclusions and Future Work

In this paper, a CA-based approach based on the method proposed in [10] for simulating lava flows was applied to the simulation of wildfires. Although the results presented here are still preliminary, such an approach seems to be able to significantly improve the accuracy of CA models based on a standard center-to-center ignition scheme. Furthermore, compared to the latter only minor implementation changes are required and no computational extra-costs are introduced. For these reasons, the proposed approach deserves more thorough investigation in order to evaluate its potential use in operational contexts.

## References

1. Finney, M.A.: FARSITE: fire area simulator-model development and evaluation. Technical Report RMRS-RP-4, USDA, Forest Service (February 2004)
2. Tymstra, C., Bryce, R., Wotton, B., Taylor, S., Armitage, O.: Development and structure of Prometheus: the Canadian wildland fire growth simulation model. Technical Report NOR-X-417, Canadian Forest Service, Edmonton, Alberta (2010)
3. Peterson, S.H., Morais, M.E., Carlson, J.M., Dennison, P.E., Roberts, D.A., Moritz, M.A., Weise, D.R.: Using HFIRE for spatial modeling of fire in shrublands. Technical Report PSW-RP-259, USDA, Forest Service, Pacific Southwest Research Station, Albany, CA (2009)

4. French, I., Anderson, D., Catchpole, E.: Graphical simulation of bushfire spread. Mathematical Computer Modelling 13, 67–71 (1990)
5. French, I.: Visualisation techniques for the computer simulation of bushfires in two dimensions. Master's thesis, University of New South Wales - Australian Defence Force Academy. Dept. of Computer Science (1992)
6. Cui, W., Perera, A.H.: A study of simulation errors caused by algorithms of forest fire growth models. Technical Report 167, Ontario Forest Research Institute (2008)
7. Johnston, P., Kelso, J., Milne, G.: Efficient simulation of wildfire spread on an irregular grid. International Journal of Wildland Fire 17, 614–627 (2008)
8. O'Regan William, G., Peter, K., Shirley, N.: Bias in the contagion analog to fire spread. Forest Science 22 (1976)
9. Trunfio, G.A., D'Ambrosio, D., Rongo, R., Spataro, W., Gregorio, S.D.: A new algorithm for simulating wildfire spread through cellular automata. ACM Trans. Model. Comput. Simul. 22(1), 6 (2011)
10. Miyamoto, H., Sasaki, S.: Simulating lava flows by an improved cellular automata method. Computers & Geosciences 23(3), 283–292 (1997)
11. Rothermel, R.C.: A mathematical model for predicting fire spread in wildland fuels. Technical Report INT-115, USDA, Forest Service, Intermountain Forest and Range Experiment Station, Ogden, UT (1972)
12. Rothermel, R.C.: How to predict the spread and intensity of forest and range fires. Technical Report INT-143, USDA, Forest Service, Intermountain Forest and Range Experiment Station, Ogden, UT (1983)
13. Vasconcelos, J., Zeigler, B., Pereira, J.: Simulation of fire growth in GIS using discrete event hierarchical modular models. Advances in Remote Sensing 4(3), 54–62 (1995)
14. Lopes, A.M.G., Cruz, M.G., Viegas, D.X.: Firestation - an integrated software system for the numerical simulation of fire spread on complex topography. Environmental Modelling and Software 17(3), 269–285 (2002)
15. Hu, X., Ntaimo, L.: Integrated simulation and optimization for wildfire containment. ACM Trans. Model. Comput. Simul. 19(4), 1–29 (2009)
16. Trunfio, G.A.: Predicting Wildfire Spreading Through a Hexagonal Cellular Automata Model. In: Sloot, P.M.A., Chopard, B., Hoekstra, A.G. (eds.) ACRI 2004. LNCS, vol. 3305, pp. 385–394. Springer, Heidelberg (2004)
17. Andrews, P.: BEHAVE: fire behavior prediction and fuel modeling system - burn subsystem, part 1. Technical Report INT-194, USDA, Forest Service (1986)
18. Anderson, H.: Predicting wind-driven wildland fire size and shape. Technical Report INT-305, USDA, Forest Service (1983)
19. McAlpine, R., Lawson, B., Taylor, E.: Fire spread across a slope. In: Proceedings of the 11th Conference on Fire and Forest Meteorology, pp. 218–225. Society of American Foresters, Bethesda (1991)
20. Blecic, I., Cecchini, A., Trunfio, G.A.: A general-purpose geosimulation infrastructure for spatial decision support. Transactions on Computational Science 6, 200–218 (2009)
21. Forthofer, J., Shannon, K., Butler, B.: Simulating diurnally driven slope winds with windninja. In: Proceedings of 8th Symposium on Fire and Forest Meteorological Society - Kalispell, MT (2009)

# A Theorem about the Algorithm of Minimization of Differences for Multicomponent Cellular Automata

Maria Vittoria Avolio[1], Salvatore Di Gregorio[1],
William Spataro[1], and Giuseppe A. Trunfio[2]

[1] University of Calabria, Department of Mathematics, Arcavacata, 87036 Rende (CS), Italy
{avoliomv,dig,spataro}@unical.it
[2] University of Sassari, DADU, P. Duomo 6, 07041 Alghero (SS), Italy
trunfio@uniss.it

**Abstract.** Multicomponent Cellular Automata, also known as Macroscopic Cellular Automata, characterize a methodological approach for modeling complex systems, that need many components both for the states (substates) to account for different properties of the cell and for the transition function (elementary processes) in order to account for various different dynamics. Many applications were developed for modeling complex natural phenomena, particularly macroscopic ones, e.g., large scale surface flows. Minimizing the differences of a certain quantity in the cell neighborhood, by distribution from the cell to the other neighboring cells, is a basic component of many transition functions in this context. The Algorithm for the Minimization of Differences (AMD) was applied in different ways to many models. A fundamental theorem about AMD is proved in this paper; it shows that AMD properties are more extended than the previous demonstrated theorem.

**Keywords:** Cellular Automata, Modeling and Simulation, Complex Systems.

## 1 Introduction

Cellular Automata (CA) [1] are a parallel computing paradigm [2] and good candidates for modelling and simulation (M&S) of complex dynamical systems, whose evolution depends mainly on the local interactions of their constituent parts (a-centric systems). Very complex behaviours emerge by relatively simple local rules. Nevertheless, CA may represent sometime an alternative approach to differential equations for a-centric complex phenomena [3].

An extension of classical Cellular Automata (CA) [4] was initially developed in order to model many complex macroscopic fluid-dynamical phenomena, which seem difficult to be modelled in other CA frames (e.g., the Lattice Boltzmann method [5]), because they take place on a large space scales [4]. In this case, the description of properties of the cells (e.g. temperature, altitude) needs a large amount of states; such states may be formally represented by means of substates, which specify the characteristics to be attributed to the state of the cell and determining the CA evolution. The Cartesian product of the sets of all substates constitutes the set of states [4]. This

G.C. Sirakoulis and S. Bandini (Eds.): ACRI 2012, LNCS 7495, pp. 289–298, 2012.

involves mostly a complicated transition function, not reducible to a lookup table; such a transition function must often account for different dynamics, that can interest the cell (e.g., temperature variation and altitude, variation by water erosion) and may involve different neighborhoods (of course the union of all the neighborhoods is the cell neighborhood) [4].

Sometimes the CA model must account for "external influences" (e.g., raining, lava flow from a crater) in particular cells or in an extended portion of the cellular space; they have to be managed by particular functions, which supplement the transition function [4]. This formalization permits in many cases, e.g., for surface flows, that quantities concerning the third dimension, i.e. the "height", may be easily included among the CA substates (e.g. the altitude), giving rise to two dimensional models, working however effectively in three dimensions [4].

Such extension of CA was named in some papers "Macroscopic Cellular Automata" (e.g. [6]), even if this label might not be appropriate in the world of Complex Systems, where the notion of "macroscopic" isn't bound to purely physical dimensions that, however, are relative to the observation frame of the system. For this reason, a proper term is "Multicomponent Cellular Automata" (MCA) in order to account for different interacting dynamics, related to the various properties attributed to the cell.

Many phenomena, involving flows of a certain substance (but not only this type of phenomena), tend to evolve to reach equilibrium conditions for some property or quantity, for which a value can be attributed (e.g., the trivial case of gas diffusion in a closed space from a opened box until the differences in gas density become insignificant). Our research group considered, as basic point for modeling the dynamics of such phenomena on level of transition function, the reduction mechanisms of the unbalance conditions, related to property values, in the cell neighborhood.

This may be performed by an algorithm, i.e., the Algorithm for the Minimization of Differences (AMD), for minimizing the differences of the property in the cell neighborhood, by substance distribution (if there is a distributable part) from the cell to the other neighboring cells. The AMD is rarely employed in its own pure version, but modalities of application or some modifications of it permit advantageously to adapt it to features of the many various considered phenomena.

The underlying intuitive ideas for MCA modeling of such situations, where a system tends to equilibrium, related to the presence of a certain substance, could be expressed by means of the following questions: If the universe is reduced to the neighborhood of only one cell and if only that cell is able to distribute to the other cells a quantity of the substance, how much must the flows of the substance be in order to minimize unbalance conditions? Then, how to regulate the amount of flows according to a MCA step that corresponds to a physical time? How may this be related to other phenomenological interactions?

Of course, answers must be proposed such that scientific principles ruling systems, e.g., conservation laws of the physics, must be observed or adequately approximated to the typology of the considered phenomena.

AMD operates on averaged MCA data; that implies necessarily a lack of information, e.g. exact determination of one or more real slopes related to a cell. In this case we may assume that all the possible slopes are considered (one for each adjacent cell), but we consider also that all the cells in the neighborhood are "communicating vessels"; one approximation in this case can "statistically" remedy for such an imprecision for the other imprecision, and viceversa.

MCA were actually used since the early '80s for modeling highway traffic (e.g. [7], [8]), then lava flows (e.g. [9] ) and flow-like landslides (e.g. [10]), while the AMD was later introduced and applied for lava flows (e.g. [11], [12]), flow-like landslides (e.g. [13], [14]) and contaminated soil bioremediation (e.g. [15]) before the official paper appearance [4], where MCA were explicitly formalized and a fundamental theorem on AMD was proved. This theorem proves that the sum of differences between the value in the cells and the minimum value in the neighborhood is minimized by AMD, but it doesn't demonstrate the stronger result that minimization holds for the sum of the value differences among all the cells. A novel theorem [16] proves such stronger result.

This paper is organized as follows. The next section defines MCA; the AMD and the novel theorem about AMD are presented in the third section. AMD applications are reported in the fourth section, while some conclusions close the paper.

## 2    Definition of Multicomponent Cellular Automata

Classical homogeneous CA evolves in a discrete infinite space-time framework; they are based on a regular division of the space in cells, each one embedding an input/output computing unit: a Finite Automaton (FA) [2]. The temporary attributes of a cell are specified by the FA state; $S$ is the finite set of states. The FA input is given by the states of $n$ neighboring cells, including the cell embedding the FA. The neighborhood conditions are determined by a pattern, which is invariant in time and constant over the cells. The FA have an identical state transition function $\tau : S^n \rightarrow S$ , which is simultaneously applied to each cell. At step 0, cells are in arbitrary states, describing the initial conditions of the system; the CA evolves by consecutive applications (steps) of $\tau$, changing the state of all cells simultaneously.

An equivalent description could be given in terms of a regular lattice, whose sites correspond to the cell centers, while neighborhood conditions are given by vectors joining a site with its neighbors.

CA M&S of real complex systems implies that a correspondence must be explicitly established between the model and the real world in order to compare phenomenon development with simulation progress. The extension, represented by MCA, meets these problems especially in the case of "macroscopic" phenomena.

Such an extension must concretely consider that:

— The cellular space does not need to be infinite; it must account only for finite region, where real phenomenon takes place. This implies also that a correspondence must be defined between cellular and real space: physical features of the cell (type of cell and dimensions, e.g., hexagonal and apothem size) must be defined so that each point of real space is individuated in a particular cell with opportune specifications.

— Comparing dynamics of the real word with the CA evolution implies that the CA step (it could be variable for computational optimization) to be related to a time value.

— The cell state must account for components that are related to different properties, so it has to be expressed by a composition of substates.

MCA are specified by the following septuple:     $< R, W, S, X, G, \tau, \gamma >$     where:

- $R = \{(x, y, z) \mid x, y, z \in \mathbb{N}, 0 \leq x \leq l_x-1, 0 \leq y \leq l_y-1, 0 \leq z \leq l_z-1\}$ is the set of points with integer co-ordinates, that individuate cells in the finite region, where the phenomenon evolves. $\mathbb{N}$ is the set of natural numbers. When space dimensions may be reduced, formulae are trivially simplified to 1 or 2 dimensions. More dimensions could be easily added for rare cases, where further dimensions could be advantageous for modeling. The case of different regular tessellation for a same dimension is solved considering mapping of such tessellation to square one [17];

- $W = W_1 \cup W_2 \cup ... \cup W_m$ is the set of cells, which undergo to the influences of the "external world"; external influences are here considered, where each one defines a subregion of the cellular space, where the influence is active. Note that $W \subseteq R$;

- $S = S_1 \times S_2 \times ... \times S_m$ is the finite set of states, given by the Cartesian product of the sets of substates;

- $X = <\xi_0, \xi_1, ... \xi_{n-1}>$, the neighborhood index, is a finite ordered set of three-dimensional vectors, that defines for a generic cell $c = <c_x, c_y, c_z>$ the set $N(X,c)$ of the neighboring cells: $<c+\xi_0, c+\xi_1, ... c+\xi_{n-1}>$, where $\xi_0$ is always the null vector (the cell $i$ itself belongs to its neighborhood by definition and is called the "central" cell). Incomplete neighborhood for border cells may be managed by a closed, but boundless surface or space, e.g., a torus, or by special states;

- $G = \{g_s, g_t, ...\}$ is the finite set of global parameters, which effect the transition function. Their value is the same for each cell in $R$ (e.g., the gravity acceleration) and could change in particular cases at different steps for optimizing computation. Two global parameters have to be always considered: the size of the cell $g_s$ (e.g., the cell edge or distance between centres of two neighbour cells) and the time corresponding to the CA transition step $g_t$.

- $\tau: S^n \to S$, $n=\#X$, is the transition function: it may be split into "elementary" processes, defined by the functions $<\sigma_1, \sigma_2 ... \sigma_p>$ with $p$ being the number of the "elementary" processes. The elementary processes are applied sequentially according a defined order. Different elementary processes may involve different neighborhoods and substates.

- $\gamma: \mathbb{N} \times W \to S$ expresses the external influences to cells of $W$ in the cellular space; it determines the variation of the state $S$ for the cells in $W$. $\mathbb{N}$ is here referred to the steps of the MCA. $\gamma$ is specified by the sequential applications of the correspondent functions: $\gamma_1: \mathbb{N} \times W_1 \to S$, $\gamma_2: \mathbb{N} \times W_2 \to S$, ... , etc.

At step 0, cells are in states, which correspond to the initial conditions of the system to be simulated; the CA evolves by applying simultaneously the function $\gamma$ to cells in

$W$, and by applying simultaneously the state transition function $\tau$ to neighborhoods of all the cells. A step is given by the consecutive application of $\gamma$ and $\tau$.

## 3    The Extended Theorem for AMD

Many complex systems evolve at a local level towards minimum unbalance conditions for some quantity $q$: the system can minimize the $q$ differences in the neighborhood of each cell by flows from the central cell to the other neighbor cells; in the CA context, this means that $\tau$ may vary "distributable" quantities only in the central cell but not in the neighbors. Of course, $\tau$ is applied simultaneously to each cells in $R$ and flows, potentially from each cell towards its neighbors, give the system evolution.

An intuitive and simple example may be represented by a fluid (e.g., lava, debris, etc.) distributed on a morphology. A substate altitude is attributed to each cell together with the substate fluid thickness. The property or quantity to be minimized is the "height" $h$, whose value is given in this case by the sum of altitude and fluid thickness. The minimization process is constituted for each cell by fluid outflows from central cell to the other neighbors, so that differences in height are minimized in the neighborhood by the contribution of the outflows.

### Explicatum of the Minimization Problem
*Definitions:*    $n = \#X$ ;

$q_d=$   distributable quantity in the central cell;

$q_0 =$   not distributable quantity in the central cell;

$q_i =$   quantity in the cell  $i$  $1{\le}i{<}n$ ;

$f_0'$ is the part of $q_d$ remaining in the central cell;

$f_i' =$   flow from the central cell towards the cell  $i$   $1{\le}i{<}n$ ;

$q_i' = q_i + f_i'$     $0{\le}i{<}n$ ;

*Bound:*    $q_d = \Sigma_{0{\le}i{<}n}\ f_i'$ ;

*Problem:*    $f_h'$ $0{\le}h{<}n$  must be determined in order to minimize the sum of all $q$ differences between all the pairs of cells in the neighborhood:

$$\Sigma_{\{(i,j)|0{\le}i{<}j{<}n\}}\left|q_i' - q_j'\right| \tag{1}$$

### Algorithm of Minimization of the Differences
*Initialization:*    a) all the neighboring cells are considered "admissible" to receive flows from the central cell, $A$ is the set of admissible cells.

*Cycle:*    b) the "average $q$" ($av\_q$) is found for the set $A$ of admissible cells: $av\_q = (q_d + \Sigma_{i \in A}\, q_i) /\, \#A$.

c) each cell $x$ with  $q_x{\ge}av\_q$  is eliminated from the set $A$. It implies that "average $q$" doesn't increase, because:

$av\_q = (q_d + \Sigma_{i \in A}\, q_i) /\, \#A = (q_d + \Sigma_{i \in A}\, q_i - av\_q) /\, (\#A - 1){\ge}$

$\qquad {\ge}(q_d\ + \Sigma_{i \in A}\, q_i - q_x) /\, (\#A - 1)$

*End of cycle:*    d) Go to step-b until no cell is eliminated.

*Result:*    e) $f_i' = av\_q - q_i$ for  $i \in A$  $(q_i{<}av\_q)$;  $f_i' = 0$  for $i \notin A$  $(q_i'{\ge}av\_q)$

*Bound conservation:* $\Sigma_{i \in A}\, f_i' = \Sigma_{i \in A}\, (av\_q - q_i) = \#A(q_d + \Sigma_{i \in A}\, q_i) /\, \#A - \Sigma_{i \in A}\, q_i = q_d$

*Properties*     P1:     $q_i' = f_i' + q_i = av\_q - q_i + q_i = av\_q$     for $i \in A$
                P2:     $q_i' = q_i$ because $f_i' = 0$     for $i \notin A$

**Theorem.** The Algorithm of Minimization of the Differences (AMD or shortly minimization algorithm) computes values of $f_h'$ $0 \le h < n$, such that (1) is minimized.

*Proof.* It will be demonstrated that each distribution $f_h''$ $0 \le h < n$, $\Sigma_{0 \le h < n} f_h'' = q_d$, different from the minimization algorithm one, with $q_h'' = q_h + f_h''$, $0 \le h < n$, involves that

$$\Sigma_{\{(i,j)|0 \le i < j < n\}} |q_i'' - q_j''| > \Sigma_{\{(i,j)|0 \le i < j < n\}} |q_i' - q_j'| \tag{2}$$

Differences $\Delta_h = q_h'' - q_h'$ $0 \le h < n$ imply $\Sigma_{0 \le h < n} \Delta_h = 0$. A different distribution $f_h''$ $0 \le h < n$ involves some (at least one) $\Delta_x > 0$ to be counterbalanced by some (at least one) $\Delta_y < 0$.

A different distribution involves that $\Delta_i \ge 0$ for $i \notin A$ because $f_i = 0$ and $f_i'' \ge 0$; $\Delta_i > 0$ for $i \in A$ implies $q_i'' > av\_q$; the value $\Delta_i < 0$ can be assumed only for cells $i \in A$ because $f_i' > 0$ and $f_i'' \ge 0$ permits cases with $f_i' > f_i''$.

Consider $C = \{r|(\Delta_r = 0) \wedge (0 \le r < n)\}$, $C' = \{s|(\Delta_s > 0) \wedge (0 \le s \le n)\}$, $C'' = \{t|(\Delta_t < 0) \wedge (0 \le t \le n)\}$ and $D = \Sigma_{s \in C'} \Delta_s$; $\Sigma_{s \in C'} \Delta_s + \Sigma_{t \in C''} \Delta_t = 0$, $\Sigma_{s \in C'} \Delta_s = -\Sigma_{t \in C''} \Delta_t$, $D = -\Sigma_{t \in C''} \Delta_t$. Note that $C'' \subseteq A$.

We may change, step by step, from the minimisation distribution to another distribution by a consecutive $q$-shift $\varsigma_{j,i} = -\Delta_j \Delta_i / D$ from each cell $j$ of $C''$ to each cell $i$ of $C'$, so that each shift is proportional both to $\Delta_i$ and $\Delta_j$. $\Sigma_{i \in C'} \varsigma_{j,i} = -\Sigma_{i \in C'} \Delta_j \Delta_i / D = -\Delta_j$ and $\Sigma_{j \in C''} \varsigma_{j,i} = -\Sigma_{j \in C''} \Delta_j \Delta_i / D = \Delta_i$.

Let $\varsigma_{u,v}$ be a shift with $u \in C''$, $v \in C'$, $^b q_h$, $^a q_h$ quantities in the cell $h$ ($0 \le h < n$) respectively before ($^b$) and after ($^a$) the shift $\varsigma_{u,v}$.

Note that $^b q_i \ge av\_q$, $i \in C'$ then $^b q_v \ge av\_q$; $^b q_j \le av\_q$, $j \in C''$ then $^b q_u \le av\_q$; $^b q_k \ge av\_q$ $k \in C$.

For $v$ and $u$ :     $|^a q_v - ^a q_u| = |(^b q_v + \varsigma_{u,v}) - (^b q_u - \varsigma_{u,v})| = |^b q_v - ^b q_u + 2\varsigma_{u,v}| > |^b q_v - ^b q_u|$
                 because $^b q_v \ge ^b q_u$;

$\{t|t \in C''\}$:     $|^a q_v - ^a q_t| = |^b q_v + \varsigma_{u,v} - ^b q_t| = (|^b q_v - ^b q_t + \varsigma_{u,v}|)$ because $^b q_v \ge ^b q_t$;
           $|^a q_u - ^a q_t| = |^b q_u - \varsigma_{u,v} - ^b q_t| \ge (|^b q_u - ^b q_t| - \varsigma_{u,v})$ ; minimum value of $|^a q_u - ^a q_t|$
           when $^b q_u = \varsigma_{u,v} + ^b q_t$ therefore $(|^a q_v - ^a q_t| + |^a q_u - ^a q_t|) \ge (|^b q_v - ^b q_t| + |^b q_u - ^b q_t|)$

$\{t|t \in C' \vee t \in C\}$:     $|^a q_u - ^a q_t| = |^b q_u - \varsigma_{u,v} - ^b q_t| = (|^b q_u - ^b q_t| + \varsigma_{u,v})$ because $^b q_t \ge ^b q_u$;
           $|^a q_v - ^a q_t| = |^b q_v + \varsigma_{u,v} - ^b q_t| \ge (|^b q_v - ^b q_t| - \varsigma_{u,v})$ ; minimum value of $|^a q_u - ^a q_t|$
           when $^b q_t = \varsigma_{u,v} + ^b q_v$ therefore $(|^a q_v - ^a q_t| + |^a q_u - ^a q_t|) \ge (|^b q_v - ^b q_t| + |^b q_u - ^b q_t|)$

$\{(u,t)|u \ne v, t \ne u\}$:     $|^a q_u - ^a q_t| = |^b q_u - ^b q_t|$

therefore     $\Sigma_{\{(i,j)|0 \le i < j \le n\}} (|^a q_i - ^a q_j|) > \Sigma_{\{(i,j)|0 \le i < j \le n\}} (|^b q_i - ^b q_j|)$

We obtain distribution $q_i''$ $0 \le i \le n$ by consecutive applications of all the shifts $\varsigma_{j,i}$ $j \in C''$, $i \in C'$ starting from distribution $q_i'$ $0 \le i \le n$; then (2) is proved.     □

# 4    Applications of the Minimization Algorithm

The Minimization Algorithm was applied in various interdisciplinary researches both by our research group, and by other research groups involved in the modeling and simulation of surface flows.

Our group, together with experts of various scientific disciplines, performed the following researches using the AMD in M&S after its publication by Di Gregorio and Serra [4]:

— M&S of lava flows by the development of the SCIARA (Simulation by Cellular Interactive Automata of the Rheology of Aetnean lava flow) model, with application regarding mainly Etnean lava flows and study about lava flow hazard in the Etnean area (see [18], [19], [20], [21], [22], [23], [6]);

— M&S of bioremediation of contaminated soil: [24];

— M&S of debris, mud, granular flows by the development of the SCIDDICA (Simulation through Computational Innovative methods for the Detection of Debris flow path using Interactive Cellular Automata) model with application regarding subaerial, subaqueous and mixed (subaerial, subaqueous) landslides (see [25], [26], [27], [28], [29], [30], [31], [32]);

— M&S of soil erosion by the model SCAVATU (Simulation by Cellular Automata for the erosion of VAst Territorial Units) (see [33]);

— M&S of pyroclastic flows by the development of the PYR model (see [34]);

— M&S of snow avalanches by the model VALANCA (Versatile model of Avalanche propagation by LAws and Norms of Cellular Automata) (see [35], [36]);

— Methodological papers about M&S of surface flows were also produced (see [37], [38]);

— M&S of attraction processes and diffusion in collective behavior (olive fruit flies and amberjacks) (see [39], [40]).

AMD based applications of other research groups to our knowledge regard the M&S of following phenomena: hot mudflows [41]; long-term soil redistribution by tillage [42]; soil surface degradation by rainfall [43]; snow avalanche [44]; density current [45] and river systems [46].

# 5    Conclusions

The AMD looks to capture fundamental processes in complex phenomena involving flows on earth surface. The MCA application in the context of M&S involves usually a type of alteration of data regarding the height dimension in order to account for directional effects regarding, e.g., momentum or run-up effects concerning kinetic energy, etc. Its straightforward coupling with other physical processes permitted to develop "simple" but robust models, which stand up to the comparison with the observation of real phenomena and permit reliable simulations for predictive purposes.

The relevance of the demonstrated theoretical result, which application may not be separated by necessary arrangements, has to be found in a semi-empirical approach to phenomenologies, where precise data are usually not accessible and where modeling items must be introduced as, e.g., the "equivalent fluid" notion [47]. It implies the necessity to carefully confine the scope of application, but it permits usually to improve the model in incremental way by introducing new substates and new elementary processes (or expanding the old ones).

The role of parameters values was crucial for a correct emergence of overall phenomena from local interactions. Genetic Algorithms resulted sometime necessary for calibrating parameters. In addition, applications on collective behavior in ecological contexts suffered because of lack of enough precise comparison data, but further chances have to be given for this topic.

In conclusion, the feeling of authors is that the AMD use may and can be extended to further M&S research areas.

**Acknowledgments.** This research was partially funded by MIUR, PON Project n. 01_01503 "Integrated Systems for Hydrogeological Risk Monitoring, Early Warning and Mitigation Along the Main Lifelines", CUP B31H11000370005.

# References

1. von Neumann, J.: Theory of self reproducing automata. Uni. of Illinois Press, Urbana (1966)
2. Ilachinsky, A.: Cellular Automata, A discrete Universe. World Scientific, New Jersey (2001)
3. Toffoli, T.: Cellular Automata as an alternative to (rather than an approximation of) differential equations in modeling physics. Physica 10D, 117–127 (1984)
4. Di Gregorio, S., Serra, R.: An empirical method for modelling and simulating some complex macroscopic phenomena by cellular automata. FGCS 16, 259–271 (1999)
5. Succi, A.S.: The Lattice Boltzmann Equation for Fluid Dynamicsand Beyond. Oxford University Press, Oxford (2001)
6. Spataro, W., Avolio, M.V., Lupiano, V., Trunfio, G.A., Rongo, R., D'Ambrosio, D.: The latest release of the lava flows simulation model SCIARA: First application to Mt Etna (Italy) and solution of the anisotropic flow direction problem on an ideal surface. Procedia Computer Science 1(1), 17–26 (2010)
7. Di Gregorio, S., Festa, D.C.: Cellular Automata for FreewayTraffic. In: Proceedings of the First International Conference "Applied Modelling and Simulation", Lyon, France, September 7-11, vol. V, pp. 133–136 (1981)
8. Di Gregorio, S., Festa, D.C.: A global model for freeway traffic simulation. In: Contributed papers of ICTS Int. Meeting Transportation Research: State of the Art, Perspectives and International Cooperation, Amalfi, Italy, November 11-14, vol. I, pp. 277–283 (1981)
9. Crisci, G.M., Di Gregorio, S., Pindaro, O., Ranieri, S.A.: Lava flow simulation by a discrete cellular model: first implementation. Int. Journal of Modelling and Simulation 6, 137–140 (1986)
10. Barca, D., Di Gregorio, S., Nicoletta, F.P., Sorriso Valvo, M.: Flowtypelandslidemodelling by cellular automata. In: Proceedings, A.M.S. International Congress Modelling and Simulation, Cairo, Egypt, pp. 3–7 (March 1987)
11. Barca, D., Crisci, G.M., Di Gregorio, S., Nicoletta, F.: Chapter Twelve of Active Lavas. In: Kilburn, Luongo (eds.) Cellular Automata Methods for Modeling Lava Flow: Simulation of the 1986-1987 Eruption, Mount Etna, Sicily, pp. 291–309. UCL Press London (1993)
12. Barca, D., Crisci, G.M., Di Gregorio, S., Nicoletta, F.: Cellular Automata for simulating lava flows: a method and examples of the Etnean eruptions. Transport Theory and Statistical Physics 23(1-3), 195–232 (1994)
13. Di Gregorio, S., Nicoletta, F., Rongo, R., Sorriso-Valvo, M., Spataro, W.: A two-dimensional Cellular Automata Model for Landslide Simulation. In: Gruber, R., Tommasini, M. (eds.) Proceedings of 6th Joint EPS-APS International Conference on Physics Computing, PC 1994, Lugano, Switzerland, August 22-26, pp. 523–526 (1994)

14. Di Gregorio, S., Rongo, R., Siciliano, C., Sorriso-Valvo, M., Spataro, W.: Mount Ontakelandslidesimulation by the cellularautomata model SCIDDICA-3. Physics and Chemistry of the Earth (A) 24(2), 97–100 (1999)
15. Di Gregorio, S., Serra, R., Villani, M.: A Cellular Automata Model of SoilBioremediation. Complex Systems 11, 31–54 (1997)
16. Avolio, M.V.: Esplicitazione della velocità per la modellizzazione e simulazione di flussi di superficie macroscopici con automi cellulari ed applicazioni alle colate di lava di tipo etneo. Ph. D. Thesis (in Italian). Dept. of Mathematics, University of Calabria (2004)
17. Weimar, J.R.: Simulation with Cellular Automata. Logos-Verlag, Berlin (1998) ISBN 3-89722-026-1
18. Crisci, G.M., Di Gregorio, S., Nicoletta, F., Rongo, R., Spataro, W.: Analysing lava risk for the Etnean area by Cellular Automata methods of simulation. Natural Hazards 20, 215–229 (1999)
19. Crisci, G.M., Di Gregorio, S., Rongo, R., Scarpelli, M., Spataro, W., Calvari, S.: Revisiting the 1669 Etnean eruptive crisis using a cellular automata model and implications for volcanic hazard in the Catania area. Journal of Volcanology and Geothermal Research 123(1-2), 211–230 (2003)
20. Crisci, G.M., Di Gregorio, S., Rongo, R., Spataro, W.: The simulation model SCIARA: the 1991 and 2001 at Mount Etna. Journal of Vulcanogy and Geothermal Research 132(2-3), 253–267 (2004)
21. Avolio, M.V., Crisci, G.M., Di Gregorio, S., Rongo, R., Spataro, W., Trunfio, G.A.: SCIARA $\gamma2$: an improved Cellular Automata model for Lava Flows and Applications to the 2002 Etnean crisis. Computers & Geosciences 32, 897–911 (2006)
22. Spataro, W., D'Ambrosio, D., Avolio, M.V., Trunfio, G.A., Di Gregorio, S.: Lava Flow Hazard Evaluation Through Cellular Automata and Genetic Algorithms: an Application to Mt Etna Volcano. Fundamenta Informaticae 87(2), 247–268 (2008)
23. Crisci, G.M., Avolio, M.V., Behncke, B., D'Ambrosio, D., Di Gregorio, S., Lupiano, V., Neri, M., Rongo, R., Spataro, W.: Predicting the impact of lava flowsat Mount Etna. Italy. J. Geophys. Res. 115, B04203 (2010), doi:10.1029/2009JB006431
24. Di Gregorio, S., Serra, R., Villani, M.: Applying cellular automata to complex environmental problems: the simulation of the bioremediation of contaminated soils. Theoretical Computer Science 217(1), 131–156 (1999)
25. Avolio, M.V., Di Gregorio, S., Mantovani, F., Pasuto, A., Rongo, R., Silvano, S., Spataro, W.: Simulation of the 1992 Tessinalandslide by a Cellular Automata model and future hazardscenarios. JAG (International Journal of Applied Earth Observation and Geoinformation) 2(1), 41–50 (2000)
26. D'Ambrosio, D., Di Gregorio, S., Iovine, G., Lupiano, V., Merenda, L., Rongo, R., Spataro, W.: Simulating the Curti-Sarno Debris Flow through Cellular Automata: the model SCIDDICA (release S2). Physics and Chemistry of the Earth 27, 1577–1585 (2002)
27. D'Ambrosio, D., Di Gregorio, S., Iovine, G., Lupiano, V., Rongo, R., Spataro, W.: First simulations of the Sarno debris flows through cellular automata modelling. Geomorphology 54(1-2), 91–117 (2003)
28. Iovine, G., Di Gregorio, S., Lupiano, V.: Debris-flow susceptibility assessment through cellular automata modeling: an example from 15–16 disaster at Cervinara and San Martino Valle Caudina (Campania, southern Italy). Natural Hazards and Earth System Sciences 3, 457–468 (2003)
29. D'Ambrosio, D., Di Gregorio, S., Iovine, G.: Simulating debris flows through a hexagonal cellular automata model: SCIDDICA S3-hex. Natural Hazards and Earth System Sciences 3, 545–559 (2003)

30. Iovine, G., D'Ambrosio, D., Di Gregorio, S.: Applying genetic algorithms for calibrating a hexagonal cellular automata model for the simulation of debris flows characterised by strong inertial effects. Geomorphology 66, 287–303 (2005)
31. Avolio, M.V., Lupiano, V., Mazzanti, P., Di Gregorio, S.: Modelling Combined Subaerial-Subaqueous Flow-Like Landslides by Cellular Automata. In: Umeo, H., Morishita, S., Nishinari, K., Komatsuzaki, T., Bandini, S. (eds.) ACRI 2008. LNCS, vol. 5191, pp. 329–336. Springer, Heidelberg (2008)
32. D'Ambrosio, D., Iovine, G., Spataro, W., Miyamoto, H.: A macroscopic collisional model for debris-flows simulation. Environmental Modelling and Software 22(10), 1417–1436 (2007)
33. D'Ambrosio, D., Di Gregorio, S., Gabriele, S., Gaudio, R.: A Cellular Automata Model for SoilErosion by Water. Physics and Chemistry of the Earth 26(1), 33–39 (2001)
34. Avolio, M.V., Crisci, G.M., Di Gregorio, S., Rongo, R., Spataro, W., D'Ambrosio, D.: Pyroclastic Flows Modelling using Cellular Automata. Computers & Geosciences 32, 876–889 (2006)
35. Avolio, M.V., Errera, A., Lupiano, V., Mazzanti, P., Di Gregorio, S.: Development and Calibration of a Preliminary Cellular Automata Model for Snow Avalanches. In: Bandini, S., Manzoni, S., Umeo, H., Vizzari, G. (eds.) ACRI 2010. LNCS, vol. 6350, pp. 83–94. Springer, Heidelberg (2010)
36. Avolio, M.V., Errera, A., Lupiano, V., Mazzanti, P., Di Gregorio, S.: A Cellular Automata Model for SnowAvalanches. To appear in Journal of Cellular Automata (2012)
37. Avolio, M.V., Crisci, G.M., D'Ambrosio, D., Di Gregorio, S., Iovine, G., Rongo, R., Spataro, W.: An extended notion of Cellular Automata for surface flows modelling. WSEAS Transactions on Computers 2(4), 1080–1085 (2003)
38. D'Ambrosio, D., Spataro, W.: Parallel evolutionary modelling of geological processes. Parallel Computing 33(3), 186–212 (2007)
39. Piscitelli, M., Badalamenti, F., D'Anna, G., Di Gregorio, S.: A Cellular Automata Model of Fish-Aggregating-Devices Performance. In: Proceedings of EUROSIM 2001 Delft, CdRom, The Netherlands, June 26-29 (2001) ISBN: 90-806441-1-0
40. Pommois, P., Brunetti, P., Bruno, V., Mazzei, A., Baldacchini, V., Di Gregorio, S.: FlySim: A Cellular Automata Model of *Bactrocera Oleae* (Olive Fruit Fly) Infestation and First Simulations. In: El Yacoubi, S., Chopard, B., Bandini, S. (eds.) ACRI 2006. LNCS, vol. 4173, pp. 311–320. Springer, Heidelberg (2006)
41. Arai, K., Basuki, A.: Simulation of Hot Mudflow Disaster with Cell Automaton and Verification with Satellite Imagery Data. International Archives of the Photogrammetry, Remote Sensing and Spatial Information Science, Part 8 38, 237–242 (2010)
42. Vanwalleghem, T., Jiménez-Hornero, F., Giráldez, J.V., Laguna, A.M.: Simulation of long-term soil redistribution by tillage using a cellular automata model. Earth Surf. Process. Landforms 35, 761–770 (2010)
43. Valette, G., Prévost, S., Laurent, L., Léonard, J.: SoDA project: A simulation of soil surface degradation by rainfall. Computers & Graphics 30, 494–506 (2006)
44. Barpi, F., Borri-Brunetto, M., Delli Veneri, L.: Cellular-Automata Model for Dense-SnowAvalanches. Journal of Cold Regions Engineering 21(4), 121–140 (2007)
45. Salles, T., Lopez, S., Cacas, M.C., Mulder, T.: Cellular automata model of density currents. Geomorphology 88(1-2), 1–20 (2007)
46. Topa, P.: A Cellular Automata Approach for Modelling Complex River Systems. In: El Yacoubi, S., Chopard, B., Bandini, S. (eds.) ACRI 2006. LNCS, vol. 4173, pp. 482–491. Springer, Heidelberg (2006)
47. Hungr, O.: A model for the runout analysis of rapid flow slides, debris flows, and avalanches. Can. Geotech. J. 32, 610–623 (1995)

# Generation of Pedestrian Groups Distributions with Probabilistic Cellular Automata

Stefania Bandini[1,2], Lorenza Manenti[1], and Sara Manzoni[1,*]

[1] CSAI - Complex Systems & Artificial Intelligence Research Center
Department of Informatics, Systems and Communication
University of Milano-Bicocca
[2] RCAST - Research Center for Advanced Science and Technology
The University of Tokyo, Japan
{bandini,manenti,manzoni}@disco.unimib.it

**Abstract.** The aim of this work is to present a model based on a Stochastic Cellular Automata to generate granulometric distribution of pedestrian groups in structured spaces. The main goal of this model is to set initial configurations for pedestrian simulations starting from plausible scenarios that consider the presence of groups within a crowd.

## 1 Introduction

The aim of this work is to introduce a model based on Cellular Automata (CA) theory for the generation of granulometric distributions of groups of pedestrians in structured space. On this model we developed *PiGro*[1] (Pilgrims Groups granulometric distribution tool) to generate plausible initial configurations of groups distributions on which perform simulations of Hajj pilgrims entering Arafat 1 train station. This station during Hajj, the annual Muslim Pilgrimage to Mecca, serves many thousands of pilgrims every day.

Granulometric distribution usually refers to the size distribution or measurement of grain sizes in sand, rock, or other deposits. We refer here to the distribution of pedestrian groups of different size and shape within a crowd. The latter within Pedestrian Dynamics research context is defined as a set of pedestrians sharing a limited spatial environment according to individual behavioral rules and goals. The study of the behaviour of crowds moving into an environment has been proposed and successfully applied to many case studies according to different computational approaches (i.e. physical models [1], agent-based models

---

\* Authors are listed in alphabetical order.

[1] PiGro is one of the software tools developed within CRYSTALS project (http://www.csai.disco.unimib.it/CSAI/CRYSTALS/), a joint research effort between the Complex Systems and Artificial Intelligence research center of the University of Milano–Bicocca, the Centre of Research Excellence in Hajj and Omrah and the Research Center for Advanced Science and Technology of the University of Tokyo, with the main aim of supporting designers and organizers involved in the management of Hajj, the annual pilgrimage to Mecca.

G.C. Sirakoulis and S. Bandini (Eds.): ACRI 2012, LNCS 7495, pp. 299–308, 2012.
© Springer-Verlag Berlin Heidelberg 2012

[2,3] and CA-based models [4]). Anyhow, the proposed models are the result of a first generation of research efforts considering individuals, their interaction with the environment and among themselves, but omitting relevant aspects that may modify the overall dynamics of the crowd [5]. In particular, this work belongs to a more recent research trend oriented towards the development of improved crowd models by taking into account the presence of *groups*.

According to anthropological and sociological studies [6,7] pedestrians that share a spatial environment can be part of a group and tend to maintain different distances with other people in respect of the kind of bond they have with them: individuals tend to stay far from individuals who do not belong to their own group (such as from physical obstacles) while tend to maintain distances from others according to proxemic rules.

Moreover, according to empirical studies [5], it is nowadays growing clearer that crowd dynamics cannot be investigated only as a collection of isolated individuals that compete on space occupation, since very often pedestrians do not move alone but as part of small groups (i.e. a set of individuals with a common goal or a common self-perceived identity that can be recognized both from involved individuals or from external observers [8]).

In particular, different pedestrian groups shapes can be defined according to their size (i.e. number of pedestrians that are components of the group) and local spatial density (i.e. number of pedestrians per spatial area) [9]. In particular, it is possible to underline three types of typical patterns for spatial distribution of small groups (i.e. groups composed by two to three individuals): line-abreast, V-like and river-like. In low density cases the preferred pattern is *line-abreast* (Fig. 1a), but when density increases, pedestrians in the middle tend to stand backwards generating a *V-like pattern* (Fig. 1b), and when a high level density situation is reached, the pattern leads to *river-like* shape (Fig. 1c). In case of larger groups composed by at least four members, other shapes can be assumed by pedestrian groups, like spherical and ellipsoidal[10]. These patterns were also confirmed in the context of CRYSTALS project.

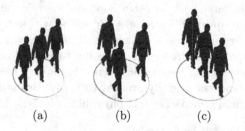

(a)             (b)             (c)

**Fig. 1.** Patterns of spatial organization for groups of three pedestrians: from the left, line-abreast, V-like and river-like shapes

Cellular Automata has already been presented in the literature as a valid approach to develop computational models for the controlled generation of granulometric distributions. For instance, in [11], [12] and [13] authors show preferences to CA techniques because of the opportunity to obtain porous medium model by exploiting the CA capability of pattern formation (in the case of carbon black filled in rubber, in the case of soil to study soil pesticides absorption, and for the construction of structures of porous medium material respectively).

The computational model we propose in this work is a *self-reproductive stochastic Cellular Automata*, an extension of CA with probabilistic rules that is able to take into account both size and morphological properties of groups into the crowd. The proper choice of CA parameters allows to obtain the crowd model with wanted pattern motifs.

The paper is organized as follows: Section 2 and Section 3 present PiGro model and its implementation in a Java-based tool respectively. Some examples of the output of the tool, in relationship with the scenario of CRYSTALS project are shown in Section 4. Ongoing and future works on model experimentation end the paper.

## 2   The Model

The aim of PiGro is to generate granulometric distributions of groups of pedestrians using a stochastic CA and following previously presented considerations on pedestrians patterns and distances. The model works on three main steps:

- the initialization of the CA according to the characteristics of walk-ability of the environment in which groups have to be distributed. Every cell assumes a state that represents its availability;
- the placement of "seeds" in the CA cells (*seeds spreading*): every seed occupies a cell and it is the starting point for the creation of a group;
- the cells reproduction. Every cell occupied by an individual of a group at any time $t$ tries to reproduce itself in one of the neighbouring cells. First a probability vector is assigned to the cell according to the shape of the group which the individual belongs to. Adjustments on probabilities values are then performed in accordance with neighbouring cells states. Then, one of the eight neighbouring cells is chosen for reproduction.

More in detailed, PiGro is defined by a stochastic Cellular Automata $\langle S, L, N, I, f \rangle$, where:

- $S$ is the the finite set of states of a cell;
- $L = \{(i,j) | 1 \leq i \leq n; 1 \leq j \leq m\}$ is a two-dimensional lattice;
- $N$ represents the neighbourhood;
- $I : L \longrightarrow S$ is the initialization function;
- $f : S \times S^{|N|} \longrightarrow S$ is the transition function defined by seeds spreading and cell reproduction.

### 2.1   States of Cells

Every *cell* $c \in L$ at any time $t$ can assume one of the following four states:

1. *Occupied by a Person* ($OP_g$), if an individual of a group $g$ is in the cell $c$;
2. *Occupied by an Obstacle* (OO), if an obstacle, or part of it, is in the space represented by the cell $c$;
3. *Near an Obstacle* (NO), if the cell is not occupied by a person or by an obstacle but at least one of the neighbouring cells is occupied by an obstacle;
4. *Free* (F), otherwise.

## 2.2   Lattice

The environment in which the granulometric distribution has to be placed is represented as a discrete approximation of the real space by means of the lattice $L$ of cells transposing it in a $n \times m$ rectangular lattice of cells. Every cell side measures 0.4 meters (according to pedestrian literature [14]). To this aim, we define a function $\omega : [0 \dots n) \times [0 \dots m) \subseteq \mathbb{N}^2 \longrightarrow S' \subset S$ (Fig. 2 on the left) that, given a cell $c$ returns all points in the space which cell $c$ is the discretization, such that $\forall c_{i,j} \in [0 \dots n) \times [0 \dots m)$

$$\omega(c_{i,j}) = \{\forall p_{x,y} \in [0.4c_i \dots 0.4(c_i + 1)) \times [0.4c_j \dots 0.4(c_j + 1))\}$$

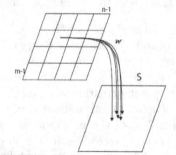

**Fig. 2.** Representation of $\omega$ function and the Moore neighborhood considering reproduction directions

## 2.3   Neighbourhood

In our model, we defined the neighbourhood as the Moore neighbourhood with radius $r = 1$: respect to the Von Neumann neighbourhood, this choice allows the representation of all the group patterns before introduced, in particular respect to V-like shape.

## 2.4   Initialization Function

The initialization for a $n \times m$ lattice $L$ is $\forall$ cell $c \in L$ is based on the previously defined states of cells and it is related to availability:

$$S(c_{x,y}) := \begin{cases} \text{NO,} & \text{if } \mathcal{A} \\ \text{OO,} & \text{if } \exists p \in \omega(c_{x,y}) : p \text{ is not F} \\ \text{F,} & \text{otherwise} \end{cases}$$

where $\mathcal{A} \equiv (\exists c' \in N(c_{x,y}) : S(c') = \text{OO} \vee x = 0 \vee x = n-1 \vee y = 0 \vee y = m-1)$ $\wedge\ S(c_{x,y}) \neq \text{OO}$. $OP_g$ state is not assigned in the initialization step because of groups are generated by means of seeds spreading and cells reproduction which change the state of $NO$ or $F$ cells into $OP_g$ state.

## 2.5   Transition Function

Every group $g$ is defined by a shape $sh$, a dimension $dim$ and a direction $dir$. More formally:

- $sh(g) \in \{spherical, ellipsoidal, line - abreast, river - like, V - like\}$;
- $dim(g) \in N$;
- $dir(g) \in \{north, south, east, west\}$.

Starting from these definitions, the transition function $f : S \times S^{|N|} \longrightarrow S$ has been defined as composition of the seeds spreading $ss(g, L)$ and cell reproduction $cr(g)$ functions.

**Seed Spreading.** Given a set of groups $G$ and a rectangular $n \times m$ lattice, *seeds spreading* creates a seeds distributions from which cell reproduction will start, following two principles: *people proxemics*, i.e. there are not two seeds in two neighbouring cells, and *obstacles proxemics*, i.e., there are not seeds near obstacles.

We propose a strategy based on approximation of the occupied space: for every seed $g \in G$ is reserved a space $A_g$ of an area equals to the area of the dimension of the group. The goal is to place all seeds so that there are no overlaps among areas of any group $g \in G$:

$$\bigcap_{g \in G} A_g = \varnothing$$

The procedure tries to place every seed starting from the one with biggest dimension proceeding in descending order.

Considering a group $g \in G$, $ss(g, L) = c$ iff $c \notin A_{g'}$, i.e. $c$ is chosen as starting point for the seed of $g$ if it does not belong to a $A_{g'}$, the reserved area for another group $g'$.

Unfortunately, this approach has a lower distribution succeed rate, but if the distribution can be generated, the following reproduction process will succeed.

**Cell Reproduction.** As this model is a self-reproducing CA, every cell occupied by a person will try to expand itself in the neighbouring cells. The expansion is governed by the function $cr(g)$ so that every group $g \in G$ will be distributed

respecting its morphology. To control the shape expansion during the reproduction process, we use stochastic CA, i.e., an occupied by a person cell $c$ will
reproduce itself towards one neighbouring cell $c' \in N(c)$ with a probability $p_{N(c)}$;
the probability vector $\boldsymbol{p}(c)$ contains all probabilities $p_{N(c)}$ (Fig. 2 on the right):

$$\boldsymbol{p}(c) = \left[p_{n(c)}, p_{s(c)}, p_{w(c)}, p_{e(c)}, p_{nw(c)}, p_{ne(c)}, p_{sw(c)}, p_{se(c)}\right]$$

where $\forall c' \in N(c), p_{c'}$ represents the probability that cell $c$ will reproduce itself
into cell $c'$. The probability vector values depend on the shape of the group that
overlaps the cell and on the group direction. We defined the following vectors
for the different shapes:

- *spherical* group: probability values are equal for all directions of the group,
  because spherical shape is symmetrical, i.e.,

$$\boldsymbol{p}(c) = \left[\tfrac{1}{4}, \tfrac{1}{4}, \tfrac{1}{4}, \tfrac{1}{4}, 0, 0, 0, 0\right]$$

- *ellipsoidal* group: the major axis is about the double of the minor axis, such
  that:

$$\boldsymbol{p}(c) = \begin{cases} \left[\tfrac{7}{20}, \tfrac{7}{20}, \tfrac{3}{20}, \tfrac{3}{20}, 0, 0, 0, 0\right], & \text{if direction is north or south} \\[2mm] \left[\tfrac{3}{20}, \tfrac{3}{20}, \tfrac{7}{20}, \tfrac{7}{20}, 0, 0, 0, 0\right], & \text{if direction is west or east} \end{cases}$$

- *line-abreast* and *river-like* group: the probability vector leads to a line shaped
  growth. In the first case the line is perpendicular to the direction of the
  group, while in the second case the line is parallel to the direction of the
  group. Probability vector is the same respect to system shown switching
  direction conditions.

$$\boldsymbol{p}(c) = \begin{cases} \left[\tfrac{1}{20}, \tfrac{1}{20}, \tfrac{9}{20}, \tfrac{9}{20}, 0, 0, 0, 0\right], & \text{if direction is north or south} \\[2mm] \left[\tfrac{9}{20}, \tfrac{9}{20}, \tfrac{1}{20}, \tfrac{1}{20}, 0, 0, 0, 0\right], & \text{if direction is west or east} \end{cases}$$

- *V-like* group: the probability vector leads to a diagonal branching with the
  acute angle of the V in the same direction of the group:

$$\boldsymbol{p}(c) = \begin{cases} \left[\tfrac{1}{200}, \tfrac{1}{200}, \tfrac{1}{200}, \tfrac{1}{200}, \tfrac{49}{100}, \tfrac{49}{100}, 0, 0\right], & \text{if direction is north} \\[2mm] \left[\tfrac{1}{200}, \tfrac{1}{200}, \tfrac{1}{200}, \tfrac{1}{200}, 0, 0, \tfrac{49}{100}, \tfrac{49}{100}\right], & \text{if direction is south} \\[2mm] \left[\tfrac{1}{200}, \tfrac{1}{200}, \tfrac{1}{200}, \tfrac{1}{200}, \tfrac{49}{100}, 0, \tfrac{49}{100}, 0\right], & \text{if direction is west} \\[2mm] \left[\tfrac{1}{200}, \tfrac{1}{200}, \tfrac{1}{200}, \tfrac{1}{200}, 0, \tfrac{49}{100}, 0, \tfrac{49}{100}\right], & \text{if direction is east} \end{cases}$$

For all $c$ that are not vertices of a V-like group, then they are in one of the two ramification of the branch: for all these cells the growth needs to continue towards the group direction. Probability vectors for $c$ is in the left and right side can be derived from the last one.

## 3   Model Development

PiGro has been implemented in a tool written in Java language. The software architecture of the tool is based on three main packages (Fig. 3a):

- *Data,* related to the management and the representation of the environment in which the distribution has to be performed;
- *Computation,* concerns the handling of seeds spreading and expansion;

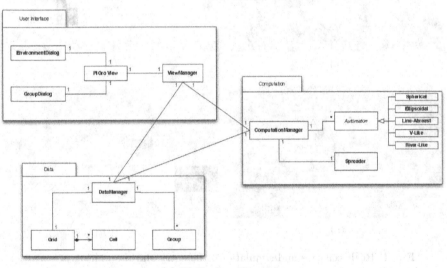

(a) UML class diagram

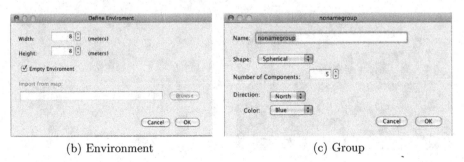

(b) Environment                           (c) Group

**Fig. 3.** User inteface and UML class diagram of PiGRo

– *User Interface*, allows user to define the number of groups with the relatives shape and dimension (see Fig. 3c), such as to load images to be defined as environment (see Fig. 3b).

## 4    Pedestrian Groups Distribution at Hajj

In this section we provide examples of the use of the model and the tool in the context of the Arafat Station 1, a station in the Al Mashaaer Al Muqaddassah

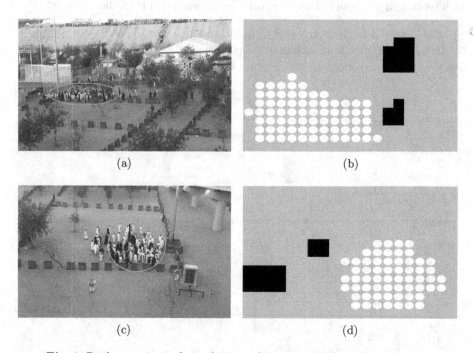

(a)                                                     (b)

(c)                                                     (d)

**Fig. 4.** Real scenarios and simulations: the entry and the waiting process

**Fig. 5.** Real scenario and simulations: the incoming process

Metro in the city of Mecca, Saudi Arabia in the context of CRYSTALS project. The attention was in particular on the process leading pilgrims from outside the station area to the train platforms. Organizers adopted waiting-box principle: groups of 250 pilgrims wait in special areas for an authorization by the station agents to move towards the ramps or elevators to reach the station.

In the following, we show how the tool developed is able to represent real scenarios with a comparison with video materials gathered during an observation activity performed in the area of the station.

We run different simulations related to the waiting box scenario: the entry process (i), the waiting process (ii), the incoming process towards station (iii). Figure 4a shows the entry process, in which a group composed of 70 individuals that are following their leader with an ellipsoidal shape. The granulometric distribution corresponding to this case is shown in Fig. 4b.

Similar to the previous case, in Fig. 4c and 4d a spherical group of 60 individuals waiting for the ingress in the station is depicted.

The last considered case is about small groups walking towards the elevator (Fig. 5 on the left). This case is different from others because small groups shape vary according to density. We have groups which dimension vary between two and four and with a line-abreast, v-like or river-like shape. Figure 5 on the right shows two possible distributions. It is possible to note that, in all these cases, distributions obtained are fairly next to the real scenarios. Moreover, proxemic distances among individuals and groups, when possible, are maintained, such as obstacle repulsions.

## 5   Future Works

The aim of this work was to present a tool based on a CA-model, able to generate granulometric distribution of groups in structured spaces in order to set initial configurations for pedestrian simulations starting from a plausible case that considers groups. Future works about the software implementation of the model concern the improvement of the tool usability allowing manual seeds spreading such as the integration of the tool with pedestrian simulation platform developed at the CSAI Research Center [15].

**Acknowledgement.** Authors want to thank Gianluca Corrado, bachelor degree in Computer Science, for his help in the development of the tool during his stage. This work is partially been funded by the University of Milano-Bicocca within the project "Fondo d'Ateneo per la Ricerca"and by the CRYSTALS project.

## References

1. Helbing, D., Molnar, P.: Social force model for pedestrian dynamics. Physical Review E 51(5), 4282 (1995)
2. Klügl, F., Rindsfüser, G.: Large-scale agent-based pedestrian simulation. Multiagent System Technologies, 145–156 (2007)

3. Manenti, L., Manzoni, S., Vizzari, G., Ohtsuka, K., Shimura, K.: An Agent-Based Proxemic Model for Pedestrian and Group Dynamics: Motivations and First Experiments. In: Villatoro, D., Sabater-Mir, J., Sichman, J.S. (eds.) MABS 2011. LNCS, vol. 7124, pp. 74–89. Springer, Heidelberg (2012)
4. Burstedde, C., Klauck, K., Schadschneider, A., Zittartz, J.: Simulation of pedestrian dynamics using a two-dimensional cellular automaton. Physica A: Statistical Mechanics and its Applications 295(3), 507–525 (2001)
5. Challenger, R., Clegg, C.W., Robinson, M.: Understanding Crowd Behaviours, vol. 1. Cabinet Office (2009)
6. Canetti, E.: Crowds and Power. Farrar, Straus and Giroux (1984)
7. Hall, E.: The Hidden Dimension. Bodley Head (1969)
8. Fabietti, U.: Enciclopedia delle Scienze Sociali: Antropologia - Gruppi. Treccani (1992)
9. Costa, M.: Interpersonal distances in group walking. Journal of Nonverbal Behavior 34(1), 15–26 (2010)
10. Moussaïd, M., Perozo, N., Garnier, S., Helbing, D., Theraulaz, G.: The walking behaviour of pedestrian social groups and its impact on crowd dynamics. PLoS ONE 5 (April 2010)
11. Bandini, S., Magagnini, M.: Pattern control in the generation of artificial percolation beds: a cellular automata approach. In: Proceedings of the Fourth International Conference on Cellular Automata for Research and Industry: Theoretical and Practical Issues on Cellular Automata, pp. 1–10. Springer, London (2000)
12. Bandini, S., Mauri, G., Pavesi, G.: Parallel Generation of Percolation Beds Based on Stochastic Cellular Automata. In: Malyshkin, V.E. (ed.) PaCT 2001. LNCS, vol. 2127, pp. 391–400. Springer, Heidelberg (2001)
13. Bandman, O.: A Lattice-Gas Model of Fluid Flow through Tortuous Channels of Hydrophilous and Hydrophobic Porous Materials. In: Malyshkin, V. (ed.) PaCT 2009. LNCS, vol. 5698, pp. 168–181. Springer, Heidelberg (2009)
14. Weidmann, U.: Transporttechnik der fussgänger. Literature Research 90, Institut füer Verkehrsplanung, Transporttechnik, Strassen- und Eisenbahnbau IVT an der ETH Zürich, ETH-Hönggerberg, CH-8093 Zürich (March 1993) (in German)
15. Bonomi, A., Manenti, L., Manzoni, S., Vizzari, G.: Makksim: Dealing with pedestrian groups in mas-based crowd simulation. In: Fortino, G., Garro, A., Palopoli, L., Russo, W., Spezzano, G. (eds.) CEUR Workshop Proceedings of the WOA, vol. 741, pp. 166–170 (2011), CEUR-WS.org

# Coupling Method for Building a Network of Irrigation Canals on a Distributed Computing Environment

Mohamed Ben Belgacem, Bastien Chopard, and Andrea Parmigiani

University of Geneva
{Mohamed.Benbelgacem,Bastien.Chopard,Andrea.Parmigiani}@unige.ch

**Abstract.** An optimal management of an irrigation network is important to ensure an efficient water supply and to predict critical situations
related to natural hazards. We present a multiscale coupling methodology to simulate numerically an entire irrigation canal over a distributed
High Performance Computing (HPC) resource. We decompose the network into several segments that are coupled through junctions. Our coupling strategy, based on the concept of Complex Automata (CxA) and
the Multiscale Modeling Language (MML), aims at coupling simple 1D
model of canal sections with 3D complex ones. Our goal is to build a
numerical model that can be run over a distributed grid infrastructure,
thus offering a large amount of computing resources. We illustrate our
approach by coupling two canal sections in 1D through a gate.

**Keywords:** irrigation canal, lattice Boltzmann models, coupling method,
distributed multiscale computing.

## 1 Introduction

Canals or rivers are important in populated area as they ensure an adequate
supply of water for agriculture and are a key component of electricity production
or transportation. An optimal management and the control of such resources
can be a critical issue for long term planning or to react to natural hazards. The
major challenge is to define appropriate actions (e.g. opening and closing gates)
that need to be taken to always guarantee an adequate water supply throughout
the canal system, whatever the external demands or perturbations can be, and
respecting constraints such as water height.

This problem can be addressed through numerical optimization methods. Usually, these methods require the simulation of different scenarios with the canal
network subject to different parameters. Therefore numerical methods able to
simulate the water flow in a full irrigation system are needed. In order to allow
canal operators to respond to real-time events, these methods should compute
fast enough, with good accuracy. Due to the size of an irrigation network and
the large variation in the flow complexity across different sections, a multi-scale,
multi-model computational approach is needed. For instance, some parts of the

G.C. Sirakoulis and S. Bandini (Eds.): ACRI 2012, LNCS 7495, pp. 309–318, 2012.
© Springer-Verlag Berlin Heidelberg 2012

system can be described with simple numerical methods, using the shallow water equation, whereas other sections need a 3D, free-surface hydrodynamic model (FS3D) to properly capture the flow properties.

In this paper we propose a methodology to achieve this goal. It follows the line proposed in the MAPPER project [2], where a set of tools, frameworks, and methodologies are developed to provide a standard way to build and run what is defined as *multiscale distributed applications*. For our specific problem, we decompose the overall canal network into segments, called submodels, that will be connected to each other through junctions. There are several reasons that make this decomposition attractive for our simulation: (i) it gives a flexibility to easily reconstruct the canal "on the fly" without the need to recode some submodels; (ii) the different components are reconfigurable and reusable; (iii) it supports multiscale coupling; (iv) the entire simulation can be efficiently carried out across distributed clusters, typically using the large computing resources of the distributed European grid infrastructure.

In this work, we use the Lattice Boltzmann (LB) approach to resolve the equations modeling a canal segment, and the MML language [11,8] to describe the coupling of the different components of the problem.

The paper is organized as follows. After a brief introduction to the LB method, we describe the coupling strategy and the distributed execution model, as specified in the CxA and MML frameworks. Then, we explain the algorithm that allows the coupling of two 1D canal sections interconnected through a gate, when using the LB method.

## 2   Lattice Boltzmann Method

We briefly present the basic equations of the LB method, which is widely used for computational fluid dynamics. Further details can be found in several papers and textbooks (see for instance [18,9]).

In the LB method, a fluid is described in terms of $q$ density distribution functions $f_i(\mathbf{x}, t)$, $i = 0, \ldots q - 1$, where $\mathbf{x}$ belongs to a Cartesian grid of spacing $\Delta x$ and $t$ is the discrete time, which varies by steps $\Delta t$. From the $f_i$, the fluid density $\rho(\mathbf{x}, t)$ and the velocity field $\mathbf{u}(\mathbf{x}, t)$ are obtained as $\rho = \sum_i f_i$ and $\rho \mathbf{u} = \sum_i f_i \mathbf{v}_i$. The $\mathbf{v}_i$ are velocity vectors associated with each $f_i$, chosen such that $\mathbf{x} + \Delta t \mathbf{v}_i$ is also a point of the computational grid. In LB modeling, the lattice is denoted as $DdQq$ where $d$ is the spatial dimension of the Cartesian lattice and $q$ the number of velocity vectors.

In the so-called BGK based LB methods, the density distribution $f_i(\mathbf{x}, t)$ are computed as a relaxation towards prescribed local equilibrium functions $f_i^{eq}$: $f_i(\mathbf{x} + \Delta t \mathbf{v}_i, t + \Delta t) = f_i(x, t) - \frac{1}{\tau}(f_i^{eq}(\mathbf{x}, t) - f_i(\mathbf{x}, t))$, where $f^{eq}$ depends on the physics of the process, and $\tau$ is a parameter called the relaxation time. The above equation can also be expressed as a succession of collision and streaming steps:

$$\text{Collision: } f_i^{out} = f_i^{in} - \frac{1}{\tau}(f_i^{eq} - f^{in})$$
$$\text{Streaming: } f_i^{in}(\mathbf{x} + \Delta t \mathbf{v}_i, t + \Delta t) = f_i^{out}(\mathbf{x}, t) \tag{1}$$

where $f_i^{in}(\mathbf{x}, t) \equiv f_i$ is the density of particles entering, at time $t$, site $\mathbf{x}$ with velocity $\mathbf{v}_i$; $f_i^{out}$ is the density of particles with velocity $\mathbf{v}_i$ at site $\mathbf{x}$ after collision.

In the shallow water (SW) model, the fluid is described as columns of water with height $h(\mathbf{x}, t)$ and velocity $u(\mathbf{x}, t)$. For solving the SW equation with a LB approach, $f_i(x, t)$ describes the part of the water column at site $\mathbf{x}$ and time $t$ that travels with velocity $v_i$.

The one-dimensional case (SW1D) is illustrated in Fig. 1(a). We use a D1Q3 lattice where grid points are separated by a distance $\Delta x$. Each lattice site is characterized by three density distributions $f_{i=0..2}(x, t)$, and three velocity vectors $v_{i=\{0..2\}}$: $v_0 = 0$, $v_1 = v$, $v_2 = -v$, with $v = \Delta x / \Delta t$. As suggested in Fig. 1(a), the water level $h$ and the velocity $u$ are then defined as $h = \sum_{i=0}^{3} f_i$ and $hu = \sum_{i=0}^{3} v_i f_i$. See for instance [17] for a more detailed description.

The SW1D is sufficient to model a simple canal section where the vertical and perpendicular flow can be neglected. For more complex simulation, a 3D free surface model is needed. An example of 3D free surface model is illustrated in Fig. 1(b), but not further described here (see [5] for more details). In our approach, such a fully resolved 3D simulation is planned to be coupled with the above SW1D model. This 1D-3D coupling will be described in a forthcoming paper. In sect. 4 we rather focus on the specific problem of coupling two 1D canal segments through a gate.

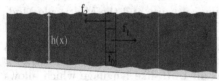     

(a) Illustration of the Lattice Boltzmann      (b) Illustration of the 3D free-surface
    1D Shallow water model (SW1D)            Lattice Boltzmann model (FS3D)

**Fig. 1.** Two numerical models needed for a multiscale simulation of an irrigation canal

## 3   Distributed Multi-scale Simulations

One of our objective is to simulate the flow in the "canal de la Bourne" in France. This irrigation network comprises a principal canal (45 km), 4 secondary canals (85 km) and 27 tertiary canals (400 km). After decomposing the entire system into segments, the whole simulation will be performed by coupling all the pieces through junctions. In order to have an acceptable computing time, it is important that the 3D free surface flow simulations are only performed for a limited number of sections, the rest being modeled within 2D or 1D shallow water models.

Such a decomposition produces a simulation involving several submodels (codes) that possibly run with different $\Delta x$ and $\Delta t$ and different spatial dimensions. Our goal is to perform the entire simulation on a distributed grid infrastructure: thus we coin our approach a *distributed, multi-scale simulation*

[8]. A specificity of this approach with respect to more standard distributed computing methods is the fact that, here, the submodels are *tightly coupled*: at each iteration, communications may be required and the coupling pattern is represented by a cyclic graph.

When dealing with tightly coupled LB based components, the main concern is to handle inlet and outlet boundaries, which depend on the temporal and spacial resolution, and to synchronize the data exchanges at the borders between canal segments.

## 3.1   MML Component

Simulating multiscale applications remains a challenge for computational sciences since it involves several temporal and spatial scales that requires an interaction of various distributed processes. Cellular automata (CA) and Lattice Boltzmann (LB) models [9] are powerful numerical and theoretical approaches for modeling various complex systems. The concept of Complex Automata (CxA) [6,14,15] provide a framework to couple them so as to obtain a multiscale model. A CxA represents a set of "single-scale" LB and/or CA systems, each representing a different physical process at a given scale. They can be coupled together to include all relevant scales and processes into the same simulation. We refer the reader to [15] for more details.

At a practical level, the theoretical CxA framework can be implemented with the MUSCLE API [13,3], a general coupling software, and the Multiscale Modeling Language (MML) [11]. Both MUSCLE and MML are further developed within the European project MAPPER [2], with the purpose of standardizing the modeling and the execution of several existing multiscale applications over large distributed HPC platforms. MML is an UML-like language which allows scientists to describe a multiscale application, its architectural diagram and its data-flow links in a standard and human-friendly way, using either an XML description (coined XMML) or a graphical tool.

The general formalism offers several components to build a multiscale application. In our case, we use the following ones: submodels, junctions and conduits:

**Sub-Model:** A canal section can be modeled either in one-dimensional shallow water (SW1D) equation or three-dimensional free surface (FS3D) model. The SW1D equation is good to describe long canal sections. We have implemented the SW1D model presented in the previous section, in the Java language. The FS3D model is needed to simulate the water flow around in a complicated geometry, for instance a fully resolved gate, a spillway, or other type of construction for which the shallow water is no longer adequate.

**Junctions:** A junction is a component that receives data from one or more submodels, performs a computation reflecting the nature of the coupling, and sends updated information back to the corresponding recipient submodels. Junctions can be: gate, spillway, pumping station, or complex structures ...etc. They can be abstracted through a phenomenological equation or actually simulated with a fully detailed flow model.

**Conduit:** A conduit is a virtual concept used to describe the data-flow links between submodels and junctions.

## 3.2 Distributed Execution

According to section 3.1, the first step to build a multiscale application consists of specifying the components and their data-flow connections. This can be done with the MML based graphical tools, as depicted in Fig. 2(a). Then the whole diagram can be exported as a virtual experiment package using the GridSpace [10] platform. GridSpace is a platform that enables the end-users to perform transparently a simulation over local or distributed grid and HPC like infrastructures. It supports interfacing with several local resources management systems (LRMS) like PBS [4] and grid middleware like QCGBroker [7].

The second step consists of executing the simulation. This can be done in two ways: local and distributed execution. In case of distributed execution, GridSpace performs the execution of the simulation by creating and scheduling jobs using QCGBroker, which facilitates secure jobs submission and management over distributed clusters. In its simple form, a job is composed of one or more canal segments or junctions running on a cluster node. In case of local simulation, GridSpace utilizes the PBS LRMS to submit jobs on the nodes of the same cluster. When the execution ends, GridSpace retrieves all the simulation results on the front-end node in both execution scenario. It is worthwhile to remind that a job uses the MUSCLE API calls to read its configuration parameters from a CxA description file [14], generated automatically in the virtual experiment package and describing the coupling schema, in order to handle all the send/receive operations among remote jobs. This is shown in the listing 1.1:

**Listing 1.1.** Example of CxA file

```
# declare kernels
cxa.add_kernel('SW1D1', 'com.unige.irigcan.kernel.d1.SW1Dkernel')
cxa.add_kernel('SW1D2', 'com.unige.irigcan.kernel.d1.SW1Dkernel')
cxa.add_kernel('Gate', 'com.unige.irigcan.junction.Gate_kernel')
# configure connection scheme
cs = cxa.cs
cs.attach('SW1D1'=>'Gate') {tie('f_out','f1_in')}
cs.attach('SW1D2'=>'Gate') {tie('f_out','f2_in')}
cs.attach('Gate'=>'SW1D1') {tie('f1_out','f_in')}
cs.attach('Gate'=>'SW1D2') {tie('f2_out','f_in')}
#parameters
cxa.env['SW1D1:dx']=0.05
cxa.env['SW1D2:dx']=0.025
cxa.env['SW1D1:dt']=0.025
cxa.env['SW1D2:dt']=0.0125
```

# 4    Coupling Techniques for Canal Sections

## 4.1    Tightly Coupled Sections

A numerical simulation of an entire irrigation canal requires to tightly couple all the submodels with each other. Besides, the multi-scale aspect of our application requires a predefined steps of exchanging boundary data between the submodels during simulation. The coupling algorithm for two submodels connected with a junction is described as follow. Each submodel obeys the CxA based formalism proposed in [6], as depicted in Fig. 2(b). In this formalism, a submodel

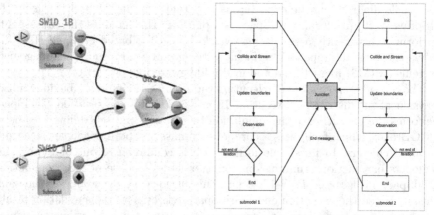

(a) The MAD [1] tool, a software part of (b) Template of the coupling algorithm
GridSpace platform, generates          for two submodels and a junction.
automatically the XMML coupling
description.

**Fig. 2.** A coupling example of two submodels with a gate

1. Initializes its parameters from the CxA coupling file, send its maximum number of iterations to the junction, and then starts execution.
2. Performs one step of computation (e.g collide and stream for a LB model)
3. Updates boundary conditions. This is done by sending data to the junction and waiting for updated information.
4. Makes an observation if needed.
5. Increments the iteration counter.
6. Repeats back to step 2 until the maximum number of iterations is reached.
7. Sends *End message* to the junction and finish the execution.

In the present case, the junction is implemented as a daemon program that keeps listening to data from the two corresponding canal sections. It is worth noting that a junction could also be modeled as a full-fledged submodel, with its generic CxA execution loop, solving the boundary condition problem at each iteration and running until the whole execution ends.

The communication process requires synchronization in the following way: the junction uses the *receive()* method, a blocking point-to-point operation of the MUSCLE framework, to receive data from each canal section. From the other side, canals send data to the junction and call the *receive()* method to wait for updated boundary information. Once data has arrived from both canal sections, the junction performs the boundary computation and sends back the updated information to the recipient submodels. This process keeps running until the maximum iteration number is reached for each submodel. The submodel will then end their execution after sending an *End* message to the junction.

In the case where the upstream and downstream canals have a different spatial and temporal resolutions, grid refinement techniques must be used for the coupling. In addition, the junction must be programmed to handle two different frequencies of send/receive operations for each side. We have implemented such a coupling using the grid refinement algorithm presented in [16]. The temporal resolution $\Delta t_c$ of the coarse grid was twice greater than the $\Delta t_f$ of the fine grid. The junction component was running on a separate computer node, thus illustrating the distributed nature of the simulation.

## 4.2  Coupling through a Gate

The information that each submodel (canal section) must send to the junction and that it will receive in return depends on the nature of this junction. Here we show which data and which computation are needed to couple two 1D canal sections that are interconnected through a gate (the junction). This coupling is based on the standard relation [12] giving the water flow $Q$ through a gate, as a function of the water height of the upstream and downstream canals.

$$Q = F(h_A - h_B) = \gamma\sqrt{h_A - h_B} \tag{2}$$

where $h_A$ and $h_B$ are the water heights before and after the gate, respectively and $\gamma$ is a coefficient depending on the gate opening.

In the LB approach to the SW equation (see section 2), one has (assuming $\Delta x/\Delta t = 1$)

$$\begin{aligned} h_A &= f_0(A) + f_1(A) + f_2(A) & Q_A &= Q = f_1(A) - f_2(A) \\ h_B &= f_0(B) + f_1(B) + f_2(B) & Q_B &= Q = f_1(B) - f_2(B) \end{aligned} \tag{3}$$

where $f_i(x)$ denotes the height distribution functions at the point $x$, and $A$ and $B$ are the points just before and just after the gate, subject to the same discharge $Q$ (see Fig. 3(a)).

Since $A$ and $B$ are at the extremity of the two canal sections, $f_2(A)$ and $f_1(B)$ are unknown. They have to be provided by the gate model which receives $f_0(A)$ and $f_1(A)$ on its left, and $f_0(B)$ and $f_2(B)$ on its right.

After eliminating $f_1(A)$ and $f_2(B)$ from eqs (3), one computes $f_2(A)$ and $f_1(B)$ as

$$f_2(A) = \frac{1}{2}\left[h_A - f_0(A) - Q\right] \qquad f_1(B) = \frac{1}{2}\left[h_B - f_0(B) + Q\right] \tag{4}$$

By subtracting these two equations, one gets

$$f_1(B) - f_2(A) = Q + \frac{1}{2}\left[h_B - h_A + f_0(A) - f_0(B)\right] \qquad (5)$$

If we assume that $h_A$ and $h_B$ are known from the previous time step (which is certainly true in a steady state), then the right-hand side of eq. (5) is known because $Q$ is a known function of $h_A - h_B$. This gives a first equation for $f_1(B)$ and $f_2(A)$.

A second equation is obtained by requesting that the total amount of water that enters the two canal sections is equal to the amount of water that leaves them. This implies that

$$f_1^{in}(B) + f_2^{in}(A) \equiv f_1(B) + f_2(A) = f_1^{out}(A) + f_2^{out}(B) \qquad (6)$$

where $f_1^{out}(A)$ and $f_2^{out}(B)$ are known from the last LB step.

Eq. (6) and eq. (5) can be solved for $f_1(B)$ and $f_2(A)$

$$\begin{cases} f_1(B) = \frac{1}{2}\left(\Delta + \bar{Q}\right) \\ f_2(A) = \frac{1}{2}\left(\Delta - \bar{Q}\right) \end{cases} \qquad (7)$$

where $\Delta = f_1^{out}(A) + f_2^{out}(B)$ and $\bar{Q} = F(h_A - h_B) + \frac{1}{2}\left[h_B - h_A + f_0(A) - f_0(B)\right]$.

Thus, the *junction component* of our model receives $f_1^{out}(A)$, $h_A$ and $f_0(A)$ from the upstream canal, and $f_2^{out}(B)$, $h_B$ and $f_0(B)$ from the downstream one. It then computes $f_2(A)$ and $f_1(B)$ according to eq. (7) and returns each of these values to each of the canals.

The physical validity of the above coupling can be demonstrated numerically as follows. We enforce the value $h_A$ and $h_B$ in $A$ and $B$ (here we chose $h_A = 0.12$ and $h_B = 0.1$) by imposing at each time step the values of $f_1(A)$ and $f_2(B)$ as

$$f_1(A, t+1) = \alpha f_1(A, t) + (1 - \alpha)(h_A(t) - f_2(A, t) - f_0(A, t))$$
$$f_2(B, t+1) = \alpha f_2(B, t) + (1 - \alpha)(h_B(t) - f_1(B, t) - f_0(B, t)) \qquad (8)$$

where $\alpha$ is a relaxation parameter (here chosen as $\alpha = 0.2$) used to smooth the way $f_1(A)$ or $f_2(B)$ reach a value that guarantees the prescribed heights $h_A$ and $h_B$. Note that eq. (8) can be seen as a way to impose a boundary condition for the water height at a chosen canal location.

We also specify the discharge $Q$ we want to impose through the gate as $Q = 0.1\sqrt{g(h_A - h_B)} = 0.044294$.

In Fig. 3(b), we show the time evolution of the discharge from arbitrary initial values for $f_2(A)$, $f_0(A)$, $f_1(B)$ and $f_0(B)$. We observe that the quantities $Q_A = f_1(A) - f_2(A)$ and $Q_B = f_1(B) - f_2(B)$ converge rapidly to the imposed value $Q$. After 20 time steps, $Q_A$ and $Q_B$ are equal to $Q$ within a precision of $10^{-5}$. After 40 iterations (not shown), the precision improves to $10^{-8}$. After convergence, the value of $\bar{Q}$ is found to be $\bar{Q} = f_1(A) - f_2(B) = 0.035138$, showing that $\bar{Q}$ is clearly different from the imposed discharge $Q$.

Also, after 40 steps, the value $f_0(A) + f_1(A) + f_2(A) - h_A$ is smaller than $10^{-8}$, showing the excellent convergence of the present gate model and the present boundary condition used to impose the heights $h_A$ and $h_B$. Note that taking $\alpha = 0$ in (8) gives a much slower convergence (oscillations).

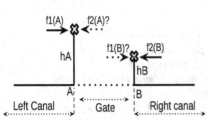

(a) The known ($f_1(A)$, $f_0(A)$, $f_0(B)$) and
    $f_2(B)$) and unknown ($f_2(A)$ and
    $f_1(B)$) distribution functions at the
    connection lattice site $A$ and $B$.

(b) Convergence of the flow $Q_A$
    (black dots) and $Q_B$ (white dots)
    to the imposed discharge
    $Q = 0.044294$. Other parameters:
    $\tau = 0.6$, $\alpha = .2$, $h_A = 0.12$,
    $h_B = 0.1$.

**Fig. 3.** A coupling example of two *SWD1* based submodels with a gate

## 5   Conclusion

We have presented a formalism to build an irrigation canal from generic and reusable components, and to simulate the water height and flow over a distributed grid infrastructure. This is obtained by decomposing the corresponding canal network into different segments and coupling them through junctions. Each canal segment can be resolved separately with either a 1D shallow water model or 3D, free-surface flow model. The coupling of these segments through junctions have been described in a "standard" way using the MML and CxA formalisms. We have also indicated that our approach can handle relatively different scales, particularly the coupling of coarse and fine LB submodels.

We have proposed an explicit implementation of a gate junction within the LB numerical method. This junction receives information from both canal sections and returns the proper boundary conditions that ensure the right discharge between the two canals.

This demonstrates that our approach of building a canal irrigation based on the MML and CxA formalism can be easily adopted to model much more complex systems. Furthermore, computing results can be sped up by running large simulation as *distributed multiscale application* over an HPC grid infrastructure.

We are currently developing the coupling of 1D and 3D models based on the LB method. Furthermore, we are working on an efficient multi-criteria algorithm to schedule jobs in an intelligent manner that will (1) assign the adequate computing resource to each canal segment accordingly to its computation requirements and (2) reduce communication time and data transfer between coupled segments.

**Acknowledgment.** This research is funded by the European project FP-7 MAPPER under grant agreement RI-261507. Numerical simulations were carried out using the European grid infrastructure. We would like to thank Daniel Harezlak, Eryk Ciepiela and Katarzyna Rycerz for their work and helpful discussions.

# References

1. MAD software, https://gs2.mapper-project.eu/mad/
2. MAPPER project, http://www.mapper-project.eu/
3. MUSCLE, http://developer.berlios.de/projects/muscle/
4. OpenPBS: Open Portable Batch System, http://www.pbsworks.com/
5. Palabos toolkit, http://www.palabos.org/
6. Hoekstra, A., Lorenz, E., Falcone, J.-L., Chopard, B.: Towards a Complex automata formalism for multuscale modeling. Int. J. Multiscale Multiscale Computational Engineering 5(6), 491–502 (2008)
7. Bosak, B., Komasa, J., Kopta, P., Kurowski, K., Mamoński, M., Piontek, T.: New Capabilities in QosCosGrid Middleware for Advanced Job Management, Advance Reservation and Co-allocation of Computing Resources – Quantum Chemistry Application Use Case. In: Bubak, M., Szepieniec, T., Wiatr, K. (eds.) PL-Grid 2011. LNCS, vol. 7136, pp. 40–55. Springer, Heidelberg (2012)
8. Borgdorff, J., Lorenz, E., Hoekstra, A.G., Falcone, J., Chopard, B.: A Principled Approach to Distributed Multiscale Computing, from Formalization to Execution. In: 2011 IEEE Seventh International Conference on e-Science Workshops (eScienceW), pp. 97–104 (December 2011)
9. Chopard, B., Droz, M.: Cellular Automata Modeling Of Physical Systems. Cambridge University Press, Aléa-Saclay (1998)
10. DICE. GridSpace2 (2011), http://dice.cyfronet.pl/products/gridspace
11. Falcone, J.-L., Chopard, B., Hoekstra, A.: MML: towards a Multiscale Modeling Language. Procedia Computer Science 1(1), 819–826 (2010)
12. Graf, W.H., Altinakar, M.S.: Hydraulique fluviale: écoulement et phénomènes de transport dans les canaux à géométrie simple. Traité de génie civil de l'Ecole polytechnique fédérale de Lausanne. Presses Polytechniques Universitaires Romandes (2008)
13. Hegewald, J., Krafczyk, M., Tlke, J., Hoekstra, A., Chopard, B.: An Agent-Based Coupling Platform for Complex Automata. In: Bubak, M., van Albada, G.D., Dongarra, J., Sloot, P.M.A. (eds.) ICCS 2008, Part II. LNCS, vol. 5102, pp. 227–233. Springer, Heidelberg (2008)
14. Hoekstra, A., Falcone, J.L., Caiazzo, A., Chopard, B.: Multi-scale modeling with cellular automata: the complex automata approach. Cellular Automata 5191, 192–199 (2010)
15. Hoekstra, A.G., Caiazzo, A., Lorenz, E., Falcone, J.-L., Chopard, B.: Complex automata: multi-scale modeling with coupled cellular automata. In: Hoekstra, A., Kroc, J., Sloot, P. (eds.) Modeling Complex Systems with Cellular Automata, vol. 3. Springer (2010)
16. Lagrava, D., Malaspinas, O., Latt, J., Chopard, B.: Advances in multi-domain lattice Boltzmann grid refinement. Journal of Computational Physics 231(14), 4808–4822 (2012)
17. van Thang, P., Chopard, B., Lefèvre, L., Ondo, D.A., Mendes, E.: Study of the 1D lattice Boltzmann shallow water equation and its coupling to build a canal network. Journal of Computational Physics 229(19), 7373–7400 (2010)
18. Sukop, M.C., Thorne, D.T.: Lattice Boltzmann Modeling: An Introduction for Geoscientists and Engineers, 1st edn. Springer (January 2007)

# Urban Cellular Automata with Irregular Space of Proximities: A Case Study

Ivan Blecic[1], Arnaldo Cecchini[1], Giuseppe A. Trunfio[1],
and Emmanuil Verigos[2]

[1] Department of Architecture, Planning and Design - University of Sassari,
Palazzo Pou Salit, Piazza Duomo 6, 07041 Alghero, Italy
{ivan,cecchini,trunfio}@uniss.it
[2] Verpa Katsouli 34, 71305 Heraklion, Crete, Greece
emverigos@teemail.gr

**Abstract.** Local interactions and influences among places in a city depend on their mutual distances in terms of accessibility to humans. That distance is hardly Euclidean, since it depends on the urban geography shaped, among others, by the network of transportation and pedestrian networks. Very little operational efforts have been undertaken in CA-based urban modelling to investigate and provide a more coherent treatment of such irregular geometries. In this paper, we propose an operational approach entirely based on cellular automata techniques for modelling of such accessibility arising from complex urban geography. We further present an example application on the city of Heraklion in Crete.

**Keywords:** urban cellular automata, land-use dynamics, proximal space, irregular neighbourhood, informational signal propagation, informational field.

## 1    Introduction

What makes the analogy between cellular automata (CA) and the city intuitively irresistible is that they both are driven by local interactions in space. This for CA is true by definition, and it is so as the matter of fact for the city, at least for many urban processes and phenomena which clearly are of that nature.

But an analogy to become a modelling paradigm needs a closer and more attentive scrutiny as to how far the analogy between the two can run. This, in the case of city means to address the question of the nature of the distance which is relevant among urban entities in urban space. In other words, what is in question is what kind of space are we to use to define the distances that are relevant for urban processes.

While the majority of, and all the most renowned CA urban models use simple Euclidean distance among cell (thus assuming that Euclidean space is an adequate representation of the urban space), this seems fairly inadequate to model all those interactions in space based on the *mutual accessibility* of urban places.

The accessibility refers here to *a measure* of how (how much, how easy, how quickly) places are mutually accessible to humans. Such accessibility depends on the

G.C. Sirakoulis and S. Bandini (Eds.): ACRI 2012, LNCS 7495, pp. 319–329, 2012.

means of transportation (pedestrian, bicycle, automobile, railway, and so on) as they all give rise to different accessibilities of places. This web of networks bringing about a highly *irregular* geometry of the accessibility type of proximity. And this type of proximity manifestly does not admit a regular representation, let alone Euclidean. Indeed, an Euclidean representation of the geometry of the accessibility-type proximity would be to a large extent inappropriate, if not fundamentally flawed.

To be fair, CA urban modellers are long aware of this, and many try to address this feature of urban processes. Hence, for example, the well-know family of Constrained CA urban models [1-3] take the (Euclidean) distance to the nearest road as a factor to calculate the transformation potential of a cell. While such an approach may be seen as a proxy of a cell's general accessibility (the underlying assumption being that we can approximate cell's overall accessibility from other cells in the city by its distance from the transportation network, which in turn is, of course, connected to all of the rest of the city), it much feels as an *ad hoc* escamotage in attempt to model that more fundamental feature of actual accessibility of that cell to *all the other* cells in the city.

Another example may the approach taken in SLEUTH [4-6]. Here again, the CA does not employ a strictly local neighbourhoods, and therefore does indeed simulate spatial interactions over greater distances, but the distance is intended exclusively in the Euclidean sense. This same general approach is taken for granted in various attempts to comprehensively present and discuss the theory and applications of urban CA (see for example [7],[8]).

Indeed, altogether little operational efforts (e.g. [9]) have been undertaken in CA-based urban modelling to investigate and provide a more consistent treatment of the irregular geometry of urban space, which is an important feature of every urban geography.

Such being the landscape of CA urban applications, to be fair there have been invitations from theoretical standpoints to develop a more appropriate understanding of the concept of nearness, to give it a deeper geographical meaning, in a way, to enrich it with a thicker geographical theory. This line of reasoning may, for instance, almost directly be derived from the notion of *proximal* space, developed within the research on 'cellular geography' [10] which set the basis for the so called *geo-algebra* approach proposed by Takeyama and Coucleis [11]. In that paper, the homogeneity of cells' neighbourhoods has been questioned by Takeyama and Coucleis precisely on the ground that every cell may have a different neighbourhood, defined by its specific relations of "nearness" with other spatial entities, where "nearness" can means both topological relation or a more generic functional influence.

In this paper, we take on the task to suggest an operational approach – entirely based on cellular automata techniques – to model the complex topology of proximities arising from urban geography, and to entangle such proximity topology with a CA model of spatial interactions. We furthermore present an experimental application of the model to the city of Heraklion in Crete.

## 2     Proximal Spaces as Informational Fields

The key element of our modelling approach is to have each cell emit information signals which propagate through a 2D cellular space. Depending on the *type* of the signal, its propagation is however not uniform in all directions, but is influenced by the "medium of propagation" the signal encounters. This means that, starting from the emitting cell, the signal is diffused in all directions, but the decay of the signal's intensity depends on the state (that is urban land use) of the cells crossed by the signal. As a consequence of such signal propagation, each cell generates an *informational field* around itself, whose shape and intensity at every cell of the cellular space depends on the states of the cells along all the paths the signal has propagated through.

To see how these general concepts may relate and be applied to urban context, we can for example think of a model in which the above described signals propagate better (i.e. with a lower rate of decay) along the roads, and that they more easily spill over to the cells surrounding the roads. Another example could be a railway transportation network. Here, the signal would propagate swiftly along the railway, but by model design would not be allowed to spill over to the surrounding cells, except at cells representing railway stations.

This method therefore generates an irregular geography-based "informational fields" around each cell. In other words, seen from the opposite perspective, every cell receives a set of signals of different type and intensity from other (potentially all) cells. Once generated, the informational fields are used in the CA transition rules, which are stated in a way to combine the received signals as the input information.

In the following section the proposed methodology will be illustrated by describing its application to the simulation of the development patterns of an urban area. However, further details on this modelling approach for simulating urban dynamics through *informational fields* can be found in [12] and [13], where some applications to ideal cases were discussed.

## 3     An Application to a CA Model

In this paper, the proposed approach is adopted for simulating the urban development of the city of Heraklion in Crete. The cellular space consists of a rectangular grid of square cells primarily characterised by their *land-use/function*. The aim of the experiment is to simulate the evolution of the urban land-use patterns between two known configurations corresponding to different years.

To this purpose, the concept of *informational fields* has been integrated into a constrained CA, in which the land-use demand is exogenous to the cellular model and assigned at each CA step  [2].

As proposed in [2], [3], the model includes three land use categories: *static, passive* and *active*. The cells having one of the static land uses will not change during the simulation, though they can influence the land-use dynamics in their neighbourhood exerting an attractive or repulsive effect on the active land uses. As mentioned above, the dynamics of the latter is driven by a demand which is generated externally to the CA model. Instead, the passive land uses represent land available to be transformed into active land uses during the simulation.

In the present application, the land uses essentially reflects the CORINE land cover classes. However, the latter have been simplified by combining those with a similar role in the model. In particular, the actively modelled land uses include: *residential dense* (RD), *residential sparse* (RS), *industrial areas* (I), *and commercial areas* (C). Passive land uses are *undeveloped land* (U), which essentially include agricultural and natural land cover classes, plus the *abandoned* state (A). Finally, static land uses include: *green urban areas and facilities* (F), *port areas* (PT), *airports* (AP), *water bodies* (W). To summarise, each cell has a *landUse* property belonging to the set {RD, RS, I, C, U, A, F, PT, AP, W}.

A further cell's property named *streetNetwork* indicates the type of link belonging to the urban transportation network that crosses the cell itself. In particular, *streetNetwork* can take one of the values in the set {0, R1, R2, R3}. The null value indicates that no relevant transportation network crosses the cell, which is the case for most cells of the automaton. The other values admitted for the *streetNetwork* property represent three different categories of speed traffic, from high (R1) to low-speed (R3).

Starting from a given initial configuration, the automaton evolves in discrete steps simulating the land-use dynamics of the area. At each simulation step, the execution of the CA model is divided into two distinct phases: (1) *informational fields propagation phase* and (2) *land-use dynamics phase*.

## 3.1   Informational Fields Propagation Phase

This phase serves to generate the informational fields around each cell. Each signal carries the following information: (1) the ID of the *source* cell, (2) the *land use* type of the source cell, (3) the *propagation rule*, and (4) the signal's intensity. During the propagation steps, every signal held by a cell is transmitted to its Moore-neighbouring cells, provided that the signal's intensity is above a predefined threshold. In particular, at the first step of this phase, the cells having RD, RS, I, C, F, W uses are made to emit two informational signals, to account for two relevant modes of spatial interaction discussed in Section 1: (1) *vicinity signal* and (2) *accessibility signal*.

The *vicinity signal* propagates regularly, in the sense that the signal decay from cell to cell is uniform in all directions and does not depend on the land uses crossed by the signal. More specifically, each source cell emits a vicinity signal of an initial intensity of $\sigma_{max}$. This intensity is subject to a constant decay when passing from one cell to another, no matter the land use. In our experimental setting, $\sigma_{max} = 1000$ and the decay constant is 25, which corresponds to the cell side of the raster representing the urban area under study. In this way, the *vicinity signal* involves cells within a circular neighbourhood of radius $\sigma_{max}$ centred on the source cell.

The *accessibility signal* uses the irregular propagation method, by which the signal decay from cell to cell depends on the land uses of the cells being crossed by the signal. Again, the source cell emits the signal with an initial intensity of $\sigma_{max}$, but the propagation rule, expressed in terms of decay of intensity on cell-to-cell basis, depends on the combination of land uses of both sender and receiver cell. This propagation rule is therefore based on a "sender-receiver land-use matrix". In our experimental setting, we use $\sigma_{max} = 1000$ and in Table 1 we report the values used for the sender-receiver land-use matrix. The decay values in this table reflect the presumed speed of movement.

**Table 1.** Sender-receiver land-use matrix used for propagation decay of accessibility information signal (N/A = "propagation not allowed")

| Receiver cell → | RD, RS, I, C | U | R1 | R2 | R3 |
|---|---|---|---|---|---|
| ↓Sender cell | | | | | |
| **RD** (Residential dense) | | | | | |
| **RS** (Residential sparse) | 100 [1] | 150 [2] | 50 [3] | 50 [3] | 50 [3] |
| **I** (Industrial Area) | | | | | |
| **C** (Commercial area) | | | | | |
| U (Undeveloped) | | 150 [2] | 50 [3] | 50 [3] | 50 [3] |
| **R1** (High-speed road) | | | 5 [4] | 10 [4] | 20 [4] |
| **R2** (Medium-speed road) | | | | 10 [4] | 20 [4] |
| **R3** (Low-speed road) | | | | | 20 [4] |

The values reflect the nature of the accessibility signal discussed in section 2. The decay of intensity is high when the signal propagates from one to another dynamic land use (residential, commercial and industrial) (1). This accounts for the fact that the effective accessibility among places is achieved using local low-speed/capacity road network (not explicitly represented on the map by road cells). The decay of the signal is even greater if propagating from one to another undeveloped cell (2), for we assume there to be even less road infrastructure. The propagation from dynamic land uses to road cells (3) are suffering somewhat minor decay, while the decay along the roads (4) is even smaller, respectful of the roads' type.

For a visual comparison of the two types of signal and propagation modes, see Fig. 1. The phase of informational fields propagation ends when no signal needs to be further propagated throughout the CA. This condition is satisfied when every cell has already emitted all its signals and all the intensities of received signals are below a predefined propagation threshold.

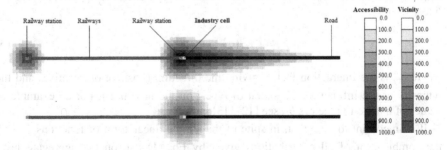

**Fig. 1.** The propagation of the two types of signal originating from the same cell (industry cell in the middle). *Above:* accessibility signal, with lower decay rate along roads and railways. *Below:* vicinity signal with uniform decay in all direction.

## 3.2 Land-Use Dynamics Phase

At the end of an informational fields propagation phase, every cell has received a series of signals from other cells. This information is used as an input in the land-use dynamics phase. The latter is based on the computation of the so-called *transition potentials* expressing the propensity of the land to be transformed into possible land uses. In [1-3], where the hereby employed concepts of transitional potentials have been developed, the cell neighbourhood is a circular region of a given radius around the cell. Therefore, we adapted the thereby presented rules to our circumstance of irregular neighbourhood patterns shaped by informational fields. Hopefully, we maintain the spirit of the spatial interaction principles inherent in the original rules.

In the present application, the transition potentials (one for each actively modelled land use) are computed as follows [3]:

$$P_j = \begin{cases} Z_j N_j & \text{if } N_j \geq 0 \\ (1 - Z_j) N_j & \text{if } N_j < 0 \end{cases} \tag{1}$$

where $Z_j \in [0, 1]$ defines the degree of legal or planning permissibility of the $j$-th land use (for example due to zoning regulations) while $N_j \in \mathbb{R}$ is the so called *neighbourhood effect*. In the canonical constrained CA approach, the *neighbourhood effect* represents the sum of all the attractive and repulsive effects of land uses and land covers within an extended Moore neighbourhood, on the $j$-th land use which the current cell may assume. In the present model, and critically different from [1-3], $N_j$ is computed using all the informational signals received by the cell:

$$N_j = \sum_t^T \sum_i^{I_t} f_{tj}(\sigma_{ti}) \tag{2}$$

where $T$ is the number of signal types; $I_t$ is the number of signals of type $t$ received by the cell; $\sigma_{ti}$ is the intensity of the single signal $i$ of type $t$; and $f_{tj}(\cdot)$ is a function yielding the component of the neighbourhood effect on the land use $j$ due to a signal of type $t$. The function $f_{tj}(\cdot)$ may in principle be of various forms. Considering that the purpose of this paper is primarily to exemplify the modelling of irregular neighbourhoods by way of informational fields, for the sake of simplicity, we use the linear form:

$$f_{tj}(\sigma) = b_{tj}\sigma \tag{3}$$

where $b_{tj}$ is the interaction factor, giving the direction (positive or negative) and the intensity of the influence of a signal of type $i$ on the land use $j$. For an example of values of interaction factors $b_{tj}$ see [12],[13].

It is important to note that, in spite of the simple linear form of functions $f_{tj}(\sigma)$, the combination of all contributions given by Eq. (1) can on the aggregate level reproduce a variety of spatial interaction patterns. An example is given in Fig. 2

where we illustrate the effect of a single industrial cell (see Fig. 1 above for its information fields) on residential potential of all the cells on the map.

Once all the transition potentials have been computed, a further stage of the CA dynamics takes place on a non-local basis and consists of transforming each cell having a non-fixed land use into the state with the highest potential, given the exogenous constraint of the overall number of cells in each state imposed for that step. Further details of this procedure can be found in [1-3].

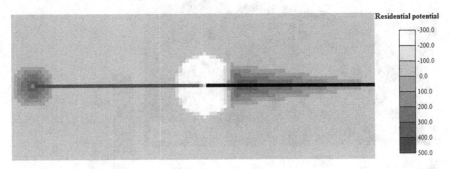

**Fig. 2.** Residential potential due to an industrial cell (cfr. Fig. 1 above). *Nota bene*, the colour scale goes from -300 to 500, so white and the two brightest shades represent negative values; the predominant background shade is used for cells with potential 0.

## 3.3    Results and Discussion

The automaton representing the urban area of Heraklion was composed of $553 \times 300$ cells with side 25 m (see Fig. 3) and was initialised with a pattern corresponding to the urbanization in 1980. The aim of our empirical assessment of the effectiveness of the proposed approach was to reproduce realistic patterns of urban development assuming as final state of the automaton the current urbanisation. The latter was obtained from the Urban Atlas EU project, which provides a sufficient level of detail for our purposes. Additional data used for the automaton were the Master Plan and the road network. The latter was obtained as a graph described by an XML document from the OpenStreetMap collaborative project, which provides free street network data with a noticeable detail and geographic coverage.

The simulation was carried out for 30 CA steps, each corresponding to one year. At each time step, the amount of cells to assign to each land use (i.e. the external constraint) was computed assuming a linear variation between the initial state (i.e. 1980) and the final state (i.e. 2010). The model implementation was based on the MAGI C++ class library described in [14] and the simulations were carried out on a desktop computer equipped with a 2.66 Ghz Intel Core 2 Quad CPU. Many runs were required to perform a preliminary rough calibration based on a trial and error process which led to the parameters already shown in Table 1. Fig. 4 shows the maps corresponding to the CA configuration after 10, 20 and 30 steps.

As it can be seen from a qualitative comparison between the maps in Fig 3. and Fig. 4., there is a reasonable overall correspondence between the real-word and the simulated scenarios. Further more formal investigation should of course be carried out to calculate metrics of map correspondences, but still, this purely qualitative comparison in this preliminary example application of the model should be able to provide some hints of the potential and the capability of our modelling approach to capture the dynamics of urban development.

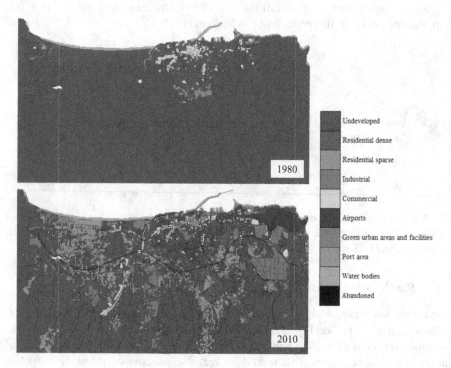

**Fig. 3.** The land cover maps adopted as initial CA configuration (1980) and the current land use data for Heraklion

Needless to say, in this application we were confronted with many uncertainties about the data fidelity and homogeneity (the information base was not on the same geographical scale, there are margins of error in Urban Atlas and OpenStreet Maps and finally issues of homogeneity and uniformity of interpretation may arise among those and the Master Plan). Furthermore, informal and illegal building practices which are not uncommon, voiding rigid prescriptions of the Master Plan, are something the model cannot account for.

All that notwithstanding, we believe that these preliminary results have shown that the model is capable of reproducing the distinctive general shape and patterns of urban development observed in the real-world.

Of no less importance, our modelling approach with respect to the conventional constrained CA models comes with a benefit. Given that some parameters - the speed of propagation of the information signals - in our model can be directly derived from physical measures, there are less parameters to be calibrated. In fact, in simplest cases of a conventional constrained CA there are usually at least four parameters to define the interaction between each couple of land uses, while in our approach there are only two parameters ($b_{tj}$ in Eq. (3) above), the rest relying on the differential of the propagation decay of vicinity and accessibility signals.

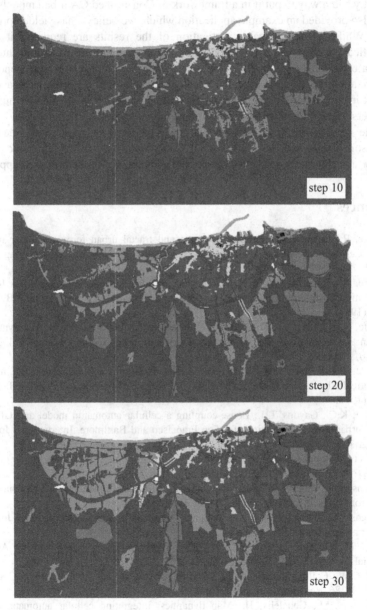

**Fig. 4.** The simulated pattern of urban development after 10, 20 and 30 steps

# 4    Conclusions and Future Work

Based on our previous empirical investigation [12,13], in this paper we proposed a specification of a CA model of proximity and proximal space arising in urban geography and a way to put it in a framework of Constrained CA urban models.

We also provided an example application which, we believe, has yielded promising results. While further formal investigation of the results are required, it was an exemplification of how existing models based on assumptions of spatial interaction may in a reasonably convenient manner be adapted to employ our more generalised, and more attentive to actual urban geography, description of the proximal space.

A not irrelevant side product of our modelling approach is the smaller number of parameters to calibrate than in a conventional constrained CA urban models.

In the future, we will take on the task to make specific and side-by-side comparison of our and the conventional Constrained CA model, in order to more formally and accurately determine the possible advantages of the proposed approach.

# References

1. White, R., Engelen, G.: Cellular automata and fractal urban form: a cellular modeling approach to the evolution of urban land-use patterns. Environment and Planning A 25(8), 1175–1199 (1993)
2. White, R., Engelen, G., Uljee, I.: The use of constrained cellular automata for high-resolution modelling of urban land use dynamics. Environment and Planning B 24, 323–343 (1997)
3. White, R., Engelen, G.: High-resolution integrated modelling of the spatial dynamics of urban and regional systems. Computers, Environment and Urban Systems 2824, 383–400 (2000)
4. Clarke, K., Hoppen, S., Gaydos, L.: A self-modifying cellular automaton model of historical urbanization in the san francisco bay area. Environment and Planning B 24, 247–261 (1997)
5. Clarke, K.C., Gaydos, L.J.: Loose-coupling a cellular automaton model and GIS: long-term urban growth predictions for San Francisco and Baltimore. International Journal of Geographic Information Science, 699–714 (1998)
6. Project Gigalopolis, NCGIA (2003),
   http://www.ncgia.ucsb.edu/projects/gig/
7. Benenson, I., Torrens, P.M.: Geosimulation: object-based modeling of urban phenomena. Environment and Urban Systems 28(1-2), 1–8 (2004)
8. Torrens, P.M., Benenson, I.: Geographic Automata Systems. International Journal of Geographical Information Science 19(4), 385–412 (2005)
9. Batty, M.: Distance in space syntax. CASA Working Papers (80). Centre for Advanced Spatial Analysis (UCL), London, UK (2004)
10. Tobler, W.: Cellular geography. In: Gale, S., Olsson, G. (eds.) Philosophy in Geography, pp. 379–386. Reidel, Dordrecht (1979)
11. Takeyama, M., Couclelis, H.: Map dynamics: integrating cellular automata and GIS through Geo-Algebra. Intern. Journ. of Geogr. Inf. Science 11, 73–91 (1997)

12. Blecic, I., Cecchini, A., Trunfio, G.A.: A Proximal Space Approach for Embedding Urban Geography into CA Models. In: Bandini, S., Manzoni, S., Umeo, H., Vizzari, G. (eds.) ACRI 2010. LNCS, vol. 6350, pp. 106–115. Springer, Heidelberg (2010)
13. Blecic, I., Cecchini, A., Trunfio, G.A.: Modelling Proximal Space in Urban Cellular Automata. In: Murgante, B., Gervasi, O., Iglesias, A., Taniar, D., Apduhan, B.O. (eds.) ICCSA 2011, Part I. LNCS, vol. 6782, pp. 477–491. Springer, Heidelberg (2011)
14. Blecic, I., Cecchini, A., Trunfio, G.A.: A General-Purpose Geosimulation Infrastructure for Spatial Decision Support. Transactions on Computational Science 6, 200–218 (2009)

# Efficient Robot Path Planning in the Presence of Dynamically Expanding Obstacles

Konstantinos Charalampous, Angelos Amanatiadis, and Antonios Gasteratos

Laboratory of Robotics and Automation,
Department of Production and Management Engineering,
Democritus University Of Thrace,
12 Vas. Sofias Str, GR-67100, Xanthi, Greece
{kchara,agaster}@pme.duth.gr,aamanat@ee.duth.gr

**Abstract.** This paper presents a framework for robot path planning based on the A* search algorithm in the presence of dynamically expanding obstacles. The overall method follows Cellular Automata (CA) based rules, exploiting the discrete nature of CAs for both obstacle and robot state spaces. For the search strategy, the discrete properties of the A* algorithm were utilized, allowing a seamless merging of both CA and A* theories. The proposed algorithm guarantees both a collision free and a cost efficient path to target with optimal computational cost. More particular, it expands the map state space with respect to time using adaptive time intervals in order to predict the necessary future expansion of obstacles for assuring both a safe and a minimum cost path. The proposed method can be considered as being a general framework in the sense that it can be applied to any arbitrary shaped obstacle.

**Keywords:** robot path planning, obstacle avoidance, cellular automata.

## 1 Introduction

The task of path planning is a subject of active research in many scientific communities. Mainly, it addresses the design of a route from a starting point to a target point, given certain operational constraints and scenarios. Some of the most common and important parameters that a path planning algorithm must hold are the ability of obstacle avoidance, the operation in static or dynamic environments and computational efficiency. A collision free path is a non tradable property that every path planning algorithm must hold. Operating in static or dynamic environments refers to whether the world model remains unchangeable during time evolution or not, respectively. Computational efficiency is another desired property to build a path planning algorithm applicable to real time applications. The above requirements of path planning design have resulted in a large amount and variations of proposed solutions, that have led to major breakthroughs especially in car navigation [1], domestic robot assistance [2], sensor fusion [3], logistics [4], and search and rescue robots [5]. However, path planning challenge can not be characterized as a solved problem.

G.C. Sirakoulis and S. Bandini (Eds.): ACRI 2012, LNCS 7495, pp. 330–339, 2012.
© Springer-Verlag Berlin Heidelberg 2012

Prior work on path planning yields different approaches dealing with most of the aforementioned constraints. Optimization approaches result in a set of inequalities and constraints which are being used to express the problem. However, in order to be accurately formed, the number of inequalities should be increased as well, producing complicated non linear functions that have to be optimized [6]. Extended use of Voronoi diagrams has be done in [7], [8] yet they lack computational efficiency. In [9] a more simple and efficient framework was introduced using Voronoi diagrams, which as yet do not satisfy the ability to deal with arbitrary shapes of mobile robots.

Methods that imitate Dubin's theorem have been proposed [10], where the exploitation of genetic algorithms provides an optimal solution in a static environments containing obstacles. Alternative approaches are based on heuristic functions [6], trying to prune possible untraversable paths considering the robot's width [11]. A wave simulation technique (Distance Transform) in the configuration space has been introduced [12], which creates into the free space a wave that carries distances from goal. An extension to Distance Transform, Path Transform [13], adds distances from near obstacles into the calculation loops.

Our algorithm guarantees a collision free path, among dynamically expanding obstacles, while it produces a path cost that is locally optimal in every time interval. The produced final trajectory lies in the neighborhood of the global optimum since it tries to attain the global optimum, in every iteration. The method can be characterized by low computational cost making it appropriate for real-time applications.

## 2   Cellular Automata

Automaton is a mathematical structure, described formally as a quintuple

$$\{I, Z, Q, \delta_1, \omega\} \tag{1}$$

where each symbol is a set according to the following definition [14]:
$I$ is a set of inputs to the defined automaton
$Z$ is a set of outputs to the defined automaton
$Q$ is a set of internal states, known as accept states
$\delta_1$ is a transition function defined as $\delta_1 : I \times Q \to Q$, that produces the corresponding internal state from the Cartesian product of an internal state and the set of inputs.
$\omega$ is a function that produces the output from the Cartesian product of an internal state and the set of inputs, defined as $\omega : I \times Q \to Z$.

Cellular automata is a subcategory of automata. CA main characteristics are that they deal with time and space in a discrete level. Using the above definition each future state is an outcome from the exact previous one, yet this can be expanded, leading to a system with memory, producing outcomes by considering numerous previous states. The neighborhood of a cell is defined as a spacial region in which a cell explores its adjacecent neighboor. The size of the neighborhood is not bounded by any restriction, but it must be the same for every cell. The most widely used types of neighborhoods are the Von Neumann and the Moore ones. Von Neumann's is a diamond shaped neighborhood in a squared grid. Given a cell $(x_0, y_0)$ in a two-dimensional plane, and range $r$, Von Neumann neighborhood is defined as [15]:

$$N_{x_0,y_0}^V = \{(x,y) : |x - x_0| + |y - y_0| \leq r\} \tag{2}$$

On the other hand, Moore's results in a squared shaped neighborhood in a squared grid. Given a cell $(x_0, y_0)$ in a two-dimensional plane and range $r$, Moore neighborhood is defined as [15]:

$$N_{x_0,y_0}^M = \{(x,y) : |x - x_0| \leq r, |y - y_0| \leq r\} \tag{3}$$

## 3   A*

A* is a search algorithm widely used in computer science, mainly in path finding and graph traversal problems. A* was introduced as an extension of Dijkstra's algorithm [16]. Originally it was proposed for two-dimensional grids, also known as state spaces, characterizing it as a discrete algorithm. A* is an algorithm that combines Dijkstra's algorithm in the sense that can it find the shortest path, but also the Greedy Best-First-Search, in the sense that it uses a heuristic function. More precisely, A* follows the path that minimizes the cost function $f(s)$, where:

$$f(s) = g(s) + h(s) \tag{4}$$

Component $g(s)$ gives the cost of the expanded path until the current state - cell $s$. The $h(s)$ component is a heuristic function providing with an assessment of cost from current state $s$ to goal. If $h(s)$ is an admissable function, i.e. $h(s)$ never overestimates the true cost from current state to goal providing a value of less or equal to real cost, then A* acquires some very desirable properties. A* having an admissable function $h(s)$ can guarantee that it will always find the shortest - optimal path [17].

Since A* was first introduced, many different heuristic functions have been proposed over the years depending on each problem's nature. Among those a common parameter exists. That is, the trade-off between heuristic's accuracy and time complexity in order to produce a result, in the form of an estimation. The challenge of making such search algorithms practical for real time implementations lies in an efficient heuristic function. Depending on each problem, the search strategy must be considered as the best trade off between global optimum path cost and fast convergence. The A* algorithm is a complete algorithm, since it always provides a path when a solution exists.

The algorithm's time complexity, as mentioned above, varies according to heuristic function $h(s)$. Complexity can be polynomial if the following assumptions hold. State space is a tree, and for a given heuristic function $h(s)$ the next condition is valid:

$$|h^*(s) - h(s)| = O(\log(h^*(s))) \tag{5}$$

where, $h(s)$ is the heuristic's value at state $s$, and $h^*(s)$ is the optimal function's value at state $s$, that is the exact cost of state $s$ to goal. This condition implies that the approximation error, which is the difference between the optimal function and the heuristic of interest, must be equal to the optimal solutions logarithmic value. However, the number of nodes could also be expanded exponentially, while deriving the path with the lower cost [18].

## 4   Proposed Approach

The proposed method is based on the A* algorithm beacuase it exploits the properties of CA theory. The purpose of this method is to derive a kinematically feasible path to a goal with fast convergence, while dynamic obstacle creation and expansion occurs. The fact that the A* search algorithm is applicable on two-dimensional grids, as well as the grounded CA properties of time and space discrete level of processing, allows a seamless merging of both CA and A* theories. As discussed before, the A* algorithm as initially proposed, holds some very intriguing properties, but it can only be applied on static and fully observable grid maps. In order to resolve the aforementioned disadvantage, the proposed approach builds on a seamless merging between A* and CA theories. The key idea is that since A* cannot be applied in dynamic grids, it will be applied on predicted grid maps where both obstacle expansion and creation properties are encapsulated.

The grid map prediction is feasible due to the discrete nature of both A* and CA theories. However, it is imposed to provide a time step. This restriction is addressed with an adaptive step usage. The proposed method iteratively defines the time step of the grid map evolution. The time step is calculated as follows:

$$D_o(i,j) = \frac{dist_o(O_i, O_j)}{2} * r_e(i) \qquad i,j = 1, \ldots, N_o, \qquad i \neq j \qquad (6)$$

$$V_r(i) = \frac{dist_r(r, O_i)}{2} * r_e(i) \qquad i = 1, \ldots, N_o \qquad (7)$$

$$T_s = min(D_o, V_r) \qquad (8)$$

where $N_o$ is the number of obstacles, $O_i$ defines the coordinates of the $i-th$ obstacle, $r_e(i)$ is the expansion rate of obstacle $i$, $dist_o$ is an operator that calculates the Euclidean distance between two obstacles and $D_o(i,j)$ is a matrix. Given a number of obstacles $N_o$, the algorithm calculates the half distance between two obstacles and then multiplies it with the expansion rate of each obstacle. In every time step, the matrix $D_o(i,j)$ will contain the time in which an obstacle $O_i$ will reach half the distance to the obstacle $O_j$. In (7), $dist_r$ is an operator that calculates the naive Euclidean distance between an obstacle and robot. Vector $V_r(i) \in \mathbb{R}^{N_o}$ stores the time in which an obstacle $O_i$ will reach half the distance to the robot. In (8), $min$ is an operator that finds the minimum time for any of the above events to happen defining the time step $T_s$.

When the time step is defined, the grip map evolves $T_s$ steps in time. Subsequently, A* is applied to the new grid map, moving the robot $T_s$ time steps.

A new time step is then recalculated. This iteration is repeated until the robot reaches the goal.

Time step calculation is justified given that in the predicted grid map obstacles will not collide, thus there will be always a kinematically feasible path for the robot between them. In case the time to impact between the robot and an obstacle is smaller than the collision time between obstacles, this time interval is selected as the new time step, ensuring that robot will avoid impact.

In the proposed methodology, each obstacle expands according to Moore's neighborhood, though this is not a constraint, since any type of neighborhood can be applied to the proposed strategy. However, Moore's neighborhood can be considered as the worst case in which an obstacle might expand, in the sense that it covers a larger part of the grid map compared to other types of expansions. Various expansion rates can be applied to each different obstacle. The proposed method allows the possibility to add obstacles during execution, as well as to alter the goal's position. This can be applied before every iteration, when the path is being recalculated, without introducing an extra computational burden.

For ensuring a safe path calculation, the A* algorithm is being applied, at a current time interval $t$, using the predicted grid map of time interval $t + T_s$. In such a way, the A* treats the obstacles on the predicted grid map as ones on the current map. This obstacle projection in time guarantees that the calculated path will be always kinematically traversable by the robot.

In order to reduce computational burden, the proposed method monitors if the following conditions hold:

1. That the imaginary line segment that joins two obstacles does not intersect with the robot path,
2. If an obstacle has a sufficiently greater expansion rate than another, leading at a time $t_o$ the second obstacle to be overlaid from the first one, then only the first obstacle needs to be taken into account from time $t_o$ onwards.

The proposed method's computational complexity varies according to the number and positioning of the obstacles. The following cases are introduced to show the A* algorithm's varies. In the worst case, where all obstacles are taken into account, computational complexity is $O((N_o)^2)$, where $N_o$ defines the number of obstacles. In the best case, where the robot distance from the goal can be traversed in less time than the time step $T_s$, then the complexity is reduced to that of A*. In the general case that $k$ obstacles meet one of the above two aforementioned conditions, then only $N_o - k$ obstacles need to be taken into account, thus the oeverall computational complexity is $O((N_o - k)^2)$.

## 5    Simulation Results

This section presents the environment as well as the simulation results of the proposed methodology. The simulation environment includes a robot, a point on the grid map marked as goal point, and expanding obstacles. The simulation depicted in Fig.1, was applied in a $100 \times 100$ grid, where both obstacles have their own expansion rates. The purpose was to demonstrate the ability of the proposed method to avoid expanding obstacles. As it can be seen, the robot's initial course is curvy in order to avoid collision. After traversing between obstacles it follows a straight line, as a result of A*'s property.   The second simulation depicted in

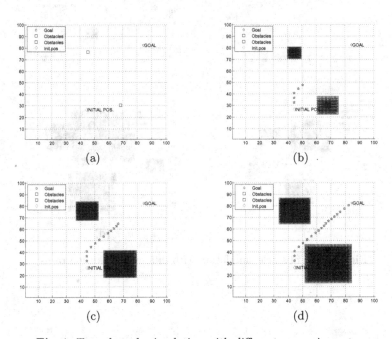

(a)

(b)

(c)

(d)

**Fig. 1.** Two obstacle simulation with different expansion rates

Fig. 2 was applied in a 100×100 grid introducing four obstacles, each one holding its own expansion rate. In this simulation we can derive the main properties of the algorithm. Firstly, it is shown that it can calculate a safe path by taking into account the predicted grids. The option to implant obstacles after the simulation start is also illustrated in Fig. 2(a), where in the north east area there is no obstacle, but in Fig. 2(b), Fig. 2(c), and Fig. 2(d) an obstacle appears in the grid. Furthermore, the distance properties between the new obstacle and its adjacent is not taken into account for the adaptive step computation, since the imaginary line segment does not intersect with the robot's path. In such a way the computational complexity of the algorithm is reduced.

In the third simulation, as illustrated in Fig. 3, a 200 × 200 grid was utilized, with six obstacles of different expansion rates. Though there were six obstacles, the overall computation burden is not significantly increased compared to the previous simulations. This is due to the fact that only two of the imaginary line segments between obstacles intersect with the robot path. As a result, the rest of the obstacles are excluded from the adaptive step computation.

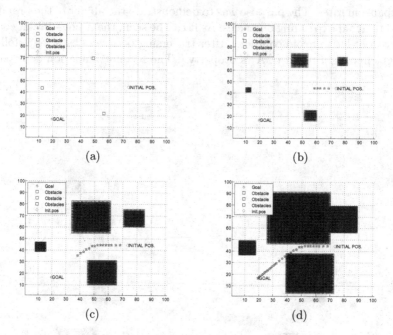

**Fig. 2.** Four obstacle simulation with different expansion rates

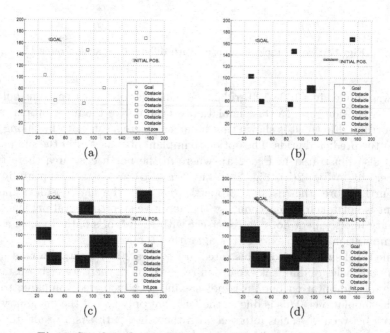

**Fig. 3.** Six obstacle simulation with different expansion rates

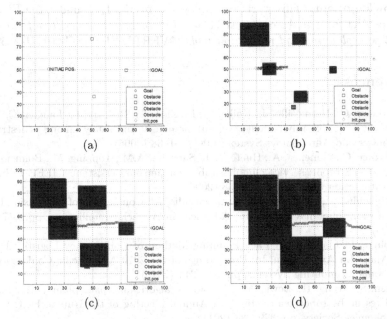

**Fig. 4.** Four obstacle simulation with additional two introduced during the simulation

In the last simulation, as depicted in Fig. 4, a $100 \times 100$ grid was used, where initially four obstacles were introduced. Subsequently, two more obstacles were added into the simulation. It can be seen that the robot initial position and the goal position are almost in a straight line. The A* part of proposed method is pointing to a path which is really close to a straight line. This path includes maneuvers in order to avoid obstacles, however the path marginally avoids collisions. The risk is not significant since the obstacles presented on the A* are predictions of their real size.

## 6   Conclusions

This paper proposes a framework for robot path planning in the presence of dynamically expanding obstacles. It guarantees a collision free and a lowest cost path to target without introducing significant computational complexity. The map prediction follows CA rules, exploiting the discrete nature of CAs for both obstacle and robot state spaces. The search strategy is based on the A* algorithm allowing a seamless merging of both CA and A* theories. The produced final trajectory lies in the neighborhood of the global optimum since it tries to attain the global optimum in every iteration. The method can be characterized by low computational cost, rendering it appropriate for real-time applications.

**Acknowledgment.** This work was supported by the E.C. under the FP7 research project for *The Autonomous Vehicle Emergency Recovery Tool to provide a robot path planning and navigation tool,* "AVERT", FP7-SEC-2011-1-285092.

# References

1. Pradalier, C., Hermosillo, J., Koike, C., Braillon, C., Bessiere, P., Laugier, C.: The CyCab: a car-like robot navigating autonomously and safely among pedestrians. Robotics and Autonomoys Systems 50(1), 51–68 (2005)
2. Balaguer, C., Gimenez, A., Huete, A.J., Sabatini, A.M., Topping, M., Bolmsjo, G.: The MATS robot: service climbing robot for personal assistance. IEEE Robotics & Automation Magazine 13, 51–58 (2006)
3. Kyriakoulis, N., Gasteratos, A., Amanatiadis, A.: Comparison of data fusion techniques for robot navigation. In: Advances in Artificial Intelligence, pp. 547–550 (2006)
4. Baohua, J., Liang, Z.: A Path Planning Method of Contingency Logistics Based on Max-Min Ant System. In: Proceedings of the 2010 Asia-Pacific Conference on Wearable Computing Systems, pp. 311–314 (2010)
5. Chien, S., Wang, H., Lewis, M.: Human vs. algorithmic path planning for search and rescue by robot teams. In: 54th Annual Meeting of the Human Factors and Ergonomics Society, pp. 379–383 (2011)
6. Hwang, Y., Ahuja, N.: Gross motion planning –A survey. ACM Comput. Surv. 24, 219–291 (1992)
7. Rao, N.S.V.: An algorithmic framework for navigation in unknown terrains. IEEE Trans. Comput., 37–43 (1989)
8. Sugihara, K.: An approximation of generalized Voronoi diagrams by ordinary Voronoi diagrams. Graphical Models and Image Processing 55, 522–531 (1993)
9. Tzionas, P.G., Thanailakis, A., Tsalides, P.G.: Collision-Free Path planning for a Diamond-Shaped Robot Using Two-Dimensional Cellular Automata. IEEE Robotics & Automation Magazine 13, 237–250 (1997)
10. Wang, C., Soh, Y.C., Wang, H., Wang, H.: A hierarchical genetic algorithm for path planning in a static enviroment with obstacles. In: Canadian Conference on Electrical and Computer Engineering, IEEE CCECE 2002, vol. 3, pp. 1652–1657 (2002)
11. Noborio, H., Naniwa, T., Arimoto, S.: A feasible motion planning algorithm for a mobile robot an a quadtree representation. In: Proc. IEEE Int. Conf. Robot. Automat., pp. 237–332 (1989)
12. Jahabin, M.R., Fallside, F.: Path planning using a wave simulation technique in the configuration space. In: Gero, J.S. (ed.) Artificial Intelligence in Engineering: Robotics and Processes. Computational Mechanics Publications, Southhampton (1988)
13. Zelinsky, A.: Using path transforms to guide the search for findpath in 2D. Int. J. Robot., 315–325 (1994)
14. Aleksander, I., Hanna, F.K.: Automata Theory: An engineerinng Approach. Crane Russak, New York (1975)
15. Gray, L.: A Mathematician Looks at Wolfram's New Kind of Science. Not. Amer. Math., 200–211 (2003)

16. Hart, P.E., Nilsson, N.J., Raphael, B.: A Formal Basis for the Heuristic Determination of Minimum cost paths. IEEE Trans. on Systems Science and Cybernetics, SSC 2004, pp. 100–107 (2004)
17. Dehter, R., Judea, P.: Generalized best-first search strategies and the optimality of A*. Journal of the ACM, 505–536
18. Pearl, J.: Heuristics: Intelligent Search Strategies for Computer Problem Solving. Addison-Wesley

# Image Encryption Using the Recursive Attributes of the eXclusive-OR Filter on Cellular Automata

Savvas A. Chatzichristofis[1], Oge Marques[2], Mathias Lux[3], and Yiannis Boutalis[1]

[1] Department of Electrical and Computer Engineering
Democritus University of Thrace, Xanthi, Greece
[2] Department of Computer & Electrical Engineering and Computer Science (CEECS)
Florida Atlantic University (FAU), Boca Raton, Florida, USA
[3] Institute for Information Technology
Klagenfurt University, Klagenfurt, Austria
{schatzic,ybout}@ee.duth.gr, omarques@fau.edu,
mlux@itec.uni-klu.ac.at

**Abstract.** A novel visual multimedia content encryption method based on cellular automata (CA) is presented in this paper. The proposed algorithm is based on an attribute of the eXclusive-OR (XOR) logic gate, according to which, its application to a square-sized CA has the ability to reconstruct the original content of a CA after a preset number of iterations. The resulted encrypted image is a lossless representation of the original/plaintext image, i.e. there is no loss of either resolution or contrast. Experimental results indicate that the encrypted image does not contain any statistical information able to reveal the original image.

## 1 Introduction

Nowadays it is often imperative to safeguard the transmission of visual multimedia information. The conventional encryption methods, e.g. the 3DES and AES, are incapable of encrypting data with patterns, like images. In order to overcome this problem, plaintext block chaining or plaintext feedback and output feedback techniques are usually applied. However, those methods only apply to problems of considerably small complexity. In recent literature though, there are numerous image encryption algorithms which may be classified according to their ability to lossless reconstruct the encrypted image or lead to loss of information after the decryption. Additionally, these methods can be classified based on the approach used to achieve the encryption, which may be divided into four categories: *SCAN*-based techniques (e.g. SCAN-based permutation of pixels) [1] [3] [15], *Chaos*-based techniques [19] [7] [11], *Structure*-based information [5], and finally algorithms where the encryption technique combine elements from the other techniques or use elements borrowed from different scientific disciplines. However, each approach is characterized by advantages and disadvantages in terms of security level and speed [3].

Several image encryption methods based on cellular automata (CA) are already reported in literature. In [14] a family of basic functions, generated from the evolving states of CA, is used to encrypt multimedia information. In [20], CA were used to produce the bit stream of the key in a Vernam cipher cryptography. An image encryption

G.C. Sirakoulis and S. Bandini (Eds.): ACRI 2012, LNCS 7495, pp. 340–350, 2012.
© Springer-Verlag Berlin Heidelberg 2012

method based on the permutation of the pixels of an image and the replacement of the pixel values is proposed in [3], where the permutation is done by SCAN patterns. The pixel values are replaced using a progressive CA substitution with a sequence of CA data that is generated from the CA evolution rules. Other CA image security methods are reported in [8] and [10].

A new lossless visual multimedia content encryption method based on CA is proposed in this paper. The proposed algorithm is based on an attribute of the eXclusive-OR (XOR) logic gate, according to which, its application to a square-sized CA has the ability to reconstruct the the original content of the CA after a preset number of repetitions. This attribute is presented in details in Section 2.

The proposed method is a symmetric-key based one, which means that it requires the same key both for encrypting and decrypting an image. Detailed description of the key construction as well as its use in encrypting and decrypting images, is presented in Section 3. Section 4 describes the encryption characteristics and evaluates several security issues regarding the application of the proposed method. Finally, the conclusions are drawn in Section 5.

## 2  The Recursive Attribute of XOR Filters

A single channel image (i.e. a grayscale or a binary image) can be considered as a CA which is comprised of a linear two-dimensional (2D) table of identical cells. Every pixel of the image corresponds to a cell of the CA and each one of these cells can be found in $k$ different states. The local state of the cell $x, y$ during time step $t$ is given by the formula:

$$s_t^{x,y} \in \sum = \{0, 1, \ldots, k-1\} \tag{1}$$

where $k = 256$ for grayscale images and $k = 2$ for binary ones.

The total state of the CA during time $t$, designated as $s_t$, is the configuration of the whole table:

$$s_t = (s_t^{0,0}, s_t^{0,1}, s_t^{0,2}, \ldots, s_t^{W-1,H-1}) \in \sum^{W \times H} \tag{2}$$

where $W, H$ designate the width and height of the 2D CA respectively.

As already mentioned, this paper is based on an attribute of the XOR filter when applied to a 2D CA, and consequently to a single channel image. According to this attribute, the CA returns in its initial state after a predefined number of applications of the filter. The implementation of the XOR gate in the CA is quite widespread in the literature, as well as the recursiveness of the resulting outcomes [4] [6] [2] [9]. The filtering process is described below:

At every time step all the cells of the CA recalculate their state concurrently according to the following rule: The values of the cells in the Moore neighborhood with radius $r = 1$, participate in the logical operation (XOR) and their result is placed in the central cell of the neighborhood.

$$S_1^{x,y} = S_0^{x-1,y-1} \oplus S_0^{x,y-1} \oplus S_0^{x+1,y-1}$$
$$\oplus S_0^{x-1,y} \oplus S_0^{x,y} \oplus S_0^{x+1,y}$$
$$\oplus S_0^{x-1,y+1} \oplus S_0^{x,y+1} \oplus S_0^{x+1,y+1}$$

After applying the filter $t$ times, the CA returns to its original state, i.e. $S_t^{x,y} = S_0^{x,y}$.

$$S_1^{x,y} = S_0^{x-1,y-1} \oplus S_0^{x,y-1} \oplus S_0^{x+1,y-1} \oplus S_0^{x-1,y} \oplus$$
$$S_0^{x,y} \oplus S_0^{x+1,y} \oplus S_0^{x-1,y+1} \oplus S_0^{x,y+1} \oplus S_0^{x+1,y+1}$$

$$S_2^{x,y} = S_1^{x-1,y-1} \oplus S_1^{x,y-1} \oplus S_1^{x+1,y-1} \oplus S_1^{x-1,y} \oplus$$
$$S_1^{x,y} \oplus S_1^{x+1,y} \oplus S_1^{x-1,y+1} \oplus S_1^{x,y+1} \oplus S_1^{x+1,y+1}$$

$$\ldots$$

$$S_t^{x,y} = S_0^{x,y}$$

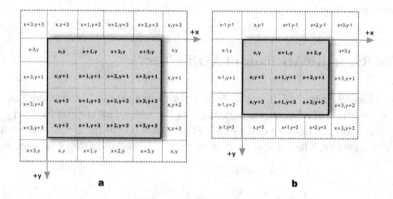

**Fig. 1.** Boundaries of the CA. (a) Periodical. (b) Pseudo-Cells

The reconstruction periodicity is based strictly on the size of the CA and on the **boundary conditions**. The proposed encryption method is based on the reconstruction periodicity which occurs under two different conditions:

**Condition 1.** *The application of an XOR filter on a CA of $N \times N$ dimensions and periodical boundaries has the ability to lossless reconstruct the CA after $t = N/2$ repetitions when $N = 2^p$ and $p \in Z$.*

Periodical boundaries of a CA are displayed in Figure 1(a). This may be visualized as taping the left and right edges of the rectangle to form a tube, then taping the top and bottom edges of the tube to form a torus (donut shape). The interested reader may find more information regarding this condition in [2] [9].

**Condition 2.** *The application of an XOR filter on a CA of $N' \times N'$ dimensions and pseudo-cells boundaries has the ability to lossless reconstruct the CA after $t = 2^p \times 2$ iterations when $N' = 2^p - 1$ and $p \in Z$. In other words, the application of an XOR filter on a CA can reconstruct the CA after $t = (N' + 1) \times 2$ steps.*

Pseudo-Cells boundaries of a CA are displayed in Figure 1(b). In this case, the data forming the boundaries belong to hypothesized neighboring cells. In other words, the $N' \times N'$ CA is regarded as a part of another $N' + 1 \times N' + 1$ CA, to the boundary conditions of which the filter is not applied. An application of a CLF (COORDINATE LOGIC FILTERS)-XOR filter to a 2D CA of $3 \times 3$ ($p = 2$) dimensions is presented in Figure 2.

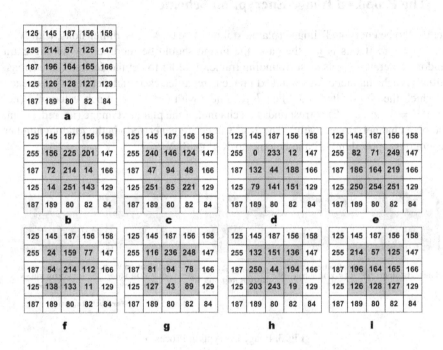

**Fig. 2.** Application of CLF-XOR to a 2D CA size of $3 \times 3$

It is crucial to emphasize that under both conditions, during intermediate time steps, the CA content and consequently the single channel image is greatly distorted in an almost unpredictable manner.

In case of color images, each channel is processed individually. More specifically, each channel is considered as a 2D CA. Hence, for a typical RGB image, 3 CAs of identical dimensions are generated. The cell values are integer numbers in $[0, 255]$, which are subsequently converted into a binary form. The XOR filter is applied on every cell of every CA, which is actually an application of the filter to every pixel of each channel of the image. Essentially, this filter executes the XOR operation to the binary form values of the 9 cells that belong to the Moore neighborhood on which the filter is applied. The application of the filter to the nine(9) 8-bit values results in an 8-bit number, and the operation outcome is placed in the central cell of the neighborhood. This procedure is repeated for every pixel/cell of every channel.

The exact same procedure should be followed when the filter is applied more than once, with new values being generated for all the CA cells after each iteration. These new values constitute the basis for the next iteration and so on. It is worth noting once more that during the interim time steps, the image is greatly distorted, making it impossible to be recognized.

## 3   The Proposed Image Encryption Scheme

Let the "to be encrypted" image (plaintext image) be of $N \times N$ dimensions, with $N = 2^p$, $p \in \mathcal{Z}$. If this is not the case, the image should be modified by adding extra random generated pixels as surrounding frame, in order to get the desired dimensions. Initially, each channel of the plaintext image is regarded as an independent CA, to each of which the XOR filter is applied $K[i]$ times, with $i \in [0, 2]$. Each value of $i$ (i.e. $i = 0$, $i = 1$, and $i = 2$) corresponds to a channel of the plaintext image (i.e. red, green, and blue channel, respectively). The $K[i]$ values are generated via the random number generator proposed in [13] and belongs to $K[i] \in [0, N/2]$.

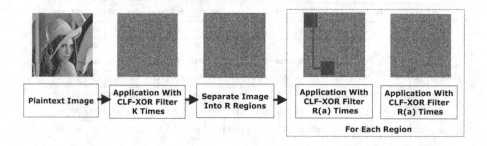

Fig. 3. Image Encryption Process

In the sequence, an integer pseudo-random number $Q$, where $Q \in [4, Y], 2^Y \le N/2$, is generated via the same random number generator. These values define the number of sub-images that the $K[i]$ times filtered plaintext image will be divided to.

Every sub-image is of $N' \times N'$ dimensions, with: $N' = 2^Q - 1$.

Given that MOD $\left(\frac{N}{N'}\right) > 0$, necessarily, some sub-images will overlap. The manner via which the plaintext image is divided may be seen in Figure 4. Note that although $Q > 4$, so that the smallest sub-image possible being of dimensions $15 \times 15$, in the given example the values $N = 8$ and $Q = 2$ are selected for ease of understanding. Hence, the dimensions of each sub-image are $N' \times N' = 3 \times 3$. As may be seen in Figure 4, the top-right and bottom-left sub-images (designated as '3' and '5'), are borrowing pixels from the neighboring sub-images

The image is divided into $R$ sub-images, each of which is regarded as an independent CA, with its boundaries being assumed as pseudo-cells. Actually, when applying the XOR filter to the sub-images' CA, the values of the cells of the neighboring CA participate to the boundary conditions. Consequently, in order to retrieve the content of each CA, no change should occur to the neighboring CA.

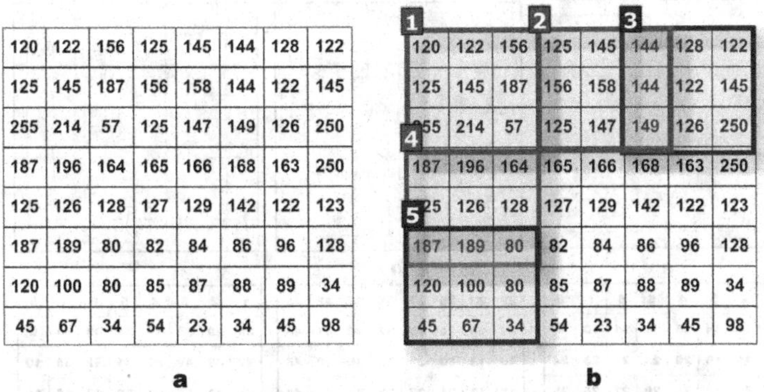

**Fig. 4.** Separating the plaintext Image into Sub Images

At this point, the random number generator generates $R$ values in $[0, 2 \times (N' + 1)]$ which are stored in the array $RA[i], i \in [0, R-1]$, as well as $R$ values in $[0, N/2]$ which are stored in array $RB[i], i \in [0, R-1]$.

Hence, in every sub-image $i$, the XOR filter will be applied $RA[i]$ times. A very important parameter of the proposed method is the ordering in which the sub-images will be filtered. Let for example a grayscale plaintext image $C$ being divided into 4 sub-images $C[i], i \in [0, 3]$ of dimensions $N' \times N'$. Let also every sub-image to be filtered with the filter XOR $RA[i]$ times. Even if $RA[0] = RA[1] = RA[2] = RA[3]$, the result depends on the order in which the sub-images are filtered, because each filtering of every sub-image utilizes information of the current state of the neighboring sub-images. Furthermore, it is worth noting that in order to reconstruct every sub-image, it has to be filtered $(2 \times (N'-1)) - RA[i]$ times, following the opposite order of the initial $RA[i]$ filter applications. For example, when an XOR filter is applied $RA[0]$ times to sub-image $C[0]$, then $RA[1]$ times to $C[1]$, then $RA[2]$ times to $C[2]$ and finally $RA[3]$ times to $C[3]$, in order to reconstruct the sub-images' content, the XOR filter must be applied $(2 \times (N' - 1)) - RA[3]$ times to $C[3]$, then $(2 \times (N' - 1)) - RA[2]$ times to $C[2]$, then $(2 \times (N' - 1)) - RA[1]$ times to $C[1]$, and finally $(2 \times (N' - 1)) - RA[0]$ times to $C[0]$.

The ordering in which the sub-images will be filtered is defined by a random integer generated by the pseudo-random number generator. This number defines which space ordering method [18] will be used. Some common examples of space ordering methods are (a) the raw order, (b) the row prime order, (c) the Mordon order, (d) the Peano Hilbert order, (e) the Cantor diagonal order, (f) the spiral order, (g) the Gray order, (h) the double gray order, (i) the $U$ order, (j) the Z-Order, and so on [17]. Of course, any other ordering method could be utilized, given that it is known to both the sender and the receiver side. An illustration of (a) the Row Prime Order, (b) the Peano Hilbert Order, and (c) the Spiral Order, for 64 sub-images, are presented in Figure 5. Furthermore, Figures 5(d),(e), and (f), present the sub-images filtering ordering if the Raw Prime, the Peano Hilbert, or the Spiral ordering method is applied, respectively.

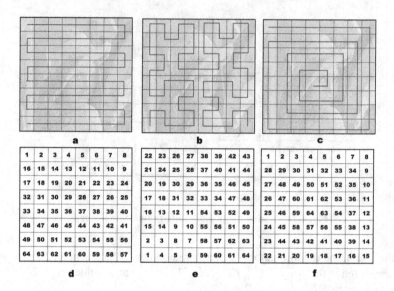

| 1 | 2 | 3 | 4 | 5 | 6 | 7 | 8 |
|---|---|---|---|---|---|---|---|
| 16 | 15 | 14 | 13 | 12 | 11 | 10 | 9 |
| 17 | 18 | 19 | 20 | 21 | 22 | 23 | 24 |
| 32 | 31 | 30 | 29 | 28 | 27 | 26 | 25 |
| 33 | 34 | 35 | 36 | 37 | 38 | 39 | 40 |
| 48 | 47 | 46 | 45 | 44 | 43 | 42 | 41 |
| 49 | 50 | 51 | 52 | 53 | 54 | 55 | 56 |
| 64 | 63 | 62 | 61 | 60 | 59 | 58 | 57 |

d

| 22 | 23 | 26 | 27 | 38 | 39 | 42 | 43 |
|---|---|---|---|---|---|---|---|
| 21 | 24 | 25 | 28 | 37 | 40 | 41 | 44 |
| 20 | 19 | 30 | 29 | 36 | 35 | 46 | 45 |
| 17 | 18 | 31 | 32 | 33 | 34 | 47 | 48 |
| 16 | 13 | 12 | 11 | 54 | 53 | 52 | 49 |
| 15 | 14 | 9 | 10 | 55 | 56 | 51 | 50 |
| 2 | 3 | 8 | 7 | 58 | 57 | 62 | 63 |
| 1 | 4 | 5 | 6 | 59 | 60 | 61 | 64 |

e

| 1 | 2 | 3 | 4 | 5 | 6 | 7 | 8 |
|---|---|---|---|---|---|---|---|
| 28 | 29 | 30 | 31 | 32 | 33 | 34 | 9 |
| 27 | 48 | 49 | 50 | 51 | 52 | 35 | 10 |
| 26 | 47 | 60 | 61 | 62 | 53 | 36 | 11 |
| 25 | 46 | 59 | 64 | 63 | 54 | 37 | 12 |
| 24 | 45 | 58 | 57 | 56 | 55 | 38 | 13 |
| 23 | 44 | 43 | 42 | 41 | 40 | 39 | 14 |
| 22 | 21 | 20 | 19 | 18 | 17 | 16 | 15 |

f

**Fig. 5.** Space Ordering Methods. (a) Row Prime Order, (b) Peano Hilbert Order and (c) Spiral Order

Finally, after the $RA[i]$ filter applications on the $i$ sub-image, the whole image is filtered $RB[i]$ times. This way, the neighboring cells states are even more altered. The procedure is completed when all the sub-images are filtered.

The proposed method can be classified as a symmetric private key security method, meaning that the same key is required for both encryption and decryption; of course, both sender and receiver must know the key. The proposed key for encrypting a single channel image is divided into the following parts. The first part is an integer number $K, K \in [0, N/2]$ which describes the number of XOR filter applications to the plaintext image. The second part describes the size $N'$ of every sub-image, whereas the third part is an integer $F$ designating the utilized space ordering method.

The final part of the key includes $R$ values $RA[i], i \in [0, R-1]$, describing the number of the XOR filter applications to every sub-image, as well as $R$ values $RB[i], i \in [0, R-1]$ for the number of filter applications to the plaintext image, after every sub-image filtering. In case of color images, 3 such keys are required, one for every channel of the image. Note that to increase the encryption security, different values for every part of each key may be selected.

Given that the length of the key alone, may reveal crucial part of the information that an attacker would need to decrypt the image, the key may be modified as follows. Although the number of sub-images equals $R$, the key may include $\frac{N}{15} + 1$ values to the arrays $RA$ and $RB$ (the value 15 corresponds to the smallest sub-image size possible). From all the values in the arrays $RA$ and $RB$, only the first $R$ correspond to the actual times the XOR filter was applied to the sub-images and the plaintext image, whereas the rest of the values are random numbers generated. Thus, for same sized images, the key length is the same irrespectively of the size of the sub-images. The procedure of exchanging the key is not a feature of the proposed method and is omitted.

For decrypting the image, the receiver follows the exact opposite procedure. The first element retrieving from the key is the $N'$ value so that the size of the sub-images is recognized, and subsequently identify which of the $RA$ and $RB$ values included in the key are useful. Then the XOR filter is applied $(N/2 - RB[i])$, $i \in [R, 0]$, times to the encrypted image, and then $(2 \times (N' + 1) - RA[i])$, $i \in [R, 0]$, times to the sub-image that is defined by the ordering method – which is known via the $F$ value of the key. It is crucial to note that during decryption, the inverse ordering of the selected space ordering method is followed. Finally, it should be reminded that the proposed method reconstructs the plaintext image in a lossless manner.

## 4   Statistical Analysis

Initially, the resistance of the method against a brute force attack is evaluated. Brute force attack is a trial and error method in which every possible combination of characters against the encrypted data is tested in an attempt to retrieve the key. Suppose an adversary possesses a cipher image with $N \times N$ dimensions, with $N = 512$. To begin with, a random value $Q \in [4, 8]$, $2^8 \leq 256$ is chosen by the adversary, say $Q = 4$. Thus the adversary assumes that the image is divided into 4 sub-images of dimensions $512/(2^Q - 1) \times 512/(2^Q - 1)$. There are 1225 sub-images in total. Then, for every sub-image $16 \times 2 = 32$ combinations are tested. For the sake of simplicity, suppose that the plaintext image is NOT filtered by $K$ times and that after filtering each sub-image, the entire image is NOT filter $RB$ times. At the beginning, the adversary would apply the filter up to 32 times to every sub-image. In one of those trials the sub-image content would be reconstructed (given that $Q$ is the correct one), and thus the 1/1225 of the image would have been revealed. If no sub-image would have been reconstructed, the adversary would choose a different $Q$. After revealing the first sub-image, the adversary has to unlock the 8 neighboring sub-images identifying the utilized space ordering method as well - with finite complexity. Then, following the inverse ordering, and after only up to 32 iterations per sub-image, the whole image is reconstructed.

By initially filtering the plaintext image $K$ times, it is impossible for the adversary to realize that a sub-image is reconstructed, because its original state is the $K$ times filtered state of the plaintext. Hence the only possible way to reconstruct the content is the following: select randomly a space ordering method and locate the last sub-image and its neighboring 8 sub-images. Adversary's goal would be to test all the possible $RA$ combinations to this neighborhood, and then to each one of these combinations test the $N/2 = 256$ filtering iterations to the whole image. Once more, in this scenario it is supposed that after filtering a sub-image, the whole image is NOT $RB$ times filtered. The complexity in this case is defined as: $256 \times 9^{32} = 8.8 \times 10^{32}$. Of course, the correct space ordering method should have been chosen at first place. Furthermore, note that there is no guaranty that a part of the plain text image is truly revealed even if the $RA$ values of the neighborhood are identified, in case the rest of the sub-images are not reconstructed as well.

By applying the filter $RA$ times to every sub-image, the complexity is intensively increased because it is impossible to isolate a neighborhood of sub-images, due to the fact that the population of the neighborhood changes. Furthermore, given that the whole procedure should be followed for every channel of the image, it is strongly believed that a brute force attack would have no result at reconstructing the plaintext image.

The difference between the plaintext image and the encrypted one is analyzed in the following. To distinguish the difference, the function of peak signal to noise ratio (PSNR) is adopted. Although PSNR is commonly used as a measure of quality of reconstruction of non-lossless encryption methods, it is a very strong tool for describing image distortion as well. PSNR is usually expressed in logarithmic decibel scale. When using 8 bit images the greatest difference between images is calculated at 0 dB, whereas for matching images the value tends to infinity.

To assess the method, the experiment proposed in [2] is conducted for 3 artificially constructed images. Furthermore, the method is applied to 3 real-life images which are well known in the literature. Then, the PSNR between the plaintext and the encrypted images is calculated. The results per channel are presented in Table 1.

**Table 1.** PSNR Values (in dB) for the Encrypted and Random Generated Images

|  | Lena | Lady | Fruits |
|---|---|---|---|
| Random Image 1 (R/G/B) | 6.87/6.98/6.54 | 7.08/6.41/6.91 | 7.24/7.30/6.94 |
| Random Image 2 (R/G/B) | 7.54/7.01/6.75 | 6.24/6.80/6.37 | 6.44/6.11/6.71 |
| Random Image 3 (R/G/B) | 6.42/6.10/6.26 | 6.96/6.37/6.92 | 7.42/7.36/6.81 |
| Encrypted Lena (R/G/B) | 7.78/7.97/7.90 | 7.21/7.45/7.12 | 8.11/8.43/8.52 |
| Encrypted Lady (R/G/B) | 8.89/8.68/8.65 | 8.69/8.33/8.12 | 8.06/8.70/8.27 |
| Encrypted Fruits (R/G/B) | 7.04/7.69/7.58 | 6.91/7.16/6.83 | 7.51/7.22/7.67 |

As may be seen, the PSNR results for the encrypted images and the random generated images are similar. This fact suggests that the encrypted artificially generated images are as distorted as the encrypted real-life images, and do not reveal information about the plaintext image content.

In addition, an important feature of the proposed method is its attribute to deteriorate elements of the encrypted image that would possibly reveal information relative with the nature of the image that was encrypted. The example of Figure 6 is provided for illustration of this fact, where the same key has been applied in order to encrypt a natural image (Lena) Figure 6(a) and a grayscale image depicting a document Figure 6(b). As may be observed, the brightness histograms of these images are quite different. Nevertheless, after the application of the method, the resulting histograms tend to coincide. The experiment was repeated twice for every image whereas some characteristics of the image histograms are presented in Table 2.

Evaluating the results in Table 2, as well as the histograms of the encrypted images, it is easily seen that in both cases the encrypted images tend to coincide. Consequently, it is impossible for an attacker to identify the nature of the image that was encrypted.

Finally, taking into account that the proposed method is based on CA, it is easily realized in hardware. In contrast to the serial computers, the implementation of the method is motivated by parallelism, an inherent feature of CA that contributes to further accelerating the method's operation. CA are perhaps the computational structures best suited for a fully parallel hardware realization [16] [12].

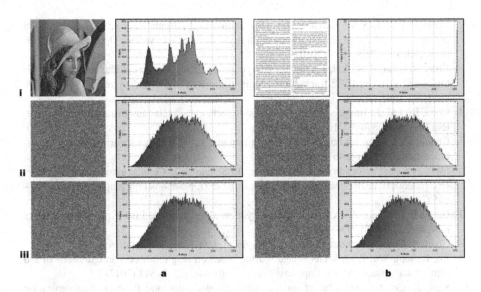

**Fig. 6.** Encrypting a (a) natural and a (b) grayscale image depicting a document using the same key

**Table 2.** Histograms Statistical Characteristics

|                      | Mean   | Median Area | Std. Dev. | Max. Prob |
|----------------------|--------|-------------|-----------|-----------|
| Lena                 | 123.56 | 128         | 47.678    | 154       |
| Encrypted Lena 1     | 127.02 | 127         | 49.444    | 102       |
| Encrypted Lena 2     | 127.22 | 127         | 49.367    | 135       |
| Document             | 228.16 | 250         | 35.414    | 255       |
| Encrypted Document 1 | 127.15 | 127         | 49.241    | 134       |
| Encrypted Document 2 | 127.21 | 127         | 49.347    | 112       |

## 5    Conclusions

This paper presented a visual multimedia content encryption method using the recursive attributes of the XOR filter on cellular automata. The decryption result is a lossless representation of the original encrypted image. Experimental results have shown that the resulted encrypted images do not contain statistical information able to reveal the source from which they originate (i.e. the plaintext image). Moreover, the proposed method appears to be able to withstand brute force attacks. Future work includes further analysis of the security of the method, by using tests such as the known plaintext - cipher text attack etc.

## References

1. Bourbakis, N.G., Alexopoulos, C.: Picture data encryption using scan patterns. Pattern Recognition 25(6), 567–581 (1992)

2. Chatzichristofis, S.A., Mitzias, D.A., Sirakoulis, G.C., Boutalis, Y.S.: A novel cellular automata based technique for visual multimedia content encryption. Optics Communications 283(21), 4250–4260 (2010)
3. Chen, R.J., Lu, W.K., Lai, J.L.: Image encryption using progressive cellular automata substitution and scan. In: IEEE International Symposium on Circuits and Systems, ISCAS 2005, pp. 1690–1693 (2005)
4. Chen, R., Lai, J.: Image security system using recursive cellular automata substitution. Pattern Recognition 40(5), 1621–1631 (2007)
5. Chung, K., Chang, L.: Large encrypting binary images with higher security. Pattern Recognition Letters 19(5-6), 461–468 (1998)
6. Dasgupta, P., Chattopadhyay, S., Chaudhuri, P., Sengupta, I.: Cellular automata-based recursive pseudoexhaustive test pattern generator. IEEE Transactions on Computers 50(2), 177–185 (2001)
7. Gaoand, T., Chen, Z.: A new image encryption algorithm based on hyper-chaos. Physics Letters A 372(4) 21, 394–400 (2008)
8. Guan, P.: Cellular automaton public-key cryptosystem. Complex Systems 1, 51–56 (1987)
9. Jin, J., hong Wu, Z.: A secret image sharing based on neighborhood configurations of 2-d cellular automata. Optics &amp; Laser Technology 44(3), 538–548 (2012)
10. Kari, J.: Cryptosystems based on reversible cellular automata. Personal communication (1992)
11. Koduru, S., Chandrasekaran, V.: Integrated confusion-diffusion mechanisms for chaos based image encryption, pp. 260–263 (2008)
12. Konstantinidis, K., Sirakoulis, G.C., Andreadis, I.: Design and implementation of a fuzzy-modified ant colony hardware structure for image retrieval. IEEE Transactions on Systems, Man, and Cybernetics, Part C 39(5), 520–533 (2009)
13. Kotoulas, L., Tsarouchis, D., Sirakoulis, G., Andreadis, I.: 1-d cellular automaton for pseudorandom number generation and its reconfigurable hardware implementation, p. 4 (2006)
14. Lafe, O.: Data compression and encryption using cellular automata transforms. Engineering Applications of Artificial Intelligence 10(6), 581–592 (1997)
15. Maniccam, S.S., Bourbakis, N.G.: Image and video encryption using scan patterns. Pattern Recognition 37(4), 725–737 (2004)
16. Nalpantidis, L., Sirakoulis, G.C., Gasteratos, A.: A Dense Stereo Correspondence Algorithm for Hardware Implementation with Enhanced Disparity Selection. In: Darzentas, J., Vouros, G.A., Vosinakis, S., Arnellos, A. (eds.) SETN 2008. LNCS (LNAI), vol. 5138, pp. 365–370. Springer, Heidelberg (2008)
17. Poullot, S., Buisson, O., Crucianu, M.: Z-grid-based probabilistic retrieval for scaling up content-based copy detection. In: CIVR, pp. 348–355 (2007)
18. Samet, H.: Foundations of Multidimensional and Metric Data Structur. Diane D. Cerra (2006)
19. Scharinger, J.: Fast encryption of image data using chaotic kolmogorov flows. Electronic Imaging 17(2), 318–325 (1998)
20. Seredynski, F., Bouvry, P., Zomaya, A.: Cellular automata computations and secret key cryptography. Parallel Computing 30(5-6), 753–766 (2004)

# Agent-Based Model to Simulate Groundwater Remediation with Nanoscale Zero Valent Iron

Davide De March[1,3], Alessandro Filisetti[2], Elisabetta Sartorato[1],
and Emanuele Argese[1]

[1] Department of Molecular Sciences and Nanosystems,
Ca' Foscari University of Venice, Dorsoduro 2137, 30121 Venice, Italy
[2] C.I.R.I. - Energy and Environment Alma Mater Studiorum - University of Bologna
via F.lli Rosselli, 107 42123 Reggio Emilia - Italy
[3] EvoSolutions S.r.l., Viale Ancona 17, 30172 Venice, Italy

**Abstract.** Soils, air and water have been deeply contaminated by anthropogenic activities continuously spread over time. One of the most dangerous pollutant in groundwater is represented by chlorinated organic solvents, which acts as a Dense Non Aquifer Phase Liquid (DNAPL) contaminant. Many laboratory experiments have shown that nZVI encapsulated into micelles could treat DNAPL pollution directly into the groundwater but very few in situ experimentations have been tested. Agent-Based Model (ABM) is a powerful tool to simulate and to gain better insights in complex systems. In this paper we present an ABM simulation of DNAPL contaminated groundwater remediation. The model simulates a dehalogenation process of Trichloroethylene (TCE) with the application of encapsulated nZVI, directly injected into the DNAPL contaminant source.

## 1 Introduction

The chlorinated organic solvents (Trichloroethylene, Tetrachloroethylene) are very common contaminants of groundwater and aquifers. Chlorinate solvents are very low soluble and more dense than water, and when released in groundwater they do not dissolved but become Dense Non Acquifer Phase Liquid (DNAPL). However, some DNAPL components are slowly and continuously released into groundwater, creating a persistent source of contamination that could last for ages. Conventional techniques to remediate contaminated groundwater are "Pump and Treat" [1] and "Permeable Reactive Barrier" (PRB)[8] but they are very inefficient when treating DNAPL. In fact, these techniques are able to remediate only a very small part of DNAPL (i.e the soluble part of the pollutant) and, in the case of PRB, the source of contamination is not directly treated. Moreover, the remediation of a DNAPL contaminated groundwater needs unsustainable time and costs.

In the last few years, a very promising technique for this kind of contamination seems to be the nano-scale Zero Valent Iron (nZVI) suspension for the reductive dehalogenation of chlorinated organic solvents. The use of colloidal suspension of nano-particles of iron allows the treatment of the DNAPL in aquifer, reaching

G.C. Sirakoulis and S. Bandini (Eds.): ACRI 2012, LNCS 7495, pp. 351–359, 2012.

also deeper contaminated areas and directly reacting into the source of contamination or into dissolved contaminant of the plume. Unfortunately, this technique has to face some problems when applied for in situ remediation. In particular, due to their high specific surface area and, consequently, their remarkably high reactivity, nano-particles tend to form bigger aggregates of micrometers size, giving a dimensional instability. In addition, the nano-particles tend to interact with non target compounds, such as nitrate, perchlorate and heavy metal, reducing their efficiency in treating the target. Therefore, it is necessary to create a formulation of nZVI able to optimise the mobility, the stability and the reactivity of the nano-particles.

The encapsulated nZVI (EZVI) into artificial membranes, obtained with the emulsification of oil and sulfactant, represents a very good compromise among stability, selectivity and reactivity [4]. The surfactant surrounds the nanoparticles, forming very small colloidal droplets. This particular emulsifier has many advantages among which to be miscible in DNAPL, to protect nZVI from other non target compounds and to enhance the mobility of the membranes. In the last few years many laboratory experimentations have shown good results in the reductive dehalogenation of chlorinated organic solvents with encapsulated nZVI, but large information gaps currently exist about their behaviour in environmental condition such as in situ remediation. A very useful tool to study in situ remediation is the application of models which are able to characterise the environment of the contaminated area and simulate possible remediation scenarios [11].

The choice of an agent-based description turns to be useful in order to simulate the reaction within different environments. In classical chemistry solver tools the simulation of different environments is a difficult tasks. Conversely, modelling the system by means of the characteristics of single entities allows to deal with different environments, e.g. different soil compositions, by changing only few proprieties, in terms of composition, boundaries and shape, of the environment where molecules react.

In this work we present an agent-based model (ABM) to study the evolution of the reductive dehalogenation of a DNAPL, composed of trichloroethylene (TCE), treated with emulsified nZVI. The paper aims to combine the information obtained from laboratory experimentations with a simulation of possible groundwater contaminated scenarios. We present, in Sect. 2, the chemical experimentation of a degradation of TCE, treated with nZVI and Palladium (Pd); in Sect. 3 we present an agent-based model, simulating the *in vitro* experimentation of the reductive dehalogenation of TCE treated with nano-particles of Fe and Pd and in Sect. 4 the application of the ABM to simulate a DNAPL remediation of a scenario of a contaminated area. Conclusion will follow in Sect. 5.

## 2    Chemical Experimentation of Trichloroethylene Remediation

The experimentation is set up in a chemical laboratory of Ca' Foscari University. We study the dechlorination of the TCE in water solution, adding nZVI with Pd, in proportion of $0.1\% \, Mol/Fe$, which enhances the reactivity and functionality of Fe and consequently accelerates the rate of the reaction kinetics [3,7,14]. The concentration of pollutant is set to $900 \, mg/L$ in a water solution where $10 \, g/L$ of Fe/Pd are dissolved. The reductive dechlorination of TCE by nZVI follows the pseudo-first-order reaction kinetic governed by Eq. 1 since the concentration of nZVI is almost 30 times the concentration of TCE and it could be considered as a constant.

$$\frac{C_t}{C_0} = e^{-k_{obs} \cdot t}, \tag{1}$$

where $C_0$ is the concentration of TCE ($900 \, mg/L$) at time 0 and $C_t$ is the concentration of the pollutant at time $t$. Experimental samples are taken every 5 minutes in the first hour and every 30 minutes up to the $5^{\text{th}}$ hour and the concentration of TCE is recorded, as shown in Fig. 1.

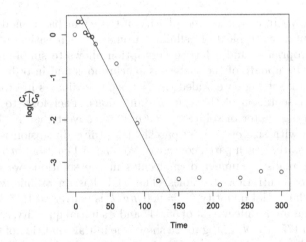

**Fig. 1.** Dechlorination kinetics of $900 \, mg/L$ of TCE in water solution with $10 \, g/L$ of Fe with 0.1% moles of Pd. The plot shows the logarithm of the concentration ratio of the pollutant at time $t$ and at $t = 0$ versus time

The reaction rate, $k_{obs}$, is calculated by a linear regression in the time interval from 10 to 120 minutes, when maximum reductive dechlorination happens. We show in Table 1 that nZVI is significant (p-value $\ll 0.001$) and the slope of

**Table 1.** Summary of the linear regression model of degradation of trichloroethylene in water solution with nZVI

|        | Coef     | SE    | T-Value | P-Value  |
|--------|----------|-------|---------|----------|
| nZVI   | -0.03227 | 0.001 | -23.06  | 2.58 e-09 |
| $R^2 = 0.98$ | | | | |

the regression is negative with a value equal to $0.0323\,min^{-1}$. The regression coefficient of determination $R^2 = 0.98$ shows the goodness of the model.

The laboratory experiment shows an effective performance of nZVI for reductive dehalogenation of trichloroethylene.

## 3   The Agent-Based Model Approach to Simulate Reductive Dehalogenation of Trichloroethylene

According to the experimental settings, we initially recreate the reaction of TCE reductive dehalogenation with Fe/Pd, in order to validate our model. The reaction is simulated with Netlogo 5.0 [15] starting from the model presented by Stieff and Wilensky[12]. NetLogo is an agent-based integrated modeling framework with two principle types of agents that are turtles (that move around in "the virtual world") and patches (square pieces of "ground" over which turtles can move).

NetLogo allows to couple the peculiarity of the agent-based models with the spatial configurations typical of cellular automata. Each entity in the system has its own proprieties and a lattice description allows to simply describe the interactions. The update of the system is synchronous and in order to recreate the experimental settings, we scaled the Netlogo coordinates in order to create a realistic representation of the system dimensions. Therefore, to represent a beaker containing a liter of solution ( $1\,dm^3$) we convert the "Netlogo world" to a 2D world with size of $20 \times 50$ patches (the third dimension is considered equal to unit) so that each patch contains a volume of $1\,cm^3 = 1\,mL$ of solution. To simulate a realistic number of molecules in the solutions we convert the experimental concentrations to moles. The TCE has an atomic weight equal to 131.79, so the initial quantity $C_0 = 900\,mg/L$ is converted to $6.83\,mMol/L$. Similarly, Fe has an atomic weight of 55.847 and its initial quantity, set to $10\,g/L$, is converted to $179\,mMol/L$. Figure 2a shows the initial condition of the solution characterised by an average concentration of $6830\,\mu M/L$ of pollutant (green coloured turtles) and of $179000\,\mu M/L$ of nZVI (red coloured turtles). Because the real experiment is performed in an well-stirred solution, we consider a random walk of length 1 patch for each turtle as a plausible diffusion movement in the beaker. The reaction time is calculated according to Eq. 1 with the reaction rate set to $k_{obs} = 0.0322\,min^{-1}$ (as calculated in the laboratory experimentation). Mimicking the dechlorination reaction of TCE due to nZVI we assume that the reaction of one particle of pollutant with one particle of nZVI creates a new product (i.e. Ethene, blu coloured in Fig. 2b) by transforming the reaction compounds [5,6].

The simulation runs until all the pollutant molecules are remediated and we observed that the degradation kinetics of the TCE, in Fig. 3, matches reasonably well the behaviour of the real experimentation. The initial settings of the laboratory test is not suitable for in situ remediation; in fact, in field experimentation we expect that pollutant and reactant do not largely differs in concentration and for that reason we cannot assume that the reaction in a contaminated

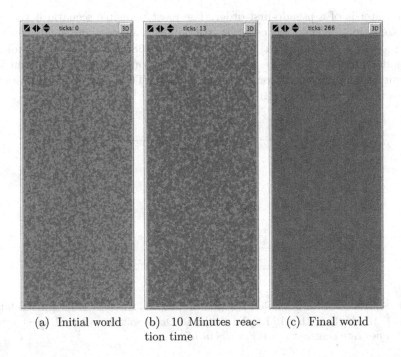

(a)  Initial world       (b)  10 Minutes reac-       (c)  Final world
                         tion time

**Fig. 2.** Simulation of the reaction of TCE in 1 Liter of water solution with Fe/Pd. In panel 2a the initial conditions of the system are represented. Red turtles stand for Fe and and green turtles stand for the pollutant molecules. In panel 2c the state of the system at the end of the simulation is represented. It is possible to observe that all pollutants have been converted into non toxic compounds such as Ethene [13] . Panel 2b shows the state of the system after a time of 10 Minutes.

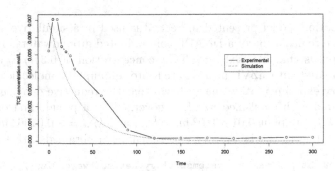

**Fig. 3.** simulation of degradation kinetics of 0.06 $Mol/L$ of TCE in water solution with 0.179 $Mol/L$ Fe with 0.1% of Pd with a fixed degradation constant $k = 0.03\,min^{-1}$. Solid line represents contaminant concentration of the real experimentation, and dotted line represents the simulation of the reaction with ABM

groundwater is of a pseudo-first-order. The most plausible scenario is that the dehalogenation follows a second-order reaction with a second order rate constant calculated as $K_s = K_{obs}/[Fe] = 0.03/0.179 = 0.168\, Mol \cdot min^{-1}$. We validate the model simulating a more realistic concentration of both contaminant and reactant, setting an equal concentration of both TCE and nZVI. Results are then compared with Dizzy [10] software[1].

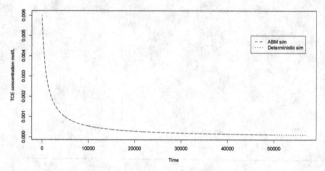

**Fig. 4.** Simulation of degradation reaction of $0.06\, Mol/L$ of TCE in water solution with $0.06\, Mol/L$ Fe with ABM (solid line) and Dizzy software (dotted lines) with a second order rate constant $k = 0.168\, Mol\, min^{-1}$

The agent-based model is able to recreate a second-order reaction of reductive dehalogenation of TCE when treated with nZVI and this model is applied in a large scale simulation of a DNAPL groundwater contaminated area.

## 4    The Study of a Dense Non Aqueous Phase Liquid (DNAPL) Contaminated Groundwater

The dechlornation model presented in Sect. 3 is used in a simulative study to investigate the remediation of a DNAPL contaminated groundwaters. The contaminated area is characterised by a TCE concentration of $6.3\, \mu g/L$ and the DNAPL is treated with nZVI, incapsulated into amphiphilic molecules. Previous laboratory experimentations have shown that the reductive dehalogenation of TCE, treated with emulsified nZVI, is governed by a pseudo-first-order kinetic with a $k_{obs}$ of about $0.01 - 0.03\, min^{-1}$ [2] and $k_{obs} = -0.01064\, min^{-1}$ is selected, according to the laboratory experimentation obtained with the same

---

[1] Available at http://magnet.systemsbiology.net/software/Dizzy/. Although Dizzy is actually developed to perform stochastic simulations, it provides also a useful tool for the simulation of deterministic systems. Once that the reactions scheme has been created, the user has the possibility to choose which kind of simulation performs. With regard to these analysis we adopted a finite difference method ODE solver, specifically the 5th-order Runge-Kutta algorithm with an adaptive stepsize controller.

settings presented in Sect. 2. Hence, we assume to use the same reaction model, presented in Sect. 3, to simulate a second-order reaction with a rate constant equal to $K_s = K_{obs}/[Fe] = 0.0106/0.179 = 0.0594\,Mol \cdot min^{-1}$. We assume that a slurry of encapsulated nZVI is injected into the contaminated area with a concentration equal to the pollutant to be treated. The groundwater horizontal hydraulic conductivity $(K_x)$ is estimated to be $1.2\,m \cdot day^{-1}$ and the contaminant area is limited into a small area. In accordance with these assumptions we set our simulator as a Netlogo world with size $100 \times 10$ patches, representing an area of $10^3\,m^3$ (the third dimension is set equal to unit).

Therefore, each patch represents $1\,m^3$ of soil. Following the same conversion used in Sect. 3, the concentration of TCE in the DNAPL is $4.79 * 10^{-2}\,\mu Mol/L$ and the simulation unit becomes $47.9\,\mu Mol/patches$. The contaminated area is simulated to be on the top-left of the represented scenario with a size of $10 \times 5 = 50$ patches (gray coloured in Fig. 5a), and the soil is considered with a 30% porosity. $47.9 \times 50 \approx 2500\,\mu Mol$ of pollutants are randomly added to the contaminated area. We, then, introduce the nZVI through a injection pump in the middle of the DNAPL with the same concentration of TCE, an initial pressure is simulated to distribute the reactant into the contaminated soil. The

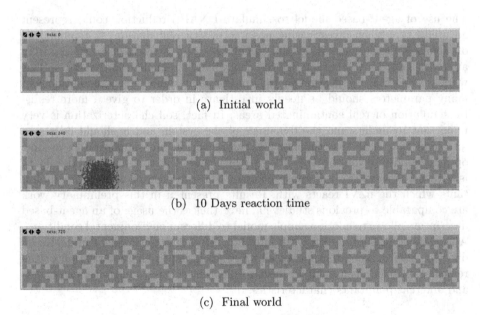

(a) Initial world

(b) 10 Days reaction time

(c) Final world

**Fig. 5.** Simulation of degradation of a Dense Non Acqueus Phase Liquid contaminated area: Panel 5a represents the initial condition where pollutant (green coloured) is spread into the DNAPL and nZVI incapsulates (red coloured) is injected in a column into the DNAPL. Panel 5b shows the movement of the DNAPL into the porous soil after 10 days and the products (blue coloured) originated by the dechlorination reaction. Panel 5c shows the simulation after 30 days where all the contaminants, nZVI and products are deposited on the bottom of the groundwater

agent movement is due to two forces, the horizontal hydraulic conductivity ($K_x$) and the infiltration conductivity ($K_y$), so that the direction ($\alpha$) of the movement is calculated as:

$$\alpha = \arctan \frac{K_x}{K_y} \tag{2}$$

Each step of the simulation ("tick" in Netlogo vocabulary) is defined as one hour and consequently $K_x = 1.2/24 = 5*10^{-2} m \cdot h^{-1}$; the infiltration conductivity, $K_y$, is set half of the horizontal hydraulic conductivity. The simulation runs for one month and the evolution of the DNAPL reduction is evaluated. Figure 5b shows the movement of the DNAPL after 10 days of simulation and a reduction of TCE and the formation of new products (blue coloured) due to the dechlorination reaction with nZVi emulsified with oil and surfactant is observed. The concentration of pollutant after 10 days is reduced of about 50%. At the end of the simulation (after 30 days in Fig. 5c) DNAPL reaches the bottom of the groundwater and the dechlorination of the TCE is almost 90%.

## 5    Conclusion

The use of agent-based model to simulate DNAPL reduction could represent an useful tool when investigating possible in situ remediation. A combination of laboratory experimentations and simulative models seems to be a promising approach in order to characterise the contaminant remediation dynamics. This work is an initial application in the contaminant remediation simulation and many parameters should be deeply investigate in order to give a more realistic simulation of real contaminated areas. In fact, soil characterization is very important to understand the dynamics of the system and it should be tested into some pilot scale experimentations. Moreover, in this simulation we assume optimal condition for the DNAPL in which only one contaminant, the TCE, is present; conversely, it is quite common the presence of many other pollutants which the nZVI reacts with. Results presented in this preliminary work are comparable to previous studies [9], nevertheless the usage of an agent-based description allows to adapt a simple model to different environmental conditions. Although we present here only an initial investigation, our model can deal with different environmental scenarios allowing an in-depth characterisation of the remediation phenomena with respect to different soils, groundwater conditions and different pollutants characteristics.

**Acknowledgement.** We would thank prof. Roberto Serra, prof. Marco Villani and Prof. Irene Poli for their helpful comments and suggestion.

## References

1. Bayer, P., Finkel, M.: Life Cycle Assessment of Active and Passive Groundwater Remediation Technologies. Journal of Contaminant Hydrology 83, 171–199 (2006)

2. Bezbaruah, A., Shanbhogue, S., Simsek, S., Khan, E.: Encapsulation of iron nanoparticles in alginate biopolymer for trichloroethylene remediation. Journal of Nanoparticle Research 13(12), 6673–6681 (2011)
3. Cho, Y., Choi, S.-I.: Degradation of PCE, TCE and 1,1,1-TCA by nanosized FePd bimetallic particles under various experimental conditions. Chemosphere 80, 940–945 (2010)
4. Kanel, S.R., Choi, H.: Transport characteristics of surface-modified nanoscale zerovalent iron in porous media. Water Science & Technology 55(1-2), 157–162 (2007)
5. Lin, C.J., Lo, S.L., Liou, Y.H.: Dechlorination of trichloroethylene in aqueous solution by noble metal-modified iron. Journal of Hazardous Materials 116(3), 219–228 (2004)
6. Liu, Y., Majetich, S.A., Tilton, R.D., Sholl, D.S., Lowry, G.V.: TCE Dechlorination Rates, Pathways, and Efficiency of Nanoscale Iron Particles with Different Properties. Environmental Science & Technology 39, 1338–1345 (2005)
7. Lowry, G.V., Reinhard, M.: Pd-catalyzed TCE dechlorination in water: effect of [H2] (aq) and H2-utilizing competitive solutes on the TCE dechlorination rate and product distribution. Environ. Sci. Technol. 35, 696–702 (2001)
8. Powell, R.M., Puls, R.W., Blowes, D.W., Vogan, J.L., Gillham Guelph, R.W., Powell, P.D., Schultz, D., Sivavec, T., Landis, R.: Permeable Reactive Barrier Technologies for Contaminant Remediation, US Environmental Protection Agency, Technical Information Office, Washington, DC. USEPA/600/R-98/125 (September 1998)
9. Quinn, J., Geiger, C., Clausen, C., Brooks, K., Coon, C., O'Hara, S., Krug, T., Major, D., Yoon, W., Gavaskar, A., Holdsworth, A.: Field Demonstration of DNAPL Dehalogenation Using Emulsified Zero-Valent Iron. Environmental Science & Technology 39(5), 1309–1318 (2005)
10. Ramsey, S., Orrell, D., Bolouri, H.: Dizzy: stochastic simulation of large-scale genetic regulatory networks. Journal of Bioinformatics and Computational Biology 3(2), 415–436 (2005)
11. Di Gregorio, S., Serra, R., Villani, M.: Applying cellular automata to complex environmental problems: The simulation of the bioremediation of contaminated soils. Theoretical Computer Science 217, 131–156 (1999)
12. Stieff, M., Wilensky, U.: NetLogo Enzyme Kinetics model. Center for Connected Learning and Computer-Based Modeling. Northwestern University, Evanston, IL (2001), http://ccl.northwestern.edu/netlogo/models/EnzymeKinetics
13. Zhang, W.-x.: Nanoscale iron particles for environmental remediation: An overview. Journal of Nanoparticle Research 5, 323–332 (2003)
14. Wei, J., Xu, X., Liu, Y., Wang, D.: Catalytic hydrodechlorination of 2,4-dichlorophenol over nanoscale Pd/Fe: reaction pathway and some experimental parameters. WaterRes. 40, 348–354 (2006)
15. Wilensky, U.: NetLogo. Center for Connected Learning and Computer-Based Modeling. Northwestern University, Evanston (1999), http://ccl.northwestern.edu/netlogo/

# Theory and Application of Restricted Five Neighborhood Cellular Automata (R5NCA) for Protein Structure Prediction

Soumyabrata Ghosh, Nirmalya S. Maiti, and Parimal Pal Chaudhuri

Cellular Automata Research Lab (CARL), CARLBio Pvt. Ltd. and Alumnus Software Ltd.
Saltlake City, Kolkata – 700091, India
soumya@carlbio.com

**Abstract.** This paper reports the theory of a special class of Cellular Automata (CA) referred to as Restricted 5 Neighborhood CA (R5NCA). Its application deals with identification of Protein Structure. Each amino acid of a protein chain is modeled with a R5NCA rule. In the process, a protein gets modeled as a R5NCA. CA Evolution models the evolution of the protein to its minimum energy folded configuration. The physical domain parameters are next mapped to CA model parameters from the analysis of known structural data available in Protein Data Base (PDB). The process of reverse mapping is implemented to identify the structure of a protein in blind test from its model parameters. The CA model achieves close to 99% correct prediction for secondary structure prediction, while for tertiary structure prediction, the average RMSD (Root Mean Square Deviation) value has been found to 1.82.

**Keywords:** Protein Structure, Amino Acid, CA Model, R5NCA, Protein modeling Cellular Automata Machine (PCAM).

## 1    Introduction

Proteins are the most vital bio-molecules of any living organism. Knowledge of structure and function of target proteins are the prerequisite for drug design. In the post–genomic era, large-scale sequencing projects have generated an abundance of protein sequence data. However, experimental determination of a protein structure from its sequence is labor intensive, time consuming and expensive. As a result, the gap between the number of protein sequences and the number of proteins with experimentally determined structure is growing rapidly. To overcome this problem, a large number of model based structure prediction methods have evolved over the past decade.

A linear chain of amino acids of a protein gets folded to a minimum energy 3D structure that determines its function. Protein structure prediction problem [1] demands investigation of  the local and global interaction of electrostatic forces among the atoms of different  amino acids; it  results in a highly complex folding relationship due to multi-body interaction [2], [3], [5]. The low resolution model is applied

G.C. Sirakoulis and S. Bandini (Eds.): ACRI 2012, LNCS 7495, pp. 360–369, 2012.

within a hierarchical ab initio approach [4]. Structure prediction procedures have been also studied extensively [6], [7]. De novo or model based prediction of protein structure has the inherent advantages - fast, unbound, and no need for physical sample. However, the associated disadvantage is the low confidence level of the user community on such prediction results.

In this background, this paper reports a model having following distinctive feature. Rather than energy minimization, the model is designed to process information modeling physical entities. The physico-chemical properties of an Amino Acid molecule is represented in Section 3 as a 32 bit pattern of a 5 neighborhood CA rule. This section also covers   a special class of CA referred to as R5NCA (Restricted 5 Neighborhood CA)   modeling the function of tRNA molecule employed for amino acid synthesis out of a codon  - a triplet of four nucleotide bases A, U, C, G. The PCAM (Protein modeling CA Machine) is presented in Section 4. PCAM evolution to its attractor basin (Fig 1) models the minimum energy 3D folded configuration of a protein chain. Preliminaries of three neighborhood CA rule employed for modeling codon is presented in next section. Detailed analysis of codon modeling is beyond the scope of the current paper.

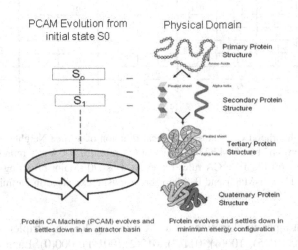

**Fig. 1.** PCAM evolution modeling folding of protein chain to minimum energy configuration

## 2     Preliminaries of Three Neighborhood CA Rules

A three neighborhood CA is shown in Fig 2(a) along with the structure of a cell storing binary state 0 or 1. It is marked as $i^{th}$ cell while its left and right neighbors are denoted as $(i - 1)^{th}$ and $(i + 1)^{th}$ cell respectively. Consequently, 8 ($2^3$) combinations exist for the triplet of current state values $< a_{i-1} \, a_i \, a_{i+1} >$ of $(i - 1)^{th}$, $i^{th}$ and $(i + 1)^{th}$ cells. The next state function of a cell is shown in Fig 2(b). It specifies how the cell evolves in the next time step. The decimal value of the 8 bits of cell next state is referred to as 'Rule' of evolution of a CA cell. There are $2^8 = 256$ such rules for a three neighborhood cell.

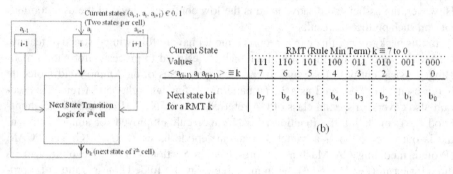

(b)

(a)

| CA Rule | 1-Major RMT | | | | 0-Major RMT | | | | (N1,N0) | δ |
|---------|---|---|---|---|---|---|---|---|---------|---|
| | 7 | 6 | 5 | 3 | 4 | 2 | 1 | 0 | | |
| | 111 | 110 | 101 | 011 | 100 | 010 | 001 | 000 | | |
| [90] | 0 | 1 | 0 | 1 | 1 | 0 | 1 | 0 | (2,2) | 0 |
| [150] | 1 | 0 | 0 | 0 | 1 | 1 | 1. | 0 | (1,3) | 0 |
| [60] | 0 | 0 | 1 | 1 | 1 | 1 | 0 | 0 | (2,2) | 2 |
| [45] | 0 | 0 | 1 | 1 | 0 | 1 | 0 | 1 | (2,2) | 1 |
| [101] | 0 | 1 | 1 | 0 | 0 | 1 | 0 | 1 | (2,2) | 1 |

(c)

**Fig. 2.** Three Neighborhood CA Rules - (a) Local function of a three Neighborhood CA Cell defining 8 bit pattern <b7 b6 b5 b4 b3 b2 b1 b0> of CA rule; (b) A CA rule represents the Rule of Evaluation (RE), (c) Example CA rules represented as 1/0 -Major bit strings; (N1, N0, δ) denote number of 1's in 1-Major and 0- Major bit strings, δ explained in Definition 5 (of the text)

Eight different input combinations of a CA rule (Fig 2(b)) is a triplet of binary bits – 111(7), 110(6), 101(5), 100(4), 011(3), 010(2), 001(1), 000(0). Each combination represents the current state of $(i - 1)^{th}$, $i^{th}$, and $(i + 1)^{th}$ cells which can be viewed as three binary variables. We refer to the combinations of three input variables as Rule Min Terms (RMTs) [9] referred to by its decimal value that varies from 0 to 7. First row of Fig 2(b) displays all the RMTs $k$ ($k = 0$ to 7), while the second row shows the cell next as $b_k$ ($b_k = 0$ or 1) for RMT $k$.

**Definition 1(a): Rule Min Term (RMT), 1-Major and 0-Major RMTs** - Out of 8 RMTS, the binary string of each of the 4 RMTs (7, 6, 5, 3) has two 1's, while RMTs (0, 1, 2, 4) has two 0's. The RMTS are classified as 1-Major and 0-Major RMTs respectively. The 4 bit string corresponding to next state values of 1-Major and 0-Major RMTs are denoted as $< b_7 b_6 b_5 b_3>$ and $< b_4 b_2 b_1 b_0>$ respectively.

Fig 2(c) reports a few rules expressed as 1-Major and 0-Major bit strings. Fourth row shows the 8 bit pattern $< b_7\, b_6\, b_5\, b_4\, b_3\, b_2\, b_1\, b_0 >$ of Rule 45(0010, 1101) rearranged as per the next state values of 1-Major and 0-Major RMTs.

**Definition 1(b): Balanced Rule (BR)** – A rule with four 1's and four 0's is referred to as Balance Rule.

**Definition 2: Balanced RMTs (BRMTs)** - A RMT for which left and right neighbor have identical value. The RMTs 7(111) and 5(101) are the 1-Major BRMTs while 0(000) and 2(010) are the 0-Major BRMTs.

**Definition 3: $N_1$, $N_0$ values of a rule (Fig. 2(c))** - Number of 1's in 1-Major, 0-Major bit strings.

**Definition 4: Transformation TR1** – The transformation TR1 on a rule $R_x$ interchanges the left and right neighbors of a cell to generate its equivalent rule $R_y$. In the process – (i) the RMT 6(110) and 3(011) gets interchanged with corresponding interchange of $b_6$ and $b_3$; and (ii) RMT 4(100) and 1(001) gets interchanged with interchange of $b_4$ and $b_1$. $(R_x, R_y)$ is an equivalent rule pair under TR1. Rule 45 (0011,0101) and 101(0110,0101) (Shown in Fig. 2(c)) is a equivalent rule pair under TR1.

**Definition 5: Critical Pair (CP), $\delta$** – The RMT pairs (6,3) and (4,1) are referred to as 'Critical Pairs' (CPs) in the sense that if $b_6 = b_3$ and $b_4 = b_1$, the rule remains unaltered under transformation TR1. If the next state value of CP differs for one or both, a rule generates its equivalent rule under TR1. The parameter $\delta$ characterizes CP - it specifies the number of CPs where next state bit for RMTs of a CP differs (Fig 2 (c)).

A set of 64 BRs models 64 codons – the 16 rule groups, each covering four equivalent rules, model the (16 x 4) codon table.

# 3    Five Neighborhood CA Rules Modeling Amino Acids

Development of an efficient model demands appropriate mapping of physical parameters to the model parameters. The physical  parameters of an amino acid are - (a) uniform back bone (BB) consisting 9 atoms divided into three functional groups (FGs) – $NH_3$, $C_\alpha H$, COO-; (b) Side Chain of varying size – 1 to 18 atoms, a subset of atoms associated with a FG of side chain; (c) Polar or Non-polar, (i) if Polar, Charged or Uncharged, and (ii) if charged, (+)ive or (–)ive; (d) number of hydrogen atoms H and non-hydrogen atoms (carbon, nitrogen, oxygen, sulpher) referred to as H´; and (e) covalent bonds between a pair of atoms. Mapping of all these physical parameters of an amino acid requires a 32 bit information pattern. Based on this guiding factor coupled with the analysis of the physical process of amino acid synthesis out of a codon (modeled with the 8 bit pattern of three neighborhood CA rule), an amino acid has been modeled with the 32 bit pattern of a five neighborhood CA rule.

## 3.1    Five Neighborhood CA Rule

Fig 3(a) shows the structure of a five neighborhood CA cell. RMT of a five neighborhood CA cell is a five bit vector. The current state bits of $(i-2)^{th}$, $(i-1)^{th}$, $i^{th}$, $(i+1)^{th}$, $(i+2)^{th}$ cells are noted as $k = < a_{(i-2)}\, a_{(i-1)}\, a_i\, a_{(i+1)}\, a_{(i+2)} >$; the next state bit of $i^{th}$ cell is noted as $b_k$ for RMT $k$. Each RMT is analyzed with reference to $i^{th}$ cell. Two of its left neighbors are $(i-2)^{th}$, $(i-1)^{th}$ cells and right neighbors are $(i+1)^{th}$, $(i+2)^{th}$ cells. Fig 3(b) displays the 32 bit pattern representing a 5 neighborhood CA rule. There are 32 RMTs $k$ $(k = 0(00000)$ to $1111(31))$ and $2^{32}$ rules for a 5 neighborhood CA cell. RMTs that do not undergo any modification on interchanging two left and right neighbors are referred to as BRMT (Balanced RMT Defn. 2). The RMT pair where one is derived out of other on interchanging two left and right neighbors is referred to as CP (Critical Pair – Defn. 5). The symbol $\delta$ denotes the number of CPs. The 32 bit patterns of 5 Neighborhood CA rules are analyzed with the procedure similar to the one adopted to analyze 3 neighborhood CA rules.

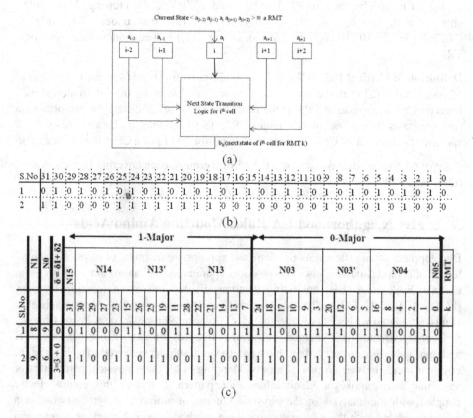

**Fig. 3.** Five neighborhood CA rules - (a) Local function of a 5 Neighborhood CA cell; (b) Two rules of a 5 Neighborhood CA Rule, (c) 5 Neighborhood CA rules (of Fig 3(b)) presented as 1-major and 0-Major next state bits and 4 subgroups of 1/0 –Major strings along with parameters $N1$, $N0$, $\delta = \delta1 + \delta0$;

**Definition 6:** $\delta_1$, $\delta_0 - \delta$ for a 5 neighborhood CA rule is defined as $\delta = \delta_1 + \delta_0$, where $\delta_1$ and $\delta_0$ are derived out of 1-Major and 0-Major RMT groups.

The 32 bit pattern of a CA rule, as shown in Fig 3(c), can be divided into next state bit strings of 1/0 major RMTs. Each group of RMTs is divided into 4 subgroups (Fig 3(c)).

**Definition 7(a): 1-Major RMT Group and its Sub-groups** – **(I)** $N_{15}$ - RMT 31(11111) has five 1's; **(II)** $N_{14}$ - RMT group with four 1's - two CPs (Defn. 7) - (i) 15(01111), 30(11110)), and (ii) 23(10111), 29(11101)) and the BRMT 27(11011); **(III)** $N_{13}$'- RMT group with three 1's and $a_i = 0$- two CPs (11(01011), 26(11010)) and 19(10011), 25(11001); **(IV)** $N_{13}$ - RMT group with three 1's and $a_i = 1$- two CPS (7(00111), 28(11100)) and (13(01101), 22(10110)) and two BRMTs 14 (01110) and 21(10101).

**Definition 7(b): 0-Major RMT Group and its Sub-groups** - **(I)** $N_{05}$ – RMT 0(00000) with five 0's- it is a BRMT; **(II)** $N_{04}$ – RMTs with four 0's: two CPs (1(00001), 16(10000)) and (2(00010), 8(01000)), and one BRMT 4; **(III)** $N_{03}$' – RMTs with three 0's and $a_i = 1$- Two CPs (5(00101), 20(10100)) and (6(00110), (12(01100); **(IV)** $N_{03}$ – RMTs with three 0's and $a_i = 0$ - two CPs (3(00011), 24(11000)), and (9(01001), 18(10010)) and two BRMTs 10(01010) and 17(10001).

Fig 4 displays mapping of two amino acids to two 32 bit parameters of 5 neighborhood CA rules - RMT assigned to an atom is shown adjacent to it. For example, in the case of amino acid Valine, RMTs 19 and 12 are assigned to $C_\alpha$ carbon and H atom covalently bonded.

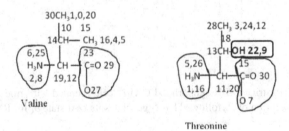

**Fig. 4.** Mapping of two amino acids to two 32 bit parameters of 5 neighborhood CA rules

In order to model the physical process of amino acid synthesis out of a codon, rather than conventional 5 neighborhood CA, a special class of CA referred to as Restricted 5 Neighborhood CA (R5NCA) is employed for generating 32 bit patterns modeling amino acids.

### 3.2    Restricted Five Neighborhood CA (R5NCA) Rules

Next state value of a CA cell for a conventional five neighborhood CA rule is evaluated in one step. For a R5NCA cell (Fig 5), the next state of $i^{th}$ cell (referred to as $b_k$

for RMT $k$) is evaluated in two steps. The rule $R$ for a R5NCA cell is represented as $<R_0\ R_1>$ - the first rule $R_0$ is employed on current states $< a_{(i-1)},\ a_i,\ a_{(i+1)} >$ of $(i-1)^{th}$, $i^{th}$, and $(i+1)^{th}$ cells to generate the Intermediate Next State (INS) of $i^{th}$ cell. Next, rule $R_1$ is employed on $< a_{(i-2)},\ INS,\ a_{(i+2)} >$ to derive the next state $b_k$ of $i^{th}$ cell for RMT $k$ . Both the rules $R_0$ and $R_1$ are 3 neighborhood CA rules. Its application to model tRNA function follows.

## 3.3     R5NCA Rule $<R_0\ R_1>$ Modeling tRNA Function

A tRNA molecule has two functions: (i) It recognizes a codon CN by its anticodon CN' through codon-anticodon pairing; and (ii) it translates CN' to link it up with the amino acid specified for the codon CN. Function of a tRNA molecule is modeled with a R5NCA rule $<R_0\ R_1>$, $R_0$ models the anticodon CN' while $R_1$ translates CN' to a 32 bit pattern identical to  that of the amino acid rule modeling its   physical and chemical parameters reported in Section 3.1. Derivation of the rule $R_0$  of anticodon CN' out of three neighborhood balanced rule of the codon CN follows the function of Watson-Creek and Wobble pairing [8].

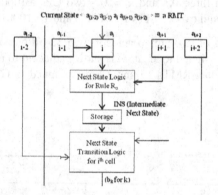

**Fig. 5.** A R5NCA (Restricted 5 Neighborhood CA) $i^{th}$ cell operated with rule $R = < R_0, R_1 >$ Note : sequential execution of $R_0$ followed by $R_1$ generates its next state $b_k$ for RMT $k = <a_{i-2}\ a_{i-1}\ a_i\ a_{i+1}\ a_{i+2}>$

# 4     PCAM (Protein Modeling CA Machine ) with R5NCA

Given the chain of n amino acids of a protein primary structure, the Rule Vector (RV) $< R_0\ R_1-----R_i------R_{(n-1)}>$ of the CA modeling the protein is derived by replacing $i^{th}$ amino acid in the chain with the R5NCA rule $R_i$, where $R_i = <R_{i0}\ R_{i1}>$, $i = 0,1,2-----$ (n-1). The CA is operated with an n bit initial state (0 for non-polar and 1 for polar amino acid) in successive time steps till it reaches an attractor basin covering a set of states the CA cycles (Fig 1). CA evolution is analyzed by four primary parameters - Static Region (SR), Dynamic Region (DR), Height (H) and Cycle Length (CL) defined next.

**Height (H)** – specifies the time step at which the cell enters in a cycle; **Cycle Length** – a CA cell enters in a cycle of specified length after elapse of H time steps of evolution; **Dynamic Region (DR)** – a region of adjacent cells where each cell runs through a cycle of specified length; **Static Region (SR)** – a Region of cycle length 1 is referred to as Static Region. CA operates till it reaches an attractor basin generating the Model Parameters (MPs) defined next.

**Definition 8: Model Parameters (MP)** – First parameter MP1 covers four factors – (i) Height (H); (ii) Cycle Length (CL); (iii) Number of times a RMT appears and number of transitions from different RMTs to the RMT during the run from the initial state to its first cyclic state. MP1 reflects the local parameters of a CA cell derived out of its evolution. The second parameter MP2 covers SR and DR locations and their width.

While MP1 captures the environment an amino acid is subjected to, the parameter MP2 captures the characteristics specific to the protein chain. It has been observed that a large number of CA model parameters converge to a unique bit pattern. This confirms the general belief that two amino acids under two different environments may behave in an identical fashion, and conversely an amino acid in two different environments may behave in a totally different way so far as the folded protein structure is concerned.

## 4.1    Mapping Physical Domain Parameters to CA Model Parameters

The Mapping Function (MF), in general, follows the following algorithmic steps. It maps a physical domain parameter (noted as Hidden State - HS) to Model Parameters MP1 and MP2. The MF is designed for a node that covers structurally relative proteins derived using PSI-BLAST tool.

**Algorithm Map (Design of Mapping Function MF)**
Input: A set of structurally equivalent proteins covered by a node derived out of Protein Data Base (PDB) and Hidden State (HS) values collected from PDB
Output: The MFI and MFII for the node expressed as Mapping Tables to map the HS values to MP1 and MP2 (Defn. 8).
Step 1: Derive the R5NCA for each protein in the node and execute Step 2.
Step 2: Run the CA and derive MP1 and MP2.
Step 3: For each of the 20 amino acids, note the MP1 and MP2 parameter and list the Hidden States (the physical domain parameter) associated with an amino acid in different proteins of the node.
Step 4: Output the mapping tables for MFI and MFII for Mapping of Hidden States (HSs)  to MP1 and MP2. Stop.

## 4.2    Prediction of Secondary Structure

As noted in Section 4.1, the MFI and MFII, derived out of a structurally relative node, are used for reverse mapping to identify the structure of target protein sequences. The

HSs for this case are Helices (H), Strands (E), Coiled (C) and Unstructured (U). The MFI generated 96% unique entries in the sense that - for average 96% entries of model parameters MP1, there is a single HS entry and so in 96% cases the prediction is correct. For remaining 4% cases there are more than one HS entry. On inclusion of both MFI and MFII the number of multiple entries comes down confirming correct prediction for average 98% for blind test of 1867 proteins from PDB database.

## 4.3    Tertiary Structure Prediction Scheme

Tertiary structure prediction scheme employs a Transform to represent the 3D coordinate value of $C_\alpha$ atom of each amino acid backbone. The Transform generates 4 parameters $d_1, d_2, d_3$, and $\alpha$ angle for alpha carbon atom as shown in Fig 6. Distances $d_1, d_2, d_3$ are the linear distances from $C_{\alpha(i)}$ to $C_{\alpha(i-1)}, C_{\alpha(i-2)}, C_{\alpha(i-3)}$ respectively. While, $\alpha$ angle is the dihedral angle between planes P1($C_{\alpha(i)}, C_{\alpha(i-1)}, C_{\alpha(i-2)}$) and P2 ($C_{\alpha(i-1)}, C_{\alpha(i-2)}, C_{\alpha(i-3)}$), where the intersection between P1, P2 goes through points $C_{\alpha(i-1)}$ and $C_{\alpha(i-2)}$.

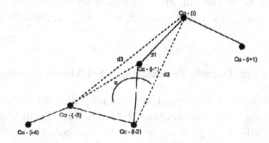

**Fig. 6.** Chain of Protein Backbone $C_\alpha$ showing $d_1, d_2, d_3$, and $\alpha$ angle

Thus the 3D coordinate values ($x_i, y_i, z_i$) of the alpha carbon atom of $i^{th}$ amino acid is represented as ($d_1^i, d_2^i, d_3^i, \alpha^i$). Here, the Hidden State (HS) is the vector $<d_1^i\ d_2^i\ d_3^i\ \alpha^i>$ of $i^{th}$ amino acid. The mapping functions MFI and MFII are generated as per Algorithm Map noted earlier. The following algorithmic steps are executed to predict tertiary structure of a protein. Sample results are reported in Table 1.

**Algorithm Predict 3D Structure**
Input: The chain of n amino acids of the protein – its 3D structure to be determined
Output: The ($x_i, y_i, z_i$) coordinates of the $C_\alpha$ carbon of $i^{th}$ amino acid, ($i = 0,1,2, …$ $(n-1)$)
Step 1: A set of structurally equivalent proteins covered by a node is derived out of Protein Data Base (PDB).
Step 2: Derive R5NCA for each protein of the node. Operate the CA to derive MP1 and MP2 (Defn. 8) for the CA model.
Step 3: Derive the R5NCA for the candidate protein and extract its model parameters.
Step 4: Identify the HS from reverse mapping of MFI and MFII.

Step 4: Generate 3D coordinates for alpha carbon of each amino acid from the HS vector $< d_1, d_2, d_3, \alpha >$ with reverse transform. Stop.

**Table 1.** Quality of Tertiary Structure Prediction. Root Mean Square Deviation (RMSD) of five candidate protein chains are shown. Lesser RMSD signifies better prediction

| PDB ID | CHAIN ID | Length | RMSD of Prediction |
|--------|----------|--------|--------------------|
| 1AOH   | A        | 147    | 0.98               |
| 1G1K   | B        | 143    | 1.67               |
| 1HR7   | E        | 475    | 2.21               |
| 1ANU   | A        | 138    | 1.89               |
| 2CCL   | C        | 158    | 2.10               |
| 2VN5   | C        | 151    | 1.69               |
| 3BQ1   | A        | 354    | 2.19               |
| 3P0D   | B        | 187    | 1.90               |

## 5     Conclusion

This paper presents a de novo CA model for predicting protein structures. PCAM ( Protein modeling CA Machine) evolution models the protein primary chain evolution to the minimum energy 3D folded structure. The results are being compiled for blind test of a protein listed in PDB employing the processing power of   Dual Core 3.5 GHz.

## References

1. Yue, K., Dill, K.A.: Sequence-structure relationships in proteins and copolymers. Phys. Rev. E 48, 2267–2278 (1993)
2. Lamont, G.B., Merkie, L.D.: Toward effective polypeptide chain prediction with parallel fast messy genetic algorithms. In: Fogel, G., Corne, D. (eds.) Evolutionary Computation in Bioinformatics, pp. 137–161 (2004)
3. Dill, K.A., Bromberg, S., Yue, K., Fiebig, K.M., Yee, D.P., Thomas, P.D., Chan, H.S.: Principles of protein folding – A perspective from simple exact models. Protein Science 4, 561–602 (1995)
4. Xia, Y., Huang, E.S., Levitt, M., Samudrala, R.: *Ab Initio* Construction of Protein Tertiary Structures using a Hierarchical Approach. J. Mol. Biol. 300, 171–185 (2000)
5. Bradley, P., Misura, K.M., Baker, D.: Toward high-resolution *de novo* structure prediction for small proteins. Science 309(5742), 1868–1871 (2005)
6. Rohl, C.A., Baker, D.: *De novo* determination of protein backbone structure from residual dipolar couplings using Rosetta. J. Am. Chem. Soc. 124(11), 2723–2729 (2002)
7. Combet, C., Jambon, M., Deleage, G., Geourjon, C.: Geno3D: automatic comparative molecular modelling of protein. Bioinformatics 18, 213–214 (2002)
8. Mizuno, H., Sundaralingam, M.: Stacking of Crick Wobble pair and Watson-Crick pair: stability rules of G-U pairs at ends of helical stems in tRNAs and the relation to codon-anticodon Wobble interaction. Nucl. Acids Res. 5(11), 4451–4462 (1978)
9. Maiti, N.S., Ghosh, S., Munshi, S., Pal Chaudhuri, P.: Linear Time Algorithm to Identify Invertibility of Null-Boundary Three Neighborhood Cellular Automata. Complex Systems 19(1), 89–113 (2011)

# Multi Agent-Based Simulation on Technology Diffusion of China

Gu Gaoxiang[1], Wang Zheng[1,2,*], and Wu Jing[1]

[1] Institute of Policy and Management Science,
Chinese Academy of Sciences, Beijing, 100080, China
[2] Key Laboratory of Geographical Information Science, Ministry of State Education of China;
East China Normal University, Shanghai 200062, China
caesarggx@163.com, wangzheng@casipm.ac.cn, wujing@casipm.ac.cn

**Abstract.** Technology plays an important role on the regional competitiveness. In this paper, we built a regional technology diffusion model based on MABS considering agents similar to irregular Cellular Automata model. The results show that under the impact of heterogeneous traffic lines, the traditional center-hinterland diffusion mode has been no longer fit. In reality technology diffusion mode complies with a hub-net structure. Traffic condition plays an important role in regional technology improvement. A preferential tax policy can be conductive to the improvement of the local technology level.

**Keywords:** MABS, Bottom-up, Technology diffusion, Policy.

## 1 Introduction

Nowadays technology plays a more and more important role on the regional competitiveness. Although social economy of China has gained a great advance, the economy development is unbalanced. Comparing the traditional 4 regions, the East has a dominated position in both technology level and economy. Therefore, it has extremely significance to research into technology diffusion mode and spatial structure in China.

In this paper, we bring agent-based simulation theory and try to simulate the trend and structure of regional economy development in China in microcosmic view. Agent-based simulation is an important approach in the field of complex system analysis and simulation. Its key idea is the Complex Adaptive System (CAS) theory which was presented by John Holland [1]. The key assumption of ABS approach is that social phenomena result from local interactions of agents Gilbert N and Troitzsch K.G [3]. As a step forward the idea of simulation agents that behave as irregular Cellular Automata is presented, Therefore, the development and evolution of social economy in macro-level as well as its trends can be given by observing the "emerging" activities of micro individuals Schilloa M  Funka P and Rovatsosb M [2].

ABS has been widely used in social science and economy simulation. The development of ABS is one of two linked reason for the major growth of the use of simulation in the social science. Zhang [4] proposed an ABS model to study the formation of high-tech

---

* Corresponding author.

G.C. Sirakoulis and S. Bandini (Eds.): ACRI 2012, LNCS 7495, pp. 370–374, 2012.

industrial clusters such as Silicon Valley. Xue L and Weng J [5] integrated economic deductive model with ABS theories for the study on the evolutional process of metropolitan commerce. Ligtenberg [6] explored how to use ABS to simulate spatial scenarios based on modeling multi-actor decision-making within a spatial planning process.

## 2    The Model

### 2.1    The Assumptions and Regulation Design of the Model

We assume that in an economic system, there are plenty of spatial notes which represent settlements like towns or cities. We use CA cells to represent those spatial notes, and, moreover, separate them into different groups. Accordingly, we abstract a complex system which is formed by CA cells with different neighborhood and an external market environment [7].

1. In this paper, 362 prefecture-level cities and autonomous prefectures in China are defined as agents. Because the map is formed by agents and every agent presents a piece of land, our model corresponds to an irregular CA model.
2. We adopt timing simulation in the model, while the 0 period is defined as the initial stage. In the 0 period, all agents are alive. One period denotes a production cycle taking a single quarter   in the real world
3. Labors will decide whether to move or not after comparing the wage rates, degree of resident crowdedness and the index of roughness and remoteness between the city he lives and the ones around it.
4. The technologies will diffuse along with the process of labor's movement.

### 2.2    The Weight of Road between Regions

The space damping coefficient $\beta = \sqrt{2T/t_{max}D}$ , where $T$ denotes the time interval from one migration to the next and $D$ is the scale of interactive regions. The space damping coefficient can be dropped by reducing the time interval between two migrations.

In the real world, the roads are divided into different kinds. We assume roads have different weights because of their different regulation speeds and load capacities.   In this paper, we assume that the road network is only formed by railways classified as "normal railway", "electrified railway" and "high-speed railway". We define the weight $w_i=\mathbf{max}(t)/t_i$, where $t_i$ means the average time spent on 1 km road $i$. Hence, the weight of the route from region $i$ to region $j$ can be given by:

$$\beta_{i,j} = \sqrt{2T/t_{max}D \cdot w_{i,j}} \tag{1}$$

### 2.3    The Behavior Design of Agent

**The Movement of Labor.** In this model, labor can move from one region to another along the routs among regions. The impetus of labor's movement and migration from one region to another is affected by various facts. We assume that the gap of wages, the density of human population, the distance and the difference of regional roughness are the impact factors of labor's movement. We use Wilson model [8, 9] to denote the labor attractiveness $TP_{ij}$ impacted by region $j$ on region $i$.

$$TP_{ij} = AL_i w_j \exp((ef_i - ef_j) - \beta_{ij} D_{ij}) \tag{2}$$

where $w_j$ denotes the wage of region $j$, $D_{ij}$ denotes the distance between region $i$ and region $j$, $P_i$ denotes the population of region $i$, $ef_i$ denotes the roughness of region $i$. We assume the labor moving from region $i$ to region $j$ is:

$$m_{i,j} = P_i \frac{TP_{i,j}}{\sum_i \sum_j TP_{i,j}} \quad i \neq j \tag{3}$$

**The Diffusion of Technology.** A diffusion of technology can be brought by the movement of labor. We assume that well educated labors transmit technology when they move from that region to another. The tech-level $h_{j,t}$ is determined by the number of emigration, the number of immigration, its own tech-level and tech-level of immigration.

$$h_{j,t} = \frac{\sum_i m_{ij} h_{i,t-1} + (P_{j,t-1} - \sum_j m_{ij}) \cdot h_{j,t-1}}{P_{j,t-1} - \sum_j m_{ij} + \sum_i m_{ij}} \tag{4}$$

where $\sum_i m_{ij}$ denotes the immigration number, $\sum_j m_{ij}$ denotes the emigration number, $P_{j,t-1}$ denotes the population of agent $j$ in the last period

The tech-level of an agent can be reverted after the progress of labor movement by education. If an agent is successful in the reverting progress of tech-level, its tech-level in period $t$ can be given by

$$he_t = \min(he_{t-1} + \kappa, he_0) \tag{5}$$

where $\kappa$ is the quantity of tech-level improvement in one period.

## 3    Agent-Based Simulation

### 3.1    The Impact of Different Geo-Structures on the Tech-Diffusion Process

For analyzing the impact of spatial structure on the tech-diffusion, we set two scenes. In Scene 1, we assume that the traffic network is formed by homogeneous road. That means all the weights of road equal 1. In Scene 2, we use the traffic network introduced in Section 2.2, assigning different weights for different kinds of roads. We set the "normal railway" has a weight equaling 1, the "electrified railway" has a weight equaling 1.8 and the "high-speed railway" has a weight equaling 2.7 based on real world. Through agent-based simulation, we obtain the outcomes as follow.

Figure 1 depicts the tech-level distribution of Scene1 and Scene 2. We can see that high-level technology diffuses from center cities to surrounding ones in Scene1. In period 100, the extent of Beijing diffusion cycle is enlarged, as well as the Yangtze River Delta diffusion cycle. Regions located between that two cycles receive larger number of tech-diffusion, producing a dense high tech-level belt. The technology gap between the common regions on the belt and the core cities is narrowed. From period 100 to period 200, technologies diffuse from high-tech belt to Middle, West and Southeast regions. Thus, a double-core center-hinterland structure for technology diffusion has been formed in Scene1.

The diffusion mode is obviously different in Scene2. Regions located on the arterial roads receive larger number of high-level technologies. In period 100, the technology gap between cities beside the arterial roads and other common ones are obvious, forming high-tech belts. From period 100, technologies begin to diffuse from arterial roads to cities along the branch roads. In period 200, the tech-level gap between center cities and cities beside the arterial roads are narrowed. The tech-level of initial center cities are almost similar with cities around them. In conclusion, technologies diffuse from one region to another along with traffic lines and a hub-net tech-diffusion mode emerges in Scene2.

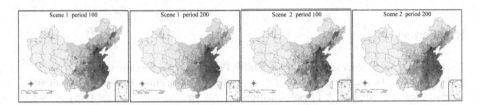

**Fig. 1.** Tech-diffusion distribution in Scene 1 and Scene 2

## 3.2    The Impact of Preferential Tax Policy on the Tech-Diffusion Process

From Figure 6 and Figure 7 we can see that northeast district has a slower speed for technology improving in both Scene 1 and Scene 2. We set Scene 3 implementing a 50% preferential tax rate for the business income tax and individual income tax, while in Scene 2, the tax rate equals 20%. Conclusions can be obtained by comparing the outcomes of Scene 3 and Scene2. We only show a part of directs in Figure 3.

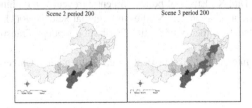

**Fig. 2.** Tech-diffusion distribution of northeast district in Scene 2 and Scene 3

We can see the tech-level of Northeast has been improved obviously with a preferential tax. In period 200, a high-tech belt along with the arterial road from Beijing to Dalian has been built up. At the same time, technologies also diffuse from high-tech belt to regions around them. It indicates the preferential tax policy holds a remarkable implication for labor's movement. Labors having higher technology begin to choose the northeast regions as their preference partly, result in an improvement of tech-level in Northeast.

## 4    Conclusion

In this paper, we build a regional economy model based on multi-agent based simulation theory. We proposed design a movement mode of labor based on Wilson model. Based on this, we present a mode of technology diffusion accompanied by the movement of labor. By using scenarios simulation, we gain conclusions as follows: The outcomes indicate that the center-hinterland diffusion mode has been no longer fit for the real world. In reality, it is a hub-net structure which technology diffusion complies with. It shows that traffic condition plays an important role in regional development. Finally, the attraction for high-tech labors of the northeast district can be improved by a preferential tax policy, which can be conductive to the improvement of the local technology level and encourage economic development consequently.

## References

1. Holland, J.: Emergence: From Chaos to Order. Perseus Books, Reading (1998)
2. Schilloa, M., Funka, P., Rovatsosb, M.: Using trust for detecting deceitful agents in artificial societies. Applied Artificial Intelligence: An International Journal 14(8), 825–848 (2000)
3. Gilbert, N., Troitzsch, K.G.: Simulation for the Social Scientist. Open University Press, New York (2005)
4. Zhang, J.F.: Growing Silicon Valley on a Landscape: an Agent-based Ap-proach to High-tech Industrial Clusters. Journal of Evolutionary Economics 13, 193–197 (2003)
5. Xue, L., Weng, J.: Dynamic Simulation on Spatial Structure of Metropolitan Commerce Based on Monopolistic Competition Model. Acta Geographica Sinica 65(8), 938–948 (2010)
6. Ligtenberg, A., Wachowicz, M., Bregt, A.K., Beulens, A., Kettenis, D.L.: A de-sign and application of a multi-agent system for simulation of multi-actor spatial planning. Journal of Environmental Management 72(1-2), 43–56 (2004)
7. Wang, Z., Liu, T., Dai, X.: Effect of policy and entrepreneurship on innovation and growth: an agent-based simulation approach. Studies in Regional Science 40(1), 19–26 (2010)
8. Wilson, A.G.: A statistical theory of spatial distribution models. Transportation Research 1, 253–267 (1967)
9. Wang, Z: Spatial interaction: A statistical mechanism model. Chinese Geography 10(3), 279–284 (2000)

# An Edge Preserving Image Resizing Method
# Based on Cellular Automata

Konstantinos Ioannidis, Ioannis Andreadis, and Georgios Ch. Sirakoulis

Department of Electrical and Computer Engineering,
Democritus University of Thrace, Xanthi, Greece
{kioannid,iandread,gsirak}@ee.duth.gr

**Abstract.** This paper introduces a novel image resizing method for both color and grayscale images. The method could be beneficial in applications where time and quality of the processed images are crucial. The basic idea of the proposed method relies on preserving the edges by partitioning the digital images into homogenous and edge areas during the enlargement process. In addition, the basic fundamentals of Cellular Automata were adopted in order to achieve better performance both in terms of processing time as well as in image quality. By creating appropriate transition rules, the direction of the edges is considered so that every unknown pixel is processed based on its neighbors in order to preserve the quality of the edges. Results demonstrate that the proposed method improves the subjective quality of the enlarged images over conventional resizing methods while keeping the required processing time in low levels.

**Keywords:** Image resizing, Color/Grayscale image enlargement, Edge-oriented method, Cellular automata.

## 1    Introduction

The main objective of the image resizing methods is to generate a high resolution image from its lower resolution version. Digital images and video sequences result in large amount of image data. Efficient manipulation of these types of data in systems with limited technical specifications is a significant issue in their overall performance. Image interpolation techniques are the most commonly adopted methods for image enlargement. Nevertheless, conventional linear interpolation schemes based on space-invariant models fail to preserve the quality of the edges and consequently produce resized images with blurred edges or annoying zigzag artifacts.

Several commonly used interpolation methods have been suggested for image resizing, such as nearest neighbor interpolation [1], bilinear interpolation [1], bicubic interpolation [2] and spline interpolation [3]. Linear approaches are the most frequently applied for the resizing process due to their low computational burden. However, those methods produces image artifacts like blurring on edges since no information related to abrupt changes of pixel values is considered. On the contrary, nonlinear methods produce better results; nevertheless, they appear larger computational burden and involve blurring, as well. Various generic approaches have been proposed to

G.C. Sirakoulis and S. Bandini (Eds.): ACRI 2012, LNCS 7495, pp. 375–384, 2012.
© Springer-Verlag Berlin Heidelberg 2012

improve the subjective quality of the interpolated images and overcome such deficiencies. In addition, the method in [4] is based on variation models with smoothing and orientation constraints. The nonlinear Partial Differential Equation (PDE) problem is simplified into a series of problems with explicit solutions. Furthermore, the area based interpolation scheme in [5] computes each interpolated pixel by proportional area coverage of a filtering window which is applied to the input image. A quadratic image interpolation method [6] has been proposed with adequate visual results nonetheless its computational cost remains in high levels. Finally, a method to estimate the model parameters piecewisely is proposed in [7] using an autoregressive image model. The method utilizes the covariance matrix of the high resolution image itself, with missing pixels properly initialized.

An alternative type of approaches has been introduced, namely edge-directed interpolation methods, in order to preserve the edges of the low resolution image and produce crisper results. Edge-directed interpolation methods apply a variety of operators according to the edge directions [8]. A fuzzy interpolation approach was proposed in [9] for two dimensional signal resampling, however, additional processing for edge identification is required. In addition, a neural network approach has been proposed in [10] to approximate the computational rules of interpolation algorithms for learning statistical inter-pixel correlation of interpolated images. The method in [11] comprises a hybrid artificial intelligence system. A fuzzy decision system was proposed to classify all the pixels of the input image into human perception nonsensitive class and sensitive class. The bilinear interpolation is applied to the nonsensitive regions while a neural network was used to interpolate the sensitive regions along the edges. Furthermore, the method proposed in [12] initially estimates local covariance coefficients from a low resolution image. These covariance estimates are used to adapt the interpolation at a higher resolution based on the geometric duality between the low-resolution and the high-resolution covariance. Despite the visually accurate resulted images, the above edge directed approaches show high levels of computational cost and thus, their application in real-time systems is restricted. In order to achieve frame rates close to real time limits while enhancing the quality of the edges, an edge-oriented method was proposed in [13]. The main idea is to discriminate the image into homogenous areas and edge areas, which are processed using different interpolation methods. The method achieves real-time image enlargement, nevertheless, the classification of the areas depends on a predefined threshold as well as two stages of process are required. Finally, Shi et al. in [14] initially expand the low resolution image using a bilinear interpolation method and a Canny edge detector [15] is applied to identify the edges of the upscaled image. The final pixel values are calculated by applying some refinement functions. Despite the satisfactory visual results and the high frame rates, the inaccuracies inserted by the initial bilinear enlargement lead to blurred edges and thus, the Canny edge detector is unable to detect significant edges.

In this paper, we introduce an edge-directed method which exploits the simplicity and the inherent parallelism of Cellular Automata [16]. Cellular automata are decentralized space-time systems where interactions are local and can be used to model physical systems. In addition, they consist of identical rectangular cells which results to a regular grid in one or more dimensions. Each cell can be marked with a finite number of states at each evolution step, which are updated synchronously according to a specified transition rule set and the states of its adjacent cells. Due to its finite nature, the cells belonging to the borders of the grid are updated based on the defined boundary conditions, i.e. periodic, fixed or reflection. Cellular automata are extensively used in a variety of applications including numerous image processing methods. In the past, they were exploited to perform pattern reconstruction tasks [17], border detection [18] and noise filtering [19]. In the proposed method, a Cellular automaton (CA) was applied to increase the resolution of digital images. The edges of a low resolution image are initially determined by applying the Canny edge detector leading to a bitwise edge map. This map is then considered as a cell grid along with a cell state which corresponds to the undefined pixel values. The CA evolves its state by applying the appropriate transition rules, which were constructed based on the orientation of the edges. Finally, a simple remapping of each cell state to pixel value is applied, which is based on the weighted summation of the adjacent pixel values. The method manages to preserve the initial edges adequately while achieving high frame rates in both color and in grayscale images. In order to evaluate the performance of the proposed method, a quantitative comparison with other related methods was applied proving its effectiveness.

The rest of the paper is organized as follows. In Section 2, the proposed method is analyzed while in Section 3, the experimental results are provided. Conclusions are drawn in Section 4.

## 2    Proposed Method

The proposed method aims at calculating the unknown pixel values, which are produced by the resizing process. The basic concept of the method is to initially classify the pixels of the initial image into two categories: homogenous areas and edge areas. The method exploits the capability of the Canny edge detector to accurately determine the edges of the image. Since the bitwise edge map is produced, the logical array is enlarged and is considered as a CA lattice. The unknown cells update their state according to the proposed transition rules. Finally, a simple transformation is applied to calculate the unknown pixel values based on the state of each CA cell. For color images, the above procedure is applied to each of the RGB vector separately. The overall process of the method is illustrated in Fig. 1.

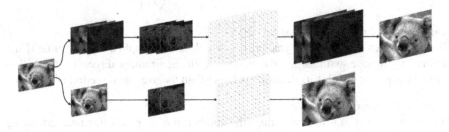

**Fig. 1.** Proposed CA based image resizing method

## 2.1 Edge Detection

The first stage of the method is the application of an edge detection technique in order to discriminate the homogeneous areas from the edge areas. Thus, any method reported in the literature could be applied. However, most of the methods which produce more accurate edges display higher computational burden. Therefore, their application in real-time systems is not permissible. In order to produce accurate edge maps with high frame rates, the Canny edge detector was incorporated. The most significant criteria of this selection are as follows:

- Correct detection: edges are detected with high probability when these exist in the real images.
- Accurate localization: marked edges are accurately close to the edges in the real images.
- Minimal response: a defined edge is detected only once, and where possible, noise should not create false edges.

The Canny edge detector is actually an optimal technique of edge detection and creation and its application relies on the criteria above: correct detection, accurate localization and minimal response. To satisfy these requirements, a technique which finds the function, which optimizes a given functional was used, namely the calculus of variations. The method produces binary edge maps by applying sequentially the following processing stages:

**Stage 1:** Filtering the image
The image is initially filtered using a 2D Gaussian filter of zero mean value and a predefined standard deviation $\sigma$ in order to eliminate possible noise. The result is a slightly blurred version of the original image.

**Stage 2:** Defining the intensity gradient of the filtered image
At this stage, elementary edge detection operators, like Sobel, are used in order to define the first derivative both in the horizontal and the vertical direction. Thus, the gradient and direction of each pixel are defined by the following equations:

$$E_g = \sqrt{I_{Gx}^2 + I_{Gy}^2}, \ E_d = \arctan\left(\frac{I_{Gy}}{I_{Gx}}\right) \tag{1}$$

**Stage 3:** Non maximum suppression
Given estimates of the image gradients, a search is then applied to determine if the gradient magnitude assumes a local maximum in the gradient direction. A pixel is defined as an edge pixel if its direction is larger than the average direction of its area.

**Stage 4:** Hysteresis thresholding
The last stage intends to further reduce the number of edge pixels that resulted during the above stages. For this purpose, two thresholds are used. The process starts by applying a high threshold and by using the directional information; edges can be

traced through the image. While an edge is traced, the lower threshold is applied in order to trace faint sections of edges. The most frequent value for the high threshold is considered to be related to the highest value of the gradient magnitude of the image while the low threshold is usually equal to *0.4\*(high threshold)*.

Once the process is completed, a binary image is produced where each pixel is marked as either an edge pixel or a non-edge pixel. Essentially, a new image with the same dimensions is produced representing the edges of the initial image.

## 2.2    CA Resizing

Motivated by the binary nature of the calculated edge maps, a CA is proposed to define the state of the additional cells that resulted after the resizing process and eventually the pixel values Without loss of generality, it is assumed that the high resolution edge map $Y_{i,j}$ of size $2(M \times N)$ directly comes from size $M \times N$. Thus, it yields $Y_{2i,2j} = X_{i,j}$. Fig. 2 gives a schematic illustration of the resulted enlarged edge map.

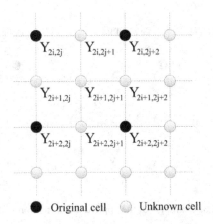

**Fig. 2.** Edge map after the enlargement

The enlarged edge map is considered to be a *2D* lattice of cells where every binary pixel is represented by a cell. Thus, the proposed CA grid has the same dimensions with the enlarged image. Moreover, in order to update the state of each cell, Moore neighborhood is applied. In addition, the set of states must be defined. Since the enlarged edge map includes non-edge cells (stated as "0"), edge cells (stated as "1") and undefined cells, we assume that the undefined cells are marked with the state "2". In concluding, the cells of the CA before its evolution can be marked with three states: "0" (non-edge cell), "1" (edge cell) and "2" (undefined cell). Taking advantage of the cellular automata flexibility, the transition rules as well as the states of the cells after the evolution are created in order to preserve the edges. The basic motive is to create states that eventually will produce crisper transitions of pixel values from non-edge pixels to edge pixels during the remapping process. By using such states, the orientation of each edge is considered. For example, based on the lattice of Fig. 2, let us assume that the cell $Y_{2i,2j}$ is marked as non-edge while the cell $Y_{2i,2j+2}$ is an edge cell. The intermediate cell $Y_{2i,2j+1}$ must be evolved to a cell that will produce a pixel value, which is closer to the value of the edge pixel and less close to the non-edge pixel. In addition, if no cell in its immediate neighbor is marked as a non-edge cell, its next state must correspond to a pixel value which leads to a homogenous area. It must be mentioned that all non-edge and edge cells of the enlarged map are surrounded by eight unknown cells and, after the evolution, they are marked with states which leads to equal pixel values with the corresponding pixels of the low resolution image. In addition, every cell stated as "2" appears either two (horizontal or vertical cells indexed as $Y_{2i,2j+1}$ and $Y_{2i+1,2j}$, respectively) or four cells (central cell indexed as $Y_{2i+1,2j+1}$) with known states in its Moore neighborhood, which will eventually designate the next state. The total number of the used states and the constructed transition rules is 24 therefore, each cell is marked with one discrete number between the range of [0,23] after the evolution of the CA. Finally, null boundary conditions are used in order to evolve the state of the frontier cells. Fig. 3 represents simple cases of the above rationality.

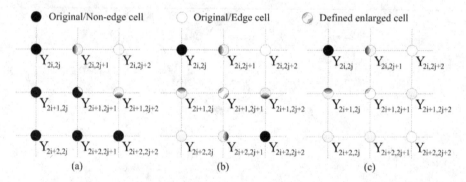

**Fig. 3.** Examples of the applied CA transition rules

## 2.3   Remapping Process

At this stage of the process, every pixel value of the resized image is defined based on the state of the corresponding cell. Let us consider that $f_{i,j}$ and $F_{2i,2j}$ corresponds to the low resolution image and the high resolution image, respectively. At the previous stage, cells indexed by $(2i,2j)$ were marked with states that simply apply the following: $F_{2i,2j} = f_{i,j}$. On the contrary, in order to keep computational cost in low levels, pixels with the indices $(2i,2j+1)$, $(2i+1,2j)$ and $(2i+1,2j+1)$ are expressed as a weighted summation of their adjacent pixel values of the low resolution image. Thus, for the remapping process of these pixels, the following expressions are introduced:

$$F_{2i,2j+1} = a_1 * f_{i,j} + a_2 * f_{i,j+1} \tag{2}$$

$$F_{2i+1,2j} = b_1 * f_{i,j} + b_2 * f_{i+1,j} \tag{3}$$

$$F_{2i+1,2j+1} = c_1 * f_{i,j} + c_2 * f_{i,j+1} + c_3 * f_{i+1,j} + c_4 * f_{i+1,j+1} \tag{4}$$

where $a_k$ and $b_k$, $k = 1,2$, corresponds to the applied weights for the $F_{2i,2j+1}$ (horizontal) and $F_{2i+1,2j}$ (vertical) pixel values of the high resolution image, respectively, while $c_m$, $m = 1,..4$, depicts the weights applied for the central pixel $F_{2i+1,2j+1}$.

Each of the above weights is defined based on the state of the corresponding cell of the CA grid. In addition, the summation of each of the factors $a_k, b_k$ and $c_k$ must be equal to one. For example, assuming that cell $(2i,2j)$ is defined as a non-edge cell and cell $(2i,2j+2)$ as an edge cell (Fig. 3(a)), weight $\alpha_2$ must be greater than $\alpha_1$ in order to produce a crisper value transition between the non-edge and the edge pixel. In addition, if both pixels are denoted as non-edge or edge pixels, the weights are equal in order to produce an expanded homogenous or edged area. Based on the case that Fig. 3(c) presents, the cell $Y_{2i,2j+1}$ is surrounded by the non-edge cell $Y_{2i,2j}$ and the edge cell $Y_{2i,2j+2}$. Thus, the cell $Y_{2i,2j+1}$ has been depicted during the CA evolution with a state, which results to the following $\alpha_k$ weights: $\alpha_1 = 0.25$ and $\alpha_2 = 0.75$. In addition, the cell $Y_{2i+1,2j}$ is surrounded by an edge cell $Y_{2i+2,2j}$, and by a non-edge cell, $Y_{2i,2j}$, thus, its state after the CA evolution will correspond to a state where the following values will be used during the mapping process, $b_1 = 0.25$ and $b_2 = 0.75$. Finally, for the central cell $Y_{2i+1,2j+1}$, values $c_1 = 0.1$ and $c_2 = c_3 = c_4 = 0.3$ are applied since cells $Y_{2i,2j}$ and $Y_{2i,2j+1}$, $Y_{2i+1,2j}$, $Y_{2i+1,2j+1}$ are non-edge and edge cells, respectively.

# 3     Experimental Results

To evaluate the performance of the tested resizing methods including the proposed method, several tested were performed. Zero – order, bilinear, bicubic, the Nedi [12], the edge-oriented [13] and the proposed method were tested on both color and grayscale images of various resolutions. All original images were initially down sample and then up sampled by the same algorithm to meet the initial dimensions. The results shown in Fig. 4 are a comparison of all the applied algorithms for the *Cameraman* image. In order to quantify the effectiveness of every method, the Peak Signal-to-Noise Ratio (PSNR) metric was calculated, as given by:

$$PSNR = 20 * \log_{10}\left(\frac{255}{\sqrt{MSE}}\right) \tag{5}$$

where MSE stands for the Mean-Squared-Error, calculated by:

$$MSE = \frac{1}{M \times N}\sum_{i=0}^{M-1}\sum_{j=0}^{N-1}[I(i,j) - F(i,j)]^2 \tag{6}$$

where $I(i,j)$ is the original image, $F(i,j)$ is the approximated version of the image and $M, N$ are the dimensions of the image respectively. For color images, the definition of PSNR is exact the same, except the MSE is the sum over all squared value differences divided by image size and by three.

**Fig. 4.** Resized Cameraman Images: (a) Original image, (b) Nearest neighbor, (c) Bilinear, (d) Bicubic, (e) Nedi, (f) Edge-oriented and (g) CA based proposed method

All resulted PSNR values for every tested image are provided in Table 1, while in Table 2, the resulted execution time for each method is demonstrated. As it is depicted in Table 1, the proposed method produces sufficiently high PSNR values. Despite their low processing times, the Nearest-neighbor method produces zigzag artifacts over the edge areas while the bilinear method results blurred edges. In addition, the Bicubic method also produces blurred edges requiring more processing time. The highest PSNR values are produced by the Nedi algorithm nevertheless; the required execution time prohibits its use for real-time applications. In addition, the edge-oriented method produces adequate PSNR values with low processing time, however, it is a threshold dependent method since it is required to determine the edge areas. On the contrary, the proposed method produces sufficiently high PSNR values preserving the edges of the initial image. Moreover, exploiting the inherit parallelism of the CA, the method displays low execution time, making it appropriate for real time systems.

**Table 1.** Resulted PSNR(dB) values. NN: Nearest; BL: Bilinear; BC: Bicubic; ND: Nedi, EO: Edge – oriented; CA-R: Proposed method

| Image | Method | | | | | |
|---|---|---|---|---|---|---|
| | NN | BL | BC | ND | EO | CA-R |
| Koala (Rgb 256×192) | 23.70 | 25.37 | 25.14 | 32.45 | 29.30 | 30.32 |
| Cam-man (Gr 128×128) | 22.37 | 23.96 | 23.70 | 30.77 | 25.80 | 26.54 |
| Lena (Rgb 150×150) | 26.93 | 28.88 | 28.77 | 34.57 | 30.90 | 31.57 |
| Box (Gr 320×240) | 28.68 | 30.19 | 29.99 | 32.1 | 29.13 | 30.02 |
| Building (Rgb 640×480) | 29.92 | 31.71 | 31.73 | 33.91 | 30.62 | 31.58 |

**Table 2.** Execution time (msec). NN: Nearest; BL: Bilinear; BC: Bicubic; ND: Nedi, EO: Edge – oriented; CA-R: Proposed method

| Image | Method | | | | | |
|---|---|---|---|---|---|---|
| | NN | BL | BC | ND | EO | CA-R |
| Koala (Rgb 256×192) | 3.6 | 19 | 21 | 44860 | 91.2 | 84.4 |
| Cam-man (Gr 128×128) | 3.1 | 8.7 | 9.7 | 4500 | 38.2 | 36.9 |
| Lena (Rgb 150×150) | 3.9 | 13.2 | 15.9 | 18600 | 41.2 | 39.3 |
| Box (Gr 320×240) | 3.6 | 9.4 | 10.6 | 5000 | 63.2 | 58.6 |
| Building (Rgb 640×480) | 5 | 26.2 | 29.5 | 65290 | 102.4 | 99.4 |

## 4    Conclusions

In this paper, a new image resizing method based on Cellular Automata and the Canny edge detector was introduced. The Canny edge detector is initially applied in order to descriminate the edge areas from the homogenous areas. The resulted binary edge map is then upscaled and processed as a CA grid. Appropriate CA states and transition rules were constructed to evolve the CA, which eventually attempt to enhance the quality of the edged areas. The orientation of the edge cells is considered in order to preserve effectively the edges of the initial image. Finally, a simple linear transformation is applied to reevaluate the value of each pixel for the final resized image. In terms of quantative comparison based on the PSNR values, the method demonstrates sufficient performance while the required processing time is kept in low levels due to the parallel nature of the CA. The method could be considered as appropriate for systems with low specifications, i.e. low resolution cameras, when further image processing is required.

## Rerefences

1. Jain, A.K.: Fundamentals of Digital Image Processing. Prentice-Hall, Upper Saddle River (1978)
2. Keys, R.G.: Cubic convolution interpolation for digital image processing. IEEE Trans. Acoust., Speech, Signal Process. 29, 1153–1160 (1981)
3. Hwang, J.W., Lee, H.S.: Adaptive image interpolation based on local gradient features. IEEE Signal Process. Lett. 29, 359–362 (2004)
4. Jiang, H., Moloney, C.: A new direction adaptive scheme for image interpolation. In: International Conference on Image Processing, Rochester, New York, USA, pp. 369–372 (2002)
5. Amanatiadis, A., Andreadis, I., Gasteratos, A.: A Log-Polar interpolation applied to image scaling. In: IEEE International Workshop on Imaging Systems and Techniques, Cracovia, Poland, pp. 1–5 (2007)
6. Muresan, D., Parks, T.: Adaptively quadratic (Aqua) image interpolation. IEEE Trans. Image Process. 13, 690–698 (2004)
7. Xiong, R., Ding, W., Ma, S., Gao, W.: Improved autoregressive image model estimation for directional image interpolation. In: 28th Picture Coding Symposium, Nagoya, Japan, pp. 442–445 (2010)

8. Cha, Y., Kim, S.: The error-amended sharp edge (EASE) scheme for imaging zooming. IEEE Trans. Image Process. 16, 1496–1505 (2007)
9. Chen, J.L., Chang, J.Y., Shieh, K.L.: 2D discrete signal interpolation and its image resampling application using fuzzy rule-based inference. Fuzzy Sets Syst. 114, 225–238 (2000)
10. Huang, Y., Fan, H.: Learning from interpolated images using neural networks for digital forensics. In: IEEE Conference on Computer Vision and Pattern Recognition, San Francisco, CA, pp. 177–182 (2010)
11. Lin, C.T., Fan, K.W., Pu, H.C., Lu, S.M., Liang, S.F.: An HVS-directed neural network based image resolution enhancement scheme for image resizing. IEEE Trans. Fuzzy Syst. 15, 605–615 (2007)
12. Li, X., Orchard, M.T.: New edge-directed interpolation. IEEE Trans. Image Process. 10, 1521–1527 (2001)
13. Chen, M.J., Huang, C.H., Lee, W.L.: A fast edge-oriented algorithm for image interpolation. Image and Vision Computing 23, 791–798 (2005)
14. Shi, H., Ward, R.: Canny edge based image expansion. In: IEEE International Symposium on Circuits and Systems, Scottsdale, Arizona, USA, pp. 785–788 (2002)
15. Canny, J.: A computational approach to edge-detection. IEEE Trans. Pattern Anal. Mach. Intell. 8, 679–700 (1986)
16. Wolfram, S.: Theory and applications of Cellular Automata. World Scientific, Singapore (1986)
17. Piwonska, A., Seredynski, F.: Discovery by genetic algorithm of Cellular Automata rules for pattern reconstruction task. In: 9th International Conference on Cellular Automata for Research and Industry, Ascoli Piceno, Italy, pp. 198–208 (2010)
18. Popovici, A., Popovici, D.: Cellular Automata in image processing. In: 15th International Symposium on Mathematical Theory of Networks and Systems, Notre Dame, Indiana, pp. 1–6 (2002)
19. Selvapeter, P.J., Hordijk, W.: Cellular Automata for image noise filtering. In: World Congress on Nature & Biologically Inspired Computing, Coimbatore, India, pp. 193–197 (2009)

# Modelling of Incident Sound Wave Propagation around Sound Barriers Using Cellular Automata

Toshihiko Komatsuzaki[1], Yoshio Iwata[1], and Shin Morishita[2]

[1] Institute of Science and Engineering, Kanazawa University, Kakuma-machi,
Kanazawa, Ishikawa, 920-1192 Japan
{toshi,iwata}@t.kanazawa-u.ac.jp
[2] Graduate School of Environment and Information Sciences, Yokohama National
University, 79-7 Tokiwadai, Hodogaya-ku, Yokohama 240-8501, Japan
mshin@ynu.ac.jp

**Abstract.** In the present study, acoustic wave propagation in the field
including sound isolation panel is simulated using Cellular Automata
(CA). CA is a discrete system which consists of finite state variables,
arranged on a uniform grid. CA dynamics is described by a local interaction rule which is used for computation of new state of each cell from
the present state at every time step. In this study a sound field is modeled using CA where the sound isolation panel exists and the numerical
simulation results are evaluated quantitatively by the insertion loss. The
results showed good correspondence with analytical solutions.

**Keywords:** Cellular Automata, Wave Propagation, Incident Sound Wave,
Diffraction, Sound Barrier.

## 1   Introduction

Not only the recent growth of roadway traffic but also the increasing number
of full-sized vehicle, high-speed running cars on highways cased serious noise
problems especially in urban regions. The noise abatement usually follows either
the reduction of noise emitted by car itself, or the absorption and the isolation
of air-borne noise within the environment. The former approach includes, for
example, the development of low-noise emitting vehicle and tires. On the other
hand, the latter uses noise-reducing porous asphalts and the construction of
sound insulation walls beside the highways. It is physically proper that the higher
sound insulation wall is preferable in order to prevent the noise leakage into
the inhabited region [1], however, the high wall adversely causes some of the
problems related to insolation, the landscape and also the radio disturbance.
Hence the high sound insulation performance should be realized while the height
of the insulation wall is kept low. The sound can be reduced by appropriately
arranging the sound transmission paths along the wall shape where the sound
waves are well diffracted and interfered with each other so that the outgoing
sound transmission characteristic is changed. Several studies have been done
for this issue devising the shape of the wall, whose noise isolation performances

G.C. Sirakoulis and S. Bandini (Eds.): ACRI 2012, LNCS 7495, pp. 385–394, 2012.

are predicted analytically and numerically [2]-[6]. The development of double y-shaped noise barrier is one typical example of these works [2], where the tip of the wall consists of y-shaped branches each possessing another y-shaped sub-branches.

It is desirable that the numerical prediction of the isolation performance would be made by more efficient, precise simulation strategies. The boundary element method (BEM) is commonly used in order to predict the sound field bounded by the insulation wall, however, the method is basically suited for the stationary analysis where the harmonic sound source is assumed. Therefore, numerous calculations are required in order to obtain frequency response characteristics for a wide range of frequencies, since a harmonic response is only calculated for respective frequencies. Additionally, the expression for the moving sound source which corresponds to the sound emitted by the moving cars is hardly introduced into the BEM model. These restrictions may limit the numerical simulation to the simplified case unlike the practical situations. Another numerical method known as the finite element method (FEM) can be used, but the considerable amount of time needed for the calculation may not be negligible depending on the number of space division into elements.

The Cellular Automata has been used for modeling wide range of phenomena including many physical processes described generally by partial differential equations [7]-[10]. The authors have also developed an acoustic wave propagation model for two dimensional acoustic problems [11]. Due to its easiness and simplicity of the modeling procedure, the Cellular Automata would be suitable for representing realistic situation of the actual problems involved. In the present study, the acoustic wave propagation model constituted by Cellular Automata is applied in order to evaluate the sound isolation performance of the sound insulation wall placed within the acoustic space. The wave model is based on past studies by authors where the two dimensional acoustic problems were solved for sound source movement, diffraction, reflection and also the sound absorption. The sound isolation performance is numerically predicted for three types of insulation walls whose geometries are different: the straight wall, the wall with single y-shaped branch installed at the top, and also the wall with double y-shaped branch. As already mentioned, the third type consists of y-shaped smaller branch subordinated by the larger main y-shaped branch, where the incident sound wave and the wave traveling along the surface of the wall are interfered each other and multiply diffracted, insomuch that the dissipation of the wave energy would be expected to some extent. In order to examine the predicted results obtained by the Cellular Automata model, the calculations are also performed for the model based on boundary element method which is generally used to analyze acoustic problems. In addition, the model is compared with the theoretical model suggested by Maekawa [12], in which the insertion loss of sound energy caused by the isolation wall is predicted. It is shown that highly compatible results with other approaches can be obtained by the Cellular Automata model, while keeping the modeling procedure simple and straightforward.

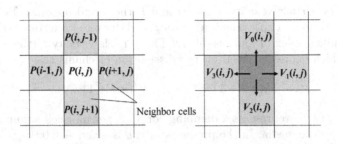

**Fig. 1.** Definition of neighbor in two dimensional acoustic model. Two state variables, sound pressure $P$ and particle velocity $V$, are placed in each cell.

## 2  The Cellular Automata Model for Wave Propagation

Cellular Automata model for simulating acoustic wave propagation is shown in this section. CA has been developed for modeling wide range of phenomena including many physical processes [7]. Specifically the wave propagation models have been studied by researchers based on Cellular Automata [7]-[11]. The simple finite difference scheme obtained by linear wave equation is referenced for developing local interaction rule, in a sense that discretized wave equation yields to an expression of local relationship of wave amplitudes. The rule is then extended to a more practical case, yet time and space are treated as discrete integers. Definitions for state variables and local interaction rules are presented in the following subsections.

### 2.1  Space Partitioning and State Definition

Two dimensional space is discretized into rectangular cells, where state of each cell is distinguished by two integers; i) zero for acoustic media, ii) one for rigid wall. Additionally, two variables which express the sound pressure and particle velocity in four neighbor directions are defined for the acoustic medium state. These variables are updated at each simulation step according to the local interaction rules which describe the relationship between a cell and its cross-located four neighboring cells as shown in Fig.1. Following Cellular Automata convention, time and space are treated as integers. In order for the model to be comparable with actual dimension, we assign unit cell length $dx = 0.001$[m], and also $c = 344$[m/s] for the sound speed.

### 2.2  Definition of Local Rules

State parameters given in each cell is updated every discrete time step according to a local interaction rule. First, the particle velocities in four directions are updated in time with respect the difference of sound pressure between adjacent cells, whose update rule is described explicitly as,

$$V'_a(\mathbf{x}, t+1) = V_a(\mathbf{x}, t) - \{P(\mathbf{x} + \mathbf{dx}_a, t) - P(\mathbf{x}, t)\} \ . \tag{1}$$

$V_a$ represents particle velocity of media and $P$ the sound pressure. Two dimensional cell position is expressed as a vector $\mathbf{x}$ and discrete time step as $t$. A suffix $a$ in (1) signifies index of four neighbors. The particle velocity further obeys the next (2), which expresses linear energy dissipation mechanism.

$$V_a(\mathbf{x}, t+1) = (1-d) \cdot V_a'(\mathbf{x}, t+1) . \tag{2}$$

In the above (2), $d$ represents a damping constant per unit cell assuming sound absorption by the media. In the present study, $d$ is given as 0.001.

The pressure is then updated according to the rule described by (3),

$$P(\mathbf{x}, t+1) = P(\mathbf{x}, t) - c_a^2 \sum_a V_a(\mathbf{x}, t+1) , \tag{3}$$

where $c_a$ denotes the wave traveling speed in CA space. Sound pressure and particle velocities are updated according to the local rule described by above three equations. In addition, if the wall is totally reflective, the sound pressure values of wall state cells are copied by those of the adjacent medium state cells so that the perfect reflective condition can be represented.

Since calculation is carried out between nearby cells that are separated only a unit length at every step, any physical quantities cannot have the transport speed exceed to this calculation limit. The maximum wave speed becomes $c_a = 1/\sqrt{2}$ for two dimensional space, therefore the wave front travels $1/\sqrt{2}$ of unit length per calculation step [11].

## 3   Simulation of Sound Field Incorporating Isolation Wall

### 3.1   Description of the Model

Numerical simulation is performed for the wave propagation within two dimensional acoustic field incorporating sound isolation wall. The sound field is calculated for the simulation space of 4[m] in height and 6[m] in width, whose boundary conditions are assumed to be infinite without any reflected wave from the boundaries. Despite the easiness in realizing infinite boundary condition in BEM modeling, the finite set of cell arrangement in CA model naturally causes boundary reflection at the cells located on four edges. Therefore, the actual size of the simulation space is set as large as threefold of the analyzed space so that the reflection problem is avoided in the course of the simulation. The unit size of a cell is assumed to be 10[mm], hence the cellular space is constituted of $1200 \times 1800$ cells. A sound insulation wall is located and extended downward vertically separating the analyzed space. On the left side, the noise source is located, and the other side the sound observation points labeled by numbers from 1 to 12 are placed. The sound isolation performance is numerically predicted for three types of insulation walls whose geometries are different, as shown in Fig.3: the straight wall (type 1), the wall with single y-shaped branch installed at the top (type 2), and also the wall with double y-shaped branch (type 3). The sound

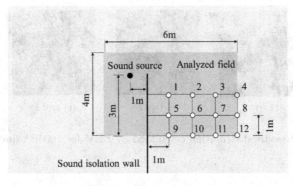

**Fig. 2.** Schematic of calculated sound field incorporating noise insulation wall. The numbers on grids signify the observation points of sound pressure passes over the wall.

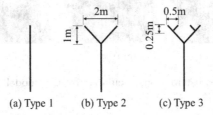

(a) Type 1    (b) Type 2    (c) Type 3

**Fig. 3.** Geometries of sound insulation walls

source assuming the air-borne noise radiated by the roadway cars is placed 1[m] apart horizontally from the tip of the wall.

In both BEM and CA models, the harmonic sound source ranging from 500[Hz] to 2[kHz] at every 100[Hz] step is given and the sound pressure distribution of the field is calculated at respective frequency. Additionally, the RMS of the propagated sound pressure transmitted beyond the wall is measured at 12 points, where each pressure is normalized by the RMS reference pressure at the source location. The normalized pressure is employed as evaluation indicator when comparing the isolation performance among three types of walls. Whereas the acoustic field response analysis is rather limited to the harmonic cases in BEM model while avoiding the formulation become complex, the transient field response is easily calculated in CA model. Therefore, the random sound source response is calculated for the CA model as an additional sound source condition. By computing Fourier transformation of the observed time histories of sound pressure at measurement points and further calculate the transfer functions to the frequency characteristics at the source location, roughly the identical evaluation of the isolation performance can be made in comparison to the sinusoidal cases with just a single computation.

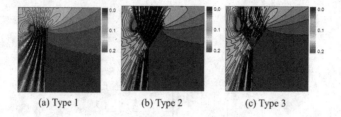

(a) Type 1          (b) Type 2          (c) Type 3

**Fig. 4.** Sound pressure distribution calculated by BEM for 1000Hz sinusoidal source

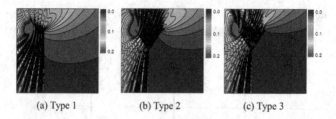

(a) Type 1          (b) Type 2          (c) Type 3

**Fig. 5.** Sound pressure distribution calculated by CA model for 1000Hz sinusoidal source

## 3.2   Sound Pressure Distribution of the Calculated Field

Examples of calculated sound field incorporating three types of isolation walls when the sinusoidal sound source frequency is set to 1[kHz] are shown respectively for BEM and CA model in Figs.4 and 5. The sound source is located on the left side of the wall, whereas the region in which the sound transmission is undesirable is assumed to be on the right side. In each type of wall and in all the frequencies given to the sinusoidal source, approximately the consistent pressure distribution can be obtained in both models. In view of the sound isolation performance, the double y-shaped wall (type 3) mostly prevents sound transmission downward the right hand side of the wall as compared to the vertically straight type wall (type 1). The sound dissipation is thought to be occurred by the interference of the outgoing direct wave and the phase-delayed diffracted sound wave transmitting along the wall shape. These numerically predicted results are qualitatively supported by the experimental observations made by the original inventor group of double y-shaped insulation wall.

## 3.3   Frequency Characteristics of the Sound Isolation Performance

The measured frequency response of the sound isolation performance measured at observation points 1 and 11 are shown for three types of walls in Figs.6, 7 and 8, respectively. The calculated results are compared for sinusoidal source case in both BEM and CA models, and also for the random source case in CA model. In these figures, the insertion loss is adopted for the isolation performance evaluation, which is defined as the difference between the sound pressure level measured at a point under the presence of the isolation wall and that without the wall. Here again it is seen that the calculation results by both models coincide well in each type of wall. What is more remarkable is that the frequency response characteristics calculated by assigning the transient sound wave in the CA model are approximately consistent with those obtained by the other two models. Despite the prediction accuracy, one could say that simulating field response of the transient sound wave incorporating multiple frequencies is useful in view of computational efficiency.

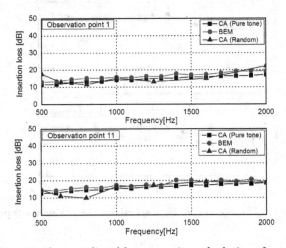

**Fig. 6.** Insertion loss predicted by respective calculations for type 1 wall

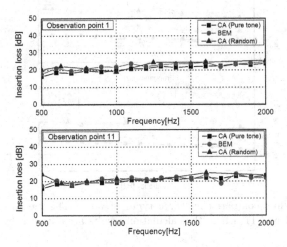

**Fig. 7.** Insertion loss predicted by respective calculations for type 2 wall

In Fig.9, the insertion loss is further compared for three types of insulation walls in which the sound pressure is measured at observation point 1 and 11. The calculations are performed for the CA model where the sinusoidal sound source at respective frequency is given. It is known qualitatively from the figure that the type 3 wall shows better noise isolation performance throughout the frequency range in comparison to the other two types. Though not shown in the figure, not much difference can be seen at any other observation points.

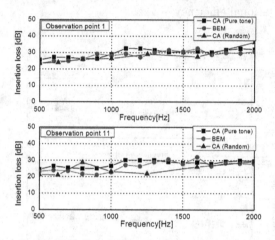

**Fig. 8.** Insertion loss predicted by respective calculations for type 3 wall

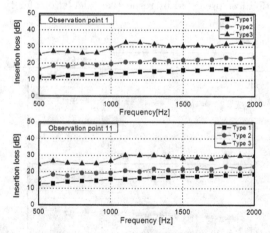

**Fig. 9.** Insertion loss compared by three types of walls. The measurement point is located at point 1 and 11, where the calculation results are obtained by CA model.

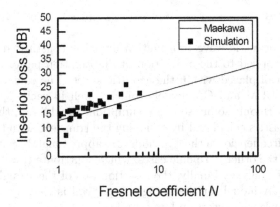

**Fig. 10.** Application of Maekawa's insertion loss chart to the calculated results obtained by CA simulation

### 3.4 Verification of the Calculated Results Using Maekawa's Insertion Loss Chart

The sound field calculated by CA model is examined based on more realistic performance criterion known as Maekawa's insertion loss chart [12]. Although limited to the straight wall case, the chart is derived from Kirchhoff's approximate diffraction theory where the formulated insertion loss is further calibrated by experimental observation. The insertion loss $[IL]$[dB] is generally plotted against Fresnel number $N$, defined as,

$$N = \frac{(A+B) - d}{\lambda/2} = \frac{2\delta}{\lambda} \ . \tag{4}$$

In (4), $A$ signifies the distance between the sound source and the vertex of the wall, $B$ the distance between the observation point and the vertex, $d$ the straight-line distance between the source and observation points, and also $\lambda$ the wavelength of harmonic sound. The Fresnel number is defined by the difference between the indirect $(A+B)$ and the direct $d$ path of transmitted sound divided by half-wavelength of the source. The transmission loss is then represented as function of Fresnel number, which is expressed as follows.

$$\lfloor IL \rfloor_h = \begin{cases} 10 \log_1 0\{N\} + 13 & N \geq 1 \\ 5 \pm \frac{8}{\sinh^{-1}} \sinh^{-1}\{|N|^{0.485}\} & -0.324 \leq N < 1 \\ 0 & N < -0.324 \end{cases} \tag{5}$$

Using the first formula for $N > 1$, Maekawa's empirical curve is shown in Fig.10 in conjunction with plots obtained by the CA model. The overall value of the plotted insertion loss exceeds the curve, one reason may be because the chart is constituted by adopting the minimum value out of empirically tested multiple data measured for each Fresnel number, based on the safe side estimation. From the figure, the CA model shows certain level of agreement with the insertion loss criterion.

# 4   Conclusions

In this study, the acoustic wave propagation model is constituted by Cellular Automata and is applied to the evaluation of the isolation performance of the sound insulation wall placed within the acoustic space. The calculation results obtained by both BEM and CA models coincide well in each type of insulation wall for the harmonic sound source assumption. In addition, the frequency response characteristics calculated by assigning the transient sound wave incorporating multiple frequencies in the CA model are approximately consistent with those obtained by the other harmonic cases, which contribute to reduce computation time for the analysis. Finally, the insertion loss of the straight type wall predicted by the CA model for the straight type wall is roughly shown to be consistent with Maekawa's insertion loss criterion.

# References

1. Morse, P.M., Ingard, K.U.: Theoretical Acoustics. Princeton University Press (1986)
2. Shima, H., Watanabe, T., Mizuno, K., Iida, K., Matsumoto, K., Nakasaki, K.: Noise reduction of a multiple edge noise barrier. In: Proc. of Internoise 1996, pp. 791–794 (1996)
3. Watts, G.R.: Acoustic Performance of a Multiple Edge Noise Barrier Profile at Motorway Sites. Applied Acoustics 47, 47–66 (1996)
4. Crombie, D.H., Hothersall, D.C., Chandler-Wilde, S.N.: Multiple-Edge Noise Barriers. Applied Acoustics 44, 353–367 (1995)
5. Jin, B.J., Kim, H.S., Kang, H.J., Kim, J.S.: Sound Diffraction by a Partially Inclined Noise Barrier. Applied Acoustics 62, 1107–1121 (2001)
6. Murata, K., Nagakura, K., Kitagawa, T., Tanaka, S.: Noise Reduction Effect of Noise Barrier for Shinkansen Based on Y-shaped Structure. QR of RTRI 47(3), 162–168 (2006)
7. Chopard, B., Droz, M.: Cellular Automata Modeling of Physical Systems. Cambridge University Press (1998)
8. Chopard, B.: A Cellular Automata Model of Large-scale Moving Objects. J. Phys. A: Math. Gen. 23, 1671–1687 (1990)
9. Chen, H., Chen, S., Doolen, G., Lee, Y.C.: Simple Lattice Gas Models for Waves. Complex Systems 2, 259–267 (1988)
10. Sudo, Y., Sparrow, V.W.: Sound Propagation Simulations Using Lattice Gas Methods. AIAA J. 33, 1582–1589 (1995)
11. Komatsuzaki, T., Iwata, Y.: Modeling of Sound Absorption by Porous Materials Using Cellular Automata. In: El Yacoubi, S., Chopard, B., Bandini, S. (eds.) ACRI 2006. LNCS, vol. 4173, pp. 357–366. Springer, Heidelberg (2006)
12. Maekawa, Z.: Noise Reduction by Screens. Applied Acoustics 1, 157–173 (1968)

# Path Tracing on Polar Depth Maps
# for Robot Navigation

Ioannis Kostavelis[1], Evangelos Boukas[1],
Lazaros Nalpantidis[2], and Antonios Gasteratos[1]

[1] Robotics and Automation Lab., Production and Management Engineering Dept.,
Democritus University of Thrace, Vas. Sofias 12, GR-671 00 Xanthi, Greece
{gkostave,evanbouk,agaster}@pme.duth.gr
[2] Computer Vision and Active Perception Lab., Centre for Autonomous Systems,
Royal Institute of Technology - KTH, SE-100 44 Stockholm, Sweden
lanalpa@kth.se
http://robotics.pme.duth.gr

**Abstract.** In this paper a Cellular Automata-based (CA) path estimation algorithm suitable for safe robot navigation is presented. The proposed method combines well established 3D vision techniques with CA operations and traces a collision free route from the foot of the robot to the horizon of a scene. Firstly, the depth map of the scene is obtained and, then, a polar transformation is applied. A v-disparity image calculation processing step is applied to the initial depth map separating the ground plane from the obstacles. In the next step, a CA floor field is formed representing all the distances from the robot to the traversable regions in the scene. The target point that the robot should move towards to, is tracked down and an additional CA routine is applied to the floor field revealing a traversable route that the robot should follow to reach its target location.

**Keywords:** cellular automata, floor field, path estimation, v-disparity image, polar transformation.

## 1 Introduction

In the past decades multiple efforts took place for the development of an efficient method for safe robot navigation. Estimating traversable routes, which the robots can safely follow in a scene, involves the detection and avoidance of obstacles. Thus, it comprises the first step towards higher level navigation algorithms, such as path planning and simultaneously localization and mapping (SLAM). CA have been proven to provide reliable solutions to a variety of robotics-related problems. They have been successfully exploited both in field of the mobile robotics [1], as well as in other manufacturing and fabrication process problems [2]. The majority of the CA applications in robotic applications suppose a cell grid workspace, where the robot and the objects are represented as points [3], [4]. In [5], an algorithm based on CA is introduced for the path

G.C. Sirakoulis and S. Bandini (Eds.): ACRI 2012, LNCS 7495, pp. 395–404, 2012.

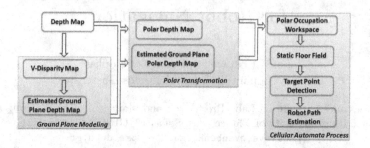

**Fig. 1.** The flow chart of the proposed methodology

planning of a simple rigid body in a planar workspace with prior knowledge of the topology of the obstacles. The mobile robot is modeled as a point moving from one cell to another, while the main limitation is that the robot moves forward on a smoothed trajectory without stopping and turning with a minimum radius of curvature. Moreover, in [6] the input space is an image obtained by a camera, which contains information about the position of each object and the locations of the starting and goal point. The CA algorithm operates in two phases exploiting Manhattan distances and reveals the shortest path between the initial and goal position. In a different approximation, [7], a CA algorithm has been utilized for the removal of the perspective-effect. This method has been embodied in a vision system of an autonomous robot designed to operate in indoor environments. Additionally, in [8], a CA method has been utilized for the development of a real time path planning of cooperative robots proving that accurate collision-free paths could be created with low computational cost. A simulation method based on CA enhancements for a qualitative description of a structured indoor environment, as a first step towards a SLAM framework is proposed in [9]. In [10] a planar CA algorithm has been employed in a SLAM algorithm. More specifically, a CA undertook the refinement of the global and local map merging step, improving the quality of the resulting map output The method proposed in this work employs 3D vision techniques and CA operations for the estimation of a collision-free robot path in a scene. Firstly, a disparity map of the scene is obtained utilizing either a stereo vision algorithm or by exploiting an appropriate sensor that retrieves immediately the depth of the scene. Then, a polar transformation is applied in the disparity map forming a polar-depth image, where the obstacles are rearranged in an angular configuration. Afterwards, the ground plane of the scenery is modeled by a v-disparity image computation processing module over the initial depth image and, consequently, a new obstacle-free depth map is calculated, which is also transformed into a polar one. The two polar depth maps are compared to produce a binary polar workspace that reveals the existence of obstacles in any possible direction. In the next step, a floor field based on CA operations is formed, which involves the calculation of the distances between the traversable regions in the scene and the robot location. The target location in the scene is then detected and after applying different CA rules over the floor field the traversable path is computed. Fig. 1 summarizes the steps of the proposed methodology.

## 2    Proposed Algorithm

### 2.1    Depth Map Acquisition

The first step of the proposed methodology requires the computation of a disparity image, which contains the depth information of the scene [11]. Although the development of a stereo vision algorithm that produces disparity images is out of the scope of this work, it should be stated that there are multiple approaches for the estimation of the depth information involving different depth cameras and computation methods. Cameras that can acquire a continuous stream of depth images such as *Microsoft Kinect* or *Time of Flight Cameras* (ToFC) are now commonly available, whilst lot of research has already taken place in this field [12], [13]. Additionally, a well known technique to obtain the depth of a scene is the utilization of a stereo correspondence algorithm, which takes as input a pair of images acquired from a stereo rig and produces a disparity map [14]. The proposed algorithm does not pose any restrictions to the selection of the methodology, as far as the selected one produces reliable and dense depth maps. In cases where a depth camera is not available, the stereo correspondence algorithm described in [15], which is suitable for robotic applications is proposed. The efficiency of this stereo algorithm has been extensively tested in real world navigation applications [10], the output of which is presented in Fig. 2(b) .

### 2.2    Obstacle Free Ground Plane Modeling

A depth map, such as the one obtained from the stereo correspondence algorithm, can be used for the computation of a v-disparity image, as shown in Fig. 2(c). The latter is a horizontal histogram of the disparity values, which encodes basic geometric features of the scene and it provides, in a direct way, an estimation of the horizon and the objects above the ground plane. In a v-disparity image each

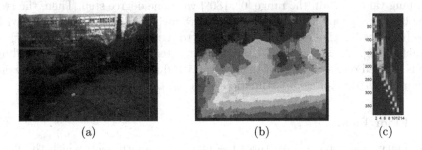

(a)                          (b)                          (c)

**Fig. 2.** a) Left reference image of the stereo pair, b) The disparity map c) The calculated v-disparity map

pixel has a positive integer value that denotes the number of pixels in the input image that lie on the same image line (ordinate) and possesses disparity values equal to its abscissa [16]. The information resulting from the v-disparity image is important as it easily distinguishes the pixels belonging to the ground plane from the ones belonging to obstacles. The ground plane in the v-disparity image can be modeled by a linear equation $f(x) = \alpha \cdot x + \beta$, where the parameters $\alpha$ and $\beta$ correspond to the slope of the camera and to the height that the ground plane meets the horizon in the scene respectively. These parameters can be computed by Hough transform [17], in case that the geometry of the camera-environment system is unknown. Then, if we use $\alpha$ and $\beta$ to reconstruct a void v-disparity image, this will correspond to an obstacle-free depth image with a basic geometry similar to the one of the initial depth map.

## 2.3   Polar Transformation of the Depth Map

The initial depth map and the estimated ground plane depth map are remapped by a polar transformation, which rearranges the depth information of the scene and places the disparity values in a radial topology around the front of the robot. Consequently, a spatial distribution of the obstacles placed in the surrounding of the robot is obtained. The output of this transformation is two distinct polar depth images. The first one is the *polar-depth* map resulted from the transformation of the initial disparity image (Fig. 3b) and the second one is the *ground plane polar-depth map* (Fig.3d) resulted from the transformation of the estimated obstacle-free depth map. Each column of the polar-depth map corresponds to a specific direction in the scene, e.g. the $90^{th}$ column corresponds to a direction at $90°$, i.e. straight ahead of the robot. The main advantage of the polar-depth map is that the depth information is conveniently rearranged to correspond to the possible directions of motion for the robot. Consequently, each column describes the spatial distribution of the obstacles lying on the respective direction. More specifically, the pole, which is the origin of the polar coordinate system, is set to the central pixel of the lowest disparity image row $O(M, \frac{N}{2})$, where $M$ and $N$ denote the number of the disparity rows and columns respectively (Fig. 3b). The selected radial resolution $\rho$ ensures that the information of the image will be uniformly distributed in the polar space, while the angular resolution $\theta$ is a variable obtaining values within the range $[0°, 180°]$ with one degree step. Then, the two polar-depth maps are subtracted (Fig. 3e) producing a binary polar image with zeros (0) placed in the regions corresponding to the ground plane and ones (1) to obstacles (Fig. 3f), respectively. Actually, an intermediate simple thresholding step is applied on the output of the subtraction due to the fact that the *ground plane polar-depth map* is an estimation based on the v-disparity image.

## 2.4   Floor Field

The binary polar image constitutes the input workspace upon which the floor field $F$ for each pixel $(i, j)$ is created [18]. The floor field is a gradient having low values nearby the robot and higher values away from it [19]. The dimensions of

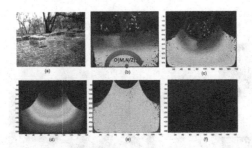

**Fig. 3.** a) The left reference image, b) the depth map, c) the polar-depth map, d) the reconstructed *ground plane polar-depth map*, e) the difference of the two depth maps, f) the binary image indicating the obstacles

the current workspace are the same as those of the initial polar-depth maps and consequently the $F_{i,j}$ space is populated as follows:

$$F_{i,j} = \begin{cases} > 0, & \text{if a distance value has been assigned} \\ = 0, & \text{if no value has been assigned yet} \\ = -1, & \text{if there is an obstacle.} \end{cases} \quad (1)$$

The computation of the floor field is a CA process exploiting the Von Neumann neighborhood. This is a diamond shaped neighborhood, which is used to define a set of cells surrounding a central one with given coordinates $(i_0, j_0)$. In the proposed method, the Von Neumann neighborhood $(N^{von})$ does not take into consideration the central cell and, therefore, it is defined as follows:

$$N(i_0, j_0)^{von} = \{(i,j) : |i - i_0| + |j - j_0| = (p)\} \quad (2)$$

where the range $p = 1$. Moreover, the CA is executed in parallel according to a specific rule, until all the cells of the $F_{i,j}$ are populated with non zero values. At each time step $t$ the CA rule is applied over every cell having zero value $F_t(i_0, j_0)$ and examines the values of neighborhood pixels $F_t(i,j)$ within its $N^{von}$. As a result, in the next time step $t+1$ the respective cell $F_{t+1}(i_0, j_0)$ is assigned with the minimum positive value of the neighborhood, increased by one as described in Eq. 3, whilst in different case the value of the cell at the current time $t$ is inherited at time $t+1$ (Eq. 4).

**IF** $F_t(i_0, j_0) = 0$ **AND** $F_t(i,j) > 0$ **THEN** $F_{t+1}(i_0, j_0) = \min F_t(i,j) + 1$ (3)

**IF** $F_t(i_0, j_0) = 0$ **AND** $F_t(i,j) \leq 0$ **THEN** $F_{t+1}(i_0, j_0) = F_t(i_0, j_0)$ (4)

where $(i,j) \in N^{von}(i_0, j_0)$. In Fig. 4(a) a traversable scene, which contains several obstacles is transformed into a polar binary one (Fig. 4(b)). The aforementioned CA rule is applied in the binary image and the calculated floor field is presented in Fig. 4(c). In the latter, the regions that correspond in obstacles have been discarded.

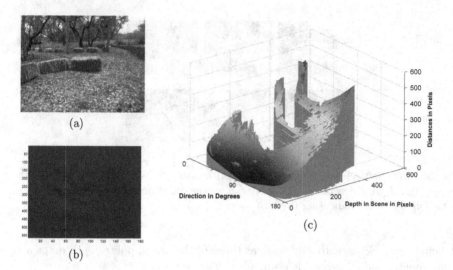

**Fig. 4.** (a) A reference image of a scene, (b) the polar workspace that contains the obstacles and the ground plane, and (c) the respective floor field

## 2.5   Path Estimation

Once the floor field has been computed the target location in the scene should be selected. The goal target is the furthest point in the scene that the robot can reach. The distance in pixels between the robot location and the target point are calculated by utilizing the binary polar workspace. More specifically, the number of the row that the target point lays, in the polar-depth map, indicates the furthest distance that the robot is able to reach in the scene. Due to the fact that this work examines only the traversable regions in the scene the search for the target location is bounded in the area which correspond up to the horizon. The latter has already been computed ($\beta$ in the v-disparity) and, therefore, the maximum number of the rows in the polar depth map that examined is equal to $\beta$ as indicated in Fig. 5(a). The next step of the proposed method comprises the detection of the route that the robot should follow in order to reach the horizon of the image plane. Towards this direction, an additional CA procedure has been adopted exploiting the precomputed floor field, which contains all the distances from the robot location to each traversable point. Thus, considering as a starting point the target location and transiting to the cells that contain lower distance values a trace which connects this point with the robot location can be computed. The indexes of this trace correspond to the selected path. This computation is undertaken by the CA employing the Moore neighborhood. This is a square shaped neighborhood, which is described as follows:

$$N(i_0, j_0)^{Moore} = \{(i, j) : |i - i_0| \leqslant (p), |j - j_0| \leqslant (p)\} \qquad (5)$$

where the range $p = 1$. The CA operation workspace comprises the previously computed floor field and the binary polar image. However, the latter is examined only up the curve that corresponds to the horizon, estimated from the v-disparity. Therefore, a new planar workspace $P_{i,j}$ is described according to Eq. 6.

$$P_{i,j} = \begin{cases} = 0, & \text{traversable region} \\ = 1, & \text{occupied region} \\ = 2, & \text{path indexes.} \end{cases} \tag{6}$$

Initially, only the target location is marked on the workspace as a *path index* and, subsequently, the path that the robot should follow in order to leave out any obstacle is propagated by applying the following CA rule:

$$\textbf{IF} \sum_{i=-1}^{1} \sum_{i=-1}^{1} P_t(i,j) < 3 \ \textbf{THEN} \ P_{t+1}(i_{min}, j_{min}) = 1 \tag{7}$$

where the $(i_{min}, j_{min})$ are the indexes that correspond to the minimum values in the respective neighborhood in the floor field, i.e $[i_{min}, j_{min}] = \text{argmin} F(i,j)$, and $(i,j) \in N^{Moore}$. Moreover, the CA procedure is executed in parallel according to the aforementioned rule, until the formation of the entire route that connects the robot with any horizon point. Fig. 5(b) presents the path that has been computed by utilizing the CA rule over the respective floor field. Additionally, the pixels that correspond to the polar route are transformed back to the Cartesian coordinate system and, therefore, the estimated path is presented in the the reference image Fig. 5(c).

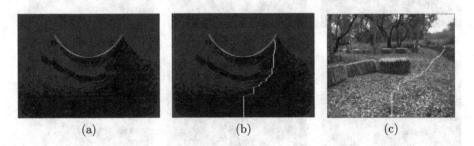

|  (a)  |  (b)  |  (c)  |

**Fig. 5.** (a) A binary polar image with the horizon, (b) the estimated path in the polar space, (c) the respective path in the Cartesian space

## 3   Algorithm Assessment

The performance of the proposed system has been assessed on a dataset captured during the DARPA "Learning Applied to Ground Robots" (LAGR) program, which involves a series of natural outdoor scenes [20]. In this dataset the reference color images are provided along with the corresponding disparity information. The geometry of the camera-environment was unknown and constantly changing. Consequently, the ground plane in the calculated v-disparity images was modeled exploiting the Hough transformation.

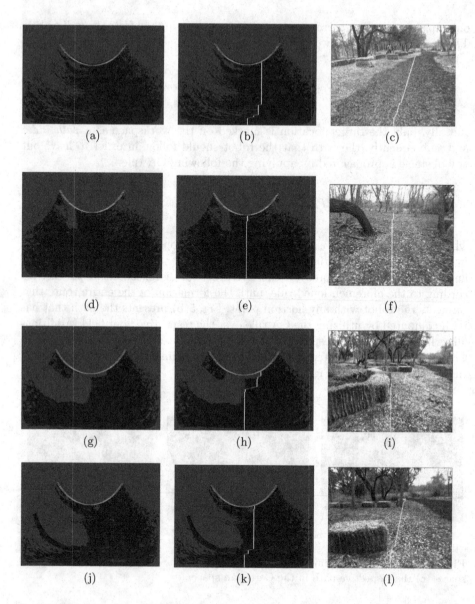

**Fig. 6.** Experimental results for four different scenarios. The first two row correspond to a fully traversable scene, whilst the second and third row correspond to a traversable scene with some obstacles around the robot.

This dataset consists of directly and indirectly traversable scenes and, therefore, the proposed algorithm has been tested for both the scenarios. More specifically, among the entire tested dataset four different cases are illustrated in Fig. 6, where the intermediate results and the final output of the algorithm are demonstrated. The first two cases comprise the assessment of the proposed method on fully traversable scenes, which contain almost no obstacles (Fig. 6(c)) or the obstacles exist in the background (Fig. 6(f)). The scene in the third case is also a traversable one, however some obstacles exist nearby the robot. The estimated path between the location of the robot and the detected target point, which lies on the horizon, bypasses all the existing obstacles in the scene (Fig. 6(i)). Furthermore, in the last scenario involving yet another non directly traversable scene, the proposed method manages to plan a route that avoids any obstacles found either close or far from the robot (Fig. 6(l)).

## 4 Conclusions

A CA-based method for robot path estimation exploiting depth maps has been presented. The proposed system consists of a stereo vision module responsible for the depth acquisition of the scene. An auxiliary modeled depth map has been calculated utilizing the v-disparity image algorithmic procedure. Then a polar transformation is applied to the depth images producing a radial rearrangement of the obstacles in the scene. After a thresholding procedure, the polar planar workspace that contains only the obstacles of the scene is further processed by CA techniques. In the latter, the floor field is computed and the estimated path is produced after an additional CA step. The main advantage of the proposed method is that the occupancy grid is formed directly in the image plane by exploiting the polar transformation, contrary to the already existed techniques that assume a planar occupation grid as a workspace for the CA. This attribute endows the proposed method with the ability to directly track the obstacle free path within the scene. The presented method has been evaluated in an outdoor dataset and has been proved capable of producing collision-free paths between the location of the robot and the selected target point, which is close to the horizon of the scene. The fact that the proposed method exhibits great performance while tested on uneven terrain, where the camera geometry is unknown, indicates even better behavior in indoor scenarios, where the geometry of the system is usually constant. As a result, we conclude that the method proposed in this work could be considered as a reliable first step towards real world robotic path planning and navigation applications. Future work will consist of the online test of the proposed algorithm in uneven terrains, as it will be integrated into an autonomous robot platform able for outdoor exploration.

## References

1. Marchese, F.M.: Multiple mobile robots path-planning with mca. In: International Conference on Autonomic and Autonomous Systems, ICAS 2006, pp. 56–56. IEEE (2006)
2. Sirakoulis, G.C., Karafyllidis, I., Thanailakis, A.: A cellular automaton for the propagation of circular fronts and its applications. Engineering Applications of Artificial Intelligence 18(6), 731–744 (2005)
3. Zhou, K., Ma, S., Zhu, X., Tang, L., Feng, X.: Improved ant colony algorithm based on cellular automata for obstacle avoidance in robot soccer. In: 3rd IEEE International Conference on Computer Science and Information Technology (ICCSIT), vol. 5, pp. 298–302 (July 2010)

4. Marchese, F.M.: A directional diffusion algorithm on cellular automata for robot path-planning. Future Generation Computer Systems 18(7), 983–994 (2002)
5. Marchese, F.: Cellular automata in robot path planning. In: Proceedings of the First Euromicro Workshop on Advanced Mobile Robot 1996, pp. 116–125. IEEE (1996)
6. Behring, C., Bracho, M., Castro, M., Moreno, J.A.: An algorithm for robot path planning with cellular automata. In: Proceedings of the Fourth International Conference on Cellular Automata for Research and Industry: Theoretical and Practical Issues on Cellular Automata, Citeseer, pp. 11–19 (2000)
7. Adorni, G., Cagnoni, S., Mordonini, M.: Cellular automata based inverse perspective transform as a tool for indoor robot navigation. In: AI* IA 99: Advances in Artificial Intelligence, pp. 345–355 (2000)
8. Ioannidis, K., Sirakoulis, G.C., Andreadis, I.: A path planning method based on cellular automata for cooperative robots. Applied Artificial Intelligence 25(8), 721–745 (2011)
9. Pradel, G., Hoppenot, P.: Symbolic trajectory description in mobile robotics. Journal of Intelligent & Robotic Systems 45(2), 157–180 (2006)
10. Nalpantidis, L., Sirakoulis, G.C., Gasteratos, A.: Non-probabilistic cellular automata-enhanced stereo vision simultaneous localization and mapping. Measurement Science and Technology 22, 114027 (2011)
11. Nalpantidis, L., Sirakoulis, G.C., Gasteratos, A.: Review of stereo vision algorithms: from software to hardware. International Journal of Optomechatronics 2(4), 435–462 (2008)
12. Khoshelham, K., Elberink, S.O.: Accuracy and resolution of kinect depth data for indoor mapping applications. Sensors 12(2), 1437–1454 (2012)
13. Castaneda, V., Mateus, D., Navab, N.: Stereo time-of-flight. In: International Conference on Computer Vision (November 2011)
14. Nalpantidis, L., Kostavelis, I., Gasteratos, A.: Stereovision-based algorithm for obstacle avoidance. In: Intelligent Robotics and Applications, pp. 195–204 (2009)
15. Kostavelis, I., Nalpantidis, L., Gasteratos, A.: Supervised Traversability Learning for Robot Navigation. In: Groß, R., Alboul, L., Melhuish, C., Witkowski, M., Prescott, T.J., Penders, J. (eds.) TAROS 2011. LNCS, vol. 6856, pp. 289–298. Springer, Heidelberg (2011)
16. Labayrade, R., Aubert, D., Tarel, J.P.: Real time obstacle detection in stereovision on non flat road geometry through v-disparity representation. In: IEEE Intelligent Vehicle Symposium 2002, vol. 2, pp. 646–651. IEEE (2002)
17. De Cubber, G., Doroftei, D., Nalpantidis, L., Sirakoulis, G.C., Gasteratos, A.: Stereo-based terrain traversability analysis for robot navigation. In: IARP/EURON Workshop on Robotics for Risky Interventions and Environmental Surveillance, Brussels, Belgium (2009)
18. Huang, H.J., Guo, R.Y.: Static floor field and exit choice for pedestrian evacuation in rooms with internal obstacles and multiple exits. Physical Review E 78(2), 021131 (2008)
19. Zheng, Y., Jia, B., Li, X.G., Zhu, N.: Evacuation dynamics with fire spreading based on cellular automaton. Physica A: Statistical Mechanics and its Applications 390, 3147–3156 (2011)
20. Procopio, M.J.: Hand-labeled DARPA LAGR datasets (2007), http://ml.cs.colorado.edu/~procopio/labeledlagrdata/

# Modeling Development and Disease in Our "Second" Brain

Kerry A. Landman[1], Benjamin J. Binder[2], and Donald F. Newgreen[3]

[1] Department of Mathematics and Statistics
University of Melbourne, Victoria 3010, Australia
kerryl@unimelb.edu.au
[2] School of Mathematical Sciences,
University of Adelaide, South Australia 5005, Australia
benjamin.binder@adelaide.edu.au
[3] Murdoch Childrens Research Institute
Royal Children's Hospital, Parkville, Victoria 3052 Australia
don.newgreen@mcri.edu.au

**Abstract.** The enteric nervous system (ENS) in our gastrointestinal tract, nicknamed the "second brain", is responsible for normal gut function and peristaltic contraction. Embryonic development of the ENS involves the colonization of the gut wall from one end to the other by a population of proliferating neural crest (NC) cells. Failure of these cells to invade the whole gut results in the relatively common, potentially fatal condition known as Hirschsprung disease (HSCR). Cellular automata models provide insight into the colonization process at both the individual cell-level and population-level. Our models generated experimentally testable predictions, which have subsequently been confirmed. The model results imply that HSCR is chiefly a NC cell proliferation defect and not, as previously thought, a NC cell motility defect. These results have important implications for HSCR; namely stochastic effects can determine success or failure of the colonization process for a certain range of NC cell proliferation rates.

**Keywords:** Cellular Automata, Motility, Proliferation, Frontal Expansion, Stochastic, Hirschsprung disease.

## 1 Introduction

The enteric nervous system (ENS), nicknamed the "second brain" [1], is a large complex network of neurons lining the wall of our gastrointestinal tract, controlling normal gut function and peristaltic contraction.

Vertebrate embryonic ENS development involves the colonization of the gut wall from the stomach to the anal end by a small population of neural crest (NC) cells which migrate from the hindbrain [2]. Hirschsprung disease (HSCR), a relatively common birth defect (1/5000 births) occurs when NC cells fail to colonize to the anal end. This causes intractable constipation and is potentially fatal unless surgically treated.

G.C. Sirakoulis and S. Bandini (Eds.): ACRI 2012, LNCS 7495, pp. 405–414, 2012.
© Springer-Verlag Berlin Heidelberg 2012

During the highly time-tabled colonization process (approximately 4 weeks in humans starting at week 3, 4-5 days in rodents and avians), there is a vast increase in NC cell numbers through cell division (proliferation). Surprisingly small numbers of initiating NC cells can populate relatively large regions of gut [3]. Conversely, reducing the initial numbers of NC cells by ablation can lead to reduced lengths of neural gut, the last section remaining aneural as in HSCR. Despite a decrease in the extent of colonization, the resulting NC cell density at any colonized region is largely independent of the initial starting numbers. Therefore, the NC cell density increases, through proliferation, to reach a preferred density, which may be regarded as a local carrying capacity.

The elongation of the intestinal tissues, within which the NC cells migrate and proliferate, complicates the net NC cell colonization of the gut. The intestinal tissue is made up of mesenchymal cells which undergo cell division, resulting in rapid tissue expansion – in the midgut this primarily causes an increase in gut length and very little radial expansion [4].

Time lapse observations of enteric NC cells colonizing avian and murine gut have emphasised that the movement of individual cells is unpredictable in speed and direction, while the wave-like spread of the entire population is predictable [5]. Cellular automata (CA) models are ideal for probing this colonization process at the cell-level. Such models naturally incorporate variability between agents (simulating cells) by assigning probabilities to agent (cell) functions such as motility and proliferation. We use a two-dimensional square lattice to represent a cylindrical shell of intestinal tissue (cut longitudinally). We simulate agent colonization on a non-growing and growing lattice. Since the lattice represents the tissue mesenchymal cells, we consider a CA method to increase the lattice length through random insertion of new lattice sites.

The CA models predict testable experimental outcomes. An *in vitro* organ culture system [6] provides a simplified experimental model of NC cell colonization, since normal tissue growth is largely suppressed while the NC cell invasion is otherwise normal. Another *in vivo* system allows NC colonization with rapid gut growth [3]. The model predictions, together with experimental confirmation, are providing major advances to our understanding of HSCR.

## 2　Cellular Automata Model

A discrete time CA model, based on exclusion processes, is used. Each NC agent excludes other NC agents from occupying the same lattice site. A regular square lattice (unit spacing) in two-dimensions is appropriate, since the NC cells are restricted to a cylindrical surface within the intestinal tissue.

Consider a two-dimensional rectangular domain with constant width $Y$ and prescribed length $L(t)$ (for a non-growing domain $L(t) = L(0)$ a constant). The domain consists of sites within a rectangular lattice $(L(t), Y)$ whose positions are located at the discrete integer points $(x, y)$, where $1 \leq x \leq L(t)$ and $1 \leq y \leq Y$. Each lattice site is occupied by a single domain agent, representing a intestinal tissue mesenchymal cell.

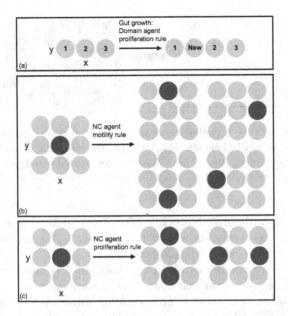

**Fig. 1.** CA mechanisms for domain agent (yellow) proliferation and NC agent (blue) motility and proliferation. (a) Domain agent proliferation rule produces a growing domain. (b) A NC agent can move to one of the four configurations shown with equal probability. (c) A NC agent can divide into two daughter agents, placed at two possible configurations (to replicate experimental observations) with equal probability.

At every time step, each of the operations of domain growth (if it is growing), NC agent movement and proliferation occur in turn.

During a single time step from $t$ to $t+1$, for each row in the lattice, a number of domain agents $n(t)$ are randomly selected to proliferate by mitotic division. Here $n(t) = \text{round}(L(t+1) - L(t))$. If a domain agent at $(x, y)$ proliferates, the original domain agent moves to $(x+1, y)$, and a new domain agent is inserted at $(x, y)$. All domain agents to the right of $(x, y)$ also move one unit in the positive $x$-direction (Fig. 1(a)).

If a NC agent lies on the proliferating domain agent at $(x, y)$, it is transported with its domain agent to $(x + 1, y)$. Similarly, all agents to the right of the proliferating domain agent are transported, along with their domain agents, a unit step to the right.

Suppose the domain contains $m(t)$ NC agents at time $t$. During a single time step from $t$ to $t + 1$, first $m(t)$ NC agents are selected randomly and given the opportunity to move, and then $m(t)$ NC agents are selected randomly and given the opportunity to proliferate. A NC agent at $(x, y)$ that is chosen to be motile attempts to move with probability $P_m$ to one of the four nearest neighbours $(x \pm 1, y \pm 1)$ each with probability $1/4$ (Fig. 1(b)). When considering a potential proliferation event, a mother cellular agent attempts to divide with probability $P_p$, and the two daughter cellular agents are either placed at $(x \pm 1, y)$

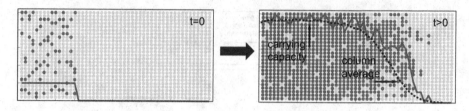

**Fig. 2.** No gut growth. A travelling wave moving to the right evolves, given by the column site occupancy of NC agents (blue line) and the average column site occupancy over 100 realizations (black line). The NC population advances only when the column site occupancy increases to approximately the carrying capacity. Here $P_m = 1$, $P_p = 1$.

or $(x, y \pm 1)$ each with probability $1/2$ (Fig. 1(c)). If the target site for any motility or proliferation event is occupied by another NC agent, then that event is aborted. These events are exclusion processes [7].

Periodic boundary conditions along the horizontal boundaries and no-flux boundary conditions along vertical boundaries are imposed.

It is worth noting that there is no overriding directional signal in the gut. Placement of the NC cells at the anal end of the gut results in reverse-direction migration [8]. In the models discussed here, no directional signal is imposed. Colonization will proceed from left to right only because the initial cell population is placed at the left-hand end.

## 3    Complete or Incomplete Colonization?

The CA algorithm is implemented to simulate various experimental situations for the non-growing and growing gut.

### 3.1    No Gut Growth

First consider the case when all NC agents are labelled the same color. Starting with a small number of agents at the left end of the domain, the agent density first increases on the left with little colonization of the uninvaded part of the domain. At a later time the population reaches its carrying capacity and moves to the right and colonizes the whole domain in finite time (Fig. 2). If the lattice-site occupancy of the NC agents is column-averaged for a single realization (blue line Fig. 2), a representation of the evolving density wave is obtained. Averaging over many realizations, a smooth density wave evolves into a travelling wave moving from left to right with a constant speed, which is dependent on the probabilities associated with agent motility and proliferation, to emulate the well-known Fisher wave [9].

If all the agents are labelled the same color, it is impossible to track the lineage or position of individual agents. In particular, we cannot ascertain whether agents at the wavefront are behaving differently from those well behind the

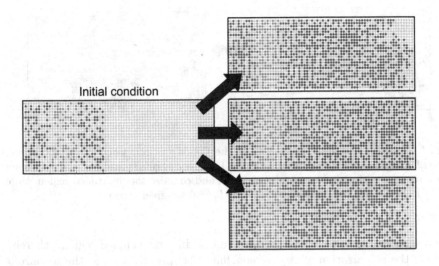

**Fig. 3.** No gut growth. Three realizations of the CA algorithm at the same time, when subpopulations of NC agents are labelled differently. The number of descendants from a single agent can differ vastly (see the two blue agents on the left), while the colonization capacity of the total population is relatively consistent. Here $P_m = 1$, $P_p = 1$ for all agents.

wavefront. Much more information is obtained if agents are labelled by different colors. In Fig. 3 we label three subpopulations of NC agents and we also color two agents right at the wavefront (blue in Fig. 3). In a proliferation event, the daughter NC agents inherit parent's color. At a later time, the agents at the front (red or blue) have been able to proliferate into the uninvaded region and thereby advance the colonization wave. Behind the wavefront, there is some mixing of green and red agent subpopulations, but there is very little proliferation, due to the agent density being already close to its carrying capacity. Therefore the colonization proceeds by *frontal expansion* of the agent population. All three realizations have the same behavior. However, the individual contributions to the increase in agent numbers is vastly different, as illustrated by the different number of blue agents in three realizations. The differences occur through the stochastic nature of the CA algorithm and the variable opportunity of the agent to encounter free space for movement and proliferation events.

In the absence of gut growth, we can determine the behavior of NC cells in different parts of the colonization wave using quail and chick NC cells, since they are functionally equivalent but label differently using antibodies. We suggested a set of experiments to test against our models. In organ culture where there is no gut growth, a segment of chick host gut tissue is removed and replaced with quail donor tissue containing NC cells. Three days later the resulting host and donor cells are identified. Donor cells can be placed at or behind the wavefront. Both models and experiments give the same results [6]. Cells at the wavefront

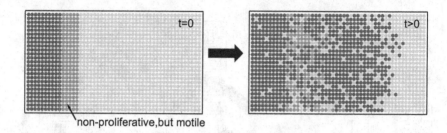

non-proliferative, but motile

**Fig. 4.** No gut growth. A realization of the CA algorithm, when wavefront agents (green) are non-proliferative but are motile. The green agents spread out, the red agents move into the region and eventually overtake and colonize the uninvaded region. Here $P_{\mathrm{m}} = 1$, $P_{\mathrm{p}} = 1$ for red agents and $P_{\mathrm{m}} = 1$, $P_{\mathrm{p}} = 0$ for green agents.

are responsible for an increase in cell numbers into unoccupied regions, thereby driving the colonization wave. We conclude that proliferation at the wavefront is the driver of colonization.

If proliferation at the wavefront is so important, then we ask: what happens if NC agent proliferation is eliminated at the wavefront? (Fig. 4). Our model predicts that the green non-proliferative wavefront agents move (but remain a constant number) and therefore leave space for the red agents to move into this region. Eventually some red agents overtake the green agents, proliferate and become the wavefront agents – these red agents are responsible for driving further colonization through frontal expansion.

This configuration can also be implemented experimentally using donor cells treated to eliminate cell division but preserving cell motility. The experimentalists thought there were two possible outcomes. Either nothing happens (stalling) or the host cells proliferate and push the donor cells forward (shunting). Therefore, the experimentalists were surprised to observe this overtaking phenomenon – their results matched the model predictions.

## 3.2   With Gut Growth

We now include domain growth into the simulations and again label three subpopulations. We observe that the population of agents still colonizes the domain by frontal expansion (Fig.5). However, since more domain agents (yellow) are being randomly inserted throughout the domain producing additional space, agents behind the wavefront are able to continue to proliferate and expand in numbers. Furthermore, there is more mixing of the various colored subpopulations (black, green, red). Note in particular that agents derived from the two blue agents now become mixed with agents of different color in contrast to the coherent blue groupings in the non-growing scenario (top two realizations in Fig. 3).

Whereas with no domain growth the colonization wave always colonizes the whole domain in finite time, this is no longer the case when the domain grows. For a choice of domain growth $L(t)$, if the agent proliferation probability $P_{\mathrm{p}}$ is

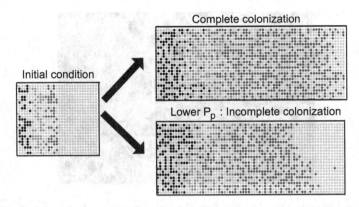

**Fig. 5.** With gut growth. Two realizations of the CA algorithm at the same time for two proliferation rates, when NC subpopulations are labelled. Note the mixing of the subpopulations and the spread out nature of the blue agents. Here $L(t) = 30 + t$ and $P_m = 1$, $P_p = 1$ (top) for all agents, $P_m = 1$, $P_p = 0.5$ (bottom) for all agents.

sufficiently large, then colonization is always successful at some time. However, if the agent proliferation rate is reduced too much, then colonization is incomplete and fails (Fig. 5). In particular, there will always be a region on the right which is unoccupied by NC agents. In this case, agent proliferation and motility cannot keep up with the growth of the domain. (We found that results were much less sensitive to the motility probability parameter $P_m$.) These predictions were confirmed experimentally [3], using highly proliferative versus less proliferative NC cells in a gut growing over a three day period. Indeed, small starting numbers of highly proliferative cells/agents overwhelmingly outperformed large starting numbers of less proliferative cells/agents in both mathematical and biological models [3].

## 4    Mesoscale Structure of the Colonization Wave

The colonization process has many other interesting features. A defining characteristic is the mesoscale structure of the colonization wave. We conclude with a brief discussion of these interesting features, and how they can be incorporated into a more complex CA model. However, the major conclusions of the previous section remains valid. We discuss the case with no gut growth.

Images show that NC cells are in close contact and form chains that intersect, forming a network which is spatially stable over many hours. However the NC cells making up the chains move independently and change neighbors unpredictably on the scale of minutes. Recent experimental observations imply that NC cells have an affinity for nerve fibres (axons) [10]. After eliminating the possibility that NC cells follow some underlying chain-like network, we proposed an alternative hypotheses which were tested using a CA model.

**Fig. 6.** Mesoscale structure (no gut growth). (a) Axons (red lines) form a connected network, NC agent (green) largely occupy sites along the axon (red) so that the NC agent form an interweaving chain-like network. The axons enclose open, often empty, spaces. If a cluster of NC agent is labeled (white and yellow), then (b) at a later time these agents will be separated.

Additional biological features must be included into the CA model [11]. NC cells progressively convert to neurons, and each neuron extends an axon. Axon elongation occurs by growth at the tip, called the growth-cone. The gut tissue produces a growth factor required for NC cell function. We propose that NC cells deplete the growth factor, thus producing a growth factor gradient across the wavefront. Since axon growth-cones are known to respond to growth factor gradients, this mechanism produces a directional forward bias to axon extension.

We translate these features into CA rules for four species of CA agents [11] (and implement on a regular hexagonal tiling). The movement of an NC agent is now biased to move to an axonal agent and follow an axonal agent. NC agents can differentiate into a non-motile and non-proliferative neuronal agent. Neuronal agents extend axonal agents led by a motile growth-cone agent. The growth-cone agent is biased to move to sites which have been recently visited by NC agents. A site may only be occupied by at most one NC agent or one neuronal agent, but can have one or more of the axonal agents or growth-cone agents.

From these simple local rules, a self-organizing network pattern emerges which is stable over time, as illustrated with a single realization in Fig. 6, starting with only a few green NC agents on the very left. There are open empty spaces, as observed experimentally. In order to determine individual NC agent trajectories, we have colored a cluster of agents (yellow and white). At a later time the NC agents become separated, but remain on the stable evolving network. Frontal expansion (not shown) is maintained, but now it is on a mesoscale structure determined by the axonal agents. Therefore, the key characteristics at both the population and cellular level are reproduced by the CA model. A second hypothesis where NC agents form chains spontaneously (by attraction and contact inhibition), while the axonal agents follow these chains, is also explored in Landman et al. [11].

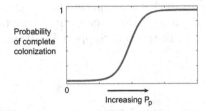

**Fig. 7.** Probability of complete colonization in a growing gut versus the proliferation probability $P_p$ of the NC agents

# 5    Conclusion

Mathematical modeling using cellular automata (CA) in collaboration with developmental biologists is providing insight into the development and disease of the ENS. While molecular investigations have had great success in identifying genes, molecules and pathways, these do not necessarily clarify how the disease is caused. However, mathematical modeling using CA has clarified this in the case of HSCR. The two-way collaboration has led to testable predictions of how the ENS develops in a normal or abnormal way.

The model results have important implications for HSCR. We now understand HSCR to be chiefly a NC cell proliferation defect and not, as previously thought, a NC cell motility defect. Furthermore, the mathematical models and experimental confirmation have identified a major but previously obscure connection between the many genes implicated in HSCR, in that they all directly or indirectly influence NC cell proliferation.

The CA models provide more information than partial differential equation continuum models [12], since they include the variability inherent in biological phenomena. They allow us to track trajectories of each agent, as well as tracking the agent descendants. Furthermore, every realization of our CA model has a different outcome. If the NC agent proliferation is sufficiently high, then all realizations will reach the end of the growing domain. Alternatively, if the NC agent proliferation is sufficiently low, then almost no realizations will reach the end of the growing domain (Fig. 7). At intermediate reductions of NC agent proliferation rate (the equivalent of a HSCR mutation) while the gut is elongating at a normal rate, there is variable success in completing colonization. The probability of success to complete colonization decreases gradually as the NC proliferation rate is lowered gradually. This probabilistic outcome is the result of the stochasticity of movement and proliferation of each NC agent in conjunction with domain growth.

Since stochastic effects can determine success or failure of the colonization process for a certain range of NC agent proliferation rates, we suggest that this mechanism may explain the existence of identical twins where only one of the pair has HSCR.

**Acknowledgments.** This work was supported by Australian Research Council and National Health and Medical Research Council grants and with Victorian Government Operational Infrastructure Support Program.

# References

1. Gershon, M.D.: The second brain: A groundbreaking new understanding of nervous disorders of the stomach and intestine. HarperCollins, New York (1998)
2. Heanue, T.A., Pachnis, V.: Enteric nervous system development and Hirschsprungs disease: advances in genetic and stem cell studies. Nat. Rev. Neurosci. 8, 466–479 (2007)
3. Zhang, D., Brinas, I.M., Binder, B.J., Landman, K.A., Newgreen, D.F.: Neural crest regionalisation for enteric nervous system formation: Implications for Hirschsprungs Disease and stem cell therapy. Dev. Biol. 339, 280–294 (2010)
4. Binder, B.J., Landman, K.A., Simpson, M.J., Mariani, M., Newgreen, D.F.: Modeling proliferative tissue growth: A general approach and an avian case study. Phys. Rev. E 78, 031912 (2008)
5. Young, H.M., Bergner, A.J., Anderson, R.B., Enomoto, H., Milbrandt, J., Newgreen, D.F., Whitington, P.M.: Dynamics of neural crest-derived cell migration in the embryonic mouse gut. Dev. Biol. 270, 455–473 (2004)
6. Simpson, M.J., Zhang, D.C., Mariani, M., Landman, K.A., Newgreen, D.F.: Cell proliferation drives neural crest cell invasion of the intestine. Dev. Biol. 302, 553–568 (2007)
7. Chowdhury, D., Schadschneider, A., Nishinari, K.: Physics of transport and traffic phenomena in biology: from molecular motors and cells to organisms. Phys. Life Rev. 2, 318–352 (2005)
8. Burns, A.J., Delalande, J.M., Le Douarin, N.M.: In ovo transplantation of enteric nervous system precursors from vagal to sacral neural crest results in extensive hindgut colonisation. Dev. 129, 2785–2796 (2002)
9. Murray, J.D., Mathematical Biology, I.: An Introduction, 3rd edn. Springer, Heidelberg (2002)
10. Hao, M.M., Anderson, R.B., Young, H.M.: Development of enteric neuron diversity. J. Cell. Mol. Med. 13, 1193–1210 (2009)
11. Landman, K.A., Fernando, A.E., Zhang, D., Newgreen, D.F.: Building stable chains with motile agents: Insights into the morphology of enteric neural crest cell migration. J. Theor. Biol. 276, 250–268 (2011)
12. Simpson, M.J., Landman, K.A., Hughes, B.D., Newgreen, D.F.: Looking inside an invasion wave of cells using continuum models: Proliferation is the key. J. Theor. Biol. 243, 343–360 (2006)

# A 2D Cellular Automaton Biofilm Detachment Algorithm

Chrysi S. Laspidou[*], Antonis Liakopoulos, and Marios G. Spiliotopoulos

Department of Civil Engineering, University of Thessaly, Pedion Areos, 38334 Volos, Greece
{laspidou,aliakop,spilioto}@uth.gr

**Abstract.** A cellular-automaton based two-dimensional biofilm detachment module is developed. The module is an improvement of previously presented methodologies for modeling biofilm detachment under the influence of hydrodynamic forces of the moving fluid in which biofilm develops. It uses biofilm mechanical properties that are variable in time and space and are determined by the percentage of each biofilm solid substance—active biomass, extracellular polymeric substance (EPS) and residual dead biomass—and pores that are contained in each cellular automaton compartment in the biofilm column. A methodology is presented that estimates wall shear stresses applied on the biofilm by the fluid for different hydrodynamic conditions and an association with the biofilm mechanical properties is created to predict its detachment. The module is applied in samples created by the UMCCA model [Laspidou and Rittmann, Water Res 38 (2004), 3362-3372].

**Keywords:** Biofilm detachment, biofilm mechanical properties, cellular automaton, biofilm wall shear stress, probability of detachment.

## 1    Introduction

A biofilm consists of microbial cells attached to a solid surface that are usually embedded in a matrix of organic polymers produced by cells, the extracellular polymeric substances (EPS). They are found everywhere in nature and are increasingly important in engineering processes used in environmental biotechnology [1]. Some biofilms are viewed as "good," such as those found in wastewater treatment fixed-film processes, or in engineered bioremediation systems of contaminated groundwater. Other biofilms are viewed as "bad," such as those fouling ship hulls, or accumulating in pipes in water distribution systems. They are highly heterogeneous systems; they can have various types of microbial species throughout, which affect the metabolic reactivity in different parts of the biofilm. Multi-species biofilms can include distinctly different microbial types, such as heterotrophs and autotrophs. But even when they include similar microbial types, they are still highly heterogeneous, as microorganisms always produce EPS and "inert" or dead biomass, thus comprising different solid species. Biofilms are also heterogeneous in terms of biomass density and physical strength. The former is the concentration of solid components that form a biofilm, while the latter determines its

---

[*] Corresponding author.

G.C. Sirakoulis and S. Bandini (Eds.): ACRI 2012, LNCS 7495, pp. 415–424, 2012.

ability to resist detachment forces. Clearly, biomass density and physical strength are related to each other.

## 1.1    The UMCCA Model

Discrete particle biofilm models represent biomass in individual units and include two general model classes: cellular automaton (CA) models, such as the Unified Multi-Component Cellular Automaton (UMCCA) model [1]—[2] and individual based models. A comparison of the two types of models is presented in [3]. UMCCA is a hybrid differential and discrete CA model; solutes are represented in a continuous field by reaction-diffusion mass balances, while solids are mapped in a discrete cell-by-cell fashion that employs a CA algorithm. It includes eight major variables: active biomass ($X_a$), extracellular polymers (*EPS*), residual inert biomass ($X_{res}$) and pores, as well as original donor substrate (*S*), two metabolic products—the utilization-associated products (*UAP*) and the biomass-associated products (*BAP*)—and oxygen. The model's general objective is to describe quantitatively the heterogeneity of bio-films. More specifically, one of the main goals of UMCCA is the prediction of varia-ble "composite biofilm density," i.e. a density that corresponds to a total solids or other dry weight measurement, since it has been documented experimentally that biofilm density varies throughout the biofilm depth. To explain such differences in density, UMCCA includes a physical explanation, postulating that biofilm *consoli-dates*, or gradually packs to a higher density, due to differential forces, such as fric-tion that develops as a result of the fluid flowing over it. The consolidation module that is implemented in UMCCA allows the simulation of biofilms that become more compact at their bottoms as they age; it simulates biofilm samples that have been observed experimentally with bottom layers having much higher densities than their "fluffy" top layers.

UMCCA uses a CA algorithm to distribute the newly formed biomass (Fig. 1). It divides the physical space into a fine grid of compartments almost as fine as a single bacterium and biomass grows in the compartments as fast as it is defined by the amount of substrate that is available, the microbial kinetics of the species and the diffusion coefficient. When a compartment fills up completely, the biomass is divid-ed into two parts to simulate cell division when cells multiply; the first part stays in the same compartment, but the second needs to be placed in another "free" compart-ment. The algorithm searches all neighboring cells to find the closest unoccupied compartment. It calculates the Euclidean distance from the center of the full com-partment to the center of all unoccupied compartments that are the closest. Once the algorithm identifies one unoccupied compartment, it keeps searching until it finds all equidistant compartments. It then randomly picks one and back-traces the path to the original overflowing compartment. This is the shortest path from the overflowing compartment to a randomly-chosen "free" compartment. The new biomass will be placed by "shoving" existing biomass along the shortest path that has been identified by the CA algorithm.

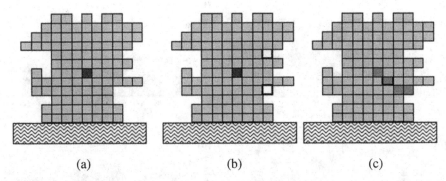

**Fig. 1.** The CA algorithm used in the UMCCA model:  (a) overflowing compartment; (b) the nearest two equidistant compartments to the overflowing compartment; (c) the algorithm randomly picks one of the two and places the new biomass in a neighboring compartment (bold compartment), while it shoves existing biomass along the path of least resistance.

Figure 2 shows some sample model outputs of composite density.  A complete analysis of the initial conditions that led to these simulations is included in [2].  The results in Figure 2 are presented in a shading format, with a shade of gray being associated with a composite density: a black compartment represents a biofilm location that is filled completely (100%) with a combination of solid species, while a white compartment represents an empty compartment.  Figure 2 shows that different conditions produce different physical structures.  Biofilms may grow in "mat" formations (Figure 2a), in "mushrooms" (Figure 2b and c) and in mat formations with "holes" close to the substratum (Figure 2d).  Figures 2b and d show biofilms with much higher densities at the bottom, while Figures 2a and c show lower and more uniform densities throughout the column of the biofilm.  Finally, UMCCA is a 2D model; when performing analyses with UMCCA, we assume that the same biofilm profile extends in the third dimension (width), which may be true for small widths, or for "thin" biofilm slices.

## 1.2     Biofilm Detachment and Mechanical Properties

Biofilm mechanical properties have a great impact on many aspects of biofilm development, such as thickness, overall density, shape, as well as biofilm detachment and its behavior under the influence of hydrodynamic forces.  It is therefore of critical importance to be able to predict biofilm behavior, deformation and detachment in response to hydrodynamics, or other external forces.  Since biofilms can be useful or detrimental, it may be desirable to either promote the former or eliminate the latter; either way, biofilm accumulation depends on its mechanical strength, or its ability to sustain forces that scour or abrade it off the surface.  Biofilm mechanical behavior depends on the composition and density of biomass, which changes in time and in space.  As described above, three solid species are found in a biofilm: active and inert (or dead) bacteria embedded in EPS, which are the bacterially-secreted "glue" that

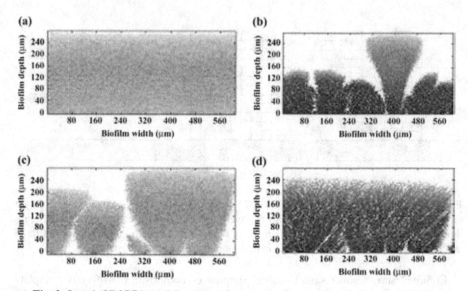

**Fig. 2.** Sample UMCCA model outputs of composite density. Details presented in [2].

binds the other two substances together. Biofilms are porous materials, so the fourth substance is the voids, or pores in the biofilm.

Recently, various researchers have reported some (difficult to measure) experimentally obtained biofilm mechanical properties, such as tensile strength, cohesive strength, elastic modulus, shear modulus, viscoelastic strength, etc. [4]—[9], most of them compiled in [10]. There is great variability between reported measurements, as discussed in Aravas and Laspidou [11], usually attributed to measurement protocols and different biofilm environments during growth and biofilm characterization. Biofilm mechanical properties are mainly affected by density and porosity, quantities that vary from one biofilm to another and also through the biofilm thickness. Porosity decreases in biofilms that are subjected to compressive forces, since the pores collapse [12] and can be reduced to almost zero; conversely, porosity increases when biofilms are under tension. Changes in porosity bring about changes in the volume fractions of all phases throughout the biofilm column [13].

Biofilm detachment, as important as it may be, remains a poorly characterized phenomenon. Researchers that have conducted experiments may report detachment kinetics of limited value since they apply only to their specific system; others use arbitrary kinetics that are not descriptive enough and do not take into account biofilm mechanical properties. Naturally, detachment rates should depend on two factors: (i) hydrodynamic forces exerted by the fluid in which biofilm grows in and (ii) on biofilm mechanical properties, such as "strength" or cohesion. Hermanowicz [14] developed a simple function that includes both hydrodynamics and biofilm cohesion and expresses the probability of cell erosion/detachment. He used the lumped parameter $\sigma$ for biofilm strength and $\tau$ for hydrodynamics, without providing a methodology on how to calculate these quantities; he presented an analysis on how biofilm development would be affected for different values of $\sigma/\tau$. This probability is suitable for use in CA biofilm models. In this paper, we advance this concept by providing a methodology on how to quantify biofilm strength and hydrodynamics and embody it in a CA model for biofilm growth. As an example for the methodology, we apply the concept on a modeling sample produced by UMCCA.

## 2     Materials and Methods

The Young's modulus (or elastic modulus) is a measure of stiffness of an elastic material and is a quantity used to characterize materials. It is measured in units of force per unit area and could therefore be used as a measure of biofilm strength. For the purpose of modeling its mechanical properties, biofilm can be presented as an elastic medium, a homogeneous composite material that is linearly elastic and isotropic. Biofilm elastic modulus is not uniform throughout the biofilm column, but changes in time and space and is a function of the fraction of the three solid components; however, it is not a weighted average of the elastic moduli of individual solid biofilm components. As presented in [12] and [13], in order to obtain a local composite Young's modulus based on the relative amounts of the three solid component materials (EPS, $X_a$ and $X_{res}$), one needs to follow a homogenization technique.

In Figure 3, the composite density of an UMCCA sample that has been presented elsewhere [2] is shown; as described above, shades of grey are used on the image with dark colors corresponding to high densities and light colors to low densities. The same idea is used in Figure 4, where fractions of each one of its three solid components, as well as its porosity, are mapped separately. Biofilm dimensions are 150 cellular automata compartments across the x direction and 70 compartments across the y direction. The dimension of each compartment is 4 by 4 μm, which makes our biofilm sample 600 μm long with a maximum depth of almost 280 μm.

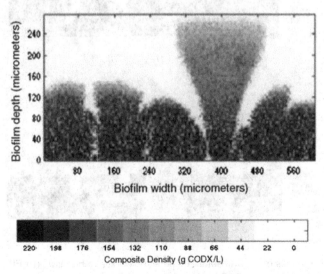

**Fig. 3.** Map of composite density of UMCCA sample; details presented in [2].

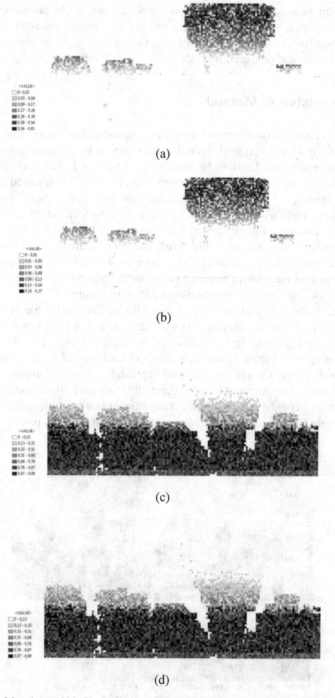

**Fig. 4.** Map of fractions of biofilm solid components: (a) active biomass, (b) EPS, (c) residual dead biomass and (d) voids in UMCCA "mushroom" sample.

**Fig. 5.** Map of Young's modulus throughout the biofilm module in UMCCA sample. Values are in Pa.

The conditions that lead to the formation of such a sample are described in [2]; the biofilm is old, thus, it has a large fraction of inerts at its bottom layers and is closely packed due to consolidation. This can be seen in Figure 4d, in which biofilm porosity is mapped: we see that porosity is almost zero in the biofilm bottom layers, while it is higher in higher layers. In Figure 5, we see a map of the composite tensile modulus throughout the biofilm column, which was calculated using the Willis methodology [13]. We see that localized elastic modulus values are high at the bottom of the biofilm, in which the fraction of inerts is really high and porosity is almost zero.

Hermanowicz [14] describes the probability of detachment by the following function:

$$P_d = \frac{1}{1+(\sigma/\tau)} \tag{1}$$

where, $\sigma$ is a lumped parameter that represents biofilm strength/cohesion and $\tau$ represents hydrodynamic shear stress. What we propose herein is a methodology on how to calculate $\sigma$ and $\tau$. For the former, we set $\sigma$ equal to the value of the localized Young's modulus $E_i$, which is calculated as in [12]—[13]. A different value of tensile modulus is calculated for each cellular automaton compartment and for each time step and is a function of individual fractions of solid components in each compartment and a function of localized biofilm composite density.

We propose to calculate the hydrodynamic shear stress $\tau_w$ as a function of the dimensionless friction factor $f$ used in the Darcy-Weisbach equation. Friction factor $f$ is a function of Reynolds number Re for laminar flow, e.g.:

$$f = \frac{64}{\text{Re}}, \text{ for Re} < 2300 \tag{2}$$

where, $\text{Re} = \dfrac{\rho \bar{V} D}{\mu}$, for flow in a circular pipe of diameter D, while for flow in pipes of different cross-sectional shape, an equivalent diameter is calculated; $\rho$ and $\mu$ are the fluid density and viscosity respectively. In this context, biofilm developing in a pipe is treated as "roughness" or rugosity, causing energy losses due to friction. To model roughness, the dimensionless ratio ε/D, called "relative roughness" is used, which relates the height of the small-scale variations in the pipe to its diameter. To calculate the ε/D ratio, we set ε equal to the average biofilm depth (or height) and D equal to the sum of the highest point of the biofilm plus the boundary layer length.

Friction factor $f$ is a function of Re and ε/D for turbulent flow in pipes as shown in the Colebrook-White equation:

$$\frac{1}{f^{1/2}} = -2.0 \log\left(\frac{\varepsilon/D}{3.7} + \frac{2.51}{\text{Re}\, f^{1/2}}\right) \tag{3}$$

and is usually obtained by reading the Moody diagram. Numerical approximations also exist, that usually have excellent results. Equation (4) is the Swamee-Jain approximation that can be used in the cellular automaton algorithm to calculate $f$.

$$f = \frac{0.25}{\left[\log\left(\dfrac{\varepsilon}{3.7D} + \dfrac{5.74}{\text{Re}^{0.9}}\right)\right]^2} \tag{4}$$

Analogous relationships are established for flat surfaces, where $\tau_w$ varies with the distance from the leading edge of the surface [15]. For more complicated surfaces, $\tau_w$ can be experimentally measured as function of position. Once $f$ is calculated, we can obtain hydrodynamic stress $\tau_w$ from the following equation:

$$\tau_w = \frac{\rho V^2 f}{8} \tag{5}$$

which includes fluid velocity V and fluid density ρ. In this methodology, we obtain a single hydrodynamic stress $\tau_w$ for each time step, i.e. $\tau_w$ does not vary with space, but only with time. At each time step, we calculate a different ε/D, as biofilm morphology and its depth change; since $\tau_w$ is calculated using average biofilm sample dimensions, it is not localized for each cellular automaton compartment.

## 3    Results and Discussion

We apply the methodology described in the previous section on the biofilm sample shown in Figure 3, in order to calculate the probability of detachment. Since this is merely a modeling sample and we do not have fluid velocity measurements to calculate Reynolds number and fluid velocity, we assume a high hydrodynamic shear stress $\tau_w$ equal to 10 Pa. For this sample, to obtain the ε/D ratio, we calculate the average biofilm depth of the sample. We average the depths of all cellular automata columns (150 columns) to find the average roughness depth (ε); for the UMCCA sample shown in Figure 2, ε is set at 176 μm (average biofilm depth). We then divide it by D, which in this case, is 280 μm (maximum biofilm depth) increased by the boundary

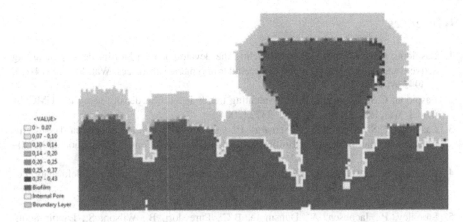

**Fig. 6.** Map of probability of detachment on the cellular automaton cells that are in contact with the fluid. Boundary layer is also shown.

layer thickness, which is assumed to be 40 μm (10 cellular automaton compartments); thus, total D is found 320 μm and the ε/D ratio is 0.55.

We calculate the probability of detachment for cellular automata compartments that are on the biofilm "front," i.e. only for biofilm compartments that are in contact with the fluid. In Figure 6, we present the results in a graphical format: In this case, we show the biofilm as a uniform body (we use a single color) and also map the boundary layer around the biofilm. Probability of detachment values are as high as 0.43, while we see that high values are observed on the top layers of the "mushroom," where biofilm is "young," "fluffy" and porous and has relatively low tensile modulus values. On the other hand, in areas where biofilm is old, lacks pores and is almost 100% inert, probability of detachment is relatively small, since biofilm has a high Young's modulus and is considered strong and stiff. Using the methodology presented in this article, we get probabilities of detachment that are consistent with what has been observed experimentally elsewhere.

## 4    Conclusions

In this article, we have presented a methodology for the calculation of a probability of detachment based on biofilm mechanical properties that are variable in time and space. Mechanical properties are based on biofilm composition and are calculated using a homogenization technique that treats biofilm as a composite solid composed of four different materials with different mechanical properties each. We also present a methodology for the calculation of hydrodynamic shear wall stress, based on Reynolds number and biofilm dimensions. The result is the calculation of a probability of detachment, which is low when biofilm is strong and stiff and high when biofilm is porous and "fluffy". This probability of detachment is suitable for use in biofilm CA models.

# References

1. Laspidou, C.S., Rittmann, B.E.: Modeling the development of biofilm density including active bacteria, inert biomass and extracellular polymeric substances. Wat. Res. 38(14-15), 3349–3361 (2004)
2. Laspidou, C.S., Rittmann, B.E.: Evaluating trends in biofilm density using the UMCCA model. Wat. Res. 38(14-15), 3362–3372 (2004)
3. Laspidou, C.S., Kungolos, A., Samaras, P.: Cellular-Automata and Individual-Based Approaches for the Modeling of Biofilm Structures. Pros. and Cons., Desalination 250, 390–394 (2009)
4. Stoodley, P., Lewandowski, Z., Boyle, J.D., Lappin-Scott, H.M.: Structural deformation of bacterial biofilms caused by short-term fluctuations in fluid shear: An in situ investigation of biofilm rheology. Biotechnol. Bioeng. 65(1), 83–92 (1999)
5. Stoodley, P., Jacobsen, A., Dunsmore, B.C., Purevdorj, B., Wilson, S., Lappin-Scott, H.M., Costerton, J.W.: The influence of fluid shear and A1C13 on the material properties of *Pseudomonas aeruginosa* PAO1 and *Desulfovibrio sp.* EX265 biofilms. Water Sci. Technol. 43, 113–120 (2001)
6. Poppele, E.H., Hozalski, R.: Micro-cantilever method for measuring the tensile strength of biofilms and microbial flocs. J. Microbiol. Methods 55, 607–615 (2003)
7. Körstgens, V., Flemming, H.-C., Wingender, J., Borchard, W.: Uniaxial compression measurement device for investigation of the mechanical stability of biofilms. J. Microbiol. Methods 46, 9–17 (2001)
8. Klapper, I., Rupp, C.J., Cargo, R., Purvedorj, B., Stoodley, P.: Viscoelastic fluid description of bacterial biofilm material properties. Biotechnol. Bioeng. 80(3), 289–296 (2002)
9. Vinogradov, A.M., Winston, M., Rupp, C.J., Stoodley, P.: Rheology of biofilms formed from the dental plaque pathogen *Streptococcus mutans*. Biofilms 1, 49–56 (2004)
10. Aggarwal, S., Hozalski, R.: Determination of biofilm mechanical properties from tensile tests performed using a micro-cantilever method. Biofouling 26(4), 479–486 (2010)
11. Aravas, N., Laspidou, C.: On the calculation of the elastic modulus of a biofilm streamer. Biotechnol. Bioeng. 101(1), 196–200 (2008)
12. Laspidou, C.S., Aravas, N.: Variation in the mechanical properties of a porous multi-phase biofilm under compression due to void closure. Water Sci. Technol. 55(8-9), 447–453 (2007)
13. Laspidou, C.S., Rittmann, B.E., Karamanos, S.A.: Finite element modeling to expand the UMCCA model to describe biofilm mechanical behavior. Wat. Sci. Tech. 52(7), 161–166 (2005)
14. Hermanowicz, S.W.: A simple 2D biofilm model yields a variety of morphological features. Math. Biosciences 169, 1–14 (2001)
15. Liakopoulos, A.: Fluid Mechanics. Tziolas Publications, Thessaloniki (2010) (in Greek)

# Creature Learning to Cross a CA Simulated Road

Anna T. Lawniczak[1,2], Jason B. Ernst[3], and Bruno N. Di Stefano[2,4]

[1] Department of Mathematics and Statistics, University of Guelph, Guelph, Ontario, Canada
alawnicz@uoguelph.ca
[2] The Fields Institute for Research in Mathematical Sciences, Toronto, Ontario, Canada
[3] School of Computer Science, University of Guelph, Guelph, Ontario, Canada
jernst@uoguelph.ca
[4] Nuptek Systems Ltd, Toronto, Ontario, Canada
bruno.distefano@nupteksystems.com, b.distefano@ieee.org

**Abstract.** Agent-based models approximate the behaviour of simple natural and man-made systems. We present a simple cognitive agent capable of evaluating if a strategy has been applied successfully and capable of applying this strategy again with small changes to a similar but new situation. We describe some experimental results, present our conclusions, and outlines future work.

**Keywords:** Agents, Cognitive Agents, Learning, Fuzzy Logic, Fuzzy Learning, Cellular Automata, Rule 184, Nagel-Schreckenberg model.

## 1    Introduction

An agent is an abstraction of an autonomous entity capable of interacting with its environment and other agents, [1], [2], [3], [4], [5]. The actual embodiment of the agent, e.g. software program in a simulated reality (e.g., virtual reality) or a stand-alone hardware, depends on the problem for which the agent has been designed. Even when the agent results in something that is actually built in a tangible form, almost always a software instantiation exists to model and simulate it before it is actually built. This makes mistakes and misunderstandings explicit, thus avoiding costly hardware modifications. In a given simulated reality, agents perform "Reflexive Acts", i.e. perceiving reality (the environment and the other agents) and responding to the actions (i.e., the dynamics) of other entities. The ability of agents to act autonomously is limited to the predefined environment and to the predefined situations to which the agent is expected to respond, because agents can only act in a situation compatible with the way they are designed. In fact the behaviour of the agent is provided by means of a finite state machine or a set of finite state machines. A problem with all finite state machines is that their design, verification, validation, coding, and testing becomes progressively harder when trying to prepare the finite state machine for all possible scenarios beyond a small number. "Cognitive agents" partially solve this problem by performing "Cognitive Acts" (i.e., a sequence consisting of all of the following acts: Perceiving, Reasoning, Judging, Responding, and Learning). The functionality and performance of cognitive agents requires replacing the finite state

G.C. Sirakoulis and S. Bandini (Eds.): ACRI 2012, LNCS 7495, pp. 425–433, 2012.
© Springer-Verlag Berlin Heidelberg 2012

machine typical of "non cognitive" agents, i.e. "reactive agents", with more complex functional blocks, built using computational intelligence methodology, i.e.: fuzzy logic, neural networks, evolutionary computation, and various types of bio-mimicry [6], [7]. In reality, also cognitive agents are implemented by means of software or a mix of hardware and software and are still far from the performance of animals and humans.

In this paper we explore what may be considered some of the simplest possible cognitive functions of a primitive cognitive agent.

The paper is structured as follows: section 2 describes the universe of the problem domain that we are studying (i.e., the environment, the population of agents, and the experiment); section 2.1 describes and discusses the learning algorithms implemented for our agents; section 2.2 describes our model and its software implementation; section 3 contains some experimental results; section 4 presents our conclusions and outlines future work.

## 2     The Environment, the Population of Agents, and the Experiment

For our research we assume that an agent is *"an autonomous entity capable of interacting with its environment and other agents"*, [1], [2], [3], [4], [5]. For simplicity and for ease of visualization as in [8], we assume that the agent is a creature with a strong instinct to forage for food. The environment is a piece of land with a long stretch of highway characterized by unidirectional vehicular traffic, without any intersection [8]. In some scenarios the highway is a single lane highway, while in other scenarios it can be a two or three lane highway. While in this paper we do not report on bidirectional traffic, bidirectional vehicular traffic is conceivable in our model. We assume that each creature must cross the highway in order to reach food. However, given the presence of vehicular traffic, crossing the highway may or may not be successful for the creature. If successful, the creature simply crosses, reaches the food and never crosses again. Otherwise if not successful, the creature is struck by a vehicle and dies. Crossing may happen at any point of the highway.

We assume that the creatures are a population of agents who can observe the outcome of the previous attempt to cross by other creatures of the same species [8]. Based on this observation each creature may decide to postpone crossing if the situation resembles one that has resulted in the death of another creature that has previously crossed. However, for realism's sake we assume that the creature cannot derive quantitative information from its observations. Thus, the creature can perceive only "fuzzy" categories for speeds such as "fast" "medium" and "slow", and proximities such as "close distance", "medium distance", and "far distance".

The experiment consists in studying how the creature can "naturally" learn to avoid being struck by vehicles after having observed a sufficient number of other creatures attempting the same or similar crossings. The creature is capable of applying several learning algorithms. We model the motion of the vehicles according to the Nagel-Schreckenberg model, [9], which can be seen as an extension of ECA (Elementary

CA) Rule 184. This rule accurately describes the motion of a vehicle at constant speed of one cell per time step and null acceleration. This is unrealistic, but is a good starting point to apply extensions to Rule 184 as it may be needed. It is important to notice that Rule 184 is deterministic and cannot simulate real traffic with accidents. The Nagel-Schreckenberg model solves the problem adding stochastic behaviour, a larger size neighbourhood that can be used to implement variable speed and non null acceleration. Nagel and Schreckenberg extend the neighbourhood from one cell (as in ECA Rule 184) to five cells. They introduce six discrete velocities. The model consists of four steps that are applied simultaneously to all cars:

- Acceleration
- Safety Distance Adjustment
- Randomization
- Change of Position

For our investigation the implementation of the Nagel-Schreckenberg model requires to modify the Cellular Automata (CA) paradigm and to make the evolution of the CA not only dependent on the state of the neighbourhood but also on the current velocity of each vehicle. This implies that each cell is characterized not only by presence or absence of a vehicle but also by a pointer to a data structure containing the current velocity of the vehicle. The motion of the creature is modeled similarly to the motion of the vehicle, with a CA-like approach. However, the creature decides if to move or not to move not only based on positional criteria, but also on reasoning dependent on what the creature has learned observing the prior experience of other creatures.

## 2.1    The Learning Algorithm

A lot of interesting research on learning algorithms has been conducted [9], [11]. Many algorithms have been developed for various situations [6], [7]. However, at this stage our interest is to start with the simplest possible algorithm, the one requiring the least complex brain [8]. We assume that our creature is not capable of detailed quantitative reasoning. We apply two main learning algorithms: a simple "naïve" algorithm and a fuzzy logic based algorithm.

**We First Describe the Simple "Naïve" Algorithm**

We assume that the creature is capable of matching simple patterns. If a set of values of distance, velocity, and crossing point resulted in success (or failure) for other creatures, the creature attempting to cross the highway will expect that a similar set of values will result in a similar outcome, i.e. success or failure as it may apply. We assume that the creature will always repeat the action that has previously resulted in success. If the set of distance, velocity and crossing point does not correspond to a known outcome, i.e. if this situation has never occurred earlier, the creature will assume that crossing is possible. At each cell where the crossing may take place the creature builds a "mental" table with all possible outcomes for all possible combinations of vehicle distance and vehicle velocity. When behaving according to the "naïve" algorithm, the creature has an optimistic approach. What is not known to have failed earlier, it is assumed to be successful. A "0" in the table means that either that situation has never occurred earlier or that it resulted in success. If crossing results in a creature being struck all other creatures will "write" a "1" for the specific (distance, velocity) combination, while if the crossing is successful a "0" will be left for the specific (distance, velocity) combination. In other words, the mental table in the beginning is populated with 0s in the assumption that all possible distance velocity combinations allow crossing.

**"Naïve" Algorithm with "Fear" and "Desire"**

The mental table described so far is the knowledgebase of the creature. The "naïve" algorithm is totally based on this knowledge-base. However, "fear" and "desire" may alter the behavior of the creature. When a creature is created, its fear and desire are both random between 0 and 1. The algorithm can use this information so that creatures which are fearless and have a strong motivation such as availability of food on the other side of the road are more likely to cross in risky situations, as opposed to fearful creatures that even under safe conditions may not cross the highway. However, it is possible to use these two parameters to make all creatures behave as fearless/fearful. In short "fear" and "desire" act as modifiers of the decision made by the creature if to cross or not to cross.

**Fuzzy Logic Based Algorithm**

Two types of fuzzy logic inference algorithms are available to the creature, one using three membership functions and the other using five membership functions to evaluate the distance and velocity of the vehicle to decide if to cross or not to cross. Currently, the membership functions are triangle shaped, but more complex shapes are possible and will be studied in the future.

## 2.2    The Model and Its Software Implementation

The simulation software implementation is based on a configuration file containing in plain ascii text all parameters of the specific experiment.

The highway traffic is modeled adopting the Nagel – Schreckenberg model, [9]. As customary in the traffic modeling literature, we model the one lane highway as a large number of adjacent cells, with each cell representing a segment of highway of 7.5m in length [12]. Such representation has been chosen because it corresponds on average to the space occupied by the typical car plus the distance to the preceding car in a situation of dense traffic jam of cars of more or less homogeneous length (i.e., trucks and busses are excluded). The simulation also supports multiple lanes.

The program is based on two loops, an "external" time loop and an "internal" space loop [12]. The time loop simulates the passing of time, assigning a number of seconds to each time step. The space loop "scans" the representation of the physical highways, where distances are converted into cells, for every cell checking if the cell is occupied by a car or not. If it is not occupied by a car the next cell is examined, while if the cell is occupied by a car the "rule of transition" (also called "rule of motion") is applied. At each time step in the simulation, for each lane, a new car may be generated with a probability specified in the configuration file as car creation probability. If there is already a car in the first lane because it hasn't sped up enough, or traffic is congested, it is added to a queue of cars waiting to enter the highway. The entrance point is always cell zero of each lane. Cars move according to the Nagel – Schreckenberg model. That is to say, they accelerate by one until they reach their maximum speed which is specified in the configuration file. With the assumption that the cells are 7.5m, a maximum speed of 10 corresponds to 99 km/h. If a car encounters another car in front of it, it slows down to match the speed to avoid a collision. The simulation also supports the idea of random deceleration of cars (as specified by the Nagel-Schrekenberg model, [9]), and can be turned on or off by setting RANDOM_DECEL to TRUE in the configuration file. So far we have not experimented with this, as we commence our investigation focusing on understanding simple experiments. It is our intention to explore more complex situations in the future.

The creatures are implemented in a fashion similar to the cars. They also use a queue so that if a creature has not yet crossed, the new creatures line up behind it. The creatures are generated with a creation probability at each time step, and at each cross point. Cross points are specified in the configuration file and can be repeated as many times as there are places for the creature to cross. When a creature crosses, it does so one lane at a time. In the presented study we consider only one fixed crossing point and one lane highway. In a single time step, the creature looks at the environment (where cars are, and with what speed they are travelling) then decides to move. If it decides to move, it moves onto the highway, then the cars move. If a car moves into the cell the creature is occupying or to a cell with coordinate number higher than the creature's cell number, then the creature is hit. In order for a creature to decide whether to move, it must consult the global "knowledgebase" derived from the creatures' past experiences. This "knowledgebase" is a table of states and results. The table has "fuzzy" categories for speed (e.g., "fast", "medium", and "slow") and proximities (e.g., "close", "med", and "far"). The values are all set in the configuration file for "fast", "medium", "slow", "close" and "far". When a creature attempts to cross under one of these conditions, if it is hit, a negative result is recorded. If the creature successfully crosses, a positive result is recorded. In a multi-lane highway, the result is propagated to all of lanes – condition pairs the creature encountered on its trip across the lanes.

# 3      Experimental Results

The software developed to simulate our model allows, among other things, to log the results of the simulation. At this preliminary stage of our research, we have produced 500 simulation plots, each consisting of 1009 time steps. In what follows, as an example, we show two sets of plots for different simulation parameters.

Figure 1 shows the "crossing success rate" for different values of vehicle creation probability, which is equivalent to the traffic density on the road. In all cases the crossing algorithm is the "naïve" algorithm. The stretch of road under examination (i.e., being simulated) is 1009 cells long (equivalent to 7567.5 m). The road consists of 1 lane only. The duration of the simulation is 1009 time steps (only 50 displayed).

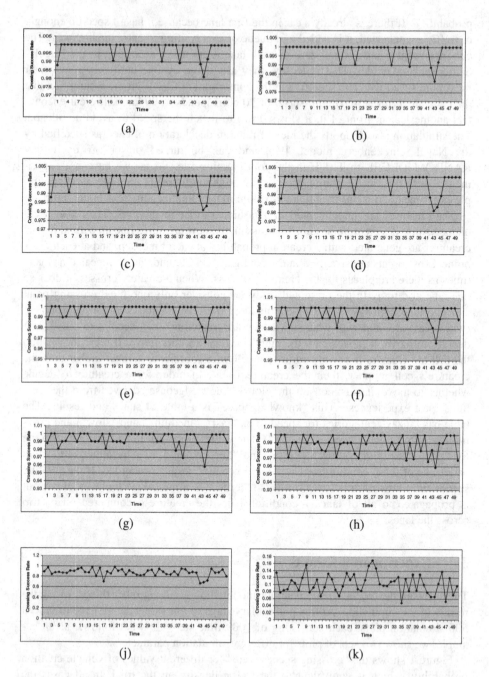

**Fig. 1.** "naïve" Algorithm; 1009 cells (equivalent to 7567.5 m); 1 lane; 1009 time steps (only 50 displayed); creature creation probability 0.1 – Vehicle creation probability: (a) 0.1, (b) 0.2, (c) 0.3, (d) 0.4, (e) 0.5, (f) 0.6, (g) 0.7, (h) 0.8, (j) 0.9, (k) 1.0

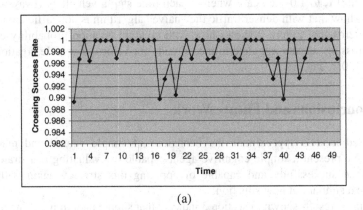

(a)

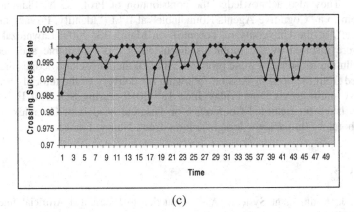

(b)

(c)

**Fig. 2.** "naïve" Algorithm; 1009 cells (equivalent to 7567.5 m); 1 lane; 1009 time steps (only 50 displayed);   creature creation probability 0.3 – Vehicle creation probability: (a) 0.1, (b) 0.2, (c) 0.3

The creature creation probability is 0.1, while the vehicle creation probability ranges from 0.1, to 1.0 (i.e., case when at each time step a vehicle is always created. The plots show that with denser traffic the "naïve" algorithm is not sufficient to allow for a safe crossing. Figure 2 shows how with creature creation probability equal to 0.3, the crossing success rate deteriorates already for values of vehicle creation probability: 0.1, 0.2, and 0.3.

# 4    Conclusions and Future Work

Agent-based models approximate the behaviour of simple natural and man-made systems. We present a simple cognitive agent capable of evaluating if a strategy has been applied successfully and capable of applying this strategy again with small changes to a similar but new situation.

Preliminary results shown in section 3 indicate that simple pattern matching as in the "naïve" algorithm is not sufficient to allow safe crossing. We suspect that "jaywalkers", as pedestrians crossing illegally between traffic lights are called in North America, have much better cognitive equipment than the little creatures of our experiment. We are planning to continue our study first by examining the outcome of the adoption of the two fuzzy inference algorithms programmed in our simulator. Later, if needed, we will apply other computational intelligence techniques such as genetic algorithm,

**Acknowledgments.** A. T. Lawniczak acknowledges partial financial support from the Natural Science and Engineering Research Council (NSERC) of Canada. B. N. Di Stefano acknowledges full financial support from Nuptek Systems Ltd., J. Ernst acknowledges full financial support from a SHARCNET Research Fellowship provided by A. T. Lawniczak. B. N. Di Stefano and A. T. Lawniczak acknowledge the hospitality of The Fields Institute for Research in Mathematical Sciences during the preparation of this manuscript. They also acknowledge the contribution of Prof. K. N. Plataniotis who invited them to a "Cognitive Agents Roundtable" at IPSI ("Identity, Privacy and Security Institute", at the University of Toronto), on March 13, 2009. Lawniczak and Di Stefano were inspired by the problems discussed at this roundtable and decided to search a solution for some of these problems. B.N.Di Stefano acknowledges the inspiration derived from the open discussion following his delivery of the tutorial "Simulation of cognitive multi-agents", on Friday June 18$^{th}$ 2010, during SOLSTICE 2010 (2nd Summer Solstice International Conference on Discrete Models of Complex Systems), LORIA laboratory (http://www.loria.fr/le-loria-1-en), Nancy, France.

# References

1. Ferber, J.: Multi-Agent Systems. An Introduction to Distributed Artificial Intelligence. Addison Wesley, London (1999)
2. Di Stefano, B.N., Lawniczak, A.T.: Cognitive agents: Functionality & performance requirements and a proposed software architecture. In: 2009 IEEE Toronto International Conference on Proc. of Science and Technology for Humanity (TIC-STH), pp. 509–514 (2009)

3. Lawniczak, A.T., Di Stefano, B.N.: Computational intelligence based architecture for cognitive agents. In: ICCS 2010, Procedia Computer Science, Amsterdam, Holland, May 31 - June 2, vol. 1(1), pp. 2221–2229. Elsevier (2010)
4. Wooldridge, M.: An Introduction to MultiAgent Systems. John Wiley & Sons, Ltd., Chichester (2009)
5. Uhrmacher, A.M., Weyns, D.: Multi-Agent Systems Simulation and Applications. CRC Press, Taylor & Francis Group, Boca Raton (2009)
6. Kasabov, N.K.: Foundations of Neural Networks, Fuzzy Systems and Knowledge Engineering. The MIT Press, Cambridge (1988)
7. Tettamanzi, A., Tomassini, M.: Soft Computing, Integrating Evolutionary, Neural, and Fuzzy Systems. Springer, Heidelberg (2001)
8. Di Stefano, B.N., Lawniczak, A.T.: Modeling a Simple Adaptive Cognitive Agent. Acta Physica Polonica, B Proceedings Supplement 5(1), 21–29 (2012)
9. Nagel, K., Schreckenberg, M.: A cellular automaton model for freeway traffic. J. Physique I 2, 2221–2229 (1992)
10. Marsland, S.: Machine Learning: An Algorithm Perspective. Chapman and Hall/CRC (2009)
11. Alpaydin, E.: Introduction to Machine Learning, 2nd edn. The MIT Press, Cambridge (2009)
12. Lawniczak, A.T., Di Stefano, B.N.: Development of CA model of highway traffic. In: Adamatzky, A., Alonso-Sanz, R., Lawniczak, A., Martinez, G.J., Morita, K., Worsch, T. (eds.) Automata-2008, Theory and Applications of Cellular Automata. Luniver Press, U.K. (2008)

# An Electro-Mechanical Cardiac Simulator Based on Cellular Automata and Mass-Spring Models

Ronan Mendonça Amorim[2], Ricardo Silva Campos[1], Marcelo Lobosco[1], Christian Jacob[2], and Rodrigo Weber dos Santos[1]

[1] Universidade Federal de Juiz de Fora, Juiz de Fora - MG, Brazil
[2] University of Calgary, Calgary, Canada
rmamorim@ucalgary.ca, {ricardo,marcelo.lobosco}@ice.ufjf.br,
cjacob@ucalgary.ca, rodrigo.weber@ufjf.edu.br
http://www.fisiocomp.ufjf.br

**Abstract.** The mechanical behavior of the heart is guided by the propagation of an electrical wave, called action potential. Many diseases have multiple effects on both electrical and mechanical cardiac physiology. To support a better understanding of the multiscale and multiphysics processes involved in physiological and pathological cardiac conditions, a lot of work has been done in developing computational tools to simulate the electro-mechanical behavior of the heart. In this work, we propose a new user-friendly and efficient tool for the electro-mechanical simulation of the cardiac tissue that is based on cellular automata and mass-spring models. The proposed tool offers a user-friendly interface that allows one to interact with the simulation on-the-fly. In addition, the simulator is parallelized with CUDA and OpenMP to further speedup the execution time of the simulations.

**Keywords:** Cardiac modeling, Cellular automata, Parallel computing.

## 1 Introduction

Cardiac diseases are a major cause of death in the world and a lot of work has been done to elucidate their causes. The heart pumps blood to the whole body and its contraction is preceded and triggered by a fast electrical wave, i.e. the propagation of the so called action potential (AP). Abnormal changes in the electrical properties of cardiac cells as well as in the structure of the heart tissue can lead to life-threatening arrhythmias and fibrillation.

Mathematical models have been widely used to study the electrical activity in the heart. In the cell level, ordinary differential equations (ODEs) are generally used to describe the electrical and mechanical behaviour.

Tissue simulation involves the simulation of thousands of cells, which make its numerical solution quite challenging. The electrical wave propagation is often modeled with partial differential equations (PDEs). Cardiac cells are connected to each other by gap junctions creating a channel between neighboring cells

G.C. Sirakoulis and S. Bandini (Eds.): ACRI 2012, LNCS 7495, pp. 434–443, 2012.

and allowing the flux of electrical current in the form of ions. An electrically stimulated cell transmits an electrical signal to the neighboring cells allowing the propagation of an electrical wave to the whole heart which triggers contraction.

This work proposes a cellular automata model to represent electrical excitation of cells propagating according to simple rules in a regular, discrete and finite network. It uses precomputed profiles of cell AP and force-development that mimics those obtained by complex models based on ODEs. Although it is less accurate than the models based on ODEs, it is much faster than PDE based-simulators, making possible real time time simulations of heart behavior. In this paper we present a 2D cellular automata (CA) simulator of the electrical activity of the heart coupled with a mass-spring system to simulate the cardiac mechanical behavior.

Our simulator was able to assess interesting cases such as the influence of ischemic cells on the generation of spiral waves and the mechanical behavior under this pathological condition. Our simulation platform is fast enough to allow the users to change the simulation setup and model parameters on-the-fly, i.e. during its execution. In order to achieve this goal the solution of the model was parallelized with OpenMP, a set of directives used to explore multi-core environments. It was also parallelized with the CUDA, so that part of the simulation runs on Graphic Processing Units. Because of the embarrassingly parallel nature of the CA and the mass-spring system, the simulator was able to allow on-the-fly simulation changes for relatively large setups, i.e. for cardiac tissues composed by large number of cells.

The work is organized as follows: Section 2 presents the application and the techniques used in its implementation, Section 3 shows how the code was parallelized and Section 2 presents the results.

## 2   The Cellular Automata

The Cellular Automata (CA) can be used to simulate macroscopically the excitation-propagation in the cardiac tissue. If the electrical potential of a cell exceeds a threshold the cell gets excited and this excitation can trigger the excitation of the neighboring cells. Therefore, an electrical stimulus will propagate through the CA grid as the time steps are computed. The following sections will describe the CA approach for simulating the anisotropic electrical propagation in the cardiac tissue and the force-development in each cell.

### 2.1   Cellular Automata Lattice States and Rules

The CA states are related to the AP and force development in a cell. To make CAs more efficient they are usually parametrized using real or simulated data from accurate models. This means that the states related to the AP in the cell will be related to a specific portion of the cardiac cell potential. Figure 1 presents how the AP of a cell can be divided into five different states. In state S0 the cell is in its resting potential where it can be stimulated, in S1 the cell

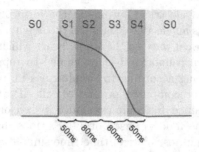

**Fig. 1.** Action potential of a cardiac cell separated into five different states (S0,S1,S2,S3,S4) for the cellular automata

was stimulated and can stimulate the neighbors. In S2 the cell is still able to stimulate the neighbors. In S3 the cell is in its absolute-refractory state where it cannot be stimulated and do not stimulate its neighbors. In S4 the cell is in its relative refractory state where it can be stimulated by more than one neighbor but it does not stimulate its neighbors. As described, the state of a cell generate rules for when a cell can stimulate a neighbor and when it can be stimulated. These rules are an important aspect which will allow the stimulus to propagate. Another important point is how the cells change their states. The AP has a predetermined period so that the states will be spontaneously changed when an AP starts, according to the timing presented in Figure 1.

Some fatty build-ups in arteries can totally or partially block the blood irrigation in parts of cardiac tissue causing it to die (not propagating stimulus, dead cells) or to behave differently (ischemic cells). The ischemic cells of the tissue present an AP with different properties than a healthy cell. Usually it has a shorter duration of the AP with different potential values. Table 1 presents the CA states, potential and times for both healthy and ischemic tissue. The contraction of a cardiac cell is coupled with the electrical potential of the cell. When the cell is stimulated it will increase the concentration of calcium ions inside the cell which will cause the cell contraction. The force development has a delay after the cell is stimulated because of its dependence on the calcium ions.

**Table 1.** Healthy and ischemic states of the cellular automata and the respective duration and potentials

| CA State | Healthy Cell | | Ischemic Cell | |
|---|---|---|---|---|
| | Duration | Potential | Duration | Potential |
| S0 | in rest | -90mV | in rest | -70mV |
| S1 | 50ms | +20mV | 50ms | 0mV |
| S2 | 80ms | 0mV | 40ms | -40mV |
| S3 | 80ms | -25mV | 25ms | -60mV |
| S4 | 50ms | -50mV | 10ms | -65mV |

The force development of a cell can be represented in states that change over time like the electrical potential states. Figure 2 presents the force development states and its relation with the electrical states. The force-development states will only pass from state F0 (no contraction force) to state F1 when the electrical state of the cell goes from state S1 to S2. After this change, force development will be time dependent but will not depend on the electrical state of the cell, i.e. will be ruled by a mass-spring model, as described in the next sections.

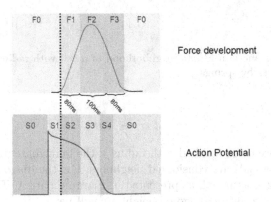

**Fig. 2.** Force development states in relation with the cell electrical states

## 2.2  Propagation Rules

The electrical propagation velocity in the cardiac tissue is dictated by the fiber direction and tissue type. Figure 3 shows typical conduction velocities for the ventricle tissue along and transversal to fiber direction. The CA is discretized in space and time. Each cell in the CA corresponds to tissue square of area $dx \times dx$, where $dx$ is the space discretization. CA states are updated at every discretized time, $dt$. Based on this information and the velocities we can calculate the time that a stimulus takes to travel from one CA cell to another. For simplification, imagine that the propagation has the same velocity $v$ in all directions (isotropic tissue). The time $t$ for a stimulus travel from the center of one cell to another is given by:

$$dx = v \times t \tag{1}$$

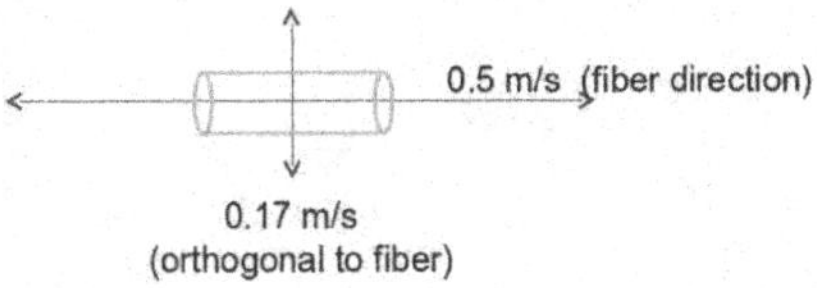

**Fig. 3.** Typical conduction velocities along and transversal to fiber directions of a ventricular tissue

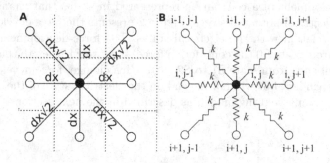

**Fig. 4.** A) The distances in Moore neighborhood of a cell with radius 1. B) Interconnected set of masses by springs.

$$t = \frac{dx}{v} \tag{2}$$

Assuming a Moore neighborhood with radius 1, the immediate top, bottom, left, right and all diagonals are considered neighbors. For the diagonals, a different distance of $dx\sqrt{2}$ is assumed, as presented in Figure 4 part A. The time for the stimulus to travel from the diagonal neighbors will be:

$$t = \frac{dx\sqrt{2}}{v} \tag{3}$$

The fiber direction is included for each cell in the CA. For including the fiber direction in the computation of the traveling time of a stimulus an angle between the neighbor and the fiber direction is calculated. The velocity of propagation will depend on this angle.

The activation of a cell will depend on the time of the activation of its neighbors. For each time step each cell checks if the neighboring cells are activated. If an activated cell is found the time of the stimulus to travel from that cell is computed and compared with the activation time of the same cell to check if there was enough time to the stimulus to travel. For the activation to take place the neighboring cells must also be in states S1 or S2, i.e. states that allow one cell to stimulate another. After a cell is stimulated it will, independently of the neighboring cells, dynamically change its state until it finally goes to the states S4 and S0, when it may be stimulated again. With this set of rules the stimulus is able to propagate through the CA simulating the electrical propagation o APs on the cardiac tissue.

## 2.3    Mass-Spring System

The modeling of cardiac tissue deformation can be simplified by the use of mass-spring systems. In such systems, masses are connected with the neighboring masses by springs and forces can be applied to the system deforming its spatial distribution. The springs of the system will try to bring the system to its initial configuration again. The cardiac tissue does not have a linear stress-strain relation. However the linear model of the Hooke's law can be used as a simplification:

$$\overrightarrow{F_s} = -k\overrightarrow{X}, \tag{4}$$

where $k$ is the spring constant and determines the stiffness of a spring and $\overrightarrow{X}$ and $\overrightarrow{F_s}$ are vectors with displacement and force, respectively. The components of these vectors are projections on $x$ and $y$ axis. From Newton's second law we have that $\overrightarrow{F} = m\overrightarrow{a}$ and equating this with the Hooke's law equation we have:

$$m\frac{d^2\overrightarrow{X}}{dt^2} + k\overrightarrow{X} = 0 \tag{5}$$

But such systems will oscillate forever. In practice there will be forces in the environment that will resist to the movement. Such forces are called damping forces $F_d$ and are proportional to the velocity of the mass:

$$\overrightarrow{F_d} = -\beta\frac{d\overrightarrow{X}}{dt}, \tag{6}$$

where $\beta$ is the damping coefficient. Other forces can be included in the system such as the contraction force of the cell. The interconnected set of masses (lattices) are depicted in Fig. 4 part B, where a black cell has nine white neighbor cells. Therefore the total $\overrightarrow{F_s}$ force on the black cell is a sum of the force between this cell and each one of its neighbors, $\sum \overrightarrow{F_s}$. Finally it is necessary to integrate the system of equations for each cell in the CA to simulate the mechanical deformation of the tissue. Using the Forward Euler's method we have

$$\overrightarrow{F}_{total} = \left(\sum \overrightarrow{F_s}\right) + \overrightarrow{F_d} + \overrightarrow{F}_{contraction} \tag{7}$$

$$\overrightarrow{a}(t) = \frac{\overrightarrow{F}_{total}}{m} \tag{8}$$

$$\overrightarrow{v}(t + dt) = \overrightarrow{v}(t) + \overrightarrow{a}(t)dt \tag{9}$$

$$\overrightarrow{P}(t + dt) = \overrightarrow{P}(t) + \overrightarrow{v}(v)dt \tag{10}$$

where $\overrightarrow{v}(t)$ and $\overrightarrow{P}(t)$ are the velocity and position of a mass at time $t$. In this way, CA and mass-spring models are coupled by $\overrightarrow{F}_{contraction}$, i.e by the force generated by the cell during the dynamically change of its AP. The contraction's amplitude depends on the CA as presented on Fig. 2 and the contraction's direction is the same as the fiber direction.

There are different approaches for modeling the electro-mechanical behavior of the heart. In [1], a method based on CA is presented that can simulate electrical propagation in 3D cardiac tissue with arbitrary local fiber orientations. In [2], a CA is used to simulate cardiac electrical propagation and a model based on the finite element method is used to simulate cardiac mechanics. In [3] the CA approach is used for the electro-mechanical simulation of the cardiac tissue. A comparison of models for cardiac tissue based on differential equations and on CA is presented in [4].

# 3   Parallel Computing

Each cell of the CA and the mass-spring model can be computed separately, which involves only the communication between neighboring cells. Two parallel computing techniques were applied in order to speedup the execution time of the simulator. OpenMP[5], an Application Program Interface (API) that is used for multi-threaded, shared memory parallelism, was used to speed up the simulations on multi-core processors. Basically, the OpenMP implementation consists of adding a directive over the loop that iterates the computation of the next state and displacement for each cell (i,j). The pseudo-code of the OpenMP version is given below:

```
#pragma omp for schedule(static)
for(int i =1; i < height-1; i++)
 for(int j=1; j<width-1; j++)
   make calculation(i,j);
```

An alternative parallel implementation was also proposed using Graphic Processing Units (GPU) with CUDA (Compute Unified Device Architecture). In this architecture, it's necessary to copy the elements' matrix that represents the CA from the CPU (host) to the GPU (device). This is done in the beginning of the computation as follows:

```
copyHostToDevice(); //copy data from CPU to GPU
dim3 threads(16, 16); //set up the number of threads to each block
dim3 grid_size; //set up the grid
grid_size.x = (width + threads.x -1)  / threads.x;
grid_size.y = (height + threads.y -1)/ threads.y;
while(stop != true){
 for(i = 0; i < nsteps; i++){
   time += dt; //increments simulations time
   simulateElectrical<<<grid_size, threads>>>();
   simulateMechanics <<<grid_size, threads>>>();
 }
 copyDeviceToHost(); //copy data from GPU to CPU
 printResults();     //display the results
}
```

In this code, the CA matrix is divided into blocks containing $16 \times 16$ threads. The distinct blocks form the matrix grid that is set up according to its dimensions, *height* and *width*. After computing in the GPU, it is necessary to copy data back to CPU in order to show the results, since application exhibits the results at every *nsteps* steps, where *nsteps* is defined by the user. This pseudo code is run in the CPU. The functions called with the triple angle bracket are invoked by the CPU but they actually are run in the GPU.

# 4   Results

Different tests with the implementation were performed. The simulations used a square tissue with $19 \times 19$ cells with a spatial discretization of $0.001m$ and a time discretization of $0.001s$. Conduction velocity is assumed to be $0.5m/s$ and $0.17m/s$ along and transversal to fiber direction, respectively. A stimulated cell is placed in the middle of the tissue and the propagation will be studied. The first test assumed horizontal fiber orientation for all cells of the tissue, and the second one the fiber direction is a $45^o$ degrees inclined. The tests' results are presented in the first and second line in Figure 5, respectively. It can be observed that the stimulus propagates through the tissue in the preferential direction of the fiber. The third test, Figure 6, uses a CA with $49 \times 49$ cells with the same configuration aforementioned. But now, ischemic and dead tissues are included in the simulation. It is possible to note that, although the stimulus propagation is blocked by the dead tissue, it finds a way around it. An interesting behavior happens with the ischemic tissue. Because of its shorter AP duration the ischemic tissue is able to be stimulated again earlier than the healthy tissue. This leads to the creation of a reentry circuit where the tissue keeps stimulating itself forever via the propagation of spiral wave. This causes arrhythmic contractions of the cardiac tissue. The fourth and fifth tests present the force-development in the cell and the deformation of the tissue. Figure 7 presents in the first line the case for horizontal fibers and in the second line, that of fibers with $45^o$ degrees of inclination. The tests imply that the cardiac tissue contracts in the direction of the fibers. Such behaviors can be observed in the figure. Finally, these tests as well as other simulations can be found in [6], where it also becomes clear that the simulator offers an user-friendly interface that allows one to interact with the simulations and to setup different simulation scenarios on-the-fly. In order to measure the impact of the implemented parallel techniques, the speedup of both parallel versions, OPENMP and CUDA, were computed. All tests were performed in an Intel i7 machine with 8 GB of RAM, Nvidia GeForce GTX 480, running Ubuntu/Linux 4.6.1 with gcc 4.6.1. The tissue used has $200 \times 200$ cells. The spatial and time discretization used are $0.01m$ and $0.0001s$, respectively.

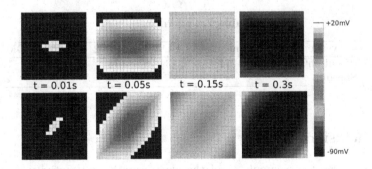

**Fig. 5.** Stimulus propagation

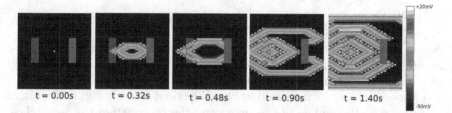

Fig. 6. Simulation including ischemic and dead tissues. The ischemic and the dead tissues are the blue and red cells, respectively, in $t = 0.00s$.

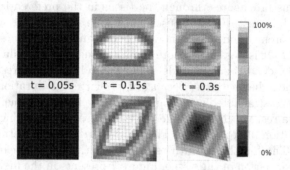

Fig. 7. Simulation of the cardiac force-development

The execution time corresponds to the simulation of 3 seconds of tissue activity. Results are displayed every 100 steps. All tests were run three times. The average execution time, in seconds, is then used to calculate the speedup. In all cases the standard deviation observed in the execution times was less than 1%. Table 2 presents the performance of a) the sequential code, b) the CUDA code and c) the OpenMP code using 2, 3 and 4 threads. CUDA achieved the best performance, 3.7 times faster than the sequential code, while OpenMP was from 1.7 to 2.2 times faster than the sequential code, varying according to the number of threads used.

Table 2. Performances

| Code version | Sequential | CUDA | OMP / 2 | OMP / 3 | OMP / 4 |
|---|---|---|---|---|---|
| Average execution time(s) | 271 | 73 | 164 | 139 | 124 |
| Speedup | - | 3.7 | 1.7 | 2.0 | 2.2 |

## 5   Conclusion

This work presented a simulator of the electro-mechanical activity of cardiac tissue via the coupling of CA and mass-spring models. Although models based on PDEs are more accurate and detailed, they are very computationally expensive. CA has been shown to be an alternative for real-time simulation because of its fast performance. The pattern of propagation obtained with CA has shown to be very similar to the patterns obtained with PDE-based models although a more detailed comparison is necessary. The tissue deformation obtained with the mass-spring system has shown to be very responsive to the force-development providing a qualitative demonstration of cardiac contraction. However, it is also necessary to further compare this model with models based in continuum mechanics.The parallel implementations sped up the simulations by almost 4 times. A linear speed up was not obtained due to the overheads introduced by both parallel versions of the code. For instance, the time spend copying data and scheduling threads consumed a substantial percentage of the execution time. As future work, we plan to make a 3D simulation of the heart with CA and to change the CUDA implementation in order to avoid data transfers by providing the routines for user interface inside the GPU. Some improvements can also be achieved in terms of parametrization of both CA and mass-spring systems, adjusting them to data obtained in experiments or from more realistic heart models.

# References

1. Feldman, A.B., Murphy, S.P., Coolahan, J.E.: A method for rapid simulation of propagating wave fronts in three-dimensional cardiac muscle with spatially-varying fibre orientations. Engineering in Medicine and Biology (2002)
2. Cimrman, R., Kroc, J., Rohan, E., Rosenberg, J., Tonar, Z.: On coupling cellular automata based activation and finite element muscle model applied to heart ventricle modelling. In: 5th International Conference on Simulations in Biomedicine - Advances in Computational Bioengineering (2003)
3. Hurmusiadis, V.: Virtual Heart: Cardiac Simulation for Surgical Training & Education. In: Workshop & Conference on Virtual Reality and Virtual Environments (2007)
4. Sachse, F.B., Bilmcke, L.G., Mohr, M., Glnzel, K., Hfner, J., Riedel, C., Seemann, G., Skipa, O., Werner, C.D., Dssel, O.: Comparison of macroscopic models of excitation and force propagation in the heart. Biomed. Tech. (Berl) 47, 217–220 (2002)
5. Mattson, T.G., Sanders, B.A., Massingill, B.L.: Patterns For Parallel Programming. Pearson Education (2005)
6. http://www.youtube.com/watch?v=UELEfV_OhwU (2012)

# Swii2, a HTML5/WebGL Application for Cellular Automata Debris Flows Simulation

Roberto Parise[1], Donato D'Ambrosio[1], Giuseppe Spingola[1],
Giuseppe Filippone[1], Rocco Rongo[2],
Giuseppe A. Trunfio[3], and William Spataro[1,*]

[1] Department of Mathematics and High Performance Computing Center,
University of Calabria, Via Pietro Bucci, I-87036 Rende, Italy
spataro@unical.it
[2] Department of Earth Sciences and High Performance Computing Center,
University of Calabria, Italy
[3] DADU, University of Sassari, Alghero, Italy

**Abstract.** We here present the preliminary release of Swii2, a web application for debris flows simulation. The core of the system is Sciddica-k0, the latest release of the Sciddica debris flow Cellular Automata family, already successfully applied to the 1997 Albano lake (Italy) debris flow. In Swii2, the Sciddica-k0 model runs server-side, while a Web 2.0 application controls the simulation. The graphical user interface is based on HTML5 and JavaScript, which permits to have a fully portable application. The client is able to control the basic Sciddica-k0 simulation functionalities thanks to asynchronous callbacks to the server. Simulation results are visualized in real time by means of a 3D interactive visualization system based on WebGL, a cross-platform application program interface used to create 3D graphics in Web browsers. Eventually, user-oriented cooperative services, which desktop applications in general do not offer, are conjectured and discussed.

**Keywords:** Scientific Computing, HTML5, WebGL, GWT, JavaScript, Debris Flow Simulation, Cellular Automata, Cooperative Services.

## 1 Introduction

The great spread of Internet and the World Wide Web has suggested since the '90s (when Sun Microsystems announced Java applets) the idea to execute programs directly inside a Web browser. In the last few years, a collection of technologies were combined to increase Web pages' interactivity, speed, functionality, and usability, making Web applications similar, if not better in some cases, to desktop ones. Such set of technologies are known as AJAX [7], which stands for Asynchronous JavaScript And XML, and essentially represents a Web development technique for creating interactive and Rich Internet Applications (RIA).

---

* Corresponding author.

G.C. Sirakoulis and S. Bandini (Eds.): ACRI 2012, LNCS 7495, pp. 444–453, 2012.
© Springer-Verlag Berlin Heidelberg 2012

Well known examples are Gmail, many blogs and wiki. Web 2.0 is the neologism that was coined for indicating these new kinds of rich Web applications.

Notwithstanding, Web applications for Scientific Computing are not diffused as expected and no significant examples can be found. Among others, one obstacle has probably been the absence of a native support for interactive 3D Graphics, which could be desirable in most cases. For instance, opening an OpenGL context was not permitted up to HTML4, and alternative solutions must be adopted. For this reason, the off-screen rendering technique (see e.g. [18]) was adopted in the first version of Swii [4], consisting in producing the graphic output as a raster image on the server (indeed by means of the off-screen rendering capability of OpenGL) and sending it to the client in order to be visualized. Obviously, such kind of solution presented great disadvantages in terms of interactivity. However, this scenario has changed thanks to the recent introduction of HTML5 and WebGL. The former, thanks to its Canvas element, allows the opening of OpenGL contexts in a Web page while the latter, which is based on OpenGL ES 2.0, permits to realize even complex 3D interactive visualization systems.

This paper aims in evaluating the possibility to create reliable and efficient Web-based scientific applications through a practical example. Accordingly, Swii2 is here presented, the second release of Swii (Sciddica Web Interactive Interface) [4] and represents an example of a HTML5/WebGL application for the Sciddica-k0 debris flows simulation model, based on the Cellular Automata computational paradigm.

The choice of AJAX for the Graphical User Interface (GUI) development has been suggested by the need to guaranty an adequate degree of interactivity to the user, exploiting asynchronous communications and data exchange between client and server. In this phase, the Google Web Toolkit (GWT) was considered in order to better control the overall development process. It essentially provides Java as reference language (instead of the less flexible JavaScript), which simplifies exceptions management, provides debug facilities and offers, in general, all the power of a high level Object Oriented Programming Language. The use of HTML5 and WebGL was imposed by the need to have an efficient and interactive 3D visualization system.

The next section briefly introduces Cellular Automata and the Sciddica-k0 debris flows simulation model. Section 3 describes the SWII2 system architecture, while both the SWII2 GUI and the 3D interactive visualization system are illustrated in Section 4. Section 5 presents the results of the preliminary, qualitative, performance analysis of Swii2, while Section 6 discusses some possible development based on cooperative features. Eventually, Section 7 concludes the paper with a general discussion about the performed work and future developments.

## 2   The Sciddica-k0 Debris Flows Simulation Model

Cellular Automata [17] are dynamical systems, discrete in space and time. They can be thought as an $n$-dimensional space partitioned in cells of uniform size (e.g. square or hexagonal for $n = 2$), each one embedding an identical finite automaton. The cell state changes by means of the finite automaton transition function, which defines local rules of evolution for the system. In fact, its input is constituted by the states of a small set of cells that, usually, includes the cell itself (called central cell) and a small number of neighboring ones. The CA initial configuration is defined by the finite automata states at time $t = 0$. The overall global behavior of the system emerges, step by step, as a consequence of the simultaneous application of the transition function to each cell of the cellular space.

CA have become increasingly utilized for modelling and simulating systems that evolve on the basis of local interactions of their constituent parts [6]. Major CA applications regard the most various scientific fields, from Physics [14] [1] [19] to Social Sciences [9] [10], from Geology [2] [16] to Medicine [15] [11]. In Physics, CA represent an alternative approach to differential equations for modeling and simulating complex fluid dynamical systems, both at microscopic (see e.g. [13]) and macroscopic levels (see e.g., [5], [12]) of description.

The Cellular Automata model here considered is Sciddica-k0, reflecting the classical modeling approaches of dynamic models. The movement of debris masses is, in fact, driven by gravitational acceleration, while resulting forces can be influenced by resisting forces. The moving material is approximated by means of an *equivalent fluid*, whose bulk properties are macroscopically similar to the real case. The computation of flows between cells is fundamentally based on the *minimization algorithm of the differences* [6], specifically adapted to manage rapid inertial flows. Sciddica-k0 introduces many improvements with respect to its predecessors, like a better management of flow energy and inertial effects. Moreover, the model does not consider mass barycenter explicitly inside the cell, which further improves computational performance without however loosing accuracy. Furthermore, it simplifies input/output management, by re-introducing a square cellular space instead of the previously adopted hexagonal one, by contextually improving simulation accuracy. The first application of Sciddica-k0 to a real case of study, namely the 1997 Albano lake (Italy) debris flow, provided encouraging results.

As its predecessors, the model includes a set of parameters whose values determine different characteristics of the modeled equivalent fluid. In general, model parameters can not be directly deduced and must be determined through calibration. With respect to lumped mass models, Sciddica-k0 allows for predicting the propagation of the flow front, besides other details about the phenomenon and the overall affected area. Yet, differently from most continuum mechanics models, it allows to simulate the propagation of the flow either onto complex topography or open slopes. The model is able to simulate the erosion of the regolith along the flow-path, as well as events of branching and re-joining of the masses. Dissipative effects are modeled in terms of a quadratic velocity-dependent mechanism. Moreover, effects of mass collisions are correctly managed by guaranteeing mass conservation. In case of no dissipation, energy and momentum conservation are also assured. Besides the specification of the values to be assigned to model's parameters, Sciddica requires further input data: the topographic map over which the debris flows will evolve must be provided, as well as the maps that specify the depth of soil that can be eroded and the location(s) of debris flow source(s). Such information is generally provided by means of standard ASCII Grid maps (supplied by GIS elaborations), and define the initial configuration of the system.

The following Section provides the formal definition of the model. However, its complete specification lies outside the aim of this paper and is thus here omitted.

## 2.1   Formal Definition of Sciddica-k0

Sciddica-k0 is formally defined as:

$$Sciddica - k0 = <R, E, X, S, P, \tau, \gamma>$$

where:

$R = \{(x,y) \in \mathbb{Z}^2 | -l_x < x < l_x, \ -l_y < y < l_y\}$ is the bi-dimensional cellular space subdivided in square cells; $l_x$ ed $l_y$ identifies the boundaries of the region where the debris flow evolves;

$E \subset R$ is the set of the cells where the phenomenon triggers (sources);

$X = \{(0,0),(0,-1),(-1,0),(1,0),(0,-1),(-1,1),(-1,-1),(1,-1),(1,1)\}$ is the Moore neighborhood relation; it identifies the central cell and its 8 surrounding ones;

$S = Q_z \times Q_h \times Q_{h_k} \times Q_d \times Q_f^9$ is the finite set of the cell states; it is expressed as Cartesian product of the following sub-states:

 - $Q_z$ is the cell altitude, expressed in meters;
 - $Q_h$ is the debris thickness, expressed in meters;
 - $Q_{h_k}$ is the flow kinetic head (i.e. $v^2/2g$, being $v$ and $g$ the flow velocity and the acceleration of gravity, respectively); it is expressed in meters;
 - $Q_d$ is the depth of regolith, i.e. the depth of the soil that can be eroded; it is expressed in meters;
 - $Q_f^9$ are the 9 debris outflows from the central cell towards its neighbors (central cell included); they are expressed in meters.

$P = \{p_c, p_{hc_{\theta_0}}, p_{dQ}, p_{mt}, p_{pef}\}$ is the set of parameters of the cellular automaton:

 - $p_c$ is the cell side, expressed in meters;
 - $p_{hc_{\theta_0}}$ is the Binghamian critical height on an horizontal plane (i.e. debris can not flow if its thickness does not overcomes $p_{hc_{\theta_0}} \cos\theta$, being $\theta$ the slope angle); it is expressed in radians;
 - $p_{dQ}$ is the quadratic mechanism of velocity drop: velocity of the flow is updated by considering the following relation: $v_{(t+1)} = v_t - p_{dQ}v_t^2$;
 - $p_{mt}$ is the soil erosion velocity threshold: erosion occurs only if flow velocity overcomes $p_{mt}$;
 - $p_{pef}$ is the progressive erosion factor: erosion depth is computed according to the formula $e_d = vp_{pef}$;

$\tau : Q^9 \to Q$ is the cell deterministic transition function; it is composed by the following elementary processes, which are applied in the following order:

1. internal transformation $T_1$: soil erosion;
2. local interaction $I_1$: computation of debris outflows and kinetic head;
3. local interaction $I_2$: updating of both debris thickness and kinetic head;
4. internal transformation $T_2$: velocity drop;
5. internal transformation $T_3$: evaluation of maximum flow velocity and time ($\Delta_t$) corresponding to the CA step.

$\gamma : E \times \mathbb{N} \times Q_d \times Q_h \times Q_{h_k} \to Q_z \times Q_d \times Q_h \times Q_{h_k}$ is the triggering function for the sources. Main sources trigger at the first step of the simulation; secondary sources can trigger at subsequent steps ($\mathbb{N}$ is the set of Natural numbers, corresponding to the CA steps).

At the beginning of the simulation, cell states specify the initial condition of the system. They are assigned as follows: $z \in Q_z$ is initialized to the topographic altitude of the surface over which the phenomenon evolves (topographic elevation of the bedrock plus the erodible stratum); $d \in Q_d$ is initialized to the depth of erodible regolith (note that $d = 0$ in the source cells); $h \in Q_h$ is zero everywhere, except for the source cells, where it is $d$; $h_k \in Q_{h_k}$ and $q_f \in Q_f$ are zero everywhere. The transition function is then applied simultaneously to each cell so that the CA global state changes and the evolution of the phenomenon is obtained.

## 3  The SWII2 System Architecture

As stated in Section 1, Swii2 was implemented by means GWT. Following the GWT development approach, the interaction between the user interface and the Sciddica-k0 computational model is guarantied by a set of client-side services which are implemented on the server (see e.g. [8]). Multi-client connections are also guarantied. Whenever a user logs in, an asynchronous request is sent to the server in order to establish a connection; here, a servlet binds the client to an individual connection-handler, which allows multiple unambiguous communications through HTTP requests and responses.

Figure 1 shows the Swii2 system architecture. Server-side, Sciddica-k0 is implemented as a static library, developed in C++ for efficiency reasons. A dynamic-link library (DLL), specifically developed in C++ for permitting the interaction between the simulation model and the Web application, receives requests by Java Native Interface (JNI) methods and provides simulation data to the application server. Data is therefore sent to the client via HTTP and stored into the Web browser cache memory. Sciddica-k0 parameters are displayed in GUI controls (in which they can also be modified), while simulation data (e.g. the topographic surface or the simulated debris flow) are visualized by means of the 3D WebGL rendering engine, which runs on a HTML5 <Canvas>. Thus, whenever the Sciddica-k0 simulation produces a debris flow, it is displayed over the surface and its dynamical behavior can be observed. All the client-server communications are managed by means of asynchronous JavaScript calls, which are able to provide the same usability level of desktop applications to Swii2.

**Fig. 1.** The Swii2 system architecture

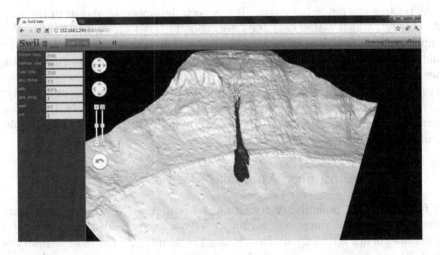

**Fig. 2.** A screenshot of Swii2 during a simulation performed by the Sciddica-k0 debris flow molel. The left panel allows to view/set both Sciddica-k0 and simulation parameters (e.g. current and visualization step).

## 4   The Swii2 GUI and the Visualization System

As previously stated, the Swii2 GUI was mainly written in JavaScript by means of the Google Web Toolkit (GWT). The graphic layout of some elements has however been modified by means of cascade stile sheets (CSS). Figure 2 shows a screenshot of Swii2.

On the upper part of the GUI, a horizontal panel shows the application name/logo and contains the controls which permit to interact with the simulation. A notification area is also present on the right side of the panel. The remaining client area is subdivided in two panels. The left one contains the controls which permits to show the current simulation step, set the graphic update interval and show/edit the Sciddica-k0 parameters. The right one contains the graphic output of the simulation. The graphic panel also contains additional controls (in Google Maps style), which allows the user to interact with the 3D model in a very simple way. Buttons have been developed for users which also adopt touch-screen devices. Moreover, application interaction is also possible through mouse based movements. In fact, like most 3D modeling applications, users can move or rotate by dragging the 3D model and zoom it by mouse wheeling. However, as the application is currently under development, the GUI is still oversimplified and some functionalities of the Sciddica-k0 simulation model cannot be used through the Swii2 user interface. For instance, it is not possible to upload configuration data to the server directly from Swii2 and the operation must be performed externally, e.g. through a FTP application, where data must be placed in a specific directory.

As regards the rendering engine, it has been developed by means of the gwt-g3d library[1], which makes easy the integration in GWT. As a matter of fact, it simplifies many development aspects like projection, matrix operations or shader binding. Data meshing has been based on triangle strips. For performance reasons, the function `drawArrays` has been used. In fact, as it represents the vertices following the order in which they appear in the vertices buffer, `drawArrays` guaranties better performance with respect to the alternative WebGL function `drawElements`, which represents the vertices by following the order of a supplementary array of indexes pointing to the vertices.

## 5   Swii2 Preliminary Analysis

So far, Swii2 was preliminary tested on a Local Area Network by only considering standard laptops, one acting as a Web server and a maximum of 3 as remote clients accessing simultaneously the former. The level of usability of the GUI resulted more than satisfactory, mainly thanks to the asynchronous communications between client and server. In fact, the activation response of any element of the user interface was practically immediate and comparable with that of desktop applications. Moreover, also data exchange between clients and server, in particular simulation data did not cause a significant slow down. Therefore, the 3D visualization system resulted to be surprisingly efficient, especially if compared with that of the first release of Swii. Moreover, thanks to the low computational requirements of the Sciddica-k0 simulation model, also the computational efficiency resulted more than acceptable on the considered server, making Swii2 comparable to standard desktop applications in terms of both efficiency and usability.

---

[1] gwt-g3d homepage: http://code.google.com/p/gwt-g3d/

# 6   Cooperative Aspects in Scientific Simulation

As mentioned in Section 3, Sciddica-k0 depends on a set of parameters which rule the system evolution. Different sets of parameters are generally needed in order to simulate different types of debris flows. Therefore, if a new debris flow must be simulated, which is different for instance, in rheological terms, with respect to all the other simulated before, Sciddica could require a calibration phase, in order to determine a new proper set of parameters to be employed. This phase can be accomplished manually or by means of an automated optimization technique (e.g. by Genetic Algorithms - see e.g. [3]). However, in both cases, calibration generally requires a large number of trials and thus great computational resources and time. While this could not be an issue in case of a desktop application, it may represent a serious limitation for a client-server system, as the server could not be able to satisfy multiple calibration requests. In addition, the problem could become as greater as the user's community increases. On the other hand, an adequate solution, which does not require high computational resources, is advisable. Without such a solution, the level of the web application's usability could result strongly penalized.

A possible solution could be inspired from the cooperative philosophy of Web 2.0. For instance, depending on some policies and on the computational power of the server(s), calibration experiments could be permitted to a restricted number of users, who are invited to share their results with the community by providing information about the performed experiment, mainly regarding debris flows technical description and calibrated parameters. Such information could then be stored in a intelligent database system for future usage.

After a transition phase, the database should reach a critical size and contain a significant number of Sciddica sets of parameters, linked to both the simulated phenomena and the obtained results. In this way, if a new event must be simulated without having a precise idea concerning parameters to be used, the user could query the intelligent database to get a useful starting point. For example, the user could execute a query by using some knowledge on the phenomenon to be simulated as search criterion, and obtain a list of sets of parameters employed in similar cases. A measure of the correspondence between the new case to be simulated and the events in the returned records should be provided, together with information about obtained fitness values.

Such kind of cooperative approach could represent an interesting innovation in the global panorama of scientific applications that, once consolidated, could significantly reduce the employment of optimization techniques. In fact, if the user is facilitated in finding immediately a good set of parameters for the simulation, which can be subsequently further refined, the calibration phase could even become unnecessary. Moreover, this feature should become the more rich and reliable, as its employment increases.

The ideas here just outlined will be better formalized and considered in the next release of SWII, as we conjecture that they could represent the basis for a different and innovative way to exploit scientific simulation models.

# 7    Discussion

We have presented Swii2, the second release of Swii, one of the first example of Web 2.0 application for Scientific Computing. With respect to its predecessor, Swii2 adopts the new debris flows simulation model Sciddica-k0 (still in a preliminary version), and improves the 3D interactive visualization system dramatically thanks to the adoption of WebGL instead of the off-screen rendering technique previously used in Swii. Concerning the Sciddica-k0 CA model, it demonstrated to be able to reproduce a real case of study, notwithstanding it is still a preliminary version and has undergone a not thorough parameters calibration. However, improvements to the computational model are currently under development, which will be considered for the definition of the final release.

An AJAX based solution was adopted for the user interface, guaranteeing both a clear separation between client and server applications, and a high degree of interactivity and usability. Among the different advantages of the considered approach, one of the most interesting consists in the possibility to easily change the computational model without the need to carry out substantial modifications to the overall application. However, even if in principle the Sciddica-k0 debris flow model could be replaced by any different computational application, extended Cellular Automata models (e.g. the lava flows model Sciara-fv2 [12]), designed in a similar way with respect Sciddica-k0, represent the simplest choice. Eventually, being a preliminary release, the Swii2 GUI must be enriched in order to be able to fully exploit the capability of the underlying computational model.

The level of usability was preliminary verified on an ideal case in which few multiple accesses to the server application were considered. Nevertheless, although results are more than satisfying and comparable with those of desktop applications. Anyway, the usage of a dedicated server with multiple GPUs could make the use of Swii2 suitable to a greater number of users.

Eventually, the idea of a cooperative system supported by an intelligent database that allows users to share experiences about the model usage has been conjectured and proposed as a future development. In principle, the introduction of a similar feature could represent a significant improvement in the field of Scientific Computing, which has so far mainly englobed *close* applications only for expert users.

**Acknowledgments.** This work was partially funded by the European Commission - European Social Fund (ESF) and by Regione Calabria.

# References

1. Chopard, B., Droz, M.: Cellular Automata Modeling of Physical Systems. Cambridge University Press (1998)
2. Crisci, G.M., Di Gregorio, S., Rongo, R., Scarpelli, M., Spataro, W., Calvari, S.: Revisiting the 1669 Etnean eruptive crisis using a cellular automata model and implications for volcanic hazard in the Catania area. J. Volcanol. Geoth. Res. 123, 211–230 (2003)

3. D'Ambrosio, D., Iovine, G., Spataro, W.: Parallel genetic algorithms for optimising cellular automata models of natural complex phenomena: an application to debris-flows. Comput. Geosci. 32, 861–875 (2006)

4. D'Ambrosio, D., Spataro, W., Rongo, R., Cirimele, C., Riccetti, E.: An Example of Web Application for Scientific Simulation. In: Proceedings of the 2008 Summer Computer Simulation Conference, Edinburgh, UK, June 16-19 (2008)

5. D'Ambrosio, D., Spataro, W., Iovine, G., Miyamoto, H.: A macroscopic collisional model for debris flows simulation. Environ. Modell. Softw. 22, 1417–1436 (2007)

6. Di Gregorio, S., Serra, R.: An empirical method for modelling and simulating some complex macroscopic phenomena by cellular automata. Future Gener. Comp. Sy. 16, 259–271 (1999)

7. Garrett, J.J.: Ajax: A New Approach to Web Applications (2005), http://www.adaptivepath.com/ideas/essays/archives/000385.php

8. Hanson, R., Tacy, A.: GWT in Action. Manning Pubblications Co. (2007)

9. Kacperski, K., Holyst, J.A.: Opinion formation model with strong leader and external impact: a mean field approach. Physica A 269, 511–526 (1999)

10. Kun, F., Kocsis, G., Farkas, J.: Cellular automata for the spreading of technologies in socio-economic systems. Physica A 383, 660–670 (2007)

11. Mallet, D.G., De Pillis, L.G.: A cellular automata model of tumor immune system interactions. J. Theor. Biol. 239, 334–350 (2006)

12. Spataro, W., Avolio, M.V., Lupiano, V., Trunfio, G.A., Rongo, R., D'Ambrosio, D.: The latest release of the lava flows simulation model SCIARA: first application to Mt Etna (Italy) and solution of the anisotropic flow direction problem on an ideal surface. In: Proceedings of the International Conference on Computational Science, ICCS 2010. Procedia Computer Science, vol. 1, pp. 17–26. Elsevier (2010)

13. Succi, S.: Lattice Boltzmann schemes for quantum applications. Comput. Phys. Commun. 146, 317–323 (2002)

14. Toffoli, T.: Cellular automata as an alternative to (rather than an approximation of) differential equations in modeling physics. Physica D 10, 117–127 (1984)

15. Ueda, H., Iwaya, Y., Abe, T., Kinoshita, T.: A cellular automata model considering diversity associated with HIV infection. Artif. Life Robot. 10, 73–76 (2006)

16. Vicari, A., Ganci, G., Behncke, B., Cappello, A., Neri, M., Del Negro, C.: Near-real-time forecasting of lava flow hazards during the 12-13 January 2011 Etna eruption. Geophys. Res. Lett. 38, L13317 (2011)

17. von Neumann, J. (Edited and completed by Burks, A.): Theory of self-reproducing automata. University of Illinois Press, Urbana (1966)

18. Wright, R., Lipchak, B.: OpenGL Supebible, 3rd edn. SAMS, Indianapolis (2004)

19. Wu, F.F., Shi, W.P., Liu, F.: A lattice Boltzmann model for the Fokker-Planck equation. Communications In Nonlinear Science And Numerical Simulation 17, 2776–2790 (2012)

# Effects of Initial Concentration and Severity of Infected Cells on Stochastic Cellular Automaton Model Dynamics for HIV Infection

Monamorn Precharattana[1,2,*] and Wannapong Triampo[1,2]

[1] Institute for Innovative Learning, Mahidol University, Thailand
[2] R&D Group of Biological and Environmental Physics (BIOPHYSICS),
Department of Physics, Faculty of Science, Mahidol University, Thailand
mprecharattana@hotmail.co.th, wtriampo@gmail.com

**Abstract.** This work is conducted to investigate how the initial concentration and the severity of HIV which spreads over the lymphoid tissues affect the dynamics of infection, and to what extent?. Therefore, we vary the initial concentration of HIV infected cells, $P_{M\_DC}$, and the severity of HIV infected cells, $P_{I\_T4}$, of a stochastic cellular automaton for HIV infection which describes the dynamics of HIV infected cells spreading over a patch of lymphoid tissues. Our results reveal that the variations of $P_{M\_DC}$ and $P_{I\_T4}$ do not change the feature of the dynamics of the model. They affect the dynamics of the model in the following ways: the greater the magnitude of $P_{M\_DC}$ and $P_{I\_T4}$, the faster the dynamics during the primary phase, and the severity parameter has greater effect on the model than does the HIV's initial concentration.

**Keywords:** AIDS, stochastic process, cellular automata, spatial structure model, epidemic infection.

## 1 Introduction

The infection by Human Immunodeficiency Virus (HIV) causing AIDS (Acquired Immunodeficiency Syndrome) has been intensively researched in many fields and a long-standing topic for more than 30 years. Although major mechanism between the virus and its host has been discovered by medical and biological research, resulting in understanding of many different aspects of the infection, some clues still remain hidden.

The courses of HIV infection can be divided into three stages involving two time scales, i.e., weekly and yearly [1]. The weekly scale concerns the primary infection. The dynamics begin when there is a rapid increase in the virus level after entering a human body, causing a fast decrease in CD4$^+$ T cells, following by a rapid decrease in the virus level due to the immune response. However, instead of being completely got rid of, HIV still

---

* Corresponding author.

G.C. Sirakoulis and S. Bandini (Eds.): ACRI 2012, LNCS 7495, pp. 454–463, 2012.
© Springer-Verlag Berlin Heidelberg 2012

persists in the immune system by hiding in the white blood cells and the lymphoid reservoirs, and thus detracts from the immune system's ability to eradicate the virus. The interplay suppresses the AIDS development, and maintains it for a period of time. This latent period may vary from 1 to 10 (or more) years. Meanwhile HIV continues to destroy the immune system, causing the latter to become weak and dysfunctional. Finally, the AIDS stage is reached which is characterized by the drop in the $CD4^+$ T cell level of the HIV infected patient to lower than 20% of the normal level. As a consequence, the patient gets infected easily by other opportunistic diseases and normally dies within two years.

Over the years, several cellular automata [2-5] have been introduced to explain the dynamics of HIV infection over the lymphoid tissues. By assuming that the tissues have a mesh structure which could be viewed approximately as a rough surface [6], the infection could spread among the cells over the lymphoid tissues according to a set of local rules which depends on the state of the cell and the states of its neighbors at each time step. Using cellular automata (CA) for HIV infection, the biological process normally begins when the virus has already infected a human body and presented by the antigen-presenting cells (APCs). During the early days of using CA for the infection, those CA models [2, 7, 8] described the dynamics of the infection by using different sets of parameters for different stages of the models, and focused on the interactions among the $CD4^+$ T cells, the $CD8^+$ T cells, the macrophages, the interleukin molecules, and the virus particles. Although, those models could reproduce different interesting dynamics of the infection, especially during the first phase; unfortunately, they could not provide the entire course of the infection in a model. Around ten years later, the use of CA became popular again when Santos et al. [3] proposed a model that could reproduce the three-phase dynamics of HIV infection by using one set of parameters in the model. However, it was found that the simulation dynamics of the entire course in the model, processed by changing the state of one kind of immune cell, i.e., the $CD4^+$ T cells, of cellular automata [9, 10].

Therefore, recently, in order to avoid the spatial properties of CA and converge into a more realistic model of the biological process, we proposed a stochastic CA model [11] which focused on the interaction among the $CD4^+$ T cells, the $CD8^+$ T cells, and the dendritic cells. We did not concern ourselves with the role of free virus particles like Pandey et al. [2] did because several experiments [12, 13] observed cell-to-cell transmission during HIV infection in the lymphoid tissues, and inferred that the cell-to-cell spread of infection was probably more important than cell-to-virus transmission. Besides, evidence [14] revealed that the number of infected cells and the number of free virus particles correlated. In fact, it is customary to assume that the viral load is simply proportional to the number of infected cells (see, for example, [4, 15]). Moreover, we assumed that the size of a free virus particle is too small to be set in a grid of the same size as that of a white blood cell. The simulation results showed that the model could reproduce the primary phase of HIV infection, and the dynamics of the infection were controlled by the dynamics of HIV-specific immune responses' parameter. However, the model still needs to be extensively researched in the future.

Therefore, herein, we focus on the model in [11] by considering the dynamics of the model when varying (i) the initial concentration, $P_{M\_DC}$, mimicking the concentration of HIV initially entering the human body, and (ii) the severity of the infected cells, $P_{I\_T4}$, mimicking the severity of HIV to the host. This is because the dynamics of the primary phase of the infection, which might depend on factors such as the initial concentration of free virus particles entering the human body according to its route of transmission, the virulence of the virus strain, etc, have a significant impact on and provide an important insight into the events in the later phases. The aim of the paper is thus to investigate how the severity of infected cells and the initial concentration affect the dynamics of the model, and to what extent?. The paper is organized as followed. In section 2, the model is presented together with a discussion of $P_{M\_DC}$ and $P_{I\_T4}$. In section 3, the obtained results are presented and discussed, and the conclusion is presented in section 4.

## 2     CA Model

Our simulation is performed by MATLAB. For conducting a cellular automaton model, a square lattice of size $L$ by $L$ is used to represent a patch of lymphoid tissue. A cell in the lattice represents a position where an immune cell in any state may locate or a space ($E$) to which an immune cell can move. The states of the immune cells are naïve CD4$^+$ T cell ($N\_T4$), effector CD4$^+$ T cell ($E\_T4$), infected CD4$^+$ T cell ($I\_T4$), naïve CD8$^+$ T cell ($N\_T8$), effector CD8$^+$ T cell ($E\_T8$), mature dendritic cell ($M\_DC$), and dead ($D$). The initial configuration is set by randomly assigning cells in the lattice to the three fundamental states of immune cells which they are $N\_T4$, $N\_T8$, and $M\_DC$, with the probabilities $P_{N\_T4}$, $P_{N\_T8}$, and $P_{M\_DC}$, respectively. To update the state of a cell in the lattice, the specify cell is updated by using CA rules according to the state of the cell and its eight nearest neighbors. Periodic boundary condition is used. Each time step represents 4 hours in real life. After all the cell states are updated, the number of each cell states is counted and noted. Then, the cells randomly move to the unoccupied neighboring cells for the next time step. The flow diagram of the algorithm in our model is shown in Fig 1.

### 2.1     Update Rules

1. If an $N\_T4$ cell comes into contact with $k$ $I\_T4$ cell, it becomes an $I\_T4$ cell with the probability $1-(1-P_{I\_T4})^k$. Otherwise, it stays unchanged. If an $N\_T4$ cell comes into contact with $k$ $M\_DC$ cell, it becomes an $I\_T4$ cell with the probability $1-(1-P_{I\_T4})^k$ or an $E\_T4$ cell otherwise. Moreover, an $N\_T4$ cell becomes a $D$ cell after $\tau_{N\_T4}$ time steps.

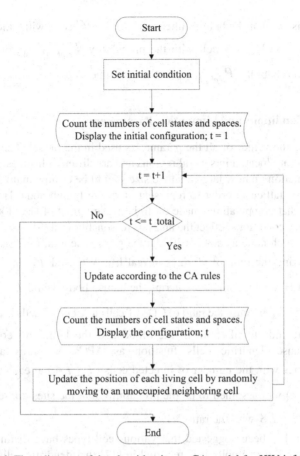

**Fig. 1.** Flow diagram of the algorithm in our CA model for HIV infection

2. If an $E\_T4$ cell comes into contact with $k$ $I\_T4$ or $M\_DC$ cells, it becomes an $I\_T4$ cell with the probability $1-(1-P_{I\_T4})^k$. Otherwise, it stays unchanged. Moreover, an $E\_T4$ cell becomes a $D$ cell after $\tau_{E\_T4}$ time steps.

3. An $I\_T4$ cell becomes a $D$ cell after $\tau_{I\_T4}$ time steps, or if it comes into contact with at least one $E\_T8$ cell.

4. An $N\_T8$ cell becomes an $E\_T8$ cell if it comes into contact with at least one $M\_DC$ cell or one $E\_T4$ cell, or becomes a $D$ cell after $\tau_{N\_T8}$ time steps.

5. An $E\_T8$ cell becomes a $D$ cell after $\tau_{E\_T8}$ time steps. Otherwise, it stays unchanged.

6. An $M\_DC$ cell becomes a $D$ cell after $\tau_{M\_DC}$ time steps, or if it comes into contact with at least one $E\_T8$ cell.

7. A $D$ cell is replenished by either an $M\_DC$ cell with the probability $P_{repl\_M\_DC}$, an $N\_T4$ cell with the probability $P_{repl\_N\_T4}$, or an $N\_T8$ cell with the probability $P_{repl\_N\_T8}$ in the next time step.

## 2.2    Initial Conditions and Simulation Parameters

Table 1 contains the values of all the parameters used in the model. The lymph nodes in a human body are located in several regions and are different in sizes, and currently there is no estimation on how large a lattice size should be or how many immune cells are located in the lattice in order to represent an entire lymph node. However, it has been suggested that computations made on finite square grids of size 300 to 800 with periodic boundary conditions reflect the analysis reasonably well [9]. We thus considered the individual lymph node as a $300 \times 300$ lattice grids. The total time step of 540 was used for mimicking the time of 90 days in real life. We used $P_{M\_DC}$ to mimic the concentration of HIV which initially entering the human body, while $P_{N\_T8}$ was taken to be a half of $P_{N\_T4}$ because the ratio of CD4$^+$ T cells to CD8$^+$ T cells is approximately 2:1 in a healthy individual (both in the blood and the lymphoid compartments) [14, 16]. Because dendritic cells function as APCs, we thus assumed that $P_{repl\_M\_DC}$ varies with the number of infected cells ($I\_T4$) at each time step and $(1 - P_{repl\_M\_DC})$ was assumed to be the probability that the sites are replenished by $N\_T4$ and $N\_T8$ with the ratio 2:1.

In addition, it has been suggested that various cell types have distinctly different half-lives in vivo. For example, it is reported in [17] that dendritic cells have a very short lifespan and may also undergo accelerated clearance from the lymphoid organs after interacting with antigen-specific T cells [18]; and naïve T cells live relatively long while lives of activated T cells are shorter [19]. Therefore, based on [15], we estimated the age of immune cells in our model according to the following inequalities.

$$\tau_{E\_T8} < \tau_{E\_T4} < \tau_{M\_DC} < \tau_{N\_T8} = \tau_{N\_T4}$$

Furthermore, although an activated CD4$^+$ T cell is more susceptible to infection than a naïve one and an activated cell in the infected state has a shorter half-life than does a cell infected while in the resting (naïve) state [20-23], we assumed that the susceptibilities and the lifespans of both infected CD4$^+$ T cells are equal ($= P_{I\_T4}$ and $\tau_{I\_T4}$ respectively). Thus the probability of a healthy CD4$^+$ T cell being infected depends on the severity of infected cell ($P_{I\_T4}$), mimicking the severity of HIV to the host, and the amount of the infected cells among the neighboring cells ($k$), that is, $1 - (1 - P_{I\_T4})^k$ [24].

**Table 1.** Values of all the parameters in the model

| Meaning & Symbols | Values |
|---|---|
| Lattice side ($L$) | 300 |
| Total time steps ($t\_total$) | 540 |
| Probability of the initial $N\_T4$ cells ($P_{N\_T4}$) | 0.5 |
| Probability of the initial $N\_T8$ cells ($P_{N\_T8}$) | 0.25 |
| Probability of the initial $M\_DC$ cells ($P_{M\_DC}$) | Vary from $10^{-3}$ to $10^{-2}$ |
| The severity of infected cells ($P_{I\_T4}$) | Vary from 0.1 to 0.2 |
| Probability that a $D$ cell is replenished by an $M\_DC$ cell ($P_{repl\_M\_DC}$) | $\left(\dfrac{I\_T4}{L^2 - E}\right)$ |
| Probability that a $D$ cell is replenished by an $N\_T4$ cell ($P_{repl\_N\_T4}$) | $\dfrac{2}{3} \times \left(1 - \left(P_{repl\_M\_DC}\right)\right)$ |
| Probability that a $D$ cell is replenished by an $N\_T8$ cell ($P_{repl\_N\_T8}$) | $\dfrac{1}{3} \times \left(1 - \left(P_{repl\_M\_DC}\right)\right)$ |
| Time delay for an $M\_DC$ cell ($\tau_{M\_DC}$) | 180 |
| Time delay for an $N\_T4$ cell ($\tau_{N\_T4}$) | 540 |
| Time delay for an $N\_T8$ cell ($\tau_{N\_T8}$) | 540 |
| Time delay for an $E\_T4$ cell ($\tau_{E\_T4}$) | 18 |
| Time delay for an $E\_T8$ cell ($\tau_{E\_T8}$) | 6 |
| Time delay for an $I\_T4$ cell ($\tau_{I\_T4}$) | 90 |

## 3    Results and Discussion

From the simulation results, it was found that the variation of initial infected cells' concentration ($P_{M\_DC}$) and the variation of infected cells' severity ($P_{I\_T4}$) do not affect the feature of infected-cell dynamics, but the variations impact the model dynamics in such a way that the greater the magnitudes of $P_{M\_DC}$ and $P_{I\_T4}$, the faster the first phase regime (see Fig. 2A and Fig. 3A). Moreover, the behaviors of two quantities are plotted (see Fig. 2B, C and Fig. 3B, C). They characterize the infected-cell dynamics, i.e., the percentage of maximum average infected cells during primary infection ($I\_T4$) and the time to that maximum ($T$) as a function of $P_{M\_DC}$ and $P_{I\_T4}$, on the double-logarithmic scale.

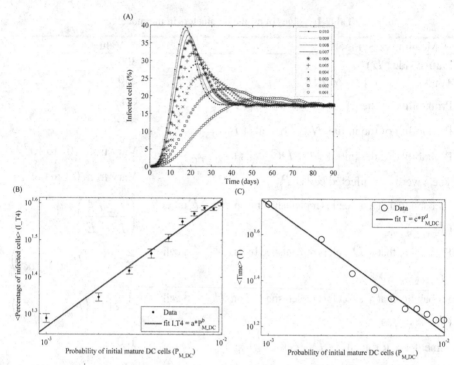

**Fig. 2.** (A) plots the average infected cells as functions of time when the probability of initial $M\_DC$ cells is varied. The severity of infected cells, $P_{I\_T4}$, is equal to 0.1 and the other values are the same as in initial conditions and simulation parameters. (B) shows the percentage of maximum average infected cells during the primary infection as a function of $P_{M\_DC}$. Similarly, (C) shows the time to that maximum during the primary infection. The results were averaged over 20 runs. Dashed lines indicate the linear fitting.

Fig. 2B and 3B seem to indicate the power-law behavior: the percentage of maximum average infected cells ($I\_T4$) varies with $(P_{M\_DC})^b$ and $(P_{I\_T4})^f$ (a healthy cell is infected by an infected cell with the probability $1-(1-P_{I\_T4})^k$) with exponents $b = 0.3446$ and $f = 0.9213$. Similarly, Fig. 2C and 3C show that the time to average maximum percentage of infected cells ($T$) varies with $(P_{M\_DC})^d$ and $(P_{I\_T4})^h$ with exponents $d = -0.5527$ and $h = -1.4760$. The mathematical relationship of these values of $b$, $d$, $f$ and $h$ represent how the initial concentration ($M\_DC$) and the severity parameter ($I\_T4$) are related to and affect the dynamics of the model. The larger of magnitudes of $b$, $d$, $f$ and $h$ the greater effects on the dynamics of the model the $P_{M\_DC}$ and the $P_{I\_T4}$.

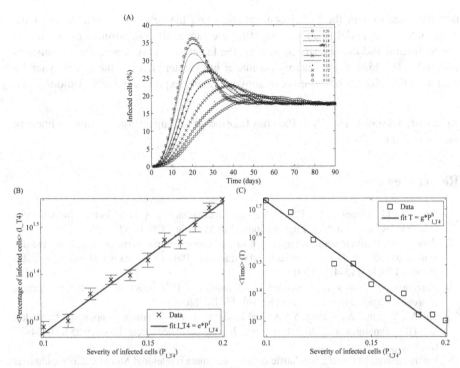

**Fig. 3.** (A) plots the average infected cells as functions of time when the severity of infected cells, $P_{I\_T4}$, is varied. The probability of initial $M\_DC$ cells, $P_{M\_DC}$, is equal to $10^{-3}$ and other values are the same as in initial conditions and simulation parameters. (B) shows the percentage of maximum average infected cells during the primary infection as a function of $P_{I\_T4}$. Similarly, (C) shows the time to that maximum during the primary infection. The results were averaged over 20 runs. Dashed lines indicate the linear fitting.

It should be noted that when the magnitude of $P_{M\_DC}$ or $P_{I\_T4}$ increases, the primary infection becomes sooner and more severe, which is similar to the results in a previous work [25]. It should also be noted that the severity parameter ($P_{I\_T4}$) has greater effect on the model dynamics than does the initial concentration ($P_{M\_DC}$) (as was observed by, $|f| > |b|$ and $|h| > |d|$). In other words, as evidenced by many infectious-disease observations, a small amount of a severe pathogen is going to be more virulent than a large amount of a pathogen that is less severe.

# 4    Conclusion

By using the stochastic CA model proposed in [11], this work was conducted to investigate how the variations in the initial concentration and the severity of infected cells affect the dynamics of the primary phase of HIV infection. The results indicated that the variations in the initial concentration and the severity parameter affect the dynamics of the model in such a way that the larger the magnitudes of the initial concentration and the severity parameter, the faster and more severe the dynamics of the model. In addition, the severity parameter has greater effect on the model dynamics than does the initial concentration, as shown in many experimental observations.

**Acknowledgement.** Thanks to Parames Laosinchai for suggestions on how to improve the manuscript.

# References

1. Pantaleo, G., Graziosi, C., Fauci, A.: The immunopathogenesis of human immunodeficiency virus infection. New England Journal of Medicine 328(5), 327–335 (1993)
2. Pandey, R.: Cellular automata approach to interacting cellular network models for the dynamics of cell population in an early HIV infection. Physica A: Statistical and Theoretical Physics 179(3), 442–470 (1991)
3. Zorzenon dos Santos, R., Coutinho, S.: Dynamics of HIV infection: A cellular automata approach. Physical Review Letters 87(16), 168102 (2001)
4. Shi, V., Tridane, A., Kuang, Y.: A viral load-based cellular automata approach to modeling HIV dynamics and drug treatment. Journal of Theoretical Biology 253(1), 24–35 (2008)
5. Precharattana, M., et al.: Stochastic cellular automata model and Monte Carlo simulations of CD4 T cell dynamics with a proposed alternative leukapheresis treatment for HIV/AIDS. Computers in Biology and Medicine 41(7), 546–558 (2011)
6. Hood, L.E., Wood, W.B., Wilson, J.H., Benbow, R.M.: Immunology. Menlo Park. Cummings Publishing Company, The Benjamin/ (1984)
7. Pandey, R., Stauffer, D.: Metastability with probabilistic cellular automata in an HIV infection. Journal of Statistical Physics 61(1), 235–240 (1990)
8. Kougias, C.F., Schulte, J.: Simulating the immune response to the HIV-1 virus with cellular automata. Journal of Statistical Physics 60(1), 263–273 (1990)
9. Burkhead, E., Hawkins, J., Molinek, D.: A Dynamical Study of a Cellular Automata Model of the Spread of HIV in a Lymph Node. Bulletin of Mathematical Biology 71(1), 25–74 (2009)
10. Precharattana, M., et al.: Investigation of Spatial Pattern Formation Involving CD4+ T Cells in HIV/AIDS Dynamics by a Stochastic Cellular Automata Model. International Journal of Mathematics and Computers in Simulation 4(4) (2010)
11. Precharattana, M., Triampo, W.: Stochastic cellular automata for HIV infection with effects of cell-mediated immunity (in press, 2012)
12. Sato, H., et al.: Cell-to-cell spread of HIV-1 occurs within minutes and may not involve the participation of virus particles. Virology 186(2), 712–724 (1992)
13. Jolly, C., et al.: HIV-1 cell to cell transfer across an Env-induced, actin-dependent synapse. The Journal of Experimental Medicine 199(2), 283–293 (2004)
14. Haase, A.: Population biology of HIV-1 infection: viral and CD4+ T cell demographics and dynamics in lymphatic tissues. Annual Review of Immunology 17(1), 625–656 (1999)
15. Bajaria, S.H., Kirschner, D.: CTL action during HIV-1 is determined via interactions with multiple cell types. Deterministic and Stochastic Models for AIDS Epidemics and HIV Infection with Interventions, 219–254 (2005)

16. Rosenberg, Y.J., Anderson, A.O., Pabst, R.: HIV-induced decline in blood CD4/CD8 ratios: viral killing or altered lymphocyte trafficking? Immunology Today 19(1), 10–17 (1998)
17. Kamath, A.T., et al.: Developmental kinetics and lifespan of dendritic cells in mouse lymphoid organs. Blood 100(5), 1734–1741 (2002)
18. Ingulli, E., et al.: In vivo detection of dendritic cell antigen presentation to CD4+ T cells. The Journal of Experimental Medicine 185(12), 2133–2141 (1997)
19. Tough, D.F., Sprent, J.: Turnover of naive-and memory-phenotype T cells. The Journal of Experimental Medicine 179(4), 1127–1135 (1994)
20. Gougeon, M.L., Montagnier, L.: Apoptosis in AIDS. Science 260(5112), 1269–1270 (1993)
21. Schnittman, S., et al.: Preferential infection of CD4+ memory T cells by human immunodeficiency virus type 1: evidence for a role in the selective T-cell functional defects observed in infected individuals. Proceedings of the National Academy of Sciences of the United States of America 87(16), 6058–6062 (1990)
22. Chun, T., et al.: Differential susceptibility of naive and memory CD4+ T cells to the cytopathic effects of infection with human immunodeficiency virus type 1 strain LAI. Journal of Virology 71(6), 4436–4444 (1997)
23. Ostrowski, M., et al.: Both memory and CD45RA+/CD62L+ naive CD4+ T cells are infected in human immunodeficiency virus type 1-infected individuals. Journal of Virology 73(8), 6430–6435 (1999)
24. Zhang, S., Liu, J.: A massively multi-agent system for discovering HIV-immune interaction dynamics. Massively Multi-Agent Systems I, 572–573 (2005)
25. Figueirêdo, P., Coutinho, S., Zorzenon dos Santos, R.: Robustness of a cellular automata model for the HIV infection. Physica A: Statistical Mechanics and its Applications 387(26), 6545–6552 (2008)

# Decentralized Method for Traffic Monitoring

Guillaume Sartoretti[1,2], Jean-Luc Falcone[1],
Bastien Chopard[1], and Martin J. Gander[2]

[1] Computer Science Department
[2] Department of Mathematics,
University of Geneva, Switzerland

**Abstract.** We propose a decentralized method for traffic monitoring, fully distributed over the vehicles. An algorithm is provided, specifying which information should be tracked to reconstruct an instantaneous map of traffic flow. We test the accuracy of our method in a simple cellular automata traffic simulation model, for which the traffic condition can be controlled and analyzed theoretically.

## 1 Introduction

Nowadays in big cities, the need for an overview of the traffic situation is critical in order to avoid queues, accidents, and establish an efficient routing strategy. Current solutions often involves a centralized node which collects information from the drivers within the traffic, and broadcast it to let everyone make reasonable decisions. While this strategy works well, it raises the question of privacy: the central node knows everything about everyone in the network, and this centralization of the information may hit back if the knowledge is in the wrong hands.

In this paper, we define a fully decentralized communication method which allows drivers to gather information and share it anonymously with the neighboring drivers throughout their journey, letting everyone have a good view of the status of the traffic. Due to this type of information distribution, the disadvantages of centralization and the privacy violation can be avoided. However, the problem is not trivial because the system must converge quickly to an accurate and stable representation of the current traffic conditions, and it must be able to detect rapid changes due to accidents or rush hours.

To test the capability of our method to build an accurate traffic map, we use a simple traffic model in which the cars accumulate information as they move, through mutual exchanges. Our goal is to produce well defined traffic conditions that can then be compared with the estimate made by each car. The paper is organized as follows. We first propose a theoretical description of the car motion, from which the traffic flow can be predicted with the knowledge of only a few quantities. Then we define how the cars communicate and how they combine the information to progressively build a global traffic map. Finally we provide some examples of simulation, showing how accurately the traffic can be estimated. More detail about this study can be found in [1].

G.C. Sirakoulis and S. Bandini (Eds.): ACRI 2012, LNCS 7495, pp. 464–473, 2012.

## 2   Traffic Model and Theoretical Framework

In order to produce simple traffic conditions suitable to test our communication method, we consider a Cellular Automata (CA) model. This approach has been widely used in traffic simulations, with excellent results (see for instance [2–6]).

### 2.1   Basic Model

Here we consider several road segments, interconnected through simple junctions. A road segment is a 1D vector of length $L$, where each component (cell) represents a possible location for a car. Let $n_i(t)$ be the value of the cell $i$ at time $t$. We define $n_i(t) = 1$ if there is a car at location $i$, at time $t$. Otherwise, we define $n_i(t) = 0$

Here we use Wolfram's rule 184 [7] to describe the motion of the cars on a road:

$$n_i(t+1) = n_{i-1}(t)(1 - n_i(t)) + n_i(t)n_{i+1}(t) \qquad \text{for } 1 < i < L \qquad (1)$$

This means that a car moves to the next cell if and only if this next cell is free; otherwise it stays still. Roads are considered as one-way lanes. The two special locations are the beginning and the end of a road. These cells obey other rules that implement the chosen boundary conditions, for instance the junction that interconnects two segments.

**Circuits.** A simple example of interconnection between two roads is the circuit shown in Fig. 1. It is composed of two side by side roads of length $L_1 = L_2 = L$. A car reaching the end of one of the roads may cross to the other road with probability $\pi$ (as if there was a stop sign, or a traffic light), and given that the beginning of the other road is free.

Accordingly, the rule for cells 1 and $L$ can be expressed as

$$n_1(t+1) = m_L(t)(1 - n_1(t)) \cdot Q(t) + n_1(t)n_2(t)$$
$$n_L(t+1) = n_{L-1}(t)(1 - n_L(t)) + n_L(t)(1 - m_1(t)) \cdot P(t)$$

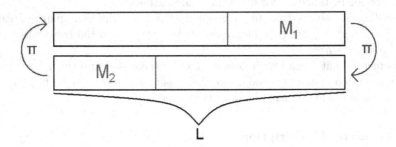

**Fig. 1.** Diagram of a two-road circuit, with an initial number $M_1$ and $M_2$ of car on each road

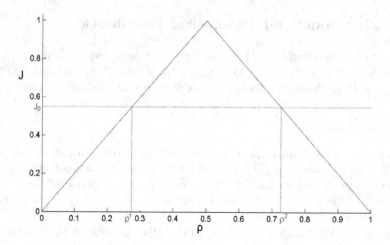

**Fig. 2.** Fundamental diagram of traffic, showing the flow $J$ according to the density $\rho$

where $n_i$ and $m_i$ denote the occupation numbers of the first and second roads, respectively. The quantities $P(t)$ and $Q(t)$ are Boolean random variables which are 1 with probability $\pi$. The equations for $m_1$ and $m_L$ are obtained by symmetry.

**Occupation Density of a Cell.** On a road segment, the car density $\rho_i(t)$ on cell $i$ is defined as $\langle n_i(t) \rangle$, the average of $n_i$ (over time or space). We can write an evolution equation for $\rho_i(t)$ by taking the average of eq. (1):

$$\rho_i(t+1) = \rho_{i-1}(t) - \langle n_{i-1}(t)\, n_i(t) \rangle + \langle n_i(t)\, n_{i+1}(t) \rangle. \tag{2}$$

Note that $\langle n_i(t)\, n_{i+1}(t) \rangle \neq \rho_i(t)\, \rho_{i+1}(t)$ in general, because $n_i(t)$ and $n_{i+1}(t)$ are highly correlated.

**Fundamental Diagram of Traffic.** The traffic flow $J(t)$ in a road segment is defined as $J(t) = \rho(t)\, v(t)$, with $v$ the average speed of the cars on that section. In a steady state, the flow obeys the *fundamental diagram of traffic* shown in Fig. 2 (see for instance [2] for a detailed calculation).

This diagram shows that for a given flow $J_0$, two different pairs of values $(\rho^1, v^1)$ and $(\rho^2, v^2)$ are possible: $J_0 = \rho^1 v^1 = \rho^2 v^2$, with the constraints $\rho^1 < \frac{1}{2} < \rho^2$ and $\rho^1 + \rho^2 = 1$.

This means that a road with flow $J_0$ may be separated into two zones, a low-density zone (a free moving zone where the density will be $\rho^1$), and a high-density zone (a queue of cars, where the density will be $\rho^2$).

## 2.2   Theoretical Description

**Queue Length.** Fig. 3 illustrates the typical density $\rho_i$ at each cell $\{1, ..., L\}$) of one section of the two-road circuit shown in Fig. 1. This figure shows that

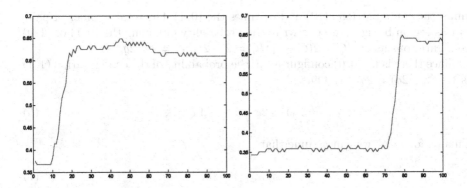

**Fig. 3.** Density plots for a road of length $L = 10$, averaged over 128 successive time iterations at different time of evolution. As we can see, the length of the queue can vary over time.

the queue length varies over time. In this section, we propose an analytical description of this behavior.

In a steady state, we can rewrite eq. (1) as

$$\rho_i = \rho_{i-1} - \langle n_{i-1}n_i \rangle + \langle n_i n_{i+1} \rangle, \tag{3}$$

In a steady state, the traffic flow $J$ is constant. Therefore the density has two possible values $p$ and $q = 1 - p$, as discussed above. Let us assume boundary conditions such that $\rho_1 = p$ and $\rho_L = q = 1 - p$, with $p < \frac{1}{2}$. Then, eq. (2) is obeyed if

$$\rho_i = \begin{cases} p \text{ if } i \le k \\ q \text{ if } i > k \end{cases} \quad \forall k \in \{1, 2, ..., L\}. \tag{4}$$

This condition means that there is a change in the car density at a cell $k$ along the road. This is interpreted as the presence of a queue that starts at position $k$.

We can check that eq. (4) obeys eq. (2) by computing the value of $\langle n_{i-1}n_i \rangle$ and $\langle n_i n_{i+1} \rangle$. Let us consider the region where $i \le k$, the low-density region. Since $\rho < \frac{1}{2}$, the cases where $(n_i, n_{i+1}) = (1,1)$ is impossible in the long run, as there is always enough space to let a free cell between two following cars. In such a case, we can only have $n_i n_{i+1} = 0$, so that

$$\langle n_i n_{i+1} \rangle = 0 \quad \text{if } \rho_i = p < \frac{1}{2} \tag{5}$$

In the high-density region, $i > k$, where $\rho_i = q = 1 - p > \frac{1}{2}$, we cannot have $(n_i, n_{i+1}) = (0,0)$ in the long run. The number of cars is too high to allow such configuration, and only the $(1,0), (0,1)$ and $(1,1)$ configurations can be observed. Let us denote $C = L - k$ the number of cells in the region of density $q$. We define $c_1 = qC$ the number of cars in this region and $c_0 = C - c_1$ the number of free cells. Since next to any free cell, there will be a car, there are $c_0$

times the configuration $(1,0)$ and $c_0$ times the $(0,1)$ The total number of pairs in this region being $C$, we can write the probability of having the $(0,1)$ or $(1,0)$ configurations as $2c_0/C = 2(C - c_1)/C = 2 - 2c_1/C = 2 - 2q$.

Since there is no $(0,0)$ configuration, the probability of the configuration $(1,1)$ is $1 - (2 - 2q) = 2q - 1$. Thus

$$\langle n_i n_{i+1} \rangle = 2q - 1 \qquad \text{if } q > \tfrac{1}{2}. \tag{6}$$

Finally, for $i = k$ we can assume that

$$\langle n_k n_{k+1} \rangle = 0 \tag{7}$$

This means that at the interface between the two regions, the configuration $(1,1)$ is impossible: if this configuration were possible, we should move the break point from $k$ to $k-1$, as $k$ would already be in the high-density region. In other word, the cell $k$ at which $< n_k n_{k+1} >$ switches to a non-zero value is defined as the start of the queue. Using eqs. 4, (5), (6), (7), it is easy to verify that eq. (3) is satisfied.

A consequence of this analysis is that the queue can a priori have any length because $k$ can be any integer between 1 and $L$. However, there is a constraint related to the total number of cars. Let $N$ be the number of car in the upper road of the circuit shown in Fig. 1. Then, we must have $N = kp + (L - k)q$. Thus, $k = (Lq - N)/(q - p)$ and the fluctuation of $k$ are related to the fluctuations of $N$. In the two-road circuit, $N$ is constrained by the maximum number of car $M_1 + M_2$ and the length $L$ of the two road segments: $\max(0, M_1 + M_2 - L) \le N \le \min(L, M_1 + M_2)$. As the queue length is a quantity which can potentially vary a lot in our circuit, it is not well suited for testing the capability of our mapping method to estimate the traffic condition. It is better to consider a quantity which is easier to control and which is more stable. A better test is to check whether the cars can accurately estimate the value of $\pi$, the probability that a car can cross the last cell of the road.

**Traffic Flow in the Two-Road Circuit.** In our circuit, there is a relation between the densities $p$ and $q = 1 - p$, and the value of $\pi$, the probability of not being stopped. In a steady state, the flow $J$ must be constant all across the system. At the end of each road, $J$ is given by the probability $q$ to have a car times the probability that this car is allowed to continue. This assumes that the first cell of the next segment is always free, which is the case as no two cars can successively enter the low density region from the high density region (there must be a free cell between moving cars). Moreover, from the fundamental diagram, the flow in the low density region is equal to $p$. Thus

$$J = q\pi = p = 1 - q, \tag{8}$$

from which we conclude that $\pi = p/q$ and $p = \frac{\pi}{1+\pi} = 1 - q$.

## 3   Decentralized Flow Estimation

We showed in the previous section that for a given flow at steady state, a road is composed of two regions, one with low density $p$ and the other with high density $q = 1 - p$. We have also shown that the flow could be reconstructed when $p$ and $q$ are known. Thus, we could estimate the flow of each road segment, if we can estimate the values of $p$ and $q$. In this section, we present a way to estimate those quantities by a decentralized exchange of information between neighboring cars.

### 3.1   Global Map

We call *global map*, the real traffic map that each car will try to estimate. According to our discussion, we can restrict this map to a few cells in the network, those which are enough to predict the traffic flow in each road segment. Here, the map is composed of the measured densities at each road end, $\hat{\rho}_2$ and $\hat{\rho}_{L-1}$. Those densities are computed as the average occupation of the cell during the last 128 iterations:

$$\hat{\rho}_i(t) = \frac{1}{128} \sum_{k=t-127}^{t} n_i(k) \tag{9}$$

The use of a "sliding time window" (of size 128 in our case) to compute the density of a cell, allows us to forget the remote past and to get a dynamic view at traffic evolutions. The size of 128 was chosen for practical implementation reasons, and provides good results as shown in the next section. If the window size is too small, fluctuations will dominate time-stable structures. If it is too large, temporary (but relevant) structures will become undetectable.

### 3.2   Local Map

Every car in the model maintains an estimated map of traffic density, termed *local map*. This map is updated at each iteration by direct observations and communications with other cars. Cars can exchange information with neighboring cars. Here, during a single iteration, each car can communicate with at most with 5 other cars, the leading and trailing ones, and the three cars in the opposite lane.

For a street map with $N_{\text{road}}$ road segments, the local map $m_v$ of a car $v \in \{1, 2, ..., M_1 + M_2\}$ at iteration $t$ is a matrix with 128 rows and $2N$road columns. The rows correspond to the 128 previous time steps and the columns contain the tracked locations (both ends of each road segment). The elements of the map defined as

$$m_v(i, j) = \begin{cases} 1 & \text{if a car was recorded by } v \text{ at location } j \text{ at time } t - i + 1 \\ 0 & \text{else.} \end{cases} \tag{10}$$

An estimate of the density of each location can be computed by averaging the corresponding column.

**Local Map Update.** All cars start with a local map filled with zeroes. At each iteration, they update the map according to the following steps: **(1)** The local map matrix rows are shifted down, eliminating the oldest row. The first row is filled with zeroes. **(2)** Each car adds 1 to the element of the first row corresponding to its current location, if it is a tracked location ($i = 2$ or $i = L-1$). **(3)** Each car sends its map to each neighboring car and receives maps from them, merging the information into its own local map with an element-wise logical **OR**.

It is easy to see that the logical **OR** of the first 128 lines of the local maps of all the cars in our circuit will produce the global map. Indeed, as all cars only put their own position at each step of the simulation in their local maps, the logical **OR** of all the local maps will give the occupation of each of the cars in the last 128 iterations. The question is whether our car to car communications will be fast enough to provide an accurate **OR** of all the local maps, and thus the global map.

## 4    Simulation Results

We present here some preliminary results demonstrating the capability of our decentralized communication method to build a reliable traffic map. Using the circuit defined in Sec. 2.1, we ran several simulations using road segments with a length of $L = 60$ cells initialized with $M_1 = M_2 = 30$ cars per road segment placed in a queue at the end. One car is chosen at random as the reference car. After $12L$ iterations of traffic update, allowing us to reach a steady state, the cars start updating their local maps and exchanging information as explained above.

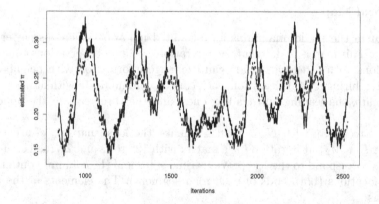

**Fig. 4.** Estimation of $\hat{\pi}$ in a circuit with $\pi = 0.2$. The solid line corresponds to the local map and the dashed line to the global map. Increasing the memory length from 128 to 1024 would smooth out the variations and give a more accurate prediction of $\pi$.

In this simulation we study how well the test car can estimate the probability $\pi = p/q$ (see eq. (8)) that a car is not stopped at the end of a segment. The estimate value $\hat{\pi}$ is computed as

$$\hat{\pi}(t) = \frac{\hat{\rho}_2(t)}{\hat{\rho}_{L-1}(t)} \tag{11}$$

This value is then compared with the value obtained from the global map using the same procedure, as well as the exact value of $\pi$ used in the simulation. We consider here two situations: (i) a circuit where $\pi$ is constant in time; (ii) a circuit where the value of $\pi$ varies suddenly.

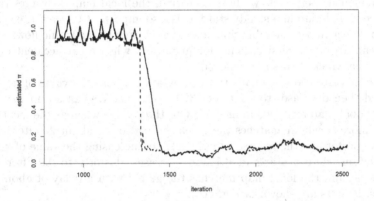

(a) Case with $\pi = 0.9$ when $t <= 1320$ and $pi = 0.1$ for $t > 1320$

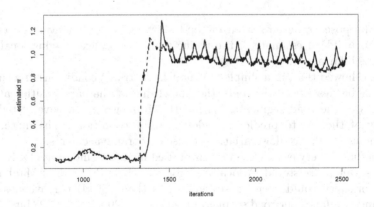

(b) Case with $\pi = 0.1$ when $t <= 1320$ and $\pi = 0.9$ for $t > 1320$

**Fig. 5.** Value of $\hat{\pi}$ computed from the local map (continuous line) and from the global map (dashed line)

## 4.1   Constant Flow

Here we analyze a circuit with $\pi = 0.2$, once then a steady flow has settled. In Fig. 4 we compare the value of $\pi$ computed from the local map of the test car and that computed from the global map. As we can see, the measured values stay around the actual value of $\pi$ for both cases. Variations, reflecting the intrinsic fluctuations of traffic and the limited lenght of the memory, are visible in both maps, though more pronounced on the local one, due to its incomplete information.

## 4.2   Flow with Abrupt Transition

In the previous experiment, we have seen than the local map converges rather well to the global map in a steady state. It is also important to see if the system is able to detect in a reasonable time a sudden change in the traffic flow. These changes can arise in real situations, for instance a when a car accident occurs and until the wrecked cars are removed.

To test this situation, we have run a simulation where the value of $\pi$ starts at 0.9 and then decreases to 0.1 after 1320 iterations. We can see in Fig. 5(a) that the global map responds immediately to the change whereas the local map re-adjust more slowly. It matches the global estimation in about 200 iterations.

We also performed the reverse experiment, i.e. increasing the value of $\pi$ during simulation. Here $\pi$ starts at 0.1 and increases abruptly to 0.9 after 1320 iterations. Again, the local map matches the global with a delay of about 200 iterations. Results are shown in Fig. 5(b).

## 5   Discussion

We have proposed a decentralized method allowing the cars traversing a road network to build an estimate of the traffic situation, by exchanging local and anonymous information.

We also showed that, in a simple CA model, the traffic conditions in a simple circuit can be described with only the knowledge of the car densities at the extremities of the road segments. Within this framework, we have tested the capability of the car to predict the global traffic conditions. The method is robust enough to detect flow variations caused by traffic accidents.

The method is very economic in terms of used memory, since only $2 \times 128$ bits per road segment are stored. A local map for the whole Borough of Manhattan in New-York city could then be stored in less than $150\,\mathrm{kB}$ (11 avenues, 220 streets, and two lanes per road segment give us $11 \times 220 \times 2 \times 2 \times 128$ bits). The computational cost is also very low: (i) most of the operations are element-wise and thus may run in parallel; (ii) bitwise **OR** operations are executed as a single instruction in all current processors.

In the current model of communication, we restrict communication with nearest neighbor cars and thus the information is propagated at the same speed than the cars. However, in a concrete implementation of the communication system, information will be exchanged via a wireless protocol, which allows the communications to be both faster and with an extended range. We expect such a system to be even better because, as stated above, the union of all local maps in a system gives the exact global map. Thus, if the communication is more efficient, the local maps of every car will be more accurate. Radio-wave transmission could nevertheless be simulated with a multi-scale CA where the communication rule is applied with smaller time-steps than the traffic rule.

We have also tested the method using a more realistic street map and promising results are described in [1].

# References

1. Sartoretti, G.: Communication method for decentralized estimation of traffic density. Technical report, University of Geneva. Master Thesis (2012)
2. Chopard, B., Luthi, P.O., Queloz, P.A.: Cellular automata model of car traffic in a two-dimensional street network. Journal of Physics A: Mathematical and General 29(10), 2325 (1996)
3. Dijkstra, J., Timmermans, H.J.P., Jessurun, A.J.: A multi-agent cellular automata system for visualising simulated pedestrian activity. In: Bandini, S., Worsch, T. (eds.) Theoretical and Practical Issues on Cellular Automata - Proceedings on the 4th International Conference on Cellular Automata for Research and Industry, pp. 29–36. Springer (2000)
4. Dupuis, A., Chopard, B.: Cellular automata simulations of traffic: A model for the city of geneva. Networks and Spatial Economics 3, 9–21 (2003), doi:10.1023/A:1022044932736
5. Nagel, K., Schreckenberg, M.: A cellular automaton model for freeway traffic. J. Phys. I France 2(12), 221–2229 (1992), http://dx.doi.org/10.1051/jp1:1992277
6. Nishinari, K., Fukui, M., Schadschneider, A.: A stochastic cellular automaton model for traffic flow with multiple metastable states. Journal of Physics A: Mathematical and General 37(9), 3101 (2004)
7. Wolfram, S.: Theory and Application of Cellular Automata. World Scientific, Singapore (1986)

# Improving a Project Management
# by Use of Cellular Automata

Kenichiro Shimura[1,2] and Katsuhiro Nishinari[1]

[1] Research Center for Advanced Science and Technology, The University of Tokyo,
4-6-1, Komaba, Meguro-ku, Tokyo, 153-8904, Japan
[2] Department of Informatics Systems and Communication, The University of Milano
Bicocca, Viale Sarca 336 - U14, 20126 Milano, Italy
shimura@tokai.t.u-tokyo.ac.jp

**Abstract.** For any project management, it is of great interest to improve the accuracy of planning since a delay in the project often causes extra cost. This paper provides a method for dynamical simulation of a project. The results provide probabilistic estimate of project time and gives project manager a chance to make preemptive action to avoid major delay.

**Keywords:** Cellular Automata, ASEP, Project Management, Scheduling, Planning, PERT.

# 1    Introduction

A calendar is often used to manage a project. Daily plans are written in a box on a calendar matrix, and then the box is crossed out after the day finishes. A classic scheduling board is also in the calendar base that the array of days is aligned in a row parallel to the work plan, which often called a Gantt chart. Again, in the end of the day, the box is crossed out. If the planed work is not completed on the day, the planning board is rewritten and the remaining work of the day is carried over to the next day. The accumulation of such small delay on the daily plan consequently cusses recalculation of the plan then the whole schedule is rewritten. Catastrophically, a project turns out to be a death march or failure of pursuance to a promised delivery date may occur. Management of time and risk appear to be key issues to avoid such negative aspects, since it is of great importance to estimate the risks that delays the schedule. The established bases to manage those factors in a project of various sectors are Program Evaluation and Review Technique (PERT) [1], Critical Path Method (CPM) [1], for time management and Fault Tree Analysis (FTA) [2], for risk management. A project often consists of number of tasks where every task are connected in a network and expressed as a graph. The PERT focuses on these connections of tasks, while Gantt chart focuses on the daily shift of the project progress. PERT provides the method to analyze the task network and giving an estimate of the project completion time. Statistical approach can also be applied to PERT. Considering the probability risk for completion of each task, the overall

G.C. Sirakoulis and S. Bandini (Eds.): ACRI 2012, LNCS 7495, pp. 474–482, 2012.
© Springer-Verlag Berlin Heidelberg 2012

project completion time can be estimated by means of Monte Carlo method. By use of this approach, the critical path in the task network can also visible. The critical path is a series of tasks which are rate limiting the overall progress in the project. Understanding the context of the critical path eventually derives efficient work diversion and planning to reduce the project completion time. Besides, the PERT provides an analysis in time domain, FTA provides a static method to analysis a probability of any event occurs in a large system. FTA often used for the evaluation of the safety in a plant. But this method is also applied to estimate the probabilistic risk of the project delay. Today, the approach of PERT has been applied to various factors in business, plant and project operation to analyze cost, reliability and manpower. And improving the accuracy of planning is of great interests in various sectors.

This paper proposes the dynamic method to analyse the project to obtain a probabilistic expression of project time by use of Cellular Automata (CA). The method is based on Asymmetical Simple Exclusion Process (ASEP) to express each task of the project. The method to employing ASEP to the scheduling problem is described then the method is applied to the real world project for evaluation.

## 2    Modelling

At first we consider the Gantt chart for project time management. In Gantt chart, the project is broken down to each task and listed vertically. Then, horizontal bar graphs that represent the expected start time, task duration and the finishing time of the corresponding task are presented in the chart. The abscissa of the chart represents the unit time of the project, which unit is often taken as one calendar day. Moreover, the estimation of the work duration for each task is calculated by the total work loading divided by the daily work capability with consideration of some operation rate. The successive presentation of such tasks in the chart creates the overall task network of the project. Another important point in the Gantt chart is the existence of the time progress, such that the calendar date shifts to the next working day when the expected work is completed. Although number of tasks are closely related each other in the real project and there exist predecessor and successor tasks, here we are focusing on a particular single task. Let the total work load is assumed as 100 work unit (wu) and the ideal daily work capability is assumed as 10 wu/day, then the duration of the task is calculated as 10 days which often called a "optimistic time" in PERT method. But it is not always the case that the daily work is carried out with full efficiency. Introducing the concept of the operation rate where the maximum efficiency is taken as unity, then the task duration can be estimated longer than 10 days. Fig. 1 illustrates the Gantt chart of this example task namely "Task A", for the case of the operation rate = 1 and the operation rate = 0.5. When the operation rate is 0.5, the average task duration is 20 which is twice longer than that for the operation rate = 1. The operation rate expresses the efficiency of the work and the factor inverse of the operation rate is multiplied to the optimistic time to deduce the average task duration.

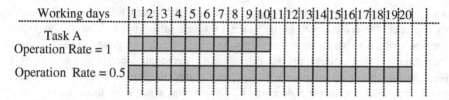

**Fig. 1.** The Gantt chart of an assumed task. Where work loading is assumed as 100 work unit (wu), daily work capability is assumed as 10 wu/day, operation rate = 1 and 0.5.

This estimation is considered lather the deterministic approach that means the operation rate of every working day is fixed as 0.5. It is also possible to understand that the operation rate is macroscopic implementation of delay risks. In order to make the estimation more accurate, realistic and practical, it is necessary to consider the microscopic context of the operation rate. In the microscopic point of view, a task is broken into smaller work units that the operational rate of each are individually evaluated. This approach is effective for planning the outdoor operations such that the work is very much affected by uncertainties such as the natural conditions. And also the effect of uncertainties on the task duration is larger as the optimistic time becomes longer. The typical example is concreting process in the construction sector that needs successive dry days. The decision of those tasks involving the natural conditions are often made on an empirical basis by the members on the project spot. But sometimes there occurs major delay caused by the harsh natural conditions. Thus the consideration of the daily operation rate is of great advantage to improve the evaluation of such risks.

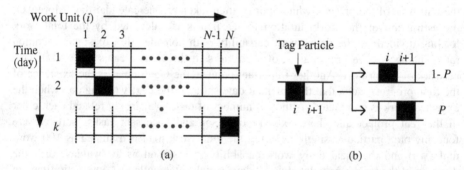

**Fig. 2.** (a) The time evolution of the task. Where $N$ denotes the optimistic time and $k$ denotes the expected time of a task. (b) The corresponding transition rues. Where $P$ denoted the transition probability.

The implementation of scheduling in CA is carried out by use of the Asymmetical Simple Exclusion Process (ASEP) with a single particle in a lattice where each cell expresses a work unit per unit time. It is convenient to consider a unit time as one calendar day and the cell size as the relevant unit amount of work. Fig. 2(a) and (b) illustrates the time evolution of the task and corresponding transition rues respectively. In Fig. 2(a) a task is broken in to smaller peace of work unit and represented in one-dimensional lattice. Each cell in the lattice represents the work unit per unit time. The length of the lattice is denoted as $N$, which represents the optimistic time of the task. The progression of the task is represented as movement of a particle namely a "tag particle", for which only one tag particle is allowed in a lattice. The tag particle shows the current state of the task and able to characterize how much of the task is finished and how much left. The tag particle moves forward when the planned work unit is finished and it stays at the same position if it is not finished. The probability of the tag particle moves forward from $i$ th to $i+1$ th cell is given as $P$ and contrary to this, the probability that the particle stays over is $1-P$ as shown in Fig. 2(b). In this expression, $P$ is the probabilistic implementation of the operation rate discussed earlier. The duration of the task is represented as $k$ unit time where in this case, referred to as calendar days when unit time is taken as one day. It is also seen that when $P = 1$ for every work unit then the task duration is equals to optimistic time such that $k = N$. Although this is an expression of a single task in a project, it is possible to connect this task model in a network to analyse a complex project. Clarification of risks in each work unit can be performed by various statistical methods. The evaluation of the risks deduces the value of the transition probability $P$. Thus determining the value of $P$ is a critical issue for accurate estimation of the project time. When the value of $P$ is resolved the simulation can be performed in a normal ASEP approach. However this approach can be applied for not only for the project time estimation but also cost estimation by changing the work unit to the cost unit.

## 3    Simulation Results and Discussion

The optimistic time calculated by given operation rate is rather a deterministic approach. This method gives more detailed understanding of the project time since every work unit is considered as a stochastic process. The result of the simulation is shown in Fig. 3. The calculation is carried out for the scenario shown in Fig. 1, where the work load is assumed as 100 work unit (wu), daily work capability is assumed as 10 wu/day, operation rate = 0.5. A tag particle starts from the first cell in the lattice which represents the stating point of a task then calculate the over all required time needed for the tag particle to reaches the end of the lattice. The context of operation rate is that, the work is most likely delay by the reciprocal of this value. Moreover, the work should never be finished earlier than optimistic time or referred to as a minimum time, which is 10 days in this case. In reality, there are cases that the planned work is finished earlier or later than expected. For example, if the operation rate is taken as 0.5, then a work supposed to be finished in one day takes most likely takes two days. But it is not always the case that it could be finished in one day or takes longer than two days. Considering to such variation, the deterministic implementation of operation rate is not capable to represent such a nature. As it is seen from Fig. 3(a), using this method, the expected time is represented as a probability density. The minimum expected time is 10 days, which means the task is carried on exactly as planned without any delay. The expected day that occurs most frequently in the simulation that is called the mode in statistics is 18 days. This value represents the case when the work is carried out with operation rate of 0.5 for all the way. In this case, the average expected day is calculated as 20 days. The origin of the different values in the average and the mode is due to the nature of an asymmetrical distribution. Fig. 3(b) illustrates the cumulative distribution. This indicates that the probability of completing the task in given expected time. For example, the probability of completing the task in 25 days is 90%. This indication is often appreciated by industries for project planning as well as the purpose of cost estimation.

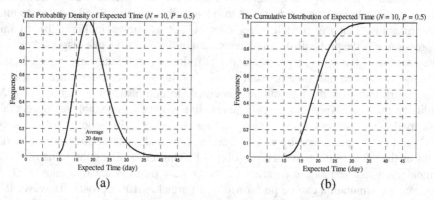

(a)                                                    (b)

**Fig. 3.** The simulation result where work load is assumed as 100 work unit (wu), daily work capability is assumed as 10 wu/day, operation rate = 0.5. (a) The probability density. Where the mode is 18 days and the average is 20 days. (b) Cumulative distribution of expected time.

Furthermore, theoretical analysis has been carried out for the probability density and is given as Eq. (1).

$$f(k) = 0 \qquad\qquad\qquad\qquad\qquad\qquad\qquad ,\text{for } k < N$$

$$f(k) = P^N (1-P)^{k-N} \frac{(k-1)!}{(N-1)!(k-N)!} \qquad ,\text{for } k \geq N \tag{1}$$

Where $f(k)$ denotes the probability density function, $k$ denotes the expected day, P denotes the operation rate or hopping probability in ASEP and N denotes the lattice length. Together with the expression for probability density function, the variance $V$ is also calculated and given in Eq. (2).

$$V = (1-P)\frac{N}{P^2} \tag{2}$$

Fig. 4 illustrates the comparison between the results obtained by numerical calculation of ASEP and Eq. (1) for various P values with the lattice length or optimistic time N is taken as 10. For every case, good agreement with theoretical analysis is seen. It is also seen from Fig. 5 and Eq. (2) that the variant tends larger as P decreases.

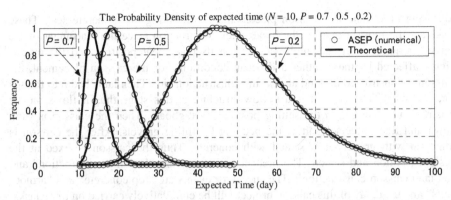

**Fig. 4.** The comparison of the probability density function obtained by numerical calculation of ASEP and theoretical result of Eq. (1) for $N = 10$ and $P = 0.7, 0.5, 0.2$.

## 4    Application to the Real World

This method is applied to evaluate the project time of a real construction project. The project is to construct a caisson breakwater at a harbour where facing to the Pacific Ocean in Japan. The work is severely affected by the weather and the ocean conditions. The weather condition affects to the concreting task and the ocean condition such as ocean swell affects the work condition of the vessels. The project had carried out by considering an empirical operation rate, but severe delay had been occurred in some tasks and in the end, the project had turned out to be a death march for pursuance to a promised delivery date. This is an example of planning failure and often results an extra cost. In this paper, the cause of the failure is revealed and the method to improve accuracy of the planning is discussed.

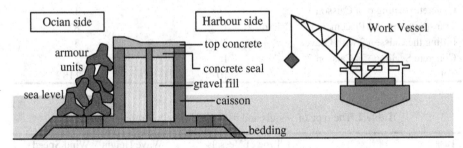

**Fig. 5.** The cross sectional diagram of the breakwater by use of the caisson. And a example of work vessels used in the construction.

Fig. 5 illustrates the cross sectional diagram of the caisson breakwater. The caisson is placed on top of the bedding that is made of relatively large rocks. The caisson is filled up with gravels and sealed with concrete. Then whole modules are decorated with top concrete. And also blocks of armour unit protect the caisson. The project to be considered in this paper is a setting of the caisson. The project consists of the following tasks that are, caisson placement, gravel filling and concrete seal. These tasks are the most critical of the breakwater construction since the placement of the caisson requires relatively high accuracy in its placement position and the task is highly affected by the weather and ocean condition. For the caisson placement, the caisson is constructed on land at near the construction site. Then launched into the sea for placement. The caisson is a hollow structure at this stage thus it flows on the water, so it is carried to the setting position by tugboats. Then the caisson is sunk down and fixed precisely on to the bedding by filling gravels. After the caisson is filled up with gravels it is sealed with concrete. Thus the caisson is fixed at the designed potion and sealed. The predecessor events are "bedding construction" and "on land caisson construction". The successor events are "top concrete" and "armour units" and the delay of this caisson project will be cumulatively carried on these tasks.

In this project, the optimistic time for placement of two caissons is 10 days. And operation rate has chosen empirically as 0.33. This means that the expected time of the project is 30days. Note that the operation rate is empirically calculated and given by Japan Ministry of Land, Infrastructure, Transport and Tourism (MLIT). Table 1 shows the optimistic, expected and actual duration of each task. It is seen that the variation of expected and actual time is fairly large. The most time consuming task is "Transportation and Placement of a Caisson". Since the nature of this construction method, transportation, filling and sealing task must be performed successively in straight days. Thus the starting of series of tasks for each caisson had been delayed due to the ocean condition had not been met to the working condition of the vessels.

Table 1. The optimistic, expected and actual time of tasks in the caisson project

| Task | Optimistic Time (days) | Expected Time (days) | Actual Time (days) |
|------|------------------------|----------------------|--------------------|
| Transportation and Placement of a Caisson 1 | 1 | 3 | 20 |
| Filling the Caisson 1 with Gravel | 3 | 9 | 10 |
| Concrete Sealing of a Caisson 1 | 1 | 3 | 1 |
| Transportation and Placement of a Caisson 2 | 1 | 3 | 82 |
| Filling the Caisson 2 with Gravel | 3 | 9 | 3 |
| Concrete Sealing of a Caisson 2 | 1 | 3 | 2 |
| Total | 10 | 30 | 118 |

Table 2. The type of vessels and its performance limit for each task

| Task | Type of Vessels | Wave Height Limit (m) | Wind Speed Limit (m/sec) |
|------|-----------------|-----------------------|--------------------------|
| Transportation and Placement of a Caisson | Tugboat | 0.6 | 10 |
| Filling the Caisson with Gravel | Sand carrier | 0.6 | 10 |
|  | Crane vessel. | 0.6 | 10 |
| Concrete Sealing of a Caisson | Cement mixer vessel | 0.6 | 10 |

As it is seen from Table 1, the actual time needed for the task is extremely exceeding to the expected value. This is caused by wrong choice and implementation of the operation rate. Here, the expected time is re-evaluated by using this method.

Various vessels are used for each task and every vessel has its own performance limit. One critical factor is the wave height that has an effect on pitching and rolling of the vessel. The construction site of this project is facing to the Pacific Ocean and the wave height is relatively high throughout a calendar year because of the direct strike of ocean swell. Type of vessels used for each task and the performance limit is listed in Table 2. The table shows the conditions that the vessel cannot be used if the weather or ocean condition exceeds the indicated values. The probability of workable condition of the vessels can be evaluated by the comparison of the past weather and wave observation data at the construction site. The weather observation data is provided by the Japan Meteorological Agency (JMA) and the wave observation data is provided by the MLIT. Note that rather than mean wave height, the significant wave height (SWH) is used in this calculation since SWH reflects more reality for the work condition of vessels. The observation data of 9 consecutive years is used to count the number of workable and unworkable days. Then the probability of workable days is obtained by the ratio of those values. This statistical method is directly applicable to obtain the operation rate. The operation rate is calculated monthly and shown in Table 3.

**Table 3.** The monthly operation rate calculated from real observation data of significant wave height and wind speed

| Jan. | Feb. | Mar. | Apr. | May. | Jun. | Jul. | Aug. | Sep. | Oct. | Nov. | Dec. |
|------|------|------|------|------|------|------|------|------|------|------|------|
| 0.065 | 0.050 | 0.046 | 0.019 | 0.012 | 0.092 | 0.131 | 0.115 | 0.019 | 0.020 | 0.10 | 0.081 |

The operation rate is calculated monthly because of the seasonal background. And also if the task crosses the season, the relevant operation rate also changes. For example there is over ten times difference in operation rate for May and July. This means that when a task is carried out in May, it takes ten times longer than the case it started in July. Such result suggests the importance for selecting an appropriate season to proceed the task. This pseudo real time approach dramatically improves the estimation of the project time. Fig. 6(a) illustrates the result of the simulation for the caisson project. The actual project was started in August and it took 118 days to finish. As it is seen from the figure, the highest possibility for the project time is 120 to 130 days. Considering the actual project time was 118 days, this simulation successfully estimating the project time. The simulation is also applied for other scenario to find shorter project time. One way is to change the season to start the project. Fig. 6(b) illustrates the probability density of expected time in case of the task is started in June. There are two peaks at 77 days and 161 days. This means that the project time is most likely 77 days. But if the project did not finished within this time, it is highly possible that the project delays to 161 days. This result is very useful for the project management, since the project manager can foresees the danger of significant delay and appropriate action can be taken in advance.

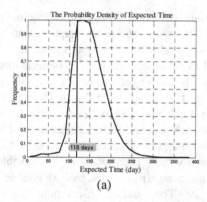
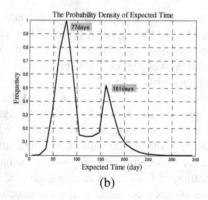

**Fig. 6.** Calculated expected time. (a) Simulated for the real construction project that is the task is started in August. 118 days was required for the real project. (b) For the scenario of if the task is started in June.

# 5    Conclusions

Scheduling method by use of ASEP is developed. This method provides the probability distribution of the expected project time. So the project manager can foresees the risk of major delay and possible to plan ahead. Appropriate evaluation of the project risk is important to evaluate the transition probability of ASEP. The comparison to the real project, it can be concluded that this method is adequate for the real world application.

# References

1. An American National Standard: A Guide to the Project Management Body of Knowledge (PMBOK Guide), 4th edn.: Project Management Institute, Inc. (2008)
2. Haasl, D.F., Roberts, N.H., et al.: Fault Tree Handbook. U.S. Nuclear Regulatory Commission (1981)

# Use of Cellular Automata to Create an Artificial System of Image Classification and Recognition

Stepan Belan[1] and Nikolay Belan[2]

[1] State Economic and Technologies Transport University, Kiev, Ukraine
bstepan@ukr.net
[2] "Transnistrian Radio and Television Center" OJSC
nickni@mail.ru

**Abstract.** The paper studies possibilities of creating an artificial system of image classification and recognition that simulates the functions of the human retina. Cellular automata are used to create such a system. A method for image recognition, rotated to any angle and in the modified scale, is proposed. The proposed methods and schematic technical decisions are simulated.

**Keywords:** cellular automata, image, contour, image classification, machine vision, image scaling, retina.

## 1    Introduction

Until recently cellular automata (CA) have been presented in different models and forms but still without any generalized definition. However, CA are most effectively used in simulating various dynamical processes, computer graphics and image processing [1-11]. In the first two cases CA are used in mechanical description of the processes necessary for computer simulation. CA are also applied in hardware implementation as homogenous discrete structures that process large data arrays online [12, 13]. In this case the use of CA allows the systems of image recognition and processing to be made more effective with regard to pre-processing and efficient preparation of images for their further recognition. Now there is a problem of effective description of the images for reliable recognition. This is especially true as the image is rotated and changes in scale. The paper solves the problem of using CA for effective processing and preliminary preparation of images. The possibility to use the main laws of construction and functioning principles of CA to simulate the functions of a human optic canal in perception of optic pictures is studied [12, 14, 15].

## 2    CA as a Biological Model for Primary Perception of Visual Pictures

Nowadays experts in the field of processing and recognitions expend their energy trying to create artificial systems that are based on the functioning principles of the

G.C. Sirakoulis and S. Bandini (Eds.): ACRI 2012, LNCS 7495, pp. 483–493, 2012.

human nervous system. All the known attempts are, first of all, based on the results of neurophysiological research while combining upwards and downwards approaches [12, 14, 15].

Each biological system is characterized by a separate intellectual peculiarity that is conditioned by its interaction in the environment for the purpose of supporting its energy as well as keeping and improving its biological species. Such a system is made of a set of cells the majority of which are nerve cells being an exact system of information processing prone to self-improvement due to self-organization.

Let us study a known biological system of retina organization and the processes that take place while transmitting and distributing a signal in the systems of retina cells. A biological scheme of horizontal retina organization is shown in figure 1 [12, 14, 15].

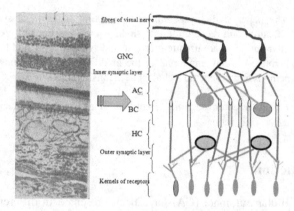

**Fig. 1.** Biological scheme of horizontal retina organization

Information is processed in the following way. A primary image comes to retina receptors (RR) that are connected with bipolar and horizontal cells (BC, HC). At the same time bipolar cells are connected with horizontal cells (HC). Information from BC is sent to ganglionic cells (GNC) interconnected by amacrine cells (AC) which act as commutators between GNC and AC. AC are also interconnected with each other to process and estimate the processed information and to process the information from bipolar cells. The given organization of cells' positioning helps to present the retina as a schematic technical description (Fig. 2).

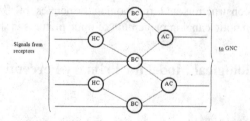

**Fig. 2.** Scheme of operating layer of preliminary processing

In the case of such an organization we can assume that BC functionally transform signals from receptors to GNC. Signals from HC are also taken into account because these cells process information from photoreceptors and BC. In the cellular synaptic outer layer of the retina the information among BC and AC is exchanged and transmitted to GNC. After processing the received information GNC create informational signals about the image in the form of impulse sequences and transmits them via the optic canal into the visual zone of the brain (Fig. 3).

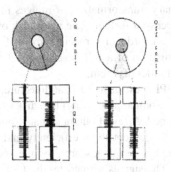

**Fig. 3.** Forms of signals from GNC

Due to the fact that synaptic connections allow two-way transmission of a signal, it is logical to assume that such an environment possesses a cellular structure consisting of numerous cellular layers and connections among cells and cellular layers. Direct connection between cells may be overlooked if one takes into account that synaptic connections function as signal transmitters. This would be unfair in relation to such a complicated system, however. So, in our opinion, it is synaptic connections where functional interconnection among all the cells takes place. Signals are exchanged in these areas according to a non-periodic principle.

Retina structure and CA construction promoted generalization and helped in choosing a direction for creating an artificial system that simulates the principles of organization and functioning of retina. As shown in fig.2, the retina can be described with the help of a CA having a multi-layer structure. Such a CA possesses a complicated organization of cell environment in each layer as well as organization of environment among the layers. The main task of the CA that simulates biological functions of retina in optic canal is effective preliminary processing and preparation of images to be transmitted via the optic canal into the brain area which is in charge of recognition.

## 3    Creation of the Geometric Type of Images for Their Efficient Classification and Identification within the Class

In a general form the system of image recognition consists of three main units [2]. These are the unit of preliminary processing and display of an image (UPI), unit of comparison (UC) and unit of memory (UM) (fig. 4).

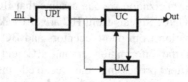

**Fig. 4.** Structure of an artificial system of image recognition

UPI carries out preliminary transformation of images in a body of signals that are projected to a CA to be processed further. The main task of the UPI is to transform a visual picture effectively in order to receive lots of output signals which if compressed, allow the acquisition of a full description of the image, bringing it to a definite class and completely identifying it.

To solve this task the UPI must have such architecture and structure which could provide the best performance (online processing) together with the least equipment used and fewest operations performed. Array of output signals from the UPI must be presented in such a form that allows to be kept them efficiently and distributed among classes. Moreover, UM structure is to ensure quick search for a template according to the output signals formed by the UPI. The signals formed by the UPI and the signals sent by the UM are compared by the UC which realizes effective comparison algorithms.

The main operations to be conducted during preliminary preparation of an image are the following:

- Separation of objects in a picture;
- Segmentation of the object images;
- Separation of a frame;
- Separation of a contour;
- Turn;
- Scaling
- Displacement;
- Interference removal.

CA are used to perform these operations effectively. Many achievements have been made while separating a contour with the help of a CA, and these successes are described in much detail in different works [2]. A wide choice of image scaling methods exists but they cannot be applied in practice using a CA. An important aspect in the process of classification and recognition of images is their effective description, which allows defining the class of this image and identifying it inside the class. An image must be described with the help of a structured set of a minimal number of characteristics which provides an opportunity to refer it to a definite class and distinguish it from other image classes.

The paper studies an attempt to describe images of an object, its geometrical shape called a geometrical type of G image. In other words, geometrical characteristics of an image are used for its basic description, and peculiarities of colour and brightness act as additional ones that enrich the relationship class. Geometrical G type is seen as an aggregate of informative elements (cells) of images and a set of relationships among them.

$$G = \{a_i, r_j\},$$

where $a_i$ is a set of informative cells that belong to the image of an object, $r_j$ is a set of relationships among $a$ elements. The main task is to distinguish $a$ and define $r$. A cell in CA is considered to be informative if the state of cells in its vicinity differs from the state of cells in the vicinity of neighbouring cells. In a polygon informative are the cells that belong to the tops. Relationships $r$ among informative cells are conditioned not only logically or by means of the distance between them. $G$ is also defined by the sequence of informative cells arrangement.

Relationships can be created with all informative cells. But such a description is superfluous. If separate cells are chosen then $G$ may be incomplete. This is why the image cells which create an optimal basis are used to get $G$. With this the information value of cells increases if the number of cell belonging to its vicinity grows. Thus, an image of an object can be described with the help of the type $G^M{}_N$, where $N$ is a class identifier and $M$ is an object identifier inside the class. A lot depends on the accurate definition of the class that determines a number of included subclasses. In this case $N$ value is represented by a set of subclasses identifiers which define a set of objects included. $M$ and $N$ parameters are variable in time and their value is constantly increasing depending on new images which belong to the class arriving in the system. The process of images classification according to G is shown in fig. 5.

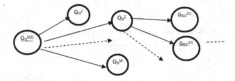

**Fig. 5.** Diagram of image classification according to $G$

This process can be described using the following model:

$$G^M_N \rhd\rhd G^{M(i)}_{N(j)}, \quad i = \overline{1,X}, \quad j = \overline{1,Y}$$

where $G_1 \rhd\rhd G_2$ is the strengthening operator which determines that $G_1$ is stronger than $G_2$, i.e. $G_2$ is a subclass of $G_1$; $X$ is a number of object images belonging to the class $N(j)$ and arriving to the input of recognition system.; $Y$ is a number of subclasses formed as a result of class $N$ images being put in. Thus, the description of images using the geometrical type provides the classifying of objects, creating new subclasses and recognizing images both of displaced objects and of those with a changed scale.

## 4    Simulation of Getting G Based on CA Taking into Account the Method of Signal Formation by Human Retina

Nowadays there exist a lot of developed methods of getting $G$ in CA, they are described in literature in great detail [2, 11]. The technique described in [2] provides the closest simulation of the processes that take place in the retina. It helps by creating an impulse sequence which, in its shape, is similar to the sequence of signals formed by ganglionic cells. The pulse sequence is formed by spreading the excitation pulse in the field of CA and the contour of the figure (fig. 6). Originally formed pulse sequences contain pulses which are formed by the vertices of the figure and impulses resulting from aliasing (fig. 7a). Use of a threshold processing in amplitude enables researchers to get the sequence with the pulses which indicate the corresponding vertex and are enlarged in scale (fig. 7c).

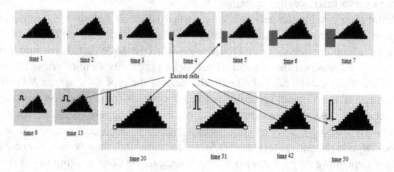

**Fig. 6.** An example of propagation of the excitation signal to generate a pulse sequence

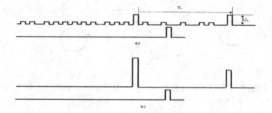

**Fig. 7.** An example of shaped pulse sequence (a - primary, b - after threshold processing)

Block diagram of the device shown in Figure 8. CA generates pulses at the outputs. The pulses are sent to a two-dimensional signal combiner (SC). SC generates a sequence of pulses. Thresholding module (TM) generates a sequence of pulses, which describes the input image. The structure of the CA is described in [2].

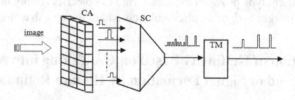

**Fig. 8.** The structure of the device to transform images into pulse sequences

The created impulse sequence (fig. 9) determines G by the number of impulses, amplitudes and duration of impulses as well as duration of pauses between them.

**Fig. 9.** An example of a created impulse sequence by a simulation program

However, this method cannot simulate signals of ganglionic cells completely and is limited by the abilities of more detailed classifications and identifications of an image. The paper offers a modified method of creating G in the form of an impulse sequence. This technique, apart from the above mentioned parameters also forms impulses of negative polarity to describe concave contour areas. The given method is simulated and experimental research is conducted. An example of a computer simulation of the modified temporal-impulse method is shown in fig. 10.

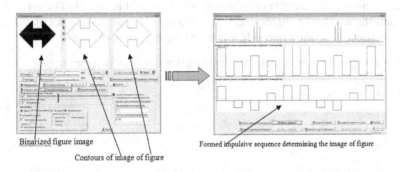

Binarized figure image                    Formed impulsive sequence determining the image of figure

Contours of image of figure

**Fig. 10.** An example of program operation using the modified temporal-impulse method

To evaluate the recognition accuracy by using the temporal-impulse method, images of a number of figures were formed on a piece of paper, each of which was rotated by $1^0$ relative to the previous ones. Then, using a video camera, they were

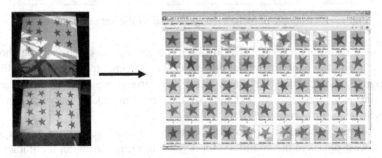

**Fig. 11.** Images of the figures obtained from a video camera and a folder which contains image files of individual figures

transformed into a graphic file (fig. 11). Each image was processed by means of filling with a specified sensitivity and binarization. Binarization was carried out with a help of developed program (fig. 12).

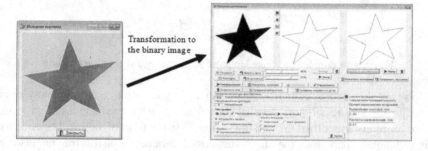

**Fig. 12.** The program's interface with the capabilities of binarization

The generated pulse sequence and the results of its processing are served in a separate window. An example of recognition is presented in fig. 13. The vertical axis represents the number of angles which describe the polygon, and the horizontal axis - a rotation angle. A straight line indicates a 100% correct recognition.

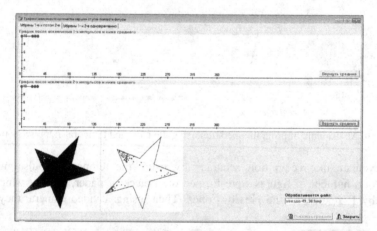

**Fig. 13.** An example of images recognition with different angles of rotation

The final recognition results with different percentage of sensitivity are shown in fig. 14. Used in the experiment and other images of figures too (fig. 15). Analysis of the program showed that the image data with the corresponding noise at 97% recognition was accurate. An example of the program, taking into account affine changes in images, is presented in fig. 16.

The functions of pulse sequences processing, considering moving of single and double lowest pulses in the amplitude for a given filtering threshold, are implemented in the program; and an adapted choice of the threshold amplitude which determines

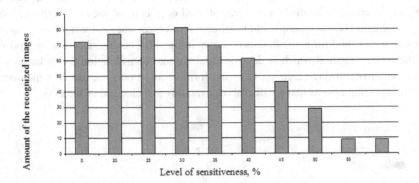

**Fig. 14.** Histograms showing the number of correctly recognized images (%) at different thresholds of sensitivity

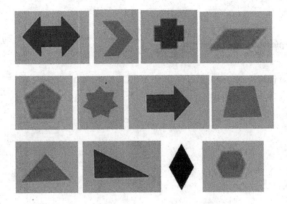

**Fig. 15.** Images of figures which were used in the experiment

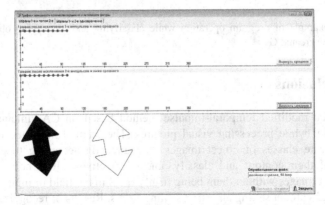

**Fig. 16.** Results of the program which simulates a method, based on time-pulse representation of the images

the highest percentage of recognition, is realized. The developed method allows the detailing of classes to be made more accurate and objects to be identified more reliably using the created $G$. An example of classification of object images for a polygon carried out using the method for plane figures is shown in fig. 17. The described example proves that the offered method which is developed taking into consideration the techniques of cellular automata ensures creating $G$ in the form of an impulse sequence which helps while recognizing objects that are displaced invariably and changed in scale.

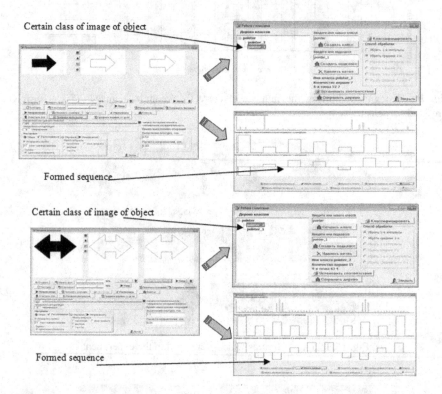

**Fig. 17.** An example of program operation while classifying and identifying object images according to the created G

## 5    Conclusions

The developed modified temporal-impulse method based on CA simulated human retina behavior while processing visual pictures. The method helps the recognition system to create classes of object images independently according to geometrical parameters of their contour and classify objects effectively. It is now possible to classify object images without them being firmly fixed in the field of input aperture of the system and without setting any strict scaling forms. Results of recognizing various types of polygons showed 97% correct recognition in the case of displaced images and those with changed scaling forms.

# References

1. Ilachinski, A.: Cellular automata: a discrete universe, 801 p. World Scientific (2001) ISBN 978-981-238-183-5
2. Belan, S.: Specialized cellular structures for image contour analysis. Cybernetics and Systems Analysis 47(5), 695–704 (2011)
3. von Neumann, J.: The general and logical theory of automata. In: Jeffress, L.A. (ed.) Cerebral Mechanisms in Behavior – The Hixon Symposium, pp. 1–31. John Wiley & Sons, New York (1951)
4. Von Neumann, J.: Theory of Self-Reproducing. In: Burks-Urbana, A.W. (ed.), 324 p. University of Illinois Press (1966)
5. Codd, E.F.: Cellular Autovata, p. 120. Academic Press, New York (1968)
6. Garzon, M.: Models of massive parallelism: analysis of cellular automata and neural networks, p. 149. Springer (1995) ISBN 978-3-540-56149-1
7. Toffoli, T.: Cellular Automata Machines as Physics Emulators. Tricate: The International Center for Nheoretical Physics, 28–36 (1988)
8. Wissner-Gross, A.D.: Pattern formation without favored local interactions. Journal of Cellular Automata 4, 27–36 (2007, 2008)
9. Wolfram, S.: A New Kind of Science. Wolfram Media. Inc. (2002)
10. Orovas, C.: Cellular Associative Neural Networks for Pattern Recognition. University of York (1999)
11. Белан, С.Н.: Система распознавания изображений с растущими клеточными слоями. Искусственный интеллект (4) 150–161 (2010)
12. Mertoguno, S., Boubakis, N.G.: Adigital Retina-Like Low-Level Vision processor. IEEE Transactions on Systems, Man. and Cybernetics-Part B: Cybernetics 33(5), 782–788 (2003)
13. Aladjev, V.Z.: Classical Cellular Automata. Homogeneous Structures. Fultus Corporation, 480 (2010)
14. Roska, B., Molnar, A., Werblin, F.S.: Parallel processing in retinal ganglion cells: How integration of space-time patterns of excitation and inhibition form the spiking output. Journal of Neurophysiology 95, 3810–3822 (2006)
15. Baddeley, R.J., Tatler, B.W.: High frequency edges (but not contrast) predict where we fixate: a Bayesian system identification analysis. Vision Research 46, 2824–2833 (2006)

# Modeling of Recrystallization with Recovery by Frontal Cellular Automata

Dmytro S. Svyetlichnyy, Jarosław Nowak, and Łukasz Łach

AGH University of Science and Technology, Faculty of Metal Engineering and Industrial
Computer Science, Kraków, Poland
{svetlich,nowak}@metal.agh.edu.pl,
lukasz-lach@wp.pl

**Abstract.** The objective of the paper is modeling of material softening after the deformation. The main problem of almost every model with digital material representation is consideration of recrystallization as the only mechanism of material softening. Static recovery is introduced into the model based on frontal cellular automata. An influence of static recovery on softening process is twofold. Static recovery effects on a decrease of dislocation density directly and on growing rate of recrystallized grain indirectly. Because of static recovery the recrystallization slows down and the time of recrystallization is extended. Simulation consists of two stages. During the deformation, distortion of the cells, evolution of dislocation density, nucleation and grain growth are considered, while after the deformation, the processes of softening are considered only. Comparison of simulation results with experimental data are presented as well.

**Keywords:** cellular automata, microstructure, softening, recrystallization, recovery.

## 1    Introduction

The prediction of the microstructure is one of the most important problems in materials science. There are different methods used for the modeling of the microstructure evolution. Cellular automata (CA) models [1], Monte Carlo Potts models [2], the finite element method (FEM) based models [3], the phase field [4-5], multi-phase-field [6] models, the front tracking method [7-8] and the vertex models [9] are among them. The application of the CA models, for the simulation of the different phenomena in the materials, has become incredibly important during the last years. CA are used for modeling of crystallization (solidification) [10-13], dynamic and static recrystallization [14-17], phase transformation [16], [18-19], cracks propagation [20], severe plastic deformation [21-23], rolling processes [19], [24] etc. One of the 3D CA modifications, known as the frontal CA (FCA) [17], which is capable to accelerate calculations, is used for the simulation of the microstructure evolution in the paper.

The history of simulation of recrystallization has begun with publication Hesselbarth and Göbel [25]. Then Davies [1] has considered influence of nucleation and growth of nuclei on recrystallization. Ding and Guo [26] simulated joint problem of

G.C. Sirakoulis and S. Bandini (Eds.): ACRI 2012, LNCS 7495, pp. 494–503, 2012.
© Springer-Verlag Berlin Heidelberg 2012

dynamic recrystallization and flow stress calculation on the base of modeling of dislocation evolution. Reviews of cellular automata in materials science were published by Raabe [27] in 2002, by Janssens [28] in 2010 and by Yang et al. [29] in 2011. Mukhopadhyay et al. [30] simulated static recrystallization accounting different types of nucleation with consideration the effect of dislocation density, temperature and grain boundaries misorientation angle on the mobility of a grain boundary.

Flow stress is usually modeled in CA on the basis of dislocation theory. In the cellular automata, evolution of dislocation density is applied to every grain or every cell. During the deformation, dislocation density effects on nucleation and grain growth rate, while after the deformation, dislocation density is considered to be constant and recrystallization acts as the only softening process. It leads to constant grain growth rate. It is not a problem for models, which do not use digital material representation methods, because softening process is treated as a single, without division into separate phenomena. Then, parameters of the model (or equations) can respond to whole process, not separate phenomenon. Methods based on digital material representation including the cellular automata take into account evolution of dislocation density and grain growth during the recrystallization in two completely different ways. For evolution of dislocation density the dislocation theory is mainly used, while recrystallization is considered from geometric point of view. Then a problem with kinetics of recrystallization appears for almost every model with digital material representation, which considers recrystallization as the only mechanism of material softening.

The objective of the paper is adequate modeling of material softening after the deformation, when kinetics of softening is close to experimental data.

## 2    The FCA Model

Frontal cellular automata (FCA) [17, 19] are used as the module of model presented in the paper. The use of the frontal cellular automata instead of conventional ones makes it possible to reduce the computation time significantly, especially for the three-dimensional models, as the large regions are excluded from the calculations in the current step and only the front of the changes is studied [17].

The multi-states cell automaton is presented schematically in Fig. 1 [19]. The set of the states $Q = \{q_0, q_1, q_2, q_3, q_4\}$ comprises the initial matrix state $q_0$, the "frontal cell" $q_1$, the "boundary cell" $q_2$, the "cell inside the grain" $q_3$ and the transient states $q_4$.

The set of conditions $\{I_0 - I_4\}$ is used by the transition rules. The transition rules define the next $q_{i+1}$ state of the cell on the basis of the current $q_i$ states of the cell and the cells in its neighborhood and the condition $I_k$. Such rules are commonly presented either in a form of a table or by description. Shortly, the conditions are of the following meanings: $I_0$ is the nucleation, $I_1$ – the time delay, which allows to control the grain growth rate, $I_2$ and $I_3$ determine whether the cells are on the boundary or inside the grain $(I_3 = I_2)$ and $I_4$ means that the growing grain reaches the current cell and involves it in the growing process.

Deformation in CA is rarely concerned. However, real deformation is the problem that cannot be avoided in CA simulations, especially when the multi-stage

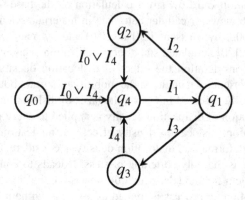

**Fig. 1.** Cellular automaton ($q$ – states, $I$ – transition conditions)

deformation is modeled. The deformed structure must be used in the further modeling. The simplest solution is an introduction of the cell distortion into the model, when the sizes and the shape of the cells are to be changed according to the strain tensor. Consideration of the deformation in FCA is described in detail elsewhere [19].

## 3    Recrystallization

In presented FCA the words $(I_0 \vee I_4)I_1(I_2 \vee I_3)$ (Fig. 1) with the initial states $q_2$ and $q_3$ describe the recrystallization. The model of recrystallization realized in FCA consists of two parts; the nucleation and the growth of recrystallized grains. They work in cooperation with the dislocation model, which is described in the next section. The microstructure evolution depends on the nucleation rate and the grain boundary migration rate. The models of nucleation and growth of recrystallized grains are described in detail elsewhere [31-32]. In this paper they are presented shortly.

The dislocation density is used for calculation of moment when recrystallization begins, as well as for calculation of the flow stress $\sigma$ and the grain boundary migration rate $v$. The critical value of the dislocation density $\rho_c$ for the nucleation initialization is of the following form (Roberts and B. Ahlblom [33]:

$$\rho_c = \frac{8\gamma}{d} = \sqrt[3]{\frac{20\gamma\dot{\varepsilon}}{3blM\tau^2}} \tag{1}$$

Number of nuclei is calculated according to:

$$N_V = a_N \varepsilon^{n_N} \exp\left(\frac{Q_N}{RT}\right) V_r \tag{2}$$

where $\varepsilon$ – strain, $T$ – temperature, $R$ – gas constant, $Q_N$ – activation energy, $a_N$, $n_N$, $Q_N$ – the material constants, $V_r$ – representative volume.

The grain growth of recrystallized grain is defined by a boundary migration rate $v$, which depends on driving force of recrystallization $p$ and grain boundary mobility $m$. The disorientation angle $\vartheta$ is taken into account as well: $v = mpf(\vartheta)$. The difference of the dislocation density of the old $\rho_{old}$ and new $\rho_{new}$ grains is the driving force are calculated on the basis of stored dislocation energy: $p = 0.5\mu b^2(\rho_{old} - \rho_{new})$. A curvature of the grain boundaries is neglected as another driving force because during the process of the recrystallization it is far smaller than the force from the difference of dislocation density. The grain boundary mobility $m$ depends on the self-diffusion coefficient and therefore, it is defined by Arrhenius' law:

$$m = a_m \exp\left(\frac{Q_m}{RT}\right)$$

(3)

where $a_m$, $Q_m$ – the material constants.

## 4    The Model of Dislocation Density

Model [31-32], [34] was developed on the basis of the Taylor dislocation theory [35]. It is used for determination of flow stress:

$$\sigma = \sigma_0 + \alpha\mu b\sqrt{\rho} ,$$

(4)

where $\sigma_0$ - stress necessary to move dislocation in the absence of other dislocations, $\alpha$ - constant, $\mu$ - shear modulus and $b$ - Burgers vector, $\rho$ – dislocation density.

It is generally assumed that during the deformation the evolution of the dislocation density is dependent on two components:

$$\frac{d\rho}{d\varepsilon} = U(\varepsilon) - \Omega(\rho) ,$$

(5)

Here, $U(\varepsilon)$ is regarded as the generation and the storage of the dislocation (hardening), while the term $\Omega(\rho)$ contributes an annihilation of the dislocation (dynamic recovery), $\varepsilon$ - strain.

When deformation ends, the left side of the equation (5) is meaningless, dynamic recovery stops, and dislocation density is considered to be constant. Then, constant dislocation density ($\rho_{old} - \rho_{new} = $ const) and constant temperature ($T = $ const) lead to the constant grain boundary mobility ($m = $ const) and boundary migration rate ($v = $ const).

When constant boundary migration rate $v$ is applied to simulation by two- or three dimensional cellular automata (2D or 3D CA), kinetics of softening, as well as recrystallization can be described by Avrami equation

$$\chi = 1 - \exp(-at^n)$$

(6)

with Avrami exponent equal to $n = 2$ (2D CA) or $n = 3$ (3D CA) only ($t$ – time, $a$ – factor depended on recrystallization conditions). But real exponent is less then 2

($n < 2$). Actually, arbitrary value of $n$ (6) is accepted in analytical model of static re-crystallization that can be obtained from experimental data. Equation (6) for static recrystallization can be rewritten in following form:

$$\chi = 1 - \exp\left(-\frac{\pi}{3} Nv^3 t^3\right).$$ (7)

Considering equation (7) it can be noted that only one element can be varied during the softening process, namely the grain boundary migration rate $v$. It is also known that apparent Avrami exponent $n$ (6) with constant rate $v$ can be differed from theoretical value of 3 if rate $v$ is a function of time $t$. On the other hand at constant temperature, when boundary mobility remains constant, only stored energy, which depends on dislocation density $\rho$, can influence on rate $v$. So, dislocation density $\rho$ of non-recrystallized grains should be changed. And, in turn, dislocation density $\rho$ can be decreased in process of static recovery only. It is the main causes why static recovery ($R$) can be introduced into the model of evolution of dislocation density (2):

$$\dot{\rho} = U(\varepsilon)\dot{\varepsilon} - \Omega(\rho)\dot{\varepsilon} - R(\rho)$$ (8)

In fact, static recovery affects the material softening in two ways, decreasing the dislocation density of non-recrystallized grains $\rho$ and reducing the grain growth rate that is changing the recrystallization fraction $\chi$.

However not all dislocations can be removed by static recovery or the process for such dislocations is too long. As a result another type of dislocations is introduced to the model. This type of dislocation can be designated $\rho_s$ – "structural" dislocations. Differential equation for $\rho_s$ is of following form:

$$\varepsilon_s \frac{d\rho_s^+}{d\varepsilon} = f\rho - \rho_s$$ (9)

where $f$ – factor, which determines fraction of dislocation that cannot be removed by static recovery, $\varepsilon_s$ – characteristic strain, sign "+" near the derivative means that dislocation density $\rho_s$ can only increase.

Thus, two types of dislocations can be taken into account and instead of $\rho$ in equation (4) it is necessary to use the sum of these two dislocations types: $\rho + \rho_s$. During the deformation all three components of (8) effect on dislocation density $\rho$, in its absence (after deformation) only the last term. After the deformation "structural" dislocations $\rho_s$ remain constant and the only recrystallization takes them away. Moreover, recrystallization removes dislocations $\rho$.

# 5     Experimental Studies

The stress relaxation method is applied to measure kinetics of material softening [36]. Here only one deformation is required. After the deformation specimen is kept in testing machine with the control of compressive force. The force changes reflect fraction of stress relaxation. It is a reliable and highly effective method which allows to receive kinetics for the given conditions in one test. The stress relaxation tests were carried out on a Gleeble3800 at IMŻ (Gliwice, Poland). The specimens were heated at a rate of 3 K/s up to the temperature of 1275, 1200 or 1100°C held 10 s. Then temperature was decreased to the deformation temperature (1000°C to 1200°C), and later compressed up to prescribed strain at constant strain rate. After the prior deformation, the strain was held constant at least 300 s and compressive force relaxed was recorded as a function of time.

A carbon steel of grade 45 was used in the tests to prevent any interference of softening with precipitation of microalloy elements.

# 6    Simulation

Simulations reflect stress relaxation test. At first, parameters of the models are identified. Microscopic studies give parameters of nucleation model. Relaxation tests allow to obtain fraction $f$ and parameters of static recovery and grain growth rate. Plastometric tests were a basis for calculation other parameters of dislocation model.

After identification of model parameters, the initial microstructure with average grain size about $d_{av} = 100$ μm (measured in studies 101.7 μm) was created according to algorithm described elsewhere [37]. The microstructure presented in Fig.2 is used in all further simulation.

Modeled material has been subjected to deformation at the specified stain rate, up to a given strain at the prescribed temperature. After deformation, modeled material was held at the deformation temperature up to complete recrystallization. Two examples of microstructure after deformation and recrystallization are presented in Fig.3. The first variant shows microstructure obtained when material was subjected to deformation at $T = 1100$°C with strain rate $\dot{\varepsilon} = 1$ s$^{-1}$ up to strain $\varepsilon = 0.18$. Time of softening was about $t_s = 7.5$ s. Average grain size is $d_{av} = 92$ μm (measured 92.4 μm). The second variant of microstructure was obtained after deformation: $T = 1100$°C, $\dot{\varepsilon} = 0.1$ s$^{-1}$, $\varepsilon = 0.18$ and $t_s = 5.5$ s. Average grain size is $d_{av} = 75$ μm (measured 78.5 μm).

Next results present kinetics of material softening after the deformation. In Fig.4 presents experimental data from stress relaxation test (symbols), simulation results obtained by new softening model, that takes into account recrystallization and static recovery (solid lines), by the previous model with the only recrystallization (solid lines with symbols) and approximation by equation (6), which is used in conventional analytical models (dashed lines).

Simulations by the model with the only recrystallization give results that can be approximated by the equation (6) with Avrami exponent equal to 3. Therefore, only time of half recrystallization can be adjusted, not all curve. It is clearly seen on Fig. 4. Such results were the main reason for development of new model.

Typically, approximation by equation (6), as observed in Fig. 4, gives good result, but when strain is low enough, recrystallization becomes very slow and effect of static

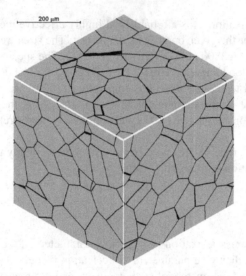

**Fig. 2.** Initial microstructure created by FCA, average grain size $d_{av}$ = 100 μm

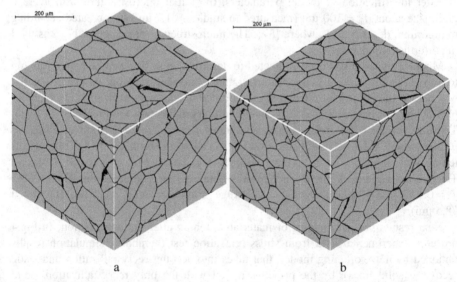

a            b

**Fig. 3.** Final microstructure after deformation at temperature $T$ = 1100°C and recrystallization: a – $\dot{\varepsilon}$ = 1 s$^{-1}$, $\varepsilon$ = 0.18, $d_{av}$ = 92 μm; b – $\dot{\varepsilon}$ = 0.1 s$^{-1}$, $\varepsilon$ = 0.18, $d_{av}$ = 75 μm

recovery can be separated from one of recrystallization. That can be seen in figure for the experimental curve with the smaller strain. Then the curve cannot be approximated by the equation (6) precisely.

The new model based on cellular automata that takes into account recrystallization and static recovery allows for proper simulation both variants, when effect of those two phenomena can be separated or they acts simultaneously. Fig. 4 confirms it.

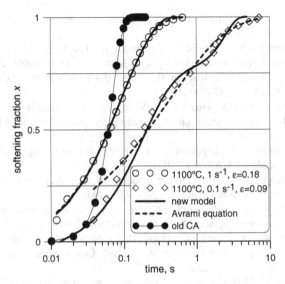

**Fig. 4.** Softening fraction

## 7 Summary

In the paper a new model based on frontal cellular automata is presented. FCA contains a module for simulation of evolution of dislocation density. The modification of dislocation model consists in accounting for static recovery. It allows to obtain curves that can be described by Avrami equation (6) with almost arbitrary Avrami exponent. It also makes possible to model processes where effect of recrystallization and static recovery can be divided into two events. Effectiveness of new model is confirmed by comparison simulation results with experimental data.

**Acknowledgements.** Support of the Polish Ministry of Education and Science is greatly appreciated (Grant Nos. N N508 620140 and 2011/01/N/ST8/03658).

## References

1. Davies, C.H.J.: Growth of nuclei in a cellular automaton simulation of recrystallization. Scr. Mater. 36, 35–40 (1997)
2. Holm, E.A., Hassold, G.N., Miodownik, M.A.: The influence of anisotropic boundary properties on the evolution of misorientation distribution during grain growth. Acta Mat. 49, 2981–2991 (2001)
3. Bernacki, M., Chastel, Y., Digonnet, H., Resk, H., Coupe, T., Loge, R.E.: Development of numerical tools for the multiscale modeling of recrystallization in metals, based on a digital material framework. Comp. Meth. Mat. Sci. 7, 142–149 (2007)
4. Fan, D., Chen, L.Q.: Computer simulation of grain growth using a continuum field model. Acta Mat. 45, 611–622 (1997)

5. Kobayashi, R., Warren, J.A., Carter, W.C.: A continuum model of grain boundaries. Physica D 140, 141–150 (2000)
6. Takaki, T., Hisakuni, Y., Hirouchi, T., Yamanaka, A., Tomita, Y.: Multi-phase-field simula-tions for dynamic recrystallization. Comput. Mater. Sci. 45, 881–888 (2009)
7. Thompson, C.V., Frost, H.J., Spaepen, F.: The relative rates of secondary and normal grain growth. Acta Metall. 35, 887–890 (1987)
8. Frost, H.J., Thompson, C.V., Howe, C.L., Whang, J.: A two-dimensional computer simulation of capillarity-driven grain growth: preliminary results. Scripta Metall. 22, 65–70 (1988)
9. Weygand, D., Brechet, Y., Lepinoux, J.: A Vertex Simulation of Grain Growth in 2D and 3D. Adv. Engng. Mater. 3, 67–71 (2001)
10. Rappaz, M., Gandin, C.-A.: Probabilistic modeling of microstructure formation in solidification processes. Acta Metal. Mater. 41, 345–360 (1993)
11. Raabe, D.: Mesoscale simulation of spherulite growth during polymer crystallization by use of a cellular automaton. Acta Mater. 52, 2653–2664 (2004)
12. Burbelko, A.A., Kapturkiewicz, W., Gurgul, D.: Problem of the artificial anisotropy in solidification modeling by cellular automata method. Comp. Meth. Mat. Sci. 7, 182–188 (2007)
13. Svyetlichnyy, D.S.: Modeling of macrostructure formation during the solidification by using frontal cellular automata. In: Salcido, A. (ed.) Cellular Automata - Innovative Modelling for Science and Engineering, pp. 179–196. InTech, Croatia (2011)
14. Hurley, P.J., Humphreys, F.J.: Modelling the recrystallization of single-phase aluminium. Acta Mater 51, 3779–3793 (2003)
15. Qian, M., Guo, Z.X.: Cellular automata simulation of microstructural evolution during dynamic recrystallization of an HY-100 steel. Mater. Sci. Eng. A 365, 180–185 (2004)
16. Kumar, M., Sasikumar, R., Kesavan Nair, P.: Competition between nucleation and early growth of ferrite from austenite – studies using cellular automation simulations. Acta Mater. 46, 6291–6303 (1998)
17. Svyetlichnyy, D.S.: Modeling of the microstructure: from classical cellular automata approach to the frontal one. Comput. Mater. Sci. 50, 92–97 (2010)
18. Macioł, P., Gawąd, J., Kuziak, R., Pietrzyk, M.: Internal variable and cellular automata-finite element models of heat treatment. Int. J. Multiscale Comp. Eng. 8, 267–285 (2010)
19. Svyetlichnyy, D.S.: Simulation of microstructure evolution during shape rolling with the use of frontal cellular automata. ISIJ Int. 52, 559–568 (2012)
20. Das, S., Palmiere, E.J., Howard, I.C.: CAFE: a tool for modeling thermomechanical processes. In: Proc. Int. Conf. on Thermomechamical Processing: Mechanics, Microstructure & Control, Sheffield, UK, pp. 296–301. University of Sheffield, Sheffield (2003)
21. Svyetlichnyy, D., Majta, J., Muszka, K.: Modeling of microstructure evolution of BCC metals subjected to severe plastic deformation. Steel Res. Int. 79, 452–458 (2008)
22. Svyetlichnyy, D.S.: Modeling of microstructure evolution in process with severe plastic deformation by cellular automata. Mater. Sci. Forum, 638–642, 2772–2777 (2010)
23. Svyetlichnyy, D., Majta, J., Muszka, K., Łach, Ł.: Modeling of microstructure evolution of BCC metals subjected to severe plastic deformation. In: AIP Conf. Proc., vol. 1315, pp. 1473–1478 (2010)
24. Svyetlichnyy, D.S.: Reorganization of cellular space during the modeling of the microstructure evolution by frontal cellular automata. Comput. Mater. Sci. (in press, 2012)
25. Hesselbarth, H.G., Göbel, I.R.: Simulation of recrystallization by cellular automata. Acta Metal. Mater. 39, 2135–2143 (1991)

26. Ding, R., Guo, Z.X.: Coupled quantitative simulation of microstructure evolution and plastic flow during dynamic recrystallization. Acta Mater. 49, 3163–3175 (2001)
27. Raabe, D.: Cellular automata in materials science with particular reference to recrystallization simulation. Annu. Rev. Mater. Res. 32, 53–76 (2002)
28. Janssens, K.G.F.: An introductory review of cellular automata modeling of moving grain boundaries in polycrystalline materials. Math. Comput. Simul. 80, 1361–1381 (2010)
29. Yang, H., Wu, C., Li, H.W., Fan, X.G.: Review on cellular automata simulations of microstructure evolution during metal forming process: Grain coarsening, recrystallization and phase transformation. Sci. China Tech. Sci. 54, 2107–2118 (2011)
30. Mukhopadhyay, P., Loeck, M., Gottstein, G.: A cellular operator model for the simulation of static recrystallization. Acta Mater. 55, 551–564 (2007)
31. Svyetlichnyy, D.S.: The coupled model of a microstructure evolution and a flow stress based on the dislocation theory. ISIJ Int. 45, 1187–1193 (2005)
32. Svyetlichnyy, D.S.: Modification of coupled model of microstructure evolution and flow stress: experimental validation. Mater. Sci. Technol. 25, 981–988 (2009)
33. Roberts, W., Ahlblom, B.: A nucleation criterion for dynamic recrystallization hot working. Acta Metall. 26, 801–813 (1978)
34. Svyetlichnyy, D.S., Nowak, J., Łach, Ł., Pidvysotskyy, V.: Numerical simulation of Flow Stress by Internal Variables Model. Steel Res. (in press, 2012)
35. Taylor, G.I.: The mechanism of plastic deformation of crystals. Part I. Theoretical. Proc. R. Soc. A. 145, 362–415 (1934)
36. Karjalainen, L.P.: Stress relaxation method for investigation of softening kinetics in hot deformed steels. Mater. Sci. Technol. 11, 557–565 (1995)
37. Svyetlichnyy, D.S., Łach, Ł.: Digital material representation of given parameters. Steel Res. (in press, 2012)

# A CA-Based Model Describing Fat Bloom in Chocolate

Pieter Van der Weeën[1,*], Nathalie De Clercq[2],
Koen Dewettinck[2], and Bernard De Baets[1]

[1] KERMIT, Department of Mathematical Modelling, Statistics and Bioinformatics,
Ghent University, Coupure links 653, Gent, Belgium
[2] Laboratory of Food Technology and Engineering, Department of Food Safety and
Food Quality, Ghent University, Coupure links 653, Gent, Belgium
{pieter.vanderweeen,N.declercq,koen.dewettinck,bernard.debaets}@ugent.be

**Abstract.** In this paper a stochastic model based on a cellular automaton (CA) for describing the spatio-temporal dynamics of fat migration in chocolate confectionery, as well as the resulting fat bloom, is conceived. Several hypotheses on the underlying mechanisms for fat migration exist, but there is no consensus on the correct ones. Although many researchers are studying this industrially important phenomenon, few models describing it have been developed. Therefore, the incorporation of different mechanisms of fat migration into a stochastic CA-based model is discussed and the model parameters are investigated for a better understanding of both the model and the complex fat migration phenomenon.

**Keywords:** capillarity, cellular automata, chocolate, fat bloom, simulation, stochastic model.

## 1 Introduction

Belgian pralines, commonly known as Belgian chocolates, were first introduced in 1912 by Jean Neuhaus II, a Belgian chocolatier. They usually contain a hard chocolate coating with a softer, for example (hazel)nut-based, filling. Today, Belgian pralines still have an excellent reputation on the international market. However, the whitish haze formed over time on the surface of chocolate, known as fat bloom, poses a worrisome problem hampering the export of these products [7]. Fat bloom occurs in all chocolate products, but the presence of a liquid filling accelerates the process as the filling oils are often completely liquid at room temperature and can therefore transfer easily through the chocolate coating to the surface [12]. Although bloomed pralines are harmless and still consumable, a softening of the chocolate coating, a hardening of the filling, a flattening of the taste and most importantly a rejection of the pralines by the consumers due to the association with inferior and expired products may occur [9]. A solution for this problem would therefore be very valuable for this multimillion dollar industry. Unfortunately, the actual mechanisms for fat bloom remain speculative and

---

* Corresponding author.

G.C. Sirakoulis and S. Bandini (Eds.): ACRI 2012, LNCS 7495, pp. 504–513, 2012.
© Springer-Verlag Berlin Heidelberg 2012

a more thorough understanding is necessary to better abate quality deterioration. Based on this, a manufacturer would know a priori the effect on the rate and amount of fat bloom when changing an ingredient or process. Therefore, there is a need to develop better models that combine mass transfer with the phase behavior to be able to accurately predict the migration process of liquid fat and the occurrence of fat bloom [1,6,11].

## 2    Preliminaries

### 2.1    Mechanisms of Fat Bloom

The phenomenon of fat bloom is presented schematically in Figure 1. A crucial step in the appearence of fat bloom is the migration of liquid fat to the surface. Several hypotheses and mechanisms have been put forward to explain fat migration in chocolate. Originally, the driving force for the migration was believed to be diffusion due to a difference in liquid fat content, but nowadays diffusion is ascribed to a gradient in triacylglycerol concentration between the chocolate coating and the filled center [1,6]. The addition of extra cocoa particles and sugar particles is said to retard the fat migration rate, because they are impenetrable to oil [6]. However, a recent study has shown that cocoa particles disrupt the formation of the cocoa butter crystal network such that the resulting crystal network is less dense and more permeable to oil [13].

Besides diffusion, capillary forces may play a significant role and have therefore been proposed as an alternate mechanism of fat migration [1,12]. Another hypothesis for fat migration states that the increase in volume when cocoa butter melts forces liquid fat to the surface through pores and micro fractures formed during crystallization [10]. Several other theories focus on the thermal stability of the different polymorphic forms of cocoa butter as the cause of fat bloom [1], but although bloom formation is accompanied by a polymorphic transition of the cocoa butter, it is by itself not sufficient to always cause visual fat bloom [12]. Although there exists no consensus on which mechanisms do actually occur and to what extent, most papers focus on the diffusion of triacylglycerols and the capillary rise or a combination of both.

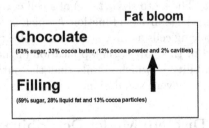

**Fig. 1.** Schematic representation of fat bloom in chocolate confectionery, with indication of the compostion of the different layers in volume percentages

## 2.2   Models Describing Fat Bloom

Many authors have described the fat bloom phenomenon, the influence of different process parameters on the degree and instant of appearance of visual fat bloom and possible causes for this blooming [6,9,11,13]. However, very few authors have attempted to develop an elucidatory or descriptive model for fat bloom. Some authors support their theories through a series of calculations based on suited physical laws and (partial) differential equations (PDEs) [1,20], but the search for a full-fledged mathematical model accurately describing fat bloom is ongoing. In this paper, a stochastic CA-based model describing fat migration is proposed, with CAs being the utter discrete counterpart of PDEs. This model takes into account gradient-driven diffusion and the chemical equilibrium between solid and liquid fat in the chocolate coating, which is regulated by melting and crystallization of the fat [5]. Further, it also incorporates capillary rise and keeps track of the spatial distribution of the fat bloom at the surface.

## 2.3   Cellular Automata

A 2D stochastic CA $\mathcal{C}$ can be represented as a quintuple $\mathcal{C} = \langle \mathcal{T}, S, s, N, \Phi \rangle$ of which the components are described next.

**Tessellation.** In this paper, a finite tessellation $\mathcal{T}^*$ consisting of squares is used, because it has the most straightforward implementation and suffices for the purpose of in this paper. The tessellation represents a vertical cross-section of the composed chocolate product (cfr. Figure 1).

**Discrete States.** Every cell $c_{i,j}$ in $\mathcal{T}^*$ takes one of the $k$ discrete states contained in the set $S$, with $s(c_{i,j}, t)$ the state of cell $c_{i,j}$ at the $t$-th discrete time step. At the beginning of each simulation, every cell is assigned a state, i.e. the initial condition of the CA.

**Neighborhood.** Different neighborhoods $N$ can be considered, such as the von Neumann and the Moore neighborhoods.

**Transition Function.** The state $s(c_{i,j}, t+1)$ of a cell $c_{i,j}$ at the $(t+1)$-th time step is determined using the transition function $\Phi$ which is based on $s(c_{i,j}, t)$ and the states of the neighboring cells at time step $t$. In stochastic CA-based models, which will be employed in this paper, the application of the transition function $\Phi$ is subject to a probability $p$, which entails that the outcome of a stochastic CA-based model differs for every simulation.

## 3   A Stochastic Discrete Model Describing Fat Bloom

In this paper a stochastic CA is used as described in Section 2, in which $\mathcal{T}^*$ is a square tessellation with periodic boundary conditions along the horizontal axis and fixed boundary conditions along the vertical axis as shown in Figure 2.

The tessellation consists of an upper part which represents the chocolate coating (500 × 50 cells) and a lower part which represents the filling (500 × 2 cells). The filling is considered as an infinite source of liquid fat which is replenished at every time step. The size of a square cell, $\Delta x$ is assumed to be 0.0001 m, which results in realistic dimensions for the confectionery.

Further, five different states are discerned, i.e. $S = \{$cavity, solid fat, liquid fat, sugar, cocoa particle$\}$, where a cell in a certain state represents a homogeneous amount of that state, which is a simple approximation intended to capture the synoptic effects of fat migration [3,17]. Although diffusion is the consequence of a gradient in triacylglycerols (cfr. Section 1), here liquid fat is considered as a state rather than the triacylglycerols, because (1) liquid fat consists mainly of triacylglycerols and (2) the future validation of the CA-based model will be based upon data for liquid fat.

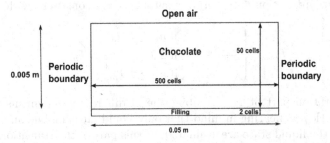

**Fig. 2.** Schematic representation of the square tessellation

To initialize the CA, every $c_{i,j} \in \mathcal{T}^*$ for the chocolate coating part is assigned a state according to the volume proportion of the cavities, cocoa butter (of which at ambient temperature around 74% is solid [14]), sugar and cocoa particles and for the filling part according to the volume proportion of liquid fat, sugar and cocoa particles as depicted in Figure 1. All states are initially randomly distributed across $\mathcal{T}^*$ except for the cavities, which together form vertical capillaries through which liquid fat can migrate. Twenty capillaries with a mean length of 25 cells are randomly distributed across the width of the chocolate coating [11]. The transition function $\Phi$ consists out of two parts that describe crystallization/melting and migration, respectively.

The first part of the transition function describes the chemical equilibrium between the amount of liquid fat and the amount of solid fat in a certain region of the chocolate coating. Wünderlich [19] states that the balance between liquid and solid fat can be written as a reversible chemical reaction with a certain forward ($r$) and backward ($r_{-1}$) reaction rate (cfr. Eq. (1)), where solid (resp. liquid) fat melts (resp. crystallizes) if the concentration of solid (resp. liquid) fat in the neighborhood is sufficiently high. This type of reaction is suited to be modeled with a CA-based model as has already been demonstrated by some of the present authors [15,16].

$$A \text{ (liquid fat)} \underset{r}{\overset{r_{-1}}{\rightleftharpoons}} B \text{ (crystalline fat).} \tag{1}$$

Two model parameters are introduced: a melting probability $P_m$ (cfr. $r_{-1}$) and a crystallization probability $P_c$ (cfr. $r$). The melting probability $P_m$ is determined by comparing the number of cells in the radius 2 Moore neighborhood in the solid state to a threshold value for melting/crystallization $T_{mc}$ and determines whether a cell in the solid state melts (i.e. gets state liquid fat) at a certain time step. Eq. (2) shows that as long as the number of neighboring cells in the solid state, $n_s$, is lower than or equal to $T_{mc}$, it holds that $P_m = 0$. If $n_s$ exceeds $T_{mc}$, $P_m \in [0, 1]$ and the higher this number of neighbors is, the closer $P_m$ is to one. A same course of reasoning is used to determine $P_c$. The cells of the chocolate coating part of $\mathcal{T}^*$ in the solid state and the liquid state are evaluated asynchronously according to the random order update method [2] in this part of the transition function $\Phi$ to obtain results that are consistent with reality.

$$P_m = \begin{cases} 0 & , \text{if } n_s \leq T_{mc}, \\ \frac{n_s - T_{mc}}{T_{mc}} & , \text{if } 2\,T_{mc} > n_s > T_{mc}, \\ 1 & , \text{if } n_s \geq 2\,T_{mc}. \end{cases} \tag{2}$$

For the migration part of $\Phi$, a combination of different mechanisms (cfr. Section 2) is employed, bearing in mind that only liquid fat is mobile and therefore only cells in the liquid state are evaluated for this part of the transition function $\Phi$. Diffusion due to a gradient in liquid fat is a first mechanism that is incorporated. A neighborhood for diffusion, $N_d$, is introduced in Figure 3(a), which is split up into eight cells which form the upper part (cells closer to the open air) and eight cells which form the lower part (cells closer to the filling) of $N_d$.

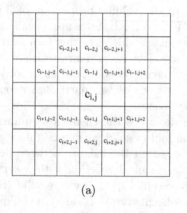

(a)

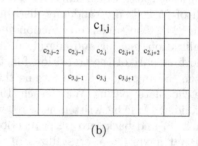

(b)

**Fig. 3.** Neighborhoods in a square tessellation for migration of: (a) a central cell $c_{i,j}$ and (b) a cell $c_{1,j}$ at the surface

The number of cells $c_{i,j}$ in the liquid state are counted in both the upper and lower part of $N_d$ and the liquid fat will move according to the vertical gradient, i.e. in the direction with the lowest number of cells in the liquid state. If both upper and lower part of $N_d$ contain the same number of cells in the liquid state, the liquid fat will move to the left or to the right with equal probability, such that liquid fat tries to move in every time step. In the CA-based model, the motion dynamics of liquid fat are simulated by switching the state of the central cell under consideration and the state of the cell it moves towards. Keeping in mind the CFL condition [4], a time step $\Delta t = 2500$ s is chosen such that the distance that liquid fat travels in one time step, is equal to one cell and that this diffusion only happens via cells that share a vertex (cfr. the von Neumann neighborhood). A special case of diffusion is depicted in Figure 3(b) for liquid fat reaching the surface. Here, a threshold $T_o$ is introduced. If the number of cells in the liquid state in the lower part of $N_d$ surpasses $T_o$, the liquid fat on the first row will reach the surface. In this paper, after expert feedback on preliminary simulation results, $T_o = 2$ is assumed.

Normally, diffusion can not occur if the liquid fat has to pass through sugar, because this is impermeable to oil (cfr. Section 2). However, to account for the possibility of fat migration by volume and thermal effects as well as the influence of cocoa particles on the crystalline structure (cfr. Section 2), the diffusion 'through sugar' is made dependent on a permeability factor $\gamma \in [0,1]$, so that this diffusion is possible in the model.

Finally, the third mechanism that is included in the CA-based model is capillary rise. It can be proven, making use of the Lucas-Washburn equation [18], that the distance that liquid fat can travel through capillarity during the time that same amount of liquid fat needs to diffuse one cell through gradient pressure, is far greater. It is therefore assumed that if liquid fat enters a capillary at a certain time step, it will reach the end of that capillary in that same time step. All cells of $\mathcal{T}^*$ in the liquid state are evaluated asynchronously according to the random independent update method [2] in the migration part of $\Phi$.

# 4  Simulation Study

## 4.1  Choice of Threshold Gradient Parameter $T_{mc}$

Although theoretically different values for $T_{mc}$ are possible, initially the amount of solid and liquid fat in the chocolate coating are in equilibrium, i.e. before fat migration from the filling to the coating that takes place. Therefore, a parameter value has to be chosen for which there is initially no rise or decrease in the amount of liquid (or solid) fat. In the radius 2 Moore neighborhood there are, with exclusion of the central cell, 28 neighbors. Initially, on average 24.5 % of the cells $c_{i,j}$ of $\mathcal{T}^*$ are in the solid state, which translates into six cells out of the 28 in the radius 2 Moore neighborhood. Figure 4 shows the average number of cells in the liquid state in the chocolate coating in function of the time step for ten simulations with the CA-based model for different values of $T_{mc}$. Bearing in mind the above argumentation, it can be seen that simulations with $T_{mc} = 6$

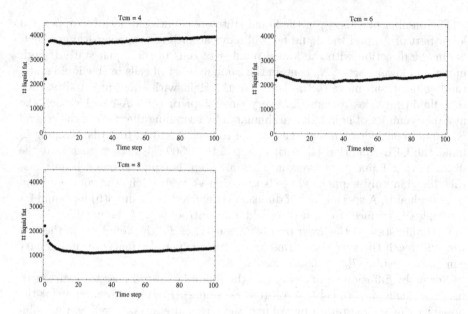

**Fig. 4.** Evolution of the number of cells in the liquid state in the chocolate coating at the beginning of the simulation for $T_{mc} = 4$, $T_{mc} = 6$ and $T_{mc} = 8$

give the desired result, whilst simulations with $T_{mc} = 4$ and $T_{mc} = 8$ result in the undesired initial steep rise and decrease in liquid fat, respectively (cfr. Figure 4).

## 4.2   Effect of Capillarity

To investigate the influence of capillary rise on the liquid fat migration, simulations are performed with the CA-based model with cracks as described in Section 3, as well as with an adapted version of the model where the cavities are not grouped into cracks, but are homogeneously distributed over the tessellation. Figures 5(a) and 5(b) show that, when capillarity is taken into consideration in the CA-based model, the capillaries serve as a highway that transports liquid fat rapidly to the surface, so that more liquid fat reaches the surface.

## 4.3   Effect of Permeability Parameter $\gamma$

The permeability parameter $\gamma$ has a great influence on the simulated outcome with the CA-based model, especially because sugar is the biggest component of the chocolate coating in terms of percentage (cfr. Figure 1). Figure 6 shows that the amount of liquid fat that reaches the surface is strongly dependent on $\gamma$, where the amount of liquid fat reaching the surface rises as $\gamma$ is closer to one. It can be seen from Figure 6 that higher values of $\gamma$ give rise to an exponential relationship between a discrete time step of the CA-based model

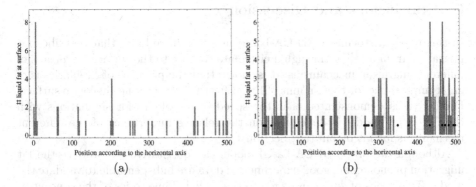

**Fig. 5.** Spatial distribution of liquid fat on the surface: (a) homogeneously distributed pores and (b) pores grouped into cracks with indication of the position of the cracks in the coating (●)

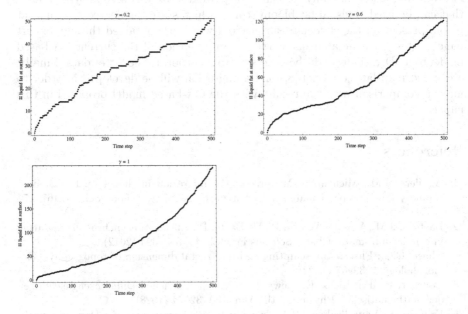

**Fig. 6.** Amount of liquid fat that reaches the surface for different values of $\gamma$

and the amount of liquid fat that reaches the surface. If the CA-based model would be parameterized using experimental data, the calibrated value for $\gamma$ would give an indication of the proportion of fat migration that can be contributed to mechanisms other than gradient-driven diffusion and capillarity, such as volume and thermal effects, as well as the final crystalline structure of the chocolate due to addition of cocoa particles and sugar. If these other mechanisms play little role, $\gamma$ is expected to be close to zero, whilst if the other mechanisms play a significant role, $\gamma$ will be larger.

# 5    Conclusions and Discussion

In this paper a stochastic 2D CA-based model is introduced that describes fat migration from a filling through a chocolate coating to the surface, by means of different migration mechanisms. It is shown that the presence of capillaries is of great importance for the amount of liquid fat that reaches the chocolate surface. Further, it is demonstrated that the speed of fat bloom for simulations with the CA-based model is dependent on the relative importance of the different mechanisms for fat bloom (cfr. Section 1).

Although the proposed CA-based model can qualitatively reproduce the fat migration phenomenon, good experimental data are indispensable to validate the model. Two types of data can be fed to the model. Time series of the concentration of liquid fat throughout the chocolate coating can be used to determine the values of $T_o$, $T_{cm}$ and $\gamma$, as well as the relationship between a discrete time step of the model and physical time if the effective diffusion coefficient can be found in literature, experimentally measured or parameterized. A second type of data that can be used is visual fat bloom scores, which state the degree of visual fat bloom present on the chocolate surface and which are obtained through expert panel scores or image analysis. However, an extension of the current CA-based model to a 3D variant might be necessary to incorporate the latter data. Finally, a coupled map lattice model [8] for fat migration will be developed in order to make a comparison with the results with the CA-based model proposed in this paper.

# References

1. Aguilera, J.M., Michel, M., Mayor, G.: Fat migration in chocolate: Diffusion or capillary flow in a particulate solid? A hypothesis paper. J. Food Sci. 69, 167–174 (2004)
2. Baetens, J.M., Van der Weeën, P., De Baets, B.: Effects of asynchronous updating in cellular automata. Chaos, Solitons Fractals 45, 383–394 (2012)
3. Chase, C.G.: Fluvial landsculpting and the fractal dimension of topography. Geomorphology 5, 39–57 (1992)
4. Courant, R., Friedrichs, K., Lewy, H.: Über die partiellen Differenzengleichungen der mathematischen Physik. Math. Ann. 100, 32–74 (1928)
5. Foubert, I., Vanrolleghem, P.A., Vanhoutte, B., Dewettinck, K.: Dynamic mathematical model of the crystallization kinetics of fats. Food Res. Int. 35, 945–956 (2002)
6. Ghosh, V., Ziegler, G.R., Anantheswaran, R.C.: Fat, moisture, and ethanol migration through chocolates and confectionary coatings. Crit. Rev. Food Sci. Nutr. 42, 583–626 (2002)
7. Hartel, R.W.: Chocolate: fat bloom during storage. The influence of structural elements. The Manufacturing Confectioner 79, 89–99 (1999)
8. Kaneko, K.: Overview of coupled map lattices. Chaos 2, 279–282 (1992)
9. Khan, R.S., Rousseau, D.: Hazelnut oil migration in dark chocolate - kinetic, thermodynamic and structural considerations. Eur. J. Lipid Sci. Technol. 108, 434–443 (2006)

10. Kleinert, J.: Etude sur la formation du blanchiment gras et les moyens propres à le retarder. Rev. Int. Choc. 16, 345–368 (1961)
11. Loisel, C., Lecq, G., Ponchel, G., Keller, G., Ollivon, M.: Fat bloom and chocolate structure studied by mercury porosimetry. J. Food Sci. 62, 781–788 (1997)
12. Lonchampt, P., Hartel, R.W.: Fat bloom in chocolate and coompound coatings. Eur. J. Lipid Sci. Technol. 106, 241–274 (2004)
13. Motwani, T., Hanselmann, W., Anantheswaran, R.C.: Diffusion, counter-diffusion and lipid phase changes occuring during oil migration in model confectionery systems. J. Food Eng. 104, 186–195 (2011)
14. Timms, R.E.: Confectionery Fat Handbook. The Oily Press, Bridgewater (2003)
15. Van der Weeën, P., Baetens, J.M., De Baets, B.: Design and parameterization of a stochastic cellular automaton describing a chemical reaction. J. Comput. Chem. 32, 1952–1961 (2011)
16. Van der Weeën, P., Baetens, J.M., Verwaeren, J., Van Doorslaer, X., Heynderickx, P.M., Dewulf, J., De Baets, B.: Modeling the photocatalytic degradation of moxifloxacin by means of a stochastic cellular automaton. Chem. Eng. J. 188, 181–190 (2012)
17. Vautrin-Ul, C., Mendy, H., Taleb, A., Chaussé, A., Stafiej, J., Badiali, J.P.: Numerical simulations of spatial heterogeneity formation in metal corrosion. Corros. Sci. 50, 2149–2158 (2008)
18. Washburn, E.W.: The dynamics of capillary flow. Phys. Rev. 17, 273–283 (1921)
19. Wünderlich, B.: Thermal Analysis. Academic Press, New York (1990)
20. Ziegler, G.R., Shetty, A., Anantheswaran, R.C.: Nut oil migration through chocolate. Manufacturing Confectioner 84, 118–126 (2004)

# Scene Text Detection on Images Using Cellular Automata

Konstantinos Zagoris and Ioannis Pratikakis

Image Processing and Multimedia Lab,
Department of Electrical and Computer Engineering,
Democritus University of Thrace, Xanthi, Greece
{kzagoris,ipratika}@ee.duth.gr

**Abstract.** Textual information in images constitutes a very rich source of high-level semantics for retrieval and indexing. In this paper, a new approach is proposed using Cellular Automata (CA) which strives towards identifying scene text on natural images. Initially, a binary edge map is calculated. Then, taking advantage of the CA flexibility, the transition rules are changing and are applied in four consecutive steps resulting in four time steps CA evolution. Finally, a post-processing technique based on edge projection analysis is employed for high density edge images concerning the elimination of possible false positives. Evaluation results indicate considerable performance gains without sacrificing text detection accuracy.

**Keywords:** Cellular Automata, Text Detection, Coord. Logic Filters.

## 1 Introduction

The mixture of the contemporary social networks and the high-performance of smart-phones with built-in cameras has sparked a tremendous increase of available images. Textual information in images constitutes a very rich source of high-level semantics for retrieval and indexing. It can be acquired as scene text that was captured by a camera as part of a scene. Although after decades of research in document image processing, it has reached a satisfactory level of success. Text detection on natural scenes is still a hard task to solve.

State of the art research on scene text detection can be roughly split in two categories: region-based and texture-based. Region-based methods group pixels that belong to the same character based on the colour homogeneity [13], the strong edges between characters and background [2] or by using a stroke filter [8]. Then, the detected characters are grouped to form lines of text according to colour, size and geometrical rules. Texture-based algorithms [9,7] scan the image at different scales using a sliding window and classify image areas as text or non-text based on features that rely on texture information.

From another perspective, text detection methods can be divided into heuristic-based and machine learning-based methods. Many heuristic based methods are

G.C. Sirakoulis and S. Bandini (Eds.): ACRI 2012, LNCS 7495, pp. 514–523, 2012.

derived from the document analysis research area focused on colour or the intensity homogeneity of characters. The core idea is to segment the image into small regions and then group them by geometrical or some other constraint in order to form words or text lines. These methods can be based on region features such as the connected component (CC) techniques [13,26,27].

The machine learning-based methods that have been the popular, use directly machine learning classifiers to detect text. In particular, Jung [11] and Kim et al. [20] use the colour and grey values of the pixels as input for a Neural Network (NN) and an SVM, respectively. Wolf et al. [29] use an SVM trained on differential and geometrical features.

In the case of scene text detection in natural images there is not an acceptable available solution yet. The heuristic techniques proved to be very efficient and satisfactory robust for specific applications with high contrast characters and relatively smooth background. However, the fact that many parameters have to be estimated experimentally condemns them to data dependency and lack of generality. Moreover, when background is really complex, they become computationally expensive.

The texture-based techniques cannot catch satisfactory text with size bigger of the sliding window. Moreover, an increase of the window make these methods quite costly. In addition, they still use empirical thresholds on specific features therefore they lack adaptability.

The proposed method address the scene text detection problem by modelling texture into cellular automata (CA) context aiming to eliminate most limitations, such as the empirical thresholds and costly operations.

CA, first introduced by von Neumann [17], are models of physical systems with local interactions, where space and time are discrete. CA are made for simulating physical systems perceiving the essential local features of systems in order to achieve global actions from the collective effect of locally component interaction [30]. Complicated CA are obtained whenever the dependence from the values of each state is nonlinear [1]. As a result, on the one hand any physical system satisfying differential equations may be approximated by a CA, by introducing finite differences and discrete variables [5,22,23], on the other hand, CAs are one of the computational structures best suited for a VLSI realization [25,24,21,15].

Therefore, the CA architecture offers a number of advantages and appealing features such as simplicity, regularity, ease of mask generation, silicon-area utilization, and locality of interconnections making them suitable for the scene text detection problem.

Two-dimensional CA have been employed extensively for image processing and pattern recognition [14,12,18,10,4]. Specifically, in [18], the author trained CA in order to perform base image processing tasks such as noise filtering, thinning and convex hulls. Ioannidis et. al [10] proposed a CA-based image interpolation algorithm that produced smaller Peak Signal-to-Noise Ratio values and quicker execution times among all the tested methods.

It is worth noting, however, that to the best of the authors knowledge there is no approach using the CA to detect text in scene images. The structure of the paper is as follows: Section 2 describes the proposed model, Section 3 discusses the evaluation of the proposed method and finally, at Section 4, we share some final thoughts.

## 2   Proposed Methodology

The proposed method encounter the scene text detection problem with an extensive use of a two-dimensional CA in order to take advantage of its speed and simplicity among other things. Figure 1 illustrates the architecture of the proposed technique. Every image is considered to be a 2-D lattice of cells where every pixel is represented by a cell. Therefore, the CA grid width and height is defined by the corresponding image width and height. Each cell can take the value of 0 or 1 since it corresponds to a pixel of a binary image.

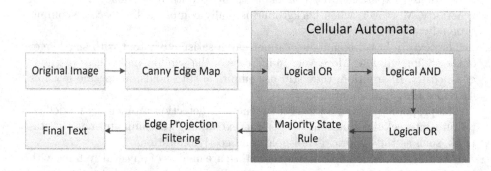

**Fig. 1.** The architecture of the proposed method

Initially, the Canny edge detector is used for the detection of the salient image edges. Canny [3] uses Sobel masks in order to find the edge magnitude of the image intensity and then he employs thresholding and non-maxima suppression(Low threshold is equal to 20 and high threshold is equal to 100). The final edge map is a binarised image with the contour pixels set to one (white) and the remainder pixels equal to zero (black). This approach exploits the fact that text lines produce strong vertical edges horizontally aligned with a high density. The use of edge information for text detection is justified by the fact that every kind of text presents strong edges, in order to be readable. Furthermore, using edges as the prominent feature of our system gives us the opportunity to detect normal or inverse characters of any colour.

For the next stage, a CA is used in order to detect the text areas on the images. Its rules partially depend on Coordinating Logic Filters (CLF) [16] and partially on the majority state rule . CLFs execute coordinate logic operations among the pixels of the image and are very efficient in various 1D, 2D, or higher-dimensional digital signal processing applications. CLFs are logic operations (AND, OR, NOT, XOR and their combinations) among the corresponding binary values of two or more signals or image pixels. The CL operations is similar to the morphological operations of erosion and dilation. Therefore the CL filters are suitable to perform the range of tasks and applications that are executed by morphological filters, achieving similar functionality [16]. Section 2.1 describes how their advantages are exploited as CAs rules.

Finally, a post-processing filtering is applied in order to discard some false positives on high edge density images. It is based on the statistics of the horizontal and vertical edge projections from the candidate text areas. Section 2.2 describes this procedure analytically.

Since the proposed algorithm depends on a precise scale we have to make some assumptions about the size range of the text. We assume that the text height deviate from $MinH = 8$ pixels to $MaxH = 25$ pixels and moreover, every text line consists of at least two characters specifying a minimum width equal to $MinW = 2 * MinH = 16$.

## 2.1  Proposed Cellular Automata Text Detection Method

The proposed CA as described before is considered to be a 2-D lattice of cells where every pixel is represented by a cell. The CA grid width and height is defined by the edge image width and height and each cell have two states as the input image is binary. Taking advantage of the CA flexibility, the transition rules are changing and are applied in four consecutive steps resulting in four time steps CA evolution. Moreover, for the proposed method three different neighbourhoods are employed. The boundaries of the CA are nullified meaning that have theirs states equal to 0 (black).

For the first time step, the 10-connection 11x1 neighbourhood (Fig. 2(a)) is employed. The values of the cells belong to this neighbourhood participates in the logical operation OR and their results is placed in the central cell of the neighbourhood:

$$S_1^{x,y} = S_0^{x-5,y} \vee S_0^{x-4,y} \vee S_0^{x-3,y} \vee S_0^{x-2,y} \vee S_0^{x-1,y} \vee S_0^{x,y} \vee$$
$$S_0^{x+1,y} \vee S_0^{x+2,y} \vee S_0^{x+3,y} \vee S_0^{x+4,y} \vee S_0^{x+5,y} \tag{1}$$

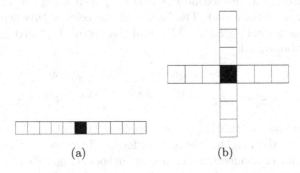

(a)                                    (b)

**Fig. 2.** The neighbourhoods for the proposed CA. (a) The 11x1 neighbourhood (b) The 7x7 neighbourhood.

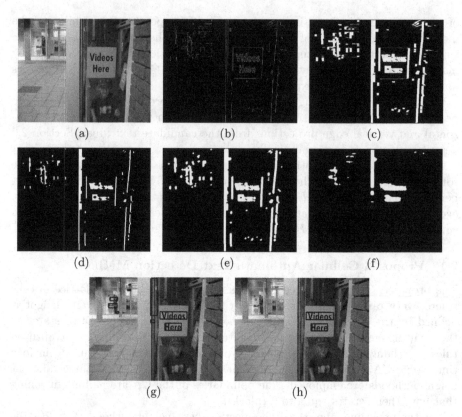

**Fig. 3.** The steps of the proposed scene text detection. (a) The original image (b) The Canny edge binary image (c) The logical OR operation (d) The logical AND operation (e) The logical OR operation (f) The majority state rule (g) Candidate text areas (h) Edge Projection Filtering.

The effect of the above logical operation is similar to the morphological dilation and links the character edges of every text line as depicted in Fig. 3(c).

In the next iteration, the second CA rule is applied using the 12-connection 7x7 (Fig. 2(b)) neighbourhood. The values of the cells of this neighbourhood participate in the logical operation AND and their result is placed in the central cell of the neighbourhood:

$$
\begin{aligned}
S_1^{x,y} = S_0^{x,y-3} \wedge S_0^{x,y-2} \wedge S_0^{x,y-1} \wedge S_0^{x-3,y} \wedge S_0^{x-2,y} \wedge S_0^{x-1,y} \wedge \\
S_0^{x,y+3} \wedge S_0^{x,y+2} \wedge S_0^{x,y+1} \wedge S_0^{x+3,y} \wedge S_0^{x+2,y} \wedge S_0^{x+1,y} \wedge S_0^{x,y}
\end{aligned}
\tag{2}
$$

In the third iteration, the third CA rule is applied. This rule is the same with the first step but now the neighbourhood is different. That means that the values of the cells of the 12-connection 7x7 neighbourhood (Fig. 2(b)) participate in the logical operation OR and their results is placed in the central cell of the neighbourhood. The transition rules this time are:

(a)                                          (b)

**Fig. 4.** Horizontal and vertical edge projections on (a) a word edge area and (b) a non word edge area

$$S_1^{x,y} = S_0^{x,y-3} \vee S_0^{x,y-2} \vee S_0^{x,y-1} \vee S_0^{x-3,y} \vee S_0^{x-2,y} \vee S_0^{x-1,y} \vee$$
$$S_0^{x,y+3} \vee S_0^{x,y+2} \vee S_0^{x,y+1} \vee S_0^{x+3,y} \vee S_0^{x+2,y} \vee S_0^{x+1,y} \vee S_0^{x,y} \qquad (3)$$

The effect of the previous two logical executions to the image is the equivalent of the opening morphological operation. It removes the noise and smooth the candidate text areas as Fig. 3(d) and Fig. 3(e) illustrates.

Following the previous iteration, a hybrid Moore neighbourhood is employed which it is defined as:

$$N_{(x_0,y_0)}^{M} = \{(x,y) : |x - x_0| \le r_1, |y - y_0| \le r_2\}, r_1 = 14, r_2 = 4 \qquad (4)$$

This huge neighbourhood is necessary in order to detect the characters/words with the defined maximum height. The transition rule is called the majority state rule and it is determined by the state of the majority cells. If the majority of those cells have state 1 then the central cell transits to state 1 else it transits to state 0. This rule and its corresponding neighbourhood are employed for one iterations and their effects to the cells and subsequently to the image as shown to Fig 3(f). They merge the areas that contains text and eliminates those that do not embody it.

## 2.2   Edge Projection Analysis

The output of the proposed cellular automata correctly identifies the text areas but in the high edge density images produces a number of false positives (Fig. 3(g)) and a post-processing filtering is required in order to remove them. The low precision originates from detected bounding boxes which do not contain text but objects with high vertical edge density. To improve precision by rejecting the false alarms we filtered them based on horizontal and vertical projections. Firstly, the areas in the edge image that corresponds to the detected areas from the cellular automata output are extracted and the horizontal and vertical projections are calculated as shown in Fig 4. Areas with mean horizontal and vertical projections below a threshold are discarded. The remaining areas are presented to the user on the original image. Fig. 5 shows some output examples of our proposed CA-based scene text detection method.

**Fig. 5.** Examples of the proposed scene text detection method

# 3    Experimental Results and Discussion

For the evaluation of the proposed method, we used a subset of the dataset that is provided from the ICDAR 2011 Robust Reading Competition [19]. There are two performance metrics, recall and precision for our evaluation needs. For the

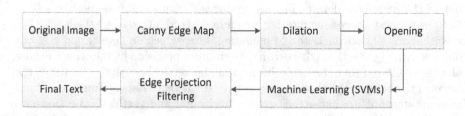

**Fig. 6.** The architecture of the machine-based scene text detection method

detected text rectangles and their corresponding ground truth rectangles, these metrics are defined as follows:

$$R = \frac{\text{Number of correctly detected rectangles}}{\text{Number of rectangles in the database}} \tag{5}$$

$$P = \frac{\text{Number of correctly detected rectangles}}{\text{Total number of detected rectangles}} \tag{6}$$

The recall metric characterize the amount of correct detected objects and precision informs about the number of false alarms. Both are better if higher. The harmonic mean of precision and recall merge the above two metrics into one by emphasizing the minimum of these two:

$$H = 2 * \frac{R * P}{R + P} \tag{7}$$

Unfortunately, for our object detection problem, the above measures are not directly applicable, since the decision whether an object has been detected or not is not a binary one. In our experiments, we used the DetEval evaluation software and its associate evaluation method [28]. It is based on the amount of overlap between the ground truth rectangles and the result rectangles and consequently deals some of the evaluation problems.

In order to showcase the advantages of our proposed method, we test it against a machine-learning edge based scene text detection system. Its architecture is depicted in Fig 6. We replace the CLF with the corresponding morphological operations (dilation and opening) and the majority state rule with the Support Vector Machines (SVMs) [6] classifier. The SVMs are chosen based on their high performance and their ability to not require large training sets.

Table 1 shows the above performance metrics for both the proposed and the machine learning-based method. Moreover, Table 2 shows the mean execution time of each of them for a set images (15 total) in a Intel Core 2 Quad CPU Q9550 (2.83GHz) machine. As Table 1 and 2 states, the proposed CA-based model exhibits better performance scores in terms of classification accuracy along with a speed-up at the execution level. It is worth to note, that the machine-learning based method needs training samples where the proposed method is not supervised.

**Table 1.** The Evaluation Metrics for both the proposed CA-based and machine learning methods

| Method | Recall | Precision | Harmonic Mean |
|---|---|---|---|
| Proposed CA-based method | 0.7942 | 0.7462 | 0.7652 |
| Machine-learning based method | 0.7134 | 0.5234 | 0.6038 |

**Table 2.** Mean Execution Time for 15 images

| Method | Mean Execution Time (sec) |
|---|---|
| Proposed CA-based method | 2.75 sec |
| Machine-learning based method | 5.96 sec |

## 4  Conclusions

In this paper a method based on the Cellular Automata was presented for the detection of scene text on natural images. Initially, the Canny edge detector is employed in order to exposed the dominant edges on the image. Then a CA is used for the calculation of the candidate text areas. Its rules depend on Coordinating Logic Filters and on the majority state rule. Finally, a post-processing technique based on edge projection analysis is employed for the high density edge images in order to eliminated the false positives. Experimental results have shown considerably performance gains besides better detection scores.

## References

1. Adamatzky, A.: Identification of cellular automata. CRC (1994)
2. Anthimopoulos, M., Gatos, B., Pratikakis, I.: Multiresolution text detection in video frames. VISAPP (2), 161–166 (2007)
3. Canny, J.: A computational approach to edge detection. IEEE Transactions on Pattern Analysis and Machine Intelligence (6), 679–698 (1986)
4. Chatzichristofis, S., Mitzias, D., Sirakoulis, G., Boutalis, Y.: A novel cellular automata based technique for visual multimedia content encryption. Optics Communications 283(21), 4250–4260 (2010)
5. Chopard, B., Droz, M., Press, C.U.: Cellular automata modeling of physical systems, vol. 122. Cambridge University Press, Cambridge (1998)
6. Cortes, C., Vapnik, V.: Support vector networks. Machine Learning 20, 273–297 (1995)
7. Crandall, D., Antani, S., Kasturi, R.: Extraction of special effects caption text events from digital video. International Journal on Document Analysis and Recognition 5(2), 138–157 (2003)
8. Epshtein, B., Ofek, E., Wexler, Y.: Detecting text in natural scenes with stroke width transform. In: 2010 IEEE Conference on Computer Vision and Pattern Recognition (CVPR), pp. 2963–2970. IEEE (2010)
9. Goto, H.: Redefining the dct-based feature for scene text detection. International Journal on Document Analysis and Recognition 11(1), 1–8 (2008)
10. Ioannidis, K., Sirakoulis, G., Andreadis, I.: Depicting pathways for cooperative miniature robots using cellular automata. In: 2011 International Conference on High Performance Computing and Simulation (HPCS), pp. 794–800. IEEE (2011)
11. Jung, K.: Neural network-based text location in color images. Pattern Recognition Letters 22(14), 1503–1515 (2001)
12. Karafyllidis, I., Andreadis, I., Tzionas, P., Tsalides, P., Thanailakis, A.: A cellular automaton for the determination of the mean velocity of moving objects and its vlsi implementation. Pattern Recognition 29(4), 689–699 (1996)

13. Lienhart, R., Effelsberg, W.: Automatic text segmentation and text recognition for video indexing. Multimedia Systems 8(1), 69–81 (2000)
14. Maniccam, S., Bourbakis, N.: Lossless image compression and encryption using scan. Pattern Recognition 34(6), 1229–1245 (2001)
15. Mardiris, V., Sirakoulis, G., Mizas, C., Karafyllidis, I., Thanailakis, A.: A cad system for modeling and simulation of computer networks using cellular automata. IEEE Transactions on Systems, Man, and Cybernetics, Part C: Applications and Reviews 38(2), 253–264 (2008)
16. Mertzios, B., Tsirikolias, K.: Coordinate logic filters and their applications in image processing and pattern recognition. Circuits, Systems, and Signal Processing 17(4), 517–538 (1998)
17. Neumann, J., Burks, A.: Theory of self-reproducing automata (1966)
18. Rosin, P.: Training cellular automata for image processing. IEEE Transactions on Image Processing 15(7), 2076–2087 (2006)
19. Shahab, A., Shafait, F., Dengel, A.: Icdar 2011 robust reading competition challenge 2: Reading text in scene images. In: 2011 International Conference on Document Analysis and Recognition (ICDAR), pp. 1491–1496. IEEE (2011)
20. Shin, C., Kim, K., Park, M., Kim, H.: Support vector machine-based text detection in digital video. In: Proceedings of the 2000 IEEE Signal Processing Society Workshop Neural Networks for Signal Processing X, vol. 2, pp. 634–641. IEEE (2000)
21. Sirakoulis, G.: A tcad system for vlsi implementation of the cvd process using vhdl. Integration, the VLSI Journal 37(1), 63–81 (2004)
22. Sirakoulis, G., Karafyllidis, I., Mardiris, V., Thanailakis, A.: Study of lithography profiles developed on non-planar si surfaces. Nanotechnology 10, 421 (1999)
23. Sirakoulis, G., Karafyllidis, I., Thanailakis, A.: A cellular automaton model for the effects of population movement and vaccination on epidemic propagation. Ecological Modelling 133(3), 209–223 (2000)
24. Sirakoulis, G., Karafyllidis, I., Thanailakis, A.: A cad system for the construction and vlsi implementation of cellular automata algorithms using vhdl. Microprocessors and Microsystems 27(8), 381–396 (2003)
25. Sirakoulis, G., Karafyllidis, I., Thanailakis, A., Mardiris, V.: A methodology for vlsi implementation of cellular automata algorithms using vhdl. Advances in Engineering Software 32(3), 189–202 (2000)
26. Sobottka, K., Bunke, H., Kronenberg, H.: Identification of text on colored book and journal covers. In: Proceedings of the Fifth International Conference on Document Analysis and Recognition, ICDAR 1999, pp. 57–62. IEEE (1999)
27. Wang, K., Kangas, J.: Character location in scene images from digital camera. Pattern Recognition 36(10), 2287–2299 (2003)
28. Wolf, C., Jolion, J.M.: Object count/area graphs for the evaluation of object detection and segmentation algorithms. International Journal on Document Analysis and Recognition 8(4), 280–296 (2006)
29. Wolf, C., Jolion, J., de Lyon, L.: Model based text detection in images and videos: a learning approach. Laboratoire dInfoRmatique en Images et Systemes dinformation, Palmas, TO (2004)
30. Wolfram, S.: Theory and applications of cellular automata (advanced series on complex systems, selected papers 1983–1986), vol. 1. World Sci., Singapore (1986)

# A Novel Cellular Automaton Model for Traffic Freeway Simulation

Marcelo Zamith, Regina Célia P. Leal-Toledo, and Esteban Clua

Federal Fluminense University, Passo da Pátria Street, 156, Niterói, Brazil
{mzamith,leal,esteban}@ic.uff.br
http://www.ic.uff.br/~medialab

**Abstract.** This work introduces a novel Cellular Automata (CA) model applied for freeway traffic. Besides its capacity for representing basic traffic proprieties, it is capable of representing different drivers behaviors as well as its fluctuation and variation, based on the combination of acceleration and anticipation policy. Both policies are based on normal probabilistic function which represents the nature of unpredictable human behavior. The simulations developed and described herein give rise to a phase diagram which resembles and enriches the fundamental diagram, in its theoretical as well as for real data. Therefore, novel feature proposed herein is normal probabilistic function invoked in both policy (acceleration and anticipation), which allows for a simple group of rules with a few parameters.

**Keywords:** Normal Probabilistic Function, Behaviors, Rejection Technique, Traffic Simulation.

## 1 Introduction

The vehicular traffic motion directly affects life of modern society. The saturation of roads, the time spent in jammed traffic as well as environment pollution contribute for deteriorating urban areas. Louis A. Pipes [1] was one of first researchers in studying the traffic motion in 1950s which describes mathematically the vehicular motion.

Several researchers have tried to describe mathematically traffic flows and understand its bottlenecks. These models are typically classified as macroscopic or microscopic. Among the microscopic models, Cellular Automata (CA) has been adopted with good results, due to the fact that it creates similar behavior features of traffic vehicular motion, such as the relation of flow-density and the metastable phase [2], [3], [4] and [5]

The model proposed herein improves previous CA models, which includes in a new manner anticipation and acceleration policies. Indeed, these models present some difficultly for adjusting the velocities of vehicles which consider the continuous movement of ahead vehicle. The proposed model herein has also the capacity to predict the movement of head vehicle.

The main motivation of this work is the challenge of describing a complex traffic vehicular motion systems. The contribution is based on the proposed CA

G.C. Sirakoulis and S. Bandini (Eds.): ACRI 2012, LNCS 7495, pp. 524–533, 2012.
© Springer-Verlag Berlin Heidelberg 2012

model which predict the velocity of head vehicle combined with a acceleration policy. This work is organized as follows: In Section 2 concepts of traffic-flow and theoretical aspects are reviewed; in Section 3, concepts of cellular automata are presented and some related work on cellular automata models applied to traffic highways is discussed; Section 4 describes in detail the model proposed in this work; Section 5 presents some test cases. Finally, concluding remarks about the proposed model are discussed in Section 6.

## 2   The Traffic-Flow Theory

The trajectories for a single vehicle is an useful tool for studying and analyzing a vehicular motion behavior, summarizing the relevant information within an understandable way. An usual case of analysis consists on tracking position of vehicles over time along a one dimensional path or freeway. This problem can be mathematically written denoting the distance traveled by $x$ related to its corresponding travel time $t$ as the corresponding travel time. Thus, the function $x(t)$ describes the trajectories of a vehicle within a specified time, and graphics representation of the function $(x(t))$ is named as the time-space diagram in the bibliography (see, e.g. Fig. 1).The graphics representation may denote when there is any invalid trajectory, as can be observed in curve 'C' of Fig. 1. The traffic behavior can be described thought three basic variables: density $(\rho)$, velocity $(v)$ and flow $(J)$. The first describes the number of vehicles per unit length on a highway at some time ( Eq. 1), where $n$ is the number of vehicles and $L$ represents the full length of the highway's segment under observation.

$$\rho = \frac{n}{L} \tag{1}$$

The average velocity, i.e., the averaged sum of velocities, is obtained with the following (Eq.2)

$$\bar{v} = \frac{\sum_{i=1}^{n} v_i}{n} \tag{2}$$

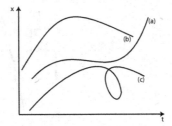

**Fig. 1.** Example of a time-space diagram

Finally, the flow is defined as the number of vehicles $(m)$ that pass through a specific point of the highway in a given time interval $(T)$, as denoted in Eq. 3.

$$J = \frac{m}{T} \tag{3}$$

The vehicular motion data can be obtained by two ways: either by an instantaneous photograph of a specific section with length $L$ or by observing the flow from a fixed location during an interval time $T$. While equations 1 and 2 describe the density and average velocity considering a continuous section of the freeway as a photograph taken at a given instant of time. On the order hand, Eq. 3 considers the counting strategy during a gap time. Finally, it is possible to build a relation among these variables, as described in the following Eq. 4 (considering a stationary traffic state).

$$J = \rho\bar{v} \tag{4}$$

The equations above describe the behavior of a traffic flow on a highway by means of vehicle counts over long periods of time at a fixed observation point. Typically, the analysis of traffic flow is performed by constructing the corresponding fundamental diagram. This depicts how flow and density are related. The theoretical model is illustrated in Fig. 2 and a fundamental diagram for real data is presented in Fig. 3. Upon inspection of the fundamental diagram (Figs. 2 and 3) it is possible to see three well defined phases: the first one represents the free-flow and corresponds to the region of low to medium density and weak interaction between vehicles. In this phase, the vehicles can move almost at the highways speed limit, and the flow increases linearly with density level, within the interval of $0 \leq \rho \leq c_1$. The second phase represents medium and high density and is also known as the synchronized flow. The flow should behave either free or jammed, i.e., the phase $c_1 < \rho < c_2$ shows a flow that is not defined only by density, but by the interaction among the vehicles. This phase is named the metastable phase. The last phase represents the jammed flow or wide-jammed flow, where an increase in density causes a decrease in the flow $(\rho > c_2)$. The relation of cellular automata and traffic theory is discussed by Kerner et al [6].

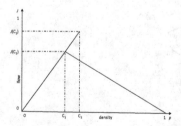

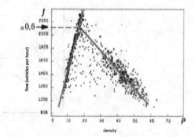

**Fig. 2.** Theoretical fundamental diagram    **Fig. 3.** Real data fundamental diagram

In their research is presented how the micro interaction makes arise a macro behavior and phases of traffic theory.

# 3  Cellular Automata

The Cellular Automata (CA) is model mathematic widely employed for describing complex system, such as traffic, crowd simulation, etc. Its concept was presented by J. Von Neumann[7]. A theoretical systematic description of CA was developed by Wolfram [8]. It is a robust and powerful mathematical model for simulating the dynamics systems, typically used for physics, biology, ecology, fluid flow, crowd behavior, among others [9], [10] and [11].

CA models applied to traffic problems can describe basic proprieties of the traffic. They are used for representing the vehicular movement across the lattice, which represents the highway. Nagel and Schreckenberg (NaSch) [12] proposed the successful model that has been widely employed, which became the basis for several developments and is referred to NaSch's model. Several others models were proposed based on NaSch's models, which create families of models.

A well known family of these solutions is named slow-to-start. This model tries to mimic the driver inertia in returning his velocity whenever he stops. It was introduced by Takayasu and Takayasu (T2) [13]. Several others works were proposed [14], [15], [16] and [17]. Despite depicting metastable region, this family model should work with more than one probability with different range of values. At last, metastable region relies on its initial condition: For free flow, the vehicles must be distributed uniformly by the CA lattice. On the other hand, jammed flow is represented by vehicles in jammed state on the CA lattice.

Another family of CA applied for traffic are related to those that include anticipation feature. These models resemble the continuity of drivers movement in the next instant time. The concept adopted in this approach is that every driver considers that his ahead vehicle will move with the same velocity as in the previous time instant. The disadvantage of this model family is given by the unpredictable driver's behavior due to correct velocity definition. Emmerich et al. [18] suggests that each vehicle may adjust its velocity considering the movement of the vehicle ahead at the next time instant, but this strategy depends on flow and the results show that the flow becomes jammed prematurely, besides not reproducing metastable phase. Another strategy considers a percentage of velocity of the ahead vehicle as proposed by Larraga et al. [19], including a safety distance among vehicles. Break light models is a subset of this family, which adopts a signalize strategy [20]. Other strategy adopted by anticipation model was proposed by Zamith et al. [21]. where a recursive procedure is added in order to correctly define each vehicle velocity. Although these models reproduce basic propriety of traffic, such as good flow-density relation and metastable region, these are done through one of following features: signalization of previous vehicle, recursive procedure for correct velocity definition and counter flow velocity adjustment. Several of them need to setup many parameters and others require a high computational power with complex data structure.

## 4  A New Cellular Automata Model

In this section, a novel and efficient probabilistic model is introduced. It is based
on an extension of the anticipatory concept proposed by Larraga et al. [19] and
Lima [22]. Typically, CA models adopt NaSch's randomness feature in order to
describe uncertainly behavior of traffic. While in this strategy all vehicles try to
increase their velocity. However, in real situation there is a probability of some
drivers do not behavior like this. Knowing that randomness of this behavior
is based on uniform probabilistic function. This work proposes a model which
considers that drivers will conduce their vehicles within customary behavior.
Thus, in order to achieve a normal behavior, the proposed model adopts a normal
probabilistic function to depict acceleration and anticipation steps.

Acceleration policy considers that all drivers try to move at the freeway's
speed limit or at the velocity allowed by the flow of vehicles. Additionally, this
stage is responsible for random driver's behavior, where all drivers try to move
at the freeway's speed limit or at the velocity allowed by the flow of vehicles,
but several drivers do not have this behavior and decrease their velocity without any logical reason. CA models adopt uniform probability function in order
to describe nature of drivers' uncertainly. Several of them employ up to three
different probabilities to define drivers' behavior.

In the proposed model, the acceleration policy, different than others models,
is defined in accordance with average value of normal probabilistic function and
the standard deviation describes the fluctuation of unpredictable behavior. The
average value depicts level aggressiveness of driver conduction. Drivers are able
to increase their own velocity in until two cells per second ($2\ cell/s^2$ or $3\ m/s^2$).
Which mens that more aggressive drivers increase velocity close to maximum rate
acceleration ($2\ cell/s^2$), whereas less aggressive drivers increase velocity slowly
or keep velocity stable. This acceleration rate adopted is based on studying of
The Highway Capacity Manual [23].

The anticipation policy adopts the same concept of acceleration policy, i.e.,
given an analyzed vehicle which believes that ahead vehicle will keep its velocity
in accordance to a normal probabilistic function, where average value defines
the level of expectancy of analyzed vehicle to the ahead one, as well as root
means square which makes analyzed vehicle take in to account the randomness
of ahead vehicle in keeping its velocity. Besides the velocity of the ahead vehicle,
the distance between an ahead vehicle and next one is taken into account in
herein model, whenever there is not enough space for the ahead vehicle to move
in the desired speed.

The freeway is modeled as a discretized lattice, divided in cells with 1.5m
($\Delta x$) of length and time is measured in seconds ($\Delta t$). The $x$ denotes a position
in the lattice, which is considered to have periodic boundary condition, where
inflow rate is equal to outflow. In the solution proposed herein is outside of the
influence area of ramps or weaving areas of the freeway. Velocity is represented
by $v$ and the speed limit by $v_{max}$. The $\alpha \in [0,1]$ parameter defines two features
of the model: The fluctuation around to acceleration value and an expectation
level of how much the next vehicle will move, being both given by a probability

distribution function. The distance between the $i^{th}$ vehicle analyzed and its leading vehicle is denoted by $d_i$. Finally, $d_{is}^t$ defines how far the $i^{th}$ vehicle can move, taking into account the movement of its ahead vehicle.

The adjustment of each vehicle's speed takes into account the distance and the velocity of its ahead vehicle. Furthermore, a mechanism is implemented to take the awareness of the analyzed vehicle's state into account where each vehicle attempts to predict the ahead vehicle motion continuity. For each time instant simulation, the analyzed vehicle takes into account an expectation level of ahead vehicle speed as well as the distance between this one and its next. With this in mind, the worst case is when ahead vehicle stops at next time instant. In this case, the analyzed vehicle stops immediately behind of its ahead vehicle, and there is not any empty cell between them. The model proposed herein is

---

**Algorithm 1.** The Proposed Algorithm - main algorithm

---

1: **for all** vehicles **do**
2:     $\alpha \leftarrow normal(\mu, \sigma)$
3:     $acc_i^t \leftarrow 2 \times (1 - \alpha)$
4:     $v_i^t \leftarrow min(v_i^{t-1} + acc_i^t, v_{max})$
5:     $\alpha_i^t \leftarrow normal(\mu, \sigma)$
6:     $d_i^t \leftarrow x_i^{t-1} - x_{i-1}^{t-1} - 1$
7:     $d_{is}^t \leftarrow d_i^t + min\left[[v_{i+1}^{t-1} \times (1 - \alpha_{i+1}^{t-1})], d_{i+1}^t\right]$
8:     **if** $v_i^t > d_{is}^t$ **then**
9:         $v_i^t \leftarrow d_{is}^t$
10:     **end if**
11: **end for**
12: **for all** vehicles **do**
13:     $x_i^t \leftarrow x_i^{t-1} + v_i^t$
14: **end for**

---

divided in three stages and described through 1. The first stage is responsible for the acceleration definition, considering the fact that the driver usually wants to increase his velocity in accordance to normal behavior.

The model proposed herein is divided in three stages and described through 1. The first stage is responsible for acceleration definition, considering the fact that the driver usually want to increase his velocity in according to normal behavior. This stage is implemented by means of

$$acc_i^t \leftarrow 2 \times (1 - \alpha) \tag{5}$$

The second stage considers how much the vehicle will effectively move when the unpredictability of its ahead vehicle is taken into account. In accordance with the Eq.:

$$d_{is}^t \leftarrow d_i^t + min\left[[v_{i+1}^{t-1} \times (1 - \alpha_{i+1}^{t-1})], d_{i+1}^t\right] \tag{6}$$

With respect to the role of the second stage, it is important to notice that the velocity definition considering an expectation level of ahead vehicle velocity or, if there is not enough space, the distance of ahead vehicle and next one. Indeed, in order to analyzed if the vehicle is able to predict the correct continuos behavior of the ahead vehicle, it is considered the minimum value between the distance and the velocity of the ahead entity. Finally, the last stage is responsible for updating vehicle position.

Aggressive rate acceleration and anticipatory expectation level are modeled by $\alpha$, which is sampled from a continuous probability function. The value selection is performed by a Monte Carlo rejection process.

Monte Carlo rejection process consists in transforming uniform to normal distribution function. Hence, given a couple of random numbers defined by ($x$, $y$) shall be discarded, since the point lies above the normal function's value, otherwise the point is accepted $x$ value is returned. This procedure is effective for both discrete and continuous probability distribution functions. Since the normal function is adopted here, the average and root mean square parameters have to be established. These are given by $\mu$ and $\sigma$, respectively.

# 5    Tests and Results

Since this work is a first approach of the model, the tests translate qualitative results. This proposed model herein needs a set of parameters in order to define what one intends to simulate: simulation time, number of cells, number of vehicles and probability of maintaining the velocity are required to define any simulation. An important feature carried out by the model is the fact that the simulations are independent of the initial state, i.e., hundreds of time steps are performed before the "memory" of the any initial state stops influencing the dynamics of the process. One refers to this as the convergence of the simulation to satisfactory result.

Each instance of test was executed with the configuration: periodic boundary condition, 10.000 cells , 25.000 simulation time steps and the first 10.000 time transient time steps. The simulations were carried out using highway densities ranging from 0.05 to 0.95. The maximum speed value allowed is 25 cells per unit time (135 $km/h$). Each vehicle has 7.5 $mts$ of length and occupies 5 cells.

Finally, three behaviors are tested: high ($\mu = 0.3$), medium ($\mu = 0.5$) and low ($\mu = 0.7$) level of aggressively. Moreover, for each one $\sigma$ is equal to $\sigma = 0.05$, $\sigma = 0.10$ and $\sigma = 0.15$.

For a high level of aggressively, drivers move almost to road speed limit with low interaction among them, even-if there are some speed fluctuation caused by different values of root mean square. This low interaction is arose from acceleration and anticipation policy as well as average values adopted to normal distribution function. Considering the fact that there is a group of drivers, all of them moves basing on aggressive behavior, i.e., increase their velocity as high as possible and moves very close to ahead one, for low values of $\sigma$, there is low velocity fluctuation among vehicles. If no driver reduces its velocity then the relation flow-density is improved. Moreover, low interaction produces a little metastable region.

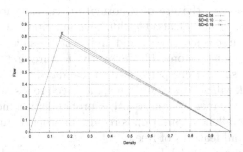

**Fig. 4.** High aggressive level with $\mu = 0.3$

Fig. 4 depicts the different values of root mean square. Despite these instances present same maximum flow (almost to 0.85 vehicles per seconds), the relation flow-density improves in according to less values of root mean square. Furthermore, different values of root mean square give arise a metastable region, but influences little in flow-density relation. Fig. 4 shows that the flow-density relation has lower value between (0.65 and 0.85) vehicles per second than the previous one, a greater metastable region also arises. As previous instance, metastable is depend on root mean square. Since both policy (acceleration and anticipation) consider average value equal $\mu = 0.5$, the relation flow-density is lower. Besides, root mean square values influences more flow-density when $\mu = 0.5$ than average higher value. At last, with a flow-density relation between 0.35 and 0.40, medium aggressive behavior is illustrated by Fig. 6. These instances present the lower flow-density relation than others instance. In face of results herein presented and as expected, lower acceleration and anticipation policy produces a low flow-density relation. Otherwise, high values improve flow density relation. A novel probabilistic model is proposed and discussed in this work. It is based on Nagel-Schreckenberg's approach. Few parameters, such as time step, number of cells, number of vehicles and empirical probability of maintaining the velocity, are required to set up a simulation which resembles the basic features of realistic highway traffic flows.

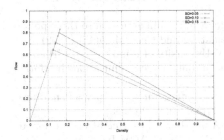

**Fig. 5.** Medium aggressive level with $\mu = 0.5$

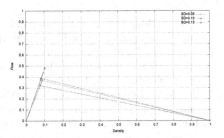

**Fig. 6.** Low aggressive level with $\mu = 0.7$

Innovative features are the use of a normal distribution for the description of drivers' behavior, either in acceleration and anticipation adjustment step. However, gaussian curve is symmetric and limits the possible values of $\mu$, due to the sum of curve area must be one. The innovative features in this work improved the adequacy of the simulations performed to real data.

Forthcoming work will address multi-lane, multi-cell roads, within the successful framework of this paper as well as other probabilistic functions. Moreover, high-performance parallel computation is require in order to guarantee real-time forecast considering all features of freeway.

At last, the proposed model herein depicts robust model. Because of basic features of freeway traffic is resembled, such as flow-density relation and metastable region in according to behavior defined. It means, low aggressive behavior yields low flow-density relation, whereas higher aggressive behavior improves flow-density relation. In addition to, the interaction among vehicles arises from combination of average and root mean square. The proposed method converges independently of initial condition or different probability values.

**Acknowlegments.**    Authors gratefully acknowledge CAPES, FAPERJ and CNPq for the financial support.

# References

1. Pipes, L.A.: An operational analysis of traffic dynamics. Journal of Applied Physics 24, 274–281 (1953)
2. Wahle, J., Neubert, L., Esser, J., Schreckenberg, M.: A cellular automaton traffic flow model for online simulation of traffic. Parallel Computing 27(5), 719–735 (2001)
3. Hafstein, S.F., Chrobok, R., Pottmeier, A., Schreckenberg, M.: A high-resolution cellular automata traffic simulation model with application in a freeway traffic information system. Computer-Aided Civil and Infrastructure Engineering 19, 338–350 (2004)
4. Nagatani, T.: Traffic states and fundamental diagram in cellular automaton model of vehicular traffic controlled by signals. Physica A: Statistical Mechanics and its Applications 8(388), 1673–1681 (2009)
5. Spyropoulou, I.: Modelling a signal controlled traffic stream using cellular automata. Transportation Research Part C: Emerging Technologies 15, 175–190 (2007)
6. Kerner, B.S., Klenov, S.L., Wolf, E.D.: Cellular automata approach to three-phase traffic theory. Journal of Physics A: Mathematical and General 35(47) (2002)
7. The general and logical theory of automata. University of Illinois Press, Urbana
8. Wolfram, S.: Computation theory of cellular automata. Communications in Mathematical Physics 96, 15–57 (1984)
9. Takai, Y., Ecchu, K., Takai, N.K.: A cellular automaton model of particle motions and its applications. The Visual Computer 11(5), 240–252 (1995)
10. Ling, C., Xiaohua, X., Yixin, C., Ping, H.: A novel ant clustering algorithm based on cellular automata. In: Proceedings of the IEEE/WIC/ACM International Conference on Intelligent Agent Technology, IAT 2004, pp. 148–154. IEEE Computer Society, Washington, DC (2004)

11. Gaylord, R.J., D'Andria, L.J.: Simulating Society: A Mathematica Toolkit for Modeling Socioeconomic Behavior, 1st edn. Springer (June 1998)
12. Nagel, K., Schreckenberg, M.: A cellular automaton model for freeway traffic. Journal de Physique I 2, 2221–2229 (1992)
13. Takayasu, M., Takayasu, H.: 1/f Noise in a Traffic Model. Factral 1 5, 860–866 (1993)
14. Benjamin, S., Johnson, N., Hui, P.: Cellular Automata Models of Traffic flow Along a Highway Containing a Junction. Journal of Physics A 5, 3119–3127 (1996)
15. Tian, R.: The mathematical solution of a cellular automaton model which simulates traffic flow with a slow-to-start effect. Discrete Applied Mathematics 157(13), 2904–2917 (2009)
16. Barlovic, R., Santen, L., Schadschneider, A., Schreckenberg, M.: Metastable states in cellular automata for traffic flow. The European Physical Journal B 5(3), 793–800 (1998)
17. Nishinari, K., Fukui, M., Schadschneider, A.: A stochastic cellular automaton model for traffic flow with multiple metastable states. Journal of Physics A 37, 3101–3110 (2004)
18. Emmerich, H., Rank, E.: An Improved Cellular Automaton Model for Traffic Flow Simulation. Journal of Physics A 234, 676–686 (1997)
19. Larraga, M.E., del Rio, J.A., Schadschneider, A.: New kind of phase separation in a ca traffic model with anticipation. Journal of Physics A: Mathematical and General 37(12), 3769–3781 (2004)
20. Knospe, W., Santen, L., Schadschneider, A., Schreckenberg, M.: Towards a realistic microscopic description of highway traffic. Journal of Physics A: Mathematical and General 33(48) (2000)
21. Zamith, M., Leal-Toledo, R.C.P., Kischinhevsky, M., Clua, E.W.G., Brandão, D.N., Montenegro, A.A., Lima, E.B.: A probabilistic cellular automata model for highway traffic simulation. Procedia CS 1(1), 337–345 (2010)
22. Lima, B.E.: Modelos micoscópios para simulação do tráfego baseados em autômatos celulares. Master's thesis, Universidade Federal Fluminense (2007)
23. Wachs, M.: Highway Capacity Manual. Transportation Research Board (2000)

# Scintillae: How to Approach Computing Systems by Means of Cellular Automata

Gabriele Di Stefano[1] and Alfredo Navarra[2]

[1] Dipartimento di Ingegneria e Scienze dell'Informazione e Matematica,
Università degli Studi dell'Aquila, Italy
gabriele.distefano@univaq.it
[2] Dipartimento di Matematica e Informatica,
Università degli Studi di Perugia, Italy
alfredo.navarra@unipg.it

**Abstract.** The paper deals with a very simple game called *Scintillae*. Like in a domino game, Scintillae provides the player with limited basic pieces that can be placed over a chessboard-like area. After the placement, the game starts in a sort of runtime mode, and the player enjoys his creation. The evolution of the system is based on few basic rules.

Despite its simplicity, Scintillae turns out to provide the player with a powerful mean able to achieve high computational power, storage capabilities and many other peculiarities based on the ability of the player to suitably dispose the pieces.

We show some of the potentials of this simple game by providing basic configurations that can be used as "sub-programs" for composing bigger systems. Moreover, the interest in Scintillae also resides in its potentials for educational purposes, as many basic concepts related to the computer science architecture can be approached with fun by means of this game.

## 1 Introduction

Scintillae is a game designed for fun to simulate a sort of domino effect on a PC.[1] Although it hides some peculiarities that cannot be realized by standard domino games with falling pieces, it is very interesting how such kind of simulator may easily realize a computing system in a sort of visual programming environment [3]. Its strength is witnessed by the high computational power that indeed can be obtained by means of the few pieces provided by the game for composing desired configurations. Instead of domino pieces falling in a sequence determined by their proximity, Scintillae provides the user with sparks that seem to move according to designed paths obtained by disposing arrows on a chessboard-like area. The rules that establish the evolving of the system are very simple.

### 1.1 Rules of Scintillae

In an unbounded area divided into squares, it is possible to place two basic pieces, at most one per square, to compose a game: *Sparks* ("Scintillae" in the

---

[1] An executable graphic version of the program along with some explanatory examples contained also in this paper can be found in [1,2].

G.C. Sirakoulis and S. Bandini (Eds.): ACRI 2012, LNCS 7495, pp. 534–543, 2012.

Latin language), and four types of *Arrows* ($\rightarrow$, $\uparrow$, $\downarrow$, $\leftarrow$), see Fig. 1. Each arrow has four neighboring squares. The square pointed by the arrow is called the *output square* while the other three squares are called *input squares*. The system is synchronous and pieces interact at each time $t$ according to the next simple operations applied sequentially, that move the system's state to time $t + 1$:

1. an arrow becomes *loaded* if among its input squares there is exactly one spark;
2. each spark disappears and leaves empty the corresponding square;
3. for each loaded arrow, a spark is placed in the output square, if empty;
4. each loaded arrow becomes unloaded.

Fig. 1 shows the available pieces and some basic configurations. By the rules above, it follows that arrows never change from their original placement. That's all! The rules are specified, now only the imagination of the user can lead to surprising results. In the implemented program, once the pieces have been placed, a running button can be pressed to enjoy the evolution. Another way to experience the evolution of the system is to press the space bar for a single clock's tick.

Clearly, Scintillae belongs to the family of *Cellular Automata* [4,5,6,7,8,9]. Similarly to such systems, in Scintillae the user is provided with an area divided into cells. Each cell may change its status according to its own one, and to the status of a limited number of neighbors. The evolution is synchronous for all the cells. Hence, Scintillae preserves the fundamental peculiarities of such kind of computational means, that are: parallelism, locality, and homogeneity. In fact, all the cells are updated synchronously in parallel, by applying the same common rule based on local peculiarities. Likewise domino games but differently from most cellular automata, in Scintillae there are predefined paths provided by the initial disposal of the arrows that determine the evolution of the sparks. It reminds the WireWorld tool [9], but it is even simpler as less rules are specified. Moreover, the composed configurations appear very neat, clear and intuitive, hence more appropriate for educational purposes. However, "unexpected" but useful behaviors may occur for particular configurations.

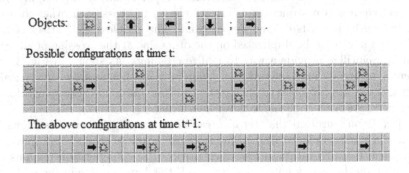

**Fig. 1.** Available pieces, and a description of the evolving synchronous system

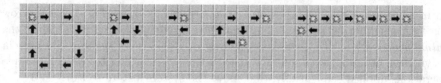

**Fig. 2.** Three possible cycles with periods 8, 4, and 2, respectively, and their application in generating infinite sparks

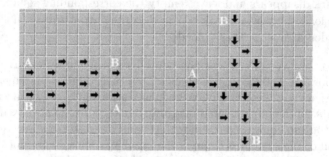

**Fig. 3.** Two possible ways of realizing crossings

## 2   Basic Configurations

One main peculiarity of Scintillae is the opportunity to obtain infinite evolutions. In fact, if the user defines a cycling sequence of arrows, and place a spark nearby one of them, the spark will be moved along the cycles infinitely often, until the user stops the run-time mode. In Fig. 2, three possible cycles are shown. Moreover, on the right, it is shown how cycles can be used as infinite generators of sparks. In particular, the size of the used cycle determines the frequency of sparks in output. Another way to decide the frequency of sparks is to insert more sparks in the cycle at the beginning during the designing mode.

Interesting basic configurations concern the appropriate placement of the pieces in order to realize desired connections. In particular, it may happen that the user requires two sequences of arrows (*lines*) to cross each other in order to move sparks towards desired destinations. The problem that arises is that sparks on a line could be duplicated on the other line at the crossing point. Surprisingly, Scintillae provide a way to realize crossings. As shown in Fig. 3, two sequences of arrows may cross in two different ways, horizontally or vertically, and it is interesting to observe during the run-time mode how the sparks follow the appropriate A or B paths, without interfering.

A useful configuration that recall a candle or an on/off switch is shown in Fig. 4. If a spark is placed nearby the leftmost arrow →, the system moves to the rightmost configuration in few clock's ticks. The configuration remains the same until another spark enters the system. If this happens, again the first configuration occurs (switching off the candle). The rational behind such a structure

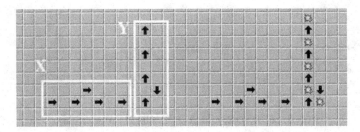

**Fig. 4.** On the left, the starting configuration representing a candle (switch) divided into two sub-structures $X$ and $Y$. On the right, the configuration obtained after placing a spark near by the leftmost arrow.

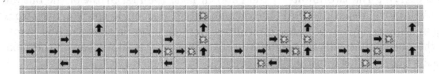

**Fig. 5.** The first configuration represents an alternative way for realizing a switch. The second and the third configurations are obtained alternately once a spark is placed near by the leftmost arrow. The last configuration can be obtained when switching off the candle, according to the time when a second spark arrives.

is provided by the two sub-structure depicted in the figure. First, an input spark is duplicated by means of the sub-structure $X$. Then, the two consecutive sparks arrive to the cycle in the sub-structure $Y$. If the candle is off (i.e., the cycle is empty), then the effect of the two sparks is that of filling the cycle, and hence the candle turns on. If the candle was on, then the two consecutive sparks remove the ones contained in the cycle since the entering arrow of the cycle will be neighbor of two sparks for two steps. Another way for realizing the candle is shown in Fig. 5. However, this configuration reveals a weird side effect. In fact, if a spark is placed near by the leftmost arrow, the system moves to an instable situation where the candle is switched on, but the configuration alternates between the second and the third ones shown in the figure. When another spark enters the system, the candle is switched off, but according to the time this new spark arrives, the configuration might become either the original one or the fourth one. Clearly, the configurations shown so far represent only few samples with respect to the potentials of Scintillae. The ability of the user to find new ways of composing the available pieces might realize surprising configurations.

## 3    From the Game to Computing

In this section, we exploit some of the potentials of Scintillae in order to realize computing systems. An interesting peculiarity of Scintillae is its nice attitude to provide a way for realizing combinatorial circuits. We now show how to implement the basic logic gates like *XOR, OR, NOT* and *AND*.

**Fig. 6.** *XOR*, *OR*, and *NOT* realized on Scintillae

The most natural logic gate obtainable by composing few lines of arrows is the *XOR*. As shown in Fig. 6, it is enough to put a line of arrows between the two lines carrying the two inputs of the gate. In fact, the first arrow of the output line will move a spark towards the output only if one single spark arrives from the input lines. When both the input lines carry on a spark, then the first arrow of the output line will be neighboring two sparks that disappear at the next clock's tick, as shown in the fifth configuration of Fig. 1.

*Remark 1.* Actually, a single arrow in Scintillae represents a *XOR* gate of three inputs, the neighboring squares not pointed by the arrow. It follows that any other logic gate obtainable by composing Scintillae's pieces is the result of composing *XOR* gates. Although the *XOR* is not a universal gate like the *NOR* and the *NAND* gates (see [10]), i.e., not all the other logic gates can be obtained from the *XOR*, we show how this problem can be overcome in Scintillae. Even tough this seems a contradiction, it will be better clarified later on.

Realizing the *OR* gate is also quite easy since it requires a little modification with respect to the *XOR*, as shown in Fig. 6. Now, if both the input lines carry on a spark, they will be both moved to the tail of the output line, where it appears like only one spark as output. In order to realize the *NOT*, a bit more understanding is required. In fact, we need to have a spark in the output line when there is nothing in input. In order to realize such a configuration, we make use of an infinite generator of sparks, as shown in the fifth configuration of Fig. 2. As shown in Fig. 6, when the input line carries on a spark, the middle arrow of that line will be neighboring with two sparks, as in the sixth configuration of Fig. 1, and then there won't be a spark at its head in the next clock's tick.

*Remark 2.* In the construction of the *NOT* gate resides the trick to obtain any other logic gate by means of *XOR* gates. In fact, once we have both the *OR* and the *NOT* gates we can obtain any other gate. The fact is that we are using also sparks to realize the *NOT* gate. In particular, we are able to generate a sequence of infinite sparks representing a line set to 1, and this is not possible when considering only *XOR* gates.

Concerning the *AND* gate, by simply applying De Morgan's rule [10], it can be realized as *NOT*(*NOT*(A) *OR* *NOT*(B)). This is shown in the first configuration of Fig. 7. In the same figure, the other configuration still realizes the *AND* gate

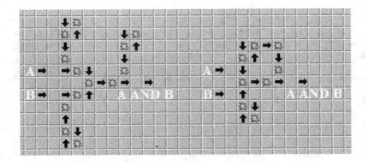

**Fig. 7.** Two configurations realizing the *AND* gate

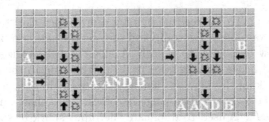

**Fig. 8.** Other two possible ways for realizing the *AND* gate

but some more insights are required for its understanding. It comes from the requirement of obtaining the "easiest" way for realizing such a gate. As part of the game, we tried to obtain the same results by means of optimized configurations in terms of used pieces. For the case of the *AND* gate, for instance, while the first configuration of Fig. 7 is quite straightforward since obtained by applying well-known rules, the other comes from our intuitions. Indeed, the rational behind it is simply to merge the infinite generators of the first configuration as much as possible. More tricky configurations that realize the *AND* gate are shown in Fig. 8. These required much more confidence with the game.

Another interesting circuit obtained by serializing some candles and appropriately connecting them with infinite generators, realizes a binary counter as shown in Fig. 9. The assumption is that 1 corresponds to the candle switched on, 0 otherwise. In the figure, it is shown a snapshot of the system after injecting eleven sparks as input (rightmost arrow ←).

In Fig. 10, we show a memory component of one byte with recorded value 11011100. The byte is contained in the cycle *M*. In order to read the value contained in the memory, one has to insert a spark in the read line *R*. For a correct reading of the byte, the input spark must arrive at line *R* synchronously with a spark that in the CLOCK cycle occupies the bottom leftmost square as in the figure.[2] Then a copy of the correct sequence describing the byte will flow

---

[2] The cycle defining the CLOCK is not really part of the memory, but is visualized only for a correct use of the memory component.

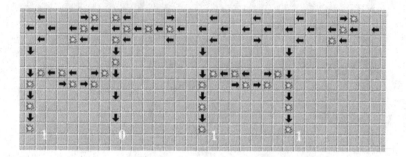

**Fig. 9.** A binary 4-bits counter

on the output line $O$. This is realized by temporarily open the "tap" $T3$ between $M$ and line $O$. A tap like $T3$ is composed of a candle and two paths that leads to the same arrow belonging to a path. A closed tap is realized by switching on the candle and hence making two sparks neighboring to the common arrow of a line, i.e., blocking the flow on that line. To open the tap, it is sufficient to switch off the candle, hence removing the block. Note that, on the way from $R$ to $T3$, the line $P2$ is used to duplicate the input spark in such a way that, after eight clock's ticks, the tap is automatically closed, hence letting flow only eight bits on the output line $O$. The input line $C$ is used to clean the memory. In fact, when a spark enters this way, it is duplicated by means of line $P1$ in such a way that the two sparks reach the tap $T1$ and make it closed for exactly eight clock's ticks. In doing so, two sparks become neighbors to a common arrow of $M$, hence obtaining the delation of the contained byte. By using the $C$ line, one obtains also another effect, that is, to open tap $T2$ for exactly eight clock's ticks. This is, in fact, used for writing in the memory. To write a new byte in the memory, the sequence of sparks describing the new byte must arrive at the input line $W$ concurrently with a spark at line $C$. Hence, $M$ is first cleaned and then refilled with the new sequence. For the synchronization of such operations we were required to carefully consider the length of the involved lines.

## 4   A Case Study

Based on some previous configurations, we might be able to simulate any combinatorial circuit. In this section, we aim to construct a circuit that counts from 0 to 3, cyclically, and displays the outcome on a standard seven-bars display. Moreover, we make also the display by means of the Scintillae's pieces. In doing so, we provide the evidence that Scintillae can be used for both computing and wider purposes more related to aesthetical factors. In Fig. 11, the mentioned configuration is shown. The snapshot is taken while the counter is displaying the number 2 on the seven-bars display realized by means of arrows. We are now going to describe all the "objects" composing the whole circuits. In order to realize the desired counter we need four main sub-circuits: (i) a clock that

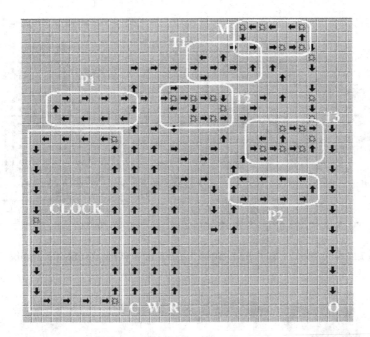

**Fig. 10.** A byte memory cell

frequently generates a signal in order to advance the counting; (ii) a counter that translates the received signal from the clock into a binary string representing how many signals have been received modulo the size of the counter (four in our case); (iii) a seven-bars display that has seven input lines for switching on the correspondent bars (see Fig. 12); (iv) a circuit able to convert the binary string representing a digit among the set $\{0, 1, 2, 3\}$ into the suitable signals that switch on the appropriate bars on the display for a correct visualization.

As discussed in the previous section, (i) and (ii) have been already realized. In fact, (i) is obtained by a cycle of arrows with one spark inside (see bottom left side of Fig. 11). In this way, we generate a spark every time the one in the cycle covers all the cycle. Clearly, the more is the length of the cycle, the less is the speed of the counter. The output of such a cycle is connected to a 2-bits counter (similar to the one shown in Fig. 9, see on the left side of Fig. 11) that provides the correct binary coding of the number of sparks received in input, modulo four. The construction realizing (iii) can be easily recognized on the right part of Fig. 11, with its seven input lines surrounding the display. This has been realized by means of a suitable disposal of the arrows, some of which are there only for aesthetical reasons. Concerning (iv), the circuit for converting the binary string into switching signals for the seven-bars display is shown in Fig. 12, along with the activation functions related to the bars of the display. Such a circuit is a bit hidden in Fig. 9, but following the lines from the counter to the display, one can easily recognize the logic gates used. Indeed, many of the arrows are used for crossing lines by means of the horizontal configuration shown

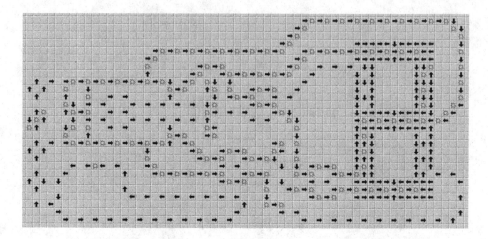

**Fig. 11.** Snapshot of a cyclic counter form 0 to 3 while displaying number 2

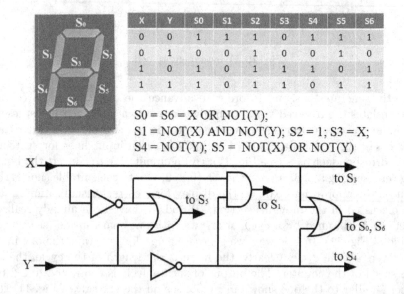

| X | Y | S0 | S1 | S2 | S3 | S4 | S5 | S6 |
|---|---|----|----|----|----|----|----|----|
| 0 | 0 | 1 | 1 | 1 | 0 | 1 | 1 | 1 |
| 0 | 1 | 0 | 0 | 1 | 0 | 0 | 1 | 0 |
| 1 | 0 | 1 | 0 | 1 | 1 | 1 | 0 | 1 |
| 1 | 1 | 1 | 0 | 1 | 1 | 0 | 1 | 1 |

S0 = S6 = X OR NOT(Y);
S1 = NOT(X) AND NOT(Y); S2 = 1; S3 = X;
S4 = NOT(Y); S5 = NOT(X) OR NOT(Y)

**Fig. 12.** The seven-bars display, the activation functions of its input lines, and the circuit used to convert a binary string of two bits XY into the appropriate signals for visualizing the input number by means of a decimal digit on a seven-bars display

in Fig. 3. Concerning, for instance the activation function of $S_1$, the *AND* gate has been realized by means of the first configuration shown in Fig. 8. Concerning $S_2$, since the specific circuit counts cyclically from 0 to 3, its activation function is always set to 1. This has been realized by embedding directly in the display an infinite generator of sparks. Moreover, it is interesting to note that, if we add more consecutive sparks in the cycle that provides the input to the counter, we may obtain the visualization of the digits corresponding to the current digit plus the number of sparks in the cycle modulo four. In particular, if we put three consecutive sparks in the cycle, we obtain a cyclic countdown from 3 to 0. Actually, the same effect might be realized by reducing the length of the cycle so much that the display is not able to visualize all the input sequence. This implies a refresh frequency of the designed display that must be carefully managed by prolonging or shortening the connecting lines.

## 5    Conclusion

We have presented Scintillae, a new and simple cellular automaton that reveals high computational power capabilities. Surprising results have been obtained by suitably placing the few pieces provided by the game. As future work, we aim to write the code of Scintillae for open source platforms, and adding further capabilities to make easier its usage. For instance, it would be very useful to exploit configurations already defined as black boxes for new configurations. This would expand the visual programming features of the game. Moreover, educational characteristics could also be exploited. In fact, Scintillae turns out to be a very good mean for experiencing sequential circuits, but also for an easy approach to low level programming languages like assembly.

**Historical Note and Acknowledgement.**    A first version of Scintillae has been implemented by Gabriele Di Stefano on a PC Olivetti M24 in the mid-eighties. Special thanks go to Gian Marco Tedesco for his great contribution in coding Scintillae with graphic libraries, for his insights and useful discussions.

## References

1. http://www.dmi.unipg.it/navarra/Scintillae/scintillae.zip
2. http://gs.ing.univaq.it/Scintillae/scintillae.zip
3. Chang, S.K.: Visual Languages and Visual Programming (Languages and Information Systems). Springer (1990)
4. Adamatzky, A.: Game of Life Cellular Automata. Springer (2011)
5. Gardner, M.: The fantastic combinations of John Conway's new solitaire game "Life". Scientific American 223, 120–123 (1970)
6. http://www.bitstorm.org/gameoflife/
7. Kari, J.: Theory of cellular automata: a survey. Theoretical Compututer Science 334, 3–33 (2005)
8. Wolfram, S.: A New Kind of Science. Wolfram Media, Inc. (2002)
9. Dewdney, A.K.: Computer recreations: The cellular automata programs that create wireworld, rugworld and other diversions. Scientific American 262, 146–149 (1990)
10. Patterson, D.A., Hennessy, J.L.: Computer Organization and Design: The Hardware/Software Interface. Elsevier Inc. (2007)

# Cellular Automata Analysis on Self-assembly Properties in DNA Tile Computing

Miki Hirabayashi[1], Syunsuke Kinoshita[2], Shukichi Tanaka[1], Hajime Honda[2], Hiroaki Kojima[1], and Kazuhiro Oiwa[1]

[1] Advanced ICT Research Institute, National Institute of Information and Communications Technology (NICT), Japan
[2] Department of Engineering, Nagaoka University of Technology, Japan

**Abstract.** An Analysis on the self-assembly process in DNA tile computing is presented using the cellular automata approach. It is known that a cellular automata model can simulate various complex systems by updating the states of calculation cells based on the local interaction rules. Generally DNA computing is operated through the local interaction between complimentary strands. Therefore the cellular automata approach is suitable to investigate qualitative features of such systems. Focusing on the cryptosystem using a DNA motif called a triple crossover (TX) tile, we construct a new cellular automata model. Our objective is to find a solution to improve the fragmentation problem in the self-assembly process of a calculation sheet of TX tiles, because the fragmentation prevents the system from realizing the sufficient performance. Our results suggest that such fragmentation occurs when the error correction function is lost due to the strong stability of local interaction. It is expected that these findings using cellular automata simulations provide effective information to solve the problems to develop practical applications of DNA-based computation.

**Keywords:** DNA computing, self-assembly, DNA cryptosystem, pattern formation.

## 1 Introduction

DNA realizes the information processing system that integrates hardware and software, and executes sophisticated biological functions based on genetic information. In the field of nanotechnology, DNA attracts attention as an intelligent material. Here we present a new cellular automaton [1] model to solve problems that we are faced with when we develop the DNA cryptosystem using a DNA motif called a triple crossover (TX) tile (Fig. 1). Connection rules are programmed in the sequence of a sticky end, which is an overhang at the end of a DNA strand as shown in Fig. 1. A TX tile that we used consists of four single-stranded DNAs. It exchanges complementary strands and forms the three double helical domains (Fig. 1). Utilizing this structural feature, we can design

G.C. Sirakoulis and S. Bandini (Eds.): ACRI 2012, LNCS 7495, pp. 544–553, 2012.

à reporter strand running through the diagonal array to associate the calculated output of the tile computing [2]. It was shown that the XOR calculation can be performed using this reporter strand [2]. Taking advantage of these features, we can construct unbreakable XOR cryptosystems without any external random source [3,4,5,6,7].

In the DNA cryptosystem, well-controlled structure growth is essential for practical use. Especially in our multi-layer model [6], DNA tiles must form many layers as shown in Fig. 2(a). Nevertheless, in fact we observe nothing but small fragments as shown in Fig. 2(b). It seems that artificial DNA structures with complex functions are subject to the fragmentation in the self-assembly process. The adequate growth of the connection of TX tiles is crucial for our DNA cryptosystem to fulfill a sufficient function. In this work, we developed a new cellular automata model to investigate the cause of this fragmentation and find a solution to improve the systems.

Cellular automata provide a discrete model that consists of lattice cells in one of finite states updated by local interaction rules. It is known that the cellular automata approach is effective to analyze on complex phenomena generated by simple local interactions. As mentioned in the previous paragraph, in DNA tile computing, connection rules are programmed in the sticky-end sequence utilizing the hybridization features between complimentary strands. Therefore the cellular automata analysis is suitable to investigate the calculation process of the DNA tile computing operated based on such simple local interactions.

Our simulation results show that the fragmentation occurs when the error correction function is lost due to the strong stability of the sticky-end connection. We can solve this fragmentation problem by improving the operating protocol or the sequence at the sticky end. The information processing by DNAs in natural systems realizes the advanced control utilizing instability. As for artificial systems

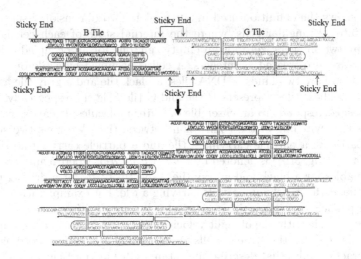

**Fig. 1.** Examples of triple-crossover DNA tiles

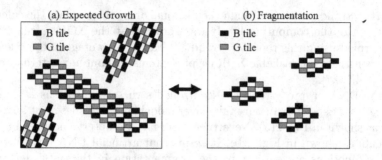

**Fig. 2.** An example of fragmentation

using TX tiles, it is expected that practical applications can be constructed by the system optimization through the introduction of the instability to avoid the fragmentation. A cellular automata approach will offer an effective tool to design practical applications of DNA-based computation.

## 2 Cellular Automata Modeling for the DNA Tile Computation

A cellular automata model to simulate the programmed assembly of a calculation sheet of DNA tiles is shown in this section. Utilizing local interactions, the following model implements the connection rules programmed in sticky ends of DNA tiles.

### 2.1 Space Partitioning and State Definition

Figure 3 shows the definition used in our model. Two dimensional space is discretized into rectangular cells, where the internal state of each cell is distinguished by two integers; zero for an empty cell, one for an occupied cell. Time and space are also treated as integers. A cell is occupied by a tile or a driving particle. There are two kinds of DNA tiles; a black tile and a gray tile as shown in Fig. 3(a). These tiles represent B tile and G tile (Fig. 1) respectively. A driving particle corresponds to an ensemble of water molecules. It carries a tile and promotes the switching of the connection between tiles. We have two states of driving particles; a particle carrying a tile and a particle carrying no tile. The internal state (Fig. 3(b)) is denoted by $S = \{b, g, d_0, d_1\}$, where $b$ and $g$ represent state valuables for a black and a gray tile respectively, $d_0$ for a driving particle with no tile, $d_1$ for a driving particle carrying a tile. For example, when there is a driving particle carrying a tile in a target cell, we can write as $S = \{0, 0, 0, 1\}$. A driving particle with one of eight velocities (Fig. 3(c)) propagates to a neighbor cell and updates the state of cells at each simulation step according to the local interaction rules that describe the action of driving particles ("put", "lift", and "keep") based on the states of neighbor cells as mentioned later. The basic

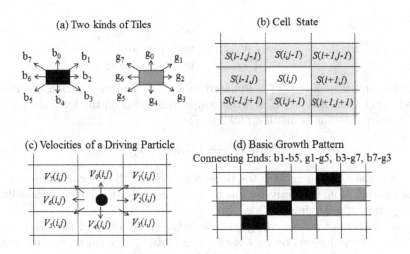

**Fig. 3.** Definition of neighbor in two dimensional model

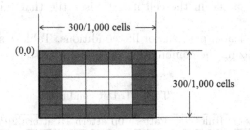

**Fig. 4.** Two-dimensional simulation field

growth pattern is shown in Fig. 3(d). The filled square represents that the cell is filled by a tile and the unfilled a vacant space. Figure 4 shows a simulation field. Filled squares represent a boundary wall area.

## 2.2   Definition of Local Rules

As mentioned above, state parameters given in each cell are updated at every discrete timestep according to local interaction rules. The update scheme consists of the collision step and the propagation step. During the propagation step, a driving particle moves to one of neighbor cells determined by the direction of own velocity. At the collision step, the internal state $S$ of a cell is updated according to the evolution rule. When a driving particle goes into a wall in a boundary area or a DNA tile, the propagation velocity is chosen with the predetermined probability based on the following rule:

$$V_i'(i = 0, 1, \ldots, 7) = \begin{cases} V_{i \, mod \, 3} & \text{with probability } p = 1/3 \; ; \\ V_{i \, mod \, 4} & \text{with probability } p = 1/3 \; ; \\ V_{i \, mod \, 5} & \text{with probability } p = 1/3 \; . \end{cases} \tag{1}$$

Thus the current velocity $V_i$ is updated to $V_i'$. By the propagation of driving particles, the internal state $S$ of a cell is updated based on the local interaction rule associated to the transition function $f$:

$$f : \{S, x, t\} \longrightarrow \{S', x, t + 1\}, \tag{2}$$

where $x$ is the position and $t$ is the time. $S$ and $S'$ are the internal states before and after transition, respectively. The update function or the local rule is defined by the action of a driving particle.

Figure 5 shows that a driving particle takes three kinds of actions ("put", "lift", and "keep") based on its tile-carrying status and local interaction rules. One sticky end of a tile can connect with a complimentary sticky end of another tile. A driving particle can put a carrying tile in the cell if there is a tile with a complimentary sticky end in a neighbor cell. A driving particle carrying no tile can lift a tile in the cell if there is a tile that fulfills the provided lift condition.

Figure 6 indicates patterns of lift conditions. Table 1 shows the applied lift conditions utilizing the combination of these lift patterns.

**Table 1.** Lift conditions

| Local Rules | Pattern 0 | Pattern 1 | Pattern 2 | Pattern 3 |
|-------------|-----------|-----------|-----------|-----------|
| Lift Condition 0 | + | - | - | - |
| Lift Condition 1 | + | + | - | - |
| Lift Condition 2 | + | + | + | - |
| Lift Condition 3 | + | + | + | + |

## 3   Model Verification

Figure 7 shows snapshots of simulation results using four lift conditions in Table 1. The calculation space is divided into $300 \times 300$ cells. Using 45 driving particles, 110 black tiles, and 110 gray tiles, we verify fundamental properties of our cellular automata model. The color coding of tiles is useful to know a correct growth block of tiles. We can distinguish a correct block in an alternate order of black and gray stripes. Convergence properties are represented by the percentage of moving tiles being carried by driving particles. Moving tiles are represented by filled circles (Fig. 5). They are not visible as tiles when they are

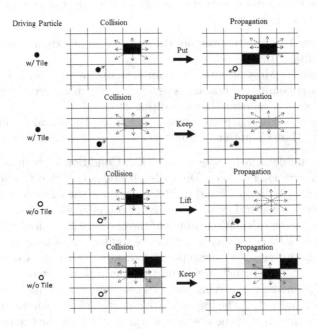

**Fig. 5.** Actions of a driving particle

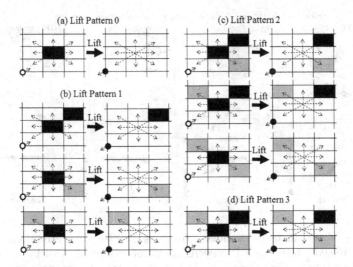

**Fig. 6.** Examples of lift patterns for a black tile by a free particle (without carrying a tile) with $V_1$ velocity. Pattern (a) target tile with no connection tile, (b) target tile with one connection tile, (c) target tile with two connection tiles, (d) target tile with three connection tiles.

moving. These results indicate that convergence patterns can be classified based on their behaviors as follows;

**(1)** Quasi-Class 1 : An initial random state converges quickly into a stable state (Lift Condition 0).
**(2)** Quasi-Class 2 : Most of initial random patterns evolve quickly into a stable state. At the boundary of patterns oscillating structures are observed. Local changes do not disappear (Lift Condition 1).
**(3)** Quasi-Class 3 : Initial patterns continue to evolve. Local changes spread indefinitely (Lift Conditions 2 and 3).

Our experimental data [3,4] suggest that "Lift Condition 1" is matched to the empirical hybridization process of DNA tiles. It is expected that the probabilistic mixture of "Lift Condition 1" and "Lift Condition 2" provides a more realistic simulation, because natural systems consist of probabilistic processes.

Figure 8 shows the calculation results of the cases with two-fold driving particles. Driving particles carry tiles and produce similar effects to water molecules. In figs. 7 and 8, convergence timesteps are indicated by arrows. Compared with both values, we can find that driving particles have the effect to accelerate the calculation. The increase of driving particles can represent the increase of kinetic energy of water molecules. The fragmentation problem is not solved here. By the investigation of the effect of the tile increase, an analysis on the fragmentation of a tile sheet is shown in the following section. We will try a relaxed lift condition, too.

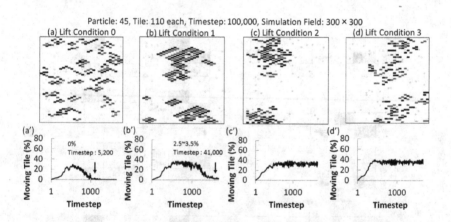

**Fig. 7.** Snapshots of simulation results of the cases in different lift conditions shown in Table 1 at 100,000 timesteps and convergence properties represented by the percentage of moving tiles (single logarithmic plot). The convergence timesteps are indicated by arrows. Moving tiles are tiles being carried by driving particles (small filled/open circles). Two colors of tiles are useful to know a correct growth block of tiles by an alternate order of black and gray stripes.

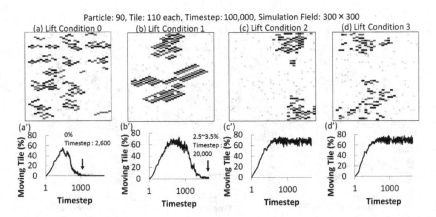

**Fig. 8.** Snapshots of simulation results of the cases with 90 driving particles and convergence properties (single logarithmic plot). The convergence timesteps are indicated by arrows. Compared with Fig. 7, driving particles have the effect to accelerate the calculation. Driving particles carry tiles and promote the switching of the connection between tiles. They can produce similar effects to water molecules. The increase of driving particles can represent the increase of kinetic energy of water molecules. The fragmentation problem is not solved.

## 4    Fragmentation Analysis

Figure 9 shows that the increase of tile numbers (from 1,000 to 2,000) does not provide the remarkable improvement of the fragmentation problem, but the relaxed lift conditions bring the growth of a fragment block. The calculation space is divided into $1,000 \times 1,000$ cells. We use 400 driving particles, 1,000/2,000 black tiles, and 1,000/2,000 gray tiles here. The relaxed lift condition is realized by the probabilistic lift actions (50%) in "Lift Condition 2". The introduction of relaxed lift conditions corresponds to the implementation of error tolerance.

These results indicate that the appropriate reconnection of a tile leads the desirable growth of a fragment, because a outer tile in a small block can move to a more preferable cell with adequate neighbors. This action reduces a small block and increases a large stable block. In the molecular biological experiment, the reconnection can be realized by the higher reaction temperature or the nucleic-acid base sequence with a low guanine and cytosine content at the connection end.

The experimental data [3,4] shows the intermediate state of Fig. 9(b) and Fig. 9(c). By the introduction of further probabilistic processes, we will be able to learn more about the optimization of tile computing systems from the cellular automata approach. For example, the holes in a block are formed due to the restriction caused by 2-dimensional movements of driving particles. This problem will be solved by the introduction of probabilistic permeable processes of driving particles. It is expected that this procedure will realize pseudo 3-dimensional actions.

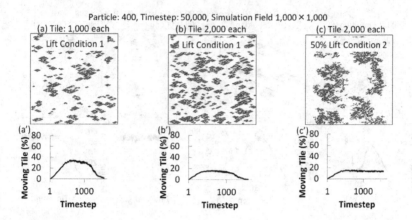

Fig. 9. Fragmentation analysis. Snapshots of simulation results of the cases with 1,000/2,000 tiles and convergence properties (single logarithmic plot) are shown. The increase of tiles does not solve the fragmentation problem remarkably. The relaxed lift conditions bring large blocks of tile assemblies. .

## 5   Conclusion

We presented a new cellular automata model to investigate the empirical problem of DNA tile computing. Focusing on the fragmentation problem that reduces the calculation performance, we find that the lost of error correction function brings this kind of fragmentation when the tile connection has the strong stability. It is expected that this problem will be solved by improving the experimental protocol and the sticky-end sequence to introduce the adequate instability. For example, we can treat samples at the higher reaction temperature or use the sequence with a low guanine and cytosine content to introduce the instability as mentioned in the previous section.

Although a cellular automata model just consider limited conditions through simple interaction rules, it is suitable to estimate characteristic features brought by target conditions. We can use simulation findings to improve the experimental design to develop the DNA cryptosystem which is a promising application of molecular computing. Shannon has proven that unbreakable cryptosystem is realized by the one-time use of a true random key at every encryption [8]. The generation of sufficient amounts of true random numbers is not easy, because mathematical algorithm can generate pseudo-random numbers only and therefore we need an intrinsic physical random process to generate true random numbers. In such a physical process, sometimes random events are too rare to provide the enough amounts of random numbers. Or the observation of random events is difficult or costs much, or destroys the randomness. The DNA cryptosystem can provide random numbers as much as necessary through the calculation process utilizing the random self-assembly events without external physical random source [3,4,6]. Thus it is expected the DNA cryptosystem can realize the unbreakable cryptosystem, because DNA calculates utilizing physical processes that can include the physical random number generation.

In this work we showed that the cellular automata approach is effective to get suggestions to solve empirical problems. Experimental investigations of all possible conditions require a financial infusion, therefore this kind of numerical simulation plays important roles in the development of new technologies. By further improvements toward the realization of practical applications, our cellular automata model will reveal the influence of other parameters and provide significant supports to design new experiments and analyze empirical data effectively.

# References

1. Chopard, B., Droz, M.: Cellular Automata Modeling of Physical Systems. Cambridge University Press, Cambridge (1998)
2. Mao, C., LaBean, T.H., Reif, J.H., Seeman, N.C.: Logical computation using algorithmic self-assembly of DNA triple-crossovermolecules. Nature 407, 493–496 (2000)
3. Hirabayashi, M., Nishikawa, A., Tanaka, F., Hagiya, M., Kojima, H., Oiwa, K.: Analysis on Secure and Effective Applications of a DNA - Based Cryptosystem. In: 6th IEEE International Conference on Bio-Inspired Computing: Theory and Applications, pp. 205–210 (2011)
4. Hirabayashi, M., Nishikawa, A., Tanaka, F., Hagiya, M., Kojima, H., Oiwa, K.: Implementation of tile sequencing for DNA logical computation toward next-generation information security. In: 5th IEEE International Conference on Bio-Inspired Computing: Theory and Applications, pp. 1296–1307 (2010)
5. Hirabayashi, M., Kojima, H., Oiwa, K.: Effective algorithm to encrypt information based on self-assembly of DNA tiles. Nucleic Acids Symposium Series, vol. 53. Oxford Press (2009)
6. Hirabayashi, M., Kojima, H., Oiwa, K.: Design of true random one-time-pads in DNA XOR cryptosystem. In: 4th International Workshop on Natural Computing, vol. 2, pp. 174–183 (2010)
7. Chen, Z., Xu, J.: One-Time-Pads Encryption in the Tile Assembly Model. In: Third International Conference on Bio-Inspired Computing: Theories and Applications, pp. 23–29 (2008)
8. Shannon, C.: Communication Theory of Secrecy Systems. Bell System Technical Journal 28(4), 656–715 (1949)

# Quantum–Dot Cellular Automata Design for Median Filtering and Mathematical Morphology Operations on Binary Images

Fotios K. Panagiotopoulos, Vassilios A. Mardiris, and Vassilios Chatzis

Department of Information Management
Technological Institute of Kavala, Greece
{fpanag,mardiris,chatzis}@teikav.edu.gr

**Abstract.** The continuing development of smaller electronic devices into the nanometer regime offers great possibilities of highly parallel computing systems, as it allows to reduce power consumption and device sizes and to increase operating speed. Quantum-dot Cellular Automata (QCA) has been proposed as an alternative for nanoelectronic devices and introduces a new opportunity for the design of highly parallel algorithms and architectures. Its benefits are the fast speed, very small size, high density and low energy consumption. These advantages can be very useful for various real time image processing applications. Complex image processing algorithms include in many cases the well-known binary median filter and mathematical morphology operations such as dilation and erosion. In this paper we propose and simulate two innovative QCA circuits which implement the dilation and the erosion.

**Keywords:** Dot Cellular Automata, circuit design, circuit simulation, nanoelectronics, median filter, mathematical morphology, binary image.

## 1 Introduction

In many image processing applications it is often required to attenuate noise while certain properties of the image should be preserved to enhance the final outcome. Nonlinear filtering techniques have been proven able to remove different types of noise, while at the same time they preserve some desired image properties. One of the well-known nonlinear filter is the median, which is able to remove impulse noise while preserving the edges in images [1-3]. Another nonlinear image processing technique is mathematical morphology [4]. Mathematical morphology is based on the shape of an object contained in an image and it is strongly related with set theory and Minkowski algebra [5]. Mathematical morphology was initially applied only on binary images, but later several generalizations and variations have been proposed in order to be applied on grey-level or colored images [6-8]. The main advantages of mathematical morphology algorithms are their efficiency to model the shape of an object and their fast hardware implementations. They have been used in various

G.C. Sirakoulis and S. Bandini (Eds.): ACRI 2012, LNCS 7495, pp. 554–564, 2012.

applications for example for edge detection, object or character recognition, shape description and reconstruction [9-11].

Although median and morphological filters have been expensively used in past, they are still used in many modern algorithms either in preprocessing steps or as parts of more complex algorithms, which support systems for computer vision, real time image or video processing, information retrieval in multimedia databases etc. During the application of complex algorithms there are intermediate results where binary images arise. Binary images are usually results of grey level or color image segmentation or thresholding techniques. So, the application of nonlinear filters on binary images is also a useful and demanding task. Besides, in many of the above mentioned systems the need for fast implementation of algorithms is imperative.

Digital image processing is an ever expanding and dynamic area with applications reaching out into our everyday life such medicine, space, exploration, surveillance, authentication and many more areas. Applications such as these involve different processes like image enhancement and object detection. Implementing such applications on a general purpose computer can be easy, but not very efficient due to additional constraints on memory and other peripheral devices [12]. Application specific hardware implementation offers much greater operation speeds than a software implementation. Implementing complex computation tasks on hardware by exploiting parallelism and pipelining in algorithms, yield significant reduction in execution times [13-15]. Because of these advantages VLSI (Very Large Scale Integrated) technology hardware implementation has become the dominant approach over the ultra-high speed image processing implementations.

Emerging nanoelectronic technologies have been the focus of extensive research while conventional VLSI technologies are reaching their limits. Computation at nano regimes is substantially different from conventional VLSI. Extremely small feature size, high device density and low power are some of the attributes that emerging technologies addresses, while implementing new computational paradigms. The international roadmap for semiconductors has enumerated several nanoelectronic alternatives including Resonant Tunneling Diodes (RTD), Quantum-dot Cellular Automata (QCA), Tunneling Phase Logic (TPL) and Single Electron Tunneling (SET) [16-18]. One of the most promising nanoelectronic technologies is QCA, which can provide high device density, low power consumption and high switching speeds [19]. Additionally, QCA introduces a new information representation approach, which provides new very interesting design characteristics and leads to the development of new design methodologies.

Several logic gates and computing devices are implemented with QCAs. Basic implementations that have been proposed are: the binary wire, the majority gate, AND gate, OR gate, NOT gate, XOR gate [20], bit-serial adder [21,22], full adder [20,21,23], multiplier [24], CAs [25], multiplexer [26-28], flip-flop [29,30], serial memory [31,32], parallel memory [33], Arithmetic Logic Unit (ALU) [34], microprocessor [34], PLA [35] etc.

Regarding the use of QCAs in image processing, weighted median filter has been reported in [36] but there are several doubts whether the proposed design is able to pass the simulation, and in [37] a directional marginal median filter has been proposed without a QCA implementation.

In this paper two morphological filter QCA circuits are designed and simulated. The circuits have been designed according to the QCA design rules [23], especially focusing on circuit functionality robustness. The new QCA implementations provide high circuit performance, very low dimension, parallel processing and very low power consumption. These characteristics makes the proposed implementations suitable for systems applied on fast growing area of mobile or autonomous devices.

In the following Section we will make a synoptic description of Binary Median Filter and Mathematical Morphology, which is the objective of our implementation. In Section 3 the background of QCA technology and design techniques will be presented. The design and simulation of the proposed circuits will be presented in Section 4. Finally, in Section 5 we will discuss the conclusion and the areas of future work.

## 2     Overview of Binary Image Processing Algorithms

### 2.1     Binary Median Filter

A median filter is a non–linear digital filter which is able to preserve sharp image changes and is very effective in removing impulse noise. Linear filters don't have ability to remove this type of noise without affecting the distinguishing characteristics of the image. Median filters have the remarkable advantages over linear filters for this particular type of noise. Therefore median filter is very widely used in digital image processing applications.

A standard median operation is implemented by sliding a window of odd size (3 x 3 pixels) over an image. At each windows position, the sampled image values are sorted and the median value of the sample, replaces the sample in the center pixel of the window. In case of binary images there are only two possible values (0, 1) and the median of the sample is always the value of the majority.

### 2.2     Mathematical Morphology Operations

"Morphology" can literally be taken to mean "doing things to shapes". "Mathematical Morphology" then, by extension, means using mathematical principles to do things to shapes. In other words, it is a theory which provides a number of useful tools for image analysis. It is based on the assumption that an image consists of structures which may be handled by set theory. The initial form of mathematical morphology is applied to binary images and usually referred to as standard mathematical morphology in the literature in order to be discriminated by its later extensions such as the grey-scale and the soft mathematical morphology.

Erosion and dilation are elementary morphological operations, which conform to Minkowski – addition and subtraction. They combine two sets $A \subseteq Z^2$ and $S \subseteq Z^2$ by the following set translation:

- Dilation :

$$A \oplus S = \bigcup_{s \in S}\{A + s\} \tag{1}$$

- Erosion :

$$A \ominus S = \bigcap_{s \in S}\{A - s\} \tag{2}$$

The operation is characterized by S which is often called "structuring element". Let us assume an image with a black object in a white background. Dilation and erosion are shown at the following example in Fig.1.

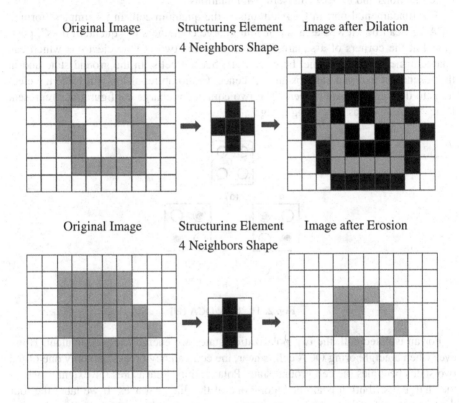

**Fig. 1.** Dilation and Erosion examples applied on binary images

At the dilation and erosion example we can see the prior form of the image and how the operations using the 4-neighbors structuring element transforms the original image. Dilation and erosion can be applied for the given structuring element by following the next steps. At the dilation if the origin of the structuring element coincides with a "black" image pixel, make black all pixels from the image covered by the structuring element. If the origin of the structuring element coincides with a 'white' image pixel just move to the next pixel. At the erosion if the origin of the structuring element coincides with a "black" pixel image, and at least one of the "black" pixels in the structuring element falls over a "white" image pixel, then change the "black" pixel in the image from "black" to "white". If the origin of the structuring element coincides with a "white" pixel in the image there is no change, move to the next pixel.

# 3    QCA Background

QCA is a nanoelectronic digital logic architecture in which information is stored as configuration of electron pairs in quantum dot arrays and have been originally proposed by Lent et al [20]. QCA use arrays of coupled quantum dots to build Boolean logic functions and to perform useful computations.

The fundamental unit in QCA circuits is the quantum cell. In its simplest form, a QCA cell can be viewed as a set of four charge containers or "quantum dots", positioned at the corners of a square. The cell contains two mobile electrons which can quantum mechanically tunnel between dots, but not cells. In the ground state and in the absence of external electrostatic influence, Coulomb repulsion will force the electrons to dots on opposite corners. The two equivalent charge configurations represent logic "1" and "0", as presenting in fig.2.

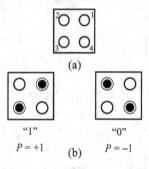

(a)

"1"
$P = +1$

(b)

"0"
$P = -1$

**Fig. 2.** The basic QCA cell

For an isolated cell, the two polarization states are energetically equivalent. However when a neighboring QCA cell is near, the equivalency breaks and only one of the two states becomes the cell ground state. Polarization, $P$ measures the extent to which the charge distribution is aligned along one of the diagonal axes. If we label the four dots from 1 to 4 anti-clockwise starting from the upper right dot of the cell, and assign $\rho_i$ as the electron density of the $i^{th}$ dot, $P$ is defined as:

$$P = \frac{(\rho_1 + \rho_3) - (\rho_2 + \rho_4)}{\rho_1 + \rho_2 + \rho_3 + \rho_4} \tag{3}$$

The polarization of a non-isolated cell is determined based on the interaction between neighboring cells [38]. Signal propagation in a QCA circuit takes place through a binary wire (fig.3). In the binary wire, a signal propagates from the input to output, since every cell in the row passes its state to the adjacent cell by Coulomb interactions.

It is possible to implement all logic functions by properly arranging cells so that the polarization of one cell sets the polarization of a nearby cell [39]. QCA circuits need four clock signals to synchronize and control the information flow. Every clock signal produces an electric field which controls the tunneling barrier between quantum-dots within a cell. When the potential barrier is low, the cell is unpolarized so the mobile electrons were released to move between the quantum dots. When the potential barrier is high, cells cannot change their state. QCA clocking includes four phases: switch phase, hold phase, release phase and relax phase and each of the four clock signals has a 90 degrees phase difference with the next one. The circuit is partitioned in clocking zones, in a way that every adjacent zone is clocked by its adjacent clock.

**Fig. 3.** Binary Wire

## 4    QCA Binary Median Filter

In general a binary median filter for image processing is implemented by sliding a window of odd size (3 x 3 pixels) over an image. At each windows position, the sampled image values are sorted and the median value of the sample, replaces the sample in the center pixel of the window. This operation can be transferred on hardware by implementing a nine input majority gate and use one input for each value of the 3x3 pixels window. The output of the majority gate will be the window's center pixel new value.

The three-input majority gate is one of the two basic logic gates implementations in QCA [20]. A three-input majority gate with the logic function of M (A, B, C) = AB+AC+BC is composed of five cells as shown in fig.4.

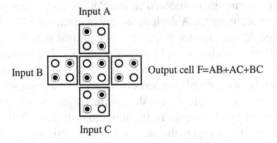

**Fig. 4.** QCA Majority gate

Five-input majority gates have been proposed in the literature [18,40-42].These implementations could be extended to design a nine input majority gate. This task will be addressed by the authors in future work.

# 5     QCA Implementation of Dilation and Erosion

## 5.1     Dilation

In this section we will present the QCA implementation of dilation operation using the 4 neighbors shape structuring element presented in example of fig.1. In general according to dilation operation, if the origin of the structuring element coincides with a "black" in the image, make black all pixels from the image covered by the structuring element and move to the next pixel. In the case of the selected structuring element, this is equivalent to: if at least one of the "black" pixels in the structuring element falls over a "black" pixel in the image, then make the pixel in the image that falls over the center pixel of the structuring element "black" and move to the next pixel.

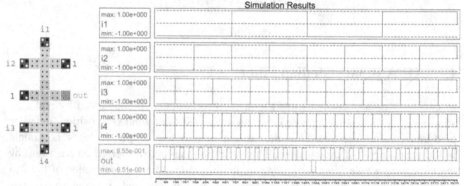

**Fig. 5.** Dilation QCA Circuit and Simulation Results

In QCA implementations it is very important to produce a design which can work with advanced stability [43]. Many times small QCA designs succeed in simulation but fail when they are used as parts of a larger design. In other cases the designers in order to manage their circuits to succeed in simulation, they tweak simulation model parameters. As a result many QCA designs are not operational.

For the proposed design in order to increase operational stability, we keep the maximum length of all wires within a clocking zone to 4 cells. The reason to do this is that as wire length grows the probability that a QCA cell will switch successfully decreases in proportion to the distance of this particular cell from a clamped (frozen) input at the beginning of the wire. Additionally, short wire lengths result in circuit operation in higher clock rates [23]. Furthermore the minimum distance between two wires is kept to 2 cells in order to minimize the undesirable interactions.

This operation can be transferred on hardware by implementing a 4-input OR gate, applying as inputs the values of the four pixels in the image corresponding to the four neighbors according to the structuring element. The output of the 4-input OR gate will be the new value of the pixel in image which corresponds to the center pixel of the structuring element. A 2-input OR gate in QCA is realized by clamping one input of the 3-input majority gate to logic '1'. In figure 5 the QCA implementation of the dilation operation is presented. In the design the maximum wire length in a clocking zone is kept to 4 cells and the minimum distance between to wires is 2 cells.

According to the QCADesigner tool [44] the design consists of 23 cells covering an area of 98 x 218 nm$^2$ that is approximately 0.021 µm$^2$. It is covering an area of 5 x 11 grids and the ratio of the area covered by QCA cells to the overall area of the layout is 0.418.

The simulation results of the design are presented in fig.5. As it is shown all possible value combinations of 4 inputs are applied to the circuit. The output is set to logic '0' only when all inputs stay at logic '0' otherwise is set to logic '1' indicating the OR gate behavior.

## 5.2    Erosion

In this section we will present the QCA implementation of erosion operation using the 4 neighbors shape structuring element presented in example of fig.1. In general according to erosion operation, if the origin of the structuring element coincides with a "black" in the image, and at least one of the "black" pixels in the structuring element falls over a "white" pixel in the image, then change the "black" pixel in the image that coincides with the origin, from "black" to "white". In other cases do nothing.

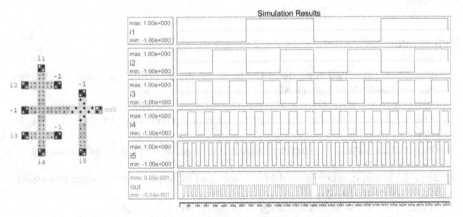

**Fig. 6.** Erosion QCA Circuit and Simulation Result

This operation can be transferred on hardware by implementing a 5-input AND gate, applying as inputs the values of the four pixels in the image corresponding to the four neighbors according to the structuring element plus the value which corresponds to the center pixel of the structuring element. The output of the 5-input AND gate will be the new value of the pixel in image which corresponds to the center pixel of the structuring element. A 2-input OR gate in QCA is realized by clamping one input of the 3-input majority gate to logic '0'. Fig.6 presents the QCA implementation of the erosion operation. In the design the maximum wire length in a clocking zone is kept to 5 cells and the minimum distance between to wires is 2 cells.

According to the QCADesigner tool the design consists of 35 cells covering an area of 198 x 218 nm$^2$ that is approximately 0.043 $\mu$m$^2$. It is covering an area of 10 x 11 grids and the ratio of the area covered by QCA cells to the overall area of the layout is 0.318.

The simulation results of the design are presented in fig.6. As it is shown all possible value combinations of 5 inputs are applied to the circuit. The output is set to logic '1' only when all inputs stay at logic '1' otherwise is set to logic '0' indicating the AND gate behavior.

## 6    Conclusion

This paper presents the design and simulation of the morphological operations of dilation and erosion on binary images with QCA. The new QCA implementations provide parallel processing, high circuit performance, very low dimension and very low power consumption compared to similar implementations with conventional VLSI technology. These advantages make the proposed implementations useful for image processing systems applied on mobile or autonomous devices. The image processing algorithms considered in this work is limited to basic algorithms which are applied only on binary images, but further work will cope with more complex algorithms.

## References

1. Huang, T.S. (ed.): Two-dimensional Digital Signal Processing II: Transforms and Median Filters. Springer, New York (1981)
2. Gallagher, N.C., Wise, G.L.: A Theoretical Analysis of the Properties of Median Filters. IEEE Transactions on Acoustic, Speech and Signal Processing, ASSP 29, 1136–1141 (1981)
3. Breveglieri, L., Piuri, V.: Digital Median Filters. Journal of VLSI Signal Processing 31, 191–206 (2002)
4. Serra, J., Soille, P.: Mathematical Morphology and its Applications to Image Processing. Kluwer, Norwell (1994)
5. Matheron, G.: Random Sets and Integral Geometry. Wiley, N.Y. (1975)
6. Chatzis, V., Pitas, I.: A Generalized Fuzzy Mathematical Morphology and its Application in Robust 2D and 3D Object Representation. IEEE Trans. on Image Processing 9(10), 1798–1810 (2000)
7. Koskinen, L., Astola, J., Neuvo, Y.: Soft morphological filters. In: Proc. SPIE Symp. Image Algebra Morphological Image Processing, vol. 1568, pp. 262–270 (1991)
8. Bloch, I., Maitre, H.: Fuzzy mathematical morphologies: A comparative study. Pattern Recognit. 28, 1341–1387 (1995)
9. Maragos, P., Schafer, R.W.: Morphological Systems for Multidimensional Signal Processing. IEEE Proceedings 78(4), 690–710 (1990)
10. Danielson, P.E., Levialdi, S.: Computer Architectures for Pictorial Information Systems. IEEE Computer Magazine, 53–67 (November 1981)
11. Reinhardt, J.M., Higgins, W.E.: Efficient morphological shape representation. IEEE Trans. Image Processing 5, 89–101 (1996)

12. Venkateshwar Rao, D., Patil, S., Babu, N.A., Muthukumar, V.: Implementation and Evaluation of Image Processing Algorithms on Reconfigurable Architecture using C-based Hardware Descriptive Languages. International Journal of Theoretical and Applied Computer Sciences 1(1), 9–34 (2006)

13. Malamas, E.N., Malamos, A.G., Varvarigou, T.A.: Fast Implementation of Binary Morphological Operations on Hardware. Efficient Systolic Architectures Journal of VLSI Signal Processing 25, 79–93 (2000)

14. Nalpantidis, L., Amanatiadis, A., Sirakoulis, G.C., Gasteratos, A.: An Efficient Hierarchical Matching Algorithm for Processing Uncalibrated Stereo Vision Images and its Hardware Architecture. IET Image Processing 5(5), 481–492 (2011)

15. Konstantinidis, K., Sirakoulis, G.C., Andreadis, I.: Design and Implementation of a Fuzzy Modified Ant Colony Hardware Structure for Image Retrieval. IEEE Transactions on Systems, Man and Cybernetics – Part C 50(3), 519–537 (2009)

16. The international technology roadmap for semiconductors: Emerging research devices 17 (2005), http://www.itrs.net/

17. Antonelli, D.A., Chen, D.Z., Dysart, T.J., Hu, X.S.: Quantum-dot Cellular Automata (QCA) circuit partitioning: Problem modeling and solutions. In: Proc. of Design Auto. Conf., San Diego, CA (June 2004)

18. Akeela, R., Wagh, M.D.: A Five-input Majority Gate in Quantum-dot Cellular Automata. NSTI-Nanotech, 2011 vol. 2 (2011), ISBN 978-1-4398-7139-3, http://www.nsti.org

19. Zhang, R., Walus, K., Wang, W., Jullien, G.A.: A majority reduction technique for adder structures in quantum-dot cellular. In: Proceedings of SPIE, vol. 5559, pp. 91–100 (2004)

20. Tougaw, P.D., Lent, C.S.: Logical devices implemented using quantum cellular automata. Journal of Applied Physics 75(3), 1818–1825 (1994), doi:10.1063/1.356375

21. Wang, W., Walus, K., Jullien, G.A.: Quantum-Dot Cellular Automata Adders. In: IEEE International Conference on Nanotechnology IEEE-NANO, vol. 2, pp. 461–464 (2003), doi:10.1109/NANO.2003.1231818.

22. Fijany, A., Toomarian, N., Modarress, K., Spotnitz, M.: Bit-serial Adder Based on Quantum Dots. NASA technical report (January 2003)

23. Kim, K., Wu, K., Karri, R.: The Robust QCA Adder Designs Using Composable QCA Building Blocks. IEEE Transactions on CAD of Integrated Circuits and Systems 26(1), 176–183 (2007), doi:10.1109/TCAD.2006.883921

24. Hänninen, I., Takala, J.: Arithmetic Design on Quantum-Dot Cellular Automata Nanotechnology. In: Bereković, M., Dimopoulos, N., Wong, S. (eds.) SAMOS 2008. LNCS, vol. 5114, pp. 43–52. Springer, Heidelberg (2008)

25. Mardiris, V.A., Karafyllidis, I.G.: Universal cellular automaton cell using quantum cellular automata. Electronics Letters 45(12), 607–609 (2009)

26. Vankamamidi, V., Ottavi, M., Lombardi, F.: Two-Dimensional Schemes for Clocking/Timing of QCA Circuits. IEEE Transactions on Computer-Aided Design of Integrated Circuits and Systems 27(1), 34–44 (2008), doi:10.1109/TCAD.2007.907020

27. Mardiris, V.A., Karafyllidis, I.G.: Design and simulation of modular quantum-dot cellular automata multiplexers for memory accessing. Journal of Circuits, Systems and Computers 19(2), 349–365 (2010)

28. Mardiris, V.A., Karafyllidis, I.G.: Design and simulation of modular 2n to 1 quantum-dot cellular automata (QCA) multiplexers International. Journal of Circuit Theory and Applications 38(8), 771–785 (2010)

29. Huang, J., Momenzadeh, M., Lombardi, F.: Analysis of missing and additional cell defects in sequential quantum-dot cellular automata. INTEGRATION, the VLSI Journal 40, 503–515 (2007), doi:10.1016/j.vlsi.2006.08.001

30. Huang, J., Momenzadeh, M., Lombardi, F.: Design of sequential circuits by quantum-dot cellular automata. Microelectronics Journal 38, 525–537 (2007), doi:10.1016/j.mejo.2007.03.013

31. Vankamamidi, V., Ottavi, M., Lombardi, F.: Tile-Based Design of a Serial Memory in QCA. In: Proceedings of the 15th ACM Great Lakes Symposium on VLSI, pp. 201–206 (2005), doi:10.1145/1057661.1057711

32. Vankamamidi, V., Ottavi, M., Lombardi, F.: A Serial Memory by Quantum-Dot Cellular Automata (QCA). IEEE Transactions on Computers 57(8), 606–618 (2008), doi:10.1109/TC.2007.70831

33. Vankamamidi, V.M., Ottavi, M., Lombardi, F.: A Line-Based Parallel Memory for QCA Implementation. IEEE Transactions on Nanotechnology 4(6), 690–698 (2005), doi:10.1109/TNANO.2005.858589

34. Niemier, M.T., Kontz, M.J., Kogge, P.: A Design of and Design Tools for a Novel Quantum Dot Based Microprocessor. In: Proceedings of the 37th Design Automation Conference, pp. 227–232 (2000), doi:10.1145/337292.337398

35. Crocker, M., Hu, X.S., Niemier, M., Yan, M., Bernstein, G.: PLAs in Quantum-Dot Cellular Automata. IEEE Transactions on Nanotechnology 7(3), 376–386 (2008), doi:10.1109/TNANO.2007.915022

36. Helsingius, M., Kuosmanen, P., Astola, J.: Quantum-dot cells and their suability for nonlinear signal processing. In: Procceding og the IEEE EURASIP Workshop on Nonlinear Signal and Image Processing, NSIP 1999, vol. 2, pp. 659–663 (1999)

37. Cardenas-Barrera, J.L., Platoniotis, K.N., Venetsanopoulos, A.N.: QCA implementation of a multichannel filter for image processing. Math. Probl. Eng. 8(1), 87–99 (2002)

38. Amlani, I., Orlov, A.O., Toth, G., Bernstein, G.H., Lent, C.S., Snider, G.: Digital Logic Gate Using Quantum-dot Cellular Automata. Science 284(5412), 289–291 (1999), doi:10.1126/science.284.5412.289

39. Lent, C.S., Tougaw, P.: A Device Architecture for Computing with Quantum Dots. Proceedings of the IEEE 85(4), 541–557 (1997), doi:10.1109/5.573740

40. Navi, K., Sayedsalehi, S., Farazkish, R., Azghadi, M.R.: Five-input majority gate, a new device for quantum-dot cellular automata. Journal of Computational and Computational and Theoretical Nanoscience 7, 1546–1553 (2010)

41. Navi, K., Farazkish, R., Sayedsalehi, S., Azghadi, M.R.: A new quantum-dot cellular automata full adder. Microelectronics Journal 7(22), 820–826 (2010)

42. Azghadi, M.R., Kavehei, O., Navi, K.: A novel design for quantum-dot cellular automata cells and full-adders. Journal of Applied Sciences 7(22), 3460–3468 (2007)

43. Amlani, I., Orlov, A.O., Kummamuru, R.K., Bernstein, G.H., Lent, C.S., Snider, G.L.: Experimental demonstration of a leadless quantum-dot cellular automata cell. Applied Physics Letters 77(5), 738–740 (2000), doi:10.1063/1.127103

44. Walus, K., Dysart, T. J., Jullien, G. A., Budiman, A.R.: QCADesigner: A Rapid Design and Simulation Tool for Quantum-Dot Cellular Automata. IEEE Transactions on Nanotechnology 3(1), 26–31 (2004), doi:10.1109/TNANO.2003.820815

# A 3-State Asynchronous CA for the Simulation of Delay-Insensitive Circuits

Oliver Schneider and Thomas Worsch

Karlsruhe Institute of Technology, Germany
mail@oli-obk.de, worsch@kit.edu

**Abstract.** We show the construction of a rotation- and reflection-invariant local function for a two-dimensional asynchronous cellular automaton with only 3 states and radius 1 Moore neighborhood in which one can implement arbitrary delay-insensitive circuits.

## 1 Introduction

The underlying assumption of a global clock in synchronous cellular automata is considered to be an obstacle for their implementation in "hardware", be it silicon or (in future) some other physical substrate.

That is at least one motivation to have a look at asynchronous cellular automata (ACA) where it is not required that all cells are updating their states simultaneously. Instead cell updates happen as, completely or at least partially, unrelated events. Usually one still assumes a discrete time scale. But in each step an arbitrary subset of all cells change their states. Some special definitions of ACA put restrictions on the subsets (or sequences of subsets) that are allowed.

In the present paper we are describing an ACA which works in all cases: For example, it works even when only one cell is active in each step; on the other hand it does not forbid the simultaneous updating of cells which are neighbors. In addition it adheres to the standard definition of CA, where the activity of one cell can by itself not change the states of its neighbors, but only its own.

It is of course trivial to obtain the local rules of such CA for any problem. One just has to take the local rule of a synchronous CA solving the problem, and apply the construction by Nakamura [4] to make it "robust" for asynchronicity. But there is at least one disadvantage. The size of the set of states increases from $k$ to $3k^2$ (which is greater than or equal to 12 for any interesting $k$).

Lee et al. [1] have described a 4-state CA which can simulate arbitrary DI circuits for any mode of asynchronous updating, and were able to use only the von Neumann neighborhood of radius 1. Other attempts to reduce the number of states required at least one of the following restrictions or changes:

- Not all updating sequences are allowed, e. g. it is forbidden to update neighboring cells simultaneously.
- A modified definition of CA is used, e. g. the update of a cell in general also changes the states of the neighbors. Examples can be found in papers by Lee et al. [2,3].

G.C. Sirakoulis and S. Bandini (Eds.): ACRI 2012, LNCS 7495, pp. 565–574, 2012.
© Springer-Verlag Berlin Heidelberg 2012

In the following sections we will describe a two-dimensional ACA with only 3 states which can simulate every delay-insensitive circuit, and which can simulate every Turing machine. Compared to [1] we are able to reduce the number of states from 4 to 3, keep the ability to work for any update sequences of cells and keep the rotation and reflection symmetry of the local rule. The price we have to pay is a larger neighborhood (Moore instead of von Neumann) and more "rules", i.e. there are more local configurations for which a cell really *changes* its state when updated. This paper is based on the diploma thesis of the first author [5].

## 2    Basics

We assume that readers know the concepts of cellular automata and their asynchronous mode of operation.

We will describe a two-dimensional CA with Moore neighborhood of radius 1. There are 3 possible states for each cell which will be denoted by □, ■, and ■. State □ will in particular serve as a quiescent "background state".

The local transition function will be described using little images as in Figure 1. On the left-hand side of each ↦ arrow a local configuration is shown and on its right-hand side the new state of the center cell. It is to be understood that each such pair is representing up to eight local rules: the one for the local configuration shown, its mirrored version and those for the local configurations resulting from rotating the shown one and its mirrored version by 90, 180 and 270 degrees. At the end we will have specified the new state of a cell only for a small fraction of all local configurations. For all the others by definition the state of the center cell doesn't change.

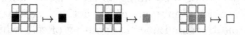

**Fig. 1.** Rules for the movement of head (left), navel (middle) and tail (right) of a signal

For the realization of Boolean logic we will use *cables* to transmit *bits* between Boolean gates. A cable consists of 3 *wires*. A bit is transmitted by a signal on either the 0-wire or the 1-wire (dual-rail encoding). Reception of the bit is acknowledged by a signal on the third wire in the opposite direction (see Figure 2). Only then may another bit be sent. Cables need to be initialized with a signal on one of its three wires. All Boolean gates can be constructed in such a way that the invariant is preserved that on each cable there is always either exactly one bit signal or an acknowledgement signal.

We will now step by step describe sets of rules for the local function and how they are used. In the rest of this section we will discuss the implementation of signals which even work in the asynchronous setting.

A signal will be composed of a *front* and a *rear*. The front is a sequence of one or more cells in state ■ and the rear is a sequence of one or more cells in

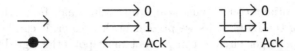

**Fig. 2.** On the left symbolic representations of a wire without a signal and a wire with a signal (black dot) are shown. The right image shows the symbolic representation of a cable with the two wires for bit transport going right and the acknowledgement wire going left. An inverter (shown on the right) can be constructed directly inside the cable by crossing the wires for transmitting the 0 and 1 signals.

state ■. The cell of the front which sees a □ cell in the direction it is moving is called the *head*. The cell of the front which sees a ■ cell in the opposite direction is called the *navel* and the "last" cell of the rear is called the *tail*.

The lengths of the front and the rear of a signal may vary due to asynchronous updating. Signals can move in "free space", i. e. in an area consisting of □ cells only. Thus a "wire" does not have an actual representation through patterns inside the CA, but is a set of either horizontally or vertically connected cells that change their state to propel a signal. In our constructions wires are only used unidirectionally. Therefore all signals travelling through a certain wire will travel in the same direction. (There are two small exceptions in the modules for resettable join and ATS.) Figure 3 shows how a signal moves to the right using the rules from Figure 1 when all cells are updated synchronously.

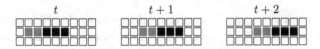

**Fig. 3.** A signal moving to the right, assuming *synchronous* updating of all cells

But our construction also works in the case of asynchronous updating. Figure 4 shows an example of what can happen to a signal. In the first step only the navel cell is updates its state. In the second step all cells except the cell in front of the head. That one is active in the third step. Front and rear can grow and shrink, but never vanish.

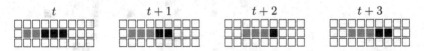

**Fig. 4.** A signal moving to the right, assuming *asynchronous* updating of some cells

In larger circuits it becomes necessary to allow wires to cross each other. A wire crossing is the one-cell intersection of a horizontal and a vertical wire. It is not allowed to have two signals pass the wire crossing simultaneously as the signals can potentially collide which can stop both signals from advancing. Due to the nature of the DI-Circuits we present in this paper, it can be shown that careful design of larger circuits can prevent most potential signal collisions. It is possible to construct a "safe" wire crossing which can handle "simultaneous" signals; see the right-hand side of Figure 14.

## 3   Pipes, Entrances, Exits, and Turns

*Pipes* are wires encapsulated by cells in state ■. Really "long" pipes are not needed anywhere, but pipes of length 2 to 4 will show up as parts of larger modules. Since the rules needed are always the same, they are described next. As for wires there is a horizontal and a vertical version. Figure 5 shows an example configuration with a signal travelling inside a pipe on the left and the rules needed to implement this behavior on the right.

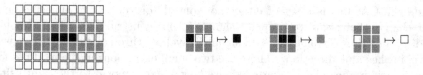

**Fig. 5.** A signal travelling inside a pipe and the rules for moving its head (left), navel (middle) and tail (right)

Advertent readers will already have noticed that something is incomplete in Figure 5. If a pipe would simply end in free space somewhere, the rule for the movement of the tail of a signal from Figure 1 would immediately destroy the ends of a pipe. Therefore they always have to be attached to "something else". Two examples are the pipe *entrance* and the pipe *exit*, described next. They are the simplest so-called *modules*. A pipe will always connect two modules. In general a module will also perform some kind of operation on the signal.

An entrance allows a signal to enter a pipe from free space. Figure 6 shows an entrance and the rules needed to allow a signal to move from the free space into the pipe. An exit allows signals to travel from inside a pipe into free space.

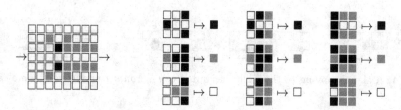

**Fig. 6.** An entrance and the rules to shift a signal through the entrance. The top (middle, bottom) rows depict the rules to move the head (navel, tail) of the signal. All rules in the same column correspond to the same location in the entrance.

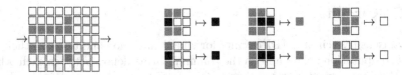

**Fig. 7.** An exit and the rules to shift a signal through the exit. The left (middle, right) columns depict the rules to move the head (navel, tail) of the signal.

Figure 7 shows its shape and the required rules. All the rules to move signals into and out of pipes have corresponding signal movement rules. Therefore signals will move in the same manner through free space, pipes, entrances and exits.

Entrance and exit have different shapes. To understand why one can for example try to send a signal from free space to an exit. Once the tail has entered the exit, a rule is needed which changes that cell back to state □. But such a rule would also destroy pipes. Similar considerations apply in other cases.

There is one more module which does not really "compute" something. The *turn* modules can be used to change the direction of signal. Turns have a direction; thus there are 8 of them (4 directions for the input directions and 2 possibilities for the turning direction). Figure 8 shows the case of a turn changing the direction from rightward to downward; the other cases are obtained by rotations and mirroring. Strictly speaking the turn modules are not necessary (the ATS module introduced later is a generalization), but it is convenient.

The head of a signal will wait inside the turn until the navel also arrives at the turn. Then the navel waits inside the turn until the tail arrives. Now both navel and tail can continue. This prevents a signal from ever colliding with itself, as it cannot stretch itself over more than three turns.

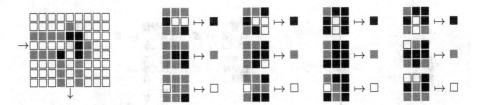

**Fig. 8.** Turn: A signal arriving from the left will be turned to travel downwards. It is not valid to have a signal entering this module from below. Rules in the top (middle, bottom) row are for the movement of the head (navel, tail).

In the next section we will describe more complicated types of modules. They can be connected by pipes, wires and turns to build any delay-insensitive circuit. Using those one can simulate any Turing machine. Modules need to be separated by at least two cells in state □ or by a two cell long pipe. Otherwise it could happen that modules are so close to each other that they are destroyed, because rules can be applied to cells whose neighborhood contains cells from both modules.

## 4    DI-Circuits

Delay-insensitive circuits (DI circuits for short) have no conditions on their internal computation delays and on the communication delays between each other. Thus they are a good match for asynchronous CA, where any cell may take an arbitrary (but finite) amount of time until it updates its state and thus the speed of signals is not fixed.

A *fork* splits an incoming signal into two separate signals. Figure 9 shows a fork, its symbolic representation used later on, and the additional rules needed for proper functioning.

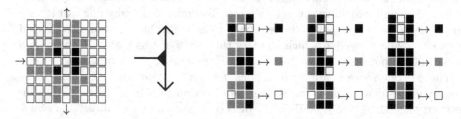

**Fig. 9.** Fork: A signal arriving from the left will be duplicated. The rules in the first (second, third) row move and split the head (navel, tail). Additional rules from the entrance and the turn are required to allow the signal to exit the module.

A *merge* module transports signals from two input wires to the same output wire. Simultaneous signals on both input wires are not allowed. Figure 10 shows a merge, its symbolic representation, and the additional rules needed.

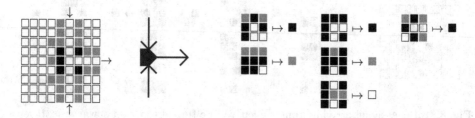

**Fig. 10.** Merge: A signal arriving from the top or bottom will be turned to exit on the right. Simultaneous signals on both the top and bottom are invalid and will cause unpredictable behavior. The first column of rules allow the head and navel of the signal to move to either one cell above or one cell below the central cell of the module. The second column concerns rules that move all parts of the signal through the central cell of the module. Several rules from the turn and entrance are required for allowing the signal to enter and exit the module.

The previous DI-Circuits have a very static behavior. To perform more interesting signal operations we now introduce a "resettable join" which has three input wires ($A$, $B$, $C$) and two output wires ($X$, $Y$). It is forbidden to send signals on all three inputs "simultaneously". Signals entering the resettable join simultaneously or in sequence at inputs $A$ and $B$ will be consumed and a signal will be output to $X$. As long as there is only one signal at either $A$ or $B$, it can be deleted by a signal on input $C$. Once a signal has been deleted, an output signal is emitted at $Y$.

Figure 11 shows the implementation of a resettable join. It basically consists of the "reset part" in the left half and a join in the right half. The two parts are connected by a short pipe which is used in both directions. This module needs quite a number of rules. The rules in Figure 12 make sure that the right half acts as a join, the rules in Figure 13 make sure that the reset works.

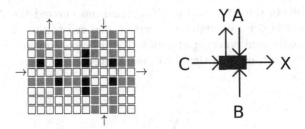

**Fig. 11.** Resettable join: Inside this module there is a short path where information travels bidirectionally. This is necessary because it is impossible to connect five wires to a single cell while ensuring a two cell distance between all wires.

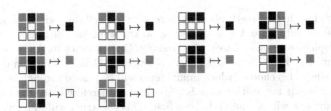

**Fig. 12.** Resettable join: The rules realizing the join. The top (middle, bottom) row is responsible for the handling of the head (navel, tail).

The resettable join, the merge and the fork form a minimal set which is universal for DI-Circuits, and hence allow for Turing universality (see Section 5).

To ease development of large circuits we also implemented a "safe wire crossing". Such a wire crossing allows signals to pass a wire crossing simultaneously while only interfering by introducing additional delays. To be able to implement the safe wire crossing, an "arbitrary test and set" (called ATS from now on) DI-Circuit is introduced, shown in Figure 14. The ATS has two input wires $A$ and $C$ and two output wires $X$ and $Y$. A signal entering at input $A$ will be turned

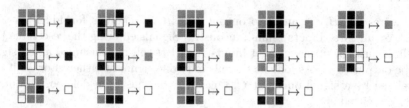

**Fig. 13.** Resettable join: The rules implementing the reset. The top row is responsible for generating the front of the signal which will leave at $Y$; the middle row for deleting the signal which had arrived at $A$ or $B$; the bottom row for moving the tail out to $Y$. The first rule in the last row fixes a "bug" in the join part of the module caused by the last rule in the first row.

to output $X$ like in the turn module. If a signal has entered the ATS through input $C$ and traveled far enough to be within one cell of the turn part of the module, the next signal entering at input $A$ will be consumed, and instead of getting passed to output $X$, a signal will be emitted at output $Y$. The rules are shown in Figure 15.

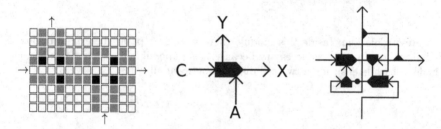

**Fig. 14.** ATS: Like in the resettable join, there are a few cell through which information travels bidirectionally. $A$ and $Y$ may also be on the same side of the module. On the right is an implementation of a safe wire crossing. One entrance to this wire crossing is at the bottom, the other on the left. There is an active signal running in cycles inside the wire crossing. This chooses which input signal will be passed through by alternately checking both inputs for waiting signals. Signals may therefore enter the wire crossing simultaneously; one will be chosen to pass first. This construct will also ensure that no signal has to wait indefinitely to pass the crossing.

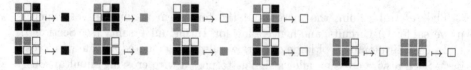

**Fig. 15.** The first row of rules moves a signal from $A$ to $X$. The second row causes a signal from $C$ to delete the next signal from $A$ and transmit a signal to $Y$.

# 5   Boolean Logic and Networks

It is well known [6] that for the computation of arbitrary complex Boolean functions it is sufficient to use NAND operations, as all other Boolean operations can be constructed by chaining NAND operations. Therefore we now present a NAND gate with two input cables and one output cable. Since we use three wires per bit the resulting module is relatively large; see Figure 16.

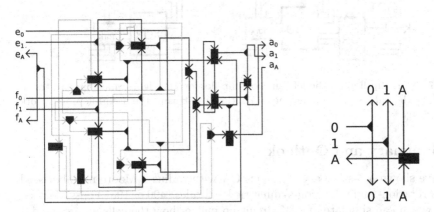

**Fig. 16.** A NAND gate. There are two input cables $e$ and $f$ on the left and one output cable $a$ to the right. There are no safe wire crossings required for this construct, as it is designed in such a way that none of the wire crossings can have two signals crossing it. To the right a fork for cables is shown. It duplicates signals entering on the input cable and passes them on to the output cables. It is guaranteed, that both outgoing cables have successfully transmitted their data signals, when an acknowledgement signal is sent back through the input cable.

The correctness of the rules for the implementation of the modules described in the previous sections can be ensured relatively easy. There are always only very few cells which can change their states, and most of the time the are not neighbors of each other. One can therefore enumerate and check all possibilities.

The situation changes for the NAND. First, the question is different: It's not about the correctness of the local rules, it's about the correctness of the interplay between the DI circuits involved. The method to prove it is adopted appropriately: One can identify different phases, during which signals can only move along certain parts of the whole circuit. Again by complete enumeration of all possibilities it can be shown that everything works. Details can be found in [5].

Of course, one can construct flip-flops from Boolean gates. But in the present setting it is possible to avoid the crossing of cables. This is shown in Figure 17 for a T-flip-flop and a JK-flip-flop. Only when receiving a 1-bit the T-flip-flop toggles its state and sends a bit containing its new state. When it receives a 0-bit it simply transmits its stored state. The cable looping back from the fork needs to be initialized with either a signal on the 0-wire or the 1-wire. The fork's input cable needs an acknowledgement signal. Cable $Q$ must not be initialized. When the JK-flip-flop receives a 1 on both input cables, its state is toggled and transmitted to cable $Q$. A 0 on both input cables directly transmits its state to $Q$. A 1 on $J$ and a 0 on $K$ sets the state to 1 and transmits this. A 0 on $J$ and a 1 on $K$ sets the state to 0 and also transmits this.

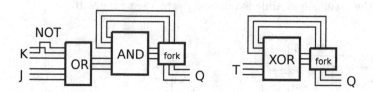

**Fig. 17.** A JK-flip-flop on the left and a T-flip-flop on the right. Since bits are transmitted on the cables in units and not a continuous stream, the T-flip-flop does work in this setup.

## 6    Summary and Outlook

We have shown a 3-state asynchronous CA with radius 1 Moore neighborhood and 82 rotation- and reflection-symmetric local rules (490 of 19683 possible fixed rules) which can simulate any DI circuit no matter how the cells are updated.

Although the details of the implementations in [1] and in this paper differ, the main reason for being able to reduce the number of states to 3 probably here is the larger neighborhood. Even with 3 states instead of 4 this allows to distinguish a sufficient number of different "local situations". It remains an open problem whether 2 states are sufficient under these constraints. Another possible direction for future research is the reduction of the necessary number of rules.

## References

1. Lee, J., Adachi, S., Peper, F., Mashiko, S.: Delay-insensitive computation in asynchronous cellular automata. Journal of Computer and System Sciences 70, 201–220 (2005)
2. Lee, J., Peper, F., Adachi, S., Morita, K.: An Asynchronous Cellular Automaton Implementing 2-State 2-Input 2-Output Reversed-Twin Reversible Elements. In: Umeo, H., Morishita, S., Nishinari, K., Komatsuzaki, T., Bandini, S. (eds.) ACRI 2008. LNCS, vol. 5191, pp. 67–76. Springer, Heidelberg (2008)
3. Lee, J., Peper, F.: Efficient Circuit Construction in Brownian Cellular Automata Based on a New Building-Block for Delay-Insensitive Circuits. In: Bandini, S., Manzoni, S., Umeo, H., Vizzari, G. (eds.) ACRI 2010. LNCS, vol. 6350, pp. 356–364. Springer, Heidelberg (2010)
4. Nakamura, K.: Asynchronous Cellular Automata and Their Computational Ability. Systems, Computer, Control 5, 58–66 (1974)
5. Schneider, O.: Schaltkreise in einem Zellularautomat mit 3 Zuständen. Diploma thesis, Karlsruhe Institute for Technology, Faculty for Informatics (2012)
6. Wernick, W.: Complete Sets of Logical Functions. Transactions of the American Mathematical Society 51, 117–132 (1942)

# On Construction by Worm-Like Agents on a Self-timed Cellular Automaton

Daichi Takata[1], Teijiro Isokawa[1], Jia Lee[2],
Ferdinand Peper[3,1], and Nobuyuki Matsui[1]

[1] Division of Computer Engineering, Graduate School of Engineering,
University of Hyogo, 2167 Shosha, Himeji, 671-2280, Japan
isokawa@eng.u-hyogo.ac.jp
[2] Chongqing University, China
[3] National Institute of Information and Communications Technology, Japan

**Abstract.** This paper presents a novel scheme to construct circuits on the cell space of an asynchronous cellular automaton that has partitioned cells. The construction process in this scheme is conducted by worm configurations that contain instructions on how to operate. Circuits are constructed by multiple worms, which move around in parallel on the cell space, resulting in an efficient process, as is shown.

## 1 Introduction

The construction of configurations in Cellular Automata (CA) has attracted the attention of researchers for a long time [1] since the proposal of von Neumann's original CA. Von Neumann aimed to formalize biological self-reproduction by creating an abstract machine that can replicate itself and conduct universal computation. A universal constructor is a configuration in the cellular space that moves around under the direction of instructions such as to place configurations on the cell space. A potential application of a (universal) constructor is the con-figuration and reconfiguration of computational circuits for CA-based computers. Such computers have become closer to reality since proposals of molecular CA [2,3] and nanometer-scaled computers (nanocomputers) [4,5,6] have been made.

There are two types of constructors explored in CA research, particularly in the context of self-reproducing CA. One type is a universal constructor [1,7,8]. A universal constructor has a writing head for placing a configuration of the cell space. This head moves around in the cell space by changing the states of its adjacent cells. Moving the head and changing the cells' states is directed by sequences of signals from the control part of the constructor to the head. The number of writing heads is typically one, and the writing head can accept one signal at a time, thus the construction is performed sequentially.

The other type of constructor is a so-called self-reproducing loop, originated by Langton [9,10,11]. A self-reproducing loop has a loop structure and typically contains a part of the sequence for creating the loop itself. This loop creates the same loop structure, called daughter loop, at its neighborhood and copies

G.C. Sirakoulis and S. Bandini (Eds.): ACRI 2012, LNCS 7495, pp. 575–584, 2012.

the sequence to the daughter loop. These procedures result in the indefinitely creation of loops accross the cell space. One loop can produce one daughter loop at once, but each loop in the cell space can conduct the reproduction process independently, thus the reproduction process can be performed in parallel.

A universal constructor needs to be able to create a large variety of configurations, but due to its sequential nature, it tends to be slow. Self-reproducing loops operate much faster than universal constructors due to their parallelism, but the resulting products are uniform, i.e. the same as the original loop. It would be useful to explore construction schemes that are conducted in parallel, while allowing a variety of configurations to be constructed, but this research is virtually unexplored. Yet, parallelism of construction ability in CA is very important, if reconfiguration of circuits is to be successfully realized in molecular CA and CA-based nanocomputers.

This paper presents a scheme for constructing configurations in the cellular space, whereby both construction universality and a high degree of parallelism is achieved. The scheme adopts the concept of a *worm* configuration, which is a combination of a writing head and sequences of instructions to control it, in accordance with the proposal by Lee [12]. The constructor uses multiple worm configurations that travel around in the cell space and place circuit elements in appropriate positions. Each worm has only a part of a configuration to be constructed, and several worms construct one circuit elements together. The proposed scheme is implemented on a Self-Timed Cellular Automaton, which is a type of asynchronous partitioned CA [4].

## 2 Preliminaries

### 2.1 Self-Timed Cellular Automaton

A Self-Timed Cellular Automaton (STCA)[4] is a two-dimensional asynchronous CA of identical cells, each of which is partitioned into four parts in a one-to-one correspondence with its neighboring cells. Each part of a cell has a state. Figure 1 shows a cell in STCA where the states of the partitions are denoted as $p_n$, $p_e$, $p_s$, and $p_w$. For simplicity the diagonal lines indicating partitions in cells are left out in the remainder of the paper. Each cell undergoes transitions in accordance with a transition function $f$, which operates on the four parts of the cell $p_n$, $p_e$, $p_s$, $p_w$ and the nearest part of each of its four neighbors $q_n$, $q_e$, $q_s$, $q_w$. The transition function $f$ is defined by

$$f(p_n, p_e, p_s, p_w, q_n, q_e, q_s, q_w) \rightarrow (p'_n, p'_e, p'_s, p'_w, q'_n, q'_e, q'_s, q'_w), \qquad (1)$$

where a state symbol to which a prime is attached denotes the new state of a partition after update (see Fig. 2). Function $f$ can be described by a finite set of transition rules on the STCA. Dummy transitions, which are transitions without any changes of the partition states, are not included in a set of the transition rules, so we assume that the left-hand side of a transition rule (Fig. 2) always differs from the right-hand side. Furthermore, we assume that transition rules

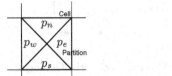

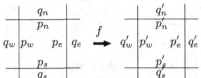

**Fig. 1.** Cell in a Self-Timed Cellular Automaton

**Fig. 2.** Transition rule in accordance with the function $f$

on an STCA are rotation-symmetric, thus each of the rules has four rotated analogues.

In an STCA, transitions of the cells occur at random times, independent of each other. Furthermore, it is assumed that neighboring cells never undergo transitions simultaneously to prevent a situation in which such cells write different values in shared partitions at the same time. Due to the random updating of cells, worm configurations can eventually undertake their journeys to their destinations, even if some of them collide with each other. This will be described in more detail in section 3.

There are several approaches to perform computation on STCAs, such as simulating synchronous CA on them, or embedding delay-insensitive circuits on them [13,14]; we will use the latter approach, because of its low overhead in terms of the number of required cell states and transition rules. We use Morita's Rotary Element [15] for conducting computation. A network of Rotary Elements can be used to construct a universal Turing machine, thus this element is computationally universal.

**Rotary Element(RE) and Its Implementation on STCA.** A *Rotary Element (RE)* [15] is a logic element with four input lines $\{n, e, s, w\}$, four output lines $\{n', e', s', w'\}$, and two states—the H-state and the V-state—which are displayed as horizontal and vertical rotation bars respectively (Fig. 3). A signal coming from a direction parallel to the rotation bar passes straight through to the opposite output line, without changing the direction of the bar (Fig. 4(a)); a signal coming from a direction orthogonal to the bar turns right and rotates the bar by 90 degrees (Fig. 4(b)).

Embedding an arbitrary RE-circuit on the cellular space of STCA can be achieved by the two states of a partition and the five transition rules shown in Fig. 5 (see [8] for details). Rule #1 defines a signal used for ordinary computation. Applying it to the successive shaded cells in Fig. 6 results in a signal proceeding northwards on a straight continuous path of cells, all bits of which are 0. Transmitting a signal towards the east, south, or west is done similarly, because of the rotation-symmetry of transition rules. Rules #2–4 are responsible for routing a signal according to the direction the signal comes from. The operation of the rotation bar in an RE is conducted by rule #5.

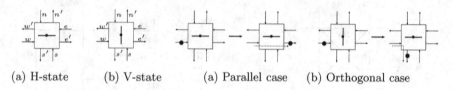

(a) H-state          (b) V-state          (a) Parallel case    (b) Orthogonal case

**Fig. 3.** Rotary Element          **Fig. 4.** The operation of an RE on a signal

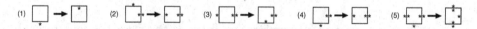

**Fig. 5.** Transition rules implementing the RE. A '∗' symbol in a partition denotes the corresponding state '∗', and a blank denotes the state '  '

A rudimentary RE is shown in Fig. 7. The input/output paths at the sides of this RE are bi-directional. Connecting so-called Input/Output Multiplexers [8] to these paths results in a regular RE with four input and four output paths, all uni-directional. Fig. 8 illustrates the traces of a signal input to a rudimentary RE from a line (a) parallel with or (b) orthogonal to the rotation bar. Since all the elements of RE-circuits can be realized by stable partition pairs, any circuit on this STCA can be represented by a certain configuration of stable partition-pairs.

## 3    Worm Configuration for Laying Out Circuits

Configuring (constructing) circuits can be accomplished by placing stable partition-pairs at desired locations. The *worm* configuration proposed in this paper has this capability. Each cell partition in the underlying STCA has one of 10 states that are represented by the symbols $\{\phi, \blacksquare, H, L, T, S, f, t, m, a\}$. The partition state '∗' in section 2 is mapped to the partition state '■', which is used to encode stable pairs as well as signals.

An example of a worm configuration is shown in Fig. 9. The structure of the worm is similar to Langton's self-reproducing loop, i.e., it is *sheathed*, but the configuration's structure is not that of a loop. The partition states 'H'(*Head*), 'T'(*Tail*), 'L'(*Leg*), 'S'(*Sense*), and 'a'(*anchor*) constitute the body of a worm, and the states 'f'(*front*), 't'(*turn*), and 'm'(*make*) are used as the instructions for the worm. Sheathed structures prevent the overlapping of worms, and through the use of *anchor* states a worm can pass through stable pairs on its journey.

Inside a worm structure, i.e., between the sheaths of the worm, the instruction states flow back and forth. The worm accepts these instruction at its head and deletes them in the process of interpreting them. During this process, the worm gradually becomes shorter while consuming instructions (see Figs. 10(a) and 10(b)), and when the worm runs out of instructions (Fig. 10(c)), it self-destructs (Fig. 10(d)), leaving no trace.

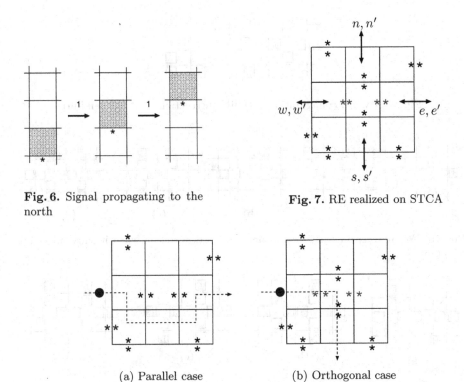

**Fig. 6.** Signal propagating to the north

**Fig. 7.** RE realized on STCA

(a) Parallel case          (b) Orthogonal case

**Fig. 8.** Signal passing through RE

The instruction 'f' makes the worm proceed by one cell toward the direction of the head. Figure 11 shows the transitions the states of the worm undergo when accepting one 'f' instruction. When an 'f' partition states arrives at the head of the worm (Fig. 11(a)), the head puts the 'S' state at its direct neighboring partition such as to extend the cell (Fig. 11(b)). Then an extension of the head is created in the cell next to the old head (Fig. 11(c)). At the final stage of moving the head forward, the old head, the 'S' state, and the 'f' instruction are changed to the quiescent state (Fig. 11(d)).

By accepting the instruction 't', a worm turns its direction to the left or the right by 90 degrees. Figure 12 shows the transitions a worm undergoes when accepting one 't' instruction. One single turn instruction makes the worm turn to the left. Turning the worm to the right requires two successive 't' instructions, as shown in Fig. 13.

To construct a stable partition pair, we use the instruction 'm'. Figure 14 shows a worm putting a stable partition pair at the left of its head. When an 'm' instruction is interpreted at the head of a worm, the worm creates an anchor state at which the stable partition pair will be placed. This anchor state becomes the stable partition pairs after the tail of the worm has passed. In the case in

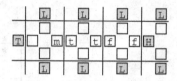

**Fig. 9.** A worm configuration with five instructions (f, f, t, t, and m)

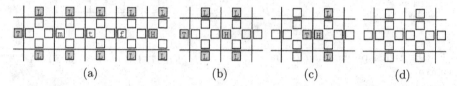

**Fig. 10.** Worm accepting instructions and its self-destruction when it runs out of instructions

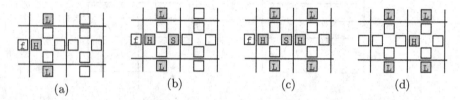

**Fig. 11.** The actions of a worm when accepting a single 'f' instruction

Fig. 14, the 'm' instruction is at the tail of the instruction sequence in the worm, thus the worm vanishes by itself.

Multiple successive 'm' instructions have different meanings for the head, in analogy to the case of the 't' instruction. Two successive 'm's give rise to two stable partition pairs at both sides of the worm, as shown in Fig. 15. This is a useful way to decrease the number of instructions in the worm.

Furthermore, three 'm' instructions give rise to another type of configuration, i.e. a computational signal (Fig. 6). Figure 16 shows the transitions taking place when a computational signal is created by three 'm' instructions. Once a computational signal is created, it is injected into the constructed circuit such as to activate the circuit.

It is necessary for worms to have the ability to pass over stable partition pairs that have already been placed on the cellular space, because several worms are moving around on the cellular space at the same time. The anchor state is used for this purpose. A worm finding stable partition pairs on its left or right changes these pair states to anchor states inside the worm (see Figs. 17(a), 17(b), and 17(c)). These anchor states are restored to the stable partition pairs after the tail of the worm passes (see Figs. 17(f) and 17(g)), following the same mechanism as the construction of stable partition pairs by 'm' instructions.

**Fig. 12.** A worm turning its direction to the left by accepting one single 't' instruction

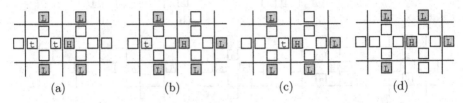

**Fig. 13.** Two successive 't' instructions make the worm turn its head to the right

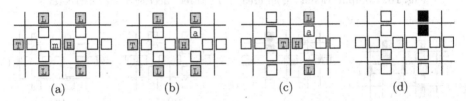

**Fig. 14.** Worm constructing a stable partition pair at the left of its head, by accepting a single 'm' instruction

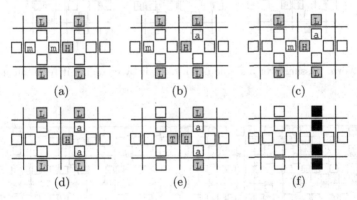

**Fig. 15.** A different type of construction of stable partition pairs, which uses two successive 'm' instructions

Finally, we show an example of a worm constructing a configuration. Figure 18 shows a worm that can construct one rotary element. The process of construction is illustrated in Fig. 19. Though this worm constructs one rotary element, it is also possible to prepare different cases, such as when one worm constructs several rotary elements or several worms construct one rotary element together.

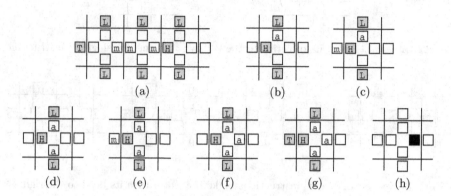

**Fig. 16.** Computational signal created by three successive 'm' instructions

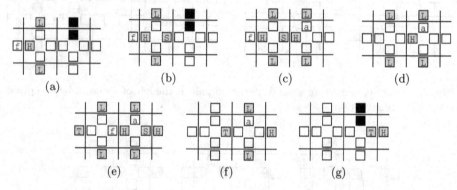

**Fig. 17.** Worm passing over a stable partition pair by changing it to an anchor state

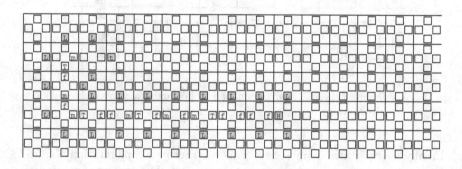

**Fig. 18.** A worm constructing a rotary element

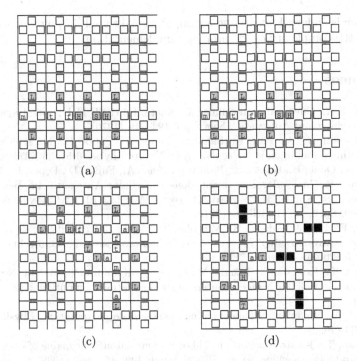

**Fig. 19.** A rotary element is constructed by the placement in cell space of stable partition pairs by the worm in Fig. 18

## 4   Conclusion

We have presented a scheme for constructing circuits in parallel and have shown its implementation on STCA. This scheme adopts worm-like agents that contain sequences of instructions in them for moving around in the cell space and placing stable partition pairs at desired locations. A number of worms can travel on the cell space simultaneously, and many collisions between worms or between a worm and pre-placed partition pairs can be avoided by the sheathed structure of the worm and the asynchronous timing of cells' updating. This scheme will be useful for cellular automaton-based reconfigurable computers, in which reconfiguration should be rapidly completed.

Because of page limitations, the example shown in this paper shows only a construction of a rotary element by one single worm. Another example is available at [16], where worms construct a network of four REs, after which a computational signal is started that passes through them. The list of the transition rules is also shown there.

The number of states of a cell partition is 10 and the number of transition rules is 400 for this implementation. A large part of the transition rules is necessary for the avoidance of collisions and for interpreting instructions at the head of a worm. Also, in the current implementation head-on collisions of worms cannot be resolved. More probabilistic behavior, like Brownian CA in which a backtracking mechanism is endowed for driving a computational signal [17], may be useful for reducing the complexity of the proposed implementation.

# References

1. Banks, E.R.: Universality in cellular automata. In: IEEE 11th Annual Symposium on Switching and Automata Theory, pp. 194–215 (1970)
2. Bandyopadhyay, A., Pati, R., Sahu, S., Peper, F., Fujita, D.: Massively parallel computing on an organic molecular layer. Nature Physics 6(5), 369–375 (2010)
3. Sahu, S., Oono, H., Ghosh, S., Bandyopadhyay, A., Fujita, D., Peper, F., Isokawa, T., Pati, R.: Molecular Implementations of Cellular Automata. In: Bandini, S., Manzoni, S., Umeo, H., Vizzari, G. (eds.) ACRI 2010. LNCS, vol. 6350, pp. 650–659. Springer, Heidelberg (2010)
4. Peper, F., Lee, J., Adachi, S., Mashiko, S.: Laying out circuits on asynchronous cellular arrays: a step towards feasible nanocomputers? Nanotechnology 14, 469–485 (2003)
5. Isokawa, T., Kowada, S., Takada, Y., Peper, F., Kamiura, N., Matsui, N.: Defect-Tolerance in Cellular Nanocomputers. New Generation Computing 25(2), 171–199 (2007)
6. Biafore, M.: Cellular automata for nanometer-scale computation. Physica D 70, 415–433 (1994)
7. Serizawa, T.: 3-state Neumann neighbor cellular automata capable of constructing selfreproducing machine. Trans. IEICE Japan J-69, 653–660 (1986)
8. Takada, Y., Isokawa, T., Peper, F., Matsui, N.: Universal Construction and Self-reproduction on Self-Timed Cellular Automata. International Journal of Modern Physics C 17(7), 985–1007 (2006)
9. Langton, C.G.: Self-reproduction in cellular automata. Physica D 10, 135–144 (1984)
10. Reggia, J.A., Armentrout, S.L., Chou, H.H., Peng, Y.: Simple systems that exhibit self-directed replication. Science 259(5099), 1282–1287 (1993)
11. Takada, Y., Isokawa, T., Peper, F., Matsui, N.: Asynchronous self-reproducing loops with arbitration capability. Physica D 227, 26–35 (2007)
12. Lee, J.: personal communication with T.Isokawa (2003) (unpublished)
13. Peper, F., Lee, J., Abo, F., Isokawa, T., Adachi, S., Matsui, N., Mashiko, S.: Fault-Tolerance in Nanocomputers: A Cellular Array Approach. IEEE Trans. on Nanotechnology 3(1), 187–201 (2004)
14. Lee, J., Peper, F., Adachi, S., Morita, K., Mashiko, S.: Reversible Computation in Asynchronous Cellular Automata. In: Calude, C.S., Dinneen, M.J., Peper, F. (eds.) UMC 2002. LNCS, vol. 2509, pp. 220–229. Springer, Heidelberg (2002)
15. Morita, K.: A Simple Universal Logic Element and Cellular Automata for Reversible Computing. In: Margenstern, M., Rogozhin, Y. (eds.) MCU 2001. LNCS, vol. 2055, pp. 102–113. Springer, Heidelberg (2001)
16. http://www.eng.u-hyogo.ac.jp/eecs/isokawa/ACRI2012/
17. Peper, F., Lee, J., Isokawa, T.: Brownian Cellular Automata. Journal of Cellular Automata 5(3), 185–206 (2010)

# Periodicity in Quantum Cellular Automata

Georgios I. Tsormpatzoglou and Ioannis G. Karafyllidis

Department of Electrical and Computer Engineering
Democritus University of Thrace 67100 Xanthi, Greece
{geortsor,ykar}@ee.duth.gr

**Abstract.** Studies of quantum computer implementations suggest cellular quantum computer architectures. These architectures are based on the evolution of quantum cellular automata, which can possibly simulate both quantum and classical physical systems and processes. It is however known that except for the trivial case, unitary evolution of one-dimensional homogeneous quantum cellular automata with one quantum bit (qubit) per cell is not possible because of the no-go lemma. In this paper, we define quantum cellular automata that comprise two qubits per cell and study their evolution using a quantum computer simulator. The evolution is unitary and its linearity manifests itself as a periodic structure in the probability distribution patterns.

**Keywords:** Quantum Computer, Quantum Cellular Automata, Simulation, Periodicity.

## 1 Introduction

Cellular Automata (CAs) were proposed by von Neumann as a model of self-replicating systems [1]. The CA model has been successfully used for the simulation of physical systems and processes and served as basis for parallel computer processor architectures [2,3,4].

One of the main issues in quantum information processing concerns the possible quantum computer architectures [5,6]. Feynman examined the possibility of using CAs both as models of quantum systems and as quantum computer architecture in 1982 [7]. Several studies of quantum computer implementations suggest that cellular architectures are the natural quantum computer architectures [8,9]. CAs that evolve according to quantum mechanics are referred to as quantum cellular automata (QCAs).

Studies revealed that, except for the trivial case, unitary evolution of one-dimensional QCAs is impossible [7,10,11]. This is known as the "no-go lemma" and presents a major obstacle for the construction of cellular quantum computer architectures. In order to overcome the obstacle, an alternative QCA structure using two qubits per cell was proposed in [12,13].

G.C. Sirakoulis and S. Bandini (Eds.): ACRI 2012, LNCS 7495, pp. 585–590, 2012.

## 2   Definition of QCAs with Two Qubits per Cell

In the QCAs that we are about to define, the same evolution rule applies to all cells at all times. The number of spatial dimensions of the QCA is one, i.e. it forms one-dimensional lattice.

Each QCA cell comprises two qubits. The first qubit is the controlled qubit (c-qubit) and the other is the state qubit (s-qubit). The state of the $j$th QCA cell at computation step $t$ is written as:

$$|s_j^t \, c_j^t\rangle = c_{0,j}^t|00\rangle + c_{1,j}^t|01\rangle + c_{2,j}^t|10\rangle + c_{3,j}^t|11\rangle \tag{1}$$

where $c_{n,j}^t$, $n = 0, 1, 2, 3$ are the basis-state probability amplitudes and therefore are complex numbers. The global state of the QCA at computation step t, $S^t$, is the tensor product of the states of all of its cells.

Three different neighborhood sets are considered for the QCAs defined here. The first set of the $j$th QCA cell neighborhood comprises the same cell and the $j + 1$ cell, the second set the same cell and the $j - 1$ cell and the third set the same cell and both the $j - 1$ and $j + 1$ cells.

The quantum computation starts with a preparation phase in which the qubits may be set in basis-state superposition and entangled states may be produced.

The QCAs defined here, evolve according to a global unitary rule $R$. The rule $R$ is applied in two phases. In the first phase, which is the interaction phase, the state of the c-qubit at each cell is changed according to the states of the s-qubits in the neighboring cells. In the second phase, which is the evaluation phase, a two-input quantum gate or a combination of quantum gates is applied to the c-qubit and the s-qubit at each cell, thus the information flow in the QCA lattice and simultaneous change of all s-qubit states. Therefore, $R$ is given as a product of the unitary operators $R_I$ and $R_E$ which correspond to the interaction and evaluation phases:

$$|S^{t+1}\rangle = R|S^t\rangle = R_E R_I|S^t\rangle \tag{2}$$

Figure 1 shows three QCA evolution rules as quantum circuits.

In the interaction phase, a quantum Controlled-NOT (CNOT) gate is applied to the two cells of each neighborhood or in the case of Fig. 1(c) a Controlled-Controlled-NOT (CCNOT) gate is applied to the three cells of each neighborhood. The CNOT gates are applied to all neighborhoods and the operator $R_I$ is given by the tensor product:

$$R_I = \cdots \otimes \text{CNOT} \otimes \text{CNOT} \otimes \text{CNOT} \otimes \cdots \tag{3}$$

During the interaction phase, the states of all s-qubits remain unaltered and the states of all c-qubits change.

In the evaluation phase, a two-input quantum gate or a combination of quantum gates is applied to the qubits of each cell, therefore the operator $R_E$ is given by the tensor product:

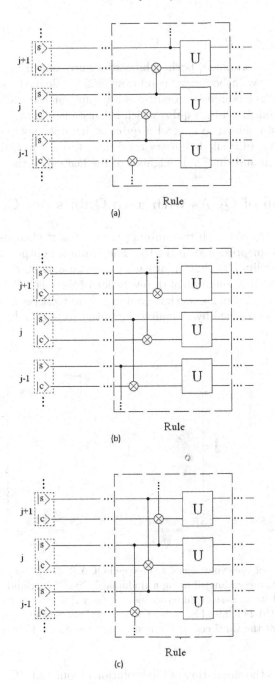

**Fig. 1.** (a) The evolution rule for the case where the neighborhood comprises the $j$th and the $j+1$ cells. (b) The evolution rule for the case where the neighborhood comprises the $j$th and the $j-1$ cells. (c) The evolution rule for the case where the neighborhood comprises the $j$th and both the $j-1$ and $j+1$ cells. Figure from [13].

$$R_E = \cdots \otimes U \otimes U \otimes U \otimes \cdots \tag{4}$$

During the evaluation phase, both qubit states may change.

Constant and cyclic boundary conditions will be defined for the QCAs. In the case of constant boundary conditions a c-qubit at the end of the lattice is assumed to be controlled by a qubit which is constantly in basis-states $|0\rangle$ or $|1\rangle$ and a s-qubit is assumed to control a qubit which does not participate in the QCA global state. In cyclic boundary conditions the $j - 1$ neighbor of the first cell is the last cell and the $j + 1$ neighbor of the last cell is the first cell.

## 3   Evolution of QCAs with Two Qubits per Cell

The evolution of QCAs with two qubits per cell was studied using a quantum computer simulator presented in [14,15]. The graphical output of the simulator shows the probability distribution at each computational step.

Figure 2 shows the simulation of the evolution of three-cell QCAs. Comparison of Fig. 2(a), 2(b) and 2(c) shows that even in the simplest case, entirely different final states can be reached by changing the initial state of only one qubit.

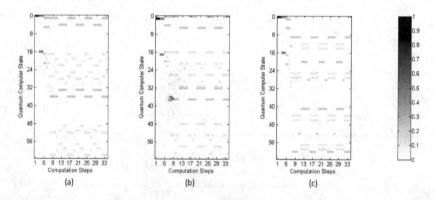

**Fig. 2.** Simulation of the evolution of a three-cell QCA. During the preparation phase, the first cell qubits are entangled using a Hadamard-CNOT gate and second and third cell qubits are set in basis-state superposition using a Hadamard gate. (a) The initial state is $|000000\rangle$. (b) The initial state is $|000001\rangle$. (c) Differs from (a) in the application of a CNOT gate at the third cell at the first evaluation phase. Figure from [12].

Figure 3 shows the simulation of the evolution of four-cell QCAs. The periodic structure of the probability distribution patterns is apparent.

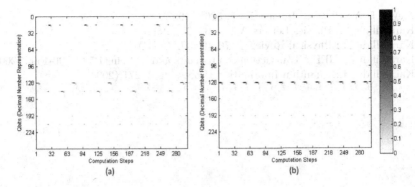

**Fig. 3.** Simulation of the evolution of four-cell QCAs. The initial state is $|10000000\rangle$. At evaluation phases a Hadamard gate acts on both qubits at each cell. (a) The rule is the one shown in Fig. 1(b). (b) The rule is the one shown in Fig. 1(c). Figure from [13].

## 4    Conclusion

Simulations of QCAs with two qubits per cell provided a strong indication for periodic evolution. Furthermore, the period of the probability distribution patterns varies with the evolution rule and the number of cells. This is an indication for possible ability to construct QCAs with desirable periods of evolution. If this is possible then many applications can be found for QCAs with two qubits per cell in quantum information processing.

The simulations, also revealed a rich behavior that stems from a high sensitivity on initial state and gate configuration at evaluation steps. This is a desirable property in computation. QCAs could be a promising architecture for the implementation of neural networks and CA using quantum computers. Another possibility of this architecture is the preparation of the state of a QR which may be used as the initial state for the application of a quantum algorithm.

## References

1. von Neumann, J.: Theory of Self-Reproducing Automata. University of Illinois Press, Urbana IL (1966)
2. Karafyllidis, I., Thanailakis, A.: Ecological Modeling 99, 87 (1997)
3. Karafyllidis, I., Hagouel, P.I., Thanailakis, A., Neureuther, A.R.: IEEE Transactions on Semiconductor Manufacturing 13, 61 (2000)
4. Karafyllidis, I.: Biosystems 45, 1 (1998)
5. Bettelli, S., Serafini, L., Calarco, T.: arXiv:cs/0103009v3
6. De Raedt, H., Hams, A., Michielsen, K., Miyashita, S., Saito, K.: arXiv:quant-ph/0008015v2
7. Feynman, R.P.: International Journal of Physics 21, 467 (1982)
8. Ferguson, A.J., Cain, P.A., Williams, D.A., Briggs, A.D.: Physical Review A 65, 034303-1 (2002)
9. Twamley, J.: Physical Review A 67, 052318-1 (2003)
10. Grössing, G., Zeilinger, A.: Complex Systems 2, 197 (1988)

11. Meyer, D.A.: Physical Review E 55, 5261 (1997)
12. Karafyllidis, I.: Physics Letters A 320, 35–38 (2003)
13. Karafyllidis, I.: Physical Review A 70, 044301 (2004)
14. Karafyllidis, I.: IEEE Transactions on Circuits and Systems I 52, 1590-1596 (2005)
15. Karafyllidis, I.: Quantum Information Processing 2, 271 (2003)

# CSHR: Selection of Cryptographically Suitable Hybrid Cellular Automata Rule

Kaushik Chakraborty and Dipanwita Roy Chowdhury

Department of Computer Science and Engineering, IIT Kharagpur, India
kaushik.chakraborty9@gmail.com,
drc@cse.iitkgp.ernet.in

**Abstract.** In this paper a new procedure has been proposed to synthesize cellular automata (CA) with hybrid rulesets which are very well suited for designing cryptographic primitives. These rulesets are analyzed with respect to nonlinearity, algebraic degree, d-monomial test etc. A new graph theoretic property has also been proposed to analyze the cryptographic strength of cellular automata rules. The randomness of the sequences generated by the rulesets has been tested by NIST test-suite. The experimental results are compared with the existing related works and have shown to be out-performed.

**Keywords:** Cryptographic properties, Hybrid Cellular Automata, Cryptographic primitives, Cellular Automata Sequences.

## 1 Introduction

Design of cryptographic primitives are the most important task in achieving security. Now a days because of the advancement of technology and also discovery of several cryptanalysis techniques, the security strength of existing cryptographic primitives become insufficient. It is not quite easy to design an entity that will satisfy all of the cryptographic properties to make it absolutely secure. Since some of them are self contradicting in nature. For example, a crypto primitive must have higher algebraic degree and higher nonlinearity but to introduce randomness it should have higher order of correlation immunity. These three properties are self contradicting, if higher algebraic degree is achieved, non-linearity will increase but the correlation immunity must be compromised.

Cellular automaton (CA) is already known as good candidate to be employed in cryptographic application. It's self reproducing nature in its cellular space allows to go forward states easily but make backward transition almost impossible. Cellular Automata has a capability of generating good pseudo random sequences [3]. A good random feature is seen only for linear CA rules. But S.R.Blackburn et al.[1] has made a cryptanalysis on linear CA. So, currently the researchers are exploring the nonlinear CA rules and their suitability in cryptography. Though the nonlinear CA rules do not posses good pseudo random properties, but due to their high algebraic degree they are resistant against linear cryptanalysis.

G.C. Sirakoulis and S. Bandini (Eds.): ACRI 2012, LNCS 7495, pp. 591–600, 2012.

Wolfram[8] has proposed *Rule 30* as a good candidate for cryptographic purpose. But because of strong correlation, *Rule 30* can easily be cryptanalyzed. *Willi Meier et al* has shown [6] that for uniform rule 30, the sequence generated by 3-neighborhood 300 cell CA is equivalent to $2^{19}$ only. So, a 300 bits 3-neighborhood CA provides a security of only 19 bits.

From the above discussion it is clear that the sequence generated by uniform linear CA rulesets may show good randomness but can't offer security. The nonlinear rules have higher algebraic degree and also nonlinearity but due to lack of correlation immunity it can be easily cryptanalized. Because of those reasons some researcher [4] has tried to make cryptographically robust hybrid CA rules by mixing the linear and nonlinear rules. In [4] *Sandeep et al* has made good effort by suggesting some cryptographically robust hybrid CA rule and also provide a way of analysis using d-monomial test. Although, the CA rules in [4] has shown good performance in d-monomial test but they have not analyzed one important property, the period of the generated sequence of the CA rulesets. Here we have analyzed the period of the rulesets reported in [4] and observed that they have very short period, hence, they can't be used for cryptographic purpose. Here, we have also studied other cryptographic properties like nonlinearity, algebraic degree, correlation immunity etc of both of the rulesets proposed in [4] and in this paper. Beside this we have provided a procedure for constructing hybrid rulesets consisting of linear and nonlinear rules. This formal procedure will lead the designers to design a cryptographically robust hybrid CA rules without making any hard effort. In this paper, it has been shown that the rulesets generated following our approach posses better cryptographic properties than that of [4]. In this work we also explore a new CA model called *one-null* instead of the conventional *null or periodic boundary CA*. This *1-null model* makes the CA rules more cryptographically robust and it provide a longer period.

## 2    CA Model

In this paper we have considered 3-neighborhood one dimensional CA. Each cells transition is determined by the corresponding state transition function $f_i$. The input bits to the CA cells are denoted by $x_0, x_1, ........, x_n$ and the output bits are denoted by $y_0, y_1, ......., y_n$. For *3-neighborhood CA*, the input of $i^{th}$ cell, $y_i = f_i(x_{i-1}, x_i, x_{i+1})$. But if multiple clock cycles(say $t$) is applied to the 3-neighborhood CA then $i^{th}$ output bit is the function of $2t + 1$ input bits.

$$y_i^t = f_i^t(x_{i-t}, ...., x_i, .....x_{i+t}) \qquad (i)$$

*Rules in Cellular Automata : Rule in Cellular Automata is the decimal representation of the output set of the Boolean function associated with a cell.*

Usually in practice two kinds of boundary cells are used one is *null boundary CA* and another is *periodic boundary CA*. But here we explore the CA rules with the following three boundary condition.

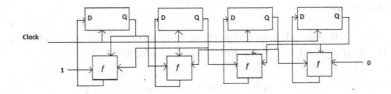

**Fig. 1.** One-null CA Boundary

*one null boundary CA* : The left most boundary is kept as logical 1 and the right most boundary is kept as logical 0.

*null one boundary CA* : The left most boundary is kept as logical 0 and the right most boundary is kept as logical 1.

*one boundary CA* : The left most boundary is kept as logical 1 and the right most boundary is kept as logical 1.

For all kind of CA models we have checked the performance of the CA rules. Among them we have found out that for *one null CA* and for *periodic CA* CA rules satisfies the criteria required for being cryptographically robust. In this paper all calculations are done by taking *one null boundary CA*.

## 3 Properties of Cryptographically Robust Cellular Automata Rules

This section describes the fundamental properties that should be possessed by cryptographic primitives. Here we have explored the tests for cryptographic properties like d-monomial test, balancedness, nonlinearity etc. In addition to these existing test methodologies, we propose a new graph theoretic property to measure the strength of the crypto primitives against the known cryptographic techniques.

### 3.1 *d-Monomial Test*

*d-Monomial test : It is a statistical test for pseudo randomness. If a Boolean function of n Boolean variables is a good pseudo random sequence generator, then it will have $\frac{1}{2}\binom{n}{d}$ d-degree monomials.*

   It is first introduced by [2],[5]. It is a simple procedure to test pseudo randomness of a sequence. Beside its simplicity it has gained a huge acceptance in cryptography community. *d-monomial test* has been used in [4] to test the pseudo randomness of the sequence generated by the CA.

### 3.2 *Balancedness*

*Balanced Boolean Function : A Boolean function of n variables is said to be balanced if for exactly $2^{n-1}$ assignments the function f will evaluate to 0 and for exactly $2^{n-1}$ assignments the function f will evaluate to 1.*

## 3.3  *Resiliency*

*Correlation Immune : A function in n variables is correlation immune of order k, $1 \le k \le n$, if and only if all of the Walsh transforms*

$$\widehat{f(w)} = \sum_{x \in V_n} (-1)^{f(x) \oplus x \cdot w}, \quad 1 \le wt(w) \le k,$$

*are equal zero.*

A Boolean function $f(x)$ in $n$ variables is correlation immune of order $k$ if its values are statistically independent of any subset of $k$ input variables.

*Resiliency : A Boolean function which is balanced and correlation immune of order k is said to be a k-resilient function. For example, resiliency of $f(x_1, x_2) = x_1 \oplus x_2$ is 1.*

## 3.4  *Nonlinearity*

*Nonlinearity : Nonlinearity of a boolean function f of n variables is the distance from f to the set of affine functions with n variables. If $A_n$ be the set of all n bit affine boolean function then $nl(f) = \min\limits_{h \in affine} d(f, h)$ Nonlinearity of an n bit boolean function f can be measured by using the following formula*

$$nl(f) = 2^{n-1} - \frac{1}{2} \max_{w \in \{0,1\}^n} |\widehat{f(w)}|$$

Where $\widehat{f(w)}$ is the Walsh-Hadamard transform of the boolean function $f$.

## 3.5  *Algebraic Degree*

*Algebraic Degree : The maximum number of literals in any conjunction of ANF of a Boolean function is called its degree. For example $f(x_1, x_2) = x_1 \cdot x_2 \oplus x_2$ has algebraic degree 2. Linear functions have algebraic degree 1.*

## 3.6  *Graph Properties of Cellular Automata Rules*

**Cycle:** In most of the cryptographic applications of the CA at first a random number called symmetric key is chosen and put it as a seed to the CA. Depending upon some rule the CA runs for several clock cycles and generates a pseudo random sequence. This sequence must have a long period, otherwise it can easily be cryptanalyzed. As the seed to the CA is random, so, for each seed the period must be long. This period is called the cycle of the CA.

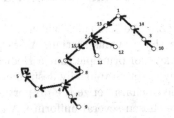

**Fig. 2.** Graph Diagram for Rule-30

We define a term, *coefficient of periodicity* or *COP* as follows,

$$COP = \frac{(max\ period\ generated\ by\ a\ ruleset\ -\ min\ period\ generated\ by\ a\ ruleset)}{max\ period\ generated\ by\ a\ ruleset}$$

The value of *COP* lies between 0 and 1. CA ruleset, having lower *COP* offers better robustness against cryptanalysis.

Consider a directed graph G(V,E) [where V= { $v_i$; all possible seeds to the CA } and E ={ $(v_i, v_j)$ ; transition from $v_j$ form $v_j$ after one clock cycle}]. For example if we consider $4 - cell\ 3 - neighborhood\ uniform\ CA$ for *Rule-30*, then the graph generated by it has the following structure.

From the above figure it is clear that if the seed is 5 or 6 then it has a very short period, but for 10 it has a long period. The short periods are not a desired property, rather a uniform period for all of the seeds may lead to a good pseudo random generator. So, the CA rule must be chosen carefully so, that its *COP* is as low as possible.

$$COP \rightarrow 0 \qquad\qquad (ii)$$

For example in fig-2 the value of *COP* is 1.

**Average Incoming Degree:** A graph having $COP \rightarrow 0$ may not be a good pseudo random generator. Consider the graphs whose $maxperiod = minperiod$, then that kind of random number generator may have bijective mapping from its domain to co-domain. This kind of random number generating function has unique inverse function. So, any sequence can easily be back traced.

Let $G(V, E)$ be a graph generated by a CA. If for any node $v \in V$ in $G$ has small number of incoming edges then for the adversary it will be easier to backtrack and guess the seed. So, the another criteria of a good pseudo random number generator is that it's average number of incoming degree to a node must be high. But this contradicts with the criteria of satisfying *equation(ii)*, because the total number of nodes and edges of that graph is fixed. If the average number of incoming edges of a graph is high then $COP \rightarrow 1$. So, there must be some trade off between those two criteria. Let $c_{min}$ be the length of minimum cycle of the generated graph and each node in that cycle has $d_i$ incoming edges, each node of the generated graph has only one outgoing edges, then for $n$ bit CA the following condition will be satisfied by $c_{min}$ and $d_i.c_{min} \times d_i = 2^n$. So, in ideal case $c_{min} = d_i = 2^{\frac{n}{2}}$

# 4   Selection of Hybrid Cellular Automata Rules

It is not trivial task to choose the CA rules which collectively satisfies all of the conditions described in the previous section. As we have discussed in the last section that it is some kind of principle that a Boolean function cannot simultaneously have too many cryptographically desirable properties. Beside this there is no method available to characterize the properties of the nonlinear CA rules. In this paper we have chosen several uniform CA rules and studied their cryptographic properties and graph theoretic properties. As uniform CA rules are either linear or nonlinear so, they don't satisfy collectively all of the cryptographic properties as well as the graph theoretic properties. But on the basis of their properties we have tried to made some hybrid CA rules which satisfies (better than uniform CA rules) all those cryptographically robustness criteria described in the last section. Here we have studied the cryptographic properties of the CA rules at the 3rd iteration.

**Table 1.** Graph Theoretic Properties of Uniform CA Rule

| Rule | ANF | Max,Min Cycle | Average incoming edges |
|------|-----|---------------|------------------------|
| 22 | $x_{i-1} \cdot x_i \cdot x_{i+1} \oplus x_{i-1} \oplus x_i \oplus x_{i+1}$ | 28,1 | 1.765517 |
| 30 | $x_i \cdot x_{i+1} \oplus x_{i-1} \oplus x_i \oplus x_{i+1}$ | 26,1 | 1.620253 |
| 60 | $x_{i-1} \oplus x_i$ | 16,16 | 1 |
| 90 | $x_{i-1} \oplus x_{i+1}$ | 28,4 | 1 |
| 120 | $x_{i-1} \oplus x_i \cdot x_{i+1}$ | 26,3 | 1.729730 |
| 150 | $x_{i-1} \oplus x_i \oplus x_{i+1}$ | 16,1 | 1.984496 |
| 180 | $x_{i-1} \oplus x_i \oplus x_i \cdot x_{i+1}$ | 30,6 | 1.882353 |
| 210 | $x_{i-1} \oplus x_{i+1} \oplus x_i \cdot x_{i+1}$ | 10,1 | 1.882353 |

**Table 2.** Cryptographic Properties of Uniform CA Rule

| Rule | Algebraic Degree | Nonlinearity(Max) | Balanced(Max) | CI(Max) |
|------|------------------|-------------------|---------------|---------|
| 22 | 7 | 45 | False | 1 |
| 30 | 5 | 40 | True | 1 |
| 60 | 1 | 0 | True | 3 |
| 90 | 1 | 0 | True | 3 |
| 120 | 5 | 48 | True | 0 |
| 150 | 1 | 0 | True | 4 |
| 180 | 4 | 32 | True | 1 |
| 210 | 4 | 32 | True | 0 |

From table 1 and table 2 it is clear that the nonlinear rules have high algebraic degree, nonlinearity but their correlation immunity is very low. This is the reason the sequences generated by rule 30, can be guessed upto certain limit[6]. Again the linear rules have correlation immunity of higher degree. On the basis of table 1 and table 2 we have chosen the CA rules and combine them to construct hybrid CA rules. While constructing the hybrid CA rules we have considered the procedure called CSHR.

---

**Selection Procedure for Cryptographically Suited Hybrid Rules 1: CSHR**

---

**input** : Set of nonlinear CA rules $NLR = \{22, 30, 120, ...\}$; Set of linear CA rules $LR = \{60, 90, 150...\}$;

**output**: Set of cryptographically robust hybrid CA rules;

1 At first consider some nonlinear CA rule from $NLR$ for the first or first few cells, which has good cryptographic properties.

2 For the remaining cells choose equal number of linear and nonlinear rules to form the hybrid rule set. It will help to get a good trade off between algebraic degree and correlation immunity.

3 To increase the algebraic degree and to satisfy the d-monomial test of higher degree put some cases two or three nonlinear rules consecutively.

4 Put one nonlinear rule and more than one linear rule alternatively to increase the order of correlation immunity.

5 Choose those CA rules which has larger period to make the period of the hybrid CA larger. As we know that (90,150) rules make the maximum length cycle so, we have chosen them as linear rules and placed them alternatively.

---

Following the stated facts in the procedure CSHR we have constructed the following hybrid CA rule sets.

- *R-1* : Rule $< 30, 90, 150, 30, 210, 30, 90, 150 >$ spaced alternatively.
- *R-2* : Rule $< 22, 90, 150, 22, 30, 22, 90, 150 >$ spaced alternatively.
- *R-3* : Rule $< 180, 90, 150, 180, 22, 180, 90, 150 >$ spaced alternatively.

## 5   Experimental Results and Comparison

In this section we have investigated the cryptographic properties along with the proposed graph theoretic properties of the hybrid rule sets for both CSHR and [4]. In [4] they have only calculated the $d - monomial$ properties of the hybrid CA rule sets. But to use the CA rules in cryptography all other properties like nonlinearity, algebraic degree, correlation immunity must be tested.

Beside this we have shown that the rules chosen on the basis of the technique described in the last section(CSHR) are better than the hybrid CA rules proposed in[4] in all aspect.

## 5.1   Characteristics of Hybrid CA rules

Some of the experiments have been done using *Mathematica 7.0 Student Edition*, frequency test and cumulative sum test has been done using the NIST's random number test suite. Each cell of the CA is assumed to be initialized with an unknown Boolean value, $x_i$. In each of the experiment we have taken 16 bit CA.

*Graph Theoretic Properties:* In table 3 graph theoretic properties of both CSHR and [4] are explored and from the table it is clear that almost all the rulesets in [4] has small cycles except for *ruleset-2* but it has very small average incoming degree. So, CSHR rulesets are better. In table 3 we have denoted *Average Incoming Degree* as *AID*

**Table 3.** Graph Theoretic Properties

| | [4] | | | | CSHR | | |
|---|---|---|---|---|---|---|---|
| Characteristics | Ruleset-2 | Ruleset-3 | Ruleset-4 | Ruleset-5 | R-1 | R-2 | R-3 |
| Max,Min Cycle | 1053,1 | 83,9 | 84,6 | 50,1 | 548,250 | 696,0 | 466,7 |
| AID | 1.33 | 1.882353 | 2 | 1.9999 | 1.771626 | 1.956766 | 1.815603 |

*Algebraic Degree:* In table 4 we have calculated the algebraic degree of both CSHR and [4] for up to three clock cycles. From the table it is clear that the maximum algebraic degree for the rulesets in [4] for the $3^{rd}$ clock cycle is 4, but in CSHR it is 7.

**Table 4.** Algebraic Degree

| | [4] | | | | | | CSHR | | |
|---|---|---|---|---|---|---|---|---|---|
| Iteration | Ruleset-1 | Ruleset-2 | Ruleset-3 | Ruleset-4 | Ruleset-5 | Ruleset-6 | R-1 | R-2 | R-3 |
| 1 | 2 | 2 | 2 | 2 | 2 | 2 | 2 | 3 | 3 |
| 2 | 2 | 2 | 3 | 3 | 3 | 3 | 3 | 5 | 5 |
| 3 | 3 | 3 | 3 | 4 | 4 | 4 | 5 | 6 | 7 |

*Correlation Immunity:* In table 5 we have calculated the correlation immunity of the CA rules for both CSHR and [4] up to three clock cycles. The correlation immunity of the CA rules decreases with the number of clock cycles for both CSHR and [4]. Though *ruleset* − 2 has higher correlation immunity but it has low algebraic degree.

*Nonlinearity:* In table 6 we have calculated the nonlinearity of the CA rules for both CSHR and [4] up to three clock cycles. By both of the rulesets we can conclude that CSHR CA rule sets has higher nonlinearity than [4].

**Table 5.** Correlation Immunity

| Iteration | [4] | | | | | | CSHR | | |
|---|---|---|---|---|---|---|---|---|---|
| | Ruleset-1 | Ruleset-2 | Ruleset-3 | Ruleset-4 | Ruleset-5 | Ruleset-6 | R-1 | R-2 | R-3 |
| 1 | 1 | 1 | 1 | 2 | 2 | 2 | 2 | 2 | 2 |
| 2 | 1 | 3 | 2 | 2 | 2 | 2 | 2 | 2 | 2 |
| 3 | 0 | 1 | 2 | 1 | 2 | 2 | 1 | 0 | 1 |

**Table 6.** Nonlinearity

| Iteration | [4] | | | | | | CSHR | | |
|---|---|---|---|---|---|---|---|---|---|
| | Ruleset-1 | Ruleset-2 | Ruleset-3 | Ruleset-4 | Ruleset-5 | Ruleset-6 | R-1 | R-2 | R-3 |
| 1 | 2 | 2 | 2 | 2 | 2 | 2 | 2 | 1 | 2 |
| 2 | 8 | 8 | 8 | 12 | 12 | 12 | 8 | 10 | 10 |
| 3 | 32 | 48 | 48 | 48 | 48 | 48 | 48 | 48 | 52 |

*d-monomial test:* In table 7 we have calculated the d-monomial test of the CA rules for both CSHR and [4] up to three clock cycles. From the tables it is clear that for higher order terms CSHR rule sets has better d-monomials than [4].

**Table 7.** d-monomial test

| Deg | Ideal | Rulesets in [4] | | | | | | CSHR | | |
|---|---|---|---|---|---|---|---|---|---|---|
| | | R-1 | R-2 | R-3 | R-4 | R-5 | R-6 | R-1 | R-2 | R-3 |
| 1-deg | 1,2,3 | 3,3,5 | 3,3,2 | 3,2,4 | 3,2,4 | 3,2,4 | 3,2,4 | 3,3,3 | 3,3,3 | 3,1,3 |
| 2-deg | 1,5,10 | 1,3,3 | 1,3,3 | 1,3,5 | 1,3,7 | 1,3,5 | 1,3,5 | 2,5,9 | 0,4,8 | 1,4,6 |
| 3-deg | 0,5,52 | 0,0,2 | 0,0,1 | 0,1,3 | 0,1,7 | 0,2,6 | 0,2,6 | 0,2,14 | 1,7,24 | 0,4,7 |
| 4-deg | 0,2,52 | 0,0,0 | 0,0,0 | 0,0,0 | 0,1,2 | 0,0,3 | 0,0,3 | 0,0,6 | 0,1,16 | 0,2,10 |
| 5-deg | 0,1,10 | 0,0,0 | 0,0,0 | 0,0,0 | 0,0,0 | 0,0,0 | 0,0,0 | 0,0,1 | 0,1,12 | 0,1,10 |
| 6-deg | 0,0,3 | 0,0,0 | 0,0,0 | 0,0,0 | 0,0,0 | 0,0,0 | 0,0,0 | 0,0,0 | 0,0,2 | 0,0,4 |
| 7-deg | 0,0,0 | 0,0,0 | 0,0,0 | 0,0,0 | 0,0,0 | 0,0,0 | 0,0,0 | 0,0,0 | 0,0,1 | 0,0,1 |

*Frequency & Cumulative Sum Test :* Frequency test and Cumulative sum test are used to test the randomness of generated sequence. Here we have run these tests on the sequence generated by the proposed rulesets using the test suite

**Table 8.** Frequency Test & Cumulative Test

| Rule set | Frequency Test P-value | Cumulative Sum Test P-value |
|---|---|---|
| R-1 | 0.066882 | 0.035174 |
| R-2 | 0.033 | 0.213309 |
| R-3 | 0.35085 | 0.350485 |

provided by NIST [7]. For each sequence we have calculated $P - value$ for both of the tests. If the $P - value < 0.01$ then the generated sequence will not be called random[7]. Our proposed rulesets have passed these tests successfully. In table 8 we have reported the $P - values$ for these tests.

# 6    Conclusion

In this paper a new graph theoretic property has been introduced to analyze the cryptographic strength of cellular automata (CA) rules. A new procedure has also described for selecting the nonlinear and linear rules to construct a cryptographically suited hybrid CA. The rulesets selected following this procedure are analyzed with respect to nonlinearity, algebraic degree, d-monomial test and the randomness test by NIST test-suite. The experimental results are compared with that of existing related results and are shown to be better.

# References

1. Blackburn, S.r., Murphy, S., Paterson, K.g.: Comments on "theory and applications of cellular automata in cryptography". IEEE Transactions on Computers 46, 637–638 (1997)
2. Filiol, É.: A New Statistical Testing for Symmetric Ciphers and Hash Functions. In: Deng, R.H., Qing, S., Bao, F., Zhou, J. (eds.) ICICS 2002. LNCS, vol. 2513, pp. 342–353. Springer, Heidelberg (2002)
3. Hortensius, P.D., McLeod, R.D., Card, H.C.: Parallel random number generation for vlsi systems using cellular automata. IEEE Trans. Computers 38(10), 1466–1473 (1989)
4. Karmakar, S., Mukhopadhyay, D., Roy Chowdhury, D.: d-Monomial Tests of Nonlinear Cellular Automata for Cryptographic Design. In: Bandini, S., Manzoni, S., Umeo, H., Vizzari, G. (eds.) ACRI 2010. LNCS, vol. 6350, pp. 261–270. Springer, Heidelberg (2010)
5. Markku-juhani, Saarinen, O.: Chosen-iv statistical attacks on estream stream ciphers. In: eSTREAM, ECRYPT Stream Cipher Project, Report 2006/013, pp. 5–19 (2006)
6. Meier, W., Staffelbach, O.: Analysis of Pseudo Random Sequences Generated by Cellular Automata. In: Davies, D.W. (ed.) EUROCRYPT 1991. LNCS, vol. 547, pp. 186–199. Springer, Heidelberg (1991)
7. NIST Pseudo Random Number Testing Suite, http://csrc.nist.gov/groups/st/toolkit/rng/documentation_software.html
8. Wolfram, S.: Random sequence generation by cellular automata. Advances in Applied Mathematics 7, 123–169

# CASTREAM: A New Stream Cipher Suitable for Both Hardware and Software

Sourav Das and Dipanwita Roy Chowdhury

Alcatel-Lucent India Ltd and Dept. of CSE, IIT, Kharagpur, India
sourav10101976@gmail.com, drc@cse.iitkgp.ernet.in

**Abstract.** A new Cellular Automata based stream cipher is proposed which is suitable for both hardware and software. It has a non-linear combiner where two non-linear blocks along with a linear block are linearly combined to produce the key-streams. Unlike Non-linear Feedback Shift Register (NFSR) based non-linear combiners, it combines 128-bit blocks using parallel evolution of Cellular Automata (CA) and small CA based S-boxes. The usage of CA prevents the correlation attack and two layers of re-usable small S-boxes prevent the algebraic attacks. The proposed stream cipher takes 128 bits Key and 128 bits of Initial Vector(IV). Theoretically, the cipher operates with an encryption speed of nearly 8 bits per cycle. The initialization process needs 96 cycles which is much faster than Grain and Trivium. This stream cipher is extensible in terms of Key size and provides configurable security and vendor specific implementation option. On implementation, the proposed cipher receives higher throughput than the existing standards.

**Keywords:** Stream Cipher, Security Properties, Cellular Automata, S-box.

## 1 Introduction

Stream ciphers have gained a lot of attention in recent years and provide fast encryption. In stream ciphers a key stream sequence is generated from a secret key. The plain-text is simply XORed with the key stream to encrypt the message at the encryption site. At the decryption site, the same key stream is generated with the same secret key. The cipher-text is XORed with the key-stream to get back the plain-text. The ESTREAM [13] project had been launched to search for a good stream cipher that can provide advantage in performance over block ciphers.

The ESTREAM project has divided the stream ciphers into two categories, namely, software oriented stream ciphers that provide fast encryption in software and hardware oriented stream ciphers that provide fast encryption with easy hardware implementation. Traditionally, the hardware oriented stream ciphers used LFSRs (Linear Feedback Shift Register) filtered with a non-linear function. But such kind of stream ciphers have been subjected to correlation attacks [10], [9], and algebraic attacks [4], [5]. Later, stream ciphers started using NFSRs,

G.C. Sirakoulis and S. Bandini (Eds.): ACRI 2012, LNCS 7495, pp. 601–610, 2012.
© Springer-Verlag Berlin Heidelberg 2012

which are LFSR with non-linear feedback. The NFSRs are linearly combined to produce the key-streams. ESTREAM finalist Trivium [3] is an example of such stream ciphers. The stream cipher Grain [8] uses a combination of linearly filtered NFSR with a non-linearly filtered LFSR. Mickey [1] is another finalist in ESTREAM hardware profiles, and it uses variable clocking method. The software oriented stream ciphers, however, in general use block oriented state transitions that help in efficient software implementation. Examples of such stream ciphers are Rabbit [2], HC-128 [16] etc.

Cellular Automata (CA) generate statistically random sequences which are necessary for stream ciphers. CA also provide parallel transformations that help to achieve more throughput which is also essential for stream ciphers. The use of Cellular Automata in stream ciphers was proposed first by Wolfram using Rule 30 [14], [15]. However, Meier and Staffelbach found weaknesses in that stream cipher [11]. But, the weaknesses of these stream ciphers may not be because of any inherent weaknesses of CA, since CA are just primitives that generate statistically random sequences. The problem was the way CA were used in those stream ciphers. If CA are used a bit differently in the construction of stream ciphers, CA can still prove to be excellent primitive for stream ciphers.

In [7] and [6], it was shown how to generate highly non-linear S-boxes using CA. These papers demonstrate CA can be effective cryptographic primitives. These S-boxes can be used in a stream cipher to enhance the security. The S-boxes are dynamically generated, scalable and secure with efficiency in implementation. In this paper, the idea of S-box generation in [6] is extended to generate the non-linear block of a stream cipher. The uniqueness of this non-linear block is that it uses CA based small non-linear generators with CA based mixing among the generators. The advantages of such a non-linear block are higher throughput, scalability and statistically random output sequences. Using two such non-linear blocks and a linear block of maximum length linear CA, a stream cipher, *CASTREAM*, with 128 bits Key and 128 bits IV is designed in this paper.

This paper is organized as follows. Section 2 describes the cipher along with the initialization process. The security properties of the cipher is analyzed in section 3. Section 4 provides the implementation aspects of the cipher which has two subsections for hardware and software implementations.

## 2    Description of the Stream Cipher

The high level block diagram of the construction is shown in Figure 1. This stream cipher has three 128 bits blocks of state which are linearly combined to produce 128 bit key-stream in each round. Two of the three blocks perform non-linear transitions and the third block performs linear transition which guarantees the period. The linear block is a 128-bit maximum length CA using rules 90/150. This CA run for sixteen cycles in each iteration. The non-linear parts are designed using a series of dynamically generated CA based S-boxes. The S-boxes are generated by using the principle of input governing the number of

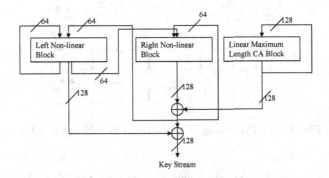

**Fig. 1.** The Stream Cipher Block Diagram

cycles of a maximum length CA with a constant initial seed as shown in [7]. Each non-linear block also has a 128-bit maximum length linear CA to achieve mixing among the S-boxes with good statistical properties. Both the non-linear blocks contain two non-linear layers with a maximum length linear CA sandwiched between them to achieve mixing. The linear CA in the non-linear block also run for sixteen cycles. The non-linear layers contain a series of 4-bit, 5-bit and 6-bit S-boxes. These S-boxes are mixed in such a way that they give rise to four 32-bit blocks of S-boxes. Two different combinations of the small S-boxes are used to form the thirty-two bits blocks. The first combination contains 5-bit, 4-bit, 5-bit, 4-bit, 5-bit, 4-bit and 5-bit S-boxes in order. The second combination contains 4-bit, 5-bit, 4-bit, 6-bit, 4-bit, 5-bit and 4-bit S-boxes in order. Each combination is repeated four times to constitute the non-linear layer. In the left hand side non-linear block, the first combination makes the first non-linear layer and the second combination constitutes the second non-linear layer as shown in figure 2. The right hand side non-linear block consists of the second combination in the first non-linear layer and the first combination in the second non-linear layer as shown in Figure 3.

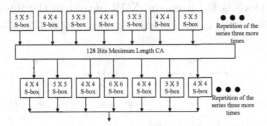

**Fig. 2.** The Processing of Left Hand Side Non-linear Block

In each iteration, the linear block feedbacks to itself. The two non-linear blocks send feedback to the other block as well as to itself as follows. Let us divide the each 128 non-linear state bits into eight 16-bits blocks. Then these blocks are

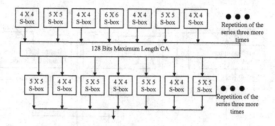

**Fig. 3.** The Processing of Right Hand Side Non-linear Block

permuted so that each alternate block is taken from the left and right hand side non-linear blocks. If we denote the left state bits $(L_1 \cdots L_{128})$, the right state bits as $(R_1 \cdots R_{128})$ and the linear state bits as $(C_1 \cdots C_{128})$, then after permutation the left state bits become:

$(L_1 \cdots L_{16}, R_1 \oplus C_1 \cdots R_{16} \oplus C_{16}, L_{17} \cdots L_{32}, \cdots, L_{49} \cdots L_{64}, R_{49} \oplus C_{49} \cdots R_{64} \oplus C_{64})$.

Similarly, the right hand side state bits become:

$(L_{65} \cdots L_{80}, R_{65} \oplus C_{65} \cdots R_{80} \oplus C_{80}, \cdots, L_{113} \cdots L_{128}, R_{113} \oplus C_{113} \cdots R_{128} \oplus C_{128})$.

The key stream is generated by XORing all the three blocks. The encryption is performed after XORing the key stream with the plain-text. The decryption is performed after XORing the key stream with the cipher-text.

## 2.1 Initialization

The initialization of the cipher uses the same method as the key stream generation. On the left hand side non-linear block, the Key bits are loaded into the state registers. On the right hand side non-linear block, the IV bits are loaded. For the linear side, XOR of Key and IV bits are loaded. After loading the Key and the IV bits, the cipher is iterated six times without generating any key stream. While initializing, the only difference from the key stream generation is that the linear block is fed from the XOR output of the internal states. Also, after the Key and the IV are loaded, the last bit in the linear CA is always

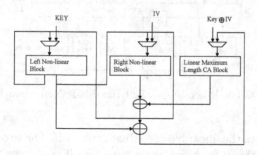

**Fig. 4.** The Cipher Initialization

kept at logic one during initialization. The key-streams are taken out from the seventh iteration. The initialization process is shown in Figure 4.

## 2.2   Parameterizations

The parameterizations of the cipher help different vendors implement the cipher in a different way. A different parameter value will result in a different key-stream sequence even with the same Key-IV pairs in the following way. Each of the S-boxes takes the seed as a parameter. There are four 128-bits layers of S-boxes in the non-linear blocks. Each layer takes a parameter of 128 bits. Hence, the total size of the parameter is $128 \times 4 = 512$ bits. However, care should be taken that none of the S-boxes is parameterized with all zeros. To make the parameterizations simple, every fourth bit of the 128-bits parameter is made to logic one. This makes the user parameter size as $96 \times 4 = 384$.

## 3   Security Analysis

In this section, we provide security analysis of the cipher.

### 3.1   An Analysis of the Cipher

Let, $f_{NL}$, $f_L$ denote the non-linear function of the S-boxes and linear function of maximum length CA, respectively. Also, let $K_i$, and $IV_i$ denote the $i$-th, ($i \in (1 \cdots 128)$), bit of the key and the initial value. $L_{i,j}$, $R_{i,j}$ and $C_{i,j}$ denote the $i$-th, ($i \in (1 \cdots 128)$), bit of the the state bits of left hand side non-linear block, right hand side non-linear block and linear CA block, respectively, during some iteration $j$. For clarity we analyze the evolution of first bit ($i=1$) for all the blocks below. The evolution of other bits can easily be extended from this analysis.

**The Evolution of the First Bit of All the Blocks.** The equation for the left hand side non-linear block after the first S-box layer transformation (denoting it as $LS1_{i,j}$) is, since the first S-box transforms five bits:

$$LS1_{1,j} = f_{NL}(L_{1,j}, L_{2,j}, L_{3,j}, L_{4,j}, L_{5,j}) \tag{1}$$

After the linear transformation (denoting the bits as $LC1_{i,j}$), the equation for the first bit becomes, since after sixteen cycles each bit in the CA will depend on itself, 16 more bits from left and 16 more bits from right:

$$LC1_{1,j} = f_L(LS1_{1,j}, \cdots, LS1_{17,j}) \tag{2}$$

Expanding, as $LS1_{17,j}$ is the part of $4 \times 4$ S-box,

$$LC1_{1,j} = f_L(f_{NL}(L_{1,j}, \cdots, L_{5,j}), \cdots, f_{NL}(L_{15,j}, \cdots, L_{18,j})) \tag{3}$$

Then occurs the second layer of S-box substitution. If $LS2_{i,j}$ denotes the output of this layer, then the expression for the first bit is:

$$LS2_{1,j} = f_{NL}(LC1_{1,j}, \cdots, LC1_{4,j}) \tag{4}$$

Expanding, since $LC1_{4,j}$ will depend on sixteen bits from right side and will also be affected by all the bits in the left hand side,

$$LS2_{1,j} = f_{NL}(f_L(LS1_{1,j}, \cdots, LS1_{17,j}), \cdots, f_L(LS1_{1,j}, \cdots, LS1_{20,j})) \tag{5}$$

Expanding, since $LS1_{20,j}$ depends on $L_{19,j}, \cdots, L_{23,j}$

$$LS2_{1,j} = f_{NL}(f_L(f_{NL}(L_{1,j}, \cdots), \cdots, f_{NL}(\cdots, L_{23,j})), \cdots) \tag{6}$$

Note that, $LS2_{i,j}$ is nothing but $L_{1,j+1}$. Also, $L_{17,j} \cdots L_{23,j}$ are $R_{1,j} \oplus C_{1,j}$ $\cdots R_{7,j} \oplus C_{7,j}$ due to the swap of bits at the end of every round. Hence, we can write, denoting $F_{NLL}$ as the transformation function of the left hand side non-linear block (which is the right hand side of the equation 6):

$$L_{1,j+1} = F_{NLL}(L_{1,j}, \cdots, L_{16,j}, R_{1,j}, \cdots, R_{7,j}, C_{1,j} \cdots C_{7,j}) \tag{7}$$

In a similar manner, we can show that in the right hand side also, the expression for the first bit is:

$$R_{1,j+1} = F_{NLR}(L_{65,j}, \cdots, L_{80,j}, R_{65,j}, \cdots, R_{71,j}, C_{65,j}, \cdots C_{71,j}) \tag{8}$$

where, $F_{NLR}$ is the transformation function of the right hand side, which is similar to the expression in equation 6, but the functions are applied in the reverse order.

Then, it is easy to derive the equation for the first bit of the linear CA block, which is, since this block runs for 16 cycles:

$$C_{1,j+1} = f_L(C_{1,j}, \cdots, C_{17,j}) \tag{9}$$

Finally, the equation for the first bit of the 128 block of key stream is:

$$KS_{i,j+1} = L_{1,j+1} \oplus R_{1,j+1} \oplus C_{1,j+1} \tag{10}$$

where, $L_{1,j+1}, R_{1,j+1}, C_{1,j+1}$ are as in equations 7, 8 and 9.

**Expression for other Bits.** Since the non-linear blocks use asymmetric S-box transformation, the expression of each bit will be different. Hence, it is difficult to write generalized expression for all the 128 bits. If we simplify the S-boxes to have only uniform 4-bits S-boxes, then we can make an attempt. In that case, the first bit is affected by four bit tuple it belongs to and another four 4-bits tuples from immediate right. It can be also be shown that another four 4-bits tuple affect each state bit from the left for the bit numbers $i \in (17 \cdots 128)$ for both left hand side and the right hand side non-linear blocks. So, we can write a generic expression for any non-linear next state bit in the simplified non-linear block, $X_{i,j+1}$ in terms of the previous state bits $X_{i,j}$, where $i$ denotes the $i$-th state bit ($i \in (33 \cdots 96)$) and $j$ denotes the iteration number.

$$X_{i,j+1} = F(X_{i-(16+(i \bmod 4)),j}, \cdots, X_{i+20-(i \bmod 4),j}) \tag{11}$$

where, $F$ denotes the transformation function of the non-linear block. Hence, each state bit will depend on at least 36 bits from the previous state.

For the linear state bits the corresponding equation is:

$$C_{i,j+1} = f_L(C_{i-16,j}, \cdots, C_{i+16,j}) \tag{12}$$

**Key and IV Mixing During Initialization.** We show now that each state bit after initialization depends on all the Key and the IV bits. We divide the left hand side non-linear block and the right hand side non-linear block into eight sixteen bits blocks. Let us denote them $L_1, L_2, L_3, L_4, L_5, L_6, L_7, L_8$ for the left hand side non-linear block and $R_1, R_2, R_3, R_4, R_5, R_6, R_7, R_8$ for the right hand side non-linear block. We use the following facts.

1. After sixteen cycles in the linear CA of the non-linear block, every bit in the each sixteen bit block depends on all the bits in that block.

2. After both the S-box transformations and linear CA transformation running for sixteen cycles, all the bits from the immediate neighboring blocks affect at least one bit in the current block. In addition, a few bits from neighbor's neighbor block affect at least one bit in the current block.

We also simplify the analysis by ignoring the XOR from the linear block. However, due to this XOR, if we prove that after the initialization the right block affects all the bits in the left block, then, it will automatically imply that the linear block also affects all the state bits in the non-linear blocks. Also, due to the XOR feedback to the linear block, the proof will also imply that the linear block is also affected by all the state bits.

Now let us see how the permutation at the end of the round takes place for different rounds during initialization.

Round 1: $L_1, L_2, L_3, L_4, L_5, L_6, L_7, L_8, R_1, R_2, R_3, R_4, R_5, R_6, R_7, R_8$

Round 2: $L_1, R_1, L_2, R_2, L_3, R_3, L_4, R_4, L_5, R_5, L_6, R_6, L_7, R_7, L_8, R_8$

Round 3: $L_1, L_5, R_1, R_5, L_2, L_6, R_2, R_6, L_3, L_7, R_3, R_7, L_4, L_8, R_4, R_8$

Round 4: $L_1, L_3, L_5, L_7, R_1, R_3, R_5, R_7, L_2, L_4, L_6, L_8, R_2, R_4, R_6, R_8$

Round 5: $L_1, L_2, L_3, L_4, L_5, L_6, L_7, L_8, R_1, R_2, R_3, R_4, R_5, R_6, R_7, R_8$

Now, if we start backtracking from round 5 for each of the blocks, we can easily see that all sixteen blocks have affected each of the block. We show this for the first block below.

After Round 1, the block $L_1$ is affected by all the bits in the block $L_2$ (plus some more bits from $L_3$, which we ignore for this example). At Round 2, $L_1$ is affected by $R_1$. But $R_1$ is already affected by all the bits in $R_2$ in Round 1. Hence, after Round 2, $L_1$ depends on $L_2, R_1, R_2$.

At Round 3, $L_1$, depends on all the bits from $L_5$. But, in Round 2 $L5$ depends on all the bits from $R_5$. In Round 1, $L_5$ depends on all the bits of $L_4$ and $L_6$.

Again, in Round 1 $R_5$ depends on all the bits of $R_4$ and $R_6$. Hence, at the end of Round 3, $L_1$ depends on $L_2, L_4, L_5, L_6, R_1, R_2, R_4, R_5, R_6$.

At Round 4, $L_1$, depends on all the bits from $L_3$. But, in Round 3 $L3$ depends on all the bits from $L_7$ which depends on $L_6$ and $L_8$ at the first round itself. In Round 2, $L_7$ depends on $R_6$ and $R_7$. In Round 1, $R_7$ depends on $R_6$ and $R_8$. Again, in round 2 $L_3$, depends on $R_2$ and $R_3$. Hence, at Round 4, $L_1$ depends on all the sixteen 16-bits blocks, namely, $L_1, L_2, L_3, L_4, L_5, L_6, L_7, L_8,$ $R_1, R_2, R_3, R_4, R_5, R_6, R_7, R_8$.

In a similar manner, it can be shown that all other blocks are affected by rest of the blocks after four round of initialization. Before the Round 1 all the blocks are initialized with the Key bits and IV bits. Hence, after four rounds of initialization, all state bits are affected by all the key bits and the IV bits.

### 3.2 Statistical Tests

The output of the stream cipher was evaluated for statistical randomness using NIST [12] statistical test tool. This test tool contains sixteen statistical tests to evaluate a random number generator. We generated 128 million bits of key streams and used the tool for the evaluation with 10 bitstreams of size 12.8 million each. The following Key and IV pairs are used:
$Key : 0xFEDCBA98765432100123456789ABCDEF$
$IV : 0x0123456789ABCDEFFEDCBA9876543210$.
The default parameters of the tools were used except for the block length of Approximate Entropy where the block length used was 4. With these inputs, the tool performed a number of statistical tests out of which 15 tests failed and 1829 tests passed. Table 1 shows the result of the statistical tests with the first bit stream. $p - value > 0.01$ implies that the tests are passed.

**Table 1.** Statistical Tests Summary

| Test | p-val | Test | p-val |
|---|---|---|---|
| Frequency | 0.032 | Longest Run | 0.782 |
| Block Freq | 0.726 | Non-overlapping Template | 0.369 |
| Runs | 0.789 | Overlapping Template | 0.356 |
| Rank | 0.564 | Random Excur | 0.065 |
| FFT | 0.664 | Random Excur Var | 0.548 |
| Universal | 0.747 | Approx Entropy | 0.247 |
| Serial | 0.560 | Lin Complexity | 0.513 |
| CuSums | 0.062 | CuSums(Reverse) | 0.050 |

## 4   Implementation and Performance

In this section we provide the architecture for hardware implementation along with the software implementation.

## 4.1   Hardware Implementation

The hardware architecture of the key stream generation algorithm of the proposed cipher is shown in Figure 5. The hardware layout is made same as the structure of the cipher. The S-boxes are implemented by using ROMs. The CA are implemented using combinational logic. There is a 128 bit flip-flop layer in each part of the state that perform the sequential part of the CA of running sixteen cycles. The flip-flops in the non-linear layer takes the input from the first S-box layer on Reset and from the output of the CA combinational circuit at each cycle. The output of the CA combinational part is sent to the second S-box layer whose output is connected to a three input XOR layer. The XOR output is fed to the Key Stream flip-flops. After running sixteen cycles, a counter enables the Key Stream flip-flops where the key-stream can be extracted. The state flip-flops are Reset again with the wire permutation of the their contents at the end of sixteen cycles. The linear block also consists of a series of flip-flops with CA combinational logic. The CA in the linear block always take their inputs from the outputs of the CA combinational logic.

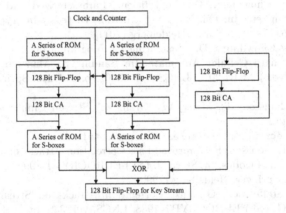

**Fig. 5.** The Hardware Architecture

The above circuit was implemented using Xilinx 7.i synthesis tool. The speed was 183 MHz and the number of slices required was 1196. Since, at each iteration it provides a key stream block of 128 bits, the throughput is $183 \times 128 = 23.4$ GBPS, which is very high and better than all the ESTREAM candidates. The throughput to area ratio is 19.4 which is again higher than all the existing stream ciphers. On post place and route (PPR) results, the area required was more and the speed was less than the synthesis results.

## 5   Conclusion

In this paper, a new stream cipher is proposed based on Cellular Automata (CA). The cipher is secure and suitable for both hardware and software. It operates at a good speed. The cipher can be used both in small and large devices. It is also extensible to a higher key size.

# References

1. Babbage, S., Dodd, M.: The stream cipher MICKEY 2.0.,
   http://www.ecrypt.eu.org/stream/mickeyp3.html
2. Boesgaard, M., Vesterager, M., Pedersen, T., Christiansen, J., Scavenius, O.: Rabbit: A New High-Performance Stream Cipher. In: Johansson, T. (ed.) FSE 2003. LNCS, vol. 2887, pp. 307–329. Springer, Heidelberg (2003)
3. De Canniere, C., Preneel, B.: Trivium Specification,
   http://www.ecrypt.eu.org/stream/triviump3.html
4. Courtois, N.T.: Fast Algebraic Attacks on Stream Ciphers with Linear Feedback. In: Boneh, D. (ed.) CRYPTO 2003. LNCS, vol. 2729, pp. 176–194. Springer, Heidelberg (2003)
5. Courtois, N., Meier, W.: Algebraic Attacks on Stream Ciphers with Linear Feedback. In: Biham, E. (ed.) EUROCRYPT 2003. LNCS, vol. 2656, pp. 345–359. Springer, Heidelberg (2003)
6. Das, S., Roy Chowdhury, D.: An Efficient, Parameterized and Scalable S-box for Stream Ciphers. In: Lai, X., Yung, M., Lin, D. (eds.) Inscrypt 2010. LNCS, vol. 6584, pp. 77–94. Springer, Heidelberg (2011)
7. Das, S., Roy Chowdhury, D.: Generating Cryptographically Suitable Non-linear Maximum Length Cellular Automata. In: Bandini, S., Manzoni, S., Umeo, H., Vizzari, G. (eds.) ACRI 2010. LNCS, vol. 6350, pp. 241–250. Springer, Heidelberg (2010)
8. Hell, M., Johansson, T., Meier, W.: Grain - A Stream Cipher for Constrained Environments,
   http://www.ecrypt.eu.org/stream/Grainp3.html
9. Johansson, T., Jönsson, F.: Improved Fast Correlation Attacks on Stream Ciphers via Convolutional Codes. In: Stern, J. (ed.) EUROCRYPT 1999. LNCS, vol. 1592, pp. 347–362. Springer, Heidelberg (1999)
10. Meier, W., Staffelbach, O.: Fast Correlation Attacks on Stream Ciphers. In: Günther, C.G. (ed.) EUROCRYPT 1988. LNCS, vol. 330, pp. 301–314. Springer, Heidelberg (1988)
11. Meier, W., Staffelbach, O.: Analysis of Pseudo Random Sequences Generated by Cellular Automata. In: Davies, D.W. (ed.) EUROCRYPT 1991. LNCS, vol. 547, pp. 186–199. Springer, Heidelberg (1991)
12. NIST Statistical Test Suit, http://csrc.nist.gov/rng/
13. The Estream Project, http://www.ecrypt.eu.org/stream/
14. Wolfram, S.: Random Sequence Generation by Cellular Automata. Advances in Applied Mathematics 7, 123 (1986)
15. Wolfram, S.: Cryptography with Cellular Automata. In: Williams, H.C. (ed.) CRYPTO 1985. LNCS, vol. 218, pp. 429–432. Springer, Heidelberg (1986)
16. Wu, H.: The Stream Cipher HC-128,
    http://www.ecrypt.eu.org/stream/p3ciphers/hc/hc128_p3.pdf

# Evolution of 2-Dimensional Cellular Automata as Pseudo-random Number Generators*

Bernard Girau[1] and Nikolaos Vlassopoulos[2]

[1] INRIA Nancy-Grand Est / LORIA
Cortex Team, F-54600, France
Bernard.Girau@loria.fr
[2] INRIA Nancy-Grand Est / LORIA
MaIA Team, F-54600, France
nvlassopoulos@gmail.com

**Abstract.** In this paper we revisit the problem of using Genetic Algorithms to evolve 2-dimensional Cellular Automata (CA) as Pseudo-random Number Generators (PRNG). Our main contribution is two-fold. First, we review the problem of using CAs as PRNGs under the scope of the newer and more demanding batteries of pseudo-random generator tests that have been developed since the introduction of DIEHARD [1]. Second, we introduce a composite fitness metric, that incorporates elements from PRNG tests, to be used in the evolution of the CAs.

## 1 Introduction

Pseudo-random number generators (PRNGs) play an important role in many diverse scientific fields. Ranging from modeling physical phenomena [2], [3], Complex Systems [4], Pattern Recognition [5] Computational Physics [6] and Markov Chain Monte Carlo methods [7], modern scientific experiments and simulations rely heavily on high quality PRNGs.

Using Cellular Automata (CA) as PRNGs is not a new concept. What makes CA particularly attractive for such a task is their regular structure and locality of interconnections that leads to more efficient hardware implementations. This became apparent really early, Hortensius et al, [8], and a substantial work has been done on the field, with applications in several different domains, e.g. PRNGs [9], Cryptography [10], [11], [12] and hardware testing [13], [14]. Similarly, using genetic algorithms to evolve CA has been applied on several different occasions and for a wide and diverse range of problems, see e.g. [15], [16] and other works from the same authors, but also [17] where the authors evolve CAs to simulate the rules of DNA evolution, [18] for an application to simulating the recrystallization process, [19] for an application in Lava flow simulation. Finally, there are several publications in the literature with respect to evolving CA as PRNGs, see for example the work by Tomassini et al, [20], [21].

---

* This work has been partly realized thanks to the support of the Région Lorraine and the CPER MISN TALC project.

G.C. Sirakoulis and S. Bandini (Eds.): ACRI 2012, LNCS 7495, pp. 611–622, 2012.

So, what is new in this work? Our motivation was two-fold. First, most of the work in the CA based PRNG literature bases its results on the DIEHARD [1] battery of PRNG tests, a long standing, *de-facto* tool. However, batteries of tests have evolved in the past years, first with the introduction of "DieHarder" [22], and lately with the introduction of "TestU01" [23], a particularly hard test-suite that "stresses" even high-quality PRNGs such as the Mersenne Twister [24]. What we wanted to investigate was the performance of CA as PRNGs under the scope of these newer tools. Second, we wanted to investigate the evolution of Cellular Automata that are based on a more generic set of rules than the additive CA, that are used in the literature, and that we present here. What we found out, as we will see in Sec. 3, is that in order to evolve more general CA, we need to introduce new metrics that specifically target and evaluate the performance of a CA with respect to PRNG batteries of tests. In this work we discuss the main direction of our research so far, i.e. the construction of a metric that is suitable for evolving CAs so as to pass specific tests from a PRNG battery of tests.

The remaining sections are organized as follows. First, in Sec. 2 we describe the CA subset that we use in our experiments. Section 3 presents our observations and comments on the use of entropy as a metric for evolving CA as PRNGs. Section 4 introduces the proposed metrics for evolving CA and what led us to the introduction of these metrics. Finally, Sec. 5 presents our results and our future work.

## 2   CA Subset and Model Description

A Cellular Automaton is a discrete, spatially extended dynamical system. A two-dimensional CA can be represented by an array of cells, $\mathcal{L} \subset \mathbb{Z}^2$, such that each cell can be in a discrete state. We denote the state of a cell, $c$, at time $t$ by $\sigma_c^t$ and its neighborhood by $\mathcal{N}_c$. The time evolution of the state of a cell is computed as a function of its state and the states of the cells in the neighborhood, so that $\sigma_c^{t+1} = f_c(\sigma_c^t, \mathcal{N}_c^t)$. In this work we consider only the subclass of additive binary CA, so that the state of each cell is $\sigma \in \{0,1\}$ and the transition function of each cell can be expressed with the combination of XOR and XNOR logical gates. Further, we consider non-homogeneous CAs, i.e. automata where the transition function may differ among different cells. Finally, we restrict ourselves to 4-connected neighborhoods, so that $\mathcal{N}_c = \{(x_i, y_i) : |x_c - x_i| + |y_c - y_i| = 1\}$ and periodic boundary conditions.

The above restrictions, i.e. binary and additive CA having only four neighbors, have as result that we need 6 bits to describe each possible rule. The final set of transition functions, or rules, and configurations of the CAs we investigate, follows closely the notation of Tomassini et al, [20], and Chowdhury et al, [13]. If $\sigma_{i,j}$ is the state of cell at $i^{\text{th}}$ row and $j^{\text{th}}$ column , then the parametric transition function is written as (according to [20])

$$\sigma_{(i,j)}^{t+1} = X \oplus (C \cdot \sigma_{(i,j)}^t) \oplus (N \cdot \sigma_{(i-1,j)}^t) \oplus (W \cdot \sigma_{(i,j-1)}^t) \oplus (S \cdot \sigma_{(i+1,j)}^t) \oplus (E \cdot \sigma_{(i,j+1)}^t)$$

$$(1)$$

where · stands for logical AND and $\oplus$ is the XOR operation. As we can see, the *control* variables $CNWSE$ determine whether the state of the current cell ($C$) or each of its neighbors is included in the computation of the next state. Further, $X$ can be considered as a "rule inverter". These 6 variables define the exact behavior of the transition function. The *genome* of each cell can be represented with 6 bits, and we will be naming the rules according to $XCNWSE$. The main differences of our work, besides the introduction of the composite metric, with respect to the CA configuration, compared to [20] are that we considered CAs with periodic boundaries and that we studied both the 4 rules suggested in [20] and the complete set of 64 additive rules.

## 2.1   Genetic Algorithm Approach

Genetic algorithms (GA) [25] are a class of heuristic algorithms that imitate natural selection. Typically, a genetic algorithm starts with a randomly initialized population of individuals that encode different solutions for the optimization problem at hand. This encoding maps a possible solution to a bitstring, that constitutes the genome of each individual. The individuals are then evaluated using a *fitness function* that measures their performance and is followed by a selection phase, where the most fitted individuals are propagated to the next generation (i.e. evolution step). The surviving individuals undergo crossover and mutation phases. The crossover operation combines the genome of two individuals so as to generate two offsprings, while the mutation mechanism randomly modifies some parts of the genome of an individual. Both of these operation serve, among others, as to not get trapped in local minima while exploring the solution space. Finally, the structure of the encoded genome depends on the problem at hand.

We encoded the structure of each CA (individual) by a string of $8 \times 8$ 6-bit genes arranged in scan-line order. Our approach differs from a standard genetic algorithm only in 2 points: First we assumed that the crossover operation can occur only on cell boundaries, i.e. without crossing the genome of a cell. This is because crossover in a random point within a rule, results in two completely new rules in the offsprings, thus adding an additional, non-controllable mutation factor. Second, we observed that performing mutation on single bits results in a slowed down evolution of the population. Therefore, mutation operates on a rule-based fashion, i.e. mutation "events" completely change an entire rule. For the *selection* operation, we used a standard elitistic rule, so that, after the evaluation of the fitness function, the individuals were sorted and only a percentage of the fittest ones was carried to the next generation for crossover and mutation.

Finally, to minimize the fluctuations in the calculation of the fitness function, we used a per-generation fixed, random initialization of the CA states, meaning that in each generation, we would select a fixed pattern and initialize all individuals with this pattern. This point is important, since, otherwise, two identical individuals would produce a different fitness value, thus producing unnecessary fluctuations.

# 3   A Critic on the Use of Entropy as Metric

Most of the previous work on the same subject was based mainly on different forms of entropy for evaluating the fitness of CAs. One such example is the sequence entropy, $S_h$ that is defined on sequences of bits of length $h$ [20]. There are $2^h$ such possible sequences, identified by the binary expansion of the integers $\{0, \ldots, 2^h - 1\}$, and $S_h$ can be calculated as

$$S_h = - \sum_{i=0}^{2^h-1} p_i \log(p_i) \tag{2}$$

where $p_i$ is the probability of appearence of the sequence corresponding to the $h$-bit expansion of $i$. Of course, entorpy alone cannot identify good PRNGs, rather it is used as a criterion which determines the individuals will be tested with a PRNG battery. One of our first experimental observations, while working with the entire 6-bit ruleset was that, it is possible to have CAs that attain high entropy values and have fixed 0 values in their configuration. Having a 0 rule, means that the specific output bit will always have the value 0, which, of course is absurd for a PRNG. Figure 1 shows a CA that has been evolved specifically to demonstrate this. An important thing to note here is that the four additive

| 5  | 43 | 27 | 6  | 13 | 57 | 57 | 38 |
|----|----|----|----|----|----|----|----|
| 59 | 21 | 61 | 10 | 32 | 25 | 0  | 37 |
| 14 | 46 | 37 | 29 | 25 | 31 | 52 | 52 |
| 34 | 61 | 44 | 43 | 4  | 63 | 46 | 2  |
| 6  | 2  | 3  | 51 | 59 | 54 | 42 | 12 |
| 47 | 61 | 63 | 36 | 33 | 24 | 45 | 5  |
| 54 | 53 | 37 | 7  | 59 | 15 | 60 | 36 |
| 55 | 28 | 25 | 19 | 44 | 22 | 49 | 39 |

**Fig. 1.** A CA using the 64 additive rules that has been evolved so as to maximize entropy and at the same time have exactly a single 0 cell. The entropy criterion was the sum of the subsequence entropies for subsequence lengths of $10, \ldots, 16$ bits, which gives a maximum value of 91 bits. The fitness value of the individual is 90.986626 bits.

rules proposed by [20], i.e. 15, 31, 47 and 63, are indeed a very particular set of rules. More specifically, and from our experiments, it appeared that any random configuration, or population, of individuals using these rules starts from a very high average entropy and is capable of achieving very good values of entropy in a very short time.

So, why is it a good thing to introduce a complex metric that includes tests from a PRNG battery? First, if one decides to work with the entire set of additive rules (i.e all 64 instead of the 4 rules), then entropy alone, as the above discussion indicates, is not sufficient. The second point has to do with the concept of *hard* tests as noted by G. Marsaglia in [26]. By including tests from a PRNG battery in the fitness value, we can, in a sense, "guide" the evolution towards individuals that pass such specific tests. Our initial experiments have shown that several such *hard* tests exist for CA, both in [22] and [23] PRNG batteries.

## 4   A Family of Metrics for Evolving CA as PRNGs

Before we describe how to construct a family of metrics that include PRNG tests from a battery, let us review how these tests evaluate a PRNG. Essentially, the idea underlying PRNG tests is to extract a set of statistics from the generated random numbers and test these statistics against a know theoretical or experimental distribution. This is done by checking the null hypothesis, $\mathcal{H}_0$, that the statistics from the experiment belong to the theoretical or expected distribution. If we accept $\mathcal{H}_0$, given the confidence interval we have selected, then the test is considered sucessful. How these statistics are generated, what they represent and what is their expected distribution depends on the specific test. L'Ecuyer and Simard [23] as well as the manuals for TestU01 provide a very extensive list of references on the most common tests, their statistics and expected distributions.

So, how would one go on in order to design a metric that includes specific tests from a battery so as to improve and guide the evolution of the CA? A direct approach is to construct a "naïve" metric that counts the number of successful tests, i.e. tests that an individual passed, and to modify the metric accordingly. As an example, of this "naïve" metric, assume that we want to include $N$ distinct tests, $t_1, \ldots, t_N$ while evaluating the fitness of each individual, possibly assigning a weight on the importance of each test, $w_1, \ldots, w_N$, a simple metric could have the form

$$H \cdot (1 + \sum_{i=1}^{N} w_i \sum_{j=1}^{r_{t_i}} s_{t_i,j}) \tag{3}$$

where $H$ is the entropy, $r_{t_i}$ is the number of repetitions of the test and $s_{t_i,j}$ result of the test (0 for failed tests and 1 for successful tests). The rationale behind such a metric is to reward the CA individuals that successfuly pass some tests. However, there is one important problem with this approach, namely:

### 4.1   How "Good" Is "Bad"?

Using the result of each test as a binary value, like in Eq. 3, does not differ that much from using only entropy as the fitness function. To explain this a bit further, consider a random population, such that all individuals fail on all of the tests in Eq. 3. Then, this metric does not give any "hint" to the fitness function, as of "how likely" is an individual to pass one or more of the tests that appear in the metric, i.e. it does not provide a measure of "how good is bad" among individuals that all fail a test. Indeed, using this metric, the evolution of such a (initially random and failing all tests) population will actually still be guided only by the entropy, such that if any individuals manage to pass one or more tests, then it is more likely to be because of a random event and is more comparable to a "random walk crossing a hyperplane". Of course passing a single test can lead to individuals passing more tests, but still, this does not change the fact that the evolution is guided mainly by the entropy. Our best bet with such a metric is to work with pre-initialized populations such that different individuals pass different tests, i.e. to merge populations from different evolutionary runs.

So, it becomes clear that we need a fitness function that rewards the individuals that are more likely to pass a test and penalizes those that are not. One approach towards this direction would be to use the $p$-value, or significance probability as this kind of metric. However, as it is discussed in, i.e., [27], $p$-values cannot be used as measures for supporting $\mathcal{H}_0$, or at least, not in the general case. In order to avoid semantic pitfalls of statistics we decided to completely avoid using $p$-values. To answer the question "how good is bad", we will start first by describing the construction of a metric that is based on the Kolmogorov-Smirnov (K-S) test. This metric can be applied in all the cases where we can build an experimental cumulative distribution function of the sample data.

## 4.2   A Fitness Metric Inspired by the Kolmogorov-Smirnov Test

The K-S test is a non-parametric method that can be used to test whether a set of sample data is drawn from a reference probability distribution. Since the properties and theory behind the K-S test can be found in most statistics textbooks (e.g. [28]), we will not go into details here. We will, however, describe what is essential for the construction of the proposed metric, i.e. the K-S statistic. Assume that we have an i.i.d. sample $X_i$ from some unknown distribution, $P$, and we want to test the hypothesis that $P$ is equal to a certain distribution $P_0$. Let the empirical cumulative distribution function of the sample be $F_n(x)$,

$$F_n(x) = P_n(X \leq x) = \frac{1}{n} \sum_{i=1}^{n} I(X_i \leq x) \tag{4}$$

and denote the c.d.f. of the test distribution by $F(x)$. Then, the statistic of the K-S test is

$$D = \sup_x |F_n(x) - F(x)| \tag{5}$$

and the test uses the K-S distribution to calculate the probability that the sample data are indeed drawn from the reference distribution. If we set

$$M_{\mathrm{KS}} = 1 - D \tag{6}$$

we see that the proposed metric is maximized when the two c.d.f.'s are identical, while it is minimized when their max absolute distance is 1. Combining this metric with entropy, using a simple composition rule, gave really good results, even for simulation runs that started with individuals that were all failing the extra tests. More specifically, in nearly all of our experiments, the best individuals of the final population of an evolution run would pass the selected tests. As we can see, this metric can be applied to every test, where we can build a c.d.f..

## 4.3  $X^2$ and Poisson Based Tests

In the case of PRNG tests that are based on the $X^2$ distribution or on the goodness of fit of two Poisson distributions we can use a different fitness metric as an alternative to the K-S metric described above. We have to stress at this point, that, the proposed alternative metric is in no case unique and any smooth function with similar properties can equally serve as a metric. Let $x^2 = \sum_{i=1}^{n} \frac{(e_i - o_i)^2}{e_i}$ be the $X^2$ test statistic, where $e_i$ are the expected and $o_i$ the observed frequencies. Similarly, let $\mu_e$ and $\mu_o$ be the expected and observed mean values for Poisson-based tests. Intuitively, we would like a fitness value to attain its maximum value when the $x^2$ statistic is 0, i.e. when the expected and observed values coincide or when the two mean values $\mu_e$ and $\mu_o$ are equal, and attain smaller values in other cases. Further, in order to be able to compare and treat the fitness functions in a uniform way (including Eq. 6), we would like the fitness function to take values in the $[0, 1]$ interval. It is easy to see that

$$M = 1 - e^{-d^2/C} \qquad (7)$$

where $d$ is a *generalized distance* ($x^2$ or $\mu_e - \mu_o$ in our cases) and $C$ is a normalizing constant has the above properties. Regarding the normalizing constant (which is related to the standard deviation), it can be calculated on a per test basis, where we can calculate the extent of the generalized distance, $d$, or it can be determined experimentally. Figure 2 shows how the choice of the normalizing constant affects the fitness function. Ideally, we would like the resulting, normalized, fitness function to behave like curve C1.

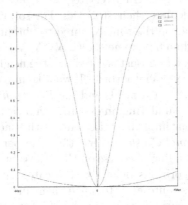

**Fig. 2.** An example of the effect of the normalizing constant on the generalized fitness function

## 4.4    Building a Composite Metric

In order to build a composite metric, we need to combine the above fitness functions into a single one, preserving at the same time their monotonicity. Apparently, this can be done using many different approaches. For our experiments we used a weighted $\mathbb{L}_2$ norm so that the resulting fitness function had the following form:

$$f = H \cdot \sqrt{1 + \sum_{i=1}^{n}(w_i M_i)^2} \tag{8}$$

where $H$ is the subsequence entropy, $w_i$ the weight (importance) assigned to test $i$ and $M_i$ the fitness function of each individual test. The term 1 under the square root serves as a means to preserve the entropy value, even when an individual fails on all the selected tests. An alternative approach would be to use an "entropy preserve term" for each fitness function individually, something that would modify the weighted terms like $(\epsilon + w_i M_i)^2$, where $\epsilon \geq 0$. In the case where we want to combine several sequence entropies into a single one, we can just replace them by their sum, i.e. $H = \sum_{i=1}^{n} H_i$. Finally, it is possible to combine the composite metric with the naïve metric (3) that we introduced earlier. More specifically, Eq. 3 can appear as a term in the sum of Eq. 8, provided that it is normalized to $[0, 1]$.

## 4.5    A Critic on the Proposed Metric

Although the proposed metric succeeds on evolving CA that pass specific tests in a PRNG battery, it has the significant drawback, that it is computationally expensive. This computational cost is due to two different factors, first from the complexity of running a test, and second and most importantly from the fact that most of the tests in a PRNG battery require a very large amount of random numbers in order to calculate their statistics. For software implementations of 2D-CA this time is linear on the time required to obtain a bit, since in order to calculate $N$ pseudo random bits we need $O(\sqrt{N}\sqrt{N}|\mathcal{N}_c|)$ iterations, where $\sqrt{N}$ is the edge of the CA and $|\mathcal{N}_c| = \text{const}$ is the size of the neighborhood, plus the time we need to combine these bits into words. If we take into account that the *Crush* battery in [23] requires $2^{35}$ such words and the *BigCrush* battery $2^{38}$ words, it is easy to understand that simulating an evolution run can be a time and resource consuming process. In our implementation and with fitness functions combining 4 or 5 tests from the *SmallCrush* battery, the time per individual could be as much as 5 minutes, depending of course on the fitness function configuration. Of course, since genetic algorithms belong to the category of *Embarrasingly Parallel* problems [29], it is quite easy to solve them in a distributed way, using, e.g. a cluster, which was our initial approach before starting to work on utilizing GPGPUs to speed up the pseudo random number generation. An optimal solution would be to use specialized hardware, i.e. a Field-programmable-gate-array (FPGA) platform to generate the pseudo-random numbers, and this is one of our future directions.

# 5    Results

To evaluate and compare the performance of the evolved CAs we needed a prototype CA that would serve as a benchmark. For this purpose, we used the CA reported by [20]. The specific configuration and set of rules perform amazingly well, even when tested with [22] and [23]. The comparison of the results was in terms of the number of tests passed by each CA by assigning the same weight on all tests. Using this approach, the prototype CA fails only 2 of the *SmallCrush* tests, namely the "MaxOft" and "MatrixRank" tests and 40 of the *Crush* tests.

We have to stress here, that in most of the cases, our evolved CAs performed equally good or marginally better with respect to the prototype CA. The main reason for this is that as we introduce new tests in the metric, the number of required random numbers increases significantly, resulting in an increased simulation time. If we could reduce the computational cost of the CA by, e.g. computing the CA state and generating the random numbers on an FPGA, then, the time required to evaluate the fitness function would decrease significantly. As it is noted in [23], the running time for *SmallCrush* on a general purpose CPU for evaluating MT19937 [24] is 14 seconds. In the case of a CA-PRNG this ranges from 8.5 minutes on a CPU to 1.5 minutes when using a GPGPU.

Finally, we would like to mention that we made, to some extent, similar observations as Marsaglia in [26]. There are several specific "hard" tests that appear to be the "milestones" for an evolved CA, so that it can perform adequately. The ones we encountered in our experiments are the "MatrixRank", "Knuth GAP", "Collisions" and "Birthday Spacing" tests, along with the "Random Walk" family of tests. These tests appear to be mutually exclusive, i.e. if one manages to successfully evolve a CA that passes, i.e. 3 out of 5 of these tests, then there is still a rather high probability that the CA will fail the remaining two. We restrain to run all of these tests in a single simulation until we have solved and optimized the random number generation "bottleneck". Finally, at an earlier stage of this work we also used some tests from DIEHARD, i.e. the "3DSpheres" and "Parking" tests, as well as the "MatrixRank" and "Gap", but with the test parameters from DIEHARD, which made them significantly easier to pass.

## 5.1    CAs and Their Performance with Respect to Different Tests

Figure 3 shows several of the evolved CA, both from experiments that utilized DieHard tests and from experiments that utilized TestU01 based tests. Of the above CA, (A) was evolved using GAP(TestU01), MatrixRank(TestU01) and it fails on BirthdaySpacings and Collisions tests. CA (B) is an older result that was evolved using mainly DieHard tests, i.e. GAP(DieHard), 3DSpheres(DieHard), Parking(DieHard), MatrixRank(DieHard) and it fails on BirthdaySpacings and MatrixRank tests. At this point we note that the specific test succeeds the version of a test from the DIEHARD battery and fails the respective version from TestU01. The CA shown in (C) is the result of an older experiment, that has been evolved using GAP(DieHard), 3DSpheres(DieHard), Parking(DieHard) and fails the SimpPoker, CouponCollector, MaxOft, WeightDistrib, MatrixRank and 1 of

| (A) | | | | | | | | | (B) | | | | | | | | | (C) | | | | | | | | | (D) | | | | | | | |
|---|---|---|---|---|---|---|---|---|---|---|---|---|---|---|---|---|---|---|---|---|---|---|---|---|---|---|---|---|---|---|---|---|---|---|
| 15 | 47 | 63 | 63 | 31 | 63 | 47 | 63 | | 31 | 47 | 15 | 63 | 15 | 31 | 15 | 15 | | 42 | 13 | 21 | 46 | 12 | 9 | 26 | 38 | | 35 | 15 | 15 | 35 | 47 | 17 | 58 | 46 |
| 15 | 47 | 47 | 31 | 47 | 15 | 63 | 15 | | 31 | 31 | 31 | 15 | 31 | 63 | 63 | 15 | | 47 | 30 | 37 | 3 | 14 | 42 | 13 | 62 | | 27 | 37 | 30 | 41 | 56 | 39 | 23 | 60 |
| 15 | 63 | 15 | 47 | 47 | 31 | 47 | 47 | | 47 | 31 | 15 | 31 | 47 | 47 | 63 | 15 | | 34 | 45 | 42 | 11 | 4 | 35 | 46 | 51 | | 60 | 17 | 23 | 29 | 29 | 10 | 26 | 43 |
| 31 | 15 | 15 | 63 | 31 | 15 | 31 | 15 | | 63 | 63 | 63 | 63 | 63 | 63 | 31 | 47 | | 7 | 55 | 19 | 60 | 53 | 8 | 19 | 13 | | 61 | 36 | 57 | 62 | 25 | 41 | 42 | 13 |
| 63 | 63 | 15 | 31 | 15 | 63 | 15 | 63 | | 47 | 47 | 63 | 63 | 31 | 31 | 63 | 15 | | 51 | 3 | 36 | 39 | 2 | 12 | 43 | 14 | | 29 | 50 | 4 | 9 | 63 | 39 | 26 | 52 |
| 15 | 63 | 31 | 15 | 47 | 31 | 15 | 63 | | 47 | 47 | 31 | 47 | 31 | 15 | 31 | 63 | | 5 | 59 | 46 | 57 | 31 | 22 | 28 | 63 | | 6 | 52 | 58 | 5 | 28 | 11 | 54 | 21 |
| 15 | 15 | 31 | 31 | 63 | 15 | 63 | 47 | | 31 | 15 | 15 | 15 | 31 | 31 | 63 | 31 | | 47 | 61 | 30 | 15 | 23 | 51 | 53 | 29 | | 31 | 60 | 11 | 35 | 43 | 46 | 29 | 52 |
| 31 | 15 | 15 | 47 | 63 | 47 | 15 | 15 | | 63 | 63 | 63 | 15 | 63 | 47 | 47 | 31 | | 40 | 5 | 30 | 20 | 51 | 12 | 22 | 45 | | 30 | 20 | 19 | 38 | 6 | 22 | 41 | 31 |

**Fig. 3.** Several evolved CAs. CAs (A) and (B) are based on the 4 rule set, while CAs (C) and (D) are based on all 64 rules

the RandomWalk tests. Finally, (D) has been evolved using a composite metric that included the BirthdaySpacing (TestU01) and Collision (TestU01) tests as well as the Rabbit battery of tests that has been included as a normalized term in Eq. 8. The specific battery consists of 26 tests and the required amount of time for the battery to complete depends on the input size. For 1 million random numbers this amounts to several seconds, so it doesn't add much overhead to the computation of the metric. Nevertheless, passing a test from the Rabbit battery does in no way ensure that the PRNG will pass the same test in the SmallCrush or Crush tests. The CA fails the MaxOft, MatrixRank, HammingIndep and 3 RandomWalk tests.

## 5.2   Conclusions and Future Work

The family of additive CA, that we considered in this work, possesses two very important properties. First, such CA can be implemented very efficiently in hardware, since they consist only of simple logic gates. Second, the restriction on the rules restricts the state space that the genetic algorithm has to explore. However, these two properties impose important limits on the properties of the family of additive CA. The most important of these limitations is related to the d-Monomial test, as introduced in [30]. The basic concept behind the d-Monomial test is to calculate the distribution of monomials in a function and compare that distribution with the expected, theoretical number of monomials of a random boolean function. The pitfall with additive CA is that the terms in each transition function are monomials of degree 1, which makes it impossible for such a CA to pass the specific test. Although the d-Monomial test is best suited for testing cryptographic functions, choosing a set of CA rules such that the d-Monomial test is important, at least on a research level. The reason for this is that, although PRNGs are not necessarily cryptographically secure, cryptographic algorithms are, on the other hand, usually good PRNGs. As an example for this, see the results table in [23]. The three cryptographic algorithms tested there have only one "weak" result in all the test-suites.

In this work we have presented a composite metric to be used in evolving CA as PRNG. The main advantages of the metric is that it allows to quantify the performance of CAs with respect to individual PRNG tests, i.e. it allows to find the CAs that are most likely to pass among a set that fails a specific PRNG test. The main disadvantage is that since PRNG tests require a large amount of random bits, this results in increased running times that are caused mainly by the time required to simulate a CA step.

One of our high priority future research directions is to further optimize the running time of the experiments by implementing the CA computations on, e.g. an FPGA and evolve CAs that pass at least the *SmallCrush* battery of tests in [23]. However, the real challenge is to investigate methods and algorithms for exploring the solution space of more generic CA. Therefore, on a second stage we will try to focus on removing the "additive" constraints from the evolved CAs and work on a larger subset (and possibly with bigger dimension CA), aiming to evolve high quality PRNGs that successfully pass the *Crush* and *BigCrush* batteries of tests in TestU01. Finally, since GPGPUs appear to be a standard in modern desktop computing, it would be worth investigating what are the perspectives of using CA based PRNGs running on GPGPUs in desktop based simulations.

# References

1. Marsaglia, G.: Diehard prng tests (1995)
2. Abarbanel, H.D.I., Brown, R., Sidorowich, J.J., Tsimring, L.S.: The analysis of observed chaotic data in physical systems. Rev. Mod. Phys. 65(4), 1331–1392 (1993)
3. Kier, L., Seybold, P., Cheng, C.K.: Modeling Chemical Systems Using Cellular Automata. Springer (2005)
4. Berry, H., Gracia Pérez, D., Temam, O.: Chaos in computer performance. Chaos 16, 013110 (2006)
5. Musti, U., Toutios, A., Ouni, S., Colotte, V., Wrobel Dautcourt, B., Berger, M.O.: HMM-based Automatic Visual Speech Segmentation Using Facial Data. In: Interspeech 2010, pp. 1401–1404 (2010)
6. Oran, E., Oh, C., Cybyk, B.: Direct simulation monte carlo: Recent advances and applications. Annual Review of Fluid Mechanics 30, 403–441 (1998)
7. Diaconis, P.: The markov chain monte carlo revolution. Bull. Amer. Math. Soc. 46, 179–205 (2009)
8. Hortensius, P., McLeod, R., Card, H.: Parallel random number generation for vlsi systems using cellular automata. IEEE Transactions on Computers 38(10), 1466–1473 (1989)
9. Kotoulas, L.G., Tsarouchis, D., Sirakoulis, G.C., Andreadis, I.: 1-d cellular automaton for pseudorandom number generation and its reconfigurable hardware implementation. In: ISCAS. IEEE (2006)
10. Nandi, S., Kar, B., Chaudhuri, P.: Theory and applications of cellular automata in cryptography. IEEE Transactions on Computers 43(12), 1346–1357 (1994)
11. Tomassini, M., Perrenoud, M.: Cryptography with cellular automata. Applied Soft Computing (1), 151–160 (2001)
12. Karmakar, S., Mukhopadhyay, D., Roy Chowdhury, D.: d-Monomial Tests of Nonlinear Cellular Automata for Cryptographic Design. In: Bandini, S., Manzoni, S., Umeo, H., Vizzari, G. (eds.) ACRI 2010. LNCS, vol. 6350, pp. 261–270. Springer, Heidelberg (2010)

13. Chowdhury, D.R., Sengupta, I., Chaudhuri, P.P.: A class of two-dimensional cellular automata and their applications in random pattern testing. J. Electron. Test. 5(1), 67–82 (1994)
14. Tomassini, M., Sipper, M., Zolla, M., Perrenoud, M.: Generating high-quality random numbers in parallel by cellular automata. Future Generation Computer Systems 16, 291–305 (1999)
15. Mitchell, M., Crutchfield, J.P., Das, R.: Evolving cellular automata with genetic algorithms: A review of recent work. In: Proceedings of the First International Conference on Evolutionary Computation and Its Applications (1996)
16. Mitchell, M., Hraber, P.T., Crutchfield, J.P.: Revisiting the edge of chaos: Evolving cellular automata to perform computations. Complex Systems 7, 89–130 (1993)
17. Mizas, C., Sirakoulis, G., Mardiris, V., Karafyllidis, I., Glykos, N., Sandaltzopoulos, R.: Reconstruction of dna sequences using genetic algorithms and cellular automata: Towards mutation prediction? Biosystems 92(1), 61–68 (2008)
18. Dewri, R., Chakraborti, N.: Simulating recrystallization through cellular automata and genetic algorithms. Modelling and Simulation in Materials Science and Engineering 13(2), 173 (2005)
19. Rongo, R., Spataro, W., D'Ambrosio, D., Vittoria Avolio, M., Trunfio, G.A., Di Gregorio, S.: Lava flow hazard evaluation through cellular automata and genetic algorithms: an application to mt etna volcano. Fundamenta Informaticae 87(2), 247–267 (2008)
20. Tomassini, M., Sipper, M., Perrenoud, M.: On the generation of high-quality random numbers by two-dimensional cellular automata. IEEE Transactions on Computers 49, 1146–1151 (2000)
21. Sipper, M., Tomassini, M.: Generating parallel random number generators by cellular programming. International Journal of Modern Physics C 7, 181–190 (1996)
22. Brown, R.: Dieharder prng tests (2009)
23. L'Ecuyer, P., Simard, R.: Testu01: A c library for empirical testing of random number generators. ACM Trans. Math. Softw. 33, 2/1–2/40 (2007)
24. Matsumoto, M., Nishimura, T.: Mersenne twister: a 623-dimensionally equidistributed uniform pseudo-random number generator. ACM Trans. Model. Comput. Simul. 8(1), 3–30 (1998)
25. Mitchell, M.: An Introduction to Genetic Algorithms. MIT Press (1999)
26. Marsaglia, G., Tsang, W.W.: Some difficult-to-pass tests of randomness. Journal of Statistical Software 7(3), 8 (2002)
27. Schervish, M.J.: P values: What they are and what they are not. The American Statistician 50(3), 203–206 (1996)
28. Boes, D.C., Graybill, F.A., Mood, A.M.: Introduction to the Theory of Statistics, 3rd edn. McGraw-Hill (1974)
29. Wikipedia: Embarrassingly parallel — wikipedia, the free encyclopedia (2012) (online, accessed April 4, 2012)
30. Filiol, E.: A New Statistical Testing for Symmetric Ciphers and Hash Functions. In: Deng, R.H., Qing, S., Bao, F., Zhou, J. (eds.) ICICS 2002. LNCS, vol. 2513, pp. 342–353. Springer, Heidelberg (2002)

# Countermeasures of Side Channel Attacks on Symmetric Key Ciphers Using Cellular Automata

Sandip Karmakar and Dipanwita Roy Chowdhury

Indian Institute of Technology, Kharagpur

**Abstract.** Side Channel Attacks (SCA) are one of the most effective means in breaking symmetric key ciphers. Generally, SCA exploits the side-channel leakages output by the implementations of ciphers or introduces defects in the system to analyze them. A number of countermeasures have been proposed to strengthen/remedy implementations of ciphers against SCA. However, none of the countermeasures, to our knowledge, are good enough towards its goal ([16], [19], [3]). In this paper, we emphasis on the necessity of randomness in designing countermeasures against SCA and propose Cellular Automata (CA) based system to thwart SCA. Our countermeasure is also analyzed against popular SCA, such as, differential power attack (DPA), scan-chain based attacks (SC-SCA) and fault attacks (FA).

## 1 Introduction

Side Channel Attacks (SCA) are cryptographic attacks on implementations of ciphers. This kind of attacks analyze the side channel leakages of the implementations of the ciphers, such as, power consumption, electromagnetic radiation, scan-chains etc. to deduce information about the key of the cipher. Fault attacks are a kind of SCA which inject faults into the implementation of a cipher in order to obtain information about the secret key exploiting the correct and faulty ciphertexts. It is shown in literature ([4], [10], [9], [13], [22], [1], [5]) that a wide variety of symmetric ciphers are vulnerable against SCA. The most important aspect of SCA is that it is completely practical i.e. it can be implemented easily in real-life applications and completes within few hours. Most block and stream ciphers have been shown to be broken by SCA. Hence, the necessity to resist SCA is obvious. A large number of countermeasures are introduced in literature aiming to thwart SCA. Most of the countermeasures are however costly and shown to be analyzable. Countermeasures using random masks are particularly effective ([16], [19], [3]).

Cellular Automata are a self-evolving system of cells which updates itself per cycle following a rule embedded into it. Linear Cellular Automaton (CA) is known for its ability to generate pseudorandom sequences needed for various applications like VLSI testing and coding theory [21]. CA shows very good pseudo-randomness ([21], [14]). Several researchers have exploited this pseudorandomness of CA to

G.C. Sirakoulis and S. Bandini (Eds.): ACRI 2012, LNCS 7495, pp. 623–632, 2012.

cryptography. The cryptanalysis of linear CA-based cryptographic techniques [18] show that nonlinearity is needed for cryptographic applications. However, nonlinear CA shows high correlation. The 3-neighbourhood nonlinear rule 30 CA has long been considered a good pseudo-random generator and studied for cryptography [20]. It passed various statistical tests for pseudorandomness with good results, until Willi Meier and Othmar Staffelbach proposed an attack, exploiting its high correlation, on pseudorandom sequences generated by rule 30 CA [17], which would break any such system of 300 cells with a complexity of about $2^{19}$. Another attack on rule 30 CA is also reported in [15]. These findings show that for cryptography, the data stream generated by CA needs to satisfy additional properties for pseudorandom sequence generation [14].

In this paper, the non-linear hybrid CA introduced in [14] is used as the random sequence generator. We test different cryptographic properties of the CA along with d-monomial to conclude that it is cryptographically robust. These cryptographically robust sequences are used as a random mask for resisting the side channel attacks. We then present the masking scheme. Finally, we analyze the masking scheme against different SCA.

This paper is organized as follows. Following the introduction, Section 2 presents basic definitions and notations regarding Cellular Automata and the related cryptographic terms. It also discusses the presently known countermeasures against SCA. In Section 3, we introduce the random masking scheme using CA and discuss its performance. Finally, the paper is concluded in Section 4.

## 2   Preliminaries

In this section, we present the basic definitions of CA and also of the cryptographic properties. The existing countermeasures against SCA are also briefly outlined in this section.

### 2.1   Cellular Automata Related Definitions

**Definition 1.** *Cellular Automata: A cellular automaton is a finite array of cells. Each cell is a finite state machine $C = (Q, f)$ where $Q$ is a finite set of states and $f$ is a mapping $f : Q^n \rightarrow Q$. The mapping $f$, is called local transition function. $n$ is the number of cells the local transition function depends on. On each iteration of the CA each cell updates itself with respective $f$.*

Adjacent cells of a cell are called the neighbourhood of CA. A 1-dimensional CA, whose rule depends on left and right neighbour and the cell itself is called a 3-*neighbourhood CA*. Similarly, if each cell depends on 2 left and 2 right neighbours and itself only, it is called 5-*neighbourhood CA*. A CA whose cells depend on 1 left and 2 right neighbouring cells is called a 4-*neighbourhood right skew CA*. A *left skewed 4-neighbourhood CA* can be defined similarly.

**Definition 2.** *Rule: The local transition function for a 3-neighbourhood CA cell can be expressed as follows:*

$$q_i(t+1) = f[q_i(t), q_{i+1}(t), q_{i-1}(t)]$$

*where, $f$ denotes the local transition function realized with a combinational logic, and is known as a rule of CA [7]. Here, $q_i(t)$ represents the value of the $i^{th}$ cell after $t$ iterations. The decimal value of the truth table of the local transition function is defined as the* rule number *of the cellular automaton.*

For one dimensional 3-neighbourhood CA the definitions of some rules are given below:

*Rule 30:* $f = q_{i-1}(t) \oplus (q_{i+1}(t) + q_i(t))$, where $+$ is the Boolean 'OR' operator and $\oplus$ is the Boolean 'XOR' operator.
*Rule 60:* $f = q_{i-1}(t) \oplus q_i(t)$.
*Rule 90:* $f = q_{i-1}(t) \oplus q_{i+1}(t)$.

A CA whose local transition function is same accross the cells is called *uniform CA*. A CA whose local transition function is *not* same for all the cells is a *hybrid CA*. Hybrid CA may be constructed by choosing different linear rules or by choosing different linear and nonlinear rules over the automaton. A CA whose first and last cells are connected to 0 is called *null-boundary* CA.

A CA whose local transition function consists of only 'XOR' operator is called a *linear CA*. A CA whose at least one local transition function consists of 'AND'/'OR' in addition to 'XOR' is *nonlinear CA*. For example, rule, $f = q_{i-1}(t) \oplus q_{i+1}(t)$ employed in each cell is a linear CA and $f = q_{i-1}(t).q_{i+1}(t)$ employed in each cell is a nonlinear CA, where, $q_{i-1}(t)$ and $q_{i+1}(t)$ denotes left and right neighbours of the $i^{th}$ cell at $t^{th}$ instance of time. A uniform CA each of whose transition function is, $f = q_{i-1}(t) \oplus (q_{i+1}(t) + q_i(t))$ is a *rule 30 uniform CA*.

## 2.2   Cryptographic Terms and Primitives

We now present definitions of related cryptographic terms and properties used in this paper.

**Definition 3.** *Pseudorandom Sequence: An algorithmic sequence is pseudorandom if it cannot be distinguished from a truly random sequence by any efficient (polynomial time) probabilistic procedure or circuit.*

A variable or its negation ($x$ or $\bar{x}$) is called a *literal*. Any number of 'AND'-ed literals is called a *conjunction*. For example, $x.y.\bar{z}$ is a *conjunction*.

**Definition 4.** *Algebraic Normal Form: Any Boolean function can be expressed as* XOR *of conjunctions and a Boolean constant, True or False. This form of the Boolean function is called its* Algebraic Normal Form (ANF).

Every *Boolean function* can be expressed in *ANF*. As an example, $f(x_1, x_2, x_3) = (x_1 \oplus x_2).(x_2 \oplus x_3)$ is not in *ANF*. Its *ANF* representation is, $f(x_1, x_2, x_3) = x_1.x_2 \oplus x_1.x_3 \oplus x_2 \oplus x_2.x_3$.

**Definition 5.** *Algebraic Degree: The maximum number of literals in any con-junction of ANF of a Boolean function is called its degree. Ciphers expressible or conceivable as a Boolean function have algebraic degree which is the same as the degree of the ANF of the Boolean function.*

Thus, $f(x_1, x_2) = x_1 \oplus x_2 \oplus x_1.x_2$ has algebraic degree 2.

### 2.3   Existing Countermeasures against SCA

In this section, we briefly discuss existing proposed countermeasures against SCA.

The countermeasures presented in literature can be broadly divided in two categories:

1. Full/Partial Duplication of the Cipher Implementation.
2. Random Masking of the Cipher Output.

**Full/Partial Duplication of the Cipher Implementation.** The most pop-ular and effective countermeasure proposed against SCA is the full or partial duplication of the cipher in its implementations ([2], [6], [3], [16], [19]). In this category, duplicate copies of the cipher is kept in the implemented system. There-fore, within the cipher there are always two ciphertexts (full/partial). A correct output is generated only when both the implementations match in output. This kind of countermeasure is particularly effective against fault attacks. The three major countermeasures proposed are discussed below:

- **Full Duplication:** The cipher implementation duplicates the cipher in two. Both the implementations are run simultaneously. A correct ciphertext is generated only if both the outputs of the implementations match. Clearly, a fault attack against such countermeasure is highly unlikely to succeed as in case of defective computations both the implementations are unlikely to give same result. DPA may however be more effective against such counter-measure. SC-SCA is unaffected by this algorithm. However, this method is costly.
- **Partial/Full Encrypt/Decrypt:** Here, the generated ciphertext from the encryption system is fully/partially decrypted through the decryption system to see for a match at an intermediate level or the plaintext. A correct output is generated only after a match. FA and DPA can be resisted using this technique, but, SC-SCA is not affected.
- **Diffusion of Defect:** Fault attacks are effective against symmetric key ci-phers mainly due the localization of defect in the computation of the cipher-text. Hence, a technique to increase the complexity of FA is to diffuse the defect in computation of the cipher. In this scenario, the the output of both the implementations are XOR-ed and run through a diffusion layer before actually generating the ciphertext. A 0 difference only generates the correct ciphertext. This clearly makes FA difficult. It also increases the complexity of DPA. SC-SCA remains unaffected through this countermeasure.

**Random Masking.** Random masking is a strong form of countermeasure ([11], [8]) against SCA targeting mainly against DPA and SC-SCA. There are many variants of masking in literature. Generally, random masking also uses some form of duplication of cipher computation. However, SC-SCA will be protected by a simple masking of the scan_out line with no . FA or DPA however, requires full duplication in general. A generic view is to mask the two computations of ciphertexts using some randomly generated masks and output correct ciphertext when at some equality. An SC-SCA may be protected using masking by giving the adversary the masked output. FA may be resisted by testing the equality of the two masked outputs. Clearly, DPA can also be thwart by an appropriate random mask. We provide an example of the random masking scheme next.

**Example:** Consider cryptosystem $S_c$. A mask generator $M_g$. A duplicate of the cryptosystem will be present in the system, $S_c'$. At any instant consider, the output from $S_c$ and $S_c'$ be the ciphertexts, $C$ and $C'$. The mask generator $M_g$ generates two masks per correct ciphertext, $M$ and $M'$ (Fig. 1). The countermeasure logic then does the following:

$a = (C + M) + M'$
$b = (C' + M') + M$
**if** $a == b$ **return** $C$
**else return** $0$
where, $+$ is the bitwise-XOR operator.

Note that, this masking scheme prevents the exact computation of $C$ and $C'$ from being leaked thus resisting DPA, also, the computation of $a$ and $b$ is symmetric which also complicates DPA. A fault attack is also difficult due to this masking scheme as, considering $S_c$ or $S_c'$ or $M_g$ being faulted at random storage places or operations used in these systems, it is highly unlikely that the equality $a == b$ will hold. It can be mentioned that a lot of security of the system depends on $M_g$ being a good pseudorandom generator. Otherwise, FA may easily find a bypass by faulting $S_c$ or $S_c'$ only or both. Pseudorandomness of $M$ and $M'$ also secures the system against DPA as the added random noise into the computation prevents predicting exact leakage of the system. Non-random masks are therefore, weakness of the system.

Although effective, most of the countermeasures have been shown to be vulnerable. The masking based countermeasure is particularly effective as it is simple to implement and much more effective against any SCA compared to the duplication based countermeasures which are mainly targeted to FA. In the following subsection we will emphasis on the necessity of randomness of the masking function and present a masking scheme using CA which we analyze against FA, DPA and SC-SCA.

# 3 Random Masking Using Cellular Automata

In this section, we introduce a countermeasure against SCA on symmetric key ciphers. As may be seen from the earlier description of existing countermeasures against SCA, the random masking scheme is an elegant and secure methodology in resisting SCA. However, most of the security of the scheme depends on the random sequence generator used in masks. The requirements of the generation of mask-bits are, security, low-cost hardware and high throughput. CA is a good choice for low-cost compact implementations and security. We discuss the CA based pseudo-random generator for masking next.

Our countermeasure assumes that there is a duplication of the original cipher structure. The masking bits are generated using the pseudo-random sequence generator $M_g$. Two sets of bits, $M$ and $M'$ are generated per output bit sequence. The design and security of $M_g$ is described in the following two subsections. The masking scheme then works as depicted next.

$a = M' \star (C \star M);$
$b = M \star (C' \star M');$
*if* $(a == b)$ *return C;*
*else return 0;*

where, $C$ and $C'$ are the two ciphertexts generated by the two cipher instances. $\star$ is a commutative operator generally taken as $\oplus$. Note that, this scheme eliminates the possibility of FA as, C and C' are not the same in that case. The complexity of DPA attacks increase as the masking introduces randomness into the power traces. SC-SCA also gets complicated as the random masks are also part of scan-chain. The operator $\star$ may be operators other than $\oplus$, such as, . or a combination of other operators.

**Table 1.** ANF of CA Rules used in Ruleset 5

| Rule # | ANF | Linear? |
|--------|-----|---------|
| 30 | $(x_2.x_3) \oplus x_1 \oplus x_2 \oplus x_3$ | No |
| 60 | $x_1 \oplus x_2$ | Yes |
| 90 | $x_1 \oplus x_3$ | Yes |
| 120 | $x_1 \oplus (x_2.x_3)$ | No |
| 150 | $x_1 \oplus x_2 \oplus x_3$ | Yes |
| 180 | $x_1 \oplus x_2 \oplus (x_2.x_3)$ | No |
| 210 | $x_1 \oplus x_3 \oplus (x_2.x_3)$ | No |
| 240 | $x_1$ | Yes |

## 3.1   Design of $M_g$

$M_g$ is a random sequence generator the output of which masks the ciphertexts. The random sequence generator $M_g$ is constructed using a hybrid non-linear cellular automata (CA) [21]. It is an CA consisting of cells with rules $30, 60, 90, 120, 150, 180, 210, 240$ spaced alternatively. The actual functions these rules operate on is given in table 1. We use a null-boundary CA of length 128 for this design. The input to the CA is a 128 bit key specified by the developer.

At each iteration the CA is run for two cycles to generate two masks $M$ and $M'$. The masks are then operated with the two generated ciphertexts, $C$ and $C'$ as discussed earlier (Fig. 1).

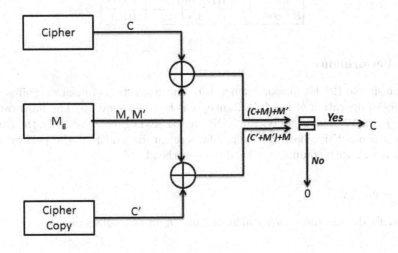

**Fig. 1.** The Pseudo-random Generator $M_g$

We present the cryptographic properties of the hybrid CA in the following subsection.

**Cryptographic Properties of $M_g$.** The hybrid CA used in construction of $M_g$, is studied in [14], it is called ruleset 5 by the authors. We briefly discuss its characteristics here.

Ruleset 5 is tested over three iterations for cryptographic properties like, balancedness, nonlinearity, resiliency and algebraic degree. It is also tested against d-monomial test [12]. The results are tabulated in tables 2 and 3.

**Table 2.** Cryptographic Properties of Ruleset 5

| Iteration | Balancedness | Nonlinearity | Resiliency | Degree |
|-----------|--------------|--------------|------------|--------|
| 1 | Balanced | 2 | 2 | 2 |
| 2 | Balanced | 8 | 2 | 3 |
| 3 | Balanced | 32 | 2 | 4 |

It can be seen that over all the iterations, the CA generates balanced output, has a fast nonlinearity growth. Resiliency of the CA is constant, it has good algebraic degree growth rate. Also, results of d-monomial test is satisfactory. Hence, it may be claimed that it will work as a good pseudo-random sequence generator.

**Table 3.** *d*-Monomial Characteristics of Hybrid Ruleset 5 CA [14]

| Rules | Number of $n^{th}$ degree terms | | | |
|---|---|---|---|---|
| | 1 | 2 | 3 | 4 |
| Ideal | 1,2,3 | 1,5,10 | 0,5,52 | 0,2,52 |
| Ruleset 5 | 3,2,4 | 1,3,5 | 0,2,6 | 0,0,3 |

## 3.2 Performance

$M_g$ is a simple 128-bit masking generator. The generation of masks requires only 2 cycles of operation of the CA. Hence, it is fast in operation. The hardware of $M_g$ requires 128 bit registers, 192 XOR and 64 AND gates.Obviously, the design requires competitive hardware. Therefore, it can be said that the performance of $M_g$ is fast with competitive hardware overhead.

## 3.3 Security

We briefly discuss the security achieved by $M_g$ in this subsection.

**Scan Based Side Channel Attacks.** Scan-chains allow the adversary to observe states of the chip-registers. Due to the presence of 128-bit CA registers, the scan-chain observation now has to derive $n + 128$ bits in order to completely break the system. Though scan-attacks may possibly be able to obtain the states of the cipher and the $M_g$ registers, it may be possible to change operation of the system such that in test mode through scan-chain the adversary is actually able to obtain only the scrambled version of the cipher states. The modification may be done as follows:

*if* (test_mode)
*return* $(C \star M) \star M'$

This way the adversary needs to guess 128 bits of $M$, leading to a complexity of $2^{128*n}$ to break the cipher. Note that the 128 registers of $M_g$ need not be disconnected from scan-chain while testing.

**Fault Attacks.** Introducing faults into the system, may due to the countermeasure induce faults in three parts, cipher state bits, duplicate cipher state bits and the masking generator $M_g$. Due to the masking scheme, the probability to actually get a faulty ciphertext is, $2^{128*2}$ due to the two masks, $M$ and $M'$ used in the scheme. Evidently, the countermeasure strengthens the cipher against fault attacks.

**Power Attacks.** According to the scheme, power attacks now have to take care of the 128-bit registers of $M_g$. Since, the AND and XOR gates of $M_g$ will introduce disturbances in the power traces of the cipher instead of having only the cipher implementation, essentially the adversary has to break a system of $2n + 128$ bits. Therefore, the attack is expected to be difficult. Further, most of the rules used in the CA are linear, therefore, power traces in breaking the mask generator are expected to be flat. Hence, it may be claimed that the countermeasure is safe against power attacks.

## 4 Conclusion

In this paper we have proposed a cellular automata based masking generator to countermeasure SCA on symmetric key ciphers. The masking generator is built using a non-linear hybrid CA. It is shown to be cryptographically robust. We have further analyzed the security of the countermeasure against popular SCA like, fault attacks, differential power attacks and scan-based side channel attack. The countermeasure does not induce much hardware overhead to the implementations and is fast in operation.

## References

1. Agrawal, M., Karmakar, S., Saha, D., Mukhopadhyay, D.: Scan Based Side Channel Attacks on Stream Ciphers and Their Counter-Measures. In: Chowdhury, D.R., Rijmen, V., Das, A. (eds.) INDOCRYPT 2008. LNCS, vol. 5365, pp. 226–238. Springer, Heidelberg (2008)
2. Akkar, M.-L., Giraud, C.: An Implementation of DES and AES, Secure against Some Attacks. In: Koç, Ç.K., Naccache, D., Paar, C. (eds.) CHES 2001. LNCS, vol. 2162, pp. 309–318. Springer, Heidelberg (2001)
3. Barenghi, A., Breveglieri, L., Koren, I., Pelosi, G., Regazzoni, F.: Countermeasures against fault attacks on software implemented AES: effectiveness and cost. In: Proceedings of the 5th Workshop on Embedded Systems Security, WESS 2010, pp. 7:1–7:10. ACM, New York (2010)
4. Berzati, A., Canovas, C., Castagnos, G., Debraize, B., Goubin, L., Gouget, A., Paillier, P., Salgado, S.: Fault analysis of GRAIN-128. In: IEEE International Workshop on Hardware-Oriented Security and Trust, vol. 0, pp. 7–14 (2009)
5. Biham, E., Shamir, A.: Differential Fault Analysis of Secret Key Cryptosystems. In: Kaliski Jr., B.S. (ed.) CRYPTO 1997. LNCS, vol. 1294, pp. 513–525. Springer, Heidelberg (1997)
6. Chari, S., Jutla, C.S., Rao, J.R., Rohatgi, P.: Towards Sound Approaches to Counteract Power-Analysis Attacks. In: Wiener, M. (ed.) CRYPTO 1999. LNCS, vol. 1666, pp. 398–412. Springer, Heidelberg (1999)
7. Pal Chaudhuri, P., Roy Chowdhury, D., Nandi, S., Chattopadhyay, S.: CA and its Applications: A Brief Survey. Additive Cellular Automata - Theory and Applications 1 (1997)
8. Coron, J.-S., Goubin, L.: On Boolean and Arithmetic Masking against Differential Power Analysis. In: Paar, C., Koç, Ç.K. (eds.) CHES 2000. LNCS, vol. 1965, pp. 231–237. Springer, Heidelberg (2000)
9. Hojsík, M., Rudolf, B.: Differential Fault Analysis of Trivium. In: Nyberg, K. (ed.) FSE 2008. LNCS, vol. 5086, pp. 158–172. Springer, Heidelberg (2008)

10. Hojsík, M., Rudolf, B.: Floating Fault Analysis of Trivium. In: Chowdhury, D.R., Rijmen, V., Das, A. (eds.) INDOCRYPT 2008. LNCS, vol. 5365, pp. 239–250. Springer, Heidelberg (2008)

11. Itoh, K., Takenaka, M., Torii, N.: DPA Countermeasure Based on the "Masking Method". In: Kim, K.-c. (ed.) ICISC 2001. LNCS, vol. 2288, pp. 440–456. Springer, London (2002)

12. Saarinen, M.J.O.: Chosen-IV Statistical Attacks on e-Stream Stream Ciphers. eS-TREAM, ECRYPT Stream Cipher Project, Report 2006/013, pp. 5–19 (2006)

13. Karmakar, S., Roy Chowdhury, D.: Fault Analysis of Grain-128 by Targeting NFSR. In: Nitaj, A., Pointcheval, D. (eds.) AFRICACRYPT 2011. LNCS, vol. 6737, pp. 298–315. Springer, Heidelberg (2011)

14. Karmakar, S., Mukhopadhyay, D., Roy Chowdhury, D.: d-Monomial Tests of Non-linear Cellular Automata for Cryptographic Design. In: Bandini, S., Manzoni, S., Umeo, H., Vizzari, G. (eds.) ACRI 2010. LNCS, vol. 6350, pp. 261–270. Springer, Heidelberg (2010)

15. Koc, C.K., Apohan, A.M.: Inversion of Cellular Automata Iterations. IEE Proceedings on Computers and Digital Techniques 144(5), 279–284 (1997)

16. Malkin, T.G., Standaert, F.-X., Yung, M.: A Comparative Cost/Security Analysis of Fault Attack Countermeasures. In: Breveglieri, L., Koren, I., Naccache, D., Seifert, J.-P. (eds.) FDTC 2006. LNCS, vol. 4236, pp. 159–172. Springer, Heidelberg (2006)

17. Meier, W., Staffelbach, O.: Analysis of Pseudo Random Sequences Generated by Cellular Automata. In: Davies, D.W. (ed.) EUROCRYPT 1991. LNCS, vol. 547, pp. 186–199. Springer, Heidelberg (1991)

18. Paterson, K.G., Blackburn, S.R., Murphy, S.: Theory and Applications of Cellular Automata in Cryptography. IEEE Transactions on Computers 46(5) (1997)

19. Sere, A.A., Iguchi-Cartigny, J., Lanet, J.-L.: Automatic detection of fault attack and countermeasures. In: Proceedings of the 4th Workshop on Embedded Systems Security, WESS 2009, pp. 7:1–7:7. ACM, New York (2009)

20. Wolfram, S.: Cryptography with Cellular Automata. In: Williams, H.C. (ed.) CRYPTO 1985. LNCS, vol. 218, pp. 429–432. Springer, Heidelberg (1986)

21. Wolfram, S.: Random Sequence Generation by Cellular Automata. Advances in Applied Mathematics 7, 123–169 (1986)

22. Yang, B., Wu, K., Karri, R.: Scan based side channel attack on dedicated hardware implementations of Data Encryption Standard. In: ITC 2004: Proceedings of the International Test Conference, Washington, DC, USA, pp. 339–344 (2004)

# First Steps on Asynchronous Lattice-Gas Models with an Application to a Swarming Rule

Olivier Bouré, Nazim Fatès, and Vincent Chevrier

Université de Lorraine – INRIA Nancy Grand-Est – LORIA
{olivier.boure,nazim.fates,vincent.chevrier}@loria.fr

**Abstract.** Lattice-gas cellular automata are often considered as a particular case of cellular automata in which additional constraints apply, such as conservation or spatial exclusion of particles. But what about their updating? How to deal with non-perfect synchrony? Novel definitions of asynchronism are proposed that respect the specificity of lattice-gas models. These definitions are then applied to a well-known swarming rule in order to explore the robustness of the model to perturbations of its updating.

**Keywords:** Asynchronous cellular automata, Lattice-Gas cellular automata, Robustness, Swarming behaviour.

## 1 Introduction

In the field of discrete dynamical systems, cellular automata (CA) are widely used as a tool for the simulation of natural phenomena and as a model of parallel computing. Their discrete and spatially-extended structure makes them a computationally simple model yet capable of displaying a wide range of complex behaviours. While initial studies only considered a simultaneous updating of all components, recent years have seen an increasing interest in asynchronous CA models, where the perfect synchrony hypothesis is relaxed. We are here particularly interested in *robustness*, which characterises the stability of the behaviour when external disturbances and structural changes are applied. In the case of asynchronism, robustness boils down to exploring how much of the CA behaviour is related to the synchronous scheme, and how much comes intrinsically from the individual rule [10]. Thus, we observed in previous works a variety of behaviours that arise from different updating schemes, including phase transitions [4,8].

In particular, studies on asynchronous CA have revealed the existence of synchrony-dependent behaviours we call *synchronous singularities*, that is, behaviours which stability depends on the synchronicity of the model. Examples include the periodic patterns of the *Game of Life* [2,7], of several Elementary Cellular Automata [8], or even the spatially-extended Prisoner's Dilemma [9]. Considering those examples, one may wonder whether such observations can be only made in systems with an ad hoc deterministic transition rule or whether it can occur for models of natural phenomena.

G.C. Sirakoulis and S. Bandini (Eds.): ACRI 2012, LNCS 7495, pp. 633–642, 2012.

Our aim here is to tackle the robustness question in the scope of lattice-gas models, in which particles travel through the lattice. As an introductionary example, consider the following pattern uncovered in a previous work [3]: particles are displaced according to a synchronous updating scheme which consists of the successive application of two rules, the interaction step (I) – which reorganises the particles within a cell to maximise their alignment with the particles of the neighbours – and the propagation step (P) – which displaces particles towards the corresponding neighbours. Paradoxically, in this pattern particles are all opposing the directions of their direct neighbours, in spite of the alignment-favouring local rule (see Fig. 1 and more details in Sec. 3).

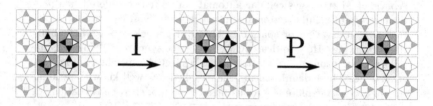

**Fig. 1.** Synchronous singularity in a lattice-gas cellular automaton. A black triangle represents one particle present in a channel, and white an empty channel.

A step-by-step look at the evolution of this pattern may let us think that this behaviour requires a deterministic updating rule. However, what is outstanding is that it has been observed to self-organise (a) with a stochastic local rule, (b) from a random initial configuration. Thus the question: if such a pattern can form outside of a deterministic model, how is it related to the perfect synchrony of the system? And how can we question this property in lattice-gas models in order to probe the robustness to asynchronism?

In Sec. 2, we confront the notion of asynchronism to the constraints and hypotheses of lattice-gas cellular automata and propose several definitions of an asynchronous updating scheme. In Sec. 3, we precise further the individual rules considered for our model and compare the observed patterns in the synchronous and asynchronous versions. Finally in Sec. 4, we briefly discuss on the role of asynchronism in discrete dynamical systems, based on our definitions and experimental results.

## 2   Defining Asynchronous Lattice-Gas Cellular Automata

There exist a wide range of interpretations and definitions given to asynchronism, and even more diverse resulting behaviours (see for example [1,4] and ref. therein). The problem we are tackling here is that the system we want to "make asynchronous" is a lattice-gas cellular automaton which, in spite of its compatibility with the classical CA definition, includes additional hypotheses that may not be conserved when changing the updating scheme. Let us now present how we tackle this problem formally.

## 2.1  Definition of Lattice-Gas Cellular Automata

The lattice-gas cellular automaton (LGCA) we are interested in is a particular CA, where:

- the *cellular space* $\mathcal{L} = \{\mathbb{Z}/L \cdot \mathbb{Z}\}^2$ is a 2-dimensional square lattice of length $L$ with periodic boundary conditions.
- the *neighbourhood* $(n_i)_{i \in [\![1,4]\!]} = \{(1,0); (0,1); (-1,0); (0,-1)\}$ associates to a cell $c \in \mathcal{L}$ the set of its 4 nearest neighbours.

In a LGCA, each cell is connected to its neighbours via *channels* through which particles can travel. Cell configurations $\boldsymbol{x}_c = (x_i(c))_{i \in [\![1,4]\!]}$ are therefore represented as a vector of the numbers of particles contained by each of its channels $x_i(c) \in \mathbb{N}$. The dynamics of LGCA is determined by the successive application of two global transitions:

1. The *interaction step* reorganises particles within cells according to a transition function $f_I$, which applies to the configuration of a cell and its neighbourhood:
$$\forall c \in \mathcal{L}, \ \boldsymbol{x}_c^I = f_I(\boldsymbol{x}_c, \boldsymbol{x}_{c+n_1}, \ldots, \boldsymbol{x}_{c+n_4}). \tag{1}$$

2. The *propagation step* displaces particles from the channels of a cell to the corresponding neighbours:
$$\forall c \in \mathcal{L}, \ \forall i \in [\![1,4]\!], \ x_i^P(c) = x_i^I(c - n_i). \tag{2}$$

In addition, we consider two fundamental constraints which we want to keep valid under an asynchronous updating scheme: the *particle exclusion* – channels may contain at most one particle, and are therefore considered as either empty (state 0) or full (1) – and the *particle conservation* – particles must always be conserved when they interact and propagate[1].

## 2.2  Which Asynchronism?

For this work, we will consider $\alpha$-*synchronism* [8,4] which follows the general definition: at any time step, each component updates according to the regular transition function with probability $\alpha$, or remains unchanged using the identity function with probability $1 - \alpha$. This updating scheme provides us with a useful control parameter, the *synchrony rate* $\alpha$, allowing for a continuous control of the updating scheme from evolution in perfect synchrony ($\alpha = 1$) to quasi-sequential updates ($\alpha \to 0$).

The global transition function of LGCA from a time $t$ to $t + 1$ is constituted of two steps, interaction and propagation, applied successively to all cells. When we want to apply asynchronism, we need to properly define the meaning of "updating" and "remaining unchanged" in terms of computation. Does

---

[1] Note that our particle-oriented interpretation of the system resembles *Totally Asymmetric Simple Exclusion Processes* [5].

asynchronism apply to the sole interaction? The propagation? Shall we consider these transitions as correlated, independent?

To address this issue, we propose as a starting point three possible implementations of asynchronism:

(1) **Asynchronous interaction:** the interaction is applied with a probability $\alpha_I$, called the *interaction rate*. The propagation is always applied.
(2) **Asynchronous propagation:** the interaction is always applied, but the propagation is applied with a probability $\alpha_P$, called the *propagation rate*.
(3) **Correlated interaction and propagation:** for each cell, interaction and propagation are both applied with a probability $\alpha_C$, otherwise none of them is applied.

However, if the asynchronous interaction (1) can be implemented without problem as the interaction rule itself is particle-conserving, desynchronising the propagation (2, 3) is not a straightforward operation and requires further reflexion.

**Conserving Particles During the Propagation.** Let us first consider the case where asynchronous propagation is simply determined as the application of the transition rule with probability $\alpha_P$, and identity function with probability $1 - \alpha_P$. In LGCA models, there is no actual means for a given cell to know whether its neighbours are selected for update or not. This is problematic as we need this type of information to decide whether to propagate the state of a channel or not (see Fig. 2-b and -c).

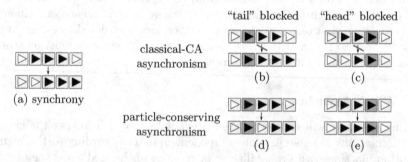

**Fig. 2.** Representation of the propagation step along one channel direction in a sample of five cells, for different updating schemes and situations of particles. Darker cells are not selected for update. (a) is the synchronous classical case, (b,c) the asynchronous case without the particle-conserving changes and (d,e) our proposition for an asynchronous propagation.

There exist several model adaptations that can solve this issue: for instance, by adding specific states which keep cells synchronized [11] or by using additional steps to perform validity checks (*e.g.* transactional CA [12]). Similarly, our proposition here consists in modifying the point of view of the asynchronous propagation function by considering no longer the cells but the channels as the base components of the system. We first select randomly the cells which are to be updated, and then determine from non-selected cells which channels are *free*, and thus updated, and which are *blocked* and remaining unchanged. We now specify the formal definitions of asynchronous interaction and propagation using selection functions.

## 2.3 Definition of an Asynchronous LGCA

**Interaction step.** We introduce a *selection function* $\Delta_I : \mathbb{N} \to \mathcal{P}(\mathcal{L})$ which associates to each time $t$ the subset of cells to be updated during the interaction step, where each cell has a probability $\alpha_I$ to be selected. The interaction transition function becomes $\forall t \in \mathbb{N}$, $\forall c \in \mathcal{L}$, $\mathcal{N} = \{n_1, \dots, n_4\}$:

$$x_c^I = f_{\Delta_I}(x_c, x_{c+n_1}, \dots, x_{c+n_4}) = \begin{cases} f_I(\dots) & \text{if } c \in \Delta_I(t) \\ x_c & \text{otherwise.} \end{cases} \tag{3}$$

When $\alpha_I = 0$, the system is ballistic, *i.e.* particles always go straight.

**Propagation Step.** First, we need to determine which cells update, and which remain unchanged. Similarly to asynchronous interaction, we introduce a *selection function* $\Delta_P : \mathbb{N} \to \mathcal{P}(\mathcal{L})$ which returns for time $t$ the subset of cells to be updated during the propagation step, where each cell has a probability $\alpha_P$ to be selected. In addition, we define $\mathcal{B}^t \subset [\![1,4]\!] \times \mathcal{L}$ as the set of *blocked channels*, which will remain unchanged between times $t$ and $t + 1$. To build this set, we state that a channel $(i, c)^t$ (channel $i$ of cell $c$ at time $t$) is *blocked* if it contains a particle ($x_i^t(c) > 0$), and if one of the two conditions is true: ($C1$) its containing cell $c$ is not selected for update, or ($C2$) its destination channel is blocked. We thus have:

$$(i,c)^t \in \mathcal{B}^t \text{ if } \left( x_i^t(c) > 0 \right) \text{ and } \begin{cases} c \notin \Delta_P(t) & (C1) \\ \text{or} \\ (i, c + n_i)^t \in \mathcal{B}^t & (C2) \end{cases}$$

The construction of $\mathcal{B}^t$ describes a general relation between particles. It can be implemented with a recursive algorithm: once a channel is blocked because of condition ($C1$), the chain of the channels that "point" to this one must be also blocked if they contain a particle because of condition ($C2$) (see Fig. 2-e). The propagation transition function therefore becomes:

$$x_i^P(c) = \begin{cases} x_i^I(c) & \text{if } (i, c) \in \mathcal{B}^t \\ 0 & \text{if } (i, c) \notin \mathcal{B}^t \text{ and } (i, c - n_i) \in \mathcal{B}^t \\ x_i^I(c - n_i) & \text{otherwise.} \end{cases} \tag{4}$$

When $\alpha_P = 0$, the particles are never propagated and thus never leave their cell.

## 3    Observation on a Swarming Rule

The model of swarming we present here is borrowed from a compilation of biological models by Deutsch *et al.* [6, ch. 8]. It describes a probabilistic swarming
interaction rule in which the particles of a cell tend to align themselves with the
neighbourhood predominant directions. The probability for a given cell configuration $\boldsymbol{x}_c$ to reorganise into $\boldsymbol{x}_c^I$ is given by:

$$P(\boldsymbol{x}_c \to \boldsymbol{x}_c^I) = \frac{1}{Z}\exp\left[\sigma \cdot \boldsymbol{J}_c(\boldsymbol{x}^I) \cdot \boldsymbol{D}_c(\boldsymbol{x})\right] \cdot \delta(\boldsymbol{x}_c, \boldsymbol{x}_c^I) \tag{5}$$

where:

- $Z$ is the normalisation factor, so that $\sum_{\boldsymbol{x}_c^I} P(\boldsymbol{x}_c \to \boldsymbol{x}_c^I) = 1$.
- $\sigma \in \mathbb{Z}$ is the alignment sensitivity.
- $\boldsymbol{J}_c(\boldsymbol{x}^I)$ is the *flux* in cell $c$, the resulting vector of particle directions.
- $\boldsymbol{D}_c(\boldsymbol{x})$ is the *director field*, the sum of cell $\boldsymbol{x}_c$ neighbours' flux.
- $\delta(\boldsymbol{x}_c, \boldsymbol{x}_c^I) = 1$ if cell configurations $\boldsymbol{x}_c$ and $\boldsymbol{x}_c^I$ have same number of particles,
  0 otherwise. This ensures conservation of particles.

Starting from a random initial configuration of density $\rho$, where $\rho$ is the probability for each channel to contain a particle, we need only to set the parameter
$\sigma$ to determine the local interaction rule. This limits the parametric space to
the $\sigma/\rho$ plane, allowing for a complete exploration of the different qualitative
behaviours that the model may display.

### 3.1    Recapitulation of the Synchronous Behaviour

The main interest of the swarming model is that, in spite of a simple and stochastic interaction rule, a variety of qualitatively different behaviours can arise. In
particular, it has been previously established that, using the two control parameters $\sigma$ and $\rho$, two phases may emerge, chaotic and organised [6]. In recent
work, we reported that the organised phase can display several stable patterns
of global particle organisation [3] (see Fig. 3):

**Checkerboard pattern (CB)** : local groups of anti-aligned particles. Typically occurs for high densities (typically $\rho \approx 0.5$).
**Diagonal stripe pattern (DS)** : a traveling compact diagonal shape of particles in two orthogonal directions, that loops over the lattice boundaries.
**Clouds pattern (CL)** : traveling competitive groups of aligned particles. Typically occurs for a high sensitivity ($\sigma \approx 3 - 4$).

It is interesting to note that these behaviours have been observed for systems of
limited size and time, and can therefore be considered as metastable attraction
basins. This means that once a behaviour is reached, the system will conserve
it until random fluctuations make the system "escape" this behaviour. We now
apply the different updating schemes to the system and try to determine whether
these patterns are robust to perturbations of the updating. More particularly we
are interested in whether their appearance depend on perfect synchrony.

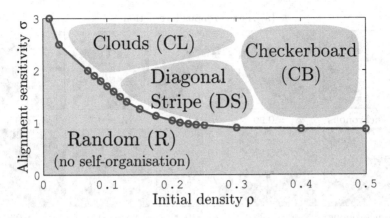

**Fig. 3.** Spatial distribution of the different patterns in the sensitivity-density parametric plane. The small rounds represent critical detections of self-organisation phenomena.

## 3.2 Exploration of the Asynchronous Behaviour

As a preliminary study, we now propose to consider each of the three patterns independently, by setting the system in adequate initial condition of size ($L = 20$) and iterating the system for a large number of steps ($t = 5000$). We then observe if the expected pattern appears, and compare the results for different values of the different synchrony rates ($\alpha_I$, $\alpha_P$, $\alpha_C$).

**Asynchronous Interaction.** Two observations can be made (see Fig. 4-a):

1. The checkerboard pattern is very sensitive to asynchronism. Indeed, a small but apparently not infinitesimal amount of asynchronism ($\alpha_I \approx 0.95$) is sufficient to switch the behaviour to a diagonal stripe pattern which covers the lattice entirely.
2. For the diagonal stripe and the clouds patterns, as long as the amount of asynchronism remains small, the only effect on the pattern is to introduce additional noise. As soon as a critical value $\alpha_I$ is reached, the clouds pattern becomes a diagonal stripe, and the diagonal strips becomes random.

**Asynchronous Propagation.** The three tested patterns displayed a sudden change of behaviour for a small amount of asynchronism (see Fig. 4-b).

1. The checkerboard pattern is very unstable and shifts to a global consensus on the directions of propagation. However, for higher the value of $\alpha_P$, it is possible for the pattern to "survive" for a few time steps.
2. The diagonal stripe still appears for high $\alpha_P$ but is soon replaced by "semi-random" patterns, where some order regularly appears in some parts of the lattice and disappears, but never stabilises.

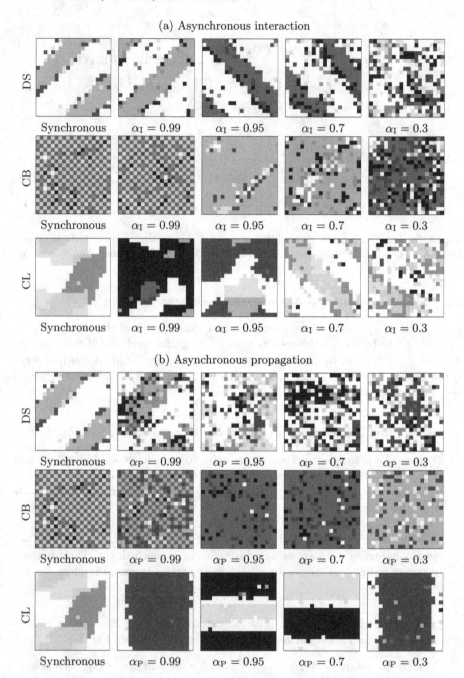

**Fig. 4.** Evolution of the main patterns for different interaction (propagation) rate values $\alpha_I$ ($\alpha_P$, respectively). Configuations are obtained from random initial configurations run for 5000 steps for typical values of $\sigma$ and $\rho$ (DS: $\{\sigma = 1.5; \rho = 0.2\}$, CB: $\{\sigma = 1.5; \rho = 0.45\}$, CL: $\{\sigma = 4; \rho = 0.2\}$). The simulations and visualisations are realised with *FiatLux*, a CA simulator in Java (http://fiatlux.loria.fr)

3. The clouds pattern is destabilised and transforms into one or several vertical or horizontal stripes of aligned particles.

These observations suggest a destructive effect of asynchronous propagation on all behaviours, even for a high propagation rate $\alpha_P \approx 0.95$. However, this observation does not seem to hold for infinitesimal values of asynchrony ($\alpha_P = 1^-$), which let us think that our patterns have a minimal degree of robustness to asynchronous propagation.

**Correlated Interaction and Propagation.** Similar experiments have been applied to the correlated updating scheme. The resulting behaviour is a mix of asynchronous interaction and asynchronous propagation:

1. For higher values of the synchronism rate ($\alpha_C \approx 0.95$), the behaviour follows the sudden changes observed in the asynchronous propagation.
2. For lower values ($\alpha_C \approx 0.5$), the swarming and identity interaction rules become equiprobable and, as particles do not gather in clusters any more, the system enters a random phase.

Considering how differently asynchronous interaction and asynchronous propagation effect on the system dynamics, and the synchrony rates for those changes were observed, this result is somehow "expected": the behaviour changes correspond more or less to the changes observed for each type of asynchronism.

**Synthesis of the Experiments.** Observations on the swarming model, which was thought rather robust in the first place due to the stochastic rule and self-organisation phenomena, highlighted the dependence between the type of asynchronism applied to the system and the stability of each pattern. For instance, we observed that there exist (1) differences between patterns in their robustness to asynchronism (*e.g.* diagonal stripe versus checkerboard under asynchronous interaction) and (2) differences between types of asynchronism in their effects on the system's behaviour (*e.g.* diagonal stripe under asynchronous interaction and propagation).

Moreover, we ask whether there exists a fundamental change of behaviour between perfect synchrony ($\alpha = 1$) and quasi-synchrony ($\alpha = 1^-$). Indeed, as our system is stochastic, it is difficult to determine experimentally whether patterns such as the checkerboard can be considered as "synchronous singularities". For now, additional experiments must be conducted in deeper details, as our simulations were limited in space and time, in order to give a proper estimation of the robustness of the behaviour of this model.

# 4   Discussion

This paper presented a first definition of an asynchronous LGCA, which intends to extract from classical CA the idea of questioning the perfect synchrony, and adapt it to the definition and hypotheses of a lattice-gas model of swarming.

Although cellular automata and lattice-gas models share strong resemblances, the introduction of asynchronism managed to reveal an intrinsic difference. Indeed, cellular automata are based on cells that are updated according to the observation of their neighbours' state, whereas lattice-gas models intend to capture a transport of information between cells.

From this example we learned that a naive expression of asynchronism – for instance reproducing the classical definition from cellular automata – could compromise the constraints of the lattice-gas model: the conservation and spatial exclusion of particles imposed us to change the modelling point of view and consider *channels* as the base components of the updating scheme. However, many issues remain unexplored. For instance, according to our definitions, a single particle can block an entire array of particles, which may contradict the idea of locality of events in spatially-distributed computing.

The next step of this approach consists in building a model where particles are considered as autonomous agents, with their own perception and decision process.

# References

1. Bandini, S., Bonomi, A., Vizzari, G.: An analysis of different types and effects of asynchronicity in cellular automata update schemes. Natural Computing, 1–11 (2012)
2. Blok, H.J., Bergersen, B.: Synchronous versus asynchronous updating in the "Game of Life". Physical Review E 59(4), 3876–3879 (1999)
3. Bouré, O., Fatès, N., Chevrier, V.: Observation of novel patterns in a stressed lattice-gas model of swarming. Tech. report, Nancy Université – INRIA Nancy–Grand-Est – LORIA (2011)
4. Bouré, O., Fatès, N., Chevrier, V.: Robustness of Cellular Automata in the Light of Asynchronous Information Transmission. In: Calude, C.S., Kari, J., Petre, I., Rozenberg, G. (eds.) UC 2011. LNCS, vol. 6714, pp. 52–63. Springer, Heidelberg (2011), Extended version, http://hal.inria.fr/hal-00658754/
5. Derrida, B.: An exactly soluble non-equilibrium system: The asymmetric simple exclusion process. Physics Reports 301(1-3), 65–83 (1998)
6. Deutsch, A., Dormann, S.: Cellular Automaton Modeling of Biological Pattern Formation. Birkhäuser, Boston (2005)
7. Fatès, N.: Does *Life* resist asynchrony? In: Game of Life Cellular Automata, pp. 257–274. Springer (2010)
8. Fatès, N., Morvan, M.: An experimental study of robustness to asynchronism for elementary cellular automata. Complex Systems 16, 1–27 (2005)
9. Grilo, C., Correia, L.: Effects of asynchronism on evolutionary games. Journal of Theoretical Biology 269(1), 109–122 (2011)
10. Ingerson, T.E., Buvel, R.L.: Structure in asynchronous cellular automata. Physica D: Nonlinear Phenomena 10(1-2), 59–68 (1984)
11. Peper, F., Isokawa, T., Takada, Y., Matsui, N.: Self-timed cellular automata and their computational ability. Future Generation Computer Systems 18(7), 893–904 (2002)
12. Spicher, A., Fatès, N., Simonin, O.: From reactive multi-agents models to cellular automata - illustration on a diffusion-limited aggregation model. In: Proceedings of ICAART, pp. 422–429 (2009)

# Synthesis of Reversible Asynchronous Cellular Automata for Pattern Generation with Specific Hamming Distance*

Sukanta Das[1], Anindita Sarkar[1], and Biplab K. Sikdar[2]

[1] Department of Information Technology
sukanta@it.becs.ac.in, anindita.sarkar10@gmail.com
[2] Department of Computer Science & Technology
Bengal Engineering & Science University, Shibpur, West Bengal, India, 711103
biplab@cs.becs.ac.in

**Abstract.** The reversibility issue of 1-dimensional asynchronous cellular automata (ACA) has been reported in [4]. The ACA rules are classified to synthesis reversible ACA. Characterization has been done to explore the update patterns of cells forming the reversible ACA. This work reports synthesis of reversible ACA for pattern generation, where specific Hamming distance between two consecutive ACA states of a cycle is maintained. A hardware realization of ACA is also reported that can effectively be utilized in VLSI circuit design, testing of asynchronous circuit, and Hamming code generation.

**Keywords:** Asynchronous cellular automata (ACA), reversibility, ACA cycle, reversible ACA rules.

## 1 Introduction

The reversibility of (synchronous) cellular automata has been studied extensively for years [1,2,5]. However, reversibility of asynchronous cellular automata (ACA) is almost an unaddressed issue. A very few works on reversibility of 2-dimensional ACA have been reported in the literature [3]. This scenario motivates us to explore the issue for 1-dimensional two-state 3-neighborhood ACA in [4].

In ACA, the cells are updated independently. So, in a single step any number of cells can be updated. Based on the updates of ACA cells, we define *update pattern* for reversibility of ACA. A number of CA 'rules' [6] has been identified as the *irreversible rules* that can not design reversible ACA for any set of update patterns. On the other hand, the *reversible rules* can synthesize reversible ACA for some set of update patterns. A scheme is developed to find an update pattern of ACA with specific cycle. In this work, we report synthesis of reversible ACA having some cycles for pattern generation, where two consecutive states maintain some specific Hamming distance. A hardware realization of ACA is also reported that can effectively be utilized in VLSI circuit design and testing of asynchronous circuit.

* This work is supported by AICTE Career Award fund (F.No. 1-51/RID/CA/29/2009-10), awarded to Sukanta Das.

G.C. Sirakoulis and S. Bandini (Eds.): ACRI 2012, LNCS 7495, pp. 643–652, 2012.
© Springer-Verlag Berlin Heidelberg 2012

## 2   Cellular Automata

A cellular automaton (CA) is the discrete spatially-extended dynamical systems. It evolves in discrete space and time. In its simplest form, as it is proposed by Wolfram [6], CA consist of a lattice of cells, each of which stores a discrete variable at time $t$ that refers to the present state of the CA cell. The next state of a cell in 1-dimensional two-state 3-neighborhood (self, left and right neighbors) CA is $S_i^{t+1} = f(S_{i-1}^t, S_i^t, S_{i+1}^t)$, where $f$ is the next state function; $S_{i-1}^t$, $S_i^t$ and $S_{i+1}^t$ are the present states of the left neighbor, self and right neighbor of the $i^{th}$ CA cell at $t$. The function $f : \{0,1\}^3 \mapsto \{0,1\}$ can be expressed as a look-up table as shown in Table 1. The decimal equivalent of the 8 outputs (next state) is called 'rule' [6]. There are $2^8$ (256) CA rules in two-state 3-neighborhood dependency. Two such rules, 60 and 51 are shown in Table 1. From the view point of *Switching Theory*, a combination of the present states (first row of Table 1) can be viewed as the *Min Term* of a 3-variable $(S_{i-1}^t, S_i^t, S_{i+1}^t)$ switching function. So, each column of the first row of Table 1 is referred to as Rule Min Term (RMT).

The collection of states of all the cells $(S_1^t, S_2^t, \cdots, S_n^t)$ at time $t$ is the state of $n$-cell CA at $t$. If the left most and right most cells are the neighbors of each other (that is, $S_0^t = S_n^t$ and $S_{n+1}^t = S_1^t$), then the CA are *periodic boundary* CA. On the other hand, in *null boundary* CA, $S_0^t = S_{n+1}^t = 0$ (null).

**Table 1.** Look-up table for rule 60 and 51

| Present state : | 111 | 110 | 101 | 100 | 011 | 010 | 001 | 000 | *Rule* |
|---|---|---|---|---|---|---|---|---|---|
| (RMT) | (7) | (6) | (5) | (4) | (3) | (2) | (1) | (0) | |
| (i) Next State : | 0 | 0 | 1 | 1 | 1 | 1 | 0 | 0 | 60 |
| (ii) Next State : | 0 | 0 | 1 | 1 | 0 | 0 | 1 | 1 | 51 |

If all the cells of a CA update their states simultaneously, the CA is *synchronous*. In *asynchronous CA* (ACA), the cells are updated independently and any number of cells can be updated in a time step.

**Fig. 1.** Partial state transition of rule 60 ACA. Cells updated are noted on the arrow

The next state of ACA depends not only on the cell rule, but also on the cells that update their states at that time instant. We denote the set of cells updated at $t$ as $u_t$. Therefore, $U = \langle u_1, u_2, \cdots, u_t, \cdots \rangle$ is the *update pattern* for the ACA. If the ACA rule, $U$ and an initial state are given, the state transitions of the ACA can be identified. A partial state transition diagram of 4-cell rule 60 ACA with null boundary condition is shown in Fig. 1. The set $U = \langle \{2\}, \{1,4\}, \{2,4\}, \{3\}, \{2,4\}, \{3,4\}, \{2\}, \cdots \rangle$ and initial state is 15.

In ACA, a single state transition diagram may not cover all the CA states. A set of update patterns can illustrate the transition of all the states.

## 3    The Reversibility of ACA

The state transition diagram classifies the CA states as *cyclic* and *acyclic* states. If a CA state lies on a cycle in state transition diagram, the state is cyclic; otherwise it is acyclic. The CA is *reversible* if all the CA states are cyclic. The reversibility, in synchronous domain, guarantees that each CA state has unique predecessor and successor.

**Definition 1.** *For a set of update patterns, an ACA is* **reversible** *if each CA state can uniquely be reached from the state itself. Otherwise, it is* **irreversible**.

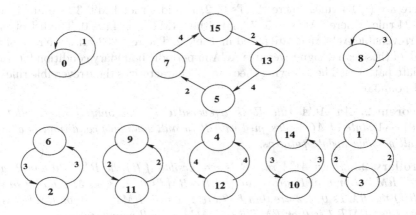

**Fig. 2.** 4-cell rule 60 reversible ACA in null boundary condition

Fig. 2 depicts the state transition diagram of 4-cell null boundary reversible ACA. The 8 update patterns (one for each cycle) are $\langle\{1\}\rangle$, $\langle\{2\}, \{4\}, \{2\}, \{4\}\rangle$, $\langle\{3\}\rangle$, $\langle\{3\}, \{3\}\rangle$, $\langle\{2\}, \{2\}\rangle$, $\langle\{4\}, \{4\}\rangle$, $\langle\{3\}, \{3\}\rangle$, and $\langle\{2\}, \{2\}\rangle$. The update patterns cover all the $2^4 = 16$ states of the ACA.

**Definition 2.** *A CA rule R is an* **irreversible rule** *if there is at least a state of ACA, designed with R, can never be cyclic for any update pattern. Otherwise, R is a* **reversible rule**.

For example, rule 77 (01001101) in null-boundary condition is an irreversible rule. The all-0 state of rule 77 ACA is acyclic for all possible update patterns. On the other hand, rule 60 is a reversible rule in null and periodic boundary condition (Fig. 2). The following theorem [4] characterizes the irreversible rules in periodic boundary condition.

**Table 2.** Irreversible ACA rules in periodic boundary

| 0 | 2 | 4 | 6 | 8 | 10 | 12 | 14 |
|---|---|---|---|---|----|----|----|
| 16 | 20 | 24 | 28 | 64 | 66 | 68 | 70 |
| 72 | 74 | 76 | 78 | 80 | 84 | 88 | 92 |
| 141 | 143 | 157 | 159 | 173 | 175 | 189 | 191 |
| 197 | 199 | 205 | 207 | 213 | 215 | 221 | 223 |
| 229 | 231 | 237 | 239 | 245 | 247 | 253 | 255 |

**Theorem 1.** *An ACA rule R is irreversible if and only if all-0 or all-1 state of ACA, designed with R in periodic boundary condition, is acyclic for all possible update patterns.*

**Corollary 1.** *[4] An ACA rule R is irreversible if (i) the RMTs 0, 2, 7, and either RMT 3 or 6 of R are 1, or (ii) the RMTs 0, 5, 7, and either RMT 1 or 4 are 0, in periodic boundary condition.*

There are (i) 24 rules where RMTs 0, 2, 7, and either RMT 3 or 6 are 1, and (ii) 24 rules where RMTs 0, 5, 7, and either RMT 1 or 4 are 0. The list of such 48 irreversible ACA rules are noted in Table 2. The rest 208 rules are reversible. Each of these can design reversible ACA in periodic boundary condition for some update patterns. The following theorem [4] characterizes the irreversible rules in null boundary.

**Theorem 2.** *An ACA rule R is irreversible if and only if all-0, all-1 or $10101\cdots1$ state of ACA, designed with R in null boundary condition, is acyclic for all possible update patterns.*

**Corollary 2.** *[4] An ACA rule R is irreversible if (i) the RMTs 0 and 2, and either RMT 3 or 6 of R are 1, or (ii) the RMTs 0, 1, 3, 4, 5, 6 and 7 are 0, or (iii) the RMTs 0 & 2 are 0, 5 & 7 are 1, and if RMT 1 is 0 or RMT 3 is 1, then either RMT 4 is 0 or RMT 6 is 1 ACA in null boundary condition.*

Therefore, in null boundary, there are (i) 48 irreversible ACA rules while RMTs 0, 2, and either 3 or 6 are 1, (ii) 2 irreversible ACA rules while RMTs 0, 1, 3, 4, 5, 6 and 7 are 0, and (iii) 9 irreversible ACA rules while RMTs 0 and 2 are 0, RMTs 5 and 7 are 1, and if RMT 1 is 0 or RMT 3 is 1, then either RMT 4 is 0 or RMT 6 is 1. All such (59) irreversible rules are listed in Table 3. The rest 197 rules are reversible in null boundary.

However, the reversibility of ACA depends not only on the rule, but also on update patterns. For example, rule 60 ACA can be irreversible (Fig. 1), as well as reversible (Fig. 2) depending on the update patterns. Since the ACA cells can update independently, it can not be predicted in advance that ACA designed with a reversible rule is reversible.

**Theorem 3.** *[4] It is impossible, in general, to synthesize reversible an 1-d ACA.*

The following section investigates the update patterns for the cycles of reversible ACA.

**Table 3.** Irreversible ACA rules in null boundary

| 0 | 4 | 13 | 15 | 29 | 31 | 45 | 47 |
|---|---|---|---|---|---|---|---|
| 61 | 63 | 69 | 71 | 77 | 79 | 85 | 87 |
| 93 | 95 | 101 | 103 | 109 | 111 | 117 | 119 |
| 125 | 127 | 141 | 143 | 157 | 159 | 160 | 168 |
| 170 | 173 | 175 | 189 | 191 | 197 | 199 | 205 |
| 207 | 213 | 215 | 221 | 223 | 224 | 229 | 231 |
| 232 | 234 | 237 | 239 | 240 | 245 | 247 | 248 |
| 250 | 253 | 255 | | | | | |

# 4   Identifying Update Pattern for a Cycle

The reversible rules require different sets of update patterns for reversible ACA. Even, for a particular reversible rule, different sets of update patterns can be identified that result in reversible ACA. The following theorem [4] characterizes the states forming a cycle of ACA.

**Theorem 4.** *A sequence of $l$ distinct $n$-bit CA states $\langle S_1, S_2, \cdots, S_l \rangle$ form a cycle of length $l \geq 2$ if, $\forall i$ ($1 \leq i \leq n$), the $i^{th}$ bit of the CA states does not flip or flips even number of times.*

To get a cycle of the reversible ACA, an update pattern along with an initial state is required. Since the states of a cycle of length $l$ are to be distinct, the update pattern should be designed in such a way that at least one bit of a state flips to get the next state. Moreover, in any sub-sequence of states, the bits of states are not to be flipped in even number of times (Theorem 4). If they flip, the $l$ states can not be distinct.

   Therefore, distinct states depend not only on the update pattern, but also on the initial state. Because, the initial state may not allow an arbitrary cell of an ACA to flip. Rule 51 (Table 1) is the only rule that always allows a cell to flip its state when updated. So, rule 51 ACA do not depend on the initial state to form a cycle. The following rule is designed to generate an update pattern for a cycle of length $2^i$ ($1 \leq i \leq n$, $n$ is the number of ACA cells) while updating a single cell at a time.
*To get a cycle of length $2^i$ ($1 \leq i \leq n$) of rule 51 ACA, we form a sequence of $i$ cells, to be updated, arbitrarily. Then we start with an arbitrary state and update $(2^{j-1})^{th}$ state by updating $j^{th}$ cell ($1 \leq j \leq i$) of the sequence. We repeat the update of $j^{th}$ cell after each $2^j$ states, where $j < i$. The next step is the update of $i^{th}$ cell after $2^{i-1}$ states to get a cycle of length $2^i$.*

*Example 1.* To design a full length cycle for 4-cell rule 51 ACA (*length* $= 2^4$), all the cells are to be updated in some sequence. Consider, the sequence of update is $SEQ = \langle 1, 2, 3, 4 \rangle$ and the initial state is 0100. Each $j^{th}$ cell of $SEQ$ is selected for the first time to update $(2^{j-1})^{th}$ state. Hence, to get the second state, the first bit of the initial state $((2^{j-1})^{th}$ state, where $j = 1$) is updated. Similarly, the second, third and fourth cells are selected for the first time to update the second, fourth and eighth states respectively. The first cell is again selected to update third, fifth, and all odd states (that is, after each $2^j$ states where $j = 1$). After the first time update, the second and third cells are selected repeatedly to update after every $2^2$ and $2^3$ states respectively. The last cell is updated for the second time after $2^3$ states ($2^{i-1}$ states where $i = 4$) to complete the cycle. Therefore, the sequence of states in the cycle is $\langle 0100, 1100, 1000, 0000, 0010,$ $1010, 1110, 0110, 0111, 1111, 1011, 0011, 0001, 1001, 1101, 0101, 0100 \rangle$. The update pattern is $\langle \{1\}, \{2\}, \{1\}, \{3\}, \{1\}, \{2\}, \{1\}, \{4\}, \{1\}, \{2\}, \{1\}, \{3\}, \{1\},$ $\{2\}, \{1\}, \{4\} \rangle$. Here, the update pattern is independent of the initial state, but depends on $SEQ$ (the update pattern and cycle of rule 51 ACA are same for both the boundary conditions).

The cycles can also be formed by updating multiple cells simultaneously.

**Theorem 5.** *Rule 51 ACA with $n$ cells can form a cycle of maximum length $2^{n-m+1}$ if $m$ cells $(1 \leq m \leq n)$ are updated simultaneously.*

In such case, the same rule of single cell update to get a cycle can be followed with an exception that each entry in the sequence of cells ($SEQ$ in Example 1) in a set of $m$ cells.

*Example 2.* Let us consider, $n = 4$ and $m = 2$. To get an 8 length $(2^{n-m+1})$ cycle of the ACA, a sequence $SEQ = \langle \{1, 2\}, \{2, 3\}, \{3, 4\} \rangle$ of cells is formed arbitrarily. Consider that the initial state is 0100. The first and second bits are updated to generate the second state (1000). Similarly, the cells of second and third entries of $SEQ$ are selected to update the second and forth states. Like Example 1, the cells of first set ($\{1, 2\}$) are repeatedly selected to update the odd states. The cells of second set ($\{2, 3\}$) are selected again to update the sixth state. Therefore, a sequence $\langle 0100, 1000, 1110, 0010, 0001, 1101, 1011, 0111,$ $0100 \rangle$ of states is obtained and the update pattern is $\langle \{1, 2\}, \{2, 3\}, \{1, 2\}, \{3, 4\}, \{1, 2\}, \{2, 3\}, \{1, 2\}, \{3, 4\} \rangle$.

The update rule, designed for rule 51 reversible ACA, guides us to develop Algorithm 1 which finds the update pattern for a cycle of the reversible ACA. It first forms a sequence of $i$ unique sets (arbitrarily). The sets are also designed arbitrarily with $m$ ACA cells per set. If no bit flips during the update of a set of $m$ cells, another set of $m$ cells is searched so that at least one bit flips. While $2^i$ states are covered but no cycle is formed, the algorithm attempts to form a cycle with fewer states.

*Algorithm 1.* FindACACycle
**Input:** $R$ (rule), $n$ (# cells), $2^i$ (cycle length, $1 \leq i \leq n$), $S$ (initial state), $m$ (# cells updated in each step)
**Output:** Update pattern with cycle length
*Step 1:* Form a sequence, $SEQ$ of $i$ unique sets of $m$ ACA cells, arbitrarily.
*Step 2:* Load the ACA, designed with $R$, with $S$.
*Step 3:* For $k = 1$ to $2^i$ repeat Step 4 to Step 9.

RMTs of Rule 123

| 111 | 110 | 101 | 100 | 011 | 010 | 001 | 000 |
|-----|-----|-----|-----|-----|-----|-----|-----|
| (7) | (6) | (5) | (4) | (3) | (2) | (1) | (0) |
| 0   | 1   | 1   | 1   | 1   | 0   | 1   | 1   |

| Update Pattern of 51 | 1 2 3 4 5 6 | Update pattern generated |
|----------------------|-------------|--------------------------|
| 1, 3 | 0 1 1 1 1 1 | 1, 3 |
| 1, 4 | 1 1 0 1 1 1 | 1, 5 |
| 1, 3 | 1 1 0 1 0 1 | 1, 3 |
| 2, 4 | 1 1 1 1 0 1 | 2, 4 |
| 1, 3 | 1 0 1 1 0 1 | 1, 3 |
| 1, 4 | 0 0 1 1 0 1 | 5, 6 |
| 1, 3 | 0 0 1 1 1 0 | 1, 3 |
| 2, 4 | 1 0 1 1 1 0 | 2, 4 |
|      | 1 1 1 0 1 0 |      |

$SEQ = \langle\{1, 3\}, \{1, 4\}, \{2, 4\}\rangle$

| | 1 2 3 4 5 6 | |
|---|-------------|---|
| | 1 1 1 0 1 0 | 4, 6 |
| | 1 1 1 1 1 1 | 2 |
| | 1 0 1 1 1 1 | 1 |
| | 0 0 1 1 1 1 | 2 |
| | 0 1 1 1 1 1 | |

**Fig. 3.** Generation of cycle for rule 123 ACA ($m = 2$)

*Step 4:* If $k = 2^{j-1}$ ($1 \leq j \leq i$), select the $j^{th}$ set of the $SEQ$.
   If $k = 2^i$, select the $i^{th}$ set of $SEQ$.
   If $k = 2^{j-1} + p * 2^j$ ($p$ is a positive integer and $1 \leq j < i$) select $j^{th}$ set.
*Step 5:* Update ACA cells of the selected set.
*Step 6:* If no cell flips during update, find a set of $m$ cells so that
   a) at least one cell flips, and b) the generated state is unique.
   Otherwise, goto Step 9.
*Step 7:* If no such set is found in Step 6, goto Step 14.
*Step 8:* Update the ACA cells according to the set, designed in Step 6.
*Step 9:* Print the ACA cells that are updated to generate the next state of $k$.
*Step 10:* If no cycle is formed, identify the bits of $2^i + 1$ state which differ from the initial state, $S$. Otherwise, go to Step 15.
*Step 11:* Update the ACA cells to flip the identified bits.
*Step 12:* If few cells flip, print those. Update the nearest cells of rest bits (one-by-one or more than one at a time) so that the $S$ is reached within few steps.
*Step 13:* If cycle is formed, goto Step 15.
*Step 14:* Print 'Cycle is not possible', and exit.
*Step 15:* Print the length of cycle and exit.

*Example 3.* Let us consider, $R = 123$, $n = 6$, cycle length $= 8$ ($2^3$), $S = 011111$ and $m = 2$. Formation of cycle following Algorithm 1 is shown in Fig. 3. Firstly, a sequence of 3 sets $SEQ = \langle\{1, 3\}, \{1, 4\}, \{2, 4\}\rangle$ is formed arbitrarily (Step 1). The ACA is designed with rule 123 in null boundary condition. To get the next state of 011111, the first and third cells are updated (Steps 4 and 5). In Fig. 3, update pattern of rule 51 ACA is noted on the left side of the states, and the update pattern generated for rule 123 is shown on the right side. To update the second state (similarly sixth state), according to the update pattern of rule 51 ACA, the set $\{1, 4\}$ is selected. Since no cell flips following RMTs of rule 123, another set $\{1, 5\}$ is searched (Step 6). After generation of 8 states, cycle is not formed. So, another 4 states are generated to form a cycle (Steps 10 – 12). Therefore, length of cycle is 12.

We have experimented with different reversible rules. It is found that for a number of reversible rules, update pattern can be extracted utilizing Algorithm 1 to get a full length cycle (by updating a single cell at a time). Few of such rules are: 3, 19, 35, 83, 115, 131, 147, 163, 179, 211, 243.

# 5    Pattern Generation by ACA

The states generated by ACA can be considered as binary patterns. So, the ACA can be treated as a pattern generator. If the ACA follow update pattern produced by Algorithm 1, it can be predicted that a specific Hamming distance between two consecutive patterns in the sequence of states is always maintained. Such patterns can be utilized in various fields, like generating Hamming code, testing VLSI circuits, etc. However, these applications demand hardware realization of ACA, so that pattern generation can be fast and cost effective.

For hardware realization of ACA, a cell is to be implemented in hardware. To do this, we need a combinational logic for implementing the next state logic (rule), and a flip-flop to store present state of the cell. Such a cell is to be

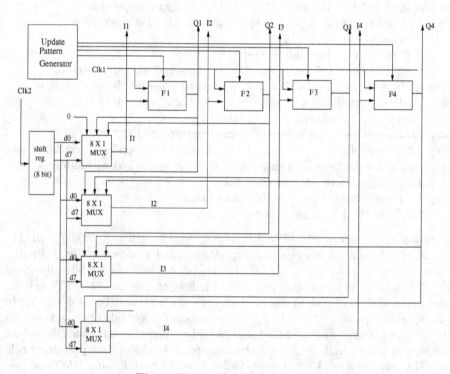

**Fig. 4.** The 4-cell ACA hardware

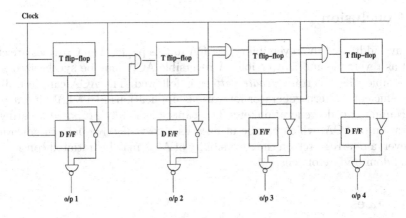

**Fig. 5.** Update pattern generator

placed into $n$ positions to realize $n$-cell ACA. However, to optimize the space requirement, we can use an 8-bit shift register to store the rule, and a multiplexer (MUX) at each cell position to output state of the cell. Such implementation also enables us to design ACA with any rule.

The detail hardware of a 4-cell ACA is shown in Fig. 4. The rule is kept in the shift register, D flip flops (F1, F2, F3 and F4) are used to store the states of cells, an $8 \times 1$ MUX selects an RMT to get the next state, and *Update Pattern Generator* generates update pattern for the ACA. The logic diagram of update pattern generator is noted in Fig. 5. The generator is designed using T and D flip-flops.

We have simulated the logic diagram (Fig. 4 and Fig. 5) of ACA in FPGA (Field-Programmable Gate Array). Device utilization of such implementation of 4-cell and 16-cell ACA is reported in Table 4.

**Table 4.** Device utilization of 4-cell and 16-cell ACA

| # cells | Name of unit | Unit Utilized | Available Unit | % of Utilization |
|---------|--------------|---------------|----------------|------------------|
|         | Number of Slices | 14 | 1920 | 0 |
|         | Number of Slice Flip Flops | 20 | 3840 | 0 |
| 4       | Number of 4 input LUTs | 25 | 3840 | 0 |
|         | Number of IOs | 8 | - | - |
|         | Number of bonded IOBs | 8 | 173 | 4 |
|         | Number of GCLKs | 2 | 8 | 25 |
|         | Number of Slices | 56 | 1920 | 2 |
| 16      | Number of Slice Flip Flops | 56 | 3840 | 1 |
|         | Number of 4 input LUTs | 108 | 3840 | 2 |
|         | Number of IOs | 20 | - | - |
|         | Number of bonded IOBs | 20 | 173 | 11 |
|         | Number of GCLKs | 2 | 8 | 25 |

# 6   Conclusion

We have addressed the reversibility of ACA in this paper. The CA rules are classified as reversible and irreversible. A reversible ACA may be synthesized with a reversible rule if certain *update pattern* is followed. The ACA can be utilized as an efficient pattern generator for various applications like VLSI circuit testing, Hamming code generation, etc. The paper has finally proposed a hardware realization of ACA, which can be utilized as a cost effective pattern generator. However, a new research on the reversibility of ACA may be initiated considering the random update of cells.

# References

1. Amoroso, S., Patt, Y.N.: Decision procedures for surjectivity and injectivity of parallel maps for tesselation structures. Journal of Computer and System Sciences 6, 448–464 (1972)
2. Das, S., Sikdar, B.K.: Classification of *CA* Rules Targeting Synthesis of Reversible Cellular Automata. In: El Yacoubi, S., Chopard, B., Bandini, S. (eds.) ACRI 2006. LNCS, vol. 4173, pp. 68–77. Springer, Heidelberg (2006)
3. Lee, J., Peper, F., Adachi, S., Morita, K., Mashiko, S.: Reversible Computation in Asynchronous Cellular Automata. In: Calude, C.S., Dinneen, M.J., Peper, F. (eds.) UMC 2002. LNCS, vol. 2509, pp. 220–229. Springer, Heidelberg (2002)
4. Sarkar, A., Mukherjee, A., Das, S.: Reversibility in asynchronous cellular automata. Accepted in Complex Systems (2012)
5. Toffoli, T.: Computation and construction universality of reversible cellular automata. J. Comput. System Sci. 15, 213–231 (1977)
6. Wolfram, S.: Theory and applications of cellular automata. World Scientific, Singapore (1986) ISBN 9971-50-124-4 pbk

# $m$-Asynchronous Cellular Automata

Alberto Dennunzio[1], Enrico Formenti[2,*],
Luca Manzoni[1], and Giancarlo Mauri[1]

[1] Università degli Studi di Milano–Bicocca
Dipartimento di Informatica, Sistemistica e Comunicazione,
Viale Sarca 336, 20126 Milano Italy
{dennunzio,luca.manzoni,mauri}@disco.unimib.it
[2] Université Nice-Sophia Antipolis, Laboratoire I3S,
2000 Route des Colles, 06903 Sophia Antipolis France
enrico.formenti@unice.fr

**Abstract.** A new model for the study of ACA dynamical behavior has been introduced. The classical properties of injectivity, surjectivity and expansivity have been adapted to the new setting. Preliminary results show that the injectivity is almost always equal to surjectivity and that both property are almost always implied by expansivity.

## 1 Introduction

Cellular automata (CA) are a well-known formal model for complex systems used in many scientific fields [5,4,14]. They essentially consist of a grid ($\mathbb{Z}$ in this paper) of identical automata, called *cells*, that update their own state according to a local rule which takes into account the state of only on a fixed number of neighbouring automata. Synchronicity is a main characteristic of classical CA. Indeed, all cells update their state in parallel at each time step.

However, when CA are used as models of physical phenomena the assumption of synchronicity can be an issue. In fact, full synchronous behaviour is a quite rare event in nature. This led researchers to consider asynchronous CA and many empirical analyses [1,2,7,17,22,23] have been carried out on them. They highlighted that the behaviour of a CA considerably changes when relaxing the synchronicity constraint. This fact motivated subsequent theoretical studies on asynchronous CA [24,18]. However, the few formal analyses of asynchronicity concern either examples or particular classes [10,11,21,8,9,16,20].

In this paper, we study a more general setting, that includes some of the previous approaches, relaxing the synchronicity constraint. Indeed, at each time step, the subset of cells to be updated is extracted using a probability measure $\mu$ on subsets of $\mathbb{Z}$. Clearly, one should put some conditions on $\mu$ to grant both a non-trivial behavior and a considerable degree of asynchronicity. We called these constraints "fairness conditions" (see Definition 2).

This new point of view asked to adapt the classical notions about dynamical behavior such as injectivity, surjectivity, expansivity, etc. In this paper, we

---

* Corresponding author.

G.C. Sirakoulis and S. Bandini (Eds.): ACRI 2012, LNCS 7495, pp. 653–662, 2012.

prove a somewhat surprising result, namely, $\mu$-almost surely surjective CA are $\mu$-almost surely injective and *vice-versa*. Curiously, this result is much similar to the case of fully-ACA (ACA in which only one cell is allowed to be updated per time step [19]) and much different different from the classical CA setting where injective CA are surjective but the *vice-versa* is false.

We also prove that almost sure injectivity has also a combinatorial facet through the classical notion of diamond (Proposition 2). The existence of diamonds is also related to almost sure expansivity (Proposition 3).

## 2   Preliminary Notions

For all $i, j \in \mathbb{Z}$ with $i \leq j$ (resp., $i < j$) let $[i,j] = \{k \in \mathbb{N} | i \leq k \leq j\}$ (resp., $[i,j) = \{k \in \mathbb{N} | i \leq k < j\}$). The set of positive integers (resp., reals) is denoted by $\mathbb{N}_+$ (resp., $\mathbb{R}_+$). Given a set $X$, $\mathfrak{P}(X)$ denotes the collection of subsets of $X$.

Let $\Sigma$ be a finite alphabet. A *configuration* is a function from $\mathbb{Z}$ to $\Sigma$. The *configuration set* $\Sigma^{\mathbb{Z}}$ is usually equipped with the metric $d$ defined as follows:

$$\forall x, y \in \Sigma^{\mathbb{Z}} \; d(x,y) = 2^{-n} \text{ , where } n = \min\{i \in \mathbb{N} \mid x_i \neq y_i \text{ or } x_{-i} \neq y_{-i}\}$$

The set $\Sigma^{\mathbb{Z}}$ is a compact, totally disconnected and perfect topological space (i.e., it is a Cantor space). For any pair $i, j \in \mathbb{Z}$, with $i \leq j$, and any configuration $x \in \Sigma^{\mathbb{Z}}$ we denote by $x_{[i,j]}$ the word $x_i \cdots x_j \in A^{j-i+1}$. Similarly, for every $u \in A^{\ell}$ and for every $i, j \in [0, \ell)$, $u_{[i,j]} = u_i \ldots u_j$ is the portion of a word inside $[i, j]$. In both the previous notations, $[i, j]$ can be replaced by $[i, j)$, with the obvious meaning. A configuration $x$ is said to be $a$-finite for some $a \in \Sigma$ if the number of positions $i$ with $x_i \neq a$ is finite.

A 1D CA is a structure $(\Sigma, \lambda, r)$ where $\Sigma$ is the *alphabet* or *set of states*, $r \in \mathbb{N}$ is the *radius*, and $\lambda : \Sigma^{2r+1} \to \Sigma$ is the *local rule* of the automaton. The local rule $\lambda$ induces a *global rule* $F : \Sigma^{\mathbb{Z}} \to \Sigma^{\mathbb{Z}}$ defined as follows:

$$\forall x \in \Sigma^{\mathbb{Z}}, \; \forall i \in \mathbb{Z}, \qquad F(x)_i = \lambda(x_{i-r}, \ldots, x_i, \ldots, x_{i+r}) \; .$$

Note that $F$ is a uniformly continuous map with respect to the metric $d$. For any CA, the pair $(\Sigma^{\mathbb{Z}}, F)$ is a (discrete time) dynamical system. From now on, for the sake of simplicity, we identify a CA with the dynamical system that it induces or even with its global rule $F$. A local rule $\lambda : \Sigma^{2r+1} \to \Sigma$ is *center-permutive* iff for any $w \in \Sigma^{2r}$ and any $b \in \Sigma$ there exists a unique $a \in \Sigma$ such that $\lambda(w_{[0,r)} a w_{[r,2r)}) = b$.

Let $\mathcal{T}$ be a monoid of continuous functions from $\Sigma^{\mathbb{Z}}$ to $\Sigma^{\mathbb{Z}}$. The family $\mathcal{T}$ is said to be *positively expansive* (or, briefly, *expansive*) if there exists a constant $\varepsilon > 0$ such that for every pair of distinct elements $x, y \in \Sigma^{\mathbb{Z}}$, we have $d(T(x), T(y)) \geq \varepsilon$ for some $T \in \mathcal{T}$.

A $\sigma$-algebra over a topological space $X$ is a non-empty collection of subsets of $X$ closed under countable union and complementation. The Borel $\sigma$-algebra on $X$ is the smallest $\sigma$-algebra containing all the closed and the open sets of $X$.

A measure $\mu$ is a function from a $\sigma$-algebra on $X$ to $\mathbb{R}_+ \cup \{+\infty\}$ such that $\mu$ is countably additive. A measure $\mu$ is said to be a probability measure if $\mu(X) = 1$. For a given set $X$ of outcomes, a $\sigma$-algebra on $X$ represents the set of events and, once introduced a probability measure $\mu$ on the $\sigma$-algebra, the probability of an event $E$ is $\mu(E)$.

For any $i \in \mathbb{Z}$, the *principal ultrafilter* $\mathcal{U}_i$ of $i$ is the collection of all subsets of $\mathbb{Z}$ containing $i$. The complement of $\mathcal{U}_i$ is denoted by $\overline{\mathcal{U}}_i$. From now on, we consider $\mathfrak{P}(\mathbb{Z})$ equipped with a topology for which the principal ultrafilters are clopen (i.e., closed and open) sets.

# 3     *m*-Asynchronous Cellular Automata

In this section we introduce the notion of *m*-ACA as a generalization both of classical CA and of fully-ACA. The basic idea is to augment the classical CA model by a measure $\mu$. Updating sequences will be generated using $\mu$. In this manner, it is possible to precisely define when a property holds for almost all updating sequences or only for a negligible set of them.

**Definition 1 (*m*-ACA).** *An* *m-ACA* $\mathcal{C}$ *is a quadruple* $(\Sigma, r, \lambda, \mu)$ *where A is a finite alphabet,* $r > 0$ *is the radius,* $\lambda : \Sigma^{2r+1} \to \Sigma$ *is the local rule and* $\mu$ *is a probability measure on the Borel* $\sigma$-algebra on $\mathfrak{P}(\mathbb{Z})$.

Given the local rule $\lambda$ and a set $U \in \mathfrak{P}(\mathbb{Z})$ define $F_U : \Sigma^{\mathbb{Z}} \to \Sigma^{\mathbb{Z}}$ as follows

$$\forall x \in \Sigma^{\mathbb{Z}}, \forall i \in \mathbb{Z} \quad F_U(x)_i = \begin{cases} \lambda(x_{i-r}, \ldots, x_i, \ldots, x_{i+r}) & \text{if } i \in U \ , \\ x_i & \text{otherwise} \ . \end{cases}$$

Given a sequence $v \in \mathfrak{P}(\mathbb{Z})^{\mathbb{N}}$ extracted using $\mu$ (all extractions are considered as independent), the *dynamics* of the *m*-ACA is described by the family of functions $\mathcal{T}_v = \{id, F_{v_1}, F_{v_2} \circ F_{v_1}, \ldots\}$. Remark that all the elements from $\mathcal{T}_v$ are continuous functions w.r.t. the metric $d$. The *orbit* of a configuration $x \in \Sigma^{\mathbb{Z}}$ is the sequence $\gamma_{x,v} = (x, F_{v_1}(x), (F_{v_2} \circ F_{v_1})(x), \ldots)$ associating with each time step $t \in \mathbb{N}$ the configuration $\gamma_{x,v}(t) = (F_{v_t} \circ \ldots \circ F_{v_1})(x)$ of the *m*-ACA at that time.

*Remark 1.* The notion of *m*-ACA includes both classical CA and fully-ACA. Indeed, the former case is obtained choosing a measure $\mu_1$ such that $\mu_1(A) = 1$ if $\mathbb{Z} \in A$, 0 otherwise. The latter is obtained by choosing $\mu_2$ such that $\mu_2(\mathcal{U}_i) > 0$ for $i \in \mathbb{Z}$ and $\mu_2(\mathcal{U}_i \cap \mathcal{U}_j) = 0$ for $i \neq j$. Note that in the last case we cannot have a shift-invariant measure.

In order to study the core behavior of the model, the "extremal" cases reported in Remark 1 should be avoided. This goal can be reached, for instance, by adding some further requirements to the measure $\mu$ used to produce the updating sequences. Therefore, the following "fairness" requirements are put on $\mu$:

1. at any time step (extraction), each single cell is updated or non updated with a positive probability. This means that events like "always updated" or "always non updated" for the same cell happen with probability 0.
2. for any cell the probability of being updated is independent from the probability of being updated of any other cell.
3. any event concerning the update/non update of an infinite number of cells has zero probability.

The following definition formalizes the above requirements.

**Definition 2.** *A probability measure $\mu$ on the Borel $\sigma$-algebra on $\mathfrak{P}(\mathbb{Z})$ is fair iff:*

1. *$\forall i \in \mathbb{Z}$, $0 < \mu(\mathcal{U}_i) < 1$.*
2. *$\forall A \subseteq \mathbb{Z}$ with $A$ finite, $\mu\left(\bigcap_{a \in A} U_a\right) = \prod_{a \in A} \mu(U_a)$, where each $U_a$ can be either $\mathcal{U}_a$ or $\overline{\mathcal{U}}_a$.*
3. *$\forall A \subseteq \mathbb{Z}$ with $A$ infinite, $\mu\left(\bigcap_{a \in A} U_a\right) = 0$, where each $U_a$ can be either $\mathcal{U}_a$ or $\overline{\mathcal{U}}_a$.*

*Remark 2.* The class of $\alpha$-asynchronous CA are an example of $m$-ACA. Indeed, each cell $i$ is updated with a fixed probability $\alpha > 0$. This is equivalent to take $\mu(\mathcal{U}_i) = \alpha$ for every $i \in \mathbb{Z}$. Note that $m$-ACA also allow the non-shift invariant case of a probability of updating a cell that depends on its position.

*Remark 3.* For both classical CA and fully-ACA it is impossible to define a fair measure to generate the correct updating sequences. In fact, for classical CA we need that $\mu(\mathcal{U}_i) = 1$ for every $i \in \mathbb{Z}$. Also, for fully-ACA we need that $\mu(\mathcal{U}_i \cap \mathcal{U}_j) = 0$ whenever $i \neq j$.

The following lemma illustrates a first consequence of the fairness requirements on the measure $\mu$: for a given cell, the probability of being updated or not can be arbitrarily close neither to 0 nor to 1.

**Lemma 1.** *Consider a fair measure $\mu$ on the Borel $\sigma$-algebra on $\mathfrak{P}(\mathbb{Z})$. There exist $h, k \in \mathbb{R}$ with $0 < h \leq k < 1$ such that $\forall i \in \mathbb{Z}$, $h \leq \mu(\mathcal{U}_i) \leq k$.*

*Proof.* Let $h = \inf \{\mu(\mathcal{U}_i) \mid i \in \mathbb{Z}\} \geq 0$. We claim that $h > 0$. By contradiction, assume $h = 0$. Then, there exists a sequence $\{a_i\}_{i \in \mathbb{N}}$ of elements of $\mathbb{Z}$ such that $\mu(\mathcal{U}_{a_i}) \leq \frac{1}{(i+2)^2}$. Remark that $\prod_{i \in \mathbb{N}} \mu(\overline{\mathcal{U}}_{a_i}) \geq \prod_{i=2}^{+\infty} \left(1 - \frac{1}{i^2}\right) = \frac{1}{2}$. This contradicts the assumption that $\prod_{i \in A} \mu(\overline{\mathcal{U}}_{a_i}) = 0$ for every infinite subset $A \subseteq \mathbb{Z}$.

Let $k = \sup \{\mu(\mathcal{U}_i) \mid i \in \mathbb{Z}\} \leq 1$. We claim that $k < 1$. Again, by contradiction, assume that $k = 1$. Then, there exists a sequence $\{a_i\}_{i \in \mathbb{N}}$ of elements of $\mathbb{Z}$ such that $\mu(\mathcal{U}_{a_i}) \geq \frac{(i+2)^3 - 1}{(i+2)^3 + 1}$. Remark that $\prod_{i \in \mathbb{N}} \mu(\mathcal{U}_{a_i}) \geq \prod_{i=2}^{+\infty} \frac{i^3 - 1}{i^3 + 1} = \frac{2}{3}$ contradicting the assumption that $\mu$ is fair. $\qquad\square$

*Remark 4.* As a direct consequence of Lemma 1, the measure of the complements of ultrafilters is also bounded between $1 - k$ and $1 - h$. Moreover, there exists $0 < p \leq q < 1$ such that for every finite set $A \subseteq \mathbb{Z}$, $p^{|A|} \leq \mu(\bigcap_{a \in A} U_a) \leq q^{|A|}$.

Denote by $\mathcal{S}$ the set of all updating sequences. In the model proposed in this paper, $\mu$ is used to extract the subset of $\mathbb{Z}$ indicating which cells are allowed to be updated. At each time step, a new extraction is performed and we made the hypothesis that extractions are independent. Therefore, it is natural to consider the product measure $\mu_s$ of the measure $\mu$ to measure sets of updating sequences i.e., subsets of $\mathcal{S}$ ($\mu_s$ always exists and is unique, see [12, Thm. B, pag. 157]).

In the sequel, the notion of control pattern will play a central role in the proofs concerning injectivity and surjectivity properties.

A *control pattern* of length $n$ is an updating mask for $n$ contiguous cells. More formally,

**Definition 3.** *A control pattern of length $n \in \mathbb{N}_+$ is a pair $B = (B_1, B_2)$ of sets such that $\{B_1, B_2\}$ is a partition of $[0, n)$.*

**Definition 4.** *Given a control pattern $B = (B_1, B_2)$ and $\tau \in \mathfrak{P}(\mathbb{Z})$, $B$ is represented in $\tau$ at position $k$ iff $\forall b \in B_1$, $b + k \in \tau$ and $\forall c \in B_2$, $c + k \notin \tau$. $B$ is represented at least $m$ times in $\tau$ if there exist $m$ distinct positions at which $B$ is represented. If $B$ is represented at least $m$ times for any $m \in \mathbb{N}_+$, then $B$ is said to be represented infinitely many times.*

**Lemma 2.** *For any fair measure $\mu$, the following statements hold.*

1. *For every $n \in \mathbb{N}_+$ and for every control pattern $B$ of length $n$, the set of all $\tau \in \mathfrak{P}(\mathbb{Z})$ in which $B$ is represented infinitely many times has measure 1.*
2. *Every countable family of subsets of $\mathbb{Z}$ has measure 0.*

*Proof.*

1. Consider a control pattern $B$ of length $n$. For any $t \in \mathbb{N}$, let $E_t$ be the set of all subsets of $\mathbb{Z}$ in which the pattern is represented at position $tn$. Note that $\mu(E_t \cap E_q) = \mu(E_t)\mu(E_q)$ whenever $t \neq q$. Each $E_t$ has a positive measure and, by Lemma 1 there exists $p > 0$ such that for all $t \in \mathbb{N}$, $\mu(E_t) \geq p^n$. Since $\sum_{i=0}^{+\infty} \mu(E_t) \geq \sum_{i=0}^{+\infty} p^n = \infty$, by the second Borel-Cantelli Lemma [3], it follows that $\mu(\limsup_{t \to \infty} E_t) = \mu\left(\bigcap_{i=1}^{\infty} \bigcup_{j=i}^{\infty} E_j\right) = 1$. Hence, $B$ is represented almost surely infinitely many times.
2. Consider $A \subseteq \mathbb{Z}$ then $\mu(\{A\}) = \mu\left(\bigcap_{a \in A} \mathcal{U}_a \bigcap \bigcap_{a \notin A} \overline{\mathcal{U}}_a\right) = p$. By Condition 3. from Definition 2, we have $p = 0$. Finally, the thesis follows by countable additivity of $\mu$.

$\square$

By Lemma 2, for every control pattern $B$, the set of $\tau \in \mathfrak{P}(\mathbb{Z})$ in which $B$ is represented infinitely many times has full measure. Moreover, for every control pattern $B$ and every position $i \in \mathbb{Z}$, the set of $\tau \in \mathfrak{P}(\mathbb{Z})$ in which $B$ is represented infinitely many times at positions greater (or smaller) than $i$ has full measure too. Furthermore, from item 2. of Lemma 2, one can deduce that the set of all $\tau \in \mathfrak{P}(\mathbb{Z})$ for which the number of updated cells is finite or cofinite (i.e., with finite complement) has null measure.

**Definition 5.** *An m-ACA $C = (\Sigma, \lambda, r, \mu)$ is surjective (resp. injective) iff $\forall U \in \mathfrak{P}(\mathbb{Z})$, $F_U$ is surjective (resp. injective). The m-ACA $C$ is $\mu$-almost surely surjective (resp., injective) iff*

$$\mu\left(\{U \in \mathfrak{P}(\mathbb{Z}), F_U \text{ is surjective (resp. injective)}\}\right) = 1 .$$

From Definition 5, it trivially follows that if an $m$-ACA $C = (\Sigma, \lambda, r, \mu)$ is surjective, the corresponding CA $(\Sigma, \lambda, r)$ is surjective. The *shift* CA $(\{0, 1\}, \sigma, 1)$ where $\sigma(a, b, c) = c$ for all $a, b, c \in \{0, 1\}$ is bijective but its corresponding $m$-ACA $(\{0, 1\}, \sigma, 1, \mu)$ is not $\mu$-surjective for any fair $\mu$.

Recall that for fully-ACA, injectivity is equivalent to surjectivity [19]. Indeed, a similar result holds also for $m$-ACA as illustrated by the following proposition.

**Proposition 1.** *Consider an m-ACA $C = (\Sigma, \lambda, r, \mu)$, where $\mu$ is fair. Then, $C$ is $\mu$-almost surely surjective iff $C$ is $\mu$-almost surely injective.*

*Proof.* Consider a control pattern $B = (\emptyset, [0, r))$ and let $\tau \in \mathfrak{P}(\mathbb{Z})$ be generated by $\mu$. By Lemma 2, $B$ is represented infinitely many times in $\tau$. Hence, $\tau$ can be decomposed in intervals separated by gaps of non updated cells of length at least $r$. Call $\mathcal{F} = \{[h_i, k_i]\}_{i \in \mathbb{Z}}$ the sequence of such intervals, namely $\forall i, j \in \mathbb{Z}$, $i < j$ implies $k_i + r < h_j$ (i.e., the intervals are ordered and the distance between the extremes is at least $r$) and $\forall j \in \mathbb{Z}$, if $j \notin \bigcup_{i \in \mathbb{Z}}[h_i, k_i]$ then $\forall x \in \Sigma^{\mathbb{Z}}$, $F_\tau(x)_j = x_j$.

Note that $F_\tau$ is injective iff $\forall i \in \mathbb{Z}$ and $\forall x, y \in \Sigma^{\mathbb{Z}}$, $x_{[h_i, k_i]} \neq y_{[h_i, k_i]}$ implies $F_\tau(x)_{[h_i, k_i]} \neq F_\tau(y)_{[h_i, k_i]}$. This is equivalent to the following condition: $\forall i \in \mathbb{Z}$ and $\forall w \in \Sigma^{(k_i - h_i + 1)}$, $\exists x \in \Sigma^{\mathbb{Z}}$ such that $F_\tau(x)_{[h_i, k_i]} = w$, that in its turn is equivalent to the surjectivity of $F_\tau$. Thus, $F_\tau$ is injective iff it is surjective.    □

*Remark 5.* By the proof of Proposition 1, it follows that every $m$-ACA that is $\mu$-almost surely injective has a center-permutive local rule for any fair measure $\mu$. Indeed, this property holds since the set of all $\tau$ in which the control pattern $B = (\{r\}, [0, r) \cup (r, 2r + 1))$ occurs has full measure for any fair measure. When $B$ occurs at some position in $\tau$, injectivity or surjectivity of $F_\tau$ holds only if the local rule is center-permutive.

*Example 1.* Consider the $m$-ACA $C = (\{0, 1\}, \lambda, 1, \mu)$ where $\mu$ is fair and $\forall a, b, c \in \{0, 1\}$, $\lambda(a, b, c) = a$ xor $b$. Since $\forall n \in \mathbb{N}_+$ and $\forall x, y \in \Sigma^{\mathbb{Z}}$, $x_{[0, n)} \neq y_{[0, n)}$ implies $F(x)_{[0, n)} \neq F(y)_{[0, n)}$, $C$ is almost surely injective and surjective. Figure 1 gives an example of evolution of $C$.

Similarly to classical CA, we introduce the concept of *diamond* and relate it to injectivity/surjectivity properties [13].

**Definition 6.** *An m-ACA $C = (\Sigma, \lambda, r, \mu)$ has a diamond if there exist a control pattern $B = (B_1, B_2)$ of length $n \in \mathbb{N}_+$ and words $z, w \in \Sigma^n$, with $z \neq w$, $u, v \in \Sigma^r$ such that $\lambda_B(uwv) = \lambda_B(uzv)$ where $\lambda_B : \Sigma^{n+2r} \to \Sigma^n$ is defined as*

$$\forall \alpha \in \Sigma^{n+2r}, \quad \forall i \in [0, n), \quad \lambda_B(\alpha)_i = \begin{cases} \lambda(\alpha_{[i, i+2r]}) & \text{if } i + r \in B_1 \\ \alpha_{i+r} & \text{otherwise} \end{cases}$$

**Fig. 1.** The space-time diagram of the probabilistic xor CA of Example 1. A black (resp., white) box stands for a 1 (resp., 0). $\mu$ is the uniform measure over $\{0,1\}^{\mathbb{Z}}$. Time goes downward.

*Notation.* For notational convenience, for any $\tau \subseteq \mathbb{Z}$ and for all $h, k \in \mathbb{N}$ with $h < k$, let $\tau_{[h,k)}$ be the pattern $(B_1, B_2)$ where $B_1 = \{i \in [0, k - h) \mid i + h \in \tau\}$ and $B_2 = \{i \in [0, k - h) \mid i + h \notin \tau\}$.

**Proposition 2.** *Consider an* $m$-*ACA* $\mathcal{C} = (\Sigma, \lambda, r, \mu)$ *with* $\mu$ *fair. Then the following statements are equivalent:*

1. $\mathcal{C}$ *is not* $\mu$-*almost surely injective.*
2. $\mathcal{C}$ *has a diamond.*

*Proof.*

1. $\Rightarrow$ 2. If $\mathcal{C}$ is not almost surely injective then there exists a collection $A$ of subsets of $\mathbb{Z}$ with positive measure such that $\forall \tau \in A$, $\exists x, y \in \Sigma^{\mathbb{Z}}$, with $x \neq y$ and $F_\tau(x) = F_\tau(y)$. Since $A$ has positive measure, there exists at least a set $\tau \in A$ in which the pattern $B = (\emptyset, [0, r))$ is represented infinitely many times. Let $x, y \in \Sigma^{\mathbb{Z}}$ be two distinct configurations such that $F_\tau(x) = F_\tau(y)$ and let $i \in \mathbb{Z}$ be a position such that $x_i \neq y_i$. Let $h, k$ be two positions such that $h + r < i < k - r$ and $B$ is represented in $\tau$ at positions $h$ and $k - r$. It is immediate that $x_{[h,h+r)} = y_{[h,h+r)}$, $x_{[k-r,k)} = y_{[k-r,k)}$, $x_{[h+r,k-r)} \neq x_{[h+r,k-r)}$, and $\lambda_{\tau_{[h,k)}}(x_{[h,k)}) = \lambda_{\tau_{[h,k)}}(y_{[h,k)})$. Thus, there exists a diamond.
2. $\Rightarrow$ 1. Suppose that there exists a diamond. Let $B = (B_1, B_2)$ and $z, w \in \Sigma^n$, $u, v \in \Sigma^r$ be the control pattern of length $n$ and the words, respectively, that define the diamond. Let $B' = (\emptyset, [0, r))$. An integer $i \in \tau \subseteq \mathbb{Z}$ is said to have property $I$ if it is a multiple of $n + 2r$ such that $B'$ is represented in $\tau$ at positions $i$ and $i + n + r$ and $B$ is represented in $\tau$ at position $i + r$. Let $\tau \in \mathfrak{P}(\mathbb{Z})$ be a set with property $I$ for an integer $i$. Consider the configurations $x, y \in \Sigma^{\mathbb{Z}}$ with $x_j = y_j$ for all $j \notin [i, i + n + 2r)$, $x_{[i,i+n+2r)} = uwv$, and $y_{[i,i+n+2r)} = uzv$. Then, $F_\tau(x) = F_\tau(y)$. Thus $F_\tau$ is not injective. Let $A$ be the collection of all subsets of $\mathbb{Z}$ having at least an integer with property $I$. By the same

idea used in the proof of Lemma 2, one can show that $\mu(A) = 1$. Thus $\mathcal{C}$ is not $\mu$-almost surely injective.

## 4   A First Exploration of Dynamical Properties

In this section, we adapt the notion of expansivity to $m$-ACA and we show that it is related to surjectivity in a similar way to classical CA [6,15].

**Definition 7.** *An $m$-ACA $\mathcal{C} = (\Sigma, \lambda, r, \mu)$ is $\upsilon$-expansive, for a sequence $\upsilon \in \mathfrak{P}(\mathbb{Z})^{\mathbb{N}}$ extracted by $\mu$, if the family $\mathcal{T}_\upsilon$ is expansive. $\mathcal{C}$ is said to be almost surely expansive, if the set of sequences $\upsilon \in \mathfrak{P}(\mathbb{Z})^{\mathbb{N}}$ such that $\mathcal{C}$ is $\upsilon$-expansive has measure 1 (w.r.t. the measure $\mu_s$).*

**Proposition 3.** *Let $\mathcal{C} = (\Sigma, \lambda, r, \mu)$ be an almost surely expansive $m$-ACA. Then, $\mathcal{C}$ is $\mu$-almost surely injective.*

*Proof.* Suppose that $\mathcal{C}$ is not $\mu$-almost surely injective. By Proposition 2, $\mathcal{C}$ has a diamond. So, there exist a control pattern $B$ of length $n$, and words $w, z \in \Sigma^n$, $u, v \in \Sigma^r$ such that $\lambda_B(uwv) = \lambda_B(uzv)$. By Lemma 2, for any $k \in \mathbb{N}$, $B$ is represented in almost all sets $\tau \subseteq \mathbb{Z}$ infinitely many times at positions greater than $k$. For every $k \in \mathbb{N}$, define now the non empty set $A_k = \{(x, y) \in \Sigma^{\mathbb{Z}} \times \Sigma^{\mathbb{Z}} \mid \exists h > k, \; \forall i \notin [h, h + 2r + n) \; x_i = y_i, \; x_{[h, h+2r+n)} = uwv, \; y_{[h, h+2r+n)} = uzv\}$. Since for almost all $\tau \subseteq \mathbb{Z}$, there are infinitely many pairs $(x, y) \in A_k$ such that $F_\tau(x) = F_\tau(y)$, the set of sequences $\upsilon$ having $\tau$ as first component has non null measure (w.r.t. $\mu_s$). This means that $\mu_s\{\upsilon \in \mathfrak{P}(\mathbb{Z})^{\mathbb{N}} \mid \mathcal{C}$ is not $\upsilon$-expansive$\} \neq 0$. By additivity of $\mu_s$, it follows that $\mu_s\{\upsilon \in \mathfrak{P}(\mathbb{Z})^{\mathbb{N}} \mid \mathcal{C}$ is $\upsilon$-expansive$\} \neq 1$, i.e., $\mathcal{C}$ is not almost surely expansive. □

*Example 2.* Let $\mathcal{C} = (\Sigma, \lambda, r, \mu)$ be an $m$-ACA with $\lambda : \{0, 1\}^3 \to \{0, 1\}$ defined as $\lambda(a, b, c) = a$ xor $c$. The local rule $\lambda$ is not center-permutive, hence $\mathcal{C}$ is not almost surely surjective. Note that $0\lambda(0, 0, 0)0 = 0\lambda(0, 1, 0)0 = 000$ (i.e., $\mathcal{C}$ has a diamond). Thus, $\mathcal{C}$ is not almost surely expansive. Remark that, in the case of fully-ACA, $\lambda$ is the local rule of an $\alpha$-expansive ACA. Figure gives an example of evolution of $\mathcal{C}$.

**Fig. 2.** Probabilistic xor CA of Example 2. A black (resp., white) box stands for a 1 (resp., 0). $\mu$ is the uniform measure over $\{0, 1\}$. Time goes downward.

# 5 Conclusions

In this paper we introduced a new model of asynchronicity for CA where the set of cells where the local rule is applied is given by a probability measure with some fairness conditions. This model represents a first step in trying to unify different approaches to asynchronicity under a common framework. We adapted to this new setting the usual notions of injectivity, surjectivity, diamond and expansivity. We found that both injectivity and surjectivity are almost always equivalent and they are related to a generalized version of the classical notion of diamond. Moreover, an almost always expansive CA is also almost always injective. This fact is a bit surprising since in the classical case, expansive CA are never injective.

The study of *m*-ACA has just been started over and as usual there are more questions than answers. For instance, in the classical CA setting, it is well known that a CA is either sensitive to initial conditions or it has equicontinuity points. It would be interesting to investigate if this dichotomy is still true or which weakened form it can take.

# References

1. Bersini, H., Detours, V.: Asynchrony induces stability in cellular automata based models. In: Proceedings of Artificial Life IV, pp. 382–387. MIT Press, Cambridge (1994)
2. Buvel, R.L., Ingerson, T.E.: Structure in asynchronous cellular automata. Physica D 1, 59–68 (1984)
3. Cantelli, F.P.: Sulla probabilità come limite della frequenza. Rend. Accad. dei Lincei 24, 39–45 (1917)
4. Chaudhuri, P., Chowdhury, D., Nandi, S., Chattopadhyay, S.: Additive Cellular Automata Theory and Applications, vol. 1. IEEE Press, New York (1997)
5. Chopard, B.: Modelling physical systems by cellular automata. In: Rozenberg, G., et al. (eds.) Handbook of Natural Computing: Theory, Experiments, and Applications. Springer (2010)
6. Fagnani, F., Margara, L.: Expansivity, permutivity, and chaos for cellular automata. Theory Comput. Syst. 31(6), 663–677 (1998)
7. Fatès, N., Morvan, M.: An experimental study of robustness to asynchronism for elementary cellular automata. Complex Systems 16(1), 1–27 (2005)
8. Fatès, N., Morvan, M., Schabanel, N., Thierry, E.: Fully asynchronous behaviour of double-quiescent elementary cellular automata. Theoretical Computer Science 362, 1–16 (2006)
9. Fatès, N., Regnault, D., Schabanel, N., Thierry, É.: Asynchronous Behavior of Double-Quiescent Elementary Cellular Automata. In: Correa, J.R., Hevia, A., Kiwi, M. (eds.) LATIN 2006. LNCS, vol. 3887, pp. 455–466. Springer, Heidelberg (2006)
10. Fukś, H.: Non-deterministic density classification with diffusive probabilistic cellular automata. Physical Review E 66(2) (2002)
11. Fukś, H.: Probabilistic cellular automata with conserved quantities. Nonlinearity 17(1), 159–173 (2004)

12. Halmos, P.R.: Measure theory. Graduate texts in Mathematics, vol. 38. Springer (1974)
13. Hedlund, G.A.: Endomorphisms and automorphisms of the shift dynamical system. Mathematical Systems Theory 3, 320–375 (1969)
14. Kier, L.B., Seybold, P.G., Cheng, C.-K.: Modeling Chemical Systems using Cellular Automata. Springer (2005)
15. Kůrka, P.: Languages, equicontinuity and attractors in cellular automata. Ergodic Theory & Dynamical Systems 17, 417–433 (1997)
16. Lee, J., Adachi, S., Peper, F., Mashiko, S.: Delay-insensitive computation in asynchronous cellular automata. J. Comput. Syst. Sci. 70, 201–220 (2005)
17. Lumer, E.D., Nicolis, G.: Synchronous versus asynchronous dynamics in spatially distributed systems. Physica D 71, 440–452 (1994)
18. Macauley, M., McCammond, J., Mortveit, H.S.: Order independence in asynchronous cellular automata. J. Cellular Automata 3(1), 37–56 (2008)
19. Manzoni, L.: Asynchronous cellular automata and dynamical properties. Natural Computing 11(2), 269–276 (2012)
20. Nakamura, K.: Asynchronous cellular automata and their computational ability. Systems, Computers, Control 5, 58–66 (1974)
21. Regnault, D.: Abrupt behaviour changes in cellular automata under asynchronous dynamics. In: Electronic Proc. of 2nd European Conference on Complex Systems, 6 pages. ECCS, Oxford, UK (2006)
22. Regnault, D., Schabanel, N., Thierry, E.: Progresses in the analysis of stochastic 2d cellular automata: A study of asynchronous 2d minority. Theoretical Computer Science 410, 4844–4855 (2009)
23. Schönfisch, B., de Roos, A.: Synchronous and asynchronous updating in cellular automata. BioSystems 51, 123–143 (1999)
24. Worsch, T.: A note on (intrinsically?) universal asynchronous cellular automata. In: Proceedings of Automata 2010, Nancy, France, June 14-16, pp. 339–350 (2010)

# Cellular Automata and Random Field:
# Statistical Analysis of Complex Space-Time Systems

Mario Di Traglia

Department EGSeI, University of Molise, Via Mazzini, 8 - 86170 Isernia, Italy
ditraglia@unimol.it

**Abstract.** In the classical approach to the mathematical model specification, for space-time complex system, the usual framework is the Partial Difference-Differential Equations system (PDEs). This approach is very hard from a mathematical point of view, and the search for the (PDEs) solutions, almost in the practical applications, often it is impossible. Our approach is based, on the contrary, on Cellular Automata methodology in the framework of Random Field models. The statistical model building methodology for the Random Fields, is based on very simple statistical and probabilistic reasoning that utilize the concept of divisible distributions and logistic non-linear model. The interaction rules for the Cellular Automata mechanism, are built thorough inferential statistics and data analysis.

**Keywords:** Random Field, Cellular Automata, space-time interactions, statistical model building, non-linear modeling, Complex space-time Systems.

## 1    Introduction

The model building methodologies, can be divided in three philosophical approach: a) hypothetical-deductive approach (mechanic models), b) inductive approach (statistical models), c) mixture of the two previous approach (statistical-mechanic models). If the relationship between the phenomena are linear (Gaussian field), there are no substantial differences between the above approach. The differences begin substantial, when the relationship are non-linear. The aim of this work is showing that mathematical models,t hat describe non linear relationship between phenomena, can be built applying cellular automata methodology in the framework of Random Field (R.F.) theory. This approach is a mixture of the above listed approach, because it utilizes the mechanic and the statistical reasoning in different step of model building procedure. In the classical mathematical modeling of physical, economics and ecological phenomena, one of the most applied methodology, is the system of PDEs (Partial Differential Equations). Unfortunately, it is not simple to find solutions for a such system [8]. Moreover, even if a solution is available, difficulties arise in the statistical parameter estimation. To avoid this problem we introduce, in our work, the Cellular Automata (CA) methodology in the framework of R.F. representation of data. The goal is to estimate a mathematical model for the conditional mean of a generic phenomenon, indicated with $Z$ *(dependent variable)*, when other variables

G.C. Sirakoulis and S. Bandini (Eds.): ACRI 2012, LNCS 7495, pp. 663–671, 2012.

(phenomena related to Z), are known. The variable Z is supposed related to other two phenomena, indicated with $X$ and $Y$ (the conditioning variables). All this phenomena are observed in the time, so the mathematical tools occurring in this case, are based on dynamic system theory. All the random systems belongs to the typology of complex systems such as the socio-economic, physical, climatic-environmental, and ecological systems. A complex system is constituted by a large set of sub-systems reciprocally related each other in a non-linear way. In the quantitative analysis of complex dynamical systems, the mathematical-statistic models, that are able to analyze the space-time statistical phenomena, are the random field models. The statistical reasoning is based on the average behaviour of the phenomena and, the results has to be considered as average values. This imply a loss of information on system dynamic and can compromises the forecast and control of the system. To avoid this difficulties we apply the *conditioning methodology*, thorough acquisition of further information to reduce the variability. Taking in mind these definitions, it is presented a methodological approach which integrates statistic modeling and 2-D cellular automata (CA) techniques.

## 2     The Random Field Model

We indicate with $Z$ a dependent phenomena and with $X$ the conditioning ones (independent variables), with $(x,t)$ a point of the Cartesian space-time $X \otimes T$, ($X$ take values in a $N$-dimensional space). The random field $Z(x,t)$ is a random function of two variables: *space* and *time*. To be more explicit, for each point $(x,t)$, the value $z(x,t)$ is a random number generated by the random variable $Z(x,t)$, located to the space-time coordinate point $(x,t)$. If such of all the Z variables of the field are statistically independents, the phenomenon shows a random patterns without hidden deterministic low. Such random field is purely stochastic (if the mean is zero, is the *noise field*) and is predictable only with the *space-time statistical mean*. Mathematically speaking, the equation of such a field is:

$$Z(x,t) = m + U(x,t) \tag{1}$$

The classic geo-statistical analysis of random fields $Z(x,t)$ (Matheron, Journel, Cressie,), is based on the space-time *Bravais-Pearson autocorrelation function*. Unfortunately, this function captures only the linear relationship between the random variables $Z(x_i,t_i)$, $Z(x_j,t_j)$; $i \neq j$; where, in the real world, a large part of the relationships between phenomena, are non-linear. In this work, we introduce a new statistical measure of space-time non-linear relationship between the variables (IOS index). In general, the *random field*, is a real valued function that maps the points of a sample space $\{\Omega, X, T\}$, into the real space $\Re$ (**X** represents a N-dimensional vector) :

$$Z(x,t):\{\Omega \otimes X \otimes T\} \to \Re \tag{2}$$

The eq. (2) implies the existence of a family of probability distribution for $Z(x,t)$ that can be derived from the relationship, between the random variables $Z(x,t)$ on the field as $x$ and $t$ varies. At first, we define the *space-time statistical mean and variance* of $Z(x,t)$ as (without loss of generality, we assume the continuity):

$$E[Z(x,t)] = \int_{\Re} Z(x,t)P[Z(x,t)]dZ(x,t)) = \mu(x,t) \tag{3}$$

The formula (3) says that the mean of a random field is a deterministic function of space and time. For what concern the variance, we have:

$$V[Z(x,t)] = E\{ Z(x,t) - E[(Z(x,t)] \}^2 =$$
$$= \int_{\Re} \{ Z(x,t) - E[Z(x,t)] \}^2 P[Z(x,t)]dZ(x,t) = \sigma^2(x,t) \tag{4}$$

The formula (4) shows that, the variance, is a deterministic function of space and time (sometime, the eqs. 3 and 4 are called *infinitesimal mean* and *infinitesimal variance* of the field). The definition of bilinear operator *Covariance* is more complicated than 3 and 4; we skip, now, its definition. The classical way to built the family of probability distributions for $Z(x,t)$ is as solution of the (Feyneman-Kac equation):

$$\frac{\partial P(Z)}{\partial t} + \sum_{i=1}^{N} \mu_i(x,t)\frac{\partial P(Z)}{\partial x_i} + \frac{1}{2}\sum_{i=1}^{N}\sum_{j=1}^{N} \sigma_{ij}(x,t)\frac{\partial^2 P(Z)}{\partial x_i x_j} - V(x,t)P(Z) = f(x,t) \tag{5}$$

In that equation, $V$ and $f$ are given function, respectively: *potential* and *forcing* functions. If that functions are zero, the (5) begins the Chapman-Kolmogorov (or Fokker-Plank or Smulokovsky-Einstein) Partial Differential Equation (PDE). The meaning of (5) is a first order relationship over the time (Markov random field) is equal to the second order relationship over the space. The specification of $\mu(x,t)$ e $\sigma(x,t)$ functions in eq. (5) determines the form of $P[Z(x,t)]$ and then, the form of the random field $Z(x,t)$. Appling the linear operator $E$ to the left and right member of equation (5), under the hypothesis $V=0$ and $f=0$, we obtain the Langevin equation:

$$dZ(x,t) = \mu(x,t)Z(x,t) + \sigma(x,t)W(x,t)dt \tag{6}$$

In that equation $W(x,t)$ is a Wiener R.F. and to solve this stochastic differential equations, we have to specify the mathematical field $\mu(x,t)$ e $\sigma(x,t)$, (it assumes to be deterministic functions). In our work, the family distribution $P$, instead, will be built without assumption on space-time relationship but only by statistical consideration on Bernoulli random field and on Poincarrè formula (*Inclusion-Exclusion Theorem*). Furthermore, we develop a measure of non-linear dependence between statistical phenomena, based on the concept of *Correlation Integral for Random Fields* (IOS-Structural Organization Index).

## 3    Model Building

We will consider a real phenomenon $Z$ whose measure takes value in a numerical space $Z$ and two real phenomena $X$ and $Y$, whose measure takes value in two numerical bounded spaces, $X$ and $Y$, without less of generality, we can consider $(Z, X, Y) \in \Re^3$. We are searching for a non-linear function $\square$ that describe the relationship between the phenomenon $Z$ and the phenomena $X$ and $Y$. Moreover, $Z$ is a random variable while $X$ and $Y$ are deterministic variables. If $X$ and $Y$ are stochastic, then $Z$ is a *quantum random field* and $P$ could be a family of quantum probability density functions [1], [10]. We indicate with $D$ the space $(X \otimes Y)$ and we suppose it is continuous furthermore, for simplicity, the space, $Z$ is a Boolean space. As a consequence, $Z(x,y)=0$ or $Z(x,y)=1$ with probability given by an unknown function $\pi$ $(Z/x,y)$. Assuming that, as of $x$ and $y$ varies, the random variables $Z(x,y)$ are statistically independent and identically distributed (the event $Z(x,y)=1$, it can arise, with the same probability in anywhere) his probability is given as:

$$\pi[Z \,/\, x, y] = \frac{\iint\limits_{xy \in D} Z(x, y)dxdy}{\iint\limits_{xy \in D} dxdy} \tag{7}$$

Under this hypothesis, the Field $Z(x,y)$ is homogeneous and isotropic. As a consequence, the random variables $Z$, overall D, is a *Bernoulli Random Field* and their probability distribution is given by: $P(Z)=\pi^Z[1-\pi]^{1-Z}$. The probability $\pi$ is constant in $D$ and, as a consequence, $P(Z)$ doesn't depend by $(x,y)$ coordinates. Then: $\forall A : A \subset D$ the field:

$$N(A) = \iint\limits_{(x,y) \in A} Z(x, y)dxdy \tag{8}$$

is a Poisson Random Field, in which:

$$P(N(A)) = \frac{\pi(A)^{N(A)}}{N(A)!} \exp[\pi(A)\mu(A)] \tag{9}$$

Where $\mu(A)$ is the area of A and $\pi(A)$ is proportional to $\mu(A)$. It means that the mean number of events in a generic area of size $\mu(A)$ is given by the product measure: $\mu(A)$ $\pi(A)$. The probability $\pi(A)$, as measure of $A$, is:

$$\pi[A] = \frac{\iint\limits_{xy \in D} Z(x, y)dxdy}{\iint\limits_{xy \in D} dxdy} \iint\limits_{xy \in A} dxdy \tag{10}$$

In this framework, the forecast of the number of events in a given region $A$, it depends only from the area of that region: *the best predictor is the mean*. Now we introduce the hypothesis that there exists some relationship between the coordinates $(x,y)$ and the variable $Z$. In this case, the form of $\pi(Z/x,y)$ arises by the relationship between the natural logarithm of the odds and the coordinate $(x,y)$; the *odds* are the ratios between the probability $P(Z=1)$ and the probability $P(Z=0)$. That is:

$$\pi(Z/x,y) = \frac{e^{F(x,y)}}{1+e^{F(x,y)}} \quad \text{from which:} \quad \pi(Z/x,y) = \frac{e^{F(x,y)}}{1+e^{F(x,y)}} \quad (11)$$

The Log-function of the *odds*, eq. (12), can be interpolated by a polynomial equation.

$$\ln\left(\frac{\pi(x,y)}{1-\pi(x,y)}\right) = F(x,y) = \sum_{ij} a_{ij} x^i y^j \quad (12)$$

The $a_{ij}$ coefficients are estimated by the non Linear Least Square Method with numerical solution of the system of normal equations. A new model, showing a high explicative ability of the *odds* variability, is given by the generalization of Poincarrè's formula in the logistic function (11). We briefly describe the general aspects of this method, which has been adopted in the framework, of exponential polynomial functions. We assume that the statistical variable $Z$ is conditioned by two deterministic variables $(X,Y)$. Appling assiomatic Kolmogorov rule for probability, we have:

$$P\big(Z(x,y)/X,Y\big) = P[\big(Z(x,y)/X\big) \cup (Z(x,y)/Y)] =$$
$$= P\big(Z(x,y)/X\big) + P\big(Z(x,y)/Y\big) - P[(Z(x,y)/X) \cap (Z(x,y/Y)] \quad (13)$$

We can get the conditional independence between $P(Z(x,y)/X)$ and $Z((x,y)/Y)$ with the spectral decomposition of the covariance matrix $COV(X,Y)$. Under the conditional independence we have: $P(Z/X \cap Z/Y)=P(Z/X)P(Z/Y)$, and then, we obtain:

$$P(Z/X,Y) = \frac{e^{F(X)} + e^{G(Y)} + e^{F(X)+G(Y)}}{1+e^{F(X)} + e^{G(Y)} + e^{F(X)+G(Y)}} \quad (14)$$

## 4    Cellular Automata and Complex Systems

We consider, as complex system, the R.F. $Z(x,y,t)$ defined on a set of referenced cells $(x,y)$ constituting a regular partition of a mathematical (or phisycal) space $D$. The CA works on the interaction among cells of $D$. The most common interaction contours are due to Von Neuman and to Moore and describes different sets of adjacent cells. In our work, we apply the first order Von Neumann CA contour (spatial influence), that can be formally given as:

$$(\Delta x, \Delta y) = [(x, y-Dy), (x, y+Dy), (x+Dx, y), (x-Dx, y)] \quad (15)$$

The contour of time coordinate is given by the sequence of time interval before the actual time $t$, having, the time, a direction from past to the future.

$$Dt = t-1, t-2, \ldots t-h.; \qquad h > 0 \tag{16}$$

In the dynamical space-time systems, we can define some theoretical function connecting the cell-field $Z(x,y,t)$ to its space-time contour $(\Delta x, \Delta y, \Delta t)$:

$$Z(x, y, t) = F[\ Z(\Delta x, \Delta y, t\ ),\ Z(\Delta x, \Delta y, Dt),\ \varepsilon(x, y, t)] \tag{17}$$

The R.F. $\varepsilon(x,y,t)$ is a planar Brownian Motion Process representing the random perturbations.

The CA approach consists in the iteration map of function (17) on the space-time neighbour $[(\Delta x, \Delta y),\ \Delta t]$ of the cell $(x,y,t)$. It does not exists any theory or methodology to build the function $F$ in the (4.3). As a consequence, we should build the function $F$ by statistical analysis of data. The simplest function, for the dynamic of the space-system Z, is the homogenous Markov process. The Markov dynamic claims that what happen at time $t$, depends linearly on what happened at time $t$-$\Delta t$. Formally:

$$Z(x, y, t) = f[Z(x, y, t - Dt)] + \varepsilon(x, y, t) \tag{18}$$

Iterating for a long number of time eq. (18), it is possible to describe the change of spatial configuration of $Z(x,y,t)$ overall the area D, without searching for a solution of the stochastic PDE (eq. 5). To estimate the parameter $\phi$ of eq. 18, we use the initial condition $Z(x,y,t_0)$ and found the constant rate of growth that works for each cell and transforms the $Z(x,y,t_0)$ in $Z(x,y,t_0+\Delta t)$. From the eqn. 18:

$$Z(x, y, t) = \phi(x, y)^{(t-t_0)} Z(x, y, t_0) \tag{19}$$

Then:

$$\phi(x, y) = \exp[(1/(t - t_0)) \ln(Z(x, y, t) / Z(x, y, t_0)]\ \tag{20}$$

If the function $\phi(x, y)$ depends on $t$,(not-homogenous Markov R.F.) the (19) isn't appropriate.

To build the time behavior of $\phi(x, y, t)$ as $t$ varies, now we apply the *Time Series Analysis* techniques of linearization (smoothing and differentiation together with the *State-Space Akaike representation* ) to get the markovianity. If $\phi(x, y, t)$ is non-linear we apply the Lotka-Volterra type models to capture the competition mechanism between the space-time cells.

## 4.1      A Simple Statistical Analysis to Build Spatial Interaction Function

In order to built the $F$ function we develop a statistical methodology called, here, *extreme discretization*. In this frame, the dependence between the variable Z and the variables $X$ and $Y$ is expressed, as:

$$P(Z = z \mid X = x, Y = y) \neq P(Z = z) \tag{21}$$

In other words, the conditional probability of the random event $(Z = z)$ is different from the unconditional one. The eqn. (4.7) must be valid for all the $z$, $x$ and $y$ values. It is necessary to know the probability distributions $P(Z \mid X, Y)$ and $P(Z)$ to verify eq. (21), but these are not known. Consequently, these probabilities, should be statistically estimated through relative frequencies of conditional and unconditional events for each $Z=z$ value of the eq. (21), derived by empirical data. Instead of compare the probability distributions; we compare the conditional mean of $Z$ with the unconditional one. In fact, if $Z$ is dependent from $X$ and $Y$, we have: $E(Z / X, Y) \neq E(Z)$ and, as a consequence, is a function of $X$ and $Y$:

$$E(Z / X, Y) = F(X, Y) \tag{22}$$

The conditional mean of $Z$ is described by the eq. (22) and specified as function of $X$ and $Y$. Thus, we build a new dichotomised random variable, $\varphi$ - which is $\varphi=0$ when the eq. (22) is false and is $\varphi=1$ when it is true. This sentence has to be read from a statistical point of view, as test of hypothesis: $Z \amalg X, Y$ (independence between Z, and (X, Y).

We perform the statistical inference for unconditional mean of $Z$ to set a threshold value of $z$ in order to define when $\varphi = 1$ or $\varphi = 0$. In this framework, $\varphi$ represents the values of $Z$ which are statistical significance different from its unconditional mean, pointing out that differences are due to the effects, of $X$ and $Y$ on $Z$, revealing thus the effect of $F(X, Y)$ (conditional mean of $Z$). We model, then, the field $\phi(X, Y)$ for each couple $(X=x, Y=y)$, because we are interested to estimate the following probability;

$$P\left(\phi = 1 \mid X = x, Y = y\right) \tag{23}$$

The probability expressed in eq. (23) as function of $X$ and $Y$ variables, we show that an universal model is the logistic one:

$$P(\varphi = 1 \mid X, Y) = \frac{e^{F(X, \Delta X)} + e^{G(Y, \Delta Y)} + e^{F(X, \Delta X) + G(Y, \Delta Y)}}{1 + e^{F(X, \Delta X)} + e^{G(Y, \Delta Y)} + e^{F(X, \Delta X) + G(Y, \Delta Y)}} \tag{24}$$

The $F$ function have been derived from the PCA polynomial analysis (which was a representation of the product space $(X, Y)$ as a discrete and finite Hilbert space).

## 5    The Building of the Statistical Indicators IOS

The statistic method used here is based on the Correlation Integral (CI) adapted to spatially extended systems. In the framework of our approach, the IOS gives information about the non-linear dependence in the spatial interactions of R.F. $Z(x,y)$. The CI is given as:

$$C(r,h) = \frac{\displaystyle\sum_{i=1}^{N-h}\sum_{j=1}^{N-h} H[Z(x_i,y_j)-Z(x_i-h,y_j-h),r]}{(N-h)^2} \tag{25}$$

where $H(x,y,r)$ is the Heaviside function. As a consequence $C(r,h)$ is a not-decreasing function of $r$ and $h$, how it is possible to demonstrate by easy calculations.

The area beneath the surface depends on the spatial relations between the $Z(x,y)$ random variables in the different points of the fields, therefore it can be used as an indicator of structural homogeneity, because integrating the function $C(h,r)$ between zero and $max(r)$ we obtain an index which we named IOS. This index, from a theoretical point of view, is defined as:

$$IOS = 1 - A^{-1} \int_0^{max(r)} \int C(h,r)drdh \tag{26}$$

It is easy to show that: $0 \le IOS \le 1$. The symbol $A$ in the equation (26) represents the volume of the minimum parallelepiped containing the surface $C(h,r)$. Therefore IOS will show low values for uniform random fields and high values for conditions characterized by large structural-weaving homogeneity.

## 6     Conclusions

The method, described in this work, has been applied for a study concerning environmental and ecological phenomena [5]. We believe that this approach can generalize the concept of statistical modeling based on nonlinear regression analysis. In fact, we introduce the local relation between the dependent and independent variables and the general model was born from this relationship, through the mechanism of cellular automata. In particular, we will consider a partition of Z into more than two intervals so as to be able to build models that follow the mechanical-statistical reasoning. In this framework, we will introduce the hypothesis of asymmetry in the calculation of the joint probabilities and the hypothesis of stochastic nature for the independent variables to build quantum-statistical models.

## References

1. Accardi, L. (ed.): Quantum information and computing. International Conference on Quantum Information 2003. Tokyo University of Science, Tokyo, Singapore, November 1-3, 2003 (2006)
2. Bellacicco, A.: A diagnostic model for distinguishing chaos from noise - Forecasting and modelling for chaotic and stochastic systems. Bellacicco, Koch, Vulpiani (ed.) (1994)
3. Cressie, N.: Statistics for Spatial Data. Wiley Series in Probability (1991)
4. Dendrinos, D.S., Sonis, M.: Chaos and Socio-Spatial Dynamics. Springer, New York (1990)

5. Di Traglia, M., et al.: Is cellular automata algorithm able to predict the future dynamical shifts of tree species in Italy under climate change scenarios? A Methodological Approach. Ecological Modelling 6070 (2011) ISSN: 0304-3800

6. Di Traglia, et al.: Analisi spaziale della copertura vegetale in zone a diverso grado di antropizzazione - Atti della II Conferenza ASITA su: Rilevamento, Rappresentazione e Gestione dei dati Territoriali ed Ambientali 1, 169–164 (1998)

7. Kaiser Mark, S.: Statistical Dependence in Markov Random Field Models. Department of StatisticsIowa State University (2007)

8. Kolesnik, A.D., Orsingher, E.: A planar random motion with infinite number of directions controlled by the dumped wave equation. Journal of Applied Probability 42, 1168–1182 (2005)

9. Ozaki, T., Iino, M.: An innovation Approach to non-Gaussian time series. Journal of Applied Probability 38A, 78–93 (2001)

10. Skeide, M.: Nondegenerate representations of continuous product systems. J. Op. Theory 65, 71–85 (2011)

# Limit Cycle Structure for Block-Sequential Threshold Systems

Henning S. Mortveit

Department of Mathematics and Network Dynamics and Simulation
Science Laboratory Virginia Tech
Henning.Mortveit@vt.edu

**Abstract.** This paper analyzes the possible limit set structures for the standard threshold block-sequential finite dynamical systems. As a special case of their work on Neural Networks (generalized threshold functions), Goles and Olivos (1981 [2]) showed that for the single block case (parallel update) one may only have fixed points and 2-cycles as $\omega$-limit sets. Barrett et al (2006 [1]), but also Goles et al (1990 [3]) as a special case, proved that for the case with $n$ blocks (sequential update) the only $\omega$-limit sets are fixed points. This paper generalizes and unifies these results to standard threshold systems with block-sequential update schemes.

**Keywords:** graph dynamical systems, finite dynamical system, automata networks, neural networks, block-sequential, cellular automata, threshold function, periodic orbit, limit cycle, sequential, parallel (37B99,68Q80).

## 1 Introduction

This paper analyzes the structure of limit sets for finite dynamical systems (also called automata networks), see for example [2, 3, 5–9], where each vertex function is a standard threshold function over the domain $\{0, 1\}$. In [2] it is demonstrated, as a special case of a more general result on neural networks (generalized threshold functions), that for the parallel update scheme standard threshold dynamical systems may only exhibit fixed points and 2-cycles as limit sets. It is shown in for example [1] that under the sequential update scheme the only limit sets are fixed points. Here we extend these results to block sequential update schemes.

Following the notation of Serre, let $X$ denote a simple graph with vertex set $v[X] = \{1, 2, 3, \ldots, n\}$, and write $S_X$ for the set of permutations over $v[X]$. We refer to the elements of a partition $\mathcal{B} = \{B_1, B_2, \ldots, B_m\}$ of $v[X]$ as *blocks* and write $S_{\mathcal{B}}$ for the set of permutations of $\mathcal{B}$. We say that a block $B \in \mathcal{B}$ is *non-trivial* if it induces a connected subgraph. Clearly, any block can be decomposed into non-trivial blocks. The main result can now be stated as follows:

**Theorem 1.** *Let $X$ be a simple graph and $\mathcal{B}$ a block partition of $v[X]$. If the largest non-trivial block of $\mathcal{B}$ has size at most three, then any block-sequential threshold finite dynamical system with update sequence $\pi \in S_{\mathcal{B}}$ only has fixed points as limit sets. If the largest nontrivial block has size at least four, then a block-sequential threshold finite dynamical system may have periodic orbits of length at least two.*

G.C. Sirakoulis and S. Bandini (Eds.): ACRI 2012, LNCS 7495, pp. 672–678, 2012.

We provide an explicit example of a 2-cycle in a threshold finite dynamical system (FDS) where the maximal non-trivial block size is four and where there are multiple blocks. In the remainder of this paper we first introduce the necessary terminology. The proof, which is based on a potential function argument, is then presented in Section 3 before we finish by discussing generalizations in Section 4.

## 2  Terminology

Let $X$ be a simple graph as above, and assign a state $x_v \in K = \{0, 1\}$ to each vertex $v \in v[X]$. Here we refer to $x_v$ as a *vertex state* and $x = (x_1, x_2, \ldots, x_n)$ as a *system state*. Whenever it is clear from the context we will simply say state for either case. Let $n[v]$ denote the sorted sequence of vertices from the 1-neighborhood of $v$ in $X$, and let $x[v]$ denote the corresponding restriction of $x$ to $n[v]$. Denoting the degree of $v$ by $d(v)$, each vertex is assigned a *vertex function* $f_v : K^{d(v)+1} \longrightarrow K$. The function $f_v$ is used to map the vertex state at time $t$ to $t + 1$, that is, $x_v(t)$ to $x_v(t + 1)$, taking $x[v]$ (at time $t$) as input.

Using the *parallel update* we obtain the finite dynamical system map $F : K^n \longrightarrow K^n$ given by

$$F(x_1, \ldots, x_n) = (f_1(x[1]), \ldots, f_n(x[n])) .$$

For a sequential application of the maps $f_v$, it is convenient to introduce the $X$-local maps $F_v : K^n \longrightarrow K^n$ given by

$$F_v(x_1, \ldots, x_n) = (x_1, \ldots, x_{v-1}, f_v(x[v]), x_{v+1}, \ldots, x_n) .$$

For a sequential update given by the permutation (or order) $\pi = (\pi(1), \pi(2), \ldots, \pi(n)) \in S_X$ we obtain the finite dynamical system map $F_\pi : K^n \longrightarrow K^n$ given by the composition

$$F_\pi = F_{\pi(n)} \circ F_{\pi(n-1)} \circ \cdots \circ F_{\pi(1)} .$$

A block-sequential update scheme generalizes both maps above. Let $\mathcal{B} = \{B_1, \ldots, B_m\}$ be a block partition as above. The map $F_{B_k} : K^n \longrightarrow K^n$ is given by

$$\left(F_{B_k}(x)\right)_v = \begin{cases} f_v(x[v]), & \text{if } v \in B_k \text{ and,} \\ x_v, & \text{otherwise.} \end{cases}$$

The block-sequential map $F_\mathcal{B} : K^n \longrightarrow K^n$ is defined by

$$F_\mathcal{B} = F_{B_m} \circ F_{B_{m-1}} \circ \cdots \circ F_{B_1} .$$

Regardless of the choice of update scheme, we write $\text{Per}(F)$ and $\text{Fix}(F)$ for the set of periodic points and fixed points of $F : K^n \longrightarrow K^n$, respectively. Of course, $\text{Fix}(F) \subset \text{Per}(F)$.

Define $\sigma_m : K^m \longrightarrow \mathbb{N}$ by $\sigma_m(x_1, \ldots, x_m) = |\{i \mid x_i = 1\}|$. The focus of this paper is on *standard threshold vertex functions*. The standard threshold function $t_{k,m} : K^m \longrightarrow K$ is defined by

$$t_{k,m}(x_1, \ldots, x_m) = \begin{cases} 1, & \sigma_m(x_1, \ldots, x_m) \geq k , \\ 0, & \text{otherwise.} \end{cases} \tag{1}$$

A finite dynamical system map is a threshold system if each of its vertex functions is a threshold function. The threshold need not be the same for all vertices.

We remark that the generalized threshold function $f\colon \{0,1\}^n \longrightarrow \{0,1\}$ of neural networks (see [2]) is defined by

$$f(x_1,\ldots,x_n) = \begin{cases} 1, & \text{if } \sum_{j=1}^{n} a_{ij}x_j < \theta_i \\ 0, & \text{otherwise} \end{cases},$$

where $\theta = (\theta_1,\ldots\theta_n) \in R^n$ and $A = (a_{ij})_{i,j=1}^{n}$ is a real symmetric matrix. The case considered in this paper additionally follows by restricting the $a_{ij}$'s to be either 0 or 1.

**Example:** The following example illustrates the concepts. As graph, take $X = \text{Circle}_4$ as shown in Figure 1. In this case we have $n[4] = (1,3,4)$, $x[4] = (x_1,x_3,x_4)$ and $F_4(x) = (x_1,x_2,x_3,f_4(x_1,x_3,x_4))$. Taking $x = (1,0,1,0)$ and threshold-2 vertex functions, we see that with the parallel update scheme $F(x) = (0,1,0,1)$, whereas with sequential update and sequence $\pi = (1,2,3,4)$ we have $F_\pi(x) = (0,0,0,0)$. Using the block partition $\mathcal{B} = \{B_1 = \{2,4\}, B_2 = \{1,3\}\}$ and update sequence $\pi' = (B_1,B_2)$ we get $F_{\pi'}(x) = (1,1,1,1)$. For the map $F$ the state $x$ is on a 2-cycle, but is not periodic under either $F_\pi$ or $F_{\pi'}$.

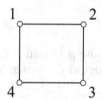

**Fig. 1.** The graph $\text{Circle}_4$

Note that for the synchronous update in this example we have a case where block-size 4 yields a 2-cycle. Later, we give another example of this where the update is neither parallel or sequential, but is instead block-sequential with three blocks.

## 3    Main Result

In this section we present the proof of the main result. The technique is an extension of the threshold function argument used in [1] and that was developed further in [4].

*Proof (Theorem 1).* For $v \in \text{v}[X]$ let $T_1(v)$ denote the threshold value for vertex $v$. Also, let $T_0(v)$ denote the smallest number of states in $x[v]$ that must be zero to ensure that $x_v$ is mapped to zero. Clearly, we have the relation $(d(v)+1) - T_0(v) = T_1(v) - 1$, or $T_0(v) + T_1(v) = d(v) + 2$. We next introduce the vertex potential function

$$P(x, v) = \begin{cases} T_1(v), & x_v = 1 \\ T_0(v), & x_v = 0 \end{cases}$$

and the edge potential function

$$P(x, e = \{v, v'\}) = \begin{cases} 1, & x_v \neq x_{v'} \\ 0, & \text{otherwise.} \end{cases}$$

We combine these and define the potential function $P \colon K^n \longrightarrow \mathbb{N}$ by

$$P(x) = \sum_{v \in \mathrm{v}[X]} P(x, v) + \sum_{e \in \mathrm{e}[X]} P(x, e) . \tag{2}$$

Clearly, there exist an integer $M \geq 0$ such that $0 \leq P(x) \leq M$ for all $x \in K^n$. We write $n_i(x, v)$ for the number of neighbors of $v$ with state $x_v = i$ with $i = 0, 1$. We then have $n_0(x, v) + n_1(x, v) = d(v)$. In the following we set $x' = F_v(x)$.

In [1] it is shown that whenever $x' \neq x$ we have $P(x') < P(x)$, which clearly implies that sequential FDS maps only have fixed points as limit sets. This covers the case where the maximal non-trivial block size is 1. In the following we prove that the same holds when the non-trivial blocks sizes are less than 4.

For a vertex state transition from $x$ to $x'$ where $x_v$ is mapped from 0 to 1 by $F_v$ we must have that $n_1(x, v) \geq T_1(v)$ or $T_1(v) - n_1(v) \leq 0$. Similarly, for the transition where $x_v$ is mapped from 1 to 0 we must have that $n_1(x, v) + 1 \leq T_1(v) - 1$ so that $n_1(x, v) - T_1(v) \leq -2$.

In the argument to follow, we will first consider block-size 2 before handling block-size 3. For a block $B$ of size $|B| = 2$ we may limit our consideration to the case where all elements $v \in B$ change their state in the transition $x \mapsto x'$. If one or more of the states do not change, we are effectively working with a smaller block-size.

When determining the difference in potential $\Delta P$ when a block $B$ is updated by $F_B$ we may also limit our attention to the vertices in $B$ and their incident edges since all other terms in the potential function $P$ are the same before and after. However, if we simply add $P_v(x) = P(x, v) + \sum_{e = \{v, v'\}} P(x, e)$ for the elements $v \in B$ we may over-count the potential of all common edges in the block. However, by the previous remark that all states in the block must change, this over-counting in edge-potential is precisely the same for $P(x)$ and $P'(x)$. Consequently, we may disregard this without any consequence and simply add up $P_v(x)$ for each vertex $v$ in the block.

To determine the potential change $\Delta P_v = P_v(x') - P_v(x)$ at vertex $v$, assume that $v \in B$ is adjacent to $\beta - 1$ other vertices in $B$, and assume that of these, $\alpha$ are in state 1 in $x$. It follows that the remaining $\beta - \alpha - 1$ other vertices in $B$ adjacent to $v$ have state 0. Since, all states are inverted, we conclude that in $x'$ we have $\alpha$ adjacent vertices in state 0 and $\beta - \alpha - 1$ in state 1.

We first consider the transition where $x_v$ is mapped from 0 to 1 in which case $n_1(x, v) \geq T_1(v)$:

$$
\begin{aligned}
\Delta P_v &= T_1(v) + n_0(x', v) - [T_0(v) + n_1(x, v)] \\
&= T_1(v) + [n_0(x, v) + \alpha - (\beta - \alpha - 1)] - [T_0 + n_1(x, v)] \\
&= T_1(v) + d(v) - n_1(x, v) + 2\alpha - \beta + 1 - [d(v) + 2 - T_1(v) + n_1(x, v)] \\
&= 2(T_1(v) - n_1(x, v)) + 2\alpha - \beta - 1 \\
&\leq 2\alpha - \beta - 1 \, .
\end{aligned}
$$

Similarly, if $x_v$ is mapped from 1 to 0, and therefore $n_1(x, v) - T_1(v) \leq -2$, we have

$$
\begin{aligned}
\Delta P_v &= T_0(v) + n_1(x', v) - [T_1(v) + n_0(x, v)] \\
&= T_0(v) + [n_1(x, v) + (\beta - \alpha - 1) - \alpha] - [T_1 + n_0(x, v)] \\
&= d(v) + 2 - T_1(v) + n_1(x, v) + \beta - 2\alpha - 1) - [T_1(v) + d(v) - n_1(x, v)] \\
&= 2(n_1(x, v) - T_1(v)) + \beta - 2\alpha + 1 \\
&\leq 2(-2) + \beta - 2\alpha + 1 \\
&= \beta - 2\alpha - 3 \, .
\end{aligned}
$$

**Block-size 2.** For any block $B = \{v, v'\}$ and state $x$ for which $x' = F_B(x) \neq x$ we have $P(x') < P(x)$.

If $\{v, v'\}$ is not an edge, we are effectively in the block-size 1 case and the statement is known to hold. Assume therefore that $v$ and $v'$ are connected. By symmetry, there are three cases to consider: (a) $(0, 0) \mapsto (1, 1)$, (b) $(1, 1) \mapsto (0, 0)$, and (c) $(1, 0) \mapsto (0, 1)$. In all three cases we have $\beta(v) = \beta(v') = 2$. For case (a) we have $\alpha(v) = \alpha(v') = 0$, so $\Delta P \leq 2(2 \cdot 0 - 2 - 1) = -6$. Similarly, for case (b) we have $\alpha(v) = \alpha(v') = 1$ so that $\Delta P \leq 2(2 - 2 \cdot 1 - 3) = -6$. Finally, for case (c) we have $\alpha(v) = 0$ and $\alpha(v') = 1$, so $\Delta P \leq -1 + (-1) = -2$, so in all cases we have $\Delta P < 0$.

**Block-size 3.** For any block $B = \{u, v, w\}$ and state $x$ for which $x' = F_B(x) \neq x$ we have $P(x') < P(x)$.

Again we may assume that $B$ is non-trivial and that $x_u$, $x_v$ and $x_w$ are all mapped non-identically since all other possibilities reduce to the block-size 1 or block-size 2 cases. There are two possibilities for the subgraph induced by $B$: (i) the 3-line with with edges $\{u, v\}$ and $\{v, w\}$ and (ii) the 3-cycle.

*Case (i):* the induced subgraph of $B = \{u, v, w\}$ is a 3-line. There are eight transitions to consider, but by symmetry, it follows that $(1, 1, 0) \mapsto (0, 0, 1)$ has the same potential change as $(0, 1, 1) \mapsto (1, 0, 0)$ and similarly for $(1, 0, 0) \mapsto (0, 1, 1)$ and $(0, 0, 1) \mapsto (1, 1, 0)$. We write $\alpha$ and $\beta$ as vectors, so that in this case $\beta = (2, 3, 2)$. This gives us the following cases listed in Tab. 1.

*Case (ii):* the induced subgraph of $B = \{u, v, w\}$ is a 3-circle. In this case, symmetry implies that there are four cases to consider: $(0, 0, 0) \mapsto (1, 1, 1)$, $(1, 0, 0) \mapsto (0, 1, 1)$, $(1, 1, 0) \mapsto (0, 0, 1)$ and $(1, 1, 1) \mapsto (0, 0, 0)$. Here $\beta = (3, 3, 3)$ with cases summarized in Table 2.

**Table 1.** Potential changes for case ($i$) where block size is 3

| Transition | $\alpha$ | Potential change |
|---|---|---|
| $(1,1,1) \mapsto (0,0,0)$ | $(1,2,1)$ | $\Delta P \leq -3 - 4 - 3 = -10$ |
| $(0,0,1) \mapsto (1,1,0)$ | $(0,1,0)$ | $\Delta P \leq -3 - 2 - 1 = -6$ |
| $(1,1,0) \mapsto (0,0,1)$ | $(1,1,1)$ | $\Delta P \leq -3 - 2 - 1 = -6$ |
| $(0,1,0) \mapsto (1,0,1)$ | $(1,0,1)$ | $\Delta P \leq -1 - 0 - 1 = -2$ |
| $(1,0,1) \mapsto (0,1,0)$ | $(0,2,0)$ | $\Delta P \leq -1 - 0 - 1 = -2$ |
| $(0,0,0) \mapsto (1,1,1)$ | $(0,0,0)$ | $\Delta P \leq -3 - 4 - 3 = -10$ |

**Table 2.** Potential changes for case ($ii$) where block size is 3

| Transition | $\alpha$ | Potential change |
|---|---|---|
| $(1,1,1) \mapsto (0,0,0)$ | $(2,2,2)$ | $\Delta P \leq -4 - 4 - 4 = -12$ |
| $(0,1,1) \mapsto (1,0,0)$ | $(2,1,1)$ | $\Delta P \leq \phantom{-}0 - 2 - 2 = -4$ |
| $(0,0,1) \mapsto (1,1,0)$ | $(1,1,0)$ | $\Delta P \leq -2 - 2 - 0 = -4$ |
| $(0,0,0) \mapsto (1,1,1)$ | $(0,0,0)$ | $\Delta P \leq -4 - 4 - 4 = -12$ |

It follows that whenever the maximal non-trivial block size in $\mathcal{B}$ is at most three, the block sequential threshold map may only have fixed points as limit cycles as claimed.

**Block-size 4.** For this case it is possible to construct systems with 2-cycles. Specifically, let $X$ be the graph displayed in Figure 2. Let the blocks be $B_1 = \{0\}$, $B_2 = \{1, 2, 3, 4\}$ and $B_3 = \{5\}$. The state $x$ obtained by assigning 0 to the even vertices and 1 to the odd vertices is clearly periodic with period 2 for any permutation update sequence of $B_1$, $B_2$ and $B_3$.

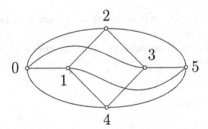

**Fig. 2.** A graph where threshold finite dynamical system maps with block size 4 can have periodic orbits of size $\geq 2$

## 4   Summary and Open Questions

We note that extending the results above to the generalized threshold functions is non-trivial and will require additional constraints on the matrix $A$, see [3].

Here we did not address the question of what is the maximal periodic orbit size when the maximal non-trivial block size $b$ falls in the range $4 \leq b \leq n - 1$. It seems plausible that it is bounded by 2, but we have no proof for this at the moment. We close with this as a conjecture and challenge the reader to settle it.

*Conjecture 1.* The periodic orbits of any block sequential threshold system have length at most 2.

**Acknowledgments.** The author thanks the Network Dynamics and Simulation Science Laboratory (NDSSL) at Virginia Tech for the support of this research which was funded under DTRA R & D Grant HDTRA1-09-1-0017, DTRA Grant HDTRA1-11-1-0016 and DTRA CNIMS Contract HDTRA1-11-D-0016-0001. The author also thanks the anonymous reviewers for corrections and constructive comments.

# References

[1]  Barrett, C.L., Hunt III, H.B., Marathe, M.V., Ravi, S.S., Rosenkrantz, D.J., Stearns, R.E.: Complexity of reachability problems for finite discrete sequential dynamical systems. Journal of Computer and System Sciences 72, 1317–1345 (2006)

[2]  Goles, E., Olivos, J.: Comportement periodique des fonctions a seuil binaires et applications. Discrete Applied Mathematics 3, 93–105 (1981)

[3]  Goles, E., Martinez, S.: Neural and automata networks: Dynamical behaviour and applications. Kluwer Academic Publishers (1990)

[4]  Kuhlman, C., Mortveit, H.S., Murrugarra, D., Anil Kumar, V.S.: Bifurcations in boolean networks. Discrete Mathematics and Theoretical Computer Science (2011), accepted, peer-reviewed article for Automata, November 21-23, Santiago, Chile (2011)

[5]  Laubenbacher, R., Paraigis, B.: Limits of sequential dynamical systems (preprint)

[6]  Laubenbacher, R., Pareigis, B.: Equivalence relations on finite dynamical systems. Advances in Applied Mathematics 26, 237–251 (2001)

[7]  Mortveit, H.S., Reidys, C.M.: Discrete, sequential dynamical systems. Discrete Mathematics 226, 281–295 (2001)

[8]  Mortveit, H.S., Reidys, C.M.: An introduction to sequential dynamical systems. Springer, Universitext (2007)

[9]  Robert, F.: Discrete iterations. a metric study. Springer Series in Computational Mathematics, vol. (6). Springer (1986)

# A Study of Stochastic Noise and Asynchronism in Elementary Cellular Automata

Fernando Silva and Luís Correia

LabMAg, Faculty of Sciences, University of Lisbon,
Lisbon, Portugal
{fsilva,luis.correia}@di.fc.ul.pt

**Abstract.** This work focuses on the set of 32 legal Elementary Cellular Automata. We perform an exhaustive study of the systems' response under: (i) $\alpha$-asynchronous dynamics, from full asynchronism to perfect synchrony; (ii) $\phi$-noise scheme, a perturbation that causes a cell to miscalculate the new state when it is updated. We propose a new classification in three classes under asynchronous conditions: $\alpha$-invariant, $\alpha$-robust and $\alpha$-dependent. We classify the 32 legal automata according to the degree of behavioural modification. We demonstrate that, in the $\alpha$-dependent class, asynchrony behaves as a form of noise in timing. We identify models tolerant to both noise and asynchrony. While the majority of the $\alpha$-invariant class is robust to noise, a subset is not able to recover its original behaviour.

**Keywords:** Elementary Cellular Automata, Asynchronism, Noise.

## 1 Introduction

Cellular Automata (CA) are a class of discrete dynamical systems widely used to model the dynamics of biological and physical systems. Modelled phenomena include, among others, pedestrian movement, the interaction between tumours and immune system, prey and predators, host and parasites, and the development of pigment patterns in molluscs. In its classic definition, CA perform with perfect synchronism. This assumption has been widely questioned since it does not reflect what happens at a microscopic level for physical and biological systems, where such synchrony is a rare event. Distinct studies focused on asynchronous updating schemes have been performed (e.g. [1,2,3,4,5,7]), including the formalization of properties of asynchronous CA [8]. These contributions highlighted that the behaviour of a CA can change considerably when synchrony is absent. Depending on the rule, the order in which the cells are updated and the degree of asynchronism can influence the dynamics of the system.

A different kind of behaviour modification is due to stochastic noise in the transition functions. This aspect has been studied in CA-related areas, such as evolutionary games [9] and boolean networks using a generalization of rule 22 of elementary cellular automata (ECA) [10]. Noise consists of a functional perturbation to a cell's state when it is updated. Noise simulates a misreading of the

G.C. Sirakoulis and S. Bandini (Eds.): ACRI 2012, LNCS 7495, pp. 679–688, 2012.

neighbours' states or a fault in the cell's computation. Contrary to asynchronism, noise has not been frequently studied in CA. In a recent contribution [11], we investigated the impact of noise on a reduced set of ECA. Results suggested that, in certain behavioural classes, the impact of noise and asynchronism on the automaton's dynamics are quantitatively similar. The fact that asynchronism can be considered as a form of noise in timing motivates a more comprehensive study on both aspects, which is performed in this contribution.

In this paper, we extend previous work and study the effects of asynchronism on the set of 32 legal CA rules, i.e., those obeying the quiescence and reflection symmetry conditions [12]. These restrictions offer interesting properties when modelling dynamical systems: (i) Quiescence blocks the *instantaneous propagation* of value-one sites; (ii) Reflection symmetry guarantees isotropy and homogeneity in CA evolution. This way, we include rules that are 0-quiescent (some of which are also 1-quiescent) and symmetric. From the set of 32 rules, the asynchrony of 16 has been studied in [13]. We use the *α-asynchronous* updating method. This updating scheme has been partially studied in [4], where authors used a density-based approach with macroscopic parameters to find robust models in a set of 88 ECA. We use Wolfram's classification [14], among other aspects, as a means for examining the behavioural effects of asynchrony. This categorization divides synchronous CA according to their observed dynamics. For other classifications see, for instance, [15,16]. We propose a new classification according to the degree of behavioural modification under asynchronous conditions.

We also investigate the impact of including different degrees of stochastic noise in the system through a parametrizable noise rate $\phi$, which in not performed in [13]. We analyse and compare the effects of asynchronism and noise in the system's dynamics. The paper is organized as follows. In Section 2, we recall and define basic notions involving the used CA models and methods. In Section 3, we study the effects of different synchrony rates on the 32 rules space and define the proposed classification of CA under asynchronous regimes. In Section 4, we investigate: (i) the impact of the noise on the behaviour of CA in the same space; (ii) common characteristics between noise and asynchrony. Finally, in Section 5 conclusions are drawn and future work is presented.

## 2    Basic Concepts and Notions

### 2.1    Asynchronism and Noise in Cellular Automata

The distinction between synchronous and asynchronous cellular automata is due to the updating method employed. A CA is *synchronous* if all cells are updated simultaneously, otherwise it is said to be *asynchronous*. We use a *step-driven* updating scheme, in which time is discrete [2]. At each time step, every cell has an independent and equal probability $\alpha$ of being updated, with $0 < \alpha \le 1$, thus satisfying a fair sampling condition. The *synchrony rate* $\alpha$ defines the *α-asynchronous dynamics* of the system. For a CA composed of N cells, we study the CA behaviour from the extreme case of $\alpha = 1$ to $\alpha = 1/N$, which approximates a sequential updating. Notice there is no local temporal synchronization constraint in this updating method. This way, results presented in [6], in which an asynchronous CA model with constraints can behave synchronously, do not apply.

The set of states of all cells in a CA, at a certain time step, is called a *configuration*. As part of this work, we also address the impact of noise on the system's orbits, i.e., the following series of configurations obtained by the iteration of the automaton. We parametrize $\phi$, the *noise rate*, that allows controlling the level of functional perturbations to the cell's state, with $0 \leq \phi \leq 1$. When updating its state (if such action occurs), $\phi$ defines an independent probability of a cell miscalculating the new state. Since we use a two-state CA (see 2.2), these perturbations can change a cell's state after update from 0 to 1 or vice-versa.

Considering an automaton composed by N cells, we define $N\alpha$ and $N\phi$ respectively as the average number of cells updated and the average number of cells subjected to noise, at each time step $t$.

## 2.2 Elementary Cellular Automata

We concentrate our study on *elementary* cellular automata (ECA). ECA are one-dimensional models in which individual cells comprise one of two possible values, $A = \{0, 1\}$. Local transition rules depend only on own and radius one neighbours' states. We consider a ring lattice of size $n$. Following [14], every ECA $e$ is described by a code, according to the employed local transition rule, as follows:

$$W(e) = f(0,0,0) \cdot 2^0 + f(0,0,1) \cdot 2^1 + \ldots + f(1,1,1) \cdot 2^7 \qquad (1)$$

An ECA $e$ with code $R = W(e)$ is denoted by ECA **R**. When considering the system's orbits, we will say that a configuration $x$ is a *fixed point* if the result of iterating over the CA is equal to $x$. We will distinguish between homogeneous and non-homogeneous fixed points. We will designate the former by 0* when all cells are 0 and 1* if they are all in state 1.

From this point on, we also adopt the following terms: (i) Classical CA, i.e., synchronous and without noise, will be referred to as ECA. (ii) Asynchronous CA not subject to noise will be mentioned as $ACA_\alpha$. (iii) CA subject to both asynchronism and noise will be designated as $ACAN_{\alpha,\phi}$.

## 2.3 Measurements

The macroscopic parameter used to evaluate the impact of noise and asynchronism is a problem-specific correlation factor denominated $\rho^* \in [-1, 1]$ [11]. It measures the differences between two CA based on a normalized Hamming Distance (HD) [17] between two configurations, *c1* and *c2*. Given the HD between *c1* and *c2*, and their cardinality N, $\rho^*$ is computed as:

$$\rho^* = 1 - \frac{2 \cdot HD}{N} \qquad (2)$$

When comparing two models, we also analyse the relation between the CA cardinality, i.e. number of cells, and the number of iterations required for models to reach a certain correlation level. This data provides a mechanism to directly relate the three involved variables: the perturbation level, the number of cells in each CA and how the first affect the latter through time. $\rho^*$ allows to determine if a CA has converged to a fixed point by calculating the differences between consecutive configurations. It also allows to determine to what extent are two CA distinct, with $\rho^* = 1$ if identical. We define as *degenerative iterations*, the number of iterations elapsed since the first difference was introduced until a low correlation threshold was reached. In this work, we use $|\rho^*| < 0.3$ as boundary, which means that the CA behaviour is rather different from its original one.

## 3     Study of Asynchronism on the 32 Rules Space

In this section, we analyse the 32 ACA's behaviour according to their response to different synchrony rates. The experimental results were obtained with a lattice size $N = 500$ and synchrony rate $\alpha \in [1/N, 1.0]$. Each ACA starts with random initial configurations. For each setup, we averaged results of 30 independent runs.

### 3.1     $\alpha$-invariant ACA

The analysis of experimental data revealed that some ACA are perfectly invariant to the synchrony rate $\alpha$. Given a specific initial condition, even extreme cases of asynchronism do not influence the final outcome of the system. Increasing asynchrony only delays the convergence to the final state by augmenting the transient time. The configurations of the asymptotic part (after the transient time is elapsed) converge to the same fixed point as the synchronous system. We define this type of ACA as invariant to asynchrony, $\alpha$-*invariant*, the class for which the behaviour of a CA is independent of $\alpha$. Table 1 shows the transient time for a subset of $\alpha$-invariant with different synchrony rates.

**Table 1.** Transient time (average iterations ± std. dev.) for a subset of $\alpha$-invariant rules. Remaining rules present a similar behaviour (see text).

| $\alpha$ | $|N\alpha|$ | ACA 32 | ACA 128 | ACA 160 | ACA 236 | ACA 254 |
|---|---|---|---|---|---|---|
| 0.9 | 450 | 9.87 ± 1.46 | 10.67 ± 2.67 | 16.97 ± 4.03 | 5.10 ± 0.96 | 10.17 ± 1.72 |
| 0.7 | 350 | 13.73 ± 2.07 | 15.10 ± 3.12 | 20.33 ± 2.88 | 9.70 ± 2.34 | 15.50 ± 3.86 |
| 0.5 | 250 | 21.00 ± 2.86 | 25.37 ± 5.28 | 30.37 ± 6.13 | 15.37 ± 2.94 | 24.03 ± 4.65 |
| 0.2 | 100 | 64.13 ± 8.87 | 71.60 ± 14.45 | 90.40 ± 19.81 | 47.97 ± 11.71 | 69.03 ± 10.73 |

Experimentally, we find that $\alpha$-invariant= {0, 32, 128, 160, 200, 204, 236, 250, 254}. All rules in this class comprise with our definition of fixed point (see 2.2). In ACA 0 (null rule), each update turns the cells into state 0 as the system evolves towards the fixed point $0^*$. This way, the updating scheme does not play any role. In ACA 32, all cells turn to state 0, unless they are in state 0 and surrounded by two 1. This leads to any configuration evolving to the fixed point $0^*$. The longest convergence takes place when the automaton starts with a configuration of interleaved 0s and 1's. For instance, the orbit from $10101 \to 00000$ consists in the series of configurations $10101 \to 01010 \to 00100 \to 00000$. In ACA 128, the only transition to a state 1 is given by the neighbourhood (1,1,1). Any initial configuration different from $1^*$ will evolve to the fixed point $0^*$. ACA 160 is a composition of both ACA 32 and 128. Initial $1^*$ maintains itself as any other configuration leads to $0^*$.

A more remarkable situation occurs in ACA 204. Any initial condition is a non-homogeneous fixed point. ACA 236 includes the set of transitions of both ACA 204 and 32. Asynchrony only affects the cells subject to the latter, which in turn will converge to $0^*$, as the remaining parts of the automaton remain stable. This way, the convergence of ACA 236 is less susceptible to asynchrony than several other ACA (see Table 1). ACA 200 includes the same set of transitions as ACA 204, except $\langle (0, 1, 0) \rangle$. Asynchronism works on this zones by delaying the change of state to 0. On its turn, ACA 250 and 254 encapsulate almost all the transitions possible in the ECA space. As a result, a configuration different from $0^*$ will always converge, in a number of iterations depending on the asynchrony level, to the fixed point $1^*$.

## 3.2   $\alpha$-robust ACA

In this section, we examine ACA considered robust to asynchronism. We define the class of models as robust to asynchrony, $\alpha$-*robust*.

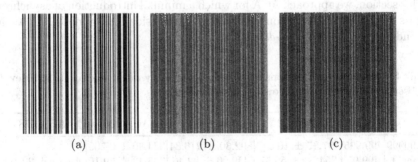

(a)                    (b)                    (c)

**Fig. 1.** Perturbations introduced by asynchrony. a) Localized modifications in ACA $232_{0.9}$ (in red), and period distortion (in blue): b) ACA $94_{1.0}$, c) ACA $94_{0.9}$. In all presented CA diagrams, time increases downwards.

$\alpha$-robust is defined as $\alpha\text{-robust}_1 \cup \alpha\text{-robust}_2$, where $\alpha\text{-robust}_1 = \{4, 36, 72, 76, 104, 132, 164, 218, 222, 232\}$ and $\alpha\text{-robust}_2 = \{94, 108\}$. Rules in $\alpha\text{-robust}_1$ are characterized as non-homogeneous fixed point under a synchronous regime.

Below a certain synchrony rate, presented in Table 2, asynchronism induces localized perturbations (see Fig. 1) from which the system does not recover. Rules in $\alpha$-robust$_2$ present a periodic repetition of a series of configurations. The behavioural class is not altered due to asynchrony. However, the periodic patterns are altered, as presented in Fig. 1. With a synchrony rate $\alpha = 0.9$, ACA in this class start to exhibit small behaviour modifications. Considering the size of the CA, such synchrony rate is quite significant: at each time step, on average, 50 cells are not updated. ACA $232_{1.0}$ is an ECA version of the "Majority Vote Rule": each cell adopts the most common state in the neighbourhood. This rule is a good example of an ACA robust to asynchrony. Behaviour modifications are contained in small regions. The CA is attracted to a certain set of configurations, in which the effects of different synchrony rates are partially overcome by the system's evolution.

**Table 2.** Tolerance to asynchrony for distinct ACA. The table shows, in 30 independent runs, the number of times each ACA managed to recover its behaviour.

| $\alpha$ | $N\alpha$ | ACA | | | | | | | | | |
|---|---|---|---|---|---|---|---|---|---|---|---|
| | | 4 | 36 | 72 | 76 | 104 | 132 | 164 | 218 | 222 | 232 |
| 0.99999 | 499.995 | 30 | 30 | 30 | 30 | 30 | 30 | 30 | 30 | 30 | 30 |
| 0.9999 | 499.95 | 29 | 29 | 29 | 28 | 19 | 30 | 27 | 27 | 28 | 30 |
| 0.999 | 499.5 | 23 | 15 | 28 | 29 | 15 | 23 | 11 | 14 | 20 | 24 |
| 0.9 | 450 | 0 | 0 | 0 | 0 | 0 | 0 | 0 | 0 | 0 | 0 |

### 3.3  $\alpha$-dependent ACA

In this section, we approach ACA for which a minimal introduction of asynchrony results in significant behavioural changes. We consider these models in a class dependent of asynchrony, $\alpha$-*dependent*.

**Table 3.** Degenerative iterations for different synchrony rates. Average $\pm$ std. dev. for a subset of $\alpha$-dependent rules over 30 independent runs.

| $\alpha$ | $N\alpha$ | ACA 22 | ACA 54 | ACA 150 | ACA 178 |
|---|---|---|---|---|---|
| 0.99999 | 499.995 | $437.87 \pm 100.47$ | $892.30 \pm 216.84$ | $334.40 \pm 37.09$ | - |
| 0.9999 | 499.95 | $254.73 \pm 56.57$ | $439.90 \pm 92.46$ | $235.43 \pm 39.10$ | $44714 \pm 20293$ |
| 0.999 | 499.5 | $98.17 \pm 10.31$ | $153.87 \pm 30.54$ | $93.23 \pm 12.00$ | $7063.3 \pm 2042.7$ |
| 0.9 | 450 | $8.13 \pm 0.90$ | $7.20 \pm 0.55$ | $7.70 \pm 0.92$ | $21.30 \pm 3.49$ |

Experimentally, we find $\alpha$-dependent= {18, 22, 50, 54, 90, 122, 126, 146, 150, 178, 182}. Under a synchronous updating method, all rules in $\alpha$-dependent are characterized by periodic patterns or the formation of triangular structures. These structures, an apparent form of self-organization, dissolve when even a

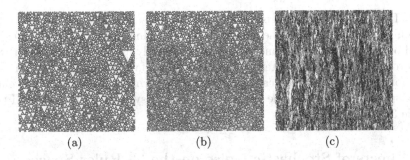

**Fig. 2.** The behavioural consequences of asynchronism in ACA 22 (first 500 iterations). a) ACA $22_{1.0}$, b) ACA $22_{0.9999}$, c) ACA $22_{0.5}$. For better comparison, the initial state is the same across all (the three) simulations.

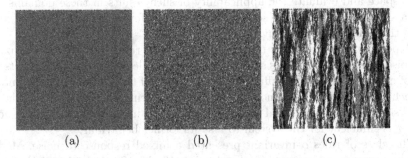

**Fig. 3.** The behavioural consequences of asynchronism (first 500 iterations). a) ACA $178_{1.0}$, b) ACA $178_{0.9}$, c) ACA $178_{0.5}$. For better comparison, the initial state is the same across all (the three) simulations.

very small amount of asynchrony is present (see Fig. 2). This effect has already been discussed in the literature [1]. The structures are characterized as arte-facts produced by the synchronization of the clocks phenomenon, i.e., perfect synchronism. Nonetheless, even with very low asynchrony, the system rapidly differentiates from the synchronous model, as presented in Table 3.

Rules in this class raise interesting behavioural exceptions as there is no unique response to asynchrony. For instance, ACA 18 and 50, with $\alpha = 0.7$ and $\alpha = 0.6$ respectively, are attracted towards fixed point $0^*$. On the other hand, rules such as ACA 178 are completely disrupted by asynchrony. The behaviour changes drastically with distinct synchrony rates, as presented in Fig. 3.

Under Wolfram's behavioural classes [14] and a synchronous regime, ACA 50 and 178 are periodic (class II), ACA 54 belongs to class IV while the remaining $\alpha$-dependent rules are part of class III. Nonetheless, it is possible to discuss the effects of asynchrony by examining how each class handles information. In class II, partial information about previous stages of the system is retained. Asynchrony affects localized spaces but, in spite of not being communicated to the other parts of the system, it is less contained than in homogeneous fixed points.

Class III shows a long range of communication. Any change introduced into the system will spread even to the most distant cells. Since local transition rules depend on each adjacent cell, modifications recursively affect each neighbourhood thus reaching the entire system. Class IV systems fall between class II and III. The long-range of communication is possible in principle. It occurs in a much more sporadic way, hence the larger resistance to asynchrony than class III (see Table 3).

## 4    Effects of Stochastic Noise on the 32 Rules Space

In a recent contribution [11], our preliminary results suggested that in class III and IV systems, noise and asynchronism can have similar effects in the CA's dynamics. As part of this contribution, we examine the impact of noise in the 32 rules space and evaluate the applicability of such results in these domains. We use a synchronous updating scheme in order to differentiate the effects of noise from those due to asynchrony.

Experimental data shows that for $\alpha$-dependent rules, the system's response to noise and asynchronism is similar. Note that while asynchronism restricts the set of cells updated, noise influences the outcome of the update. In this context, asynchronism is a form of noise in timing, inhibiting the cells from updating their state. Results presented in Table 4 show that introducing a minimal noise rate $\phi$ is sufficient for the system to *lose* its former behaviour.

The class of rules $\alpha$-invariant presented a mixed response to noise. Models that converge to a homogeneous fixed point, $\{0, 32, 128, 160, 250, 254\}$, class I systems, demonstrate high tolerance and robustness to both asynchronism and noise. When noise is present, these ACA are able to forget perturbations *instantaneously* and evolve into the same uniform state. The remaining set of rules in $\alpha$-invariant, $\{200, 204, 236\}$, characterized by evolving into a non-homogeneous fixed point, are not able to recover from noise. In opposition to their tolerance to asynchronism, local modifications due to noise typically remain in the system. To confirm this effect, we performed 30 independent runs in which a single random local perturbation was induced in the initial configuration. On the long run, this perturbation is maintained and affects, on average, 2.67, 2.00 and 2.73 cells on ACANs $200_{1.0}$, $204_{1.0}$ and $236_{1.0}$, respectively. These results confirm that in this domain, noise perturbations remain but are contained in the neighbourhood. Table 5 shows the effects of distinct $\phi$ rates and the system's languishing rhythm. High standard deviation in ACANs such as 200 and 236 indicates not only the low significance of averaged values, but also the system's intermittent behaviour in response to small noise rates.

The containment of noise that occurs in a subset of the $\alpha$-invariant class is also present in $\alpha$-robust models. Each perturbation remains contained to a small portion of the space and thus does not spread to the rest of the system. Contrary to what happens when asynchrony is present, results indicate that the class II systems considered respond equally to noise. The noise rate required to achieve a low-correlation with a noise-free system varies from $0.2 \geq \phi \geq 0.0001$. ACANs 72

**Table 4.** Degenerative iterations for distinct ACANs under a synchronous regime. Average ± std. dev. for a subset of $\alpha$-dependent rules over 30 independent runs. See Table 3 for comparison with the effects of asynchrony.

| $\phi$ | $\lvert N\phi \rvert$ | ACAN 22 | ACAN 54 | ACAN 150 | ACAN 178 |
|---|---|---|---|---|---|
| 0.00001 | 0.005 | 387.20 ± 119.37 | 829.57 ± 314.31 | 308.67 ± 53.47 | - |
| 0.0001 | 0.05 | 204.33 ± 43.45 | 330.83 ± 56.91 | 188.37 ± 29.83 | 42942 ± 21261 |
| 0.001 | 0.5 | 70.73 ± 10.05 | 119.33 ± 18.93 | 68.80 ± 10.95 | 6444.7 ± 2421.9 |
| 0.1 | 50 | 5.50 ± 0.68 | 5.47 ± 0.73 | 5.07 ± 0.25 | 16.50 ± 2.52 |

**Table 5.** Degenerative iterations for distinct synchronous ACANs. Average ± std. dev. over 30 independent runs for $\alpha$-invariant rules incapable of tolerating noise.

| $\phi$ | $\lvert N\phi \rvert$ | ACAN 200 | ACAN 204 | ACAN 236 |
|---|---|---|---|---|
| 0.0001 | 0.05 | 23816 ± 10809 | 11352 ± 913.00 | 25604 ± 13368 |
| 0.001 | 0.5 | 3982.4 ± 5293.5 | 1134.8 ± 102.08 | 2984.9 ± 2989.4 |
| 0.01 | 5 | 226.80 ± 64.45 | 111.20 ± 7.98 | 226.63 ± 90.75 |

and 104 are the most resilient models, demonstrating the capability to often forget perturbations. As so, they require the larger $\phi$ values to degenerate from the noise-free system. For instance, ACAN 232, that in a synchronous and noise-free system represents the "Majority Vote Rule", is robust to asynchrony. Nonetheless, when noise is present, it degenerates in approximately 43625.00 ± 18947.98 iterations, with $\phi = 0.0001$. When modelling certain phenomena, this result can have important implications. If elements have a slight probability of adopting the rarest state in their neighbourhood, for instance due to misreading the state of its neighbours, the system's behaviour will slowly degenerate.

## 5  Conclusions

In this work, we analysed the behaviour of the 32 legal ECA under asynchronous update and with stochastic noise in the local transition function. We proposed a new classification in three classes under asynchronous conditions: $\alpha$-invariant, $\alpha$-robust and $\alpha$-dependent. We classified the 32 ECA into those classes based on ECA robustness to asynchrony. We also analysed the behaviour of these ECA under noise. The majority of $\alpha$-invariant systems are completely invariant to both noise and asynchrony. In the second proposed class, $\alpha$-robust, systems are capable of sustaining a moderate degree of asynchrony. Their response to noise is weak as induced perturbations remain throughout the system's evolution. The $\alpha$-dependent class exhibited high susceptibility to asynchrony and noise. The impact of both aspects is similar, thus indicating that asynchronism acts as form of noise in timing. This has important implications when modelling natural systems. By using synchronous and noise-free CA, we introduce an artificiality that may produce results seldom found in nature, where there is no perfectly timed nor noise-absent system.

The next step will be to analyse the ECA behaviour under both asynchronism and noise, simultaneously. We will also extend this study to more rules and explore the adequacy of our classification in other types of CA.

# References

1. Ingerson, T.E., Buvel, R.L.: Structure in Asynchronous Cellular Automata. Phys. D 10, 59–68 (1984)
2. Schönfisch, B., de Roos, A.: Synchronous and Asynchronous Updating in Cellular Automata. BioSystems 51(3), 123–143 (1999)
3. Bersini, H., Detours, V.: Asynchrony Induces Stability in Cellular Automata Based Models. In: Artificial Life IV, pp. 382–387. MIT Press, Cambridge (1994)
4. Fatès, N., Morvan, M.: An Experimental Study of Robustness to Asynchronism for Elementary Cellular Automata. Complex Syst. 16, 1–27 (2005)
5. Regnault, D., Schabanel, N., Thierry, É.: Progresses in the Analysis of Stochastic 2D Cellular Automata: A Study of Asynchronous 2D Minority. Theoret. Comput. Sci. 410, 4844–4855 (2009)
6. Nehaniv, C.: Asynchronous Automata Networks can Emulate any Synchronous Automata Network. Int. J. of Algebra and Comp. 14, 719–740 (2004)
7. Kanada, Y.: The Effects of Randomness in Asynchronous 1D Cellular Automata. Technical Report, Tsukuba Research Center (1997)
8. Manzoni, L.: Asynchronous Cellular Automata and Dynamical Properties. Nat. Comp. (2012), doi: 10.1007/s11047-012-9308-y
9. Grilo, C., Correia, L.: Effects of Asynchronism on Evolutionary Games. J. of Theor. Bio. 269, 109–122 (2011)
10. Beck, G.L., Matache, M.T.: Dynamical Behaviour and Influence of Stochastic Noise on Certain Generalized Boolean Networks. Phys. A 387(19), 4947–4958 (2008)
11. Silva, F., Correia, L.: Noise and Intermediate Asynchronism in Cellular Automata with Sampling Compensation. In: 15th Portuguese Conference on Artificial Intelligence, pp. 209–222 (2011)
12. Wolfram, S.: Statistical Mechanics of Cellular Automata. Rev. of Mod. Phys. 55(3), 601–644 (1983)
13. Fatès, N., Regnault, D., Schabanel, N., Thierry, É.: Asynchronous Behavior of Double-Quiescent Elementary Cellular Automata. In: Correa, J.R., Hevia, A., Kiwi, M. (eds.) LATIN 2006. LNCS, vol. 3887, pp. 455–466. Springer, Heidelberg (2006)
14. Wolfram, S.: A New Kind of Science. Wolfram Media, Illinois (2002)
15. Fatès, N.: Experimental Study of Elementary Cellular Automata Dynamics using the Density Parameter. Disc. Math. and Theoret. Comput. Sci. AB, 155–166 (2003)
16. Cattaneo, G., Finelli, M., Margara, L.: Investigating Topological Chaos by Elementary Cellular Automata Dynamics. Theoret. Comput. Sci. 244, 219–241 (2000)
17. Hamming, R.: Error Detecting and Error Correcting Codes. Bell System Tech. J. 29(2), 147–160 (1950)

# (Intrinsically?) Universal Asynchronous CA

Thomas Worsch

Karlsruhe Institute of Technology, Germany
worsch@kit.edu

**Abstract.** We consider asynchronous one-dimensional cellular automata (CA). It is shown that there is one with von Neumann neighborhood of radius 1 which can simulate each asynchronous one-dimensional cellular automaton. An analogous construction is described for $\alpha$-asynchronous CA (where each cell independently enters a new state with probability $\alpha$. We also point out some generalizations for other updating schemes.

## 1 Introduction

Asynchronous cellular automata (ACA) are cellular automata where not all cells are updating their states simultaneously. Several variants and special cases are considered in the literature. In this paper we will investigate two of them (see [1, 2] for more details and references): In "'pure"' asynchronous CA during a global step an arbitrary subset of all cells make a state transition while the others retain their current states. In $\alpha$-asynchronous CA, $\alpha \in ]0; 1]$, one requires that all cells independently make a transition during a step with probability $\alpha$.

This paper is organized as follows: In Section 2 we review the basic definitions and a few results as far as they are relevant in the present context. The core of the paper is Section 3 where the overall construction is sketched and the main technical tool explained which give rise to the following results:

**Theorem 1.** *There is a purely asynchronous deterministic CA which is able to simulate all purely asynchronous deterministic CA.*

**Theorem 2.** *For each $\alpha \in ]0; 1]$ there is an $\alpha$-asynchronous deterministic CA which is able to simulate all $\alpha$-asynchronous deterministic CA.*

The precise definition of "simulation" needed in the theorems can be seen from the constructions below. We consider this to be a reasonable approach, but admittedly the situation is more complicated than in the synchronous deterministic case. In addition until a satisfying definition is agreed upon we use the adverb "intrinsically" informally: For a set of automata $\mathcal{M}$ a member $M \in \mathcal{M}$ is intrinsically universal for $\mathcal{M}$, if it can simulate each $M' \in \mathcal{M}$. It should be pointed out, that an extension of the precise notion of intrinsic universality for S-DCA, as proposed e. g. by [3], to CA which are *not* S-DCA is still missing.

The main technical problem is that on one hand despite asynchronous updating the universal simulator has to work reasonably (this is easy) while on the

G.C. Sirakoulis and S. Bandini (Eds.): ACRI 2012, LNCS 7495, pp. 689–698, 2012.

other hand one has to exploit the asynchronicity of the simulator to generate the different possibilities for global steps of the simulated asynchronous CA. A closer inspection of the construction reveals that the same ideas can be one applied in several other situations. These possibilities are discussed in Section 4. We conclude with a summary and a short outlook in Section 5. The present paper is an improvement of a "short contribution" presented at Automata 2010 [4].

## 2   Basics

### 2.1   General Notation

We write $\mathbf{Z}$ for the set of integers, $B^A$ for the set of all total functions from $A$ to $B$, and $2^M$ for the powerset of a set $M$. The cardinality of a set $M$ is $|M|$.

In this paper we are interested in one-dimensional cellular automata. The set of states of one cell is denoted as $Q$; the set of all configurations is $Q^{\mathbf{Z}}$. A neighborhood is a finite set $N = \{\nu_1, \ldots, \nu_k\}$ of integers. A *local configuration* is a mapping $\ell : N \to Q$. A tuple $(q_1, \ldots, q_k, q')$ with $q' \in f(q_1, \ldots, q_k)$ is called a *rule*. The local configuration $c_{i+N}$ observed by cell $i \in \mathbf{Z}$ in the global configuration $c$ is defined as $c_{i+N} : N \to Q : n \mapsto c(i + n)$.

The behavior of a single cell of a *nondeterministic CA (NCA)* is described by the local transition function $f : Q^N \to 2^Q$. An NCA is a *deterministic CA (DCA)* iff for all $\ell \in Q^N$ holds: $|f(\ell)| = 1$. For a *probabilistic CA (PCA)* the local transition function is of the form $p : Q^N \to [0;1]^Q$, where $p(\ell)(q)$ is the probability that a cell enters state $q$ if it observes $\ell$ in its neighborhood. For PCA it is required that for all $\ell \in Q^N$ the sum $\sum_{q \in Q} p(\ell)(q) = 1$.

To each PCA there is a corresponding NCA with local transition function $f : Q^N \to 2^Q : \ell \mapsto \{q \mid p(\ell)(q) > 0\}$.

The triple $(Q, f, N)$ is called the *local structure* of a CA.

### 2.2   Updating Schemes

In general a local structure $(Q, f, N)$ together with a prescription how cells are updated induce a global transition relation $\mathcal{R} \subseteq Q^{\mathbf{Z}} \times Q^{\mathbf{Z}}$ describing the possible global steps. We will mostly use the infix notation $c \ \mathcal{R} \ c'$ (possibly with sub- and/or superscripts for further clarification) to indicate that it is possible to reach configuration $c'$ in one step from configuration $c$.

In a global step each cell has two possibilities: to be *active* and make a state transition (according to a rule) or to be *passive* and not to change its state. Restrictions made by different updating schemes lead to different possible behaviors, i.e. different relations $\mathcal{R}$, of CA.

A (finite or infinite) sequence $(c_0, c_1, c_2, \ldots)$ of configurations is a *computation*, iff for all pairs $(c_i, c_{i+1})$ within the sequence it is true that $c_i \ \mathcal{R} \ c_{i+1}$.

*Synchronous Updating.* Synchronous updating means that in a global step all cells are active and we use $\mathcal{S}$ to denote the corresponding one step relation. Hence for an NCA $c \ \mathcal{S} \ c'$ holds iff $\forall i \in \mathbf{Z} : c'(i) \in f(c_{i+N})$. For DCA $\mathcal{S}$ is in fact a function. The prefix S- indicates synchronous updating (S-NCA etc.).

*Purely Asynchronous Updating.* The first version of asynchronous updating has been considered for many years now [5, 6]. In order to distinguish it from the other forms mentioned below we call this version *purely asynchronous* updating. In this case there are no restrictions on whether a cell may be active or passive. Thus in each step there is a subset $M$ of "active" cells which do make a transition while the cells in the complement simply remain in their current state.

For an NCA $c \mathcal{A} c'$ holds iff there is a $M \subseteq \mathbf{Z}$ such that $c'(i) \in f(c_{i+N})$ if $i \in M$ and $c'(i) = c(i)$ if $i \notin M$. We may sometimes write $c \mathcal{A}_M c'$ to indicate the set $M$ of active cells. Therefore $\mathcal{S} = \mathcal{A}_{\mathbf{Z}}$.

Obviously, even for deterministic CA purely asynchronous updating can lead to many different possible computations starting with the same configuration. See Section 2.3 below for further remarks on this.

We will use the prefix A- to indicate asynchronous updating (A-NCA etc.) and use the term *asynchronous CA* (ACA) for A-DCA (with a deterministic local function!).

We note that each A-NCA with local function $f : Q^N \to 2^Q$ can be considered as a slightly modified S-NCA: One uses $N' = N \cup \{0\}$ and the local function $f' : Q^{N'} \to 2^Q$, where $f'(\ell') = f(\ell'|_N) \cup \{\ell(0)\}$.

*α-Asynchronous Updating.* Recently α-asynchronous CA have attracted some attention. Here, $\alpha \in {]}0; 1]$ is a positive probability. Similar to PCA one considers the behavior (active or passive) of each cell during a global step as a random variable, and $\alpha$ is the (uniform) probability of a cell to be active.

We quickly mention the fully asynchronous updating scheme, where in each global step only exactly one cell is active. An analogue to Theorem 1 has been proven. Due to page limitations the construction is deferred to a follow-up paper.

## 2.3   Relations between Different Types

We will now review some known relations between different types of CA. This quickly leads to the notion of *simulation*. In the following we will speak about *guest CA* and *guest cells* and about *host CA* and *host cells*. The host is the simulating CA and the guest is the simulated CA.

*The Obvious.* It should be clear that ACA, i.e. A-DCA, are a special case of S-NCA in the following sense: Assume that $A$ is an ACA with local structure $(Q, f_A, N_A)$. Define an NCA $B$ with local structure $(Q, f_B, N_B)$ as follows: the set of states is the same and the neighborhood is $N_B = N_A \cup \{0\}$ (may be the same, too). For each local configuration $\ell : N_B \to Q$ one requires $f_B(\ell) = \{\ell(0)\} \cup f_A(\ell|_{N_A})$. (Here $f|_M$ is the restriction of $f$ to the subset $M$ of its domain.)

Then $\mathcal{A}_A$ is the same as $\mathcal{S}_B$. This is so, because given $c \mathcal{A}_A c'$, a cell $i$ in configuration $c'$ of $A$ has the possibilities $c(i)$ and $f_A(c_{i+N_A})$ (by definition of asynchronicity); and given $c \mathcal{A}_A c'$ in configuration $c'$ a cell $i$ in $B$ has the possibilities $c(i)$ and $f_A(c_{i+N_A})$ (by definition of $f_B$) as well.

So in a very strong sense each A-DCA $A$ can be simulated by a S-NCA $B$: the induced global step relations are exactly the same. In general the reverse simulation, in the same sense, of S-NCA by A-DCA is impossible since a cell of an S-NCA may enter one of three or more different states while a cell of an A-DCA has at most two choices. Analogously one can consider $\alpha$-asynchronous DCA as a special case of PCA, but not vice versa.

*Golze's Construction.* Golze [6] has shown how for each S-NCA $B$ one can construct an A-DCA $A$ simulating $B$. Besides the obstacle of different numbers of choices just mentioned, there is another problem. Whenever one uses some kind of asynchronous updating, there are infinite computations in which only a constant number of cells is ever active. Such computations are not useful at all. Roughly speaking, the solution proposed by [6] is to consider equivalence classes of space-time diagrams where for example computations as just mentioned are equivalent to the trivial computation where nothing at all has happened.

The simulations described in Section 3 are reasonable in the sense that the overall approach is along the lines already proposed by several authors.

It should be noted that in Golze's construction the size of the neighborhood of the host cannot be bounded by a constant. We point out that the construction in Section 3 can be used to achieve the same while only using von Neumann neighborhood of radius 1 in *all* cases.

*Nakamura's Construction.* Nakamura [5] has described how an S-DCA $D$ can be simulated (again in a specific sense) by an A-DCA $A$. The problem to overcome is that uncontrolled active state changes of one cell may lead to totally "irrelevant" configurations if neighboring cells do not become active at all. We briefly sketch the idea (citing [7]). There is a more complicated construction which only needs a total of $k^2 + 2k$ states instead of $3k^2$ in order to simulate a $k$-state CA [2].

As the set of states for $A$ one uses $Q_A = Q_D \times Q_D \times \{0, 1, 2\}$. Let $c^t$ denote the configuration reached by $D$ after $t$ steps from some initial configuration $c$. If in a given configuration $c_A$ of $A$ cell $j$ of $A$ has already simulated $t$ transitions of cell $j$ of $S$ then $c_A(j) = (c^t(j), c^{t-1}(j), t \bmod 3)$. Therefore we denote by $current(q)$, $old(q)$, and $time(q)$ the first, second, and third component of a state $q \in Q_A$ respectively. $time(q)$ is also called the time stamp of the cell.

To maintain this invariant, given $q_1, \dots, q_k$, the local function $f_A(q_1, \dots, q_k)$ is defined as follows (assuming without loss of generality that $\nu_1 = 0$):

– If for all $i$: $time(q_i) = time(q_1)$ or $time(q_i) = time(q_1) + 1 \pmod 3$, then
$f_A(q_1, \dots, q_k) = (f_D(q_1', \dots, q_k'), current(q_1), time(q_1) + 1 \pmod 3)$, where

$$q_i' = \begin{cases} current(q_i) & \text{if } time(q_i) = time(q_1) \\ old(q_i) & \text{if } time(q_i) = time(q_1) + 1 \pmod 3 \end{cases}$$

– otherwise $f_A(q_1, \dots, q_k) = q_1$.

If a cell is updated according to the first alternative, we will say, that it *makes progress*. As in Golze's construction also in this case different guest CA are simulated by different host CA. Below we will describe *one host* being able to simulate *all guests* (from an infinite set of CA).

# 3   Universal Simulation of Purely Asynchronous DCA

In this section we will describe the construction of a purely asynchronous DCA able to simulate each purely asynchronous DCA.

Since we are interested in *one host* being able to *simulate different guests* for different initial configurations it is necessary to provide the host with an encoding of the local structure of the guest and an encoding of the initial guest configuration. These are described in Sections 3.1 and 3.2. The simulation is described as a sequence of refinements in Sections 3.3 to 3.6. This will be done in such a way that it can not only be used in the purely asynchronous setting, but with no modifications for $\alpha$-asynchronous updating as well (see Section 4).

The description will make use of so-called *"asynchronous coins"*. For the moment these can be considered as black boxes consisting of two adjacent cells. A "toss of the coin" can be requested by a signal from outside and the result will be a 0 or a 1 (once the cells have been active a constant number of times). In Section 3.7 it will be explained how to implement such an asynchronous coin.

## 3.1   Encodings of Local Structures

For convenience we will use the alphabet $\{0, 1, [, ]\}$ for representing all the pieces of a guest CA on the host. Without loss of generality $Q = \{0, \ldots, n-1\}$. The encoding of a single guest state is $cod_Q(q) = [\, bin(q)\,]$ where $bin(q) \in \{0,1\}^+$ is the binary representation of $q$, all of them having the same length $\lceil \log_2 |Q| \rceil$.

Members of the neighborhood $N = \{\nu_1, \ldots, \nu_k\}$ are encoded as

$$cod_N(\nu_i) = \begin{cases} [\, 10 \, [\, bin(-\nu_i)\,]\,] & \text{if } \nu_i < 0 \\ [\, 00 \, [\, bin(\nu_i)\,]\,] & \text{if } \nu_i = 0 \\ [\, 01 \, [\, bin(\nu_i)\,]\,] & \text{if } \nu_i > 0 \end{cases}$$

(where all $bin(\nu_i)$ have the same length.) That allows to find out easily whether a neighbor is to the left or to the right and how far. The complete neighborhood is encoded as the word $cod(N) = [\, cod_N(\nu_1) \cdots cod_N(\nu_k)\,]$. Without loss of generality we assume that $\nu_1 = 0$, i.e. a cell may make use of its own state during a transition and it as listed as the first state in the rules below.

For the simulation of asynchronous DCA it is useful to encode a single local rule $(q_1, \ldots, q_k, q')$ as two words which we will call encoded rules:

$$[\, cod_Q(q_1) \cdots cod_Q(q_k) \, [0] \, cod_Q(q_1)\,] \; [\, cod_Q(q_1) \cdots cod_Q(q_k) \, [1] \, cod_Q(q')\,] \, .$$

In addition to the states in the neighborhood an "activity flag" as introduced as a pseudo neighbor. If it is 1, the new state of a cell will be read off as prescribed by the local rule, and if it is 0 the state does not change (remember that $\nu_1 = 0$). The whole local transition function is encoded as

$$cod(f) = [\, \langle \text{concatenation of encodings of all local rules} \rangle \,]$$

and the whole local structure of a guest CA as $[\, bin(|Q|) cod(N) cod(f)\,]$ .

## 3.2 Encodings of CA Configurations

Given a guest CA $G$ with its encoding a guest configuration $c \in Q^{\mathbf{Z}}$ is encoded by mapping each cell $i$ to a *block* $b_i \in \{0, 1, [, ]\}^+$ which consists of four segments:

$$\langle block \rangle = [\ \langle encoding\ segment \rangle\ \langle state\ segment \rangle\ \langle activity\ bit \rangle\ \langle coin\ segment \rangle\ ]$$

The $\langle encoding\ segment \rangle$ will simply store the encoding of the guest CA. The $\langle state\ segment \rangle$ of $b_i$ will store the encoding of the current state $c_i$ of one guest cell. The $\langle activity\ bit \rangle$ will be used to choose between an active and passive cell. The symbols of each block are stored in adjacent host cells and the blocks corresponding to consecutive guest cells are stored consecutively in the host.

## 3.3 Simulation Overview

For the description of the simulation assume that the host is started in an initial configuration which is the encoding of a guest configuration as just described. The operation of the host will be explained using notions like "mark", "signal" and "moving counter". It is helpful to imagine that the local set of states of the host is subdivided into several *registers*. The complete array of cells then consists of several *tracks*; one contains the encoding of the guest configuration, while others are used for specific signals, counters, etc.

The construction/explanation of the host is successively refined in three steps:

- Sect. 3.4: review of a construction for synchronous deterministic CA
- Sect. 3.5: simple modification to get a host with asynchronous updating
- Sect. 3.6: possibility to simulate guests which use asynchronous updating

## 3.4 Synchronous Simulation of S-DCA

The following algorithm is similar to the simulation described by [7]. As long as everything is deterministic one may assume that the $\langle activity\ bit \rangle$ of each block is always 1 and the $\langle coin\ segment \rangle$ is not used. Global steps of the guest are simulated one after the other. For each of them the host uses four phases:

P1. *Collect (the encodings of) the current states of the neighbors of the guest cell to be simulated.*

Signals are sent to neighboring blocks. They have to know how many blocks to travel (and they have to travel as many blocks back to the origin). One uses signals of constant speed (smaller than 1 for the algorithms described below to work) and attach to it a pair of binary numbers $(d, D)$, which initially are both the number of blocks the signal has to travel. The distance of the blocks is given by the encoded offsets of the guest neighborhood.

When a signal arrives at the correct block of a neighboring guest cell the encoding of its current state is copied and sent back to the origin.

P2. *Use these information to select rules of the guest transition function.*
Upon arrival of a guest state in the block that had requested it, corresponding rules of the transition table are marked as possibly relevant. If a state $q_j$ could be obtained from neighbor $j$, state $q_j$ in the encodings of rule $[q_1, \ldots, q_j, \ldots, q_k, q']$ is marked. The fact that all signals have returned a valid state can be recognized by the fact that in two encoded local rules *all* $q_1, \ldots, q_k$ are marked. This is checked each time a state is marked.

P3. *Use the ⟨activity bit⟩ to select that one of the two remaining encoded rules with the same ⟨activity flag⟩.*
Since for deterministic guest CA the ⟨activity bit⟩ is always 1, a guest cell will always be updated according to its local rules.

P4. *Update the state segment of the block.* The encoding of the new state of the guest cell is read off the local rule $[cod_Q(q_1) \cdots cod_Q(q_k)[1]cod_Q(q')]$ in which *all* of $q_1, \ldots, q_k$ have been marked and it is stored in the state segment. Also, all the marks attached to the encoded rules are removed.

### 3.5   Asynchronous Simulation of S-DCA

It is easy to realize the simulation of synchronous DCA guests on an *asynchronous* DCA *host*. One just has to apply Nakamura's transformation to the CA described in the previous Section 3.4. But now it is a different type of simulation. In the asynchronous host CA one can now have computations which are completely useless. As an extreme example consider the infinite computation where in each step only host cell 0 is active. On the other hand the computation during which in each step all host cells active is identical to the computation of the synchronous CA described in the previous subsection.

Assume that $m$ steps of the synchronous host are necessary to simulate one step of the guest CA. Then those computations of the asynchronous host where each host cell makes progress (in the sense of Section 2.3) exactly $m$ times correspond very closely to the $m$-step computations of the synchronous host.

The more general approach by [6] is to look at (equivalence classes of) space-time diagrams. If one is interested in the new states of only a finite number of guest cells, one can be even less restrictive. These topics will be discussed in another paper.

### 3.6   Asynchronous Simulation of A-DCA

As a third step we now want to generalize the construction above in such a way that it is possible to simulate *asynchronous guest* DCA. For each encoding $c'$ of an initial configuration $c$ of an asynchronous guest DCA $G$, and for each computation of $G$ starting with $c$ there is a computation of $H$ starting with $c'$ which simulates the above.

One has to exploit the nondeterminism inherent to the asynchronicity of the *host* $H$ to systematically choose whether a *guest* cell should be passive or active.

Now the ⟨activity bit⟩ and the ⟨coin segment⟩ in each block become relevant. The implementation of an asynchronous coin will be explained in detail in the next subsection. The behavior visible from outside is the following:

- Initially the two coin cells are in a waiting state $w$.
- A signal can be sent to the coin from the left, requesting a bit 0 or 1.
- Both coin cells become "alerted" and after a certain number of steps when they have been active sufficiently often, the will have entered 00 or 11.
- The cell to the left then has to change the request signal to a corresponding result signal which does not yet start to travel back.
- When the left coin cell (is active and) observes that the result bit has been copied it returns to the waiting state.
- Once the result signal observes this, it starts traveling back.

Assuming for the moment that this indeed can be implemented, it is used as follows for the simulation of asynchronous guests. Once all prerequisites $q_1, \ldots q_k$ of two encoded local rules $[cod_Q(q_1), \ldots, cod_Q(q_k)[f] q']$ (with $f \in \{0, 1\}$) have been marked (phases P1 and P2 above), a request signal is sent to the coin. The result returned is stored in the $\langle activity\ bit \rangle$. Then phases P3 and P4 follow, comparing the $\langle activity\ bit \rangle$ to $f$ choosing between the simulation of an active guest cell or a passive one. In the latter case case the state segment is not changed; the marks at the local rules are removed nevertheless.

## 3.7   The "Asynchronous Coin"

The asynchronous coin consists of two adjacent cells. Without loss of generality they are specially marked so that each of them can easily identify itself as the left or right cell of such a pair. Instead of a description of the local transition function Figure 1 captures the essence of the possible transitions of the pair. We use possible states $w$, $a$ and $b$, and 0 and 1 (and ignore the fact that the coin cells have additional registers for moving signals etc. as all other cells). Initially both coin cells are is state $w$, waiting for a request to produce a bit. For the figure we assume that the request comes from the left and that the result also will be consumed (carried away) to the left.

An edge indicates a possible transition from one pair of states to the next. The label of the edge shows which cells have to be active in order to realize this transition. 'L' means that only the left cell is active, 'R' that only the right cell is active and 'LR' that both cells are active. The trivial loops have been omitted.

The gray ww pair at the top of Figure 1 is the start, where the coin is waiting for a request to produce a 0 or 1. When the (same) gray ww pair at the bottom has been reached, one tossing cycle has been finished. Edges which are straight lines indicates transitions which happen without exceptions. Starting from the top ww pair one can reach 00 as well as 11. This is the result of the coin toss.

The dashed edges indicate that cells leave a state only under certain circumstances. The transition from ww to aw only happens when the left coin cell sees a request for a "coin toss" arriving from the left. And once the cells have entered states 00 or 11 they start to return to ww only when the left coin cell observes that its left neighbor has copied the bit produced.

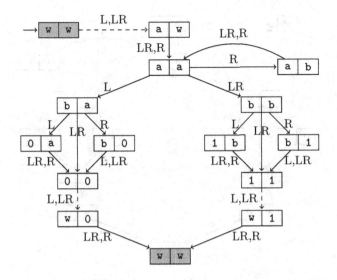

Fig. 1. The purely asynchronous coin

## 4    Universality for $\alpha$-Asynchronous CA

One might have wondered why we did not choose a more symmetric approach in the previous section, exchanging the roles of 'bb' and 'ab' in Figure 1. But for the construction for $\alpha$-asynchronous CA this "asymmetry" is vital; see Figure 2.

The goal is an $\alpha$-asynchronous host which is able to simulate all $\alpha$-asynchronous guests; note the same probability for guests and host. A cell is active with probability $\alpha$ and passive with probability $\beta = 1 - \alpha$.

Figure 2 results from Figure 1 by replacing the label 'L', 'R', 'LR', etc. with the corresponding probabilities. An edge labeled 'L' (or 'R') represented the case that exactly one of the two cells is active. In $\alpha$-asynchronous CA this happens with probability $\alpha\beta$. An edge labeled 'LR' represented the case that both cells are active. In $\alpha$-asynchronous CA this happens with probability $\alpha^2$. An edge labeled 'L,LR' (or 'LR,R') represented the case that either exactly one of the two cells is active or both. This happens with probability $\alpha\beta + \alpha^2 = \alpha(\beta + \alpha) = \alpha$.

It is now easy to see that 00 will happen with probability $\alpha\beta/(\alpha\beta + \alpha^2) = \beta$, while 11 will happen with probability $\alpha^2/(\alpha\beta + \alpha^2) = \alpha$. Thus Theorem 2 holds.

## 5    Outlook

We have shown that there is one purely asynchronous DCA which can simulate all purely asynchronous DCA, and similarly for $\alpha$-asynchronous DCA. One can generalize the construction to even simulate all asynchronous *nondeterministic* CA, improving an earlier construction by Golze. This will explained in another paper.

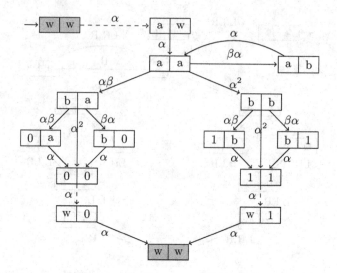

**Fig. 2.** The $\alpha$-asynchronous coin. For clarity self loops are not shown.

We have restricted ourselves to one-dimensional CA, but only in order keep the descriptions and notations a little bit simpler. The generalizations of the above results to higher dimensions are straight forward.

In our opinion one major interesting open problem is: Can a definition and concepts of intrinsic universality as proposed by [3, 8] be generalized to CA which are not synchronous and deterministic?

# References

[1] Bandini, S., Bonomi, A., Vizzari, G.: What Do We Mean by Asynchronous CA? A Reflection on Types and Effects of Asynchronicity. In: Bandini, S., Manzoni, S., Umeo, H., Vizzari, G. (eds.) ACRI 2010. LNCS, vol. 6350, pp. 385–394. Springer, Heidelberg (2010)

[2] Lee, J., Adachi, S., Peper, F., Morita, K.: Asynchronous game of life. Physica D 194(3-4), 369–384 (2004)

[3] Ollinger, N.: Universalities in cellular automata; a (short) survey. In: Durand, B. (ed.) Proceedings JAC 2008, pp. 102–118 (2008)

[4] Worsch, T.: A note on (Intrinsically?) universal asynchronous cellular automata. In: Fatès, N., Kari, J., Worsch, T. (eds.) Proceedings Automata 2010, pp. 339–350 (2010)

[5] Nakamura, K.: Asynchronous cellular automata and their computational ability. Systems, Conputers, Control 5(5), 58–66 (1974)

[6] Golze, U.: (A-)synchronous (non-)deterministic cell spaces simulating each other. Journal of Computer and System Sciences 17(2), 176–193 (1978)

[7] Worsch, T., Nishio, H.: Achieving universality of CA by changing the neighborhood. Journal of Cellular Automata 4(3), 237–246 (2009)

[8] Delorme, M., Mazoyer, J., Ollinger, N., Theyssier, G.: Bulking II: Classifications of cellular automata. Theoretical Computer Science 412(30), 3881–3905 (2011)

# Data Collection for Modeling and Simulation: Case Study at the University of Milan-Bicocca

Mizar Luca Federici[1], Andrea Gorrini[2],
Lorenza Manenti[3], and Giuseppe Vizzari[3,*]

[1] CROWDYXITY s.r.l. - Crowd Dynamics and Complexity
Via Ventura 3, 20134 - Milano, Italy
m.federici@crowdyxity.com
[2] INFORMATION SOCIETY Ph.D. Program
University of Milan-Bicocca
Via Bicocca degli Arcimboldi 8, 20126 - Milano, Italy
a.gorrini@campus.unimib.it
[3] CSAI - Complex Systems and Artificial Intelligence Research Center
University of Milan - Bicocca
Viale Sarca, 336, 20126 - Milano, Italy
{manenti,vizzari}@disco.unimib.it

**Abstract.** The investigation of crowd dynamics is a complex field of study that involves different types of knowledge and skills, and, also from the socio-psychological perspective, the definition of crowd is still controversial. We propose to investigate analytically this phenomenon focusing on pedestrian dynamics in medium-high density situations, and, in particular, on proxemic behavior of walking groups. In this work we will present several results collected during the observation of the incoming pedestrian flows to an admission test at the University of Milano-Bicocca. In particular, we collected empirical data about: levels of density and of service, group spatial arrangement (degree of alignment and cohesion), group size and composition (gender), walking speed and lane formation. The statistical analysis of video footages of the event showed that a large majority of the incoming flow was composed of groups and that groups size significantly affects walking speed. Collected data will be used for an investigative modeling work aimed at simulating the observed crowd and pedestrian dynamics.

**Keywords:** Crowd, Pedestrian Dynamics, Groups, Proxemics.

## 1 Introduction

The investigation of crowd dynamics is a complex field of study, and it involves different types of knowledge and skills. Its scientific relevance is related to the growing need of applicative results, strictly linked to the management of large events (e.g., celebrations, concerts, sports events) and to the design of public

---

* Authors are listed in alphabetical order.

G.C. Sirakoulis and S. Bandini (Eds.): ACRI 2012, LNCS 7495, pp. 699–708, 2012.
© Springer-Verlag Berlin Heidelberg 2012

spaces (e.g., squares, stadiums, stations). From the socio-psychological perspective the definition of crowd is still controversial. Moreover, it is difficult to establish standard guidances for the empirical investigation of the phenomenon due to its variability among size and typology.

Early interest in studying crowd behavior started from the pioneering study of Gustave Le Bon [1] who defined a crowd as a potential threat to society: as members of a crowd people display an altered state of consciousness, with a consequent loss of sense of self-awareness and an increase of irrational and violent behaviors. Far from this approach the ESIM-Elaborated Social Identity Model [2] proposes a social-normative conception of collective behavior, claiming that social norms continue to shape behavior of people also within the crowd, by means of the spontaneous transition from an individual identity to a common social identity [3]. Starting from these divergent theoretical assumptions, the most accepted definition of crowd cites:

> "A crowd can be defined as a gathering of 20 people (at least), standing in close proximity at a specific location to observe a specific event, who feel united by a common social identity, and who are able to act in a socially coherent way, despite being strangers in an ambiguous or unfamiliar situation"[4, p.43].

Because of the difficulty to reach an exhaustive definition of what a crowd is, we propose to analytically investigate the phenomenon focusing on pedestrian dynamics in medium-high density situation. In particular, we focus on: groups[1], which are the basic constitutive elements of the crowd, and proxemics [5], chosen as an analytical indicator of crowd behavioral dynamics, thanks to its ability to model social relationships among people and groups in the crowd, by means of the dynamic regulation of interpersonal distances[2].

Proxemic behavior reveals the psychological bonding among group members, and, in high-density situation, it represents an adaptive stress-reducing behavior to crowding[3], by producing spatial boundaries that shield group members from the invasion of personal space. In motion situation, group proxemic behavior generates typical patterns (see Fig. 1), which allow communication and spatial cohesion among members [9].

At low density, group members tend to walk side by side, forming a line perpendicular to the walking direction (line-abreast pattern); as the density increases, the linear walking formation turns into a V-like pattern, with the middle individual positioned slightly behind in comparison to the lateral individuals; in situation of high density, the spatial distribution of group members

---

[1] A group can be defined as two or more people who interact for a shared goal, perceiving a membership based on a shared social identity [3].

[2] The regulation of spatial distances (intimate, personal, social, and public distances) is influenced by age, gender, culture, and personality [6]. Previous studies in the pedestrian dynamics literature confirm that culture is an important factor that influence the dynamics of crowds and pedestrian flows [7].

[3] Psycho-physiological responses of arousal and stress, cognitive performance decrements, and aggressive response [8].

**Fig. 1.** The typical patterns of walking groups (from the left: line-abreast, V-like, river-like pattern)

leads to river-like pattern and lane formation, characterized by the presence of a leader that coordinates the group members to cross the space [10].

To further investigate pedestrian dynamics in medium-high density situations, we propose to detect the behavior of walking groups, focusing on the relation among: level of density, proxemic spatial arrangement (degree of alignment and cohesion), walking speed, group size and composition (gender). In particular, in this work we will present several results collected during the observation of the incoming pedestrian flows to the admission test of the Faculty of Psychology at the University of Milano- Bicocca, which was performed in September 1st, 2011. In the context of crowd studies carried out by the CSAI research center, the survey was aimed at enhancing existing knowledge and results achieved from several early observations [11,12], and at formalizing a first modeling proposal [10,13,14].

This work is organized as follow: after a brief description of the scenario and of the methodological approach (Sec. 2), a preliminary analysis will be proposed (Sec. 3); in particular we will focus on flow composition (Sec. 3.1) and on walking speed analysis (Sec. 3.2); then previous results on modeling and simulation of the entry process will be presented (Sec. 4). The paper ends with some final remarks and some suggestions for future developments (Sec. 5).

## 2  Scenario Analysis and Methodological Approach

About two thousand of people attended the admission test to the Faculty of Psychology at the University of Milano-Bicocca[4]. The survey was aimed at observing individual and group behavior during the inflow and entry processes into the Building U6, one of the venues of the admission test (see Fig. 2a). In particular, data collection was focused on levels of density, group composition (size and gender), group spatial arrangement and group walking speeds.

---

[4] The subscription list of the participants to the admission test was composed of 2094 students, including 437 males (29%), and 1657 females (79%), on average 19 years old.

The size and the composition of unidirectional incoming pedestrian flow were measured every minute. The identification of groups in the streaming of participants was assessed on the basis of: visual contact, body orientation, gesticulation and talk and, in particular, on spatial arrangement and cohesion of members (in reference to typical proxemic patterns). A topographical analysis of the environment was performed to support the detection of the level of density, of the levels of service and of the walking speed analysis.

The team was composed of two supervisors and six observers (distributed on different counting locations). Each counter was equipped with: a pre-printed blank table that was necessary to note data, a people counter and a chronograph. Several preliminary inspections were performed to define the best counting locations, trying not to hinder the activities of the organizers, and not to influence the behavior of observed subjects. To ensure more validity to the research video-recording tools were employed in addiction to headcounting. The equipment for video footage consisted of full HD video cameras with stands. Existing legislation about privacy was also consulted to exceed some ethical issues about the video recording of the event.

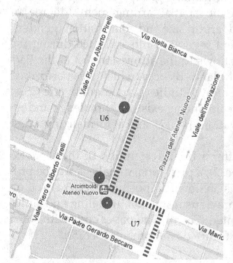

(a) The buildings U6 and U7; the counting points (circles); unidirectional incoming flow (dotted line)

(b) The area of the bidirectional flow between the building U6 and U7; the entry area of the building U6 (dotted line)

**Fig. 2.** Scenario analysis: the incoming pedestrian flow and the entrance of building U6

## 3   Data Analysis

The starting point of data analysis consisted of a preliminary investigation about these data (e.g., charts and tables of frequency). Then, a blind codification of the video-recorded images was performed by two independent coders to achieve average results. A preliminary comparison of the results obtained by the two techniques (head-counting and video analysis activities) showed that the video analysis, although time spending, is a useful technique to monitor human error, ensuring more validity to the research. Even if expert counters were employed during the activities, from the video footages analysis emerged the presence of an error of over estimation of the size and group composition of the incoming flow by counters, quantifiable around 4% in relation to its size and more than 10% in relation to groups detection. For this reason we decided to rely on the video footages[5] of the event. In the following, we will introduce several analysis performed taking into account video footages of the event: flow size and composition, and walking speed analysis.

### 3.1 Flow Size and Composition

The incoming pedestrian flow was composed of 1897 persons, which reached the venues of the admission test between 7:35 a.m. and 8:40 a.m.. The 34% of them arrived alone, while the 66% arrived in groups: 77% of groups were couples, 19% triples and 4% larger groups. In relation to the average low-level of density observed (0,05 pers/m$^2$), the analysis of the typical spatial patterns of walking groups shows that (see Tab. 1):

- 97% of couples is characterized by line-abreast pattern, 3% by river-like pattern;
- 66% of triples is characterized by line-abreast pattern, 33% by V-like pattern, and 1% by river-like pattern;
- groups with four members were usually split into subunits of dyads, triads, and single individuals: 30% of four-person groups is characterized by rhombus-like pattern (one person heading the group, followed by a dyad and a single person), 21% of the groups split into two dyads, 21% line-abrest pattern; 14% triads followed by a single person, 7% single individual followed by a triad, 7% by V-like pattern.

### 3.2 Walking Speed Analysis

In this section an analysis of a selected portion of the incoming flow is proposed, considering people that reached building U6 between 7:52 a.m. and 8:15 a.m. (39% of the total incoming flow - 745 persons). We propose below a data analysis of the walking speed of single pedestrians and groups, and, in particular, we focused on: level of service (referred to a precise area of 146,4 m$^2$, see Fig. 2b), group size, group spatial arrangement and gender of individuals and group members.

---

[5] The use of people tracking tools although it constitutes a useful contribution in detecting spatial movements of pedestrian within the crowd, is not enough calibrated to recognize proxemic indicators among group members.

**Table 1.** Percentages related to the typical spatial patterns of walking groups

|                       | Couples | Triples | Four Person Groups |
|-----------------------|---------|---------|--------------------|
| Line abreast pattern  | 97%     | 66%     | 21%                |
| River-like pattern    | 3%      | 1%      |                    |
| V-like pattern        |         | 33%     | 7%                 |
| Rhombus-like pattern  |         |         | 30%                |
| Two-dyad pattern      |         |         | 21%                |
| Triad + single pattern|         |         | 14%                |
| Single + triad pattern|         |         | 7%                 |

According to the existing HCM Walkway Level of Service Criteria [15], the flow rate was measured as the relationship among pedestrian/minute/meter: the average flow rate (5,09 ped/min/m) belongs to A-level, while several time intervals belong to B-level. It has to be underlined that the available space was huge in relation to the flow and, therefore, the level of service of the free flows were as low as expected. LOS-B were further analyzed in relation to flow composition: considering time intervals belong to B-level, we extracted a subset of 201 pedestrians. Because of large groups were not regularly detected, we focused the analysis on singles (50 single pedestrians - 25% of the subset), couples (50 couples - 50%) and triples (17 triples - 25%). A first statistic analysis was devoted to the identification of the average walking speed for singles (M = 1,38 m/s), couples (M = 1,30 m/s) and triples (M = 1,21 m/s). Moreover, a one-way analysis of variance (ANOVA see Tab. 3) showed that the size of groups affects walking speed in situation of medium density (p<0,05). More in detail, the differences in walking speed between singles and couples, singles and triples, couple and triples, were confirmed by a T-test analysis (p<0,01). In conclusion, the results showed that, at a low level of social density, the more the size of the pedestrian groups, the lower the walking speed was. Several further T-test analyses showed the following results:

- spatial patterns: no significant differences in walking speed (p>0,05) between line abreast and river-like couples, and among line-abreast, V-like and river-like triples;
- gender: no significant differences in walking speed (p>0,05) between females and males walking alone (i), same and mixed gender's couples (ii), same and mixed gender triples (iii).

## 4   Towards Entry Process Simulation

The last part of observation was related to the pedestrian dynamics of the entry process to the Building U6, in order to collect empirical data in different levels of density. In fact, the entry process consisted of two phases, the first being the incoming flow at the entrances of the Building U6 and gathering before the opening of the entrances of the venue; and the second being the access of

**ANOVA**

Walking_Speed

| | Sum of Squares | df | Mean Square | F | Sig. |
|---|---|---|---|---|---|
| Between Groups | ,435 | 2 | ,218 | 9,678 | ,000 |
| Within Groups | 2,563 | 114 | ,022 | | |
| Total | 2,998 | 116 | | | |

**Post Hoc Tests**

**Multiple Comparisons**

Walking_Speed
LSD

| (I) N_people | (J) N_people | Mean Difference (I–J) | Std. Error | Sig. | 95% Confidence Interval | |
|---|---|---|---|---|---|---|
| | | | | | Lower Bound | Upper Bound |
| 1 | 2 | ,08660* | ,02999 | ,005 | ,0272 | ,1460 |
| | 3 | ,17386* | ,04210 | ,000 | ,0905 | ,2573 |
| 2 | 1 | -,08660* | ,02999 | ,005 | -,1460 | -,0272 |
| | 3 | ,08726* | ,04210 | ,040 | ,0039 | ,1707 |
| 3 | 1 | -,17386* | ,04210 | ,000 | -,2573 | -,0905 |
| | 2 | -,08726* | ,04210 | ,040 | -,1707 | -,0039 |

*. The mean difference is significant at the 0.05 level.

**Fig. 3.** ANOVA analysis of the difference of walking speeds among singles, couples and triples (the analysis was performed by means of IBM SPSS Statistics v.18)

the participants to the building according to a scheduling managed by the University Authorities. Participants were sub-divided into groups accordingly to the classrooms where they had to perform the admission test. Groups of about twenty people at time where called and allowed to access the venue, this on the basis of the availability of the assigned classrooms. The entry process, therefore, was not homogeneous as entrances in use and waiting times could vary. During the entry process the density in proximity of the doors varied from high levels (4,4 p/m²) to low levels (<1 p/m²) in relation to the phases of the process. Considering the existing HCM queueing LOS [15], the level of service in proximity of the entrance varied from E-Level to A-level. Moreover, local variations of the level of density were detected in the environment, because of the dynamics triggered by called participants that needed to reach the doors crossing the standing crowd. This latter phenomenon is related to the emergence of lane formation, i.e., when groups of people move in opposite directions in a crowded environment, they spontaneously organize themselves into different lanes for each direction of travel [16].

The modeling of this specific dynamic is an on-going work. An agent based model has been implemented to simulate the scenario of the entry process. Simulation has been informed by observed data and it is now undergoing a validation phase. In Fig. 4a and Fig. 4b the real and simulated phenomenon of lane formation are shown. The platform used for the simulation is based on an agent based model in which the environment is discretized and managed according to Cellular Automata approach (see [17] for a complete explanation of the model): the floor field method is used to guide agents towards their goal, according to the behavioral rule related to avoid contact with obstacles and other agents. Fig. 4c, Fig. 4d, and Fig. 4e show respectively: the grid obtained by the discretization of the environment (the pentagonal blue shape represents the destinations of agents (external and inside the building), the green areas represent generation points of agents and red areas represents obstacles in the environment), the path grid obtained with floor field method and related to the blue rectangular shape that represent the area inside building U6, and the composition of the path field grids related to both destinations (external and internal area).

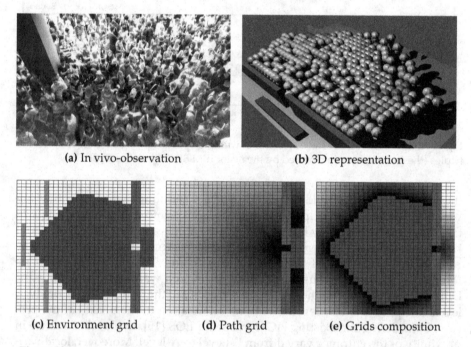

(a) In vivo-observation          (b) 3D representation

(c) Environment grid     (d) Path grid     (e) Grids composition

**Fig. 4.** Observation, modeling and simulation of the entry process to the Building U6

## 5   Discussion and Future Works

The analysis of the video footages of the event showed that: the incoming flow to the admission test was composed of almost two thousands of people and that a large majority of it was composed of groups (couples, triples, and groups of four members). The results achieved can be compared to others similar observations [9], taking into account the different context where the observations took place. These preliminary results point out that it can be useful to further investigate the pedestrian dynamics starting from groups, which constitute the basic elements that compose the crowd. Results show that at a low level of density the larger is the size of the pedestrian groups, the lower is the walking speed. At a high level of density, it was possible to detect lane formation, an emergent phenomenon related to pedestrian dynamics in crowded environments.

Moreover, it would be interesting to further investigate if overestimation error of counters was occasional or if it can be considered as systematic, considering different results achieved by observations performed in different contexts [18]. In the latter hypothesis, the specific percentage of error could be estimated by means of further investigations. This would help to apply correction to future data collection campaigns based on manual head counts.

Future works would be aimed to collect empirical data about the relationship between walking speed and proxemic spatial arrangement of walking groups in high-density situation (taking into account also age and gender differences, and larger groups). In high-density scenarios, the degree of freedom of spatial distribution of walking groups would be affected by the lack of space and the need to avoid physical contact with other individuals or groups. The entry process represents a typical scenario of high-density situation in which different and competitive behaviors between individuals and impromptu collectives (lanes) which are strictly linked with emergent complex dynamics that are difficult to be detected. For these reason those scenario can be supported by using simulation techniques.

Moreover, with the grant of the University Authority, the final aim of the survey will be the design of applicative strategies related to a more efficient management of people who attend every year the admission test. The use of simulation tools for pedestrian dynamics would be an useful approach to deeply investigate the phenomenon, and to study innovative strategies to support the management of entrance of people during this kind of test. To exceed this objective, we will collaborate with the University Authority to the development of planning standards related to pedestrian circulation dynamics, and physical layout of the environment in congested situations (such as the reduction of the entry queues to the venues, and the reduction of the delay in transfer times or ingress/egress, by means of the use of barriers or signposting).

**Acknowledgement.** This work is partially been funded by the University of Milano-Bicocca, within the project "Fondo d'Ateneo per la Ricerca - anno 2010/2011.

# References

1. Le Bon, G.: The crowd: A study of the popular mind. Macmillian (1897)
2. Reicher, S.: The psychology of crowd dynamics. Blackwell handbook of social psychology, pp. 182–208. Group processes (2001)
3. Turner, J.: Towards a cognitive redefinition of the social group. Cahiers de Psychologie Cognitive/Current Psychology of Cognition (1981)

4. Challenger, R., Clegg, C.W., Robinson M.: Understanding Crowd Behaviours, vol. 1. Cabinet Office (2009)
5. Hall, E.: The Hidden Dimension. Bodley Head (1969)
6. Aiello, J.: Human spatial behavior. Handbook of Environmental Psychology 1, 389–505 (1987)
7. Chattaraj, U., Seyfried, A., Chakroborty, P.: Comparison of pedestrian fundamental diagram across cultures. Arxiv preprint arXiv:0903.0149 (2009)
8. Baum, A., Paulus, P.: Crowding. In: Handbook of Environmental Psychology, vol. 1, pp. 533–570 (1987)
9. Costa, M.: Interpersonal distances in group walking. Journal of Nonverbal Behavior 34(1), 15–26 (2010)
10. Moussaïd, M., Perozo, N., Garnier, S., Helbing, D., Theraulaz, G.: The walking behaviour of pedestrian social groups and its impact on crowd dynamics. PLoS ONE 5 (April 2010)
11. Peacock, R., Kuligowski, E., Averill, J.: Pedestrian and evacuation dynamics. Springer (2011)
12. Kachroo, P., Al-Nasur, S., Wadoo, S., Shende, A.: Pedestrian dynamics: Feedback control of crowd evacuation. Springer (2008)
13. Bandini, S., Manzoni, S., Vizzari, G.: Situated cellular agents: A model to simulate crowding dynamics. IEICE Transactions on Information and Systems e Series D 87(3), 669–676 (2004)
14. Was, J.: Crowd Dynamics Modeling in the Light of Proxemic Theories. In: Rutkowski, L., Scherer, R., Tadeusiewicz, R., Zadeh, L.A., Zurada, J.M. (eds.) ICAISC 2010, Part II. LNCS, vol. 6114, pp. 683–688. Springer, Heidelberg (2010)
15. Milazzo, II., Rouphail, N., Hummer, J., Allen, D.: Transportation research board. National Research Council, Washington, DC 113 (2000)
16. Katsuhiro, N., Schadschneider, A., Kirchner, A.: CA approach to collective phenomena in pedestrian dynamics. In: International Conference on Cellular Automata for Research and Industry, pp. 239–248 (2002)
17. Bandini, S., Rubagotti, F., Vizzari, G., Shimura, K.: An Agent Model of Pedestrian and Group Dynamics: Experiments on Group Cohesion. In: Pirrone, R., Sorbello, F. (eds.) AI*IA 2011. LNCS, vol. 6934, pp. 104–116. Springer, Heidelberg (2011)
18. Diogenes, M., Greene-Roesel, R., Arnold, L., Ragland, D.: Pedestrian counting methods at intersections: a comparative study. Transportation Research Record: Journal of the Transportation Research Board 2002(-1), 26–30 (2007)

# Cellular Model of Room Evacuation
# Based on Occupancy and Movement Prediction

Pavel Hrabák*, Marek Bukáček, and Milan Krbálek

Faculty of Nuclear Sciences and Physical Engineering,
Czech Technical University in Prague, Czech Republic
{pavel.hrabak,bukacma2,milan.krbalek}@fjfi.cvut.cz

**Abstract.** The rule-based CA for simulating the evacuation process of single room with one exit is presented. Analogically to the Floor-Field model, the presented model is based on the movement on rectangular lattice, driven by the potential field generated by the exit. Several ideas of decision-making allowing the agent to choose an occupied cell are implemented, to reflect the observed behaviour in high densities. The velocity of pedestrians is represented by the updating frequency of the individuals. To calibrate model parameters, an experiment "leaving the room" was organized. Based on the observed behaviour, the influence of parameters is discussed and several modifications are suggested.

**Keywords:** Evacuation model, shape of pedestrian cloud, movement prediction.

## 1 Introduction

The model presented in this article is primarily designed to support the experimental study of pedestrian cloud formation in front of the exit during non-panic evacuation of single room without obstacles. Such a model should reflect important features observed in the real system ([6]). Several ways of describing pedestrian interaction by the so called "social force" appeared in [3], being suitable not only for evacuation purposes ([2]), but for other crowd features as well ([13]). Such approach is very attractive but mostly not applicable for fast, ideally real-time simulations. In this case, the computational power of Cellular Automata should be used. For elaborate summary of CA phenomena in pedestrian dynamics we refer the reader to [10] or [12].

The inspiration for the model presented in this article is the Floor-Field model ([5], [11]) and its implementation in F.A.S.T ([9], [10], [13]). Similarly to this model, the potential field is considered, but unlike these models the desired line formation is reached using "bounds" rather then the dynamical field. This is closely related to the possibility of choosing an occupied cell ([4]). To handle the problem of the diagonal movement symmetrization (discussed e.g. in [7], [9], [14], or [18]) the time penalization of diagonal movement is implemented.

---

* Corresponding author.

G.C. Sirakoulis and S. Bandini (Eds.): ACRI 2012, LNCS 7495, pp. 709–718, 2012.

Inspired by [8], [16], and [17], simple movement prediction is taken into account. Furthermore, essential change in the potential iso-curves solves elegantly the problem of wall repulsion mentioned in [1].

## 2    Description of the Model

The presented model is designed to describe and simulate the following situation: Consider a rectangle room with one exit (see Figure 1), containing given number of persons. People inside the room are motivated to exit the room as fast as possible.

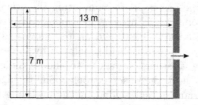

**Fig. 1.** Experiment was performed in a rectangle room 13 m long and 7 m wide

### 2.1    Space

The operational space of the simulation is divided in square-shaped cells with the edge length corresponding to 0.5 m. Each cell $x = (x_{\text{column}}, x_{\text{line}})$ may be either empty or occupied by one agent, which is indicated by the *occupation number* $n(x)$, where $n(x) = 0$ if the cell is empty and $n(x) = 1$ otherwise. Here we note, the exit cell $e$ is presented as always empty, keeping the rule that only one agent can enter the cell at the time. Each cell carries the *potential* $U(x)$ indicating the attractiveness of the cell for the agent (see [5] for details), which can be defined as

$$U(x) = -F \cdot \varrho(e, x) , \tag{1}$$

where $F$ is the constant determining the potential strength and $\varrho$ is a "distance" of the cell $x$ to the exit cell, being often chosen es Euclidian metric, i.e.

$$\varrho(e, x) = \left( |e_{\text{column}} - x_{\text{column}}|^2 + |e_{\text{line}} - x_{\text{line}}|^2 \right)^{\frac{1}{2}} . \tag{2}$$

For illustration purposes the coordinates of the exit in presented Figures are set to $e = (0, 0)$. To the static properties of the cell belongs the *cell type number* $t(x)$, which determines, whether the agent can enter the cell ($t(x) = 1$), e.g. floor cell, exit, or not ($t(x) = 0$), e.g. wall, barrier.

Besides the occupation number, the dynamical status of the cell is determined by the *prediction number* $r(x) \in \{0, 1, \ldots\}$, which denotes the number of pedestrians being predicted to enter the cell $x$. As we will see in (4), the maximum number of entering agents is 8. The principle of prediction will be explained below.

## 2.2   Decision Process – Choosing the Target Cell

The essence of the CA dynamics lies in the rules, according to which the agent chooses next target cell. In this project, the agent decides stochastically, i.e. the probability $p_d(x)$ of choosing the cell $x + d$ from the "target" surrounding $S_T(x)$ depends on the current state of the "reaction" surrounding $S_R(x)$:

$$p_d(x) = \Pr\{x + d | S_R(x)\} \ . \tag{3}$$

In this article, the surrounding according to Moore's definition with range 1 is chosen for both, the target and the reaction surrounding, i.e. $S_T(x) = S_R(x) = x + S_M$, where

$$S_M = \{(-1,1); (0,1); (1,1); (-1,0); (1,0); (-1,-1); (0,-1); (1,-1)\} \tag{4}$$

(see Figure 2). Here, $d \in S_M$ is referred to as *direction*. The definition (4) implies that the agent cannot choose his current position $x$ during the decision process (it does not mean that he *has* to move; see subsection 2.3).

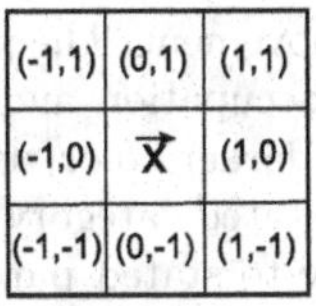

| (-1,1) | (0,1) | (1,1) |
|--------|-------|-------|
| (-1,0) | ⤩ | (1,0) |
| (-1,-1) | (0,-1) | (1,-1) |

**Fig. 2.** Moore's surrounding with range 1 of cell $x$, with indexation used in this article

Let us now denote $d_r(i)$ the currently predicted direction of the agent $i$. The movement prediction from the view of the agent $i$ then is

$$r_i'(d) = r(x + d) - \delta_{d, d_r(i)} \ , \tag{5}$$

where $\delta_{i,j}$ is the Kronecker's symbol. For all $d \in S_M$ the indicator $\tilde{r}_i(d) = \delta_{0, r_i'(d)}$ indicates, whether the cell $x + d$ is predicted to be entered by another agent than $i$. Using the notation presented above, the probability that the agent $i$ sitting in the cell $x$ chooses the direction $d$ is given as

$$p_d(x) = \mathcal{N} \cdot t(x + d) \cdot \exp\{\alpha \cdot U(x + d)\} \times$$
$$\times [1 - \beta \cdot n(x + d)] \cdot [1 - \gamma \cdot \tilde{r}_i(d)] \ , \tag{6}$$

where $\mathcal{N}$ is the normalization constant ensuring that $\sum_{d \in U_M} p_{d(x)} = 1$, and coefficients $\alpha$, $\beta$, $\gamma$, are coefficients of sensitivity to the potential, occupation number, and prediction number. These parameters are to be determined later and their influence is demonstrated in Figure 3.

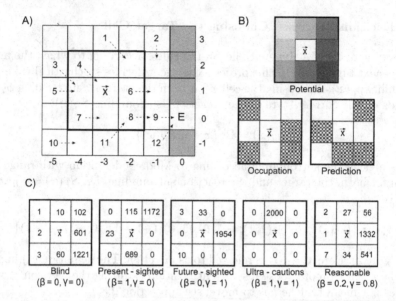

**Fig. 3.** Example illustrating principle of decision of one pedestrian. Subfigure A visualized wider surrounding of an agent in the cell $x$. Integer numbers represent agents and dashed arrows their predicted movement. The probability distribution $p_d(x)$ given by (6) is determined by potential, occupation and conflict prediction. The subfigure B visualizes these parameters. The darker color the higher potential (closer to exit), hatched area means penalization in stated category. The final cell attractivity strongly depends on coefficients of sensitivity to stated parameters. While potential represent static conditions, occupation and prediction of conflict reflect agent strategy. Final probabilities for different settings of sensitivity parameters $\beta, \gamma$ are shown in subfigure C. For each of them, 2000 decisions were divided into the cells according to (6). The values of potential strength is $F = 3$, and the potential sensitivity $\alpha = 1$. The potential sensitivity plays an important role in the heterogenous system ($\alpha_i$ differs from agent to agent), which is not the demonstrated case.

## 2.3   Agent Movement and Conflicts

The goal of this subsection is to explain the interaction of all agents within considered time period as a whole. One update of the system can be divided in four phases:

1. Selection of active agents
2. Decision process
3. Conflicts solution and motion
4. Time actualization

1. *Selection of active agents* means that only agents that are supposed to move at the considered time according to their frequency are activated (similar approach has been applied in [14] to handle the diagonal movement symmetrization). Each agent $i$ has its own updating frequency $f_i$ giving the number of

updates during one time unit. In principle, whenever the agent moves, or tries to move, at the time $t$, the time of his next activation is set to $t + f_i^{-1}$. The only situation, when this rule changes, is after the diagonal movement. Because the diagonal movent (i.e. in directions $(-1,1)$, $(1,1)$, $(-1,-1)$, or $(1,-1)$), is $\sqrt{2}$-times longer, it takes $\sqrt{2}$-times more time. This leads to the diagonal movement time-penalization, and the next activation time is set to be $t + qf_i^{-1}$, where $q$ is the rational approximation of $\sqrt{2}$, e.g $q = 3/2$. The rational approximation of $\sqrt{2}$ is necessary, if we want to keep "sufficiently" discrete structure of time for long period.

2. *Decision process* of each agent $i$ proceeds independently and consists in choosing the direction according to given rules explained in section 2.2. If the target cell is empty, the agent is added to the *waiting list* of the cell. If the target cell is occupied by another agent $j$ the *bound* of $i$ to $j$ is created. Agent $j$ is called the *blocker* and agent $i$ becomes *bounded*. The bound holds until the next update of the bounded agent $i$ or until the motion of the blocker $j$.

3. *Conflict solution and motion.* It is obvious that the two-dimensional structure of the problem connected to the independent decision of agents leads to variety of conflicts.

a) More agents choose the same unoccupied cell (the waiting list of some cell contains more then one agent). In this case, with probability $\mu$, playing role of the *friction parameter* (taken from [13]), the movement of all agents is disabled – non of the agents enters the cell. Otherwise, i.e. with probability $(1-\mu)$, one of the waiting agents is chosen randomly to enter the cell, the others don't move.

b) The agent chooses an occupied cell. In this case, the agent $i$ predicts the movement of the blocker $j$ and wants to take his place. If the blocker $j$ moves (i.e. is the single agent to enter the target cell or wins the conflict described in a)), the bounded agent $i$ tries to enter his target cell. Again, if he is the only bounded agent to $j$, there is no conflict. If more then one agent are bounded to $j$, the occurring conflict is solved analogically to the conflict a). This rule is applied recursively to all bounded agents.

Here we note, that during the conflict solution of type b) even a non-active agent can move, if he is bounded to the blocker. This is illustrated by an example in Figure 4. The principle of conflict solution and bounds during one update is illustrated in Figure 5.

# 3    Calibration of the Parameters

For parameters calibration, an experiment "leaving the room" was organized. 28 participants were arranged in a room with area 13m × 7m according to specific setting (see fig 6). After initiation, everyone started to move towards the doors.

Participants were only briefly instructed to follow three basic rules:

– leave the room as fast as possible
– do not run, just walk
– avoid physical contact

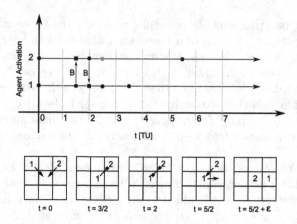

**Fig. 4.** Example illustrating principle of bounds. Two agents 1 and 2 with frequencies $f_1 = 1$, $f_2 = 1/2$ are activated in time t=0 and decide to enter the same cell $(0,0)$, agent 1 wins. Next update-time of agent 1 is set to $t = 3/2$ because of the diagonal movement; agent 2 waits until t=2. At $t = 3/2$ agent 1 decides to enter the cell $(1,1)$ occupied by agent 2 and gets bounded to 2. At $t = 2$ agent 2 decides to enter $(0,0)$ and gets bounded to agent 1. At $t = 5/2$ agent 1 cancels his bound and moves to $(1,0)$. Due to the bound, agent 2 moves to $(0,0)$ and his next-update time is set to $t = 5/2 + 2(3/2)$. The multiplication by $3/2$ is due to diagonal movement penalization.

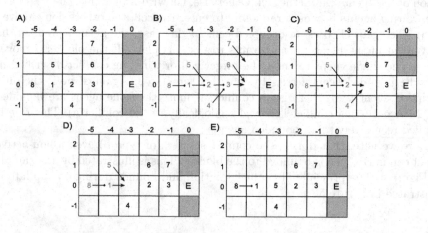

**Fig. 5.** Example illustrating principle of waiting lists and bounds during one update. 8 agents are depicted at their positions in subfigure A; every agent chooses the target cell and is either added in waiting list (triangles) or bounded to the blocker (squares) as shown in subfigure B. In this case, the agent 7 is in the waiting list of cell $(-1,1)$, agents 3 and 6 in the waiting list of cell $(-1,0)$, agent 4 and 2 are bounded to agent 2 etc.. After conflict solution in waiting lists (subfigure C) the bounds induce conflict in cell $(-3,0)$, which is solved analogically (subfigures D and E).

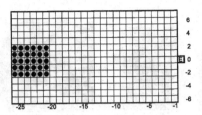

**Fig. 6.** Initial setting of the experiment, black circles represent pedestrians

These restrictions protected the participants from injuries, they were not motivated to furious evacuation. Following phenomenons were observed (see left part of Figure 7):

1. Pedestrians hold the initial formation and wait rather than walking around the crowd $\to$ occupation is not important ($\beta = 0.2$), but the prediction and bounding principle is significant ($\gamma = 0.8$).
2. Pedestrians are not forced to form a cluster near exit; multi-line (chaotic) queue is formed instead.
3. Unsolved conflicts appeared only rarely $\to$ low friction parameter $\mu$.
4. The movement is relatively deterministic ($F = 3$).

Furthermore, considering the essence of the experiment, strong moral barriers connected to social conventions avoided the participants to create semi-spherical cluster in front of the exit, which is expected in panic-like situations (see e.g. [2], [12], etc.). The participants were not motivated to leave the room earlier than others, therefore there has not been observed any drastic fight at the door. Such behaviour inspired us to deform the spherical form of potential iso-value curves to

$$\varrho(e, x) = \sqrt{\frac{10(e_{\text{line}} - x_{\text{line}})^2}{e_{\text{column}} - x_{\text{column}}} + (e_{\text{column}} - x_{\text{column}})^2} \ . \tag{7}$$

These potential iso-value curves are presented in Figure 8. Here we note that the equation (7) is applicable to define the required potential modification only for normal conditions without obstacles, where the average direction of pedestrian cloud centre towards exit is in the positive $x$ direction. The generalization to more complex geometries requires more detailed experimental study and further discussion.

At the end of experiment, running was allowed. Physical contact was still forbidden, but participants were not able to keep it. These physical forces caused that more than one pedestrian occupied one cell sometimes. On the other hand, expected phenomenons as the spherical shape of cluster near the exit and the inability to hold formation were observed (see right part of Figure 7). The movement under such panic-like conditions is described well using spherical potential (equations (1), (2)). To avoid conflict, runners were quite cautious; both occupation and prediction numbers were significant ($\beta = 0.95$, $\gamma = 0.95$).

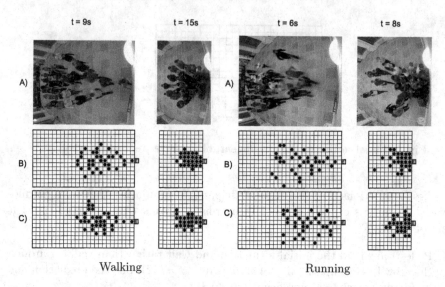

**Fig. 7.** Visualization of progress of one round, pedestrians walked (left) and run (right). Pictures A come from frontal camera, 9 (resp. 6) seconds after initialization, when first person approaches the exit and 15 (resp. 8) seconds after initialization, when compact cluster is developed. Subfigures B project previous pictures to lattice representation and subfigures C represent corresponding realization of the simulation. One time unit of the simulation corresponds to 0.7 s. The time interval between creating the cluster and completing the evacuation was used to create the time-span of the model, because this article focuses on the shape of the cluster in front of the exit. Mean actualization frequency was set to 1 time unit.

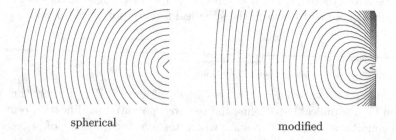

**Fig. 8.** Demonstration of suggested potential

## 4   Conclusion

A concept of CA model of pedestrian crowd modeling has been introduced, which brings new elements in Floor Field model. The principle of waiting list and bounds has been defined. This allows the agent to choose an occupied cell. The innovative idea of creating bound to the blocking agent reflects the observed line formation and spontaneous queuing typical for the crowd movement with negligible effect of panic. We believe that the proposed mechanism of bounds is very close to the unconscious behaviour of pedestrians in high densities.

The pedestrian velocity is represented by the updating frequency being in this article defined in time discrete way. Nonetheless, it is possible to generalize it in the time continuous way, which meets the presumption that the pedestrian desired velocity is Gaussian distributed.

For the calibration of model parameters the experiment "leave the room" has been performed. Key information has been found to calibrate model parameters to the non-panic simulation of room evacuation. Based on the measured data, the shape of the potential iso-value curves needs to be modified due to the effect of moral barriers connected to social conventions, when the situation is not intensely panic, e.g. controlled evacuation. Proposed rules including bounds and prediction improve the model in spontaneous line formation, but only the simulation with modified potential corresponds to the observed non-spherical shape of the pedestrian cloud in front of the exit.

Here we note that only the macroscopic behaviour represented by the shape and velocity of the pedestrian "cloud" was considered for the calibration of parameters. The microscopic behaviour of single individuals slightly differs from the observed behaviour during the experiment. Although the model has been designed to describe important phenomena of one specific experimental study, we believe that ideas presented here can be used for simulating the movement in more complex situations.

**Acknowledgements.** This work was supported by the grant SGS12/197/ OHK4/3T/14 and by the MSMT research program under the contract MSM 6840770039. We would like to thank to members of research Group of Applied Mathematics and Stochastics, especially Juraj Panek, for significant help with the experiment preparation and data processing.

# References

1. Georgoudas, I.G., Koltsidas, G., Sirakoulis, G.C., Andreadis, I.T.: A Cellular Automaton Model for Crowd Evacuation and Its Auto-Defined Obstacle Avoidance Attribute. In: Bandini, S., Manzoni, S., Umeo, H., Vizzari, G., et al. (eds.) ACRI 2010. LNCS, vol. 6350, pp. 455–464. Springer, Heidelberg (2010)
2. Helbing, D., Farkas, I., Vicsek, T.: Simulating dynamical features of escape panic. Nature 407, 487–490 (2000)
3. Helbing, D., Molnar, P.: Social force model for pedestrian dynamics. Phys. Rev. E 51(5), 4282–4286 (1995)
4. Henein, C.M., White, T.: Macroscopic effects of microscopic forces between agents in crowd models. Physica A 373, 694–712 (2007)
5. Kirchner, A., Schadschneider, A.: Simulation of evacuation processes using a bionics-inspired cellular automaton model for pedestrian dynamics. Physica A 312, 260–276 (2002)
6. Klüpfel, H., Schreckenberg, M., Meyer-König, T.: Models for Crowd Movement and Egress Simulation. In: Traffic and Granular Flow 2003, pp. 357–372 (2005)

7. Klüpfel, H.: A Cellular Automaton Model for Crowd Movement and Egress Simulation. PhD. thesis, Universität Duisburg-Essen, Germany (2003)
8. Kretz, T., Kaufman, M., Schreckenberg, M.: Counterflow Extension for the F.A.S.T.-Model. In: Umeo, H., Morishita, S., Nishinari, K., Komatsuzaki, T., Bandini, S. (eds.) ACRI 2008. LNCS, vol. 5191, pp. 555–558. Springer, Heidelberg (2008)
9. Kretz, T., Schreckenberg, M.: The F.A.S.T.-Model. In: El Yacoubi, S., Chopard, B., Bandini, S. (eds.) ACRI 2006. LNCS, vol. 4173, pp. 712–715. Springer, Heidelberg (2006)
10. Kretz, T.: Pedestrian Traffic, Simulation and Experiments. PhD. thesis, Universität Duisburg-Essen, Germany (2007)
11. Nishinari, K., Kirchner, A., Namazi, A., Schadschneider, A.: Extended floor field CA model for evacuation dynamics. IEICE Trans. on Inf. and Syst. E87-D, 726–732 (2004)
12. Schadschneider, A., Chowdhury, D., Nishinari, K.: Stochastic transport in complex systems. Elsevier Science, Amsterdam (2010)
13. Schadschneider, A., Seyfried, A.: Empirical results for pedestrian dynamics and their implication for cellular automata models. In: Timmermans, H. (ed.) Pedestrian Behavior: Models, Data Collection and Applications. Emerald Group Publishing, Bingley (2009)
14. Schultz, M., Lehmann, S., Fricke, H.: A discrete microscopic model for pedestrian dynamics to manage emergency situations in airport terminals. In: Waldau, N., Gattermann, P., Knoflacher, H., Schreckenberg, M. (eds.) Pedestrian and Evacuation Dynamics 2005, pp. 369–375. Springer, Heidelberg (2007)
15. Seyfried, A., Portz, A., Schadschneider, A.: Phase Coexistence in Congested States of Pedestrian Dynamics. In: Bandini, S., Manzoni, S., Umeo, H., Vizzari, G., et al. (eds.) ACRI 2010. LNCS, vol. 6350, pp. 496–505. Springer, Heidelberg (2010)
16. Steffen, B.: A Modification of the Social Force Model by Foresight. In: Klingsch, W.W.F., Rogsch, C., Schadschneider, A., Schreckenberg, M. (eds.) Pedestrian and Evacuation Dynamics 2008, pp. 677–682. Springer, Heidelberg (2010)
17. Sumaa, Y., Yanagisawab, D., Nishinari, K.: Anticipation effect in pedestrian dynamics: Modeling and experiments. Physica A 391, 248–263 (2012)
18. Yamamoto, K., Kokubo, S., Nishinari, K.: Simulation for pedestrian dynamics by real-coded cellular automata (RCA). Physica A 379, 654–660 (2007)

# On Validation of the SIgMA.CA Pedestrian Dynamics Model with Bottleneck Flow

Ekaterina Kirik[1,2] and Tat'yana Vitova[1]

[1] Institute of Computational Modelling SB RAS,
Krasnoyarsk, Akademgorodok, Russia, 660036
kirik@icm.krasn.ru
[2] Siberian Federal University, Krasnoyarsk, Russia

**Abstract.** In this paper a connection of a width of a bottleneck and unidirectional virtual people flow by the SIgMA.CA pedestrian movement model (stochastic Cellular Automata model) is investigated. Specific and full flow rates for different model parameters, initial densities, and bottleneck width are presented and discussed.

**Keywords:** bottleneck, (specific) flow rate, pedestrian dynamics, cellular automata, transition probabilities.

## 1 Introduction

Bottlenecks on pedestrian facilities gives the most considerable contribution to the upper limit of evacuation way capacity. Bottlenecks are reasons of jams. Up to now literature on pedestrian dynamics does not give one quantitative answer on bottleneck questions. Qualitative descriptions have common points. Many authors investigated bottleneck flows in experimental environments [6]. They observed a changing capacity of the bottleneck with changing width, trajectories of pedestrians passing the bottleneck, and corresponding self-organization phenomenon. Figure 1 presents empirical data by different authors for unidirectional flow under normal conditions, some initial densities and geometry[1]; data were taken from the web resource http://ped-net.org. Diagrams show a common feature that is an increasing of the flow rate with the bottleneck width increasing. But specific flow rates behavior differs with respect to author.

Figure 2 presents flow rate and specific flow rate versus width of the bottleneck for different densities from Predtechenskii and Milinskii [4].

One can see qualitatively the same behavior of the flow rate, it goes up with the bottleneck width increasing. The specific flow rate is given almost independently on the bottleneck width. Lines only differ with respect to the density in front of the bottleneck.

Here we present investigations of our SIgMA.CA model dynamics in the bottlenecks. The model is stochastic discrete CA model and supposes short-term

---

[1] It was shown that exact geometry of the bottleneck is of only minor influence on the flow [5].

G.C. Sirakoulis and S. Bandini (Eds.): ACRI 2012, LNCS 7495, pp. 719–727, 2012.

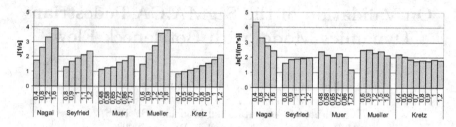

**Fig. 1.** Empirical flow rate (left) and specific flow rate (right) versus bottleneck width, [m], for different authors

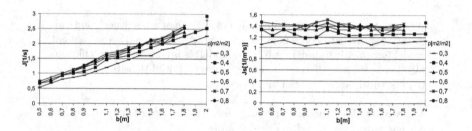

**Fig. 2.** Flow rate (left) and specific flow rate (right) versus bottleneck width, [m], of Predtechenskii and Milinskii

decisions made by the pedestrians [1,2]. A possibility to move according the shortest path and the shortest time strategies are implemented to the model. From the comprehensive theory of pedestrian dynamics [6] such model may be refereed to tactical level.

We investigated flow rate under different conditions: constant initial densities (in front of the bottleneck) versus different widths of the bottleneck, constant widths of the bottleneck versus different initial densities, model parameters versus different widths of the bottleneck and different initial densities.

In the next section the model is presented. Section 3 contains description of the case study and results obtained. We conclude with a summary.

## 2    Description of the Model

### 2.1    Space and Initial Conditions

The space (plane) is known and sampled into cells $40cm \times 40cm$ in size which can either be empty or occupied by one pedestrian (particle) only (index $f_{ij} = \{0, 1\}$). Cells may be occupied by walls (index $w_{ij} = \{0, 1\}$) and other nonmovable obstacles[2].

---

[2] Here and below under "obstacle" we mean only nonmovable obstacles (walls, furniture). People are never called "obstacle".

The model imports idea of a map (static floor field $S$) from floor field (FF) CA model [7] that provides pedestrians with information about ways to exits. Our field S increases radially from exit cells. It doesn't evolve with time and isn't changed by the presence of the particles.

A target point for each pedestrian is the nearest exit. Each particle can move to one of four its next-neighbor cells or to stay in present cell (the von Neumann neighborhood) at each discrete time step $t \to t+1$; i.e., $v_{max} = 1[step]$.

A direction of the movement of each particle at each time step is random and determined in accordance with the distribution of transition probabilities and transition rules.

## 2.2 Update Rules and Transition Probability

A scheme typical of the stochastic CA models is used. At the first stage, some preliminary calculations are made. Then, at each time step the transition probabilities are calculated, and the directions are selected. In the case, when there are more than one candidate to occupy a cell, a conflict resolution procedure is applied. Finally, a simultaneous transition of all the particles is made.

In our case, the *preliminary step* includes the calculation of FF $S$. Each cell $S_{i,j}$ stores the information on the shortest discreet distance to the nearest exit.

The probabilities of movement from cell $(i, j)$ to, e.g., up neighbor is[3]

$$p_{i-1,j} = \frac{\tilde{p}_{i-1,j}}{N_{i,j}} = N_{i,j}^{-1} \exp\left[k_S \triangle S_{i-1,j} - k_P F_{i-1,j}(r_{i-1,j}^*) - \right.$$
$$\left. - k_W(1 - \frac{r_{i-1,j}^*}{r})\tilde{1}(\triangle S_{i-1,j} - \max \triangle S_{i,j})\right](1 - w_{i-1,j}); \quad (1)$$

where

- $N_{i,j} = \tilde{p}_{i-1,j} + \tilde{p}_{i,j+1} + \tilde{p}_{i+1,j} + \tilde{p}_{i,j-1}$;
- $\triangle S_{i-1,j} = S_{i,j} - S_{i-1,j}$, $k_S \geq 0$ is the (model) field $S$ sensitive parameter (the higher $k_S$, the better directed the movement);
- $\max \triangle S_{i,j} = \max \triangle S_{i-1,j}, \triangle S_{i,j+1}, \triangle S_{i+1,j}, \triangle S_{i,j-1}$;
- $r > 0$ is the visibility radius (model parameter) representing the maximum distance (number of cells) at which the people density and obstacles influence on the probability in the given direction;
- $r_{i-1,j}^*$ is the distance to the nearest obstacle in the given direction ($r_{i-1,j}^* \leq r$);
- $F_{i-1,j}$ is people (dimensionless) density in this direction which lies within $[0, 1]$, see [2];
- $k_P$ is the (model) people sensitivity parameter which determines the effect of the people density, the higher parameter $k_P$, the more pronounced the shortest time strategy;
- $k_W \geq k_S$ is the (model) wall sensitivity parameter which determines the effect of walls and obstacles.

---

[3] Probabilities $p_{i,j+1}, p_{i+1,j}, p_{i,j-1}$ are calculated similarly. $p_{i,j} = 0$: the probability of retaining the current position is not calculated directly. Nevertheless, the decision rules are organized so that such opportunity could be taken.

**The decisions rules** are the following:

1. If $N_{i,j} = 0$, motion is forbidden.
2. If $N_{i,j} \neq 0$, target cell $(l, m)^*$, $(l, m)^* \in I = \{(i - 1, j), (i, j + 1), (i + 1, j), (i, j - 1), (i, j)\}$ is chosen randomly using the transition probabilities.
3. (a) If $N_{i,j} \neq 0$ and $(1 - f_{l,m}^*) = 1$, then target cell $(l, m)^*$ is fixed.
   (b) If $N_{i,j} \neq 0$ and $(1 - f_{l,m}^*) = 0$, then the cell $(l, m)^*$ is not available as it is occupied by other particle. In such case $p_{i,j} = \sum\limits_{(y,z) \in I : (1 - f_{y,z}) = 0} p_{y,z}$
   and $p_{y,z} = 0 \forall (y, z) \in I : (1 - f_{y,z}) = 0$. Again, the target cell is chosen randomly using the transformed probability distribution.
4. Whenever two or more pedestrians have the same target cell, movement of all the involved pedestrians is denied with probability $\mu$. One of the candidates moves to the desired cell with the probability $1 - \mu$. The pedestrian allowed to move is chosen randomly.
5. The pedestrians that are allowed to move perform motion to the target cell.
6. The pedestrians that appear in the exit cells leave the room.

The above rules are applied to all the particles at the same time; i.e., parallel update is used.

## 2.3   Discussion on the Model Parameters

The simplest shape of the way, the strait corridor, supposes that strategy of the shortest path coincides with the shortest time strategy for the whole way. Geometry of the way does not influence on the movement, and the shape of the flow and velocity are only determined by the density. To realize only the shortest path strategy the model density sensitive parameter $k_P$ has to be low ($k_P < k_S$).

If there are turns on the way, congestions appear before turns (depending on density), and some people start to use detours facilities (that means to follow the shortest time strategy) and not to wait when the shortest path will free. In the model the shortest time strategy is pronounced under $k_P \gg k_S$. The mechanism is the following. If the shortest path direction has a high density, $F(r^*) \approx 1$, the probability of this direction goes down. At the same time, the probability ($F(r^*) \ll 1$) of direction that is more favorable for movement rises. In this case detours around high-density regions has the largest probability. One can say that the model is density adjustable.

Low visibility radius $r$ may be interpreted like a moving in dark or smoke conditions. The higher $r$ the more sensitive model to the nearest people density and obstacles.

## 3   Numerical Experiments

### 3.1   Experimental Setup

To investigate the SIgMA.CA model's flow rate through the bottleneck under different conditions there was used a geometry in the figure 1 presented. This geometry was adopted from [5].

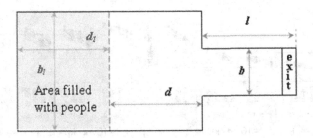

**Fig. 3.** Geometry set up. Constant parameters are: $b_l = 4\,m$, $l = 0.4\,m$, $d = 0\,m$

Initially $N$ people filled grey area of length $d_l$, $[m]$, with initial density $\rho_0$, then they leave the geometry through the bottleneck of width $b$, $[m]$.

There were made different numerical experiments under different initial conditions (density, $N$, $b$, model parameters [4]). For each set of conditions (parameters) 500 runs were made. As an estimate of the evacuation time ($T_{st}$, [step]) a mode of a time density distribution was used. Full flow rate $J = \frac{N}{T_{st}}$, $[\frac{pers}{step}]$, and specific flow rate $J_s = \frac{N}{T_{st}*b}$, $[\frac{pers}{step*m}]$, were investigated [5].

## 3.2 Constant Initial Densities $\rho_0 = 0.5$ and Different Widths of the Bottleneck $b$

In this experiment there were placed 20, 40, 60, and 120 particles with constant initial density $\rho_0 = 0.5$, $[\frac{m^2}{m^2}]$, that is approximately $\rho_0 \approx 3.125 = 0.5/0.16$, $\frac{pers}{m^2}]$. This means that geometry parameter $d_l$ was increased with changing $N$: 1.6 m, 3.2 m, 4.8 m, 6.6 m correspondingly.

Figure 4 presents dependance of the flow rate and specific flow rate versus number of particles. One can see that sensitivity of the flow rate to $N$ grows gradually with increasing $b$. Note that after start congestion appears in front of the bottleneck, density of congestion depends on $b$. The smallest width $b = 0.8$ m gives the highest density, and the flow rate is independent on initial number of particles. The lower density after start in front of the bottleneck, the dependent on $N$ the flow rate.

Width $b = 4$ gives the most pronounced dependence. In this case bottleneck is absent in fact ($b_l = b = 4$ m), and initial density ($\rho_0 = 0.5$) is approximately

---

[4] In all experiments we investigated the directed movement with $k_S = 4$; the attitude to walls was "loyal", $k_W = k_S$, $\mu = 0$. The following parameters were varied: $k_P = 2, 4, 10$; $r = 1, 10$. Combinations of these parameters reproduce the different people movement: from using only one strategy (the shortest path) when $k_P < k_S$ to combining both strategies if $k_P > k_S$.

[5] Pure CA model's units $[\frac{pers}{step}]$ and $[\frac{pers}{step*m}]$ are used here. It is motivated by a fact that to present flows in usual physical units $[\frac{pers}{s}]$ and $[\frac{pers}{s*m}]$ time scaling procedure is necessary. But time scaling for CA models is not close problem nowadays, examples one can see in [3]. And each time scaling procedure gives additional noise. Thus in this investigation our goal is to operate and estimate pure results of the model.

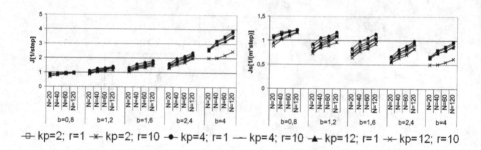

**Fig. 4.** Flow rate (left) and specific flow rate (right) versus initial number of people $N$ ($\rho_0 = 0.5$) for different $b$. Variety of curves corresponds sets of model parameters.

maintained during all simulation [6]. One can expect independent on $N$ flow rate but stochasticity of the model gives contribution; and for small $N$ it is pronounced most of all. An expected (one may say theoretical) flow rate value is $5\left[\frac{pers}{step}\right]$ [7]. For $N = 20$ the highest flow rate is $2.7\left[\frac{pers}{step}\right]$ and is given by average evacuation time $T_{st} = 7, 4$ steps; at the same time the minimal theoretical evacuation time for this case is 4 steps [8]. Specific flow rate for $N = 120$ and $b = 4$ (see fig. 4 (right)) corresponds results presented in [3].

Figure 5 presents the same results but in other way. Flow rate (left graphic) and specific flow rate (right graphic) are given versus bottleneck width for each $N$. Such presentation makes clear a fact that model dynamics is sensitive to bottleneck. On can observe that (for each $N$) for equal $\Delta b$ (pairs $b = 0.8$, $b = 2.4$ and $b = 2.4$, $b = 4$) the largest flow rate increment is given by pair $b = 2.4$ and $b = 4$ (recall that the width of the corridor $b_l = 4$).

For each $N$ specific flow rate goes down with the increasing $b$ except maximal width $b = 4$, see fig. 5 right. Case $N = 120$ gives the lightest dependence of specific flow rate versus $b$.

This simulation experiments show that stochasticity of the model gives some contribution to the evacuation time. If the expected time is comparable with stochastic contribution that varies from 4 to 7 steps in each experiment then model dynamics could not be catched carefully [9]. Experimental data [5] gives similar results. For small $N = 20$, $N = 40$ specific flow independently varies with increasing $b$. The bigger $N$, the more reliable simulation results and real experiments data.

As for model parameters, the worst set for such geometry is $k_p = 12$, $r = 10$ that gives the lowest flow rate.

---

[6] It is due to exclusive principle that is used in the model and initial particles positions as on a chessboard.

[7] Initially there were 5 particles in one row; and recall initial density was $\rho_0 = 0.5$.

[8] For $N = 120$ the highest flow rate is given by average evacuation time $T_{st} = 30$ steps; the minimal theoretical evacuation time for this case is 24 steps.

[9] It is true for small $N = 20$, $N = 40$.

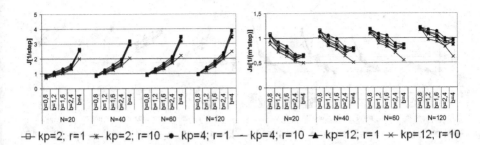

**Fig. 5.** Flow rate (left) and specific flow rate (right) versus bottleneck width $b$ for different $N$ ($\rho_0 = 0.5$). Variety of curves corresponds sets of model parameters.

## 3.3 Different Initial Densities $\rho_0$ and Different Widths of the Bottleneck $b$

A set of initial densities, $[\frac{m^2}{m^2}]$, was considered: 0.25, 0.5, 0,75, 1. There were placed 30, 60, 90, 120 particles correspondingly in the initial area.

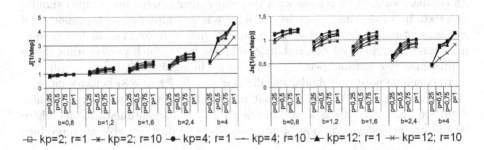

**Fig. 6.** Flow rate (left) and specific flow rate (right) versus initial densities for different bottleneck width $b$. Curves are for different sets of model parameters.

Figure 6 presents dependance of the flow rate and specific flow rate versus initial density $\rho_0$. One can see that sensitivity of the flow rate to initial density grows gradually with the increasing $b$. For those $b$ which give real bottlenecks graphics are very close to the previous case (compare with fig. 4 left). This fact shows that situations (congestions) in front of the bottleneck develop according to similar scenarios, and there is a capacity of each bottleneck width. For $b = 4$ specific flow rate coincides qualitatively [10] with results in [3] for the same model.

Figure 7 presents the same results but in other way. Flow rate (left graphic) and specific flow rate (right graphic) are given versus bottleneck width for each initial density $\rho_0$. Such presentation confirms statement on bottleneck capacity: shapes of the flow rate and specific flow rate are almost independent on initial density ($\rho_0 = 0.5, 0.75, 1$).

---

[10] Low numbers of particles make model stochasticity pronounced.

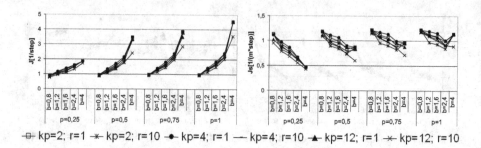

**Fig. 7.** Flow rate (left) and specific flow rate (right) versus bottleneck width $b$ for different initial densities $\rho_0$. Curves are for different sets of model parameters.

## 4    Conclusion

The experimental data that are presented in the Introduction show flow rate increasing and approximately constant specific flow rate with increasing bottleneck width. Density in front of the bottleneck is supposed more or less constant. To compare simulation results with this experimental data we grouped simulation data in a following principle: changing $b$ is accompanied with proportional changing of initial density. By this means we may rely on more or less permanent conditions in front of the bottleneck, see fig. 8. Such presentation shows approximately constant specific flow rate with increasing bottleneck width.

To conclude note that model specific flow rate (see figure 8) behaves more or less permanent with increasing $b$ that quantitatively agrees with experimental data, see fig. 1, 2. This is a confirmation that cellular automata model where people are considered as noncompressible hard bodies are able to reproduce

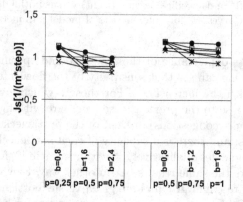

**Fig. 8.** Specific flow rate under comparable conditions in front of the bottleneck. Curves are for different sets of model parameters.

people movement phenomena in a congested area. Time scaling task (to deal with physical units like [pers/m/s]) is still waiting to be solved.

**Acknowledgment.** This work is supported by the Integration project of SB RAS, number 49/2012.

# References

1. Kirik, E., Yurgel'yan, T., Krouglov, D.: The Shortest Time and/or the Shortest Path Strategies in a CA FF Pedestrian Dynamics Model. Journal of Siberian Federal University, Mathematics and Physics 2(3), 271–278 (2009)
2. Kirik, E., Yurgel'yan, T., Krouglov, D.: On realizing the shortest time strategy in a CA FF pedestrian dynamics model. Cybernetics and Systems 42(1), 1–15 (2011)
3. Kirik, E., Yurgel'yan, K., Krouglov, D.: On Time Scaling and Validation of a Stochastic CA Pedestrian Dynamics Model. In: Peacock, R.D., Kuligowski, E.D., Averill, J.D. (eds.) Proceedings of the International Conferenc "Pedestrian and Evacuation Dynamics", pp. 819–822 (2011)
4. Predtechenskii, V.M., Milinskii, A.I.: Planing for foot traffic flow in buildings. American Publishing, New Dehli; Translation of "Proektirovanie Zhdanii s Uchetom organizatsii Dvizheniya Lyudskikh potokov. Stroiizdat Publishers, Moscow (1969, 1978)
5. Seyfried, A., Rupprecht, T., Passon, O., Steffen, B., Klingsch, W., Boltes, M.: New insights into pedestrian flow through bottlenecks. Transportation Science 43, 395–406 (2009)
6. Schadschneider, A., Klingsch, W., Kluepfel, H., Kretz, T., Rogsch, C., Seyfried, A.: Evacuation Dynamics: Empirical Results, Modeling and Applications. In: Encyclopedia of Complexity and System Science. Springer, vol. 3, pp. 3142–3192 (2009)
7. Schadschneider, A., Seyfried, A.: Validation of CA models of pedestrian dynamics with fundamental diagrams. Cybernetics and Systems 40(5), 367–389 (2009)

# Modeling of Walking through Pathways and a Stairway by Cellular Automata Based on the Guideline for Evacuation

Shigeyuki Koyama, Nobuhiko Shinozaki, and Shin Morishita

Yokohama National University
Graduate School of Environment and Information Sciences
79-7 Tokiwadai, Hodogaya-ku, Yokohama 240-8501 Japan
mshin@ynu.ac.jp

**Abstract.** Walking through a pathway, a T-junction, and a stairway was modeled by Cellular Automata, introducing local neighbor and transition rules based on the Public Guideline for Evacuation. Setting two types of "personal space" for each pedestrian in one direction and 45° inclined direction, a person moves to the next cell at some probability in 24 directions by interpolation of these two patterns. The moving probability was evaluated just for the crowd flow through a straight pathway so that the relationship between density and flow rate might agree with that proposed by the Guideline. It is shown that these flow models can be applied to inclined 24 direction pathways. As the combination of straight pathways, the crowd flow through T-junction was simulated, which showed good agreement with the estimated results according to the Guideline. The flow in a stairway was also simulated in the present paper.

**Keywords:** Evacuation, Modeling, Guideline, Inclined pathway, Stairway.

## 1 Introduction

An Evacuation simulation is very important to evaluate the duration time required to rush away from a room to outside of buildings. Especially in Japan, we encountered the earthquake disaster followed by tsunami on March 11, 2011. More than 15,800 died and 26,000 were injured. 3,000 people were not discovered yet. In addition we were damaged by a big earthquake occurred in Kansai district (west part of Japan) on January 17,1995. At that time, more than 6,400 people were died and 43,000 were injured. Even without these kinds of natural disaster, we always encounter various risks in case of fire of houses or buildings. In such cases, quick escape may be most important to survive.

There have been numerous studies on evacuation simulation as an application of Cellular Automata (CA) or Multi-Agent Simulation [1]-[6]. Yuichiro Naka simulated the passenger flow in the concourse of stations on macroscopic and also microscopic point of view by introducing several local neighbor rules in the early 1970s [1]. Dirk Helbing, et al. presented a model of pedestrian behavior to study the mechanisms of

G.C. Sirakoulis and S. Bandini (Eds.): ACRI 2012, LNCS 7495, pp. 728–737, 2012.

panic and jamming by uncoordinated motion in crowds [3]. One of the authors proposed several local neighbor rules for evacuation simulation by Cellular Automata [4]. Nishinari, et al. presented the floor field model for pedestrian dynamics introducing wall potentials and simulated evacuation flow from a room with several exits [6].

Though Cellular Automata model may be a strong tool for pedestrian flow simulations, the local neighbor rules or state transition rules introduced in the simulation might include subjectivity of the program engineer who completed the simulation. As a guarantee of the accuracy of simulation results, some of the previous authors demonstrated experiments where many voluntary subjects walked along several paths and the required time and position in a space were recorded.

In the present paper, the local neighbor and transition rules for a pedestrian to step forward were determined as simple as possible, in the way that a person may choose the next cell to proceed by just physical interaction among the other persons surrounding him/her. Peculiar characteristics of a person were excluded and all the people were adapted by the same rules. All the people may evacuate from the buildings through halls or stairs in good order without any personal troubles. The flow of crowds were adapted to the density-flow rate diagram and density-velocity diagram provided by the government by adjusting the probability introduced to settle the velocity of a person [7]-[9]. Several typical examples of flow patterns; through the inclined straight pathway, through a T-junction of pathways and through stairway were presented.

## 2    Cellular Automata Model

### 2.1    Cell Division

The floor plan was divided into cells of 30 x 30 cm, and at most one person was permitted to stay on one cell. The unit length of "30 cm" is very important in Japan, because typical width of doors or pathways is designed by multiple of 30 cm. Two persons were not permitted to stand on the adjacent cells to each other, because the cross sectional area of a body was estimated 60 x 30 cm. Then the maximum density in this model was about 5.5 persons/m$^2$. The typical state variable of each cell was "pedestrian, "vacant" or "obstacle" (such as wall, pillar or furniture), and a little more precise state variable were added.

### 2.2    Direction Vector

A person on a cell had the direction vector which indicated the direction of movement. A pedestrian on a cell could move in the eight directions including forward, backward, right, left and every 45 degree directions. When the direction of a pedestrian was not coincide to the eight directions mentioned above, the pedestrian should choose one of the eight directions according to the probability calculated by the following equations

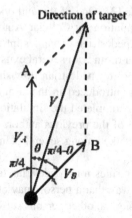

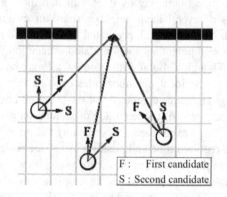

**Fig. 1.** Direction vector          **Fig. 2.** Cells to proceed

$$prob(A) = a/(a+b)$$
$$prob(B) = b/(a+b)$$
$$a = \sqrt{2}|V|\cos(\pi/4+\theta), \quad b = \sqrt{2}|V|\cos(\pi/4-\theta)$$

where, $prob$(A) and $prob$(B) was the probability to select direction A and B. The direction vector $V_A$ and $V_B$ are shown in Fig. 1. The vector $V$ was divided into two vectors coinciding to two directions from prescribed eight directions. The length of the vector $V_A$ and $V_B$ might be determined by direction of the original vector $V$. As shown in Fig. 2, each pedestrian had the cells to proceed by the first and second priority.

## 2.3    Walking Velocity

When a pedestrian walks along a free space without any constraint, the velocity is estimated as up to 1.3 m/s, the value of which has been supported by several documents edited by the Japanese government. As a person was set to proceed one cell in each time step, then the time step was estimated as 0.3/1.3 = 0.23 s in physical meaning. The process of walking, a person moved to the next cell or not, was governed by probability. When the walking velocity was less than 1.3 m/s, the probability of movement was calculated as v/1.3. Furthermore, when the direction vector was inclined to 45 degree, the probability was decreased as $1/\sqrt{2}$, to keep the free velocity as 1.3 m/s.

As described in section 2.2, a person should select one of the eight directions to proceed in each time step. According to the fact that an average stride of adult men was 75-80 cm, and 2 or 3 time steps in this simulation corresponded to the time for one walking step of pedestrians, it was possible for a pedestrian to proceed 8 x 3 = 24 directions in one actual walking step at maximum as shown in Fig. 3. In this case, the velocity of a person in eight directions; forward, backward, right, left, and every 45

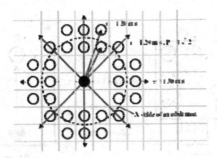

**Fig. 3.** Walking directions and speed of a pedestrian

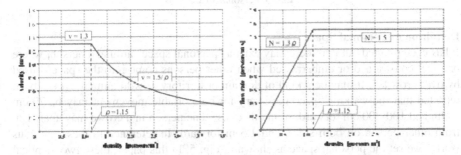

**Fig. 4.** Density-velocity diagram and density-flow rate diagram

degree directions was 1.3 m/s, while that was 1.2 m/s in other directions, which was considered as almost the same velocity.

### 2.4    Crowd Flow

**Typical Idea of Modeling**
In the crowd flow, the velocity of pedestrians may decrease as the density of crowds increased. According to the previous papers, the following tendency were observed.

- The transition of crowd flow state from free walking state may appear when the density exceeds 1 person/m$^2$.
- The relation among the parameters flow rate (f), velocity (v), and density ($\rho$) may be described as f = $\rho$ x v, when the density of crowd is up to 4 persons/m$^2$.
- Under the condition above, the flow rate becomes almost 1.5 person/m s.
- The flow rate at narrow passages like exits my be around 1.5 person/m s.

In the present paper, the crowd flow was simulated under the condition of density from 1.0 to 4.0 persons/m$^2$, which follows that $\rho$ x v = 1.5 persons/m s. The typical relation among density, velocity and flow rate is shown in Fig. 4.

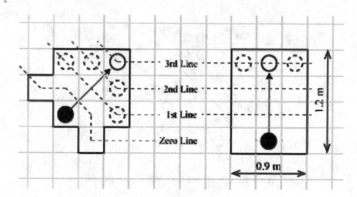

**Fig. 5.** Personal space

## Definition of Personal Space

It has been pointed out that there may exist a "personal space" around a person, where one feel constrained or embarrassed when other persons come into the space caused by over-crowded. It may be a kind of domain or territory as wild animals. It has been reported that the walking space necessary for comfortable movement may be 70 cm width and 100-200 cm forward, or in other case, one person in a crowd may apart 1 m from other person on both sides, and 1.5 m forward. In reference to these previous works, we set the personal space as shown in Fig. 5. In this paper, these two identical patterns of personal space were used to find the moving space.

## Local Neighbor Rules for Movement

In this paper, the local neighbor rules were applied as simple as possible, so that the simulated crowd flow might satisfy the typical velocity-density diagram and flow rate diagram provided in the guideline. When there was no person inside of the personal space, the pedestrian continued to walk straight forward at the free walking speed of 1.3 m/s. In case that more than one person existed in the personal space, the movement of the pedestrian was expressed by "transfer probability" considering the location and the number of other person in the space so that the simulated crowd flow might adjust the density-velocity diagram and flow rate diagram provided in the government rule as shown in Fig. 4. The transfer probability was calculated as follows according to the state of the personal space.

$$\text{transfer probability} = (1.0 - P_{stop} \times C_{dens}) \times C_{dir}$$

where $P_{stop}$ is "stop probability", $C_{dens}$ is "density coefficient" determined by the location of other person in the personal space, and $C_{dir}$ is "direction coefficient". $P_{stop}$ was determined as

0.0 : no person in the personal space
1.0 : at least one person exists in the 1st line in Fig. 5
0.4 : at least one person exists in the 2nd line in Fig. 5
0.2 : at least one person exists in the 3rd line in Fig. 5

The density coefficient was determined as

1.0 : 0 - 2 persons in the personal space
0.6 : 3 persons in the personal space
0.3 : 4 persons in the personal space
0.0 : more than 5 persons in the personal space

The direction coefficient is set to 1.0 to the forward cell, and $1/\sqrt{2}$ to aslant cell.

The order of calculation for a pedestrian to decide the space to proceed at next time step was at random, and the movement for all pedestrians in simulation space was conducted all at once. Transfer probability to the cells where other person existed and the adjacent cells was zero. The probability to move was increased due to $C_{dens}$ as the density increased, because the simulated crowd flow should adjust the flow-rate density diagram in high density region.

## 2.5    Movement through a Stairway

According to previous works, the velocity of pedestrians through a stairway corresponds to the number of steps per unit time on horizontal movement. Moreover, the velocity at a standard stairway on a projected horizontal plain may be as half as that through a horizontal passage according to the report edited by the Building Center of Japan. Based on the document on Evacuation Safety Performance Evaluation Manual, the velocity was set 0.45 times at up-stairway and 0.6 times at down-stairway as that at horizontal passages.

On the other hand, the velocity of passengers would decrease as the density of crowd is increased. The flow coefficient at a stairway is 1.3 persons/m s in the guideline of Japanese Ministry of Land, Infrastructure, Transport and Tourism, and 80 persons/m min (=1.33 persons/m s). In the present paper, the velocity of a person is evaluated by multiplying the transfer probability by "stair coefficient". The stair coefficient is determined as

0.6 : down flow, less than 2 persons in the personal space
0.8 : down flow, more than 3 persons in the personal space
0.4 : up flow, less than 2 persons in the personal space
0.9 : up flow, more than 3 persons in the personal space

# 3    Simulation Results and Discussions

## 3.1    One Directional Flow

Simulations were conducted for crowd flow on four types of inclined pathways as shown in Fig. 6; (a) orthogonal (0°), (b) 1/3 inclination ($\tan^{-1}(1/3) = 18.4°$), (c) 1/2 inclination ($\tan^{-1}(1/2) = 26.6°$), and (d) 1/1 inclination ($\tan^{-1}(1/1) = 45°$). These simulations were conducted to show that the crowd flow in each direction was adjusted to the density-flow rate diagram in the evacuation guideline and to show the results

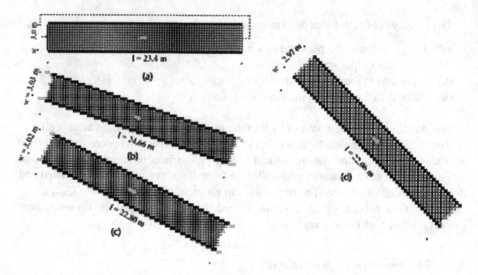

**Fig. 6.** Inclined pathways

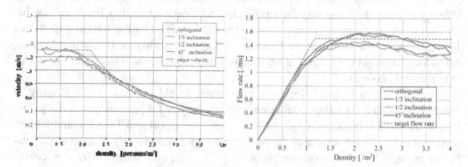

**Fig. 7.** Density-velocity diagram          **Fig. 8.** Density-flow rate diagram

could be applied in two dimensional simulation. For each case study, pedestrians came into the pathway from the density of 0.1 to 4.0 persons/m$^2$ at initial state, and started the simulation at free walking speed of 1.3 m/s in one direction. Simulations were carried out ten times and averaged flow rate was estimated. Free walking state and also the crowd flow state were simulated corresponding to the flow density. The flow rate was estimated at each flow density as an average in 60 s. Periodical boundary condition for pedestrians was introduced in this simulation, where the pedestrians walking out from the exit was introduced from the inlet to get constant flow density on the pathway.

The results are shown in Figs. 7 and 8. The relation between the flow density and velocity is shown in Fig. 7, and flow density and flow rate in Fig. 8. As shown in Fig. 7, the free walking state was simulated under the density from 0.1 to 1.1 persons/m$^2$, and the velocities were almost 1.2 - 1.3 m/s in each case. The velocity of pedestrians began to decrease when the flow density exceeded about 1.1 persons/m$^2$

in each case. The flow rate, as shown in Fig. 8, increased as the density was increased by 1.1 persons/m². After the flow rates were saturated around 1.5 persons/m s, it began to decrease from the density of 2.0 persons/m².

## 3.2    Flow around a T-Junction

Flow simulation was conducted around a T-junction, as shown in Fig. 9, where pedestrians coming into the gates A and B, joined at T-junction C, and flew out from the exit D. The pedestrians were placed on the pathway at a certain density randomly, and they walked in one direction at the free speed of 1.3 m/s. Two different cases of density, 0.3 and 0.7 persons/m², were set in the simulation.

The simulation result is shown in Table 1. When the flow density was 0.3 persons/m², the pedestrian flow remained as free walking state, because the total flow density at the junction was estimated about 0.6 persons/m², which was less than the transient density from free walking to crowd flow, 1.15 persons/m².

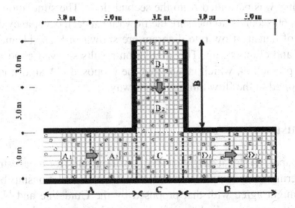

**Fig. 9.** Simulated area around T-junction

**Table 1.** Simulation results for T-junction flow

| Inlet flow | | Interval | A1 in | A1 out | A2 out | B1 in | B1 out | B2 out | C out | D1 out | D2 out |
|---|---|---|---|---|---|---|---|---|---|---|---|
| Low | Density [ /m²] | 0~60s | 0.32 | 0.32 | 0.40 | 0.30 | 0.30 | 0.36 | 0.69 | 0.69 | 0.68 |
| | | 60~120s | 0.31 | 0.30 | 0.38 | 0.30 | 0.30 | 0.36 | 0.66 | 0.68 | 0.61 |
| | Flow rate [ /m·s] | 0~60s | 0.41 | 0.42 | 0.40 | 0.38 | 0.39 | 0.40 | 0.81 | 0.79 | 0.77 |
| | | 60~120s | 0.41 | 0.39 | 0.39 | 0.39 | 0.39 | 0.38 | 0.79 | 0.81 | 0.78 |
| | Velocity [m/s] | 0~60s | 1.28 | 1.29 | 0.99 | 1.28 | 1.31 | 1.12 | 1.18 | 1.16 | 1.12 |
| | | 60~120s | 1.33 | 1.30 | 1.03 | 1.30 | 1.29 | 1.06 | 1.20 | 1.19 | 1.27 |
| Inlet flow | | Interval | A1 in | A1 out | A2 out | B1 in | B1 out | B2 out | C out | D1 out | D2 out |
| High | Density [ /m²] | 0~60s | 0.70 | 0.69 | 1.54 | 0.68 | 0.75 | 2.06 | 2.09 | 2.09 | 1.72 |
| | | 60~120s | 0.74 | 0.78 | 3.05 | 0.73 | 0.83 | 2.96 | 2.83 | 2.83 | 2.21 |
| | Flow rate [ /m·s] | 0~60s | 0.90 | 0.89 | 0.88 | 0.86 | 0.90 | 0.87 | 1.65 | 1.61 | 1.58 |
| | | 60~120s | 0.92 | 0.86 | 0.78 | 0.92 | 0.84 | 0.74 | 1.54 | 1.49 | 1.49 |
| | Velocity [m/s] | 0~60s | 1.28 | 1.29 | 0.57 | 1.27 | 1.21 | 0.42 | 0.79 | 0.77 | 0.92 |
| | | 60~120s | 1.24 | 1.10 | 0.26 | 1.25 | 1.02 | 0.25 | 0.54 | 0.53 | 0.68 |

On the contrary, when the initial density was set to 0.7 persons/m², the total density exceeded the transient density. As shown in Table 1, the density at C and D was increased as time passed, and the density at A was affected to be increased even though the point A was located at the upper stream of pedestrian flow. The velocity of pedestrians decreased corresponding to the elevation of flow density.

When the initial density was high, and the density exceeded 2.0, the flow rate at C and D was estimated around 1.5, which means that the flow rate in crowd flow maintained around 1.5 persons/m s as was appointed for target flow rate.

### 3.3    Flow through a Stairway

As shown in Fig. 10, flow simulation was also conducted for a stairway in one direction of a three-story building. People were placed at random at the density from 0.1 to 4.0 persons/m² to demonstrate the free walking as well as crowd flow state, and went down the stairs at 0.78 m/s and climbed up at 0.585 m/s as the free walking speed. After they walked out from the exit, they flew into the inlet so that steady-state flow may be realized. No entry was permitted from the second floor. The simulation was performed and averaged in 60 seconds, to measure the flow rate at each occupancy density.

The results of density-flow rate diagram are shown in Figs. 11 and 12, in case of walking down and climbing up. The simulation results showed good agreement with the theoretical prediction, which means that the proposed CA algorithm of pedestrian flow can be applied to the flow through a stairway.

## 4    Conclusions

In the present paper, the local neighbor and transition rules for a pedestrian to step forward were determined as simple as possible, so that the relationship between density and flow rate might agree with that proposed by the Guideline and Notification. The proposed algorithm was applied to one directional flow of orthogonal and inclined

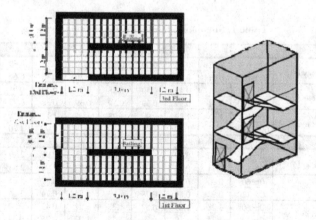

**Fig. 10.** Simulation model for a stairway

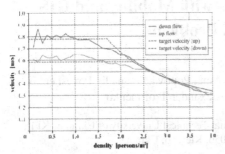

**Fig. 11.** Density-velocity diagram  for a stairway

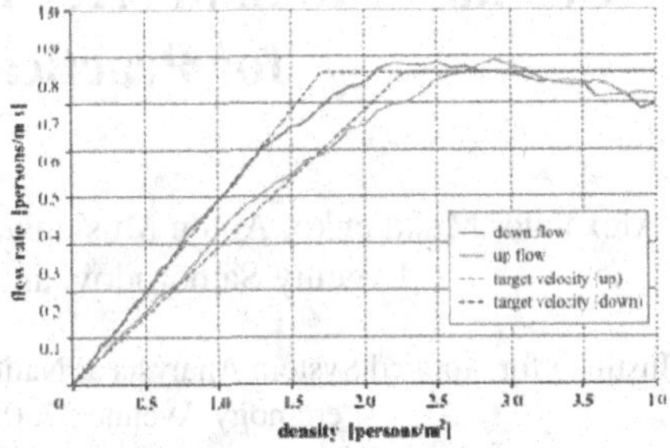

**Fig. 12.** Density-flow rate diagram  for a stairway

pathways, T-junction pathway and a stairway. The results show good agreement with predicted values based on the Guideline, and furthermore, the time history of pedestrians flow revealed the precise mechanism of jamming around junction of pathways.

# References

1. Naka, Y.: Study on Complicated Passenger Flow in a Railway Station, Railway Technical Research Report, No.1079 (1978)
2. Kato, K., Uehara, T., Nakamura, K., Yoshioka, M.: Analysis of Pedestrian Movement in Bi-directional Flow. Bulletin of Architectural Institute of Japan (289), 119–129 (1980)
3. Helbing, D., Farkas, I., Vicsek, T.: Simulating dynamical features of escape panic. Nature 407, 487–490 (2000)
4. Morishita, S., Nakatsuka, N.: Simulation of Emergency Evacuation by Cellular Automata. In: Proceedings of 6th International Conference on Complex Systems, pp. 92–97 (2002)
5. Narimatsu, K., Shiraishi, T., Morishita, S.: Acquisition of Local Neighbor Rules in the Simulation of Pedestrian Flow by Cellular Automata. In: Sloot, P.M.A., Chopard, B., Hoekstra, A.G. (eds.) ACRI 2004. LNCS, vol. 3305, pp. 211–219. Springer, Heidelberg (2004)
6. Nishinari, K., Kirchner, A., Namazi, A., Schadschneider, A.: Extended Floor Field CA Model for Evacuation Dynamics. IEICE Transaction of Information & Systems E87-D(3), 726–732 (2004)
7. Building Center of Japan, Comprehensive Fire Safety Design for Buildings, vol. 3 (Evacuation Safety Method) (1989)
8. Building Center of Japan, Introduction to Building Fire Safety Engineering (2002)
9. Ministry of Construction Notification, No. 1441 & 1442 (2000)

# Cellular Automata, Agents with Mobility and GIS for Practical Problems

Alexander Makarenko, Anton Musienko, Anna Popova, Gennadiy Poveshenko, Evgeniy Samorodov, and Alexander Trofimenko

Institute for Applied System Analysis at National Technical University of Ukraine "KPI', Peremogy Avenue 37, 03056, Kiev-56, Ukraine
makalex@i.com.ua

**Abstract.** Some real applications of improved cellular automata models are considered. Considered improvement of models concerned the using real data applications from GIS and incorporating the concepts from other methodologies – especially neural networks and learning. We describe models which allow considering different processes in the case of Ukrainian capital Kyiv. Migration processes and voting processes have been considered. New ways of cellular automata development are discussed.

**Keywords:** Cellular automata, urban planning, multiagents, GIS, opinion formation.

## 1    Introduction

Since the origin at 50th years of past century cellular automata had many developments and applications in physics, biology, mathematics, technique (see the books J. Von Neumann, Toffoli T.&Margolus S., Chopard B.&Droz M., Langton C., Wolfram S., Illiachinski A., L. Chua etc.). But now new fields of cellular automata theory and applications are in the processes of intensive development.

Although the papers with applications of cellular automata to the social systems have been proposed at 80th – 90th years recently many questions still are open. For example, important and prospective are idea on binding cellular automata approach with multi-agent approach (especially of moving agents) (see [1, 2]); idea of incorporating learning approaches for deriving the parameters of transition functions in cellular automata; investigations of the role of anticipation in cellular automata models of social systems ([3, 4]). The development and merging of such concepts are still continuing. But the formal classical frames of existing approaches and tools sometimes restrict the applications of concepts to real systems and problems. The strict abstract frames also involve frequently the difficulties in interpretation of received results in the common for practical user's descriptions of social systems (for example, by maps, useful tables, networks structures etc.). As the authors suppose the solution of such problems will be find in the using recent practical tools for data representation [5]: special data bases, geo-information systems (GIS), 3D visualization in time. So in the

G.C. Sirakoulis and S. Bandini (Eds.): ACRI 2012, LNCS 7495, pp. 738–742, 2012.

next subsection of proposed paper we at first will describe some problems, which has a practical importance and which use combination cellular automata models with some kind of mobility accounting. At first we describe the modeling of scenarios of harmful manufacturing remouting from the city. Then we remark the problem of migration scenarios of country population and epidemic modeling for Ukraine. Also we describe the problem of modeling political preferences of population (especially of political election) in the case of Ukraine.

Then in the last subsection of the paper we discuss some ways of cellular automata development which follows from analysis of current state of investigations and from our experience of solving real practical problems. Opinion formation problem, political elections and team sportive games are proposed as the background for investigation the problems with multi-agents nature of the systems.

## 2    Examples of Cellular Automata Modeling for Real Problems

### 2.1    Modeling of the Isolating of Harmful Manufactures Out of the Borders of the City of Kiev

Here we briefly reproduce the main concept of models from ([6]). The model is made so that it shown as spatial distribution depends on preferences of agent situated on the grid. In simplest variant the agent (the people or company) lives on lattice $N \times N$. Irregular lattice (and special Voronoy cells) may be used for actual geography. The set of agents is $M = \{1,2,...,m\}$. The agents choose the locations. More than one agent can occupy the same location on lattice. The level to usefulness of the agent and need of its using the site depends on distribution agent on lattice and many other parameters: social, economical, geographical and cultural. Allow $F$ to mark distribution an agent on set of the locations. $F_{ij}$ has marked the number an agent, living in $i$-th row and $j$-th row of the lattice. Utility function $u : N \times N \times F \to R$ is one of the key components of current approach. Considering identical agents, initial distribution $F$, the final distribution should be determined which maximize usefulness $F_{ij} \times u(i, j, F)$. Usefulness of the agent depends of all factors: population in its initial location and average distance from its initial location before the other agent.

We have applied the models for different processes. We had considered in details one of the important problem – the scenarios of harmful manufacturing relocation from the city with use the real data [5]. In such case each agent corresponds to single harmful manufacturing. Using such improved models we had considered the processes of relocating of harmful manufacturing in Kiev in dependce on ecological, financial, infrastructure conditions. Scenarios correspond to different utility functions.

### 2.2    Modeling of Migration Scenarios at Ukraine

Other important class of problems is investigation of migration processes of large scales – regional, country, trans-regional. Fortunately the approach from previous subsection allows also considering such problems, for example modeling of migration scenarios, different attitudes of population, merging of multiagent and cellular models. All such models allow using of Geoinformational systems and real data base.

## 2.3    Modeling of Epidemic Scenarios by Cellular Automata

In some previous work (see [7]), it is proposed to use the Stochastic Cellular Automata paradigm to simulate an infectious disease outbreak. The simulation facilitates the study of dynamics of epidemics of different infection diseases, and has been applied to study the effects of spread vaccination cells izolation. Fundamentally the simulator loosely simulates the SIR (Susceptible Infected Removed) and SEIR (Susceptible Exposed Infected Removed) models.

Then, a Cellular Automata model for disease spreading have been developed, implemented and studied in some details. This has been performed on abstract level, but nevertheless with some surprising results: even a simple spreading model can exhibit a sharp transition between controlled situation and devastating epidemics.

## 2.4    The Problem of Opinion formation and Political Elections

Other very important part of real society is different social and political processes. Here we very shortly describe the problem which is interesting for cellular automata applications. Very important part of social structure is election of different representative authorities and governmental structures. Our implementation of such services had been concentrated mainly around the elections at Ukraine. During our research and information system development we had used different models for election considering: simple algebraic; neural networks; differential equations of diffusive type; models with associative memory; cellular automata.

The choice of models for implementation in the information system depends on the goals of modeling, the processes under investigation, complexity of the models, existing of computer and financial resources etc. One of the basic models of system is the model for the dynamics of voter preferences. Simplest models already had been used in forecasting of last president election campaign in Ukraine at 2010 year.

Remark that the next useful step at improving the solutions of such problems consists in using cellular automata models but with the cells which have non-square shape and which correspond to the real distribution of populations in geographical environment.

## 3    Discussions

Described above results are interesting as the examples of important problems solutions. But analysis of such examples (and other investigations and papers) allows considering some already existing tendencies and anticipating the new possibilities for cellular automata development.

The first tendency consists in merging the cellular automata approach with using real data base. This will follow to weakening the useful requirement on regularity and homogeneity structures accompanied by adjusting real data from geoinformational system (GIS).

The second tendency is related to the idea of considering moving elements on the regular space subdivision. Following [1, 2] it is useful to name it 'situated moving agents' where 'agent' understands as some elements which have own preferences. Remark that traffic and pedestrian movements are the good examples of such systems. Also many such problems supply ecology, political and social sciences, economy.

Now also relatively new tendency may be found in the theory and applications of cellular automata approach – namely, correct accounting of different properties of the objects of modeling on the base of cellular automata approach.

First of all we should remark the spreading ideas from the field of artificial intelligence, especially the different kinds of learning, including reinforcement learning. Of course some investigations in this field exist more then third years (especially in social modeling: emerging of social norms, rules, order and power). But now new possibilities emerges for cellular automata models by more extensive use of recent data mining approaches, multi-agent modeling, decision-making theory and computational neuroscience, including using of computer models for brain processes.

Because of such presumable expanding of cellular automata modeling more involved models will be useful. Here we remark only some evident possibilities. The first consists in using more complex structure of cellular automata – especially by hierarchical models. The second tendency is using more complex dynamics for each cell states evolution, by the rules for transition of cells states for the next moments of time. This may include as the models for internal dynamics of cell's states as the modified internal descriptions of the environment and neighbor cell's dynamics. Remark that for these goals (description, dynamics and reinforced models) may be useful the neural networks models with internal representation of the systems in elements (see [4]). The next direction for cellular automata models improvement consists in more detailed accounting of evolutionary aspects of dynamics in the rules of the models. Following the general outlines from physic the first example consist in accounting the memory (delay) effects in cellular automata. Relatively few papers on such investigations have been published before.

But recently the accounting of strong anticipatory property by D. Dubois in cellular automata opens the new prospects in the theory and applications of cellular automata. Since the of 90-th by D.Dubois [8] the idea of strong anticipation had been introduced: "Definition of an incursive discrete strong anticipatory system ...: an incursive discrete system is a system which computes its current state at time $t$, as a function of its states at past times $,...,t-3,t-2,t-1$, present time, $t$, and even its states at future times $t+1, t+2, t+3, ...$

$$x(t+1) = A(..., x(t-2), x(t), x(t+1), x(t+2), ..., p)$$

where $x$ at future times $t+1,...$ is computed in using the equation itself".

We already had been investigating some such effects in game 'Life' models and in some traffic problems [3, 9]. The main new peculiarity by accounting strong anticipation is the possibility of multivaluedness of element's state at given moment of time. Remark that recently we have found the way for using such multivaluedness for description of intrinsic uncertainty in the traffic problems.

# 4    Conclusions

Thus in proposed paper we have discussed some presumable ways for development of cellular automata which follows from analysis of some concrete models and applications. May be the most interesting is the intensive using of real geography and geometry of considered objects and systems especially with geoinformational systems; exploiting idea of situated cellular agents and using more complex representation of cellular automata structure, description of rules and states and more complex dynamics of cells, especially with accounting memory and anticipation.

# References

1. Bandini, S., Manconi, S., Vizzari, G.: Agent based Modeling and Simulation. In: Encyclopedia of Complexity and System Science, pp. 184–197 (2009)
2. Bandini, S., Manconi, S., Vizzari, G.: Situated Cellular Agents a Model to Simulate Crowding Dynamics. Special Issues on Cellular Automata E87-D, 669–676 (2004)
3. Goldengorin, B., Makarenko, A., Smelyanec, N.: Some Applications and Prospects of Cellular Automata in Traffic Problems. In: El Yacoubi, S., Chopard, B., Bandini, S. (eds.) ACRI 2006. LNCS, vol. 4173, pp. 532–537. Springer, Heidelberg (2006)
4. Makarenko, A.: Anticipating in modeling of large social systems - neuronets with internal structure and multivaluedness. International Journal of Computing Anticipatory Systems 13, 77–92 (2002)
5. ISGEO 2012 WWW Intelligence Systems GEO (2012), http://www.isgeo.kiev.ua
6. Page, S.: On the emergence of cities. Working Paper Santa- Fe Institute n. 98 -08- 075e, 28 p (1998), http://www.santa-fe.edu/sfi/publications/working-papers/98-08-075E.ps
7. Venkatachalam, S., Mikler, A.R.: Towards Computational Epidemiology Using Stochastic Cellular Automata in modeling spread of diseases, Department of Computer Science and Engineering, University of North Texas, Denton, TX - 76207, USA (2005), http://www.cerl.unt.edu/publications/2005/ps/Paper_hawaii.ps
8. Dubois, D.: Introduction to computing Anticipatory Systems. International Journal of Computing Anticipatory Systems (Liege) 2, 3–14 (1998)
9. Makarenko, A., Krushinski, D., Goldengorin, B.: Anticipation and Delocalization in Cellular Models of Pedestrian Traffic. In: Proceed. of INDS 2008, Klagenfurt, Austria, pp. 61–64. Shanker-verlag, Aachen (2008)

# Evacuation Simulation from Rooms through a Pathway and a Stairway by Cellular Automata Based on the Public Guideline

Nobuhiko Shinozaki, Shigeyuki Koyama, and Shin Morishita

Yokohama National University
Graduate School of Environment and Information Sciences
79-7 Tokiwadai, Hodogaya-ku, Yokohama 240-8501 Japan
mshin@ynu.ac.jp

**Abstract.** Evacuation simulation was conducted by Cellular Automata in which the local neighbor and state transition rules for movement of pedestrians were satisfied with the occupancy density-flow rate diagram proposed in the Public Guideline for evacuation. As case studies of the proposed algorithm, evacuation from a room with several exits, from three rooms connected to a pathway and a stairway were simulated. The simulation results were compared with the estimated evacuation time calculated by flow rate, number of people, and width of the exits. The simulation results showed good agreement with the estimated evacuation time, and furthermore, it showed precise movement of each person to evacuate from rooms caused by the flow rate change in the process.

**Keywords:** Evacuation, Crowd Flow, Guideline, Flow rate-Density diagram, Pathway, Stairway.

## 1 Introduction

Evacuation simulation is getting serious attention to evaluate the duration time required to rush away from a room of office to outside of buildings, especially in Japan after the great earthquake on March 11, 2011. The number of exits of a building, width and location of exits of a room and width of pathways or stairways should be designed by construction rules or notification of the government.

There have been numerous studies on evacuation simulation as an application of Cellular Automata (CA) or Multi-Agent Simulation [1]-[6]. Yuichiro Naka simulated the passenger flow in the concourse of stations on macroscopic and also microscopic point of view by introducing several local neighbor rules in the early 1970s [1]. Dirk Helbing, et al. presented a model of pedestrian behavior to study the mechanisms of panic and jamming by uncoordinated motion in crowds[3]. One of the authors proposed several local neighbor rules for evacuation simulation by Cellular Automata, and furthermore, proposed an algorithm in which the local neighbor rules could be determined automatically in the process of simulation [4],[5]. Nishinari, et al. presented the floor field model for pedestrian dynamics introducing wall potentials and simulated evacuation flow from a room with several exits [6].

G.C. Sirakoulis and S. Bandini (Eds.): ACRI 2012, LNCS 7495, pp. 743–751, 2012.
© Springer-Verlag Berlin Heidelberg 2012

In the present paper, CA was applied to evacuation simulation, in which the local neighbor rules were determined so that the simulated crowd flow might be adapted to "Density-velocity diagram" and "Density-flow rate diagram" provided by the government [7]-[9]. The local neighbor rules were determined as simple as possible just by introducing the transfer probability for the movement in the next time step [10]. As case studies of the proposed algorithm, evacuation from a room with several exits, from three rooms connected to a hall, and from the rooms connected with a hall and a stairway were simulated. The simulation results were compared with the estimated evacuation time calculated by flow rate, number of people, and width of the exits. Peculiar characteristics of a person were excluded and all the people were adapted by the same rules. All the people might evacuate from the buildings through halls or stairs in good order without any personal troubles.

## 2 Cellular Automata Model

### 2.1 Cell Division and State Variables

The floor plan was divided into cells of 30 x 30 cm, and at most one person was permitted to stay on each cell. Two persons could not stand on the adjacent cells to each other, because the cross sectional area of a body was estimated 60 x 30 cm. The typical state variable of each cell was "pedestrian", "vacant" or "obstacle (wall, pillar or furniture)". The unit length of 30 cm is important in Japan, because the width of pathways or stairs is designed by multiple of this unit length.

A person on a cell had the direction vector and could move in the eight directions including forward, backward, right, left and every 45 degree directions. When the direction of a pedestrian was not coincide to the eight directions, the pedestrian would choose one of the eight directions. According to the fact that an average stride of adult men was 75-80 cm, and 2 or 3 time steps in this simulation corresponded to the time

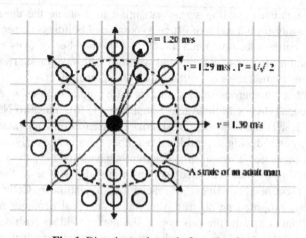

**Fig. 1.** Direction and speed of a pedestrian

for one walking step of pedestrians, it was possible for a pedestrian to proceed 8 x 3 = 24 directions in one actual walking step at maximum as shown in Fig. 1.

When a pedestrian walked along a free space without any constraint, the velocity was estimated as up to 1.3 m/s, the value of which had been supported by several documents edited by the Japanese government. The process of walking was governed by transfer probability. When the walking velocity was less than 1.3 m/s, the probability of movement was calculated as v/1.3. Furthermore, when the direction vector was inclined to 45 degree, the probability was decreased as $1/\sqrt{2}$, to keep the free velocity as 1.3 m/s.

## 2.2    Crowd Flow Model

In the crowd flow, the velocity of pedestrians may decrease as the density of crowds is increased. In the present paper, the crowd flow was simulated under the condition of density from 1.0 to 4.0 persons/m². The relation among the parameters; flow rate (f), velocity (v), and density ($\rho$), might be described as $f = \rho \times v$, when the density of crowd was up to 4 persons/m². In reference to these previous works, we set the personal space as shown in Fig. 2. In this paper, these two identical patterns of personal space were used to find the moving space in the same way as the other article prepared by the authors [10].

When there was no person inside of the personal space, the pedestrian continued to walk straight forward at the free walking speed of 1.3 m/s. In case that more than one person existed in the personal space, the movement of the pedestrian was expressed by "transfer probability" considering the location and the number of other person in the space so that the simulated crowd flow might adjust the density- flow rate diagram provided in the government rule. The transfer probability was calculated as

$$\text{transfer probability} = (1.0 - P_{stop} \times C_{dens}) \times C_{dir}$$

where $P_{stop}$ is "stop probability", $C_{dens}$ is "density coefficient" determined by the location of other person in the personal space, and $C_{dir}$ is "direction coefficient". These parameters were determined according to the state of the personal space [10].

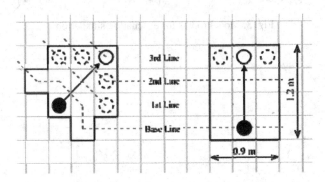

**Fig. 2.** Personal space of a pedestrian

As described previously, all the pedestrians might walk in good order without being stricken by a serious panic even in the evacuation state and all the people were adapted by the same rules. All the people might evacuate from the buildings through halls or stairs in good order without any personal troubles due to panic, for example.

# 3    Simulation Results and Discussions

## 3.1    Evacuation from a Room

Two case studies were performed to evaluate the applicability of the present algorithm of CA to evacuation from a room as shown in Fig. 3. In Case-1, the area of room was 54 m$^2$ with single exit, whereas the area was twice as much, 108 m$^2$, with two exits in Case-2. At the initial state, the total number of persons were 10, 30, or 50 for Case-1, and 20, 60, or 100 for Case-2, placed uniformly at random. When the simulation started, each person moved toward the nearest exit at the speed of 1.3 m/s. Because there were two exits in Case-2, each person would select at each time step of simulation one of the exits. In this selection, one estimated to be able to evacuate as soon as possible, based on the information of flow speed through the exit and the number of persons waiting for evacuation around the exit. During the evacuation process, one could change the exit based on the information. Time history of evacuation from a room with two exits (Case-2) is shown in Fig. 4, as an example of simulation.

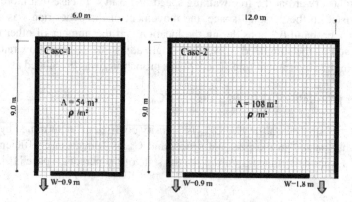

**Fig. 3.** Model rooms for evacuation simulation

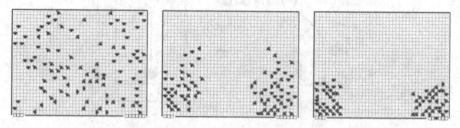

**Fig. 4.** Time history of evacuation from a room with two exits

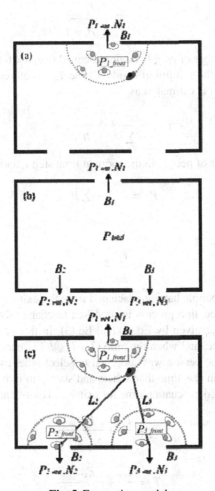

**Fig. 5.** Evacuation model

**Estimation of Evacuation Time**

Suppose that people evacuate from a room with three exits as a general case. Total number of people in the room at initial state is $P_{total}$, and the width of exits are $B_1$, $B_2$, and $B_3$ as shown in Fig. 5. When a person in the room escapes from the exit-1, and the number of people in the area around the exit-1 closer to the person is $P_{1\_front}$ as shown in Fig. 5(a), the required time $T_1$ for the person to escape from the room at the simulation time step t is estimated as,

$$T_1 = \frac{P_{1\_front}}{N_1 \times B_1} \tag{1}$$

where $N_1$ is flow ratio, which is derives as,

$$N_1 = \frac{P_{1\_out}}{B_1 \times t} \tag{2}$$

Where $P_{1\_out}$ is the number of people having escaped from exit-1 at time step $t$.

On the other hand, the minimum residual time $T_{min}$ required for evacuation of all the people at time step $t$ is estimated as

$$T_{min} = \frac{P_{in}}{\sum_i (N_i \times B_i)} \tag{3}$$

where $P_{in}$ is the number of people in the room at time step t, and calculated as

$$P_{in} = P_{total} - \sum_i P_{i\_out} \tag{4}$$

and flow rate $N_i$ is

$$N_i = \frac{P_{i\_out}}{B_i \times t} \tag{5}$$

$P_{i\_out}$ is the number of people having evacuated from the exit-i.

A person in the evacuation process is supposed to change the exit according to the difference of $T_1$ and $T_{min}$ given by Eq.(1) and Eq.(3). In this paper, the change of exit was carried out just once, and when the ratio $(T_1 - T_{min})/ T_{min}$ exceeded 0.1. When a person changed the exit, the person was supposed to select other exit which might permit the person to evacuate in less time than others and started to move toward the new exit. For example, the required evacuation time for exit-2 and exit-3, namely $T_2$ and $T_3$, are

$$T_2 = \frac{L_2}{v} + \frac{P_{2\_in}}{N_2 \times B_2} \tag{6}$$

$$T_3 = \frac{L_3}{v} + \frac{P_{3\_in}}{N_3 \times B_3} \tag{7}$$

where $L_2$ and $L_3$ are the distance between the person and each exit, as shown in Fig. 5.

The simulation results are shown in Table 1. Simulation was performed 10 times for each case at different initial state, and maximum as well as minimum required

Table 1. Simulation results for Case-1 and Case-2

| The number of pedestrian | | CASE-1 | | | CASE-2 | | |
|---|---|---|---|---|---|---|---|
| | | 10 | 30 | 50 | 20 | 60 | 100 |
| Walking time $t_1$ [s] | | 8.32 | | | 8.32 | | |
| Transit time of exit $t_2$ [s] | | 7.41 | 22.22 | 37.04 | 5.56 | 16.67 | 27.78 |
| Evacuation time $t$ [s] | | 8.32 | 22.22 | 37.04 | 8.32 | 16.67 | 27.78 |
| Simulation Result | Max. [s] | 10.12 | 24.15 | 39.56 | 10.12 | 20.93 | 34.50 |
| | Min. [s] | 8.74 | 20.16 | 32.20 | 8.97 | 17.63 | 28.06 |
| | Ave. [s] | 9.48 | 22.38 | 36.92 | 9.58 | 19.08 | 30.38 |

evacuation time were evaluated. As a reference, the moving time $t_1$, which was calculated by speed and walking distance to the exit, and transit time $t_2$ calculated by the flow rate, exit width and the number of people are shown. The longer time of $t_1$ and $t_2$ was regarded as the evacuation time regulated by the guideline of Japanese Government. The evacuation time might be the moving time in lower density case (10 persons in Case-1 or 20 persons in Case-2), and it might be the transit time in high density case (30-50 in Case-1, and 60-100 in Case-2).

As shown in Table 1, the simulation results showed good agreement with the evacuation time regulated by the guideline. For the results in Case-2, the evacuation time for different initial density was 2.6-2.8 s longer than the guideline, which might be caused by the number of exit.

### 3.2     Evacuation from Rooms through a Pathway and a Stairway

As a little more complex case study, evacuation from three different type rooms through a straight pathway and a stairway at the end of the pathway was simulated. The floor plan is shown in Fig. 6. The number of people at initial state in each room (a, b, c) were (5, 3, 4) for Case-3, (25, 15, 20) for Case-4, and (50, 30, 40) for Case-5. These persons were placed uniformly in each room at random, and in addition, one person was placed at the largest distance point from the exit in each room. Evacuation started at the same time in each room, and people moved toward the exits. After passing through the exits, they walked along the straight pathway to the stairway placed at the end of the pathway, and completed their evacuation from the floor.

The time history of evacuation from each room is shown in Fig. 7. These are the snapshot from the simulation of Case-5, that is, total number of persons was 120 at initial state. After 6 seconds, the people in each room evacuated quite smoothly to the pathway as shown in Fig. 7(b). But, the evacuating crowd began to jam on the pathway close to the exits of Rooms-A and B, as shown in Fig. 7(c). At this time, when around 20 seconds had already passed since the evacuation started, the people in Room-A could not pass the exits because of the traffic jam just outside of the exit. It took almost 60 seconds for all the people in the rooms to get out of the room as shown in Fig. 7(d).

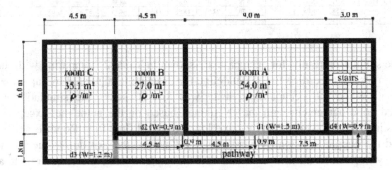

**Fig. 6.** Simulation model for evacuation from rooms with a pathway and stairway

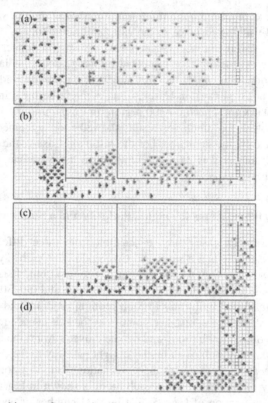

**Fig. 7.** Time history of evacuation from three rooms with a pathway and stairway

**Table 2.** Simulation results for Case-3, Case-4, and Case-5

| The number of pedestrian | CASE-3 (0.1 pedestrians/m²) | | | | CASE-4 (0.5 pedestrians/m²) | | | | CASE-5 (1.0 pedestrians/m²) | | | |
|---|---|---|---|---|---|---|---|---|---|---|---|---|
| | Room A | Room B | Room C | Entire floor | Room A | Room B | Room C | Entire floor | Room A | Room B | Room C | Entire floor |
| | 5 | 3 | 4 | 12 | 25 | 15 | 20 | 60 | 50 | 30 | 40 | 120 |
| Walking time $t_1$ [s] | 5.77 | 5.77 | 6.92 | | 5.77 | 5.77 | 6.92 | | 5.77 | 5.77 | 6.92 | |
| Transit time of exit $t_2$ [s] | 2.22 | 2.22 | 2.22 | | 11.11 | 11.11 | 11.11 | | 22.22 | 22.22 | 22.22 | |
| Evacuation time $t$ [s] | 5.77 | 5.77 | 6.92 | 19.61 | 11.11 | 11.11 | 11.11 | 50.90 | 22.22 | 22.22 | 22.22 | 95.35 |
| Simulation Result — Max. [s] | 7.59 | 7.13 | 7.59 | 21.62 | 26.22 | 14.49 | 12.42 | 61.87 | 66.47 | 28.75 | 22.85 | 103.50 |
| Simulation Result — Min. [s] | 5.29 | 5.06 | 6.44 | 19.78 | 17.02 | 10.81 | 9.66 | 48.53 | 51.52 | 25.30 | 19.09 | 96.37 |
| Simulation Result — Ave. [s] | 6.58 | 6.05 | 6.95 | 20.70 | 22.91 | 13.55 | 11.59 | 54.26 | 57.09 | 27.03 | 21.31 | 100.51 |
| Simulation Result — Error (%) | | | | 5.56 | | | | 6.60 | | | | 5.41 |

The simulation results for each case are shown in Table 2, comparing with the calculation results according to the Guideline for evacuation regulated by Japanese government. When the occupancy density was low (Case-3), the simulation results showed good agreement with the calculation based on the guideline, except for the results in Room-A. This might be caused by the crowd flow from Room-B and Room-C, and the people in Room-A were congested around the exit due to the jam in the pathway in front of the exit of Room-A. This tendency was more remarkable as the population density was increased as shown in the results for Case-4 and Case-5.

# 4    Conclusions

Evacuation simulation was conducted by CA in which the local neighbor and state transition rules for movement of pedestrians were satisfied with the occupancy density-flow rate diagram proposed in the Public Guideline for evacuation. As case studies, the evacuation from a room with several exits were simulated and the evacuation time was compared with the simple calculation based on the Guideline. Furthermore, evacuation from three rooms with a common pathway and a stairway was also simulated. The results showed that it needed more evacuation time for this case than the simple calculation based on the Guideline because of the jam on the pathway just in front of the exit of the room. Because the simulation by CA presented in this paper can reveal the precise movement of evacuation process, it is important to design a room, a floor or a building to consider the movement of crowd for higher safety.

# References

1. Naka, Y.: Study on Complicated Passenger Flow in a Railway Station, Railway Technical Research Report, No.1079 (1978)
2. Kato, K., Uehara, T., Nakamura, K., Yoshioka, M.: Analysis of Pedestrian Movement in Bi-directional Flow. Bulletin of Architectural Institute of Japan (289), 119–129 (1980)
3. Helbing, D., Farkas, I., Vicsek, T.: Simulating dynamical features of escape panic. Nature 407, 487–490 (2000)
4. Morishita, S., Nakatsuka, N.: Simulation of Emergency Evacuation by Cellular Automata. In: Proceedings of 6th International Conference on Complex Systems, pp. 92–97 (2002)
5. Narimatsu, K., Shiraishi, T., Morishita, S.: Acquisition of Local Neighbor Rules in the Simulation of Pedestrian Flow by Cellular Automata. In: Sloot, P.M.A., Chopard, B., Hoekstra, A.G. (eds.) ACRI 2004. LNCS, vol. 3305, pp. 211–219. Springer, Heidelberg (2004)
6. Nishinari, K., Kirchner, A., Namazi, A., Schadschneider, A.: Extended Floor Field CA Model for Evacuation Dynamics. IEICE Transaction of Information & Systems E87-D(3), 726–732 (2004)
7. Building Center of Japan, Comprehensive Fire Safety Design for Buildings, vol. 3 (Evacuation Safety Method) (1989)
8. Building Center of Japan, Introduction to Building Fire Safety Engineering (2002)
9. Ministry of Construction Notification, No. 1441 & 1442 (2000)
10. Koyama, S., Shinozaki, N., Morishita, S.: Modeling of Walking through Pathways and a Stairway by Cellular Automata Based on the Guideline for Evacuation. In: Sirakoulis, G.C., Bandini, S. (eds.) ACRI 2012. LNCS, vol. 7495, pp. 728–737. Springer, Heidelberg (2012)

# Follow-the-Leader Cellular Automata Based Model Directing Crowd Movement

Christos Vihas, Ioakeim G. Georgoudas*, and Georgios Ch. Sirakoulis

Democritus University of Thrace, Department of Electrical & Computer Engineering,
Laboratory of Electronics, GR-67100 Xanthi, Greece
{cvihas,igeorg,gsirak}@ee.duth.gr

**Abstract.** This paper describes a model that simulates crowd movement incorporating an efficient follow-the-leader technique based on cellular automata (CA). The scope of the method is to derive principal characteristics of collective motion of biological organisms, such as flocks, swarms or herds and to apply them to the simulation of crowd movement. Thus, the study focuses on the massive form of the movement of individuals, which is lastingly detected macroscopically, during urgent circumstances with the help of some form of guidance. Nevertheless, on a lower level, this formation derives from the application of simple local rules that are applied individually to every single member of the group. Hence, the adoption of CA-based formation has allowed the development of a micro-operating model with macro-features. Furthermore, the model takes advantage of the inherent ability of CA to represent sufficiently phenomena of arbitrary complexity. The response of the model has been evaluated through different simulation scenes that have been developed both in two and three dimensions.

**Keywords:** Cellular automata, Crowd movement, Follow-the-Leader.

## 1 Introduction

Safe crowd movement in case of emergency involves the immediate and fast redirection of individuals. Urgent instances vary from small to large scale ones. The first category includes mass departure from a building due to bomb or fire threat. The second one takes place in metropolitan areas due to mass catastrophes, such as heavy floods or earthquakes. Focusing on movements inside a building, the process is more likely to be completed successfully in case that some characteristics accommodate the activation of appropriate routes. Such features could be structural, e.g. multiple exits, alarms, sound and optical signals or human-based, e.g. guidance provided by well skilled personnel.

Algorithmically, it is desirable the development of a generic approach that could be applied to a variety of different cases. Plans of facing emergent circumstances are developed in order to reassure the most effective movement of people away from the

---

* Corresponding author.

G.C. Sirakoulis and S. Bandini (Eds.): ACRI 2012, LNCS 7495, pp. 752–762, 2012.

dangerous area. Thus, for each different case, a corresponding critical, temporal boundary is defined. Such boundaries can be effectively derived from appropriate simulation schemes. The latter are developed on the basis of computational models that try to emulate behaviours under emergent conditions.

According to the method that has been adopted, the crowd is approached as comprised individuals that follow their own rules of behaviour. In the past, crowd was modeled as homogeneous mass characterised by properties of a moving fluid. The main constraint was the large number of required computations. Nowadays, the advanced capabilities of computational systems sidestepped such difficulties. A step forward towards a more effective modeling of such processes is the incorporation of intelligent computational techniques, such as Cellular Automata [1].

Furthermore, it is a distinct feature of moving processes people to act together as forming a compound set. The, so called, herding or swarm or flocking behaviour arises, especially, in cases of emergency. Then people tend not to move autonomously but prefer to move in groups also due to psychological factors. In Physics, a flock is defined as the coherent motion of a group of self-propelled particles emerging from a simple set of interactions between the constituents of that group [2]. Flocking behaviour was initially simulated in 1986 by C.W. Reynolds [3]. He introduced the notion of boids, which are defined as self-propelled particles that have the ability to move according to a predefined set of rules. The initial pattern was created to emulate the behaviour of birds that form swarms but it can also be applied in cases of fishes or other biological organisms that present similar behaviours. In 1995, Vicsek et al. introduced the notion of flocking in the community of physicists by developing a model that presented physical mechanisms. This resulted in the creation of flocking formations [4]. They proved that a group of self-propelled particles, which is modeled with the use of a simple set of parameters, presents behaviour similar to that of a ferro-magnetic system. Airline companies have also applied routing methods of airplanes based on ants' behaviour and the theory of swarm intelligence [5]. Furthermore, in marketing, principles of flocking behaviour are used to explain the dependencies of human consuming tendencies [6].

The scope of this paper is to present a CA-based model that has been developed to simulate crowd movement deriving its theoretic principles from the collective behaviour of biological organisms (e.g. school of fishes, flock of birds etc). Although macroscopically, the individuals that form the crowd move like a mass towards a certain direction, the motion of each individual is independently adjusted by local rules. To that point, the adoption of CA approach allows the development of a microscopically-induced model with macroscopical characteristics. The driving mechanism of the model stems from two inter-dependent rules that are applied at different levels. At the local level of the restrained neighbourhood, individuals move towards the closest free cell that may lead to an exit. At a broader level each individual tries to stay bonded to other members of the crowd, in order not to be isolated. In literature, similar systems are called follow-the-leader systems and highlight the role of leaders in the evacuation. Though crowd evacuation simulation has been thoroughly investigated recently, little research focuses on simulating the evacuation process with Leader-Follower models [7], [8].

## 2     Related Work

Many different simulation approaches of crowd dynamics have been reported in the literature. Thus, methods based on CA are presented [9-11] as well as lattice-gas and social force models [12]. There are also fluid-dynamic [13] and agent-based [14] models or methods related to game theory [15] and experiments with animals [16]. In some models, pedestrians are considered as homogeneous individuals, whereas in others, they are treated as heterogeneous groups. There are methods that describe pedestrian dynamics in a microscopic scale, thus collective phenomena emerge from the complex interactions among individuals. There are also approaches that model crowd dynamics on a macroscopic scale. Moreover, there are models discrete in space and time and others spatial-temporally continuous.

Further focusing on CA, literature reports also a variety of CA-based models investigating crowd behaviour. CA based methods model human behaviours, such as inertial effects, unadventurous effect and group effect [17] or treat pedestrians as particles subject to long-range forces [18]. Furthermore, the impact of environmental conditions [19] and bi-directional pedestrian behaviour [20] has been studied with the use of CA as well as interactions among pedestrians, friction effects [21] and herding behaviour [12].

The presented model introduces the concept of a dynamically defined leader that is perceived as an exit by all other individuals. Thus, they adapt their movement towards the leader-exit. The idea of a leader as a moving exit facilitates the movement of a crowd towards a specific target, as for example towards an exit during evacuation. The leader itself follows a given strategy; it moves towards the nearest exit. The flexibility in the definition of the leader further accommodates the movement of the crowd. In case that a given leader is blocked or another member of the group moves faster then the role of the leader passes to another entity. Hence, the movement of the group is prevented from possible limitations.

## 3     Model Description

### 3.1     Basic Structure

A CA-based computational model has been developed that simulates the movement of a crowd formed by individuals, following some of the basic principles of [22]. The driving mechanism of the model is based on the assumption that each member of the crowd moves independently. Whenever possible, a group of individuals approaches the closest exit following the shortest route. Thus, each member is supposed to have a complete knowledge of the space topology and acts completely rational.

According to the CA modeling structure, the space is divided into rectangular parts that correspond to the cells of the lattice. The state of the cell is described by a value that is assigned to it from a predefined set of values. Specifically, value 0 (zero) indicates an empty cell, while value 1 (one) an occupied one. Value 2 (two) is assigned to cells that correspond to a part of a wall or an obstacle and value 3 (three) represents an exit. The structure of the algorithm is based on two arrays *start* and *final*. They represent the state of each cell at the beginning and at the end of each time step respectively. Assuming that the limits of the space correspond to walls, the boundary conditions of the CA model are constant. The simulation mechanism of the model is matrix-driven, discretising a floor area into a grid. The grid of the automaton is homogeneous and isotropic, whereas the CA cells are able to exist in two possible states; either free or occupied by exactly one particle. Each cell corresponds to the minimum area that a person could occupy [9]. During each time step, an individual chooses to move in one of the eight possible directions of its closest neighbourhood. Each particle moves towards the direction that is closer to an exit.

## 3.2    Crowd Movement in Two- or Three-Dimensions

The model has been developed to simulate crowd movement both in two- and three-dimensions, according to flocking principles and incorporating the Follow-the Leader technique. Results presented by J. Tourma et al. have also been taken under consideration [23]. As soon as a single member of the group is assigned the role of the leader, all other individuals adapt their moving attributes to the leaders'. Specifically, all other members try to follow the route of the leader by executing similar movements, thus forming and maintaining the collective pattern.

Following nature's practice, the model allows dynamical transitions of the role of the leader among the members of the group. Particularly, in case that a member of the group appears in front of the leader also following the same direction of movement, then a leader's role transition occurs. The member in front becomes the leader, whereas the leader turns into a simple member. An individual follows the leader until it reaches the target, e.g. the exit. Furthermore, the model enables the creation of different groups in the crowd, assigning to each group a leader and the corresponding members. It favors the dynamic grouping rather than the static one [8]. Instead of forming inflexible groups, the members of each group may change as the process evolves. Besides, dynamic grouping is more realistic than static.

Algorithmically, the model adopts a method of movement similar to closest-exit method. In fact, its functionality is extended by incorporating leaders as well. A value greater than value three (3) that has been used to indicate an exit is assigned to a cell that is occupied by a leader. Thus the leader is also treated as an exit as well, which a group of individuals tries to approach. Furthermore, alike the motion of a school of fishes in a fishbowl, the model is able to simulate the case of movement in a blocked (or non-exit) area. Hence, another one parameter is assigned to the leader, the internal clock. According to the value of the clock the leader makes a predefined movement. For example, the clock of a leader can be assigned values in the space of [1, 200]. Particularly, when the value of the clock lies in-between [1, 49], the leader moves to the North, [50, 99] to the West, [100, 149] to the South and [150,200] to the East respectively, thus defining an anti-clockwise route.

As far as the members of the group concern, their movement is defined by the same set of rules as the one that defines the movement of individuals towards an exit.

The new property that has been incorporated in the model relies on the fact that now the members of a group perceive their leader as a moving exit that they want to approach. This attribute enables the formation of the group and its persistence, without any computational overhead. In the case of the simplified simulation process, the velocities of the members have been adopted as unary. Hence, individuals can hardly pass their leader. Though, the model is provided with the option of an increased velocity of the leader.

From a mathematical point of view, the direction of movement of the individuals relies on a potential field. It derives from the negative gradient of a function that involves the distance (Manhattan) of each point of the area from the position of the leader. In the case of two-dimensions, the function $f(x,y)$ is defined as follows:

$$f(x, y) = abs(x - x_o) + abs(y - y_o) \tag{1}$$

where $(x_o, y_o)$ correspond to the coordinates of the leader.

The corresponding gradient of the function $f(x,y)$ is defined as:

$$-\nabla f(x, y) = -\left( \frac{\partial f(x, y)}{\partial x} \vec{i} + \frac{\partial f(x, y)}{\partial y} \vec{j} \right)$$

$$-\nabla f(x, y) = -\left( \frac{\partial abs(x - x_o)}{\partial x} \vec{i} + \frac{\partial abs(y - y_o)}{dy} \vec{j} \right) \tag{2}$$

It can be thought of as a collection of vectors pointing in the direction of decreasing values of $f(x,y)$.

Spatially, the whole process is divided in eight sub-sections, i.e. for the case that the leader moves i) downwards $(y>y_o)$, ii) upwards $(y<y_o)$, iii) to the left $(x>x_o)$, iv) to the right $(x<x_o)$, v) downwards and to the right $(y>y_o)$ and $(x<x_o)$, vi) downwards and to the left $(y>y_o)$ and $(x>x_o)$, vii) upwards and to the left $(y<y_o)$ and $(x>x_o)$ and viii) upwards and to the right $(y<y_o)$ and $(x<x_o)$. For instance, in the case that the leader moves downwards and to the right (i.e. case (v)), the corresponding potential field that is derived from equation (2), is depicted in Fig. 1.

Moreover, an additional modification has taken place, as far as obstacles concerns. In general, the leaders tend to move in sectors rather than following an internal clock. The latter is only adopted in the special case of a totally blocked area (fishbowl case). Thus, the movement of the leaders turns out to be more flexible and the obstacles' avoidance becomes more effective. Particularly, the two-dimensional space has been divided in 17 sectors (16 peripherals and a central one) and the leaders move among these sectors (Fig. 2). In the case of a clockwise movement, the sectors' changing sequence is 1-2-3-4-..-15-16-1, whereas the sequence becomes 16-15-...-2-1-16 to realise the anti-clockwise movement. The way that the leader moves depends on its value. In the case that the value is divided exactly with 2 then the leader moves clockwise, otherwise the leader moves anticlockwise.

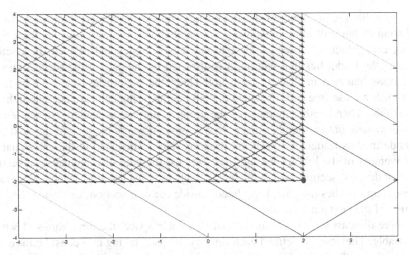

**Fig. 1.** The corresponding potential field in the case that the leader is positioned at ($x_o$=2, $y_o$=-2) and moving downwards and to the right. All individuals within blue-arrows area follow the leader (red spot).

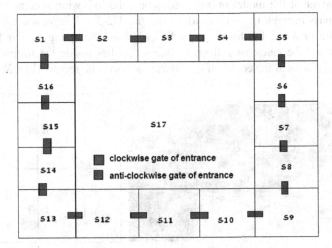

**Fig. 2.** Planar sections and gates of sections. For example, green gate that lies inside section 2 is used by leaders that tend to move from section 1 towards section 2. As soon as the leader enters section 2 starts to move towards green gate that lies inside section 3 (clockwise).

The adoption of sectors is based on the simple fact that even in real life bounded areas are divided to multiple sub-areas with their own formation and their own exits. Each sub-area shares the same properties with the total area, thus enabling the use of the property of the superposition. Hence, the scalability of the method is reassured, allowing its application in more complicated areas.

The movement of the leaders through sections takes place as follows: depending on the direction of the leaders' motion, each section is supplied with two gates that the leaders use to enter the section. The leaders move towards the exits following the same rules that the members of the flock use to follow the leader; they calculate the Manhattan distance of all neighbouring cells and choose to move towards the neighbouring cell, which is closer to the exit and it is not occupied as well. In a sense, whenever the leader lies in a section, it is attracted by the gate of the successive section. In case that also an obstacle exists in the area, the leader tries to avoid it by moving towards a close free cell. Provided that all neighbouring cells are occupied, this is not possible. Then another member of the group is defined as leader. The same process is repeated, until a member that is free to move towards the gate of the next section is defined as leader. A significant property that is attributed to the gates enables the movement of the leaders through the sections; the gate of reference of a section resides at the next section, which the leader tends to move towards. Hence, as soon as the leader approaches the gate, it is already inside the new section, i.e. inside the field of action of the next gate.

In three dimensions, the CA is defined in a cubic space, the dimensions of which are variable. They can be defined each time by the user, taking into consideration that each cell needs three coordinates $(i, j, k)$ to be properly defined. The neighbourhood of each cell is shaped by its 26 closest cells, whereas there are four (4) sectors that divide the space in four rectangular parallelepipeds (Fig. 3a). In case that we wish to test the behavior of the model in 3-d dimensions, the following scheme takes place; the leaders pass through the sectors following the 1-2-3-4-1 sequence for the clockwise direction or 4-3-2-1-4 for the anti-clockwise one. Adopting similar logic as in two-dimensions, the gate that influences one sector lies inside the following sector. The gates are placed at the center of the internal sides of the sectors (Fig. 3b).

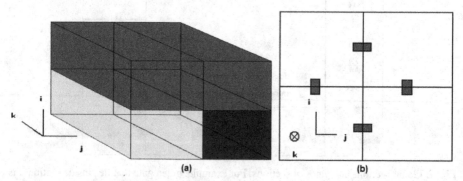

**Fig. 3.** (a) Four sectors in 3-D (b) Gates placed at the center of the internal sides of the sectors

## 4     Simulation Results

In order to validate the proposed model and evaluate its functionality a couple of different simulation schemes took place. The first one studied the case of obstacle avoidance. Solid obstacles were spread within the area of movement. It was observed that whenever a flock met an obstacle, it was divided into two smaller flocks that moved along the obstacle and they were unified again at the back of the obstacle. This is a response identical to nature's response. According to the second scheme, the leaders were forced to move faster than the members of the flock. The response of the model proved that even under such conditions, the members of the flock try to follow the leader, as it is naturally expected.

Furthermore, in all scenarios members of a flock were free to move from one flock to another. Thus, for example, in the case that two flocks approached each other very closely or a member of a flock could not follow its initial group, individuals tended to change groups. This is also a natural response that further validates the operation of the proposed model. The initial two-dimensional approach included a scheme with two groups of people that make a circling movement, each following a leader. The leaders initially followed the same direction and then moved to reverse directions in order the behaviour of the flocks to appear when they met each other. When moving reversely, there was a time span that the two groups merged until they separated again, each following its direction. The latter is also an expectable behaviour that is naturally defined. In all simulations, individuals moved within a restrained area with the walls forming the boundaries, thus adopting zero boundary conditions. Below, characteristic simulation scenarios are demonstrated that contain all above discussed attributes of crowd movement.

## 4.1     Two Leaders Move in Opposite Directions

This scenario includes two leaders moving in an opposite direction and it has taken place in 120 time steps. One group follows a leader that moves clockwise and another one trails a leader that moves anti-clockwise. This simulation has taken place so as the behaviour of two flocks in direction of collision to be studied. As the leaders approach each other, the two flocks follow the same direction until they merge (Fig. 4b). While the two leaders continue to move in opposite directions, the two groups divide again (Fig. 4c,d) depicting a behaviour that is also apparent in nature. This result enforces the efficiency of the model. In the meanwhile, some members of the first group have been incorporated into the other and vice versa. Such a transition is naturally expectable as well. Finally, as derived by the simulation process, the density of the crowd increases as the group turns in order to change its direction of motion. The latter observation is also confirmed by real life experiences.

## 4.2     Two Leaders Move in an Area with Obstacles

This scenario includes two leaders moving in an area with obstacles and it has taken place in 80 time steps. It demonstrates the way that the groups react when facing an obstacle that hinders their route. In any case, each group tries to follow its leader. Furthermore, depending on the area layout, a group may overcome an obstacle by moving along its perimeter or it may squish itself, adapting its shape to the free area between two obstacles (Fig. 5). Macroscopically, the flock adopts characteristics of a fluid, though the emerging behaviour derives from simple rules that they are applied locally. Finally, the simulation process affirms that the speed of the group decreases as it moves in an area that its members have to overcome obstacles.

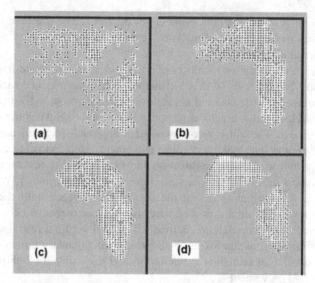

**Fig. 4.** Two leaders move in opposite directions. The two flocks that follow the leaders meet (a), merge (b) and split again after having passed the one through the other (c, d), respectively.

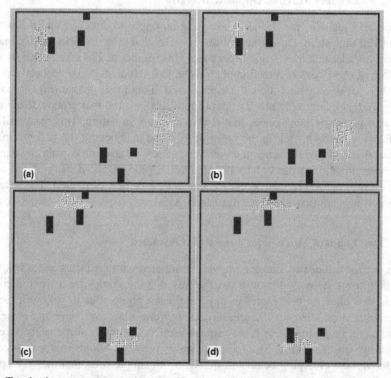

**Fig. 5.** Two leaders move among obstacles. The corresponding groups try to follow the leaders. Thus, they may move along the perimeter of an obstacle (a, b), or even squish themselves to move among obstacles (c, d).

# 5     Conclusions and Future Work

A CA-based computational model has been presented that aims at simulating qualitatively crowd behaviour. Particularly, various simulation scenarios demonstrated distinct features of crowd movement, thus enhancing the efficiency of the model. There have been presented phenomena such as flocking, increasing crowd density in turnings and crowd movement deceleration as self-organised groups try to pass obstacles. Furthermore, significant features of crowd dynamics, such as transition from a random to a coordinated motion during crowd movement as well as arching in front of exits have also been detected during simulations. Considerable modifications in crowd movement are observed when crowd density fluctuates, as congestions may lead to immobility. Such behaviour is also apparent during simulations, further validating the response of the model.

The driving mechanism of the model could be referred as biologically-inspired, since it derives from a naturally detected behaviour of biological organisms, i.e. follow-the-leader behaviour. The latter technique has been incorporated into the model and triggers the herding formations of crowd during mass collective motion. This lastingly detected macroscopical behaviour of crowds, especially during urgent circumstances, has been modeled on a lower level. It took place with the development of a CA and the application of simple local rules that define the moving options of every single member that forms the crowd. The number of acquired leaders is not fixed and depends on the layout of the evacuation area as well as on the dense of the crowd.

The serial access of array-structures that is adopted by the computational resources constraints the response of the model, especially as far as its depiction potentialities concerns. Undesirable co-ordinations appear when individuals move towards certain directions. Such problems could be moderated by adopting the use of parallel programming or parallel processing. The latter can be implemented with a graphical processing unit (GPU). Such a solution could enable a more effective utilisation of the intrinsic parallel characteristics of CA. Such a modification could certainly accelerate the response of the model and improve it qualitatively.

# References

1. Burks, A.W.: Theory of Self-Reproducing Automata JOHN VON NEUMANN. University of Illinois Press, Urbana and London (1966)
2. Smith, J.A.: Martin A.M., Comparison of Hard-Core and Soft-Core Potentials for Modelling Flocking in Free Space, University of Melbourne, Parkville, arXiv:0905.2260v1 (2009)
3. Reynolds, C.W.: Flocks, herds and schools: A distributed behavioral model. In: Computer Graphics, Los Angeles (1987)
4. Vicsek, T., Czirok, A., Ben-Jacob, E., Cohen, I., Shochet, O.: Novel Type of Phase Transition in a System of Self-Driven Particles. Phys. Rev. Lett. 75, 1226 (1995)
5. Lawson, D.: Planes: Trains and Ant Hills: Computer scientists simulate activity of ants to reduce airline delays. Science Daily, April 1 (2008)

6. Swarming the shelves: How groups can exploit people's herd mentality to increase sales. The Economist, 90 (November 11, 2006)
7. Fisher, L.: The perfect swarm: the science of complexity in everyday life. Basic Books, New York (2009)
8. Qingge, J.I., Can, G.A.O.: Simulating Crowd Evacuation with a Leader-Follower Model. IJCSES International Journal of Computer Sciences and Engineering Systems 1(4) (October 2007)
9. Burstedde, C., Klauck, K., Schadschneider, A., Zittartz, J.: Simulation of pedestrian dynamics using a two-dimensional cellular automaton. Physica A 295, 507–525 (2001)
10. Bandini, S., Federici, M.L., Vizzari, G.: Situated Cellular Agents Approach to Crowd Modeling and Simulation. Cybernetics and Systems 38, 729–753 (2007)
11. Bandini, S., Manzoni, S., Redaelli, S.: Towards an Ontology for Crowds Description: A Proposal Based on Description Logic. In: Umeo, H., Morishita, S., Nishinari, K., Komatsuzaki, T., Bandini, S. (eds.) ACRI 2008. LNCS, vol. 5191, pp. 538–541. Springer, Heidelberg (2008)
12. Helbing, D., Farkas, I., Vicsek, T.: Simulating dynamical features of escape panic. Nature 407, 487–490 (2000)
13. Goldstone, R.L., Janssen, M.A.: Computational models of collective behavior. Trends in Cognitive Sciences 9(9), 424–430 (2005)
14. Bonabeau, E.: Agent-based modeling: Methods and techniques for simulating human systems. Proc. of the National Academy of Sciences of the USA (PNAS) 99(suppl.3), 7280–7287 (2002)
15. Lo, S.M., Huang, H.C., Wang, P., Yuen, K.K.: A game theory based exit selection model for evacuation. Fire Safety Journal 41, 364–369 (2006)
16. Altshuler, E., Ramos, O., Nunez, Y., Fernandez, J., Batista-Leyva, A.J., Noda, C.: Symmetry breaking in escaping ants. The American Naturalist 166(6), 643–649 (2005)
17. Aubé, F., Shield, R.: Modeling the Effect of Leadership on Crowd Flow Dynamics. In: Sloot, P.M.A., Chopard, B., Hoekstra, A.G. (eds.) ACRI 2004. LNCS, vol. 3305, pp. 601–611. Springer, Heidelberg (2004)
18. Yuan, W.F., Tan, K.H.: An evacuation model using cellular automata. Physica A 384, 549–566 (2007)
19. Varas, A., Cornejo, M.D., Mainemer, D., Toledo, B., Rogan, J., Munoz, V., et al.: Cellular automaton model for evacuation process with obstacles. Physica A 382, 631–642 (2007)
20. Li, J., Yang, L.Z., Zhao, D.L.: Simulation of bi-direction pedestrian movement in corridor. Physica A 354, 619–628 (2005)
21. Kirchner, A., Klupfel, H., Nishinari, K., Schadschneider, A., Schreckenberg, M.: Simulation of competitive egress behavior: comparison with aircraft evacuation data. Physica A 324, 689–697 (2003)
22. Georgoudas, I.G., Sirakoulis, G.C., Andreadis, I.: A Simulation Tool for Modelling Pedestrian Dynamics during Evacuation of Large Areas. In: The Proceedings of the 3rd IFIP Conference on Artificial Intelligence Applications, & Innovations (AIAI 2006), Athens, Greece, June 7-9. IFIP, vol. 204, pp. 618–626 (2006)
23. Touma, J., Shreim, A., Klushin, L.I.: Self-Organisation in two-dimensional Swarms. Physical Review E 81, 066106 (2010), arXiv:1103.2551v1

# A Spatially Explicit Migration Model for Pike

Steffie Van Nieuland[1,*], Jan M. Baetens[1], Ine S. Pauwels[2], Bernard De Baets[1], Ans M. Mouton[3], and Peter L.M. Goethals[2]

[1] KERMIT, Department of Mathematical Modelling, Statistics and Bioinformatics, Ghent University, Coupure links 653, Gent, Belgium
[2] Laboratory of Environmental Ecotoxicology and Aquatic Ecology Ghent University, J. Plateaustraat 22, Gent, Belgium
[3] Research Institute for Nature and Forest, Kliniekstraat 25, Brussels, Belgium
steffie.vannieuland@ugent.be

**Abstract.** Pike (*Esox lucius* L.) populations have been suffering from habitat degradation and the increasing number of restoration programs had only limited success. In order to set up more effective restoration programmes in the future, it is important to gain insight into the spatio-temporal dynamics of pike. Because no efforts have been spent to develop a spatially explicit model that enables a better understanding of the observed patterns of movement, and actually as a first step towards an integrated spatially explicit model for describing pike dynamics, a model mimicking the movement of pike in the river Yser, Belgium, is proposed.

**Keywords:** spatially explicit, migration, northern pike, rivers.

## 1 Introduction

Pike populations have been suffering from the degradation of the environment and, taking into account its role as a top predator and its recreational value, several attempts were undertaken to reintroduce pike in Belgium. However, a rehabilitation was mostly not achieved since the primary causes leading to a relapse of the pike populations, such as poor water quality and habitat deterioration, largely remained. The spatio-temporal distribution of pike in both rivers and still waters was investigated thoroughly throughout the last decade [4], but no efforts have been spent to develop a spatially explicit model for gaining better understanding of the observed patterns of movement. The use of spatially explicit models in ecology is manifold and their contribution to a full understanding of the spatio-temporal dynamics has long been considered promising [6].

Motivated by the lack of a spatially explicit model for describing the movement of pike, we propose a model to mimic the spatial distribution of pike within one of Belgium's principal rivers, namely the river Yser. The actual study area covers a 10 km stretch of the river and contains three artificial spawning grounds. This stretch was conveniently represented by a rectangular region in which the position of the individuals could be identified unambiguously by means of a Cartesian

---

* Corresponding author.

G.C. Sirakoulis and S. Bandini (Eds.): ACRI 2012, LNCS 7495, pp. 763–767, 2012.

coordinate system centered halfway the river at the downstream boundary of the study area. As a means to quantify the habitat suitability, a map of the habitat suitability index (HSI) was composed [5] based upon a survey of the vegetation type and the naturalness of the bank reinforcements [1].

## 2   Model Development

### 2.1   Equations of Motion

Basically, the spatio-temporal dynamics of a pike individual $i$ is governed by a vector equation that was proposed originally to simulate the motion of interacting particles in a plane [7]. This vector equation allows to describe the position $p_i(t) = (x_i(t), y_i(t))$ of the $i$-th pike that belongs to a population of size $N$ through time and is given by

$$\mathbf{x}_i(t + \Delta t) = \mathbf{x}_i(t) + v_i(t) \frac{\mathbf{W}_i(t)}{\|\mathbf{W}_i(t)\|} \Delta t \,, \tag{1}$$

where $\mathbf{x}_i(t) = [x_i(t), y_i(t)]^{\mathrm{T}}$ (the location) and $v_i(t)$ is the swimming speed of the $i$-th individual. Further, $\mathbf{W}_i(t)$ is a weighted average, $i.e.$

$$\mathbf{W}_i(t) = \big(1 - \alpha_i(t)\big) \mathbf{P}_i(t) + \alpha_i(t) \mathbf{Q}_i(t) \,, \tag{2}$$

of two unit vectors $\mathbf{P}_i$ and $\mathbf{Q}_i$ that steer the direction in which pike $i$ moves depending on the presence of other individuals in its neighborhood and the season ($\mathbf{P}_i$), and the attraction to spawning grounds ($\mathbf{Q}_i$). The swimming direction $\theta_i$ of a given pike $i$, which is defined by the angle between the horizontal axis of an orthogonal coordinate system centered in $(x_i(t), y_i(t))$ and the vector of motion, can be obtained from

$$\begin{bmatrix} \cos \theta_i(t) \\ \sin \theta_i(t) \end{bmatrix} = \frac{\mathbf{W}_i(t)}{\|\mathbf{W}_i(t)\|} \,. \tag{3}$$

Essentially, the weighing coefficient $\alpha_i(t)$ in Eq. (2) allows to alter the relative contribution of $\mathbf{P}_i(t)$ and $\mathbf{Q}_i(t)$ in the determination of $\mathbf{W}_i(t)$. Hence, it enables a periodization of the individuals' behaviour through time. Yet, the formulation of the unit vectors $\mathbf{P}_i(t)$ and $\mathbf{Q}_i(t)$ has to be modified in order to mimic the behaviour of pike.

### 2.2   Seasonal Behaviour

Three periods during which pike show distinct migratory behaviour are distinguished in one annual cycle. A spawning season (February 15 - May 15) with long distance migration [3], a passive sedentary period that runs from the end of the spawning season until the start of the winter (December 1) with long stationary periods, interchanged with short-lasting movements to catch their preys [4] and finally, an active sedentary season that differs from the passive one as the individuals have to look for their potential preys more actively [4].

Fuzzy sets are used to make a distinction between the different behavioural periods. The weighing function $\alpha_i(t)$ in Eq. (2) can be contemplated as a trapezoidal fuzzy set with parameters $(45, 73, 104, 134)$ to distinguish between the spawning and the sedentary period, where it should be noticed that the first of January is labeled as day number one. Similarly to the weighing function $\alpha_i(t)$, a weighing function $\beta_i(t)$ that grasps the transition between periods in which pike individuals display distinct degrees of activity can be defined as a trapezoidal fuzzy set with parameters $(104, 104, 304, 334)$ [4].

## 2.3   Swimming Direction

The swimming direction is determined by the unit vectors $\mathbf{P}_i(t)$ and $\mathbf{Q}_i(t)$. The first vector $\mathbf{P}_i(t)$ embodies the direction outside the spawning period and is defined as

$$\mathbf{P}_i(t) = \begin{bmatrix} \cos \varphi_i(t) \\ \sin \varphi_i(t) \end{bmatrix}. \tag{4}$$

Since numerous papers report that pike exhibit territorial behaviour outside the spawning period [2,3,4], every individual $i$ is assigned a circular territory that is centered at $c_i = (x_i^\tau, y_i^\tau)$, has radius $r_i$, and through which pike $i$ can swim freely. During the passive sedentary season $r_i$ is set to 50 m. On the other hand, preliminary findings in the framework of an ongoing telemetry study have shown a considerably larger home range during the active sedentary season, namely $r_i = 2000$ m.

Taking this and the behaviour of pike into consideration, $\varphi_i(t)$ in Eq. (4) is a $\beta$-weighted sum of the behaviour during the passive sedentary season and the one during the active sedentary season. The behaviour during the passive sedentary season is defined in such a way that a pike $i$ flees in the direction of its territory center if it encounters a congener or crosses the outskirts of its territory ($r_i = 50$ m). During the active sedentary season, pike $i$ only flees if it crosses the outskirts of its territory ($r_i = 2000$ m) seen the absence of cannibalism.

## 2.4   Swimming Speed

On the basis of preliminary findings in the framework of an ongoing telemetry study, the swimming speed, expressed in meter per day, of every individual $i$ was supposed to be distributed normally, $i.e.$ $N(1230, 650)$. Yet, in order to account for discrepancies that have been observed between the degrees of activity during different seasons [4], both $\alpha_i(t)$ and $\beta_i(t)$ are used to stipulate that the mean swimming speed during the spawning season is 1230 m day$^{-1}$, whereas it is supposed to be only $1230/3$ m day$^{-1}$ during the active sedentary season [4]. Further, since it is to be expected that pike are even less active during the passive sedentary season, a mean swimming speed of 123 m day$^{-1}$ is assumed.

## 3   Simulation Results

We chose $\Delta t = 3600$ s and reflecting boundaries. Initially, each of the 50 pikes are assigned a territory that is located within the concerned river stretch. These

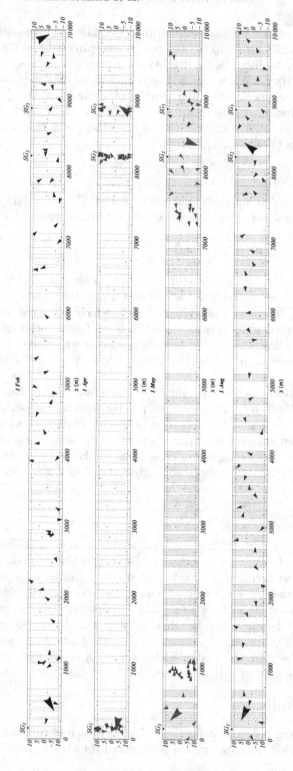

**Fig. 1.** Simulated spatial distribution of the individuals (arrowheads) within the study area at the beginning of four different days during an annual cycle together with the territories (dotted lines) determined by minimization of the overlap between its own territory and the one of individuals in its vicinity and the maximazation of the habitat HSI. They are colored gray with an opacity proportional to beta (if homing is important, the territories are colored). The individuals, of which two are shown by large arrowheads for tracking purposes, are represented by black arrowheads if $\alpha_i(t) = 0$ (outside the spawning season) and gray arrowheads if $\alpha_i(t) > 0$ (during the spawning season). The spawning grounds are indicated as $SG_k$.

territories cannot be randomly distributed across the river stretch, but it is natural to assume that a pike individual will try to minimize the overlap between its own territory and the one of individuals in its vicinity because it is a solitary and cannibalistic species [2], while, at the same time, it will try to maximize the suitability (HSI) of its habitat.

Figure 1 shows just one possible realization of the annual cycle and depicts snapshots of the simulated spatial pike distribution within the study area at the beginning of four different days during an annual cycle. The dates at which snapshots are shown, were selected such that the movement patterns during both the sedentary and spawning season can be inferred. From the first snapshot it is obvious that all members of the population are residing within their large territory ($r_i = 2000$ m) prior to the start of the spawning season, whereas on March 1, pike are colored gray and have migrated towards the spawning grounds. By the first of May the spawning season has finished, pike become territorial and return to their territories ($r_i = 50$ m) where they can be retrieved from the summer on.

## 4    Conclusions

The developed spatially explicit model allows for mimicing the seasonal behaviour of pike. Even though it is presented in the framework of attempts for understanding the spatio-temporal dynamics of pike in the river Yser, it is generic in the sense that it can be tuned easily if another fish species or other regions is at stake by tuning its parameters using species-specific data.

## References

1. Bry, C.: Role of vegetation in the life cycle of pike. Pike: Biology and Exploitation, pp. 45–68. Chapman and Hall, Londen (1996)
2. Craig, J.F.: Pike biology and exploitation. Chapman and Hall, Londen (1996)
3. Harvey, B.: A Biological Synopsis of Northern Pike (*Esox lucius*). Canadian Manuscript Report of Fisheries and Aquatic Sciences 2885 (2009)
4. Koed, A., Balleby, K., Mejlhede, P., Aarestrup, K.: Annual movement of adult pike (*Esox lucius* L.) in a lowland river. Ecol. Freshw. Fish 15, 191–199 (2006)
5. US Fish and Wildlife Service: Standards for the development of habitat suitability index models. Tech. rep., US Fish and Wildlife Service (1981)
6. Van Winkle, W., Rose, K.A., Chambers, R.C.: Individual-based apporach to fish population dynamics: an overview. Trans. Am. Fish. Soc. 122, 397–403 (1993)
7. Vicsek, T., Czirok, A., Ben-Jacob, E., Cohen, I., Shochet, O.: Novel type of phase transition in a system of self-driven particles. Phys. Rev. Lett. 75, 1226–1229 (1995)

# Proxemics in Discrete Simulation of Evacuation

Jarosław Wąs, Robert Lubaś, and Wojciech Myśliwiec

AGH University of Science and Technology
al. Mickiewicza 30, 30-059 Kraków, Poland
jarek@agh.edu.pl

**Abstract.** The article deals with a proxemic approach to evacuation modeling. Proxemics is interpreted as a process of acquisition of space. The authors propose a new, discrete model, based on a more detailed representation of space (taken from the Social Distances Model) and the idea of floor fields. The presented model allows for efficient, real time simulation of evacuation from large facilities using more detailed representation of spatial relations.

## 1 Introduction

The term *proxemics* was introduced by an American anthropologist Edward T. Hall in 1959 to describe *a set of measurable distances among people as they interact.*

According to [7],the etymology of the word refers to as a combination of two elements: prox(imity) + -emics (as in phonemics). The term *proxemics* is defined as: *the study of the cultural, behavioral, and sociological aspects of spatial distances between individuals.*

Recently, the application of the theory of proxemics is becoming an important issue in crowd dynamics modeling. In [5] the idea of space acquisition process in inflow process using proxemic floor field is proposed. Whilst [4] deals with the influence of groups in crowd in the context of spatial relations (proxemics).

One of the possible keys to the understanding of pedestrian behavior and dynamics in different situational contexts is using the theory of proxemics. It is worth noting that the idea of the optimal use of space and pedestrian comfort is described in the Fruin's work [1]. Fruin introduces the term *Level of service* (dedication of a given area of public space to a statistical pedestrian). The originally reffered to a free movement of pedestrians on the streets, but it is also useful for other scenarios.

It should be stressed, that problems related to space acquisition are valid in free movement and also in evacuation situations (resources include time and space). Thus the authors suggested that the concept of *proxemics* in crowds modeling should be interpreted both in normal and emergency situations.

G.C. Sirakoulis and S. Bandini (Eds.): ACRI 2012, LNCS 7495, pp. 768–775, 2012.

## 2    Adaptation of Social Distances Model for Emergency Evacuation

The starting point is Social Distances model described in [10], but actually we do not take into account a force component in pedestrian algorithm movement, because the aim is to create an effective model for large facilities.

### 2.1    Geometrical Representation of Pedestrian

In the simplest case, a pedestrian in the model is represented by an ellipse, whose center coincides with the center of the cell occupied by that person. The size of each ellipse equals $a = 0.225$ m (semi-major axis) and $b = 0.135$ m (semi-minor axis) which is assumed to be the average size of a person (according to WHO data), while cell size is equal $0.25m$ [10]. A pedestrian can transfer to another cell in Moore neighborhood of radius 1. Each ellipse can be rotated around by: $\pm 0$, $\pm 45$, $\pm 90$ and $\pm 135$ degrees.

The crucial issue is to establish the set of forbidden and allowed positions for all cells in Moore neighborhood of radius 1, each cell being occupied by one person. The calculation of the allowed/forbidden positions is based upon simple geometrical dependencies [10]. It takes into account the following: the orientations of two ellipses occupying two adjacent cells and the size of their cross-section. It is assumed that the position is allowed if the ratio of the calculated crossection (for this position) to the size of the ellipsis is smaller than imposed tolerance $\epsilon_N \in [0, 1]$.

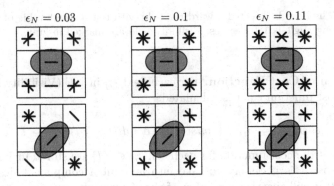

**Fig. 1.** Allowed neighborhood configurations for different tolerance parameters

Fig. 1 presents allowed states for neighbor-cells for different tolerance parameters. Lines represents allowed configurations of different agents in an agent neighborhood.

With this approach, we can consider the fluctuations of density and crowd compressibility more accurately, than in classical CA based models (where a pedestrian is represented as a special state of square-shaped cell sized $0.4m$).

It should be stressed, that elliptic representation of pedestrians, taking into account forbidden/allowed states in the neighborhood, make the modeling of proxemics rules during evacuation possible.

## 2.2 Movement Rules

Applied movement algorithms are based on three ideas known from other CA based models [2,3]: static floor field, dynamic floor field and a cost function. The implementation of ideas were modified to apply in the Social Distances Model environment.

The execution of a single-step of the simulation includes choosing the next destination cell by pedestrians. The following steps are realized:

**Calculation of *Visibility Fields* (VF).** Visibility field is determined by head position Fig 2. It is calculated on the base of a static field $S$ in Moore neighborhood.

**Fig. 2.** (a) The head is directed toward the field with the smallest value of static field $S$. (b) Viewing angle is 180 degrees. Visibility field are marked in gray.

**Calculation of Cost Function.** For each field $f_{ij}$ in $VF$ (Visibility Field) the following cost function eq. 1 is calculated:

$$cost(f_{ij}) = S_{ij} + (dens(f_{ij}) + \alpha * dist(s, f_{ij})) * W * I \qquad (1)$$

The values of the cost function for each cell $c_{ij} \in VF$ are stored in $VF_{cost}$.

Afterwards, it is necessery to take into account a component described in equation (2) It will give rise of number of parallel lanes in moving crowd (Fig. 3). Different colors of pedestrians in Fig. 3 represent different maximal velocities of pedestrians.

$$dens(f_{ij}) = e^{\delta * D_{ij}} \qquad (2)$$

where:

$D_{ij}$ - value of dynamic field,
$\delta \in [0, \infty)$ – chosen empirically.

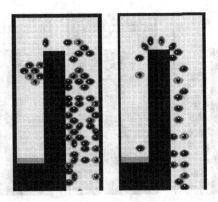

**Fig. 3.** Simulation with parameters $\delta = 3.5$, $\alpha = 1.3$, $diag = 3.0$, $straight = 0$, $rad_1 = 0.14$, $rad_2 = 0.07$, $I = 0.55$ - overtaking is possible (a) and in (b) are the same parameters except $\delta = 0$, thus $dens(f_{ij}) = 1$ - the shortest path is preferred

Next, we have to take into consideration the distance component [12] to improve obstacle avoidance.

$$\alpha * dist(s, f_{ij}) = \begin{cases} diag & \text{for diagonal movement direction} \\ straight & \text{for straight movement direction} \end{cases} \quad (3)$$

where:

$\alpha \in [0, \infty)$,
$s$ - is the cell occupied by a pedestrian.

Wall force - avoiding wall component is simalar to [2].

$$W = 1.0 + \sigma_W \quad (4)$$

$$\sigma_W = \begin{cases} rad_1 + rad_2 \in (0, 1] & \text{if an obstacle is located in the von Neumann} \\ & \text{neighborhood of radius 1} \\ rad_2 \in (0, 1] & \text{if an obstacle is located in the von Neumann} \\ & \text{neighborhood of radius 2} \\ 0 & \text{otherwise} \end{cases}$$

Inertia component - we use inertia factor $I$, thanks to which pedestrians keep their direction as long as possible.

**Selection of the most attractive field (new destination) $f_{best}$ from $VF_{cost}$**

$$f_{best} = min(VF_{cost}) \quad (5)$$

In the end, when two or more pedestrians want to chose the same cell a mechanism of conflicts resolving is applied by random function or by the selection

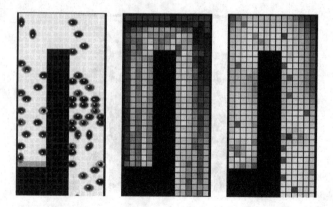

**Fig. 4.** View of pedestrians represented by ellipses (a), view of frequency matrix (b), view of dynamic fields

of a pedestrian who is waiting the longest to adjust the allowed neighborhood configuration Fig.1.

Fig. 4 presents different views from simulation based on the described model: simulation, frequency matrix and dynamics field. While a view on evacuation of a stadium tribune is presented in Fig 5

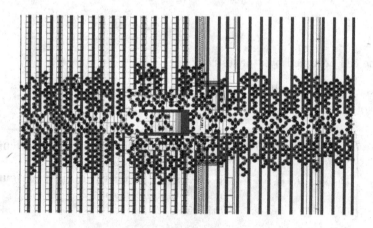

**Fig. 5.** Simulation of a stadium tribune

The presented model is actually validated. Exemplary fundamental diagram (flow/density relation) is presented in Fig. 6.

## 2.3   Performance

A performance test was executed on a unit with the following specification: Intel CPU q6600 $3.2GHz$, 4GB RAM and Microsoft Windows 7 Pro 64-bit. Test object

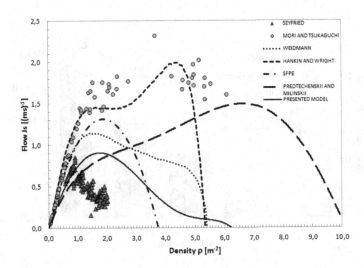

**Fig. 6.** Fundamental diagram of presented model compared with fundamental diagrams by SFPE Handbook [13], Predtechenskii & Milinskii [14], Weidmann [16], Hankin & Wright, Seyfried [9], Mori i Tskukaguchi

is defined as an empty space with dimensions of $176.5m$ x $176.5m$ ($31152.25m^2$). The number of pedestrians in the simulation were $100, 1000, 10000, 25000, 50000$. The graph 7 shows the dynamics of memory usage and the average execution time of one iteration of the algorithm.

Execution time of a single iteration is the average of 500 trials.[1]

The run-time complexity for the avarage-case scenario of presented algorithm is quasilinear: $O(n \log n + m)$, where $n$ – number of pedestrians in simulation and $m$ – number of emergency exits. The reason for that class of complexity is the sorting algorithm used to sort list of agents. It is worth mentioning, that the time complexity is not dependent on the size of grid, but only on the number of agents.

Memory complexity is directly related to the size of grid in the model. If we denote in this case $n$ as the grid size ($m$ - is still number of emergency exits), the memory complexity will be estimated as $O(n^2m)$ class. One can observe increasing of memory usage in dependence on the number of emergency exits in the grid. This is due to the structure of static fields.

## 3 Concluding Remarks

The issue of proxemics, understood as the process of acquisition space by individuals, requires a different approach to normal and emergency situations in the modeling of crowd behavior.

---

[1] SysInternals Process Explorer was used to measure the memory consumption. The value refers to the Private Working Set.

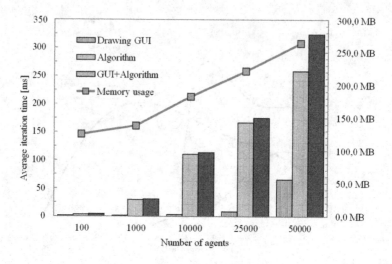

**Fig. 7.** Results of performance tests.

In a normal situation, we can observe *territoriality* and *classical social zone* around individuals or groups of people. On the other hand in evacuation situation, pedestrians want to leave the occupied facility. In this case, the process of achieving the aims (like exits or safe places) is realized dynamically using different strategies such as: fastest path, shortest path, etc depending on specific conditions.

The proposed model allows for more accurate modeling of spatial relations than models based on classical cellular automaton. We do not consider the zones around an individual, but we take into account different configurations in neighborhood, that allow for more precise modeling of the occupation of space.

The model was tested for large facilities and we obtained encouraging results. The proposed model works in real time, but it is a necessity to carry out further, comprehensive performance tests. The model is being validated. Some procedures and scenarios are successfully finished like the scenario described in [9,8,15], but the validation process is in progress.

**Acknowledgment.** This work is partially supported under the FP7 ICT program of the European Commission under grant agreement No 231288 (SOCIONICAL).

# References

1. Fruin, J.J.: Pedestrian and Planning Design. Metropolitan Association of Urban Designers and Environmental Planners (1971)
2. Nishinari, K., Kirchner, A., Namazi, A., Schadschneider, A.: Extended Floor Field CA Model for Evacuation Dynamics. IEICE Trans. Inf. & Syst. E87-D, 726–732 (2004)

3. Kirik, E., Yurgelyan, T., Krouglov, D.: On realizing the shortest time strategy in a CA FF. Pedestrian Dynamics Model Cybernetics and Systems 42, 1–15 (2011)
4. Manzoni, S., Vizzari, G., Ohtsuka, K., Shimura, K.: Towards an agent-based proxemic model for pedestrian and group dynamics: motivations and first experiments. In: AAMAS 2011, pp. 1223–1224 (2011)
5. Ezaki, T., Yanagisawa, D., Ohtsuka, K., Nishinari, K.: Simulation of space acquisition process of pedestrians using Proxemic Floor Field Model. Physica A 391(1), 291–299
6. Okada, M., Motegi, Y., Yamamoto, K.: Human swarm modeling in exhibition space and space design. IEEE Intelligent Robot and Systems, 5021–5026 (2011)
7. The American Heritage Dictionary of the English Language. Term: Proxemics (2011)
8. Schadschneider, A., Seyfried, A.: Validation of CA models of pedestrian dynamics with fundamental diagrams. Cybernetics and Systems 40, 367–389 (2009)
9. Zhang, J., Klingsch, W., Schadschneider, A., Seyfried, A.: Transitions in pedestrian fundamental diagrams of straight corridors and T-junctions. Journal of Statistical Mechanics: Theory and Experiment 6 (June 2011)
10. Wąs, J., Gudowski, B., Matuszyk, P.J.: Social Distances Model of Pedestrian Dynamics. In: El Yacoubi, S., Chopard, B., Bandini, S. (eds.) ACRI 2006. LNCS, vol. 4173, pp. 492–501. Springer, Heidelberg (2006)
11. Wąs, J., Myśliwiec, W., Lubaś, R.: Towards realistic modeling of crowd compressibility. In: Richard, D., Peacock, E.D., Kuligowski, J.D. (eds.) Pedestrian and Evacuation Dynamics PED 2010: the Fifth International Conference on: Gaithersburg Maryland, pp. 527–534. Springer, New York (2011)
12. Kotulski, L., Sędziwy, A.: Parallel Graph Transformations Supported by Replicated Complementary Graphs. In: Dobnikar, A., Lotrič, U., Šter, B. (eds.) ICANNGA 2011, Part II. LNCS, vol. 6594, pp. 254–264. Springer, Heidelberg (2011)
13. National Fire Protection Association and Society of Fire Protection Engineers, SFPE handbook of fire protection engineering (2002)
14. Predtechenskii, V.M., Milinskii, A.I.: Planning for foot traffic flow in buildings, Amerind (1978)
15. Wąs, J.: Experiments on Evacuation Dynamics for Different Classes of Situations. In: Pedestrian and Evacuation Dynamics 2008, pp. 225–232. Springer, Heidelberg (2010)
16. Weidmann, U.: Transporttechnik der Fussgänger - Transporttechnische Eigenschaften des Fussgängerverkehrs (Literaturstudie), Institut füer Verkehrsplanung, Transporttechnik, Strassen- und Eisenbahnbau IVT an der ETH Zürich (1993)

# Metastability in Pedestrian Evacuation

Takahiro Ezaki[1] and Daichi Yanagisawa[2]

[1] Department of Aeronautics and Astronautics, School of Engineering,
The University of Tokyo, 7-3-1, Hongo, Bunkyo-ku, Tokyo 113-8656, Japan
ezaki@jamology.rcast.u-tokyo.ac.jp
[2] College of Science, Ibaraki University,
2-1-1, Bunkyo, Mito, Ibaraki, 310-8512, Japan
daichi@mx.ibaraki.ac.jp

**Abstract.** We investigate the behavior of evacuation process with steady inflow using the floor field model. By simulations, the metastable state induced by conflicts of pedestrians is observed. The system is controlled by parameters of the inflow and competitiveness of the pedestrians, and large inflow leads to a congested situation. The critical condition of the transition is theoretically derived.

**Keywords:** cellular automata, pedestrian dynamics, evacuation process, floor field model.

## 1 Introduction

Study of crowd behavior has attracted many physicists over the last decades [1,2]. The motion of pedestrians can be regarded as a many-body system of 'self-driven' particles, and the perfect understanding of its dynamics is still remain open. In order to investigate the collective phenomena of the systems, many microscopic models have been developed: the social force model [3], the floor field (FF) model [4,5,6,7,8], the lattice gas model [9], and etc. In addition to the simulations, much effort has been devoted also to experimental studies [10].

In this study field, evacuation of pedestrians has been vigorously studied since it is of great importance to design buildings properly for the case of emergency, in the context of risk management. One of the prominent phenomena observed in the evacuation is clustering of pedestrians at bottlenecks such as exits. When more than one pedestrian tries to move to the same place, the *conflict* occurs, decreasing the outflow of pedestrians. The effect of the conflict is a dominant factor of total evacuation time; however, only a few theoretical analyses have been performed so far [6,7,8]. In the previous studies, the evacuation process from a single room has been investigated. On the other hand, in actual emergency, the pedestrian flow experiences many bottlenecks and merges together toward the exit. Up to authors' knowledge, no theoretical approach to the evacuation from complex buildings has been proposed. This study gives a first step towards the understanding about the problem by focusing on a single segment of the bottlenecks.

G.C. Sirakoulis and S. Bandini (Eds.): ACRI 2012, LNCS 7495, pp. 776–784, 2012.

In this paper, the overall argument is based on the FF model, which is one of the well-established cellular automata model for describing the pedestrian dynamics. The effect of the conflict was first implemented in the FF model by introducing the friction parameter in Refs. [5,6]. In the present study, we use a more general version of the friction parameter, namely, the friction function which was first proposed in Ref. [8]. The motion of pedestrians involved in the conflict is cancelled with a certain probability determined by the friction function, which controls the strength of clogging and sticking among pedestrians. Different from other studies, in addition to exits, we set an entrance providing pedestrians stochastically in the system. This entrance enable us to control the inflow of pedestrians, and by regarding it as inflow from the exit of the previous bottleneck, we can evaluate the effect of connectivity of bottlenecks.

The rest of this paper is organized as follows. Section 2 gives the definition of the model. In Sec. 3, simulation results are shown. To explain the phenomena analytically, we propose the second order cluster approximation in Sec. 4. Finally, we summarize the argument in Sec. 5.

## 2    Model

### 2.1    Floor Field Model

We consider a two-dimensional lattice representing a room with an entrance and exit, consisting of $N \times N$ sites. Each site can contain only one pedestrian at most. Every time step pedestrians choose one destination site out of five neighboring sites: $(i, j)$, $(i+1, j)$, $(i-1, j)$, $(i, j+1)$, and $(i, j-1)$ (see Fig. 1), according to two types of FFs. One of the FFs is the static FF $S_{ij}$ describing the shortest distance to the exit site, and the other is the dynamic FF $D_{ij}$ expressing the total number of pedestrians who has visited the site. The dynamic FF has the dynamics of diffusion and decay, unlike the static FF. The transition probability $p_{ij}$ for a jump to the neighboring site $(i, j)$ is determined by the following expression:

$$p_{ij} = N\xi_{ij} \exp\left(-k_s S_{ij} + k_d D_{ij}\right), \tag{1}$$

where $k_s$ and $k_d$ are non-negative sensitivity parameters, and $N$ stands for the normalization factor. $\xi$ returns 0 for forbidden transitions such as to a wall, an obstacle, and neighboring occupied sites, and returns 1 for other transitions. In this paper, the static FF is given by the $L^2$ norm as

$$S_{ij} = \sqrt{(x_{ij} - x_{ex})^2 + (y_{ij} - y_{ex})^2}, \tag{2}$$

where $(x_{ij}, y_{ij})$ and $(x_{ex}, y_{ex})$ are the coordinates of the site $(i, j)$ and the exit site, respectively. Moreover, we ignore the effect of the dynamic FF ($k_d = 0$) since it does not greatly affect the arguments in this work.

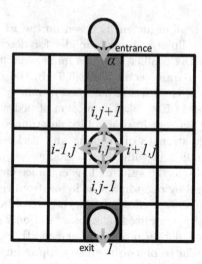

**Fig. 1.** Update rules. Each pedestrian can hop to its neighboring sites or stay at its present site in a time step. Pedestrians enter the area from the entrance with the probability $\alpha$, and leave the area from the exit with the probability 1.

## 2.2 Conflict Resolution

Due to the use of parallel update it happens that more than one pedestrian tries to choose the same site, which is called the *conflict*. The simplest solution of the conflict is to choose one pedestrian randomly to move to the site, and keep other pedestrians at their present sites. However, in actual situations, conflicts sometimes remain unsolved for a while. To model this effect, the friction parameter has been introduced [6,5], and many significant results have been obtained. In a recent study [8], the friction function has been proposed to describe the effect more precisely. In the friction function, the number of pedestrian $k$ involved in the conflict is reflected to its resolution probability. In this paper, we assume $\phi$ in the following form as in Ref. [8]:

$$\phi(\zeta, k) = 1 - (1 - \zeta)^k - k\zeta(1 - \zeta)^{k-1}. \tag{3}$$

Here, $\zeta \in [0, 1]$ is the friction coefficient representing the strength of the clogging irrelevant to $k$. This $\phi$ is a monotonically increasing function of $k$ and $\zeta$. Note that this choice of $\phi$ is one of the possible expressions. If one takes the friction function independent of $k$, it coincides with the friction parameter.

Each conflict is resolved with probability $1 - \phi(\zeta, k)$, and one of $k$ pedestrians is randomly selected to move to the site, otherwise, the conflict remains.

## 2.3 Entrance and Exit

In each time step, a pedestrian is provided to each entrance site with the probability $\alpha \in [0, 1]$ if the site is empty, and pedestrians at exit sites are removed with probability 1. (See Fig. 1.)

# 3    Simulations

In the following, we set $k_s = 10, k_d = 0$. The dimensions of the simulation area are $25 \times 25$, and one entrance site and one exit site are set at $(13, 25)$ and $(13, 1)$, respectively. In this section we see some simulation results, varying the inflow probability $\alpha$ and the conflict coefficient $\zeta$.

## 3.1    Metastability of Pedestrian Flow

In Fig. 3, the average pedestrian outflow through the exit, $q$, is plotted. Here, the density $\rho$ is defined as the number of pedestrians in the room divided by the number of sites in the area, $25 \times 25$. The flux and density are averaged over 100 time steps. The relation between the flux and density is often referred to as the *fundamental diagram* in the context of traffic flow, and interestingly, the *metastable* state is observed also in this problem. While, in the traffic flow, the metastability comes from the effect of inertia of vehicles, in this case, the conflict plays an important role. The occurrence mechanism of the metastable state is as follows. First, the free-flow phase (see Fig. 2) can be observed for every $\alpha$ and $\zeta$. In this phase, large $\alpha$ directly leads to large flux, corresponding to a linear relation between $q$ and $\rho$. In addition, for large $\alpha$ and $\zeta$, a congested situation is observed. The congested situation is caused by the effect of conflict. Once the conflict occurs at the exit, the outflow shrinks. If this outflow is smaller than inflow, the density of pedestrians increases to the congestion. In contrast, if the inflow is not enough large, the conflict disappears, recovering the free flow.

If we take $\alpha$ as a controllable parameter for a given $\zeta$, we can answer "how can we optimize the inflow parameter?" The answer is to keep the inflow lower than the critical rate, which prevents the conflict at the exit from growing. We discuss this argument in the following sections in detail.

## 3.2    Critical Phenomenon Related to $\alpha$ and $\zeta$

In this subsection, we see minutely the phase transition from the free flow to the congestion. Fig. 4 shows the density and flux in the steady state and *transient* state. Here, the transient state is defined as the state of the system with free-flow initial conditions (the room with no pedestrian) at finite time steps and introduced to include the probability of the phase transition. Even in the parameter regime of the congestion, the system might keep the metastable state. In this case, the probability of finding the system in the free-flow phase decreases as the time step grows.

In the simulations, each plot of the transition state (tr.) is obtained by averaging the flux or density over $t_{max} = 100000$ time steps and 100 samples[1]. On the other hand, plots for the steady state (st.) are calculated by averaging

---

[1] Strictly speaking, this quantity corresponds to the 'averaged' transient state, rather than the transient state at timestep $t_{max}$. The quantity is dependent on $t_{max}$ and converges to that of the steady state in the limit of $t_{max} \to \infty$.

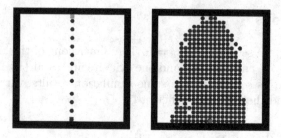

**Fig. 2.** Schematic view of the system. Green and red sites indicate the entrance and exit sites, respectively. With the same inflow rate, one can observe the free-flow phase (left) and congestion phase (right) of pedestrians represented by blue circles.

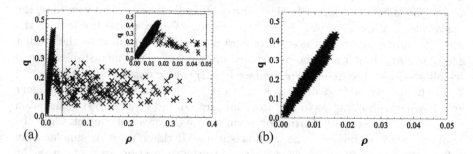

**Fig. 3.** Fundamental diagram of the system in competitive parameter regime [(a)$\zeta = 0.8$] and corporative parameter regime [(b)$\zeta = 0.0$]. Each plot is obtained by setting the inflow probability $\alpha = 0.1, 0.2, \cdots, 0.6$ and averaging the flux and density over 100 time steps.

over 1000000 time steps from $t = 100000$ to $t_{max} = 1100000$. For the st. plots, we adopted the initial condition that pedestrians occupy all the available sites to ensure the occurrence of the congested situation in corresponding parameter regime. In the free-flow phase, the flux is determined only by the inflow probability as shown in the next section. As mentioned in the previous section, the density jumps at a critical $\alpha$, which corresponds to the occurrence of the congestion. In the parameter regime of the congestion, the flux is determined by the outflow, not by the inflow. The simulation results of steady states imply the situation near the exit can be assumed to be independent of the inflow probability in the congested situation. On the other hand, one can see the peak of the flux in the transient state. Since the system does not always cause the congestion even in the congestion regime of parameters (metastability), the expected flux is higher than the jammed flux, if the evacuation is started with uncrowded initial condition.

# 4 Theoretical Analyses

## 4.1 Free-Flow Phase

In the free-flow phase, the pedestrian flux is evaluated by the inflow. First, we consider a balance equation at the entrance site:

$$\alpha(1 - \rho_{en}) = \rho_{en}. \tag{4}$$

Here, $\rho_{en}$ is the probability of finding a pedestrian at the entrance site. Since we set $k_s = 10$, a pedestrian at the entrance site surely leaves the site (with probability 1) in the next time step. By solving the equation, we can evaluate the flux $q_f$:

$$q_f \simeq \alpha(1 - \rho_{en}) = \frac{\alpha}{1 + \alpha}. \tag{5}$$

This expression is shown in Fig. 4 (a) and well agrees with the simulation results.

## 4.2 Congestion Phase

In the congested situation, the area near the exit is almost fully occupied. This fact enables us to estimate the outflow. In the previous studies, the pedestrian density at the neighboring sites of the exit is approximately assumed to be 1 [6,7,8]. However, when the effect of the conflict is strong, this assumption does not give a good estimation. Especially in this paper, since the effect of the conflict depends on the number of pedestrians involved, we have to take the configuration of pedestrians at the exit into consideration. Therefore, we adopt a second order approximation here. In the approximation, we assume the density of pedestrians at the sites where the exit is accessible with two jumps (the second neighboring sites) to be 1 (see Fig. 5). Then, the states of the neighboring sites are characterized by four occupation numbers which take 0 (empty) or 1 (occupied). By considering transition probabilities among these states, we can obtain the probability distribution $P$ of finding each state. To reduce the dimension of the transition matrix, we use the following facts. First, we can easily find $P^0_{000} = 0$ and $P^1_{111} = 0$ since no configuration of pedestrians can result in these states in the next time step. Here, the superscript corresponds to the occupation number of the exit, and the subscripts indicate ones of its neighboring sites as shown in Fig. 5. Furthermore, by symmetry of the system, the following equations

$$P^0_{100} = P^0_{001}, \tag{6}$$
$$P^0_{110} = P^0_{011}, \tag{7}$$
$$P^1_{100} = P^1_{001}, \tag{8}$$
$$P^1_{110} = P^1_{011}, \tag{9}$$

are satisfied. With the nomalization condition, the transition matrix is summarized as follows:

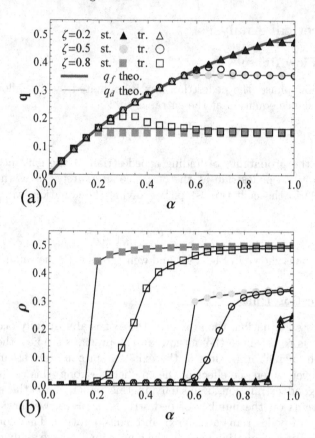

**Fig. 4.** Pedestrian flux and density in the steady state (st.) and transient state (tr.) vs $\alpha$. Eq. (5) and (12) derived in Sec. 4 are also shown as $q_f$ theo. and $q_d$ theo., respectively. The curves are added to improve visibility in the right figure (b).

$$
\begin{pmatrix}
P_{100}^0 \\
P_{010}^0 \\
P_{110}^0 \\
P_{101}^0 \\
P_{111}^0 \\
P_{000}^0 \\
P_{100}^1 \\
P_{010}^1 \\
P_{110}^1 \\
P_{101}^1
\end{pmatrix}
=
\begin{pmatrix}
0 & 0 & 0 & 0 & 0 & \frac{1}{4}\phi_2^2 & \frac{1}{2}\phi_2^2 & 0 & 0 & 0 \\
0 & 0 & 0 & 0 & 0 & \frac{1}{4}\phi_2^2 & 0 & \phi_2^2 & 0 & 0 \\
0 & 0 & \phi_2^2 & 0 & 0 & \frac{1}{2}\phi_2\tilde\phi_2 & \frac{1}{2}\phi_2\tilde\phi_2 & \phi_2\tilde\phi_2 & \phi_2 & 0 \\
0 & 0 & 0 & \phi_2\phi_3 & 0 & \frac{1}{4}\phi_3+\frac{1}{2}\phi_2\tilde\phi_2 & \phi_3+\phi_2\tilde\phi_2 & 0 & 0 & \phi_3 \\
0 & 0 & 2\phi_2\tilde\phi_2 & \phi_2\tilde\phi_3 & \phi_3 & \frac{3}{4}\tilde\phi_2^2+\frac{1}{4}\tilde\phi_3 & \tilde\phi_2^2+\tilde\phi_3 & \tilde\phi_2^2 & 2\tilde\phi_2 & \tilde\phi_3 \\
\phi_2^2 & \phi_2^2 & 0 & 0 & 0 & 0 & 0 & 0 & 0 & 0 \\
\frac{1}{2}\phi_3+\frac{1}{2}\phi_2\tilde\phi_2 & \phi_2\tilde\phi_2 & \frac{1}{2}\phi_2\tilde\phi_2 & \frac{1}{2}\tilde\phi_2\phi_3 & 0 & 0 & 0 & 0 & 0 & 0 \\
\frac{1}{2}\phi_2\tilde\phi_2 & 0 & \phi_2\tilde\phi_2 & 0 & 0 & 0 & 0 & 0 & 0 & 0 \\
\frac{1}{2}\tilde\phi_2^2+\frac{1}{2}\tilde\phi_3 & 0 & \frac{1}{2}\tilde\phi_2^2 & \frac{1}{2}\tilde\phi_2\tilde\phi_3 & \frac{1}{3}\tilde\phi_3 & 0 & 0 & 0 & 0 & 0 \\
0 & \tilde\phi_2^2 & \tilde\phi_2^2 & 0 & \frac{2}{3}\tilde\phi_3 & 0 & 0 & 0 & 0 & 0
\end{pmatrix}
\begin{pmatrix}
P_{100}^0 \\
P_{010}^0 \\
P_{110}^0 \\
P_{101}^0 \\
P_{111}^0 \\
P_{000}^0 \\
P_{100}^1 \\
P_{010}^1 \\
P_{110}^1 \\
P_{101}^1
\end{pmatrix}
,\ (10)
$$

$$2P_{100}^0 + P_{010}^0 + 2P_{110}^0 + P_{101}^0 + P_{111}^0 + P_{000}^1 + 2P_{100}^1 + P_{010}^1 + 2P_{110}^1 + P_{101}^1 = 1. \quad (11)$$

Note that abbreviated notations $\phi_2 = \phi(\zeta,2), \phi_3 = \phi(\zeta,3), \tilde\phi_2 = 1 - \phi_2$, and $\tilde\phi_3 = 1 - \phi_3$ are used. Then, the pedestrian flux is given by

$$q_d = P_{000}^1 + 2P_{100}^1 + P_{010}^1 + 2P_{110}^1 + P_{101}^1. \quad (12)$$

This expression is illustrated with simulation results in Fig. 4(a). When the effect of the conflict is dominant, the error becomes large. In this parameter region, pedestrians are not provided smoothly to the second neighboring sites due to the strong friction, and thus, the assumption of the approximation is not satisfied. On the other hand, when the effect of the conflict is not strong, the approximation gives good evaluation.

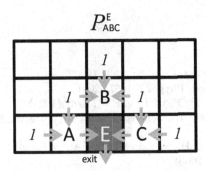

**Fig. 5.** Cluster approximation. The probability of finding a pedestrian on the second neighboring sites of the exit is assumed to be 1.

### 4.3   Critical Conditions

In the previous subsections, we have evaluated pedestrian flux in the free-flow situation $q_f$ and congested situation $q_d$. When $q_d$ is smaller than $q_f$, the system cannot maintain the congested situation; therefore, we can obtain the critical condition regarding the inflow probability for a given $\zeta$ from the condition, $q_d = q_f$:

$$\alpha_c = \frac{q_d}{1 - q_d}. \tag{13}$$

This argument can be easily extended to systems with multiple entrances. Using this expression, we can control the inflow, preventing from the occurrence of the congestion. For example, by keeping the total inflow lower than the outflow in the congested situation, the clustering at the exit can be avoided, which may shorten the total evacuation time.

## 5   Conclusions

In this paper, we have given a first step to treat the problem of multiple bottlenecks in evacuation process. To consider the problem, we focused on a single segment of the bottlenecks, using a stochastic entrance. By simulations, the metastable states of pedestrian flow, arising from phase transitions from the free flow to the congestion, is demonstrated. Supported by approximate analyses we have derived the expressions for the pedestrian flux in the free-flow phase and congestion phase, and a critical condition of the inflow to prevent the congestion. The methods shown in this paper can be applicable to many problems dependent on the number of entrance and exit, exit width, etc. without a substantial change.

**Acknowledgement.** We appreciate the useful feedback offered by Katsuhiro Nishinari.

# References

1. Nagatani, T.: Rep. Prog. Phys. 65, 1331 (2002)
2. Helbing, D.: Rev. Mod. Phys. 73, 1057 (2001)
3. Helbing, D., Molnar, P.: Phys. Rev. E 51, 4282 (1995)
4. Burstedde, C., Klauck, K., Schadschneider, A., Zittartz, J.: Physica A 295, 507 (2001)
5. Kirchner, A., Klüpfel, H., Schadschneider, A., Nishinari, K., Schreckenberg, M.: Physica A 324, 689 (2003)
6. Kirchner, A., Nishinari, K., Schadschneider, A.: Phys. Rev. E 67, 056122 (2003)
7. Yanagisawa, D., Nishinari, K.: Phys. Rev. E 76, 061117 (2007)
8. Yanagisawa, D., Kimura, A., Tomoeda, A., Nishi, R., Suma, Y., Ohtsuka, K., Nishinari, K.: Phys. Rev. E 80, 036110 (2009)
9. Song, W., Xu, X., Wang, B.H., Ni, S.: Physica A 363, 492 (2006)
10. Kretz, T., Grünebohm, A., Schreckenberg, M.: J. Stat. Mech., 10014 (2006)

# Modeling and Simulation of a Car Race

Rolf Hoffmann[1] and Maurice Margenstern[2]

[1] Technische Universität Darmstadt
[2] Université de Lorraine, campus de Metz-Saulcy
hoffmann@informatik.tu-darmstadt.de, margens@univ-metz.fr

**Abstract.** This paper was motivated by an old car racing game played in French schools. The objective of this paper is to model such a car racing system and to find a strategy that allows to move the cars automatically. First the rules of the racing game are given. Then it is modeled as a multi-agent system by GCA-w, a CA related model. An automatic driving strategy is presented in detail. A car moves from the starting line to the arrival line from one temporary goal to the next. The car first searches for the remotest convex point at a border and fixes the next goal nearby it. Then it moves to it stepwise, first accelerating and then decelerating. It is shown that this strategy allows the cars to move automatically around the circuit without bumping against a border.

**Keywords:** MAS, GCA-w, Car Race, Autonomous Driving Strategy.

## 1 Introduction

Car races are an important event, not only from the point of view of sightseeing and their social impact, but also for the technological impact on ordinary cars by the challenge to reach the highest performance. In addition, controlling the car motions on actual roads automatically, especially in order to reduce the number of accidents and to maximize the traffic flow, the simulation of car races are of great practical relevance. Another application is the simulation of moving robots in an area without predefined paths in order to find the fastest routes for the transportation of goods. Last but not least car racing can be played as a game, e.g. a human player may contest against an autonomous vehicle.

The objectives of this research are: (*i*) find a car racing scheme (*functional model*), (*ii*) describe and simulate the system by a CA related model, and (*iii*) find an automatic moving strategy. Note that it was not aimed to find an optimal moving strategy, which is subject to further research.

As functional model, we have taken an old game played in French schools which used an ordinary sheet of paper which happen to have a grid on it, as in many notebooks for school people. Below, in Sect. 2, we describe this game in detail. Then we show in Sect. 3 how this game can be described by a CA related model (*GCA-w, Global Cellular Automata with write access*). In Sect. 4, the car racing system and the automatic moving strategy are described in detail. We show an experiment with one and two cars in Sect. 4.5. In Sect. 5, we conclude and indicate further work.

G.C. Sirakoulis and S. Bandini (Eds.): ACRI 2012, LNCS 7495, pp. 785–794, 2012.

## 2  An Old Game

In high school where the second author spent a few years during his youth, a few pupils spent leisure time between lectures with a strange game which they called the *car race*. They took a page from a note book where a grid was printed, to facilitate the hand writing. It was a true square grid, each square with sides of half a centimeter. First, one of the players drew a circuit for the race (like Fig. 1). It had to be what geometers call a *Jordan closed curve*. In fact, there were two such curves, the borders, more or less 'parallel' so that their midpoints should be on a Jordan closed curve. Two lines were drawn, being normal to the borders, the starting line and the arrival line. An order was fixed between the players, and at each step, each player placed the new position of his car, one after the other, according to the order. The steps were repeated until a first car crossed the arrival line: this car was designated as winner. The game had a single rule. At time 0, the cars were all on the starting line, each player putting his car on a square of the line each one after the other, according to the order, the cars being on pairwise different squares. At time 1, each player could choose the new position of his car, again according to the order and on a position not already taken by another car. At time $t+2$, knowing the positions of the car at times $t$ and $t+1$, say $p_0$ and $p_1$ respectively, the player drew on the paper the 'theoretical' position $p_2^0$ which is the reflection of $p_0$ in its position $p_1$ (Fig. 2). Then, the player was allowed to choose as the new position $p_2$, either $p_2^0$ or one of the 8 neighbours around $p_2^0$, provided that the new position lies within the borders and that it is not already occupied by a car at the time $t+2$. If no new position satisfied these conditions, the corresponding player was ruled out of the race as his car was forced to cross one of the borders. Usually, there were up to five players, and most often two or three of them.

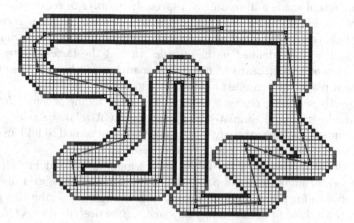

**Fig. 1.** The circuit. The outer and inner border enclose the track. A car starts from the starting line and stops after one round after the arrival line. The red arrows depict segments, which the driver travels through. Each end of a segment is a temporary goal.

# 3    How to Describe this Scheme by a CA Related Model

Basically, we take this scheme and implement it with agents situated on cells. We keep the frame indicated above: a square grid, each square being a kind of CA-like cell. But now, we consider that the contents of a cell can move on the grid, from one square to another one, not necessarily a close neighbour one: this is why we introduce *agents*. The cars are represented by agents which are cells' data which we allow to move from one square to another. The moving distance is restricted by the speed of the car, and a driver has a local view, he can see until the next turn in the road. We use a discrete clock, and the time intervals between two consecutive ticks of the clock are considered equal.

When modeling a multi-agent system (MAS), we are faced with three problems: (*i*) how can the movement of an agent be described from position A (source) to target position B (target), and (*ii*) how can conflicts be resolved. Another problem (*iii*) arises in MAS: The number of agents usually is relatively small compared to the number of all cells, and therefore the number of active cells changing their state becomes low. In order to reduce the computational effort, it is advised to avoid the computation of inactive cells, e.g. empty cells that will not change their state.

In order to describe a movement, two operations have to be performed: (*1*) copy the agent to the target and (*2*) delete it on the source. In classical CA, two rules have to be used to describe a movement, a *copy rule* and a *delete rule*. A conflict can be solved by the target cell, it selects and copies an agent. The agent situated on the source cell has to be aware of being selected, this can be accomplished by replicating the target's decision, or by testing the target cell decision in a second phase. In classical CA, the movement and conflict resolution becomes computationally expensive when the distance between source and target is not very small, because each possible target cell is trying to copy an agent situated somewhere in the large neighborhood. Conflict resolution becomes very expensive, too.

There is a lot of literature about modeling and simulation of MAS (e.g. [1,2,3]). We will focus on a relatively simple CA related model, that allows to write information onto neighbors, the GCA-w (Global Cellular Automata with write-access) model ([7,9]). In this model three types of cells are distinguished, *dead* (constant), *active*, and *passive* cells. An active cell can write information to another non-constant cell. Thereby passive cells can be turned into active cells, and active cells can also be deactivated. The movement of an agent from A to B can be described as follows: The cell at A (*i*) writes ("beams") the agent to B and at the same time activates cell B, and (*ii*) cell A deletes the agent and turns itself into the passive state.

Dead cells are used to describe the static environment, the borders and the area enclosed by the borders. Active cells are used for the agents. Passive cells are used for cells that can be agents' targets, e.g. the cells inside the borders. The GCA-w model is very appropriate for applications that are inherently conflict-free as shown in [9,8]. In case of a target conflict, several methods to resolve the conflict can be applied, e.g. all agents are blocked, one agent is selected to move and the others are blocked, and so on. For the car race, another method is required: each car has always to move, otherwise it is ruled out of the game if it cannot find a legal position.

How can conflicts be resolved in the GCA-w model? One way is that the agents observe each other whether they have chosen the same target. In case of a conflict each agent applies a local procedure by itself in order to solve it. Another way is that each possible target observes all agents which are candidates to move to it. Then the target cell selects an agent, copies it and deletes it on the source. The other unsuccessful agents are informed or even directly modified (e.g. change speed, direction, or even rule out of the game). Another method is that the agents send first moving requests to the target cell, which solves the conflict. Then an acknowledge signal is send back to the winner, or all agents test the result of the conflict resolution. Then the winner moves. Usually several phases are used, e.g. (select target), (resolve the conflict, maybe in sub-phases), (let the winner move and choose another action for the loosers).

We have used the following simulation model based on GCA-w:

**REPEAT** // *start time step t*
**FOR** car $i = 1, 2, \dots n$ **DO** // *asynchronous microsteps within each time step*

*Operation 1.* Car $i$ chooses its next favorite position (under certain restrictions depending on speed, distance to the next goal, etc.) within a 3 x 3 window. Positions within this windows which are outside the track, or are border cells, or are occupied by another previous car are discarded. If the car cannot find any free position, it is ruled out of the game. Already occupied positions of the cars with identifiers $< i$ are taken into account, thereby conflicts are solved in a sequential way.

*Operation 2.* Car $i$ moves from current position to next position. This is done by the cell the car is situated on (beam to next position, delete on current p.).
**ENDFOR**, $t \leftarrow t + 1$
**UNTIL** *a car crossed the arrival line.*

If the number of cars is low and conflict situations are rare, the FOR loop can run in parallel with a barrier synchronization at the end. But then a conflict handler has to be implemented that can detect and solve conflicts in a semantically equivalent way as described above. – The order of processing the cars could also be changed from $t$ to $t + 1$ (random order, next permutation, etc.).

## 4    The Whole System and the Driving Strategy

### 4.1    The Cell Field and the Circuit

First we have to define how to describe the circuit and the agents in the discrete grid. The position of a cell is $(x, y)$, where $x$ is the column and $y$ is the line. In order to simplify the simulation, we use two layers, ENV and AGT. The ENV layer describes the environment, and the AGT layer describes the agents. An ENV cell (EC) can be either an empty cell (E), a track cell (T), or a border cell (B), formally:

$EC \in \{E, T, B\}, \quad T \in \{free, starting, arrival\}$

$B = (inout, direction, curvature), \quad inout \in \{inner, outer\}$

$direction \in \{0, 1, ...7\}, \quad curvature \in \{flat, concave, convex\}.$

*Empty* cells are used to mark the cells that don't belong to the circuit. *Track* cells are used to mark the free track cells, the starting line and the arrival line.

*Border* cells store information about the border's shape that can be observed by the driver. This information is computed in a preprocessing step, and it is possible to do it by CA by successive substitutions (this method is not described here), but it can also be done by ordinary computation through a comparison of the border cells with their neighbors.

We go counter-clockwise around the borders, starting with index zero at the start line and assigning to each border cell a consecutive index. We use the index during the computation of the border information, and it also helps the driver to facilitates the processing of the information he observes.

Each border cell contains information about the *position* (which is also given implicitly by the indices of the array), whether the point is on the *inner* or the *outer* border, the *direction* to the next point on the border, and the kind of *curvature* of the border at this point. The preprocessing upon the borders allows to mark the extremal points: *convex* or *concave* ones, which is indicated by the curvature information. The curvature is defined by comparing the direction of the just obtained next point with that of the current point. If the directions are the same, the curvature is `flat`. Otherwise, it depends on which border we are. On the inner border, if the new direction is more counter-clockwise the curvature is `convex`, otherwise it is `concave`. The rule is just the opposite on the outer border. This information is also marked on the border in the visualization by an appropriate colour, see Fig. 1.

Formally an AGT cell (AC) is given by: $AC \in \{agent, empty\}, \quad agent = (speed, nextgoal)$. In the implementation, an AGT cell first contains a flag, declaring if there is an agent on the cell's position or not. If there is a an agent on a cell, then the supplied record for the agent's data is valid. The record consists of the *position* (implicitly given by the array coordinates), the *speed*, and the coordinates of the next *goal* (Sect. 4.3). – Note that the two layers ENV and AGT can technically be joined into one layer in order to have uniform cells. Having a separate layer for the agents has the advantage that the programmer may easier apply optimization techniques in order to reduce the execution time, e.g. by using lists.

## 4.2   Position, Speed, and Distance

The square where an agent $A$ is at the time $t$ is called the **position** of the agent, and we denote it by $p(A, t)$ or $p_{A,t}$. We consider that the squares have two coordinates, fixed once for all, which are integers and the couple of coordinates of a square is also called the **position** of the agent: this allows us to identify the position of an agent with its coordinates. If $p_0$ and $p_1$ are two positions with coordinates $(a_0, b_0)$ and $(a_1, b_1)$ respectively, we denote by $\overrightarrow{p_0 p_1}$ the vector with coordinates $(a_1 - a_0, b_1 - b_0)$. Accordingly, we shall write that $p_1 = p_0 + \overrightarrow{p_0 p_1}$. In

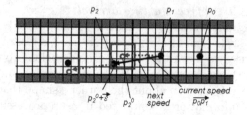

**Fig. 2.** The next speed is the current speed $\overrightarrow{p_0 p_1} + \overrightarrow{\epsilon}$ (variation in 3 x 3 window)

this frame, we also say that a vector $\overrightarrow{p_0 p_1}$ is a **speed**. This allows us to say that if we are at a position $p$ with a speed $\overrightarrow{v}$, the new position of the agent at the next tick of the clock will be $p + \overrightarrow{v}$.

If the agent is at the position $p_0$ at time $t$ and at the position $p_1$ at time $t+1$ (Fig. 2), we say that the **current speed** of the agent at time $t+1$ is $\overrightarrow{p_0 p_1}$. Accordingly, from what we have said in Sect. 2, the **theoretical position** $p_2^0$ of the agent at time $t+2$ is $p_2^0 = p_1 + \overrightarrow{p_0 p_1}$. Now, the **actual next position** is $p_2 = p_2^0 + \overrightarrow{\epsilon}$ where $\overrightarrow{\epsilon}$ is one of the nine vectors, $(\eta_x, \eta_y)$ with $\eta_x, \eta_y \in \{-1, 0, 1\}$. This means that the next position can be varied within the Moore-neighborhood of $p_2^0$. Then the **next speed** at time $t+2$ is given by the vector $\overrightarrow{p_1 p_2}$. Depending on $\overrightarrow{\epsilon}$ the current speed remains unchanged, or is reduced (deceleration) horizontally and/or vertically by one, or is increased by one (acceleration).

The parameters on which the driver takes its decisions are based on the notion of **distance** we define. Of course, we could take the Euclidean distance. However, this would entail unnecessary computational complications due to the fact that we are in a portion of the grid $\mathbb{Z}^2$ on which the coordinates of the cells are integers. Accordingly, we should take a distance computed with integers only. There are two main distances in this situation, and we express them in terms of the distance to $(0,0)$ in order to simplify the expressions. The first distance of $(x, y)$ to $(0,0)$ is $\max(|x|, |y|)$ and the second one is $|x| + |y|$. Taking the mean is a good approximation to the Euclidean norm. Now, in order to get integers, we take the sum of these two distances.

Call **braking distance** the distance, on a straight line road, needed for a car to stop when it is at an initial speed $v$. As $v$ is an integer and can decrease at least by 1 at each time, it can be seen that the breaking distance is around $v^2/2$ while it takes $v$ steps to stop. E.g., if the current speed is 5, then the partial travel distances are (5-1, 4-1, 3-1, 2-1, 1-1), the total travel distances are (4, 4+3, 4+3+2, 4+3+2+1, 4+3+2+1+0), the braking distance is 4+3+2+1=4*5/2, and the number of time steps is 5. A partial travel distance is also called **section**.

## 4.3   The Driving Strategy

We have to define a way to choose which square between $p_2^0$ and its eight neighbours will be taken as the next position. We call **strategy** a finite set of rules which allow us to choose the next position among the 9 of them which are possible. For this, we have mainly two solutions: either to find a deterministic way to choose a single square as the next position, or to choose the next position by a non-deterministic process, either at random or by applying rules defined by a genetic algorithm, for instance. In this paper, we aim at a deterministic strategy.

For this purpose, we analyze how a driver would determine the next step, and then, how to implement that in the discrete setting of our grid. In fact, a driver always looks at the remotest point (or an appropriate point nearby) he can see on the road and he tries to reach it as fast as possible without overshooting. Call this point the current **goal** (Fig. 3). In reality, this goal changes dynamically when the car moves forward. In our setting we have simplified this a bit. After having fixed the next goal it is kept constant until it is reached within a Moore-neighborhood. In principle a car moves from the current goal to the next goal, and then to the next next goal and so on, segment by segment. We call **segment** the vector between two successive goals. The distance of a segment is covered by the car section by section. The length of a section depends on the speed of the car. It is assumed that the car starts with $v = 0$ at the beginning of a segment and stops with $v = 0$ at the end of the segment. In between the car accelerates in order to cover the distance as fast as possible, and decelerates in order not to overshoot.

Note that the driver has always two parameters to fix: the direction of the car and its speed. A constant speed is possible, but only on a long straight portion of the road. Otherwise, the driver has to slow down when he approaches a turn, and to speed up again when the car leaves the turn. Now, we decide that as long as the driver is far from the current goal, he chooses to increase the speed, when it is not too close to the goal it keeps the same speed and when it is close to the goal, it reduces the speed, until it almost reaches the goal. When it is at the goal, a new goal is defined and the process is repeated.

### 4.4    The Rules of the Strategy in More Detail

The rules are executed within a **cycle** which consists of a sequence of actions from defining the goal to the next time when a new goal is to be fixed after having reached the end of the segment. The first step of a cycle consists in defining the goal (Sect. 4.4.A). Then we see how the driver defines the trajectory to the goal (Sect. 4.4.B). In Sect. 4.4.C we indicate the behaviour of the driver in the turns.

**A. Fixing the Next Goal.** Fixing the next goal is rather simple. The drivers looks at the remotest point he can see on the track. Let $(a, b)$ be the position of the car at the beginning of the cycle. The driver looks at both borders, looking for the remotest **convex** point (Fig. 3). Remember that a convex point of a boundary is a point where the arriving direction and the leaving one are different and such that there intersection with the cells in the track makes a reflex angle at this point. By contrast, at a **concave** point, the arriving and leaving directions are different and their angle of intersection with the tracks makes an obtuse or a right angle. The fact that the driver must see this point means that the line segment which goes from the driver to the point does not meet any point outside the tracks and the borders. At least one such point exists, otherwise the circuit

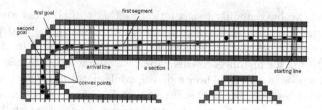

**Fig. 3.** The driver searches for the next convex point, and then computes the nearby next goal. Then the car travels to it, from the start to the end of each segment, section by section. The black dots represent the cars proceeding counter-clockwise.

cannot be defined by closed curves. If we find two such points, one on the inner border and one on the outer border, we take the remotest one.

Now the driver has detected a convex point on the border. In order to make it easier to find a distant goal in the following next cycle we tune a bit the position of the goal. We go from the border where the convex point was found to the other border, along a kind of normal line with respect to the border until we reach a point such that the line segment from the driver to that point does not intersect with the border. (The goal then lies inside the track and not far from the convex point at a safe distance from the border.)

We have to make it precise what we call a line. As we are in a discrete context, our line is a discrete line. It is defined by inequalities of the form $d \leq a.x + b.y < d + c$ where $a$, $b$, $c$, $d$, $x$ and $y$ are integers and $c = \max(|a|, |b|)$. A line which satisfies these inequalities is called a **naive discrete** line, see [4,5,6], we shall later say a **discrete line**.

Let $(a_0, b_0)$ be the position of the driver at the beginning of the cycle. Let $(x_0, y_0)$ be the remotest convex point on a border seen by the driver. This means that the segment of the discrete line going from $(a_0, b_0)$ to $(x_0, y_0)$ contain cells of the track or of the border but no other kind of cell. The tuning defines a point $(x, y)$ such that the segment of the discrete line joining $(a_0, b_0)$ to $(x, y)$ contains points of the track only.

**B. Defining the Trajectory.** Once the goal is defined, the driver tries to stick to the segment of the discrete line going from its initial position $(a, b)$ at the beginning of the cycle to its goal $(x, y)$. Acceleration, braking or keeping the speed are defined within this constraint. Remember that a segment will be divided into sections, where the length of a section is given by the speed (Fig. 3). Note that the number of sections should be kept as small as possible in order to move as fast as possible from the beginning to the end of a segment.

Consider a position $P_0$ of the car, assuming $P_0$ to be the starting point of a sector on the discrete line which joins $(a, b)$ to $(x, y)$. Let $\overrightarrow{v_0}$ be the speed of the car. We know that the theoretical next position is $P_1 = P_0 + \overrightarrow{v_0}$ and the driver chooses among the points $P_1 + \overrightarrow{\epsilon}$ where $\overrightarrow{\epsilon} = \overrightarrow{(\xi, \eta)}$ with $\xi, \eta \in \{-1, 0, 1\}$. Now, the driver rules out the values of $\overrightarrow{\epsilon}$ such that $P_1 + \overrightarrow{\epsilon}$ are not on the track.

Depending on the orientation of $\overrightarrow{v_0}$, there are always points which allow to accelerate or to brake or to keep the pace. We know that the decision is defined

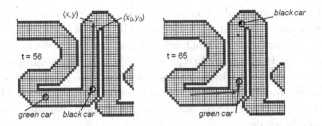

**Fig. 4.** Two cars are approaching a hairpin, at time $t = 56$ and $t = 65$

by the value $\delta$ of dist $(P, (x, y))$, where $P$ is the candidate position of the car. If $\delta$ is bigger than twice the braking distance, the driver accelerates. Otherwise, if $\delta$ is bigger than the braking distance, the driver keeps the pace. If this is not the case, the driver brakes.

**C. The Turns.** This strategy allows the driver to take turns without any problem. The driver reduces its speed almost until 0 when it reaches the goal, usually at the entry of a turn. This allows to have a trajectory which will pass close to a convex point near a point inside the turn or close to the exit from the turn, depending on the shape of the turn. The circuit of Fig. 1 gives a collection of very different turns, including hairpin ones, which allow to test the proposed strategy. – In Fig. 4, we have an illustration of the behaviour of the leading black car at a hairpin. On the left-hand side figure, the driver of the black car has fixed its goal at the previous step. The convex point on the border is $(x_0, y_0)$ and the goal is $(x, y)$. On the right-hand side figure, the black car has reached its goal and the green car has turned to the left. The goal of the green car is now near to the previous goal of the leading black car. This shows us that the strategy allows the driver to safely negotiate the turn.

### 4.5  The Simulation

Each of the authors implemented a simulation program: one program is written in *Ada95*, the other one in *Pascal*. Both programs can create a picture of the circuit for each tick of the clock. This allows us to visualize the behaviour of the driver. We can observe the signalling of the borders in Figs. 1, 4. Horizontal line segments are delimited by red squares. Convex points which are not already occupied by a red square are marked with a green square. Concave points are marked by two purple squares before and two other ones after. For a few concave points, the point where the concavity is reached is occupied by a red square.

*Simulation with one car.* As shown in Fig. 1, a car can drive around the circuit automatically, segment by segment. The car first fixes the next goal, and then moves to it, section by section (time-step per time-step). The sections are short when the car drives slowly, and they are longer when the car drives faster. In order to drive fast, the driver tries to accelerate as much as possible under the restriction not to shoot over the next goal. The speed and the sections (as shown in Figs. 2, 3) are automatically computed by the car. The number of time steps was 133 to cross the arrival line (pink line in the figures).

*Simulation with two cars.* A black and a green car are performing a race, the asynchronous order is black car first, then green car. The results show us that the winner is the black car which crosses the arrival line at time 133. The green car crosses the arrival line at time 145. One reason that the green car is slower is, that it cannot use a preferred position in a 3 x 3 window, because it was already occupied by the black car.

## 5   Conclusion

We have presented a functional racing model following the scheme of an old French game. We used the GCA-w model to describe the whole multi-agent system. This model facilitates the movement of agents by beaming them to their targets. We defined a strategy that allows a car automatically to move safely from the starting line to the arrival line. The car fixes the next goal, which is nearby the remotest convex point the driver can see at a border, and he moves to it section by section, first accelerating and then decelerating. There are several topics for further research. We could use the same strategy with different temperaments, having a more daring or a more wiser driver. We could improve this handcrafted strategy, e.g. by varying the position of the goals or by dynamically updating the goals more often. A genetic algorithm could be applied in order to find a better strategy. The performance of the strategies could be evaluated by a properly defined fitness function for a set of different circuits and for a varying number of cars. Cars with different strategies could compete against each other. This shows us that there is room for a lot of promising work.

## References

1. Wooldridge, M.: An Introduction to MultiAgent Systems. Wiley & Sons (2009)
2. Weyns, D., Holvoet, T.: Model for Simultaneous Actions in Situated Multi-agent Systems. In: Schillo, M., Klusch, M., Müller, J., Tianfield, H. (eds.) MATES 2003. LNCS (LNAI), vol. 2831, pp. 105–118. Springer, Heidelberg (2003)
3. Fatès, N., Chevrier, V.: How important are updating schemes in multi-agent systems? An illustration on a multi-turmite model. In: Proc. 9th Int. Conf. on Autonomous Agents and Multiagent Systems, AAMAS 2010, vol. 1 (2010)
4. Reveillès, J.-P.: Géométrie discrète, calculs en nombre entiers et algorithmique., Thèse d'état, Université Louis Pasteur, Strasbourg (1991)
5. Debled-Rennesson, I., Reveillès, J.: A linear algorithm for segmentation of digital curves. Int. J. of Pattern Recognition and Artificial. Intell. 9, 635 (1995)
6. Debled-Rennesson, I., Margenstern, M.: Cellular Automata and Discrete Geometry. In: Int. Conf. on High Perf. Comp. and Sim (HPCS), CAAA spec. session (2011)
7. Hoffmann, R.: The GCA-w Massively Parallel Model. In: Malyshkin, V. (ed.) PaCT 2009. LNCS, vol. 5698, pp. 194–206. Springer, Heidelberg (2009)
8. Hoffmann, R.: GCA-w Algorithms for Traffic Simulation. Acta Phys. Pol. B Proc. Suppl. 4, 183 (2011), Summer Solstice Int. Conf. 2010
9. Hoffmann, R.: Rotor-routing Algorithms Described by CA-w. Acta Phys. Pol. B Proc. Suppl. 5, 53 (2012), Summer Solstice Int. Conf. 2011

# Construction of Cellular Automata Lattice Based on the Semantics of an Urban Traffic Network

Vedran Ivanac[1], Bojana Dalbelo Bašić[2], and Zvonimir Vanjak[1]

[1] Telegra, Software R&D Department,
Plesivicka 3, Sveta Nedelja, Croatia
{vedran.ivanac,zvonimir.vanjak}@telegra-europe.com
[2] Faculty of Electrical Engineering and Computing
University of Zagreb, Unska 3, 10000 Zagreb, Croatia
bojana.dalbelo@fer.hr

**Abstract.** In this paper, we propose a construction process that enables the transformation of an urban traffic network using a cellular automata lattice. An abstract network hierarchy is defined which allows us to describe the important properties of an urban traffic network layer by layer. The cellular automata lattice is extended with three additional types of cells that permit the modelling of conflict points at intersections. A supporting model of vehicle behaviour based on traffic cellular automata is also extended with rules that allow vehicles to move properly within the extended cellular automata lattice.

**Keywords:** cellular automata, construction, intersection, urban traffic network, cellular lattice, conflict points.

## 1 Introduction

Traffic simulation is used to model and simulate the flow of vehicles in a road network. Traffic simulators are most commonly applied in the planning stages of the construction of transportation networks, the prediction of traffic flow characteristics, traffic signal optimisation, the analysis of environmental impacts, and the evaluation of transportation scenarios [1]. Depending on the level of detail, simulation models may be macroscopic, mesoscopic, or microscopic. Microscopic models describe traffic flow with a high level of detail by modelling the behaviour of each vehicle in the flow [2]. Traffic microsimulation based on cellular automata is very effective in simulating vehicular traffic [3, 5–7]. Traffic cellular automata (TCA) models are capable of reproducing elementary events in traffic flow, such as the breakdown of free flow, stop and go waves, and traffic jams. The main component of cellular automata is the cellular lattice that is used to represent the road surface. Most analyses focus on defining the rule set of TCA models and evaluation of these TCA models on simple road network configurations. However, problems arise when traffic microsimulation based on

G.C. Sirakoulis and S. Bandini (Eds.): ACRI 2012, LNCS 7495, pp. 795–806, 2012.

cellular automata is used to simulate traffic flow on real traffic networks. Unlike simple traffic networks in the shape of a single straight road or a circular road, highway and urban traffic networks include many additional elements that affect the flow of traffic. Moreover, urban traffic networks contain junctions, traffic lights, roundabouts, and bus stops that make them more complex then highway traffic networks. Therefore, TCA microsimulation that enables the simulation of traffic flow on urban traffic networks must have the following components:

- **A semantically correct network representation** – All important characteristics and properties of the urban traffic network are contained in the definition of the cellular lattice.
- **Vehicle behaviour supporting model** – A model that understands the characteristics and properties of urban traffic networks contained in thenetwork representation.

An optional but desirable feature of network representation is the ability to be described on a higher level of abstraction, enabling the cellular lattice to be derived instead of constructed manually.

This paper is organised in seven sections. Following this introduction, Section 2 discusses the related works, while Section 3 defines basic traffic cellular automaton. Section 4 describes the important characteristics and properties of urban traffic networks. Section 5 presents an abstract network hierarchy with an extended definition of the cellular lattice and a behaviour model. Section 6 presents an example of the transformation of a real urban traffic network into a cellular lattice. This is followed by the conclusions in Section 7.

## 2   Related Works

In the field of traffic simulation, a broad scope of models describes the behaviour of traffic flows [2]. Maerivoet and De Moor [4] categorised TCA as deterministic, stochastic, and slow-to-start, depending on the ability to simulate different types of vehicle behaviour. Nonetheless, traffic microsimulation based on TCA that is capable of representing a complex traffic network as a cellular lattice has been successfully implemented [5, 6]. Chopard et al. [5] applied TCA to the city of Genova, representing roads with a set of one dimensional (1-D) cellular lattices and intersections with rotaries. Esser and Schreckenberg [6] described a road network as a composition of nodes and edges representing crossings and roads. Edges enable the modelling of multi-lane roads with turning sections, and transfer edges enable the merging of traffic flows to be modelled. A node describes only the connections between edges, modelling the intersections as black boxes. A similar network representation is used in TRANSIMS [7]. Ruskin and Wang [8] focused on simulating traffic flows on unsignalised intersections, which they represented as the intersection of two 1-D cellular lattices. Zhang and Chang [10] extended this idea by representing an intersection with a 2-D lattice that enables the simulation of a mixed traffic flow of vehicles and people in an intersection.

# 3   Definition of a Basic Traffic Cellular Automaton

Traffic cellular automata (TCA) are based on a theory of cellular automata (CA) introduced by Wolfram [11]. The cellular automaton is defined as the following 4-tuple [4]:

$$CA = (\zeta, \Sigma, \Omega, \delta), \tag{1}$$

where the cellular lattice is represented by $\zeta$, the set of possible cell states by $\Sigma$, the cell neighbourhood by $\Omega$, and the transition rules by $\delta$. The cellular lattice represents the space on which the CA is computed. This underlying structure can be finite or infinite in size, consisting of cells in rectangular, hexagonal, or other topologies. The dimensionality of the lattice can be 1 (an array of cells), 2 (a grid of cells), or higher. The cells are all equal in size, and each cell can be in only one state from the set of possible states at one time step. Transition rules define the evolution of a cell through discrete time steps based on the current cell state and the states of the cell's neighbourhood. The CA evolve in time and space as the rules are subsequently applied to all the cells in parallel.

Nagel and Schreckenberg [9] introduced a stochastic traffic cellular automaton (STCA) model that is capable of reproducing the important properties of real traffic flow. The forward motion of vehicles is described by the following set of rules:

1. Acceleration: $v_i(t) \leftarrow min(v_i(t-1) + 1, v_{max})$;
2. Deceleration: $v_i(t) \leftarrow min(v_i(t), gap_i(t-1))$;
3. Randomisation: $\xi(t) < p \implies v_i(t) \leftarrow max(v_i(t) - 1, 0)$;
4. Movement: $x_i(t) \leftarrow x_i(t-1) + v_i(t)$.

Each cell $i$ is either empty or occupied by one vehicle with a discrete speed $v_i \in \{0, ..., v_{max}\}$. The variable $gap_i$ defines the number of empty cells in front of the vehicle at cell $i$. $\xi(t)$ is a uniform random generator, and $p$ is the probability that defines the level of stochastic noise, which is important for reproducing speed fluctuations due to human behaviour or external conditions.

The analogy of the cellular automaton to vehicular road traffic flow is based on representing a physical road with the cellular lattice. A 1-D lattice of cells represents one traffic lane in which cells may either be empty or occupied by a vehicle. For each traffic cellular automaton model, a discretisation scheme is defined in accordance with space and time.

# 4   An Urban Traffic Network

An urban traffic network is a traffic network in a city area featuring different types of roads, intersections, and interchanges in which traffic flow is regulated by traffic signs and traffic signals. The elements of an urban traffic network [12–15] define spatial topology, signalisation and basic traffic rules. For the purpose of defining semantically correct network representations, the following important characteristics and properties of these three elements are selected:

- **Spatial topology**
  - **Roads** – There are different types of roads, including freeways, arterial roads, collector roads, and local roads. Roads have length, traffic lanes with spatial configurations, and assigned signalisation. Roads connect two junctions and can be uni- or bi-directional.
  - **Intersections** – Areas in which two or more roads intersect. The important properties of intersections include the spatial configurations of lanes and of conflict points, roads connected to intersections, and the level of control. Control in an intersection may be maintained by basic traffic rules, traffic signs, or traffic lights.
  - **Interchanges** – Points of access for vehicles to enter or leave a freeway. The important properties of interchanges include the length of enter/exit lanes and the location of interchanges on roads.
- **Signalisation**
  - **Traffic signs** – Traffic signs may be classified into the three main categories of regulatory, warning, and informative signs. The important properties of these signs are their class, meaning, and location within the network.
  - **Traffic signals** – Traffic signals solve the problems at conflict points in intersections using the principle of time sharing. Traffic signals are defined by cycle, cycle length, phases in cycle, the location of each traffic signal relative to the intersection and the traffic lanes in the intersection.
- **Basic traffic rules** – Elementary rules that apply to traffic without signalisation.

## 5   A Cellular Lattice for Urban Traffic Networks

In the Nagel and Schreckenberg model [9], the network representation is one traffic lane in the shape of a 1-D array of cells, but this is not particulary applicable to urban traffic networks. In this section, a cellular lattice for urban traffic networks is presented as part of an abstract network hierarchy representing urban traffic networks as cellular lattices with extensions.

### 5.1   Abstract Network Hierarchy

Traffic networks may be viewed at different levels of abstraction. In this way, the network representation may be modelled layer by layer until the cellular lattice on the last layer is defined. Each layer has more detail and defines additional semantics of the urban traffic network. From top to bottom, there are five layers, including the network, the graph, the segment, the inner segment, and the cell layer. The benefit of an abstract network hierarchy is that it requires definition only in the upper layers of the hierarchy, while transformation algorithms can generate the cellular lattice in the cell layer.

- **Network layer** – The network layer is the top layer that represents the grounds of the abstract network hierarchy. It holds all the entities below it and describes the network as a black box.

- **Graph layer** – The graph layer is the layer below the network layer that describes the traffic network as a graph. The graph layer consists of nodes and links that represent vertices and edges. The nodes describe the semantics of the junctions, and the links describe the semantics of the roads between the junctions.
- **Segment layer** – The segment layer describes the network as a collection of connected segments. Every node and link from the graph layer is built from segments so that connections from the graph layer become connections between segments. The main purpose of the segment layer is to achieve uniformity and create logical entities that have the same rules and semantics. Fig. 1 shows how the nodes and links from the graph layer are presented in the segment layer. Each node always has one segment, and each link may have at least one segment, depending on the road configuration and the traffic rules.

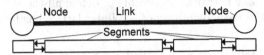

**Fig. 1.** Segments of the segment layer

- **Inner segment layer** – The inner segment layer defines semantics in more detail than simply the connections between junctions. Each segment is comprised of lanes, connectors, signs, and conflict points. Fig. 2 presents an example of inner segment structures, where the segment on the left is a typical example of a segment in a link, and the segment on the right is a typical example of a segment in a node. The lanes represent traffic lanes from a real traffic network so that each lane has its own length and neighbouring lanes. The number of lanes in the segment is the same as the number of lanes in the part of the real traffic network that the segment represents. Connectors facilitate the connections of lanes from different segments. Each connector has one or more pins where each lane in the segment may connect with its beginning and end. Connectors mediate between the defined connections of segments in the segment layer and the lane connections from the inner segment layer. Lanes from two different segments are then connected based on the information in the connectors during the process of abstract network construction. Conflict points describe lane overlaps and enable the modelling of traffic regulation within the abstract traffic network. The three types of conflict points are divergent points, cross points, and merge points. A divergent conflict point describes a situation where two or more lanes begin at the same point, a merge conflict point describes a situation where two or more lanes end at the same point, and a cross conflict point describes a situation where two or more lanes cross each other. Every traffic rule that affects traffic flow can be defined by the signs in a particular segment.
- **Cell layer** – The cell layer contains a cellular lattice that uses the semantics defined in the upper layers for its construction. Every lane within the inner

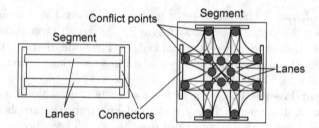

**Fig. 2.** Examples of the inner structure of segments

segment layer has a 1-D array of cells that are interconnected. Each cell represents a part of the physical road surface in a traffic lane. Information about the connections between lanes is used to connect the cells outside the array so that all cells in the cell layer are connected in a lattice that defines a real urban traffic network. To be able to define all the semantics from the upper layers, the basic definition of a cellular lattice has been extended.

## 5.2   Extended Definition of a Cellular Lattice

The basic definition of a cellular lattice defines it as a collection of cells of a single type that each have a state and a neighbourhood. The extended definition of a cellular lattice extends the definition of the cell type and its neighbourhood. The neighbourhood of the cell type varies, but it allows every cell to be its neighbour, regardless of the cell type. Apart from the existing type of cell, the road cell, there are three new types of cells called conflict point cells, resulting in the following list of cell types:

- **Road cell** – The road cell represents a cell type from the basic definition of a cellular lattice and enables modelling of a plain road surface. Fig. 3(a) presents a road cell with its von Neumann neighbourhood in the front-back and left-right directions.
- **Diverge cell** – The diverge cell enables the modelling of a diverge conflict point. It has a neighbourhood only in the front-back direction and more than one front neighbour, as shown in Fig. 3(b). It has one front neighbour cell with a key $d_i$ for every possible direction; it provides information about the destination node of the leading direction of that cell so that a vehicle can select a front cell based on its preferred route.
- **Merge cell** – The merge cell enables the modelling of a merge conflict point. It has one back cell for each direction and one front cell, as shown in Fig. 3(c). The merge cell also regulates the priorities of merging vehicle flows.
- **Cross cell** – The cross cell enables the modelling of a cross conflict point. Each lane is represented with a direction containing a pair of front and back cells relative to the cross cell, as shown in Fig. 3(d). Those cells are the neighbours of the cross cell. The priority of passing through the cross cell is determined by the position of the direction relative to the other directions of the cross cell.

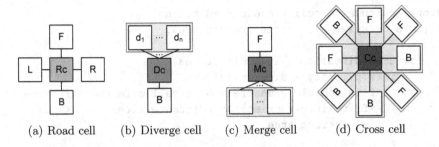

(a) Road cell        (b) Diverge cell        (c) Merge cell        (d) Cross cell

**Fig. 3.** Type of cells in an extended cellular lattice

### 5.3    Vehicle Behaviour Supporting Model

In urban traffic networks, vehicles must be able to change lanes, navigate through the network, comply with traffic signs and rules, and choose directions at intersections that correspond with their routes. In this case, the STCA model is used as a base for the extensions. A lane change extension enables a vehicle to change lanes on multi-lane [7, 16] or bi-directional roads [17, 18]. It enables the simulation of situations including passing a slower vehicle, changing lanes before an intersection in accordance with the route of the vehicle, and entering or exiting a highway [6, 7]. When simulating vehicles complying with traffic lights, an abstract flag [6] or traffic control algorithm [7] is used. The same concepts of lane changes and compliance with traffic lights are used in this paper, but different concepts are presented in the case of traffic rules.

Traffic rules are divided into basic rules and rules modelled through traffic signs that override and extend the basic rules. These rules can also be divided by the layers on which they are defined; for instance, on the segment layer, rules that limit speed and lane changes are defined, while on the cell layer, rules that prioritise vehicle passing are defined. Priority rules are defined at the conflict points on an intersection. The priority of direction in conflict points depends on the spatial position of direction relative to other directions and on traffic signs, such as stop and yield signs. Based on these concepts, each vehicle must evaluate an occupied status for cells in front of the vehicle when calculating the front gap in a forward movement model. If the cell is a conflict point cell, the occupied status requires the following additional calculation:

- **Diverge cell** – A diverge cell does not have defined priorities. If a stop sign is placed within the diverge cell, then the cell is occupied if the speed of the vehicle that evaluates the status of cell occupation is greater than zero.
- **Merge cell and cross cell** – In merge cells and cross cells, the cell's status of occupation is based on a pass acceptance algorithm.

*Pass acceptance algorithm (PAA)*

```
Input: (c, d, s) conflict point cell c, direction d in which is
the vehicle that evaluates PAA, and the zone of the conflict s.
```

```
Output: calculated cell's c occupied status.
if (c is occupied by vehicle) return true;
else
    for each(direction z in c.directions)
        if(z.priority > d.priority){
            find vehicle v upstream of a cell c in the direction z;
            if((vehicle v exist) && (distance(v.cell, c) <= s))
                return true;
        }
return false;
```

The addition of traffic signs changes the priorities of the directions in conflict point cells. Yield and stop signs reduce the priority of a particular direction. The pass acceptance algorithm does not offer a logical solution for preventing and resolving the deadlocks, that may occur between cross cells. Such deadlocks may be prevented by applying deadlock resolvers [19, 20].

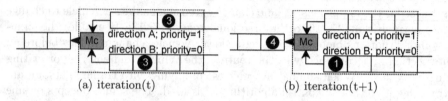

(a) iteration(t)             (b) iteration(t+1)

**Fig. 4.** Example of using the pass acceptance algorithm in a merge cell

Fig. 4(a) depicts part of a cellular lattice with a merge cell and two directions with different priorities. Each vehicle has a speed of 3 cells per iteration and must pass a merge cell. During the vehicle's process of calculating a new position for the next iteration, it uses the pass acceptance algorithm (PAA) to determine the occupied status of a merge cell. In this case, the vehicle $v_2$ travelling in direction B has a lower priority than the vehicle $v_1$ travelling in direction A. Therefore, the PAA will return true for $v_2$ and false for $v_1$, and $v_2$ will slowdown and $v_1$ will pass a merge cell, as shown in Fig. 4(b).

# 6   An Example of the Transformation of a Real Traffic Network into an Extended CA Lattice

This section will demonstrate how a real traffic network is transformed into an extended cellular automata lattice by using an abstract network hierarchy. In this example, the network part (Fig. 5(a)) comprises two bi-directional roads that cross at a signalised intersection. The horizontal road has an interchange with one entry ramp and has priority over the vertical road. Lines with arrows at the intersection and arrows on lanes show the possible directions of vehicle movement.

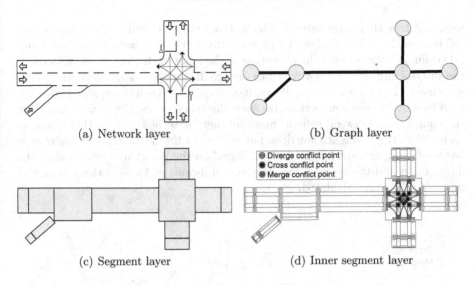

(a) Network layer  (b) Graph layer

(c) Segment layer  (d) Inner segment layer

**Fig. 5.** Upper layers within the abstract network hierarchy

The next step includes using a graph layer to describe part of a real traffic network. Fig. 5(b) presents a description of the traffic network in a graph layer, in which roads are represented by links, while intersections and interchanges are represented by nodes. The boundaries of the network are also represented by nodes.

The entire network is then described as a set of interconnected segments. Every node is represented by one segment, and each link is represented by one or more segments, depending on road configuration. Fig. 5(c) presents a description of the network in a segment layer, where the connections between segments are based on the connections in the graph layer.

In the inner segment layer, each segment's inner structure is defined with connectors, signs, conflict points and lanes. The number and position of these connectors depend on the number of the segment's neighbours. The graph and segment layers describe the connections in the traffic network, but the space dimension is described with lanes in the inner segment layer. Each segment has lanes whose number and length depend on the space that the segment represents in the real traffic network. On the inner side of the segment, a connector links the lanes, but on the outer side of the segment it connects with the other connector. Conflict points describe overlaps between the lanes and the priorities of the lanes. Fig. 5(d) shows the inner structure of segments with connectors, conflict points, and lanes.

The cell layer does not require description because it can be produced from the information defined in the upper layers and the discretisation scheme. Information from the upper layers describes the number and type of cells that are used and how they interconnect. Fig. 6 shows the extended cellular lattice in a cell layer with a zoomed view of an intersection. The lanes were transformed into 1-D cellular lattices, with the exception of the lanes in the intersection. Because the intersection was defined by lanes and conflict points, special types of cells were used. Gaps between the cells are used to present a cell layer, and arrows are used to describe the connections between the spaced cells. Fig. 6 does not show the connections between cells in neighbouring lanes; however, in this example, each cell in the segment that does not belong to the intersection segment also has a left and/or right neighbour cell. Based on the position of the lanes in the intersection and the signs at the intersection, priorities for directions in special types of cells were calculated.

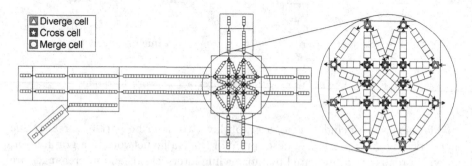

**Fig. 6.** Cell layer

## 7    Conclusion

We have successfully defined a methodology for representing urban traffic networks in traffic cellular automata (TCA) by using an abstract network hierarchy and extending the definition of a cellular lattice. We have also defined and selected the important properties of an urban traffic network and defined how these are incorporated into the layers of an abstract network hierarchy. In our example, an abstract network hierarchy is used to describe the important properties of an urban traffic network. An extended cellular lattice was built using the information from layers in the abstract network hierarchy. This offered us the option of using graphical tools that accurately describe the layers of the abstract network hierarchy and allow for the automatic creation of an extended cellular lattice. By extending a cellular lattice with three additional types of cells, we showed how the semantics of intersection and conflict points can be presented in TCA. A simulation tool is in the process of a development that will validate and calibrate the proposed model of an urban traffic network.

**Acknowledgments.** The authors would like to thank Edouard Ivanjko, Hrvoje Gold, Matija Piskorec and Jan Snajder for their helpful comments and suggestions. This work has been supported by Telegra-Europe and the Ministry of Science, Education and Sports, Republic of Croatia, under Grant 036-1300646-1986.

# References

1. Boxill, S., Yu, L.: An Evaluation of Traffic Simulation Models for Supporting ITS Development. Technical Report 167602-1, Texas Southern University (2000)
2. Hoogendoorn, S.P., Bovy, P.H.L.: State-of-the-art of Vehicular Traffic Flow Modelling. Special Issue on Road Traffic Modelling and Control of the Journal of Systems and Control Engineering, 283–303 (2001)
3. Hafstein, S.F., Chrobok, R., Pottmeier, A., Wahle, J., Schreckenberg, M.: Cellular Automaton Modeling of the Autobahn Traffic in North Rhine-Westphalia. In: Troch, I., Breitenecker, F. (eds.) Proc. of the 4th MATHMOD, North Rhine-Westphalia, pp. 1322–1331 (2003)
4. Maerivoet, S., De Moor, B.: Cellular Automata Models of Road Traffic. Physics Reports 419, 1–64 (2005)
5. Chopard, B., Dupuis, A., Luthi, P.: A cellular automata model for urban traffic and its application to the city of Geneva. In: Proc. of Traffic and Granular, pp. 154–168. Springer (1997)
6. Esser, J., Schreckenberg, M.: Microscopic Simulation of Urban Traffic Based on Cellular Automata. International J. of Modern Phys. C 8, 1025–1036 (1997)
7. Nagel, K., Stretz, P., Pieck, M., Donnelly, R., Barrett, C.L.: TRANSIMS traffic flow characteristics (1997)
8. Ruskin, H.J., Wang, R.: Modelling Traffic Flow at an Urban Unsignalised Intersection. In: Sloot, P.M.A., Tan, C.J.K., Dongarra, J., Hoekstra, A.G. (eds.) ICCS-ComputSci 2002, Part I. LNCS, vol. 2329, pp. 381–390. Springer, Heidelberg (2002)
9. Nagel, K., Schreckenberg, M.: A cellular automaton model for freeway traffic. J. Phys. I France 2, 2221–2229 (1992)
10. Zhang, X., Chang, G.L.: A CA-based Model for Simulating Vehicular-Pedestrian Mixed Flows in a Congested Network. In: The 90th Annual Meeting of the Transportation Research Board, vol. 16, pp. 1–20 (2011)
11. Wolfram, S.: Statistical Mechanics of Cellular Automata. Rev. of Modern Phys. 55, 601–644 (1983)
12. AASHTO, A Policy on Geometric Design of Highways and Streets, American Association of State Highway and Transportation Officials, Washington, DC (2001)
13. Mahmoud El-Sherbiny, Y.: Design of urban traffic areas. Journal of Engineering and Applied Sciences 6 (2011)
14. Evans, H.K.: Traffic engineering handbook, Institute of traffic engineers, New Haven, Connecticut (1950)
15. Mathew, T.V., Krishna Rao, K.V.: Introduction to Transportation Engineering. NPTEL (May 2006)
16. Nagel, K., Wolf, D., Wagner, P., Simon, P.: Two-lane traffic rules for cellular automata: A systematic approach. Phys. Rev. E 58, 1425–1437 (1998)

17. Simon, P.M., Gutowitz, H.A.: A Cellular Automaton Model for Bi-Directional Traffic. Phys. Rev. E 57, 2441 (1998)
18. Moussa, N.: Simon-Gutowitz bidirectional traffic model revisited. Phys. Letters A 372, 6701 (2008)
19. Chopard, B., Luthi, P.O., Queloz, P.A.: Cellular automata model of car traffic in a two-dimensional street network. Journal of Phys. A 29, 2325–2336 (1996)
20. Doniec, A., René, M., Espié, S., Piechowiak, S.: Dealing with multi-agent coordination by anticipation: Application to the traffic simulation at junctions. In: EUMAS, pp. 478–479 (2005)

# Calibration of Traffic Simulation Models Using Vehicle Travel Times

Pavol Korcek, Lukas Sekanina, and Otto Fucik

Brno University of Technology
Faculty of Information Technology
IT4Innovations Centre of Excellence
Bozetechova 1/2, 612 66 Brno, Czech Republic
{ikorcek,sekanina,fucik}@fit.vutbr.cz
http://www.fit.vutbr.cz

**Abstract.** In this paper, we propose an effective calibration method of the cellular automaton based microscopic traffic simulation model. We have shown that by utilizing a genetic algorithm it is possible to optimize various model parameters much better than a human expert. Quality of the new model has been shown in task of travel time estimation. We increased precision by more than 25 % with regard to a manually tuned model. Moreover, we were able to calibrate some model parameters such as driver sensitivity that are extremely difficult to calibrate as relevant data can not be measured using standard monitoring technologies.

**Keywords:** traffic, simulation, cellular automaton model, calibration, travel time.

## 1 Introduction

A very important stage of development of any traffic model is its comparison with reality, namely calibration and validation. In [1], authors proposed an effective three-step process for the microscopic traffic model calibration. Another paper [2] gives some basic guidelines for calibration of microscopic simulation models in form of framework and applications. The developers usually calibrate and validate the model on their own using some data sets that they have access to and publish the results obtained. For example, in paper [3] authors tried to perform a simple calibration of ten microscopic traffic simulation models in a way that the models were calibrated and compared to each other with the GPS based field data from year 2004 in Japan. But it should be noted, that in almost all previous calibration approaches, some real data are desired in a form, which is generally not available. It was shown that it is important to find a few basic parameters for the model calibration [4]. Namely a driver sensitivity (e.g. reaction time), a jam density headway and free-speed (maximum speed when vehicle is not constrained) have to be determined. It was also stated that this process is neither a straight-forward nor an easy task. For example, while the free-speed is relatively easy to estimate in the field and generally lies between the

G.C. Sirakoulis and S. Bandini (Eds.): ACRI 2012, LNCS 7495, pp. 807–816, 2012.

speed limit and the design speed of the roadway, the jam density headway is more difficult to calibrate but typically ranges between 110 to 150 vehicles/km/lane. The driver sensitivity factor is extremely difficult to calibrate because it can not be measured using standard monitoring technologies (e.g. detection loops that work on magnetic-induction principle).

In this work we propose to utilize our cellular automaton (CA) based microscopic traffic simulation model, which was shown not only to be extremely fast to achieve multiple in real-time simulations (e.g. [6]), but also updated to eliminate unwanted properties of ordinary CA based models. The quality of this updated model has been previously evaluated by comparison with *Van Aerde* fundamental diagram [5]. Then we will also try to calibrate parameters of this model to field data that can be obtained from standard monitoring technologies. We will show, that it is possible to achieve a better precision on travel time estimation for a given road segment. Moreover, except CA model parameters, we will also optimize some parameters such as driver sensitivity which, as stated for example in [4], are extremely difficult to calibrate with other common techniques. The optimization/calibration will be performed by genetic algorithm (GA).

The rest of the paper is organized as follows. Section 2 introduces an updated cellular automaton based traffic simulation model. Then, in Section 3, the process of optimization of the model with selected GA is described in detail with all simulation model parameters. Experimental evaluations for our field data sets are then presented in Section 4. Finally, conclusions and suggestions for future work are given in the last Section 5.

## 2    Updated Local Transition Function

In our previous work [5], we updated the original local transition function [7] to a new form, where some brand new parameters can be found. The traffic simulation model is extended to eliminate unwanted properties of ordinary CA based models, such as stopping from maximum vehicle speed to zero in one time step. This is possible due to storing the previous (or the leading) vehicle velocity $v_v(i+1)$. When there is such vehicle, the following vehicle $(i)$ is able to determine its positive or negative acceleration with $acc(i+1)$. According to Alg. 1, it is firstly determined, if investigated vehicle could accelerate (i.e. vehicle velocity $v_v(i)$ is not greater than maximal vehicles speed $p_4$ or given vehicle speed limit $v_{max}(i)$). If so, its speed-up is accomplished with probability $p_7$, so not all vehicles tend to always accelerate as in the original model [7]. Then, if there is a plenty of room for vehicle to get in (i.e. $gap(i) + acc(i+1) > v_v(i)$) or there is no previous vehicle in the same lane, collision avoidance mechanism is not performed. Similarly to the original CA local transition function, only deceleration based on probabilities could be applied in this situation. In case of small vehicle speeds ($v_v(i) < p_6$), deceleration is performed with probability $p_5$, otherwise ($v_v(i) > p_6$) with probability $p_8$.

Collision avoidance occurs only when there is no free room for vehicle $i$ in the same lane to get in (i.e. $gap(i) + acc(i+1) <= v_v(i)$). Two basic situations may

**Algorithm 1.** Updated local transition function

---

**if** $v_v(i) < p_4$ and $v_v(i) < v_{max}(i)$ **then**
  $v_v(i) := v_v(i) + 1$ with probability $p_7$
**end if**
**if** $(gap(i) + acc(i + 1)) > v_v(i)$ **then**
  **if** $v_v(i) < p_6$ **then**
    $v_v(i) := v_v(i) - 1$ with probability $p_5$
  **else**
    $v_v(i) := v_v(i) - 1$ with probability $p_8$
  **end if**
**else**
  **if** $acc(i + 1) > 0$ **then**
    $v_v(i) := 1/p_9 \times (gap(i) + acc(i + 1))$
  **else**
    $v_v(i) := 1/p_{10} \times (gap(i) + acc(i + 1))$
  **end if**
**end if**

**Ensure:** Each vehicle $i$ is advanced $v_v(i)$ times and $v_{prev}(i) := v_v(i)$.

---

occur. If the leading vehicle tends to accelerate ($acc(i+1) > 0$), the actual vehicle speed $v_v(i)$ is reduced to $1/p_9 \times (gap(i) + acc(i+1))$. Otherwise, ($v_v(i+1) <= 0$), actual vehicle speed $v_v(i)$ is reduced more strictly to $1/p_{10} \times (gap(i) + acc(i+1))$. It can be seen that these two parameters are more driver-based parameters than model oriented. We will try to find out if these ones could be determined statistically for a given road segment. Finally, each vehicle is advanced $v_v(i)$ sites and velocity updates must be also performed.

## 3    Optimization of the Model

Genetic algorithms (GA) are widely used in various areas of science and engineering to find solutions to optimization and design problems [8]. The main idea is to evolve a population (set) of candidate solutions to find better ones. A candidate solution is encoded as a chromosome which is an abstract representation that can be modified with standard genetic operators such as mutation and crossover. In this work, GA is used to find all parameters of the CA model in order to maximize the precision of the traffic simulator.

### 3.1    Parameters Encoding

In order to simplify GA, all simulation model parameters, which will be optimized, are encoded in binary form. In case of real numbers from a given interval (e.g. $[1, 0]$), the interval is divided into the $N$ pieces of the same size. The value $N$ depends on the number of bits used for encoding of the parameter.

Using a 6-bit value and the minimal length of the cell 0.125 $m$ the maximal cell length is 8 $m$ (64 × 0.125). The cell length is the first model parameter – $p_1$. One vehicle always occupies as many such cells as it fits into the 5.5 $m$ (or nearer, but not smaller). For example, for the smallest cell length (0.125 $m$) it is exactly 44 cells. Bigger vehicles, such as trucks, occupy only two times bigger place (11 $m$). The second model parameter, $p_2$, is the simulation time-step (also the reaction time) with the minimal value of 0.05 and maximum value of 3.2 seconds encoded again using 6 bits. The cell neighbor, $p_3$, is encoded using 12 bits (e.g. when the cell length is at minimum then the maximum neighbor is 0.125 × 4096 = 512 $m$). The next parameter is maximal vehicles speed $p_4$ (encoded on 11 bits, i.e. 2048 possible values for a chosen reaction time and cell lenght) giving, as in the original model [7], the number of cells per simulation step. The probability of slowing down is represented by $p_5$ (encoded on 8 bits) and slow speed boundary is encoded as $p_6$ (1 – 512 cells per simulation step on 9 bits). Then, the speed-up probability is denoted as $p_7$. The parameter $p_8$ is probability of vehicles slowing down in case of a vehicle speed greater than the slow speed $p_6$. Further model constants $p_9$ and $p_{10}$ are coefficients of vehicle approximation in case of previous vehicle acceleration and previous vehicle slowing-down. Both parameters have minimal value of 1 and maximal value of 32 (encoded on 5 bits). All parameters with their respective minimal values, maximal values and step, are briefly summarized in Tab. 1.

**Table 1.** CA model parameters and values

|  | Bits used [#] | Min. value | Max. value | Step |
|---|---|---|---|---|
| $p_1$ | 6 | 0.125 | 8.000 | 0.125 |
| $p_2$ | 6 | 0.05 | 3.20 | 0.05 |
| $p_3$ | 12 | $p_1$ | $2^{12} \times p_1$ | $p_1$ |
| $p_4$ | 11 | $p_1/p_2$ | $2^{11} \times p_1/p_2$ | $p_1/p_2$ |
| $p_5$ | 8 | 0.00392 | 1.00000 | 0.00392 |
| $p_6$ | 9 | $p_1/p_2$ | $2^9 \times p_1/p_2$ | $p_1/p_2$ |
| $p_7$ | 8 | 0.00392 | 1.00000 | 0.00392 |
| $p_8$ | 8 | 0.00392 | 1.00000 | 0.00392 |
| $p_9$ | 5 | 1 | 32 | 1 |
| $p_{10}$ | 5 | 1 | 32 | 1 |
| $p_m$ | 10 | 0.00097 | 1.00000 | 0.00097 |
| $p_c$ | 4 | 0.06667 | 1.00000 | 0.06667 |

## 3.2 Chromosome

The proposed GA has an auto-evolution or also self-adaptation capability, which means that parameters of the algorithm (the probability of mutation $p_m$ and crossover $p_c$) are also part of the chromosome. Hence the user is not forced to set them. The whole set of parameters is represented using one 92-bit number. It is important to note that each parameter of the chromosome is encoded using *Gray encoding* to ensure that the maximal Hamming distance between two successive values is only one. This setup does not allow big jumps between values in case of a single bit change. The first population $(X(0))$ consists of 60 such chromosomes $(|X(0)| = 60)$ generated randomly.

## 3.3 Fitness Function

All chromosomes from population $X_i$ are separately evaluated using the same fitness function. Firstly, a candidate CA road segment is constructed using the parameters obtained from a candidate chromosome. Then simulation is performed for that model. Incoming vehicles are generated depending on their time of arrival based on measurements from the field. Vehicles outgoing from the simulated road segment are simply removed and their travel time is recorded. Depending on the facility type, various vehicle types could be generated where possible. Whole simulation is executed until the same number of simulated vehicles as the number of vehicles in the field data is reached ($N_x$). After that, the fitness function $F$ (see Eq. 3) is calculated as a sum of two functions. The error function $E$ is defined as

$$E = \sum_{i=1}^{M} \left( \frac{|x_{mi} - x_{f_i}|}{x_{f_i}} \right),$$
(1)

where $M$ is time interval (e.g. travel times of 50 to 51 seconds – in the scope of 1 second), $x_{mi}$ and $x_{f_i}$ are frequencies (or occurrence) of $i$-th travel time measured from the calibrated model and from the field data respectively. Then the penalty function $P$ is

$$P = (cel\_length)^{-8}.$$
(2)

This penalization ensures that the solutions where the cell length is very small are not preferred due to noticeable slower simulation runtime. Moreover, it is multiplied by the number of vehicles – $N$ (to add a constant error to every vehicle). Thus the fitness function is

$$F = E + (N \times P).$$
(3)

Finally, GA tries to minimize this fitness function $F$ as better solutions are always with lower fitness value.

## 3.4 Creating a New Population

**Selection:** After evaluation of all chromosomes from the population $X(i)$ is complete, some of them are selected for next operations using a tournament selection with base 2 giving a new population $X_S(i)$, where $|X_S(i)| = 30$.

**Crossover:** Two-point crossover is applied between two randomly selected individuals giving a new set $X_C(i)$ (where $X_C(i) \subset X_S(i)$ and $|X_C(i)| = 30$). The first point of crossover operation is between the $p_3$ and $p_4$ parameter and the second one right after $p_{10}$ parameter, to allow alternation of the model and the GA parameters individually. This operator is applied with the average probability calculated from two chosen chromosomes ($p_c$).

**Mutation:** On all chromosomes from $X_C(i)$ a mutation operator (i.e. changing bit $0 \rightarrow 1$ or $1 \rightarrow 0$) is applied with the probability ($p_m$) taken from evaluated individual, which gives a brand new population $X_M(i)$ of the same size.

**Population Recovery:** Finally, a new population of 60 individuals $X(i + 1)$ is selected from the previous population $X(i)$ and the $X_M(i)$ population. This ensures that the best solution will always survive (i.e. elitism is present) [8].

## 4    Experimental Results

### 4.1    Field Data

In order to evaluate proposed method, field data have been utilized. Our field data comes from 2431 meters long road segment between two bigger villages in the Slovak Republic with a maximum allowed speed of 50 km/h. This segment is a bit crocked one and there is no allowance for another vehicle advancement due to the local restrictions. The particular segment is on the way to the country seat, so the road is utilized mostly by drivers going to work and back on ordinary business days, but traffic is not strictly homogenous here. This road segment is also a part of the route between two biggest cities in the region and statistically given 5% of traffic comes from bigger vehicles (e.g. busses, trucks, etc.).

Data set was obtained using standard monitoring technology (i.e. detection loops and detection cameras) for every day and night of the year 2010. Therefore, it was possible to measure travel time for vehicles on given road segment. To be able to get frequency of individual travel times (that is used for model comparison), we decided to round these travel times to 1 second scope. Based on this, it is possible to get frequencies of travel times for different intervals (e.g. morning travel times, one day travel times, week travel times, etc.). We utilized two such data sets, where travel time for every single vehicle is present. Frequencies of travel time from ordinary business day (Tuesday, 18/5/2010) (1) and from the last business day (Friday, 21/5/2010) (2) of the same week has been selected. First data set (1) has average travel time of 197.74 seconds for 6702 vehicles ($N_1$). Second data set (2) has about 11.21 seconds greater average travel time for 8511 vehicles ($N_2$). It is also important to note that there were sometimes short-term traffic jams during the second selected day. Both data sets for different week day are shown in Fig. 1.

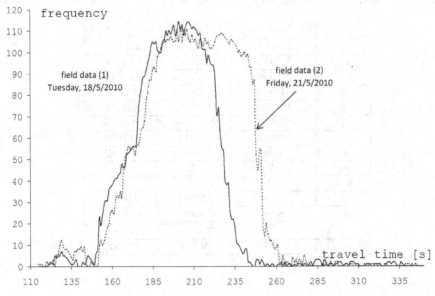

**Fig. 1.** Frequencies of travel times for two days

## 4.2   Calibrated Model

All parameters of the CA based microscopic traffic simulation model
($p_1 \ldots p_{10}, p_m$ and $p_c$), which were evolved for our data sets separately are shown
decoded as real values in Tab. 2. All come from the best solution of the last generation (220 000) of GA. Tab. 2 also shows parameters of our previously manually
tuned and updated CA model as introduced in [5] and in [6] (in the first column
of the table). Some of those manually updated values, are generally not available
(GA parameters) or have a bit different meaning in our previous model. Such
an example is the low speed boundary value $p_6$, which is identical with maximal
vehicles speed $p_4$. This is caused by absence of the first parameter in the updated
model, because slowing down was performed for all available vehicles (with probability $p_5$). Also all vehicles in the updated model tend to always accelerate, so
$p_7 = 1.0$.

In order to check whether all evolved values are not only a result of stochastic
nature of GA we made a simple convergence test and it was discovered, that all
parameters tend to evolve to one particular value during generations of GA. Due
lack of space we do not illustrate this test results here.

The cell length parameter ($p_1$) is nearly 2 times less in contrast to our previously manually updated model. This also means that single vehicle is represented
using two such cells. The evolved reaction time ($p_2$) of 1.5 seconds corresponds to
the minimal increment of 7.43 km/h ($p_1/p_2$ as seen in Tab. 1). This parameter is
also slightly different compared to our previous model. However, very important
finding is that these parameters ($p_1$ and $p_2$) converged to the same value for both
data sets as they are strictly model oriented. All other parameters ($p_3 \ldots p_{10}$)

**Table 2.** Parameters and errors for updated model and models evolved for data sets

| | Updated model | Model for (1) | Model for (2) |
|---|---|---|---|
| $p_1$ | 5.500 $m$ | 2.375 $m$ | 2.375 $m$ |
| $p_2$ | 1.200 $s$ | 1.15 $s$ | 1.15 $s$ |
| $p_3$ | 60.5 $m$ | 194.75 $m$ | 166.25 $m$ |
| $p_4$ | 181.5 $\frac{km}{h}$ | 81.78 $\frac{km}{h}$ | 89.22 $\frac{km}{h}$ |
| $p_5$ | 0.3000 | 0.1059 | 0.4118 |
| $p_6$ | 181.5 $\frac{km}{h}$ | 29.74 $\frac{km}{h}$ | 59.48 $\frac{km}{h}$ |
| $p_7$ | 1.00000 | 0.8314 | 0.7569 |
| $p_8$ | $n/a$ | 0.1451 | 0.4549 |
| $p_9$ | 12 | 2 | 2 |
| $p_{10}$ | 12 | 2 | 3 |
| $p_m$ | $n/a$ | 0.00196 | 0.00293 |
| $p_c$ | $n/a$ | 0.66667 | 0.66667 |
| $E_t$ on (1) | 28.19% | **7.63%** | 15.21% |
| $E_t$ on (2) | 36.40% | 19.23% | **6.35%** |

are a bit different in between two given data sets. The first such parameter is cell neighbor ($p_3$). It is 194.75 m (i.e. 82 cells) for the first data set (1) and 166.25 m (i.e. 70 cells) for the second data set (2). The maximum allowed speed ($p_4$) is for both models higher than a local speed restrictions. This represents the real situation at the road segment as some drivers do not keep the maximum speed limit here.

For the model calibrated to (1), the probability of slowing down ($p_5$) is 0.1059 for vehicle speeds lower than the evolved boundary ($p_6$) of 29.74 km/h. The same slowing down (in case of speed lower than 59.48 km/h) occurs for 41.18% in the model calibrated to (2). On the other hand, the probability of acceleration ($p_7$) is higher for (1). The parameter ($p_8$) of slowing down in case of speeds greater than the evolved boundary speed ($p_6$) is nearly the same as the previous one ($p_5$). This could indicate that it would be possible to somehow interoperate both of these parameters and simplify the simulation model.

Parameters $p_9$ and $p_{10}$ are surprisingly very small and also quite similar. However, based on their convergence tests, we claim that these parameters (i.e. driver sensitivity) can be also statistically obtained for a desired road segment and/or time.

Tab. 2 also shows the average travel time error $E_t$ for one time interval computed as

$$E_t = \frac{E}{M}, \qquad (4)$$

where $M$ is the number of time intervals for a given data set. We also measured this error for our manually updated model with additional maximal speed readjustment for exact local conditions (e.g. maximal speed). It can be seen that all three new calibrated models, which were obtained using described GA, are significantly better on a particular data set in comparison to our manually updated model (compared previously only with fundamental diagrams). Moreover, all new models are also better when compared to different data sets. This finding is very important for future travel time estimation using simulations.

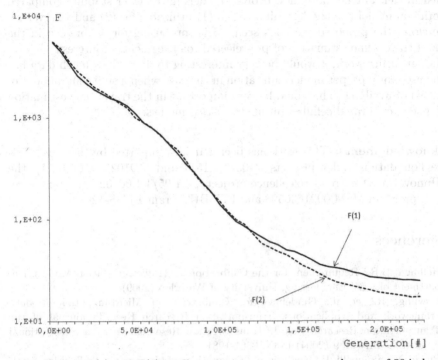

**Fig. 2.** Fitness $F(1)$ and $F(2)$ in all generations as an average value out of 50 independent runs when calibrating to data set (1) and (2) respectively

It is also important to note, that completing all runs for one data set (50 runs of 220 000 generations) takes more than three days running at *Intel Xeon CPU5420 @ 2.5 GHz* due to need for performing simulations. Fig. 2 shows the average fitness value $F(1)$ and $F(2)$ for 50 successive runs and for data set (1) and (2) respectively. Note that y-axis is in the logarithmic scale. It can be also seen, that quality tends to increase (lower fitness) during evolution of 220 000 generations which is ensured by elitism. After that number of generations, the quality of population is not changing dramatically. Our genetic algorithm was tuned to always find a reasonable solution after this number of generations. The whole tuning process will be described in the forthcoming paper.

## 5   Conclusions

In this work, we proposed an effective calibration method for a simple microscopic traffic simulation model. The proposed model is based on the cellular automaton, which can easily be accelerated. We utilized genetic algorithm for model parameters optimization, that was able to find all parameters of the CA model for a given field data. We increased the precision of simulator in average by more than 1/4 in comparison with our previously updated and manually tuned model. Furthermore, new evolved models have better stability compared to original model (i.e. model calibrated to (1) utilizable for (2) and vice versa). Therefore, the proposed methods seem to be promising for calibration in the task of travel time estimation of pre-selected road segments of interest.

In our future work, it would be very interesting to derive how much data has to be used for a proper model calibration in the case when a sufficient amount of data is not available. This could be very important in the travel time estimation using such calibrated cellular automaton based models.

**Acknowledgments.** This work has been partially suported by the Czech Science Foundation under projects P103/10/1517 and GD102/09/H042, by the IT4Innovations Centre of Excellence project CZ.1.05/1.1.00/02.0070, by the research program MSM 0021630528 and FIT BUT grant FIT-S-12-1.

# References

1. Hellinga, B.R.: Requirement for the Calibration of Traffic Simulation Models. Department of Civil Engineering, University of Waterloo (2009)
2. Dowling, R., et al.: Guidelines for Calibration of Microsimulation Models: Framework and Applications. Transportation Research Record: Journal of the Transportation Research Board, Transportation Research Board of the National Academies 1876, 1–9 (2004) ISSN: 0361-1981
3. Punzo, V., Simonelli, F.: Analysis and Comparison of Microscopic Traffic Flow Models with Real Traffic Microscopic Data. Transportation Research Record: Journal of the Transportation Research Board, Transportation Research Board of the National Academies 1934, 53–63 (2005) ISSN: 0361-1981
4. Van Aerde, M., Rakha, H.: Multivariate Calibration of Single Regime Speed-Flow-Density Relationships. In: Vehicle Navigation and Information Systems (VNIS) Conference, Seattle (1995)
5. Korcek, P., Sekanina, L., Fucik, O.: A Scalable Cellular Automata Based Microscopic Traffic Simulation. In: IEEE Intelligent Vehicles Symposium 2011 (IV11), pp. 13–18. IEEE ITSS, Baden-Baden (2011) ISBN 978-1-4577-0889-3
6. Korcek, P., Sekanina, L., Fucik, O.: Cellular automata based traffic simulation accelerated on GPU. In: 17th International Conference on Soft Computing (MENDEL 2011), Brno, CZ, UAI FSI VUT, pp. 395–402 (2011) ISBN 978-80-214-4302-0
7. Nagel, K., Schreckenberg, M.: A cellular automaton model for freeway traffic. Journal de Physique I 2(12), 2221–2229 (1992)
8. Goldberg, D.E.: Genetic Algorithms in Search, Optimization and Machine Learning, 1st edn. Addison-Wesley (1989) ISBN: 0201157675

# Cellular Automata Model Properties:
# Representation of Saturation Flow

Ioanna Spyropoulou

National Technical University of Athens, School of Rural and Surveying Engineering,
9 Heroon Polytechniou st., 15780 Zografou, Greece
iospyrop@central.ntua.gr

**Abstract.** The current study investigates the way in which the saturation flow of a traffic lane is represented through widely used cellular automata models. In particular, following a literature search specific cellular automata models that have been developed to simulate mainly urban traffic are selected for this study. The values of the saturation flow as these are produced via model simulations with the modification of relevant model parameters including maximum desired speed and probability are defined through appropriate statistical values.

**Keywords:** saturation flow, capacity, probability p, TOCA, microsimulation.

## 1    Introduction

Cellular automata models, which have been developed initially for physics domain applications, are now being extensively used in several other domains including vehicle movement simulation in the traffic engineering domain. Initially, they were designed to simulate freeway traffic conditions and have since been further modified to cater also for urban road networks The first model that was used to simulate vehicle movement was the NaSch model [1], which comprises the basis for several updated cellular automata traffic models that have been developed to fill-in the gaps of the initial one. Hence, a great number of models that reproduce elements of vehicle movement in a more realistic manner have been proposed; using more complex rules, but under the same simplistic approach such as the velocity dependant randomization (VDR) [3] which incorporates the slow-to-start concept and the time-oriented Cellular Automata (TOCA) [4]. Smaller modifications have also taken place to develop suitable models for urban traffic simulation [5]-[12]. A significant element when simulating traffic networks is their capacity, which is a representation of traffic network supply – treating the traffic flow that will be simulated to enter the network as the demand. However, little attention has been paid, to determine the resulting capacity, although it has a crucial role in the resulting vehicle movement and the evaluation of traffic control strategies.

This study attempts to investigate how saturation flow is represented in different models through establishing the values that each model may achieve under different scenarios. The paper is formed as follows. In the following chapter the traffic

G.C. Sirakoulis and S. Bandini (Eds.): ACRI 2012, LNCS 7495, pp. 817–826, 2012.

quantities that comprise road capacity at signal controlled junctions are introduced. In chapter 3, the investigated cellular automata models are described. In chapter 4, the produced values of saturation flow are determined in respect to different simulation scenarios. In the last chapter a discussion of the performance of the investigated model parameters takes place and a critical review between the models on the basis of their performance is presented.

## 2    Investigated Traffic Quantities

The maximum rate of traffic flow, and in the case of microscopic models, the maximum number of vehicles that may pass through a road section/approach is of crucial importance when simulating traffic networks. In particular, if the supply of the simulated approach is not determined an infinite number or a specific number (depending on the inherit model properties) of vehicles can pass through the approach in the unit of time. Hence, this quantity determining supply needs to be quantified. The quantity that denotes the supply of a road is capacity. However, one has to start by another traffic quantity – namely, the saturation flow. The saturation flow of a traffic lane, stream or approach involves the maximum number of vehicles that may pass from this lane, stream or approach under the prevailing geometrical and traffic conditions, assuming that vehicle movement is not interrupted by any means of traffic control. Hence, saturation flow is a quantity that is not influenced by the type of control that is present in the simulated approach. Traffic flow that may pass through a lane, stream or approach under the prevailing traffic control conditions is capacity. In cases of signalized approaches the capacity depends on saturation flow, the signal timings (cycle and green timings) and on two other properties the start and end lag. Saturation flow is a quantity that is determined through specific parameters, and there is a number of approximation formulae through which saturation flow is calculated, and differ for freeways and urban networks. In addition, there is a number of more accurate methodologies through which saturation flow can be estimated using field measurements. Several measurable parameters are included in the approximation formulae [13]-[15].  Examples include lane width, road gradient, turning traffic, proportion of heavy goods vehicles.

There is a variety of methods for calculating and estimating the saturation flow, start and end lag at signal-controlled approaches. For the needs of this study the estimation methods are suitable, which describe the way to measure the aforementioned quantities using field - and in our case, simulated - data. The most common methodologies include the so-called British [16], US [14] and Australian [15] methods, the headway ration methods [17] and synchronous and asynchronous regression methods [18]. In the present study the Road Research Laboratory method is employed, through which the saturation flow, and both the start and end lag can be estimated. Capacity can then be calculated and is a function of the saturation flow, the start and end lag as well as the duration of the red indication and the signal period.

In cellular automata models, the saturation flow is a property that is produced by the model. In deterministic cellular automata the saturation flow that the model produces is fixed – and is a function of maximum speed (and hence cell width and time-step) [19]. In stochastic cellular automata the saturation flow may be indirectly determined through the manipulation of a model parameter – namely, the probability p [2]. Capacity, however, is determined in different ways depending on the type of approach control. In signal controlled junctions, there are two approaches to determine capacity. One involves the manipulation of the green indication that is provided as input in the model taking into account the movement dynamics, the simulated green timings as well as the desired values for the start and end lag. With this approach if the values of the start and end lag are known, one may always simulate the desired value of capacity, but will interfere with model dynamics. The second approach is to allow the model produce the value of capacity, which could however differ from the desired simulated one. The advantage of the second approach is that one may also test the model's dynamics in respect to achieved capacity. Both approaches are valid and their selection depends upon the objective of the simulation.

## 3    Cellular Automata Models

### 3.1    The NaSch Model

The cellular automata model is a development of particle hopping models in which each particle/unity is assumed to hop between cells at each unit of time. Each cell may be occupied by one unity or be empty. From the aforementioned definition it is evident that the adaptation of the cellular automata models in the simulation of traffic flow involves each unity being a vehicle. Hence, the cellular automata models are microscopic models where both time and space are treated as discrete parameters. The rules that define vehicle movement at the NaSch model are as follows:

- Find number of empty sites ahead $(= gap)$ at time $t$. If $u > gap$ (too fast), then slow down to $u := gap$ . (rule 1)

- Else if $u < gap$ (enough headway) and $u < u_{max}$, then accelerate by one: $u := u + 1$. (rule 2)

- If after the above steps the velocity is larger than zero $(u > 0)$, then, with probability $p$ , reduce $u$ by one. (rule 3)

- Each particle moves $u$ sites ahead: $x := x + u$ (rule 4)

The network is represented through links that are divided in segments that are equal to the cell length which represents the length of a vehicle plus a safety distance. The rules are applied at each time-step which also denotes the driver reaction time. Vehicle dynamics illustrate several deviations from those encountered in real traffic, as all vehicles have the same properties including maximum speed, size (effective length and width), acceleration, deceleration and reaction time. In addition, acceleration can only increase speed by one unit per time-step, whereas deceleration can be rather high since a vehicle may come to a complete stop from its maximum speed in one time-step. Last, vehicle properties (acceleration/deceleration and speed) are a factor only of the space headway between vehicles at the unit of time. Several modifications of the model have since been proposed to overcome the model's simplicity and to represent vehicle movement in urban environments by including more realistic elements of vehicle movement without losing the gain cellular automata simulations have in computational time over other microscopic simulations.

## 3.2    The TOCA Model

Brilon and Wu introduced a modification to the NaSch to cater for the asymmetric car-following behaviour that the model produced. The time-orientated cellular automaton model introduced parameter $t_H$ representing the average headway in a convoy which they set as the threshold of changing speeds replacing the NaSch value which was equal to the time-step. They also introduced two types of probabilities: an acceleration and a deceleration one, thus also modifying the model stochasticity. The rules that define vehicle movement at the TOCA model are as follows:

- Find number of empty sites ahead $(= gap)$ at time $t$. If $u > gap$ (too fast), then slow down to $u := gap$. (rule 1)

- Else if $u * t_H < gap$ (enough headway) and $u < u_{max}$, then accelerate by one: $u := u + 1$ with probability $p_{ac}$ (rule 2)

- If after the above steps the velocity is larger than zero $(u > 0)$ and $u * t_H > gap$, then, with probability $p_{dc}$, reduce $u$ by one. (rule 3)

- Each particle moves $u$ sites ahead: $x := x + u$ (rule 4)

Both in rules 2 and 3 the time threshold $t_H$ is introduced which initialises speed oscillations randomly to the simulated vehicles. The values proposed by Brilon and Wu are 1.1 for $t_H$ and 0.9 for both $p_{ac}$ and $p_{dc}$. However, probabilities for acceleration and deceleration may differ allowing a greater flexibility to the model.

# 4    Analysis

## 4.1    Simulation Scenarios

The simulated scenarios involve the parameters that will be modified in the study simulations and are maximum speed (1,2,3,4), probability $p/ p_{ac}/ p_{dc}$ (0-0.99, step 0.01) and $t_h$ (1.1, 1.2, 1.3, 1.4, 1.5). For the needs of this study and to avoid complexity, the deceleration and acceleration probabilities of the TOCA model receive the same value. The simulated network consists of one link which is controlled by traffic signals and the arrivals are randomly generated and the selected time-step is 1sec.

## 4.2    Results

**The NaSch Model.**
In NaSch model the limit values of probability p are 0 and 1. In the first case the model becomes deterministic and the saturation flow and start lag can be obtained

through specific formulae [19] and in the latter case vehicles would not progress. Saturation flow as a function of maximum vehicle speeds is presented in Figure 1.

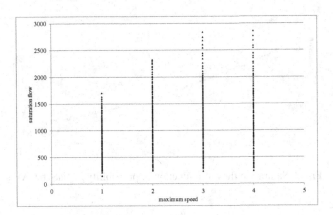

**Fig. 1.** Saturation flow as a function of maximum speed (NaSch CA)

The values of produced saturation flow only differ partially for the different simulated speeds. In particular, the minimum values remain the same and the difference mainly lies at the maximum values that the saturation flow can obtain. Higher values of simulated maximum speeds can accomplish higher values of saturation flow.

However, the main cloud of produced saturation flows is more or less within the same range, and the higher values of saturation flow produced for the values of maximum speed equal to 3 and 4 are only accomplished under a small sample. It must also be noted that these values of saturation flow are somewhat unrealistic in respect to the actual traffic network scenarios. In particular, the simulated values of maximum speed 1, 2, 3 and 4 represent the values of free flow speed of 23.4, 46.8, 70.2 and 93.6km/h respectively. Saturation flow - depending on several prevailing junction characteristics - can reach values close to 2000PCH/hour at urban streets and not more than about 2600PCU/hour at freeways [20]-[21].

Urban streets can be represented with maximum speed being set equal to 2 - in which case saturation flow can reach the value of 2400PCU/hour. In addition, for maximum speeds being set equal to 2 and 3, the produced values of saturation flow exceed 2800PCU/hour. Hence, the model allows for high - rather unrealistic - flow to depart from the junction than in reality for small values of probability $p$, i.e. with reduced randomness. The saturation flow as produced by the model with different values of probability $p$ is illustrated in Figure 2.

Saturation flow decreases with the increase of the value of probability $p$. The decrease is quite smooth and only a few oscillations that were not found to be statistically significant (a=0.05) are observed. The decrease is smoother for higher values of probability. Saturation flow values differ between speeds, with the difference being higher with low values of probability $p$, i.e. when the frequency of random vehicle deceleration is reduced. The combined impact of the maximum speed and probability $p$ on the model's produced saturation flow is illustrated in Figure 3.

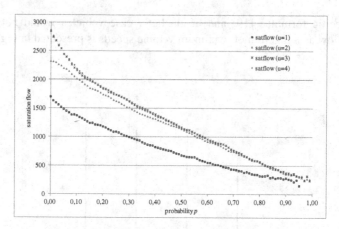

**Fig. 2.** Saturation flow as a function of probability $p$ (NaSch CA)

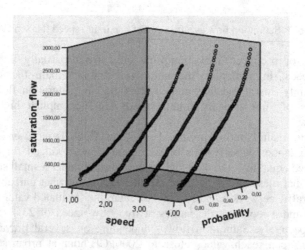

**Fig. 3.** Saturation flow as a function of maximum speed and probability $p$ (NaSch CA)

**The TOCA Model.**

The TOCA model simulated in this study is such that both the acceleration and deceleration probabilities receive the same values. Moreover, analysis was conducted for a range of time headways and results indicated that the difference is quite small. The reason for the small impact of the different $t_H$ values lies in the discrete character of the model. The model parameters can only be integer numbers and hence the resulting relationship between the gap and speed*$t_H$ is similar for several $t_H$ values. The time headway value that is used for the following analysis is $t_H=1.1$. Saturation flow as a function of maximum vehicle speeds is presented in Figure 4.

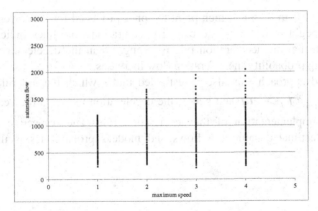

**Fig. 4.** Saturation flow as a function of maximum speed (TOCA)

The model's produced saturation flow values differ only slightly with different values of maximum speed, especially considering speed values of 2, 3 and 4. The main cloud of points seems to be within the same range of saturation flow values. In addition, the maximum produced saturation flows receive realistic values and range between about 1700 and 2100PCU/hour. The saturation flow values produced under maximum speed equal to 1, are considered to be quite low. The saturation flow as a function of the different values of the acceleration and deceleration probabilities is illustrated in Figure 5.

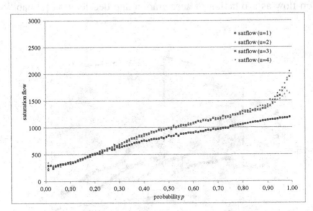

**Fig. 5.** Saturation flow as a function of acceleration and deceleration probabilities (TOCA)

The TOCA model produces rather different relationships between the saturation flow and acceleration and deceleration probabilities. In particular, the saturation flow increases with the increase of the probability value rather than its decrease. The increase is quite smooth, except for probabilities ranging between 0,90 and 0,99 where the increase is sharp, for maximum speed taking the values of 2, 3 and 4. Small oscillations are observed, however they are not statistically significant (a=0.05). The values of saturation flow are more or less equal between speeds for probabilities ranging from 0.01 to 0.25 at which point the ones produced for the lowest maximum speed (u=1) begin to differ to the rest. The saturation flow lines indicate that the model is such that the acceleration rule is stronger than the deceleration one, since with increasing probability the saturation flow increases.

A modified approach was also investigated under which the 3rd rule of TOCA considered $u_{i-1} * t_H > gap$ and hence, the deceleration involved the vehicles speed prior to the implementation of the acceleration rule. The respective relationship between the estimated saturation flows and model's probabilities is illustrated in Figure 6.

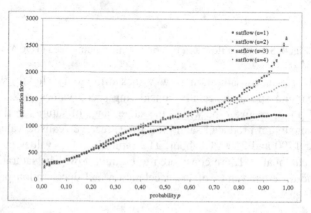

**Fig. 6.** Saturation flow as a function of acceleration and deceleration probabilities (modified TOCA)

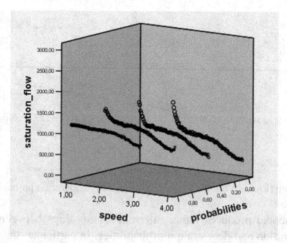

**Fig. 7.** Saturation flow as a function of maximum speed and acceleration and deceleration probabilities (TOCA)

The saturation flow relationship differs in several ways. In particular, the produced saturation flow values are higher. There is also a different effect between the estimated values for maximum speeds 3 and 4 and maximum speed 2. The difference appears for probabilities values higher than 0.70. Last, the saturation flow lines are less smooth to the ones produced using the original TOCA model.

The combined effect of the maximum speed, and acceleration and deceleration probabilities values on the saturation flow as produced by the original TOCA model is illustrated in Figure 7.

# 5    Discussion

In this study, the relationship between the saturation flow as produced by the NaSch CA model and the time-oriented cellular automaton model was investigated. Significant model parameters - in particular, the vehicle maximum speed, the probability p which is a measure of the model's stochasticity but is also incorporated to represent random oscillations in vehicle speed and a threshold value for changing vehicle speeds in the TOCA model were modified and the produced saturation flow was estimated. Results indicated that both the choice probabilities and maximum vehicles speeds influence the models' produced saturation flows, but in a different manner and also for specific value ranges. The effect of the choice of the set threshold in the TOCA model was not found to be significant.

Ongoing work includes the estimation of the TOCA produced saturation flow assigning different values to the acceleration and deceleration probabilities. In addition, sensitivity analysis is being performed to assess the size of the impact on the model's saturation flow with the different values of the models parameters. The same analysis is also performed for the traffic quantities of start and end lag. Similar work using other CA models that have been proposed for the simulation of urban road networks could also be of interest. Future work may also involve the modification of the time-step and of the cell length. In addition, the effect of heterogeneous traffic and the way in which the produced saturation flow is affected could also be investigated.

# References

1. Nagel, K., Schreckenberg, M.: A cellular automaton model for freeway traffic. J. Phys. I 2, 2221–2229 (1992)
2. Spyropoulou, I.: Modelling a signal controlled traffic stream using cellular automata. Transp. Res. C 15(3), 175–190 (2007)
3. Barlovic, R., Santen, L., Schadschneider, A., Schreckenberg, M.: Metastable states in cellular automata. Eur. Phys. J. B 5(3), 793–800 (1998)
4. Brilon, W., Wu, N.: Evaluation of Cellular automaton for Traffic Flow Simulation on Freeway and Urban Streets. In: Brilon, W., Huber, F., Schreckenberg, M., Wallentowitz, H. (eds.) Traffic and Mobility, pp. 163–180. Springer, Berlin (1999)
5. Chopard, B., Luthi, P.O., Queloz, P.A.: Cellular automat model of car traffic in two-dimensional street networks. J. Phys. A 29, 2325–2336 (1996)
6. Esser, J., Schreckenberg, M.: Microscopic simulation of urban traffic based cellular automata. Int. J. Modern Phys. C 8(5), 1025–1036 (1997)

7. Chowdhury, D., Schadschneider, A.: Self-organization fo traffic jams in cities: Effects of stochastic dynamics and signal periods. Phys. Rev. E 59(2), 1311–1314 (1999)
8. Ruskin, H.J., Wang, R.: Modeling traffic flow at and urban unsignalized intersection. In: Proceedings of the International Conference on Computational Science, pp. 381–390. Springer, London (2002)
9. Wu, Q.-S., Li, X.-B., Hu, M.-B., Jiang, R.: Study of traffic flow at an unsignalized T-shaped intersection by cellular automata model. Eur. Phys. J. B 48, 265–269 (2005)
10. Jiang, R., Wu, Q.-S.: A stopped time dependent randomization cellular automata model for traffic flow controlled by traffic light. Phys. A 364, 493–496 (2006)
11. Płaczek, B.: Fuzzy Cellular Model for On-Line Traffic Simulation. In: Wyrzykowski, R., Dongarra, J., Karczewski, K., Wasniewski, J. (eds.) PPAM 2009, Part II. LNCS, vol. 6068, pp. 553–560. Springer, Heidelberg (2010)
12. He, H.D., Lu, W.Z., Dong, L.Y.: An improved cellular automaton model considering the effect of traffic lights and driving behaviour. Chin. Phys. B 20(4), 040514-1–040514-7 (2011)
13. Kimber, R.M., McDonald, M., Hounsell, N.: Passenger car units in saturation flows: concept, definition, derivation. Transportation Research 19B(1), 39–61 (1985)
14. Transportation Research Board: Highway Capacity Manual. Special Report 209. National Research Council, Washington D.C. (2000)
15. Akcelik, R.: Traffic signals: Capacity and timing analysis. Australian Road Research Board Research Report, APR 123. Australian Road Research Board, Hawthorne (1981)
16. Road Research Laboratory: A method of measuring saturation flow at traffic signals. Road Note 34, Department of the Environment. Road Reasearch Laboratory, Harmondsworth (1963)
17. Greenshields, B.D., Shapiro, D., Erickson, E.L.: Traffic performance at urban intersections. Bureau of Highway Traffic, Technical Report, 1. Yale University, New Haven, Conn (1947)
18. Branston, D., Van Zuylen, H.: The estimation of saturation flow, effective green time and passenger car equivalents at traffic signals by multiple linear regression. Transportation Research 12(1), 47–53 (1978)
19. Spyropoulou, I.: Modelling a signal controlled traffic stream using cellular automata. Transportation Research Part C 15(3), 175–190 (2007)
20. Fellendorf, M., Vortisch, P.: Validation of the Microscopic Traffic Flow Model VISSIM in Different Real-World Situations. In: Proceedings of the 80th Annual Meeting of the Transportation Research Board, TRB, Washington D.C. (2001)
21. Laufer, J.: Freeway capacity, saturation flow and the car following behavioural algorithm of the VISSIM microsimulation software. In: 30th Australasian Transport Research Forum, Melbourne, Australia (2007)

# A Traffic Cellular Automaton with Time to Collision Incorporated

Yohei Taniguchi[1] and Hideyuki Suzuki[2]

[1] Department of Advanced Interdisciplinary Studies (AIS)
Graduate School of Engineering, The University of Tokyo,
Meguro, Tokyo 1538904, Japan
[2] Institute of Industrial Science, The University of Tokyo,
Meguro, Tokyo 1538505, Japan

**Abstract.** We present a new traffic CA model focused on an estimated time for a following vehicle to catch up with the one ahead (Time-to-Collision: TTC) , and investigate characteristics of the model with the simulation. We also analyze analytically the possibility of a collision between two cars in this model. The model is simulated under open boundary conditions and each car is parallel-updated. We draw some fundamental diagrams of the traffic flow with the simulation. In this figure, we find two distinct phases: a free flow and wide moving jam. And between the two phases, the region where the dots spread sparsely is seen clearly. In addition to this, by using different values of an important parameter, we can see the several patterns of the trajectory of vehicles. Based on these findings, we believe it is possible for this model to reproduce synchronized flow.

**Keywords:** TTC, Time-to-Collision, CA, cellular automaton, synchronized flow.

## 1  Introduction

Many researchers have studied the dynamics of traffic scientifically and proposed number of statistical physics models. Traffic flow is a complex system that can show asymptotic behaviors such as self-organized criticality and a phase transition from free flow phase to congestion phase. Due to its flexibility for modifying capability of capturing its self-organized criticality, the cellular automaton (CA) has been used successfully in modeling real behavior of traffic flow, and has become a popular tool for management of traffic [1,2,3].

The NaSch (Nagel-Schreckenberg) model [1] and the VDR (Velocity-Dependent-Randomization) model [2] were proposed in 1992 and 1998 respectively. The NaSch model is known as the model which is able to reproduce both a free flow and congestion state by increasing the possible sets of velocity value that vehicles can take. The VDR model can display a meta-stable state by introducing the slow-to-start effect. In addition to this, S-NFS model [4] proposed in 2006 shows a meta-stable state more clearly by forecasting a possible movement

G.C. Sirakoulis and S. Bandini (Eds.): ACRI 2012, LNCS 7495, pp. 827–834, 2012.

of a car ahead. And of course, there are many other mathematical models that reproduce such a behavior in a traffic flow.

In 2002, Kerner [5,6,7] proposed "Three-phase theory", which states that traffic flow has three phases; a free flow, synchronized flow and wide moving jams. He observed the existence of these three phases, and also proposed the models which can show all the phases [8].

Synchronized flow can be characterized as a sparsely clustered dots in the fundamental diagram of density and flow rate, while other phases, such as a free flow and wide moving jams are shown as dense packed clusters. Therefore, in synchronized flow, the average values of density and flow rate largely vary in time, and the average velocity can be spread from 20 km/h to 60 km/h. In the synchronized flow state, there are both the section where some small sized traffic jam occur and the section of cars moving smoothly. Synchronized flow is visualized as a phenomenon that these sections run waving through backward.

A concept of Time-to-Collision (TTC) was suggested by Lee [9] in 1976. The formula of TTC is described by the distance between a vehicle and the vehicle in front divided by the relative velocity of the two vehicles. It has been often used as the reference index for the risk of crash in a traffic model. However, TTC is rarely used to study a phenomenon of traffic jams but instead used to evaluate a safety of the traffic system as a whole [10,11]. In this paper, we regard TTC as a time allowance until the driver catches up to the car in front. Since TTC has a simpler formulation, it is easier to model behaviors of human drivers in real driving situation.

In this paper, we explain how vehicles run in the model considering the idea of TTC and also explain what is the condition of the parameters of the model to avoid any collision of vehicles in section 2. In section 3, we discuss the reproducibility of synchronized flow with figures of fundamental diagrams and time-space diagrams obtained by a few numerical simulations. Then, we conclude the findings and list what need to work in the section 4.

## 2   The Model with Time to Collision Incorporated

### 2.1   The Algorithm of the Model

We construct a model in which TTC is considered. The procedure is written as follows.

**R0** random braking parameter: $@p = \begin{cases} p_0 \ (d_n^{t-1} = 0) \\ p_d \ (d_n^{t-1} > 0 \text{ and } v_n^t < v_{\max}) \\ p_s \text{ otherwise} \end{cases}$

**R1** acceleration: $v_n^{t+1} \leftarrow \begin{cases} v_n^t + 1 \ (v_n^t < v_{\max} \text{ and } v_n^t < d_n^t) \\ v_n^t \qquad \text{otherwise} \end{cases}$

**R2** aim velocity: $\tilde{v}_n^{t+1} \leftarrow \begin{cases} v_{n+1}^t + \lfloor \frac{d_n^t}{c} \rfloor + 1 \ (v_n^t < d_n^t \text{ and } rand() < \frac{d_n^t}{c} - \lfloor \frac{d_n^t}{c} \rfloor) \\ v_{n+1}^t + \lfloor \frac{d_n^t}{c} \rfloor - 1 \ (v_n^t \geq d_n^t \text{ and } rand() > \frac{d_n^t}{c} - \lfloor \frac{d_n^t}{c} \rfloor) \\ v_{n+1}^t + \lfloor \frac{d_n^t}{c} \rfloor \qquad \text{otherwise} \end{cases}$

**R3** deceleration: $v_n^{t+1} \leftarrow \min\left(v_n^{t+1}, \tilde{v}_n^{t+1}\right)$
**R4** random braking $v_n^{t+1} \leftarrow \max\left(v_n^{t+1} - 1, 0\right)$ with probability $p$
**R5** moving: $x_n^{t+1} \leftarrow x_n^t + v_n^{t+1}$

$x_n^t$ and $v_n^t$ are the location and velocity of the $n$ th vehicle at time $t$ respectively, and the $n+1$ th vehicle represents the vehicle in front of $n$ th vehicle. $d_n^t$ is the gap between the $n$ th car and the $n+1$ th car, that is $d_n^t = x_{n+1}^t - x_n^t - 1$. Figure 1 shows a schema for the variables in the model. $\lfloor \cdot \rfloor$ is floor function.

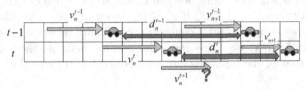

**Fig. 1.** schema for the variables. $v_n^{t+1}$ is determined by $x_n^t$, $v_n^t$ and $d_n^t$

In this model slow-to-start effect [2,4,13] is considered by making $p$ to have three possible different values at R0. Cars accelerate gradually not to exceed a limiting speed at R1. In addition, we consider a drivers' mind that they tend to avoid a collision. When the distance to the car in front is short for their own velocity $v_n^t \geq d_n^t$, they don't accelerate. Likewise, when the distance between two cars is short at R2, they take an aim velocity that is 1 smaller value than it is not. We take the idea of TTC into R2. At R2, each driver adjusts the velocity to make sure that one has more than $c$ seconds to catch up to a car in front. Suppose a time to catch up the car in front is $t_{TTC}$. Then using relative velocity $(v_n^t - v_{n+1}^t)$, we can write

$$\left(v_n^{t+1} - v_{n+1}^t\right) t_{TTC} = d_n^t. \tag{1}$$

From this equation, the range of $v_n^{t+1}$ that makes $t_{TTC}$ more than $c$ (second) is

$$v_{n+1}^t \leq v_n^{t+1} \leq v_{n+1}^t + \frac{d_n^t}{c}. \tag{2}$$

Therefore, the velocity of each car is within this range. Each driver looks at the velocity of the car in front one time step (1 second) ahead. It is just the update time step of CA.

Drivers follow the optimal velocity $v_n^{t+1} = v_{n+1}^t + \frac{d_n^t}{c}$ at R2. This model only uses integer, so rational numbers like $\frac{d_n^t}{c}$ is linearly interpolated in this model. If a car applies brakes, then a velocity $\tilde{v}_n^{t+1}$ is again computed in R2, then used in R3. In this model the maximal acceleration is one cell per one step (7.5 m/s$^2$). Therefore, even if acceleration more than one cell per one step is required in order to reach the optimal velocity, cars can't accelerate up to the value. This is why we use the value $\tilde{v}_n^{t+1}$ only when $\tilde{v}_n^{t+1}$ becomes less than $v_n^{t+1}$ at R3. Drivers apply brakes randomly at R4 and the finally, cars advanced at the step R5.

## 2.2  Risk of Collision

If the velocity is larger than the distance to a car in front, the danger of collision increases. In this situation, if the car ahead does not move at the next time ($v_{n+1}^{t+1} = 0$), a collision occurs. However, it is possible to have $v_n^{t+1} \geq d_n^t$ because there is no condition between $v_{n+1}^t + \frac{d_n^t}{c} + 1$ and $d_n^t$. Therefore, it is not clear if this model is a collision free or not.

For a car not to collide with a car in front at time $t$, it is sufficient if a condition $v_n^{t+1} \leq d_n^t$ is satisfied. Therefore, for the model to be collision free, we find the sufficient condition is "$v_n^{t+1} \leq d_n^t$ if $v_n^t \leq d_n^{t-1}$" at any possible values of $n$ and $t$. In addition, we suppose initial conditions of all cars satisfy $v_n^1 \leq d_n^0$ for all $n$.

Before going further, we write down the relation between the velocity of the front car and that of the following car. We reduce R1, R2 and R3 into the form of

$$
v_n^{t+1} = \begin{cases} \min\left(v_n^t + 1, v_{n+1}^t + \lfloor \frac{d_n^t}{c} \rfloor + 1\right) & (v_n^t < v_{max} \text{ and } v_n^t < d_n^t) \\ \min\left(v_n^t, v_{n+1}^t + \lfloor \frac{d_n^t}{c} \rfloor + 1\right) & \text{otherwise.} \end{cases} \tag{3}
$$

Then, the changes of a distance between two cars is equal to the relative velocity, that is, $d_n^t - d_n^{t-1} = v_{n+1}^t - v_n^t$ always holds (Fig 1 helps you understand easier). Now, we denote $d_n^t - d_n^{t-1}$ by $\Delta d_n^t$. Then, we substitute these equations into a equation (3) and obtain

$$
v_n^{t+1} = \begin{cases} v_n^t + 1 + \min\left(0, \Delta d_n^t + \lfloor \frac{d_n^t}{c} \rfloor\right) & (v_n^t < v_{max} \text{ and } v_n^t < d_n^t) \\ v_n^t + \min\left(0, \Delta d_n^t + \lfloor \frac{d_n^t}{c} \rfloor + 1\right) & \text{otherwise.} \end{cases} \tag{4}
$$

Actually there is the case of a driver slowing down one cell per second speed at R4, but in this subsection, consider only the case that no car brakes at R4. Since no car brakes at R4, it increases the risk of collision when a speed value increases. Thus, if we look at the case with the highest risk and find that no collision between vehicles occurs, then there will be no collision among vehicles in any other cases. Supposing the equation (4) holds, we discuss a statement if $v_n^{t+1} \leq d_n^t$ when $v_n^t \leq d_n^{t-1}$ at any $n$ and any $t$. First, in addition to the equation (4), if $v_n^t < d_n^t$ is satisfied, the statement is true. Because $v_n^{t+1} \leq v_n^t + 1$ for any $t$ and any $n$, and then, $v_n^t < d_n^t \Leftrightarrow v_n^t + 1 \leq d_n^t$.

Secondly, we discuss the case $v_n^t = d_n^t$. In this case, we can obtain the following: $v_n^{t+1} = v_n^t + \min\left(0, \Delta d_n^t + \lfloor \frac{d_n^t}{c} \rfloor + 1\right) \leq v_n^t$. Using this inequality, it is easy to see that $v_n^{t+1} \leq v_n^t = d_n^t$.

Finally, we look at the case $v_n^t > d_n^t$. In this case, whether it is possible to crash to the vehicle ahead depends on a condition of a parameter $c$. Figure 2 shows the relevance of $d_n^t$ and $v_n^t$. Drivers can take the combination of { $d_n^t$, $v_n^t$ } within the region colored in gray. In the black region, the condition that $v_n^{t+1} > d_n^t$ when $v_n^t \leq d_n^{t-1}$ is satisfied because of the following reason. The inequalities $v_n^t \leq d_n^{t-1}$ and $v_n^{t+1} > d_n^t$ can be put into $v_n^t \leq d_n^t - \Delta d_n^t$ and $v_n^t > d_n^t - \Delta d_n^t - \lfloor \frac{d_n^t}{c} \rfloor$, respectively. In the black region, both $v_n^t \leq d_n^{t-1}$ and $v_n^{t+1} > d_n^t$ are satisfied. So, the sufficient condition to be collision free "$v_n^{t+1} \leq d_n^t$ if $v_n^t \leq d_n^{t-1}$" is not satisfied. In order to know the condition of $c$, we see whether there exists a common region between the gray and black area. As the case there are no such region, the sufficient condition $v_n^{t+1} > d_n^t$ when $v_n^t \leq d_n^{t-1}$ always holds in the gray region, therefore we find any collision does not occur. To check that, it is sufficient to focus on a line $v_n^t = v_{\max}$ and the point $(c, c - \Delta d_n^t)$, which is the coordinate both $d_n^t$ and $v_n^t$ are smallest in the black region (the bigger point in Fig 2). We get the condition by comparing the value $c - \Delta d_n^t$ and $v_{\max}$, as follows:

$$c > \Delta d_n^t + v_{\max} = v_{\max} - 1. \tag{5}$$

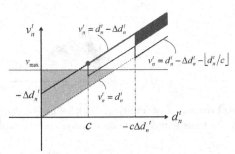

**Fig. 2.** The relevance of $d_n^t$ and $v_n^t$: It shows the region of the combination of $\{\ d_n^t,\ v_n^t\ \}$ drivers can take (colored in gray), and also shows the region where it is possible to crash to the vehicle ahead, that is, $v_n^{t+1} > d_n^t$ when $v_n^t \leq d_n^{t-1}$ (colored in black)

## 3   Simulation Results

We simulate this model with the parameter $L = 2000$ cells (15 km), open boundary, inflow ratio $\alpha = 0.5$, outflow ratio $\beta = 0.5$, $v_{\max} = 5$ (= 135km/h), $p_0 = 0.75$, $p_d = 0.375$, $p_s = 0.05$, the target of TTC $c = 4.1, 5, 7, 15$, and the calculation time step is 54000 (1 step = 1 second). From the subsection 2.2, using the condition 5, it is found that all cases are collision free. In the case of a car not running out from the end of the course in probability $\beta$, the car is on the edge of the road at this time and goes out at the next time. In this situation, we can understand that a new car is entering from branch road. Figure 3 shows the fundamental diagram of this traffic model. The density and the flux observed at the observation points ($l$) located at every 100 cells. The density is the number of cars located on the points averaged over 300 seconds. The flux is the average number of cars that pass the observation points per time step. The equations are given as follows:

Density: $\frac{1}{T}\sum_t^T \sum_n \mathbf{1}\,(x_n^t = l)$

Flow: $\frac{1}{T}\sum_t^T \sum_n \mathbf{1}\,(x_n^t \le l \cap x_n^t > l)$.

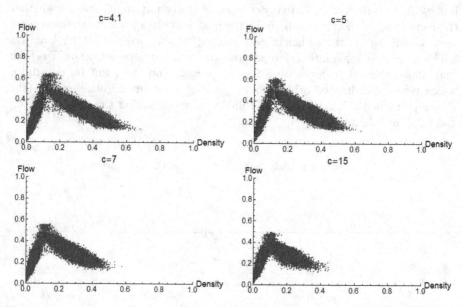

**Fig. 3.** The fundamental diagrams of identical vehicles in the proposed model. These diagrams are drawn on the same simulation condition except the values of parameter $c$.

We can see both the free flow and congestion phase in all of diagrams of figure 3. In addition to this, the meta-stable state is seen clearly. It may be derived by the slow-to-start effect. Furthermore, not only these two phases, but also there are dots spread sparsely in the boundary of two phases. They are seen especially in the case of $c = 4.1$ and $c = 5$. In general, the average velocity of vehicles in synchronized flow is between 20 km/h and 60 km/h. In order to calculate the average value in this system, we use the gradient between each of the dots and origin. The gradients just correspond to the average velocity of vehicles. For $c = 4.1$ and $c = 5$ (Fig 3), the average velocity of vehicles at the dots spread sparsely, for example the point in the area $[0.15,0.2] \times [0.3,0.4]$, is surely between 20 km/h and 60 km/h. The result suggests the reproducibility of synchronized flow in this model.

Figure 4 shows the plot of cars' position among the amount of time. In all of diagrams, each car's speed is fluctuated, and there are both the spot where cars have each short distance to the car in front and the spot where cars have each long distance. In this state, the points in the two-dimensional of car's density and flux are ranged widely by time and space. These facts obtained by the traffic simulation using this proposed car following model are some of the characters of the synchronized flow. Moreover, there are different patterns by the value of parameter $c$. In the upper left panel ($c = 4.1$) of figure 4, the shape of whole

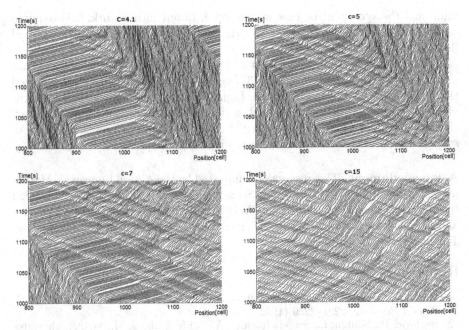

**Fig. 4.** Time-space diagrams: These figures show the trajectories of vehicles which run between 800 cell and 1000 cell from 1000 seconds to 1200 seconds. The horizontal and vertical axes represent the position and time of vehicle, respectively. Inflow ratio is $\alpha = 0.5$ in all the results. Several patterns of traffic flow are seen in these space-time diagrams.

trajectory of vehicles looks like so-called general pattern (GP) [8]. The other cases of $c$ don't show the pattern like GP, but show several ones that are different from each other. The findings suggest that the model can reproduce some patterns of synchronized flow by changing the parameter $c$.

## 4  Conclusion

In this paper, we presented a new CA model considering TTC and performed traffic simulations of identical vehicles in the model. We found that a free flow, meta-stable state and congestion state, which are some of the fundamental properties of traffic flow, were clearly observed in the simulation of this model. In addition to this, we find another area. We calculated the average velocity of vehicles in the area and looked at the the trajectory of vehicles on a inflow parameter. As the consequence, we successfully reproduced some characteristics of the synchronized flow. Furthermore, by using different values of the parameter $c$, we can see the several patterns of the trajectory of vehicles. It suggests that the proposed model can show different synchronized patterns by changing the parameter $c$. $c$ is a physically meaningful parameter based on the human mind in safety driving. Thus, we hope that the study about the relevance between these mind and the synchronized flow will proceed. In our future work, it is required to investigate whether it is possible for this model to reproduce the synchronized flow phase in detail.

In addition to this, it is also required to investigate the relation between a model proposed by HK Lee et al. [13] and our proposed model. They reported their model based on the BL iBrake Lightj model reproduces several patterns of the synchronized flow phase which can be seen in real traffic flow [14]. Furthermore, Kerner et al. presented a CA model which explains the physics of synchronized flow [15]. We are interested in comparing with this model.

**Acknowledgment.** This research is supported by the Aihara Innovative Mathematical Modeling Project, the Japan Society for the Promotion of Science (JSPS) through the "Funding Program for World-Leading Innovative R&D on Science and Technology (FIRST Program)," initiated by the Council for Science and Technology Policy (CSTP).

# References

1. Nagel, K., Schreckenberg, M.: A cellular automation model for freeway traffic. J. Phys. I France 2, 2221–2229 (1992)
2. Barlovic, R., Santen, L., Schadschneider, A., Schreckenberg, M.: Metastable states in cellular automata for traffic flow. J. Phys. B 5, 793–800 (1998)
3. Brockfeld, E., Barlovic, R., Schadschneider, A., Schreckenberg, M.: Optimizing traffic lights in a cellular automaton model for city traffic. Physical Review E 64 (2001)
4. Sakai, S., Nishinari, K., Iida, S.: A new stochastic cellular automaton model on traffic flow and its jamming phase transition. J. Phys. A: Math. Gen. 39 (2006)
5. Kerner, B.S., Klenov, S.L., Wolf, D.E.: Cellular automata approach to three-phase traffic theory. J. Phys. A: Math. Gen. 35, 9971 (2002)
6. Kerner, B.S.: Three phase traffic theory. In: Traffic and Granular Flow 2001 (2003)
7. Kerner, B.S.: Three-phase traffic theory and highway capacity. Physica A: Statistical and Theoretical Physics 333, 379–440 (2004)
8. Kerner, B.S.: Empirical macroscopic features of spatial-temporal traffic patterns at highway bottlenecks. Physical Review E 65, 046138 (2004)
9. Lee, D.N.: A theory of visual control of braking based on information about time-to-collision. Perception 5(4), 437–459 (1976)
10. Minderhoud, M., Bovy, P.: Extended time-to-collision measures for road traffic safety assessment. Accident Analysis and Prevention 33, 89–97 (2001)
11. Vogel, K.: A comparison of headway and time to collision as safety indicators. Accident Analysis and Prevention 35, 427–433 (2003)
12. Krauss, S., Wagner, P.: Metastable states in a microscopic model of traffic flow. Physical Review E 55 (1997)
13. Neubert, L., Santen, L., Schadschneider, A., Schreckenberg, M.: Towards a realistic microscopic description of highway traffic. J. Phys. A: Math. Gen. 33, 477 (2000)
14. Lee, H.K., Barlovic, R., Schreckenberg, M., Kim, D.: Mechanical restriction versus human overreaction triggering congested traffic states. Phys. Rev. Lett. 92, 23 (2004)
15. Kerner, B., Klenov, S., Schreckenberg, M.: Simple cellular automaton model for traffic breakdown, highway capacity, and synchronized flow. Physical Review E 84, 046110 (2011)

# A Cellular Automata-Based Network Model for Heterogeneous Traffic: Intersections, Turns and Their Connection

Jelena Vasic and Heather J. Ruskin

Dublin City University, Dublin, Ireland
{fjvasic,hrusking}@computing.dcu.ie

**Abstract.** The pedal bicycle as a means of transport is gaining new popularity in a world of growing environmental and health concerns. Research relating to bicycles is generally in the area of planning and behaviour, however, flow models that include this non-motorised modality have also been defined, especially for developing-world scenarios. This paper describes a cellular-automata based model for mixed bicycle and motorised traffic on city networks where roads are shared through 'positional discipline', as in Dublin and other old city centres. The paper analyses the spatial properties of a particular instance of the model in some detail and presents results that demonstrate them. It also looks at a number of considerations relating to the the model's implementation.

**Keywords:** traffic cellular automata, transportation network, non-motorised modes, heterogeneous traffic.

## 1 Introduction

Since the early nineties, powered by the accelerated increase in available machine processing capabilities, computing-oriented models, and among them cellular automata (CA) ones, gained popularity in many scientific disciplines. The ever-growing number of vehicles in both developed and developing countries and related problems of congestion and planning for the future made vehicular traffic a ready candidate and the seminal papers by [2] and [17] sparked a widespread and continuing employment of CA for the simulation and study of diverse traffic systems and a variety of qualitative and quantitative properties of traffic, including freeway dynamics [14] and those pertaining to intersections and entire urban networks. The study of intersections can be of value for understanding isolated crossroads, however, they are also of interest as constituent parts of wider networks. All types of intersection conflict resolution have been modelled with CA: signalisation [8,1]; roundabouts [7,24] and priority rules. For example, [12] use a stochastic crash avoidance method where two vehicles that are in conflict are treated as a subgroup with sequential update within the wider context of parallel updates for the whole system, producing an effectively hybrid sequential-parallel update approach. [23] use a 'minimum acceptable space' method, which takes into account individual driver characteristics.

G.C. Sirakoulis and S. Bandini (Eds.): ACRI 2012, LNCS 7495, pp. 835–844, 2012.

An early CA network model was presented by [16], where the use of the asymmetric simple exclusion process (ASEP) removes conflicts from simulations. [5] distinguish between latices representing streets and those representing intersections, which are all connected to form the model's geometric space, where intersections were represented by 4-cell rotaries. Aspects of this model were studied by other authors [3,10,20]. Larger-scale and topologically more realistic models, employing the [17] rules, were described in [6], [19], and [22]. The first and last of those are based on the same detailed cellular models of network elements such as intersections and motorway on-ramps. Conflicts are handled by employing acceptable gaps and intersections do not have a cellular structure i.e. vehicles cannot be positioned within them but only on connecting edges in the network. While [6] define this fairly complex model, [22] explore an agent-based framework for traffic predictions based on that model. The model used by [19] is simpler, in that one-dimensional latices are used for all roads, while different capacities are modelled using a probability of passage through a 'stochastic transition' point. [18] use [17] rules on a network as a base for agent-based simulation with routing based on local knowledge of traffic parameters.

The traffic mix of bicycles with motorised vehicles also has representative CA models. In [4], interference of bicycles with the adjacent car flow is expressed through a higher probability of cars slowing down in the face of 'friction' or 'blockage' caused by the bicycles. 'Cross-flow' interactions are instances of motorised and bicycle flows crossing each other, especially where the two flows initially belong to the same road. In [13] the interaction of straight-moving bicycles and right-turning cars is investigated with the cellular automaton model of [11]. The latter treats bicycles 'in bulk', allowing multiple bicycles to occupy a single cell of the CA space. Here the conflicts between vehicles on the intersecting flows are resolved using the sequential subgrouping of updates within a synchronous model, a method mentioned above. 'Diffusive' mixed traffic is modelled with CA in [9] and in [15] . Although they do not include pedal-cycles, these models would easily do so, since they include a large number of very different vehicles.

Our own model was developed for the type of bicycle traffic found in Dublin, where bicycle-specific facilities are scarce and roads are shared with motorised vehicles by 'positional discipline', which means that bicycles keep to the left[1]. Its focus is on accommodating heterogeneity and on enabling simulation of network traffic. In this paper, a cellular automata model that handles the complexity of heterogeneous traffic interactions on a network is presented and discussed, together with a number of implementation considerations and results produced by simulations. Section 2 describes the model and its features. Section 3 discusses implementation issues and solutions and 4 summarises the work done and discusses work planned for the future.

---

[1] This is the inner side of the road. "Left" and "right" are referred to in this paper as they apply to left-hand-side driving practiced in Ireland and the UK, without any loss of generality.

## 2    Model Description

The model has been described already in [21]. Its basic building block is a one-dimensional traffic cellular automata model. Vehicles move along a one dimensional cellular automata (CA) lattice at all times during the simulation. The one-dimensional CA lattices, called *tracks* from here on, merge and diverge to form the entire network, eliminating the need for 'special' cells at intersections and infrastructure elements other than a straight road. While rules need to be defined for negotiating the network, including conflict resolution and routing decisions, the essential movement along the one-dimensional CA lattice does not change. This reduces the number of scenarios that need to be handled by update rules: all conflicts can be specified in a unique form and dealt with accordingly, rather than different infrastructural elements having to be 'learnt' and incorporated explicitly into the rules. The different features of the model are discussed in the following sections.

### 2.1    Network Structure and Routing

The model views the network as a collection of tracks that can diverge and merge, allowing for any number of tracks to be joined at a merge point and any number of tracks to fork out at a divergence point. Figure 1 illustrates a merging point and a divergence of routes.

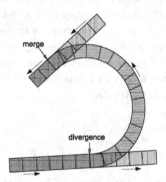

**Fig. 1.** Illustration of a merging point and a divergence of tracks

All vehicles in the model move along tracks according to some update rules. Since the collection of tracks that constitute the model merge and diverge in expression of the network's topology, a choice of route must be made at each divergence encountered by a vehicle. The end-to-end route on which a vehicle will travel is decided at a higher level of abstraction from the rules representing physical movement. The routing intelligence is not an integral part of the flow model and can be changed to suit the purpose for which the model is used.

## 2.2  Spatial Model

The spatial aspect of the model is expressed in terms of a number of constructs. It is envisaged that the extraction of a model description expressed using these constructs could be automated, with a sketch of the tracks as input. An example of a topological element's spatial model, a one-lane-per-direction intersection, is shown in Figure 4a.

Vehicle heterogeneity is handled simply by allowing *differently sized tracks* for different vehicle types, each with an appropriate cell length. Figure 2 shows a stretch of one-directional one-lane road shared by bicycles and cars through 'positional discipline'. It is represented with two tracks, each consisting of cells of an appropriate size. *Merges and divergences*, which have already been mentioned as network-topology defining element, and *crossings* between tracks feature in the model in two ways: (1) through cell overlaps, each instance of which contributes to the definition of the model's simulation space, and (2) through the conflicts that arise from merges and crossings, which also must be incorporated into the definition of that space. *Intra-track cell overlaps* are allowed and should be noted as part of the model. For example, each left-turning car track in Figure 4a), e.g. CSL, has two overlapping cells. The purpose of this is to model the slowing down caused by a sharp turn. *Turns* have a special place in the model, as they affect the dynamics of the flow in that vehicles slow down before turning, and should be noted within the model space definition. *Track relationships* indicate that two tracks are not just any two tracks in the network but that they have a special relationship. So, two tracks may be adjacent lanes on a two-lane road; or the bicycle track and the car track that constitute a narrow road shared by the two modalities. These relationships must be specified as part of the model, since they influence behaviour. If a car on a narrow road is travelling on its track and the model specifies an adjacent bicycle track, the car must 'look out' for bicycles. Similarly, in the case of multi-lane roads (which are not dealt with further in this paper), adjacent lanes have a special relationship, which allows 'lane changing' as a behaviour over the pair of tracks.

**Fig. 2.** The spatial model of a single-lane one-way stretch of road accommodating bicycles and cars by *ad hoc* sharing through *positional discipline*. The car track has 50 cells, while the bicycle track has 100 cells.

## 2.3  Behaviour

The behaviour of vehicles is specified using a set of update rules, which are applied at each time step. The rules prescribe how a new velocity should be calculated and stipulate the vehicles' movement along the track by the number of cells equal to the number representing the velocity. A real vehicle corresponds to two artefacts of the model: 1) the observable vehicle as part of the environment, which is inspected by other vehicles during application of the update rules; 2) the decision-making agent, the behaviour of which is embodied in the rules.

Any cellular automata rules for forward movement of vehicles can be used. While some investigation as to the most suitable rule-set should be carried out, the original [17] - N-S - update rules are used for the moment as a basis for expansion with network- and heterogeneity-related elements. The N-S rules, applied to each vehicle at each time-step, can be expressed as follows:

1. Acceleration: if $v_i < v_{Li}$, $v_i \rightarrow v_i + 1$
2. Slowing: if $v_{Li} < v_i$ , $v_i \rightarrow d_i$
3. Randomisation: with probability $p_R$, $v_i \rightarrow v_i - 1$
4. Vehicle motion: each vehicle is advanced $v_i$ cells

where $v_i$ is the $i^{th}$ vehicle's velocity, $d_i$ is the number of empty cells between the $i^{th}$ vehicle and the vehicle ahead of it, $v_{Li} = \min(v_{MAX}, d_i)$ is the velocity limiting value for the $i^{th}$ vehicle, $v_{MAX}$ is the maximal velocity achievable by the vehicle and $p_R$ is the randomisation parameter. The $\rightarrow$ symbol represents the transform of the vehicle's velocity from $v_i$ to its value at the next time-step. During simulations the updates are made in parallel, that is, steps 1-3 are performed on all the vehicles in the system and then step 4 is applied to all vehicles. The variables are dimensionless (length is in cells, velocity in cells per time-step), but are assigned real-world equivalents e.g. 7.5m for the length of a car cell and 1s for a time step. The same rules are applied to all vehicle types, but the value of $v_{MAX}$ is different for different vehicles.

In our model, these rules are extended in two ways: (a) the value of $v_{Li}$ is calculated to include limits imposed by close turns and conflicts (the velocity limit imposed by an unresolved conflict being 0) and by vehicles in adjacent tracks (we assume that the presence of a bicycle sharing a narrow road with a car will slow down the car but not vice versa); and (b) the value of $d_i$ is renamed the "number of *unimpinged* cells between the $i_{th}$ vehicle and the vehicle ahead. A cell is unimpinged if no overlapping cell, including itself, is occupied.

Conflicts are resolved by using traffic lights or by assigning higher priority to one of the tracks in the conflict. A vehicle on the higher-priority track moves ahead unimpeded. The vehicle on the lower priority track must check if a vehicle is arriving on the higher priority track and wait until there is not one, in order to venture ahead into the conflict area. Vehicles are assigned an acceptable gap, which can be different depending on the inspecting vehicle's type and the type of vehicle approaching on the conflicting track. A gap of 1 time step is sufficient for the avoidance of collisions, and may correspond to the real behaviour of some drivers, however, greater gaps are more realistic.

For the successful handling of network conflicts information other than the position of the observed vehicle is required. Gaps depend directly on observed vehicle velocities and knowledge of their routes is also useful. For example, let us say a car is in the cell preceding the first cell of CER track in Figure 4a) and a bicycle is at the cell preceding the first cell of track BER. Just from the position of the car, the cyclist cannot tell whether the car is going right (taking route CER) or not. It must assume that it is facing an unresolved conflict in order to avoid collision, and is unnecessarily delayed. Situations like this are avoided by making immediate route information available as part of the observable vehicle. This is reasonable, considering that in real traffic a turning indicator would be visible to trafficparticipants near a turning vehicle.

## 3    Implementation Notes

One of the features of our model that differs greatly from usual traffic cellular automata is **cell overlap**. It allows for easy extraction of the abstract model from its graphical representation and the addition of spatial features to simulation scenarios without redefinition of vehicle update rules. Areas of intensive overlap such as intersections have bit-wise cell occupation indicators, which can be read to check impingement in conjunction with cell overlap masks, defined for the topological element type. These are placed in a cell overlap table during model extraction from the graphical representation, for use by the implementation. Figure 3 shows the cell overlap table for the single lane two way intersection.

A **conflict** is unresolved either (a) if a vehicle travelling on the conflicting track is in a cell overlapping with the given track or (b) if a vehicle travelling on the conflicting track has the potential to enter the conflicting zone in the number of time-steps defined by the acceptable gap. The checking of the first condition can 'piggy-back' on the impingement checking: appropriate additional bits are simply

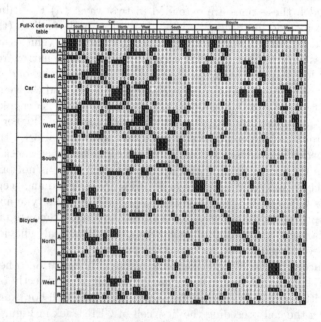

**Fig. 3.** Cell overlap table for the single-lane two-way intersection. Each cell is represented by both a column and a row. The table value for each cell pair is either 1 (with black background), indicating overlap, or 0.

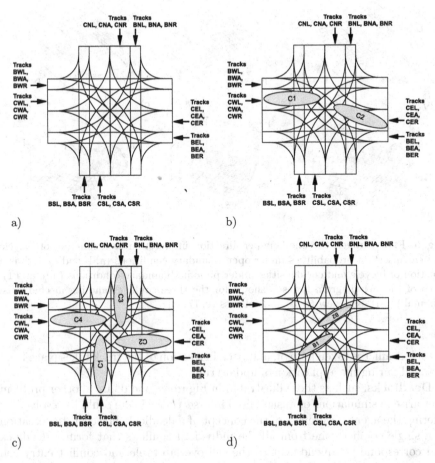

**Fig. 4.** The tracks of a one-lane-per-direction full intersection (a), an example of an unhandled conflict (b) and two deadlocks (c and d). Divergences are shown with arrows and names of associated tracks. Each name has tree letters: $C|B$ (car or bicycle), $S|E|N|W$ (south, east, north and west) and $L|A|R$ (left, ahead or right). All car tracks have two cells, which overlap in the case of left turns. The bicycle tracks have 4 cells (A and R) or 2 cells (L), none overlapping. The cell start/end lines are not shown so as not to clutter up the picture.

set in the cell overlap table. An example of a situation where this is required is illustrated in Figure 4b. Here vehicle C1 is in the first cell of track CWA and C2 is in the first cell of track CER. They are both advancing based on the *literal* (exclusive of additional bits for conflict handling) cell overlap table. Even though their current cells do not overlap, both vehicles are impinging on the other's track, which results either in a deadlock or a crash. The problem is solved by introducing virtual impingement between these two cells. The second condition for an unresolved conflict can be checked if the first conflict zone cell (*conflict entry cell*) of each track

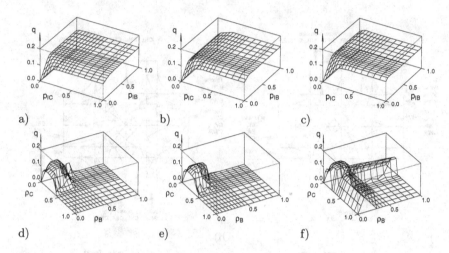

a)    b)    c)

d)    e)    f)

**Fig. 5.** Flow through the one-lane-per-direction intersection as a function of bicycle and car insertion probabilities under open boundary conditions (a, b and c) and as a function of bicycle and car densities under periodic boundary conditions (d, e and f). Each of the two diagram types is shown for the three conflict handling mechanisms: minimal (a, d), one-view (b, e) and cell-less (c, f)

in each conflict is taken note of, and back inspection of the track takes place from that cell during the application of update rules.

**Deadlocks,** such as those illustrated in Figure 4c and d, are another problem that arise in simulations of unsignalised intersections. These could be resolved by offering the agents awareness of the concept of a deadlock, however, the creation of a single conflict zone from all the individual conflicts that form a deadlock and corresponding amendment to the cell overlap table and conflict entry cell information is more straightforward since it uses existing mechanisms. With the deadlocks removed, the model provides minimal conditions for simulations of the unsignalised intersection to run.

Also implemented are the *one view* intersection negotiation approach and a *cell-less* intersection. The former requires all conflicts of the intersection to be resolved in order for a vehicle to venture into it. Here the cell overlap table and conflict entry cell information are changed so as to reflect the view, from each track, of the entire intersection as a single conflict zone. The cell-less approach eliminates the cells of the intersection and views all the conflicts as if occurring in the zero-length part of track between the last cell before entry into the intersection and first cell after exit from it.

All the manipulations described here, except the implementation of the cell-less intersection, have been generated automatically from only a track list and cell overlap table. Flow results for the three conflict resolution approaches under open and periodic boundary conditions are shown in Figure 5. In these simulations all routes at any divergence were made equally probable. As expected, the overall flows are somewhat higher for the one-view case (b, e) than for the minimal case (a, d), as they are for the cell-less (c, f) case in comparison with one-view. The most dramatic difference exists for the cell-less periodic boundary case (f), where the flow of a particular vehicle type is only limited by the density levels for that type of vehicle. This indicates that the flow cross-limitation between vehicle types is predominantly caused by direct obstruction (which is absent in the cell-less case).

## 4   Conclusion

A model for heterogeneous traffic has been presented on the case of an intersection of two-way single-lane streets. Three different approaches for conflict resolution and avoidance of deadlocks are investigated and were found to have similar run-times, which vary randomly by up to 10%, and to produce similar average flows. Further work in the immediate area will involve more detailed study of the intersection interaction handling approaches and their properties as compared to real scenarios. On a more general plane, further work on the model will be done with the aim of developing it as a tool for the study of mixed traffic including bicycles.

**Acknowledgements.** This work is funded by the Irish Research Council for Science, Engineering and Technology (IRCSET), through an 'Embark Initiative' postgraduate scholarship.

## References

1. Belbasi, S., Foulaadvand, M.: Simulation of traffic flow at a signalized intersection. J. Stat. Mech., P07021 (2008)
2. Biham, O., Middleton, A., Levine, D.: Self-organization and a dynamical transition in traffic-flow models. Phys. Rev. A 46, R6124–R6127 (1992)
3. Brockfeld, E., Barlovic, R., Schadschneider, A., Schreckenberg, M.: Optimizing traffic lights in a cellular automaton model for city traffic. Phys. Rev. E 64, 056132 (2001)
4. Cheng, S.H., Yao, D.Y., Zhang, Y., Su, Y.L., Xu, W.D.: A ca model for intrusion conflicts simulation in vehicles-bicycles laminar traffic flow. In: Proceedings of the 11th International IEEE Conference on Intelligent Transportation Systems Beijing, China, October 12-15 (2008)
5. Chopard, B., Luthi, P., Queloz, P.: Cellular automata model of car traffic in a two-dimensional street network. J. Phys. A 29, 2325–2336 (1996)
6. Esser, J., Schreckenberg, M.: Microscopic simulation of urban traffic based on cellular automata. Int. J. Mod. Phys. C 8, 1025–1036 (1997)
7. Fouladvand, M., Sadjadi, Z., Shaebani, M.: Characteristics of vehicular traffic flow at a roundabout. Phys. Rev. E 70, 046132 (2004)
8. Fouladvand, M., Sadjadi, Z., Shaebani, M.: Optimized traffic flow at a single intersection: traffic responsive signalization. J. Phys. A 37, 561–576 (2004)
9. Gundaliya, P.J., Mathew, T.V., Dhingra, S.L.: Heterogeneous traffic flow modelling for an arterial using grid based approach. J. Adv. Transport 42, 467–491 (2008)

10. Huang, D., Huang, W.: Traffic signal synchronization. Phys. Rev. E 67, 056124 (2003)
11. Jia, B., Li, X.G., Jiang, R., Gao, Z.Y.: Multi-value cellular automata model for mixed bicycle flow. Eur. Phys. J. B 56, 247–252 (2007)
12. Li, X.G., Gao, Z.Y., Jia, B., Zhao, X.M.: Cellular automata model for unsignalized t-shaped intersection. Int. J. Mod. Phys. C 20, 501–512 (2009)
13. Li, X.G., Gao, Z.Y., Jia, B., Zhao, X.M.: Modeling the interaction between motorized vehicle and bicycle by using cellular automata model. Int. J. Mod. Phys. C 20, 209–222 (2009)
14. Maerivoet, S., De Moor, B.: Cellular automata models of road traffic. Phys. Rep. 419, 1–64 (2005)
15. Mallikarjuna, C., Rao, K.R.: Cellular automata model for heterogeneous traffic. J. Adv. Transport 43, 321–345 (2009)
16. Nagatani, T.: Shock formation and traffic jam induced by a crossing in the 1d asymmetric exclusion model. J. Phys. A 26, 6625–6634 (1993)
17. Nagel, K., Schreckenberg, M.: A cellular automaton model for freeway traffic. J. Phys. I 2, 2221–2229 (1992)
18. Scellato, S., Fortuna, L., Frasca, M., Gómez-Gardeñes, J., Latora, V.: Traffic optimization in transport networks based on local routing. Eur. Phys. J. B 73, 303–308 (2010)
19. Simon, P.M., Gutowitz, H.A.: Cellular automaton model for bidirectional traffic. Phys. Rev. E 57, 2441–2444 (1998)
20. Tonguz, O.K., Viriyasitavat, W., Bai, F.: Modeling urban traffic: A cellular automata approach. IEEE Commun. Mag. 47, 142–150 (2009)
21. Vasic, J., Ruskin, H.J.: Cellular automata simulation of traffic including cars and bicycles. Physica A 391, 2720–2729 (2012)
22. Wahle, J., Schreckenberg, M.: A multi-agent system for on-line simulations based on real-world traffic data. In: Hawaii International Conference on System Sciences, vol. 3, p. 3037 (2001)
23. Wang, R., Ruskin, H.J.: Modelling Traffic Flow at a Multilane Intersection. In: Kumar, V., Gavrilova, M.L., Tan, C.J.K., L'Ecuyer, P. (eds.) ICCSA 2003, Part I. LNCS, vol. 2667, pp. 577–586. Springer, Heidelberg (2003)
24. Wang, R., Ruskin, H.J.: Modelling traffic flow at multi-lane urban roundabouts. Int. J. Mod. Phys. C 17, 693–710 (2006)

# A Metaphor of Complex Automata in Modeling Biological Phenomena

Rafał Wcisło[1] and Witold Dzwinel[1,2]

[1] AGH University of Science and Technology, Department of Computer Science,
Al.Mickiewicza 30, 30-059 Kraków, Poland
[2] WSEiP School of Economics and Law, Kielce, Poland
{wcislo,dzwinel}@agh.edu.pl

**Abstract.** We demonstrate that Complex automata (CxA) - a hybrid of a Particle method (PM) and Cellular automata (CA) — can serve as a convenient modeling framework in developing advanced models of biological systems. As a proof_of_concept we use two processes of pathogenic growth: cancer proliferation and *Fusarium graminearum* wheat infection. The ability of mimicking both mechanical interactions of tumor with the rest of tissue and penetration properties of *F.graminearum,* confirms that our model can reproduce realistic 3-D dynamics of complex biological phenomena. We discuss the scope of application of CxA in the context of its implementation in CUDA GPU environment.

**Keywords:** modeling, tumor growth, *F. graminearum* invasion, CUDA GPU.

## 1    Introduction

New challenges in systems biology involve searching for new modeling paradigms which allow for simulating multi-scale systems within a unified computational framework. In his seminal book [1] Wolfram advocates that Cellular automata paradigm can be treated as a universal computational metaphor of reality. However, the robustness of CA is still mostly qualitative. Although some CA clones such as lattice gas and lattice Boltzmann gas [2] are able to describe many dynamical properties of physical systems, they simulate mechanical interactions in a very simplistic way.

Meanwhile, for the model of interacting particles or particle model (PM) (e.g. [3,4]) mechanical interactions are its intrinsic property. PM is a discrete, off-grid and very general paradigm of modeling, which has its roots in N-body simulations and well known Molecular Dynamics (MD) method (also the Non-equilibrium Molecular Dynamics NEMD). The system of discrete particles is defined by system boundary, initial conditions and by interactions between particles represented by a collision operator. The particle system evolves according to the Newtonian equations of motion.

Despite of its conceptual simplicity, the method is computationally demanding, when used for modeling macroscopic phenomena involving large number of particles. The state_of_the_art supercomputers allow for simulating more than a trillion atoms in a million time-steps by exploiting highly efficient MD parallel codes [5]. This

G.C. Sirakoulis and S. Bandini (Eds.): ACRI 2012, LNCS 7495, pp. 845–855, 2012.

particle ensemble corresponds to spatial 3-D scales of a few micrometers and time scales of ten nanoseconds. Certainly, as shown in (e.g. [6-8]), Molecular Dynamics can be used as an efficient modeling framework also in larger scales employing various definitions of "particle". However, the main weakness of PM is the difficulty to represent important microscopic and macroscopic degrees of freedom only in the form of particle interactions. The problem becomes especially serious in modeling intrinsically complex biological systems. For example, assuming that a particle represents a cell, the microscopic processes such as chemical signaling, chemotaxis, haptotaxis, oxygen and proteins diffusion influencing cell behavior and its functions cannot be mimicked by a simple mechanical force. On the other hand, just mechanical interactions between cells can be a crucial factor influencing many types of growth.

Instead of developing multi-scale model which consists of many submodels representing various scales coupled by complicated and unreliable scale-bridging mechanisms, we propose here a uniform coarse grained model in which information about finer scales is inscribed both in CA rules and particle interactions. We demonstrate that by coupling cellular automata and particle model we can develop a new computational framework which possesses the advantages of the two. By using as examples two modeling targets, proliferation of cancer and invasion of a pathogen attacking cereal crops (*Fusarium graminearum*) we demonstrate how the concept of CxA works when applied to modeling the realistic phenomena. At the end of the paper we discuss the methods of speeding up the computations by using GPU and CUDA technologies.

## 2    Complex Automata

As it was shown in thousands of papers, the cellular automata (CA) is advantageous over other modeling approaches in simulating systems where interactions between individuals can be represented by a language instead of mathematical equations. Using more rules, i.e., more complicated language, one can simulate finer scales using coarse-grained CA representations [9]. The same property holds the particle model. The TC-DPD collision operator in macroscale - much more complicated than conservative MD force in atomistic scales (see [3,10]) - encapsulates in a consistent way averaged degrees of freedom from atomistic scales represented by Wiener stochastic terms. Concluding, the particle model reconstructs in a natural way mechanical interactions while cellular automata performs better when information exchange between individuals cannot be described only in terms of positions, velocities and forces. Therefore, by coupling the particle model with cellular automata, one can obtain the possibility to reconstruct both mechanical interactions and finer intercellular processes mimicked by CA rules. The overall CxA concept consists of the following principal simulation steps.

1.   The simulated system is made of a set of particles $\Lambda_N=\{O_i: O(\mathbf{r}_i,\mathbf{v}_i,\mathbf{a}_i), i=1,...,N\}$ where: $i$ - particle index, $N$ - the number of particles, $\mathbf{r}_i,\mathbf{v}_i,\mathbf{a}_i$ - particle position, velocity and attributes, respectively. The vector of attributes $\mathbf{a}_i$ is defined by the particle type, size, and its current states.

2. The particle state may depend on time $t$, concentration of diffusive substances and total pressure exerted on particle $i$ from its closest neighbors.

3. The collision operator $\Omega_i(\ldots)$, which is equal to the sum of particle-particle vector interactions $F_{ij}(|r_i-r_j|, v_i-v_j, a_i, a_j)$ between the central particle $i$ and all the particles $j$ confined in the sphere of radius $r_{cut}$, defines the total force acting on particle $i$. The type of particle-particle interaction, $F_{ij}$, may depend on the current attributes of particles $i$ and $j$.

4. The particle dynamics is governed by the Newtonian laws of motion. Particle positions are shifted just after computing collision operators acting on every particle $i$. The Newtonian equations are integrated numerically in discrete time-steps $\Delta t$.

$$\Delta P_i^n = \sum_j^{N_{rcut}} F_{ij} \cdot e_{ij}^n \Delta t, \qquad \Delta r_i^n = \frac{P_i^n}{m} \Delta t, \qquad (1)$$

where $r_i$ is the position of particle, $P_i$ is its momentum $N_{rcut}$ is the number of particles in the interaction range.

5. The attributes of particles $i$ are updated according to its history and the state of particles in its neighborhood according to prescribed CA rules.

6. The particles attributes may also depend on current solutions of other large-scale models formulated in terms of PDEs (partial differential equations) such as reaction-diffusion or hydrodynamics equations.

In the following subsections we present two examples employing CxA metaphor.

## 2.1  Tumor Growth Using CxA

By skipping the complex genetic processes influencing the appearance of the first tumor cells we assume that a small cluster of cancerous cells is placed inside a healthy tissue. Typically, solid tumor proliferation consists of three phases: avascular growth, angiogenesis, vascular growth, and metastasis (e.g., [11]). Avascular tumor (see Fig.1a) develops due to nutrients diffusion (e.g. $O_2$) throughout the tissue from neighboring blood vessels. Due to short $O_2$ diffusion path some of cancer cells located far from the closest blood capillary are in the chronic state of oxygen shortage - hypoxia. The hypoxic cells produce and release chemical species - called tumor angiogenic factors (TAFs) [11]. They diffuse throughout the tissue to neighboring blood capillaries and trigger a cascade of events stimulating the growth of vasculature towards the tumor cluster. Vascularized tumor (see Fig.1b) having access to unlimited resources of nutrients dramatically accelerates its growth. Moreover, the tumor secretes cancerogenic material forming metastases through the blood system.

There exist numerous mathematical models of tumor progression in all its phases (e.g. [12]). However, only a few consider mechanical factors of growth though tumor squeeze through the tight body is a purely mechanical phenomenon. The tissue and vasculature remodeling due to tumor push on influences both the speed and character of its growth. Just tumor remodeling is responsible for its heterogeneity influencing the drug dosage/rate in chemotherapy. As shown in [13], CxA can be used as a robust metaphor which closes up this gap.

We assume that a fragment of tissue, is made of a set of $N$ particles $\Lambda_N$. Each particle represents a single cell with a fragment of ECM (extracellular matrix). The vector of attributes $\mathbf{a}_i$ is defined by the particle type {*tumor cell (TC), normal cell (NC), endothelial cell (EC)*}, cell life-cycle state {*newly formed, mature, in hypoxia, after hypoxia, apoptosis, necrosis*}, cell size, cell age, *hypoxia* time, concentrations of $k$=TAF, $O_2$ (and others) and total pressure exerted on particle $i$ from its closest neighbors. The particle system is confined in the cubical computational box with a constant external pressure. For the sake of simplicity the vessel is constructed of tube-like "particles" – EC-tubes – made of two particles connected by a rigid spring. We define three types of interactions: particle-particle, particle-tube, and tube-tube. The forces between particles mimic both mechanical repulsion from squashed cells and attraction due to cell adhesiveness and depletion interactions cause by both ECM matrix and the cell. We postulate the heuristics – two-body interaction potential $V(d_{ij})$ - in the following form:

$$V(d_{ij}) = \begin{cases} a_1 d_{ij}^2, \text{ for } d_{ij} < 0 \\ a_2 d_{ij}^2, \text{ for } 0 < d_{ij} < d_{cut} \\ a_2 d_{cut}^2, \text{ for } d_{ij} \geq d_{cut} \end{cases} \quad \text{where } a_1 > a_2$$

(2)

where $d_{ij} = |\mathbf{r}_{ij}| - (r_i + r_j)$ and $r_{ij}=|\mathbf{r}_{ij}|$ is the distance between particles while $r_i$ and $r_j$ are their radiuses.

We assume that the interactions between spherical particles and EC-tube particles have similar character. However, as shown in [13], additional rules have to be introduced to enable appropriate growth of the vascular network. The particle dynamics is governed by the Newtonian dynamics while DPD (dissipative particle dynamics) collision operator [3,4] is used for simulating particle-particle interactions.

In dissipative particle dynamics [3,4] the two-body interactions between two fluid particles $i$ and $j$ are assumed to be central and short-ranged. The collision operator, $\Omega(r_{ij}, \mathbf{p}_{ij})$, can be defined as a sum of a conservative force $\mathbf{F}_C$, dissipative component $\mathbf{F}_D$ and the Brownian force $\mathbf{F}_B$. The Brownian factor represents the coarse grained equivalence of thermal fluctuations. The equations below show the basic formula describing the two-body forces.

$$\mathbf{F}_C = -\pi \cdot \nabla V(r_{ij}) \cdot \mathbf{e}_{ij}, \quad \mathbf{F}_D = \gamma \cdot m \cdot \omega^2(r_{ij}) \cdot (\mathbf{e}_{ij} \circ \mathbf{v}_{ij}) \cdot \mathbf{e}_{ij}, \quad \mathbf{F}_B = \frac{\sigma \cdot \theta_{ij}}{\sqrt{\Delta t}} \cdot \omega(r_{ij}) \cdot \mathbf{e}_{ij}$$

(3)

$$\omega(r_{ij}) = \frac{3}{n \cdot \pi \cdot r_{cut}^2} \left(1 - \frac{r_{ij}}{r_{cut}}\right) \quad \theta_{ij} \in (-1,1) \text{ - random number; } n \text{ - particle density}$$

$$\Omega(r_{ij}, \mathbf{p}_{ij}) = \mathbf{F}_C + \mathbf{F}_D + \mathbf{F}_B \quad \text{for } r_{ij} < r_{cut} \quad \Omega(r_{ij}, \mathbf{p}_{ij}) = 0 \text{ for } r_{ij} > r_{cut}$$

The value of $r_{cut}$ is the cut-off radius which represents the range of interaction between two interacting DPs.

Both normal and tumor cells change their states from *new* to *apoptotic* (or *necrotic*). The living cell changes its state to *hypoxic* (being the source of TAFs) when oxygen concentration drops below a given threshold. The cell dies and becomes *necrotic* if it remains in *hypoxia* state too long. The life-cycle for EC-tube is different. It can grow both in length and in diameter. Reduced blood flow, the lack of VEGF (*vascular endothelial growth factor*), dilation, perfusion and solid stress exerted by the tumor can cause their rapid collapse. Because the EC-tube simulates a cluster of EC cells, its division onto two adjoined tubes does not represent the process of *mitosis* but is a computational metaphor of vessel growth. The tube can form a sprout of newly created capillary growing from existing vessels. The new sprout is formed when the TAFs concentration exceeds a given threshold. Its growth direction is parallel to the local TAF concentration gradient.

The distribution of hematocrit is the source of oxygen, while the distribution of tumor cells in *hypoxia* is the source of TAFs. We assume that the cells of any type consume oxygen with the rate depending on both cell type and its current state, while TAFs are absorbed by EC-tubes only. TAFs are washed out from the system due to blood flow. The blood circulation is slower than diffusion but still faster than *mitosis* cycle. These facts allow for employing fast approximation procedures for both calculation of blood flow in capillaries and solving reaction-diffusion equation (see [13]).

Summing up, the basic procedures of our CxA particle model consist of: the model initialization phase, i.e., definition of initial and boundary conditions, and its evolution driven by the following phenomena: the Newtonian dynamics of interacting cells, diffusion of oxygen and TAF, cellular life cycle modeled by CxA rules, vessels sprouting and growth, vessels remodeling due to blood flow, vessel maturation and degradation.

**Fig. 1.** The snapshots from 3-D CxA simulations displaying two phases of tumor growth: a) avascular and b), c) vascular ones. In a) one can see hypoxic and necrotic parts of cancer globule. The network remodeling process is shown in c) where immature vessels (shown in red) collapse. The tissue cells are invisible in figures a) and c).

In the context of tumor modeling, the main advantage of CxA over other models, consists in more realistic and strightforward simulation of the influence of mechanical remodelling process on tumor growth dynamics. For example, in [13] we show that inward motion of tumor cells in avascular tumor, which results in production of necrotic centre (see white arrow in Fig.1a), is a purely mechanical process. It stabilizes its size in this incipient stage of growth. Similarly, in the following angiogenic phases mutual interactions between tumor body, vascularization, healthy tissue, and bones may be an important factor of temporar tumor stabilization, or converseley, its rapid growth.

The newly created blood vessel become functional, when they form closed loops (anastomoses) and are covered with adequate quantity of mural cells. Mural cells are vascular support cells that range in phenotype from pericytes to vascular smooth muscle cells [14]. As displayed in Figs.1a,c, the structures of vasculature become very complex and dynamic due to continual vessel maturation and degradation caused also by mechanical interactions. Therefore, the newly created vascular system inside the tumor is very fragile, vulnerable to rapid changes in blood pressure and the speed of volumetric growth. This very dynamic situation influencing majority of the tumor system makes it globally unstable. Very different situation is observed for *F.graminearum* infection in wheat, where mechanical factor is very local.

## 2.2    Fusarium Graminearum Infection

CxA model can be also applied for simulation of cereal infection by parasite fungi called *Fusarium graminearum* (*F.graminearum* - Fg). Fg is one of the main causal agents of Fusarium head blight (FHB) infection. It attacks cereal crops what results in significant crop losses. Another effect of this plague is the contamination of grain with mycotoxins, which is extremely harmful for animals and humans.

According to [15], we can distinguish four types of *Fusarium* cells namely: tip cells, active cells, inactive cells and spores. Tip and active cells are involved in nutrient uptake, branching and translocation. Additionally, the tip cells are responsible for growth and its direction. Active cells secrete also the acid substances and toxins used for breaking mechanical barriers (such as cellular wall) and disarming plant immunological system. The necrotic cells and spores are inactive cells i.e. the cells that are no longer directly involved in translocation, branching or uptake. Meanwhile the spores are reproductive structures that are adapted for dispersal and surviving for extended periods of time in unfavorable conditions.

*F.graminearum* is well adapted for growth in vascularized tissue due to their network structure and filamentous growth nature. This growth process is the forward and lateral movement stimulated by the extension of hyphal tips and branching respectively. As a result of tip movement, the hyphae are able to penetrate plant tissue and break hard obstacles such as cell or chitin walls. Breaking cell wall the hyphae secrete enzymes devastating its interior by leaching nutrients. The nutrients are absorbed then by the hyphae cells. Nutrient translocation is the crucial process for *Fusarium* expansion and function in heterogeneous environments. It allows the redistribution of internal metabolites throughout the mycelium by using at least two translocation mechanisms: diffusion and active movement of nutrients. We assume that:

1.  Every *Fusarium* and plant cell is modeled by a particle which interacts with other particles (cells) in their closest neighborhood.
2.  Every cell has a number of attributes that evolve in time.

3.  The concentration of nutrients is uniform in a single cell and constant in the specific time step.
4.  Nutrients circulation in the fungi body, which allows *Fusarium* to proliferate, is the effect of diffusion and translocation mechanism [15].
5.  Each *Fusarium* and plant cell is in one out of three discrete states which models cell-life cycle.

The laboratory experiments from Fig.2a,b were conducted *in vitro* in artificial conditions. This means that no nutrients were produced in the course of experiments and the initial amount of food was only consumed by *F.graminearum*. The experiments were performed on flat surfaces on so called Petri dishes. Two types of environment were tested: PDA which is nutrient-rich and SNA which is nutrient-poor. Both substances are water solutions. This allows for two important assumptions: the fungus does not encounter much strain from the environment and diffusion does not need to be modeled directly. We may safely assume that the diffusion in water is fast enough to keep uniform nutrients concentration in the whole volume. As the result all fungi cells have identical external nutrients level and there is also no need to model diffusion inside the fungus. In this early modeling stage only model of the hyphae growth and physical behavior has been developed. Due to the absence of plant cells in experiments interactions with environment were not modeled.

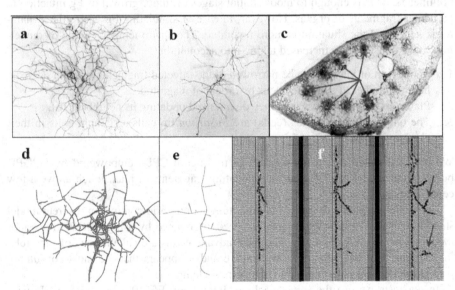

**Fig. 2.** The development of *F.graminearum* in *in vitro* - nutrient rich (a) and nutrient poor (b) - and *in vivo* (c) environments. Figure c displays the cross-section of stem of wheat head. Experimental results (a,b,c) (courtesy of Dr Shea Miller and Dr Margaret Balcerzak from Agriculture and Agri-*Food* Canada, ECORC, *Ottawa*) are compared to corresponding snapshots from CxA simulations (d,e,f). As shown in (c) and (f), *F.graminearum* (black stains pointed by arrows) proliferate mainly in vascular bundles and rachis, i.e., nutrient poor environment.

As shown in Fig.2d,e, the comparison of simulation results with experimental data is cautiously optimistic. The qualitative character of growth is very similar. However, the structural characters of networks produced by *F.graminearum* and and CxA model are clearly different. This artifact can be improved, by using higher resolution (smaller Fg cells) and playing the parameters responsible for the sprouting. Another confrontation of simulation with experiment, displayed in Fig.2c,f, also shows a good qualitative agreement of the two. *F.graminearum* spreads mainly through vascular bundles (vertical growth), penetrating also the closest neighborhood (lateral growth) [16]. When pathogen finds the nutrient rich part of the plant, it shifts the type of growth from vertical to lateral one completely devastating attacked plant organ.

## 3    GPU Acceleration of CxA Model

In general, CxA modeling approach in which a particle represents a single cell is computationally demanding [17,18]. Assuming that plant cell perimeter is about 20μm and taking into account the intercellular space and blood vessels, one can estimate that it is about $10^8$ cells of order in tissue volume of $1 \text{ cm}^3$. Assuming computational power of modern laptop processors, the Complex Automata can be used for simulating in a reasonable time the fragments of tissue not larger than a few cubic millimeters. This is enough to model initial stages of tumor growth or Fg infection in particular fragments of organs. However, in case of simulating Fg where the dynamics is very local the situation is more favorable. The spatio-temporal scale of modeling can be considerably increased taking into account that:

1.  The region of interest can be narrowed to the infected fragments of plant decreasing the number of simulated cells by orders of magnitude.
2.  Plan cells are motionless thus they do not need updating its neighbors list.
3.  The only moving particles (cells) are *Fusarium* tip cells and fungi cells in their closest vicinity.

We have estimated that using clusters of multi-core CPUs empowered by GPGPU boosters our model can be used for simulating fragments of plant much above a few centimeters of size.

For modeling global dynamics of large tumors, a hybrid continuum-discrete model should be used. We have estimated the speedup obtained by using GPGPU for tumor modeling using CxA approach. The most advantageous are calculations of tube-tube interactions. However, there are rather rare and it appears that the most consuming part of calculations is connected with tube-particle interactions.

In our tests we use the same machine: Intel Xeon E5540 at 2.53GHz CPU with Nvidia GeForce GTX 295 (containing 240 CUDA cores). Machine runs Red Hat Enterprise Linux Server release 6.0. CUDA version was 3.2.16. We compare performance of a single core of the CPU processor with GPU board. The simple (naive) GPU version of cell-cell interactions runs 6 times faster than its CPU counterpart. By use of advanced CUDA mechanisms such as shared memory, textures, atomic operations, and tailoring algorithms to GPUs, we managed to increase the speedup of our

CUDA kernel up to 60 times. The entire simulation runs 10-20 times faster than the single threaded CPU version. In Fig.3 we collected our averaged timings. In the extreme case, tubes are so dense that their interactions considerably affect overall performance. When the number of tubes reaches 9996, tube-tube interactions take 29% of the total execution time. Normally, blood vessels are sparse and hardly ever interact with each other so we can expect much better results than these shown in Fig.3.

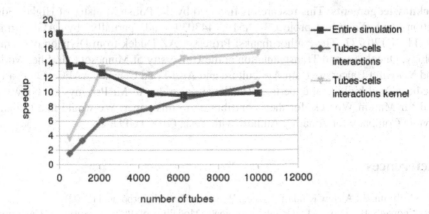

**Fig. 3.** Speedups for the most intensive calculations compared to the entire simulation

## 4     Conclusions and Discussion

We have introduced here a novel modeling concept, called Complex Automata, which integrates the two types of modeling techniques, namely, particle method and cellular automata. We have shown that the particle method decides about the mechanical properties of the system. Microscopic phenomena involving fluctuations and dissipative behavior can also be added in a consistent way exploiting widely known modeling techniques such as DPD or TC-DPD [4,10]. Apart from system properties resulting from simple Newtonian mechanics, other microscopic biological processes can be encapsulated in CA rules. These rules depend on the current configuration of the nearest neighbors and other phenomena, e.g., described by the continuum fields obtained from integrating PDEs. We have also presented a proof-of-concept of our approach by employing CxA as a metaphor in modeling of two different biological phenomena. The ability of mimicking both mechanical interactions of tumor with the rest of tissue and penetration properties of *F.graminearum*, shows that our model can reproduce realistic 3-D dynamics of these complex biological systems.

The model presented is only a pure phenomenological metaphor of *F.graminearum* and tumor growth being a proof-of-concept of Complex Automata paradigm application in these domains. Only basic principles of growth were taken into account. However, including more sophisticated processes to the framework of CxA model such as tissue defense mechanisms and toxines devastating effects should be straightforward.

To make our model functional the crucial task is to incorporate to the model a data assimilation module. Up to now the model parameters were matched coarsely using very general data which bases mainly on the results of analysis of microscopic pictures. We believe that using Complex Automata computational framework with data assimilation module will allow for attacking many biological problems in a more systematic and focused way.

**Acknowledgements.** This research is financed by the Polish Ministry of Higher Education and Science, project NN519 443039 and partially by AGH grant No.11.11.120.777. The Author thanks: Professor AZ Dudek from Division of Hematology, Oncology, and Transplantation at the University of Minnesota, dr. Shea Miller and Margaret Balcerzak from Agriculture and Agri-Food Canada (AAFC), Ottawa for mediacal and biological expertise. Thanks are also due to Mr Przemysław Głowacki and Mr Marcin Worecki for their contribution to this paper. We would like to thank Nvidia Company for donating Authors with Tesla C1060 GPU.

# References

1. Wolfram, S.: A New Kind of Science. Wolfram Media Incorporated (2002)
2. Chopard, B., Droz, M.: Cellular Automata Modeling of Physical Systems. Cambridge University Press, Cambridge (1998)
3. Dzwinel, W., Yuen, D.A., Boryczko, K.: Bridging diverse physical scales with the discrete-particle paradigm in modeling colloidal dynamics with mesoscopic features. Chemical Engineering Sci. 61, 2169–2185 (2006)
4. Espanol, P.: Fluid particle model. Phys. Rev. E 57, 2930–2948 (1998)
5. German, T.C., Kadau, K.: Trillion-Atom Molecular Dynamics Becomes a Reality. International Journal of Modern Physics C 19(9), 1315–1319 (2008)
6. Dzwinel, W.: Virtual Particles and Search for Global Minimum. Future Generation Computer Systems 12, 371–389 (1997)
7. Pelechano, N., Badler, N.I.: Improving the Realism of Agent Movement for High Density Crowd Simulation,
   http://www.lsi.upc.edu/~npelechano/MACES/MACES.htm
8. Helbing, D., Farkas, I.J., Vicsek, T.: Simulating Dynamical Features of Escape Panic. Nature 407, 487–490 (2000)
9. Israeli, N., Goldenfeld, N.: Coarse-graining of cellular automata, emergence, and the predictability of complex systems. Phys. Rev. E 73(2), 026203 (2006)
10. Serrano, M., Espanol, P.: Thermodynamically consistent mesoscopic fluid particle model. Phys. Rev. E 64(4), 46115 (2001)
11. Folkman, J.: Tumor angiogenesis, Therapeutic implications. N. Engl. J. Med. 285, 1182–1186 (1971)
12. Cristini, V., Lowengrub, J.: Multiscale Modeling of Cancer: An Integrated Experimental and Mathematical Modeling Approach. Cambridge University Press, Cambridge (2010)
13. Wcisło, R., Dzwinel, W., Yuen, D.A., Dudek, A.Z.: A new model of tumor progression based on the concept of complex automata driven by particle dynamics. J. Mol. Mod. 15(12), 1517–1539 (2009)

14. Raza, A., Franklin, M.J., Dudek, A.Z.: Pericytes and vessel maturation during tumor angiogenesis and metastasis. Am. J. Hematol. 85(8), 593–598 (2010)
15. Boswell, G.P., Jacobs, H., Ritz, K., Gadd, G., Davidson, F.: The Development of Fungal Networks in Complex Environments. Bulletin of Mathematical Biology 69, 605–634 (2007)
16. Dzwinel, W.: Complex Automata as a Novel Conceptual Framework for Modeling Biomedical Phenomena. In: Byrski, A., Oplatková, Z., Carvalho, M., Dorohnicki, M.K. (eds.) Advances in Intelligent Modelling and Simulation. SCI, vol. 416, pp. 269–298. Springer, Heidelberg (2012)
17. Worecki, M., Wcisło, R.: GPU Enhanced Simulation of Angiogenesis. Computer Science 13(1), 35–38 (2012)
18. Wcisło, R., Dzwinel, W.: Particle Model of Tumor Growth and Its Parallel Implementation. In: Wyrzykowski, R., Dongarra, J., Karczewski, K., Wasniewski, J. (eds.) PPAM 2009, Part I. LNCS, vol. 6067, pp. 322–331. Springer, Heidelberg (2010)

# Author Index

Adachi, Susumu   83
Adamopoulos, Adam   151
Amanatiadis, Angelos   330
Amorim, Ronan Mendonça   434
Andreadis, Ioannis   375
Argese, Emanuele   351
Avolio, Maria Vittoria   273, 279, 289

Baetens, Jan M.   1, 763
Bagnoli, Franco   204
Bandini, Stefania   299
Belan, Nikolay   483
Belan, Stepan   483
Ben Belgacem, Mohamed   309
Benedettini, Stefano   244
Bidlo, Michal   214
Binder, Benjamin J.   405
Blecic, Ivan   319
Boukas, Evangelos   395
Bouré, Olivier   633
Boutalis, Yiannis   340
Bukáček, Marek   709

Calidonna, Claudia Roberta   273
Campos, Ricardo Silva   434
Cecchini, Arnaldo   319
Chakraborty, Avik   11, 63
Chakraborty, Kaushik   591
Charalampous, Konstantinos   330
Chatzichristofis, Savvas A.   340
Chatzis, Vassilios   554
Chaudhuri, Parimal Pal   360
Chevrier, Vincent   633
Chopard, Bastien   309, 464
Chowdhury, Dipanwita Roy   591, 601, 623
Clua, Esteban   524
Correia, Luís   679

Dalbelo Bašić, Bojana   795
D'Ambrosio, Donato   444
Das, Sourav   601
Das, Sukanta   11, 63, 234, 643
De Baets, Bernard   1, 504, 763
De Clercq, Nathalie   504

De March, Davide   351
Dennunzio, Alberto   653
Désérable, Dominique   20
Dewettinck, Koen   504
Di Gregorio, Salvatore   273, 279, 289
Di Stefano, Bruno N.   425
Di Stefano, Gabriele   534
Di Traglia, Mario   663
dos Santos, Rodrigo Weber   434
Dzwinel, Witold   845

Ernst, Jason B.   425
Ezaki, Takahiro   776

Falcone, Jean-Luc   464
Fatès, Nazim   633
Federici, Mizar Luca   699
Filippone, Giuseppe   444
Filisetti, Alessandro   351
Formenti, Enrico   653
Fucik, Otto   807

Gander, Martin J.   464
Gasteratos, Antonios   330, 395
Georgoudas, Ioakeim G.   752
Ghosh, Soumyabrata   360
Girau, Bernard   611
Goethals, Peter L.M.   763
Gorrini, Andrea   699
Gu, Gaoxiang   370
Guazzini, Andrea   204
Gwizdałła, Tomasz M.   91

Hirabayashi, Miki   544
Hoffmann, Rolf   785
Honda, Hajime   544
Hrabák, Pavel   709

Ichikawa, Takanori   73
Imai, Katsunobu   83
Inokuchi, Shuichi   32
Ioannidis, Konstantinos   375
Ishida, Toshikazu   32
Isokawa, Teijiro   83, 575
Ivanac, Vedran   795
Iwata, Yoshio   385

Jacob, Christian    434

Karafyllidis, Ioannis G.    585
Karmakar, Sandip    623
Kayama, Yoshihiko    224
Khan, Nasiruddin    234
Kinoshita, Syunsuke    544
Kirik, Ekaterina    719
Kojima, Hiroaki    544
Komatsuzaki, Toshihiko    385
Korcek, Pavol    807
Kostavelis, Ioannis    395
Koyama, Shigeyuki    728, 743
Krbálek, Milan    709
Kubo, Keisuke    171
Kutrib, Martin    42

Łach, Łukasz    494
Landman, Kerry A.    405
Lane, David    244
Laspidou, Chrysi S.    415
Lawniczak, Anna T.    425
Leal-Toledo, Regina Célia P.    524
Lee, Jia    83, 575
Liakopoulos, Antonis    415
Lobosco, Marcelo    434
Lubaś, Robert    768
Lupiano, Valeria    273, 279
Lux, Mathias    340

Maignan, Luidnel    101
Maiti, Nirmalya S.    360
Maity, Ilora    234
Maji, Pradipta    63
Makarenko, Alexander    738
Malcher, Andreas    42
Manenti, Lorenza    299, 699
Manzoni, Luca    653
Manzoni, Sara    299
Mardiris, Vassilios A.    554
Margenstern, Maurice    785
Marques, Oge    340
Massaro, Emanuele    204
Matsui, Nobuyuki    575
Mauri, Giancarlo    653
Michail, Dimitrios    263
Morishita, Shin    385, 728, 743
Mortveit, Henning S.    672
Mouton, Ans M.    763
Mukhopadhyay, Debdeep    52

Musienko, Anton    738
Myśliwiec, Wojciech    768

Nalpantidis, Lazaros    395
Naskar, Nazma    63
Navarra, Alfredo    534
Newgreen, Donald F.    405
Nishinari, Katsuhiro    194, 474
Nowak, Jarosław    494

Ohi, Fumio    73
Oiwa, Kazuhiro    544
Oliveira, Gina M.B.    111

Pagliara, Tiziano Maria    273
Panagiotopoulos, Fotios K.    554
Parise, Roberto    444
Parmigiani, Andrea    309
Pauwels, Ine S.    763
Peper, Ferdinand    83, 575
Piwonska, Anna    121
Popova, Anna    738
Poveshenko, Gennadiy    738
Pratikakis, Ioannis    514
Precharattana, Monamorn    454

Roli, Andrea    244
Rongo, Rocco    444
Rose, Marco Delle    273
Ruskin, Heather J.    835

Samorodov, Evgeniy    738
Sarkar, Anindita    643
Sartorato, Elisabetta    351
Sartoretti, Guillaume    464
Scarlatos, Stylianos    141, 151
Schneider, Oliver    565
Sekanina, Lukas    807
Semprevira, Anna Maria    273
Seredynski, Franciszek    121
Serra, Roberto    244
Sharifulina, Anastasiya    161
Shimura, Kenichiro    474
Shinozaki, Nobuhiko    728, 743
Sidiropoulos, Epaminondas    131
Sikdar, Biplab K.    11, 234, 643
Silva, Fernando    679
Sirakoulis, Georgios Ch.    263, 375, 752
Spataro, William    289, 444
Spiliotopoulos, Marios G.    415

Spingola, Giuseppe    444
Spyropoulou, Ioanna    817
Suzuki, Hideyuki    827
Svyetlichnyy, Dmytro S.    494
Szaban, Miroslaw    121

Takata, Daichi    575
Tanaka, Shukichi    544
Taniguchi, Yohei    827
Triampo, Wannapong    454
Trofimenko, Alexander    738
Trunfio, Giuseppe A.    279, 289, 319, 444
Tsormpatzoglou, Georgios I.    585

Umeo, Hiroshi    171

Van der Weeën, Pieter    504
Vanjak, Zvonimir    795
Van Nieuland, Steffie    763
Vasic, Jelena    835
Vasicek, Zdenek    214
Verigos, Emmanuil    319

Vidica, Paulo M.    111
Vihas, Christos    752
Villani, Marco    244
Vitova, Tat'yana    719
Vizzari, Giuseppe    699
Vlassopoulos, Nikolaos    611
Voorhees, Burton    254
Vourkas, Ioannis    263

Wang, Zheng    370
Wąs, Jarosław    768
Wcisło, Rafał    845
Widemann, Baltasar Trancón y.    184
Worsch, Thomas    565, 689
Wu, Jing    370

Yanagisawa, Daichi    776
Yunès, Jean-Baptiste    101

Zagoris, Konstantinos    514
Zamith, Marcelo    524
Zawidzki, Machi    194